# JEWISH DIFFERENCE AND THE ARTS IN VIENNA

# JEWISH DIFFERENCE AND THE ARTS IN VIENNA

## *Composing Compassion in Music and Biblical Theater*

Caroline A. Kita

INDIANA UNIVERSITY PRESS

This book is a publication of

Indiana University Press
Office of Scholarly Publishing
Herman B Wells Library 350
1320 East 10th Street
Bloomington, Indiana 47405 USA

iupress.indiana.edu

 The paper used in this publication meets the minimum requirements of the American National Standard for Information Sciences—Permanence of Paper for Printed Library Materials, ANSI Z39.48-1992.

Manufactured in the United States of America

Cataloging information is available from the Library of Congress.

ISBN 978-0-253-04053-4 (cloth)
ISBN 978-0-253-04056-5 (ebook)

1 2 3 4 5 23 22 21 20 19

*For Dan,*
*with love and gratitude.*

# CONTENTS

# PREFACE

THERE ARE TWO STORIES ABOUT THE BEGINNING OF this book. The first story is told by my father. It involves a car ride from Boston to Buffalo when I was nine years old, during which he played for me one of his favorite recordings of Gustav Mahler's Second Symphony. According to his account, I fell asleep. I prefer the second story.

This one starts on a fateful winter evening, when I first walked into Vienna's famed concert hall, the Musikverein. I had arrived in the Austrian capital with a smattering of German, my viola in tow, and dreams of walking the streets that Beethoven and Mozart had once roamed. Within the first few weeks it become clear to me that I would spend more time in the concert hall than in the practice room. And that is how I found myself on a Thursday evening in the standing room section of the *Großer Saal*, listening with breathless urgency to the opening bars of Mahler's Second. This time, I was hooked.

There is an oft-quoted anecdote from Mahler that he struggled for a long time to find the proper conclusion to this work. It was only at the funeral of the conductor Hans von Bülow, when he heard Friedrich Klopstock's hymn *Resurrection*, sung by the church choir that it struck him, he claimed, "like the immaculate conception!" To say that this book came to me in a similar strike of inspiration would be adding a bit too much poetic license to this story. But the evening left a lasting impression on me. I couldn't stop thinking about the powerful questions Mahler was asking in this work: *What is life? What is death? Have we any continuing existence? Is it all an empty dream, or has this life, this death, a meaning?* And even more compelling to me was another question: *how was music telling this story*?

My fascination for the intersections of music and narrative, philosophy and religious quests, sparked that night in Vienna, has led me on an incredible journey. It inspired my application for a Fulbright Grant, which gave me the opportunity to undertake in-depth study of Mahler's world and his intellectual friendship with the poet and philosopher Siegfried Lipiner. This project led me back to Vienna, and later on to Berlin, Marburg, and Stockholm in search of Lipiner's lost archive. And it eventually led to this book, which draws their works into conversation with the music and biblical dramas of three other German-Jewish artists, Arnold Schoenberg, Richard Beer-Hofmann, and Stefan Zweig, who shared with Mahler and Lipiner a passionate belief in the power of music to transform the individual and society.

As I began to write about this book, I was struck by how the underlying message in these works still resonates today, in a world that is so deeply divided on religious, cultural, and ideological grounds. To the question that each of the artists in this book asks, how do we live on in the face of suffering, there is only one answer: community. This project has been a constant and comforting reminder to me of how art can create a space to see beyond differences and to recognize our shared humanity.

# ACKNOWLEDGMENTS

I AM DEEPLY GRATEFUL TO ALL THE PEOPLE who have supported me throughout this book's many stages and to the institutions whose financial support made this project possible, beginning first of all with Indiana University Press and the Leo Baeck Institut London, sponsor of the German Jewish Cultures Series. To Dee Mortensen, Paige Rasmussen, Rachel Rosolina, and series editors Kerry Wallach, Sam Spinner, Matthew Handelman, Iris Idelson, and Joshua Teplitsky, thank you for guiding me through the process and making this book a reality. To Kate Aid, thank you for helping me bring the pieces together.

Research for this book was supported by a Franz Werfel Grant from the Österreichischer Austauschdienst (OeAD). I am indebted to Konstanze Fliedl and Monika Meister of the University of Vienna for their support during my grant period and to the dedicated "Werfelianer" who offered such helpful feedback during my workshop. Thank you to Klemens Renoldner of the Stefan Zweig Centre, Salzburg, for pointing me toward helpful sources during my research. To Arthur Spiegler and Ingemar Söderberg, thank you for your personal insights into Lipiner's life during the early stages of my research.

I am very appreciative of the guidance I received in libraries and archives while writing this book. Thank you to Eike Fess and Therese Muxeneder of the Arnold Schoenberg Centre for the assistance with Schoenberg's archive and for the opportunity to present parts of this project at the Schoenberg Symposium in October 2015. I am also grateful to the Schoenberg family, Bernd Reifenberg of the University of Marburg, Alena Parthonnaud of the Médiathèque Musicale Mahler, Paris, and to the staff of the Wienbibliothek im Rathhaus, the Austrian Theater Museum, the Music Collection of the Austrian National Library, and the Houghton Library at Harvard University for their assistance in procuring the images that appear in this book.

Thank you to my advisors at Boston College and Duke University who shaped this project in its very beginnings, Michael Resler, Jeremiah McGrann, Bryan Gilliam, James Rolleston, Bill Donahue, and Daniel Foster. My study of Lipiner and his relationship to Mahler benefited greatly from conversations with Morten Solvik, Stephen Hefling, and Jason Starr. To the many colleagues in the field of German Studies who generously gave their time to read my work and offer helpful advice—especially Carl Niekerk, Abigail Gillman, and Jonathan Hess—thank you for your willingness to discuss this project with me as it took shape and for supporting my research in so many ways. I also extend my gratitude to Ann Marie Rasmussen, for your practical advice on the publication process and to Sylvia Schmitz-Burgard and my many wonderful colleagues at the College of the Holy Cross for your enthusiasm and guidance in my first years out of grad school.

I also feel fortunate to have such thoughtful and generous colleagues at Washington University in St. Louis. To Lynne Tatlock, Matt Erlin, Jennifer Kapcyznski, Erin McGlothlin, Gerhild Williams, Paul Michael Lützler, Kurt Beals, and Christian Schneider, thank you for your mentorship, encouragement and helpful advice. To Anne-Marie McManus and Melanie Micir, who provided invaluable feedback on my writing and moral support (virtually and in person!) over the last few years, I am so very grateful. Thank you to Patrick Goff and Amy Braun for your meticulous work in helping me keep this project organized. Finally, I extend my appreciation to the Center for the Humanities for sponsoring the summer writing retreats and proposal writing workshops that introduced me to such a welcoming and supportive community of scholars here at Wash U.

To my amazing cohort at Duke and especially the band, Michelle Eley, Johanna Schuster-Craig, and Molly Knight, thank you for being a sounding board for all of my wacky ideas, for sharing in the excitements and disappointments along the way, and for inspiring me with your creativity and brilliance. Person, you know this book inside and out. Thanks for helping me see it through.

To dear friends on both sides of the Atlantic and to my family for all of your love and encouragement on this long journey: especially my parents, Bill and Kathy, for being such incredible models of hard work and dedication and for believing in me every step of the way; my sister Kate for always being just a phone call away, no matter what time zone we were in; and my brothers, Matt and Kevin—the chapter book is finally done! I am forever grateful to you all.

Finally, to my husband Dan, who has been so supportive of me from the moment we met and unfailingly patient with this project. With deepest love and gratitude, I dedicate this book to you.

* * *

My analysis of Mahler's Second Symphony in chapter 2 appeared in a different context in "The Revolutionary, the Artist, and the Heroic Martyr: Tracing the Evolution of Sacrifice in Mickiewicz's *Dziady* and the Texts of Mahler's Second Symphony," in *"Making Sacrifices": Visions of Sacrifice in European Cultures—Essays from the Salzburg Institute Symposium* (Vienna: New Academic Press, 2016), 33–50. Chapter 3 updates and expands upon ideas in "Between Instinct and the Law: Dionysian Dissonance and Polyphonic Poetics in Arnold Schoenberg's Totentanz der Prinzipien," *Journal of the Arnold Schoenberg Center* 13 (2016), 35–48. Chapter 4 develops an earlier reading of Beer-Hofmann's *Jaákobs Traum*, published in "Richard Beer-Hofmann's Die Historie von König David: Jewish Biblical Drama and the Limits of Epic Theater," *The German Quarterly* 89, no. 2 (2016), 133–149.

# NOTE ON TRANSLATION

THIS BOOK IS CONCERNED WITH A PARTICULAR DISCOURSE of compassion, or *Mitleid*, which emerged in the nineteenth-century German philosophical and aesthetic tradition, primarily in the writings of Arthur Schopenhauer and Richard Wagner, and which refers to the feeling of solidarity and community that comes from recognizing and sharing in another person's suffering. This meaning is captured both in the German, a composition of the noun *Leid*, or suffering, and the preposition *mit* (with), and in the Latin roots *com* (with, together) and *pati* (suffer). Mitleid can also be translated as pity; however, pity, as Christopher Janaway notes in his translation of Schopenhauer's texts, implies "a sense of distance from or even superiority over those whose suffering one recognizes."[1] Because Schopenhauer's very notion of Mitleid involves the dissolution of the differences between the sufferer and the one observing her suffering, I follow Janaway in translating this term as compassion, which captures more accurately the relationship that defined the utopian communities envisioned in the works I discuss in this study.

Another term that recurs with some frequency in this text is "the Law," which refers to both *das Gesetz* or *die Gebote*. I have translated it here with a capital L to indicate its idiosyncratic meaning in this context. In antisemitic discourses of this time, das Gesetz, referring to rabbinic law, and die Gebote, referring to Mosaic Law or the Ten Commandments, are often used interchangeably to denote a stereotype of Judaism as rigid, old-fashioned, and unmodern. It also implicitly references a false understanding that Jewish laws promote justice through vengeance. In anti-Jewish and antisemitic aesthetic discourses of this time, devotion to the Law is understood as preventing the Jew from becoming a truly compassionate (and artistic) being. For each of the writers and composers studied in this book, creating compassionate art is intrinsically linked to transcending or redefining this stereotype.

# INTRODUCTION

THIS IS A BOOK ABOUT A PHILOSOPHICAL AND aesthetic discourse of compassion that emerged in mid-nineteenth-century German culture and that became the focal point of a movement toward cultural renewal in Vienna between 1876 and 1918. It traces the influence of the idea that art, in particular music and theater, could awaken compassionate understanding by encouraging the audience's identification with the suffering subject onstage and, in so doing, transform society. This vision of cultural renewal through compassion claimed to restore a communal consciousness in the fragmented modern world, but, in reality, it was predicated on the exclusion of the Jew, a figure deemed incapable of compassion or of creating compassionate art. This book reveals how five German-Jewish artists in Vienna responded to the construction of Jewish difference at the heart of this discourse of compassion in their symphonic, choral, and dramatic works. Mobilizing the universal language of music, these artists destabilize the binaries of German and Jew and reenvision compassion as the basis for an inclusive community.

As the capital of the vast Habsburg Empire that dominated eastern and central Europe at the end of the nineteenth century, Vienna was the seat of an aging monarchy and a Catholic culture defined by deeply ingrained traditions of religious theatricality and Baroque grandeur. It was also home to a diverse population, including a large number of Jews from the empire's eastern provinces. At the turn of the century, this multinational state became increasingly divided along political, religious, cultural, and class lines. Yet amid the sense of impending dissolution, "fin-de-siècle Vienna," as it became immortalized in the writings of historian Carl Schorske, attracted vibrant communities of artistic creativity and intellectual innovation.[2] Many found inspiration in a discourse of religious-artistic cultural renewal derived from the writings of Arthur Schopenhauer, Richard Wagner, and Friedrich Nietzsche.[3] A focal point of their desire for a cultural rebirth was the aesthetic and ethical ideal of compassion. In compassion, awoken through the transcendent powers of myth, drama, and music, they found an empowering force for spiritual revitalization and social change.

Yet within the "temple of art" the signs of fracture were many. With the exclusion of Austria from the formation of Germany in 1871, and the economic upheaval of the stock market crash of 1873, powerful mass political movements began to form in Vienna, shaking the core of these utopian visions of a renewed society. The rise of German nationalism and the election of Mayor Karl Lueger in 1897 in particular brought deeply ingrained religious, cultural, and racial prejudices against Jews to the forefront of public discourse. Moreover, as Lueger's popular dictum, "Wer Jud' ist, bestimm' ich" (I'll determine who is a Jew) reveals, the definition of who or what was considered to be Jewish was a shifting target. The state of precarity facing persons of Jewish heritage, regardless of their degree of identification or affiliation with the Jewish religion or the Jewish community in Vienna, left an indelible mark on this generation.[4]

*Jewish Difference and the Arts in Vienna* investigates these tensions through the musical and dramatic works of five German-Jewish artists who shaped the language, forms, and cultural products of Viennese Modernism's spiritual awakening: Siegfried Lipiner, Gustav Mahler, Arnold Schoenberg, Richard Beer-Hofmann, and Stefan Zweig. To do so, it engages the framework of Jewish difference, which, according to Lisa Silverman, describes the "dialectical, hierarchical framework that encompasses the relationship between the socially constructed categories of 'Jew' and 'non-Jew.'"[5] This lens acknowledges Jewishness not as a fixed category but rather as a constantly evolving process of defining and redefining borders between insiders and outsiders, belonging and Otherness. The works examined in this study, which each reflect deeply personal engagements with questions of identity and community, provide prime case studies for exploring the idea of Jewish difference. On the one hand, these works were shaped by a shared language and cultural idea of Germanness that was also inflected by the ideals of totality and theatricality found in Austria's Catholic Baroque culture.[6] On the other, they drew on a common spiritual language drawn from their authors' and composers' Jewish heritage: the idea of being Chosen, the shared values of critical thought and commentary, a common history of diaspora, transience, and homelessness, and a passionate commitment to the principles of justice. Their negotiations of identity, myth, and history remain highly idiosyncratic and distinct from those emerging in Vienna's Orthodox Jewish community and political and cultural Zionist movements. Instead, under the guise of their biblical alter egos, Abel, Cain, Jacob, and Jeremiah, these writers and composers articulate their experience as mediators between Christian and Jewish faith traditions, caught between two worlds and yet resisting complete identification with either one.

Finally, these writers and composers shared an understanding of their experiences as German-Jews as deeply *musical*—at times dissonant and cacophonous, but fundamentally in tune with a universal human spirit. Thus, while their works engage in the construction of the Jew in opposition to the Austrian/German/Christian, they also seek to dissolve difference through musical-poetic languages based on polyphony and antiphony and forms such as the lied and the oratorio. Emerging from deeply personal spiritual quests, these works offer a new framework for reading fin de siècle Viennese culture—one that reflects the complex negotiations behind the construction and performance of religious and cultural identity.

## Compassion, Difference, and the Jewish Question

Compassion has roots in ancient Greek philosophy and in almost all modern religious traditions.[7] It defines how humans of different standings and situations are able to relate to one another through the universal experience of suffering. Martha Nussbaum claims it as "a basic social emotion," for to feel compassion, we must recognize the inherent value of the Other, believe that their pain was unwarranted or unjust, and be able to put ourselves in their place, to imagine this same suffering inflicted upon us.[8] The final stage of compassion is the most complex, for it calls for a creative response to the observation of another's pain, the ability to conceive of hypothetical situations and radically alternate futures. Thus, compassion encapsulates not just the *feeling* of sympathy but also the *action* that it inspires, the spark toward inner transformation. It is an experience *created* by particular circumstances and *performed* by individual actors.

The performative aspect of compassion is the basis for Aristotle's theory of tragic art.[9] In his *Poetics*, Aristotle claimed that the identification with the plight of the tragic hero inspires pity (*eleos*) and terror (*phobos*), which in turn engenders a moment of catharsis through which the audience is "purified" and transformed. Philosophers of the German Enlightenment, most notably Gotthold Ephraim Lessing, offered a critical reassessment of Aristotle's views on compassion and the theater. In his *Hamburgische Dramaturgie* (1767–1769), Lessing wrote that it is not terror (*Schrecken*) but fear (*Furcht*) that the audience feels. This fear, he claims, is self-driven; in identifying with another person, one's own anxieties are brought to the surface:

> [Aristotles] Furcht ist durchaus nicht die Furcht, welche uns das bevorstehende Übel eines anderen, für diesen andern, erweckt, es ist die Furcht, welche aus unserer Ähnlichkeit mit der leidenden Person für uns selbst entspringt; es ist die Furcht, daß die Unglücksfälle, die wir über diese verhängt sehen, uns selbst betreffen können; es ist die Furcht, daß wir der bemitleidete Gegenstand selbst werden können. Mit anderen Worten: Diese Furcht ist das auf uns selbst bezogene Mitleid.
>
> [(Artistotle's) fear is by no means the fear excited in us by misfortune threatening another person. It is the fear which arises for ourselves from the similarity of our position with that of the sufferer; it is the fear that the calamities impending over the sufferers might also befall ourselves; it is the fear that we ourselves might thus become objects of pity. In a word, this fear is compassion referred back to ourselves.][10]

By identifying compassion as the intersection of the ethics and aesthetic affect, Lessing set a powerful precedent for the theater as a space of personal and communal self-discovery. Ruth HaCohen describes the complex relationship between the sufferer and the observer of suffering evoked in this tradition of tragic art in terms of a spiral metaphor. She claims that theater enacts compassion when the internal protagonists of an artwork and the external audience are drawn to view the object of compassion not as a direct reflection of themselves (the mirror image) but as developing along a similar trajectory.[11] For HaCohen, the "sympathetic worlds" that emerge from these dynamics of compassion blur the lines between reality and fiction yet can also encourage critical awareness. The writers and artists examined in this study all aspired to compose works that might mobilize this dual effect of compassion, ultimately envisioning that the consciousness created through compassionate art might inspire the realization of inclusive community in their own time.

Lessing's comments also reveal compassion to be a concept fraught with contradictions. Indeed, critics of compassion claim that its subjective nature, while positing a deeper, more primal emotive connection between humans beyond their rational capabilities, make it an insufficient basis for determining the morality of actions. From the position of the suffering figure, Lessing notes, compassion can be read as pity. Pity, understood as a superficial or false sense of sympathy, does nothing to alleviate the sufferer, only insulting his or her dignity.[12] It is Mitleid translated as pity that

Friedrich Nietzsche critiques when he describes it as a manipulation of the emotions of the Other, a power play by the weak to contaminate the strong and healthy spirits.[13]

The idea of Mitleid most directly passed down to the writers and composers examined in this study emerged from a philosophical discourse found in the writings of Arthur Schopenhauer and Richard Wagner. I follow Christopher Janaway in translating this term as "compassion" not "pity," because it was based in the desire to dissolve difference.[14] In *Die Welt als Wille und Vorstellung* (1818/1819), Schopenhauer wrote that the ability to feel with the suffering of the other was the true basis of all ethical human action. He identified compassion, along with aesthetic contemplation and ascetic resignation, as the means by which individuals temporarily free themselves from worldly suffering and gain insight into the deeper truths beyond the phenomenal world.[15]

Despite its universal claims, Schopenhauer's understanding of compassion was also marked by an anti-Jewish discourse deeply ingrained in the German idealist philosophical tradition. In his essay, "Über die Religion," (On Religion), published in *Parerga und Paralipomena* in 1851, Schopenhauer maintained that Jews were beholden to the law of a distant, vengeful God and must therefore be composed of a different essential substance than Christians. In this way, he continued what Michael Mack has identified as a "pseudotheological" form of antisemitism in the German idealist tradition, which, employed a "secularized and politicized Christian theology" over and against an essentialized idea of Judaism.[16] Drawing on the writings of Kant, Hegel, and Feuerbach, who envisioned Jewish obedience to God's commandments as evidence of their "imagined immutability" (incapacity for change) and "enslavement to the objects of material life," Schopenhauer used narratives from the Hebrew Bible to construct an idea of the Jewish worldview as "realistic," materialistic, and optimistic — in direct opposition to his own philosophy of religion.[17] Over the course of the nineteenth century, these ideas found resonance in the emerging scholarly discipline of Comparative Mythology, which employed similar readings of the violence and tragedies of the Hebrew Bible to claim an innate Jewish incapacity for sympathetic understanding.[18] In the aesthetic realm a similar discourse emerged, which claimed the art of "the uncompassionate Jew" reflected an uncompassionate nature—artificial and derivative, rather than authentic. In particular, Jews were seen to be incapable of producing true music and could only imitate or create sounds that were maligned as noisy and cacophonous rather than musical and harmonious, a discourse Ruth HaCohen has identified as the "musical libel against the Jews."[19]

The case studies presented in each chapter of this book trace how Lipiner, Mahler, Schoenberg, Beer-Hofmann, and Zweig critically engaged with these paradigms of compassion and compassionate art in their musical and dramatic works. By returning to key stories of the Hebrew Bible, the brotherly conflicts of Cain and Abel and Jacob and Esau, and the personal struggles of Jacob and Jeremiah, these writers and composers deconstruct modern categories of Jewish Otherness and offer new models of community that integrate and include the Jewish subject.

## Music and Biblical Theater as Compassionate Art

This book investigates musical and dramatic works that evoke the legends of Hebrew Bible and Christian Scriptures to reflect critically on compassion as a means of transcending religious and cultural difference. In presenting the genesis of these symphonies, oratorios, and dramas, I reveal how these writers and composers seized upon the modernist impulse to discover new modes of art, merging traditional forms in some cases and radically fragmenting others. That many of these works remained unfinished demonstrates the quixotic nature of their authors' and composers' visions, but, however incomplete, they remain a critical documentation of the experimental impulses in music and theater at this time.

In each of these works, the Bible serves as a kind of "primal text," or origin story, although they reflect various degrees of fidelity to this source. As Henry Bial notes, biblical dramas can encompass a range of dramatic works, including those intended as explicit dramatization of episodes from the sacred Scriptures of the Christian and Jewish tradition; to those in which the Bible and its characters served as inspiration for new narratives; to those that employ a biblical setting with essentially invented stories and characters.[20] Remaining relatively close to their Hebrew Bible sources, Lipiner, Beer-Hofmann, and Zweig's works fall into the second category—what Bial terms biblical "fan fiction." Schoenberg's oratorio, which takes as its inspiration the story of Jacob from the book of Genesis while quoting from the Gospels of Luke and Matthew and alluding to the Book of Revelations in the Christian New Testament, is closest to the third category. Biblical references in Mahler's Second and Third Symphony appear primarily in his programs and published texts *about* these works. Yet, when his song settings are read alongside Lipiner's biblical drama, *Adam*, they reflect a complex, intertextual, and intermedial interchange between poet and composer on compassion and religious difference. Mahler's symphonies played a critical role in translating Lipiner's theories of compassion into a musical idiom that would greatly impact the next generation of writers and composers, who likewise found in the stories of the patriarchs and prophets compassionate heroes and antiheroes rooted in both modern Jewish and Christian mythologies. For Lipiner, Mahler, Schoenberg, Beer-Hofmann, and Zweig, these biblical figures came to represent their own complex, modern identities as mediators of Christian and Jewish traditions.

That these biblically inspired works were all written, composed, or performed in Vienna is unsurprising given the long tradition of biblical theater in Austria, dating back to the Middle Ages. Performances of biblical texts in the form of miracle and mystery plays had often served as a highlight of Christian feast days. By bringing the scriptures to life, these works served both to educate and to instill a sense of community through the enactment of ritual as public spectacle. Much like Greek tragedy, from which they drew inspiration, music played a primary role in these performances, serving both to intensify the dramatic effect of the work and to encourage audience participation.

The modern rebirth of biblical drama in Vienna at the end of the nineteenth century drew on this tradition of religious theatricality found in Austria's Baroque Catholic culture and appeared in a variety of forms. On Vienna's opera stages at this time, works such as Carl Goldmark's *Queen of Sheba* (1875) and Richard Strauss's *Salome* (1905) emphasized an idealized, sensualized, and romanticized Orient, while the city witnessed at the same time a boom in large-scale amateur choral dramas and communal biblical theater that promoted a largely conservative, Catholic cultural agenda.[21] A leading figure in the amateur theater movement was the poet Richard von Kralik, who is most well-known for his cofounding of the short-lived Sagengesellschaft (Saga Society) with Siegfried Lipiner and Gustav Mahler. His *Weihnachtsspiel* (Christmas Play 1893) and *Osterfestspiel* (Easter Festival Play 1895), along with his revival of the Spanish Baroque playwright Pedro Calderón de la Barca's Corpus Christi play, *Das große Welttheater* (The Great Theater of the World) in 1897, were performed in venues from the city hall plaza to the Musikverein, and played an important role in garnering public interest in biblical theater in Vienna at this time.

However, *Jewish Difference and the Arts in Vienna* examines the musical and dramatic works of Lipiner, Mahler, Schoenberg, Beer-Hofmann, and

Zweig in a different light, reading them as reflections on pseudotheologies of antisemitism that can be traced to their critical readings of Schopenhauer and Wagner. Because the idea of the uncompassionate Jew that they were seeking to deconstruct was based in selective readings of the Hebrew Bible, they returned to this very text as inspiration for their own works. In so doing, they recast the prophets and patriarchs as icons of the shared tradition of Judaism and Christianity, as models of resistance to dualistic thinking, and ultimately as embodying the seeds of a modern German-Jewish identity.

Finally, while Vienna also witnessed the emergence of a Yiddish theatrical scene through the establishment of the Jewish Stage, the Jewish Artists' Cabaret, and the Jewish Art Theater at this time, the writers and composers in question were not directly engaged in the endeavor to establish a Jewish National Theater, nor were they writing primarily for a Jewish public.[22] Their works were written in German, draw broadly from the Hebrew and Christian Bible, and cannot be classified as focusing on an exclusively Jewish narrative of the biblical text.[23] They did, however, seek new ways of articulating Jewishness that both recognized the distinct cultural contribution of Judaism and viewed it as part of a shared tradition that could be reconciled with their German cultural heritage.

## Wagnerian Trauma and Jewish Difference

The artist who set the standard for epic festival theater and who also defined compassionate art for these writers and composers was the composer Richard Wagner. The pivotal role of the Wagnerian legacy in European culture writ large and in fin de siècle Vienna in particular has been the subject of numerous monographs and studies over the course of the past several decades.[24] Wagner offered a language and form for capturing the desire for community outside the confines of religious dogma or tradition. His monumental four-part operatic cycle *Der Ring des Nibelungen* (1848–1876) staged the apocalyptic downfall of the gods and a new society based on love, while *Parsifal* (1880), a *Bühnenweihefestspiel,* or consecration play for the stage, reimagined the dramatic potential of religious ritual, presenting a compelling narrative of community redeemed through compassion. Wagner's paradigm of compassionate art was widely admired and adopted by the next generation of writers and composers, particularly among German-Jews, who found in his call for a rebirth of German culture a unique opportunity for cultural assimilation.[25]

*Jewish Difference and the Arts*, however, seeks to probe further the engagement of German-Jews in the production, dissemination, and critique of the composer's ideology for the theater. In particular, it focuses on how five German-Jewish writers and composers, living in Vienna at a highpoint of antisemitic sentiment, responded to the language of Wagner's cultural critiques, which popularized Schopenhauer's configuration of the Jews as uncompassionate and merged these discourses with popular cultural stereotypes of the Jews as unartistic and unmusical.

In tracing these responses to Wagner and Schopenhauer's writings on compassion and the Jews, this book suggests that these writers and composers were operating in response to a kind of "Wagnerian Trauma," which Michael Steinberg has identified as a crisis in the theater and music that resulted from the composer's merging of "ideologies of nationhood, cultural homogenization and aesthetic totalization."[26] A critical component of Wagner's ideology was the weeding out of what he defined as the decadent, foreign, Jewish, Other from the pure German artwork. As Assaf Shelleg has noted, German-Jewish artists encountering this language found themselves in a double-bind, compelled either to appropriate the exclusionary rhetoric of Wagner or to invert his message and create a self-defined Jewish art that then reified his very binaries of Jew and non-Jew.[27] Indeed, many German-Jewish writers in Vienna such as Otto Weininger, whose 1903 dissertation, *Geschlecht und Charakter* (Sex and Character), claimed that Judaism was a "psychic constitution" that must be overcome, adopted Wagner's antisemitic language at this time.

The authors and composers examined in this work encountered and responded to this "trauma" in a variety of ways. At times, they evoke the same stereotypes that Wagner used and proliferated, staging Jewish voices as noisy and unmusical and Jewish bodies as deformed or contorted. Moreover, in focusing primarily on masculine minds and bodies, they appear fixated on recuperating Jewish masculinity in the face of antisemitic categorizations of the Jew as weak and effeminate.[28] In classifying the highly contradictory depictions of Jewish subjects in these artworks, one should be wary of moving too quickly to claim them as projections of Jewish "self-hatred," a term that risks reducing to absolute negative terms experiences and perceptions of Jewishness.[29] In the cases of Lipiner, Mahler, Schoenberg, Beer-Hofmann, and Zweig examined in this book, I identify the figures coded Jewish as fruitful sites for probing more deeply questions of cultural and religious identity at the turn of the century.

This book takes as its point of departure the idea that these German-Jewish artists were well aware that they lived and acted in a world that was shaped by Jewish difference, and it claims that they engaged this idea directly in their musical and dramatic works. Drawing on theories of gender performance, Silverman's paradigm of Jewish difference proposes that the project of defining "the Jew" (and, by contrast, "the Austrian") was one to which both Jews and non-Jews contributed and reflects varying and shifting degrees of self-identification with these two cultural ideals.[30] By employing a cultural language of compassion in which particular categories of "the Jew" and "Jewishness" were already embedded, the artists examined in this study were certainly implicated in this process. Yet, I identify the construction of Jewish Otherness in their works as a means both to draw attention to the limits of the binaries of Jew and non-Jew, Jew and Catholic/Christian, and Jew and German/Austrian and to problematize and transform stereotypes of the Jews in their time.

To aid understanding of these unique characterizations of German-Jewish experience, *Jewish Difference and the Arts in Vienna* also draws on the framework of Jewish subjectivity. While Jewish difference reads as the ways in which Jewishness was performed, constructed, and perceived in the public sphere, Jewish subjectivity emphasizes the experiences and interior perceptions of individuals and their expression through aesthetic modes. It focuses in particular on what Scott Spector describes as the "intricate, complex, and self-contradictory ways in which historical actors perceive their place in the world *in contrast* to how they are perceived by others, or how they are ordered within relatively rigid external systems."[31] The works examined in this study, many of which were described by their authors as deeply personal confessions, uniquely capture their own shifting understanding of Jewishness, which was often in the public sphere a hindrance but served in their private lives as a source of creative energy. Tracing the genesis and evolution of these works in the context of their artist's developing views on compassion offers, I claim, a more nuanced picture of how German-Jewish artists navigated their role as cultural mediators. Theirs was not a one-way street of acculturation or assimilation but rather a continual process of "blurring and redrawing borders."[32]

A leading figure in the critique of Wagner's paradigm and the reconfiguration of compassionate art to reflect the voice of the German-Jewish subject was the poet and philosopher, Siegfried Lipiner. Best known today for his close friendship and intellectual exchange with the composer Gustav Mahler,

Lipiner was a prolific writer and speaker in Viennese intellectual circles at the turn of the century. His writings on artistic-religious renewal were written in conversation with Richard Wagner and Friedrich Nietzsche, and he played a significant role in shaping both Wagner's essay *Religion und Kunst* (Religion and Art 1880) and Nietzsche's philosophical novel *Also sprach Zarathustra* (Thus spoke Zarathustra 1883–1886), two texts that would profoundly influence intellectual and artistic discourses in the twentieth century.[33] In his speeches, poetry and drama, Lipiner offered a powerful vision of community through a rebirth of religious spirit outside the dogma and ritual of the church and synagogue, and affirmed the role of theater and music in creating the experience of compassion through representations of Promethean struggle and self-sacrifice. For Lipiner, tragic art was a space of reconciliation, where the shared origins of the Jewish and Christian faiths might be celebrated along with their common values. Moreover, it provided a paradigm for expanding Wagnerian compassion to include the subjective perspective of the suffering Jew. Drawing on Lipiner's philosophy of compassion, Mahler, Schoenberg, Beer-Hofmann, and Zweig sought to find new modes of giving voice to the German-Jewish subject by engaging the emotive power of music. By appealing to the essentially creative and performative nature of compassion as a formal principle of tragic art, they adapted Wagner's dramatic paradigms, such as the Gesamtkunstwerk, to allow for the resistance to absolute claims of identity, staging instead German-Jewish subjectivities in motion.[34]

In its exploration of debates surrounding compassion and the Jewish Question, this book traces a key generational shift. While Lipiner and Mahler's visions of compassion call for a reconciliatory vision in which the suffering Jewish subject is integrated as an equal member of a compassionate community, an *overcoming* of Otherness, Schoenberg, Beer-Hofmann, and Zweig imagine a more heterogeneous *synthesis* of Jewish and Christian culture. In their works of music and biblical theater, their protagonists are models of cross-cultural exchange that resist the always incomplete paradigm of assimilation. Thus, while Mahler and Lipiner sought primarily to evoke sympathy for the Jew in their works, Schoenberg, Beer-Hofmann, and Zweig redefine their Jewish protagonists as artists who create sympathetic understanding in the modern world. Their adaptable and transformable nature, devotion to the concept of unity in the form of monotheism, and innate understanding of faith as struggle are recast as the unique attributes of the Jew as compassionate soul and creator of compassionate art. To articulate this message, they turned to the language and forms of music.

## Making Musical, Jewish Subjectivities

The idea that music can communicate, listen, and perform is a trope that played an important role in the cultural production of modernity. Music's significance as a unique language and expressive form has always found particular resonance in Vienna, where performance, composition, and appreciation of music was elevated to the premiere mark of culture. To claim oneself as Viennese was to be a patron and participant in music both publicly and privately. Music became for many Viennese Jews, the *Eintrittskunst* par excellence, a point of entry into German culture.[35]

Musical subjectivity is grounded in the idea that music, like a human subject, attains a sense of "self" or ability to articulate meaning, through dialogue. For music to exist it must have a listener and interpreter. Lawrence Kramer suggests that this dialogic aspect of the musical subject makes it inherently instable, always calling into question its own legitimacy.[36] Steinberg has claimed that because of this instability, music bears a particular likeness to the modern Jewish experience. He writes that, music, like the German-Jewish subject, experiences an "anxiety of articulation," a desire to project a version of itself and at the same time to embody its opposite.[37] For many members of literary and artistic avant-garde at the fin de siècle, music's unique ability to express both subjective-individual experiences and universal emotions made it an ideal means to circumvent the *Sprachkrise* or crisis of language, a way of transcending the limitations of the word in the elusive search for communication among isolated and alienated individuals. While Leon Botstein has identified the connection between music and *Sprachkritik*, or the critique of language, for Jewish composers such as Mahler and Schoenberg, I argue that music served a similar purpose for the dramatists Lipiner, Beer-Hofmann, and Zweig.[38] Mobilizing music's subjectivity was for them not only the key to a new expressive language but also a dramatic provocation, a means of challenging the audience to critically engage with forms of artistic representation.[39]

In the works examined in this study, musical subjectivity emerges precisely at moments in which exclusionary discourses of compassion are called into question. Thus, while these works on the one hand aim to inspire the cathartic experience of compassion in the audience by employing musical paradigms of totality such as the Gesamtkunstwerk, the symphony, and the oratorio to create transcendent, harmonious visions of community, their poetic language and musical forms also reveal acoustic markers of difference that challenge and destabilize such models. The voices of subjects coded

Jewish in these works appear cacophonous and dissonant, accentuating their outsider status. In this way, they appear to evoke what Ruth HaCohen has identified as the correlation between musical harmony and religious difference, an idea of the imagined Christian heaven as sonically stable, an idealized community of like-minded souls, while Jews remain outside it as a discordant and noisy element.[40] Yet through musical-narrative strategies of polyphony, antiphony, and leitmotif the writers and composers in this book reimagine compassionate community as heterogeneous musicality. In this way, these works of biblical theater recuperate Jewish Otherness, not through the suppression of dissonance or difference but rather through its dialectical emancipation. By calling on music's alterity and "embodied critique of discursive authority," they create new forms of compassionate art based in the dissonant origins of a shared Jewish and Christian cultural myth.[41]

* * *

Chapter 1 establishes Lipiner as a central interpreter of Schopenhauer and Wagner's reading of compassion in fin de siècle Vienna. Lipiner believed that art that evoked a compassionate response in the audience would renew religion by uniting society in acknowledgment of the universal nature of suffering. This response would in turn break down the boundaries between individuals and pave the way for an empowering vision of collective spiritual renewal. This chapter further examines how a personal conversation with Wagner led to Lipiner's development of a more nuanced vision of compassion that would focus particularly on the suffering subject, eventually identifying this subject as the Jew. In *Adam*, the prelude to a planned tetralogy of biblical dramas he called *Christus*, Lipiner reenvisions the story of Cain and Abel to investigate antisemitic stereotypes of the Jews as subservient to an antiquated moral code of punishment and revenge. In Lipiner's play, Cain's strict adherence to the Lord's commands appears to make him incapable of feeling compassion. Yet in refocusing this story through Cain's perspective, Lipiner recasts him as a tragic figure deserving of the audience's sympathy. In his drafts for the other dramas in his tetralogy that remained incomplete, Lipiner planned to engage a surprising revision of Nietzsche's philosophy of the Dionysian as the center for his new vision of compassionate art. This empowering image of self-definition and becoming, crystallized in the Übermensch, would offer new possibilities for imagining the integration of the Jewish subject in his vision for cultural renewal.

Chapter 2 reveals how Lipiner's philosophy of compassion achieved musical expression in the symphonies of Gustav Mahler. By engaging the subjective perspective offered by the lied, or art song, in his Second (1888–1894) and Third (1893–1896) symphonies, Mahler presents three critical stages of Lipiner's vision in the musical-dramatic form of the symphony: the experience of the suffering subject, the transformation of the sufferer into one who feels compassion, and, finally, the birth of a new religious-spirit in the compassionate Übermensch, who embodies the Will to Love. Mahler's texts, programs, and song settings reveal striking correspondences with Lipiner's early writings on religious renewal and his *Christus* trilogy, suggesting that his two symphonies might be read as companion pieces to Lipiner's biblical drama. Most significant for Mahler's confrontation with the philosophical discourse of compassion and the antisemitic rhetoric therein are the fourth and fifth movements of the Third Symphony, in which Mahler evokes all three of Lipiner's key philosophical interlocutors, Schopenhauer, Nietzsche, and Wagner, to examine the conflict between compassion and the Law. In these movements, Mahler's alto soloist vocalizes the plight of the Jewish subject, a dissonant outsider who is beholden to the Lord's command and deaf to the angels' redemptive choir. Musical and textual references to Nietzsche's *Also sprach Zarathustra*, Schopenhauer's philosophical writings and Wagner's music drama *Parsifal* highlight the failure of their accounts of compassion to offer solace to the abject figure of the Jew. In the finale of the Third Symphony, Mahler follows Lipiner in merging Nietzsche's life-affirming impulse of the Dionysian with the model of compassionate love, Christ, in his vision of redemption for all beings.

The chapters that follow reveal how Lipiner's vision of compassionate art and its musical interpretation through Mahler came to impact three other German-Jewish Viennese artists, whose works were composed in the midst of World War I. Chapter 3 examines Arnold Schoenberg's monodrama *Totentanz der Prinzipien* (1915) and his unfinished oratorio, *Die Jakobsleiter* (1917), both originally planned as movements in a choral symphony modeled after Mahler's work. It reveals how the composer developed a polyphonic poetics, a language that complemented his own experiments with atonality and the twelve-tone method of composition, to voice the Jew's conflicted relationship to the Law. This chapter proposes that Schopenhauer's characterization of the Jew as beholden to the Law of the distant, vengeful, and jealous God in his essay "On Religion" inspired Schoenberg to develop a polyphonic poetic language to express the paradox of divine representation found in the Ten Commandments. In *Die Jakobsleiter*, Schoenberg's poetics reach their culmination in the figure of the Chosen One, who embodies the musical principle of theme and variation and through whom Schoenberg reenvisions divine revelation from *Gebot* (command) to the dialogic form of *Gebet* (prayer). The finale's chorus of a multitude of voices united in prayer reflects Schoenberg's understanding of the many-sided nature of the one true God and affirms compassion as the means by which all beings, Jew and Christian, will come to know this revelation.

Chapter 4 reveals how Richard Beer-Hofmann redefines the Wagnerian Gesamtkunstwerk as a new form of compassionate theater in his play *Jaákobs Traum* (1915). Written as the prelude to a cycle of biblical dramas about the life of King David, *Jaákobs Traum* reexamines the story of the biblical patriarch Jacob, whose struggle with God, and with figures representing Others to the Jewish experience, inspires him to imagine a new relationship with the divine based on justice, compassions and mutual responsibility. Beer-Hofmann intended to employ musical leitmotifs to articulate Jaákob's inner struggle with the Jewish legacy of suffering and blessing, and his eventual development into a compassion hero. While the integration of these musical themes united with verbal and visual gestures suggests that Beer-Hofmann envisioned his play to enact the compassionate merging of audience and actor found in Wagner's paradigm of theater, music serves also to highlight moments of rupture in the text. These disruptive moments indicate that Beer-Hofmann ultimately sought to question the immersive experience of music drama, to engage his audience in critical reflection on the nature of Jewish Otherness, and to reinscribe the Jews as a mythical, musical people.

The fifth and final chapter investigates the role of compassion in building a Jewish community in exile in Stefan Zweig's biblical drama *Jeremias* (1915–1917). It reveals how Zweig's belief in music's ability to transcend time and to speak to a collective spirit shaped his vision for Jewish spiritual unity, a concept he refers to as *Discursion*. In *Jeremias*, Zweig evokes such ideas through his development of a musical language of *Ekstase* to articulate the divinely inspired voice of the prophet, and through the integration of formal musical models, namely the oratorical aria and the communal prayer, to create compassionate community onstage and in the audience. In the final scene, the Jewish people of Zweig's play realize their spiritual unity by voicing their shared experience of suffering through the call and response of antiphony. In *Jeremias*, the Jews become a model community of unity in difference.

Utopian both in the scope of their production and in the idealist reconciliation of German-Jewish culture that they envisioned, these works nearly all failed to achieve their grandiose visions and were left unfinished, unperformed, or otherwise abandoned. Yet, they reveal fascinating, until now unexplored connections and correspondences between five artists who each turned to the philosophical and aesthetic concept of compassion to counter the discourse of antisemitism in Vienna in their time. These writers and composers sought, through their engagement with musical forms and styles, to capture the dynamic and evolving nature of the German-Jewish subject. Through their dialectical meditations and mediations, they reclaimed Jewish Otherness as a critical dynamic within the Austrian-German aesthetic tradition. When read together, these works shed new light on mediations and negotiations of cultural and religious identity in Viennese music and theater in the twilight years of the Habsburg Empire.

## Notes

1. Schopenhauer, *World as Will and Representation*, vol. 1, li.
2. Schorske, *Fin-de-Siècle Vienna*, 5–6.
3. McGrath, *Dionysian Art and Populist Politics*, 89.
4. Beller, *Vienna and the Jews*, 12–13.
5. Silverman, *Becoming Austrians*, 7.
6. Steinberg, *Meaning of the Salzburg Festival*, 2.
7. See Davies, *Theology of Compassion*, for the tradition of compassion primarily through the Christian perspective. In the Jewish tradition, discussions of compassion appear in the writings of Maimonides and Spinoza, although both philosophers generally reject it as the sole basis for determining ethical action. In modern Jewish philosophy, compassion is often linked to the writings of Hermann Cohen. Cohen takes up this idea in *Die Nächstenliebe im Talmud* (Love of Neighbor in the Talmud 1888), and specifically in a Kantian framework in his later essays in *Deutschtum und Judentum* (1915).
8. Nussbaum, "Compassion," 28.
9. Husain, *Ontology and the Art of Tragedy*, 123.
10. Lessing, *Hamburgische Dramaturgie*, 356 [Lessing, From *The Hamburg Dramaturgy*, 14].
11. R. HaCohen, *Music Libel against the Jews*, 11.
12. Nussbaum, "Compassion," 41.
13. Bamford, "Virtue of Shame," 244–245.
14. See Note on Translation.
15. Shapshay, "Schopenhauer's Aesthetics."
16. Mack, *German Idealism and the Jew*, 9–10.
17. Mack, 8, 11. See also Cartwright, who claims that Schopenhauer's "contempt for Judaism was philosophical, directed at its early biblical form, where it appeared to have no doctrine of immortality for the faithful, a doctrine he thought essential for a religion." Cartwright, *Schopenhauer*, 542–543.
18. See Williamson on critiques of Hebrew monotheism as evidence of the Jew's supposedly "intolerant and elusive nature." Williamson, *Longing for Myth in Germany*, 224.
19. R. HaCohen, *Music Libel against the Jews*, 1. See also, Gilman, "Are Jews Musical?"

20. Bial, *Playing God*, 5–7.

21. For more on amateur festival theater and the highly politicized nature of the Baroque tradition in Austria, see Beniston, *Welttheater*, 11, 78–84.

22. Bayerdörfer, "Jewish Self-Presentation," 154–155.

23. Eli Rozik describes a theater-text as Jewish if it reveals a configuration of five elements: (1) the medium of theater; (2) a Jewish or Judaized narrative; (3) a Jewish set of beliefs or values; (4) Jewish language, including nonverbal codes; and (5) a Jewish author. Rozik, *Jewish Drama and Theatre*, 2.

24. See Karnes on the Viennese context and Vazsonyi, Koss, and Large et al. on the larger European context. Karnes, *Kingdom Not of This World*; Vazsonyi, *Self-Promotion*; Koss, *Modernism after Wagner*; Large, Weber, and Sessa, *Wagnerism*.

25. This topic has been discussed in depth by a number of scholars, including: Botstein, "German Jews and Wagner"; Borchmeyer, Strasser-Vill, and Maayani, *Richard Wagner und die Juden*; Brener, *Richard Wagner and the Jews*.

26. Steinberg, *Listening to Reason*, 16.

27. Shelleg, *Jewish Contiguities*, 18.

28. The claim that these works focus on masculine minds and bodies is drawn from my reading of these works as projections of their composers' own German-Jewish subjectivities. Although a study of how gender is treated in each of these works is beyond the scope of this study, it can generally be noted that Lipiner, Mahler, and Zweig largely marginalize the feminine in their works as embodiments of an idealized "eternal feminine." Abigail Gillman has written about a potential "feminine poetics of Jewish memory," in Beer-Hofmann's *Jaákobs Traum* (Gillman, *Viennese Jewish Modernism*, 168). Jennifer Shaw has demonstrated the role of androgyny in Schoenberg's *Die Jakobsleiter* (Shaw, "Androgyny and the Eternal Feminine"). For more on the dynamics of Jews and gender stereotypes in turn-of-the-century Vienna, see Geller, *On Freud's Jewish Body*, 5–6.

29. See Paul Reitter for the complex history of the term "self-hatred," which does not enter the larger cultural discourse until after World War I. Reitter, *Origins of Jewish Self-Hatred*, 35. The application of the term "self-hatred" for Weininger has also been problematized by authors such as Sengoopta, in *Otto Weininger*, 41–44.

30. Silverman, *Becoming Austrians*, 7.

31. Spector, *Modernism without Jews?* xiii.

32. Hoedl, "Blurring of Distinction," 243.

33. R. Wagner, *Dichtungen und Schriften*, vol. 10, 117–163; Nietzsche, *Werke in drei Bänden*, vol. 2, 275–562.

34. Shelleg, *Jewish Contiguities*, 44.

35. Botstein, *Judentum und Modernität*, 123.

36. Kramer, *Classical Music and Postmodern Knowledge*, 24.

37. Steinberg, *Judaism Musical and Unmusical*, 222, 229.

38. Botstein, *Judentum und Modernität*, 54.

39. Botstein, 54.

40. R. HaCohen, *Music Libel against the Jews*, 2.

41. Kramer, *Classical Music and Postmodern Knowledge*, 100.

# JEWISH DIFFERENCE AND THE ARTS IN VIENNA

# 1

## A CASE FOR COMPASSION: SIEGFRIED LIPINER'S *ADAM*

Wenn ich, in der Dichtung, selbst das Größte vollbrächte, (ich muss es mir zutrauen, um nur existieren zu können), wenn ich—was ich anstrebe—die fernsten Zonen der darstellbaren Welt, das Tiefste und Wurzelhafteste erreichte,—was wär's? Wirken wird's immer nur auf Wenige, auf diejenigen, die's nicht so sehr nötig haben; aber die Armen und Elenden, die zugleich Geliebten und Verachteten? Die gehen leer aus, sie verstehen unsere Sprache nicht. . . . Wie führt man das Höchste in die Hütten der Niedrigsten, wie presst man den Himmel mit allen Gestirnen in die engen Schädel der Armen im Geiste?—das ist die Frage meines Lebens.

[If in poetry, I achieve the greatest (I must think myself capable of this in order to exist), if I reach—that which I strive for—the deepest and most rooted, the furthest zones of the representable world, what if? It will only affect the few, those who don't really need it; but the poor and miserable, the beloved as well as the scorned? They are left out in the cold. . . . How does one bring the highest into the hovels of the lowliest, how does one force heaven with all its stars into the narrow skulls of the poor in spirit? That is the question of my life.]

Siegfried Lipiner to Malwida von Meysenbug, 1878

In October 1878, the poet Siegfried Lipiner revealed his ardent mission to create art that would provide hope in the face of human suffering and enable compassionate understanding. Lipiner believed that compassion reflected a communal spirit of love that would counter the isolation of the individual in the modern world, inspiring a collective spiritual rebirth of society. While he was only twenty-two years old when he wrote this letter, the young poet had already made a name for himself as a promising scholar, an engaging public speaker, and a prominent intellectual in

Vienna. An authority on German idealist philosophy, Romantic literature, and the Bible, Lipiner also had his finger on the city's spiritual pulse in other arenas, participating in mythic, spiritualist societies and establishing close contact with writers and dramatists who, like himself, were seeking to redefine the function of music and theater.

Lipiner's vision for religious renewal involved a unique synthesis of the writings of three key thinkers of his time: Arthur Schopenhauer, Richard Wagner, and Friedrich Nietzsche. Following Schopenhauer, Lipiner claimed that compassion is the true basis of all ethical activity. It allows for the dissolution of the boundaries between the self and the Other, enabling solidarity in suffering. Echoing Wagner and the early writings of Nietzsche, Lipiner also asserted that compassion is the aesthetic principle at the core of tragic art and drama. In viewing the tragic fate of a protagonist onstage, the audience undergoes an inner transformation that could inspire a larger societal transformation. In his philosophical and poetic writings, Lipiner adopted the redemptive language of Schopenhauer and Wagner and their use of secularized and aestheticized Christian myth and symbol. He later sought to merge their aesthetic theories of compassion with socialist ideology, claiming that art must have a direct, ameliorating impact on those who suffer.

Lipiner's idiosyncratic reading of compassion was ultimately rejected by Wagner, leading to an intellectual crisis in which the poet attempted to establish himself as the "poet-priest" of his generation by modeling himself after his idol. Surrounding himself with like-minded artists and scholars, and shifting his creative output from poetry and speeches to cultural commentary and librettos, Lipiner also adopted Wagner's antisemitic rhetoric for a time. Yet, co-opting this language did not exempt Lipiner from becoming the target of antisemitic attacks, nor did it emancipate him from Wagner's shadow.

In the 1890s Lipiner began to withdraw from public intellectual life to work on a dramatic project that would define compassion on his own terms. In his *Christus* tetralogy, Lipiner claims compassion as a universal principle that emerges from the shared essence, or *Geist*, of all living things. Lipiner believed that despite the impulses of animalistic instinct (*Trieb*), all human beings are capable of compassion; it is society (and, in particular, dogmatic religion) that limits our ability to look beyond differences to recognize our commonality with all living things. The goal of tragic art, therefore, is to communicate the inner psyche of the sufferer so that the audience is inspired to identify with him or her, forcing a shift in the audience's own perspective.

In the prelude to his *Christus* tetralogy, *Adam*, Lipiner focused on a particular suffering subject, the Jew. Rejecting Schopenhauer and Wagner's idea of redemption through resignation, Lipiner turned instead to Friedrich Nietzsche's idea of the Übermensch as a framework for a new language of compassion. For Lipiner, the Übermensch captures the potential of all individuals to transform themselves through active striving and to sublimate suffering into an empowering affirmation of life. In a striking revision of Nietzsche's philosophy, Lipiner reconciles the spirit of the Übermensch with compassion (which Nietzsche had condemned as selfishly motivated) and God's love, as the basis for his new spiritual community.

This chapter traces the development of Lipiner's theory of compassion from its roots in the writings of Schopenhauer and Wagner, to his eventual revision of these ideas by turning to the later writings of Nietzsche. *Adam*, his interpretation of the biblical myth of Cain and Abel, represents the culmination of this endeavor. In his drama, Lipiner casts Cain as the prototypical Jew as outlined in Schopenhauer's philosophy of religion and Wagner's essay *Das Judentum in der Musik* (1850, 1869).[1] Cain's Otherness is marked by his blind fidelity to the Law (*Gesetz*) and the Lord's commands (*Gebote*). In placing the Law at the center of his biblical drama, Lipiner draws on an antisemitic stereotype, passed down to Schopenhauer and Wagner from Kant, of Jews as tied to an immutable religious worldview and a set of principles that keep God distant from humankind. In the play, Cain's strict adherence to the Law makes him incapable of feeling compassion for other beings. His lack of compassion is also made manifest in his physical appearance and voice; following Wagner's pathology of the Jewish body, Cain is described as deformed and contorted and his language is cacophonous and unmusical. In accordance with his understanding of compassionate art, Lipiner places his focus in the drama on the suffering figure of Cain. Through Cain's monologues, Lipiner probes the inner conscience of the Jewish subject who cannot feel compassion for others, not because he is innately different from his brother but because he is obeying the commands passed down to him from his father, Adam. At fault, therefore, is a broken system of ethics at the core of both Judaism and Christianity that must be transcended in order for a new Law of Love to be embraced and the community restored.

Lipiner's criticism of the Law, which is linked to Adam, the father of both religious traditions, is an attempt to draw attention to the false dichotomies of Jew and Christian found in Schopenhauer's philosophy of religion. Through the voice of his protagonist, Lipiner draws attention instead to the "shared substance" between Cain, the abject Jew, and Abel, the embodiment of the Übermensch and prototype of Lipiner's vision of a new religious spirit. Lipiner's unfinished drafts of the *Christus* tetralogy suggest that in the remaining dramas he hoped to explore how the Übermensch's affirmation of suffering might provide a model for the transformation of the suffering subject and the rebirth of compassionate community. His response to the discourses of antisemitism of his time offered an important model for an inclusive revelation of compassion that would embrace, rather than exclude, the Jew.

## Compassion as Active Love: Lipiner's *Der entfesselte Prometheus*

Already by the age of eighteen, Siegfried Lipiner had sealed his reputation as a gifted orator and voice of the Viennese Zeitgeist by drawing connections between secular philosophy, tragic art, and religious myth. As a leading voice in Vienna's spiritual awakening, he wrote poetry, speeches, and essays emphasizing the need for religious rebirth in the modern world. Despite his early successes, Lipiner has largely been forgotten in the history of German literature. One reason for this neglect lies in the relative scarcity of information on the poet's life and works; Lipiner left many of his writings unpublished and what remained of his literary estate was sold or destroyed when his family fled Austria in 1938. Although the correspondence and memoirs of mutual friends and contemporaries attest that composer Gustav Mahler sought the poet's counsel and looked up to him as a mentor, Lipiner has largely been relegated to a footnote in history and his creative oeuvre dismissed as derivative.[2] However, as this chapter reveals, Lipiner's engagement with key philosophical, theological, and cultural debates of the fin de siècle exerted a much wider impact on his generation than previously assumed.

Like many assimilated Jews of his generation, Lipiner came to Vienna as a youth to pursue the cultural ideal of Bildung (education and formation of character) with an almost religious zeal. Born Salomo Lipiner on October 24, 1856, to a Jewish family in Jarosław, Galicia, he moved in 1862 with his mother to the larger town of Tarnów before coming to Vienna in 1871. There he attended the Leopoldstädter Gymnasium in the second district with Sigmund Freud and completed his exams with distinction in 1875.[3] Lipiner's breakthrough work was an epic poem entitled *Der entfesselte Prometheus*, which was composed in 1876 and published that year with Breitkopf and Härtel in Leipzig.

*Prometheus* represents Lipiner's first attempt to articulate his vision of compassionate art. Drawing on classical forms of epic poetry, his poet-narrator is a mediator and conduit between the characters in the poem and the audience, urging them to embrace a spirit of compassion through struggle, striving, and self-overcoming. In his later dramatic works, Lipiner would abandon the narrator for the dramatic monologue. Yet, throughout his oeuvre, the poet employed forms of direct address as well as musical models to engage his public. *Der entfesselte Prometheus* is an epic poem consisting of five *Gesänge* (songs) with a prelude or *Vorgesang*. Lipiner's *Adam*, composed in rhythmic free verse, was intended for musical accompaniment by the poet's close friend, Gustav Mahler—a point that will be discussed in further detail in chapter 2.

In *Prometheus*, Lipiner claims compassion, the capacity of the individual to *feel with* the Other in solidarity with the Other's suffering, as the focal point of his vision for spiritual renewal in the modern world. Lipiner's poem picks up where the Greek myth leaves off—Prometheus is chained to a rock as punishment for having created humankind. In the opening canto, the Titan hero is freed from his imprisonment by the Fates and returns to the world where he observes the terror, hopelessness, and existential anguish of the human race that he created. Prometheus begins to doubt his ability to save them, when suddenly Christ appears to him with a crown of thorns on his head. In a dramatic struggle, Christ condemns Prometheus for his hubris in creating humanity.[4] He demands that the Titan prostrate himself before God. In this moment, Prometheus experiences an immense and overwhelming pain, which he identifies with the pain of the suffering Christ. Christ reveals to Prometheus that in order to redeem humanity he must learn compassion by taking their suffering upon himself. The final canto describes this compassionate act as an embrace of pain:

> Umschlingt den Schmerz, umschlingt ihn,
> Und nah und näher zieht
> Ihn bis an's Herz—dann stirbt er hin
> Und Tod und Hölle flieht.

> [Embrace the pain, embrace it,
> and pull it closer and closer
> Until it reaches your heart—then it dies
> And death and hell flee.][5]

The confrontation with Christ and acceptance of pain reflects a powerful reimagining of the relationship between the human and the divine as one of struggle and resolution in shared suffering. The unique synthesis of Christian and Greek myth in Lipiner's poem and his transformation of Promethean struggle as a journey toward compassionate understanding synthesized key images from the philosophies of Arthur Schopenhauer, Richard Wagner, and Friedrich Nietzsche. It is perhaps unsurprising that Nietzsche greatly admired Lipiner's poem, recognizing in it images that he had evoked in *Die Geburt der Tragödie aus dem Geiste der Musik* (The Birth of Tragedy Out of the Spirit of Music), originally published in 1872.[6] Upon receiving a copy of the text, Nietzsche wrote enthusiastically to his friend Erwin Rhode,

> wenn der Dichter nicht ein veritables "Genie" ist, so weiß ich nicht mehr, was eins ist: alles ist wunderbar, und mir ist als ob ich meinem erhöhten und verhimmlischten Selbst darin begegnete. Ich beuge mich tief vor einem, der so etwas in sich erleben und herausstellen kann.
>
> [when the poet is not a veritable "Genius," then I no longer know what one is: everything is wonderful and it is as though I encounter my own elevated and divine self in it. I bow deeply before one who can experience and create such a thing.][7]

With the widespread popularity of *Der entfesselte Prometheus* and the laudatory comments of Nietzsche, Lipiner achieved admiration and recognition in Viennese intellectual circles. The next several years would mark his dramatic rise and even more dramatic fall from grace. However, his brief moment in the sun would open the door for radical new visions of compassion and their articulations through music and biblical drama.

## "The Holiest Wonder": Compassion and Religious Spirit in Lipiner's *Über die Elemente einer Erneuerung religiöser Ideen in der Gegenwart*

The success of *Prometheus* propelled Lipiner to the center of intellectual life at the University of Vienna. In January 1878, he was invited to give a speech to the Leseverein der deutschen Studenten Wiens (Reading Society for German Students of Vienna) synthesizing the philosophical underpinnings of his theory of compassion, which he had expressed poetically in *Der entfesselte Prometheus*. In his speech, entitled *Über die Elemente einer Erneuerung religiöser Ideen in der Gegenwart* (On the Elements of a Renewal of Religious Ideas in the Present Time), Lipiner brings together the writings of Schopenhauer and Nietzsche with the libretto of Wagner's music drama *Parsifal* to propose tragic art as the cure for the problem of the modern fragmented self. Published by the Leseverein and reprinted in Vienna's German nationalist periodical, *Deutsche Zeitung*, Lipiner's speech proposed that only a revolutionary reawakening of religious feeling, inspired by the model of Christ's suffering, would pave the way for a new spiritual community.

In his speech, Lipiner makes his case for compassion by positioning himself as a fervent opponent of materialism and "scientific" understandings of religion, formulating a harsh critique of the empiricist philosophical tradition that dominated the intellectual debates at the University of Vienna at this time. For Lipiner, feeling (*Gefühl*) is the true spirit of religion that must be revived to overcome the modern crisis of faith. Feeling represents the very core of religion, while attempting to apprehend religion through rational explanation (*Vernunft*) leads only to its degeneration.[8] The primacy of feeling for Lipiner's understanding of religion in this opening statement suggests that his speech was likely directed at his professor Franz Brentano (1838–1917), who lectured at the University of Vienna from 1874–1880. Among Brentano's great achievements was his *Religionsphilosophie*, in which he attempted to ground his religious beliefs with methods of reasoning based in his study of theology, metaphysics, and positive science.[9] Brentano was a vocal opponent of Schopenhauer, who claimed that humans are driven not by reason but rather by an unseen, irrational force, known as the Will. Lipiner had already established himself as an authority on Schopenhauer among his peers with an essay, "Transzendente Spekulation über das Erhabene und das Tragische aus Schopenhauer'sche Principien" (Transcendental Speculation on the Sublime and the Tragic in Schopenhauer's Principles), composed in 1875.[10] He was also well versed in Friedrich Nietzsche's interpretation of Schopenhauer's philosophy and had presented a talk to the Leseverein on Nietzsche's 1876 essay "Schopenhauer als Erzieher" (Schopenhauer as Educator) from *Unzeitmäßige Betrachtungen* (Untimely Meditations) on April 28, 1877. Lipiner's audience, well informed of such debates, would have recognized that in his attempts to define the nature of humanity as essentially "religious" (beyond the phenomenal world), Lipiner was speaking in distinctly Schopenhauerian (and Kantian) terms. In so doing, Lipiner signaled his alliance with the tradition of German idealism against Austrian empiricism, a radical position among his contemporaries at the University of Vienna.[11]

Drawing on Schopenhauer's theories of compassion, Lipiner claimed that feeling, not reason, would lead humanity to rediscover its inner essence. In *Die Welt als Wille und Vorstellung*, Schopenhauer had asserted that human compassion springs from the fact that we are all part of one world Will, separated only by the *principium individuationis*, the illusionary perception of ourselves as individual and separate beings, as phenomena. We are able to feel compassion with others because we share this common substance.[12] According to Schopenhauer, only those who see through the principle of individuation can comprehend justice, because at that point the line of demarcation between subject and object and between the inflictor of suffering and the sufferer is dissolved: "der Quäler und der Gequälte sind eines" (the tormented and the tormentor are one).[13] In *Über die Grundlagen der Moral* (On the Basis of Morality, 1840), Schopenhauer elaborated on these ideas, claiming that compassion alone "ist die wirkliche Basis aller *freien* Gerechtigkeit und aller *echten* Menschenliebe" (is the real basis of all voluntary justice and all genuine loving-kindness).[14] At the center of Schopenhauer's vision of compassion is a longing for community. Compassionate emotion, he claims, inspires the individual to feel sympathy with the plight of another and to recognize in their suffering a common experience of humanity. It is this recognition of a shared essential substance that makes compassion the ethical basis of collective life.

In his speech to the Leseverein, Lipiner claimed that compassion, not the artificial trappings of dogma and theology, lay at the core of a true religious spirit. For this reason, the Bible should not be read as a historical document but rather as a source of the great myths of compassion:

> So lange eine Religion auf die historische Wahrheit ihrer kanonischen Schriften Werth legt, ist sie unwirksam und nichtig. Hell und leuchtend steht der nackte Kern da, wenn die modernen Fetzen von ihm gefallen sind. Der abgeschmackten und flachen physischen Wunder beraubt, flieht das Gemüth zum unvergänglichen Wunder, das nie die Pfeile der Wissenschaft zu fürchten hat, zum Wunder des heiligsten Mitleids, zum Wunder der Überwindung des Selbst.
>
> [As long as a religion places value in the historical truth of its canonical scripture, it is ineffective and void. Bright and glowing stands the naked core when the moldering tatters have fallen from it. Robbed of tasteless and insipid

> physical wonders, the soul flees to the undying wonder that never need fear the arrows of science, to the wonder of holiest compassion, to the wonder of self-overcoming.][15]

For Lipiner, myths of compassion, crystallized in tragic art, represent the "undying wonder" that sows the seeds for cultural renewal, for in the experience of tragic art individuality is dissolved, enabling the audience to perceive the essential truth behind appearances. In so doing, tragedy becomes a religious act:

> Die Tragödie ist Religion, und vor der tragischen Kunst wird der Mensch religiös. Denn in der tragischen Kunst sieht er sich selbst, wie er die Wirklichkeit vernichtet und als Erscheinung freudig vergeht—freudig, denn eben in diesem Vergehen und nur in ihm fühlt er, was nicht vergehen kann, und als Mensch dahinsterbend, fühlt er seine Auferstehung als Gott.
>
> [Tragedy is religion and in the presence of tragic art, man becomes religious. For in tragic art he sees himself, sees how he negates reality and as phenomenon joyfully passes away, and only in it does he feel what cannot pass away, and as a man dying away, he feels his resurrection as God.][16]

The reference to the individual's "resurrection as God," recalls both the Dionysian intoxication of Nietzsche's *Die Geburt der Tragödie* and Lipiner's own *Der entfesselte Prometheus.* As discussed in the previous section, the Titan of Lipiner's poem learns from Christ's compassionate self-sacrifice and is able to *feel with* suffering humanity, inspiring his own inner renewal and enabling a communal regeneration. Like Prometheus, who feels the pain of Christ as an open wound on his soul, Lipiner claims that tragic art reminds us of the "ewige Wunde des Menschen" (the eternal wound of humanity). In tragedy, pain and suffering are ultimately justified for, in recognizing the pain of others, we overcome our individuality and recognize in the Other the same eternal essence as exists in ourselves. Lipiner's description here echoes Schopenhauer's claim that compassion is the "great mystery of ethics" because it enables us not to feel our own pain but the Other's *as our own.* All difference is eliminated.[17]

Lipiner's references to the "wonder of holiest compassion" and the "eternal wound of humanity" form a bridge to the work that he holds up in this text as the ultimate synthesis of compassionate philosophy and tragic art, Wagner's music drama, *Parsifal.*[18] While the opera itself was not performed until 1881, the libretto was published in 1877, shortly before Lipiner's speech, and was widely discussed among the members of the Leseverein. In Wagner's music drama, Parsifal is a "pure fool," an orphan who stumbles upon the community of knights at Monsalvat who are entrusted with protecting the Holy Grail, the chalice used by Christ at the Last Supper, and the spear that pierced his side. In the beginning of the drama, the knights are in crisis and unable to perform the ritual of the Grail. Their leader, Titurel, has become too old and weak to officiate and his successor, Amfortas, has succumbed to the temptations of the flesh, a trap set for him by the sorcerer Klingsor. Wounded by the holy spear, Amfortas cannot complete the ritual because his wound bleeds at the sight of the sacred object. Only Parsifal, the pure fool, can redeem the knights of the Grail and restore the sacred ritual. Yet, he can only complete this task by learning compassion. At the climax of the dramatic action, Parsifal, like Amfortas before him, is seduced by the pagan temptress Kundry. In rejecting her kiss, he denies eros, erotic love, for caritas, compassionate love. In this moment, he feels a great pain that he associates with the wound of Amfortas and also with the suffering of the entire world. This experience of Mitleid enables Parsifal's transformation. In the triumphant conclusion, Parsifal returns to Monsalvat to redeem the knights. The chorus proclaims the final lines of the libretto, "Höchsten Heiles Wunder" (Highest Wonder of Salvation), as Parsifal lifts the chalice at the Last Supper, restoring the ritual of the Grail.

The reference to compassion as the "Heiles Wunder" echoes in Lipiner's speech, revealing the significance of Wagner's music drama for his conception of compassionate tragic art. By engaging the powerful language of music in *Parsifal*, Wagner had formed a bridge between Schopenhauer's ethics of compassion and his own principles of drama. By observing compassion (Mitleid) onstage, according to Wagner, the audience should be moved to sympathy (*Mitgefühl*), to identify with the tragic hero.[19] This feeling of sympathy would transform the audience, and with it the entire German *Volk*, to embrace a new sense of community.

Yet the conclusion of Lipiner's speech points toward his departure from the philosophy of Schopenhauer and the representation of compassion in Wagner's music drama. In his speech, Lipiner turns his focus to Kundry, the example of suffering humanity. She, not Parsifal, is the figure with whom the suffering individual identifies, for he recognizes in her his own "Schmerz, Angst, und Begier" (pain, anxiety, and desire).[20] Lipiner's lengthy quote from Kundry and Parsifal's meeting in the second act of Wagner's music drama points toward the centrality of the suffering figure for Lipiner's vision of compassionate art. Moreover, in his conclusion Lipiner suggests that the key to discovering compassion is not the ascetic *self-denial* described by

Schopenhauer and embodied in Wagner's protagonist Parsifal but rather the process of *self-overcoming.* In his speech to the Leseverein, Lipiner calls again upon the image of Promethean struggle that he had evoked in his epic poem, *Der entfesselte Prometheus.* Welcoming all to partake in the "tragic battle," he calls to all individuals to discover the divine within themselves through an embrace of pain and compassionate love:

> in diesem Glauben und in dieser Hoffnung werden wir die Liebe üben in schrankenloser Hingebung und in rastlosem Schaffen; und in dieser Liebe werden wir fühlen, wie das heisse Gebet um Glück erfüllt ist, und das Gebet selbst wird nur ein Bewusstwerden dieses Glückes sein, ein Bewusstwerden der Lust an unserem eigenen ewigen Wesen.
>
> [in this faith and in this hope we will practice love in boundless devotion and in tireless creativity; and in this love we will feel how the fervent prayer for happiness is fulfilled, and the prayer itself will be the becoming consciousness of this happiness, a becoming conscious of the desire in our own *eternal* being.][21]

Lipiner's speech ends with a powerful message of hope that rejects the pessimism of Schopenhauer's denial of the Will in favor of the affirmation of the creative spirit. Yet, at the time he gave the speech, the fissures between Lipiner and his idols were not yet apparent to his audience. Many believed that his new cultural religion, inspired by compassionate art, would fulfill the spiritual longings of their generation.

## Sympathy for the Sufferer: Lipiner contra Wagner and Schopenhauer

Lipiner's speech to the Leseverein sealed his reputation as Vienna's premiere interpreter of Schopenhauer's metaphysics of compassion and Wagner and Nietzsche's philosophies of tragic art. The text of the speech was published and widely distributed, eventually finding its way into the hands of Wagner, who extended an invitation to Lipiner to visit him at Villa Wahnfried in Bayreuth. The invitation further augmented the young poet's reputation, particularly as rumors circulated that he would become the next voice of Wagner's polemical journal, the *Bayreuther Blätter.* However, disagreements surrounding Lipiner's belief in the inclusive nature of compassion and in the role of tragic drama in achieving this ideal jeopardized this opportunity, perhaps permanently altering the trajectory of Lipiner's career. In a series of letters written to Malwida von Meysenbug in October 1878, Lipiner recounted in detail his visit with Wagner. Their correspondence reveals that Lipiner and Wagner engaged in a debate about art and social justice and the wider impacts of Schopenhauer's philosophy of compassion.[22] Lipiner's disagreement with Wagner on these issues eventually led him to articulate a more nuanced vision of compassionate art, which focuses on the suffering subject. Thus, Lipiner's visit to Bayreuth played a pivotal role in shaping the poet's concept for *Christus,* the tetralogy of biblical dramas in which he planned to realize his theory of compassion through tragic drama.

In a letter written a little over a week after his return from Bayreuth, Lipiner expressed his concerns to Meysenbug about a conversation he had had with Wagner about the mission of art. The subject of his critique was Wagner's tetralogy of music dramas, *The Ring of the Nibelungen.* Lipiner wrote to von Meysenbug:

> Wagner einmal sagte: "Was hat das Volk davon?" (Er sprach von den "Literaturgedichten"). Nun, ich frage: was hat das Volk von diesem volkstümlichsten aller deutschen Werke, von diesem Nibelungenring? Ich stelle in Abrede, dass, Das, das bis jetzt dem "Volk" von Wagner gesagt und offenbart wurde, irgendwie in nennenswerter Weise gewirkt hat.
>
> [Wagner at one point said, "What does the Volk know of that?" (He spoke of "literary poetry"). But I ask: what does the Volk know of this most popular of all German works, of this Ring of the Nibelung? I deny that, that which until now has been spoken of and revealed to the "Volk" has somehow, in a noteworthy way, taken effect.][23]

In his letter, Lipiner criticizes Wagner's *Ring* dramas for failing to enact the social change that had inspired their creation. Indeed, Wagner's first drafts of the dramatic tetralogy based on Old Norse and Germanic sagas dates to the revolutions of 1848, when the composer, inspired by the socialist and anarchist writings of Ludwig Feuerbach and Pierre-Joseph Proudhon, sought to inspire a cultural and political revolution through art.[24] Lipiner's reference to the Volk reveals his reference point to be Wagner's revolutionary writings, such as his 1849 essay *Das Kunstwerk der Zukunft* (The Artwork of the Future), in which Wagner describes the Volk as an ideal cultural community, the creator of the communal artwork.[25] The narrative of the *Ring* also reflects the composer's radical roots, presenting the fall of the gods and the promise of a new order based on love.

Lipiner endeavored to inspire a similar revolution in his own time. As a member of the Pernerstorfer Circle, one of the many intellectual societies in which he took part at the University of Vienna, Lipiner became close friends with Victor Adler, the later founder of the Social Democratic Workers Party in Vienna.[26] Lipiner's engagement with socialism is evident from his letters to Meysenbug, in which he reiterates his claims that art should be written for the most marginalized individuals. He also believed that art, by enabling compassionate understanding with the sufferer, could serve a transformative function. Lipiner's interest in these ideas, drawn from Wagner's early writings, reveals that he saw in his own contemporary situation a parallel to the revolutionary moment of 1848 and longed, like Wagner at that time, to find a resolution for social and political ills in the transcendent experience of art.

Given this particularly socialist imprint on his vision of compassion, Lipiner sought to engage Wagner in a discussion about how tragic art might depict suffering in such a way as to incite the compassionate response of the audience. In his letter to Meysenbug, Lipiner writes of tragic art, "Es muss dem Menschen *ad oculos* demonstriert werden, dass das Heil im Leiden und nicht im 'Wohlstande' liegt" (It must be made readily apparent to the Volk that salvation lies in suffering, not in wealth).[27] In his opinion, Wagner's *Ring* dramas had failed to provide a figure with whom the suffering Volk could identify.

Lipiner's radical vision of compassionate art sought to recapture the revolutionary spirit of Wagner's early writings and music dramas to inspire a religious and cultural rebirth. To do so, he conflated Wagner's socialist-anarchist and philosophical-religious worldviews, bringing together Wagner's essays on the revolutionary spirit of art, dating from the late 1840s, with the ideas from his later works, such as his 1870 essay *Beethoven*, which reflected the composer's later turn away from nationalist politics to a metaphysics of music, inspired by Schopenhauer's philosophy of pessimism.[28] This conflation is key to understanding Lipiner's reception of *Parsifal* as a potentially radical socialist work. While, for Wagner, *Parsifal* imagined an aesthetic-transcendent cultural unity to be achieved in music and the theater, Lipiner was still trying to imagine how this spiritual vision might produce true social transformation in his own time.[29]

Lipiner's attempt to convey his interpretation of Wagner's music dramas as insufficiently socialist was not well received. He claims to Meysenbug that Wagner dismissed his vision of socialist art as "flache Optimismus" (shallow optimism), an insult with clear anti-Jewish overtones.[30] In his essay "On Religion," Schopenhauer had claimed that the Jewish religion was defined by optimism and realism, and was thus incompatible with the transcendent, pessimistic, and idealistic nature of Buddhism and Christianity.[31] In her diary, Wagner's wife Cosima wrote her own account of the conversation between her husband and Lipiner, in which she claims that Wagner became angry with the young poet, telling him that socialism could only lead to destruction.[32] The only true solution, Wagner claimed, was to deny the will in a spirit of resignation, as he had illustrated in *Parsifal.*

Wagner and Lipiner's conversation, captured in these accounts, reveals the common roots but also the stark differences in their theories for the political and spiritual function of dramatic art. Lipiner sought to apply Schopenhauer's ideal of compassion to his own (socialist-inspired) vision of religious renewal, thus transforming the idea of resignation and denial of the will—a salvation to be found in an abstract, transcendent, metaphysical realm—into an active redemption, achieved through the struggle of "tireless creativity" that he had proclaimed in his *Prometheus* poem. Lipiner and Wagner also held different opinions on the significance and effect of experiencing compassion. As Ruth HaCohen has noted, a critical component of Wagnerian compassion is its focus not on the sufferer but rather on the individual who recognizes suffering in another. Thus, it is motivated not by the individual object (or the prompting to relieve that object's suffering) but rather by the recognition of suffering as an abstract category and philosophical ideal. HaCohen identifies this shift away from the suffering object and toward the subject who *feels with* them as a strategy of "elevating the compassionate while diminishing those who deserve compassion."[33] For Lipiner, on the other hand, the experience of the suffering individual *as subject* held primary importance. In order for drama to serve an ethical function, he concluded, the audience must be drawn to sympathize with the plight of the sufferer.

## Lipiner's "Wagnerian Trauma"

In the years following his visit in Bayreuth, Lipiner continued to develop his vision of compassionate art, fervently attempting to retain his place as the heir to Wagner's cultural legacy in Vienna. Adopting a strategy of self-promotion, borrowed from Wagner, Lipiner found his ersatz *Bayreuther Blätter* in the feuilleton page of the *Deutsche Zeitung*, where he published cultural commentaries to promote his own artistic and philosophical agenda.[34] He also turned his own creative output from poetry to tragic drama and even wrote an opera libretto. Finally, he created his own circle of artists and intellectuals in Vienna to further proliferate his artistic vision. Lipiner's writings from this period reveal, however, his difficulty in defining his own language; he even adopted for a time antisemitic stereotypes of Jews in his writings.[35] Lipiner's attempt to create a cohesive philosophical and aesthetic framework for his artistic vision might reflect a kind of "Wagnerian Trauma." In his work, Michael Steinberg uses this term to refer specifically to the crisis of musical integrity that resulted from Wagner's mobilization of ideology in the opera.[36] Following Assaf Shelleg, I also read this "trauma" in terms of the larger impact of Wagner's specific anti-Jewish ideology and the struggles of Jewish artists to reconcile the revolutionary potential of his music with the exclusionary nature of its message.[37] This period of crisis in Lipiner's development as an artist eventually led him to reformulate his idea of compassionate art through the voice of the Jewish subject.

After his departure from Bayreuth, Lipiner returned to Vienna to establish a circle of like-minded artists whom he hoped would help spread his ideas to the wider public. In 1880, he formed the Sagengeselleschaft (Saga Society) with the young composer Gustav Mahler and poet Richard von Kralik, both member of the Pernerstorfer Circle at the University of Vienna.[38] The goal of the society was, according to von Kralik, "so zu leben und zu denken und zu arbeiten in Mythen, in Göttern, und Helden" (to live, think and work in myths, gods and heroes).[39] Among the group's activities were the readings of myths and legends, such as the *Nibelungenlied*, *Gudrun*, and the *Edda*.[40]

Lipiner used the Saga Society as an opportunity to promote his own works, which in the period between 1880 and 1890 shifted from epic poetry to drama. At one session, Lipiner read aloud from an opera libretto he had written for the composer Carl Goldmark, *Merlin* (1881). *Merlin* was undoubtedly Lipiner's greatest success from this period. Its performance at the Vienna Court Opera in 1886 received largely favorable reviews, notably by the music critic Eduard Hanslick. However, there were still vocal detractors who dismissed the text as a poor attempt to imitate Wagner's style. In *Die Presse*, Max Kalbeck wrote that the work was too dependent on Wagner's language, claiming that it borrowed almost to the word from *Der Ring der Nibelungen*, *Tristan*, and *Parsifal* "ohne von dessen im Theaterhandwerk erprobter Routine etwas zu profitieren" (without profiting from the tried and true routine of their theatrical handiwork).[41] Robert Hirschfeld, a notable antisemite, who was also one of the most outspoken critics of Gustav

Mahler, acknowledged the public's warm response to the performance but claimed the second act's duet between Merlin and Viviane was a poor imitation of Tristan and Isolde's *Liebestod*.[42]

Lipiner's Saga Society was likewise not entirely free from Wagner's influence. In 1880, the same year the group was founded, Wagner published his treatise *Religion und Kunst* (Religion and Art) as the theoretical companion to his music drama *Parsifal*. The opening lines of this essay, interestingly, echo Lipiner's own critiques of religion found in his speech to the Leseverein, proclaiming the denigration of spirituality by dogmatism and the belief that art will revive religion through myth.[43] In his essay, Wagner expanded on this vision of redemption by promoting vegetarianism as a means of cleansing the body to promote inner regeneration and as a gesture of respect toward the shared inner substance with animals. It is significant that Wagner's arguments for vegetarianism are deeply intertwined with antisemitic stereotypes of Jewish cruelty to animals, an idea that he adopted from Schopenhauer and interpreted as another sign of a Jewish lack of compassion.[44] That Lipiner and his friends (many of them Jews) so enthusiastically embraced this text, reflects both the continued influence of Wagner's writings in Vienna at this time and the increasing acceptance of Wagner's pseudotheological antisemitism.[45]

Schopenhauer and Wagner's stereotypes of the Jewish people as uncompassionate, immutable, and beholden to the Law made their way into Lipiner's cultural essays, composed at this same time. After he failed to publish in the *Bayreuther Blätter*, Lipiner earned a coveted role as a regular feuilleton writer for the Viennese newspaper, the *Deutsche Zeitung*.[46] Between December 1880 and July 1881, Lipiner published seventeen essays, primarily reflections on the works of prominent past and present cultural figures, including Adalbert von Chamisso, Henrik Ibsen, Gottfried Keller, Friedrich Hölderlin, and Immanuel Kant. As with his essays intended for the *Bayreuther Blätter*, Lipiner used his profiles of other authors and their works to highlight his larger philosophical and aesthetic vision. While many of these essays elaborate on ideas that he had laid out in his speech to the Leseverein, they also co-opt the language of antisemitism. For example, in the essay entitled "Weihnachten" (Christmas), which appeared on December 19, 1880, Lipiner presents a vision of compassion in opposition to the Law (das Gesetz). Lipiner associates das Gesetz with rabbinic law, which he identifies with the hypocrisy of Jewish "philistines." Compassion, he claims, must transcend this "Sklaverei der Morale" (slavery of morals) and replace it with a new compassionate Law of Love, embodied in the figure of Christ.[47] He explains his vision with a short anecdote from the Gospel of John, when Jesus forgives the sinning woman who washes his feet and condemns the priests for their hypocrisy in judging her. Similar condemnations of the Jewish religion appear in a later essay, "Einiges über Verbrechen und Strafe" (A Few Comments on Crime and Punishment) in which Lipiner describes the "Jewish God" as one who only wishes "rächen und strafen und dreinschlagen" (to avenge, punish and strike down).[48] Lipiner's description of the tyrannical God echoes Wagner's *Religion und Kunst* in which he describes the Jewish creator as "the wrathful God of Punishment."[49] Lipiner's adoption of such stereotypes of the Jewish religion appear as an internalization of what Shelleg calls the "doctrine of aversion" nourished by the exclusionary nature of anti-Jewish rhetoric.[50]

Lipiner's realization that he might never emerge from his idol's shadow coincided with a growing shift in antisemitism in Vienna, which began to impact Lipiner on a personal level.[51] In 1885, he revealed his frustration privately to the journalist Moritz Necker, encouraging his friend to convert in order to free himself from his "verfluchtes Judentum" (accursed Judaism). Lipiner's comments to Necker, "sei es in Salzburg oder in Wien oder wo immer, ist deine scheußliche 'Confessions'-rubrik verhängnisvoll" (be it in Salzburg, Vienna, or wherever else, your cursed 'Confessions rubric' is ill-fated), suggest that antisemitic attacks were becoming more prevalent at this time.[52] Lipiner withdrew from the Viennese *Israelitische Kultusgemeinde*, the Jewish community, that same year.[53] In his letter to Necker, Lipiner refers to Jewishness as a "Confessions-rubrik," a socially constructed category disconnected from his own sense of spirituality. A short time later, after his dalliances with nationalism, socialism, and antisemitism, Lipiner began to articulate a new vision of compassionate art that would address the problem of religious difference. Responding to the aesthetic and metaphysical frameworks established by Schopenhauer and Wagner, Lipiner sought to assert his own vision of universal redemption regardless of creed or cultural background, which would inspire compassion for the Jewish subject.

Lipiner's desire for cultural renewal through compassion become the guiding force of the project he began a short time later, the *Christus* tetralogy. Designed to be performed over four consecutive nights, like Wagner's *Ring of the Nibelung*, Lipiner's drama nonetheless marks a break from his "traumatic" attempts to recast himself as Wagner's successor in the immediate post-Bayreuth years. In turning to the Bible, Lipiner not only affirms his belief in these sacred texts as a source of powerful religious myths that might redeem society; he also precisely identifies a systemic crisis in Christianity that had served as the basis for both Schopenhauer's ethics and Wagner's aesthetics of compassion: the discourse of Jewish Otherness. In *Adam*, the first play in the cycle, Lipiner's focus on Cain's suffering gives voice to the plight of the Jew. In so doing, he sought to pave the way for a new religious spirit that would absolve difference through loving compassion.

## The Tragedy of Difference—Lipiner's *Adam*

From the early 1890s until his death in 1911, Lipiner worked almost exclusively on *Christus*. Sources claim that although he twice finished the complete cycle, both times he destroyed his drafts and began again.[54] Lipiner's *Christus* begins with a prelude, *Adam*, and is followed by *Maria Magdalena*, *Judas Ischariot*, and a final work, referenced in some drafts as *Ahasver*, and in others as *Paul in Rom*. In 1899, Lipiner finally completed a draft of *Adam* that he shared with Mahler and their circle of friends. At the time of his death, multiple fragments of the second drama, *Maria Magdalena*, remained, as well as two versions of *Judas Ischariot*.[55]

*Adam*, a dramatic revision of the story of Cain and Abel, reveals that, to fashion his vision of religious renewal, Lipiner felt compelled to grapple with the legacy of Judaism and the social constructs of religion and cultural difference. Cain and his brother Abel articulate two sides of Lipiner's own German-Jewish subjectivity, the creative and perceptive artist-creator, Abel, and Cain, the Jew who is an outsider and tragic inheritor of the failures of dogmatic religion. The play's open-ended conclusion confronts the audience with the injustice of Cain's suffering, forcing a sympathetic engagement with the plight of the Jewish subject.

Lipiner's *Adam* elaborates on the biblical narrative from Genesis 4:1–16 by imagining the story of brotherly discord as a generational conflict in which Cain and Abel must grapple with the legacy of their parents' (Adam and Eve's) sin of eating the fruit of the tree of knowledge, recorded in Genesis 3. To grant the biblical myth modern resonance and to draw attention to discourses of Jewish Otherness in his own time, Lipiner casts Cain as the embodiment of contemporary anti-Jewish stereotypes. This dynamic serves a dual purpose: first, it brings to light the very arbitrary nature of the difference between the two brothers, and, second, it sheds light on the injustice faced by Cain, creating out of one of the most maligned figures in the Hebrew Scriptures a sympathetic character worthy of compassion.

Cain's dramatic monologues, marked by their expressive nature and dissonant language, shed further light on the character's inner struggle, compelling the audience to reconsider the ways in which anti-Jewish rhetoric breeds hatred and violence. By picking up on key motives from Wagner's music drama, *Parsifal*, Lipiner makes clear his goal, to reclaim compassion through the voice of the Jewish subject.[56]

The typology of the Jew manifests in Cain's strict adherence to his duties (*Pflichte*) prescribed to him by his father and the Lord's commands (*Gebote*) and by his inability to feel compassion. It also reveals itself on physical and linguistic levels in his deformed body and dissonant speech. While such stereotypical images of the Jew were widespread in Lipiner's time, Cain appears to be drawn directly from Schopenhauer's description of Judaism and the Jew in his essay, "On Religion." In this text, Schopenhauer differentiates Jews and Christians by their relative ability (or inability) to be compassionate, a trait that manifests itself primarily in their relationship to animals. In his account, Schopenhauer identifies Jews as the primary practitioners of animal sacrifice and claims that they commit this unconscionable act because they do not recognize animals as part of the one world Will, and therefore they are incapable of compassion.[57]

Accordingly, in Lipiner's *Adam*, Cain refuses to come into contact with animals because the Law has declared them unclean. He feels no sympathy with the suffering of animals, and, when Abel returns home followed by two animal companions, an eagle and a wolf, Cain chastises his brother:

> So sprach der Vater: Scheut euch vor den Tieren! Geschieden hat der Ew'ge sie und euch! Stumm sind sie, taub,— und fremd ist ihrer Art das Wort, darin der Geist sich offenbart. Blind sind sie: durch ihr Aug' blickt nicht der Geist . . . Fühlsam, ohne Seele, Regsam, nicht lebend, Blättern gleich im Wind, hintreiben sie, wohin der Trieb sie reißt . . . sie kennen nicht den Herrn und sein Gebot, sie wissen nicht, was Bös und Gut.
>
> [Thus spoke the father: avoid animals! The Eternal has divided you from them! They are mute, deaf—and the word in which the spirit reveals itself is foreign to their way. They are blind, through their eyes the spirit does not shine . . . feeling—without a soul, active—not living, like leaves in the wind, they are driven wherever their desire pulls them . . . they know not the Father and his Law, they do not know what is evil and what is good.][58]

Rather than feeling a connection to these animals, and to the instinct, or *Trieb*, within himself, Cain claims: "Ich habe ausgetilgt die Sünd' aus meinem Blut, und ausgetan das Tier aus meinem Leibe" (I have wiped out the sin from my blood, and driven the animal from my body).[59] In this way,

Cain embodies the supposedly Jewish disconnection from animals, which according to Schopenhauer marks his incapacity for compassion.

Lipiner's Cain not only embodies the stunted morality of Schopenhauer's typology of the Jew but also recalls the antisemitic tropes of the Jews' language and body popularized by Wagner's essay *Das Judentum in der Musik*. In this essay, Wagner describes the Jewish mode of speech as dissonant and unmusical, "Eines unerträglich verwirrten Geplappers" (an intolerably jumbled blabber). Aesthetically displeasing language corresponds, moreover, with emotional incapacity. Wagner describes the Jew as incapable of a "gemeinsamen Austausche der Empfindungen" (mutual interchange of feelings).[60] For Wagner, the Jews' deformed language is evidence of their lack of a shared substance or common spirit with the rest of humanity.[61] Lipiner strategically adopts elements of Wagner's portrayal of Jews in his descriptions of Cain's appearance and mode of speech. When, at the moment of the murder, Cain tries to tell Abel that he loves him, Abel remarks, "Wie deine Rede klingt! Seltsam! Und wie dein Mund sich zwingt" (How your speech sounds! How strange! And how your mouth forces itself).[62] Cain's words are identified as disingenuous by their sound—they have a false ring. Moreover, when Abel cries out: "Wie er sich bückt! Wie er die Lippen regt! . . . Grauenhaft verzogen der bebende Mund" (How he stoops down! How his lips are animated . . . the quivering mouth is gruesomely distorted), his description of the movement of Cain's mouth is anthropomorphic, as though it had a mind of its own, bursting out words of hate even as he tries to hold it back.[63] Ultimately, Cain is unable to repress his physical compulsions, and, in a fury, he strikes his brother down and kills him. Yet, Cain's inability to recognize Abel as his brother is motivated, Lipiner implies, by the fact that in his own heart, he sees only the capacity for violence that has been passed down to him by the Law.

While this scene, taken on its own, appears to affirm contemporary antisemitic stereotypes, Lipiner's depiction of Cain is in fact much more complex, revealing the author's deep ambivalence toward these typologies of the Jew and his determination to create a theatrical work that would produce compassion more effectively than Wagner's *Parsifal*. By laying bare Cain's psychological suffering, Lipiner in fact carves out a new role for the modern assimilated Jew who wishes to embody the new religious spirit that Lipiner had defined in his essay to the Leseverein. Therefore, it is not Cain's murder of Abel that serves as the focal point of Lipiner's ethical argument but rather the struggle of the Jew to overcome the antisemitic stereotypes of

Jewish immutability and submission to the Law and the arbitrary nature of discourses of difference.

To do so, Lipiner must articulate the source of this difference: their father, Adam. It is the father's "arbitrariness of preference" that shatters the unity and innocence of the brotherly bond, introducing difference into the primal myth of humanity.[64] In Lipiner's rendition of the biblical story, Cain's murder of Abel is not spurred on by the fact that the Lord prefers Abel's offering but rather by Adam's differential treatment of his sons. Adam is lenient with Abel, whom he sees as embodying a naïveté that he also possessed before eating from the tree of knowledge. Yet despite Cain's obedience to the Law, Adam rules over him with a heavy hand. Moreover, Cain is aware of his father's preference and questions it openly. When Adam demands that Cain prepare a sacrifice while allowing Abel to wander free, Cain remarks bitterly: "Warum darf ich nicht tun, wie er? Was legst du deine Hand auf mich so schwer? Bin ich nicht rein, gleich wie der reine Tag?" (Why may I not do as he does? Why do you lay your hand so heavily upon me? Am I not pure, just as the pure day?).[65] Later, when Adam attempts to warn Cain that he may one day be unable to hold his passions in check: "Hab' acht der ungetanten Sünden! Hab' acht, was nächtlich dir dein Herz vertraut" (Beware the undone sin! Beware what your heart confides in you at night!), Cain, who knows of his father's own transgressions of the Lord's commands, points out the very hypocrisy of this statement with the retort, "Bist du's von dem du sprichst?" (Are you speaking about yourself?).[66] In enforcing difference between his sons, and by arbitrarily denying compassion to Cain, Adam serves as the instigator for his sons' tragedy.

Lipiner further undermines the stereotype of Cain as the uncompassionate Jew by reimagining the murderer as the tragic antihero, the agent who challenges his father's unequal treatment. The father's arbitrary preference is institutionalized in the Lord's commands, to which Cain feels morally and psychically bound, yet which he also longs to escape.[67] The emphasis on Cain's subjectivity is evident by the fact that he is the primary self-reflective character in the work. In the opening to Act II, Cain pleads with his mother for compassion and reproaches his father for his selective treatment. His innocence and vulnerability before his mother, Eve, reveal his desire for her compassionate love.[68] He asks of her:

Und wenn wir Knaben,—den schon lang' ist's her,—
Herzig-einig sprachen: nie mit solcher Macht

War Lieb in uns, als wenn wir dein gedacht . . .
Liebst du mich, Mutter? liebst du Cain auch,
Nicht Abel bloß?

[And when we were young boys—such a long time ago
Speaking from a heart that was one, never with such force
There was love in us, as when we thought ourselves yours . . .
Do you love me, mother? Do you love Cain
and not just Abel?][69]

Cain's plea reveals his yearning for their lost childhood, when he and Abel cared for one another through a love passed down to them by their mother's warm embrace. His vulnerability in this scene provides a sharp contrast to his caustic reproach of his father's unjust treatment in the previous scenes and reveals the suffering figure's depth of character.

While Cain's dialogues draw attention to his outsider status in the context of the other characters, Lipiner seeks to provoke further compassion for Cain by unveiling his inner conflict between the desire for vengeance and his longing for love, acceptance, and compassion. Lipiner constructs these monologues through a dissonant stream of consciousness that reflects rapid shifts in perspective and the degeneration of coherent syntax. A telling example is found in the second act, when Adam attempts to rectify the damage he has done by proclaiming to his son a new law, to love his brother as himself.[70] Cain's struggle finds expression in a chaotic burst of conflicting emotions:

Du sollst ihn lieben, sollst! Sollst lieben!
Ein neu Gebot—aber ich will nicht! nein!
Könnt' ich's? . . .
Ihn lieben, wie mich selbst—: Ich aber hasse
mich selbst—und wie mich selbst, so hass' ich ihn! . . .
Ja, ich will, ich soll, Will lieben, lieb' ihn, hab' ihn nie gehaßt—
Hör' es, du Gott!

[You should love him, should! Should love!
A new Law—but I don't want to! No!
Could I? . . .
Love him, as myself—: But I hate
myself—and as myself, so do I hate him! . . .
Yes, I will, I should, will love,
love him, have never hated him—
Hear it, o God!][71]

In this monologue, Lipiner co-opts the broken language of the stereotypical unmusical Jew as an emotional form of speech, intended to provoke a powerful response of sympathy from the audience. Cain's broken language is the physical manifestation of the same conflict facing his father, Adam; the pull between instinct and feeling, and subservience to the old Law. In translating the outer conflict with the Law into Cain's broken speech, Lipiner encourages sympathy with his plight, revealing him to be a victim of arbitrary categories of difference, a suffering subject worthy of redemption.

In its conclusion, *Adam* enacts the first stage of Lipiner's revolutionary vision of religion that he had outlined in his speech to the Leseverein: the overthrow of the old moral code so that a new compassionate spirit might be reborn. In his speech, Lipiner claimed: "Und muss ich etwas von der heiligen Dreifaltigkeit opfern, so opefere ich gern den Gott-Vater und den heiligen Geist, den Gott-Sohn aber opfere ich nicht" (if I must sacrifice something from the Holy Trinity, I would gladly sacrifice the god-father and the Holy Spirit, but the god-son, I would not sacrifice).[72] Therefore, Adam, the father figure who represents the antisemitic stereotype of Jehovah as the "God of vengeance" and the discourse of difference that the Law engendered, must be sacrificed. In the final act of the play, Adam seeks to avenge Abel's death. However, as he attempts to strike down Cain for his deeds, wild animals emerge from the wilderness and attack and kill him. With Adam's death, the Law that held Cain captive is finally broken. The play ends with the fate of Cain hanging in the balance. His final monologue leaves the audience with the voice of the suffering Jewish subject ringing in their ears:

> Schwer trag ich's, schwer.
> und keine Hand, die's von mir nimmt?
> Niemand im Himmel? Niemand auf der Erde?
> Niemand—Niemand—
>
> [With difficulty, I carry (my sin), with difficulty.
> And no hand that will take it from me?
> No one in heaven? No one on earth?
> No one—No one—][73]

At the end of *Adam*, Lipiner grants Cain the final word, allowing him to voice the plea for a new ethical society. By laying bare his soul, Lipiner encourages sympathy with this suffering subject, casting doubt on Schopenhauer and Wagner's denigration of the Jewish subject as incapable of compassion.

## The Compassionate Übermensch—Lipiner's Revision of Nietzsche

In the following episodes of the *Christus* tetralogy, Lipiner had intended for the coming of Christ to usher in a new era of compassionate understanding. Although he was unable to complete the final three plays, *Mary Magdalene*, *Judas Iscariot*, and *Paul in Rome*, Lipiner's *Adam*, lays the groundwork for the emergence of a new model for religious rebirth: the compassionate Übermensch, Abel. The characterization of Abel in this text as a counterpart to Friedrich Nietzsche's prophet, Zarathustra, suggests that Lipiner intended to use this figure in response to Schopenhauer and Wagner's mobilization of Jewish difference. To do so, however, Lipiner radically revises Nietzsche's antimetaphysical stance. In his collection of aphorisms, *Die fröhliche Wissenschaft* (The Joyful Science), first published in 1880, and philosophical novel, *Also sprach Zarathustra,* composed between 1883 and 1886, Nietzsche had proclaimed the death of God and critiqued compassion as superficial and manipulative. However, in *Adam*, Lipiner claims the Übermensch as a figure uniquely capable of feeling with the suffering of others and of inspiring a new community of compassionate understanding.

To understand how Lipiner developed this unorthodox reading of Nietzsche's works, it is helpful to look back to the early interactions between the young poet and the philosopher. Lipiner first came into contact with Nietzsche's writings as a student at the Leopoldstädter Gymnasium in Vienna in the early 1870s and quickly established himself as an authority on the philosopher's works. As previously discussed, Lipiner admired Nietzsche's dissertation, *Die Geburt der Tragödie*, which inspired his poem *Der enfesselte Prometheus.* Moreover, Nietzsche's description of Dionysian *Rausch*, or intoxication, and the merging of subject and object, audience and performer in this text appear in Lipiner's 1878 speech to the Leseverein as the foundations of compassionate art. The admiration was not entirely one-sided, either. While they never met personally, Lipiner and Nietzsche carried on a correspondence and exchanged manuscripts with each other. Although Nietzsche expressed aversion to Lipiner's preoccupation with religion, he followed Lipiner's career from a distance and perhaps was even influenced by his poetic forms.[74] Lipiner was initially highly critical of Nietzsche's break with Wagner, writing to the philosopher a thirty-two-page letter critiquing his work *Menschliches Allzumenschliches.*[75] However, he appears to have returned to the philosopher in the early 1890s, in particular to the novel, *Also sprach Zarathustra*, as he began to write his *Christus* tetralogy. In the prelude, *Adam*, Lipiner envisions the Übermensch as a new model of compassion and of the overcoming of false dualisms. The Übermensch does not, for Lipiner, proclaim the death of God but rather the death of the Law, the marker of difference. By bringing down the Law, the Übermensch paves the way for a compassionate society based on love, in which all beings, even the Jew, would be welcome.

Lipiner's incorporation of the Übermensch into his vision for the rebirth of religious spirit based on compassionate love was likely grounded in Nietzsche's writings on the Christian religion and his evolving concept of the Dionysian. Lipiner's return to Nietzsche occurred at a moment as the poet was coming to an increased awareness of the challenges that his Jewish identity posed for him as an artist. Thus, he may have found in Nietzsche's criticism of Christianity a language for countering the hypocrisy of religious antisemitism. In aphorism 99 of *Die fröhliche Wissenschaft*, Nietzsche gave a withering critique of such language in Wagner's writings, remarking: "Schopenhauerisch ist Wagner's Hass gegen die Juden, denen er selbst in ihrer grössten That nicht gerecht zu werden vermag: die Juden sind ja die Erfinder des Christenthums" (Wagner is Schopenhauerian in his hatred of the Jews, to whom he is unable to do justice even in their greatest deed; after all, the Jews are the inventors of Christianity).[76] In his fragment, Nietzsche calls for the "disciples" of Wagner to remain true to his original spirit and not to be led astray by Schopenhauer's anti-Jewish rhetoric.

It must be noted that Nietzsche also employed antisemitic and anti-Jewish stereotypes throughout his works—why, then, would Lipiner turn to his philosophy while rejecting Wagner and Schopenhauer on the same grounds?[77] Clues to Lipiner's contradictory reading of Nietzsche may be found in the philosopher's highly ambivalent comments on Jews and Judaism in his later works, such as *Zur Geneologie der Morale* (On the Genealogy of Morality 1887).[78] In this essay, Nietzsche condemned "priestly Jews," while also imagining the Jews as a whole as a source of untapped potential, capable of self-overcoming and overthrowing their "slave morality." [79] Such constructions of Jewish Otherness are highly problematic, yet the idea of self-transformation, at its core, finds a degree of resonance in Lipiner's vision of redemption through active striving. Seeking a language to express his own break the Schopenhauer and Wagner, and in particular their arguments for the fixed and immutable nature of the Jews, Lipiner found in

Nietzsche's characterization of the dynamic Jewish nature powerful imagery for his vision of cultural rebirth.

The spirit of tenacity and self-transformation that Nietzsche attributes to the Jewish people also finds resonance in the spirit of the Dionysian. As previously discussed, the idea of Dionysian intoxication, the merging of self and Other, described in *Die Geburt der Tragödie* was a critical component of Lipiner's theorization of compassion. Yet after Nietzsche's break with Schopenhauer and Wagner's metaphysics and rejection of a God-centered universe, his concept of the Dionysian transformed. No longer merely one side of a dual nature, balanced by its complementary force, Apollonian clarity, the Dionysian in Nietzsche's later writings balances and masters itself.[80] The Übermensch, through the Will to Power, channels this spirit of self-mastery as a creative force.[81] While Lipiner was not willing to completely dispense with the idea of the loving God, he did believe that through the spirit of self-overcoming, all beings could come closer to the divine. In this way, the Übermensch could inspire, in Lipiner's mind, a new religious community to counter the isolation, individuation, and suffering of the modern world.

In Lipiner's *Adam*, the figure of Abel serves as the first iteration of the compassionate Übermensch, who would reappear in the later episodes of the cycle in the form of Christ. That Abel was intended as a parallel to Nietzsche's Übermensch, Zarathustra, is evident in his relationship to nature and, in particular, animals. While Zarathustra appears in Nietzsche's novel with an eagle and a serpent, Abel is followed home from the wilderness by a wolf and an eagle. Moreover, his embodiment of a Dionysian spirit of community and oneness with nature finds expression in the first act, when he wanders into the wilderness and partakes in a raucous dance with the animals.[82] However, there are also key differences. Abel is a shepherd, yet, unlike the shepherd of Nietzsche's Zarathustra who bites off the head of the serpent and spits it out, initiating his transformation from man to Übermensch, Lipiner's Abel struggles with the violent pull of instinct. For Nietzsche, the serpent becomes an image of Eternal Recurrence and affirmation of the Earth, an acceptance of the circularity of time and the cycle of life and death. However, Lipiner's Abel is deeply disturbed by the violence of human nature. When he stumbles upon the Garden of Eden, Abel also has a vision of a serpent, but here it is devouring an innocent bird.[83] This powerful image inspires Abel's prayer to God for compassion, in which he asks, "muss Eins durchs Andere sterben?" (must one die by another?).[84]

Abel's prayer parallels Cain's appeal to God at the end of the play—how do we live in a world marked by suffering and death? Is there any hope for redemption?

In his plans for the continuation of the biblical tetralogy, Lipiner intended to introduce Christ as the new incarnation of the compassionate Übermensch, tracing his interactions with the most maligned figures found in Christian biblical accounts—Mary Magdalene, Judas Ischariot, and Paul (originally the violent persecutor of Christians, Saul). While he was unable to complete this project, Lipiner's vision of compassionate art found resonance in the symphony works of his friend and intellectual protégé, the composer Gustav Mahler. In Mahler's interpretation, the compassionate Übermensch transforms the Will to Power into the Will to Love. Love, understood as the recognition of the shared substance of all beings and willingness to feel compassion for others, is ultimately the key to the rebirth of religious spirit that both poet and composer envisioned.

## Conclusion

Lipiner's *Adam* was read and discussed in intellectual circles in Vienna, yet the poet refused to publish it in his lifetime. The philosopher Paul Natorp, Lipiner's good friend who served as executor of his literary estate, finally arranged for its publication in 1913, two years after the poet's death. It received its first and only known performance at the Albert-Theater in Dresden on November 14, 1915. (See fig. 1.1.) The character of Cain, performed by a young, at the time unknown, actor, Ernst Deutsch, was considered the highlight of the afternoon event.[85] In his essay on the performance, Natorp praises Deutsch for his ability to bring Cain's "inner wretchedness" to full "outer expression" in the fratricidal act. Indeed, the shrill voice, nervous energy, and twitching, twisted body that Lipiner called for in his characterization of Cain resonated with the figures of Expressionist theater that Deutsch would come to epitomize in his long career on the stage and screen.[86] This anecdote of the first performance offers one of the few glimpses into how Lipiner's dramas might have been received and interpreted on stage. Moreover, *Adam*'s affinities with Expressionist theater suggest that Lipiner's philosophical program and its dramatic realization were remarkably forward looking for his time.

Lipiner's attempt to establish a framework for Schopenhauer, Wagner, and Nietzsche's ideas through the lens of compassion were highly

Sonntag den 14. November 1915

**Aufführung des Albert-Theaters Dresden**

Direktion: Edgar Licho

# Adam

Vorspiel in 3 Akten von **Siegfried Lipiner.**

Spielleitung: **Dr. Max Alberty.**

Personen:

| | |
|---|---|
| Adam . . . . . . . . . . . . . . . . . | Max Alberty |
| Eva . . . . . . . . . . . . . . . . . | Fanny Ritter |
| Kain . . . . . . . . . . . . . . . . . | Ernst Deutsch |
| Abel . . . . . . . . . . . . . . . . . | Günther Hadank |

**Nach dem zweiten Akt findet eine Pause statt.**

Anfang 11½ Uhr. Ende 1½ Uhr.

**Preis des Programmes 20 Pfg.**

Figure 1.1. Poster for the premiere of *Adam* in Dresden, November 14, 1915. Universitätsbibliothek Marburg, Nachlass Paul Natorp.

contradictory, yet his writings capture the profound influence of these philosophies at the turn of the century and the desire to transform these models and find language and form for their program of cultural renewal. Lipiner led this charge by probing the fissures between Schopenhauer and Wagner's redemptive claims and exclusionary rhetoric. Modeling his biblical drama on their writings and music dramas, Lipiner also undermined the antisemitic typologies in their vision of compassion by evoking sympathy for the Jewish subject. Exposing the psychological repercussions of excluding the Jewish subject from narratives of compassionate redemption, Lipiner confronted deep-seated anxieties surrounding the figure of the Jew at the turn of the century and offered a new model for the German-Jewish subject to embody the transformative potential of the Übermensch as compassionate spirit.

Siegfried Lipiner believed that compassion could unite society by acknowledging the universal nature of suffering and encouraging sympathy for the Other, dissolving differences between individuals. As the following chapters reveal, his writings opened the door for later revisions of the philosophy and aesthetics of compassion and offered new models of compassionate art for Mahler, Schoenberg, Beer-Hofmann, and Zweig, in which biblical myth would be mobilized to give voice to the suffering Jewish subject and to shape empowering visions of collective spiritual renewal.

## Notes

1. Wagner's essay *Das Judentum in der Musik* was originally published under a pseudonym in the *Neue Zeitschrift für Musik* in 1850. Wagner published the piece again in 1869 in an expanded form under his own name. Fischer, *Das Judentum in der Musik*, 89.

2. Exceptions include William J. McGrath (*Dionysian Art and Populist Politics*), Constantin Floros (*Gustav Mahler*), Carl Niekerk (*Reading Mahler*), and Stephen Hefling ("Siegfried Lipiners 'Über die Elemente'"), who have undertaken in-depth analyses of Lipiner's works and their influence on Mahler.

3. Lipiner and Freud published a journal together during their time at the Leopoldstädter Gymnasium. Although intrigued by Lipiner's idealism, Freud was skeptical of the poet's metaphysical leanings and even critiqued an essay by Lipiner on teleology, which was published in the second issue of their journal. Boehlich, *Sigmund Freud*, 85.

4. Lipiner, *Prometheus*, 110.

5. Lipiner, 174.

6. Nietzsche, *Werke in drei Bänden*, vol. 1, 57.

7. Nietzsche, "Brief an Erwin Rohde." http://www.nietzschesource.org/#eKGWB/BVN-1877,656. Accessed October 12, 2018.

8. Lipiner, *Über die Elemente*, 2.

9. Burgess, "Brentano as Philosopher of Religion."

10. Hartungen, "Der Dichter Siegfried Lipiner," 2.

11. See Luft's "Schopenhauer, Austria" on Schopenhauer's reception in Austria. On the tradition of Austrian empiricism through Zimmerman, see M. Hacohen, "Culture of Viennese Science."

12. It was this claim that led Schopenhauer to believe his ethics of compassion to lack the egoism of Kant's categorical imperative. See Cartwright, *Historical Dictionary of Schopenhauer's Philosophy*, 31.

13. Schopenhauer, *Die Welt als Wille und Vorstellung*, vol. 1, 488 [Schopenhauer, *World as Will and Representation*, vol. 1, 384].

14. Schopenhauer, "Preisschrift über die Grundlage der Moral," 253 [2009 edition]. [Schopenhauer, *On the Basis of Morality*, 144].

15. Lipiner, *Über die Elemente*, 8 ["On the Elements" 131].

16. Lipiner, *Über die Elemente*, 11 ["On the Elements" 137].

17. Cartwright, *Schopenhauer*, 491.

18. This image also appears in Lipiner's *Prometheus* poem, when he describes the pain that Prometheus feels upon identifying with the suffering Christ as "a blazing wound." It is difficult not to draw connections to *Parsifal*, although Lipiner's poem was written two years before the libretto was published.

19. According to HaCohen, for Wagner, sympathy and compassion complement one another. She writes: "Whereas compassion is a response to a particular condition of a suffering object, a moral reelection to real or fictional situations, sympathy mediates the transference of compassion from the theater onto the outer world." R. HaCohen, *Music Libel against the Jews*, 251.

20. Lipiner, *Über die Elemente*, 12 ["On the Elements," 139].

21. Lipiner, *Über die Elemente*, 17 ["On the Elements," 149].

22. Meysenbug was a close friend of Wagner and Nietzsche. Her memoir, *Memoirs of an Idealist*, which reflects her interpretation of Schopenhauer's philosophy, was a work that Lipiner greatly admired; he even quotes a section in his speech to the Leseverein of 1878. Lipiner looked up to the baroness, highly valued her opinion, and even referred to her by the affectionate title "Tante Malwida."

23. Stummann-Bowert, *Malwida von Meysenbug—Paul Rée*, 224–225.

24. Magee, *Tristan Chord*, 56.

25. R. Wagner, *Dichtungen und Schriften*, vol. 6, 17.

26. On Adler and Lipiner and their early associations through the University of Vienna's *Rede Klub*, see McGrath, *Dionysian Art and Populist Politics*, 62–64.

27. Stummann-Bowert, *Malwida von Meysenbug—Paul Rée*, 225.

28. R. Wagner, *Dichtungen und Schriften*, vol. 9, 38–109.

29. In merging his socialist views with Christian symbolism, Lipiner was in fact following in the footsteps of the young Wagner, who had in 1848–1849 begun composing an opera on the life of Jesus of Nazareth inspired by the writings of Ludwig Feuerbach, which he never completed. Williamson, *Longing for Myth in Germany*, 194.

30. Stummann-Bowert, *Malwida von Meysenbug—Paul Rée*, 225.

31. Stummann-Bowert, 225; Schopenhauer, *Parerga und Paralopomena: Kleine philosophische Schriften*, vol. 2, 405 [1878 edition].

32. "Abends Herr Lipiner, welcher R. in ein Gespräch über den Sozialismus verwickelt; R. betont, daß die Kraft dieser Bewegung nur in der Zerstörung liegen könne," C. Wagner, *Die Tagebücher*, vol. 2, 181.

33. R. HaCohen, *Music Libel against the Jews*, 250.

34. On Wagner's "self-branding," see Vazsonyi, *Self-Promotion*.

35. Another key influence on Lipiner's use of antisemitic rhetoric was the German theologian, Paul de Lagarde. Lagarde's search for a modern spirituality outside of the confines of dogmatic religion struck a chord with Lipiner, who read his works enthusiastically in the early 1880s. It was Lipiner's admiration of Lagarde, however, that also jeopardized his relationship with Wagner. See Stummann-Bowert, *Malwida von Meysenbug—Paul Rée*, 229.

36. Steinberg, *Listening to Reason*, 194.

37. Shelleg, *Jewish Contiguities*, 41.

38. For more on the Pernerstorfer Circle and Saga Society, see McGrath, *Dionysian Art and Populist Politics*.

39. Kralik, *Tage und Werke*, 98.

40. McGrath, *Dionysian Art and Populist Politics*, 99.

41. Kalbeck, "Merlin von Karl Goldmark," 1.

42. Hirschfeld, "Merlin," 2.

43. "Religion has sunk into an artificial life, when she finds herself compelled to keep on adding to the edifice of her dogmatic symbols." R. Wagner, *Prose Works*, vol. 6, 213. Such lines echo Lipiner's essay, in which he describes religion's denigration to dogmatism and fetishism (Lipiner, *Über die Elemente*, 2).

44. In *Religion und Kunst*, Wagner calls on the biblical story of Cain and Abel in his discussion of vegetarianism. He interprets the Lord's preference for Abel's calf as "suspicious evidences of the character of the Jewish tribal god." R. Wagner, *Prose Works*, vol. 6, 242; R. Wagner, *Dichtungen und Schriften*, vol. 10, 150.

45. See Introduction and Mack, *German Idealism and the Jew*, 8, on the pseudotheology of antisemitism from Kant through Schopenhauer and Wagner.

46. The *Deutsche Zeitung* was considered the "Organ of German nationalism" in Vienna. Founded in 1871, it hoped to be a rival of the *Neue Freie Presse*. Heinrich Friedjung, a member of the Pernerstorfer Circle, served as its editor from 1886–1887. See Brodbeck, *Defining Deutschtum*, 212.

47. Lipiner, "Weihnachten," 1–2.

48. Lipiner, "Einiges über Verbrechen und Strafe," 1.

49. R. Wagner, *Prose Works*, vol. 6, 217; R. Wagner, *Dichtungen und Schriften*, vol. 10, 122.

50. Shelleg, *Jewish Contiguities*, 41.

51. See McGrath on the impact of antisemitic agitation on the program of Lipiner and his colleagues at the University of Vienna. McGrath, *Dionysian Art and Populist Politics*, 241.

52. Lipiner, "Letter to Moritz Necker."

53. Lipiner did not convert to Christianity until almost seven years later and even briefly returned to the *Kultusgemeinde* between 1890 and 1892. When he finally did convert, it was not to Catholicism (which would have been more politically advantageous in Vienna) but to Protestantism. And even then, his conversion appears to have been more pragmatic (to marry his second wife, Clementine Spiegler) than a profound declaration of faith.

54. Natorp, "Vorwort zu 'Adam'" 10.

55. Unfortunately, these documents have gone missing. Ida Schein, who had access to these drafts when writing her dissertation in 1934 claimed of these fragments, "They are all wholly unsuited for publication, with the only exception being the three-act 'Maria Magdalena,' which, although remaining a fragment, is completely ready for press. The three-act, and the five-act 'Judas Iscariot,' as well as the two five-act 'Maria Magdalena' versions

are at the most unconnected compositions, for the most part just sketched in mere isolated, abrupt words." Schein, "Gedanken- und Ideenwelt Siegfried Lipiners," 1 [translation C. K.].

56. Floros claims that the suspicion that *Parsifal* was meant to reflect the conflict between Christianity and Judaism appeared in numerous commentaries on the work shortly after its premiere, including texts by Anton Rubenstein, Max Kalbeck, and Arthur Seidl. Constantin Floros, "Studien zur *Parsifal*-Rezeption," 26–27.

57. Schopenhauer further claims that the Jews' inability to recognize the injustice of their actions toward animals is attributed to their *foeter Judaicus*, the "foul stench" of the Jews. This image of the Jew, which dates back to medieval times, reflects antisemitic notions of the Jew as "disease, parasite, filth and source of death." Bhatt, "Primordial Being"; Schopenhauer, *Parerga und Paralopomena: Kleine philosophische Schriften*, vol. 2, 375–377.

58. Lipiner, *Adam, Ein Vorspiel*, 32. (Hereafter cited as *Adam*.)

59. Lipiner, *Adam*, 25.

60. Fischer, "*Das Judentum in der Musik*," 151; R. Wagner, *Prose Works*, vol. 3, 85.

61. In a letter to his then lover Mathilde Wesendonck in 1858, Wagner revealed his abhorrence for those whose "underdeveloped" natures make them incapable of feeling compassion for animals. R. HaCohen, *Music Libel against the Jews*, 249.

62. Lipiner, *Adam*, 60.

63. Lipiner, *Adam*, 61.

64. Quinones, *Changes of Cain*, 9.

65. Lipiner, *Adam*, 25.

66. Lipiner, *Adam*, 53. Cain refers here to Adam's nightly escapes to commune with the animals, despite his insistence that Cain adhere to the Law and distance himself from the animals.

67. Cain's rebelliousness aligns him with popular revisions of the Cain and Abel story in the Romantic era, particularly George Gordon Byron (Lord Byron)'s *Cain* (1821), from which Lipiner likely drew inspiration. Natorp, "Siegfried Lipiner's Adam," 807.

68. While the figure of Eve is not fully developed in Lipiner's text, she appears here both as a symbol of the mother Mary and of the concept of the Eternal Feminine. Lipiner would explore the idea of the redemptive power of the feminine in his dissertation on Goethe's *Faust* and in his play, *Hippolytos*, completed in 1900, shortly after *Adam*. See Kita, "Myth, Metaphysics and Cosmic Drama."

69. Lipiner, *Adam*, 46–47.

70. Lipiner, *Adam*, 55.

71. Lipiner, *Adam*, 57–58.

72. Lipiner, *Über die Elemente* 12 [Lipiner, *On the Elements*, 139].

73. Lipiner, *Adam*, 80.

74. According to Andrzej Walicki, Nietzsche came to know and admire the works of the Polish poet Adam Mickiewicz's works, which he read in Lipiner's translation. The writings of the Polish Romantics greatly influenced his idea of the Übermensch and the philosophical-poetical literary style of *Zarathustra*. Walicki, *Nietzsche in Poland*, 59.

75. Stummann-Bowert, *Malwida von Meysenbug—Paul Rée*, 222.

76. Nietzsche, *Werke in drei Bänden*, vol. 2, 103 [Nietzsche et al., *Gay Science*, 97–98].

77. See Holub, who maintains that Nietzsche had an ambivalence toward Jews throughout his life and often co-opted antisemitic "ethnography, linguistics, and history, even while maintaining his opposition to contemporary anti-Semitism." Holub, *Nietzsche's Jewish Problem*, 206–207.

78. Nietzsche, *Werke in drei Bänden*, vol. 2, 779–780.

79. See Yovel, who has noted that for Nietzsche there was no *Jewish essence*, and he understood Jewish history as a "changing evolving entity." Yovel, "Nietzsche, the Jews and Ressentiment," 214–236. Holub challenges Yovel's argument, claiming that even in his positive comments on Judaism, Nietzsche continues to employ antisemitic stereotypes. Holub, *Nietzsche's Jewish Problem*, 191.

80. Hollingdale, *Dithyrambs of Dionysus*, 17.

81. Hollingdale, *Dithyrambs of Dionysus*, 18.

82. Hollingdale, *Dithyrambs of Dionysus*, 33–34. This scene clearly mirrors the moment of bacchic revelry that Nietzsche describes in *Die Geburt der Tragödie*, when man overcomes his individuality and feels his reconciliation with nature: "Singend und tanzend äussert sich der Mensch als Mitglied einer höheren Gemeinsamkeit." Nietzsche, *Werke in drei Bänden*, vol. 1, 25.

83. Lipiner, *Adam*, 37.

84. Lipiner, *Adam*, 43.

85. Natorp, "Lipiner's *Adam* auf der Bühne."

86. Deutsch's breakout performance in Walter Hasenclaver's *Der Sohn* would take place in Dresden a year later. Malkin, "Transforming in Public," 156, 162.

# 2

# VOICING COMPASSION: GUSTAV MAHLER'S SECOND AND THIRD SYMPHONIES

"Vater sieh an die Wunden mein! Kein Wesen laß verloren sein!"

Verstehst du also, um was es sich da handelt? Es soll damit die Spitze und die höchste Stufe bezeichnet werden, von der aus die Welt gesehen werden kann. Ungefähr könnte ich den Satz auch nennen: "Was mir Gott erzählt!" Und zwar eben in dem Sinne, als ja Gott nur als "Liebe" gefasst werden kann.

["Father, look upon my wounds! Let no being be lost!"

Now do you understand what it is about? It is an attempt to show the summit, the highest level from which the world can be surveyed. I could equally well call the movement something like: "What God tells me!" And this in the sense that God can, after all, only be comprehended as "love."]

Gustav Mahler to Anna von Mildenburg, 1896

In July 1896, Mahler completed his Third Symphony, an epic six-movement work, which he described as expressing God and the universe as well as his deeply personal experience. While composing the work, he wrote to the opera singer Anna von Mildenburg that he had assigned an epitaph to the final movement, a quotation from a poem, "Erlösung" (Redemption) found in the early nineteenth-century folksong collection, *Des Knaben Wunderhorn* (Youth's Magic Horn). The section that Mahler quotes are the words of Christ on the cross appealing to the heavenly father for compassion. Yet this was not Mahler's first reference to Mitleid in his works. Sketches of the Third Symphony date back to the summer of 1893, when Mahler was completing his Second Symphony and composing another song of compassion from the *Wunderhorn* collection, "Urlicht" (Primeval Light), in which an individual begs for entrance at the gates of heaven. Both the Second and Third Symphonies represent a critical stage in Mahler's development of the dramatic potential of the symphonic form. Their descriptive programs and titles as well as the texts of the song settings within them, reveal the significance of compassion for his philosophical, religious, and aesthetic worldview.

This chapter examines the dramatic narratives of compassion in Mahler's Second (1888–1894) and Third (1893–1896) symphonies. Like Lipiner, Mahler sought to evoke compassion for the suffering subject and he found a unique means to do so, by inserting lieder into the symphonies as dramatic episodes. These episodes enact three critical stages of Lipiner's philosophical and aesthetic vision of compassion: (1) the articulation of the experience of the suffering subject, (2) the suffering subject's transformation into a compassionate figure, and (3) the compassionate subject's acceptance of the world's suffering and embodiment of the Will to Love. The Will to Love merges the spirit of Dionysian self-overcoming of Nietzsche's Übermensch with the all-encompassing spirit of compassion represented in the figure of Christ. This Dionysian-Christ figure is critical to the transcendence of limited visions of compassion, such as those presented in Schopenhauer and Wagner's writings, which depict the Jewish subject as an outsider deemed unworthy and incapable of empathy.

In the lieder found in the fourth movements of his Second and Third Symphonies, Mahler creates dramatic narratives of compassionate transformation. Paralleling one another in structure, both songs present a lone protagonist who reflects on the world's suffering and pleads to a divine spirit for compassion. In the Second Symphony, the individual is transformed into the compassionate comforter of others. However, the Third Symphony presents a more complex confrontation with compassion through textual and musical references to Schopenhauer, Wagner, and Nietzsche, in which Mahler reflects on the inability of their philosophies to offer solace to the abject figure of the Jew. In the finale of the Third Symphony, a dramatic adagio that Mahler entitled "Was mir die Liebe erzählt" (What Love Tells Me), Mahler merges the musical motives of the suffering subject's struggle with a reformulation of the "faith" motive from Wagner's *Parsifal*, pointing toward a new form of compassionate love, the basis for an inclusive community in which "no being will be lost."

The language of Mahler's programs and his textual choices reveal a close correspondence to Lipiner's writings on religious renewal and his biblical drama, *Adam*. While Lipiner was unable to complete his cycle of dramas, Mahler's symphonies fulfill the poet's ideal of compassionate art, that it should foster community by focusing on the sufferer and granting a voice to those most marginalized. By engaging music's ability to articulate subjective voices while at the same time transcending them to embody universal feelings and emotions, Mahler's dramatic symphonic episodes illuminate the Jewish subject's inner struggle and evoke sympathy for her plight. In so doing, he recasts the suffering Jew as a musical subject and creator of compassionate community.

## Mahler's Jewish "I"—Subjectivity and the Symphony

In order to understand how Mahler might have translated Lipiner's philosophy of compassion into a musical idiom in his symphonic works, one must first examine the composer's unique style of composition, the role of subjective voices in his work, and his complex relationship to his Jewish heritage. Mahler, like Lipiner and many other German-Jews of their generation, seldom spoke openly about Judaism or of his relationship to Jewish culture. Instead, he referred more generally to the experience of viewing the world from the position of an outsider. Yet, the layers of intertextual and intermedial references that he employed as a hallmark of his compositional style can bring us closer to an understanding of how Mahler might have conceived of Jewishness in his own time. In particular, the Second and Third Symphonies point toward the composer's complex and evolving relationship to a particular construction of Jewishness that was part of the dominant cultural narrative of his time: the idea of the uncompassionate Jew.

Born on July 7, 1860, in the town of Kalsicht (Kaliště) in Bohemia, Mahler spent his early years in the larger town of Iglau (Jihlava) in Moravia. His family was not particularly religious, however the composer did recall attending temple as a child.[1] Although his wife Alma liked to emphasize her husband's fascination with Catholicism, his conversion in 1897 was primarily a political move, to secure his position as director of the Vienna Court Opera.[2] And even though he neither engaged in traditional religious practices nor held any ties to the local Jewish community, Mahler was continually confronted with antisemitic attacks from the press during his ten-year tenure at the opera, eventually leading him to resign his post in 1907.[3] According to Mahler's longtime collaborator at the Vienna Court Opera, the set designer Alfred Roller, for the composer, Jewishness was inextricably linked to the idea of compassion:

> Was ihn vorwiegend an das Judentum band, war Mitleid. Die Gründe hierfür hat er wohl reichlich an sich selbst erfahren, obgleich er hierüber selten sprach und immer nur ruhig konstatierend, nie verbittert, nie sentimental. Aber: "Unter den ärmsten Menschen ist immer der noch ärmer, der dabei auch noch Jude ist."
>
> [What predominantly connected him to Judaism was compassion. He had plenty of reasons for this from his own experience, although he seldom spoke about it, and only calmly verified it, never embittered, never sentimental. But, "among the poorest of humans there is always one who is poorer, who is also a Jew."][4]

Roller's comment, while intriguing, poses many questions—what particular experiences might have shaped this connection between Judaism and compassion? And if he never spoke of these events directly, might his musical works offer a clearer picture?

The temptation to use the composer's works to decode his biography and worldview has captivated scholars for decades. Indeed, Mahler once claimed to his close friend, Natalie Bauer-Lechner that his first two symphonies "erschöpfen den Inhalt meines ganzen Lebens . . . wenn einer gut zu lesen verstünde, müßte ihm in der Tat mein Leben darin durchsichtig erscheinen" (contain the inner aspect of my whole life . . . To understand these works properly would be to see my life transparently revealed in them).[5] The Third Symphony, which shares with the First and Second a deeply personal, programmatic narrative, might also be read as Mahler's own personal religious confession.[6]

Mahler's symphonic programs may provide the listener with signposts of his encounters and struggles with faith and spirituality, but they are hardly transparent statements of religious identity. These narratives, refracted through many layers of literary and musical references, reveal a wide variety of religious and cultural influences.[7] Mahler's ambivalence toward identification with any one nation or creed is captured in his oft-cited comment: "Ich bin dreifach Heimatlos . . . als Böhme unter den Österreichern, als Österreicher unter den Deutschen, und als Jude unter der ganzen Welt" (I am thrice homeless . . . as a native of Bohemia in Austria, as an Austrian among Germans, and as a Jew throughout the world; everywhere an intruder, never welcomed).[8] Such ambiguous statements have led scholars to describe the Jewish nature of Mahler's music in terms of absence rather than presence. Theodor Adorno writes that the Jewish in Mahler is tangential to the "Folk" element in his music; it does not articulate it directly, yet it "speaks through all its mediations as an intellectual voice, something non-sensuous and yet perceptible in the totality."[9] Similarly, Talia Pecker-Berio refers to a "virtual Jewish aesthetics" in Mahler's music, which manifests itself by means of distance and commentary.[10] Jewishness was thus one of many modes through which the composer experienced feelings of alienation in his life, and it was always deeply intertwined with questions of local, national, and religious-cultural identity.

The present study does not aim to completely disentangle Mahler's Jewish "I" from this complex nexus. However, it suggests that Jewish difference and Jewish subjectivity may be productive frameworks for understanding the sense of *Heimatlosigkeit* that so indelibly shaped the sound and structure of his works and the vision of compassion that he believed to be the ultimate goal of art. As Lisa Silverman writes, Jewish difference existed as a kind of "invisible framework" in Austria that shaped understandings of belonging or of being an outsider.[11] Mahler's obsession with composing "intrusive" voices in his symphonic works, suggest that constructs of difference deeply shaped his worldview and music language. Moreover, the fact that Mahler so often claimed these outsider voices as projections of his own experience suggest that we might think of Mahler's understanding of Jewishness in terms of subjectivity, what Spector refers to as a "complex of questions, rather than a clear and decisive answer."[12] For indeed Mahler's Jewish "I" (and with it, his musical "I") is constantly being shifted and reformulated. It is always, in a word, "performed." Therefore, to understand Mahler's Jewish voice, one must look to the intersection of the musical, the narrative, and the theatrical in his works.[13]

The analysis of the composer's Second and Third Symphonies in this chapter unpacks the connection between Mahler's understanding of Jewishness and its relationship to discourses of compassion by examining the dramatic form of these works and the articulation of voice within them. To examine Mahler's critique of compassion on the level of form, I draw upon Michael Steinberg's thesis on the legacy of opera after Wagner. According to Steinberg, Wagner's music dramas merged ideology with word, gesture, and musical symbol so as to "command" that individuals perform identity by existing and acting in prescribed ways. Post-Wagnerian opera, he suggests, pushed back against ideology by focusing on "the regeneration of voice," a voice that extends *beyond* identity positions, "giving movement, elasticity and resonance to its subject."[14] Mahler's Second and Third Symphonies, for which he wrote explicit programs and integrated lieder, follow such theatrical models in that they create musical protagonists, whose rise, tragic fall, and rebirth articulate the dramatic arc of his works, and whose "intrusive" nature unsettle the immersive experience of the audience, resisting absolute discourses of identity and ideology.

However, Mahler's deviation from Wagner's dramatic models in the Second and Third Symphonies also can be read more specifically as part of his critique of the exclusion of the Jewish subject from an ethics and aesthetics of compassion. When the voices in these symphonies are analyzed in the context of stereotypes of the uncompassionate Jew, they appear to be coded Jewish—they are marked by their exclusion from and "deafness" to the symphonies' larger messages of redemption.[15] By using dialogue (between instruments or voice and instruments) and staging (creating the impression of the subject's distance or isolation from a collective body), as well as abrupt shifts in tone, dynamic, and character, Mahler calls into question these stereotypes, encouraging the listener to sympathize with the Jewish subject.[16]

To further understand how Mahler's musical voices emerged in the Second and Third Symphonies as a response to, and extension of, philosophies of compassion in his time, we must now return to Lipiner, who offered the composer a powerful template for challenging Wagner and Schopenhauer's discourse of Mitleid and creating an alternative vision of inclusive, compassionate community.

## In Lipiner's Words: Mahler's Programs for the Second and Third Symphonies

On August 1, 1896, Mahler met the poet Siegfried Lipiner in Steinbach am Attersee near Salzburg on a summer holiday. Mahler had just completed the draft of his Third Symphony and Lipiner was in the midst of composing the tetralogy of biblical dramas that he planned to entitle *Christus*. According to Natalie Bauer-Lechner, who accompanied them that day, Lipiner spoke with Mahler about his project in detail for four hours, not to be deterred even by a torrential rain shower that came upon them suddenly. Her description of Lipiner wildly gesticulating under the umbrella and Mahler listening intently and stamping his foot occasionally "like a wild boar," provides a fascinating and comical anecdote of the composer and poet's friendship, and it reveals that Mahler possessed detailed knowledge of Lipiner's biblical dramatic project.[17]

Yet Mahler and Lipiner's meeting in Steinbach was not their first intellectual and creative exchange. Poet and composer met as students at the University of Vienna in the late 1870s through a mutual friend, Albert Spiegler. They soon became drawn into a close-knit circle of artists, philosophers, politicians, and activists called the Pernerstorfer Circle. The members of the group engaged in critiques of liberal politics as well as discussions about German nationalism and folk culture.[18] In 1880, Lipiner and Mahler founded the Sagengesellschaft (Saga Society) with Richard von Kralik, a fellow university student. The members of the Saga Society dabbled in the occult and spiritualism at this time and undertook pilgrimages to Bayreuth and to view the annual Passion Play at Oberammergau. Although Lipiner was only four years older than Mahler, correspondence and memoirs of their mutual friends attest that the composer often sought the poet's counsel and looked up to him as a mentor. The influence of this relationship is most strongly reflected in Mahler's first four symphonies, which all focus on themes close to Lipiner's own heart: the idea of redemption, the limitations of dogmatic religion, and the desire for a direct encounter with the divine. Both poet and composer believed that through art, individuals come to feel and experience the suffering of others. All human beings are worthy and capable of compassion, but the Law (embodied in the Commandments and represented in dogmatic religion) had created a distance between humanity and God. Thus, compassion must be demanded by a devout, yet rebellious outsider, who becomes the prophet of a new religion of life-affirming love. In this "transvaluation of values," compassion serves as the great unifier of all souls.

Although both the Second and Third Symphonies evoke the redemption mythology of Christianity, Mahler distanced himself from biblical sources, preferring literary, lyrical formulations of redemption and compassion synthesized by Lipiner in his poetic and philosophical writings.[19] His program for the Second Symphony, relayed to Bauer-Lechner in 1896, provides evidence that Lipiner's mobilization of religious imagery served as an important model for Mahler as he set out to articulate his vision of compassion. In these notes, Mahler claimed that the symphony evokes the "titanic struggles of a mighty being," grappling with death, reflecting back on his life and its senselessness, and representing the soul's "striving and questioning attitude toward God and its own immortality."[20] The finale presents a dramatic vision of the end of days, in which there are "keine

Begnadeten und keine Verdammten; kein Guter, kein Böser, kein Richter!" (no souls saved and none damned: no just man, no evil-doer, no judge!).[21] Mahler's vision of Judgment Day without judgment echoes the narrative of Lipiner's *Prometheus* poem, discussed in chapter 1, in which the Titan's existential struggle reaches its climax in a verbal battle with Christ, whom he challenges with the words, "Wer will mich richten?" (Who wishes to judge me?).[22] Connections to Lipiner's works can also be found in the programs of the Third Symphony, which Mahler began sketching in the summer of 1893 and completed during the summers of 1895 and 1896.[23] Mahler's earliest notes on the Third Symphony refer to it as a hymn to nature, and his first program drafts entitled it, "Das glückliche Leben: Ein Sommernachtstraum" (The Happy Life: A Summer Night's Dream), inspired by the pantheistic language of "Der Sommer" (Summer), a feuilleton that Lipiner wrote for the *Deutsche Zeitung* in the summer of 1881.[24] As the program for the work developed, Mahler began to view this work as an origin story, tracing the emergence of life from dull and lifeless matter, through the emergence of plants and animals, to the evolving consciousness of humanity, to the angels, finally culminating in love, a theme that is also reflected in "Genesis," a poem from Lipiner's 1880 collection, *Buch der Freude* (Book of Joy).[25]

Just as the First and Second Symphonies "contained the inner aspect of his own life," Mahler's Third Symphony was similarly conceived on deeply personal terms and can be read even more explicitly as an articulation of his own subjectivity. The titles of the movements underwent several revisions over the course of the summer of 1895, but, by the following year, the composer had decided on a six-movement symphony divided into two parts. The dramatic first movement, which he entitled "Pan erwacht! Der Sommer marschiert ein!" (Pan Awakes! Summer marches in!) would compose the first section, lasting a grandiose thirty minutes in performance. The second part would feature his hierarchical vision of the universe beginning with "Was die Blumen auf der Wiese mir erzählen" (What the Flowers in the Meadow Tell Me), "Was die Tiere im Walde mir erzählen" (What the Animals of the Forest Tell Me), "Was der Mensch mir erzählt" (What Mankind Tells Me; a setting of the Midnight Song from Friedrich Nietzsche's philosophical novel, *Also sprach Zarathustra*), "What the Angels Tell Me" (the setting of a folksong from *Des Knaben Wunderhorn*), and concluding with an adagio finale, "What Love Tells Me."[26] To Friedrich Lohr, Mahler wrote in August 1895 that he conceived of the symphony as: "Die Betonung meines *persönlichen* Empfindungslebens" (the emphasis on my *personal* experiences).[27] In addition to introducing his own subjective persona into the symphony with the indication that nature is speaking "to him," the very mention of "telling," draws the listener's attention to the fact that the music will be embodying vocal subjectivities that have a story to convey.

The following analysis of Mahler's textual choices and musical settings of his vocal movements reveals how the composer translated Lipiner's dramatic vision of compassionate art into a musical idiom. Although Mahler claimed that the Third Symphony was to be much broader in scope than the Second Symphony, both works share a common narrative arc: the representation of human suffering through the perspective of the individual, the struggle to find meaning in suffering by turning to religion and philosophy, and, finally, the resolution of this conflict in an all-encompassing vision of compassionate love.[28] The first stage in the development of this theme, the representation of the suffering subject, finds unique articulation in Mahler's song settings of "Urlicht" in the Second Symphony and in "Was mir der Mensch erzählt" (The Midnight Song from *Also sprach Zarathustra*) in the Third Symphony. In these movements, the composer creates parallel scenes in which a protagonist, speaking on behalf of suffering humanity, pleads for compassion. In the Second Symphony, this setting serves as the impetus for a transformation of the suffering subject from the one in need of compassion to the compassionate comforter of others. In the Third Symphony, however, the individual struggle of the suffering subject is further complicated by her coding as a Jewish subject, who is bound to the Law and for whom compassion appears tragically out of reach. Musical and textual references to *Parsifal* in this movement and the adagio finale of the Third Symphony indicate that this movement was intended as a commentary on Wagner's limited vision of compassion. Ultimately, in the final movement, all beings are embraced through the transformative potential of Nietzsche's Dionysian spirit, which for Mahler embodies compassionate love. In this way, Mahler's Second and Third Symphonies reveal how the question of compassion, as a philosophical and aesthetic concept, might be realized in the musical form of the symphony.

## The Voice of the Suffering Subject

In both his Second and Third Symphonies, Mahler follows a similar symphonic structure to create a dramatic narrative that culminates in the form of a musical interlude, a song setting, in which the human voice articulates the need for compassion. In the Second Symphony's "Urlicht" and the Third's "Was mir der Mensch erzählt," Mahler's musical idiom for Otherness can be deciphered both through text and music, form and tone. In both movements, Mahler's vocal Others emerge as single voices from multivocal "chaos" and struggle against instrumental voices that embody opposition and resistance to the individual's integration into the musical whole.[29] Both lieder are followed in the symphony by choral movements, suggesting that the question of compassion for Mahler, as for Lipiner, is both an existential question confronting the individual and a critical dynamic of social life.[30] Mahler's voices demand compassion, but the question remains, will they be heard? The conclusions of the Second and Third Symphonies propose two very different answers to this question. Put in "Lipinerian" terms: Mahler's Second proposes a "Promethean" ending, an affirmative yes, in which the sufferer is reborn as compassionate subject, while his Third problematizes this narrative by exploring the possibility of a "Cain" ending, in which the suffering subject, marked as Jewish Other, is left tragically outside of the narrative of redemption. Yet this conflict also opens the door for a new vision of compassion in which the suffering subject embraces the world's suffering to create a new inclusive community that transcends dogmatic religion as well as the constructs of Christian and Jew.

The insertion of the lied, a genre defined by its ability to relay the inner thoughts and feelings of the subject, into the symphonic form as interludes allows Mahler to articulate the nature of human suffering and the central theme of compassion.[31] The texts that Mahler chose for these two movements draw from widely different sources, a traditional folksong and the highly stylized philosophical language of Friedrich Nietzsche, yet, their narrative trajectories reveal fascinating similarities. In both cases, the soloist begins with an appeal for compassion and both encounter resistance. In "Urlicht," this resistance takes the form of the angel who wants to turn the subject away, while in "Was mir der Mensch erzählt," the voice of all-powerful *Weh*, or sorrow threatens to dissolve all hope. Yet, this resistance is not met with defeat or resignation. Mahler makes this point in both movements by creating moments of dialogue between the voice and the solo violin, and the voice and the oboe.

Mahler's musical dialogues are a highlight of his use of dramatic techniques in his symphonies. First, these dialogues are staged through the creation of a musical mise-en-scène that is distinct from the sonic world that came before it. Raymond Knapp notes that both movements disrupt the course of the symphony by creating a sense of suspended time, which accentuates the sense for the listener that the musical subject is at a "moment of crossroads, in which something of tremendous import hangs in the balance."[32] In both symphonies, the movement immediately preceding the lied is marked by hurried time, which articulates the world's suffering. Mahler described the third movement of his Second Symphony as relaying an idea of the world "distorted and crazy—as if reflected in a concave mirror."[33] This feeling is expressed musically through the perpetual, circular motion of the sixteenth-note melody voiced by the strings, which is punctuated by the syncopated rhythm of the clarinets. In the third movement of the Third Symphony, the strings lead a similar charge by means of a running sixteenth-note motive, accompanied by frantic triplet rhythms and trills in the winds. In both symphonies, this chaotic movement is interrupted by what Adorno identifies as a moment of breakthrough (*Durchbruch*).[34] Mahler articulates the significance of these breakthroughs in his programmatic descriptions of "the appalling shriek of the tortured soul" (in the Second Symphony) and "the heavy shadow of lifeless nature" (in the Third Symphony). In both cases, the scream presents the most primal expression of suffering.

In the Second and Third Symphonies, breakthroughs mark the introduction of the human voice into the symphonic form, and, in both cases, it is a female voice, an alto soloist (or in some performances, a mezzo-soprano). In contrast to the previous movements, the song episodes of "Urlicht" und "Was mir der Mensch erzählt" are strikingly calm and contemplative. Mahler creates an acoustic stage for these voices through a similar structure and orchestration. They begin with an appeal ("O Röschen Rot!"; "O Mensch!") that vocalizes suffering. (See table 2.1.) This appeal is followed by a horn chorale (in the Second Symphony, three trumpets in F; in the Third Symphony, three horns in F). The dramatically slower tempi of these movements and their reduced orchestration create an expansion of time that simultaneously evokes an expansion of space, a hallmark of Mahler's pastorale style.[35] Mahler's musical scene, out of time and place, sets the stage for the dialogue between musical characters, the human voice and two instruments, the violin and the oboe.

Mahler's musical dialogues in "Urlicht" and "Was mir der Mensch erzählt," appear in the second section of each movement, after the articulation

Table 2.1 Mahler's Vocal Movements, Symphony No. 2 and Symphony No. 3

| Symphony No. 2, Movement 4 | |
|---|---|
| **"Urlicht" (from *Des Knaben Wunderhorn*)[1]** | **"Primeval Light" (from *Youth's Magic Horn*)** |
| O Röschen rot! | O little Red Rose! |
| Der Mensch liegt in größter Not! | Man lies in great need! |
| Der Mensch liegt in größter Pein! | Man lies in great pain! |
| Je lieber möchte' ich im Himmel sein! | O how I would rather be in heaven! |
| Da kam ich auf einem breiten Weg | Then I came along a wide pathway |
| Da kam ein Engelein und wollt' mich abweisen! | A little angel came and wanted to turn me away! |
| Ach nein! Ich ließ mich nicht abweisen! | O no! I will not be turned away! |
| Ich bin vom Gott und will wieder zu Gott | I am from God and will return to God |
| Der liebe Gott wird mir ein Lichtchen geben | Dear God will give me a little light |
| Wird leuchten mir bis in das ewige, selig Leben! | Will light me to eternal, blessed life! |
| Symphony No. 3, Movement 4 | |
| **"Was mir der Mensch erzählt" (from *Also sprach Zarathustra*)[2]** | **"What Man tells Me" (from *Thus Spoke Zarathustra*)** |
| O Mensch! Gib acht! | O Man! Take heed! |
| Was spricht die tiefe Mitternacht? | What does deep midnight speak? |
| Ich schlief! | I slept! |
| Aus tiefem Traum bin ich erwacht | I awoke from a deep dream, |
| Die Welt ist tief und tiefer als der Tag gedacht | The world is deep and deeper than day had been aware |
| O Mensch! Tief, tief ist ihr Weh! | O Man! Deep, deep is her woe! |
| Lust, tiefer noch als Herzeleid! | Longing, deeper still than the heart's suffering! |
| Weh spricht, vergeh! | Woe speaks, be gone! |
| Doch alle Lust will Ewigkeit | Yet, all longing wants desire! |
| Will tiefe, tiefe Ewigkeit! | Wants deep, deep desire! |

1. G. Mahler, *Symphonies Nos. 1 and 2*, 378 [Translation C. K.].
2. G. Mahler, *Symphony No. 3*, vi.

of suffering. The impending confrontation is signaled in both works by a musical cue reminiscent of the unsettling previous movements. In "Urlicht," it is the circular triplet figure in the clarinets that reminds the listener of the perpetual motion motive of the world "reflected in a concave mirror" (mm. 37–40). In "Was mir der Mensch erzählt," it is the oboe's rising third, marked in Mahler's music as "Wie ein Naturlaut" (Like a sound of nature), which hearkens back to the unbridled sound of nature presented in the first movement of the symphony (mm. 32–35).[36] These musical leitmotifs link the impending encounter with the vocal protagonist's past, suggesting that we are being granted a glimpse into the psyche and long-repressed traumas.

Mahler's musical dialogues between the voice and instrument draw attention to the contentious nature of this encounter by creating a "call and answer" effect, the impression of dialogue. In "Urlicht," after the voice sings "da kam ich auf einen breiten Weg" (I came upon a wide path) the violin responds with a playful dance-like melody, transitioning from the key of B-flat minor to A major (mm. 41–45). The optimistic tone of the major key dissolves in the next line as the voice sings of the rejection at heaven's gates: "da kam ein Engelein und wollt' mich abweisen" (then a little angel came and wanted to turn me away). The violin responds with two glissando figures from A to F#, a sighing motif that indicates resignation (mm. 49–50). Yet the alto voice rebels, demanding to be let into heaven. With the words, "ach nein, ich liess mich nicht abweisen" (oh no, I will not let myself be turned away) the tempo quickens and the word "abweisen" is echoed by the rising line of the oboe, a questioning gesture that seems to ask if these demands will indeed be answered (mm. 54–55). A similar pattern can be found in "Was mir der Mensch erzählt," where the violin reacts to the alto soloist singing "Tief ist ihr Weh!" (Deep is her sorrow!) with a rising quintuplet motif (m. 101). Like the oboes in "Urlicht," the violin line in "Was mir der Mensch erzählt" appears to question the vocal line, rather than affirming it or offering resolution.

At this point, however, the two song settings diverge, as "Urlicht" concludes with an assertion of faith in God's eternal love, while the call for compassion in "Was mir der Mensch erzählt" remains unresolved. In "Urlicht," the violin's tied quarter and two eighth notes first echo the alto line, creating a sense of urgency and suspense (mm. 56–60). In the final lines of the poem, "wird leuchten mir bis in das ewig, selig Leben!" (will light me to eternal, blessed life), violin and voice come together (mm. 65–69), returning to the home key of D-flat minor. In "Was mir der Mensch erzählt," the speaker's struggle with the violin initially resolves on the words "Ewigkeit" (mm. 121–122, recalling the "ewig, selig Leben" line of "Urlicht"). However, the return of the oboe's disturbing, questioning voice in the final bars of the movement destabilize this apparent resolution (mm. 132–136).

Mahler's setting of this text from Nietzsche's *Also sprach Zarathustra* is highly ambivalent. The words are taken from a chapter entitled "The Other Dancing Song" in Part III of the novel, which marks a moment of deep indecision and self-doubt as Zarathustra contemplates the possibility of the Eternal Return of the same. Mahler's setting suggests that he intended not a blind affirmation of Nietzsche's doctrine of *amor fati,* the love of fate, but rather a reflection on the moral quandary that it proposes. The questioning "Naturlaut" of the oboe mirrors the vocal protagonist's own questioning—how can one reconcile great joy and great woe (*Weh*)? How can one *live* in the face of such suffering? Or, to echo what Mahler's wife Alma once claimed was a guiding principle of Mahler's works, "How should I be happy so long as anywhere some other creature suffers?"[37]

Mahler's song settings in the fourth movements of his Second and Third Symphonies, therefore, dramatically stage the first stage of Lipiner's vision for compassionate art, the depiction of the suffering subject. Through the lied, a musical form associated with the articulation of subjective experience, he offers insight into the psyche of the suffering individual. These moments of introspection lead in both symphonies to the individual's encounter with the world's suffering. In the Second Symphony, this encounter resolves in the suffering subject's transformation into compassionate comforter. In the Third Symphony, however, Mahler meditates on the possibility of a Nietzschean resolution, the willing of Dionysian joy in the face of suffering, by juxtaposing it with a Wagnerian resolution of resignation and denial of the Will, articulated through musical references to the transfiguration scene in *Parsifal.* In this next lied setting, "Was mir die Engeln erzählen," Mahler follows Lipiner's depiction of Cain in *Adam* by staging the isolation of the Jewish subject from such narratives of compassion.

## Mahler's Dramas of Compassion

In both the Second and Third Symphonies, Mahler follows his contemplative solo movements with choral movements, further probing the problem of compassion and its implications for the individual in society. In the Second Symphony, Mahler enacts the second stage of Lipiner's vision of compassionate art, the transformation of the suffering subject into a compassionate subject, one who expresses the ability to "suffer-with" others. In the Third Symphony, however, he explores the implications of the suffering subject deemed unworthy or incapable of compassion, the Jew. Both movements engage choral and solo voices to stage a confrontation between the individual and the social order. Mahler's Second Symphony resolves in an affirmation of redemption for all in a revolutionary dissolution of judgment. In the choral movement of the Third Symphony, however, the isolation of the penitent harkens to the stereotypical depiction of the Jew in Lipiner's *Adam*, the subject who suffers because he is beholden to the Law and to the whim of a distant, uncompassionate God.

The transformation of the sufferer into compassionate subject is intoned by Mahler in the final movement of his Second Symphony. For this choral finale, Mahler claimed to have searched "die ganze Weltliteratur bis zur Bibel" (the whole of world literature through to the Bible) to find the right text. In the end, he settled on two verses from Friedrich Klopstock's hymn "Auferstehung" (Resurrection), and concluded the chorus with his own words. (See table 2.2.) His own words, as it turns out, were largely drawn from the redemption scene of Lipiner's *Prometheus* poem. In this dramatic final "scene" of the symphony, Mahler's suffering protagonist from the previous movement is transformed from sufferer into a compassionate subject. He creates this transformation by bringing back the alto soloist of "Urlicht" who demanded to be let into heaven. With the lines of the third verse, "O glaube, mein Herz, O glaube," the one who refused to be turned away by the angel now speaks to all of suffering humanity, proclaiming a message of compassion: "Es geht dir nichts verloren!" Mahler's form of musical dialogue returns in this movement, but this time the alto is not alone but accompanied by a solo soprano, whose words, "Du warst nicht umsonst geboren, hast nicht umsonst gelebt, gelitten," affirm the alto's comforting words, while the violin echoes her lines with a descending variation in the same key (mm. 602–604). The soloists' message of compassion recalls the words of Lipiner's *Prometheus* poem,

> Heil dir! Preis dir!
> Ehre und Liebe dir!
> Der du leidest, der du schaffst,
> Der du ringst und bebst und zweifelst—
> Und, tausendfach gekreuziget,
> Aus ungezählten Wunden blutest,
> Und ewig stehst in ungebeugter Hoheit
> Und nimmermüde streitest
> Und schaust mit allsehendem Blick
> Die Sonne des Siegs!
>
> [Restore thee! Praise thee!
> Worship and love thee!
> You who suffers, you who creates, you who wrestles, trembles and doubts—
> and who a thousand times crucified,
> bled out of innumerable wounds and eternally stands in unbending highness
> and tirelessly strives
> and looks with an all-seeing glance
> at the sun of victory!][38]

Table 2.2 Gustav Mahler, Symphony No. 2, Movement 5, "Auferstehen"[1]

| | |
|---|---|
| *Chor:* | *Chorus:* |
| Aufersteh'n, ja aufersteh'n wirst du, | You will rise again, yes rise again |
| Mein Staub, nach kurzer Ruh! | My dust, after brief rest! |
| Unsterblich Leben | Immortal life |
| Wird der dich rief dich geben. | Will be granted to you by the one who called you. |
| Wieder aufzublüh'n wirst du gesät! | You were sown in order to bloom again! |
| Der Herr der Ernte geht | The Lord of the Harvest goes |
| Und sammeln Garben | And collects like sheaves |
| Uns ein, die starben. | Those of us who died. |
| *Friedrich Klopstock* | |
| *Alt:* | *Alto:* |
| O glaube, mein Herz, o glaube: | Oh believe, my heart, o believe: |
| Es geht dir nichts verloren! | Nothing is lost to you! |
| Dein ist, was du gesehnt! | What you long for is yours! |
| Dein, was du geliebt, gestritten! | What you have loved and fought for is yours! |
| *Sopran:* | *Soprano:* |
| O glaube: | Oh believe: |
| Du warst nicht umsonst geboren! | You were not born in vain! |
| Hast nicht umsonst gelebt, gelitten! | Have not lived, suffered in vain! |
| *Chor:* | *Chorus:* |
| Was entstanden ist, das muss vergehen! | What was created, must die away! |
| Was vergangen, auferstehen! | What has died away, must rise again! |
| Hör auf zu beben! | Cease trembling! |
| Bereite dich zu leben! | Prepare yourself to live! |
| *Alt und Sopran:* | *Alto and Soprano:* |
| O Schmerz, du Alldurchdringer! | Oh Pain, you all-penetrator! |
| Dir bin ich entrungen, | I have wrested myself free of you, |
| O Tod, du Allbezwinger! | Oh death, you all-conqueror! |
| Nun bis du bezwungen! | Now you are conquered! |
| *Chor:* | *Chorus:* |
| Mit Flügel, die ich mir errungen | With wings that I have one myself |
| In heißem Liebesstreben | In fervent strivings of love |
| Werd' ich entschweben | I will soar |
| Zum Licht kein Aug' gedrungen! | To the light no eye has seen! |
| Sterben werde ich um zu leben! | I will die, to live! |
| Aufersteh'n, ja aufersteh'n wirst du, | You will rise again, yes rise again |
| Mein Herz in einem Nu! | My heart, in an instant! |
| Was du geschlagen, | What you have fought for, |
| Zu Gott wird es dich tragen! | Will carry you to God! |
| *Gustav Mahler* | |

1. G. Mahler, *Symphonies Nos. 1 and 2*, 378–379 [Translation C. K.].

Moreover, the image of confronting and overcoming suffering, found in the verses "O Schmerz! Du Alldurchdringer! Dir bin ich entrungen! O Tod! Du Allbezwinger! Nun bist du bezwungen!" paraphrases the final verse of Lipiner's poem: "Umschlingt den Schmerz, umschlinget ihn, und nah und näher zieht ihn bis an's Herz—dann stirbt er hin, und Tod und Hölle flieht!" (Grasp the pain, grasp it and draw it near and nearer to your heart, then it dies and death and hell flee).[39] In Mahler's musical setting, this dialogue of comfort and compassion gives way to a triumphant redemptive vision, in which the solo voices, struggling to overcome one another, become louder and more powerful, and then finally resolve, coming together at the lines "werd' ich entschweben zum Licht, zu dem kein Aug' gedrungen." Mahler's setting of the text emphasizes the image of soaring as the voices in the various ranges of the chorus join in one after another and gradually become louder as the tempo increases (mm. 561–586). This image of soaring is also found in Lipiner's *Prometheus* poem, as the Titan is redeemed by Christ:

> Und stärker fasst' ihn
> Des Sturmwinds Flügel,
> Ueber die Flammen aufgeschleudert,
> Fühlt er sich schwebend
> Zwischen Himmel und Erde.
>
> [And the wings of the stormy winds held him
> steadily above the flames.
> Spinning upwards he felt himself soaring
> between heaven and earth].[40]

Mahler's Second Symphony ends with a triumphant conclusion, an affirmation of resurrection and return to God, as the rebellious outsider is transformed into compassionate comforter. However, the Third Symphony complicates this compassionate transformation by directly engaging with the pseudo-Christian narrative of redemption found in Wagner's *Parsifal.*

In the fifth movement of the Third Symphony, a setting of "Es sungen drei Engeln," from the collection of Romantic folksongs, *Des Knaben Wunderhorn*, Mahler comments on the categorization of the Jew as uncompassionate in the works of Wagner and Schopenhauer by presenting a dramatic narrative of a suffering sinner who has transgressed the Law and must beg for forgiveness.[41] Mahler's setting of the poem employs a number of his signature dramatic elements—dialogue, staging, and role-playing—to emphasize the alienation of the penitent figure in the song's narrative. The scene is structured as a frame story with a dramatic episode in the middle. It opens with a joyous choir of angels singing of the redemption of St. Peter. Then the narration shifts to a lost soul approaching Jesus, who is sitting at table with his disciples. The unnamed figure (the alto soloist of "Was mir der Mensch erzählt") is weeping bitterly because she has broken the Ten Commandments and has come to seek forgiveness. Jesus responds that if the penitent falls on her knees and prays to God, she will find salvation and heavenly joy. The episode closes with the return of the angelic choir, proclaiming salvation for the sinner. The three musical characters are delineated through the use of distinct vocal ranges: the angels (a boys' choir), the narrator/Jesus (a women's choir), and the penitent (the contralto soloist). Moreover, by framing the penitent episode with the angelic choir, Mahler creates two musical worlds, the heavenly and the earthly, distinguished from one another by their tone. In the opening and closing chorales, the high register of the boys' choir imitates the sound of bells to the words "Bimm Bamm" and the lively women's choir represents the jubilant voices of "heavenly joy." Their bright sounds sharply juxtapose the tone of the "earthly" dialogue between the choir playing the role of Jesus and the penitent, which descends into a minor mode.

Mahler's dramatic setting is significant because in establishing a frame narrative, he also creates distance between the figures taking part in the dramatic action and the angels who are telling the story itself. This distance is reflected in what might be termed diegetic (text-internal) and extradiegetic (text-external) music. The angelic choir sings of salvation not to the penitent but rather to the audience. While the women's choir shifts between the heavenly and the earthly realms (at times narrating to the accompaniment of the boy's bell sounds), the penitent is located squarely in the central (earthly) narrative. Mahler's indications in the score (his "stage directions") call for the boys' choir to be positioned "in der Höhe" (aloft), further emphasizing their distance from the penitent. (See table 2.3.)

The positioning of the boys' choir is also significant for a reading of compassion in this text, because it directly references Wagner's *Parsifal*. Like Mahler's boys' choir, the *Knaben und Jünglinge* in the first act of *Parsifal* sing from "halfway up" (aus der mittleren Höhe).[42] In *Parsifal*, the boys' choir proclaims the words, "Durch Mitleid wissend, der reine Tor" (The innocent fool, enlightened through compassion). This is the prophesy of the hero Parsifal, who will come to redeem Amfortas and the knights of the Grail. In Mahler's song, the boys sing of another prophesy of redemption, the

Table 2.3 Gustav Mahler, Third Symphony, Movement 5—Structural Outline[1]

| | | |
|---|---|---|
| Es sungen drei Engel einen süßen Gesang; | **Frame** | Three angels were singing a sweet song: |
| mit Freuden es selig in dem Himmel klang, | **(extradiegetic)** | With joy it resounded blissfully in heaven, |
| sie jauchzten fröhlich auch dabei, | **Heavenly Realm** | They rejoiced also |
| dass Petrus sei von Sünden frei, | | That Peter was free from sin, |
| er sei von Sünden frei | Opening Chorale | He was free from sin. |
| und als der Herr Jesus zu Tische saß, | | And when the Lord Jesus sat at table, |
| mit seinen zwölf Jüngern das Abendmal aß | Boys' Choir: Angels | With his twelve disciples ate the supper, |
| da sprach der Herr Jesus: | | There spoke the Lord Jesus: |
| | Women's Choir: Angels/Narrator | |
| Was stehst du denn hier? | **Episode (diegetic)** | What are you doing? |
| Wenn ich dich anseh', so weinest du mir! | **Earthly Realm** | Whenever I look at you, I find you weeping! |
| Und sollt' ich nicht weinen, du gütiger Gott. | | And should I not weep, you gracious God. |
| (*Du sollst ja nicht weinen! Sollst ja nicht weinen!)* | Women's Choir: Angels/Jesus | *(You should truly not weep! Should truly not weep!)* |
| Ich hab übertreten die zehn Gebot | | I have broken the Ten Commandments. |
| Ich gehe und weine ja bitterlich | Penitent: Contralto | I go and weep most bitterly. |
| (*Du sollst ja nicht weinen! Sollst ja nicht weinen!)* | | *(You should truly not weep! Should truly not weep!)* |
| Ach komm und erbarme dich über mich! | | Ah, come and have mercy on me! |
| Hast du den übertreten die zehn Gebot | | If you have broken the Ten Commandments, |
| so fall auf die Knie und bete zu Gott! | | Then fall on your knees and pray to God! |
| *Liebe nur Gott in alle Zeit*! | | *Only love God forever*! |
| So wirst du erlangen die himmlische Freud' | **Frame** | So you will attain heavenly joy, |
| die himmlische Freud', die selige Stadt | **(extradiegetic)** | Heavenly joy, the holy city, |
| die himmlische Freud; war Petro bereit't | **Heavenly Realm** | Heavenly joy was prepared for Peter |
| durch Jesum und allen zur Seligkeit | Boys' Choir: Angels | By Jesus and for all for their salvation. |
| | Women's Choir: Angels | |

1. G. Mahler, *Symphony No. 3*, vi.
*Italics* mark changes by Mahler to original text.

heavenly joy of the holy city. However, despite the boy's joyful proclamation, there are a number of elements of Mahler's setting that call into question a reading of this song as a *Parsifal*-ian transfiguration. First, there is the identity of the penitent. The angels' introductory chorus, which sings of St. Peter's salvation, suggests that the penitent episode might be a flashback to Simon Peter's confrontation with Jesus at the rendition of Last Supper recorded in the Gospel of Luke (22:31–34), when Jesus informs Simon Peter that he will betray him. In another reading, the singer's female identity and the appearance at supper suggests that she might be read as the penitent woman, Mary Magdalene, the parallel to Wagner's Kundry, who Lipiner planned to feature in the title role of the second drama of his *Christus* tetralogy.[43] In a third interpretation, considering the title of the movement, "What the Angels Tell *Me*," the penitent may be Mahler himself. In all three of these readings, however, the association of the singer with the Mosaic Law and the partitioning from the angel's choir suggests that Mahler envisioned the figure as the Jew.[44]

Second, the troubled nature of the penitent's dialogue with Jesus, played out between the women's choir and the alto soloist, undermines the jubilant redemptive vision of the angels. Jesus's first response upon seeing the penitent is clearly ambivalent. The highest register of the women's choir's line, "Was stehst du denn hier?" (Why are you standing here?) is marked in the score as *grob* (rude), before they ameliorate the question with the *sanft* (gentle) remark, "Wenn ich dich anseh' so weinest du mir" (When I look at you, you weep). Up to this point, the music has retained its lively energy; yet following this response, the tempo slows as the penitent enters the acoustic stage of the song. Her vocal line is lyrical, but notably dissonant in this movement, shifting to D minor: "Und soll ich nicht weinen du gütiger Gott?" (And should I not weep, you gracious God?) The chorus, in the meantime, remains in the key of F major, attempting to soothe the fears of the penitent with the response, "du sollst nicht weinen!" (you should not weep).[45] However, the penitent appears not to hear them, continuing, "Ich habe übertreten die zehn Gebot" (I have transgressed the Ten Commandments). The penitent's confession, that she has sinned against God's Law, casts a dark shadow on the movement. Following her plea, "Ach komm und erbarme mich" (Ah come and have mercy on me) the playful bell sounds of the women and boy's choirs shift to the minor mode, where the sound of "bimm, bamm" imitates not the joyful bells of transfiguration but the lurching beat of a funeral march, accompanied by the tam tam. When all seems lost, however, the women's choir, speaking on behalf of Jesus, offers a solution, "Fall auf die Kniee und bete zu Gott. Liebe nur Gott in alle Zeit" (Fall on your knees and pray to God. Only love God forever!). The song ends with a return to the opening theme sung by the boys' and women's choirs in unison, thus closing the frame narrative of the story.

The dramatic tension of the episode lies in the isolation of the penitent Jew in the diegetic, earthly realm of the text. This isolation reads as evidence of the penitent's deafness or inability to hear the joyful words of redemption.[46] According to Carolyn Abbate, deafness in Mahler's music points to a kind of disjuncture between form and content, a rupture in our expectation for a cohesive narrative. Thus, it is also tied to the idea of intrusion, a musical gesture that, Abbate claims, "can be interpreted culturally as a trace of nineteenth century fears (and obsessions) with the notion of otherness."[47] In the fifth movement of the Third Symphony, the penitent is positioned as an intruder, through the contrast of her subjective voice with the choir and its articulation in a minor mode. The juxtaposition of her somber pleas with the joyful choir, marked in the score as "Lustig im Tempo und keck im Ausdruck" (Cheerful in tempo and cheeky in expression), draw further attention to her outsider status. The penitent's deafness points toward the stereotype of Jewish fidelity to the Law, displayed by Cain in Lipiner's *Adam*, a devotion that ultimately leads to tragedy. What, then, are we to make of the penitent's failed transfiguration? Is there still hope for the compassionate redemption that Lipiner had envisioned in his *Christus* tetralogy?

Mahler's isolation of the penitent in the fifth movement of the Third Symphony, and her apparent deafness to the joyful message of redemption draws attention to the legacy of suffering brought about by the Law that Lipiner highlighted in *Adam*. The use of the same alto soloist from the fourth movement suggests that Mahler was contemplating two alternate paths for the protagonist, one Nietzschean and one Wagnerian/Schopenhauerian, neither of which appears able to provide solace and comfort in the face of the Jewish subject's isolation and despair. Yet in the finale of the Third Symphony, Mahler resolves this conflict in a dramatic catharsis. The musical voices that have drawn us in to the tragic narrative of the suffering subject, will, in the final movement, be integrated into a harmonic cadence that creates a moment of empathy and encourages the audience to sympathize with the sufferer's plight. This alternative conclusion that Mahler proposes follows Lipiner's unorthodox reading of Nietzsche in reclaiming the Übermensch as the prophet of a new religious spirit. For Mahler, as for Lipiner, the Dionysian inspires the Will to Love, a communal redemptive spirit that embraces all beings, regardless of confession or creed.

## What Love Tells Me: Compassionate Love and Dionysian Dissonance

In the adagio finale of the Third Symphony, Mahler's voices are transformed into musical gestures that offer resolution to the problems posed in the earlier movements, the tragedy of world suffering and the inability of exclusive philosophies of compassion to provide comfort to those most marginalized. After allusions to the "faith" motif from Wagner's *Parsifal* and to the penitent's plea for compassion from the Nietzschean fourth movement, Mahler's Third Symphony, like Lipiner's *Adam,* presents a new compassionate resolution, that merges the passionate striving of the Dionysian Übermensch with a vision of all-embracing, redemptive love.

That Mahler's developed his aesthetic and ethical idea of compassion in the final movement in response to Wagner and Schopenhauer is evident from musical references to *Parsifal* and allusions to *Die Welt als Wille und Vorstellung* in his programmatic comments to friends. The opening bars of the Third Symphony's finale begin with a hymnlike melody in the strings, marked in the score as *sehr ausdrucksvoll gesungen* (sung very expressively). The motive, a rising fourth followed by a descending scale, mirrors the pattern of the "Faith" or *Glaubensmotiv,* from Wagner's *Parsifal.* This motive appears at several points in the drama, most notably after the morning prayer of the knights of the Grail, in the first act, and at the conclusion of the final act, when Parsifal heals Amfortas, and then raises high the Grail as the knight's proclaim the words, "Redemption to the Redeemer!"[48] To Natalie Bauer-Lechner, Mahler referred to the adagio in Schopenhauerian terms, claiming that in this movement, "ist alles aufgelöst in Ruhe und Sein; das Ixionsrad der Erscheinung ist endlich zum Stillstand gebracht" (everything is resolved into quiet being; the Ixion-wheel of appearances has at last been brought to a standstill).[49] In *Die Welt als Wille und Vorstellung,* Schopenhauer had written that the Will is the cause of all human suffering and that the suffering subject feels as though he is the "eternally thirsting Tantalus" who is "lying on the revolving wheel of Ixion, always drawing water in the sieve of the Daniads."[50] Mahler's near-quotation of *Parsifal*'s faith motive and reference to Schopenhauer thus might appear to affirm this idea of redemption through resignation and compassion as denial of the Will.

Yet, if we accept that Mahler's vision of compassion and compassionate art was guided by Lipiner, we would do well to not take these references at face value. For in his conversation with Wagner in Bayreuth, Lipiner had debated this very idea of resignation. As Lipiner explained to Meysenbug, resigning to suffering cannot offer a solution, for as long as people suffer under the "Zuchthausarbeit des Willens" (the servitude of the will) they will never find peace. Art, he claimed, must demonstrate that true redemption lies in the *willing* of suffering, not in the denial of it.[51]

That Mahler sought to relay a similar embrace of suffering in his Third Symphony is evident from the musical gestures in the final movement, which incorporate motives from the suffering subject in the fourth movement, "Was mir der Mensch erzählt." As in the Second Symphony, Mahler's incorporation of voices from his lied movements into the finales reflects the transformation of his musical subjects. The "suffering passage" in the final movement begins at measure 125 with the entrance of two violins, recalling the voice of "Weh," or woe, from the fourth movement who struggled with the singing protagonist. The recollection of the protagonist's inner struggle culminates in a musical quotation of the alto soloist's line "Tief ist ihr Weh" (deep is her sorrow!) in the horns at measure 180.

Mahler ultimately believed that this sorrow could inspire hope in offering an *inclusive* vision of compassionate love, one that, according to the failed transfiguration of the penitent in the fifth movement, had been withheld from the Jewish subject. Evidence of this program can be found in Mahler's letter to Fritz Löhr in 1895, that the final movement was to express "ein Zusammenfassen meiner Empfindung *allen Wesen* gegenüber" (a summary of my feelings toward all creatures).[52] Such ideas are echoed in the motto from the *Wunderhorn* folksong collection that Mahler assigned the final movement found at the opening of this chapter, "Vater, sieh an die Wunden mein! Kein Wesen laß verloren sein!" (Father look upon my wounds, let no creature be lost).[53] The text for this poem is a dialogue between Mary, Christ, and God, as Christ hangs from the cross. In response to his son's plea for redemption, the Father answers "Sohn, lieber Sohn mein, Alles was du begehrest, das soll sein" (Son, my dear son, all that you desire shall be done).[54] The Father's promise to let no creature be lost affirms the resolution of the previous movement's struggles in the image of a loving, compassionate father figure, who represents the absence of judgment and redemption for all. Musically, this inclusive gesture appears in the final bars of the symphony, where the voice of suffering, who previously appeared as the alto soloist and the "intruder" in fifth movement, is integrated into a harmonic resolution. The final gesture of affirmation is articulated by the chorale of horns playing in the "one tonality" of D major (mm. 304–309).[55]

While Mahler's turn to Christ in the epitaph for the conclusion of the Third Symphony appears to point toward a desired resolution for the "Jewish Question" in Christian mythology, this redemptive figure must also be closely examined. In the fall of 1896, after speaking to Lipiner about his *Christus* tetralogy, Mahler revised his description of the final movement, writing to Annie Mincieux that his finale represented "Es ist die letzte Stufe der Differenzierung: *Gott!* Oder wenn Sie wollen der Übermensch" (the last stage of differentiation: God! Or if you will, the Übermensch).[56] Mahler's equation of God with the Übermensch, the figure who represents the overcoming of a God-centered metaphysics, is further complicated by his earlier comments to friend Fritz Löhr that the final movement should be called "die *fröhliche* Wissenschaft."[57] What are we to make of Mahler's equation of God and Übermensch, and the titling of a movement about compassion after Nietzsche's collection of aphorisms in which he declares Mitleid the "grössten Gefahren" (the greatest danger)?[58]

Again, Lipiner's *Adam* can help us decode this complex nexus of references. In his biblical drama, Lipiner sought to elevate the suffering of the Jewish subject to a shared communal experience that could form bonds across religious and cultural divisions. To do so, he turned to Nietzsche's Übermensch and the concept of the Dionysian. Martha Nussbaum writes that the Dionysian is a "highly intellectual, heightened sense of freedom, harmony and unity," which embraces immense suffering, in order to be open to the possibility of great joy.[59] Nietzsche also equated the Dionysian with the musical term of dissonance, which he understood as articulating the empowering force of creativity. In *Zarathustra*, dissonance is linked to self-overcoming and the establishment of new values, both of which can only be achieved by the loving of fate, *amor fati*, and the willing of Eternal Return. Dionysian dissonance, therefore, points toward a refashioning of one's inner drives, recalling humanity's continual process of being or becoming. In his plans for the *Christus* tetralogy, Lipiner had indicated that the sufferings of Cain would be redeemed through a new figure who would embody both this Promethean power of active love and the spirit of compassion.

The Christ figure that Mahler refers to in the epitaph of his conclusion, therefore, reflects the merging of the outsider turned compassionate martyr with the Dionysian Übermensch that Lipiner proposed in his *Christus* tetralogy. This mediating figure encompasses the essence of their vision of compassion: the recognition of suffering in the Other and the transformation of pain into life-affirming joy. By radically fusing Übermensch and

God, Dionysus and Christ (subsuming Nietzsche's opposition of these two figures as the "life-affirming" and "life-dying" spirits), Lipiner and Mahler found a means to articulate their own subjectivity as German-Jews and a counterfigure to antisemitic stereotypes of the uncompassionate Jew. While this move appears surprising, Lipiner and Mahler were only the beginning of a long line of artists and philosophers who would likewise appropriate Nietzsche's language in the service of cultural renewal and religious rebirth.[60] In reclaiming the Übermensch as a compassionate figure, Mahler and Lipiner found a model of capturing the spirit of struggle and the demand for empathy, with their ardent belief that humanity needed the image of a loving God to inspire true community. For Mahler and Lipiner, God is not dead but only the old moral code of the Law—the commands "thou shalt" and "thou shalt not" that keep humanity at a distance from the divine being and from one another.

That Mahler envisioned himself and Lipiner as the poet-priests of this utopian religious spirit embodied in Christ, the Dionysian Übermensch, is evident from comments he made in the summer of 1896, while composing the Third Symphony, and in 1898, in response to Lipiner's *Adam*. In 1896 to Natalie Bauer-Lechner, Mahler compared his experience of capturing human suffering in his symphony to Christ on the Mount of Olives:

> Heute ist mir . . . plötzlich blitzartig aufgegangen: Christus auf dem Ölberg, der den Leidenskelch bis zur Neige leeren mußte und—wollte. Wem dieser Kelch bestimmt ist, der kann und will ihn nicht zurückweisen, doch muß ihn zu Zeiten eine Todesangst überkommen, wenn er denkt, was ihm noch bevorsteht.
>
> [So today it came to me in a flash: Christ on the Mount of Olives, compelled to drain the cup of sorrow to the dregs—and willing it to be so. No one for whom this cup is destined can or will refuse it, but at times a deathly fear must overcome him when he thinks of what is before him.][61]

In his biblical allusion to Christ's martyrdom, Mahler refers here to the *Leidenskelch*, or cup of sorrow. In a letter to Lipiner two years later, referring to *Adam*, he evoked the draining of a different cup, the wine of Dionysus:

> Das ist ein wahrhaft dionysisches Werk! . . . Was ist es denn, was alles Lebende in die Gewalt des Dionysos gibt? Der Wein berauscht und erhöht der Zustand des trinkenden. *Was* aber ist der Wein?—Der Darstellung ist es bis jetzt noch nie gelungen, wie sich in der Musik in jeder Note von selbst ergibt. In Deiner

> Darstellung weht *diese* Musik! . . . Sie erzählt nicht vom Wein und schildert seine Wirkungen—sondern sie ist der Wein, sie ist Dionysus!
>
> [This is a truly Dionysian work! . . . *What* ever is it that delivers all living creatures into the power of Dionysus? Wine intoxicates, intensifying the drinker's condition. But *what* is wine?—No visual representation has ever yet succeeded in capturing what flowers spontaneously from every note of music. *This* music lives and breathes throughout your poetry in this work of yours. It is really unique.—Instead of telling of wine or describing its effects, it *is* wine, it *is* Dionysus!][62]

Here, the cup that Mahler refers to is one of intoxication, of wine that "elevates the condition of the drinker."[63] For Mahler, Christ's cup of sorrow, symbolizing the world's suffering, and Dionysus's wine, the intoxication experienced by "all living creatures" in community, mirror one another. These two images capture how the compassionate artist transforms sorrow into a powerful communal experience in the transcendent language of music and musical-poetics. In another letter to Lipiner, written a month later, Mahler writes:

> Eins ist mir wieder groß aufgegangen in Deiner Art: ein neuer tiefer Zusammenhang Deines Schaffens mit Deinem musikalischen Wesen . . . Mein lieber Siegfried: Du musizierst ja! Dich wird nie jemand besser verstehen können als ein Musiker, und ich kann wohl speziell hinzufügen, als ich! Es ist mir manchmal geradezu lächerlich zumute, wie verwandt meine "Musik" der Deinen ist. Besonders im "Adam."
>
> [There is something else that has become grandly clear to me about your essential nature: a new and deep connection between your creativeness and the musical side of your being. . . . My dear Siegfried: you do make music! No one will ever be able to understand you better than a musician, and I may specifically add: than *myself.* It is sometimes to me quite a joke how closely my "music" is related to yours. This has become particularly clear to me from *Adam*.][64]

This deep connection that Mahler recognized between his and Lipiner's works lay in their ability to evoke both sides of the artistic-creative and compassionate spirit of Christ-Dionysus. This dual figure embodied their vision of a new religious spirit that found expression in their symphonic and dramatic works, a life-affirming impulse that would serve as the basis for inclusive community.[65]

## Conclusion

In 1897, shortly after Mahler arrived in Vienna to take over as director of the Court Opera, the press was abuzz with the rumor that Lipiner was writing the libretto for an opera, to which Mahler would compose the music.[66] The text in question was undoubtedly *Adam*, which the poet completed in 1898. This collaboration, however, never came to fruition, and Lipiner abandoned his *Christus* project sometime later.[67] As the drafts for the last three dramas have gone missing, one can only speculate how Lipiner might have planned the conclusion of his biblical *Meisterwerk*. His early feuilleton articles suggest that the final stage of compassion would be embodied in the voice of the child. In his essay, "Weihnachten," of 1880, Lipiner wrote of the child as the symbol of a new redemptive spirit.[68] Mahler was also drawn to this idea, for he had originally intended for his Third Symphony to end with a movement entitled "Was mir das Kind erzählt" (What the Child Tells Me) a setting of another *Wunderhorn* folksong, "Das himmlische Leben" (The Heavenly Life) that he had first composed in 1892. When he decided instead on the adagio finale, this song eventually formed the final movement of his Fourth Symphony.[69] For Mahler and Lipiner, the child represents the beginning of a new compassionate relationship between humanity and the divine, a community of *Gotteskinder*, or God's children, in which even they, as Jews, would be welcomed.[70]

Mahler's marriage to Alma Schindler caused a rift between the two friends for a period of nearly seven years (1902–1909) and for this reason it is unknown if Lipiner attended the premiere of Mahler's Third Symphony in Vienna, which took place in December 1904.[71] (See figs. 2.1a and 2.1b.) This premiere is significant in that it marks the first major success Mahler experienced performing one of his own compositions in Vienna. Although Mahler publicly rejected explanatory program notes in a published account to the music critic Max Marschalk in 1901, he did provide the audience with the text of the lieder.[72] Moreover, the remarks of music critics such as Julius Korngold, writing for the *Neue Freie Presse*, suggest that the movement titles and descriptions were likely well known to many audience members. In his review, Korngold identified the vocal movements as an evocation of Mahler's own faith struggle:

> Nun da das Wort eintritt, umschwirren uns wieder dringlicher die Fragen des poetischen Programms. Gelangt der Mensch, der vielleicht Gustav Mahler heißt, nachdem er die Natur belauscht hat zu spekulativer Einkehr in sich selbst? Flüchtet er dann im fünften Satze zur Religion, um sechsten und letzten zu der tröstenden und versöhnenden Menschenliebe?
>
> [Only as the word appears, does the question of the poetic program whir around us again more urgently. Does the man, who perhaps is called Gustav Mahler, after he listens to nature achieve a speculative retreat into himself?

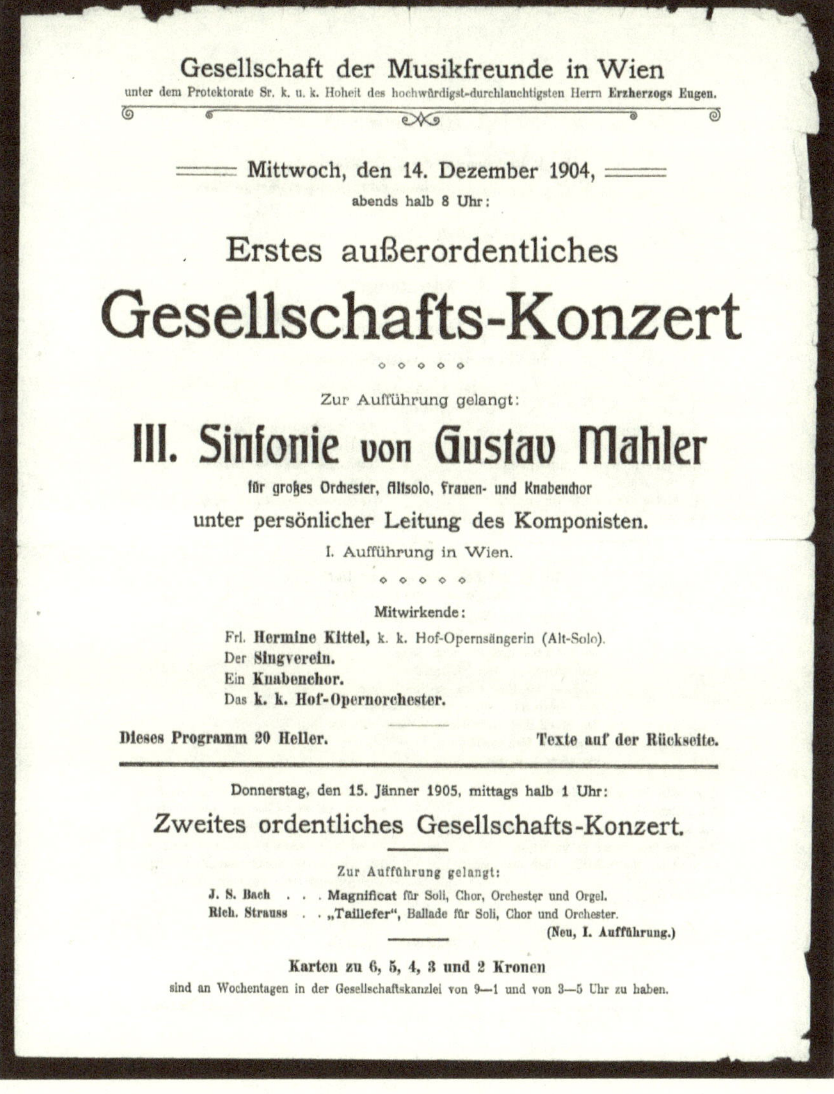

Gesellschaft der Musikfreunde in Wien

unter dem Protektorate Sr. k. u. k. Hoheit des hochwürdigst-durchlauchtigsten Herrn **Erzherzogs Eugen.**

Mittwoch, den 14. Dezember 1904,

abends halb 8 Uhr:

Erstes außerordentliches

# Gesellschafts-Konzert

Zur Aufführung gelangt:

**III. Sinfonie von Gustav Mahler**

für großes Orchester, Altsolo, Frauen- und Knabenchor

unter persönlicher Leitung des Komponisten.

I. Aufführung in Wien.

Mitwirkende:

Frl. **Hermine Kittel,** k. k. Hof-Opernsängerin (Alt-Solo).
Der **Singverein.**
Ein **Knabenchor.**
Das **k. k. Hof-Opernorchester.**

**Dieses Programm 20 Heller.** **Texte auf der Rückseite.**

Donnerstag, den 15. Jänner 1905, mittags halb 1 Uhr:

Zweites ordentliches Gesellschafts-Konzert.

Zur Aufführung gelangt:

**J. S. Bach** . . . **Magnificat** für Soli, Chor, Orchester und Orgel.
**Rich. Strauss** . . **„Taillefer"**, Ballade für Soli, Chor und Orchester.
(**Neu, I. Aufführung.**)

**Karten zu 6, 5, 4, 3 und 2 Kronen**

sind an Wochentagen in der Gesellschaftskanzlei von 9—1 und von 3—5 Uhr zu haben.

Figure 2.1a and 2.1b. Program for the Vienna premiere of Gustav Mahler's Third Symphony, December 14, 1904. Fonds Henry-Louis de La Grange, Médiathèque Musicale Mahler, Paris.

> Does he escape in the fifth movement to religion and in the last to the consolation and reconciliatory human kindness?][73]

Yet not all reviews were positive. Max Vancsa writing for the *Neue Musikalische Presse*, claimed that the work's ironic tone "corrodes and destroys the listener."[74] Alex Winterberger of the *Leipziger Neueste Nachrichten*, referred to it as an "oriental symphony," betraying his own

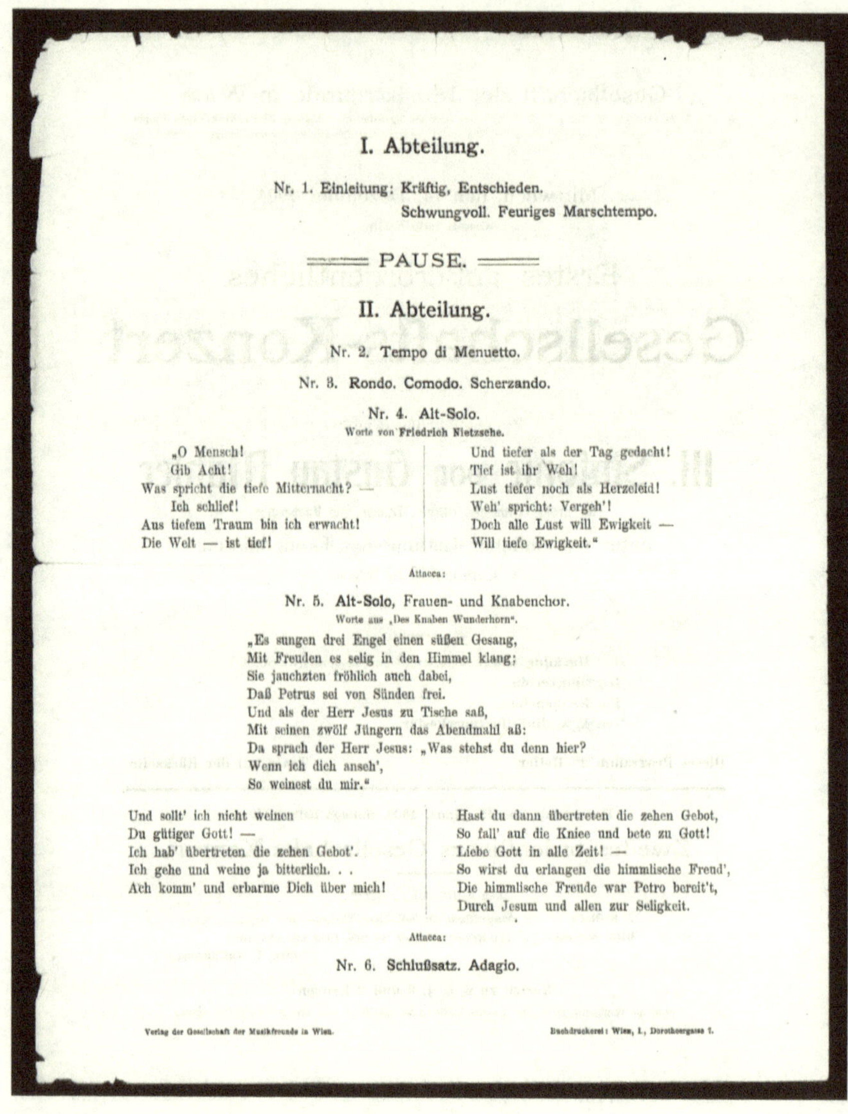

**I. Abteilung.**

Nr. 1. **Einleitung: Kräftig, Entschieden.**
**Schwungvoll. Feuriges Marschtempo.**

═══ PAUSE. ═══

**II. Abteilung.**

Nr. 2. **Tempo di Menuetto.**

Nr. 3. **Rondo. Comodo. Scherzando.**

Nr. 4. **Alt-Solo.**
Worte von **Friedrich Nietzsche.**

„O Mensch!
Gib Acht!
Was spricht die tiefe Mitternacht? —
Ich schlief!
Aus tiefem Traum bin ich erwacht!
Die Welt — ist tief!

Und tiefer als der Tag gedacht!
Tief ist ihr Weh!
Lust tiefer noch als Herzeleid!
Weh' spricht: Vergeh'!
Doch alle Lust will Ewigkeit —
Will tiefe Ewigkeit."

Attacca:

Nr. 5. **Alt-Solo,** Frauen- und Knabenchor.
Worte aus „Des Knaben Wunderhorn".

„Es sungen drei Engel einen süßen Gesang,
Mit Freuden es selig in den Himmel klang;
Sie jauchzten fröhlich auch dabei,
Daß Petrus sei von Sünden frei.
Und als der Herr Jesus zu Tische saß,
Mit seinen zwölf Jüngern das Abendmahl aß:
Da sprach der Herr Jesus: „Was stehst du denn hier?
Wenn ich dich anseh',
So weinest du mir."

Und sollt' ich nicht weinen
Du gütiger Gott! —
Ich hab' übertreten die zehen Gebot'.
Ich gehe und weine ja bitterlich. . .
Ach komm' und erbarme Dich über mich!

Hast du dann übertreten die zehen Gebot,
So fall' auf die Kniee und bete zu Gott!
Liebe Gott in alle Zeit! —
So wirst du erlangen die himmlische Freud',
Die himmlische Freude war Petro bereit't,
Durch Jesum und allen zur Seligkeit.

Attacca:

Nr. 6. **Schlußsatz. Adagio.**

Verlag der Gesellschaft der Musikfreunde in Wien.

Buchdruckerei: Wien, I., Dorotheergasse 7.

Figure 2.1a and 2.1b. (*continued*)

antisemitic prejudices, and explicitly denounced it as a Wagnerian derivation: "Whenever he tries to plumb the depths of his own heart, as in the fourth, fifth and sixth movements, and especially in the last, he is enmeshed in a Wagnerian net which holds him so tightly that he tosses and turns in every direction in order to escape, but in vain."[75] These would not be the last attacks against Mahler, his compositions, or his directing style. Three years later, the rising antisemitic sentiments in Vienna would drive him from his post as the director of the Court Opera. Yet, at least one person in the audience at the Third's premiere would be profoundly affected by Mahler's musical-dramatic vision, the composer Arnold Schoenberg, who would begin shortly afterward to sketch out plans for a dramatic work integrating song and symphony, a work that would eventually become his oratorio, *Die Jakobsleiter*, discussed in the following chapter.

Mahler's Second and Third Symphonies form the musical corollary of Lipiner's biblical dramatic works and relay, through a musical idiom, the struggle for faith and understanding at the core of compassionate art. Interestingly, both Mahler and Lipiner referred to the same biblical figure to describe their experience as outsiders desiring to belong, their demand for justice and compassion from God, and their adamant belief that art could provide hope in the face of suffering: the Hebrew patriarch Jacob. Shortly after completing his Third Symphony and following his discussion with Lipiner about the *Christus* project in August 1896, Mahler spoke of Jacob as the symbol of the artist-creator. According to the composer, "wenn die Juden nichts als das erfunden hätten, müßten sie kolossale Leute gewesen sein" (if the Jews had been responsible for nothing but this image, they would still inevitably have grown to be a formidable people).[76] Paul Natorp, the executor of Lipiner's literary estate, claims that Lipiner also identified with the Hebrew patriarch as a representation of the struggle to "capture the problems of Christianity" and to "bring it to the height of perfection."[77] Lipiner envisioned a rebirth of religious spirit through compassionate art that would transcend the categories of religious difference and offer new hope for community and understanding in the modern world. In the end, this vision became known to the world through Mahler's symphonies, particularly the Second and Third, which employ dissonant musical voices and dramatic ruptures to challenge the underlying hypocrisy of dogmatic religion and narratives of compassion that excluded the Jewish subject. As the following chapters reveal, Mahler's model of compassionate art attained new heights of expression in the writings and musical compositions of the next generation of artists: Schoenberg, Beer-Hofmann, and Zweig. In their works of biblical theater, they do not just define the German-Jewish subject as worthy of compassion but also identify the co-constituative role of the German-Jewish subject in the making of compassionate art.[78] Their Jewish protagonists embody the dynamic nature of musical motives, ever-changing and evolving, while their revisions of biblical narratives articulate the transcendent power of community.

## Notes

1. Fischer, *Gustav Mahler*, 33.
2. A. Mahler, *Memories and Letters*, 101.
3. Knittel, *Seeing Mahler*, 5.
4. Roller, *Bildnisse von Gustav Mahler*, 25–26.
5. Bauer-Lechner, Killian, and Martner, *Erinnerungen*, 26 [Bauer-Lechner and Franklin, *Recollections*, 30].
6. Walter, *Gustav Mahler*, 127.
7. Monelle, *Sense of Music*, 155.
8. A. Mahler, *Erinnerungen an Gustav Mahler*, 137 [A. Mahler, *Memories and Letters*, 109].
9. Adorno, *Mahler: A Musical Physiognomy*, 149.
10. Pecker-Berio, "Mahler's Jewish Parable," 94, 96.
11. Silverman, *Becoming Austrians*, 172.
12. Spector, "Forget Assimilation," 356.
13. Toews suggests that Mahler's narrative "I" acts and interacts in a performative manner, much like characters in a drama. Its voice is made apparent "through encounter, dialogue and reflection within the constantly shifting horizons of memory and expectation." Toews, "Road into the Open," 81–82.
14. Steinberg, *Listening to Reason*, 199.
15. That Mahler viewed his own musical legacy as a response to Wagner's ideology is supported by an anecdote relayed by Natalie Bauer-Lechner, who recalls a conversation during rehearsals for a performance of the *Ring* cycle in September 1898, in which the composer references the Jewish characteristics that Wagner intentionally attributed to the character of Mime. Mahler identified with this character, commenting, "Ich weiß nur *einen* Mimen . . . und der bin *ich*!" (I know only one Mime . . . and that is me!). Bauer-Lechner, Killian, and Martner, *Erinnerungen*, 122.
16. Charles Maier also identifies the shift in tone and character in Mahler's symphonies, which "intensifies or stylizes mood and emotive stance," as evidence of the composer's theatricality. Maier, "Mahler's Theater," 76.
17. Bauer-Lechner, Killian, and Martner, *Erinnerungen*, 68.
18. McGrath, *Dionysian Art and Populist Politics*, 101.
19. Additional references to Lipiner can be found in the title for Mahler's First Symphony (composed 1887–1888): *Titan*, an homage to the Titan hero of Lipiner's poem, *Der entfesselte Prometheus*, and in the title of Mahler's symphonic poem *Totenfeier* (Funeral Rites), which refers to Lipiner's translation of a dramatic poem by Adam Mickiewicz, published in 1887. *Totenfeier* became the first movement of the Second Symphony. See Kita, "The Revolutionary, the Artist, and the Heroic Martyr," and Hefling, "Mahler's Totenfeier."
20. Bauer-Lechner, Killian, and Martner, *Erinnerungen*, 40 [Bauer-Lechner and Franklin, *Recollections*, 43–44].

21. Bauer-Lechner, Killian, and Martner, *Erinnerungen*, 40 [Bauer-Lechner and Franklin, *Recollections*, 43–44].

22. Lipiner, *Prometheus*, 111.

23. The evidence from the summer of 1893 includes a few sketched bars of themes dated "1893 Steinbach" that Mahler gave to Bauer-Lechner, although Franklin suspects that undated early outlines for the symphony might also have been written at this time. Franklin, *Mahler, Symphony No. 3*, 41–45.

24. Lipiner, "Der Sommer," 1–2. In 1896, Mahler made a reference of Hölderlin's poem "Der Rhein" to Bauer-Lechner when describing the "Summer marches in" program of the first movement; Lipiner quotes the same poem in his feuilleton article, "Der Sommer." Bauer-Lechner, Killian, and Martner, *Erinnerungen*, 56.

25. Constantin Floros has noted many of Mahler's notes in the score of the first movement of the Third Symphony, composed in the summer of 1896, draw on the imagery from Lipiner's poem "Genesis," from *Buch der Freude*, in 1880, in particular "das Gesindel," "die Schlacht beginnt," and "Der Südsturm." Floros, *Gustav Mahler*, 82–83.

26. G. Mahler and Blaukopf, *Gustav Mahler Briefe*, 150.

27. G. Mahler and Blaukopf, *Gusgav Mahler Briefe*, 146 [G. Mahler, A. Mahler, and Martner, *Selected Letters*, 164].

28. See Mahler's comments to Natalie Bauer-Lechner, "Die höchsten Menschheitsfragen, die ich in der Zweiten stellte und zu beantworten suchte . . . sie können mich hier nicht bewegen. Denn was hat das im All zu bedeuten, wo *alles* lebt und leben *muß* und *wird*?" Bauer-Lechner, Killian, and Martner, *Erinnerungen*, 62.

29. See Knapp, who refers to Mikhail Bakhtin's term, heteroglossia, to describe multivocality in Mahler's music. Knapp, *Symphonic Metamorphoses*, 30, 272.

30. Nussbaum, "Compassion," 28.

31. Gramit, "Circulation of the Lied, 307.

32. Knapp, *Symphonic Metamorphoses*, 121.

33. Bauer-Lechner and Franklin, *Recollections*, 44.

34. Adorno, *Mahler: A Musical Physiognomy*, 41. While there is not room in the present study to interrogate the third movements of the Second and Third Symphonies, it is significant that both are also derived from *Wunderhorn* songs, "Des Antonius von Padua Fischpredigt" in the Second Symphony and "Ablösung im Sommer" in the Third Symphony; thus, the development from the lied as the melodic core of a symphonic movement to the lied inserted as an independent movement also represents a critical aspect of Mahler's form. See Knapp, *Symphonic Metamorphoses*, chapters 3 and 4.

35. Johnson, "Mahler and the Idea of Nature," 30.

36. Franklin, *Mahler, Symphony No. 3*, 68.

37. "Wie kann ich den glücklich sein, wenn irgendwo ein anders Geschöpf leidet?" G. Mahler and Blaukopf, *Gustav Mahler Briefe*, xvii. Alma attributes this question to one of Mahler's favorite authors, Fyodor Dostoyevsky.

38. Lipiner, *Prometheus*, 154.

39. Lipiner, *Prometheus*, 174.

40. Lipiner, *Prometheus*, 117–118. For another intertext for Mahler's final movement, see Kita, "The Revolutionary, the Artist, and the Heroic Martyr."

41. The original title in the collection *Des Knaben Wunderhorn* is "Armer Kinder Bettlerlied." Arnim and Brentano, *Knaben Wunderhorn*, 674.

42. Floros, "Studien zur Parsifal-Rezeption," 50.

43. The identity of Mary Magdalene has long been disputed and over time she has come to be conflated with various Mary figures in the Bible. It is likely, from the reference in the "Weihnachten" essay, and from the fragments of the *Christus* trilogy analyzed by Helmut von Hartungen in his 1932 dissertation, that Lipiner identified her as the sinful woman who washed Jesus's feet and therefore also envisioned her as a parallel figure to Wagner's Kundry, who washes the feet of Parsifal in the drama's final act. Hartungen, "Dichter Siegfried Lipiner," 59.

44. Carl Niekerk notes that a number of songs in the *Wunderhorn* collection are openly antisemitic or feature texts about "Jews interfering with Christian rituals." Niekerk, *Reading Mahler*, 67.

45. Franklin, *Mahler, Symphony No. 3*, 70. The penitent's echoing responses were an addition by Mahler to the original text.

46. As Carl Niekerk notes, the penitent does not respond to the words of Jesus, or join in the final choir, casting doubt on whether the message of redemption was actually heard. Niekerk, *Reading Mahler*, 109.

47. Abbate, *Unsung Voices*, 152.

48. Solvik, "Culture and Creative Imagination," 327. Solvik refers to this theme as the "Redemption" motive.

49. Bauer-Lechner, Killian, and Martner, *Erinnerungen*, 68 [Bauer-Lechner and Franklin, *Recollections*, 67].

50. Schopenhauer, *World as Will and Representation*, 220.

51. Stummann-Bowert, *Malwida von Meysenbug—Paul Rée*, 225.

52. G. Mahler and Blaukopf, *Gustav Mahler Briefe*, 150; G. Mahler, A. Mahler, and Martner, *Selected Letters*, 164.

53. G. Mahler and Blaukopf, *Gustav Mahler Briefe*, 189.

54. Arnim and Brentano, *Knaben Wunderhorn*, 753.

55. Bauer-Lechner, Killian, and Martner, *Erinnerungen*, 66.

56. G. Mahler, *Unbekannte Briefe*, 127.

57. G. Mahler and Blaukopf, *Gustav Mahler Briefe*, 150.

58. Nietzsche, *Werke in Drei Bänden*, vol. 2, 159.

59. Nussbaum, "Transfigurations of Intoxication," 95.

60. See Jacob Golomb, who claims that Nietzsche's philosophy had a particular attraction for *Grenzjuden*, or marginal Jews who found themselves caught between two worlds and found in his writings encouragement on their "search for authenticity," "Nietzsche and the Marginal Jews," 164. Paul Mendes-Flohr, meanwhile, reveals that for Martin Buber and many members of the Jewish Renaissance, Nietzsche "represented the possibility of regeneration of Jewish cultural and spiritual life," see "Zarathustra's Apostle," 240.

61. Bauer-Lechner, Killian, and Martner, *Erinnerungen*, 59 [Bauer-Lechner and Franklin, *Recollections*, 62].

62. G. Mahler and Blaukopf, *Gustav Mahler Briefe*, 264 [G. Mahler, A. Mahler, and Martner, *Selected Letters*, 236].

63. G. Mahler and Blaukopf, *Gustav Mahler Briefe*, 264 [G. Mahler, A. Mahler, and Martner, *Selected Letters*, 236].

64. G. Mahler and Blaukopf, *Gustav Mahler Briefe*, 272 [G. Mahler, A. Mahler, and Martner, *Selected Letters*, 243].

65. Dionysus also appears in their works under the guise of Pan, to whom Mahler referred in the program of the Third Symphony in the first movement, which he entitled "Pan

marches in." In his speech to the Leseverein, Lipiner had referred to Pan as "das All-Eine," while in his essay, "Der Sommer," written for the *Deutsche Zeitung* in 1881, Pan represents the feeling of the true loss of self ("Selbst-losigkeit").

66. "Lipiner an einem Opernlibretto gedichtet, das der Director des k.k. Hofoperntheaters Herr v. Mahler . . . bei ihm bestellt hat" ("Theater, Kunst und Literatur: Coulissenschau," 4). "Direktor Mahler componiert an einer Oper, zu welcher ihm der Goldmark'sche Merlin-Librettist Siegfried Lipiner den Text geschrieben" (H. W. "Aus dem Souffleurkasten," 3).

67. G. Mahler and Blaukopf, *Gustav Mahler Briefe*, 150; G. Mahler, A. Mahler, and Martner, *Selected Letters*, 164.

68. Lipiner, "Weihnachten," 1.

69. La Grange, *Years of Challenge*, 768–769.

70. In their fascination for the child, Lipiner and Mahler draw on Nietzsche, who wrote in the chapter "The Three Metamorphoses" in *Also sprach Zarathustra* of the child who embodies the final stage of this transformation: "Vergessen, ein Neubeginnen, ein Spiel, ein aus sich rollendes Rad, eine erste Bewegung, ein heiliges Ja-sagen" (Forgetting, a new beginning, a game, a self-rolling wheel, a first movement, a holy yes). Nietzsche, *Werke in drei Bänden*, vol. 2, 294.

71. On the break between Mahler and Lipiner, see Kita, "Jacob Struggling with the Angel," 221–223.

72. Marschalk, "Gustav Mahler," 375.

73. Korngold, "Musik," 3.

74. Quoted in Franklin, *Mahler, Symphony No. 3*, 30.

75. Quoted in La Grange, *Triumph and Disillusion*, 63.

76. Bauer-Lechner, Killian, and Martner, *Erinnerungen*, 76 [Bauer-Lechner and Franklin, *Recollections*, 76].

77. Natorp, "Vorwort zu 'Adam,'" 7.

78. See Aschheim, who refers to the role of Jews in German culture as "not simply contributory, but co-constitutive," Aschheim, *In Times of Crisis*, 87.

# 3

# POLYPHONY AS A POETICS OF COMPASSION: ARNOLD SCHOENBERG'S *DIE JAKOBSLEITER*

Ich will seit langem ein Oratorium schreiben, das als Inhalt haben sollte: wie sich der Mensch von heute, der durch den Materialismus, Sozialismus, Anarchie, durchgegangen ist, der Atheist war, aber sich doch ein Restchen alten Glaubens bewahrt hat (in Form von Aberglauben), wie dieser moderne Mensch mit Gott streitet (siehe auch "Jakob ringt" von Strindberg) und schließlich dazu gelangt, Gott zu finden und religiös zu werden.

[For a long time I have been wanting to write an oratorio on the following subject: modern man, having passed through materialism, socialism, and anarchy and, despite having been an atheist, still having in him some residue of ancient faith (in the form of superstition), wrestles with God (see also Strindberg's "Jacob Wrestling") and finally succeeds in finding God and becoming religious.]

Arnold Schoenberg to Richard Dehmel, 1912

In December 1912, the composer Arnold Schoenberg wrote to the poet Richard Dehmel about his plans to compose an oratorio. Schoenberg's letter is one of the first references to the project that would eventually become *Die Jakobsleiter* (Jacob's Ladder), one of the most perplexing works in the composer's oeuvre. The project began as a plan for seven-movement choral symphony comprising musical settings of modern and ancient poetry as well as biblical verses.[1] This massive work would combine several musical-theatrical genres, including a monodrama, entitled *Totentanz der Prinzipien* (Death Dance of the Principles) and an oratorio finale, entitled *Der Glaube des Desillusionierten* (The Faith of the Disillusioned).[2] By 1917,

Schoenberg abandoned his plans for the choral symphony and decided to compose the final movement as an independent work, which he retitled, *Die Jakobsleiter.* Although this work remained a fragment upon his death in 1951, frequent references to *Die Jakobsleiter* in Schoenberg's correspondence and in his later theoretical essays suggest that this work, in particular the libretto, retained a personal significance for the composer throughout his life.[3]

*Die Jakobsleiter* and the monodrama from the choral symphony that inspired it, *Totentanz der Prinzipien,* provide evidence of Schoenberg's attempts to inspire collective spiritual renewal through compassionate art, following the musical models of Mahler and inspired by the aesthetics of Schopenhauer, Wagner, and Nietzsche. These works laid the critical groundwork not only for Schoenberg's twelve-tone method of composition but also for his "aesthetic theology" that shaped his entire musical oeuvre from this point forward.[4] Many of the key ideas in *Totentanz* and *Die Jakobsleiter* relating to the limits of the Word as revelation and the ineffable nature of God would be expanded and elaborated in Schoenberg's later opera, *Moses und Aron* (1927–1932).

Schoenberg's musical compositions were deeply interconnected with his philosophical and religious views. As his correspondence and essays on music, from *Die Harmonielehre* (Theory of Harmony 1911) to *Stil und Gedanke* (Style and Idea 1947), attest, he believed that his search for a new musical language constituted a divine mission. For this reason, scholars have often interpreted the evolution of Schoenberg's musical style as reflections of concurrent shifts in his relationship to his religious faith.[5] His break with the Late-Romantic style of Mahler and Wagner roughly corresponds to the time of his conversion to Protestantism in 1898, while his experiments with atonality occurred during his turn to mysticism in the first decades of the twentieth century. Finally, his discovery of serial composition and the twelve-tone method emerged concurrently with his forays into Zionist politics in the 1920s and his eventual return to the Jewish faith in 1933. However, a closer look at the composer's unfinished works from 1915–1917 suggest that during this earlier period, Schoenberg's interest in spiritualism overlapped with his critical reflection on the Jewish Question and inspired an often-overlooked aspect of the composer's artistic development: his search for a new *poetic* language.[6] The libretti of *Totentanz der Prinzipien* and *Die Jakobsleiter* reveal that at the same time Schoenberg sought to free himself from the Western tonal system through the emancipation of musical dissonance, he was developing a philosophy and aesthetics of compassion, grounded in new poetic modes that would express the relationship between humanity and God as a reflection of a multiplicity and heterogeneity united in a single spirit.

The libretto of *Die Jakobsleiter* is attributed most often to the spiritual writings of the Swedish philosopher Emanuel Swedenborg and their poetic expression found in August Strindberg's dramas and Honoré de Balzac's philosophical novel, *Séraphita* (1834). Indeed, in addition to the mention of *Jakob ringt* in his letter to Dehmel, Schoenberg had planned in 1912–1913 to set Balzac's text to music and even included a quote from the novel in the final libretto for *Die Jakobsleiter.*[7] However, this chapter reads the text of the oratorio and its companion piece, *Totentanz der Prinzipien*, in light of another important work that shaped Schoenberg's worldview at this time: Schopenhauer's essay "On Religion" (1850).

In both *Die Jakobsleiter* and *Totentanz*, Schoenberg reflects on the limitations of the Mosaic Law (*die Gebote*) as a form of revelation. As his unpublished notes reveal, Schoenberg interprets the Law, embodied in the words "Du sollst," with a stereotype of Jews as blindly devoted to Jehovah and his laws; a stereotype that Schopenhauer had claimed served as evidence of Jewish immutability and their inability to feel compassion.[8] This chapter explores how Schoenberg probed the paradoxes of Law by experimenting with a musical-poetic language based on the principles of polyphony. In the monodrama *Totentanz*, he employs alliteration and rhythmic syntax to establish correspondences between words based on their sounds. This musical-poetics of revelation problematizes the one-sided nature of the Law and its inability to represent the many-sidedness of the divine spirit, which always remains just beyond human comprehension.

In *Die Jakobsleiter*, Schoenberg offers a resolution to the paradoxes of the Law posed in *Totentanz* by introducing *Gebet* (prayer) as an alternative to *Gebote*. Prayer resolves the conflict between the God who demands obedience and the compassionate God. The figure who exemplifies this new relationship between the human and the divine is the Chosen One. Like the Hebrew patriarch Jacob, the Chosen One struggles with his destiny. Like Schoenberg, he is a figure who embodies multiple subjectivities, and he is described in the text through the metaphor of a musical form: variation on a theme. His role is that of a mediator—first, he must demonstrate compassion to the "lower souls" in this heavenly hierarchy, and then he must teach them to pray, to recognize their "shared substance" with the divine. Thus, through the Chosen One, Schoenberg recasts the image of the Jewish subject from the slave of the Law to the revealer of the indivisibility, unity, and eternity of the divine spirit.

Lipiner's vision of compassion, realized by Mahler in his Second and Third Symphonies, served as an important framework for Schoenberg's compassionate musical-poetics. Like Lipiner's Cain and Mahler's penitent in the Third Symphony, Schoenberg's musical voices in *Totentanz der Prinzipien* and *Die Jakobsleiter* resist the Law and demand compassion from the divine spirit. While Mahler integrated lieder into the symphonic form as dramatic interludes, Schoenberg turned to explicit dramatic forms, the monodrama and the oratorio, and sought a more complex and deeper revelation of compassion in a new form of composition that finds its inner logic outside of the tonal language of the Western classical music tradition.

This analysis of *Totentanz der Prinzipien* and *Die Jakobsleiter* draws attention to a shift occurring in the reception of discourses of compassion by German-Jewish writers and composers in Vienna around the beginning of World War I. While Lipiner and Mahler were ultimately invested in overcoming Jewish Otherness by dissolving difference, Schoenberg's works seek a productive synthesis of Christianity and Judaism through new musical-dramatic modes that embrace multifaceted subjectivities in the form of musical heterogeneity. Thus, in their provoking and unsettling musical and poetic languages, Schoenberg's *Totentanz der Prinzipien* and *Die Jakobsleiter* offer a new means of expressing the conflicted nature of the German-Jewish subject that mirror similar developments in the writings of two contemporary playwrights composing biblical theater at the very same time: Richard Beer-Hofmann and Stefan Zweig.

## Schoenberg in Defense of Judaism: Difference, the Law, and the Un-representable

Schoenberg's search for a new poetic language to articulate the compassionate nature of the Jewish faith emerged concurrently with his explorations into theosophy and spiritualism and his engagement with antisemitic rhetoric found in the writings of Arthur Schopenhauer. Schoenberg's letters to the Expressionist painter Wassily Kandinsky from 1912 and his notes dated 1914 and 1922, found in a copy of Schopenhauer's essay "On Religion," from *Parerga und Paralopomena*, suggest that around the time he was composing *Totentanz der Prinzipien* and *Die Jakobsleiter*, Schoenberg was thinking critically about the dualisms and essentialisms found in the Law and, in particular, in the constructed category of the Jew in Schopenhauer's philosophy. These documents reveal that Schoenberg was searching for a mode of expression that would embrace his own complex and multifaceted sense of self that identified both as Jew and Christian. It was this dual identity that led Schoenberg to develop a form of compassionate art that transcended the boundaries of traditional religion, a deeper sense of spirituality that could only find expression in music and musical poetics.

Schoenberg's journey to "become religious" is often read as a circular path, yet this reading tends to oversimplify the composer's complex relationship to his Jewish heritage that he expressed in various ways, poetic and musical, throughout his life. Born in 1874, Schoenberg was raised in a Jewish family, descended on his mother's side from a family of Prague synagogue cantors. He converted to Protestantism in 1898, yet turned to mysticism and theosophy in the 1910s.[9] Schoenberg's first public experience of antisemitism while on vacation in Mattsee in 1921 is believed to have sparked his open engagement with Jewish culture in his music and writings, which eventually led, after several years of increased activism in Zionist politics, to his return to the Jewish community in 1933.[10] However, his private correspondence, poetry, and notes suggest that between 1912 and 1917, Schoenberg was thinking critically about his own German-Jewish subjectivity, his gradually evolving sense of self in relation to the socially constructed categories of German and Jew.

In the 1910s, Schoenberg had already begun seeking alternate forms of spirituality and artistic expression as a way of reconciling paradoxes of his dual Jewish-Christian identity. One of Schoenberg's most significant interlocutors at this time was the painter Wassily Kandinsky. Author of the treatise, "Über das Geistliche in der Kunst" (On the Spiritual in Art 1911) and cofounder of the Munich-based Expressionist group, *Der blaue Reiter*, Kandinsky's own spiritual and artistic views were indebted to a number of sources, including the writings of Helena Blavatsky and Rudolph Steiner, both of whom associated with the theosophical movement. A form of esoteric philosophy based largely on gnostic writing, theosophy attained widespread popularity in Europe at the end of the nineteenth century. The theosophists envisioned man, nature, and God as bound in a primal unity and sought direct knowledge of God through the world.[11] Schoenberg's letters to Kandinsky reveals that the composer's vision for a new musical language that would overthrow the old laws of harmony coincided with his desire for a new spirituality that would offer a "way out" of the paradoxes posed by Mosaic Law. In this way, Schoenberg's interest in theosophy can be understood not as a wholesale rejection of Judaism or Christianity but rather an attempt to find in his own dual identity a language to express these contradictions.

Schoenberg's correspondence with Kandinsky, particularly the letters composed just three months before he began to plan his choral-dramatic project, reveals the composer's search for a poetic language to express humanity's relationship to the divine. On August 19, 1912, Schoenberg wrote that he believed that art should be the manifestation of an "inner vision," which he describes as a whole made up of different integrated components. The true artwork should be a puzzle, "ein Abbild das Unfaßbaren" (an image of the ungraspable). According to Schoenberg, our goal should not be to solve the puzzle but rather to attempt to decipher it. In doing so, one gains something much greater than the solution to the puzzle—a method of decoding:

> Aber wenn wir durch [die Rätsel] nur lernen, das Unfaßbare für möglich zu halten, nähern wir uns Gott, da wir dann nicht mehr verlangen, ihn verstehen zu wollen. Da wir dann nicht mehr ihm mit unserem Verstand messen, ihn kritisieren, ihn ableugnen, weil wir ihn nicht auflösen können in jene menschliche Unzulänglichkeit, die unsere Klarheit ist.
>
> [But if we can only learn from (the puzzles) to consider the ungraspable as possible, we get nearer to God, because we no longer demand to understand him. Because then we no longer measure him with our intelligence, criticize him, deny him, because we cannot reduce him to that human inadequacy which is our clarity.][12]

In this letter, Schoenberg connects the goal of his art to his search for faith and points already toward an idea that would continue to occupy him for the rest of his life—how to represent the unrepresentable, the divine revelation, in artistic form.

In his response to Schoenberg's letter, Kandinsky responded by further developing the connections between art and the search for spiritual understanding. The artist replied to Schoenberg's "Abbild das Unfaßbaren" paradox by claiming that the essence of all things is *vielseitig* (many-sided) and thus human language and reasoning will always fail to understand it in its completeness. Everything, Kandinsky claims, has at least two sides but only a few can grasp this truth. In his explanation, he recalls the Ten Commandments, which he claims are *einseitig* (one-sided) in demanding "Thou Shalt, Thou Shalt Not." Christ transformed the Mosaic Law when he said, "das weiter könnt ihr heute nicht fassen" (the rest you cannot grasp today).[13] Kandinsky concludes that this statement reveals the limits of human perceptions of God, religion, science, and art. We sense only one side, when in reality, "die *Entwicklung* besteht nur darin, daß alles vielseitig, *compliziert* erscheint" (evolution consists only of this, that everything appears many-sided, complicated).[14] This early correspondence with Kandinsky while he was conceiving his choral symphony project reveals that Schoenberg was already grappling with limits of representing the divine and thinking about how a revolution of the laws of harmony might also relate to a reassessment of the Law, which appeared too limited to reveal the true nature of the divine spirit.

Just a few years later, Schoenberg would return to the idea of Mosaic Law in a very specific context, the writings of Arthur Schopenhauer. His notes on Schopenhauer's essay "On Religion" in the volume *Parerga und Paralopomena,* written just weeks before he began composing the libretti for *Totentanz der Prinzipien* and *Die Jakobsleiter*, reveal that Schoenberg's encounter with the antisemitic rhetoric in this work served as the impetus for his deeper engagement with the Law as a unique facet of the *Jewish* faith. Copies of Schopenhauer's works, found in Schoenberg's library, contain extensive markings, including underlining, comments in the margins, and handwritten notes.[15] These notes appear in various shades of pen and pencil, suggesting that Schoenberg may have reread these sections multiple times. Moreover, two loose-leaf pages, taped into the volume, contain the composer's commentary on the text as it relates to specific ideas of Jewish Otherness, in particular, the idea of Jewish fidelity to the Law, and their lack of compassion. These notes, dated 1914 and 1922, bookend the creative period of *Totentanz der Prinzipien* and *Die Jakobsleiter*, indicating that Schoenberg was reflecting on critiques of the Jewish religion while composing these works. They also reveal a shift in perspective that ultimately led to his desire to create a musical-dramatic work that would relay the paradox underlining the one-sided perspective of the Law and the necessity for a new form of revelation to express a far more complex relationship between the human and the divine.

In his examination of Schopenhauer's essay, "On Religion," Schoenberg highlights three characterizations of Judaism that he identifies as false representations of the Jewish faith and its historical legacy. First, Schopenhauer claims that the Jewish god is a distant figure, separate from his creation. Second, he claims that the Jewish god is jealous, for demanding that his people have no other gods before him. Third, he identifies the Jewish religion as abstract, materialistic, and optimistic, meaning that it shares no belief in the afterlife and denies the ability of God to be represented.[16] Schopenhauer aimed to disassociate Christianity from its origins in Judaism to reclaim Christianity as a descendent of Buddhist self-denial, a central tenet of his philosophy of pessimism. Drawing on a term central to his philosophical paradigm, "Mitleid," Schoenberg casts Judaism as uncompassionate and thus incompatible with his own philosophy, which he believes will eventually supersede religion.

In his notes on the essay, Schoenberg responds to Schopenhauer's comments by recasting Jewish monotheism (and its embodiment in Mosaic Law) as an achievement and by defending the subjective experience of the Jewish people against a flawed theology. Most important, he directly attacks Schopenhauer's pseudotheological reasoning, identifying in his argument a biased logic, which is just as limited or one-sided as the religious doctrine against which he claims to argue. In his examination of two chapters in Schopenhauer's essay, entitled "Über Theismus" (On Theism) and "A. und N.T." (Old and New Testament), Schoenberg challenges the philosopher's views of the Jewish religion in key ways that he would revisit in composing the texts for *Totentanz der Prinzipien* and *Die Jakobsleiter.* In these chapters, Schopenhauer claims Judaism as the origin of theism and criticizes the idea of a God separate from the universe who created the world out of nothing. For Schopenhauer, theism cannot explain the existence of evil, the moral insensitivity of the monotheistic God, and the need for compassion or the feeling of moral responsibility that humans feel toward each other.[17] In the chapter, "Old and New Testament," Schopenhauer claims Judaism as a materialist religion that denies the afterlife and thus condemns its followers to an eternity of suffering. Christianity, he writes, finds its true roots in "indischer Weisheit" (Indian wisdom) and in Buddhism's idealism and pessimism, while Judaism is fundamentally realist and optimistic.[18] He differentiates Christianity from Judaism in the following way,

> Die Welt ist nicht mehr Zweck, sondern Mittel: das Reich der ewigen Freuden liegt jenseits der selben und des Todes. Entsagung in dieser Welt und Richtung aller Hoffnung auf eine bessere ist der Geist des Christenthums. Den Weg zu einer solchen aber öffnet die Versöhnung, d.i. die Erlösung von der Welt und ihren Wegen. In der Moral ist an die Stelle des Vergeltungsrechtes das Gebot der Feindesliebe getreten, an die des Versprechens zahlloser Nachkommenschaft die Verheißung des ewigen Lebens, und an die des Heimsuchens der Missethat an den Kindern bis ins vierte Glied der Heilige Geist, der Alles überschattet.

> [The world is no longer an end, but a means; the kingdom of eternal joys lies beyond it and beyond death. Renunciation in this world and directing all hope to a better one are the spirit of Christianity. But the way to such a world is opened by reconciliation, i.e., the redemption from the world and its ways. In morality the right to retaliate has been replaced by the command to love one's enemy, the promise of innumerable progeny by the promise of eternal life, and visitation of the misdeed upon the children into the fourth generation, by the holy spirit who overshadows everything.][19]

Schopenhauer's description of Christianity as diametrically opposed to the message and ethics of Judaism focuses on what he claims to be the "earthly" nature of the Jewish religion, the Jewish adherence to the law of vengeance over the law of compassionate love, and on the legacy of sin passed down over generations, rather than the redemptive love of the Christian spirit.

In his notes in the margins of the text and on a separate sheet of paper, dated December 5, 1914 (just a little over a month before he began composing *Totentanz der Prinzipien*), Schoenberg formulated several responses to Schopenhauer's work, repudiating this depiction of Judaism. This passage suggests that Schoenberg believed that Schopenhauer's anti-Jewish sentiment undermined the validity of his vision of compassion. In his note, Schoenberg accuses Schopenhauer of bias, claiming that his philosophy of religion is shaped by prejudice. He writes: "Die Äußerungen Schopenhauers über (die) Juden und ihre Religion sind zweifellos von Abneigung diktiert, sind also keine unmittelbaren Erkenntnisse, sondern Gedanken zu einem Gegenstand, der (von ihm) gewertet war, ehe er ihn untersuchte." (Schopenhauer's comments about the Jews and their religion are clearly dictated by repulsion; they are thus not intuitive insights but rather thoughts about an object that was being judged by him before he began to investigate it.)[20] Schoenberg takes particular offense at Schopenhauer's criminalization of the Jews. Indeed, in his essay, Schopenhauer had claimed that monotheism is responsible for the all violence and intolerance in the world. He wrote in the chapter, "Ein Dialog," "In der Tat ist Intoleranz nur dem Monotheismus wesentlich: ein alleiniger Gott ist, seiner Natur nach, ein eifersüchtiger Gott, der keinem anderen das Leben gönnt" (intolerance is essential only to monotheism; a lone God is by his nature a jealous God who does not allow another to live).[21] Schoenberg's marginal notes to the essay "On Religion," question Schopenhauer's accusations by criticizing the philosopher's selective understanding of compassion. In a note marked with multiple exclamation points for emphasis, Schoenberg writes: "!!!Diese Roheit vom Philosophen des Mitleids! Aber sie ist ja vor aller Welt dadurch entschuldigt, dass sie sich nur gegen die Rasse 'Mauschel' richtet" (This crudeness from the philosopher of compassion! But it is publicly excused because it is against the "Mauschel" race (!!!).[22] Schoenberg's response is significant because it reveals the extent to which the composer associated compassion specifically with Schopenhauer's writings and challenged the philosopher's denial of compassion to the Jewish religion.[23]

Schoenberg then goes on to challenge Schopenhauer's critique of monotheism, recasting it as the *achievement* of the Jewish people:

> Wenn man sich ganz auf seinen Standpunkt zur Religion stellt, so steht die jüdische Religion in einer Hinsicht gewiss um soviel höher als die griechische, als der monotheistische Gedanke höher steht, als der polytheistische. Denn der Gedanke der Unteilbarkeit, Einheit und somit Unendlichkeit in jeder Richtung ist als Erkenntnis an sich eine Leistung; und seine Symbolisierung eine zweite.
>
> [If one takes his (Schopenhauer's) position on religion, the Jewish religion stands in a manner of speaking high above the Greek religion, as the monotheistic idea prevails over the polytheistic. For the idea of indivisibility, unity and with that, eternity, in every respect is an achievement; first as knowledge and secondly as symbol.][24]

Schoenberg's response here emphasizes the unique contribution of the Jewish people to the tradition of monotheism.[25] Moreover, Schoenberg's mention of the characteristics of indivisibility, unity, and eternity link his understanding of the threefold nature of the divine in the Jewish faith to what he would later identify as *Gedanke*, the unity of musical idea, which would form the basis for his musical concept of twelve-tone composition.

Finally, in his note of December 1914, Schoenberg attacks Schopenhauer's charges by making a case for Jewish subjectivity. Regarding Schopenhauer's claims of Jewish materialism and worldliness, Schoenberg responds that while Jewish theology may deny an afterlife, the Jewish people "kann mit einer abstrakten Theologie nichts anfangen, sondern braucht fühlbares" (have no use for abstract theology, rather they need something tangible).[26] Schoenberg's distinction between Jewish theology and the Jewish people suggests that he sought to carve out a space for a more complex understanding of Jewishness rooted in subjectivity or self-experience.[27]

While Schoenberg's notes in his copy of *Parerga and Paralipomena* were never published, they provide fascinating insight into the composer's state of mind when he sat down to compose *Totentanz* and, eventually, *Die Jakobsleiter*. In these texts, Schoenberg fuses the idea of Mosaic Law that he discussed with Kandinsky as a reflection of the limitation of human understanding with the antisemitic stereotype of the Law as a reflection the Jew's uncompassionate and materialistic nature. While *Totentanz* unpacks the paradoxical layers of these one-sided views of the Mosaic Law through a musical-poetic language, *Die Jakobsleiter* poses a mode of decoding this puzzle through prayer, Gebet. For Schoenberg, prayer reflects a compassionate relationship through which individual subjectivities come to realize the many-sidedness of the divine spirit. Moreover, prayer enables a new understanding of the Jewish relationship to the Law, one that is not fixed and immutable but rather dynamic and ever-changing, a covenant. In the language of polyphony, Schoenberg found a mode of expressing Judaism's belief in the indivisibility, unity, and eternity of God, the idea at the core of his philosophical, religious, and aesthetic vision of compassion.

## The Birth of the Law out of the Language of Difference: The Polyphonic Poetics of *Totentanz der Prinzipien*

Schoenberg's correspondence from the earliest phase of the symphony-oratorio-festival drama project reveals that he was searching for a mode of expression that would express the shared inner nature of all beings through their many-sidedness and correspondence. Schoenberg's understanding of correspondence was drawn initially from the writings of the Swedish philosopher and mystic, Emanuel Swedenborg. As Jack Boss notes, Swedenborg wrote in his *Theory of Correspondences* that every object in the material world has a correspondent or referent in the world beyond.[28] Prayer, Swedenborg claimed, could serve as the means to uncover these correspondences, revealing a new mode of insight into the nature of God. However, Schoenberg also mobilized the ideas of correspondence and prayer in his defense of Judaism against Schopenhauer. As the following analyses of *Totentanz der Prinzipien* and *Die Jakobsleiter* demonstrate, correspondence and prayer become a means for Schoenberg to reclaim compassion for the Jew and to reinscribe the idea of the unity, indivisibility, and eternal nature of the divine as a uniquely Jewish contribution to a modern religious spirit.

In *Totentanz der Prinzipien*, Schoenberg developed a musical-poetics of correspondence based in polyphony. Schoenberg's fascination for the principle of polyphony emerged from his study of the music of the Baroque and, in particular, his lifelong admiration for the musical language of Johann Sebastian Bach.[29] Schoenberg, who once jokingly called Bach the first twelve-tone composer, often remarked on the connections between Bach's use of polyphony and his own. Yet Schoenberg sought to expand polyphony beyond the binaries of consonance and dissonance, experimenting with a mode of composition in which there is no stable tonal center. For Schoenberg, polyphony embodies a productive form of dissonance, in which each tone, emancipated from the chord structure, becomes more differentiated and acquires its own voice. As Adorno notes, the goal of Schoenberg's polyphony is not the homogeneous resonance of the collective tones, in which dissonant sounds are suppressed or annihilated, but rather the exploration of the dynamic relationship between sounds.[30]

Composed on January 15, 1915, Schoenberg's *Totentanz der Prinzipien* was conceived as a monologue with orchestra accompaniment, which the composer planned to include as the third movement in his choral symphony.[31] Mahler's symphonies served as an important model for Schoenberg's integration of a monodrama into the symphonic form. As discussed in chapter 2, Mahler's Second and Third Symphonies incorporated art song, or lieder, as well as large-scale choirs and multiple soloists. The Third Symphony had a significant impact on Schoenberg. He wrote to Mahler after attending its premiere performance in Vienna in 1904:

"Ich fühlte das Kämpfen um die Illusionen; ich empfand den Schmerz des Desillusionierten, ich sah böse und gute Kräfte miteinander ringen, ich sah einen Menschen in qualvoller Bewegtheit nach innerer Harmonie sich abmühen; ich spürte einen Menschen, ein Drama, Wahrheit, rücksichtsloseste Wahrheit." (I felt the struggle for the illusion, I perceived the pain of the disillusioned, I saw evil and good powers wrestling with each other, I saw a human being in agonizing emotion laboring toward inner harmony; I sensed a being, a drama, truth, uncompromising truth.)[32] For Schoenberg, Mahler's expansion of the symphony allowed this musical form to relay a new kind of dramatic arc, one that would be capable of addressing the metaphysical questions of mankind's struggle to become religious. Moreover, his reference to the "pain of disillusion," finds a corollary in the plans for his own choral dramatic symphony, in which the monodrama *Totentanz der Prinzipien* would be followed by an oratorio finale entitled "Der Glaube des Desillusionierten" (The Faith of the Disillusioned), the movement that would eventually become *Die Jakobsleiter.* These references testify to the significance of Mahler's musical language and form for Schoenberg's composition.

*Totentanz der Prinzipien* is Schoenberg's creation myth, describing the emergence of language from sound. The speaker's creation myth begins at midnight with the words, "Im Anfang war das Dunkel, immer war es und wird immer sein" (In the beginning there was darkness that always was and always will be).[33] The conflation of the darkness of Genesis with the primacy of the origins of language in the Gospel of John, "In the beginning there was the Word and the Word was with God and God was the Word" (John 1:1), points immediately toward the shared origins of Judaism and Christianity. As the monologue continues, the speaker describes the revelation of the divine in the form of language (the Word) and its devolution into contradictions and dualities, to its ultimate one-sided expression in Mosaic Law, signified in the words, "Thou Shalt." The speaker's inability to avoid the Law or to understand it results in a cry of despair. Language appears always inadequate to represent the nature of the divine.[34]

This crisis of language, which is also a crisis of faith, is expressed by the speaker, whose single voice embodies the principles of polyphony. The illusion of multivocality is created through fluctuations in the speaker's vocal register and through his cacophonous, musical language. For example, the stage directions call for the speaker to alter the quality of his voice, varying from "ein höhnisches Getöse" to "mit ironischem Pathos" to "gläubiger" ("a mocking deafening noise" to "with ironic pathos" to "more devoutly").[35] The speaker's language also creates dramatic sound effects by varying the length and rhythm of his phrases and juxtaposing sentence fragments with run-on sentences. Addressing questions to invisible interlocutors and interrupting himself with desperate appellations, the speaker appears to be speaking for or with many voices at once.

While this language appears disorienting and nonsensical at first, it does reflect, upon closer examination, an inner logic. The speaker's words are connected here not through semantic meaning but rather through their sound. Alliterative word pairs, such as "wohl und weh" (joy and pain); "niedlich, neckisch" (pretty, playful), enact *Anfangsklang*, a connection based in their beginning sounds.[36] The speaker also employs end rhymes such as "Fahle und Schale" (paleness and flatness ), and onomatopoetic verbs such as *toben*, *stürmen*, and *brausen* to further evoke dissonance and upheaval:

> Alles lebt; alles Tote ist lebendig;
> Das jagt, tobt, stürmt, braust;
> Es sticht, brennt, schmerzt,
> Tut wohl und weh,
> Ist gleichgültig und erlogen.

[Everything is alive; everything dead is living,
It races, rages, storms, roars;
It pricks, burns, pains
Gives pleasure and pain,
Is indifferent and exciting,
True and invented.][37]

Contradiction lies at the core of language and thus as each idea is presented, it is immediately called into question by its opposite. Darkness is met with light, order with disorder, sound with silence. These experiences evoke opposing emotions in the speaker: pleasure and pain, excitement and indifference. Life is loud, it is brilliant and it is musical, manifesting as the simultaneous sounds of monophony and polyphony, of single and multiple tones: "Jetzt singt es; jeder singt etwas anderes, meint, daß er dasselbe singt und tatsächlich klingt es in einer Richtung einstimmig, (staunend) in einer anderen mehrstimmig, in einer dritten und vierten klingt es noch anders; aber das kann man nicht ausdrücken." (Now it sings; each sings something different thinking that it sings the same thing; and, in fact, sounds in one dimension together, [surprise] in another diverse. In a third and fourth it sounds still otherwise, which one cannot express.)[38] In *Totentanz*, the rhythmical nature of the words and the correspondence of sounds through alliteration and onomatopoeia evoke a primal *musical* language as the first attempts to express divine revelation.

For Schoenberg, the comprehensibility of this text, its understanding as a whole, must be gleaned through the sounds of language and the acoustic relationship between words.[39] Yet the complex nature of Schoenberg's poetics ultimately poses a problem that the audience must confront: How can we grasp a divine being that we cannot conceive either in word or image?

Schoenberg's introduction of Mosaic Law into his creation myth through the words "Du sollst" relates not only to his correspondence with Kandinsky in 1912 but also to his commentary on Schopenhauer's essay, "On Religion," suggesting that he identified the paradox of the Law as resonating uniquely in the Jewish faith. Its significance in the text is emphasized by the fact that "Du sollst" is the only phrase that appears in quotation marks in Schoenberg's libretto and is followed by the only first-person statement in the text, "aber ich mag nicht, ich muss nicht!" (but I do not want to, I don't have to!).[40] The speaker seeks to negate God's commands, as all things have been negated thus far in the text, but here the oppositions grind to a halt. To borrow Kandinsky's terms from his letter to Schoenberg, the Law is one-sided, and thus it obscures the many-sided nature of the divine unity that it represents. Yet, the speaker's claims that the Law cannot be negated, that it permeates his body—it is "inner and outer being"—suggests that his protest of the one-sidedness of the Law has deeper implications for the Jewish subject. According to Jeffrey Librett, Schopenhauer's critique of Judaism is directly related to what he perceives as its fidelity to the "dead letter" of the Law; a Law that he believes to embody the failure of representation, the inability of the Word to "produce immediacy."[41] Schoenberg's own confrontation with the Law stands at the center of the conflict in *Totentanz*, for as much as the speaker wants to proclaim his independence from the Lord's commands, it is also an innate part of him ("der Urschleim, von dem wir ein Teil sind!").[42] At the conclusion of the monodrama, the speaker's encounter with the Law and inability to fathom its many-sided nature appears irreconcilable.[43]

Further evidence that this episode in the monodrama was part of the composer's reflection of the Jewish Question emerges when it is read in conversation with Mahler's Second Symphony. The acknowledgment of the Mosaic Law as a representation of the shared inner substance between the human and divine is reflected in the speaker's words in *Totentanz*, that the Law "lässt sich nicht abweisen" (will not let itself be turned away) because it is a part of his inner being.[44] The phrase echoes the words of Mahler's song setting in his Second Symphony, "Urlicht," discussed in chapter 2. In Mahler's setting, the alto voice sings of a being that struggles with an angel and refuses to be turned away ("Ach nein, ich ließ mich nicht abweisen"). Mahler referred to this movement as the "struggle for naive faith" and later, in an anecdote relayed by Schoenberg's pupil, Egon Wellesz, as "the wrestling of Jacob and the Angel . . . and Jacob's cry to the angel, I will not let thee go, except that thou bless me."[45] Schoenberg's reference to Mahler at this critical moment in his monodrama thus draws attention to the connections between both composers' quests for faith, their interpretation of this quest as struggle, and their acknowledgment of the legacy of the Mosaic Law as a barrier to the realization of an art-religion of compassion. That this theme was a guiding principle of Schoenberg's artistic vision at this time is evident from the fact that he chose to evoke the same image of the biblical patriarch Jacob in the companion work to *Totentanz*, the oratorio, *Die Jakobsleiter.*

Thus, Schoenberg's polyphonic poetics in *Totentanz der Prinzipien* serve as a meditation on the limitation of Mosaic Law, its apparent immutability, its legacy in creating the idea of a distant uncompassionate God, and its contradictions with feeling or instinct, the true basis of compassionate understanding. At the time, Schoenberg was a converted Protestant, yet he was actively engaging with philosophical constructions of Jewishness and thus rethinking and questioning the limits of these identities. In his notes on Schopenhauer, Schoenberg envisioned a Jewish people, or, better stated, a Jewish *character*, separate from a Jewish theology. By tracing the roots of Law to language, the always inadequate form of revelation, and language's origins in sound, *Totentanz* represents the composer's own struggle to return to the original "shared substance," a basis for compassionate understanding *prior* to the Word. It was in primal sound that he believed a Jewish character, separate from a one-sided theological view, might be articulated.

While *Totentanz* articulates the crisis facing the German-Jewish subject, the speaker's dance on the edge of losing his faith and succumbing to despair also relays a creative energy that will be realized in new ways in the figure of the Chosen One in *Die Jakobsleiter*. The speaker's dynamic and shifting language evokes not a dance for the already dead but rather the potentiality to be attained from the suspended state of floating between multiple points.[46] His dissonant poetics thus create a "multi-sensory experience" that points toward new modes of perception.[47] Indeed, the vibrant nature of Schoenberg's polyphonic poetics, and the possibilities offered by reconfiguring aesthetic expression through acoustic correspondence, suggests that the inner dissonance of the German-Jewish subject might provide a unique insight into the many-sidedness of the relationship between the human and the divine. As the following reading of *Die Jakosbleiter*, the companion work to *Totentanz* reveals, this insight finds articulation in a new musical language of Gebet, prayer, which allows for a reenvisioning of the Jewish relationship to the Law as compassionate covenant.

## The Emancipation of Difference in Prayer: Reenvisioning the Law in *Die Jakobsleiter*

In *Die Jakobsleiter*, Schoenberg finds a resolution to the limitation of the Law to represent the divine by proposing prayer as the articulation of the compassionate covenant between humanity and God. In his libretto, Schoenberg revisits the question of the Law through a series of dialogues between various souls seeking redemption and the angel Gabriel, who serves as the gatekeeper of heaven. Schopenhauer's claims that the Jewish Law is a reflection of their immutability and devotion to a jealous God are recalled in *Die*

*Jakobsleiter* by the Rebellious One and the Struggling One. However, while the apparent irreconcilable nature of the Law, articulated in the words "Du sollst," resulted in *Totentanz* in the speaker's bitter resignation, in *Die Jakobsleiter*, the Chosen One personifies the spirit of the Law as compassionate covenant. The Chosen One is a musical being, embodying the principle of variation on a theme. In the oratorio, he ultimately redefines the Jewish relationship to the divine through prayer (Gebet), the articulation of a multitude of voices speaking with and for their God. Through the Chosen One, Schoenberg recasts the Jewish relationship to God as a compassionate exchange that recognizes the shared substance of all beings in one eternal spirit. While prayer does not solve the paradoxes of divine representation, it provides what Schoenberg referred to in letters to Kandinsky as a "mode of decoding" the many-sidedness and evolving nature of this compassionate relationship.

The first draft of the text that would become the libretto for *Die Jakobsleiter* is dated January 18, 1915, three days after Schoenberg completed the text for *Totentanz der Prinzipien*.[48] At this point, the text was still intended as a movement within the choral symphony; thus, the top of the first page of the 1915 draft is marked as "IV. Satz" (fourth movement).[49] (See fig. 3.1.) Schoenberg worked on this text between January and April 1915, before enlisting in the Austrian Army in the spring of that year.[50] He was discharged six months later due to poor health but did not take up the text again until May 1917. The title, *Die Jakobsleiter*, appears for the first time in Schoenberg's correspondence in June 1917, likely around the time that Schoenberg made the decision to complete the oratorio as a separate work.[51] Part I features a series of souls who appear before the angel Gabriel presenting their case for entrance into heaven. Part II, for which Schoenberg never completed the musical score, is framed by two lengthy speeches by Gabriel and two dramatic episodes involving multiple choirs. The souls of Part I reappear in Part II but this time as disembodied voices, surrounded by a variety of different figures, both natural and supernatural. Their outcries and exclamations are ultimately answered by Gabriel's final monologue, which proposes prayer, a direct appeal to the eternal unity, as a means to reenvision the relationship of these souls to God as compassionate covenant.

Schoenberg's vision of modern man's quest for faith as compassion finds its articulation in the language of *Die Jakobsleiter*'s libretto and in its musical composition. Like the cacophonous opening of *Totentanz*, the first several bars of Schoenberg's *Die Jakobsleiter* evokes immediate unease.

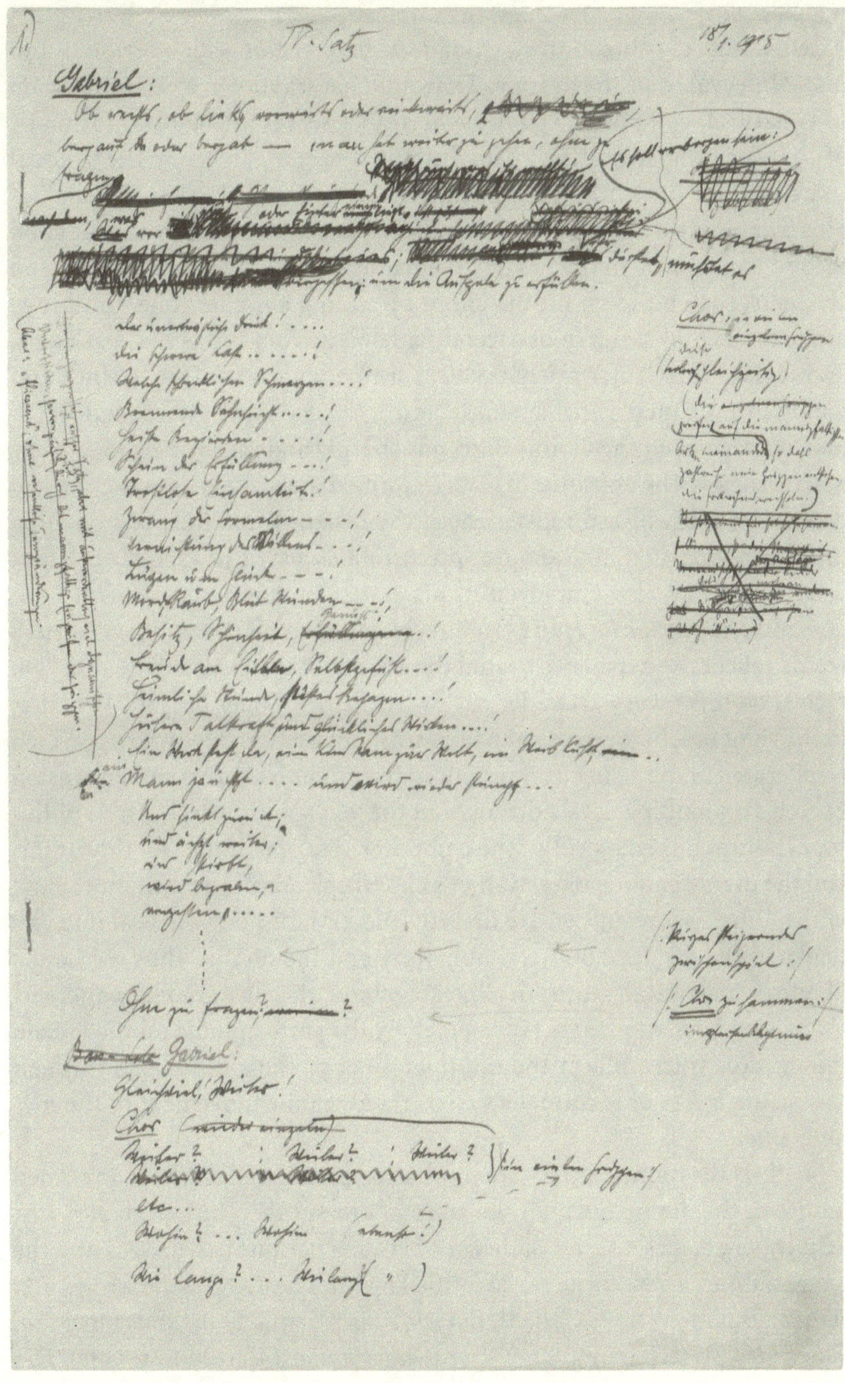

Figure 3.1. First draft of *Die Jakobsleiter* libretto (marked as fourth movement), dated January 18, 1915. Used by permission of Belmont Music Publishers, Los Angeles.

A celli and bass ostinato in startling *fortissimo* begins with a series of dramatic interval leaps, from C# to D, from F natural down to E from G# up to G natural, composing the hexachord that serves as the basis for many of the work's later motifs.[52] This tumult is accompanied by the gradual thickening of the underlying harmonic texture: the third trombone begins by holding a long C, which is followed a measure later by the first and second trombones, in the next by the trumpets, and then by the flutes and clarinets, each building on the chord by adding a higher tone, until they are overtaken by a flurry of ascending triplets from the oboes, bassoons, and violas. These instrumental voices merge with rest of the strings and winds in ever-increasing dynamic and intensity until a final sixteenth-note passage from the violins descends sharply and ascends again to a climactic shriek. The entrance of Gabriel immediately challenges the vertical upward and downward movement of the instrumental line. His opening lines are articulated in dramatic *Sprechstimme*, a style of song-speech that Schoenberg had also employed in his earlier monodramas, *Pierrot Lunaire* and *Die glückliche Hand*, and likely intended for *Totentanz*. Gabriel's words reflect the expansive spatial dimension of this heavenly realm: "Ob rechts, ob links, vorwärts oder rückwärts, bergauf oder bergab" (whether to the right or left, forwards or backwards, upwards or downwards), which is reiterated in the echo effect produced by the choirs.[53] This spatial tension operates on multiple levels throughout the text—musically, but also philosophically and theologically. The composer's staging of the "earthly" souls and the divine choir evokes Mahler's choral episode in the fifth movement of the Third Symphony, where diegetic and extradiegetic musical lines articulated the distance between humanity and the divine. Thus, while the libretto's "narrative" moves in a linear fashion, through gradually increasing levels of consciousness represented by the various souls on the ladder, the musical voices reflect the multiplicity of possible directions through increasing layers of texture, as well as the dynamic movement of the melodic line.

While the monodrama *Totentanz* attempted to reflect the many-sided nature of the divine through the voice of one speaker, in *Die Jakobsleiter*, Schoenberg stages a series of debates between various personages and the angel Gabriel. The soloists are identified by titles describing their roles: *Ein Berufener* (One Who Is Called), *Ein Aufrührischer* (A Rebellious One), *Ein Ringender* (A Struggling One), *Der Auserwählter* (The Chosen One), *Der Mönch* (The Monk), and *Der Sterbende* (The Dying One). Each approaches Gabriel seeking guidance and confessing his struggles and weaknesses.

In the dialogues of a Rebellious One and a Struggling One, Schoenberg revisits the question of the Law posed in *Totentanz* and finds a new resolution in the figure of the Chosen One, who embodies a true compassionate spirit.

Schoenberg's Rebellious One embodies resistance to the Law. He openly scoffs at the idea of obeying the command of a distant, abstract god.[54] To obey the commandments, he claims, is to be deaf to instinct. He challenges Gabriel with the reproach: "es kann nicht derselbe Gott sein, der durch Trieb uns den einen, durch Gebote den anderen Weg weist!" (it cannot be the same god, who through instincts shows us one way, and through commandments shows us the other way!)[55] His depiction of the "Herr der Gebote" (Lord of Commandments) as cruel, heartless, and powerless appears to echo Schopenhauer's critique of the Law as a product of an uncompassionate and jealous Jewish God. Moreover, his defiance recalls the words of the speaker in *Totentanz*, whose response to the command, "Thou Shalt," was "I won't! I don't have to!" as well as the arguments of Lipiner's Cain, who also challenged the contradictions between the Law and the pull of Trieb or instinct.[56] However, in *Die Jakobsleiter*, the Rebellious One is sharply rebuked by Gabriel on the basis of his limited view: "Dieses Entweder und dies Oder, eins und zwei, wie Kurzsichtigkeit und Anmaßung, eins durchs andere bedingt, ebendarum keins: der Heber deiner Empörung!" (This Either and this Or, one and two, like shortsightedness and arrogance, one depending on the other, and consequently nothing but the lever for your indignation).[57] The Rebellious One's argument against the commandments is dismissed as failing to see the many-sided revelation that the Law represents.

The next figure, a Struggling One, presents two possible responses to the Rebellious One's "one-sidedness": resignation and religious piety. Resignation refers to Schopenhauer's philosophy of pessimism and denial of the Will and thus again picks up directly where Schoenberg's notes on "On Religion" left off. While Schopenhauer posited his philosophy of religion as the answer to the paradoxes and ultimate failures of monotheism, the Struggling One claims that resignation fails to provide comfort:

> Alter Weisheit, Gesagtem,
> Geschriebenem und Selbstgesehenem,
> Das alles banal mir schien, zutrotz
> Sucht' ich ahnungslos das Glück.
> Als es sich mir versagte, strebt' ich "Schmerzlosigkeit" (Schopenhauer) an
> Durch Entsagung, was auch mißlang.

> [In spite of ancient wisdom
> That which I've heard, read and seen myself
> Which all seemed banal to me,
> I searched naively for happiness.
> When I failed to attain it, I strove for "painlessness" (Schopenhauer)
> Through abnegation which also failed.][58]

Next, the Struggling One claims, he sought to follow the path of religious piety, strictly obeying the Law in order to avoid sin:

> "Ich weiß die Gebote wohl" (Luk. 18/20)
> "Du sollst nicht—!"—ich habe es nie getan!
> "Du sollst—!"—ich tu es seit jeher!
> "Das alles habe ich gehalten von Jugend auf!" (Luk. 18/21)
>
> ["I know the commandments:" (Luke 18/20)
> Thou shall not—!—I have never done it!
> Thou shalt—!—I have always done it!
> I have kept all these since my youth! (Luke 18/21)].[59]

Here Schoenberg again evokes the idea of Mosaic Law as a barrier to a compassionate relationship between humanity and the divine. The Struggling One, like the Rebellious One before him, remains frustrated by the ineffability of the Lord's commandments. Moreover, his final plea "warum ward uns kein Sinn gegeben, ungesagte Gesetze zu ahnen, kein Auge, da zu sehn, kein Ohr, da zu hören?" (why were we not given a sense to intuit unspoken laws, no eye to see, no ear to hear?) highlights his intuition that the Law is the sign of a deeper relation between humanity and the divine that is "ungesagt" because it cannot be expressed in words.[60] The Law is therefore not just the moral precept by which one should abide but also the deeper inner essence of the relationship between the human and the divine; it is, as the speaker in *Totentanz* claims, "der Urschleim, von dem wir ein Teil sind." It is one's very identity. The question for the Struggling One and the Rebellious One is ultimately the same: How does one negotiate a compassionate relationship to the divine being when it cannot be articulated in language; when any formulation in words is doomed to misinterpretation?

The answer to the Struggling One's question lies in the Chosen One, the next figure in Schoenberg's hierarchy of souls, who will learn to embody the spirit of compassionate understanding and teach it to the others. As yet unaware of the role he is to play, the Chosen One inquires of Gabriel, "Bin ichs, der Ihre Stunde und den Ablauf zeigt, / Der Peitsche und Spiegel, Leier und Schwert vereint, / Der ihr Herr und Diener ist, ihr Weiser und Narr zugleich?" (Am I the one who shows them the hour and the course of time, / who is at the same time the scourge and the mirror, lyre and sword, / both their master and servant, their wise man and fool?)[61] He describes himself as robbing, stealing, and despising what he has inherited, a reference that likens him to the figure of Jacob, who stole his brother's blessing from their father Isaac and then proceeded to question it in his struggle with the angel.[62] The Chosen One's in-between status is key; he finds himself simultaneously drawn to and repulsed by the others, resisting their pull, and yet conscious that he also embodies their fears, hopes, and desires. In Part II of the libretto the Chosen One will learn the true nature of this relationship, that he must have compassion for these suffering souls, recognizing their fears and struggles as his own.

In his libretto, Schoenberg expresses the unique nature of the Chosen One and his capacity for compassion by portraying him as a musical being. This is first reflected in Gabriel's introduction of the Chosen One, which introduces a shift in tone. First the angel sings, rather than using *Sprechgesang*, and his vocal line is accompanied by the choir. Gabriel decrees that the Chosen One resides in a middle stage in the heavenly hierarchy; however, he relates to the other spirits on a much higher level, "wie dem Grundton der ferne Oberton" (like the fundamental to the distant overtone).[63] The Chosen One also differentiates himself from the Struggling One and the Rebellious One by his melodic singing voice. His description of himself as relating to the lower souls as a variation to their theme ("Sie sind Thema, Variation bin ich"), points toward a unique aspect of his musical nature that draws on a concept central to Schoenberg's own compositional technique.[64] Walter Frisch has described variation for Schoenberg, particularly the form of developing variation that he discussed in the essays, "Folkloristic Symphonies" (1947) and "J. S. Bach" (1950) as a "flexible procedure whereby the different elements of a basic idea or shape—what he called a *Grundgestalt*—are successively modified."[65] Variation, in this sense, does not just imitate a theme in a different form but rather embodies the principles of expansion, dynamism, and action, a forward movement whose goal is yet unknown.[66] Developing variation also serves to emphasize the relationship of the whole to its part. Thus, Schoenberg's musical aesthetics find resonance with his desire to reevaluate the relationship between the human and divine as a compassionate covenant that is continually developing toward a higher goal.

Variation plays a key role in Part II of the oratorio, where Schoenberg poses a solution to the limited, one-sided expression of die Gebote in the idea of prayer, the compassionate dialogical relationship with the divine. The Chosen One appears again, this time to provide resolution to the fragmented and alienated souls by affirming their origins in one shared spirit. This part of the libretto, which Schoenberg was never able to set to music, includes a lengthy monologue that returns to the paradoxes of the law expressed in *Totentanz*. Gabriel recounts the Genesis story of *Totentanz*; however, this time his speech begins not with darkness but with God, understood as a dynamic and evolving creative spirit.[67] In *Totentanz*, Schoenberg attempted to express the many-sided nature of the divine spirit and its division and fragmentation In *Die Jakosleiter*, he reaffirms the relation of these parts to the indivisibility, unity, and eternity of God as the greatest legacy of the Jewish religion. The conclusion of Gabriel's monologue includes one final defense of this tradition. Recalling Schopenhauer's condemnation of monotheism as a product of a vengeful God, Gabriel proclaims: "Der Ewige, Euer Gott, ist kein eifernder Gott, der rächt, sondern ein Gott, der mit euer Unvollkommenheit rechnet, dem euer Unzulänglichkeit bekannt ist, der weiß, dass ihr versagen müsst, und dass euer Weg weit ist" (The Eternal One, Your God, is no jealous god who seeks revenge, but a god who consistently considers your imperfection, one to whom your shortcomings are known, who knows that you must fail and your path is a long one).[68] Thus, according to Gabriel, the contradictions of the material world and the failings of the individual souls do not lead to hopeless damnation but rather are intrinsic to the imperfect human form. The acknowledgment of the unity of spirit is the first step toward overcoming the disillusionment and sorrows of the world, to be able to feel with the Other in compassionate solidarity, and in so doing to come closer to knowing God.

In the conclusion of *Die Jakobsleiter*, Gabriel proposes a new vision of the Law based in prayer, a mode of dialogue that expresses the relationship between the human and the divine. In *Totentanz*, the commandments are rejected with the claim "Thou Shalt, But I do not want to!"; in Part I of *Die Jakobsleiter*, the Law is called into question by a Struggling One. In the finale of the oratorio, Schoenberg points toward Christ's claims at his Sermon on the Mount in the Gospel of Matthew, that he has come to fulfill the Law by positing a new law of love.[69] Yet, this form of compassion, is only one stage in a deeper revelation for Schoenberg. In *Die Jakobsleiter*, when "Der Gott" tells the Chosen One that he must suffer with the lower souls, carrying their burdens within himself—"Du leidest mit ihnen: Hab Mitleid für sie" (You suffer with them: have compassion for them)—Gabriel responds that the true overcoming of the differences that divide humans from one another and from God is achieved through prayer.[70] For Schoenberg, compassion is the "earthly" recognition of the shared substance with the Other, while prayer gives voice to the subject, articulating the compassionate relationship between the human and divine.

The allusions to Schopenhauer in this speech and Gabriel's recuperation of the image of the Jewish "jealous God" as a compassionate figure affirm that the concept of prayer was profoundly shaped by Schoenberg's experience as a Jew, his reaction to the antisemitic rhetoric in the religious philosophy of Schopenhauer, and his desire to find resolution to the conflicts of religious and cultural identity in art. Moreover, although Schoenberg also follows Mahler and Lipiner in calling upon images and scenes from the Christian scriptures to formulate his vision of compassion, he does so not to claim Christianity as the resolution to the paradoxes of Jewish history. Rather, his call for a multifaceted and many-sided understanding of the divine reflects the Jewish reverence for the Word, and the understanding of the Scripture in the Jewish tradition as continually evolving through human interpretation.[71] Alexander Ringer has noted the centrality of dialectics to Jewish thought, particularly the overcoming of oppositions of "freedom and constraint, universal law and human creativity."[72] Indeed, for Schoenberg, prayer is an activity that channels the vacillating *schwebende* forces of *Totentanz*, the conflict and tension of instinct and the Law, and the dualities of the material and spiritual, subsumed into a higher form.[73] Thus, Schoenberg's vision of prayer sought to reïnterpret and redefine faith in the modern world by illuminating the pivotal role that Judaism played in establishing both the idea of the indivisibility, unity, and eternity of God and the spirit of commentary and critique through which the human relationship to the divine is continually reimagined and reevaluated. The struggle with God, manifested in the Law renewed as covenant, stands at the heart of his vision of compassionate religion and compassionate art.

Finally, for Schoenberg, prayer embodies the plurality of the voices appealing to their God in a poetics of polyphony. Such a spirit is embodied in the final chorus of *Die Jakobsleiter*, as the chorus sings:

> Vieltausend Stimmen, tausendfach verscheiden,
> In Wunsch und Klage, in Bangen und Hoffen,
> In Freud und Leid, in Wut und Angst,
> Streben zu Gott, dringen zu ihm,
> Der sie alle hört, sie einzeln aufnimmt,

Wie sie gefühlt, gedacht und gesagt.
Und die Stimmen all die verschiedenen
Verschieden in Anlaß und Ausdruck,
Ergeben zusammen den einen Klang nur.

[Many thousand voices, thousand-fold different,
In wish and complain, in worry and hope,
In joy and suffering, in rage and fear,
Strive toward God, press toward him,
Who hears all, receives them individually,
As they felt, thought and said.
And all the voices of all the different ones,
Different in motives and expression,
Give together only one sound.][74]

This final chorus articulates the capacity for compassionate understanding to be found in the return to the primal unity of sound. The choir of voices, "thousand-fold different," articulate their shared substance in the one, true God.[75] Prayer thus embodies a vibrant relationship with the divine that stands at the heart of a modern compassionate faith, a dialogical mode of communication that transcends the dichotomies of difference.

## Conclusion

Schoenberg's *Totentanz der Prinzipien* and *Die Jakobsleiter* probe the paradoxes facing the religious subject in the modern world, the tensions between theology and experience, and the abstract nature of the divine and its unrepresentability. His polyphonic poetics find compelling parallels in dodecaphony, his later attempt to find a new mode of composition that would reconfigure the hierarchical harmonic structures of the Western tonal musical tradition.[76] At the core of his complex and multifaceted languages, Schoenberg maintained his belief in the unity and totality both of the musical idea and of the shared substance of all beings possessing an equal capacity for compassionate understanding.

Given the biblical reference in its title, *Die Jakobsleiter* is often read as an ideological precursor to Schoenberg's later dramatic works associated with his affirmation of his Jewish heritage, including the Zionist drama, *Der biblische Weg* (The Biblical Way 1925–1926) and the unfinished opera, *Moses und Aron* (1927–1932).[77] Of these three works, *Moses und Aron* presents by all accounts the most explicit musical-dramatic setting of a biblical narrative. Yet it is important to acknowledge *Die Jakobsleiter*'s roots as a dramatic work, for it was only ever performed in Schoenberg's lifetime as a dramatic recitation. The premiere performance of the text of *Die Jakobsleiter* took place in Vienna under the auspices of Schoenberg's *Verein für musikalische Privataufführungen* (Society of Musical Private Performances) on May 22, 1921. (See fig. 3.2.) This was followed by a performance in Prague at the *Mozarteum* on February 27, 1923. Wilhelm Klitsch, an actor and member of the Deutsches Volkstheater ensemble performed on both occasions. It was also published and read widely as a literary work, appearing in print in 1917 and again in 1926 in a collection that included the libretto for his monodrama, *Die glückliche Hand*, a poem entitled *Requiem*, written for his late wife Mathilde, and *Totentanz der Prinzipien*. Thus, while Schoenberg always intended to complete the musical score for *Die Jakobsleiter*, and would never have designated the work as a purely literary text, in his lifetime it was also widely received as a poetic-dramatic work.

Moreover, *Totentanz der Prinzipien* and *Die Jakobsleiter* also provide insight into the composer's relationship to Judaism at a critical moment in the development of his religious and philosophical worldview. Schoenberg's turn to the story of Jacob in the Hebrew Scriptures reflects a mode of mediation between Christianity and Judaism, the Law and compassion. The patriarch Jacob and his struggle with the angel serve as the focal point for his spiritual quest to recast the Jewish legacy of monotheism as the origin of compassionate spirituality. In later works, Schoenberg would further develop a number of key ideas from *Die Jakobsleiter* in a more explicitly Jewish context.[78] In particular, the idea of the Law, understood as the revelation of the ineffable God, and its musical articulation in the twelve-tone row, would play a central role in both the musical composition and the aesthetic theology of *Moses und Aron*. Yet, while *Moses und Aron* reflects the standpoint of the composer having already publicly affirmed his Jewish faith and support of the Zionist cause, *Totentanz* and *Die Jakobsleiter* reveal the views of a still uncertain Schoenberg, engaging in the construction of Jewish difference, while also seeking to transcend these constructed categories.

Schoenberg was well aware of the association of his music with the idea of Jewishness as an acoustic Other—as cacophonous, noisy, and dissonant. Several years later, the composer's development of dodecaphony and his compositions would be declared "degenerate" under National Socialism. Yet, for Schoenberg, dissonance was a positive force, the motivating drive on the path toward revelation. Dissonance's empowerment is enacted in *Totentanz der Prinzipien* and *Die Jakobsleiter* through both his musical

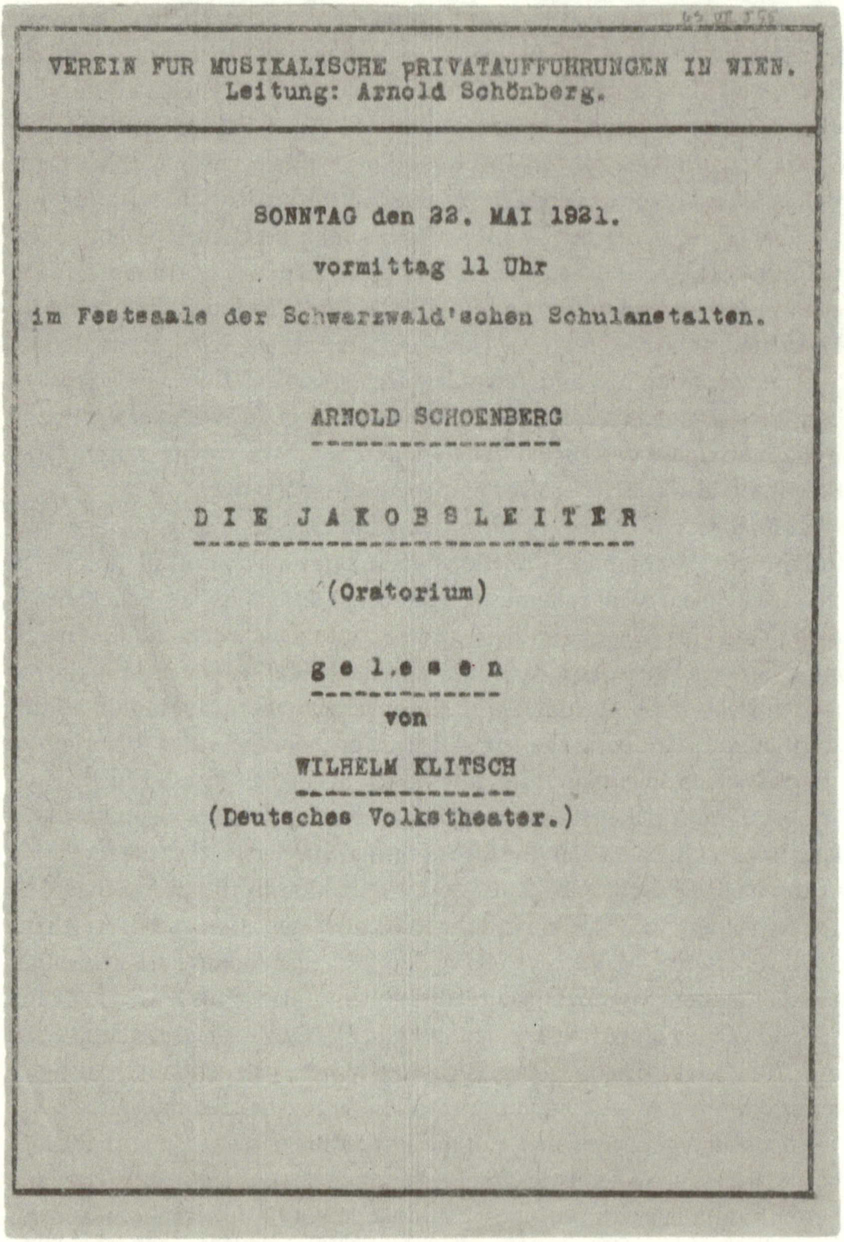

VEREIN FUR MUSIKALISCHE pRIVATAUFFUHRUNGEN IN WIEN.
Leitung: Arnold Schönberg.

SONNTAG den 22. MAI 1921.

vormittag 11 Uhr

im Festsaale der Schwarzwald'schen Schulanstalten.

ARNOLD SCHOENBERG

D I E J A K O B S L E I T E R

(Oratorium)

g e l e s e n

von

WILHELM KLITSCH

(Deutsches Volkstheater.)

Figure 3.2. Program for the spoken performance of *Die Jakobsleiter*. Vienna, May 22, 1921. Used by permission of Belmont Music Publishers, Los Angeles.

language and polyphonic poetics, through which he sought to encourage critical mediation on modes of "one-sided thinking" and their institutionalization in theology and philosophy. Schoenberg believed in music's ability to speak directly to the human heart, augmenting and ultimately transcending the limited capabilities of the word. The word remains incomplete, but when reimagined in new correspondences and variations, responding to its inner musical nature, it might shed light on the many-sidedness of human experience. The diverse, dissonant, and heterogeneous nature of humanity's common inner substance stands at the core of his belief in the unity of being with the one ineffable and ephemeral God.

The centrality of the idea of unity of being for *Totentanz der Prinzipien* and *die Jakobsleiter* also suggests that these works must also be understood in relation to a central principle of Schoenberg's "aesthetic theology": *Gedanke*, the musical idea.[79] Although Schoenberg would not formally compose his manuscript on *Gedanke* until 1923, he dated the concept of basing a musical work consciously on a unifying idea to 1915, just after he wrote his defense of monotheism in response to Schopenhauer and the same year that he composed the libretti to *Totentanz der Prinzipien* and *Die Jakobsleiter*.[80] The fact that the concept of musical unity and its corollary in the divine unity is conceptualized in *Totentanz der Prinzipien* and *Die Jakobsleiter* as a response to the Law provides further evidence for *Gedanke*'s origins in Schoenberg's aesthetics of compassion.

Schoenberg's musical language and the unique dramatic form of *Totentanz* and *Die Jakobsleiter* reveal the composer's experiments with new dramatic models of compassionate art that would provoke critical reflection as well as a powerful communal experience. Like Lipiner, Schoenberg formulated his vision for compassionate art in part as a response to Schopenhauer's anti-Jewish polemics. Modeling his original vision for a choral symphony on Mahler's compositions (and the title for his oratorio on the image of Jacob struggling, also borrowed from the composer), Schoenberg sought to create an epic work of compassionate art that would take the dramatic vocalization of the suffering subject to new heights through a dissonant polyphonic poetics. Emancipating difference through the musical models of polyphony and variation, Schoenberg found a new mode of articulating the compassionate, prayerful relationship between the human and the divine and a mode of decoding the many-sidedness of the ineffable nature of God. In so doing, he created a vision of community that celebrates diversity within an immortal, and eternal unity and recasts the

Jewish subject, the Chosen One, as an integral constituent of this heterogeneous harmonic synthesis.

*Totentanz der Prinzipien* and *Die Jakobsleiter* form important transitions between the early engagements of Lipiner and Mahler with the question of Jewish difference and its representations in the works of biblical theater by Richard Beer-Hofmann and Stefan Zweig, examined in the following chapters. In his biblical drama, *Jaákobs Traum*, Beer-Hofmann similarly attempts to recast the relationship between humanity and God as one of dialogue and mutual understanding, while in *Jeremias*, Zweig employs the oratorio form to portray the evolution of the Jewish community from a collection of dissonant voices to a musical choir, united in one shared spirit. The correlations between these works, all composed between 1915 and 1918, provide evidence of a renewed interest in the discourse of compassion and its construction of the Jewish subject during World War I.

## Notes

1. The actual date of the symphony sketch has not been determined. In his letter to Dehmel, Schoenberg requests a libretto, which the poet declined to write. However, he did send Schoenberg a poem, "Schöpfungsfeier: Oratorium natale," in his response, which Schoenberg included as a possible text for the third movement of his symphony plan; thus, the sketch could have been written as early as December 1912. Bailey, *Programmatic Elements*, 82–83.

2. For the complete outline of the Symphony, see Bailey, 85.

3. See multiple references to the work in correspondence with Alban Berg and Alexander Zemlinsky between 1920 and 1923, as well as a series of letters from the mid-1940s onward in which he attempted to secure funds in America to finish the project. Schoenberg and Stein, *Ausgewählte Briefe*, 84, 267, 294, 299.

4. Dahlhaus, *Schoenberg and the New Music*, 82.

5. Newlin claims that Schoenberg's major religious works (including *Die Jakobsleiter*) "present his spiritual autobiography in vivid and unambiguous language." Newlin, "Self-Revelation and the Law," 204.

6. The "Quest for Language" is a paradigm introduced by Alexander Ringer in *Arnold Schoenberg—Composer as Jew*.

7. For more on Schoenberg's Balzac music drama, see Kandinsky, Schönberg, and Hahl-Koch, *Der Briefwechsel*, 68–69; Nono-Schoenberg, *Arnold Schoenberg 1874–1951*, 125; Lessem, *Works of Arnold Schoenberg*, 178.

8. See Mack on the concept of Jewish immutability. Mack, *German Idealism and the Jew*, 8.

9. Ringer claims that Schoenberg's conversion was "nominal" and that he never changed his attitude toward the spiritual ideals of the Jewish people (Ringer, *Arnold Schoenberg—Composer as Jew*, 36). According to White, Schoenberg only transferred "the object of affiliation" but not the essential need to believe in a divine spirit. White, *Schoenberg and the God-Idea*, 53.

10. Stuckenschmidt, *Arnold Schonberg*, 249.

11. Schoenberg met Kandinsky in Berlin between 1911 and 1913, yet it is possible that the composer was introduced to such ideas during his first Berlin venture between 1901 and 1903, through his contact with the *Klub der "Kommenden"* where Rudolph Steiner gave several lectures. Föllmi, "Schönberg als Theosoph," 57–58.

12. Kandinsky, Schönberg, and Hahl-Koch, *Der Briefwechsel*, 69 [Schoenberg, Kandinsky, and Hahl-Fontaine, *Arnold Schoenberg, Wassily Kandinsky*, 55].

13. Kandinsky, Schönberg, and Hahl-Koch, 72 [Schoenberg, Kandinsky, and Hahl-Fontaine, 57].

14. Kandinsky, Schönberg, and Hahl-Koch, 72 [Schoenberg, Kandinsky, and Hahl-Fontaine, 58].

15. For a detailed study of Schoenberg's relationship to Schopenhauer, see White, "Schoenberg and Schopenhauer."

16. As discussed in chapter 1, these stereotypes of the Jewish religion were likely passed to Schopenhauer from Kant, who, as Mack has shown, developed a pseudotheology of antisemitism that conflated the Jewish religion with the Jewish "nation," a concept opposed to his ideal of "German" rationality and autonomous selfhood. Mack, *German Idealism and the Jew*, 17.

17. Cartwright, *Historical Dictionary of Schopenhauer's Philosophy*, 170–171.

18. Schopenhauer, *Parerga und Paralopomena: Kleine philosophische Schriften*, vol. 2, 405 [Schopenhauer, *Parerga and Paralipomena: Short Philosophical Essays*, vol. 2, 341].

19. Schopenhauer, *Parerga und Paralopomena: Kleine philosophische Schriften*, vol. 2, 408. [Schopenhauer, *Parerga and Paralipomena: Short Philosophical Essays*, vol. 2, 343].

20. Julia Bungardt, "Die Bibliothek Arnold Schönbergs," 170.

21. Schopenhauer, *Parerga und Paralopomena: Kleine philosophische Schriften*, vol. 2, 383–384 [Schopenhauer, *Parerga and Paralipomena: Short Philosophical Essays*, vol. 2, 322].

22. Criticisms of Schopenhauer's prejudice toward Jews can also be found in Schoenberg's note dated April 1922, "Der Philosoph des Mitleids zeigt jedenfalls gegen die Juden nicht einmal Nachsicht" (The philosopher of compassion is not once generous to the Jews). Bungardt, "Die Bibliothek Arnold Schönbergs," 169.

23. Further evidence that Schoenberg's critiques of Schopenhauer were focused on his interpretation of Mitleid, or compassion, can be found in one of his Bibles. Schoenberg underlined the subtitle of Deuteronomy 22, "Vermischte Vorschriften, besonders der Menschenliebe und des Mitleidens mit Tieren Gesetze wegen Sünden und Unkeuschheit" and marked a passage on the following page with the note "Siehe Schopenhauer!" (White, *Schoenberg and the God-Idea*, 49).

24. Bungardt, "Die Bibliothek Arnold Schönbergs," 170.

25. Schoenberg's reference to the dichotomy between Hellenism and Judaism in Schopenhauer's writings reflects a discourse found in the writings of the German Romantics such as Friedrich Schelling. See Williamson, *Longing for Myth in Germany*, 71.

26. Bungardt, "Die Bibliothek Arnold Schönbergs,"170.

27. Julie Brown also makes note of this distinction; however, she claims that Schoenberg still views Jewishness at this point "as a set of negative characteristics from which a penitent might turn." J. Brown, "Schoenberg's Early Wagnerisms," 60. Yet, in the larger context of criticizing Schopenhauer, Schoenberg's comments suggest not his desire to overcome Judaism but rather to further unravel the contradictions embedded in the Law as *Gebot*, how it leads to one-sidedness and misunderstanding.

28. Boss, *Schoenberg's Twelve-Tone Music*, 22.

29. Schoenberg and Vojtek, *Stil und Gedanke*, 448. Rudolph Stephan claims that Bach is the composer most cited in Schoenberg's *Theory of Harmony* (1911), his first major treatise on composition. Stephan, "Schoenberg and Bach," 127.

30. Adorno, *Philosophy of New Music*, 49.

31. In early sketches for the symphony, it was intended to be the sixth of seven movements; however, by 1915, when he began to compose the texts, he had whittled down the symphony to four movements. The first draft of *Totentanz* is marked as the third movement. Schoenberg, "Totentanz der Prinzipien."

32. Schoenberg, "Letter to Gustav Mahler."

33. Schoenberg, *Texte*, 23. The scene of the lone speaker at midnight with bells ringing in the background also recalls the "Midnight Song" of Friedrich Nietzsche's *Also sprach Zarathustra*, which Mahler set to music in his Third Symphony. See Kita, "Between Instinct and the Law."

34. Schoenberg addresses this idea again in *Moses und Aron*, where *das Wort* is explicitly linked to *Darstellung*, or representation. White, *Schoenberg and the God-Idea*, 73.

35. Schoenberg, *Texte*, 24–25 [Bailey, *Programmatic Elements*, 98–99].

36. In his essay, "Der Verhältnis zum Text," written in 1912, Schoenberg claimed that he had composed many songs based solely on the sounds of the first words of the text and had only discovered later the "real poetic content" of the song. Schoenberg und Vojtek, *Stil und Gedanke*, 5.

37. Schoenberg, *Texte*, 23–24 [Bailey, *Programmatic Elements*, 98].

38. Schoenberg, 25 [Bailey, 98–99].

39. Schoenberg differentiates comprehensibility from coherence in his *Gedanke* manuscript of August 1923. According to Carpenter and Neff, the composer's conception of coherence "addresses the question of what holds together an object made of sound and time. Comprehensibility addresses the question: how can such an object be apprehended as a whole?" Coherence, however, does not always lead to a work being comprehensible, for there will always be relationships that the listener cannot grasp. Schoenberg, Carpenter, and Neff, *Musical Idea*, 22–24.

40. Schoenberg, *Texte*, 27; Bailey, *Programmatic Elements*, 101.

41. Librett, *Orientalism*, 192.

42. Schoenberg, *Texte*, 27.

43. Schoenberg, 28

44. Schoenberg, 27.

45. Lebrecht, *Mahler Remembered*, 224.

46. Goehr, "Adorno, Schoenberg and the Prinzipien," 623.

47. Mattes, "Arnold Schoenberg's Death Dance," 125.

48. Although a detailed analysis of the various drafts of the libretto is beyond the scope of this study, the close correspondence between the original drafts and the final libretto published in the fall of 1917 reveals that already Schoenberg's drafts from 1915 contain the majority of the central ideas for this work.

49. This version is labeled DICH 7 or T07 in the archives of the Arnold Schönberg Centre Wien. In her dissertation, Jean Christensen refers to a missing nineteen-page version of the libretto—DICH 7 includes eleven of these pages. See Christensen, "Arnold Schoenberg's Oratorio *Die Jakobsleiter*."

50. Drafts dated April 12, 1915, are included in folder T56, ASC Wien.

51. See Christensen for a more detailed chronology. Christensen, "Arnold Schoenberg's Oratorio *Die Jakobsleiter*," vol. 1, 48. The title *Die Jakobsleiter* in reference to this work appears for the first time in Schoenberg's correspondence in June 1917 in a letter to Adolf Loos. Glück, "Briefe von Arnold Schönberg an Adolf Loos," 10.

52. Berry, *After Wagner*, 73. According to Berry, the triplets also reference the emergence of life in two other musical-dramatic works depicting the origins of the world: Josef Haydn's oratorio *The Creation* (1797–1798) and Richard Wagner's *The Rhinegold* (1854). However, Schoenberg dispenses with the image of eternal harmonic stasis evoked by the long opening tones in these works.

53. Schoenberg, *Texte*, 39.

54. His speech follows that of Ein Berufener, who sacrificed everything for beauty but is reprimanded by Gabriel for being too "pleased with himself" for never having suffered (Schoenberg, 42).

55. Schoenberg, 43 [Christensen, "Arnold Schoenberg's Oratorio *Die Jakobsleiter*," vol. 2, 35].

56. See Lipiner, *Adam*, 53.

57. Schoenberg, *Texte*, 43 [Christensen, "Arnold Schoenberg's Oratorio Die Jakobsleiter," vol. 2, 36].

58. Schoenberg, 44 [Christensen, 36].

59. Schoenberg, 44 [Christensen, 36].

60. Schoenberg, *Texte*, 45 [Christensen, "Arnold Schoenberg's Oratorio *Die Jakobsleiter*," vol. 2, 37].

61. Schoenberg, 45 [Christensen, 37].

62. "Ihr Bestes ist mein, wie ihr Ärgstes, ich raub es stehle, entwind es, verachte Erworbenes, Ererbtes, raffe zusammen, reiße an mich, es zu fassen" (Schoenberg, *Texte*, 46); "I rob it from them, steal, take it away, despise what I have acquired, inherited, gather it together, grab it, in order to get a hold of it" [Christensen, "Arnold Schoenberg's Oratorio *Die Jakobsleiter*," vol. 2, 37].

63. Schoenberg, 45 [Christensen, 37].

64. Schoenberg, 46.

65. Frisch, "Brahms, Developing Variation," 216.

66. Dahlhaus suggests that for Schoenberg, developing variation encapsulates both entelechy "the goal directed process of development—and the notion of musical space in which all the motivic shapes and relationships that serve to present an idea are collected together in imaginary simultaneity." Dahlhaus, *Schoenberg and the New Music*, 133.

67. "Immer war Gott. Aber im Anfang war der Geist und der mußte schaffen" (Schoenberg, *Texte*, 59); "God was always there. But in the beginning there was the Spirit and he had to create" [Christensen, "Arnold Schoenberg's Oratorio *Die Jakobsleiter*," vol. 2, 46].

68. Schoenberg, 62 [Christensen, 48].

69. Schoenberg, 59.

70. Prayer is also a key concept for Swedenborg and Balzac, as Schoenberg's citation of *Sérephita*, with the words, "Wer betet ist mit Gott eins geworden" (The one who prays is one with God), reveals.

71. Dahlhaus, *Schoenberg and the New Music*, 91–92.

72. Ringer, *Arnold Schoenberg—Composer as Jew*, 71.

73. See Kita, "Between Instinct and the Law."

74. Schoenberg, *Texte*, 64 [Christensen, "Arnold Schoenberg's Oratorio *Die Jakobsleiter*," vol. 2, 49].

75. Dika Newlin has claimed that this chorus paraphrases two prayers from the Jewish Day of Atonement ("Self-Revelation and the Law," 210).

76. Schoenberg's first attempt at composing with the twelve-tone method was the scherzo of the vocal symphony of which *Die Jakobsleiter* was to be a part. According to Newlin, *Die Jakobsleiter* reveals a "quasi-serial" method of composition wherein a variety of themes are created from the six tones of the *basso ostinato* of the opening theme. Newlin, "Self-Revelation and the Law," 207.

77. See Ringer, *Arnold Schoenberg—Composer as Jew*, 53–54. Berry, "Arnold Schoenberg's 'Biblical Way,'" 85.

78. The phrase "Du sollst" in reference to the commandments can also be found in the Four Pieces for mixed Choir, Op. 27 (1925) and *Moses und Aron*. In both of these works, the reference is specifically the second commandment, "Du sollst dir kein Bild machen." Shelleg refers to Op. 27 as Schoenberg's "first explicit and personal paraphrase of the second commandment at a period when his twelve-tone idiom was already in fully evolved form" (Shelleg, *Jewish Contiguities*, 47).

79. As Covach writes, Schoenberg's *Gedanke* was not a systematic theory but a term that he continually referred to in a variety of contexts to express his goal of art. Covach, "Sources of Schoenberg's Aesthetic Theology," 255–256.

80. In a letter to Nicholas Slonimsky of June 3, 1937, Schoenberg wrote that his first steps toward composing with twelve tones happened "about December 1914 or the beginning of 1915" when he sketched the scherzo of the symphony project. He continued, "After that I was always occupied with the idea to base the structure of my music consciously on a unifying idea." Schoenberg, "Letter to Nicholas Slonimsky." See also Schoenberg's essay, "Kompositionen mit zwölf Tönen," in Schoenberg and Vojtek, *Stil und Gedanke*, 382.

# 4

# DIALOGUES OF COMPASSION: RICHARD BEER-HOFMANN'S *JAÁKOBS TRAUM*

**Was dem Zuschauer zugespielt wird, was der Leser zu lesen erhielt, ist ein zweihändiger, leichtspielbarer Klavierauszug, meistens Klaviermässig gedacht, am Klavier ersonnen und niedergeschrieben. Dass man das Leben in seiner Fülle redender und stummer Stimmen partiturel einzufangen versuchen muss, davon ist kaum eine Ahnung zu verspüren.**

**[What is performed for the audience, what the reader receives to read is a two-handed, easy-to-play piano score, mostly "piano-esque" conceived, contrived and written down at the piano. That one must try to capture life as a score, in all of its abundant voices, both spoken and silent, not a trace of this is noticeable.]**

Richard Beer-Hofmann to Erich Kahler, 1933

In 1933, the poet Richard Beer-Hofmann wrote to his friend Erich Kahler, comparing his process of creating drama to that of composing an intricate musical score. When he wrote this letter, Beer-Hofmann had just completed the text for his drama, *Der junge David* (The Young David), the second installment of his planned biblical tetralogy, *Die Historie von König David* (The History of King David). His description corresponds to anecdotes from his daughter Naemah, who claims that her father composed sections of this work while seated at the piano.[1] Until the end of his life, music remained central to the Beer-Hofmann's conception of his art. As he remarked to Werner Vortreide in 1944, "Die Leute nennen mich wohl einen Dramatiker. Ich bin gar keiner. Ich bin nur ein verschlagener Symphoniker" (people call me a dramatist. I'm not one at all. I'm only a devious symphonist).[2]

The reception of *Die Historie von König David*, which Beer-Hofmann began in 1898 and left unfinished at his death in 1945, suggests that audiences were indeed attuned to the musicality of his dramatic works. Reviews of the cycle's prelude, *Jaákobs Traum*, which premiered in Vienna in April 1919, repeatedly refer to the play as an oratorio.[3] A reviewer for the *Frankfurter Zeitung* claimed that the characters "spoke arias," while Felix Salten, writing for the *Berliner Tageblatt*, claimed that: "man hörte eine Ouvertüre, in der wundervolle Leitmotive aufklingen, hat die Melodienfülle eines Meisters in Andeutung kennengelernt und verlangt nun nach dem Meisterwerk" (one hears an overture ringing forth in wonderful leitmotifs, has become acquainted with the fullness of melody of a master and longs for the masterwork).[4] The "masterwork" was to be a cycle of plays on the life of the biblical patriarch, David: *Der junge David*, *König David* (King David), and *Davids Tod* (David's Death). The epic and mythical content of the work, its scope as a tetralogy to be performed over four nights, and the musicality of the work's conception led another reviewer writing for the *Hamburger Fremdenblatt* to claim this work as formally and thematically evocative of Wagner's music dramas, describing it as "ein jüdischer *Ring des Nibelungen*" (a Jewish *Ring of the Nibelungen*) or "ein Mittelding zwischen ein jüdischer *Faust* und ein jüdischer *Parsifal*" (a middle thing between a Jewish *Faust* and a Jewish *Parsifal*).[5] Indeed, a study of the form and content of Beer-Hofmann's work reveals its affinities with the Wagnerian theory of drama that achieved widespread popularity in Europe at the turn of the century, the Gesamtkunstwerk, or total work of art.

The Gesamtkunstwerk permeated Beer-Hofmann's vision for his biblical tetralogy in three critical ways: ideologically, in its claims toward the regeneration of the collective by inspiring compassion for the hero protagonist; philosophically, in its employment of myth to overcome or reimagine history, and aesthetically, in its vision for an integrative, intermedial approach to drama. Beer-Hofmann's fascination for this artistic paradigm was fostered through his connections to leading members of Vienna's artistic avant-garde, including cultural critic Hermann Bahr, composer Gustav Mahler, and the artist and stage designer Alfred Roller.

However, unlike Wagner's vision of total art, which was predicated on the exclusion of the Jewish subject, Beer-Hofmann envisioned his dramatic works as modes of mediating between Jewish culture and the German-Austrian theater tradition that he also embraced as his own. Like Lipiner, Beer-Hofmann believed that art should give voice to marginalized subjects, inspiring a compassionate response from the audience. In his biblical tetralogy, Beer-Hofmann integrates an artistic portrayal of subjective interiority with the powerful unity of musical, verbal, and visual gestures to offer a new model of compassionate art rooted in his own experience as German-Jew.

To create a dramatic work that would represent German-Jewish identity as a reflection of the evolving nature of the Jewish covenant with God, Beer-Hofmann evokes a style of subjective Expressionist drama that focuses on reflection and dialogue to reveal the inner transformation of the protagonist. In *Jaákobs Traum*, the dramatic narrative traces Jaákobs journey from a naive and rebellious youth to a spokesperson for the Jewish community, a transformation that can only occur after he has learned compassion and become a proud and defiant *Exculpator Dei*, an advocate for (and challenger of) God.[6] In the play, Jaákob comes to understand compassion through his encounters with three figures who force him to question his own identity through reflection on the legacy of Jewish blessing and suffering in the past, present, and future time. The pagan slave Indibaál, Jaákob's brother Edom (coded here as Christian) and the fallen angel Samáel each present a challenge to Jaákob to reexamine suffering from another perspective and to respond compassionately. Jaákob's ability to *feel with* the suffering of these characters emboldens him to challenge God and reclaim his blessing. For Beer-Hofmann, the Jewish part of his identity is a dynamic state between free will and destiny, between choosing and being chosen. In affirming his destiny as the Chosen One, Jaákob emerges as a model of a modern German-Jewish subject, who understands the Jewish legacy as "the Chosen people" as not a static ideal but rather as a process reflecting the lived experience of individual subjects.

In the finale, the poet elevates Jaákob's individual struggle to an affirmation of compassionate community by employing the unity of musical, verbal, and visual gestures. By assigning musical leitmotifs to two key symbols in the play—the stone, which represents Jewish suffering, and the spring, the embodiment of Jewish blessing—Beer-Hofmann employs a Wagnerian technique of using musical gestures to augment the symbolic and ritualistic aspects of myth. However, these musical gestures also serve to denote moments of rupture or transition in the work, reflecting the dynamic nature of Jaákobs relationship to God. By casting Jaákob as one able to mold the dissonant themes of Jewish blessing and suffering into a harmonious affirmation of faith, Beer-Hofmann reveals the role of music as a guiding principle of his conceptions of creation and identity. The modern German-Jewish subject is, for Beer-Hofmann, like a musical motive; a figure always in the process of development. Beer-Hofmann's adaptation of Wagner's total dramatic vision employs the power of mythic art to stage the subjective interiority of the German-Jewish individual, whose dynamic and evolving nature will ultimately strengthen a fractured diasporic community.

## "Durchaus Jude . . . durchaus Österreicher"

Richard Beer-Hofmann's vision for *Die Historie von König David*, and, in particular, the first drama, *Jaákobs Traum*, emerged from the poet's engagement with his Jewish faith and with Jewish culture in Vienna around the turn of the century. Although Beer-Hofmann resisted political engagement throughout his life, he defined his relationship to Jewish identity as one of deep respect for Jewish myth. After dabbling with these themes in poetry and prose, he eventually began to compose the tetralogy of biblical dramas that would bring the legacy of Jewish culture to dramatic realization onstage. In drama, Beer-Hofmann finally found a medium to express both the subjective voice of his lyrical "I" and the noble mythical nature of Jewish culture.

Born on July 11, 1866, in Brünn in Moravia, Beer-Hofmann was adopted by his aunt and uncle after the death of his parents and raised in a secular Jewish household.[7] The family moved to Vienna in 1880, where Beer-Hofmann completed his secondary studies, followed by a law degree at the University of Vienna. Around this time, he made the acquaintance of Arthur Schnitzler, who introduced him to the circle of writers and artists who would become known as *Jung Wien* (Young Vienna), including Hermann Bahr, Jakob Wassermann, Felix Salten, Peter Altenberg, and Hugo von Hofmannstahl.[8] Beer-Hofmann's early poetry and novellas reflect the influence of the subjective lyricism and symbolism of this group of aesthetes.

In the mid-1890s, however, Beer-Hofmann also became increasingly engaged with his Jewish heritage. Correspondence with Theodor Herzl in 1896 reveals Beer-Hofmann's sympathies with the Jewish community, which he admired as "der legitime Erbe uralter vornehmer Cultur" (legitimate heirs of an ancient venerable culture).[9] Around this same time, Beer-Hofmann's poetic and prose works began to reflect his gradual shift toward Jewish themes. His poem "Lullaby for Miriam" (Schlaflied für Mirjam 1898), written after the birth of his daughter, draws on the symbolism linking Jewish blood to *Ahnen* or ancestry, the familial ties at the heart of Jewish community. These images are emphasized in the poem's final stanza:

> Ufer nur sind wir, und tief in uns rinnt
> Blut von Gewesenen—zu Kommenden rollts,
> Blut unserer Väter, voll Unruh und Stolz.
> In uns sind Alle. Wer fühlt sich allein?
> Du bist ihr Leben—ihr Leben ist dein—

[We are but shores, and blood in us deep
Flows from those passed to those yet to be
Blood of our Fathers, restless and proud.
All are within us, who feels alone?
You are their life—their life is your own.][10]

Similar themes also appear in Beer-Hofmann's novella, *Der Tod Georgs* (Georg's Death 1900). In a narrative that parallels Beer-Hofmann's own development as an artist at this time, the protagonist Paul rejects the narcissistic life of the aesthete, after discovering a link to his Jewish heritage in a dream vision.[11] These images reveal the influence of Jewish Renaissance leader, Martin Buber, as well as the *Jungjüdische Bewegung* (Young Jewish Movement) on Beer-Hofmann, a group with whom Stefan Zweig was also loosely affiliated at the turn of the century. Focusing on themes of Jewish suffering and images of a return to the Jewish homeland, many of these writers sought to create a new poetic language inspired by ancient biblical sources.[12]

Despite his connections to these key figures of the Zionist movement and the Jewish Renaissance, however, Beer-Hofmann largely distanced himself from the political realm, maintaining only marginal associations with Jewish nationalism.[13] He was strongly against chauvinism of any kind, and forcefully denied critics who claimed his biblical dramas were intended to promote nationalist themes.[14] His claim, "Meiner Substanz nach bin ich durchaus Jude . . . funktionell durchaus Österreicher" (By nature I am a Jew through-and-through . . . but in functional terms, I am totally an Austrian), reveals his complex relationship toward Jewishness, which he never sought to deny, staunchly believing it to be fully reconcilable with his Austrian cultural heritage.[15]

Around the turn of the century, Beer-Hofmann felt increasingly compelled to examine the dynamics of religious and cultural identity in his art and it was in the theater that he found a means of expressing the inner conflicts he experienced as a German Jew. His first major dramatic success was the play *Der Graf von Charolais* (The Count of Charolais), completed in 1904 and premiered in Berlin under the direction of Max Reinhardt in 1905. Set in the Middle Ages, *Der Graf* features der Rote Itzig (Red Ike), a moneylender who is marked as an outsider not only by his profession and name but also by his crude and dialect-inflected language.[16] The depiction of der Rote Itzig is highly ambivalent; while he embodies many of the antisemitic stereotypes of the time (including a lack of compassion, in holding the body of the dead count as collateral for debts), he also draws attention to the stigmatization and scapegoating of Jews. When Charolais appeals to Itzig's humanity, the Jew responds: "Ein Mensch? Wie ihr? Seit wann bin ich e Mensch? Mei Lebtag hat man mich's nicht fühlen lassen, daß ich e Mensch bin; heut' grad soll ich's sein? Weil's euch so paßt?" (A human being? Like you? Since when? All my life people have not made me feel that I am a human being; just today I'm to be one? Because it suits you?)[17] With the figure of Itzig, who challenges negative Jewish stereotypes as a product of a culture of discrimination, Beer-Hofmann probes the subjective interiority of the German-Jewish subject.[18] *Der Graf von Charolais* marks a new transition in the development of Beer-Hofmann's artistic style from decadent lyricism to drama. In the dialogic exchange of the theater, he found a means to examine contemporary political and cultural issues facing the German-Jewish subject. In *Jaákobs Traum*, he would focus in particular on how the myths of the Hebrew Scriptures and their conflicted narrative of compassion continued to impact perceptions of the Jew in his own time.

## The Gesamtkunstwerk as Compassionate Art

In his biblical tetralogy, *Die Historie von König David*, Beer-Hofmann sought to empower the modern German-Jewish subject and the Jewish diasporic community through compassionate art. To do so, he turned to a popular dramatic paradigm, the Gesamtkunstwerk, or total work of art. A central figure in the popularization and dissemination of the total work of art at the turn of the century was the composer Richard Wagner. Wagner's essays on the Gesamtkunstwerk from the 1840s offered a compelling model for drama for that would engage all of the audience's senses and emotions through a unity of musical, visual, and verbal gestures. In Wagner's vision, the unity of the arts would emphasize the transtemporal impact of myth. Moreover, as a collective production of musicians, painters, and poets, composed both by and for the Volk, the total work of art would inspire a sympathetic response from the audience and thus inspire the formation of new communities. The Gesamtkunstwerk was widely discussed and employed among the artistic avant-garde in Vienna, particularly by members of the Viennese Secession, Hermann Bahr and Alfred Roller, close friends of Beer-Hofmann. Through Bahr, Roller, and the composer and director Gustav Mahler, who realized Wagner's vision in his productions at the Vienna Court Opera at this time, Beer-Hofmann came to view the Gesamtkunstwerk as an ideal model for his biblical tetralogy, *Die Historie von König David*.

In his early essays, *Das Kunstwerk der Zukunft* (The Art-Work of the Future 1849) and *Oper und Drama* (1851), Wagner developed a theory of drama that he believed would inspire a renewed German cultural community through the power of compassion. These essays were written during the composer's period of political activism and thus reflect a revolutionary vision of the ability of art to effect social change. In *Das Kunstwerk der Zukunft*, Wagner claimed that art had become corrupted, fragmented, and disintegrated, like the society of his time. The reintegration of all art forms, music, dance, and visual art, would make possible the merging of performer and audience, a fusion that would, in turn, inspire the rebirth of a German cultural community.[19] The source material of Wagner's total artwork is myth, and in his vision, the promise of a collective redemption is predicated on the ability of myth to transcend history, creating a sense of continuity and community over generations.[20] In *Oper und Drama*, Wagner defines myth as the "poem of a life view in common," which "reaches into the heart of actual life, giving shape and measure . . . and kindling men to deeds."[21] Moreover, it makes the audience aware of their shared origins, encourages the identification of the audience with the plight of the tragic hero, and prompts their compassionate response. As discussed in chapter 1, Wagner's essays were widely read and discussed in turn-of-the-century Vienna and played a formative role in shaping Siegfried Lipiner's vision of compassionate art.

Wagner's vision for a regeneration of art also proved particularly enticing to the avant-garde of fin de siècle Austria and shaped their innovative approaches to the visual, literary, musical, and dramatic arts. Three key figures who influenced Beer-Hofmann's reception of these ideas were the writer and cultural critic Hermann Bahr, the composer and theater director Gustav Mahler, and the artist and stage designer Alfred Roller. Beer-Hofmann came to know Bahr through the Young Vienna circle, and the two developed a close friendship and intellectual exchange. Roller and Bahr were both leading members of the Vienna Secession at the turn of the century, and Roller served as Mahler's right hand at the Vienna Court Opera during their production of a number of Wagner's music dramas in the first decade of the twentieth century.

Hermann Bahr was an essayist, poet, journalist, theater director, and leading figure of Vienna's artistic avant-garde and served as one of the most vocal promoters of the Wagnerian model of the Gesamtkunstwerk in his time. In a 1904 review of a production of Friedrich Schiller's *Wilhelm Tell* at the Burgtheater, Bahr affirmed his vision of the total work of art, which should unite the physical movement of the actors and the musical gestures of the orchestra with the total visual effect. For Bahr, the movements of the actor, his gestures, "speak" to the audience, yet the individual remains a stranger to us until music incites a compassionate response:

> Dazu genügt das Wort nie, es ist zu weit, es ist ja doch immer nur ein Zeichen in der Ferne, wie eine wehende Fahne, die uns anzeigt, daß dort drüben, dort draußen etwas vorgeht, aber nicht: was. Dies wird erst durch die Gebärde des Schauspielers bestimmt, der an seinem Körper das Wort individualisiert. Die Gebärde des Schauspielers verstehen wir schon besser, aber er bleibt doch immer ein fremder Mensch für uns, ein anderer: wir erleben sein Schicksal, nicht unseres. Erst indem nun die Musik aus Geheimnissen heraufdringt, welche für alle Menschen diesselben sind, können wir am einzelnen Falle die gemeinsame Sache der ganzen Menschheit, am Falle des anderen unsere eigene Sache erkennen. Und erst wenn diese Töne, wie aus unserem eigenen Munde gequollen, um unsere tiefsten Heimlichkeiten zu verraten, nun plötzlich wieder draußen als Farben unseren Augen sichtbar werden, geht uns des Lebens höchstes Wunder auf: daß unsere innere Welt und jene äußere Welt dieselbe sind und wir . . . immer nur in einen Spiegel schauen.

> [The word is not enough for this, it is too far, it is still just a sign in the distance, like a flag blowing, that announces to us, that over there, out there something is advancing, but not what it is. This is affirmed only first by the gesture (*Gebärde*) of the actor, who individualizes the word with his body. We understand the gesture of the actor even better, but he remains still a stranger to us, another: we experience his fate, not our own. Only when music penetrates from the mysteries below, which are the same for all men, only then can we in the specific case recognize the shared destiny of humanity, and in the case of the other recognize our own destiny. And only when these tones, as if welled out of our own mouths to betray the deepest secrets, suddenly are made visible outside of us as colors before our eyes, appears life's highest wonder: that our inner world and this outer world are the same and that . . . we have been looking in a mirror all along.][22]

Bahr's language in this passage, in particular the reference to life's "höchstes Wunder," recalls the Wagnerian aesthetics of compassion that had infiltrated Viennese theater at this time through the writings of figures such as Siegfried Lipiner.[23] The union of the arts, Bahr claims, excites the sympathy of the audience, who then recognize in the hero the shared destiny of humanity, the mysteries that are "the same for all men."

The most prominent practitioner of the form of "total art" that Bahr described in Vienna at this time was the composer Gustav Mahler. Mahler's production of Richard Wagner's *Tristan und Isolde*, which premiered at the Vienna Court Opera in 1903, featured the stage design work of Alfred Roller, an artist who had served as president of the Vienna Secession. Under Mahler and Roller's direction, the Court Opera become a site of "total theater," transforming stage design away from realist backdrops to the innovative use of lighting to create mood and atmosphere.[24] Mahler and Roller's *Tristan* collaboration marked a watershed moment in the history of Wagner interpretation and theater as a whole in Europe. In breaking free from the traditions established at Bayreuth, Mahler and Roller redefined the cult status of the artistic director and stage designer, placing new emphasis on the role of creative interpretation.[25] Mahler and Roller would go on to stage other Wagner productions including *Das Rheingold* (1905), *Lohengrin* (1906), and *Die Walküre* (1907). Their staging of the complete *Ring* cycle was never achieved, due to Mahler's departure from Vienna in 1907 under pressure from the antisemitic press and other intrigues in the Opera administration.

Even after Mahler's tenure at the court opera came to an end, Roller continued to promote their vision of total art in the Viennese theater scene. In a 1909 essay entitled "Bühnenreform" (Stage Reform), published in the musical journal, *Der Merker: Österreichische Zeitschrift für Musik und Theater*, Roller called for the poets of his time to compose works that reflected the "Gleichstrebigkeit aller auf der Bühne tätigen Elemente" (the equal striving of all active elements of the stage).[26] Roller hoped that the Gesamtkunstwerk would inspire a new generation of "theaterlebendige" productions (works that "bring the theater to life") through the coordination of musical, verbal, and visual gestures. Moreover, Roller believed, like Wagner, that only through the "volle Einheitlichkeit der szenischen und der dichterischen Absicht" (full unity of scenic and poetic purpose) could this new vision of theater be realized.[27] Its goal was to offer the audience a glimpse into another world that would excite, inspire, uplift, unsettle, and entertain them. The engagement of the audience that Roller envisioned resonates with Bahr's writings on the theater and with the fusion of artist and spectator in Wagner's model of compassionate art.

The meticulous stage directions found in the text of Beer-Hofmann's *Jaákobs Traum* reveal that the poet was drawing on a theory and praxis of total art developing in the Viennese theater scene at this time. These notes indicate in precise detail the setting and lighting, the characters' clothing, and even their gestures and glances.[28] It is no surprise, therefore, that it was Roller who was enlisted as stage designer for the premiere performance of *Jaákobs Traum* at the Burgtheater in Vienna in 1919, for he understood uniquely the importance of integrating the stage design with the music, language, and physical movements of the actors in a coordinated form of gesture.[29] In a later essay to his friend Erich Kahler in 1933, Beer-Hofmann defined his vision of the total unity of art as an attempt to engage all the senses of the audience: "So versuch ich, eine gesündere dem Leben ähnlichere, organischere, Gottgewolltere Relation zwischen allem Geschautem, Geatmetem, Gerochenem, Getastetem, Geschwiegenem, Getanem und dem schliesslich Gesprochenem herzustellen." (In this way I attempt to create a healthier, closer to life, more organic and god-willed relation between everything seen, breathed, smelled, touched, silenced, enacted and finally, spoken).[30] Beer-Hofmann's understanding of his role as dramatist therefore extended far beyond the composition of the text to the creation of compassionate art, a total theatrical effect that would engage and transform the audience.

Yet, Beer-Hofmann also sought to rupture the experience of total theater through dissonant and disruptive voices. In his letter to Kahler, he wrote of the need to strike a balance between the epic plot and the dynamic "Rede und Gegenrede" (speech and counterspeech) of dialogue.[31] As the following analysis of *Jaákobs Traum* reveals, voices challenge the audience to consider new perspectives, yet ultimately resolve in ritualistic gestures that create the powerful effect of compassion that he sought in the Gesamtkunstwerk paradigm.

In *Jaákobs Traum*, the dynamics of dialogue serve to recast the figure of the Jew, suggesting that Beer-Hofmann's interpretation of the Gesamtkunstwerk developed in part as a response to the exclusionary rhetoric underlying the Wagnerian paradigm, which excluded the Jewish subject. Such ideas appear in essays such as *Opera and Drama*, in which Wagner claimed that the Jew, exemplified by composer Giacomo Meyerbeer, is the figure "without a mother tongue," whose deficiencies for instinctual speech made him incapable of creating true mythical art.[32] The idea of the Jews as a people without myth echoed in the writings of linguists and historians such as Ernest Renan (not to mention philosophers such as Schopenhauer, discussed in the previous chapter) who claimed that Judaism lacked mythology because its roots lay in monotheism, not polytheism. These scholars recast Judaism, which had previously been associated with a backward, unenlightened, and superstitious civilization, as the bearer of the "urban, commercial, secular, and (hence) antimythical culture of modernity."[33]

That Beer-Hofmann received the total work of art paradigm with skepticism is evident from his remarks to his wife Paula after a visit to Bayreuth, in which he wrote "one sees nowhere else so much artistic hypocrisy."[34]

In *Jaákobs Traum* Beer-Hofmann realized a new form of Gesamtkunstwerk which responded to these exclusionary discourses by staging the German-Jewish subject as mediator between conflicting cultures and traditions. Through his signature poetic lyricism and the unity of musical, verbal, and visual gestures, Beer-Hofmann transforms the story of the Hebrew patriarch Jacob into the epic myth of reconciliation in modern culture. In so doing, he recuperates the vision of the Jews as a people of music and myth, the creators of compassionate art.

## Composing Compassion through Dialogues of Difference

In *Jaákobs Traum*, the first installment of the *Historie* cycle, Beer-Hofmann traces Jaákob's quest to rediscover compassion and understand his status as "The Chosen One," through encounters with the Jewish past, present, and future. Beer-Hofmann began *Jaákobs Traum*, the first installment of the *Historie* cycle, in 1908 and completed it in 1915. *Jaákobs Traum* focuses on several episodes from the patriarch's life that appear in the book of Genesis: Jacob's stealing of his brother Esau's blessing (Genesis 27); his dream of a ladder leading up to heaven (Genesis 28:10–22), his wrestling with the angel (Genesis 32:22–23), and his fear of his brother and their eventual reconciliation (Genesis 32:1–21, 33). In his play, Beer-Hofmann condenses these episodes into two acts. The first act focuses on Edom (as with Jaákob, Beer-Hofmann uses the Hebrew name for Esau) and is primarily a narrative retelling of the theft of the blessing. The second act of *Jaákobs Traum* is organized according to a tripartite structure, divided into Jaákob's encounters with three figures, the pagan slave Indibaál, Edom, and the fallen angel Samáel. Through his dialogues with these characters, Jaákob comes to understand that his calling as the Chosen One requires him to feel compassion for those different from himself, to overcome the barriers between them. Through these compassionate encounters, Jaákob reevaluates the traumatic past of Jewish history and the experience of Otherness in the present moment and comes to accept the future suffering of his people. These three confrontations follow a similar pattern. First, Jaákob recognizes a central point of difference with his interlocutor, which leads him to pose a challenging question to himself about the nature of Jewish suffering and eventually to come to a deeper understanding of this calling. The scene concludes with a ritualistic gesture. These dialogues thus constitute compassionate engagements with the Other that play a critical role in Jaákob's *Bildung*, or self-education. The first two encounters, examined in this section, reveal Jaákob's journey from self-alienation to self-knowledge, from difference to compassionate understanding. The final encounter results in his affirmation of compassion, which will be examined in the concluding section.

Beer-Hofmann's vision of compassionate art draws on the techniques of the subjective theater of Expressionism. In subjective theater, the relationship between the subjective and objective "manifests itself temporally as a rapport between the present in the past," that is, the past appears as present, embodied in characters who appear to the protagonist as foreign Others.[35] In staging Jaákob's encounters with three characters who represent Jewish Otherness in past, present, and future, Beer-Hofmann creates the circumstances for theatrical compassion: first, the consciousness of difference, second, the recognition of sameness (seeing oneself in the Other, recognizing their pain as one's own), and, finally, the envisioning of a future in which the initial difference is dissolved. Like many of the Expressionist dramatists, Beer-Hofmann aimed to initiate a larger cultural transformation in which the dramatic protagonist's self-education serves as a catalyst for social change. That Beer-Hofmann and Zweig (as the next chapter will demonstrate) mobilized elements of Expressionist drama in their works to articulate their own German-Jewish subjectivity in response to a specific discourse of antisemitism attests to a fascinating overlap between the philosophical and aesthetic discourse of compassion that emerged in Vienna as well as the larger cultural movements in Europe at this time.[36]

Jaákob's dialogue with the pagan slave Indibaál represents the first stage in the hero's journey of compassion through his reconciliation with a central moment in Jewish history, Abraham's sacrifice of Isaac. The encounter begins with a confrontation with Otherness, as Indibaál tells Jaákob his culture's origin story. On the rock of Uru-Shalim, he recalls, the gods overthrew the monster that gave birth to them, tearing apart the earth. The violent death of the monster was marked by fallen star, a stone that fell from the sky and became a glowing seal. This dark past continually threatens to rise up again and engulf the world darkness.[37] It is because of this legend, Indibaál claims, that the priests make sacrifices upon this rock. At first, Jaákob's probing questions to the slave's stories "es schützen die Götter *ihren* Diener nicht?" (don't the gods protect *their* servants?) and, as he points to the precipice of the mountain, "liegt dort ein Abgrund, der *euch* heilig ist?" (is there a chasm there that is holy to *your* people?) highlight his perceived foreignness of the origin myth of Indibaál's people.[38] However, as Indibaál tells his story, Jaákob realizes that their cultural myths intersect at this sacred place. Uru-Schalim is Mount Moriah, the location of the Akedah, the near-sacrifice of Jaákob's father, Isaac, by his father, Abraham.

As a pagan and a slave, Indibaál is foreign to Jaákob, yet he also initiates his master's confrontation with an event that serves as a crucial stumbling block in the Jewish narrative of compassion. As Abigail Gillman notes, Beer-Hofmann emphasizes the conflicted image of the stone as a site of primal trauma.[39] While God ultimately spares Isaac, he does so only after taking Abraham to the very brink of inhumanity. In Beer-Hofmann's drama, Jaákob must confront this legacy of the Jewish God as the cruel and uncompassionate father in order to understand his blessing. Gazing upon the mountain, he comments to his pagan slave Indibaál that the God who appeared to Abraham was "ein fremder, unerschauter Gott—ein namensloser" (a foreign, unseen God, a nameless one) who demanded that he slay upon Moriah the one that he loved.[40] He recounts the story to his slave in the first person, placing himself in the position of his father. Jaákob questions how his father could continue to believe in God after such a trauma and wonders why he must also blindly follow the bidding of a God who would demand such violence of his own children.

Jaákob's questions remain unanswered in this scene, yet the reflection on the legacy of trauma passed on to him by his father sparks in him the feeling of compassionate understanding for the plight of Indibaál, who has been separated so long from his family and homeland that he no longer remembers them. Jaákob comforts his slave by foreseeing his return to the land of his people on the shore of a massive, mighty sea, the symbol of "primal holy creation."[41] This time, however, Jaákob describes the scene as though he were seeing this land through Indibaál's eyes. His ability to also describe the very feelings that Indibaál might experience reveals his ability to feel compassion with his slave. Indibaál responds to this vision in words of shock and awe,

> *Wer* bist du—wer? Der solches weiß zu sagen! Als Herr geboren—und weißt, wie dem Knecht ist? Sahst meine Heimat nie—und kündest sie? Fühlst mit dem Tier—has nie noch leiden müssen, und weißt um alles Leid . . . du Knabe—wer hat dir gesagt, was Altsein heißt? Wer gab dir Macht, daß du ins Innerste mir greifst?

> [Who are you—who? That knows such things to say?
> You, born a Lord—yet know the heart of slaves?
> Have never seen my home—and speak of it?
> Feel with the beasts—you who have never suffered,
> Know of all suffering . . . you, boy—who told you
> What it means to be old? Who gave you the power
> To seize the inmost in me?] [42]

Jaákob cannot undo the traumas of his own past, yet, his ability to *feel with* the sufferings of Indibaál, signals a key transition for him as he comes to understand Jewish suffering through a new light. In Indibaál, he no longer sees an Other, but an equal, a companion in suffering. This realization is marked by a ritualistic gesture, in which he tears the slave's old garments and gives him a new cloak, setting him free.[43] Jaákob's encounter with the sacrifice of Isaac reveals a point of deep rupture in the Jewish narrative of compassion but also sets the stage for deeper revelations about the paradox of blessing and suffering that will lead in the end to a renewed compassionate understanding and an affirmation of community.

Jaákob's second encounter is with his brother Edom, who appears in this scene as the Christian Other. In this scene, Jaákob again must grapple with the legacy of blessing and suffering, this time through the tenuous relationship between Christians and Jews in the present time. Like Lipiner's rendition of the story of Cain and Abel, the confrontation between Jaákob and Edom employs the trope of brotherly discord to articulate a discourse of difference.[44] In the play, the narrative of Christian-Jewish antagonism is enacted as Edom hunts Jaákob down with the intention of killing his brother and reclaiming his blessing. However, in this story, tragedy is averted. When Edom attempts to shoot Jaákob with an arrow he misses his brother but hits instead the lamb that Jaákob was raising as his own. The symbolism of lamb (an allusion to Christ in the Christian New Testament) also harkens back to the Abraham's sacrifice of Isaac, marking a reconciliatory moment between New Testament and Hebrew Scriptures, Christianity and Judaism, in narratives of sacrifice and suffering.

This near violent encounter with Edom sparks Jaákob's reconciliation with his brother and serves as the catalyst for his next stage of his self-education. In Beer-Hofmann's play, Edom embodies a hostile Christianity whose antagonism toward Jaákob (the Jew) is born of misunderstanding; he is convinced that his brother stole his blessing in order to do him harm. To rectify this image, Jaákob must display compassion, reconciling with his brother by identifying with his suffering. Having lost his blessing to his brother, Edom feels himself to be "verworfen," or cast out, by God. However, Jaákob appeals to his brother by recalling the myth of Isaac's sacrifice that he discussed with Indibaál, but this time reinterpreting it not as a site of trauma but as evidence of the blessing for *all* people. He recalls, "so sprach Er auf Moriah zu Abraham: 'Durch deinen Samen sollen alle Völker gesegnet sein!'" (Thus on Mount Moriah he spoke to Abraham: "In thy seed shall all the nations of the earth be blessed!")[45] The inclusive nature of this blessing for "all nations," is emphasized by Edom's question, "Die Fremden . . . ?" (The Foreigners . . . ?) to which Jaákob replies "Ja! *Gesegnet*—Durch *uns* gesegnet—*alle* sein!" (Aye! Blest and through us—all shall be blest!)[46] In his response to Edom's concern that Jaákob thinks less of him because he is different, Jaákob replies, "Nein! Gott braucht much *so*—und *anders* dich! Nur weil du, Edom bist—darf ich, Jaákob sein!" (No! Never! God wants me *thus* and wants you *otherwise*! Only because you Edom are—may I be Jacob!)[47] This scene thus rehabilitates the image of the Jew as unworthy and incapable of compassion, emphasized by the figure of Cain in Lipiner's *Adam*, by recasting the Jew as the original compassionate figure. According to Jaákob, difference is not a question of preference or judgment but rather articulates the unique role that each being is called to play. Despite these differences, the brothers share an "inner substance" that enables compassionate understanding. This is the blessing that the Jews have passed down to Christianity. Thus, the Christian doctrine of compassion is inconceivable without Jewish blessing.

As in the previous scene with Indibaál, a ritual of reconciliation concludes Jaákob's confrontation with Edom. Seizing his brother's hand with the same forceful gesture as he used with Indibaál ("mit raschem Griff"), Jaákob again performs a ritual cut. This time, however, it is not fabric but his brother's skin that the knife pierces, so that their blood might flow together.[48] The brothers then drink from the same cup. In both rituals, Jaákob's compassionate actions sets these men free, Indibaál from his servitude and Edom from his anger and resentment toward his brother and God. In their newly found freedom, new bonds have been established, those of Mitleid, or brotherhood in suffering.

Jaákob's encounters with Indibaál and Edom reflect on how the recognition of the self in the other leads to the strengthening of community. These encounters reveal Jaákob's capacity to turn the traumas of his past into self-empowering experiences that will enable him to challenge God, demanding of the divine father figure compassion for all of his children. Thus, Jaákob's journey to learn compassion must lead to a struggle that will, in the end, reimagine the relationship of the human and divine as one of mutual responsibility and compassionate understanding. Beer-Hofmann carries this narrative of compassion to completion by returning to the principles underlying the Gesamtkunstwerk, unity of musical, verbal, and visual gestures. Through the use of musical leitmotifs, Beer-Hofmann draws lines of continuity between Jewish past, present, and future, reclaiming the Jews as a mythical, musical, and compassionate people.

## Jaákob's Struggle with the Angels: Musical Mediations of Past, Present, and Future

In his aspiration to integrate the subjective experience of Jaákob into a visual of total, communal, compassionate art that would revive Jewish myth, Beer-Hofmann employs a technique of the Wagnerian Gesamtkunstwerk by which musical, verbal, and visual gestures serve to make the audience attuned to the significance and meaning of key symbols. Symbolism is a critical component of myth, which as Roberts claims, gives meaning to history, by reviving a "sacred conception of time, space and place."[49] In *Jaákobs Traum*, the symbols that define the Jewish experience are the *Quell* (spring) and the *Stein* (stone), which serve as points of continuity throughout the text to represent the dual legacy of blessing and suffering. These symbols are introduced to the audience in the opening act in Beer-Hofmann's text and appear again in the second act where the text is augmented through the musical technique of leitmotif. As the following analysis of these scenes, supplemented with drafts from the poet's archive, reveal, Beer-Hofmann had planned for these symbols to be represented musically through specific instruments and vocal registers. Moreover, Jaákob is assigned his own leitmotif, the shepherd's pipe, which appears at both the beginning and the end of the second act to mark the protagonist's personal development. Music, however, also marks points of rupture in the text. In Jaákobs encounter with the angels, dramatic musical climaxes are used to mark stages in his acceptance of his destiny as the Chosen One. These events culminate in Jaákob's ritual offering to God, revealing Beer-Hofmann's unique interpretation of the Gesamtkunstwerk in which the voice of the musical German-Jewish subject instigates the creation of compassionate community.

The symbols of the *Stein* and the *Quell*, interwoven into each of the key scenes, mark the link between the Jewish past, present, and future: The stone stands for Jewish suffering, while the wellspring represents the Jewish blessing and the covenant with God. The contrast between the fluidity and dynamism of the spring and the stasis and permanence of the stone reflect a tension in the collective Jewish consciousness between the transient history of exile and the longing for a stable homeland as well as the pull between fate and the freedom to choose one's own destiny. The image of the spring appears in the text of the opening act, as the servants recount Jaákob's theft of Edom's blessing. Basmath describes Isaac as possessing suddenly a powerful strength. The blessing, he recalls, "*aus* ihm bricht" (burst from him) like a dammed-up stream let loose.[50] This potent imagery appears again when Edom confronts their mother Rebekah, questioning why she did not intervene or attempt to undo the blessing. Rebekah's response, "*Kein* Bronnen strömt zurück!" (no stream flows backward to its source!), intensifies this idea of the Jewish blessing as a mystical force that is also one-directional.[51] It cannot be undone by any force. The stone, on the other hand, represents Jewish suffering and the traumatic experience of the *Adekah*, Abraham's sacrifice of Isaac. Whereas the spring points toward development, the stone marks pain and rupture. It represents both the powerful weight of the past and a literal stumbling block for moving forward, a challenge to the narrative of compassion.

In the second act, Beer-Hofmann augments his symbolic interweaving of these symbols in the text through their musical representation in the form of leitmotifs. For Wagner, leitmotifs or *Grundmotive* served as a means of organizing musical ideas. In his music dramas, these motives replaced the traditional operatic structures of aria, recitative, and chorus, allowing the music to play a critical function in the development of dramatic action.[52] He assigned these musical motives to a particular character, concept, or key symbolic object in the drama so that, when interwoven into the musical composition at different points, they could serve to emphasize their significance in the present moment, recall a past memory, or signify a future event. In this way, leitmotifs deepen the audiences understanding of the dramatic action and providing further cohesion for the total work of art. A folder of papers related to *Jaákobs Traum* in Beer-Hofmann's *Nachlass* reveals musical motives assigned to the spring and the stone. Credited to Beer-Hofmann's close friend, Leo Van Jung, another member of the *Jung Wien* circle, these motives reveal that Beer-Hofmann intended to employ musical gesture to emphasize and highlight the significance of these symbols at a critical moment in the dramatic action. (See fig. 4.1.)

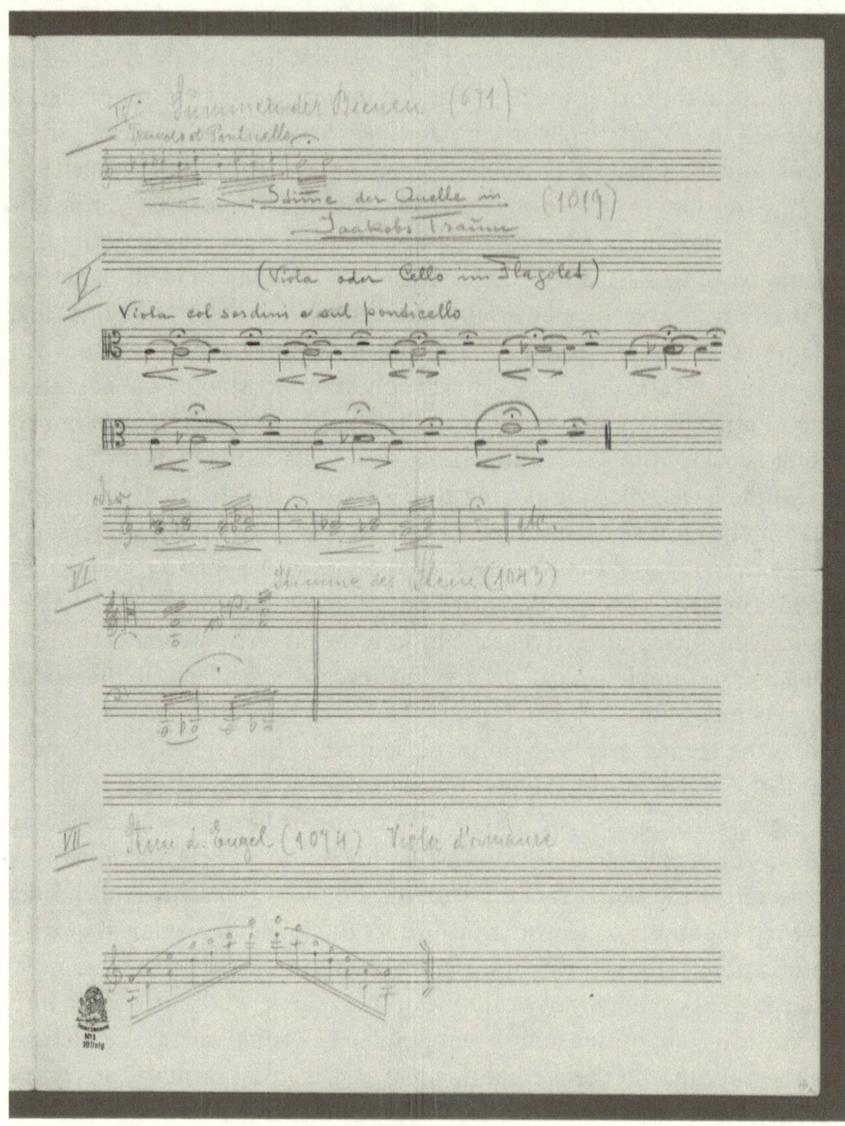


Figure 4.1. Musical notation by Leo Van Jung for Act II of *Jaákobs Traum*. MS Ger 131 Folder 70(2), Houghton Library, Harvard University.

In *Jaákobs Traum*, the musical motives of the spring and the stone appear as outer manifestations of Jaákobs own inner conflict as well as a reminder to the audience of the central role of blessing and suffering in shaping the Jewish community as a whole over time. Van Jung's notation re-creates Jaákob's inner turmoil by voicing the stone and the spring with the two contrasting registers in the viola and cello, aligning with Beer-Hofmann's descriptions in his stage directions. The alternating tremolo tones in the treble clef line articulate the spring's babbling and gurgling clarity, while the stone's "menacing growl," is composed for the lower instrumental voices in the bass clef line. In his notes, Van Jung indicates that viola or celli should play both single held notes and those marked tremolo, alternating between two tones as harmonics ("im Flageolette"). The sostenuto style of these passages is emphasized by fermatas, indicating that the notes and rests should be held for an indefinite amount of time. The composition of these motives suggest that Van Jung had in mind a primal, elemental sound, recalling the opening of Wagner's *Das Rheingold* prelude, the first drama of his *Ring* tetralogy, which opens with the held notes of the bass and bassoon. While Van Jung's music was not used for the official performance at the Burgtheater, there is a remarkable correspondence between these sketches and the stage music composed by Ernst Pfriemer, which can be found in the Austrian National Library's Music Collection. Pfriemer arranged for the voice of the spring to be played by the viola d'amour, accompanied by the woodblock and repeated arpeggios in the xylophone. The ostinato whole notes of the bass and the rumbling roll of the kettledrum provide the voice the stone. (See figs. 4.2a and 4.2b.)

In the final scene of his drama, Beer-Hofmann employs the unity of gesture central to the total work of art to provoke the audience's sympathetic understanding, elevating Jaákob's subjective experience to a shared myth of compassionate community. The previous two encounters with Indibaál and Edom led Jaákob to contemplate the Jewish past and its influence on his own journey in the present moment. In the culmination of the play, the dream scene, Jaákob completes his journey of personal development, through his confrontation with the fallen angel, Samáel. This dream vision is the final stage in Jaákob's education. Emboldened by the compassion that he has learned from the past and present, he chooses his own future by demanding compassion of God, reenvisioning their relationship as one of mutual understanding and responsibility. This reevaluation of the relationship between humanity and God rewrites Jaákob as a model for a modern

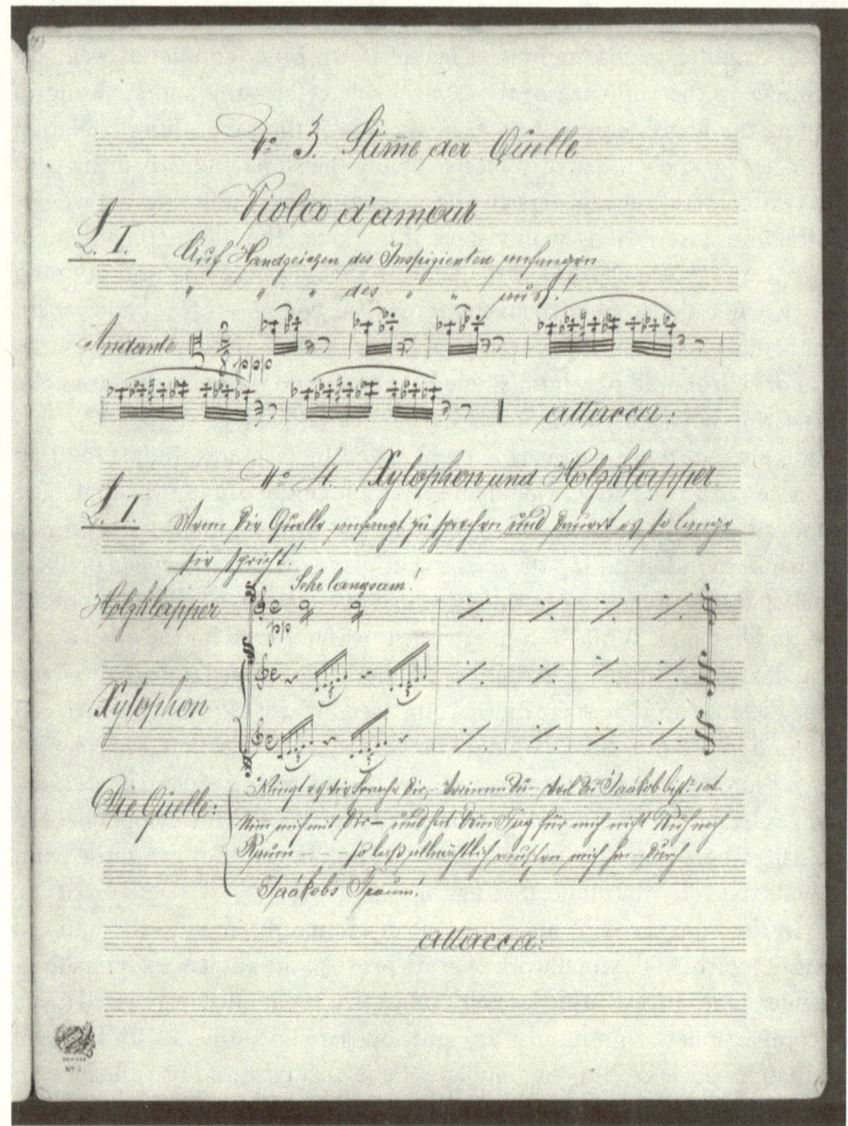


Figure 4.2a and 4.2b. Fragment of Ernst Pfriemer's musical score for performance of *Jaákobs Traum* at Vienna's Burgtheater, April 1919. Austrian National Library, Music Collection, F19. BA.57.Mus.

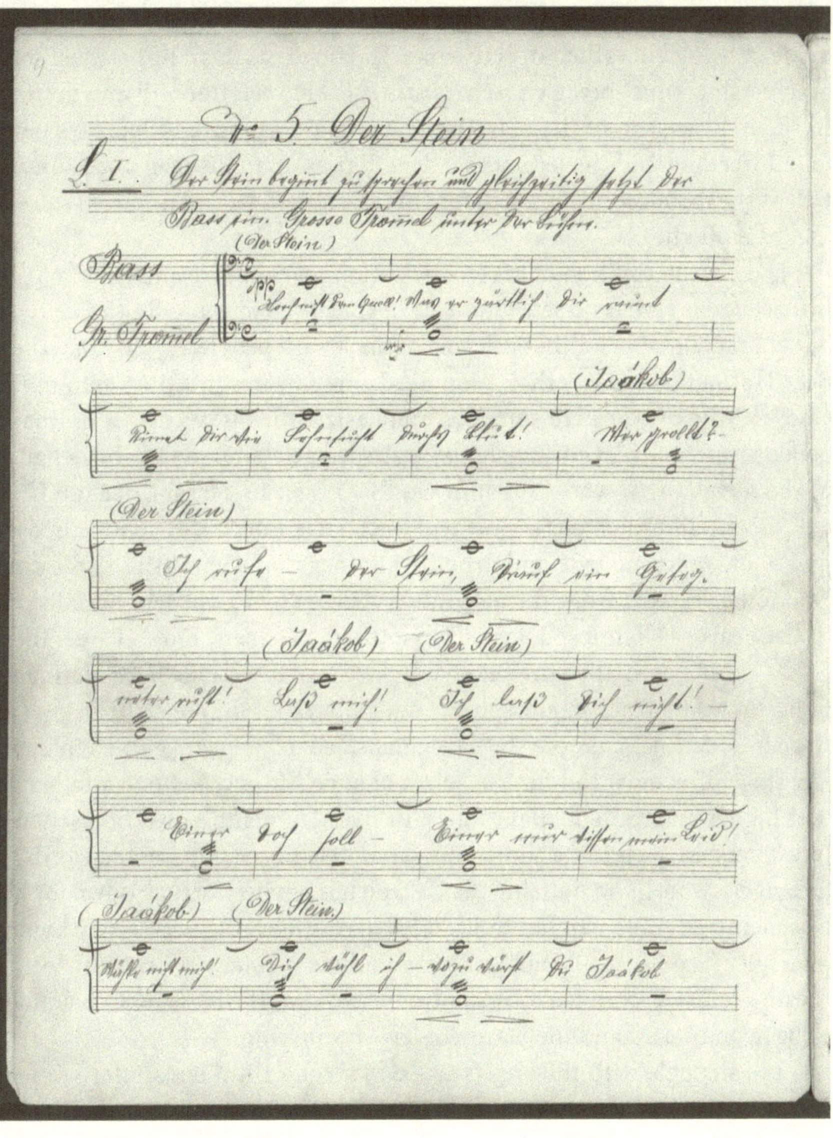


Figure 4.2a and 4.2b. (*continued*)

German-Jewish subject, whose status as the Chosen One is not a static mode of being but rather an active one. Jaákob exists in an in-between state of "choosing" and "being chosen," a struggle between free will and destiny. In the final section of the play, music marks the rupture of Jaákob's newfound freedom and the legacy that he will pass on to his own ancestors, as well as the dynamic, evolving nature of the modern German-Jewish subject that he embodies.

Jaákob's declaration of his emancipation marks the dramatic climax of this scene, in which he sets God free of the covenant, forcing the deity to be held accountable for the suffering of the Jewish people. As Elstun writes, Beer-Hofmann's view is that "God needs man just as much as man needs God."[53] This provocative stance is emphasized in the text by a dramatic breakthrough, achieved through visual spectacle and sound. In defiance of the angel Uriel, who calls him God's *Knecht*, or servant, Jaákob calls out "Gott wählt mich aus—Gott will mich stolz und wahr!" (God chooses me—Got wants me true and proud!)[54] Rather than submitting, or asking God to be released from the painful struggle of being chosen, he calls out to the heavens, "Ich lose Dich—Du Gott—aus Deinem Eid!" (I free Thee, God—Thou may'st Thy vow deny!)[55] In his stage directions Beer-Hofmann indicates that a black cloud appears, and a burst of thunder, throwing the stage into darkness. As the stage brightens, Jaákob appears bathed in light. The stage directions call for the voices of angels to succeed one another in ever higher and more jubilant tones. In Beer-Hofmann's own notes, dated July 8, 1915, he sketched a short musical motive to accompany the words of the angels, who, upon noticing that Jaákob has not been struck down for his blasphemy, begin to call out to Jaákob: "hear" (höre) at successively higher intervals. (See fig. 4.3.) This musical interlude signifies a key shift in the dream sequence from Jaákob's confrontation over the blessing to his inner struggle to understand the nature of Jewish suffering.

The struggle with the angels sets up Jaákob's third encounter with an Other to the Jewish experience, the fallen angel Samáel, who will challenge Jaákob once again to reconcile the Jewish legacy of suffering with the demands of an uncompassionate God. Samáel responds to the angel Micháel's prophesy of the Jews as God's witnesses with the warning of the life of pain, despair, and exile that awaits Jaákob's ancestors. The fallen angel plays the role of devil's advocate, at times even taunting the hero for his foolhardy acceptance of a legacy and future of suffering.[56] Samáel claims:

> *Wohl* neigt man deinem Wort sich—
> Doch blutig schlägt den Mund man, der es sprach!

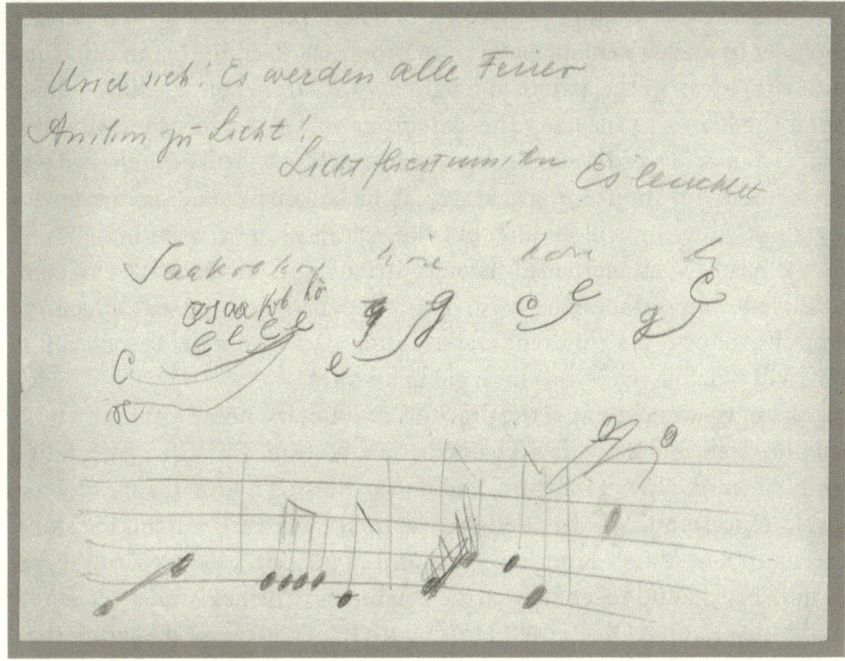

Figure 4.3. Musical notation in Beer-Hofmann's sketches for *Jaákobs Traum*. MS Ger 131 Folder 68, Houghton Library, Harvard University.

*Wohl* darfst du wandern! Aber rasten? Heimat?
Sie wird dir Wort—du sinnst ihm ewig nach!
Volk wirst du, d'raus sich alle Beute holen—
An dir zu freveln? Wem wär's *nicht* erlaubt?
Die Erde eisern unter deinen Sohlen, . . .
Heimloses Volk—sie weisen dir die Tür,
Der räudige Bettler höhnt—und rühmt und preist sich,
Daß er nicht *eines* Stammes ist mir dir!

[Men will bow before thy word,
But strike the bleeding mouth from whence it came!
True, thou shalt wander! But a rest? A home?
Mere words to thee—words pondered oft and deep!
A people shalt thou be whence all their plunder fetch—
To sin 'gainst thee? Whom is not allowed?
The earth shall be as iron beneath they foot . . .
Thou homeless people—driven from place to place
The mangy beggar turns to sneer and scoff
And prides himself that he's not of thy race.][57]

The other angels attempt to disavow Samáel's prophesy, but in a parallel moment to Jaákob's emancipatory proclamation, Beer-Hofmann calls for a dramatic break in the action, as a light appears from above, shining down upon the hero and silencing the clamorous voices. An offstage voice proclaims Samáel's word true; the descendants of Jaákob will be maligned and persecuted. Yet the voice also responds to Jaákob's demands: the Jewish legacy of suffering will endure, but the relationship between human and divine has been strengthened through struggle. In an affirmation of compassionate understanding, the divine father declares himself "indebted" (verschulden) to his children, reasserting a pact of mutual responsibility that will redefine the Jewish faith going forward.

As in the conclusion of the previous encounters, Beer-Hofmann marks this final encounter with a reconciliatory gesture, this time integrating unity of word, physical gesture, and music. Raising high a chalice of wine, a skin of milk, and a horn of oil, Jaákob pours them down upon the stone, the symbol of Jewish suffering, proclaiming his own blessing: "Mit dieses Landes Frucht und Segen salb ich dich Stein—mit meines Landes—Wein . . . und Milch . . . und Öl—!" (With this land's fruit and blessing I anoint thee, stone, with my land's wine—and milk—and oil—!)[58] In this gesture, Jaákob unites the two symbols of the spring and the stone, confirming his acceptance of his suffering and claiming his blessing as his choice. Significantly, it is not the angel who names him Israel, as in the biblical narrative; rather it is Jaákob who names himself: "Nicht—Jaákob! Nieder zu Euch steigt—der mit Gott rang—Jisro-El!" (No not 'Jacob'! Down to thee come—who with God strove—Yisro-el!)[59] According to Van Jung's fragmentary score, these words and gestures were to be accompanied by woodwind instruments playing from behind the stage, suggesting a technique from Wagner's Bayreuth Theater, in which the orchestra remains hidden from the viewers. In Pfriemer's score for the performance at the Burgtheater, this final scene was to close with Jaákob's leitmotif, a melody composed for solo flute. The flute imitates the sound of the shepherd's pipe, which appears at the opening of the second scene, when Jaákob first appears onstage.[60] (See fig. 4.4.) In its first sounding in the opening of the second act, Jaákob does not recognize the flute; it is Indibaál who informs him that this is the sound of the shepherd Schua, playing on his pipe to awaken the camp. When Jaákob awakens from his dream, he hears the flute again, but here it emphasizes that he has awakened not only from sleep but also to an understanding of his calling as the Chosen One. He calls out, "Mein Hirt da drunten, willst du

Figure 4.4. Shepherd's leitmotif. Fragment of Ernst Pfriemer's musical score for performance of *Jaákobs Traum* at Vienna's Burgtheater, April 1919. Austrian National Library, Music Collection, F19.BA.57.Mus.

wach mich spielen mit deinem Lied? Hirt—ich *bin* erwacht!" (My shepherd down there, with thy son's delight, woud'st thou waken me? Shepherd—I am awake!)[61] Thus, the shepherd's pipe serves as a musical gesture pointing toward Jaákob's spiritual awakening and defiant claim to forge his own path, having reenvisioned his relationship to the divine as one of dialogue, negotiation, compassion, and mutual responsibility.

*Jaákobs Traum* presents confrontations with Otherness that lead Jaákob to a deeper understanding of his own identity and enable him to express compassionate solidarity with those different from him. The ritualistic gestures of independence in the drama point toward compassion as an emancipatory process, a dialectical *Aufhebung*, or sublimation of suffering and blessing. Gillman elaborates on this idea by suggesting that Jaákob's dialogues and emancipatory acts reflect the process of countermemory, a rewriting of narrative from the past to "reroute the individual as well as the collective discourse."[62] In the figure of Jaákob, Beer-Hofmann's drama captures the performance of subjectivity, understood as the forging of an identity in motion, continually reevaluating itself to adapt to the present moment.[63] Through his dialogues with Indibaál, Edom, and Samáel,

Jaákob deconstructs the abstract category of "the Jew" and transforms the blessing as object into a dynamic, evolving essence that expresses Jaákob's very being.[64]

Beer-Hofmann's use of musical voices and musical symbolism in his play thus functions as a bridge between the drama's articulations of the mythical-collective and the individual-subjective. By employing both musical gestures of continuity (leitmotif) and of rupture, Beer-Hofmann posits a new model of the Gesamtkunstwerk that he hoped would reacquaint the audience with the mythical, musical nature of Judaism. Moreover, Jaákob's inclusive gestures in the final scene, which point toward a new covenant with God based in mutual responsibility, replace the image of Jews as the servants of a vengeful God with the heroic German-Jewish mediator, who offers a new model for inclusive, compassionate community.

## Conclusion

Beer-Hofmann had hoped to complete his *David* trilogy before publishing *Jaákobs Traum*, but the end of World War I and the ensuing revival of antisemitic sentiment led friends such as Martin Buber and theater critic Julius Bab to encourage him to publish it as an independent work in 1918.[65] The first performance took place on April 5, 1919, in Vienna's Burgtheater. (See fig. 4.5.) That spring, Beer-Hofmann received a letter from a woman named Nina Spiegler. In her letter, Spiegler praises *Jaákobs Traum* for its depiction of the Jewish blessing, noting how it evolves in strength as the Chosen One makes his way along the path to God. The work, Spiegler writes, reminded her of another drama published less than a decade before: Lipiner's *Adam*. In her letter, Spiegler offers to send a copy to Beer-Hofmann, with the comment, "Es dürfte Ihnen da, meiner Vermuthung nach, sowohl in dem Grundprobleme, als auch in der Art der künstlerischen Behandlung, manch Wahlverwandtes begegnen." (I suspect you may encounter in the basic problems as well as in the mode of artistic treatment some elective affinities.)[66] Beer-Hofmann's archive contains no reply; however, the fact that he preserved it among his letters suggests that it may have held significance for him. Indeed, it is clear that both works shared a common epic scope modeled on the Wagnerian festival drama. Moreover, both *Jaákobs Traum* and *Adam* offer an idea of how compassionate art might overcome the legacy of Judaism as the religion of "obedience to the law" (Religion des Gesetzesgehorsams).[67] While in Lipiner's *Adam*, Cain's confrontation with this legacy is revealed through his troubled inner monologues,

Jaákob's struggle manifests itself through dialogue. Dramatically, Beer-Hofmann's dialogue does not serve the typical function of moving forward a narrative plot. Rather, as Neumann notes, the poet employed dialogue as a "meeting-place" in which figures reveal themselves as individuals and bearers of fate.[68] Dialogue thus enables the revelation of character, in this case, Jaákob's journey to become a compassionate leader of the community.[69] Moreover, in employing musical leitmotifs to trace Jaákob's development and engagement with the sorrows and blessings of Jewish history, Beer-Hofmann, the "devious symphonist" as he called himself to Werner Vortreide, casts his protagonist as a musical figure. Like Mahler's penitent and Schoenberg's Chosen One, Jaákob's subjectivity manifests itself outwardly in musical forms, in an unfolding of being, that develops through its interplay with other characters, like a melody is enriched through its encounter with other musical lines.

Beer-Hofmann's vision for *Die Historie von König David* and realization in *Jaákobs Traum* reflect how the Wagnerian ideal of the union of the arts could be adapted to speak to a more inclusive community, encouraging understanding for the Jew as a compassionate, musical subject. He completed the second part of the tetralogy, *Der junge David* in 1932. However, this work, with its lengthy monologues and vast cast of characters proved unfit for the stage. The beginning of the third installment, *Vorspiel auf dem Theater zu König David* was published as a fragment in 1935. The inability of these works to be performed reflects the poet's growing disillusionment with the paradigm of Wagnerian theater and perhaps also the increasingly tenuous political situation for Jews in Europe at this time. Beer-Hofmann and his family fled Austria in 1938 and his beloved wife Paula died in Switzerland while awaiting their exit visas to the United States. He devoted his final years in the United States to memoirs dedicated to her and eventually abandoned the *David* project. Yet the story of Jacob was one that Beer-Hofmann claimed was very close to his own heart and remained so throughout his life.

By evoking the transhistorical power of myth through the Gesamtkunstwerk, Beer-Hofmann hoped to instill pride in Jewish heritage and culture at a time in which this community was increasingly persecuted and misunderstood. He transformed the biblical myth of Jacob into a holistic vision of compassionate art, in which the unity of visual, verbal, and musical gestures would enable the merging of the audience's inner world with the outer world onstage, creating an image of Jewish culture that

# Burgtheater

**Samstag den 5. April 1919**

Im Jahres-Abonnement — 1. Viertel — 64. Vorstellung im Saison-Abonnement

Bei erhöhten Preisen

Zum ersten Male:

# Jaákobs Traum

Von Richard Beer-Hofmann

| | | |
|---|---|---|
| Rebekah | | Fr. Bleibtreu |
| Jaákob | die Söhne Rebekahs | Hr. Gerasch |
| Edom | | Hr. Höbling |
| Basmath, Tochter Elons, des Chittiters | die Frauen Edoms | Fr. Medelsky |
| Oholibamah, Tochter Anas, des Choriters | | Fr. Wohlgemuth |
| Shamártu, der Babylonier | zwei Sklaven Edoms | Hr. Herterich |
| Zahor, der Kanaaniter | | Hr. Moncza |
| Idnibaal, der Phönikier, ein Sklave Jizchaks | | Hr. Siebert |

| | | | | |
|---|---|---|---|---|
| Die Stimme | | Hr. G. Reimers | Engel | Fr. Haeberle |
| Michael | die Erzengel | Hr. Devrient | | Fr. Osten |
| Gabriel | | Hr. Frank | | Frl. Mayer |
| Raphael | | Hr. E. Reimers | Die Stimme des Quells | Frl. Mayen |
| Uriel | | Hr. Schott | Die Stimme des Steins | Hr. Lackner |
| Samáel | | Hr. Walden | Stimme vieler Engel | |

Zeit: Die der Partriarchen — Der Ort: Zuerst Jizchaks Hof in Béer-Scheba am Rande der Wüste, dann eine Höhe (später Beth-el genannt)

Bühnenentwürfe: Alfred Roller

Ein Zwischenakt

**Abendkassen-Eröffnung vor 4½ Uhr — Anfang fünf Uhr — Ende vor 8 Uhr**

**Der Kartenverkauf findet heute statt für obige Vorstellung und für:**

Sonntag den 6. Nachmittags **halbzwei** Uhr: Renaissance. Außer dem Jahres- und Saison-Abonnement und zu halben Abendpreisen
Abends **halbsechs** Uhr: Jaákobs Traum

Weiterer Spielplan:

Montag den 7. Geschlossen
Dienstag den 8. Geschlossen
Mittwoch den 9. Dies irae (Anfang fünf Uhr)
Donnerstag den 10. Der einsame Weg (Anfang fünf Uhr)
Freitag den 11. Jaákobs Traum (Anfang **halbsechs** Uhr)

Im Falle einer Abänderung der angekündigten Vorstellung gilt das Billett auch für die Ersatz-Vorstellung, oder es kann der hiefür entrichtete Betrag zurückverlangt werden. Die Rückzahlung dieses Betrages erfolgt jedoch nur bis spätestens am Tage der Vorstellung, und zwar an der Tageskassa I. Bräunerstraße 14, von 9 Uhr früh bis 4 Uhr nachmittags, ferner an der Abendkassa des Burgtheaters bis eine Viertelstunde vor Beginn der Vorstellung. Eine Änderung der Rollenbesetzung gilt nicht als Abänderung im obigen Sinne.

Die Besichtigung des Burgtheaters ist täglich von 9 bis 12 und von 2 bis 4 Uhr (Sonn- und Feiertage nachmittags ausgenommen) gestattet. Eintrittsgebühr per Person 60 Heller

Preis 30 Heller

Figure 4.5. Poster for the premiere of *Jaákobs Traum* at the Vienna Burgtheater, April 5, 1919. KHM-Museumsverband, Theatermuseum Vienna.

would also resonate with a non-Jewish audience. He sought to employ the theater to evoke sympathetic understanding for the noble history of the Jewish people, their affirmation of community in suffering, and their commitment to self-transformation through dialogue. In this way, Beer-Hofmann follows Lipiner, Mahler, and Schoenberg in reinscribing the Jews as a compassionate collective and as a modern, musical, and mythical people.

## Notes

1. Kleinewefers, *Problem der Erwählung*, 53.
2. Vortreide, "Gespräche mit Beer-Hofmann," 185.
3. Klinenberger, "Wiener Theater"; Bach, "Das Drama der Juden."
4. "Beer-Hofmanns 'Jaákobs Traum' im Burgtheater"; Salten, "Beer-Hofmann's 'Historie von König David.'"
5. "Beer-Hofmann: Jaákobs Traum."
6. Elstun, "Poet as Exculpator Dei."
7. Biographies of Beer-Hofmann provide few details about his religious cultural upbringing. Stefan Scherer speaks of the poet's "Hinwendung," or "steering toward" Judaism around 1896, after reading Theodor Herzl's *Die Judenstadt*. Scherer, "Richard Beer-Hofmann und das Judentum," 15.
8. Elstun, *His Life and Work*, 6.
9. Beer-Hofmann, *Briefe*, 9. [translation C. K.]
10. Quoted in Elstun, *His Life and Work*, 12.
11. Le Rider, *Modernity and Crises of Identity*, 290.
12. Gelber, "Interfaces," 65.
13. Scherer, *Richard Beer-Hofmann und die Wiener Moderne*, 385. See Bunzl, however, regarding Beer-Hofmann's response to the Balfour Declaration. Bunzl, "Poetics of Politics and Politics of Poetics."
14. See, in particular, Beer-Hofmann's correspondence with Hugo von Hofmannsthal regarding the Edom and Jaákob confrontation in *Jaákobs Traum*. Hofmannsthal and Beer-Hofmann, *Briefwechsel*, 144–146.
15. This quote was reported by the literary historian Harry Zohn and is cited in Pyrah, *Burgtheater and Austrian Identity*, 94.
16. Ritchie Robertson describes Itzig's speech as "a modified form of *Mauscheldeutsch* . . . given the dignity of blank verse." Robertson, *"Jewish Question" in German Literature*, 454. Stefan Scherer cites that the name Itzig is a particularly pejorative term for Jews. Scherer, *Richard Beer-Hofmann und die Wiener Moderne*, 61.
17. Beer-Hofmann, *Der Graf von Charolais*, 57–58. [Elstun, *His Life and Work*, 115.]
18. Elstun, *His Life and Work*, 119.
19. R. Wagner, *Dichtungen und Schriften*, vol. 6, 128–120; Borchmeyer, *Richard Wagner: Theory and Theatre*, 67.
20. Roberts, *Total Work of Art*, 71.
21. R. Wagner, *Prose Works*, vol. 2, 156, 161.

22. Bahr, *Glossen zum Wiener Theater*, 50 [Trans. C. K. Unless otherwise noted, all translations in this chapter are my own].

23. "Höchstes Wunder" recalls the final words of the chorus in Wagner's *Parsifal*. Lipiner used similar language in his speech to the Leseverein at the University of Vienna, discussed in Chapter 1.

24. Maier, "Mahler's Theater," 70.

25. Carnegy, *Wagner and the Art of the Theater*, 163–165.

26. Roller, "Bühnenreform?" 196.

27. Roller, 197.

28. Accounts of the premiere of *Jaákobs Traum* in Berlin reveal that Beer-Hofmann was also involved in the production of the drama, indicating the correct appearance of "jede Sandale, jenen Kostümstoff, jede Perücke, jede Wolke, jeden Fels, jeden Blitz." Mayer, *Richard Beer-Hofmann und das Wien*, 110.

29. A comparison of Beer-Hofmann's own sketches for stage and costumes and Roller's designs attest to the collaborative work of poet and artist. Kita, "Beer-Hofmann's *Die Historie von König David*," 138.

30. Beer-Hofmann, "Über szenische Angaben," 2.

31. Beer-Hofmann, "Über szenische Angaben," 3.

32. R. Wagner, *Prose Works*, vol. 2, 87.

33. Williamson, *Longing for Myth in Germany*, 223. Renan's writings were highly influential for Stefan Zweig's play, *Jeremias*, discussed in chapter 5.

34. "Soviel Kunstheuchelei sieht man wohl sonst nirgends auf einem Fleck zusammen," Beer-Hofmann, *Briefe*, 90.

35. Szondi, *Theory of the Modern Drama*, 26.

36. Beer-Hofmann's drama is one of a relatively few examples of a work composed in the Expressionist style that was performed at the Burgtheater in Vienna, a stage generally known for its cultural conservatism. See Pyrah, *Burgtheater and Austrian Identity*, 54.

37. Beer-Hofmann, *Historie von König David*, 42. (Hereafter cited as *Historie*.)

38. Beer-Hofmann, *Historie*, 39, 41. Emphasis C. K.

39. Abigail Gillman suggests that in this story of trauma, Isaac is the "crippled survivor," psychologically debilitated by his near death, whose "inheritance of the Abrahamic legacy was stunted at the moment he became a scapegoat." Gillman, *Viennese Jewish Modernism*, 157.

40. Beer-Hofmann, *Historie*, 46.

41. Beer-Hofmann, *Historie*, 55–56; Beer-Hofmann, *Jacob's Dream: A Prologue*, 100. (Hereafter cited as *Jacob's Dream*.)

42. Beer-Hofmann, *Historie*, 58–59 [Beer-Hofmann, *Jacob's Dream*, 104].

43. Beer-Hofmann, *Historie*, 60–61 [Beer-Hofmann, *Jacob's Dream*, 106].

44. Simon Lutz describes Edom as the "unjewish opposite" (unjüdisches Gegenstück) of Jaákob, while Daniel Hoffmann reads him a materialist, a "profane Mensch," who represents the foe of Israel (Rome or Christianity). Carina Heer, on the other hand, claims that Edom is an incarnation of modern persecutors of the Jews. Lutz, "Du aber halte meinen Bund"; Hoffmann, "Die Gewißheit des Glaubens"; Heer, *Gattungsdesign in der Wiener Moderne*.

45. Beer-Hofmann, *Historie*, 70 [Beer-Hofmann, *Jacob's Dream*, 119].

46. Beer-Hofmann, *Historie*, 70. The English version by Ida Benison actually translates "Foreigners" as "Gentiles," solidifying Edom's role as non-Jewish Other in this text.

47. Beer-Hofmann, *Historie*, 77 [Beer-Hofmann, *Jacob's Dream*, 130].

48. Beer-Hofmann, *Historie*, 75 [Beer-Hofmann, *Jacob's Dream*, 127]. The image of the blood recalls Beer-Hofmann's early poetry, *Schlaflied für Mirjam*, as well as the transformation of Paul in *Der Tod Georgs*.

49. Roberts, *Total Work of Art*, 103.

50. Beer-Hofmann, *Historie*, 13.

51. Beer-Hofmann, *Historie*, 21.

52. The term "leitmotif" was actually first used by Hans von Wolzogen, the editor of Wagner's newspaper, the *Bayreuter Blätter*. H. M. Brown, *Leitmotiv and Drama*, 48.

53. Elstun, *His Life and Work*, 136.

54. Beer-Hofmann, *Historie*, 98 [Beer-Hofmann, *Jacob's Dream*, 159].

55. Beer-Hofmann, *Historie*, 98 [Beer-Hofmann, *Jacob's Dream*, 159].

56. Eke, "Rettung des Sinns," 135.

57. Beer-Hofmann, *Historie*, 101 [Beer-Hofmann, *Jaákobs Traum*, 164].

58. Beer-Hofmann, *Historie*, 109 [Beer-Hofmann, *Jacob's Dream*, 173].

59. Beer-Hofmann, *Historie*, 109 [Beer-Hofmann, *Jacob's Dream*, 173].

60. Beer-Hofmann, *Historie*, 32.

61. Beer-Hofmann, *Historie*, 108 [Beer-Hofmann, *Jacob's Dream*, 171].

62. Gillman, *Viennese Jewish Modernism*, 161.

63. Steinberg, *Listening to Reason*, 5.

64. See Hoffmann who describes this tension between "Offenbarung" or revelation, and the dynamic process of creation. Hoffmann, "Die Gewißheit des Glaubens," 111.

65. See Beer-Hofmann's letter to Martin Buber of March 6, 1917, in Beer-Hofmann, *Briefe*, 34.

66. Spiegler, "Letter to Richard Beer-Hofmann."

67. Peters, *Richard Beer-Hofmann*, 178.

68. "Ort der Begegnung . . . in der sich die Figuren als Individuen und Träger eigenen Schicksals offenbaren." Neumann, *Richard Beer-Hofmann: "Historie von König David,"* 173–174.

69. Beer-Hofmann's recognition of the centrality of dialogue to the modern Jewish faith finds resonance in the later writings of his friend and mentor, Martin Buber. Robertson, *German-Jewish Dialogue*, xxi.

# 5

# COMPASSION AS COMMUNAL SONG: STEFAN ZWEIG'S *JEREMIAS*

Es ist eigentlich meine erste wirkliche Arbeit, die erste, die ich innerlich ganz anerkenne, weil sie über das Maß meines Willens hinausgewachsen ist, weil sie—wohl aussichtslos in jedem zweckdienlichen Sinne—mir die ganzen inneren Probleme der Zeit und meines persönlichen Erlebens erlösend aufgelöst hat.

[It is in fact my first true work, the first work that I internally acknowledge, for it has surpassed the measure of my own will, for it—although futile in every practical sense—cathartically resolved the inner problems of the time and of my personal experience.]

Stefan Zweig to Arthur Schnitzler, 1916

On September 25, 1916, Stefan Zweig revealed to Arthur Schnitzler the deep personal significance of his latest dramatic project, *Jeremias* (*Jeremiah*). This letter, along with Zweig's diary entries from this time, attest to the young poet's close, personal identification with the Hebrew prophet. Indeed, Jeremiah's unheeded warnings about the destruction of Jerusalem resonated deeply with Zweig's own experiences as a journalist during World War I. For although he played his part in the propaganda machine of the Austro-Hungarian Empire as a correspondent for the *Neue Freie Presse*, Zweig privately confessed to haunted visions of Europe's downfall.[1] *Jeremias*, therefore, was Zweig's passionate appeal for pacifism at a time when he was unable to publicly speak out against the war.

Yet, the poet's interest in the biblical story also suggests his engagement with another "inner problem of the time": the Jewish Question. Although

Zweig was not an active member of the Jewish religious community in Vienna, in the years leading up to the composition of *Jeremias*, he became increasingly fascinated with Jewish culture and Jewish aesthetics through his associations with the *Jungjüdische Bewegung* (Young Jewish Movement) and correspondence with Martin Buber. Moreover, his letters and diaries recount how traveling on the eastern front during World War I led him to question his relationship to his Jewish cultural heritage.

This chapter examines Zweig's *Jeremias* as a drama of compassion, inspired by the poet's search for a model of collective belonging rooted in his own experience as a German-Jew and expressed through a musical poetics. Like Lipiner, Mahler, Schoenberg, and Beer-Hofmann, Zweig viewed his Jewish identity as a dynamic and fluid aspect of his being that was ever-evolving and redefining itself and expressed skepticism toward the image popularized in antisemitic discourses of the Jews as beholden to the commands of a distant, uncompassionate God. Thus, in *Jeremias*, Zweig casts the Jewish community as the embodiment of a modern Jewish spirit of *Discursion*. Discursion embodies the transformative potential of a collective united not through language, nation, or ethnicity but rather through a common spirit, a common myth, a common faith, and, above all, a common song. The musical nature of the Jewish community is captured in the prophet's ecstatic, divinely inspired musical poetics. It is Jeremiah's destiny to mold the people from fragmented, noisy *Stimmen*, or voices, into a jubilant choir, who recognize their common history and destiny and express this unity through music.

To understand how Zweig fashioned this vision of Jewish community, one must look to the text's musical structure, which draws upon the model of the Passion oratorio, a musical retelling of Christ's death and resurrection, and the musical form of antiphony, common to both Jewish and Christian sacred music, in which an ensemble divided into groups of distinct vocal pitches and timbres sing repeating or oppositional phrases. This chapter demonstrates how Zweig employs these musical forms and language to highlight the common origins of Judaism and Christianity in mythologies of collective suffering and communal musical practices. Allusions to arias from Johann Sebastian Bach's *St. Matthew's Passion* (1727) and *St. John's Passion* (1724) and Felix Mendelssohn's *Elijah* (1846) reveal Zweig's desire to align his work with musical dramatizations of suffering and redemption in the Hebrew and Christian Scriptures. These references appear at a key moment that marks the beginning of Jeremiah's transformation from a suffering individual to a compassionate leader of a renewed spiritual community. In the dramatic finale of the play, Zweig employs the call and answer of antiphony to express the modern Jewish diasporic identity as Discursion, sowing the seeds for a compassionate community that will overcome the tragedy of individual suffering.

Zweig's idea of Discursion finds parallels in discourses of musical metaphysics, which claim music as a language capable of speaking directly to the human heart, possessing the power to inspire collective spirit. By framing the tragedy of the Jewish Diaspora as Discursion and expressing this principle through musical poetics in *Jeremias*, Zweig transforms the image of the Jews as the wandering people without homeland into a transcendent and transnational collective whose spiritual unity finds expression in a harmonious choir composed of a multitude of voices. Ultimately, for Zweig, to be Jewish was to be a member of a musical community unbound by the political hierarchies of nation and state and above the soulless machinations of war. *Jeremias* reveals how the poet's musical German-Jewish subjectivity helped shape his cosmopolitan vision for Europe.

## Discursion and Jewish Subjectivity

Today, *Jeremias* is considered a minor work, often forgotten amid Zweig's biographical essays, novellas, and his oft-cited memoir, *Die Welt von Gestern* (The World of Yesterday 1942). Yet Zweig's diaries, as well as his correspondence with the Jewish philosopher and leader of the Jewish Cultural Renaissance, Martin Buber, reveal it to be a compelling document of Zweig's engagement with his Jewish heritage. In composing *Jeremias*, Zweig began to develop a concept of Jewish communal belonging as Discursion, a spiritual collective that transcends language, nationality, ethnicity, and modes of religious practice. Discursion emerged from Zweig's own complex and evolving relationship to his Jewish heritage and his resistance to socially constructed categories of Jewishness. Through his protagonist, Jeremiah, Zweig recasts the legacy of exile and transience as the unique attributes of a modern cosmopolitan community united in a shared faith and history of suffering. For Zweig, Jewish Discursion would serve as a blueprint for his future vision of a transnational European community.

Zweig was born on November 28, 1881, to an assimilated Jewish upper middle class in Vienna at the turn of the century. His father, who came to Vienna from a Jewish community in Moravia, was a successful textile manufacturer and his mother came from a cosmopolitan banking family. Although Zweig appears to have been familiar with Jewish traditions and religious practices, it is unlikely that he regularly took part in religious services during his childhood.[2] In his memoirs, he claims never to have experienced the sting of antisemitic prejudice at school or at the university. That the rise of Vienna's antisemitic mayor, Karl Lueger, receives but a passing mention in his memoir attests to Zweig's apolitical nature and to his relative naïveté toward the deeply rooted cultural and economic schisms within his self-proclaimed "World of Security."[3]

However, Zweig's association with the Young Jewish Movement and his correspondence with Martin Buber reveals that in the process of composing *Jeremias*, Zweig came to a much more nuanced understanding of his Jewish identity. The Young Jewish Movement emerged in Vienna and Berlin around the turn of the nineteenth century alongside the political movement of Zionism. This loose association of writers and poets composed works on modern and ancient Jewish themes and sought above all to establish a common cultural vocabulary and aesthetic style to define a modern Jewish cultural identity. In 1901–1902, Zweig published several poems and a novella in journals associated with the Young Jewish Movement.[4] Although Zweig, unlike other members of this group, resisted association with Zionist politics, these publications are significant because they reveal the poet's engagement with the effort to define a particularly Jewish aesthetic. Furthermore, they brought Zweig into contact with the leading figure of the Jewish Renaissance, Martin Buber. Zweig and Buber maintained a correspondence for over thirty years in which they discussed in detail their respective positions regarding the Zionist project and the Jewish people as a cultural community.

In Zweig's correspondence with Buber about *Jeremias*, the poet began to articulate his understanding of Judaism as a cultural identity and faith, which would eventually develop into his idea of Discursion. In May 1916, Zweig described *Jeremias* to Buber in the following way:

"Es ist Tragödie und der Hymnus des jüdischen Volks als des auserwählten—aber nicht im Sinn des Wohlergehens, sondern des ewigen Leidens, des ewigen Niedersturzes und der ewigen Erhebung aus solchem Schicksal sich entfaltenden Kraft." (It is the tragedy and the hymn of the Jewish people as the chosen ones—but not in the sense of prosperity rather in the sense of eternal suffering, eternal downfall, and eternal rising up and the strength that unfolds from this destiny.)[5] In this same letter, however,

Zweig attempts to explain his resistance to associating with Zionist organizations or publications (such as Buber's own journal, *Der Jude*), by claiming to Buber that his inner nature is "ganz auf Bindung [,] auf Synthese gestellt" (entirely situated on engagement, on synthesis). Being Jewish, he claims, is something personal and intimate: "ich fühle es ebenso wie ich meinen Herzschlag fühle, wenn ich daran denke" (I feel it just as I feel my heartbeat, when I think about it).[6] Such comments resonate with Mark Gelber's reading of Zweig's Jewishness as a *sensibility*, an empathetic understanding of or capacity for emotional solidarity.[7] Yet, only a few months earlier, Zweig had described the Jewish ghettos he had observed on his trip to the eastern front in stereotypical, exoticized terms. Zweig's visions of the ghetto as "seltsam . . . schmutzig und jede Hütte schwarz wie ein Sargtruhe" (strange . . . dirty and each hut black like a casket) suggest a romanticized "Othering"—a feeling of foreignness, and the emotional distance of a detached spectator—and indicate his own alienation from orthodox Jewish religious communities at this time.[8]

By 1917, Zweig had begun to refine his understanding of Jewishness. In a letter written in January of that year, in which he also included a copy of the final scene of *Jeremias*, Zweig describes Jewishness to Buber as a mode of being between the material and the spiritual, a space between borders that resists articulation. The Jewish sense of community could be understood, he claimed, as "Einssein ohne Sprache, ohne Bindung, ohne Heimat, nur durch das Fluidum des Wesens" (unity without language, without commitment, without homeland, only through the fluidity of being).[9] Zweig further elaborated on this idea six months later, when he wrote of the spiritual superiority of the Jews not as *Organisation* (in the sense of a united nation state) but rather as Discursion. Discursion, Zweig claims, can be understood as the "Ablösung von Ja und Nein des ganzen Seins und Wesens" (dissolution of the yes and no of the whole existence and substance).[10] For Zweig, the Jewish community finds strength in a faith that floats or hovers (*schwebt*) between the two poles of the sensual and the spiritual.[11] For Zweig, schweben is a uniquely Jewish attribute, reflecting a dynamic and evolving sense of self and community that resonated with his own German-Jewish subjectivity. Using subjectivity as a lens to read Zweig's attitude toward Jewishness emphasizes the poet's own experience as reflecting "constant renegotiations of the boundaries between self and the world," and evolving in tension with the idea of the "Jew," as a culturally constructed category.[12] For Zweig, who identified as a European and citizen of the world, the Jewish sense of common belonging rooted in Discursion could serve as a template for overcoming religious difference, nationalism, and chauvinism.

In *Jeremias*, Zweig attempted to realize his concept of Discursion by presenting the Jewish community as the embodiment of aesthetic and spiritual ideals that transcended the limited category of the Jew as it was defined by antisemites as well as Jewish nationalists. While Zweig's play on the one hand constructs an image of the Jews as "Other" or "different," he ultimately seeks to carve out a space for a modern Jewish identity that exists in harmony with Christianity by drawing on the shared roots of both faiths in the Hebrew Scriptures and, in particular, in their common musical practices. In this way, *Jeremias* can be read as a reconciliation of two increasingly polarizing aspects of Zweig's own identity but also as an attempt to the use musical forms and language to reveal how individual experience and collective belonging might function for the modern Jewish subject.

## Zweig's Musical Poetics of Ekstase

In *Jeremias*, Zweig employs a musical poetics to voice the prophet's struggle to understand his role as compassionate mediator and leader of the Jewish community in exile. Jeremiah's feelings of alienation and isolation are evoked through his distinct prophetic voice, which resounds in sharp contrast to the noisy, fragmented voices of the Jewish community. Zweig employs the term *ekstatisch*, borrowed from Expressionist poetics, to describe Jeremiah's divinely inspired musical language. However, the narrative in the first two-thirds of the play is ultimately one of failed prophesy, for Jeremiah has not learned compassion. Through two transformative musical moments, which draw on the Passion oratorio of the Christian tradition and the communal prayer of the Jewish tradition, Jeremiah becomes attuned to the depths of Jewish suffering and feels it as his own. In the final act of the play, Jeremiah and the people transform into a compassionate community, a development that culminates in a final musical act, an antiphonic singing.

*Jeremias* is divided into nine scenes that reflect Zweig's unique interpretation of this biblical narrative as a story of compassionate transformation. The central plot is pieced together from episodes in the Book of Jeremiah, chapters 27–28, 30, 34, 37–39, focusing primarily on Zedekiah's reign, the siege of Jerusalem by Nebuchadrezzar II and the Babylonians, the destruction of the Temple, and the exile of the Jews. A number of scenes, such as Jeremiah's confrontations with King Zedekiah and the false prophet Hananiah, are drawn directly from the Christian and Hebrew Scriptures. Moreover, each scene in the play opens with an epigraph from the Book of Jeremiah, Ezekiel, Isaiah, or Job that set the tone for the scene and reorient the reader back to the biblical source, so that it appears to be a faithful interpretation of the original narrative.[13]

Nonetheless, Zweig takes considerable liberties with the text in order to create his own dramatic arc for the work. The first scene, "Die Erweckung des Propheten" (The Awakening of the Prophet), introduces Jeremiah and his first conflict with his mother.[14] He tells her of his visions of the fall of Jerusalem and she begs him not to reveal this prophesy to the people. Jeremiah refuses and she curses him and banishes him from their home. In scene 2, "Die Warnung" (The Warning), Jeremiah confronts the false prophet, Hananiah, who preaches to the people of Jerusalem that it is God's will that they go to war. Jeremiah denounces Hananiah, but the people see Jeremiah as the real traitor and turn on him instead. Scene 3 "Das Gerücht" (The Rumor) serves as interlude—instead of focusing on the prophet, it reveals the disorientation and confusion among the people, as false reports begin to spread that Judah has defeated the Babylonians. In fact, the walls of the city have been breached, and the people must rush to arm themselves in their defense. In scene 4, "Die Wachen auf dem Walle" (The Watch at the Ramparts), Jeremiah warns of Jerusalem's impending defeat again, this time to King Zedekiah. Zedekiah refuses to heed the prophet; he spares Jeremiah's life but banishes him. The prophet returns to face his dying mother in scene 5, "Die Prüfung des Propheten" (The Prophet's Ordeal). In this episode, Jeremiah tries to deny his role as prophet in the hopes of sparing his mother the terrifying visions of Jerusalem's fall. However, he cannot hold back the words—his ecstatic visions burst forth from his lips and his mother dies in fear and agony. In scene 6, "Stimmen um Mitternacht" (Voices in the Night), King Zedekiah begs Jeremiah to tell him whether he should submit to the Babylonian king. If he does so, and agrees to give up his crown and march through the city with a yoke upon his shoulders, his people and city will be spared. Jeremiah tells the King to bow down before the foreign king for the sake of peace, yet Zedekiah cannot bring himself to concede to the enemy.

In these first six scenes, Jeremiah is portrayed as a conflicted character; while he is the Chosen One, selected to receive the visions of God, he is unable to convince the people to hear his message. The scenes of confrontation between Jeremiah and the people follow a similar structure. First, a conflict is presented—articulated piecemeal through the fragmented utterances of the crowd. Then, Jeremiah attempts to reveal to the crowd his warnings in a language that evolves from impassioned speech to ecstatic verses, but he is ultimately stifled by the crowd or by individual characters who cannot, or will not, listen to him. In each of these scenes, Jeremiah fails to communicate his prophecies to the Jewish community or to their leadership; his words fall on deaf ears.

Zweig evokes this breakdown in communication by distinguishing the prophet's speech through a variety of musical-poetic styles that increase in intensity and lyrical character when experiencing divine inspiration, while the Jewish people, identified not as individual characters but only as "Stimmen" (voices), become increasingly fragmented. Jeremiah begins by speaking in prose dialogue, which eventually gives way to short lyrical verses with notable assonance, and then to longer lines marked by a rhythmic pattern of speech (frequently employing the dactylic meter). This dramatic effect serves to distinguish the poet from the people and eventually to indicate his critical role in molding the Jews' disparate voices into a chorus, the aural manifestation of their rediscovered spiritual unity.

The musical amplification of Jeremiah's dramatic speech is achieved through an intricately developed musical poetics that draws on models of speech found in the biblical source texts. Examples such as those found in the first scene, when Jeremiah is seized by a vision in the presence of his mother, reveal the striking contrast between his prose speech and the concise syntax, appellatory cries, and alliterative language of his ecstatic prophesy:

> Mutter! Mutter! Hörst du es nicht:
> Schwert klirrt im Wind,
> Räder rollt die rauschende Welle,
> Lanze blinkt und Harnisch die Nacht,
> Krieger und Krieger, unendliche Scharen
> Schüttet der Sturmwind über das Land.
>
> [Mother! Mother! Do you not hear it?
> Swords clash in the wind,
> Loud roar the chariot wheels,
> The night flashes with lances and with armor;
> Warrior upon warrior, countless in number,
> The whirlwind scatters over the land.][15]

As the visions become more intense, Jeremiah's phrases become longer and more lyrical, formed through repeating relative or subordinate clauses:

> Der König von Mitternacht . . .
> Den Er erwählte,
> Als harten Vollstrecker
> Härtesten Spruchs,
> Daß er strieme das Volk um all seiner Fehle,
> Daß er mahle die Mauer und berste die Türme,
> Daß er lösche das Licht und das Lachen der Häuser,
> Daß er tilge die Stadt und den Tempel von Erden
> Und pflüge die Straßen Jerusalems.
>
> [The king from the north! . . .
> Whom the Lord has awakened
> That he may scourge the people for all its transgressions,
> That he may crumble the walls and throw down the towers,
> That he may quench the light and the laughter of homes,
> That he may raze the city and the temple to the ground,
> And that he may plough up the streets of Jerusalem.][16]

Jeremiah's monologues repeatedly personify war as the "König von Mitternacht" or as a rapacious animal, "ein bös' und bissig' Tier," that devours the flesh of the people and stamps out their land with its hooves.[17] Visions of the walls and gates of the city falling, of the Temple's altar burning, of the mauling or laceration of the body, recur in leitmotific fashion throughout the subsequent scenes. The bold imagery of these passages evokes the powerful language of the Book of Lamentations, also attributed to the prophet Jeremiah.[18] However, the poet's development of alliterative speech and his conscious effort to compose in a consistent meter and rhyme scheme throughout each passage suggest that Zweig was creating his own poetic interpretation of the scriptural language, perhaps emulating the techniques of the Young Jewish poets that he had associated with a decade earlier.

Another influence on Zweig's impassioned, emotional poetic language was literary Expressionism, in which the poet dabbled briefly in the years leading up to World War I.[19] In an article that appeared on the title page of the first issue of *Das neue Pathos*, an Expressionist journal published by Paul Zech and Ludwig Meidner in 1913, Zweig articulated his views on the pathos of modern poetry as a revival of an original musical language. He begins his essay with a vision of the *Urgedicht*, the primal poem, which has its origins in the scream, the primal vocal utterance: "Das Urgedicht, jenes, das längst entstand vor Schrift und Druck, war nichts als ein modulierter, kaum Sprache gewordener Schrei, aus Luft oder Schmerz, aus Trauer oder Versagung, aus Erinnerung oder Beschwörung gewonnen, aber immer aus dem Ueberschwang einer Empfindung" (the original poem, that which appeared long before script or print, was nothing other than a modulated scream, barely become language, out of the air or pain, out of grief or refusal, won out of memory or exorcism, but always out of the abundance of sentiment).[20] Here, Zweig links poetry both to performance and to an "abundance" of feeling, an expression of emotion that appears first as sound before it finds articulation in human language. As John Warren and others have noted, the trope of poetry as the primal scream was common in contemporary Expressionist dramas, such as Georg Kaiser's *Der Bürger von Calais* (The Citizens of Calais 1914) and later in Ernst Toller's *Die Wandlung* (The Transformation 1919).[21] Like Schoenberg's creation story in *Totentanz der Prinzipien*, Zweig's vision of the origins of language manifests as a cacophonic outburst of noise. Moreover, Jeremiah's style of speaking evokes *Sprechstimme*, or *Sprechgesang*, vocal techniques that intertwine modes of speaking and singing, which Schoenberg employed in *Die Jakobsleiter* and *Totentanz*, suggesting the poet's familiarity with modes of musical Expressionism.[22] With their musical poetics, Zweig and Schoenberg wished to push the boundaries of Expressionist language and musical sound. By locating the origins of language in noise, both sought to find a form of expression prior to language, reclaiming the dissonant potential of sound to stir the masses to compassionate understanding.

The stage directions in *Jeremias* also point toward Zweig's poetic theories in *Das neue Pathos*. In the text, Zweig frequently marks the prophet's visions with the note, *ekstatisch*. "*Ekstase*" is a term that was often associated with the impassioned speech and movement of Expressionist drama, and indeed, in his essay in *Das neue Pathos*, Zweig described the goal of his new poetic language as "Ekstase zu erzeugen" (to generate ecstasy).[23] However, Ekstase also bore a very concrete meaning for Zweig in terms of the development of musical poetics and the renewal of spiritual community. He wrote to Richard Dehmel in 1917, describing Ekstase as both the language of protest and the language of the Chosen, in his words, the "höchste Triebkraft des Menschen gegen seinen Gott" and "den vulcanischen Urwillen des berufenen Menschen" ("the greatest impetus of man against his God" but also as "the vulcanic primal Will of the one who is called").[24] According to Zweig, Ekstase stands in sharp contrast to the "irdischen, zweckstrebigen kleinen Willen des Kraftmenschen, der zu allen Dingen der Welt, aber nie zu Gott gelangt" (earthly, goal-oriented small Will of the strongman, who reaches for everything in the world but never for God).[25] In another letter, to his childhood friend Ami Kaemmerer, Zweig sought to distinguish this language of protest and prophesy from "falsche Ekstase," which he identified with the warmongers and those who are easily swayed by the opinions of others.[26] In *Jeremias*, such "false ecstasy" is embodied in the false prophet Hananiah, who claims to speak for God but seeks only to convince the crowd to support the war. In scene 2, "Die Warnung" (The Warning), Hananiah uses similar rhetorical techniques to Jeremiah's and echoes his apocalyptic images.[27] However, Hananiah cannot speak in verse, and therefore cannot lay claim to true prophetic visions. Zweig reserves the effective use of emotional, evocative verse forms for the prophet who will ultimately succeed in assembling a Jewish community.

Zweig's vision for a "new pathos" in poetic language suggests that his knowledge of music's emotional affect informed his idea of Jewish Discursion. While scholarship on Zweig's relationship to music has focused on his collaboration with the composer Richard Strauss for the opera *Die schweigsame Frau* (The Silent Woman 1934), the poet composed his first opera libretto for Max Reger in 1907, and amassed an impressive collection of music manuscripts and artifacts over the course of his life.[28] Moreover, his correspondence with his friend Romain Rolland reveal his familiarity with discourses of musical aesthetics circulating at this time that identified music's ability to prompt an empathetic response, elevating the individual subject to a universal character and promoting a mode of compassionate understanding among its listeners. In a 1912 review of Rolland's novel, *Jean-Christophe* (1904–1912), Zweig identifies music as a mode of expression prior to reason, as a "Sprache über den Sprachen," that "überfliegt . . . die Grenzen der nationalen Beschränktheiten, Stimme des Gefühls, macht sie sich auch verständlich, wo der Intellekt nicht mehr zu ergänzen weiß" ("language above languages" that "soars above the borders of national limitations, as language of feeling it makes itself understandable where the intellect cannot express itself").[29] This description of music's emotional immediacy and transcendent power finds parallels in Zweig's idea of Jewish Discursion, a spiritual unity defined by its dynamic "fluidity of being."[30]

The connections between Zweig's musical poetics and his theory of Jewish spiritual community converge in *Jeremias*, where the prophet's musical language is not just a stylized mode of speaking but also plays an integral role in the dramatic arc of the play. In *Jeremias*, the prophet must overcome his isolation, the cause of his failed prophesy, by learning compassion. Only then will his ecstatic musical voice inspire the rebirth of the Jews as a modern, musical community. To enact this transformation, Zweig follows Lipiner and Beer-Hofmann in calling upon dramatic musical models that relay the significance of transcending individuality to the listening and viewing audience. Structuring his text on the sacred musical form of the Passion oratorio and the communal musical practice common to both Jewish and Christian traditions, antiphony, Zweig reenacts and memorializes suffering in order to relay his vision of a compassionate community that embraces both Christian and Jew.

## Jeremiah's Passion

Zweig's musical poetics reach their apotheosis in the final three scenes of the play, in which the prophet learns compassion and rediscovers the collective power of communal suffering. In the beginning of the text, Jeremiah, like Beer-Hofmann's Jaákob, is a man of faith, but one without community. Similarly, the Jewish people, who are depicted in the text up to this point only as *Stimmen* or voices, are a fragmented and disparate mass. To achieve this vision of community in which these voices transform into a triumphant choir, Zweig draws upon the form of the oratorical Passion and the practice of antiphony to structure his drama. In so doing, he reveals music's universalizing language as an articulation of his own German-Jewish identity and as the unifying expression of the modern Jewish diasporic community. In his play, Zweig reconstructs Christ's Passion scene with the Hebrew Prophet, inviting Jeremiah's association with the crucified Christ. This dramatic scene serves as a catalyst for his transformation from failed prophet to compassionate leader of a new spiritual community. While the associations of the prophet and Christ point toward tropes of Expressionist poetics, and potentially suggest a Christian "solution" to the play's conflict, Zweig ultimately had another goal in mind. Jeremiah's identification with Christ is but one stage in his own transformation as mediator between Jewish and German-Christian culture, which concludes in his affirmation of belonging with the Jewish community. In the finale, the shared spirit of compassion central to both Jewish and Christian traditions is articulated in the mode of antiphony. The call and response of antiphony serves as the apotheosis of the ecstatic poetics Zweig described in *Das neue Pathos*. The prophet's ability to mold the fragmented voices of the Jewish people into a choir attests to Zweig's belief in music's power to transcend the boundaries of language, ethnicity, and religious difference. The choral finale of *Jeremias* thus reveals the power of a communal musical act to transform suffering (Leid) into compassion (Mitleid).

Just as Beer-Hofmann turned to the Gesamtkunstwerk as a theatrical form to synthesize the expression of Jewish subjectivity and his aspirations to an idealized collective, Zweig found a similar dramatic potential in the Passion oratorio. As Ruth HaCohen notes, in the oratorio, vocal parts not only take on specific roles within the narrative of the biblical legend but also provide commentary and reflection on the scene, through lyrical arias that articulate subjective, emotional responses to the action. HaCohen identifies these "oratorical moments" as "nonrealistic, transhistorical chronotopoi," which introduce voices from out of time that form "recursive nets," revealing layers of meaning by linking the past to the present.[31] Oratorical voices thus draw the audience into the action by evoking compassion and stimulating feelings of sympathy with the narrative's protagonists. The popularity of oratorios among assimilated Jewish audiences in Zweig's time suggests that they saw in the imaginary inclusive space created by this musical form the possibility of a utopian spiritual community in which all would be welcome.[32]

In *Jeremias*, Zweig evokes such an "oratorical moment" at a critical turning point of the play: in the seventh scene, "The Supreme Affliction," in which the prophet enacts Christ's Passion. As the scene opens, the people are in despair. It is clear now that they will lose the war and they are hungry, suffering, and afraid. They believe that their last hope is for Jeremiah to perform a miracle. The people, described first as the crowd and later as a menacing and turbulent mob, call out in half-heard sentence fragments and repetitions that produce an empty echo effect:

Die Menge:

> Heiliger . . . Jeremias . . . rette uns . . . Gesalbter . . . rette die Stadt . . .
> Unser König sei . . . tue ein Wunder. . . .

Jeremias:

> Ich verstehe eure Worte nicht. Was wollt ihr von mir?

Die Menge: *chaotisch durcheinander*

> Moria . . . die Burg . . . rette Jerusalem . . . ein Wunder . . . wir sind
> verloren . . . Unser Hort bist du . . . errette uns . . . rette Jerusalem . . .

Jeremias:

> Einer rede, nicht alle!

[The Crowd:
Save us, Jeremiah, anointed of the Lord.—Save the city.—Be our king.—
Show a miracle

Jeremiah:
Your words are dark to me. What is your will?

The Crowd: *chaotic, confused*
Moria.—The fortress of Zion.—Save Jerusalem.—A miracle.—We are
lost.—You are our shepherd.—Save us.—Save Jerusalem.

Jeremiah:
Speak one at a time!][33]

In this scene, Zweig portrays the people as an anonymous collective of voices, a noisy, unmusical element in the play, who can only mimic, murmur, or shout and are deaf to the *melos* of Jeremiah's prophesy. Zweig's text recalls here the antisemitic discourse of Jews as loud, cacophonous, and distinctly unmusical, popularized in such writings such as Wagner's essay, *Das Judentum und die Musik*.[34] That the Jewish voices are incomprehensible to the prophet and their ears are deaf to his message further emphasizes their Otherness and the apparent futility of his mission. In the scene's dramatic climax, the crowd's desperation leads to frustration, resentment, and, finally, revolt. They surround the prophet, crying out "crucify him!" Their inability to communicate, and Jeremiah's inability to feel compassion for their plight, appears destined to lead to violence.

However, Zweig's use of antisemitic stereotypes of Jews must be examined more closely, for, by setting up this opposition between Jeremiah and the crowd, Zweig creates the very circumstances for these binaries to be dissolved. As Jeremiah stands above the tumult with hands outstretched, he breaks out into an ecstatic speech. This vision is different from his previous prophetic dreams, particularly because it recalls not the source text of the Hebrew Scriptures but rather the libretto of Johann Sebastian Bach's *St. Matthew's Passion*. Zweig attended a performance of this work at Vienna's most revered musical venue, the Musikverein, on March 29, 1915, shortly before he began work on *Jeremias*.[35] In Zweig's version of the monologue, Jeremiah's perspective pans out of the dramatic moment and he speaks as though he were an observer at Christ's crucifixion:

Der am Kreuze hinstirbt in irdischer Pein,
Wird der selige Mittler und Fürbitter sein.
Seine Arme, die brechend am Kreuzholz hangen,
Werden liebend die Seele der Welt einst umfangen,

> Seine Lippen, die schmachtend verlöschen und brechen,
> Das erlösende Wort des Friedens aussprechen,
> Seine Seufzer werden zu Wohllaut werden,
> Seine Qual die ewige Liebe auf Erden.
>
> [Who hangs on the cross in mortal pain,
> The world's eternal welfare shall gain,
> Saviour and intercessor, he,
> With arms outstretched on the cruel tree.
> His lips, trembling with anguish till death bring release,
> Shall speak the redeeming message of peace;
> His signs to melody shall give birth,
> His torment, to love everlasting on earth.][36]

The oratorical nature of this scene is emphasized by Jeremiah's lines "seine Arme . . . werden liebend die Seele der Welt erst umfangen," a nod to the alto aria of the *St. Matthew's Passion*: "sehet, Jesus hat die Hand, uns zu fassen, ausgespannt, kommt" (see, Jesus has held his hand out to grasp us, come!).[37] Further, when the prophet holds out his arms in a mirror image of Christ on the cross, begging the Lord that his will be done—"Dein Wille geschehe," his words recall Christ's prayer on the Mount of Olives, in particular the aria, "es ist vollbracht" (it is finished), featured in Bach's *St. John's Passion*.[38] Jeremiah's words can be read as an "oratorical moment," a reflective, lyrical event that takes place out of time with the surrounding narrative. His declaration of solidarity with the suffering Christ—"Oh, daß ich es wäre, / oh, daß ich es würde, / Meine Seele verzehrt und verlodert sich!" (Oh, if it were only me, oh if only I would be it / my soul consumes itself, flares up and extinguishes itself)—recalls what HaCohen refers to as the "subjunctive proclamations" of oratorical voices, whose "would-be" status serves to transpose the speaker (and with him or her, the listener) from the present moment to a future time.[39] Jeremiah's lyrical reflection in this scene recalls how oratorios dramatized religious narratives through music to engage the audience in reflection on biblical stories. By linking Jeremiah to recognizable portrayals of Christ with his open arms, Zweig establishes a connection between his play and this tradition of sacred music dating back to the Baroque period that he cherished as a member of the educated, acculturated German-Jewish bourgeoisie. Finally, this scene serves as a climactic moment in Zweig's ecstatic musical poetics, a further evolution from a kind of rhythmic song-speech evident in his earlier prophesies to a consciously composed musical-poetic aria intended to both reflect the compassionate transformation of Jeremiah and to inspire a sympathetic response from the audience.

Zweig's portrayal of the prophet through the lens of the Passion story also references another popular oratorio of the nineteenth century, one written by a German-Jew like himself: Felix Mendelssohn's *Elijah* (1846). Mendelssohn (1809–1847), grandson of the founder of the Jewish Enlightenment, Moses Mendelssohn, was particularly revered for the role he played in reviving Bach's *St. Matthew's Passion* in Berlin in 1829. Like Zweig, Mendelssohn struggled throughout his life to define his relationship to his Jewish heritage and engaged with this theme in a number of his works. Zweig's portrayal of his Hebrew prophet as the Christ of Bach's Passions, mirrors Mendelssohn's *Elijah*, which was also modeled on Bach's works. For example, Mendelssohn's setting of Elijah's aria "es ist genug" (it is enough), as the prophet stands before the judgment of Obadiah and the people, references the same crucifixion aria from Bach's *Johannes Passion* found in Zweig's *Jeremias*, suggesting that Zweig may have looked to Mendelssohn as a model for developing his "oratorical moment."[40]

Like Mendelssohn's *Elijah*, Zweig's *Jeremias* reveals an ambiguous portrayal of his Jewish subject. By intersecting the most musical moment in the text with a near reenactment of the crucifixion, Zweig appears to emphasize antisemitic stereotypes proliferated throughout Christian communities for centuries, which demonized the Jewish people for their rejection of Christ. However, Zweig takes his cue from Mendelssohn in this scene and stops short of tracing a direct line from the prophet to Christ.[41] Jeremiah is not crucified; rather the crowd disperses upon hearing the news that Jerusalem has fallen. The scene's focus remains on the prophet, who has felt compassion for the suffering Christ but has not yet felt true suffering in communion with the Jews, from whom he still feels alienated. Only when he learns to suffer with the Jewish people will he be able to lead them toward compassionate community.

In the next scene, entitled "Die Umkehr" (The Conversion) Zweig makes this distinction by shifting the focus back to the Jewish community, following the prophet's "oratorical moment" with the interjection of Jewish sacred music. The scene opens on the Jews hiding in a vaulted cellar. No longer the angry mob of the previous scene, they appear timid and defeated. A few huddle around an elderly man who reads from the Torah. In sharp contrast to the ecstatic, oratorio-like aria of the previous scene, the old man speaks in a faint, monotone voice, rocking back and forth in rhythm with his prayer, while the people respond by murmuring their response in unison. The passage he reads aloud is from the book of Psalms, chapter 80, which tells the Jewish history of exile.[42] The community responds to the rabbi's verses by repeating the refrain, "Erscheine! Erwecke deine Gewalt!" (Appear! Awaken your might!).[43] By following the oratorio with a prayer ceremony, Zweig points toward resonances between the two faiths, their common origins in myths of suffering and the expression of solidarity through communal musical practice. He also uses this musical moment to introduce the narrative of Jewish exile. It is the Diaspora, the basis of Zweig's concept of Jewish spirit as Discursion, that will emerge as the central theme of the triumphant finale, when the final expression of Jewish unity in spirit will be achieved through the call and response of antiphony.

Like Lipiner, Mahler, Schoenberg, and Beer-Hofmann before him, Zweig evokes the discourse of Mitleid through a delicate mediation of Christian and Jewish mythologies. In the beginning of the play, Jeremiah suffers because of his inability to communicate his visions of destruction to the people and to make them understand his warnings. Like Beer-Hofmann's Jaákob, he knows that as the Chosen One he is God's instrument, but he feels isolated in this experience, a passive receptor, and not an active agent with the ability to choose his destiny. Zweig ultimately sees Leid, or suffering, as the instigator for Mitleid, or compassion, the source of communal rebirth. Zweig appears to reference here the active striving and willing of suffering of Mahler and Lipiner's compassionate Übermensch. In order to realize this transformation, Jeremiah, like Schoenberg's Chosen One and Beer-Hofmann's Jaákob, must actively choose to claim compassion *for* and solidarity *with* the Jewish people.

The "suffering with" the Other in solidarity that Zweig envisions is a mode of spiritual unity that he finds to be exemplified by the Jewish community in exile. In scene 8, "The Conversion," Jeremiah transforms from a passive receptor of suffering to the compassionate leader of the Jewish community of the Diaspora—a community not demoralized but rather, emboldened through the collective experience of suffering. In rage at the plight of his people, forced into hiding as the city of Jerusalem burns around them, the prophet calls out to God:

> Wie du dein Volk, so hab' ich dich verstoßen,
> Den harten Hasser, den Mitleidslosen,
> Denn ein Gott, der Hohn anstatt Hilfe gibt,
> Ist nicht wert mehr, daß man ihn kündet und liebt!

Nur wer das Leiden wendet, ist Gott allein,
Nur wer Trost ausspendet, darf Allmacht sein! . . .
Mein Herz erhört sie—es hat sich gewendet: . . .
Zu ihnen, den Schwestern, zu ihnen den Brüdern

[Thou spurnedst thy people, so thee too I reject'
No merciless God shall compel my respect!
For why is it seemly that reverence be paid
To a god who gives scorn when his children seek aid?
He only is God who turns sorrow aside,
Almighty but he who can solace provide! . . .
As I hearken, perforce I must turn my head . . .
To thee, my brothers, my sisters][44]

In these verses, Jeremiah addresses God as the *Mitleidslosen*, the merciless, or literally, compassion-less one. His declaration of solidarity with his brothers and sisters is a triumphant proclamation of community in the face of suffering. Refusing the request of the Babylonian king to serve as his oracle, Jeremiah instead chooses exile with the Jewish community. It is this act of compassion that leads him to be seized by a new vision of God's mercy. In a poetic improvisation on Psalm 137, "By the Waters of Babylon," the prophet recalls the story of exile in Egypt and foretells the future return to Jerusalem. Jeremiah's musical affirmation of community with the Jewish people marks his transformation from sufferer to compassionate mediator, from failed prophet to leader of the Jewish people. His musical, ecstatic voice has finally found captive listeners. Thus, in scenes seven and eight of his play, Zweig creates a narrative arc in which evocations of compassionate love found in both Christian and Jewish musical traditions enable Jeremiah to overcome his failed prophesy to join, communicate with, and contribute to a Jewish community.

So, what were audiences to take away from this drama of a Jewish-Christian prophet claiming solidarity with the Jewish community in exile? Jeremiah's oratorical aria is at once a subjective proclamation, the sign of inner transformation, and a message to the audience intended to provoke compassion for Jewish suffering. HaCohen writes that the textual mediations on the biblical texts found in the oratorio were intended to "enhance the active role of the contemporary believer" and create "emotional bridges" between the audience and the suffering protagonist on stage.[45] By evoking Bach's Passions and Mendelssohn's *Elijah*, Zweig found a unique mode of engaging his audience in contemplating the Jewish Question in their own time. In the final scene, Zweig further develops the call and response of antiphony to solidify links between Jewish and Christian musical traditions. In the finale, music serves both as a meditation on communal suffering and ultimately as an expression of the spiritual homeland of the modern Jewish Diaspora.

## Creating Communal Voice: The Call and Response of Antiphony

In the conclusion of *Jeremias*, Zweig draws again the musical traditions he references in the previous scenes, the oratorical aria and the communal prayer, to inscribe compassion as a foundational principle of the Jewish spiritual community. The final scene, entitled "Der ewige Weg" (The Everlasting Road) comprises six musical episodes that draw on three oratorical styles: dramatic episodes, which focus on dialogue and character development; epic episodes, which relay narrative; and reflective episodes, which express personal emotion.[46] In the second episode as well as the finale, both of which I identify as epic-narrative, Zweig employs the musical form of the antiphon, creating the sound of voices joining in a choir. While in the previous scenes, Jeremiah and the people were divided by their different musical voices, ecstatic speech and noisy clamor, in the finale, they sing together, gradually building up to the final episode where they join in a triumphant chorus. However, Zweig's use of musical form not only makes manifest the gradual coming together of the community in a musical-poetic expression of their spiritual unity but the episodes represent shifts from past to present to future times, evoking the transtemporal unity of the Jewish community. In this way, Zweig expresses the idea that communal music is the means by which the Jews come to know their spiritual homeland, linking his understanding of Jewish Discursion to the expression of communal voice.

In "The Everlasting Road" Zweig deploys the ability of music to transcend time and space to express the enduring resonance of the Jewish history of exile and suffering and their spirit of compassionate unity. The scene is composed of a prelude that sets the scene, followed by six interactions between Jeremiah and the people that trace the evolution of their communal, musical spirit, and a choral finale. As a structural outline of this scene reveals, dramatic or dialogic scenes (A) feature a conversation between the prophet and the people (in groups or represented by individual voices); epic-narrative scenes (B) retell a past event or foretell the future

Table 5.1 Stefan Zweig, *Jeremias*, Scene 9: "Der ewige Weg": Structural Outline[1]

| | Passage | Content | Form |
|---|---|---|---|
| Prelude | *Der gleiche große Platz vor dem Tempel...* [The same great square in front of the temple] | The people assemble, await Jeremiah | |
| 1 | *Jeremias (aus dem Kreise vortretend an die höchste der Stufe).* [Jeremiah, (leaving his companions and going to the top of the step)] | Jeremiah convinces the people to join him | A |
| 2 | *Das Volk gerät in mächtige Erregung. Aus den einzelnen Stimmen heben sich rhythmisch die Chöre* [A wave of enthusiasm answers his words. The confused medley of voices gradually gives place to rhythmical choruses] | The story of exile | B |
| 3 | Die Stimme Zedekias: Wehe, wehe! Wer wird mich führen? [Zedekiah: Alas, alas! Who will lead me?] | Jeremiah and Zedekiah | A |
| 4 | Jeremias *gewaltig auf der Höhe der Stufen aufgerichtet* [Jeremiah with confident mien, strides up the steps once more] | Jeremiah's Solo Arias | C |
| 5 | Einer *vortretend:*... schauen wir wieder Jerusalem? [The People: Shall we ever see Jerusalem again?] | Jeremiah as teacher | A |
| 6 Finale | *Die Menge gerät in mächtige Bewegung... Ihre Blicke sind aufwärtsgerichtet, sie singen im Schreiten* [The march begins... they gaze heavenward, singing as they march] | Exit of the Jews from Jerusalem | B |

1. A: Dialogic/Dramatic, B: Epic/Narrative, C: Reflective

in lyrical verse; and reflective scenes (C) serve as "oratorical moments," subjective, contemplative meditations on these events. The episodes follow the pattern ABACAB. (See table 5.1.) The dialogic episodes follow the play's dramatic arc, tracing the development of Jeremiah's relationship to the Jewish people. The epic-narrative episodes focus on the larger question underlying the play, the significance of suffering for the Jews and the continuity of their spiritual community in the past, present, and future. The reflective episode serves as an interlude. Zweig's use of antiphony in the epic-narrative episodes represents the culmination of his musical poetics of Ekstase. In his essay *Das neue Pathos*, Zweig had written that poetry lost its expressive potential when the poet no longer spoke his works aloud, anticipating the raucous response of the crowd. Instead, he wrote for the page and his verses became only "lonely conversations" and monologues.[47] The new poetic voice, Zweig claimed, would recapture the performative nature of its origins, inspiring its audience to action. Thus, with his work's chorale finale, Zweig sought to encourage compassionate connection with the Jewish community onstage, creating a powerful theatrical experience that he hoped would ultimately transform the society of his time into a more open, cosmopolitan community.

Episode one is dialogic (A) and marks the first communicative exchange between Jeremiah and the people and their first affirmation of his message of unity in suffering. After a short prelude in which groups of people express their doubt, uncertainty, and despair, Jeremiah appears onstage with his followers, accompanied by drums, cymbals, and jubilant voices. As the uncertain voices meet the celebratory chorus, a dramatic dialogue develops between them, in which Jeremiah persuades the voices to join the choir. Their conversation is carried out in a series of exchanges in which the voices gradually begin to repeat and affirm the prophet's words, following the model of the communal prayer in the previous scene. When Jeremiah proclaims, "Nur die Geprüften hat er erwählet, und nur den Leidenden gilt seine Liebe. So lasset uns die Geprüften sein und lieben sein Leid, ihr Brüder!" (Only those whom he has tested has he chosen, and only those who suffer are worthy of his love. So let us be the tested and love his suffering you brothers!), the voices of the people respond affirmatively: "Geben wir uns hin seinem Willen . . . gepriesen die Prüfung . . . Oh, Wahrheit des Wortes" (Let us give in to his will, blessed be the test . . . Oh truth of the word).[48] In repeating and affirming his words, the people acknowledge a legacy of shared suffering that binds them together. Suffering, Jeremiah proclaims, is Israel's strength and buttress ("Kraft und der Sturz seine Stufe").[49] At the conclusion of this episode, the prophet has succeeded in gathering the people and uniting their disparate voices in affirmation of a common experience of suffering, *Leiden*.

Before they can move forward, however, the community must come to affirm their shared history. In the next episode, which recounts Moses leading the Jews out of Egypt, Zweig turns to an epic-narrative style (B), organized into four verses that loosely follow a common antiphonic structure in which alternating choruses sing successive verses of a Psalm, repeating the melody at increasingly higher octaves.[50] According to Zweig's stage directions, individual voices emerge from the crowd until they eventually speak rhythmically as one.[51] Each round is composed for alternating choirs singing verses in increasing brightness or emotion. First the voices, marked as *Stimmen*, begin by speaking in short, clipped verses. They are then superseded by *hellere Stimmen*, who take over the story by speaking in lengthy, more lyrical verses, and eventually give way to *jubelnde* (joyful) or *jauchzende* (exultant) voices, who end their verse with an appellatory cry. Thus, each round gradually increases in intensity until Jeremiah's solo voice breaks in with a repetitive refrain: "Entsinnet sie, entsinnet die brennenden Tage der Bitternis! Entsinnet sie!" (Remember them, remember the burning days of bitterness! Remember them!).[52] Jeremiah's interruption and call to remember provides the transition to the next round, which begins again with the *Stimmen* and continues to gradually amplify through the different choruses. In the final verse, all the voices join together to sing a proclamation of faith in God:

> Immer waren wir Pflüger im Joche,
> Immer gebeugt und in Dienstbarkeit,
> Doch ewig hat er das Joch uns zerbrochen,
> Aus allen Kerkern uns heimbefreit,
> Wo immer sie Not und Drängung uns schufen
> Immer hat er uns heimgerufen,
> Und unsern Samen zur Blüte erneut!
>
> [Again and again have we been yoked to the plough,
> Necks bowed; again and again enslaved:
> But never has he failed to break our yoke,
> To free us from captivity and exile:
> From all our afflictions, all our privations,
> Never has he failed to deliver us,
> To summon us home at last,
> To grant us a renewed flowering.][53]

In this chorus, the word *immer* (always) serves as the connecting point between past and present suffering. These words are a call for renewed community united in compassion and sown from the seeds of a common history.

In the third episode (A), Zweig brings us back to the present, staging a dramatic scene of reconciliation between Jeremiah and Zedekiah that marks the transformation of the Jewish people from the suffering people to the compassionate people. Zedekiah, the King of Judah who refused to heed Jeremiah's warnings and thus led the people into war with the Babylonians, appears before the people as a decrepit blind man. In this scene, Jeremiah identifies Zedekiah, as "des Leidens König" (the King of Suffering). By crowning Zedekiah as the suffering King, Jeremiah alludes back to the image of the suffering Christ in Jeremiah's oratorical episode in the seventh scene.[54] Zweig's reference to the crucifixion marks another moment of reconciliation of Jewish and Christian faiths, recognizing in their shared mythologies of suffering an affirmation of the symbolic power of compassionate sacrifice.

The fourth episode introduces a new form, the reflective, lyrical passage sung by Jeremiah (C). While in the second episode, Jeremiah's calls to remember and recall signaled the transtemporal nature of the Jewish people, this reflective episode establishes their *transnational* nature. In his speech, Jeremiah elevates Jerusalem, their homeland, and the earth beneath their feet to a spiritual essence, the lost land that will permeate their being and live on in their hearts wherever they wander in the world. Jeremiah's solo arias are, as in earlier passages in which he was overtaken by the power of Ekstase, marked by alliteration, repetition, and powerful imagery. As he sings, the people gather around him, swaying in time with his lyrical speech.

The fifth episode returns to the dramatic mode (A) and, as in the first episode (the crowd's first affirmations of Jeremiah's prophesy) and the third episode (Jeremiah's encounter with Zedekiah in which the prophet proclaims him the king of suffering), this scene's dialogue marks another shift in the development of Jeremiah's relationship with the people. Whereas earlier in the text, they dismissed his prophesies as the ravings of a madman, here Jeremiah has become the teacher, to whom they turn for guidance. The dialogic nature of the episode, in which the crowd not only affirms but repeats and reformulates Jeremiah's words, indicates that the broken lines of communication that separated them earlier have been repaired. In the scene, three individuals from the crowd pose questions to Jeremiah, whose responses are enthusiastically affirmed by the crowd. The episode's use of response and affirmation reflects the crowd's increasing confidence in Jeremiah's words. In this episode, Zweig highlights the transnational and mythical nature of the Jewish people, their pride in their history, and the strength found in communal suffering that will serve to unite them in the future.[55] The repetition of "wir glauben" (we believe) in this episode reveals that a crucial transition has occurred: the people's despair has been replaced by hope. In the final scene, the individual voices will unite as joyous choirs, signaling their final transformation into a powerful community, joined together in song.

In the finale, Zweig returns to the epic form (B), in which he first introduced the antiphonic mode in episode two. Now, however, instead of competing voices, repeating their verses at ever higher intervals, the voices are marked in the score as one group of voices, the *Stimmen der Schreitenden*, the voices of those marching in step together, and with each verse the choir grows in strength and number. In the end, the masses are marked as the *Stimmen der Ausziehenden*, the voices of those departing. In the previous narrative episode, the Jewish community sang of their past sufferings and the resonance of suffering in the present moment. In this final episode, they reveal the future vision of their community:

> Auf fremden Straßen werden wir fahren,
> Durch Land und Länder stößt uns der Wind
> Heimat um Heimat reißen die Völker
> Uns von den brennenden Sohlen fort
>
> [We shall journey by unfamiliar roads;
> The wind will carry us afar, through many lands;
> Weary shall we be, footsore and weary,
> As the nations drive us from home after home][56]

The people sing of living in foreign lands, of eternal wandering. But in adopting the choral pronoun "we," they acknowledge that as a group they possess a greater force, a communal spirit. As they march out of the city in a seemingly endless procession, their captors watch them curiously, fearing this mass demonstration as a sign of resistance. But, as one of the soldiers reports, the people are not grumbling or murmuring. Nor are they lamenting. Instead, they are singing. In the final chorus, the people proclaim that Jerusalem cannot truly be defeated because "man kann das Unsichtbare nicht besiegen" (one cannot defeat, that which cannot be seen).[57] The city, their homeland, lives on in their heart and their song.

The musical structure of the final scene presents the apotheosis of Zweig's musical poetics of Ekstase, creating a dramatic intensification through the construction of musical episodes that vary in intensity as single voices respond to one another, build on one another, and eventually develop into a triumphant choir. This conclusion reiterates Zweig's idea that Judaism and Christianity are rooted in foundational myths of redemption through suffering and reaffirms his claim that the Jews as a people embody the principle of Discursion, a spiritual unity that finds expression in music. In *Jeremias*, Zweig realized a musical poetics that reflects an idea he wrote about to Romain Rolland in 1914 after attending a performance of Beethoven's *Missa Solemnis*. In this letter, Zweig wrote that music had the ability to achieve the outer realization of the inner harmony of humanity, bringing "die Wort und Tat jetzt in Einklang" (word and action now into accord).[58] By representing the Jewish community through music, Zweig depicts them as an unconquerable spiritual community, whose "inner musical harmony" finds expression in the active engagement of individual voices that transcend individual suffering through compassionate song. In *Jeremias*, Zweig recasts the Jews as a musical people, capable and worthy of compassion and as a model community that embodies the spiritual unity he envisioned in his brotherhood of humanity.

## Conclusion

In 1917, Zweig wrote to Buber that he saw the Jewish people as the epitome of the "übernationale[s] Gefühl der Freiheit" (supranational feeling of freedom) that he felt was the key to the end of world conflict.[59] For Zweig, the Jewish homeland existed not as a political state defined by geographic borders but instead as a community united in faith and in song. Thus, he found in music both the expression of communal belonging and the homeland itself, an imaginary space in which his idealized Jewish spirit could exist, unrestricted by political, cultural, or linguistic differences.

Zweig's intensely personal relationship to this work and his identification with Jeremiah indicate that the musical element in *Jeremias* was not simply a rhetorical technique but rather an articulation of Zweig's own voice and a reflection of his own experience. In portraying the prophet at times as both Christian and Jewish, Zweig drew on his own dual identity as both a poet of the German (Christian) cultural tradition and as a Jew. Zweig's conflicted relationship to these two poles of his existence emerge in scenes such as the oratorical aria, where Zweig appears to reify antisemitic stereotypes of noisy, unmusical Jews and casts his prophet as a Christ figure. However, Jeremiah's identification with the suffering Christ also makes him acutely aware of his solidarity with and compassion for the suffering of the Jewish people. Moreover, the finale ultimately rectifies this depiction by portraying the Jewish as a noble community united by a history of shared suffering; they are the founders of a spiritual and musical tradition that would later be adopted by Christianity.

Zweig claimed that he never expected *Jeremias* to be performed, and indeed the complete drama has never successfully been staged. However, in a letter to the poet Richard Dehmel in September 1917, Zweig admitted that he had in mind something like a festival play ("etwas Festspielhaftes") and a month later he wrote to his friend Ami Kaemmerer that he wished for Alfred Roller to design the stage for the performance.[60] His choice of designer indicates that Zweig knew of Mahler's collaborations with Roller at the Vienna Court Opera to stage Wagner's music dramas and was hoping to align his own work with this vision. Roller did not, in the end, work with Zweig on *Jeremias*, although he did serve as stage designer for Richard Beer-Hofmann *Jaákobs Traum*, which premiered at the Burgtheater just two years later, in April 1919.

Despite his grandiose visions, Zweig was forced to make considerable cuts, ultimately limiting his ability to stage his work in its original, musical form. Three scenes were left out at the premiere of *Jeremias* at the Zurich State Theater on February 27, 1918, and four from performances in Nuremberg and Vienna the following fall and winter. These alterations were primarily made to improve dramatic flow, yet there were also more practical concerns to accommodate. Such was the case during the performance at Vienna's Deutsches Volkstheater, when the city was still facing curfews for fuel shortages and could not afford to light the theater's lamps.[61] (See fig. 5.1.) As the program reveals, the performance had to begin at 5:30 p.m. and was cut to five scenes, eliminating scenes 3 (The Warning), 5 (The Prophet's Ordeal), and 7 (The Supreme Affliction) from the original text. The notice on the front also announces that with the author's permission, the prelude "The Awakening of the Prophet" would also be omitted for the performance. Zweig knew that the work's length was a hindrance. Still, he felt that in shortening the work, he was "selling his soul for freedom."[62] For the Vienna performance he attempted to organize with the dramaturge of the Deutschen Volkstheater, Heinrich Glücksmann, a separate performance in which the scenes that had been cut would be read aloud; however, this event does not appear to have come to fruition.[63] Yet the cuts did not dampen the work's popular reception. *Jeremias* was a rousing success for Zweig in book sales and on the stage. Moreover, the audiences of Zweig's time recognized the work's aspirations toward totalizing art forms and musical models. In similar language to that used to describe Beer-Hofmann's *Jaákobs Traum*, a

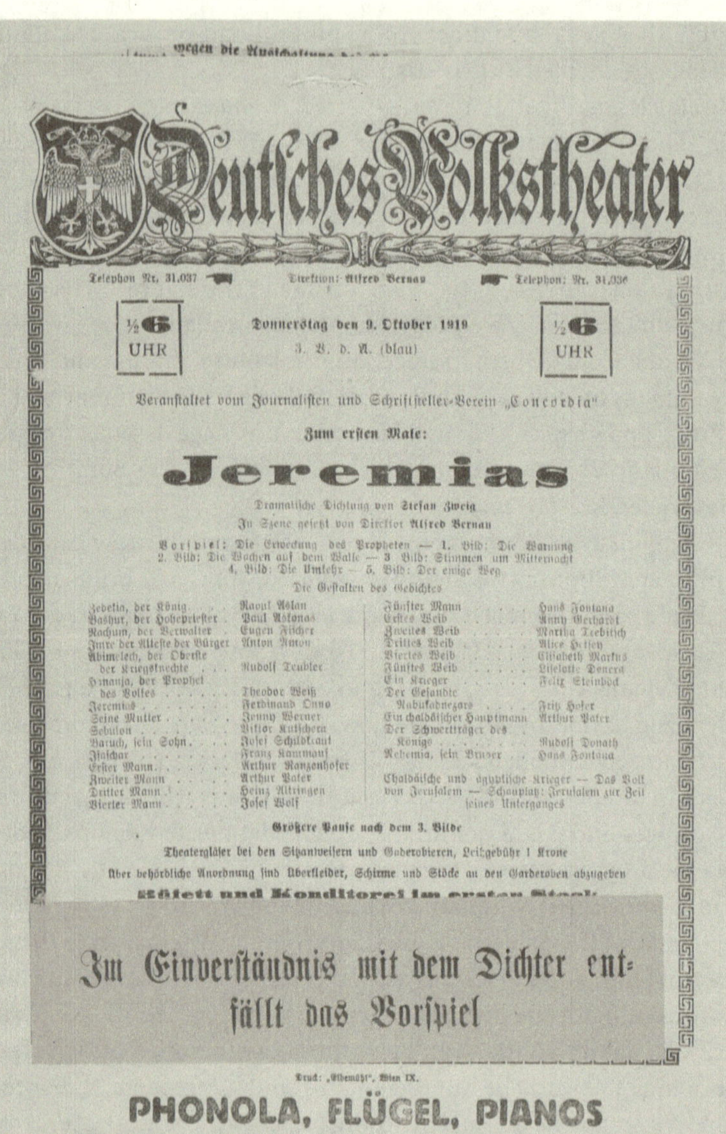

Deutsches Volkstheater

Telephon Nr. 31.037 — Direktion: Alfred Bernau — Telephon: Nr. 31.036

½6 UHR

Donnerstag den 9. Oktober 1919

3. V. d. A. (blau)

½6 UHR

Veranstaltet vom Journalisten und Schriftsteller-Verein „Concordia"

Zum ersten Male:

**Jeremias**

Dramatische Dichtung von **Stefan Zweig**

In Szene gesetzt von Direktor **Alfred Bernau**

Vorspiel: Die Erweckung des Propheten — 1. Bild: Die Warnung
2. Bild: Die Wachen auf dem Walle — 3 Bild: Stimmen um Mitternacht
4. Bild: Die Umkehr — 5. Bild: Der ewige Weg

Die Gestalten des Gedichtes

| | |
|---|---|
| Zedekia, der König | Raoul Aslan |
| Pashur, der Hohepriester | Paul Askonas |
| Nachum, der Verwalter | Eugen Fischer |
| Imre der Älteste der Bürger | Anton Amon |
| Abimelech, der Oberste der Kriegsknechte | Rudolf Teubler |
| Hananja, der Prophet des Volkes | Theodor Weiß |
| Jeremias | Ferdinand Onno |
| Seine Mutter | Jenny Werner |
| Sebulon | Viktor Kutschera |
| Baruch, sein Sohn | Josef Schildkraut |
| Isaschar | Franz Kammauf |
| Erster Mann | Arthur Ranzenhofer |
| Zweiter Mann | Arthur Pater |
| Dritter Mann | Heinz Altringen |
| Vierter Mann | Josef Wolf |
| Fünfter Mann | Hans Fontana |
| Erstes Weib | Anny Gerhardt |
| Zweites Weib | Martha Trebitsch |
| Drittes Weib | Alice Hetsey |
| Viertes Weib | Elisabeth Markus |
| Fünftes Weib | Liselotte Denera |
| Ein Krieger | Felix Steinböck |
| Der Gesandte Nabukadnezars | Fritz Hofer |
| Ein chaldäischer Hauptmann | Arthur Pater |
| Der Schwertträger des Königs | Rudolf Donath |
| Nehemia, sein Bruder | Hans Fontana |

Chaldäische und ägyptische Krieger — Das Volk von Jerusalem — Schauplatz: Jerusalem zur Zeit seines Unterganges

Größere Pause nach dem 3. Bilde

Theatergläser bei den Sitzanweisern und Garderobieren, Leihgebühr 1 Krone

Über behördliche Anordnung sind Überkleider, Schirme und Stöcke an den Garderoben abzugeben

Im Einverständnis mit dem Dichter entfällt das Vorspiel

Druck: „Elbemühl", Wien IX.

PHONOLA, FLÜGEL, PIANOS
LUDWIG HUPFELD, WIEN, VI., Mariahilferstraße 3.

Figure 5.1. Program for the Vienna premiere of Zweig's *Jeremias* at the *Deutsches Volkstheater* on October 9, 1919. KHM-Museumsverband, Theatermuseum Vienna.

reporter for the *Neue Freie Presse* wrote of Zweig's *Jeremias* in 1917 that the work could have been called "ein dramatisches Epos in neun Gesängen" (a dramatic epic in nine songs) likening the choral finale to a "mächtig zusammenklingendes Orchester" (powerful symphonious orchestra).[64] These comments reveal the pervasiveness of the musical idiom for theatrical audiences of Zweig's time and the powerful effect of his musical language and dramatic vision, despite the work's incomplete production.

Drawn to his heritage as a source of empowerment, Zweig viewed the Jewish people as a cosmopolitan community. Yet he sought this community on a spiritual and aesthetic not a political level.[65] He viewed his own Jewish subjectivity through the lens of Discursion and saw his role as a poet to serve as mediator between the German-Christian culture that he identified with as an artist and the noble history and mythology of his German-Jewish forefathers. In music, he found a supranational, humanist poetics to articulate the connections and contradictions that defined his own Jewish subjectivity. The chorale finale of *Jeremias* expresses this complex vision by returning to the common origins of human expression in the chorus, the expression of compassionate community united in harmonious song.

## Notes

1. Steiman, "Stefan Zweig: Legacy of World War I," 75.

2. Mark H. Gelber suggests that Zweig likely celebrated his Bar Mitzvah and that references to Jewish religious practices in his later works suggest that he could follow services in Hebrew. Gelber, *Stefan Zweig: Judentum und Zionismus*, 11.

3. Zweig, *Die Welt von Gestern*, 5.

4. Zweig's poems "Das Gericht" and "Spinoza" and his novella "Im Schnee" appeared in *Die Welt* in 1901 as well as in the *Jüdischer Almanach* in 1902. "Das Gericht" was reprinted in *Junge Harfen*. Gelber, "Interfaces," 72. See also Berlin, "Response and Impression," 315.

5. Zweig et al., *Briefe 1914–1919*, 106 [Translations of Zweig's *Briefe* C. K.].

6. Zweig et al., 107–108.

7. Gelber, *Stefan Zweig: Judentum und Zionismus*, 13.

8. Zweig and Beck, *Tagebücher*, 192 [Translation C. K.].

9. Zweig et al., *Briefe 1914–1919*, 130.

10. Zweig et al., 147.

11. Zweig et al., 147.

12. Steinberg, *Listening to Reason*, 7.

13. Another, more contemporary, source than the biblical Scripture for Zweig was *The History of the People of Israel* (1888–1895) by the French Orientalist and philologist Ernest Renan.

14. The English scene titles are taken from the 1939 reprint of the translation by Eden and Cedar Paul and are marked [Zweig, *Jeremiah*]. Paul and Paul effectively capture the

rhythm and rhyme of Jeremiah's prophetic speech, if at time taking liberties with the literal translation; thus, in places where the translation is not indicated, I have included my own rendition in English.

15. Zweig, *Tersites; Jeremias: zwei Dramen*, 126 (hereafter as *Jeremias*) [Zweig, *Jeremiah*, 15–16].

16. Zweig, *Jeremias*, 127 [Zweig, *Jeremiah*, 16–17].

17. Zweig, *Jeremias*, 145. Eden and Cedar Paul's translation "King of the North" is taken from the King James Bible and refers to the apocalyptic vision of the end of days in the Book of Daniel

18. Rovagnati, *Umwege auf dem Wege zu mir Selbst*, 110.

19. Macris, "Zweig as Dramatist," 190; Warren, "Stefan Zweig's *Jeremias* in Context," 45–46.

20. Stefan Zweig, "Das neue Pathos," 1.

21. Warren, "Stefan Zweig's *Jeremias* in Context," 48.

22. Zweig likely knew of these techniques from his friendship with Alban Berg, Schoenberg's student and the Italian composer, Ferrucio Busoni, whose works Zweig greatly admired.

23. Zweig, "Das neue Pathos," 5.

24. Zweig et al., *Briefe 1914–1919*, 153.

25. Zweig et al., 153.

26. Zweig et al., 139.

27. An example can be found in Hananiah's references to the yoke of captivity and the trumpets of war. Hananiah reads them as a call to arms: "So werfet ab das Joch, reißt euch los von den Ketten, die Posaune laßt schallen und erklirren das tödliche Erz; Gott hat euch wach geschrien, so kämpfet für ihn." Hananiah evokes these images as a call to war, in contrast to Jeremiah's visions of apocalyptic destruction. Zweig, *Jeremias*, 142.

28. Arens, *Stefan Zweig: Im Zeugnis seiner Freunde*, 190.

29. Rolland and Zweig, *Briefwechsel 1910–1940*, vol. 1, 47.

30. Zweig et al., *Briefe, 1914–1919*, 130.

31. R. HaCohen, *Music Libel against the Jews*, 90.

32. R. HaCohen, 80.

33. Zweig, *Jeremias*, 264. [Zweig, *Jeremiah*, 249].

34. Fischer, "*Das Judentum in der Musik*," 151. Indeed, an article in the *New York Post*, following a performance in 1939, described the mob scenes as "full of unco-ordinated voices that never seemed to convey anything beyond a confused babble, and a great deal of male mumbling through long beards and shrill female yipping." Waldorf, "Stefan Zweig's *Jeremias*," 3. The references to long beards and animal-like sounds resonate with antisemitic stereotypes of Jewish noise in Zweig's time.

35. Zweig and Beck, *Tagebücher*, 152.

36. Zweig, *Jeremias*, 270 [Zweig, *Jeremiah*, 257].

37. Paul and Paul's translation, in its attempt to retain meter and rhyme scheme, sacrifices the clear parallel to the libretto of St. Matthew's Passion. In German, both texts emphasize the image of Christ's arms stretched out on the cross to clasp (*umfangen*) or grasp (*fassen*) his people in loving embrace.

38. Zweig, *Jeremias*, 269.

39. R. HaCohen, *Music Libel against the Jews*, 90.

40. Smither, *History of the Oratorio*, vol. 4, 174.

41. See Ruth HaCohen on Mendelssohn's resistance to casting Elijah as a Christ figure. R. HaCohen, *Music Libel against the Jews*, 223.

42. In a letter to the Insel-Verlag in Leipzig from August 2, 1915, shortly after he began writing *Jeremias*, Zweig requested a copy of the Psalms in the Großherzog Wilhelm Ernst-Ausgabe, translated by Martin Luther. Zweig et al., *Briefe 1914–1919*, 80, 384.

43. Zweig, *Jeremias*, 272.

44. Zweig, *Jeremias*, 285 [Zweig, *Jeremiah*, 282].

45. R. HaCohen, *Music Libel against the Jews*, 88, 96.

46. Smither identifies oratorios by Bach and Mendelssohn as including all three elements, narrative, reflective, and dialogic. Smither, *History of the Oratorio*, vol. 4, 5.

47. Zweig, "Das neue Pathos," 4.

48. Zweig, *Jeremias*, 311.

49. Zweig, 312.

50. Apel, *Harvard Dictionary of Music*, 42. Antiphony is generally performed by two choirs, alternating back and forth.

51. Zweig, *Jeremias*, 312.

52. Zweig, 313.

53. Zweig, *Jeremias*, 315. [Zweig, *Jeremiah*, 323].

54. Zweig, *Jeremias*, 317.

55. This episode is shortened considerably in the English translation. Paul and Paul remove the individual figures that approach Jeremiah so that the questions are posed by "The People."

56. Zweig, *Jeremias*, 324 [Zweig, *Jeremiah*, 332].

57. Zweig, *Jeremias*, 327 [Translation C. K.].

58. Rolland and Zweig, *Briefwechsel 1910–1940*, vol. 1, 114.

59. Zweig et al., *Briefe 1914–1919*, 143.

60. Zweig et al., 153, 164.

61. See Zweig's letter to Rolland, October 8, 1919, in which he reports that the theaters in Vienna had to close at nine o'clock. Zweig et al., 609.

62. Dehmel claimed that if Zweig tried to perform *Jeremias* in full it would last five hours, and no audience would bear it. Zweig et al., 442.

63. See Zweig, "An die Direktion des Deutschen Volkstheaters."

64. Zifferer, "Jeremias," 3.

65. Botstein, "Illusion of the Jewish European," 90.

# EPILOGUE

*Jewish Difference and the Arts in Vienna* has traced how compassionate art provided a means to challenge and reimage religious and cultural difference in a time of great political, economic, and social instability. Siegfried Lipiner, Gustav Mahler, Arnold Schoenberg, Richard Beer-Hofmann, and Stefan Zweig engaged with the construction of Jewish difference in their time by giving voice to the German-Jewish subject, whose radical affirmations of alterity, difference, and free agency also shaped their visions of inclusive community. To capture this dynamic, they turned to the musical languages of the lied and the leitmotif, polyphony, and antiphony and to the dramatic forms of the oratorio and song-symphony, the festival play, and subjective theater. Challenging antisemitic stereotypes of the Jew as materialistic, unmusical, and devoted to the supposed "dead letter" of the Mosaic Law, they recast the Jewish subject as a compassionate Übermensch, capable of feeling with the suffering of others and of sublimating this suffering into an artistic energy. In so doing, their musical and dramatic works shift the Jewish subject from the periphery to the center. No longer the outsiders looking in, these figures play a critical role in the creation of compassionate community that is not just "contributory" but rather, as Steven Aschheim claims, "co-constitutative."[1] Reflecting their authors' and composers' unique and complex experiences as German-Jews, these works imagined utopian reconciliations of Jewish and German-Christian culture at a time when such a symbiosis appeared no longer tenable.

Although the authors and composers fell short of achieving the larger social impacts that they envisioned in their own time, their works live on in unexpected ways. Lipiner died in 1911, leaving many of his works unfinished. The executor of his literary estate, the philosopher Paul Natorp, tried with little success to secure the poet's legacy, publishing *Adam* and two other dramas, *Hippolytos* and *Der neue Don Juan* in 1913.[2] The loss of Lipiner's

*Nachlass* when his family was forced to flee Austria in the 1930s doomed the remaining fragments of his *Christus* project to obscurity. Mahler's Second and Third Symphonies have, in contrast, been performed to popular acclaim. Yet, by shedding new light on the correspondence between their works, this book reveals the fascinating and largely unacknowledged role that Lipiner played in shaping Mahler's worldview. Mahler's musical gifts may have outshined Lipiner's dramatic talents, but it is impossible to untangle the complex network of references in the programs of his symphonies without turning to the poet whom he admired to the end of his life and whose language and aesthetic vision of compassion shaped so many of Mahler's most enduring works.

The three artists in this study who lived beyond World War I, Schoenberg, Beer-Hofmann, and Zweig, encountered a shifting political landscape. With the dissolution of the Habsburg Empire and the establishment of the First Republic, the desire to create a coherent national identity gave new urgency to the project of defining the "Austrian" over and against "the Jew." Music and theater continued to play a critical role in shaping this agenda; however, it was not these utopian visions of Jewish-Christian synthesis through compassion that took center stage but rather a new ideology that took as its primary focus the symbolism and ritual of Catholicism, elevating it to a national ideal.

The clearest articulation of this Catholic national vision was the founding of the Salzburg Festival in 1920. Like the works examined in this book, the festival developed in response to the paradigm of festival theater established in Wagner's Bayreuth and was largely shaped by two artists of Jewish heritage, Hugo von Hofmannsthal and Max Reinhardt. As Steinberg notes, Hofmannsthal and Reinhardt employed the Wagnerian total art paradigm to create Austria's own ideology of totality, a "dialectic of power, identity and coherence that united nation, monarch and God."[3] This mobilization of Catholicism's pomp and circumstance and its "spiritual, dramatic gestures toward redemption" were intended to create continuity between the empire and the new republic.[4] In its aspirations toward community, the Salzburg festival fulfilled in many ways the spiritual longings identified by Lipiner and Mahler decades earlier and by Schoenberg, Beer-Hofmann, and Zweig at the same time. However, while the works examined in this study envisioned the compassionate inclusion of Jewish voices, the Salzburg Festival's unifying ideology and cultural coding for its performances largely repressed the Jewish element in the service of its Catholic-Baroque ideal.

Still, the Salzburg Festival echoes the longing to create a communal theater experience already imagined decades earlier, suggesting that these works of music and biblical theater form an important, until now overlooked, prehistory to the festival, one that, grounded in its idiosyncratic vision of heterogeneity, would fade with the fall of the empire.

The histories of Schoenberg's *Die Jakobsleiter*, Beer-Hofmann's *David* tetralogy, and Zweig's *Jeremias* in the interwar period reveal the challenges of creating a Jewish-Christian total art synthesis under these circumstances. Schoenberg sought in vain in the final years of his life in the United States to secure funding for the completion of *Die Jakobsleiter*. In the end, it remained a fragment. However, this oratorio did form the foundation for his two major dramatic works of the interwar period, the *Der biblische Weg* and the opera *Moses und Aron*, both of which reflect Schoenberg's move toward a more explicit Jewish cultural and religious framework. In *Der biblische Weg*, Schoenberg attempted once again to create a kind of festival theater, this time for a Zionist audience but still following the modes of compassionate theater he had first explored with *Die Jakobsleiter*.[5] *Moses und Aron*, like *Die Jakobsleiter*, remained unfinished but is still read today by many as the apotheosis of Schoenberg's aesthetic theology. The search for a musical language to articulate the paradoxes of the word and its representation and what he believed to be the greatest contribution of the Jewish faith, fidelity to the one, true God, remain the composer's lasting legacy.

Although Beer-Hofmann was unable to complete the *David* tetralogy, *Jaákobs Traum* continued to be performed throughout the interwar period to widespread acclaim.[6] The play was performed twenty-nine times in three separate runs between 1919 and 1925 at Vienna's Burgtheater, making it one of the most popular postwar productions.[7] From the mid-1920s onward, *Jaákobs Traum* became increasingly performed and interpreted as a Jewish nationalist drama. In 1926, it was staged by Habima, the renowned Russian-based Hebrew theater troupe. Attending one of the Habima performances of *Jaákobs Traum*, Beer-Hofmann responded with admiration that the work had indeed taken on a life of its own:

> Bei dieser Aufführung der Habima habe ich etwas Sonderbares erlebt . . . Ich selbst hatte das merkwürdige Gefühl, etwas bei lebendigem Leib zu erleben, was sonst nur Schicksal von Toten ist: Daß ein Werk sich loslöst, sein eigenes Leben lebt, seinen eigenen Weg geht, unbekümmert um den, der es schuf.

> [At this performance, I experienced something quite extraordinary . . . I myself had the strange feeling of experiencing live what otherwise is the fate of the dead: that a work detaches itself, lives its own life, goes its own way, regardless of he who created it.][8]

Interestingly, it was the music of the third act that captured the poet's attention most acutely, engendering the compassionate response that he had sought to create through the use of musical leitmotifs in his original text. Beer-Hofmann described the experience of viewing the play as an uncanny experience of foreignness and familiarity: "Was da sonderbar fremdartig von obern erklang, in einer Sprache, die ich nicht verstand, aber in einer Musik, die mir irgendwie von alther vertraut erschien—war doch in seiner Gesamtheit mir und meinem Blut verwandt" (What rang forth from above, strangely foreign in a language that I did not understand, but in a music that appeared somehow long familiar—was somehow in its totality related to me and my blood).[9] For Beer-Hofmann, the musical rendition of his own play in the Hebrew language gave him the opportunity to discover a new aspect of his Jewish identity. The recognition that Beer-Hofmann describes, of experiencing through music something innately part of him for the first time, reflects the precepts of compassionate art that served as a driving force behind the works examined in this study. Music, in its abstract language that yet still speaks "directly to the human heart," inspires a compassionate response that transcends the boundaries of difference, offering new possibilities for community and mutual understanding.

Likewise, Zweig's *Jeremias* was also widely adapted in his time, achieving powerful resonance in Jewish communities from Tel Aviv to Berlin to New York. In 1934, the Hebrew Ohel Ensemble performed *Jeremias* in Israel. That same year, it was performed for another Jewish audience; however, the context was quite different. The performers were the Jewish Kulturbund, a cultural organization founded in 1933 and sanctioned by the National Socialist government as a part of their tactics to isolate and expunge "Jewish" influence from German art and its audience.[10] As in previous performances, the text was subjected to multiple cuts; however, these were primarily politically motivated. They included the majority of the final scene, the references in the play that compared Jeremiah to Christ, and those scenes believed to encourage "Jewish communal resistance."[11] Yet, even in its truncated form, the powerful effect of the final scene, created through the communal choir, was still captured in reviews of the performance, which described it as "oratoriorianhaft" (oratorio-like) and referred to the work as a "dramatische Symphonie" (dramatic symphony).[12] The premiere of *Jeremias* in New York five years later provides further evidence of the refashioning of this work for a German-Jewish community in exile, featuring incidental music by Chemjo Vinaver (1895–1973), whose *Anthology of Jewish Music*, shaped the revival of Jewish music and folk culture in the second half of the twentieth century. That *Jaákobs Traum* and *Jeremias* adapted so easily to these new contexts provides evidence that the language of suffering and compassion in these works continued to resonate with the generation of the interwar period seeking to shape new communities in the face of a new wave of exile and oppression.

The artists and composers whose works are examined in this study sought both to acknowledge the unique contributions of the Jewish community and its noble history and traditions and to create compassionate art that would speak to all humanity through music, the language that would transgress the boundaries of national, ethnic, religious, and cultural difference. In her work on compassion, Martha Nussbaum has claimed that the emotive response to another's suffering can "provide an essential bridge to justice."[13] It reminds us of the enduring value of other people's experiences, which we see as intimately related to our own. Most important, however, it engages the imagination and creativity of the soul, fulfilling a deep human need to make sense of the world and to share this experience with others in community. Without a "compassionate training of the imagination," Nussbaum writes, we will not become a compassionate nation.[14] Today, as the world continues to be polarized by discourses of difference, these works remain testaments to the spaces that art can provide to transcend these divides, offering hope and comfort in our shared humanity.

## Notes

1. Aschheim, *In Times of Crisis*, 89.

2. *Hippolytos*, a work deeply indebted to Goethe's *Faust*, takes up the problem of compassionate love again, this time as an opposite pole to Eros, or erotic love. This work had a profound influence on Mahler's Eighth Symphony. See Kita, "Myth, Metaphysics and Cosmic Drama."

3. Steinberg, *Meaning of the Salzburg Festival*, 7.

4. Silverman, *Becoming Austrians*, 142.

5. Schoenberg, "Letter to Franz Werfel"; Schoenberg, "Letter to Max Reinhardt."

6. See Kita, "Beer-Hofmann's *Historie von König David*."

7. Pyrah, *Burgtheater and Austrian Identity*, 4, 93.

8. Nussenblatt, "Beer-Hofmann über die Habima."
9. Nussenblatt, "Beer-Hofmann über die Habima." 91.
10. Rovit, *Jewish Kulturbund Theatre*, 56.
11. Rovit, *Jewish Kulturbund Theatre*, 59.
12. Lachmanski, "Die künstlerische Leistung," 14.
13. Nussbaum, "Compassion," 37.
14. Nussbaum, "Compassion," 58.

# BIBLIOGRAPHY


Abbate, Carolyn. *Unsung Voices: Opera and Musical Narrative in the Nineteenth Century.* Princeton, NJ: Princeton University Press, 1991.

Adorno, Theodor W. *Mahler: A Musical Physiognomy.* Chicago, IL: University of Chicago Press, 1992.

———. *Philosophy of New Music.* Translated by Robert Hullot-Kentro. Minneapolis: University of Minnesota Press, 2006.

Apel, Willi. *Harvard Dictionary of Music.* Cambridge, MA: Belknap Press of Harvard University Press, 1969.

Arens, Hanns. *Stefan Zweig: Im Zeugnis seiner Freunde.* Munich: Langen Müller, 1968.

Arnim, L. Achim von, and Clemens Brentano. *Des Knaben Wunderhorn: Alte deutsche Lieder.* [1805, 1808]. Munich: Winkler, 1957.

Aschheim, Steven E. *In Times of Crisis Essays on European Culture, Germans, and Jews.* Madison: University of Wisconsin Press, 2001.

Bach, D. F. "Das Drama der Juden." *Volksstimmen.* April 26, 1919. MS Ger 131 Folder 76. Houghton Library, Harvard University.

Bahr, Hermann. *Glossen zum Wiener Theater (1903–1906).* Berlin: S. Fischer, 1907.

Bailey, Walter B. *Programmatic Elements in the Works of Schoenberg.* Ann Arbor, MI: UMI Research Press, 1984.

Bamford, Rebecca. "The Virtue of Shame: Defending Nietzsche's Critique of Mitleid." In *Nietzsche and Ethics,* edited by Gudrun von Tevenar, 241–261. Oxford: Peter Lang, 2007.

Bauer-Lechner, Natalie, and Peter Franklin. *Recollections of Gustav Mahler.* Cambridge: Cambridge University Press, 1980.

Bauer-Lechner, Natalie, Herbert Killian, and Knud Martner. *Gustav Mahler in den Erinnerungen von Natalie Bauer-Lechner.* Hamburg: K. D. Wagner, 1984.

Bayerdörfer, Hans-Peter. "Jewish Self-Presentation and the 'Jewish Question' on the German Stage from 1900 to 1930." In *Jewish Theater: A Global View,* edited by Edna Nahshon, translated by Josephine Riley, 153–173. Leiden: Brill, 2009.

Beer-Hofmann, Richard. *Briefe: 1895–1945.* Edited by Alexander Košenina. Oldenburg: Igel, 1999.

———. *Der Graf von Charolais ein Trauerspiel und andere dramatische Entwürfe.* Paderborn: Igel, 1994.

———. *Der Tod Georgs.* Edited by Alo Allkemper. Paderborn: Igel, 1994.

———. *Die Historie von König David und andere dramatische Entwürfe.* Edited by Norbert Otto Eke. Paderborn: Igel, 1996.

———. "Jaakobs Traum: Beleuchtung, Musik, Dekorierungsentwürfe." MS Ger 131 Folder 70–71. Houghton Library, Harvard University.

———. "Jaákobs Traum: Skizzen, Entwürfe, 1915." MS Ger 131 Folder 68. Houghton Library, Harvard University.

——. *Jacob's Dream: A Prologue*. Edited by Solomon Liptzin. Translated by Ida Bension Wynn. Philadelphia, PA: Jewish Publication Society of America, 1946.

——. "Über szenische Angaben: Teil eines Briefes an Erich Kahler (Anlässlich der Junge David)." 1933. MS Ger 183. Houghton Library, Harvard University.

"Beer-Hofmann: Jaákobs Traum." *Hamburger Fremdenblatt*, November 7, 1919.

"Beer-Hofmanns 'Jaákobs Traum' im Burgtheater." *Frankfurter Zeitung*, April 10, 1919. MS Ger 131 Folder 76. Houghton Library, Harvard University.

Beller, Steven. *Vienna and the Jews, 1867–1938: A Cultural History*. Cambridge: Cambridge University Press, 1989.

Beniston, Judith. *Welttheater: Hofmannsthal, Richard von Kralik, and the Revival of Catholic Drama in Austria: 1890–1934*. Texts and Dissertations/Modern Humanities Research Association 46. Leeds: Maney, 1998.

Berlin, Jeffrey B. "Response and Impression: Encountering Concepts of Judaism and Zionism in the Unpublished Correspondence between Martin Buber and Stefan Zweig (1902–1931)." *Germanisch-Romanische Monatsschrift* 30, no. 3 (2000): 333–360.

Berry, Mark. *After Wagner: Histories of Modernist Music Drama from Parsifal to Nono*. Woodbridge, Suffolk, UK: Boydell, 2014.

——. "Arnold Schoenberg's 'Biblical Way': From 'Die Jakobsleiter' to 'Moses und Aron.'" *Music and Letters* 89, no. 1 (February 2008): 84–108.

Bhatt, Chetan. "Primordial Being: Enlightenment and the Subject of Postcolonial Theory." In *Philosophies of Race and Ethnicity*, edited by Peter Osborne and Stella Sandford, 40–62. London: Continuum, 2002.

Bial, Henry. *Playing God: The Bible on the Broadway Stage*. Ann Arbor: University of Michigan Press, 2015.

Boehlich, Walter. *Sigmund Freud: Jugendbriefe an Eduard Silberstein 1871–1881*. Frankfurt am Main: S. Fischer, 1989.

Borchmeyer, Dieter. *Richard Beer-Hofmann: "zwischen Ästhetizismus und Judentum."* Paderborn: Igel, 1996.

——. *Richard Wagner: Theory and Theatre*. Oxford: Clarendon, 1991.

Borchmeyer, Dieter, Susanne Strasser-Vill, and Ami Maayani, eds. *Richard Wagner und die Juden*. Stuttgart: Metzler, 2000.

Boss, Jack Forrest. *Schoenberg's Twelve-Tone Music: Symmetry and the Musical Idea*. Cambridge: Cambridge University Press, 2014.

Botstein, Leon. "The German Jews and Wagner." In *Richard Wagner and His World*, edited by Thomas S. Grey, 151–197. Princeton, NJ: Princeton University Press, 2009.

——. *Judentum und Modernität: Essays zur Rolle der Juden in der deutschen und österreichischen Kultur, 1848 bis 1938*. Vienna: Böhlau, 1991.

——. "Stefan Zweig and the Illusion of the Jewish European." In *Stefan Zweig: The World of Yesterday's Humanist Today*, edited by Marion Sonnenfeld, 82–110. Albany: State University of New York Press, 1983.

Brener, Milton E. *Richard Wagner and the Jews*. Jefferson, NC: McFarland, 2006.

Brodbeck, David Lee. *Defining Deutschtum: Political Ideology, German Identity, and Music-Critical Discourse in Liberal Vienna*. New Cultural History of Music. New York: Oxford University Press, 2014.

Brown, Hilda Meldrum. *Leitmotiv and Drama: Wagner, Brecht, and the Limits of "Epic" Theatre*. Oxford: Clarendon, 1991.

Brown, Julie. "Schoenberg's Early Wagnerisms: Atonality and the Redemption of Ahasuerus." *Cambridge Opera Journal* 6, no. 1 (1994): 51–80.

Bungardt, Julia. "Die Bibliothek Arnold Schönbergs: mit einem kommentierten Katalog des nachgelassenen Bestandes sowie einer Edition seiner Glossen in den Büchern." PhD diss., Universität für Musik und darstellende Kunst Wien, 2014.

Bunzl, Matti. "The Poetics of Politics and the Politics of Poetics: Richard Beer-Hofmann and Theodor Herzl Reconsidered." *German Quarterly* 69, no. 3 (1996): 277–304.

Burgess, Anthony. "Brentano as Philosopher of Religion." *International Journal of the Philosophy of Religion* 5, no. 2 (1974): 79–90.

Carnegy, Patrick. *Wagner and the Art of the Theatre.* New Haven: Yale University Press, 2006.

Cartwright, David E. *Historical Dictionary of Schopenhauer's Philosophy.* Lanham, MD: Scarecrow, 2005.

———. *Schopenhauer: A Biography.* Cambridge: Cambridge University Press, 2010.

Christensen, Jean. "Arnold Schoenberg's Oratorio *Die Jakobsleiter.*" 2 vols. PhD diss., University of California, Los Angeles, 1979.

Cohen, Hermann. *Die Nächstenliebe im Talmud; ein Gutachten dem Königlichen Landgerichte zu Marburg.* Marburg: R.G. Elwert'sche Verlagsbuchhandlung, 1888. The Internet Archive. https://archive.org/details/dienchstenlieboocohe/page/n3. Accessed October 12, 2018.

———. *Deutschtum und Judentum, mit grundlegenden Betrachtungen über Staat und Internationalismus.* Gießen: Verlag von Arthur Töpelmann, 1915.

Covach, John R. "The Sources of Schoenberg's Aesthetic Theology." *19th Century Music* 19, no. 3 (1996): 252–262.

Dahlhaus, Carl. *Schoenberg and the New Music: Essays.* Cambridge: Cambridge University Press, 1987.

Davies, Oliver. *A Theology of Compassion: Metaphysics of Difference and the Renewal of Tradition.* London: SCM Press, 2001.

Eke, Norbert Otto. "Rettung des Sinns: Jaákobs Traum und das Projekt einer Geschichtestheodizee." In *Richard Beer-Hofmann (1866–1945): Studien zu seinem Werk*, edited by Norbert Otto Eke and Günter Helmes, 128–155. Würzburg: Königshausen and Neumann, 1993.

Elstun, Esther. *Richard Beer-Hofmann, His Life and Work.* University Park: Pennsylvania State University Press, 1983.

———. "Richard Beer-Hofmann: The Poet as Exculpator Dei." In *Protest-Form-Tradition: Essays on German Exile Literature*, edited by Joseph B. Strelka, Robert Bell, and Eugene Dobsen, 123–132. Tuscaloosa: University of Alabama Press, 1979.

Fischer, Jens Malte. *Gustav Mahler—Der fremde Vertraute: Biographie.* Vienna: P. Zsolnay, 2003.

———. *Richard Wagners "Das Judentum in der Musik": eine kritische Dokumentation als Beitrag zur Geschichte des Antisemitismus.* Originalausg., 1. Aufl.. Insel Taschenbuch; 2617. Frankfurt am Main: Insel, 2000.

Floros, Constantin. *Gustav Mahler—1: Die geistige Welt Gustav Mahlers in systematischer Darstellung.* 2nd ed. Wiesbaden: Breitkopf and Härtel, 1987.

———. "Studien zur Parsifal-Rezeiption." *Musik-Konzepte* 25, *Richard Wagner: Parsifal* (1982): 14–57.

Föllmi, Beat. "Schönberg als Theosoph. Anmerkungen zu einer wenig beachteten Beziehung." *International Review of Aesthetics and the Sociology of Music* 30, no. 1 (1999): 55–63.

Franklin, Peter. *Mahler, Symphony No. 3.* Cambridge: Cambridge University Press, 1991.

Frisch, Walter. "Brahms, Developing Variation, and the Schoenberg Critical Tradition." *19th-Century Music* 5, no. 3 (1982): 215–232.

Gelber, Mark H. "Interfaces between Young Vienna and the Young Jewish Poetic Movement. Richard Beer-Hofmann and Stefan Zweig." In *Jüdische Aspekte Jung-Wiens im Kultukontext des Fin de Siecle*, edited by Sarah Fraiman-Morris, 61–74. Tübingen: M. Niemeyer, 2005.

———. *Stefan Zweig: Judentum und Zionismus*. Schriften des Centrums für Jüdische Studien Bd. 24. Innsbruck: Studien, 2014.

Geller, Jay. *On Freud's Jewish Body: Mitigating Circumstances*. New York: Fordham University Press, 2007.

Gillman, Abigail. *Viennese Jewish Modernism: Freud, Hofmannsthal, Beer-Hofmann, and Schnitzler*. University Park: Pennsylvania State University Press, 2009.

Gilman, Sander. "Are Jews Musical? Historical Notes on the Question of Jewish Musical Modernism and Nationalism." *Modern Judaism* 28, no. 3 (2008): 239–256.

Glück, Franz. "Briefe von Arnold Schönberg an Adolf Loos." *Österreichische Musikzeitschrift* 16, no. 1 (January 1961): 8–20.

Goehr, Lydia. "Adorno, Schoenberg and the Prinzipien—in Thirteen Steps." *Journal of the American Musicological Society* 56, no. 3 (2003): 595–636.

Golomb, Jacob. "Nietzsche and the Marginal Jews." In *Nietzsche and Jewish Culture*, edited by Jacob Golomb, 158–192. London: Routledge, 1997.

Gramit, David. "The Circulation of the Lied: The Double Life of an Artwork and a Commodity." In *The Cambridge Companion to the Lied*, edited by James Parsons, 301–314. Cambridge: Cambridge University Press, 2004.

H. W. "Aus dem Souffleurkasten." *Wiener Sonn- und Montags-Zeitung*. December 6, 1897, 49th ed.

Hacohen, Malachi Haim. "The Culture of Viennese Science and the Riddle of Austrian Liberalism." *Modern Intellectual History* 6, no. 2 (2009): 369–396.

HaCohen, Ruth. *The Music Libel against the Jews*. New Haven, CT: Yale University Press, 2011.

Hartungen, Helmut von. "Der Dichter Siegfried Lipiner (1856–1911)." PhD diss., University of Munich, 1932.

Heer, Carina. *Gattungsdesign in der Wiener Moderne: Traditionsverhalten in Dramen Arthur Schnitzlers und Hugo von Hofmannsthals; mit Vergleichsanalysen zu Hermann Bahr, Felix Salten und Richard Beer-Hofmann*. Munich: Utz, 2014.

Hefling, Stephen E. "Mahler's 'Todtenfeier' and the Problem of Program Music." *19th-Century Music* 12, no. 1 (1988): 27–53.

———. "Siegfried Lipiner's 'Über Die Elemente einer Erneuerung religiöser Ideen in der Gegenwart.'" In *Mahler im Kontext / Contextualizing Mahler*, edited by Morten Solvik and Erich Wolfgang Partsch, 115–152. Vienna: Böhlau, 2011.

Hirschfeld, Robert. "Merlin." *Allgemeine Theater-Chronik*, no. 47 (November 20, 1886): 1–2.

Hoedl, Klaus. "The Blurring of Distinction: Performance and Jewish Identities in Late Nineteenth Century Vienna." *European Journal of Jewish Studies* 3, no. 2 (2009): 229–249.

Hoffmann, Daniel. "Die Gewißheit des Glaubens: Richard Beer-Hofmann and Moritz Heimanns Jüdische Dramen." In *Richard Beer-Hofmann: "Zwischen Aesthetizismus und Judentum,"* edited by Dieter Borchmeyer, 101–118. Paderborn: Igel Wissenschaft, 1996.

Hofmannsthal, Hugo, and Richard Beer-Hofmann. *Briefwechsel*. Frankfurt am Main: S. Fischer, 1972.

Hollingdale, R. J. *Friedrich Nietzsche: Dithyrambs of Dionysus.* London: Anvil Press Poetry, 2001.

Holub, Robert C. *Nietzsche's Jewish Problem: Between Anti-Semitism and Anti-Judaism.* Princeton, NJ: Princeton University Press, 2016.

Husain, Martha. *Ontology and the Art of Tragedy: An Approach to Aristotle's Poetics.* Albany: State University of New York Press, 2002.

Johnson, Julian. "Mahler and the Idea of Nature." In *Perspectives on Gustav Mahler*, edited by Jeremy Barham, 23–36. Aldershot: Ashgate, 2005.

Kalbeck, Max. "Merlin von Karl Goldmark." *Die Presse* 39, no. 321 (November 21, 1886): 1–2.

Kandinsky, Wassily, Arnold Schönberg, and Jelena Hahl-Koch. *Der Briefwechsel.* Stuttgart: Hatje, 1993.

Karnes, Kevin. *A Kingdom Not of This World: Wagner, the Arts, and Utopian Visions in Fin-de-Siècle Vienna.* New York: Oxford University Press, 2013.

Kita, Caroline A. "Between Instinct and the Law: Dionysian Dissonance and Polyphonic Poetics in Arnold Schoenberg's Totentanz der Prinzipien." *Journal of the Arnold Schoenberg Center*, 2016.

———. "Jacob Struggling with the Angel: Siegfried Lipiner, Gustav Mahler and the Search for Aesthetic-Religious Redemption in Fin-de-siècle Vienna." PhD diss., Duke University, 2011.

———. "Myth, Metaphysics and Cosmic Drama: The Legacy of Faust in Lipiner's Hippolytos and Mahler's Eighth Symphony." *Monatshefte* 105, no. 4 (2014): 543–564.

———. "The Revolutionary, the Artist, and the Heroic Martyr: The Evolution of Sacrifice from Mickiewicz's Dziady to Gustav Mahler's Second Symphony." In *Making Sacrifices—Opfer Bringen Visions of Sacrifice in European and American Cultures*, edited by Nicholas Brooks and Gregor Thuswaldner, 33–50. Symphilologus 1. Vienna: New Academic Press, 2016.

———. "Richard Beer-Hofmann's *Die Historie von König David*: Jewish Biblical Drama and the Limits of Epic Theater." *German Quarterly* 89, no. 2 (2016): 133–149.

Kleinewefers, Antje. *Das Problem der Erwählung bei Richard Beer-Hofmann.* New York: Olms, 1972.

Klinenberger, Ludwig. "Wiener Theater." *Breslauer Zeitung*, April 16, 1919. MS Ger 131 Folder 76. Houghton Library, Harvard University.

Knapp, Raymond. *Symphonic Metamorphoses: Subjectivity and Alienation in Mahler's Re-Cycled Songs.* Middletown, CT: Wesleyan University Press, 2003.

Knittel, Kay M. *Seeing Mahler: Music and the Language of Antisemitism in Fin-de-Siècle Vienna.* Burlington, VT: Ashgate, 2010.

Korngold, Julius. "Musik: Außerordentliches Gesellschaftskonzert. Mahlers Dritte Symphonie." *Neue Freie Presse*, December 17, 1904, 1–3.

Koss, Juliet. *Modernism after Wagner.* Minneapolis: University of Minnesota Press, 2010.

Kralik, Richard. *Tage und Werke: Lebenserinnerungen.* Vienna: Vogelsang, 1922.

Kramer, Lawrence. *Classical Music and Postmodern Knowledge.* Berkeley: University of California Press, 1995.

Lackminski, Hans. "Die künstlerische Leistung." *C. V. Zeitung*, October 11, 1934, 14.

La Grange, Henry-Louis de. *Gustav Mahler—Vienna: Triumph and Disillusion (1904–1907).* Oxford: Oxford University Press, 1999.

———. *Gustav Mahler—Vienna: The Years of Challenge (1897–1904).* Oxford: Oxford University Press, 1995.

Large, David Clay, William Weber, and Anne Dzamba Sessa. *Wagnerism in European Culture and Politics.* Ithaca, NY: Cornell University Press, 1984.

Lebrecht, Norman. *Mahler Remembered.* New York: Norton, 1988.

Le Rider, Jacques. *Modernity and Crises of Identity: Culture and Society in Fin-de-Siècle Vienna.* New York: Continuum, 1993.

Lessem, Alan Philip. *Music and Text in the Works of Arnold Schoenberg: The Critical Years, 1908–1922.* Ann Arbor, MI: UMI Research Press, 1979.

Lessing, Gotthold Ephraim. "From the *Hamburg Dramaturgy.*" In *Essays on German Theater,* edited by Martin Esslin and Margaret Herzfeld-Sander, 3–19. New York: Continuum, 1985.

———. *Hamburgische Dramaturgie.* Leipzig: Bibliographisches Institut, 1902.

Librett, Jeffrey S. *Orientalism and the Figure of the Jew.* New York: Fordham, 2014.

Lipiner, Siegfried. *Adam, Ein Vorspiel; Hippolytos, Eine Tragödie.* Stuttgart: W. Spemann, 1913.

———. *Der entfesselte Prometheus: Eine Dichtung in fünf Gesänge.* Leipzig: Breitkopf und Härtel, 1876.

———. "Der Sommer." *Deutsche Zeitung,* July 17, 1881, 1–2.

———. "Einiges über Verbrechen und Strafe." *Deutsche Zeitung,* July 24, 1881, 1–2.

———. Letter to Moritz Necker. August 26, 1885. H.I.N. 142540. Wienbibliothek im Rathaus. Handschriftensammlung. Vienna.

———. "On the Elements of a Renewal of Religious Ideas in the Present." In *Mahler im Kontext / Contextualizing Mahler,* edited by Morten Solvik and Erich Wolfgang Partsch, 117–151. Translated by Stephen E. Hefling. Vienna: Böhlau, 2011.

———. *Über die Elemente einer Erneuerung religiöser Ideen in der Gegenwart.* Vienna: Leseverein des deutschen Studenten Wiens, 1878.

———. "Weihnachten." *Deutsche Zeitung.* December 19, 1880, 1–2.

Luft, David S. "Schopenhauer, Austria, and the Generation of 1905." *Central European History* 16, no. 1 (1983): 53–75.

Lutz, Simon. "Du aber halte meinen Bund: Die Bibel als Paradigma jüdischer Identität in Beer-Hofmanns Jaákobs Traum." In *Judenrollen: Darstellungsformen im Europäischen Theater von der Restauration bis zur Zwischenkriegszeit,* edited by Hans-Peter Bayerdorfer and Jens Malte Fischer, 221–235. Tübingen: Max Niemeyer, 2008.

Mack, Michael. *German Idealism and the Jew: The Inner Anti-Semitism of Philosophy and German Jewish Responses.* Chicago, IL: University of Chicago Press, 2003.

Macris, Peter J. "Zweig as Dramatist." In *Stefan Zweig: The World of Yesterday's Humanist Today,* edited by Marion Sonnenfeld, 186–194. Albany: State University of New York Press, 1983.

Magee, Bryan. *The Tristan Chord: Wagner and Philosophy.* New York: Metropolitan Books, 2000.

Mahler, Alma. *Erinnerungen an Gustav Mahler.* Edited by Donald Mitchell. Berlin: Propyläen, 1971.

———. *Gustav Mahler: Memories and Letters.* Translated by Basil Creighton. London: John Murray, 1968.

Mahler, Gustav. *Gustav Mahler: Unbekannte Briefe.* Edited by Herta Blaukopf and Kurt Blaukopf. Vienna: P. Zsolnay, 1983.

———. *Symphonies Nos. 1 and 2 in Full Score.* Mineola, NY: Dover Publications, 1987.

———. *Symphony No. 3 in D Minor for Alto Solo, Choirs and Orchestra*. Mineola, NY: Dover Publications, 2002.

Mahler, Gustav, and Herta Blaukopf. *Gustav Mahler Briefe*. Vienna: P. Zsolnay, 1996.

Mahler, Gustav, Alma Mahler, and Knud Martner. *Selected Letters of Gustav Mahler*. New York: Farrar, Straus, Giroux, 1979.

Maier, Charles S. "Mahler's Theater: The Performative and the Political in Central Europe, 1890–1910." In *Mahler and His World*, edited by Karen Painter, 55–86. Princeton, NJ: Princeton University Press, 2002.

Malkin, Jeanette R. "Transforming in Public: Jewish Actors on the German Expressionist Stage." In *Jews and the Making of German Theater*, edited by Jeanette R. Malkin and Freddie Rokem, 151–173. Iowa City: University of Iowa Press, 2010.

Marshalk, Max. "Gustav Mahler: Eine Studie von Max Marshalk," *Die redenden Künste*. December 19, 1896, 13th ed.

Mattes, Arnulf Christian. "Arnold Schoenberg's Death Dance of the Principles and the Transformation of Colours in His Atonal Music." *Studia Musicological Norvegica*, no. 36 (2010): 122–132.

Mayer, Anton. *Richard Beer-Hofmann und das Wien des fin de siècle: Biographie und Werkauswahl*. Vienna: Edition Atelier, 1993.

McGrath, William J. *Dionysian Art and Populist Politics in Austria*. New Haven, CT Yale University Press, 1974.

Mendes-Flohr, Paul. "Zarathustra's Apostle: Martin Buber and the Jewish Renaissance." In *Nietzsche and Jewish Culture*, edited by Jacob Golomb, 233–241. London: Routledge, 1997.

Mickiewicz, Adam. *Todtenfeier (Dziady)*. Translated by Siegfried Lipiner. Leipzig: Breitkopf und Härtel, 1887.

Monelle, Raymond. *The Sense of Music: Semiotic Essays*. Princeton, NJ: Princeton University Press, 2010.

Natorp, Paul. "Lipiners *Adam* auf der Bühne." Nachlass Paul Natorp, Folder 2. University of Marburg.

———. "Siegfried Lipiners *Adam*." *Die Christliche Welt*, June 29, 1921.

———. "Vorwort zu 'Adam.'" Leipzig: Breitkopf and Härtel, 1913.

Neumann, Hans-Gerhard. *Richard Beer-Hofmann: Studien und Materialien zur "Historie von König David."* Munich: Fink, 1972.

Newlin, Dika. "Self-Revelation and the Law: Arnold Schoenberg in His Religious Works." *Yuval* 1 (1968): 204–220.

Niekerk, Carl. *Reading Mahler: German Culture and Jewish Identity in Fin-de-Siècle Vienna*. Rochester, NY: Camden House, 2010.

Nietzsche, Friedrich. "Brief an Erwin Rohde 28.8.1877." *Digitale Kritische Gesamtausgabe Werke und Briefe*. Edited by Paolo D'Iorio. *Nietzsche Source*. 2009. http://www.nietzschesource.org/#eKGWB/BVN-1877,656. Accessed October 12, 2018.

———. *Werke in drei Bänden*. 3 vols. Munich: Carl Hanser, 1960.

Nietzsche, Friedrich Wilhelm, Bernard Williams, Josefine Nauckhoff, and Adrian Del Caro. *The Gay Science: With a Prelude in German Rhymes and an Appendix of Songs*. Cambridge: Cambridge University Press, 2001.

Nono-Schoenberg, Nuria. *Arnold Schoenberg 1874–1951: Lebensgeschichte in Begegnungen*. Klagenfurt: Ritter, 1992.

Nussbaum, Martha. "Compassion: The Basic Social Emotion." *Social Philosophy and Policy* 13, no. 1 (1996): 27–58.

———. "The Transfigurations of Intoxication. Nietzsche, Schopenhauer and Dionysus. *Arion: A Journal of Humanities and the Classics* 1, no. 2 (1991): 75–111.

Nussenblatt, Tulo. "Richard Beer-Hofmann über die Habima." In *Quellenedition zur Geschichte des jüdischen Theaters in Wien*, edited by Brigitte Dalinger, 88–92. Tübingen: M. Niemeyer, 2003.

Pecker-Berio, Talia. "Mahler's Jewish Parable." In *Mahler and His World*, 87–110. Princeton, NJ: Princeton University Press, 2002.

Peters, Ulrike. *Richard Beer-Hofmann: zum jüdischen Selbstverständnis im Wiener Judentum um die Jahrhundertwende.* Frankfurt am Main: P. Lang, 1993.

Pfriemer, Ernst. "Bühnenmusik zu Jaákobs Traum," n.d. Österrischische Nationalbibliothek Musiksammlung.

Pyrah, Robert. *The Burgtheater and Austrian Identity: Theatre and Cultural Politics in Vienna, 1918–38.* London: Legenda, 2007.

Quinones, Ricardo J. *The Changes of Cain: Violence and the Lost Brother in Cain and Abel Literature.* Princeton, NJ: Princeton University Press, 1991.

Reitter, Paul. *On the Origins of Jewish Self-Hatred.* Princeton, NJ: Princeton University Press, 2012.

Renan, Ernest. *History of the People of Israel.* Translated by Joseph Henry Allen and Elizabeth Latimer, 3rd ed. London: Chapman and Hall, 1891.

Ringer, Alexander L. *Arnold Schoenberg—the Composer as Jew.* New York: Oxford University Press, 1990.

Roberts, David. *The Total Work of Art in European Modernism.* Ithaca, NY: Cornell University Press, 2011.

Robertson, Ritchie. *The German-Jewish Dialogue: An Anthology of Literary Texts, 1749–1993.* New York: Oxford University Press, 1999.

———. *The "Jewish Question" in German Literature, 1749–1939: Emancipation and Its Discontents.* New York: Oxford University Press, 1999.

Rolland, Romain, and Stefan Zweig. *Briefwechsel 1910–1940.* Edited by Waltraud Schwarze. 1 Aufl. Berlin: Rütten and Loening, 1987.

Roller, Alfred. "Bühnenreform?" *Der Merker* 1, no. 5 (1909): 193–197.

———. *Die Bildnisse von Gustav Mahler.* Leipzig: E. P. Tal, 1922.

Rovagnati, Gabriella. *Umwege auf dem Wege zu mir Selbst: Zu Leben und Werk Stefan Zweigs.* Abhandlungen zur Kunst-, Musik und Literaturwissenschaft, Bd. 400. Bonn: Bouvier, 1998.

Rovit, Rebecca. *The Jewish Kulturbund Theatre Company in Nazi Berlin.* Iowa City: University of Iowa Press, 2012.

Rozik, Eli. *Jewish Drama and Theatre from Rabbinical Intolerance to Secular Liberalism.* Eastbourne, UK: Sussex Academic Press, 2013.

Salten, Felix. "Beer-Hofmanns 'Historie von König David.'" *Berliner Tageblatt*, April 7, 1919. MS Ger 131 Folder 76. Houghton Library, Harvard University.

Schein, Ida. "Die Gedanken- Und Ideenwelt Siegfried Lipiners." PhD diss., University of Vienna, 1934.

Scherer, Stefan. "Richard Beer-Hofmann und das Judentum." In *Richard Beer-Hofmann (1866–1945): Studien zu seinem Werk*, edited by Norbert Otto Eke and Günter Helmes, 13–33. Würzburg: Königshausen and Neumann, 1993.

———. *Richard Beer-Hofmann und die Wiener Moderne*. Tübingen: M. Niemeyer, 1993.

Schoenberg, Arnold. *Die Jakobsleiter*. Original manuscript, January 18, 1915. T07.01 / DICH 7. Arnold Schoenberg Centre Wien.

———. "Die Jakobsleiter." Typoscript, July 6, 1917. T08.01 / DICH 14. Arnold Schoenberg Centre Wien.

———. *Die Jakobsleiter: Oratorium (Fragment) für Soli, Chöre und Orchester*. Edited by Ulrich Krämer. Wien: Universal Edition AG, 2018.

———. "Letter to Franz Werfel," 1933, T78.8. Arnold Schoenberg Centre Wien.

———. "Letter to Gustav Mahler," December 12, 1904. T60.08. Arnold Schoenberg Centre Wien.

———. "Letter to Max Reinhardt," May 24, 1933, T15.10. Arnold Schoenberg Centre Wien.

———. "Letter to Nicholas Slonimsky," June 3, 1937. L6S13. Arnold Schoenberg Centre Wien.

———. *Texte*. Vienna: Universal-Edition, 1926.

———. "Totentanz der Prinzipien," 1915. T07_06. Arnold Schoenberg Centre Wien.

Schoenberg, Arnold, Patricia Carpenter, and Severine Neff. *The Musical Idea and the Logic, Technique, and Art of Its Presentation*. New York: Columbia University Press, 1995.

Schoenberg, Arnold, Wassily Kandinsky, and Jelena Hahl-Fontaine. *Arnold Schoenberg, Wassily Kandinsky: Letters, Pictures, and Documents*. London: Faber and Faber, 1984.

Schoenberg, Arnold, and Erwin Stein. *Ausgewählte Briefe*. Mainz: B. Schott's Söhne, 1958.

Schoenberg, Arnold, and Leonard Stein. *Style and Idea: Selected Writings of Arnold Schoenberg*. New York: St. Martin's Press, 1975.

Schoenberg, Arnold, and Ivan Vojtek. *Stil und Gedanke*. Frankfurt am Main: S. Fischer, 1976.

Schopenhauer, Arthur. *Die Welt als Wille und Vorstellung* [1818/1819]. 2 Bd. Frankfurt am Main: Insel, 1996.

———. *On the Basis of Morality*. Translated by E. F. J. Payne. Rev. ed. Providence, RI: Berghahn Books, 1995.

———. *Parerga and Paralipomena: Short Philosophical Essays*. 2 vols. Translated by Adrian Del Caro and Christopher Janaway. Cambridge: Cambridge University Press, 2015.

———. *Parerga und Paralopomena: Kleine philosophische Schriften* [1851]. 2 Bd. Leipzig: F. A. Brockhaus, 1878.

———. "Preisschrift über die Grundlage der Moral (1840)" In *Philosophie der Morale: Texte von der Antike bis zur Gegenwart*, edited by Robin Celikates and Stefan Gosepath. Frankfurt am Main: Suhrkamp, 2009.

———. *The World as Will and Representation*. 2 vols. Translated and edited by Judith Norman, Alistair Welchman, and Christopher Janaway. Cambridge: Cambridge University Press, 2010.

Schorske, Carl E. *Fin-de-Siècle Vienna: Politics and Culture*. New York: Knopf: Distributed by Random House, 1979.

Sengoopta, Chandak. *Otto Weininger: Sex, Science and Self in Imperial Vienna*. Chicago, IL: University of Chicago Press, 2000.

Shapshay, Sandra. "Schopenhauer's Aesthetics." In *Stanford Encyclopedia of Philosophy*, edited by Edward N. Zalta, summer 2012 ed. https://plato.stanford.edu/archives/sum2012/entries/schopenhauer-aesthetics/. Accessed January 20, 2018.

Shaw, Jennifer. "Androgyny and the Eternal Feminine in Schoenberg's Oratorio Die Jakobsleiter." In *Political and Religious Ideas in the Works of Arnold Schoenberg*, edited by Charlotte M. Cross and Russell A. Berman, 61–83. New York: Garland, 2000.

Shelleg, Assaf. *Jewish Contiguities and the Soundtrack of Israeli History.* Oxford: Oxford University Press, 2014.

Silverman, Lisa. *Becoming Austrians: Jews and Culture between the World Wars.* New York: Oxford University Press, 2012.

Smither, Howard E. *A History of the Oratorio, Vol. 4: The Oratorio in the Nineteenth and Twentieth Centuries.* Chapel Hill: University of North Carolina Press, 2000.

Solvik, Morten Olsen. "Culture and Creative Imagination: The Genesis of Mahler's Third Symphony." PhD diss., University of Pennsylvania, 1992.

Spector, Scott. "Forget Assimilation: Introducing Subjectivity to German-Jewish History." *Jewish History* 20, no. 3–4 (2006): 349–361.

———. *Modernism without Jews? German-Jewish Subjects and Histories.* Bloomington: Indiana University Press, 2017.

Spiegler, Nina. "Letter to Richard Beer-Hofmann," May 20, 1919. MS Ger 183 Folder 547. Houghton Library, Harvard University.

Steiman, Lionel B. "Stefan Zweig: The Legacy of World War I and the Tasks of Exile." In *Zweig: Exil und Suche nach dem Weltfrieden*, edited by Mark H. Gelber and Klaus Zelewitz, 73–87. Riverside, CA: Ariadne, 1995.

Steinberg, Michael P. *Judaism Musical and Unmusical.* Chicago, IL: University of Chicago Press, 2007.

———. *Listening to Reason Culture, Subjectivity, and Nineteenth-Century Music.* Princeton, NJ: Princeton University Press, 2004.

———. *The Meaning of the Salzburg Festival: Austria as Theater and Ideology, 1890–1938.* Ithaca, NY: Cornell University Press, 1990.

Stephan, Rudolph. "Schoenberg and Bach." In *Schoenberg and His World*, edited by Walter Frisch, 126–140. Princeton, NJ: Princeton University Press, 1999.

Stuckenschmidt, Hans Heinz. *Arnold Schonberg.* Zurich: Atlantis, 1974.

Stummann-Bowert, Ruth. *Malwida von Meysenbug—Paul Rée: Briefe an einen Freund.* Würzburg: Königshausen and Neumann, 1998.

Szondi, Peter. *Theory of the Modern Drama: A Critical Edition.* Minneapolis: University of Minnesota Press, 1987.

"Theater, Kunst und Literatur: Coulissenschau." *Extrapost.* 1898, 843rd ed.

Toews, John. "The Road into the Open: From Narrative Closure to the Endless Performance of Subjectivity in Mahler and Freud at the Turn of the Century." In *The Oxford Handbook of the New Cultural History of Music*, edited by Jane F Fulcher, 81–116. New York: Oxford University Press, 2011.

Vazsonyi, Nicholas. *Richard Wagner: Self-Promotion and the Making of a Brand.* Cambridge: Cambridge University Press, 2010.

Vinaver, Chemjo. *Anthology of Jewish Music.* New York: E. B. Marks, 1955.

Vortreide, Werner. "Gespräche mit Beer-Hofmann." In *Richard Beer-Hofmann: "Zwischen Ästhetizismus und Judentum,"* edited by Dieter Borchmeyer, 163–188. Paderborn: Igel Wissenschaft, 1996.

Wagner, Cosima. *Die Tagebücher.* 2 vols. Munich: Piper Verlag, 1978.

Wagner, Richard. *Richard Wagner: Dichtungen und Schriften.* 10 Bd. Edited by Dieter Borchmeyer. Frankfurt am Main: Insel, 1983.

———. *Richard Wagner's Prose Works.* 6 vols. Translated by William Ashton Ellis. New York: Broude Brothers, 1966.

Waldorf, Willela. "Stefan Zweig's *Jeremias* Is Produced by the Guild." *New York Post*, February 4, 1939.

Walicki, Andrzej. *Nietzsche in Poland (before 1918)*. New York: East European Monographs; Columbia University Press, 1998.

Walter, Bruno. *Gustav Mahler*. Translated by Lotte Walter Lindt. London: Quartett Books, 1990.

Warren, John. "Stefan Zweig's Jeremias in Context." In *Stefan Zweig and World Literature*, edited by Birger Vanweesenbeck and Mark H. Gelber, 35–55. Rochester, NY: Camden House, 2004.

White, Pamela. *Schoenberg and the God-Idea: The Opera Moses und Aron*. Ann Arbor, MI: UMI Research Press, 1985.

———. "Schoenberg and Schopenhauer." *Journal of the Arnold Schoenberg Institute* 8, no. 1 (1984): 39–57.

Williamson, George S. *The Longing for Myth in Germany: Religion and Aesthetic Culture from Romanticism to Nietzsche*. Chicago, IL: University of Chicago Press, 2004.

Yovel, Yirmiyahu. "Nietzsche, the Jews and Ressentiment." In *Nietzsche, Genealogy, Morality: Essays on Nietzsche's on the Genealogy of Morals*, edited by Richard Schacht, 214–236. Berkeley: University of California Press, 1994.

Zifferer, Paul. "Jeremias." *Neue Freie Presse*, September 28, 1917.

Zweig, Stefan. "An die Direktion des Deutschen Volkstheaters," September 3, 1919. Literatur Archiv Salzburg.

———. "Das neue Pathos." *Das neue Pathos* 1, no. 1 (1913): 1–6.

———. *Die Welt von Gestern: Erinnerungen eines Europäers*. Vienna: Mono, 2013.

———. *Jeremiah: A Drama in Nine Scenes*. Translated by Eden and Ceder Paul. New ed. with a preface by the author. New York: Viking, 1939.

———. *Tersites; Jeremias: zwei Dramen*. Frankfurt am Main: Fischer, 1982.

Zweig, Stefan, and Knut Beck. *Tagebücher*. Frankfurt am Main: S. Fischer, 1984.

Zweig, Stefan, Knut Beck, Jeffrey B. Berlin, and Natascha Weschenbach-Feggeler. *Briefe 1914–1919*. Frankfurt am Main: S. Fischer, 1995.

# INDEX

Page numbers in *italics* indicate figures.

CAROLINE A. KITA is Assistant Professor in the Department of Germanic Languages and Literatures at Washington University in St. Louis.

*fulfill his promise to Abraham, namely that his posterity would someday be established in the Holy Land*], which God had sworn [*promised*] to Abraham, the people [*the children of Israel, slaves in Egypt*] grew and multiplied in Egypt,

18 Till another king arose, which knew not [*who had no respect for*] Joseph.

19 The same [*the new Pharaoh*] dealt subtilly [*treacherously*] with our kindred [*ancestors*], and evil entreated [*mistreated, abused*] our fathers [*ancestors*], so that they cast out their young children, to the end they might not live. [*The new Pharaoh, king of Egypt, commanded that every male child born to Israelite slaves be killed. See Exodus 1:15–16.*]

20 In which time Moses was born, and was exceeding fair, and nourished up in his father's house three months: [*Moses' parents successfully hid him for three months after he was born. See Exodus 2:1–2.*]

21 And when he was cast out [*when baby Moses was put in a tiny little waterproof basket and hidden in the bulrushes along side the river; Exodus 2:3–10*], Pharaoh's daughter took him up [*discovered baby Moses and kept him*], and nourished him for her own son.

22 And Moses was learned [*taught*] in all the wisdom of the Egyptians, and was mighty in words and in deeds.

23 And when he was full forty years old, it came into his heart [*he had a desire*] to visit his brethren the children of Israel.

24 And seeing one of them [*the Israelite slaves*] suffer wrong [*he was being beaten by an Egyptian; Exodus 2:11*], he defended him, and avenged him that was oppressed [*made things fair for the slave being beaten*], and smote [*killed*] the Egyptian:

25 For he supposed his brethren would have understood how that God by his hand would deliver them: but they understood not.

Verse 25, above, gives us a very significant insight regarding Moses. It informs us that he knew that he was to deliver the children of Israel out of slavery and bondage in Egypt. While we don't know for sure how Moses came to know this about himself, we would strongly believe that his mother taught him as she raised him in Pharaoh's household under the protection of Pharaoh's daughter (see Exodus 2:5–10). It is highly likely that his mother taught him about the prophecy made by Joseph who was sold into Egypt. Part of this prophecy is as follows: ". . . for a seer will I raise up to deliver my people out of the land of Egypt; and he shall be called Moses. And by this name he shall know that he is of thy house (he will know that he is an Israelite); for he shall be nursed by the king's daughter and shall be called her son." See JST Genesis 50:29, at the back of our LDS Bible. See also 2 Nephi 3:9–10.

26 And the next day he shewed [*showed*] himself unto them [*some Israelite slaves*] as they strove [*as one hit the other; see Exodus 2:13*], and would have set them at one again [*tried to get them to make peace with each other*], saying, Sirs, ye are brethren; why do ye wrong one to another?

27 But he that did his neighbour wrong [*the Israelite slave who was hitting the other slave*] thrust him away [*pushed Moses away*], saying, Who made thee a ruler and a judge over us?

28 Wilt thou kill me, as thou diddest the Egyptian yesterday? [*Are you going to kill me like you did the Egyptian slave driver yesterday?*]

This had to have been a terrible disappointment to Moses. It was also a reminder that during the centuries of slavery in Egypt, the Israelites had become a hardened, rough, people, who, for the most part, were spiritually lacking.

29 Then fled Moses at this saying [*Moses ended up having to flee for his life from Egypt because he defended a Hebrew slave and killed an Egyptian in the process*], and was a stranger in the land of Madian [*Midian, just east of Sinai*], where he begat [*had*] two sons.

30 And when forty years were expired [*at the end of another forty years, when Moses was 80 years old*], there appeared to him in the wilderness of mount Sina [*Sinai*] an angel of the Lord [*JST Exodus 3:2 "The presence of the Lord"*] in a flame of fire in a bush. [*The premortal Christ appeared to Moses in the burning bush.*]

31 When Moses saw it, he wondered at the sight: and as he drew near to behold it, the voice of the Lord [*Christ*] came unto him,

32 Saying, I am the God of thy fathers, the God of Abraham, and the God of Isaac, and the God of Jacob. [*In other words, Jesus Christ, as a spirit, was the God of the Old Testament, usually referred to as Jehovah.*] Then Moses trembled, and durst not behold [*didn't dare even look*].

33 Then said the Lord to him, Put off thy shoes from thy feet: for the place where thou standest is holy ground.

34 I [*Christ*] have seen, I have seen the affliction of my people [*the Israelite slaves*] which is in Egypt, and I have heard their groaning, and am come down to deliver them. And now come, I will send thee into Egypt.

Moses, in effect, led three lives, namely, forty years as a prince in Egypt, forty peaceful years as a shepherd in Midian, and forty years as a mighty prophet to the children of Israel. At age one hundred and twenty, he was translated and taken up without dying (see Bible Dictionary under "Moses"). He ministered to the Savior on the Mount of Transfiguration, about six months before the crucifixion (Matthew 17:1–3,) and was resurrected with the Savior (D&C 133:55).

35 This Moses whom they [*the Israelite slaves*] refused [*rejected*], saying, Who made thee a ruler and a judge? the same did God send to be a ruler and a deliverer by the hand of the angel [*the Lord, see JST Exodus 3:2*] which appeared to him in the bush.

36 He brought them out, after that he [*Moses*] had shewed wonders and signs [*including the ten plagues*] in the land of Egypt, and in the Red sea, and in the wilderness forty years.

Remember that Stephen is on trial before the Sanhedrin (Acts 6:12) and is still answering the high priest's question in verse one of this chapter. He is laying a foundation for bearing testimony to them of Christ. Moses was probably the most important prophet in the eyes of the Jews at this time, and Stephen, with wonderful, inspired skill, has laid a strong foundation, leading up to the fact that Moses prophesied about Jesus, which Stephen says in verse 37, next.

37 ¶ This is that Moses, which [*who*] said unto the children of Israel, A prophet [*Christ*] shall the Lord your God raise up unto you of your brethren, like unto me; him [*Christ*] shall ye hear [*listen to and obey*].

38 This is he [*Moses*], that was in the church in the wilderness with the angel which spake to him in the mount Sina, and with our fathers [*our ancestors, the children of Israel*]: who received the lively oracles [*revelations from the living God; see D&C 90:4, footnote a*] to give unto us:

39 To whom our fathers would not obey [*the children of Israel did not want to obey Moses*], but thrust him from them [*rejected him while he was up on Mount Sinai; see Exodus 32*], and in their hearts turned back again into Egypt,

**JST Acts 7:39**

39 Whom our fathers would not obey, but thrust him from them, and in their hearts turned back again into Egypt,

40 Saying unto Aaron [*Moses' brother*], Make us gods [*the gold calf*] to go before us [*to lead us*]: for as for this Moses, which brought us out of the land of Egypt, we wot not [*don't know*] what is become of him. [*Moses had been gone for many days on Mount Sinai, receiving commandments from the Lord, written on stone tablets. See Exodus 32:1–6.*]

**JST Acts 7:40**

40 Saying unto Aaron, Make us gods to go before us; for as for this Moses, which brought us out of the land of Egypt, we know not what is become of him.

41 And they made a calf [*the golden calf*] in those days, and offered sacrifice unto the idol, and rejoiced in the works of their own hands.

42 Then God turned, and gave them up to worship the host of heaven [*to worship idols*]; as it is written in the book of the prophets [*Amos 5:25–27*], O ye house of Israel, have ye offered to me slain beasts and sacrifices by the space of forty years in the wilderness?

43 Yea, ye took up the tabernacle of Moloch [*you worshiped the idol, Moloch (probably Molech "a fire god, worshiped by passing children through or burning them in fire; Deuteronomy 18:10") see Bible Dictionary under "Molech"*], and the star of your god Remphan, figures which ye made to worship them: and I will carry you away beyond Babylon [*the Babylonian captivity, about 600 B.C.*]

44 Our fathers [*ancestors*] had the tabernacle of witness in the wilderness, as he [*God*] had appointed [*instructed*], speaking unto Moses, that he should make it [*the Tabernacle*] according to the fashion that he had seen [*that the Lord had shown him in vision*].

**JST Acts 7:44**

44 Our fathers had the tabernacle of witness in the wilderness, as he had appointed, speaking unto Moses, that he should make it according to the pattern that he had seen.

The tabernacle, spoken of in verse 44, above, was a portable temple. See Bible Dictionary under "Tabernacle." It was about 45 feet long, 15 feet wide, and 15 feet tall, and was a very elaborate tent, which allowed it to be moved as needed. It was used for sacred worship by the children of Israel during their wanderings in the wilderness. It continued to be used until the building of Solomon's Temple.

Next, Stephen tells these Jewish religious leaders that, after Moses had been taken up, the children of Israel brought the Tabernacle into the Holy Land with them, under the direction of Joshua, who had taken Moses' place.

45 Which [*the Tabernacle*] also our fathers that came after [*after Moses was translated and taken up*] brought in with Jesus [*the Greek form of Joshua—see Bible Dictionary under "Jesus"*] into the possession of the Gentiles [*into the Holy Land, which was inhabited by Gentiles at that time*], whom God drave [*drove*] out before the face of our fathers [*ahead of the children of Israel, as they crossed over the Jordan River into the promised land*], unto the days of David [*until King David's time*];

46 Who found favour before God, and desired to find a tabernacle for the God of Jacob. [*King David wanted to build a permanent temple for the Lord, but was not allowed to. See 1 Kings 5:3–5. King Solomon, David's son, built the temple in Jerusalem. See 1 Kings, chapter 6.*]

47 But Solomon built him an house [*a temple*].

Next, in verse 48, Stephen will quote the prophet Isaiah, reminding them

that even though they and their ancestors made a big fuss about building and maintaining a temple for God, he doesn't actually live in the temple. We know that God can and does come to His temples, and that they are built for our benefit. The point Stephen is making here is that these religious leaders and their ancestors, who built Solomon's Temple, claim to be righteous followers of God and take great pride in the temple, yet they live corrupt lives and persecute and kill the righteous. They are just like their wicked ancestors!

48 Howbeit [*however*] the most High [*God*] dwelleth not in temples made with hands; as saith the prophet [*Isaiah 66:1–2*],

49 Heaven is my throne, and earth is my footstool: what house will ye build me? saith the Lord: or what is the place of my rest?

50 Hath not my hand made all these things?

51 ¶ Ye stiffnecked [*proud*] and uncircumcised [*unrighteous, wicked*] in heart and ears, ye do always resist the Holy Ghost: as your fathers [*ancestors*] did, so do ye. [*You are just like your wicked ancestors.*]

52 Which of the prophets have not your fathers persecuted? and they have slain them which shewed [*prophesied*] before [*in times past*] of the coming of the Just One [*Christ*]; of whom ye have been now the betrayers and murderers [*whom you murdered by crucifixion*]:

53 Who have received the law [*the Law of Moses*] by the disposition [*ministering*] of angels, and have not kept it. [*In other words, you claim to follow Moses' laws and teachings exactly, yet, he prophesied of Christ, and you rejected Christ; therefore, you have rejected Moses.*]

54 ¶ When they heard these things, they were cut to the heart [*the truth cut them deeply and made them furious*], and they gnashed on him with their teeth [*they bit Stephen*].

55 But he, being full of the Holy Ghost, looked up stedfastly [*steadily*] into heaven, and saw the glory of God, and Jesus standing on the right hand of God,

56 And said, Behold, I see the heavens opened, and the Son of man [*Jesus*] standing on the right hand of God.

Verses 55–56, above, are wonderful scriptures to use to teach that the Godhead consists of three distinct, separate beings. Jesus is standing to the right of the Father, and the Holy Ghost is upon Stephen.

57 Then they cried out with a loud voice [*they shouted*], and stopped their ears [*plugged their ears because they didn't want to hear his testimony*], and ran upon him with one accord [*rushed upon him with the same objective in mind*],

58 And cast him out of the city, and stoned him [*killed him with rocks*]: and the witnesses [*the men who killed Stephen*] laid down their clothes [*so they wouldn't get dirty while they killed Stephen*] at a young [*under 40 years of age*] man's feet, whose name was Saul. [*Saul will be converted and his name will be changed to Paul. He will become the Apostle Paul.*]

59 And they stoned Stephen, calling upon God, and saying, Lord Jesus, receive my spirit.

**JST Acts 7:59**

59 And they stoned Stephen; and he, calling upon God, said, Lord Jesus, receive my spirit.

60 And he kneeled down, and cried with a loud voice, Lord, lay not this sin to their charge [*allow these men, who are killing me, to repent*]. And when he had said this, he fell asleep [*he died*].

# ACTS 8

In verse one of this chapter, Luke will introduce us to Saul, a devout Pharisee who felt that the followers of Jesus Christ were a real threat to established Jewish religion. In fact, Saul was authorized by the highest Jewish religious authorities to persecute the Christians, including rounding them up and putting them in prison. After his conversion, Saul's name will be changed to Paul, and he will eventually become the Apostle Paul. We will read of his conversion in chapter 9.

In the meantime, in chapter 8, we see the spread of the gospel to other areas. Luke tells us about Philip and his successful missionary work. One of the better-known converts in this chapter is Simon the Sorcerer, who will try to buy the priesthood.

1 AND Saul was consenting unto his death [*Saul felt that it was right to stone Stephen*]. And at that time [*at the time Stephen was killed*] there was a great persecution against the church which was at Jerusalem; and they [*the members of the Church*] were all scattered abroad throughout the regions of Judæa and Samaria, except the apostles.

2 And devout men [*faithful members*] carried Stephen to his burial, and made great lamentation over him [*mourned his death*].

3 As for Saul, he made havock of the church [*caused terrible trouble for the Church*], entering into every house, and haling [*arresting*] men and women committed them to prison.

4 Therefore they [*the members*] that were scattered abroad went every where preaching the word.

This terrible persecution of members, which scattered them everywhere, actually resulted in the gospel being spread and much missionary work being done.

5 Then Philip [*one of the seven chosen, along with Stephen, to assist the Apostles in ministering to the temporal (physical) needs of the Saints; Acts 6:5*] went down to the city of Samaria, and preached Christ unto them. [*As instructed in Acts 1:8, they were to take the gospel to Samaria and to all the world.*]

6 And the people with one accord [*unitedly*] gave heed [*paid close attention*] unto those things which Philip spake, hearing and seeing the miracles which he did.

7 For unclean spirits [*evil spirits*], crying with loud voice, came out of many that were possessed with them: and many taken with [*sick with*] palsies, and that were lame [*crippled*], were healed.

8 And there was great joy in that city.

9 But there was a certain man, called Simon, which beforetime [*in the past*] in the same city used sorcery [*used Satan's power along with superstition*], and bewitched [*deceived*] the people of Samaria, giving out that himself was some great one [*building himself up in the eyes of the people*]:

10 To whom they all gave heed, from the least to the greatest, saying, This man is the great power of God. [*Simon had great influence among the people, who believed that his power came from God.*]

11 And to him they had regard [*fear and respect*], because that of long time he had bewitched them with sorceries [*because, for a long time, he had exercised unrighteous influence over them with his evil powers and pretending*].

12 But when they believed Philip preaching the things concerning the kingdom of God, and the name of Jesus Christ, they were baptized, both men and women.

13 Then Simon [*the Sorcerer*] himself believed also: and when he was baptized, he continued [*traveled*] with Philip, and wondered [*was amazed*], beholding [*seeing*] the miracles and signs which were done.

14 Now when the apostles which were at Jerusalem heard that Samaria [*many people in Samaria*] had received the word of God [*had been baptized*], they sent unto them Peter and John:

15 Who, when they were come down, prayed for them, that they might receive the Holy Ghost:

16 (For as yet he was fallen upon none of them: only they were baptized in the name of the Lord Jesus.) [*None of those baptized had yet been confirmed and given the Gift of the Holy Ghost.*]

17 Then laid they [*the Apostles Peter and John*] their hands on them, and they received the Holy Ghost.

18 And when Simon saw that through laying on of the apostles' hands the Holy Ghost was given, he offered them money [*offered to buy the Melchizedek Priesthood from them*],

19 Saying, Give me also this power, that on whomsoever I lay hands, he may receive the Holy Ghost.

20 But Peter said unto him, Thy money perish with thee, because thou hast thought that the gift of God may be purchased with money. [*The priesthood is not for sale.*]

21 Thou hast neither part nor lot in this matter: for thy heart is not right in the sight of God. [*You can't participate in the priesthood because you have wrong motives for wanting it.*]

22 Repent therefore of this thy wickedness, and pray God, if perhaps the thought of thine heart may be forgiven thee.

23 For I perceive [*know*] that thou art in the gall of bitterness [*you are a bitter man*], and in the bond of iniquity [*caught up in wickedness*].

24 Then answered [*responded*] Simon, and said, Pray ye to the Lord for me, that none of these things which ye have spoken come upon me.

25 And they [*Peter and John*], when they had testified and preached the word of the Lord, returned to Jerusalem, and preached the gospel in many villages of the Samaritans.

26 And the angel of the Lord spake [*spoke*] unto Philip, saying, Arise, and go toward the south unto the way that goeth down from Jerusalem unto Gaza, which is desert [*go down to the Gaza Strip*].

27 And he arose and went: and, behold, a man of [*from*] Ethiopia [*a nation in eastern Africa, south of Egypt*], an eunuch [*a man, who had been surgically rendered incapable of fathering children; see Bible Dictionary under "Eunuch"*] of great authority under Candace queen of the Ethiopians, who had the charge of all her treasure, and had come to Jerusalem for to worship,

28 Was returning [*the eunuch was returning home to Ethiopia from Jerusalem*], and sitting in his chariot read Esaias [*Isaiah*] the prophet.

29 Then the Spirit said unto Philip, Go near, and join thyself to this chariot [*go over to the chariot where the man is reading the scriptures*].

30 And Philip ran thither [*there*] to him, and heard him read the prophet Esaias [*Isaiah*], and said, Understandest thou what thou readest?

31 And he said, How can I, except some man should guide me? [*How can I understand Isaiah, unless someone helps me*?] And he desired Philip that he would come up and sit with him.

32 The place of the scripture which he read [*the verse of Isaiah he was reading*] was this [*Isaiah 53:7–8*], He was led as a sheep to the slaughter; and like a lamb dumb before his shearer, so opened he not his mouth:

33 In his humiliation his judgment was taken away: and who shall declare his generation? for his life is taken from the earth.

34 And the eunuch answered [*asked*] Philip, and said, I pray thee, of whom speaketh the prophet this? of himself, or of some other man? [*Please tell me. Was Isaiah speaking of himself or of some other man?*]

35 Then Philip opened his mouth [*started talking*], and began at the same scripture, and preached unto him Jesus. [*Philip used the Isaiah verses to teach the eunuch about Jesus.*]

> We will take a moment and give a few brief explanations of the verses from Isaiah about the Savior, which the eunuch was trying to understand (in verses 32–33, above):
>
> 32 He was led as a sheep to the slaughter [*the Savior went peacefully to His trial and crucifixion*]; and like a lamb dumb [*does not make noise*] before his shearer, so opened he not his mouth [*Christ refused to answer most of the questions put to him during His illegal trial*]:
>
> 33 In his humiliation, his judgment was taken away [*He was subject to humiliation, ridicule, and mocking and did not get a fair or legal trial*]: and who shall declare his generation [*who will even care about Him or what happens to Him*]? for his life is taken from the earth [*He is killed and is gone*].

36 And as they went on their way, they came unto a certain water [*a body of water*]: and the eunuch said, See, here is water; what doth hinder me to be baptized [*is there any reason why I shouldn't be baptized*]?

37 And Philip said, If thou believest with all thine heart, thou mayest. And he answered and said, I believe that Jesus Christ is the Son of God.

38 And he commanded the chariot to stand still [*the eunuch commanded the chariot driver to stop*]: and they went down both into the water, both Philip and the eunuch; and he baptized him.

> Here is another reminder (verse 38, above) that baptism was done by immersion in the Bible.

39 And when they were come up out of the water, the Spirit of the Lord caught away Philip, that the eunuch saw him no more: and he went on his way rejoicing. [*The eunuch went home to Ethiopia rejoicing that he was now baptized.*]

40 But Philip was found at Azotus [*about 20 miles north of Gaza*]: and passing through he preached in all the cities, till he came to Cæsarea [*about 80 miles north of Gaza, on the coast of the Mediterranean Sea*].

# ACTS 9

As mentioned in the note at the beginning of Acts, chapter 8, in this study guide, Saul approved of the stoning of Stephen and was a major leader in persecuting the Church (see Acts 7:58 and 8:1–3). In chapter 9, we will see the conversion of this misguided man of integrity and watch as he enters the path to becoming one of the most influential Apostles ever. His name will be changed to Paul, and he will become the Apostle Paul, who became "the Apostle to the Gentiles" and who wrote fourteen of the books of the New Testament.

Just a note about the JST quotes provided in this chapter as well as elsewhere in this study guide. As you will notice, some of the JST changes are not major doctrinal or information changes. We included them to demonstrate that the Prophet Joseph Smith, under the direction of the Lord, paid attention to "smaller matters" as well as "weightier matters."

1 AND Saul [*whose name will be changed to Paul, when he is converted*], yet

breathing out threatenings and slaughter against the disciples of the Lord [*against the members of the Church*], went unto the high priest [*the chief religious leader among the Jews*],

2 And desired of him letters [*letters of permission to empower him to arrest Christians*] to Damascus [*a major city in Syria, north and a bit east of Israel*] to the synagogues, that if he found any of this way [*any members of the Church*], whether they were men or women, he might bring them bound unto Jerusalem. [*Saul got permission to arrest any Christians he found as he traveled to Damascus, and to put them in chains and bring them back to Jerusalem.*]

3 And as he journeyed, he came near Damascus: and suddenly there shined round about him a light from heaven:

4 And he fell to the earth, and heard a voice saying unto him, Saul, Saul, why persecutest thou me? [*Why are you fighting against Me by persecuting My Saints?*]

5 And he said, Who art thou, Lord? And the Lord said, I am Jesus whom thou persecutest: it is hard for thee to kick against the pricks.

A prick was a goad, a sharp stick or pointed instrument of any type which could be used to poke animals when herding them along or keeping them moving when pulling a cart, etc. The tendency of many animals, when poked with the goad, was to stubbornly kick back against it, thus driving it deeper into their hide. The imagery here seems to be that Saul's conscience has begun to bother him, as he rounds up Christians, breaks up families, etc. He has been kicking against the pricks of his conscience and perhaps has been feeling more and more miserable about what he is doing to members of the Church.

6 And he trembling and astonished said, Lord, what wilt thou have me to do? And the Lord said unto him, Arise, and go into the city, and it shall be told thee what thou must do.

7 And the men which journeyed with him stood speechless, hearing a voice, but seeing no man.

As you will see, the JST of verse 7, above, makes a significant change.

**JST Acts 9:7**

7 And they who were journeying with him saw indeed the light, and were afraid; but they heard not the voice of him who spake to him.

8 And Saul arose from the earth; and when his eyes were opened, he saw no man [*he was blind*]: but they led him by the hand, and brought him into Damascus.

9 And he was three days without sight, and neither did eat nor drink.

10 ¶ And there was a certain disciple [*faithful member of the Church*] at Damascus, named Ananias; and to him said the Lord in a vision, Ananias. And he said, Behold, I am here, Lord [*tell me what you need me to do, Lord*].

11 And the Lord said unto him, Arise, and go into the street which is called Straight, and enquire [*ask*] in the house of Judas for one called Saul, of Tarsus: for, behold, he prayeth,

12 And hath seen in a vision a man named Ananias coming in, and putting his hand on him, that he might receive his sight.

This had to have been a startling request from the Savior to Ananias. He knew how dangerous Saul was to the members of the Church, and how much damage had already been caused by him. It would seem to be a blessing that Saul had been struck blind and perhaps would not persecute the Saints any more. Watch, beginning in verse 13, next, as Ananias expresses concern about using the priesthood to restore Saul's sight.

13 Then Ananias answered, Lord, I have heard by many of this man [*Saul*],

how much evil he hath done to thy Saints at Jerusalem:

14 And here [*in Damascus*] he hath authority from the chief priests to bind [*arrest*] all that call on thy name [*all who are members of the Church*].

15 But the Lord said unto him, Go thy way [*go ahead and do what I have asked*]: for he is a chosen vessel [*servant*] unto me, to bear [*carry*] my name before the [*to the*] Gentiles, and kings, and the children of Israel:

16 For I will shew [*show*] him how great things [*how many things*] he must suffer for my name's sake [*as he serves Me*].

17 And Ananias went his way, and entered into the house; and putting his hands on him [*Saul*] said, Brother Saul, the Lord, even Jesus, that appeared unto thee in the way [*on the road*] as thou camest, hath sent me, that thou mightest receive thy sight, and be filled with the Holy Ghost.

18 And immediately there fell from his [*Saul's*] eyes as it had been scales: and he received sight forthwith [*immediately*], and arose, and was baptized.

19 And when he had received meat [*food*], he was strengthened. Then was Saul certain days with the disciples [*Saul stayed with members of the Church for a few days*] which were at Damascus.

20 And straightway [*immediately*] he preached Christ in the synagogues, that he is the Son of God. [*After the few days with members, Saul went to the Jewish church buildings and began to teach about Christ.*]

### *A Description of Paul*

Saul, whose name will be changed to Paul (Acts 13:9,) was a very loyal, energetic, humble man who did things thoroughly. When he felt that the Christians were a threat to the church Moses had set up, he did everything he could to destroy the Christian movement. But as soon as he found out he was wrong, and that Jesus was indeed the promised Messiah, he immediately began using his full energy to preach the gospel of Christ. The Prophet Joseph Smith gave a physical description of Paul as follows: "He is about five feet high; very dark hair; dark complexion; dark skin; large Roman nose; sharp face; small black eyes, penetrating as eternity; round shoulders; a whining voice, except when elevated, and then it almost resembled the roaring of a lion. He was a good orator, active and diligent, always employing himself in doing good to his fellow man." (*Teachings of the Prophet Joseph Smith*, p. 180.)

21 But all that heard him [*Saul*] were amazed, and said; Is not this he that destroyed them [*members of the Church*] which called on this name [*who were loyal followers of Jesus*] in Jerusalem, and came hither [*here to Damascus*] for that intent [*purpose*], that he might bring them bound [*arrest them and bring them in chains*] unto the chief priests?

22 But Saul increased the more in strength [*continued growing in the gospel*], and confounded the Jews which dwelt at Damascus, proving that this is very Christ. [*Paul successfully debated the Jews in Damascus, showing them that Jesus was indeed the Christ, the promised Messiah.*]

23 ¶ And after that many days were fulfilled [*after many days*], the Jews took counsel to kill him [*the Jews plotted to kill Saul*]:

24 But their laying await was known of Saul [*Saul was aware of their plans to ambush him*]. And they watched the gates [*the city gates*] day and night to kill him.

**JST Acts 9:24**

24 But their lying in wait was known of Saul. And they watched the gates day and night to kill him.

25 Then the disciples took him by

night, and let him down by the wall in a basket.

26 And when Saul was come to Jerusalem, he assayed [*attempted*] to join himself to the disciples: but they were all afraid of him, and believed not that he was a disciple [*a follower of Christ*].

27 But Barnabas took him, and brought him to the apostles, and declared [*explained*] unto them how he [*Saul*] had seen the Lord in the way [*on the way to Damascus*], and that he [*the Lord*] had spoken to him, and how he [*Saul*] had preached boldly at Damascus in the name of Jesus.

28 And he was with them coming in and going out at Jerusalem. [*And so, Saul was permitted to associate with the members of the Church in Jerusalem.*]

29 And he spake boldly in the name of the Lord Jesus, and disputed against [*debated with*] the Grecians [*the Grecian Jews*]: but they went about to slay him.

30 Which when the brethren knew [*found out*], they brought him down to Cæsarea [*about 60 miles north of Jerusalem, on the coast of the Mediterranean Sea*], and sent him forth to Tarsus [*Saul's home town, in southern Turkey*].

**JST Acts 9:30**

30 When the brethren knew this, they brought him down to Caesarea, and sent him forth to Tarsus.

31 Then had the churches [*wards and branches*] rest [*because Saul wasn't persecuting them any more*] throughout all Judæa and Galilee and Samaria, and were edified [*strengthened and built up*]; and walking in the fear [*respect and knowledge*] of the Lord, and in the comfort of the Holy Ghost, were multiplied [*continued growing*].

32 ¶ And it came to pass, as Peter passed throughout all quarters [*as Peter traveled throughout the Church*], he came down also to the saints which dwelt at Lydda [*about 20 miles northwest of Jerusalem*].

**JST Acts 9:32**

32 And it came to pass, as Peter passed throughout all these regions, he came down also to the saints which dwelt at Lydda.

33 And there he found a certain man named Æneas, which had kept his bed eight years [*who had been bedridden for eight years*], and was sick of the palsy.

34 And Peter said unto him, Æneas, Jesus Christ maketh thee whole: arise, and make thy bed. And he arose immediately.

35 And all that dwelt at Lydda and Saron saw him [*the man who had been healed*], and turned to the Lord.

36 ¶ Now there was at Joppa [*about 12 miles northwest of Lydda and 35 miles northwest of Jerusalem*] a certain disciple named Tabitha, which by interpretation is called Dorcas: this woman was full of good works and almsdeeds [*helping the poor*] which she did.

37 And it came to pass in those days, that she was sick, and died: whom when they had washed [*prepared her body for burial*], they laid her in an upper chamber [*an upstairs room*].

38 And forasmuch as [*since*] Lydda was nigh [*near*] to Joppa, and the disciples [*the members in Joppa*] had heard that Peter was there, they sent unto him two men, desiring him that he would not delay to come to them.

**JST Acts 9:38**

38 And forasmuch as Lydda was nigh to Joppa, and the disciples had heard that Peter was there, they sent unto him two men, desiring that he would not delay to come to them.

39 Then Peter arose and went with them. When he was come [*when he arrived in Joppa*], they brought him into the upper chamber: and all the widows stood by him weeping, and shewing the

coats and garments [*clothing*] which Dorcas made, while she was with them [*while she was alive*].

40 But Peter put them all forth [*had them all leave the room*], and kneeled down, and prayed; and turning him to the body [*turning toward Tabitha's body*] said, Tabitha, arise. And she opened her eyes: and when she saw Peter, she sat up.

> **JST Acts 9:40**
> 40 But Peter put them all forth, and kneeled down, and prayed; and turning to the body said, Tabitha, arise. And she opened her eyes; and when she saw Peter, she sat up.

41 And he gave her his hand, and lifted her up, and when he had called the saints and widows, presented her alive.

> **JST Acts 9:41**
> 41 And he gave her his hand, and lifted her up; and when he had called the saints and widows; he presented her alive.

42 And it was known throughout all Joppa; and many believed in the Lord.

43 And it came to pass, that he [*Peter*] tarried [*stayed*], many days in Joppa with one Simon a tanner [*a man who made his living by making leather goods*].

# ACTS 10

One of the major messages which the Savior gave to His Apostles after He was resurrected was that the gospel was now to be taken to all the world—see Mark 16:15. For the Jewish members of the Church, this was a major change and went against their cultural traditions and upbringing. In this chapter, we will see the rather well-known account of a Roman soldier, a Gentile named Cornelius, who is ministered to by an angel in preparation for his conversion to the gospel of Jesus Christ. The angel tells Cornelius to send for the Apostle Peter. In the meantime, Peter is prepared by a vision to preach the gospel to the Gentiles, and specifically to Cornelius and his household. Watch now as the work of the Lord is extended to the Gentiles.

1 THERE was a certain man in Cæsarea [*about 30 miles north of Joppa, on the coast*] called Cornelius, a centurion [*a Roman soldier in charge of one hundred soldiers*] of the band called the Italian band,

2 A devout man, and one that feared [*respected*] God with all his house [*along with all the people in his household*], which gave much alms [*financial assistance*] to the people, and prayed to God alway.

3 He saw in a vision evidently about the ninth hour of the day [*about 3:00 PM*] an angel of God coming in to him, and saying unto him, Cornelius.

4 And when he looked on him, he was afraid, and said, What is it, Lord? And he said unto him, Thy prayers and thine alms are come up for a memorial before God. [*God has heard your prayers and knows of your contributions to the poor.*]

5 And now send men to Joppa, and call for one Simon, whose surname is Peter:

6 He lodgeth with [*is living with*] one Simon a tanner, whose house is by the sea side: he shall tell thee what thou oughtest to do.

7 And when the angel which spake unto Cornelius was departed [*had left*], he called two of his household servants, and a devout soldier of them that waited on [*served*] him continually;

8 And when he had declared all these things unto them, he sent them to Joppa.

9 ¶ On the morrow [*the next day*], as they went on their journey, and drew nigh [*near*] unto the city, Peter went up upon the housetop [*remember that the*

*houses in the Holy Land had flat roofs and were commonly used for living quarters when weather permitted*] to pray about the sixth hour [*about noon*]:

10 And he became very hungry, and would have eaten: but while they made ready [*while lunch was being prepared*], he fell into a trance [*the Spirit came upon him and his physical surroundings faded out of his mind*],

11 And saw heaven opened, and a certain vessel descending [*coming down*] unto him, as it had been [*like*] a great sheet knit [*held*] at the four corners, and let down to the earth:

12 Wherein [*on the sheet*] were all manner of [*all kinds of*] fourfooted beasts of the earth, and wild beasts, and creeping things, and fowls of the air.

The Jews had a very detailed "word of wisdom," telling them what they should and should not eat, as faithful followers of the Law of Moses. For instance, they were allowed to eat any animals which had cloven hoofs and chewed the cud, such as sheep, goats, and cows. However, they were not allowed to eat blood, camels, rabbits, pigs, eagles, vultures, ravens, owls, storks, bats, mice, tortoises, ferrets, lizards, snails, moles, etc. All of these were considered "unclean" under the Law of Moses. They were permitted to eat locusts, bald locusts, beetles, and grasshoppers, but no other bugs. For more details, see Leviticus, chapter 11. This "word of wisdom" for them was a great blessing because it prevented them from getting many diseases carried by such creatures. With this as background, the sheet in Peter's vision contained many "unclean" creatures, eating of which was against Peter's religious background, training, and commitments. Peter is startled when told by the voice to eat these "unclean" things.

13 And there came a voice to him, Rise, Peter; kill, and eat.

14 But Peter said, Not so, Lord; for I have never eaten any thing that is common or unclean.

15 And the voice spake unto him again the second time, What God hath cleansed, that call not thou common. [*Do not say that what the Lord has made clean is still unclean.*]

16 This was done thrice [*three times*]: and the vessel was received up again into heaven.

17 Now while Peter doubted in himself what this vision which he had seen should mean [*as Peter was wondering what the meaning of this vision was*], behold, the men which were sent from Cornelius [*the Roman centurion, who was a Gentile, not a Jew*] had made enquiry for Simon's house [*had asked directions for and finally found Simon's house*], and stood before the gate,

18 And called, and asked whether Simon, which was surnamed Peter, were lodged there [*asked whether or not Simon Peter was staying there*].

19 ¶ While Peter thought on the vision [*while Peter was still trying to figure out the meaning of the vision*], the Spirit said unto him, Behold, three men seek thee.

20 Arise therefore, and get thee down [*go downstairs*], and go with them, doubting nothing [*don't question My instructions*]: for I have sent them.

21 Then Peter went down to the men which were sent unto him from Cornelius; and said, Behold, I am he whom ye seek: what is the cause wherefore ye are come [*why have you come to see me*]?

22 And they said, Cornelius the centurion, a just man [*a righteous man; one who lives his beliefs with exactness*], and one that feareth God, and of good report [*good reputation*] among all the nation of the Jews, was warned from God by an holy angel to send for thee into his house [*was told by an angel to ask you to come to his*

*house*], and to hear words of thee.

23 Then called he them in, and lodged them [*then Peter invited them in and had them stay overnight*]. And on the morrow Peter went away with them, and certain brethren from Joppa accompanied him.

24 And the morrow after [*the day after*] they entered into Cæsarea. And Cornelius waited for them, and had called together his kinsmen [*relatives*] and near friends.

25 And as Peter was coming in, Cornelius met him, and fell down at his feet, and worshipped him.

26 But Peter took him up, saying, Stand up; I myself also am a man. [*In other words, don't worship me; I am just a man.*]

27 And as he talked with him, he went in [*into Cornelius' house*], and found many that were come together [*and met many who had gathered there*].

> Peter now understands the meaning of the dream or vision of the sheet with unclean animals, birds, etc., which he was commanded to eat. Jewish law made it illegal to closely associate with Gentiles (non-Jews), or go into their homes. The message of the vision was that he was no longer to follow this law. The time had now come to take the gospel to all people and to associate with them freely.

28 And he said unto them, Ye know how that it is an unlawful thing for a man that is a Jew to keep company [*associate with*], or come unto one of another nation; but God hath shewed [*showed*] me that I should not call any man common or unclean.

29 Therefore [*for this reason*] came I unto you without gainsaying [*without opposing what God told me*], as soon as I was sent for: I ask therefore for what intent ye have sent for me?

30 And Cornelius said, Four days ago I was fasting until this hour; and at the ninth hour [*about 3:00 PM*] I prayed in my house, and, behold, a man [*angel*] stood before me in bright clothing,

31 And said, Cornelius, thy prayer is heard, and thine alms [*contributions to the poor*] are had in remembrance in the sight of God.

32 Send therefore to Joppa, and call hither [*invite to come to your home*] Simon, whose surname is Peter; he is lodged in the house of one Simon a tanner by the sea side: who, when he cometh, shall speak unto thee.

33 Immediately therefore I sent to thee; and thou hast well done that thou art come [*it was good of you to come*]. Now therefore are we all here present before God [*now this is why we are all here*], to hear all things that are commanded thee of God.

> Verse 34, next, has a rather well-known and oft-quoted doctrine. It is "God is no respecter of persons."

34 ¶ Then Peter opened his mouth, and said, Of a truth I perceive that God is no respecter of persons: [*In other words, I understand for sure that God will treat all people equally.*]

35 But in every nation he that feareth him [*he who has respect and reverence for God*], and worketh righteousness, is accepted with him.

36 The word which God sent unto the children of Israel, preaching peace by Jesus Christ: (he is Lord of all:)

37 That word, I say, ye know [*you are familiar with*], which was published throughout all Judæa, and began from Galilee, after the baptism which John [*the Baptist*] preached;

38 How God [*the Father*] anointed [*prepared*] Jesus of Nazareth with the Holy Ghost and with power: who went about doing good, and healing all that were oppressed of the devil; for God was with him.

39 And we are witnesses of all things

which he [*Jesus*] did both in the land of the Jews, and in Jerusalem; whom they slew [*killed*] and hanged on a tree [*crucified*]:

40 Him God raised up [*resurrected*] the third day, and shewed him openly [*had the resurrected Jesus appear to many*];

41 Not to all the people, but unto witnesses chosen before of God [*Jesus didn't appear to everyone, but to many who serve as witnesses*], even to us, who did eat and drink with him after he rose from the dead [*as recorded in Luke 24:36–43 and elsewhere*].

42 And he commanded us to preach unto the people, and to testify that it is he which was ordained of God to be the Judge of quick [*the living*] and dead.

43 To him give all the prophets witness [*all the Old Testament prophets bore witness of Christ*], that through his name whosoever believeth in him shall receive remission [*forgiveness*] of sins.

44 ¶ While Peter yet spake these words, the Holy Ghost fell on all them which heard the word [*all the people who were listening to Peter in Cornelius' house*].

45 And they of the circumcision which believed [*the Jewish members of the Church who had accompanied Peter from Joppa to Cornelius' house in Caesarea*] were astonished, as many as came with Peter, because that on the Gentiles also was poured out the gift of the Holy Ghost. [*They were shocked that the Holy Ghost actually came upon non-Jews.*]

46 For they heard them speak with tongues, and magnify God. Then answered Peter [*Peter responded by saying*],

47 Can any man forbid water, that these should not be baptized [*would any of you dare to forbid baptism for these Gentiles*], which have received the Holy Ghost as well as we [*who have received the Holy Ghost just like we have*]?

48 And he commanded them to be baptized in the name of the Lord. Then prayed they him to tarry certain days. [*Then these new converts asked Peter to stay with them for a few days.*]

# ACTS 11

As you will see in this chapter, the fact that the gospel, including baptism, had actually been taken to Gentiles, stirred up strong feelings among Jewish members of the Church. They had grown up in a culture and tradition that Israelites were superior in the eyes of God and that Gentiles, no matter how righteous, would always be second class people as far as the kingdom of God is concerned.

Even though the Savior instructed that the gospel be taken to all the world (Mark 16:15 and elsewhere), it has not sunk in yet in the heads and hearts of Jewish members that the ordinances and rituals of the Law of Moses, including circumcision, are no longer required in the Church Jesus Christ established. Thus, you will see a rather heated debate when Peter and his fellow travelers return to Jerusalem. The debate is about the fact that Peter has actually associated with Gentiles and baptized Cornelius and his household.

As mentioned earlier, there are always growing pains as the Church and gospel are taken to other cultures and nations. We see a considerable amount of this today, so it ought to be relatively easy for us to be patient with these folks as they go through some rather painful growth toward becoming Zion people.

1 AND the apostles and brethren that were in Judæa heard that the Gentiles [*people who were not Jews*] had also received [*accepted*] the word of God.

2 And when Peter was come up to [*had arrived in*] Jerusalem, they that were of the circumcision contended with him [*Jewish members of the Church, who believed strongly that male converts should be circumcised according to the Law of Moses in order to join the Church (see "Circumcision" in the Bible Dictionary), criticized Peter*],

3 Saying, Thou wentest in to men uncircumcised, and didst eat with them [*you not only went into the homes of uncircumcised men (or in other words, Gentiles) but you actually ate with them; that is terrible!*].

4 But Peter rehearsed the matter [*explained everything*] from the beginning, and expounded it by order unto them [*explained the events, in order, which led up to his actions*], saying,

5 I was in the city of Joppa praying: and in a trance I saw a vision [*see Acts 10:10–16*], A certain vessel descend, as it had been [*as if it were*] a great [*large*] sheet, let down from heaven by four corners; and it came even to me [*it came right down to me*]:

6 Upon the which when I had fastened mine eyes, I considered, and saw [*when I looked closely, I saw*] fourfooted beasts of the earth, and wild beasts, and creeping things, and fowls of the air.

7 And I heard a voice saying unto me, Arise, Peter; slay and eat.

8 But I said, Not so, Lord: for nothing common or unclean hath at any time entered into my mouth. [*I can't do it, Lord. I have never broken the Law of Moses by eating unclean things.*]

9 But the voice answered [*said to*] me again from heaven, What God hath cleansed, that call not thou common.

10 And this was done [*repeated*] three times: and all were drawn up again into heaven [*all the things in the vision were taken back up into heaven*].

11 And, behold, immediately there were three men already come unto [*already arrived at*] the house where I was, sent from Cæsarea unto me.

12 And the Spirit bade me go [*told me to go*] with them, nothing doubting [*without questioning the instructions*]. Moreover these six brethren [*six Jewish members of the Church*] accompanied me, and we entered into the man's [*Cornelius'*] house:

13 And he shewed [*told*] us how he had seen an angel in his house, which stood and said unto him, Send men to Joppa, and call for Simon, whose surname is Peter;

14 Who shall tell thee words [*who will preach the gospel to you*], whereby thou [*through which you*] and all thy house shall be saved.

15 And as I [*Peter*] began to speak, the Holy Ghost fell on them [*the Gentiles in Cornelius' house*], as on us at the beginning [*just like it did upon us when we first heard of the gospel*].

16 Then remembered I the word of the Lord, how that he said, John [*the Baptist*] indeed baptized with water; but ye shall be baptized with the Holy Ghost.

17 Forasmuch then as [*therefore, since*] God gave them [*Cornelius and his family and friends*] the like gift [*the same manifestation of the Holy Ghost*] as he did unto us, who believed on the Lord Jesus Christ; what was I, that I could withstand God [*do you really think I should have told God He made a mistake*]?

18 When they heard these things, they held their peace [*they quit criticizing Peter*], and glorified [*praised*] God, saying, Then hath God also to the Gentiles granted repentance unto life. [*So, the fact is, God allows Gentiles to repent and attain eternal life also.*]

19 ¶ Now they which were scattered abroad upon the persecution that arose about Stephen [*members of the Church,*

*who had been scattered far and wide by persecutions which started with the stoning of Stephen,*] travelled as far as Phenice, and Cyprus, and Antioch, preaching the word to none but unto the Jews only [*taught the gospel only to Jews*].

20 And some of them were men of Cyprus and Cyrene, which, when they were come to Antioch, spake unto the Grecians, preaching the Lord Jesus. [*Now, they taught the gospel to some citizens of Greece, who were Gentiles.*]

21 And the hand of the Lord was with them: and a great number believed, and turned unto the Lord [*many Greeks were converted to Christ*].

22 ¶ Then tidings [*news*] of these things came unto the ears of the church which was [*to members of the Church who were*] in Jerusalem: and they sent forth Barnabas [*who will later become one of Paul's missionary companions*], that he should go as far as Antioch.

23 Who, when he came, and had seen the grace of God [*had seen the work of conversion among Gentiles there*], was glad, and exhorted [*counseled*] them all, that with purpose of heart [*with deep determination*] they would cleave unto [*stay true to*] the Lord.

24 For he [*Barnabas*] was a good man, and full of the Holy Ghost and of faith: and much people was added unto the Lord [*many converts were added to the Church*].

25 Then departed Barnabas to Tarsus, for to seek Saul [*Barnabas then left Antioch to go to Tarsus to try to find Saul*]:

26 And when he had found him, he brought him unto Antioch. And it came to pass, that a whole year they assembled themselves with the church, and taught much people. [*Barnabas and Saul stayed for a whole year with the Saints and did much teaching.*] And the disciples were called Christians first in Antioch. [*Antioch was the first place where people began referring to members of the Church as "Christians."*]

27 ¶ And in these days came prophets from Jerusalem unto Antioch.

28 And there stood up one of them [*one of the prophets*] named Agabus, and signified by the Spirit [*and prophesied by the power of the Holy Ghost*] that there should be great dearth [*that there would be a wide-spread famine*] throughout all the world: which came to pass [*happened*] in the days of Claudius Cæsar.

29 Then the disciples [*members in Antioch*], every man according to his ability, determined to send relief unto the brethren which dwelt in Judæa [*the Jerusalem area*]:

30 Which also they did, and sent it to the elders by the hands of Barnabas and Saul. [*Members in Antioch sent relief to the leaders of the Church in Jerusalem for them to distribute to needy members during the famine.*]

# ACTS 12

In this chapter, Luke will tell us about the persecution of the Church by King Herod. James, the brother of John, will be martyred. Peter will be placed in prison but will be set free by an angel. Just like in our day, the Church will continue to grow in spite of opposition.

1 NOW about that time Herod the king stretched forth his hands to vex certain of the church [*King Herod started persecuting members of the Church*].

2 And he killed James the brother of John with the sword. [*James was one of the original Apostles.*]

3 And because he saw it pleased the Jews, he proceeded further to take [*arrest*] Peter also. (Then were the days of unleavened bread.) [*This was during the Passover season, and would be*

*around our Easter season. See Bible Dictionary under "Feasts".*]

4 And when he had apprehended him [*had arrested Peter*], he put him in prison, and delivered him to four quaternions of soldiers [*four teams of four soldiers each*] to keep him; intending after Easter [*Passover*] to bring him forth to the people [*intending to have a public trial for Peter*].

5 Peter therefore [*for that reason*] was kept in prison: but prayer was made without ceasing of the church unto God for him. [*Members of the Church prayed constantly for Peter.*]

6 And when Herod would have brought him forth [*the night before King Herod was to have Peter brought to him from the prison*], *the same night* [*that night*] Peter was sleeping between two soldiers, bound with two chains: and the keepers before [*in front of*] the door kept the prison.

As we continue our study, you will notice that we refer occasionally to word definitions given by Strong's *Exhaustive Concordance of the Bible*. This reference work lists Biblical words by number and gives helpful alternate definitions for many words used in the Bible. It is highly respected among Bible scholars, including LDS Bible scholars. You will see an example in verse 7, next.

7 And, behold, the angel of the Lord came upon him, and a light shined in the prison: and he smote [*tapped; Strong's #3960*] Peter on the side, and raised him up, saying, Arise up quickly. And his chains fell off from his hands.

**JST Acts 12:7**

7 And, behold, the angel of the Lord came unto him, and a light shined in the prison; and he smote Peter on the side, and raised him up, saying, Arise up quickly. And his chains fell off from his hands.

8 And the angel said unto him, Gird thyself [*get dressed*], and bind on thy sandals [*put on your sandals*]. And so he did. And he [*the angel*] saith unto him, Cast thy garment about thee [*put on your robe*], and follow me.

9 And he went out, and followed him; and wist [*knew*] not that it was true which was done by the angel; but thought he saw a vision. [*Peter didn't realize this was actually happening to him, rather, thought he was seeing it in a vision.*]

10 When they were past the first and the second ward [*when they had passed the first and second sets of guards in their assigned stations*], they came unto the iron gate [*the main gate to the prison*] that leadeth unto the city; which opened to them of his own accord [*which opened by itself*]: and they went out, and passed on through one street; and forthwith [*at that point*] the angel departed from him.

11 And when Peter was come to himself [*when Peter realized he wasn't dreaming or seeing a vision*], he said, Now I know of a surety [*for sure*], that the Lord hath sent his angel, and hath delivered me out of the hand of Herod, and from all the expectation of the people of the Jews. [*Peter now knew for sure that this was actually happening and that the Lord had sent an angel to free him from Herod and from the public trial expected by the Jews the next day.*]

12 And when he had considered the thing [*had decided what to do*], he came to the house of Mary the mother of John, whose surname was Mark; where many were gathered together praying.

The member of the Church named Mark, referred to in verse 12 above, was the Mark to whom the writing of the Gospel of Mark is attributed. Peter came to Mark's mother's house directly from the prison and had a bit of difficulty getting in, as seen in the next verses.

13 And as Peter knocked at the door of the gate, a damsel [*a young lady*] came

to hearken [*came to where she could hear the person at the gate*], named Rhoda.

14 And when she knew [*recognized*] Peter's voice, she opened not the gate for gladness [*she was so happy she forgot to open the gate*], but ran in, and told how Peter stood before the gate [*she ran to the others who had gathered at Mary's house to pray for Peter, and told them Peter was standing outside*].

15 And they said unto her, Thou art mad [*You are crazy!*]. But she constantly affirmed that it was even so [*she insisted that it was true*]. Then said they, It is his angel. [*In other words, Peter is dead, and it must be his spirit standing out there.*]

16 But Peter continued knocking: and when they had opened the door, and saw him, they were astonished.

17 But he, beckoning unto them with the hand to hold their peace [*Peter signaled for them to quiet down*], declared [*explained*] unto them how the Lord had brought him out of the prison. And he said, Go shew [*show*] these things unto James [*perhaps James, the Savior's half-brother (see Mark 6:3) or James, son of Alpheus (see Luke 6:15) who was also an Apostle*], and to the brethren. And he departed, and went into another place.

18 Now as soon as it was day, there was no small stir among the soldiers, what was become of Peter [*the soldiers who had been guarding Peter in prison were very worried because he was gone*].

19 And when Herod had sought [*sent*] for him, and found him not, he examined the keepers [*questioned the prison guards*], and commanded that they should be put to death. And he [*Peter*] went down from Judæa to Cæsarea, and there abode [*and stayed there*].

At the beginning of verse 20, below, if you are using the King James Version of the Bible (the one English-speaking members of the Church use, as authorized by the Church), you will notice a "¶" which looks like a fancy backwards P. It is a symbol which means that this verse starts a new topic. There are many ¶'s in our Bible, and each one signals the beginning of a different topic.

20 ¶ And Herod was highly displeased [*very angry*] with them of Tyre and Sidon: but they came with one accord [*united in purpose*] to him, and, having made Blastus the king's chamberlain [*personal servant*] their friend, desired peace; because their country was nourished by [*was receiving aid from*] the king's country.

21 And upon a set day Herod, arrayed in royal apparel [*dressed in fine royal robe, etc.*], sat upon his throne, and made an oration [*gave a speech*] unto them.

22 And the people gave a shout, saying, It is the voice of a god, and not of a man.

23 And immediately the angel of the Lord smote him, because he gave not God the glory: and he was eaten of worms, and gave up the ghost [*he died*].

24 ¶ But the word of God grew and multiplied [*the gospel continued to spread*].

25 And Barnabas and Saul returned from Jerusalem, when they had fulfilled their ministry [*when they had finished their assignment*], and took with them John, whose surname was Mark. [*Mark will later write the Gospel of Mark.*]

## ACTS 13

In this chapter, Paul (called "Saul" until verse 9) is sent on a mission with Barnabus. It will be the first of three major missionary journeys for Paul. As you will see, Paul is a master teacher. Watch as he gives a history of God's dealings with Israel in Old Testament times,

setting the stage for teaching these people about the coming of Jesus Christ in fulfillment of the Law of Moses.

1 NOW there were in the church that was at Antioch [*a city in Syria, about 300 miles north of Jerusalem*] certain prophets and teachers; as [*including*] Barnabas, and Simeon that was called Niger, and Lucius of Cyrene, and Manaen, which had been brought up with Herod the tetrarch, and Saul.

2 As they ministered to the Lord, and fasted, the Holy Ghost said [*in other words, Christ told them through the Holy Ghost*], Separate me [*set apart*] Barnabas and Saul for the work whereunto I have called them [*send Saul and Barnabas on a mission*].

> This mission, started probably in the spring of AD 48, will be the first of three major missionary journeys for Paul over the next several years. This first mission will take him from Antioch (in Syria) to the Island of Cyprus, and then to what is known today as southern Turkey, where the Galatians lived. Paul will become known as the missionary to the Gentiles. This first missionary journey is reported in Acts 13:1 through Acts 14:26. See Bible Dictionary under "Paul."

3 And when they had fasted and prayed, and laid their hands on them [*set them apart by the laying on of hands*], they sent them away.

4 ¶ So they, being sent forth by the Holy Ghost [*by the Savior, through inspiration of the Holy Ghost*], departed unto Seleucia [*near Antioch*]; and from thence they sailed to Cyprus.

5 And when they were at Salamis [*on the east coast of Cyprus*], they preached the word of God in the synagogues [*church buildings*] of the Jews: and they had also John to their minister [*someone named John was their assistant*].

6 And when they had gone through the isle [*island*] unto Paphos [*on the southwest coast of Cyprus*], they found a certain sorcerer, a false prophet, a Jew, whose name was Bar-jesus [*also called Elymas; see verse 8, below*]:

7 Which was with [*who associated with*] the deputy of the country [*a powerful Roman official*], Sergius Paulus, a prudent [*wise*] man; who called for Barnabas and Saul, and desired to hear the word of God.

8 But Elymas the sorcerer (for so is his name by interpretation) withstood them [*tried to stop them*], seeking to turn away the deputy [*Sergius Paulus*] from the faith [*the gospel*].

> In verse 9, below, we note that Saul's name has now been changed to "Paul." He will be called Paul during the rest of Acts. Later, he will be called to be an Apostle.

9 Then Saul, (who also is called Paul,) filled with the Holy Ghost, set his eyes on him [*looked straight at Elymas*],

10 And said, O full of all subtilty [*deception*] and all mischief [*dishonesty*], thou child of the devil [*you follower of Satan*], thou enemy of all righteousness, wilt thou not cease to pervert [*plot against*] the right ways of the Lord?

11 And now, behold, the hand of [*the power of*] the Lord is upon thee, and thou shalt be blind, not seeing the sun for a season. And immediately there fell on him a mist and a darkness; and he went about seeking some to lead him by the hand.

12 Then the deputy [*the Roman official, Sergius Paulus*], when he saw what was done, believed, being astonished at the doctrine of the Lord.

13 Now when Paul and his company [*group*] loosed [*departed*] from Paphos, they came to Perga in Pamphylia [*in southern Turkey, northwest of Cyprus*]: and John [*Mark*] departing from them returned to Jerusalem.

John Mark (or Mark) sailed with Paul, Barnabas, and the others to Pamphylia [*see Acts 15:38*], in what today is southern Turkey. Then, for whatever reason, Mark left them and returned to Jerusalem. This irritated Paul and he refused to take Mark with him on his second missionary journey. See Acts 15:36–41.

14 ¶ But when they departed from Perga, they came to Antioch in Pisidia [*this Antioch is in southern Turkey, and is not the Antioch from which Paul started on this journey in Acts 13:1–3*], and went into the synagogue on the sabbath day, and sat down.

15 And after the reading of the law and the prophets [*the reading of the Old Testament scriptures*] the rulers of the synagogue sent unto them [*sent word to Paul and Barnabas*], saying, Ye men and brethren, if ye have any word of exhortation [*instruction, encouragement*] for the people, say on [*go ahead and talk to us*].

16 Then Paul stood up, and beckoning [*motioning*] with his hand said, Men of Israel, and ye that fear God, give audience.

17 The God of this people of Israel chose our fathers [*ancestors*], and exalted [*blessed*] the people when they dwelt as strangers in the land of Egypt, and with an high arm [*with power*] brought he [*God*] them [*the children of Israel*] out of it [*Egyptian bondage*].

18 And about the time of forty years suffered he their manners in the wilderness [*Israel wandered in the wilderness for about forty years because of their wickedness*].

**JST Acts 13:18**

18 And about the time for forty years suffered he their manners in the wilderness.

19 And when he [*God*] had destroyed seven nations in the land of Chanaan [*in what is now Palestine*], he divided their land to them by lot [*He divided up the land of Canaan among the twelve tribes of Israel in a fair manner*].

20 And after that he gave unto them judges about the space of four hundred and fifty years, until Samuel the prophet. [*Israel had a loose system of judges to rule over them for about 450 years, after Joshua and up until Samuel.*]

21 And afterward they desired a king: and God gave unto them Saul the son of Cis, a man of the tribe of Benjamin, by the space of forty years. [*King Saul ruled Israel for 40 years.*]

22 And when he [*God*] had removed him [*Saul*], he raised up unto them David to be their king; to whom also he gave testimony [*God said that David was a righteous man, at the time He made him king*], and said, I have found David the son of Jesse, a man after mine own heart, which shall fulfil all my will.

23 Of this man's seed [*from King David's descendants*] hath God according to his promise raised unto Israel a Saviour, Jesus: [*Jesus, as prophesied, was a descendant of David.*]

24 When John [*the Baptist*] had first preached before his [*Christ's*] coming the baptism of repentance to all the people of Israel.

25 And as John fulfilled his course [*as John the Baptist fulfilled his mission*], he said, Whom think ye that I am? I am not he [*I am not Christ*]. But, behold, there cometh one after me, whose shoes of his feet I am not worthy to loose [*whose sandals I am not worthy to take off His feet*].

26 Men and brethren, children of the stock of Abraham [*you descendants of Abraham*], and whosoever among you feareth God, to you is the word of this salvation sent [*this message of salvation through Jesus is directed at you*].

27 For they that dwell at Jerusalem

[*the inhabitants of Jerusalem*], and their rulers, because they knew him not [*refused to accept Jesus for who He was*], nor yet the voices of the prophets which are read every sabbath day [*they refused to acknowledge the prophecies about Jesus, which they read every Sabbath in their meetings*], they have fulfilled them in condemning him [*they fulfilled the prophecies that they would condemn Jesus to death*].

28 And though they found no cause of death in him [*they could not come up with a valid reason to kill Jesus*], yet desired they Pilate [*the Roman governor*] that he [*Jesus*] should be slain.

29 And when they had fulfilled all that was written of him [*when they had fulfilled all the prophecies about Christ's crucifixion*], they took him down from the tree [*the cross*], and laid him in a sepulchre [*tomb*].

30 But God raised him from the dead:

31 And he [*Jesus*] was seen many days of them which came up with him from Galilee to Jerusalem, who are his witnesses unto the people. [*His disciples saw Jesus many times after His resurrection, and are now teaching others about Him.*]

> Paul is now going to refer to scriptures, which the Jews in this meeting in the synagogue know well, to explain to them that Jesus fulfilled those prophecies and thus was truly the promised Messiah.

32 And we declare unto you glad tidings [*good news*], how that the promise which was made unto the fathers,

33 God hath fulfilled the same unto us their children [*the promise which God made to our ancestors has been fulfilled among us in our day*], in that he hath raised up Jesus again; as it is also written in the second psalm [*Psalm 2:7*], Thou art my Son, this day have I begotten thee [*I have become your father*].

34 And as concerning that he [*the Father*] raised him [*Jesus*] up from the dead [*resurrected Him*], now no more to return to corruption [*Jesus will never die again*], he said on this wise [*in these words*], I will give you the sure mercies [*blessings*] of David.

35 Wherefore he saith also in another psalm [*Psalm 16:10*], Thou shalt not suffer thine Holy One to see corruption. [*Christ's body will not die again.*]

36 For David, after he had served his own generation by the will of God, fell on sleep [*died*], and was laid unto his fathers [*was buried with his ancestors*], and saw corruption [*his body rotted in the grave*]:

37 But he [*Christ*], whom God raised again [*resurrected*], saw no corruption [*did not decompose in the tomb*].

38 ¶ Be it known unto you therefore, men and brethren, that through this man [*through Jesus*] is preached unto you the forgiveness of sins [*through Christ's Atonement, you can be forgiven of sins*]:

39 And by him [*through Christ*] all that believe are justified [*saved*] from all things, from which ye could not be justified [*redeemed*] by the law of Moses.

> Did you catch the vital message that Paul led into in verse 39, above, concerning the Law of Moses? These people to whom Paul is speaking have been taught the false doctrine all their lives that salvation comes through the Law of Moses. This is not so. The Law of Moses in its pure form was designed to lead people to Jesus Christ, through whom salvation comes. Watch now to see where Paul goes from here with his inspired message.

40 Beware therefore, lest that come upon you, which is spoken of in the prophets [*watch out that what the prophet Habakkuk said doesn't happen to you, quoting Habakkuk 1:5*];

41 Behold, ye despisers [*watch out, you skeptics and mockers*], and wonder,

and perish [*marvel at Christ's life and teachings but still reject Him and die spiritually*]: for I [*God*] work a work in your days, a work which ye shall in no wise believe, though a man declare it unto you. [*I will do something so marvelous in your day that, even if someone explains it to you, you still won't believe it, referring to Christ's gospel and His Atonement.*]

42 And when the Jews were gone out of [*had left*] the synagogue, the Gentiles [*non-Jews*] besought [*requested*] that these words [*this same message from Paul*] might be preached to them the next sabbath.

43 Now when the congregation was broken up [*was dismissed to go home*], many of the Jews and religious proselytes [*devout converts to Jewish religion*] followed Paul and Barnabas: who, speaking to them, persuaded [*encouraged*] them to continue in the grace of God [*continue to be faithful to God*].

44 ¶ And the next sabbath day came almost the whole city together to hear the word of God.

45 But when the Jews saw the multitudes [*the large crowds coming to hear Paul and Barnabas*], they were filled with envy, and spake [*spoke*] against those things which were spoken by Paul, contradicting and blaspheming [*speaking abusively against what he was preaching*].

46 Then Paul and Barnabas waxed [*grew*] bold, and said, It was necessary that the word of God should first have been spoken to you [*the Jews who are now criticizing them*]: but seeing ye put it from you [*since you are rejecting it*], and judge yourselves unworthy of everlasting life, lo, we turn to the Gentiles.

47 For so hath the Lord commanded us, saying, I have set thee to be a light of the Gentiles, that thou shouldest be for salvation unto the ends of the earth [*to all the world*].

48 And when the Gentiles heard this, they were glad, and glorified [*praised*] the word of the Lord: and as many as were ordained to eternal life believed.

**JST Acts 13:48**

48 And when the Gentiles heard this, they were glad, and glorified the word of the Lord; and as many as believed were ordained unto eternal life.

49 And the word of the Lord was published [*preached*] throughout all the region.

50 But the Jews stirred up the devout [*loyal*] and honourable [*leading*] women, and the chief men of the city, and raised persecution against Paul and Barnabas, and expelled them out of their coasts [*region*].

51 But they [*Paul and Barnabas*] shook off the dust of their feet against them [*as a testimony that they had tried to teach them the gospel; see D&C 60:15*], and came unto Iconium [*about 70 miles to the east*].

52 And the disciples were filled with joy, and with the Holy Ghost.

# ACTS 14

This is an action-packed chapter in which you feel the energy and determination of Paul, as he and Barnabus preach despite mounting opposition. They will be declared gods by the people in one place, and Paul will be stoned and left for dead in another.

1 AND it came to pass in Iconium, that they [*Paul and Barnabas*] went both together into the synagogue [*church building*] of the Jews, and so spake, that a great multitude both of the Jews and also of the Greeks believed.

2 But the unbelieving Jews stirred up the Gentiles [*people who were not Jews*], and made their minds evil affected [*prejudiced*] against the brethren [*Paul and Barnabas*].

3 Long time therefore abode they speaking boldly in the Lord [*Paul and Barnabas spent quite a long time preaching boldly under the direction of the Spirit*], which gave testimony unto the word of his grace [*which bore witness of the gospel of Christ*], and granted signs and wonders to be done by their hands [*the Spirit blessed them such that they did a number of miracles*].

4 But the multitude of the city was divided: and part held [*took sides*] with the Jews, and part with the apostles.

5 And when there was an assault [*an attack against Paul and Barnabas*] made both of [*by*] the Gentiles, and also of the Jews with their rulers, to use them despitefully [*to abuse them*], and to stone them [*kill them by stoning*],

6 They were ware of it [*they became aware of it*], and fled unto Lystra [*south of Iconium, about 20 miles*] and Derbe [*about 20 miles southeast of Lystra*], cities of Lycaonia, and unto the region that lieth round about:

7 And there they preached the gospel.

8 ¶ And there sat a certain man at Lystra, impotent [*crippled*] in his feet, being a cripple from his mother's womb [*from birth*], who never had walked:

9 The same heard Paul speak: who stedfastly beholding him [*Paul looked straight at the crippled man for several moments*], and perceiving [*knowing*] that he had faith to be healed,

10 Said with a loud voice, Stand upright on thy feet. And he [*the crippled man*] leaped [*jumped up*] and walked.

11 And when the people saw what Paul had done, they lifted up their voices, saying in the speech [*language*] of Lycaonia, The gods are [*have*] come down to us in the likeness [*form*] of men.

12 And they called Barnabas, Jupiter [*the chief of the Roman gods; see Bible Dictionary under "Jupiter"*]; and Paul, Mercurius [*Mercury, the speaker for the Roman gods; see Bible Dictionary under "Mercurius"*], because he was the chief speaker [*Paul did most of the speaking as Paul and Barnabas preached*].

13 Then the priest of Jupiter, which was before their city [*the priest of the temple of Jupiter, which was just outside the city walls*], brought oxen and garlands unto the gates, and would have done sacrifice with the people [*and wanted to offer sacrifices to Barnabas and Paul, with the crowds*].

14 Which when the apostles, Barnabas and Paul, heard of, they rent [*tore*] their clothes, and ran in among the people, crying out,

> **<u>JST Acts 14:14</u>**
>
> 14 When the apostles, Barnabas and Paul, heard this, they rent their clothes, and ran in among the people, crying out,
>
> In the culture of these people, tearing one's clothing was a sign of deep distress and extreme emotion.

15 And saying, Sirs, why do ye these things? We also are men of like passions with you [*we are not gods, rather, just ordinary mortals like you*], and preach unto you that ye should turn from these vanities unto the living God, which made heaven, and earth, and the sea, and all things that are therein [*our message is that you should turn away from such worthless worship of Jupiter, Mercury, etc., and worship the living God instead*]:

16 Who in times past suffered [*allowed*] all nations to walk in their own ways.

17 Nevertheless he left not himself without witness [*evidence*], in that he did good, and gave us rain from heaven, and fruitful seasons, filling our hearts with food and gladness. [*Even though people left the true God and worshiped as they pleased, there is much evidence of His kindness in giving rain and crops to all.*]

18 And with these sayings scarce

restrained they the people, that they had not done sacrifice unto them. [*It was all Paul and Barnabas could do, even with such strong words, to stop the priest and the people from worshiping them.*]

19 ¶ And there came thither [*to Lystra*] certain Jews from Antioch and Iconium [*who had already tried to kill Paul and Barnabas*], who persuaded the people [*who talked the people in Lystra into stoning Paul*], and, having stoned Paul, drew [*dragged*] him out of the city, supposing he had been dead [*thinking he was dead*].

20 Howbeit [*however*], as the disciples [*members of the church*] stood round about him, he rose up, and came into the city: and the next day he departed with Barnabas to Derbe.

> We gain additional insights into Paul's personality as he continues on this first missionary journey. Once he has made up his mind to do something, he is unstoppable! He seems to have no fear, and, in defiance of the Jews who stoned him and left him for dead, goes right back through their cities and ministers to new converts there, as you will see beginning with verse 21, next.

21 And when they had preached the gospel to that city, and had taught many, they returned again to Lystra, and to Iconium, and Antioch,

22 Confirming [*strengthening*] the souls of the disciples, and exhorting [*urging*] them to continue in the faith, and that we must through much tribulation enter into the kingdom of God. [*We can only get to celestial glory by staying faithful in spite of trials and troubles which stand in our way.*]

23 And when they had ordained them elders in every church [*ward or branch*], and had prayed with fasting, they commended them to the Lord, on whom they believed. [*After Paul and Barnabas had organized priesthood leadership in each ward and branch, they turned the new converts over to the Lord and continued their missionary journey.*]

24 And after they had passed throughout Pisidia, they came to Pamphylia [*both are regions in what is now east-central Turkey, near the coast of the Mediterranean Sea*].

25 And when they had preached the word in Perga, they went down into Attalia [*on the coast*]:

26 And thence [*from there*] sailed to Antioch, from whence they had been recommended to the grace of God for the work which they fulfilled [*from which they had been sent on this mission*].

27 And when they were come [*when they arrived*], and had gathered the church together, they rehearsed [*told*] all that God had done with them, and how he had opened the door of faith unto the Gentiles [*how the gospel was taking hold among the Gentiles*].

28 And there they abode long time with the disciples [*they stayed in Antioch for a long time with the members of the church*].

## ACTS 15

Remember that when Stephen was stoned to death (Acts 7:55–60,) it signaled the beginning of intense persecution against the Church. Consequently, many faithful Jewish members fled from Jerusalem and settled far away in foreign cities. Thus, the stage was set for many Gentiles to hear the gospel and join the Church. Antioch (in northern Syria, over 300 miles north of Jerusalem and near eastern Turkey today) was one of these cities. Paul and Barnabas have just returned to Antioch from a very important mission, in which the gospel was successfully taken to the Island of Cyprus, plus many cities in what is now south central Turkey. Along with

a number of Jews, many Gentiles have also been converted and have joined the Church. Antioch has become a significant gathering place for members and new converts, including a large number of Gentile converts (see Acts 11:20–21).

As we begin our study of chapter 15, we find that some Jewish members, men from Church headquarters in Jerusalem, have come to Antioch and are disturbed that the male Gentile converts have been allowed to join the Church without being required to be circumcised according to the requirements of the Law of Moses (see Bible Dictionary under "Circumcision"). Paul and Barnabas are angry with these Jerusalem brethren for imposing cultural Judaism upon Gentile converts as a requirement for church membership. Lest we be too critical of these Jerusalem brethren, who are still learning, we might note that members of the Church today should be careful not to mix "cultural Mormonism" in with actual doctrines and ordinances required for exaltation.

1 AND certain men which came down from Judea [*from Church headquarters*] taught the brethren, and said, Except ye be circumcised after the manner of Moses [*unless you are circumcised, as taught by Moses*], ye cannot be saved.

2 When therefore Paul and Barnabas had no small dissension and disputation with them [*after Paul and Barnabas had argued strongly that these Jerusalem brethren were wrong*], they determined that Paul and Barnabas, and certain other of them, should go up to Jerusalem unto the apostles and elders about this question [*it was decided that Paul and Barnabas, with some other members, should go to Church headquarters in Jerusalem and check with the leaders of the Church on this matter*].

3 And being brought on their way by the church [*as they headed toward Jerusalem on this official business of the Church*], they passed through Phenice and Samaria, declaring [*telling about*] the conversion of the Gentiles: and they caused great joy unto all the brethren.

4 And when they were come to Jerusalem, they were received of the church, and of [*by*] the apostles and elders, and they declared [*explained*] all things that God had done with them.

5 But there rose up certain of the sect of the Pharisees which believed [*some Pharisees who had joined the Church, stood up*], saying, That it was needful to circumcise them, and to command them to keep the law of Moses.

The Pharisees (see Bible Dictionary under "Pharisees," for more about these men) had been very influential in getting Jesus crucified. They were powerful political and religious leaders among the Jews, and constantly accused Christ of violating the Law of Moses. Now, apparently, some of them had been converted and had joined the Church. They want Peter and the brethren to command that the Law of Moses be kept by the Church, even though Jesus had taught that He came to fulfill the Law of Moses, and such things were no longer required.

6 ¶ And the apostles and elders came together [*met together*] for to consider of this matter.

7 And when there had been much disputing [*after much debate*], Peter rose up [*note that Peter is now presiding as the President of the Church*], and said unto them, Men and brethren, ye know how that a good while ago God made choice among us, that the Gentiles by my mouth should hear the word of the gospel, and believe [*you know that some time ago (see Acts, chapter 10), God told me that we should now take the gospel to the Gentiles*].

8 And God, which knoweth the hearts, bare them witness, giving them the Holy Ghost, even as he did unto us [*God*

*has born witness to the Gentiles and given them the Holy Ghost, just like us*];

9 And put no difference between us and them [*God has shown us that there is no difference between them and us*], purifying their hearts by faith.

10 Now therefore why tempt ye God [*why do you want to try God's patience with you*], to put a yoke [*burden*] upon the neck of the disciples [*Gentile converts*], which neither our fathers nor we were able to bear [*which neither our ancestors nor we Jews could fully live ourselves? In other words, circumcision is not necessary for exaltation.*]

11 But we believe that through the grace of the Lord Jesus Christ we shall be saved, even as they.

12 ¶ Then all the multitude kept silence, and gave audience [*turned their attention*] to Barnabas and Paul, declaring [*who began explaining*] what miracles and wonders God had wrought among the Gentiles by them [*on their missionary journey*].

13 ¶ And after they had held their peace [*after Paul and Barnabas were through talking*], James answered [*responded*], saying, Men and brethren, hearken [*listen*] unto me:

We understand that James, in verse 13, above, is the brother of Jesus, and is one of Mary and Joseph's own children. See Bible Dictionary under "James." Paul informs us that James became an Apostle. See Galatians 1:19.

14 Simeon [*Peter*] hath declared [*explained*] how God at the first did visit the Gentiles, to take out of them a people for his name. [*Peter has explained to you that the "chosen people" originally came from the Gentiles.*]

Abraham was the beginning of the "chosen people" referred to in verse 14, above. He and his posterity were chosen to carry the wonderful and often heavy burden of carrying the gospel and the priesthood ordinances to all people of the earth. See Abraham 2:9–11.

15 And to this agree the words of the prophets [*the words of the prophets in the Old Testament agree with what Peter has told you about this*]; as it is written [*in Amos 9:11–12*],

16 After this I will return, and will build again the tabernacle of David, which is fallen down; and I will build again the ruins thereof, and I will set it up: [*The Lord will gather Israel back and restore the gospel to them.*]

17 That the residue of men [*the people who remain*] might seek after the Lord, and all the Gentiles, upon whom my name is called [*that the Gentiles also may join the Church and take My name upon them*], saith the Lord, who doeth all these things.

18 Known unto God are all his works from the beginning of the world. [*The Lord knows what He is doing.*]

19 Wherefore my sentence [*recommendation*] is, that we trouble not them, which from among the Gentiles are turned to God: [*I recommend that we do not require Gentile converts to live the Law of Moses, including circumcision, in order to join the Church.*]

20 But that we write unto them, that they abstain from pollutions of idols, and from fornication, and from things strangled, and from blood. [*I recommend that we put our decision in writing and also tell them to avoid idol worship, sexual immorality, and other things associated with idol worship.*]

21 For Moses of old time hath in every city them that preach him, being read in the synagogues every sabbath day. [*It is likely that James is referring here back to what he said in verse 19, and warning that there is still a lot of pressure for all Jews to live the Law of Moses, which was done away with by Christ.*]

22 Then pleased it the apostles and

elders, with the whole church [*the unanimous decision was then made*], to send chosen men of their own company [*from the Church leadership in Jerusalem*] to Antioch with Paul and Barnabas; namely, Judas surnamed [*whose family name was*] Barsabas, and Silas, chief men [*men who had much authority*] among the brethren:

23 And they wrote letters by them after this manner [*this is what they wrote in their letters of instruction to Gentile converts*]; The apostles and elders and brethren send greeting unto the brethren which are of the Gentiles [*to the brothers who are Gentile converts*] in Antioch and Syria and Cilicia:

24 Forasmuch [*inasmuch*] as we have heard, that certain which went out from us [*that some members who came from here*] have troubled you with words [*have given you instructions which worried you*], subverting your souls [*damaging your testimonies*], saying, Ye must be circumcised, and keep the law: to whom we gave no such commandment [*we did not authorize them to give you such instructions*]:

**JST Acts 15:24**

24 Forasmuch as we have heard, that certain men which went out from us have troubled you with words, subverting your souls, saying, Ye must be circumcised, and keep the law; to whom we gave no such commandment;

25 It seemed good unto us, being assembled with one accord [*having met and come to unity on this matter*], to send chosen men unto you with our beloved Barnabas and Paul,

26 Men that have hazarded their lives [*men who have put their lives in danger*] for the name of our Lord Jesus Christ.

27 We have sent therefore Judas and Silas, who shall also tell you the same things by mouth [*verbally*].

28 For it seemed good to the Holy Ghost, and to us [*the Holy Ghost approves of this*], to lay upon you no greater burden than these necessary things;

29 That ye abstain from meats offered to idols, and from blood, and from things strangled, and from fornication [*see explanation in verse 20, above*]: from which if ye keep yourselves, ye shall do well. Fare ye well.

30 So when they were dismissed, they came to Antioch: and when they had gathered the multitude together, they delivered the epistle [*the letter from Peter and the Brethren*]:

31 Which when they [*the Gentile converts in Antioch and the surrounding areas*] had read, they rejoiced for the consolation [*because it was very comforting*].

32 And Judas and Silas, being prophets also themselves, exhorted [*taught and explained things to*] the brethren [*the Gentile converts*] with many words, and confirmed them [*and verbally confirmed what had been written in the letter*].

33 And after they [*Judas, Silas, and others who had accompanied them from Church headquarters*] had tarried there a space [*had stayed for a while in Antioch*], they were let go in peace from the brethren unto the apostles [*they left, in peace, and returned to Church headquarters in Jerusalem*].

34 Notwithstanding it pleased Silas to abide there still [*however, Silas chose to remain in Antioch*].

35 Paul also and Barnabas continued [*stayed*] in Antioch, teaching and preaching the word of the Lord, with many others also.

Beginning with verse 36, next, Paul will make preparations and leave on what is known as his second missionary journey. It is reported in Acts 15:36 through Acts 18:22. See Bible Dictionary under "Paul."

36 ¶ And some days after Paul said unto Barnabas, Let us go again and visit our brethren in every city where we have preached the word of the Lord [*let's visit the converts in every city we went to on our first missionary journey*], and see how they do.

37 And Barnabas determined to take with them John, whose surname was Mark [*Barnabas wanted to take Mark with them*].

38 But Paul thought not good to take him with them, who departed from them from Pamphylia, and went not with them to the work. [*But Paul didn't want to take Mark with them because he considered Mark to be a quitter, because he left them and went home from Pamphylia (see Acts 13:13) while they were on their first missionary journey*].

39 And the contention was so sharp between them, that they departed asunder one from the other [*Paul and Barnabas disagreed with each other so sharply that they parted company over the issue*]: and so Barnabas took Mark, and sailed unto Cyprus [*the first destination on the first missionary journey of Paul and Barnabas*];

40 And Paul chose Silas, and departed, being recommended by the brethren unto the grace of God. [*The Brethren wisely sent Paul and Silas in a different direction than Barnabas and Mark.*]

The above contention between Paul and Barnabas is a reminder that these great men were still human, and still had some growing to do. Fortunately for us all, God is patient and allows us to grow also.

41 And he [*Paul*] went through Syria and Cilicia, confirming [*strengthening*] the churches.

As mentioned previously, this is the beginning of what is known as Paul's second missionary journey. He and Silas will head north from Antioch, through the northern part of Syria, then west through what is known as Turkey today, then west to what is modern-day Greece, preaching to many, including the Philippians, the Thessalonians, the Corinthians and the Ephesians, and finally ending up in Jerusalem, after traveling thousands of miles.

# ACTS 16

Paul continues his energetic missionary work as he boldly returns to the sites of previous persecution. Timothy will join him as a missionary companion and will no doubt be taught much to prepare him for his ministry.

1 THEN came he [*Paul*] to Derbe and Lystra [*remember that Paul was stoned and left for dead in Lystra during his first missionary journey; see Acts 14:8–20*]: and, behold, a certain disciple [*member of the Church*] was there, named Timotheus [*Timothy*], the son of a certain woman, which was a Jewess, and believed [*was a member of the Church*]; but his father was a Greek [*a Gentile and apparently not a member of the Church*]:

Timothy will join Paul and Silas on their missionary journey as they leave Lystra. Timothy will become a very important assistant to Paul. First and Second Timothy are letters written to Timothy by Paul. For more about him, see Bible Dictionary under "Timothy."

2 Which was well reported of by the brethren that were at Lystra and Iconium. [*The local leaders of the Church at Lystra and Iconium told Paul that Timothy was a very faithful young man*].

3 Him would Paul have to go forth with him [*Paul wanted him to accompany him on this mission*]; and took and circumcised him because of the Jews [*so that he could work more effectively with Jewish members of the Church*] which were in those quarters [*in that region*]: for they knew all that his father was a Greek [*a Gentile*].

4 And as they went through the cities, they delivered them the decrees for to keep, that were ordained of the apostles and elders which were at Jerusalem [*they delivered instructions from the Brethren at Church headquarters in Jerusalem*].

5 And so were the churches [*wards and branches*] established [*strengthened*] in the faith, and increased in number daily [*received new converts daily*].

6 Now when they had gone throughout Phrygia [*west-central Turkey today*] and the region of Galatia [*north-central Turkey today*], and were forbidden of the Holy Ghost to preach the word in Asia [*the Spirit prompted them not to preach in Asia, which would be in western Turkey today*],

7 After they were come to Mysia [*far northwestern Turkey today*], they assayed to go [*discussed the possibilities of going*] into Bithynia [*extreme north-central Turkey today*]: but the Spirit suffered them not [*did not permit it*].

8 And they passing by Mysia came down to Troas [*on the extreme northwestern tip of Turkey today*].

9 And a vision appeared to Paul in the night; There stood a man of Macedonia [*northern Greece today*], and prayed [*urgently asked*] him, saying, Come over into Macedonia, and help us.

10 And after he had seen the vision, immediately we [*Luke has now joined them*] endeavoured [*made plans*] to go into Macedonia, assuredly gathering [*knowing for sure*] that the Lord had called us for to preach the gospel unto them.

The use of "we" and "us" in verse 10, above, is interesting. As mentioned in the note at the beginning of Acts, Luke is the author of Acts. Up to Acts 16:10, Luke has used the pronoun "they" in describing what is happening. Now, he uses the pronoun "we"—thus informing us that he has joined Paul, Silas, and Timothy at this point of Paul's second missionary journey.

11 Therefore loosing [*sailing*] from Troas, we came with a straight course to Samothracia [*an island in the northern part of the Aegean Sea*], and the next day to Neapolis [*in extreme north eastern Greece today*];

12 And from thence [*there*] to Philippi [*in northeastern Greece today*], which is the chief [*main*] city of that part of Macedonia, and a colony [*a colony planted by the Roman Empire under Octavius*]: and we were in that city abiding certain days [*staying for several days*].

13 And on the sabbath we went out of the city by a river side, where prayer was wont to be made [*where it was customary for citizens of the city to come to pray*]; and we sat down, and spake unto the women which resorted thither [*who came there*].

**JST Acts 16:13**

13 And on the Sabbath we went out of the city by a river side, where the people resorted for prayer to be made; and we sat down, and spake unto the women which resorted thither.

14 ¶ And a certain woman named Lydia, a seller of purple [*a merchant who sold purple cloth*], of [*from*] the city of Thyatira [*in modern-day western Turkey*], which worshipped God [*who believed in God*], heard us: whose heart the Lord opened [*the Spirit touched her heart*], that she attended [*paid close attention*] unto the things which were spoken of Paul.

15 And when she was baptized, and her household [*along with members of her household*], she besought [*asked*] us, saying, If ye have judged me to be faithful to the Lord [*if you consider me worthy*], come into my house, and abide there [*come stay at my home*]. And she constrained us [*convinced us to stay with her*].

16 ¶ And it came to pass, as we went to prayer, a certain damsel [*young woman slave*] possessed with a spirit of divination [*possessed by an evil spirit which helped her tell fortunes and predict the future*] met us, which brought her masters much gain by soothsaying: [*Her fortune-telling earned her owners much money.*]

17 The same [*the young slave girl*] followed Paul and us, and cried [*shouted*], saying, These men are the servants of the most high God, which shew [*who will show*] unto us the way of salvation.

18 And this did she many days. But Paul, being grieved [*saddened by this*], turned and said to the spirit [*the evil spirit who possessed her*], I command thee in the name of Jesus Christ to come out of her. And he came out the same hour [NIV, *"at that moment"*].

19 ¶ And when her masters [*owners*] saw that the hope of their gains [*that their source of income*] was gone, they caught Paul and Silas, and drew [*dragged*] them into the marketplace unto the rulers,

20 And brought them to the magistrates [*city judges*], saying, These men, being Jews, do exceedingly trouble our city,

21 And teach customs, which are not lawful [*legal*] for us to receive [*to accept*], neither to observe [*to practice*], being Romans [*since we are Roman citizens*].

22 And the multitude rose up together against them [*joined in attacking Paul and Silas*]: and the magistrates rent off their clothes, and commanded to beat them. [*The judges tore off Paul and Silas' clothes and ordered that they be beaten.*]

23 And when they had laid many stripes upon them [*when they had beaten them with several lashes of the whip*], they cast them into prison, charging [*commanding*] the jailor to keep them safely [*to make sure they didn't get away*]:

24 Who, having received such a charge, thrust them into the inner prison, and made their feet fast in the stocks. [*The jailor, having received such strict orders, put Paul and Silas in the inner dungeon and locked their feet in the stocks, so that there was no chance they would escape.*]

25 ¶ And at midnight Paul and Silas prayed, and sang praises unto God: and the prisoners heard them.

26 And suddenly there was a great earthquake, so that the foundations of the prison were shaken: and immediately all the doors were opened, and every one's bands were loosed [*every prisoner's shackles were unlocked so they could escape*].

27 And the keeper of the prison awaking out of his sleep, and seeing the prison doors open, he drew out his sword, and would have killed himself, supposing that the prisoners had been fled [*assuming that all the prisoners had escaped*].

28 But Paul cried with a loud voice, saying, Do thyself no harm [*don't hurt yourself*]: for we are all here.

29 Then he [*the jailor*] called for a light, and sprang in [*ran into the dungeon*], and came trembling, and fell [*bowed*] down before Paul and Silas,

30 And brought them out, and said, Sirs, what must I do to be saved?

31 And they said, Believe on the Lord Jesus Christ, and thou shalt be saved, and thy house [*and your family too*].

32 And they spake unto him the word of the Lord, and to all that were in his house [*they taught him and his family the gospel*].

33 And he took them [*Paul and Silas*] the same hour of the night [*immediately*], and washed their stripes [*washed their wounds from their whipping*]; and was baptized, he and all his [*family*], straightway [*immediately*].

34 And when he had brought them [*Paul and Silas*] into his house, he set meat [*food*] before them, and rejoiced, believing in God with all his house.

35 And when it was day [*in the morning*], the magistrates [*judges, city officials*] sent the serjeants [*sergeants to the jailor*], saying, Let those men go [*release Paul and Silas from jail*].

36 And the keeper of the prison [*the jailor*] told this saying to Paul [*gave Paul the following message*:], The magistrates have sent to let you go: now therefore depart, and go in peace.

37 But Paul said unto them, They have beaten us openly [*in pub*lic] uncondemned [*without a proper trial according to Roman law*], being Romans [*and we are Roman citizens*], and have cast us into prison; and now do they thrust us out privily [*very quietly*]? nay verily [*absolutely not*!]; but let them come themselves and fetch us out [*let them come personally and release us*!].

Again, we gain more insights into Paul's personality. He is feisty!

38 And the serjeants told these words unto the magistrates: and they feared [*were very worried because they themselves could get into serious trouble for abusing Roman citizens without due process of law*], when they heard that they were Romans.

39 And they came and besought them [*begged their forgiveness*], and brought them out [*personally escorted them out of the prison*], and desired them [*asked them*] to depart out of the city.

40 And they went out of the prison, and entered into the house of Lydia and when they had seen the brethren, they comforted them, and departed [*left town*].

# ACTS 17

This chapter contains Paul's masterful sermon about the "Unknown God" (see verse 23). It was given in Athens and is an excellent example of Paul's skill as a speaker. You will also see one of the best references in the Bible teaching clearly that we are literally spirit children of God (verses 28–29).

1 NOW when they had passed through Amphipolis and Apollonia [*both cities were in what is known as northeastern Greece today*], they came to Thessalonica [*in northeastern Greece, on the coast of the Aegean Sea*], where was a synagogue [*church building*] of the Jews:
2 And Paul, as his manner [*custom*] was, went in unto them, and three sabbath days reasoned with them out of the scriptures [*taught and discussed the scriptures with them each Sabbath day for three weeks*],

3 Opening and alleging [*presenting to them*], that Christ must needs have suffered [*that it was necessary for Christ to suffer for our sins*], and risen again from the dead [*and be resurrected*]; and that this Jesus, whom I preach unto you, is Christ [*that Jesus, about whom I am teaching you, is the Messiah (Christ) as promised in the scriptures*].

4 And some of them [*Jews who belonged to this synagogue*] believed, and consorted [*joined*] with Paul and Silas; and of the devout Greeks [*Gentiles*] a great multitude [*a large number joined*], and of the chief women not a few [*many prominent, influential women joined the Church also*].

Often, the word "Greeks," as used in verse 4, above, refers to Gentiles rather than just Greeks. In Strong's *Concordance*, under word #1671, it says the following regarding the word "Greek": "In a wider sense the name embraces all nations not Jews that made the language, customs, and learning of the Greeks their own . . ."

5 ¶ But the Jews which believed not [*who did not believe Paul and refused to join the Church*], moved with [*motivated by*] envy, took unto them [*gathered up*] certain lewd [*evil, wicked*] fellows of

the baser sort [*who were vulgar idlers, hanging around the market place*] and gathered a company [*a mob*], and set all the city on an uproar [*caused a riot*], and assaulted [*attacked*] the house of Jason [*Romans 16:21 informs us that Jason was one of Paul's relatives*], and sought to bring them [*Paul and Silas*] out to the people [*to turn them over to the mob*].

It appears that Jason was a Thessalonican citizen who had joined the Church and that Paul and his associates visited in Jason's home. This incident took place about AD 48.

6 And when they found them not, they drew [*dragged*] Jason and certain brethren unto the rulers of the city, crying [*shouting*], These that have turned the world upside down are come hither also [*Paul, Silas and their group, who have stirred things up everywhere they have been, have come to our city too*];

7 Whom Jason hath received [*Jason accepted them and their teachings*]: and these all do contrary to the decrees of Cæsar, saying that there is another king, one Jesus [*Paul and his people are undermining Caesar and the Roman government by saying that there is another king, namely Jesus*].

8 And they troubled [*stirred up*] the people and the rulers of the city, when they heard these things.

9 And when they had taken security of Jason, and of the other, they let them go. [*When they had made Jason and other members pay bail, they released them.*]

10 ¶ And the brethren immediately sent away Paul and Silas by night unto Berea [*about 40 miles west of Thessalonica*]: who coming thither [*having arrived there*] went into the synagogue of the Jews.

11 These were more noble than those in Thessalonica, in that they received the word with all readiness of mind, and searched the scriptures daily, whether those things were so. [*The Jews in Berea were more receptive to the gospel than those in Thessalonica, and sincerely searched the scriptures to see if what Paul and Silas said was true.*]

12 Therefore many of them believed; also of honourable women which were Greeks, and of men, not a few [*many Gentile men and women were converted also*].

13 But when the Jews of Thessalonica had knowledge [*became aware*] that the word of God was preached of [*by*] Paul at Berea, they came thither [*there*] also, and stirred up the people.

14 And then immediately the brethren sent away Paul to go as it were to the sea [*to catch a ship and get away*]: but Silas and Timotheus abode there still [*stayed in Berea*].

15 And they that conducted [*the sailors who escorted*] Paul brought him unto Athens [*in southeastern Greece*]: and receiving a commandment unto Silas and Timotheus for to come to him with all speed [*receiving instructions from Paul to tell Silas and Timothy to join him in Athens as soon as possible*], they departed [*the sailors left for Berea*].

16 ¶ Now while Paul waited for them [*Silas and Timothy*] at Athens, his spirit was stirred in him, when he saw the city wholly given to idolatry [*completely involved in idol worship*].

17 Therefore disputed he [*he debated*] in the synagogue with the Jews, and with the devout [*religious*] persons, and in the market daily with them that met with him.

18 Then certain philosophers of the Epicureans, and of the Stoicks [*Stoics*], encountered [*met with Paul*] him. And some said, What will this babbler say? other some [*others said*], He seemeth to be a setter forth of strange gods [*he is preaching about some strange gods*]: because he preached unto them Jesus, and the resurrection.

Epicureans and Stoics, as mentioned in verse 18, above, taught Greek

philosophies that were opposite each other. The Epicureans basically believed in pleasure and materialism as the source of true happiness in life. The Stoics, on the other hand, taught their followers to completely ignore pleasure, pain, and all external good or evil. They taught that the desired goal was complete independence from all external, physical influences.

19 And they took him [*Paul*], and brought him unto Areopagus [*a rocky hill in Athens, known as Mars Hill*], saying, May we know what this new doctrine, whereof thou speakest, is?

**JST Acts 17:19**

19 And they took him and brought him unto the Areopagus, saying, May we know what this new doctrine is, whereof thou speakest?

20 For thou bringest certain strange things to our ears: we would know therefore [*we would like to know*] what these things mean.

21 (For all the Athenians [*citizens of Athens*] and strangers [*foreigners*] which were there spent their time in nothing else, but either to tell, or to hear some new thing.)

Paul's sermon at Mars Hill, beginning with verse 22, next, is one of the more famous of his addresses. You can get a good feel for his inspired skill as a teacher as he sets the stage for preaching about the true God.

22 ¶ Then Paul stood in the midst of Mars' hill, and said, Ye men of Athens, I perceive that in all things ye are too superstitious [*you are very religious; see Acts 17:22, footnote a*].

23 For as I passed by, and beheld [*saw*] your devotions [*your sacred statues, etc.*], I found an altar with this inscription, TO THE UNKNOWN GOD. Whom therefore ye ignorantly [*without understanding*] worship, him declare I unto you. [*I am going to explain to you who the UNKNOWN GOD is.*]

24 [*He is the*] God that made the world and all things therein [*in it*], seeing that he is Lord of heaven and earth, dwelleth not in temples made with hands [*He does not actually live in temples built by people*];

25 Neither is worshipped with men's hands, as though he needed any thing [*you don't have to fix or repair Him like you would a damaged statue (see Strong's #2324, definition 2) because He doesn't need such things*], seeing he giveth to all life, and breath, and all things [*The true God gives life to everything; D&C 88:41*];

26 And hath made of one blood [*from Adam and Eve*] all nations of men [*we are all brothers and sisters*] for to dwell on all the face of the earth, and hath determined the times before appointed [*"God sends his spirit children to earth on a regular, organized schedule. There is nothing haphazard or accidental about the peopling of the earth . . ." McConkie,* Doctrinal New Testament Commentary, *Vol. 2, p. 159*], and the bounds of their habitation [*God has planned that certain races would inhabit certain lands*];

27 That they should seek the Lord [*God planned all this so that He would be available to help us as we seek Him*], if haply [*if perhaps*] they might feel after him [*seek Him*], and find him, though he be not far from every one of us [*it doesn't take much looking because He is close by and anxious to help us*]:

**JST Acts 17:27**

27 That they should seek the Lord, if they are willing to find him, for he is not far from every one of us;

28 For in him we live, and move, and have our being [*God is everything to us*]; as certain also of your own poets have said, For we are also his offspring.

Verse 28, above, and verse 29, below, contain simple, clear doctrine, namely, that we are the offspring of God. In most verses in scripture, we are referred to as "creations" of God, which, of course, we are. But the word "offspring" is even more specific. It means that we were

born as spirit sons and daughters of our Heavenly Parents. See Proclamation on the Family, paragraph two. It means that we are not "creations" in the sense that trees, mountains, cows, horses, sheep, birds, etc., are. Rather, we are literally children of God, and thus, through righteousness, can become like Him and become gods. (See D&C 132:19–20.) To have this correct doctrine right in the Bible can be helpful to us as we teach our nonmember friends who they really are.

29 Forasmuch then as we are the offspring of God, we ought not to think that the Godhead is like unto gold, or silver, or stone, graven by art and man's device. [*Since we are God's literal children, and we are not made of gold, silver, or stone, carved or sculpted by some artist, then it follows that the Godhead is composed of real people like us, not of statues made by man.*]

30 And the times of this ignorance God winked at [*God has been patient up to now with such foolish notions about who He is*]; but now commandeth all men every where to repent [*but now you know the truth about Him and who you are, and it is time to repent and begin worshiping the true God*]:

31 Because he [*the Father*] hath appointed a day [*Judgment Day*], in the which he will judge the world in righteousness by that man [*by Jesus who is the Christ*] whom he hath ordained [*sent*]; whereof he hath given assurance unto all men, in that he hath raised him from the dead [*the fact that the Father raised Jesus from the dead is proof that Jesus is indeed the promised Messiah*].

**JST Acts 17:31**

31 Because he hath appointed a day, in the which he will judge the world in righteousness by him whom he hath ordained; and he hath given assurance of this unto all men, in that he hath raised him from the dead.

32 ¶ And when they heard of the resurrection of the dead, some mocked [*made fun of it*]: and others said, We will hear thee again of this matter [*we would like to hear more about this from you*].

33 So Paul departed from among them.

34 Howbeit [*however*] certain men clave unto him [*joined Paul*], and believed [*and were converted*]: among the which was Dionysius the Areopagite [*a member of the Supreme Court of Athens; see Strong's #0697*], and a woman named Damaris, and others with them.

# ACTS 18

In this chapter, Paul will visit Corinth, a city widely known for its wealth and wicked lifestyle. He will meet a faithful couple named Aquila and Priscilla and they will form a life-long friendship.

1 AFTER these things Paul departed from Athens, and came to Corinth [*a wealthy, worldly, wild seaport city in Paul's day, in southern Greece*];

2 And found a certain Jew named Aquila, born in Pontus, lately [*recently*] come from Italy, with his wife Priscilla; (because that Claudius had commanded all Jews to depart from Rome:) and came unto them.

3 And because he was of the same craft [*Aquila and Paul were both skilled in making fabric for tent-making*], he abode [*stayed*] with them, and wrought [*worked*]: for by their occupation they were tentmakers.

After a year and a half, Paul will leave Corinth, and Aquila and Priscilla will leave with him.

4 And he reasoned [*taught and discussed the gospel*] in the synagogue every sabbath, and persuaded [*taught*] the Jews and the Greeks [*Gentiles*].

5 And when Silas and Timotheus [*Timothy*] were come [*finally arrived; see Acts 17:10–15*] from Macedonia, Paul was pressed in the spirit [*strongly felt the urgency to teach of Christ*], and

testified to the Jews that Jesus was Christ.

6 And when they [*the Jews*] opposed themselves [*angrily resisted*], and blasphemed [*reviled and insulted Paul*], he shook his raiment [*he took his robe off and shook it in front of them, a sign of extreme disgust, grief, etc., in Jewish culture*], and said unto them, Your blood be upon your own heads; I am clean [*I have tried, therefore I am no longer responsible for you*]: from henceforth [*from now on*] I will go unto the Gentiles. [*I've had it with you Jews! From now on, I will preach to the Gentiles.*]

> Paul's feisty personality shows strongly here. He apparently felt that all the Jews in that synagogue had rejected him, but as it turns out, the leader of the synagogue and all his family believed and were converted, as shown in the next verses, below. This is a good reminder to all of us that we sometimes don't know when someone has been helped by our efforts to bring them to Christ, even though it appears hopeless at the time.

7 ¶ And he departed thence [*from those Jews*], and entered into a certain man's house, named Justus, one that worshipped God [*one who believed in God*], whose house joined hard [*was right next door*] to the synagogue [*the building where the Jews worshiped*].

8 And Crispus, the chief ruler of the synagogue, believed on the Lord [*Christ*] with all his house [*along with his whole family*]; and many of the Corinthians hearing [*that Crispus had joined the Church*] believed, and were baptized.

9 Then spake the Lord [*the Savior*] to Paul in the night by a vision, Be not afraid, but speak, and hold not thy peace [*don't hold back, go ahead and preach to these people*]:

10 For I am with thee, and no man shall set on thee to hurt thee [*I will protect you here in Corinth*]: for I have much people in this city [*I have many people here in Corinth who will join the Church*].

11 And he continued there a year and six months, teaching the word of God among them.

12 ¶ And when Gallio was the deputy [*the Roman governor*] of Achaia [*southern Greece*], the Jews made insurrection with one accord [*joined together*] against Paul, and brought him to the judgment seat [*brought him to Gallio*],

13 Saying, This fellow persuadeth men to worship God contrary to the law [*which is against our law*].

14 And when Paul was now about to open his mouth [*was about to start speaking in his defense*], Gallio said unto the Jews, If it were a matter of wrong or wicked lewdness [*crime against our laws*], O ye Jews, reason would [*logic would dictate*] that I should bear with you [*that I would hear this case*]:

15 But if it be a question of words and names, and of your law [*but if it is a matter of your wanting me to enforce your religious laws for you*], look ye to it [*you take care of it*]; for I will be no judge of such matters [*I want nothing to do with such matters*].

16 And he drave them [*had them driven out*] from the judgment seat [*from his court room*].

17 Then all the Greeks took Sosthenes, the chief ruler of the synagogue, and beat him before [*within sight of*] the judgment seat [*Gallio's courtroom*]. And Gallio cared for none of those things [*payed no attention to it*].

18 ¶ And Paul after this tarried [*stayed*] there yet a good while, and then took his leave of the brethren [*said goodbye to the members in Corinth*], and sailed thence into Syria, and with him Priscilla and Aquila [*members of the Church; see Acts 18:2–3*]; having shorn his head [*cut his hair off*] in Cenchrea [*just a*

*few miles south of Corinth*]: for he had a vow.

We do not know what Paul's vow or promise was. The cutting off of his hair was a sign in his culture and reminder to him that he had made a promise that he was determined to keep.

19 And he came to Ephesus [*near the coast of the Aegean Sea in southwestern Turkey*], and left them [*Aquila, and Priscilla, his wife*] there: but he himself entered into the synagogue, and reasoned [*discussed the gospel*] with the Jews.

20 When they desired him to tarry longer time [*to stay longer*] with them, he consented not [*he did not agree to*];

21 But bade them farewell [*said "Goodbye"*], saying, I must by all means keep this feast that cometh in Jerusalem [*I must at all costs, keep my vow to attend the feast that is coming up in Jerusalem*]: but I will return again unto you, if God will. And he sailed from Ephesus.

We don't know which feast it was, in Jerusalem, that Paul was so anxious to attend, but he was absolutely determined not to arrive late to it.

22 And when he had landed at Cæsarea [*on the coast, about 50 miles northwest of Jerusalem*], and gone up [*to Jerusalem*], and saluted the church [*greeted the members of the Church there*], he went down to Antioch [*about 350 miles north of Jerusalem, in northern Syria*].

Starting in verse 23, next, Paul will begin what is known as his third missionary journey. His travels on this journey are reported in Acts 18:23 through Acts 21:15. See Bible Dictionary under "Paul." This missionary journey will be his last (about four years), and he will travel farther on this journey than he did on either of his first two.

23 And after he had spent some time there, he departed, and went over all the country of Galatia and Phrygia in order [*he traveled back to visit his converts in what would be central Turkey today*], strengthening all the disciples [*members*].

24 ¶ And a certain Jew named Apollos, born at Alexandria [*probably about a hundred miles north of Antioch in northern Syria*], an eloquent man [*an excellent speaker*], and mighty in the scriptures [*who knew the scriptures very well*], came to Ephesus.

25 This man was instructed in the way of the Lord; and being fervent in the spirit, he spake and taught diligently the things of the Lord, knowing only the baptism of John. [*Apollos had considerable gospel knowledge and was a spiritual man, but was only acquainted with the teachings of John the Baptist, not of Jesus.*]

26 And he began to speak boldly in the synagogue: whom when Aquila and Priscilla [*faithful members from Corinth, who had followed Paul to Ephesus, and stayed there while he went to Jerusalem*] had heard, they took him unto them, and expounded [*explained*] unto him the way of God more perfectly [*taught him about Christ and his teachings*].

27 And when he [*Apollos*] was disposed to pass into [*decided to go to*] Achaia [*the region of southern Greece, where Athens and Corinth were*], the brethren wrote, exhorting [*urging*] the disciples [*the members in southern Greece*] to receive [*accept*] him: who, when he was come, helped them much which had believed through grace: [*When Appolos arrived among the Saints in southern Greece, he taught them much and strengthened their knowledge of the gospel.*]

28 For he mightily convinced the Jews, and that publickly [*he was very successful in public debates with the non-believing Jews*], shewing by the scriptures that Jesus was Christ [*proving from their scriptures that Jesus was indeed the Messiah promised by Old Testament prophets*].

# ACTS 19

One of the more famous incidents recorded by Luke in this chapter is the account of the seven sons of Sceva who try without priesthood authority to cast out an evil spirit (verses 13–16).

1 AND it came to pass [*it so happened*], that, while Apollos was at Corinth, Paul having passed through the upper coasts [*having passed through the upper regions of what is today Turkey*] came to Ephesus: and finding certain disciples,

Did you notice Corinth and Ephesus in verse 1, above? They probably sound familiar to you. Paul wrote letters to the Saints living in these and other cities (such as Galatia in Acts 18:23) where he had taught and baptized. These letters or epistles became the New Testament books of 1 Corinthians, 2 Corinthians, Galatians, and so forth.

2 He said unto them, Have ye received the Holy Ghost since ye believed [*since you were converted*]? And they said unto him, We have not so much as heard whether there be any Holy Ghost [*we haven't even heard of the Holy Ghost*].

3 And he said unto them, Unto what then were ye baptized? And they said, Unto John's [*John the Baptist's*] baptism.

4 Then said Paul, John verily [*indeed*] baptized with the baptism of repentance, saying unto the people, that they should believe on him [*Christ*] which should come after him [*John the Baptist*], that is, on Christ Jesus.

5 When they [*the disciples at the end of verse 1*] heard this, they were baptized in the name of the Lord Jesus.

6 And when Paul had laid his hands upon [*confirmed*] them, the Holy Ghost came on them; and they spake [*spoke*] with tongues, and prophesied.

7 And all the men were about twelve [*there were about twelve who were baptized and confirmed*].

8 And he went into the synagogue, and spake boldly for the space of three months, disputing [*reasoning with them*] and persuading [*teaching*] the things concerning the kingdom of God.

9 But when divers [*various Jews there*] were hardened [*hard-hearted*], and believed not, but spake evil of that way [*severely criticized Paul's teachings about God's kingdom*] before the multitude [*in front of the crowds*], he departed from them [*he left that synagogue*], and separated [*set apart*] the disciples, disputing [*reasoning and debating*] daily in the school of one Tyrannus.

Scholars presume that Tyrannus (a name which means "sovereign") was a Greek philosopher who taught philosophy in a public school setting in Ephesus. He obviously allowed Paul to meet with his students.

10 And this continued by the space of [*for*] two years; so that all they which dwelt in Asia heard the word of the Lord Jesus, both Jews and Greeks [*Gentiles*].

11 And God wrought [*performed*] special miracles by the hands of Paul:

12 So that from his body were brought unto the sick handkerchiefs or aprons, and the diseases departed from them, and the evil spirits went out of them. [*The power of God was upon Paul so much that people were able to take handkerchiefs or aprons, which had touched Paul, to sick people, including those possessed by evil spirits, and they were healed.*]

13 ¶ Then certain of the vagabond Jews, exorcists [*wandering Jews who went around trying to cast out evil spirits*], took upon them [*took upon themselves*] to call over them which had evil spirits the name of the Lord Jesus [*decided to try using the name of Jesus Christ in their attempts to cast evil spirits out of people*], saying [*to the evil spirits*], We adjure [*command*] you by Jesus whom Paul preacheth.

14 And there were seven sons of one Sceva [*a name meaning "mind reader"*], a Jew, and chief of the priests, which did so. [*A Jew who was high in authority had seven sons who tried to cast an evil spirit out of a man in the name of Jesus Christ.*]

15 And the evil spirit answered and said, Jesus I know, and Paul I know; but who are ye?

16 And the man in whom the evil spirit was [*the man whom the evil spirit controlled*] leaped on them [*attacked them*], and overcame them, and prevailed against them [*beat them up*], so that they fled out of that house naked and wounded.

17 And this was known [*word of this spread rapidly*] to all the Jews and Greeks also dwelling at Ephesus; and fear fell on them all, and the name of the Lord Jesus was magnified [*became much more famous and honored*].

18 And many that believed [*who were converted*] came [*to Paul and his brethren*], and confessed, and shewed their deeds [*and openly confessed their sins and evil deeds*].

19 Many of them also which used curious arts [*magic, sorcery, witchcraft, etc.*] brought their books together [*gathered together their books about sorcery, etc.*], and burned them before all men [*burned them in public*]: and they counted the price of them, and found it fifty thousand pieces of silver [*they figured the cost of the books they burned to be about 50,000 pieces of silver*].

20 So mightily grew the word of God and prevailed [*had much success*].

21 ¶ After these things were ended, Paul purposed in the spirit [*felt prompted by the Spirit*], when [*after*] he had passed through Macedonia and Achaia [*modern Greece today*], to go to Jerusalem, saying, After I have been there, I must also see Rome.

22 So he sent into Macedonia [*northern Greece*] two of them that ministered unto him, Timotheus [*Timothy*] and Erastus; but he himself stayed in Asia [*the Ephesus region in what is western Turkey today*] for a season.

23 And the same time there arose no small stir [*in the region around Ephesus*] about that way [*the way of living taught by the gospel*].

24 For a certain man named Demetrius, a silversmith, which made silver shrines for Diana, brought no small gain [*profit*] unto the craftsmen;

Diana, also known as Artemis, was a Greek goddess and was worshiped by many people in that region. See Bible Dictionary under "Diana." A temple to honor her had been built at Ephesus, and silversmiths in the area made an excellent living making statues of Diana, models of the temple, etc., to sell to worshipers of this false god.

25 Whom he called together with the workmen of like occupation [*Demetrius called an emergency meeting of the silversmiths*], and said, Sirs, ye know that by this craft [*making things to sell to worshipers of Diana*] we have our wealth.

26 Moreover [*furthermore*] ye see and hear, that not alone at Ephesus [*not only at Ephesus*], but almost throughout all Asia, this Paul hath persuaded and turned away much [*many*] people, saying that they be no gods, which are made with hands: [*In other words, Paul is ruining our business by convincing people everywhere that the idols we make are not real gods.*]

27 So that not only this our craft [*our occupation*] is in danger to be set at nought [*to be ruined*]; but also that the temple of the great goddess Diana should be despised, and her magnificence should be destroyed, whom all Asia and the world worshippeth. [*Not only is Paul ruining our very profitable business, but he is convincing people*

*not to respect and worship Diana nor her temple.*]

28 And when they heard these sayings, they were full of wrath [*anger*], and cried out, saying, Great is Diana of the Ephesians.

29 And the whole city was filled with confusion [*a riot started*]: and having caught Gaius and Aristarchus, men of Macedonia, Paul's companions in travel [*missionary companions of Paul*], they [*the mob*] rushed with one accord [*together*] into the theatre [*a place where large events, games, etc., were held. This theater was capable of holding 25,000 to 30,000 spectators and was the largest built by the Greeks, according to information given in conjunction with Strong's #2181.*]

30 And when Paul would have entered in unto the people, the disciples suffered him not [*Paul wanted to go in and speak to the mob, but the members of the Church would not let him*].

31 And certain of the chief of Asia [*leading government officials*], which were his friends, sent unto him [*sent a message to him*], desiring him that he would not adventure himself into the theatre [*telling him not to go in where the mob was*].

32 Some [*members of the mob*] therefore cried one thing, and some another: for the assembly was confused; and the more part knew not wherefore they were come together.

This seems to be typical mob mentality. Many of them have joined in the uproar but don't even know what it is all about, as stated at the end of verse 32, above.

33 And they drew Alexander [*most likely one of Paul's followers*] out of the multitude, the Jews putting him forward [*the Jews pushed him out where he could be heard*]. And Alexander beckoned [*motioned for quiet*] with the hand, and would have made his defence unto the people.

34 But when they [*the mob*] knew [*discovered*] that he was a Jew, all with one voice about the space of two hours cried out, Great is Diana of the Ephesians [*they shouted for about two solid hours, "Great is Diana of the Ephesians"*] and wouldn't listen to Alexander.

35 And when the townclerk [*a public official*] had appeased the people [*had settled the mob down sufficiently*], he said, Ye men of Ephesus, what man is there that knoweth not how that the city of the Ephesians is a worshipper of [*is the host city for*] the great goddess Diana, and of the image which fell down from Jupiter [*doesn't everybody know that Diana came from Zeus, in other words, directly from heaven*]?

36 Seeing then that these things cannot be spoken against, ye ought to be quiet, and to do nothing rashly. [*There is nothing to worry about. No one can successfully speak against Diana. So, you ought to settle down and not do anything rash.*]

37 For ye have brought hither [*here to the theater*] these men [*disciples of Paul*], which are neither robbers of churches, nor yet blasphemers of your goddess [*these men have not committed any crimes*].

38 Wherefore if Demetrius, and the craftsmen which are with him, have a matter against any man, the law is open [*our courts are available to them*], and there are deputies [*judges*]: let them implead one another [*let Demetrius and the silversmiths bring formal charges against these men if they so desire, in proper manner in our public courts*].

39 But if ye enquire any thing concerning other matters, it shall be determined in a lawful assembly. [*If you have any other matters to bring up, do it legally.*]

40 For we are in danger to be called in question for this day's uproar [*we could get in big trouble with the Romans because of the riot you caused today*], there being no cause whereby we may give an account of this concourse [*we would not have a good excuse to the Romans for what happened*].

41 And when he had thus spoken, he dismissed the assembly [*he sent the crowd home*].

# ACTS 20

Sometimes we are challenged as to why Sunday is our holy day and Sabbath rather than Saturday, which was the Sabbath in Old Testament times. This chapter explains why. After the crucifixion and resurrection of the Savior, the members of the Church began meeting on the first day of the week, which was Sunday, rather than Saturday. (See verse 7.)

1 AND after the uproar was ceased [*after the riot had been settled down*], Paul called unto him the disciples [*the members of the Church in Ephesus*], and embraced them, and departed for to go into Macedonia [*northern Greece today*].

2 And when he had gone over those parts [*when he had visited the members in those regions*], and had given them much exhortation [*counsel and teachings*], he came into Greece [*southern Greece today*],

3 And there abode [*stayed*] three months. And when the Jews laid wait for him, as he was about to sail into Syria [*when he discovered that the Jews had plans to attack him as he set sail for Syria*], he purposed to [*decided instead to*] return through Macedonia.

4 And there accompanied him into Asia [*Turkey today*] Sopater of Berea [*Sopater was apparently a member of the Church from the city of Berea, in the northeastern region of central Greece*]; and of the Thessalonians [*from among the members in Thessalonica–northeastern Greece*], Aristarchus and Secundus; and Gaius of Derbe [*in southern Turkey today*], and Timotheus [*Timothy*]; and of [*from*] Asia, Tychicus and Trophimus.

5 These going before tarried [*waited*] for us [*Luke, Paul, and whoever else was with Paul*] at Troas.

6 [*The seven men mentioned in verse 4, above, who were members of the Church from the various cities mentioned, went ahead and waited for Paul, Luke, and their companions at Troas, a coastal city in what is northwestern Turkey today.*] And we sailed away from Philippi [*northeastern Greece today*] after the days of unleavened bread [*after Passover; see Bible Dictionary under "Feasts"*], and came unto them to [*met them in*] Troas in five days; where we abode [*stayed*] seven days.

As mentioned in the note at the beginning of this chapter, in verse 7, next, we see that the members of the Church were now meeting on Sunday, the first day of the week, for their sacrament meetings, etc. After the Savior's resurrection, Sunday became the Sabbath, the holy day of the week for the Saints.

7 And upon the first day of the week [*on Sunday*], when the disciples [*members*] came together to break bread [*to partake of the sacrament*], Paul preached unto them, ready to depart on the morrow; and continued his speech until midnight. [*Paul kept speaking until midnight because he knew he was leaving in the morning.*]

8 And there were many lights in the upper chamber, where they were gathered together.

9 And there sat in a window a certain young man named Eutychus, being fallen into a deep sleep [*who fell sound asleep*]: and as Paul was long preaching, he sunk down with sleep, and fell down from the third loft, and was taken up dead. [*As Paul continued talking, Eutychus sunk into even deeper sleep and fell from the third story window and was killed. See heading to Acts, chapter 20 in our Bible.*]

10 And Paul went down, and fell on him [*bent down to him*], and embracing him said, Trouble not yourselves; for his life is in him. [*Paul brought him back to life and told the people not to worry because he was alive again.*]

11 When he [*Paul*] therefore was come up again, and had broken bread, and eaten, and talked a long while, even till break of day, so he departed. [*After bringing Eutychus back to life, Paul went back upstairs, had something to eat and then talked until dawn. Then he left and continued his journey.*]

12 And they brought the young man alive, and were not a little comforted. [*The people were very comforted because Eutychus had been brought back to life.*]

13 ¶ And we [*Luke and some of the others*] went before to ship [*went ahead of Paul to the ship*], and sailed unto Assos [*on the seacoast, about 25 miles south of Troas*], there intending to take in Paul: for so had he appointed, minding himself to go afoot. [*We planned to pick Paul up there in Assos, according to his instructions. He, himself, wanted to travel to Assos on foot.*]

14 And when he met with us at Assos, we took him in [*aboard the ship*], and came [*sailed*] to Mitylene [*about 30 miles south of Assos*].

15 And we sailed thence [*from there*], and came the next day over against Chios [*the next day we sailed along close to the shores of the island of Chios—about 60 miles south of Mitylene*]; and the next day we arrived at Samos [*an island off the western coast of Turkey, about 40 miles southeast of Chios*], and tarried [*stayed*] at Trogyllium; and the next day we came to Miletus [*a distance of about 50 or 60 miles, to the southwestern coast of what is Turkey today*].

16 For Paul had determined to sail by [*past*] Ephesus, because he would not [*didn't want to*] spend the time in Asia [*what we know as western Turkey today*]: for he hasted [*was in a hurry*], if it were possible for him, to be at Jerusalem the day of Pentecost.

Luke seems to be anxious to explain why Paul didn't stop to visit the Saints at Ephesus, which would have been a logical stop en route from Chios to Miletus. Earlier, during Paul's third missionary journey, which is close to over at this point in Acts, he had spent about three years in Ephesus, ministering, teaching, and writing letters to the Saints in Corinth (First and Second Corinthians) and to the Saints in Rome (Romans) and Galatia (Galatians). Luke explains that Paul didn't have time to do justice to a visit in the Ephesus region. Paul was very anxious to get to Jerusalem for the Feast of Pentecost (see Bible Dictionary under "Feasts"), which was held 50 days after the Feast of Passover. Remember, in verse 6, above, that Paul had spent Passover ("the days of unleavened bread") in northeastern Greece. Thus, he only had about 50 days to make the journey from Philippi (in northeastern Greece today) to Jerusalem.

17 ¶ And from Miletus he sent [*a message*] to Ephesus, and called the elders of the church [*asked church leaders in Ephesus to meet him in Miletus*].

18 And when they were come to him [*when they arrived in Miletus*], he said unto them, Ye know, from the first day that I came into Asia, after what manner I have been with you at all seasons [*as you know, I have spent a lot of time with you previously*],

19 Serving the Lord with all humility of mind, and with many tears, and temptations [*trials, troubles*], which befell me by the lying in wait of the Jews [*which came upon me because of the plots of the Jews to ambush me*]:

20 And how I kept back nothing that was profitable unto you [*I spared no effort in bringing you the gospel*], but have shewed [*showed*] you, and have taught you publickly, and from house to house,

21 Testifying both to the Jews, and also to the Greeks [*Gentiles*], repentance toward God, and faith toward our Lord Jesus Christ.

**JST Acts 20:21**

21 Testifying both to the Jews, and also to the Greeks, repentance toward God, and faith on the name of our Lord Jesus Christ.

22 And now, behold, I go bound in the spirit unto Jerusalem [*I am required by the Spirit to go to Jerusalem*], not knowing the things that shall befall [*happen to*] me there:

23 Save [*except*] that the Holy Ghost witnesseth in every city, saying that bonds and afflictions abide me [*the Holy Ghost tells me everywhere I go that prison and persecutions await me*].

24 But none of these things move me [*none of these things make me want to change my mind about going to Jerusalem*], neither count I my life dear unto myself, so that I might finish my course with joy, and the ministry, which I have received of the Lord Jesus, to testify the gospel of the grace of God. [*If I lose my life as a result of finishing the work to which the Lord called me, so be it.*]

25 And now, behold, I know that ye all, among whom I have gone preaching the kingdom of God, shall see my face no more [*I know that none of you will see me again*].

26 Wherefore [*therefore*] I take you to record this day [*you are my witnesses*], that I am pure from the blood of all men [*since I have done my best, I am free from accountability for the sins of all people*].

27 For I have not shunned [*hesitated*] to declare unto you all the counsel of God [*I have not held back anything as I taught you the gospel*].

28 ¶ Take heed [*pay close attention to your responsibilities*] therefore unto yourselves, and to all the flock [*members*], over the which the Holy Ghost [*the Savior directs the work through the Holy Ghost*] hath made you overseers [*leaders*], to feed [*take care of*] the church of God, which he hath purchased with his own blood [*Christ "purchased" us from the law of justice, in other words, "redeemed" us from our sins, with His Atonement*].

29 For I know this, that after my departing [*after I leave*] shall grievous [*vicious*] wolves [*people who will try to tear the Church apart*] enter in among you, not sparing the flock.

30 Also of [*from*] your own selves shall men arise [*some among you will step forward*], speaking perverse things [*teaching false doctrines; twisting the truths of the gospel*], to draw away disciples [*followers*] after them.

31 Therefore watch, and remember, that by the space of three years I ceased not to warn every one night and day with tears. [*Stick firmly to what I have unceasingly taught you with deep*

*emotion and conviction over these past three years.*]

32 And now, brethren, I commend you to God [*I turn you over to God*], and to the word of his grace [*and to the gospel and Atonement of Christ*], which is able to build you up, and to give you an inheritance among all them which are sanctified [*which can give you exaltation among those who are made holy and clean and fit to be in the presence of God*].

33 I have coveted no man's silver, or gold, or apparel [*I have not desired other peoples' wealth or support for me*].

34 Yea, ye yourselves know, that these hands have ministered unto my necessities, and to them that were with me. [*You know that I have worked with my own hands to support myself and others traveling with me.*]

35 I have shewed you all things [*I have been an example to you*], how that so labouring [*working*] ye ought to support the weak, and to remember the words of the Lord Jesus, how he said, It is more blessed to give than to receive.

36 ¶ And when he had thus spoken, he kneeled down, and prayed with them all.

37 And they all wept sore [*much*], and fell on Paul's neck [*hugged him*], and kissed him,

38 Sorrowing most of all for the words which he spake, that they should see his face no more [*saddened most by his telling them that they would not see him again*]. And they accompanied him unto the ship.

# ACTS 21

We know from the use of "we" in verse 1, that Luke is again traveling with Paul. These "we passages" continue through Acts 28:16, indicating that Luke is with him all this time.

As you will see, Paul continues taking a direct course for Jerusalem. When he arrives, he will be persecuted and arrested. You will probably smile a bit in admiration of Paul at the end of this chapter when, after a mob has beaten him and he is rescued in the nick of time by Roman soldiers, he stands in chains on the stairs and requests permission to preach to the mob, while under the protection of the soldiers. His sermon will be recorded in chapter 22.

1 AND it came to pass, that after we were gotten from them, and had launched [*after Paul, Luke, and the other traveling companions of Paul had sailed from Miletus* (*see Acts 20:15*)], we came with a straight course unto Coos [*we sailed straight to the island of Coos (about 50 miles south of Miletus)*], and the day following unto Rhodes [*an island about 60 miles east of Coos*], and from thence unto Patara [*about 70 miles east of Rhodes* (*this would be the coast of southern Turkey today)*]:
2 And finding a ship sailing over unto Phenicia [*east to Phoenicia, which would be on the eastern coast of the Mediterranean Sea today*], we went aboard, and set forth.

3 Now when we had discovered Cyprus, we left it on the left hand [*we sailed south of the Island of Cyprus*], and sailed into Syria, and landed at Tyre [*about 100 miles north of Jerusalem*]: for there the ship was to unlade [*unload*] her burden.

4 And finding disciples [*Church members*], we tarried [*stayed*] there seven days: who said to Paul through the Spirit, that he should not go up to Jerusalem [*members at Tyre told Paul that they felt inspired to tell him not to go to Jerusalem*].

5 And when we had accomplished those days [*after the seven days*], we departed and went our way; and they all brought

us on our way [*they all accompanied us*], with wives and children, till we were out of the city: and we kneeled down on the shore, and prayed.

6 And when we had taken our leave one of another [*said goodbye to each other*], we took ship [*boarded a ship*]; and they returned home again.

7 And when we had finished our course from Tyre, we came to Ptolemais [*about 25 miles south of Tyre*], and saluted [*greeted*] the brethren, and abode [*stayed*] with them one day.

8 And the next day we that were of Paul's company [*we who were traveling with Paul*] departed, and came unto Cæsarea [*about 30 miles south of Ptolemais*]: and we entered into the house of Philip the evangelist, which was one of the seven [*one of the seven in Acts 6:5 who were chosen to assist the Apostles in ministering to the members as the Church grew*]; and abode [*stayed*] with him.

The word "evangelist" used in verse 8, would likely mean "patriarch." See Ephesians, 4:11, footnote d. Also see McConkie, *Doctrinal New Testament Commentary*, Vol. 2, p. 181. Philip, along with Stephen who was killed by stoning (Acts 7:57–60), was chosen to assist the apostles (Acts 6:1–7). It would appear that by the time Paul and his traveling companions arrive at Caesarea, Philip has been given the added responsibility of being ordained a patriarch.

9 And the same man [*Philip*] had four daughters, virgins [*who were not married*], which did prophesy [*who had the gift of prophesying, as mentioned in D&C 46:22 and elsewhere in the scriptures*].

10 And as we [*Luke, who wrote Acts, and Paul's other missionary companions*] tarried [*stayed*] there many days, there came down from Judæa [*from the Jerusalem area*] a certain prophet, named Agabus.

We don't know who Agabus was except that he prophesied that there would be a severe famine (see Acts 11:28) and that he prophesied in verse 11, next, that Paul would be imprisoned in Jerusalem. See Bible Dictionary under "Agabus."

11 And when he was come unto us [*when Agabus came to where we were staying*], he took Paul's girdle [*belt*], and bound [*tied up*] his own hands and feet, and said, Thus saith the Holy Ghost, So shall the Jews at Jerusalem bind [*tie up; put in chains; arrest*] the man that owneth this girdle, and shall deliver him into the hands of the Gentiles. [*The Jews at Jerusalem will arrest Paul and turn him over to the Gentiles.*]

12 And when we heard these things, both we, and they of that place [*the local members in Caesarea*], besought him [*begged him*] not to go up to Jerusalem.

13 Then Paul answered, What mean ye to weep and to break mine heart [*do you think you can stop me by breaking my heart*]? for I am ready not to be bound only, but also to die at Jerusalem for the name of the Lord Jesus.

14 And when he would not be persuaded [*when we saw that we could not persuade him to stay away from Jerusalem*], we ceased [*stopped trying*], saying, The will of the Lord be done.

15 And after those days we took up our carriages [*we packed our bags*], and went up to Jerusalem.

16 There went with us also certain of the disciples of [*members of the Church from*] Cæsarea, and brought with them one Mnason of Cyprus [*originally from Cyprus*], an old disciple [*member*], with whom we should lodge.

17 And when we were come to [*when

*we arrived at*] Jerusalem, the brethren [*leaders of the Church there*] received us gladly.

18 And the day following Paul went in with us unto James [*one of the Apostles*]; and all the elders were present.

19 And when he [*Paul*] had saluted [*greeted*] them [*the Brethren*], he declared [*reported*] particularly what things God had wrought [*done*] among the Gentiles by his ministry [*as a result of his missionary efforts*].

20 And when they heard it, they glorified [*praised*] the Lord, and said unto him [*Paul*], Thou seest, brother, how many thousands of Jews there are which believe [*you have obviously noticed that thousands of Jews have joined the Church*]; and they are all zealous of the law [*and they still keep the Law of Moses*]:

21 And they are informed of thee [*they know about you*], that thou teachest all the Jews which are among the Gentiles to forsake Moses, saying that they ought not to circumcise their children, neither to walk after the customs. [*They know that you teach Jewish converts in Gentile nations that they don't have to keep the Law of Moses, including circumcision, and that you teach them that they don't have to live according to our Jewish customs.*]

22 What is it therefore [*what shall we do now*]? the multitude must needs come together: for they will hear that thou art come [*no doubt many of our Jewish members here will assemble together to discuss this when they find out that you are in town*].

23 Do therefore this that we say to thee [*therefore, do what we say in order to try to resolve this problem*]: We have four men which have a vow [*covenant*] on them [*we have four men who have made a vow according to Jewish custom in keeping with the Law of Moses*];

24 Them take [*take them to the temple*], and purify thyself with them [*participate in the Law of Moses purification ritual along with them*], and be at charges with them [*pay their expenses*], that they may shave their heads [*according to Moses' instructions in Leviticus 14:8–9*]: and all may know that those things, whereof they were informed concerning thee, are nothing [*so that those local Jewish members who have heard troubling things about you will stop worrying*]; but that thou thyself also walkest orderly, and keepest the law [*rather, they will understand that you are keeping the Law of Moses yourself*].

25 As touching the Gentiles [*non-Jews*] which believe [*as far as the Gentile converts are concerned*], we have written and concluded that they observe no such thing [*we have written to them and instructed them that they do not need to keep these laws of Moses or customs of the Jews*], save only that they keep themselves from [*except that they must avoid*] things offered to idols [*idol worship*], and from blood [*eating blood*], and from strangled [*eating birds or animals which were strangled so that their blood is still in the meat*], and from fornication [*from sexual immorality*].

The situation described in verses 24 and 25 above can seem rather strange at first. Obviously, Paul has stirred up some bad feelings among the Jewish converts in the Jerusalem area, who still have not caught the vision that the Law of Moses has been fulfilled by the Savior, and it is no longer necessary to keep the law of circumcision, nor does one have to keep the customs and traditions of the Jews in order to be a good member of the Church. The Church leaders in Jerusalem are anxious to keep the peace and to not have things stirred up unnecessarily. Realizing

that change comes slowly (see Jacob 5:65–66) and the Jewish members in Jerusalem are no exception, they ask Paul to soothe feelings of local members by participating in a Law of Moses cleansing ritual, which he does as seen in verse 26, next. Knowing Paul's feisty personality, as we do, we see it as a credit to him that he did follow the counsel of his leaders.

26 Then Paul took the men, and the next day purifying himself with them entered into the temple, to signify the accomplishment of the days of purification, until that an offering should be offered for every one of them. [*Paul followed counsel and participated in the Law of Moses cleansing ritual.*]

27 And when the seven days were almost ended, the Jews which were of Asia [*anti-Christian Jews from what is Turkey today, who fought against Paul in Asia*], when they saw him in the temple, stirred up all the people, and laid hands on him [*grabbed him*],

28 Crying out [*shouting*], Men of Israel, help: This [*Paul*] is the man, that teacheth all men every where against the people, and the law, and this place [*this is the man who is teaching everybody, everywhere, not to believe in our Jewish customs nor in the Law of Moses, nor in what we have been doing in this temple under Moses' law*]: and further brought Greeks also into the temple, and hath polluted this holy place [*furthermore, Paul has taken Gentiles into our temple and has thus polluted it*].

29 (For they had seen before with him in the city Trophimus an Ephesian, whom they supposed that Paul had brought into the temple.)

30 And all the city was moved [*a mob formed*], and the people [*the mob*] ran together: and they took Paul, and drew [*dragged*] him out of the temple: and forthwith the doors were shut [*and immediately shut the gates of the temple*].

31 And as they went about to kill him [*as they dragged him off to kill him*], tidings [*news of the riot*] came unto the chief captain of the band [*the leader of the Roman soldiers*], that all Jerusalem was in an uproar.

32 Who [*the Roman military leader*] immediately took soldiers and centurions [*Roman leaders of 100 Roman soldiers each*], and ran down unto them [*the Jews who were beating Paul to kill him*]: and when they saw the chief captain and the soldiers, they left beating of Paul [*they quit beating Paul*].

33 Then the chief captain came near, and took him [*Paul*], and commanded him to be bound with two chains; and demanded who he was, and what he had done.

34 And some cried [*shouted*] one thing, some another, among the multitude [*mob; crowd*]: and when he could not know the certainty for the tumult [*when the commander of the Roman soldiers could not get a clear answer from the mob*], he commanded him [*Paul*] to be carried into the castle [*the castle of Antonia in Jerusalem, where the Roman soldiers had their barracks*].

35 And when he came upon the stairs [*when he got to the stairs of the castle*], so it was, that he was borne of the soldiers for the violence of the people [*he had to be carried by the soldiers and protected from the violence of the mob*].

36 For [*because*] the multitude [*mob*] of the people followed after, crying [*shouting*], Away with him.

37 And as Paul was to be led into the castle [*at the top of the stairs*], he said unto the chief captain [*the Roman commander*], May I speak unto thee? Who said, Canst thou speak Greek? [*The*

*Roman commander was surprised that Paul could speak Greek.*]

38 Art not thou that Egyptian, which before these days madest an uproar, and leddest out into the wilderness four thousand men that were murderers? [*I thought you were the Egyptian who recently caused trouble by leading 4,000 assassins and cutthroats out into the wilderness.*]

39 But Paul said, I am a man which am a Jew of [*from*] Tarsus, a city in Cilicia [*southeastern Turkey today*], a citizen of no mean city [*by no means a small city*]: and, I beseech [*ask*] thee, suffer [*allow*] me to speak unto the people [*to the mob*].

40 And when he [*the Roman commander*] had given him licence [*permission*], Paul stood on the stairs, and beckoned with the hand [*motioned for silence*] unto the people. And when there was made a great silence, he spake [*spoke*] unto them in the Hebrew tongue, saying,

# ACTS 22

As Paul defends himself to the mob, he will recount the story of his conversion, which includes seeing the resurrected Christ in vision.

You will gain additional insight into Paul's personality after his sermon, when the Roman officer commands that he be whipped. At exactly the right moment for dramatic effect, Paul will casually mention that he is a Roman citizen (see verse 25) which makes what the Roman soldiers were going to do to him illegal.

1 MEN, brethren, and fathers [*honored men*], hear ye my defence which I make now unto you [*listen carefully while I defend my actions to you*].

Among other talents, Paul also speaks several languages. The fact that he speaks Hebrew, both surprises and impresses the mob and they settle down to listen to him, as mentioned in verse 2, next.

2 (And when they heard that he spake in the Hebrew tongue to them, they kept the more silence: and he saith,)

3 I am verily a man which am a Jew [*I am actually a Jew*], born in Tarsus [*a coastal town in what is southeast Turkey today*], a city in Cilicia, yet brought up in this city at the feet of Gamaliel [*I was taught here in Jerusalem by Gamaliel (a prominent Pharisee and respected Jewish teacher of the day); see Bible Dictionary under "Gamaliel"*], and taught according to the perfect manner of the law of the fathers [*I was taught and trained in the Law of Moses, and am a Pharisee; see Acts 23:6*], and was zealous [*faithful*] toward God, as ye all are this day.

The Pharisees were powerful religious leaders among the Jews, and played a strong role in getting Jesus crucified. See Bible Dictionary under "Pharisee."

4 And I persecuted this way [*this way of living, in other words, the Christians*] unto the death, binding [*arresting them*] and delivering into prisons both men and women.

5 As also the high priest [*the chief religious leader of the Jews*] doth bear me witness, and all the estate of the elders [*your religious leaders here know me and will tell you I am telling you the truth*]: from whom also I received letters unto the brethren [*I obtained letters from your leaders here to the Jewish religious leaders in Damascus, giving me permission to arrest Christians there*], and went to Damascus [*a major city in southern Syria today*], to bring them [*the Christians*] which were there bound [*who had been arrested in Damascus*] unto Jerusalem, for to be punished.

6 And it came to pass, that, as I made my journey, and was come nigh [*had come near*] unto Damascus about noon, suddenly there shone [*shined*] from heaven a great light round about me.

7 And I fell unto the ground, and heard a voice saying unto me, Saul, Saul, why persecutest thou me?

8 And I answered, Who art thou, Lord? And he said unto me, I am Jesus of Nazareth, whom thou persecutest.

9 And they that were with me [*the people traveling with me*] saw indeed the light, and were afraid; but they heard not the voice of him that spake to me.

This is one of those places in the Bible where one verse conflicts with a verse in another place. Verse 9, above, says that Paul's traveling companions saw the light but did not hear the voice of Jesus. However, in Acts 9:7, it says that Paul's companions heard the voice. The Joseph Smith Translation of the Bible (the JST) straightens this out by correcting Acts 9:7 to read "And they who were journeying with him saw indeed the light, and were afraid; but they heard not the voice of him who spake to him." This is another testimony of the calling of the Prophet Joseph Smith, and a reminder that the Bible is not always translated correctly as indicated in our eighth article of faith.

10 And I said, What shall I do, Lord? And the Lord said unto me, Arise, and go into Damascus; and there it shall be told thee of all things which are appointed for thee to do.

11 And when I could not see for the glory of that light [*I had become blind because of the brightness of the light*], being led by the hand of them that were with me, I came into Damascus.

12 And one Ananias [*a faithful convert and priesthood holder in the Church in Damascus*], a devout man according to the law, having a good report [*a good reputation*] of all the Jews which dwelt there,

13 Came unto me, and stood, and said unto me, Brother Saul, receive thy sight. And the same hour I looked up upon him [*immediately my blindness was healed and I could see Ananias*].

14 And he said, The God of our fathers [*our ancestors, including Abraham, Isaac, and Jacob*] hath chosen thee, that thou shouldest know his will, and see that Just One [*Christ*], and shouldest hear the voice of his mouth.

15 For thou shalt be his witness unto all men of what thou hast seen and heard.

16 And now why tarriest thou [*what are you waiting for*]? arise, and be baptized, and wash away thy sins, calling on the name of the Lord.

17 And it came to pass, that, when I was come again to Jerusalem, even while I prayed in the temple, I was in a trance [*I had a vision*];

18 And saw him [*Jesus*] saying unto me, Make haste [*hurry*], and get thee quickly out of Jerusalem: for they will not receive [*accept*] thy testimony concerning me.

19 And I said, Lord, they know that I imprisoned and beat in every synagogue them that believed on thee [*these people in Jerusalem know that I rounded up Christians from every synagogue and had them beaten and put in prison*]:

20 And when the blood of thy martyr Stephen was shed [*when Stephen was killed; Acts 7:55–60*], I also was standing by, and consenting unto his death [*I agreed that he should be killed; Acts 8:1*], and kept the raiment of them that slew him [*I kept watch over the robes, clothing that the men who killed Stephen had taken off while they stoned him*].

21 And he [*Jesus*] said unto me, Depart:

for I will send thee far hence unto the Gentiles [*I will send you far away from here to the Gentiles*].

22 And they [*the Jerusalem mob to whom Paul was speaking while standing at the top of the stairs leading into the Roman barracks; see Acts 21:40*] gave him audience unto this word [*listened to him while he spoke*], and then lifted up their voices [*shouted out*], and said, Away with such a fellow from the earth: for it is not fit that he should live [*kill him*].

23 And as they cried out [*screamed and yelled*], and cast off their clothes, and threw dust into the air [*a sign of deep emotion in Jewish culture of the day*],

24 The chief captain [*the Roman commander*] commanded him to be brought into the castle, and bade [*requested*] that he should be examined by scourging; that he might know wherefore they cried so against him. [*The commander of the Roman soldiers commanded that Paul be whipped to get the truth out of him as to why the Jewish mob was so angry with him.*]

As mentioned previously, Paul is indeed an interesting character and a master of strategy! In the middle of all this uproar and life-threatening situation, he has not yet mentioned to the Roman soldiers that he himself is a Roman citizen. As we see in the next verses, he waits until the timing is perfect to mention this fact.

25 And as they bound [*tied*] him with thongs, Paul said unto the centurion [*the Roman soldier*] that stood by, Is it lawful [*legal*] for you to scourge [*whip*] a man that is a Roman, and uncondemned [*a man who is a Roman citizen and who has not had a proper trial*]?

26 When the centurion heard that, he went and told the chief captain [*the Roman commanding officer*], saying, Take heed what thou doest [*be careful what you do*]: for this man is a Roman [*a Roman citizen*].

27 Then the chief captain came, and said unto him [*Paul*], Tell me, art thou a Roman? He said, Yea [*Yes, I am*].

28 And the chief captain answered, With a great sum obtained I this freedom [*I had to buy my Roman citizenship with a large sum of money (implying "So* how did somebody like you obtain citizenship?")]. And Paul said, But I was free born [*I was born a Roman citizen*].

29 Then straightway [*immediately*] they departed from him which should have examined him [*the Roman soldiers who planned to ask him questions while whipping him left in a big hurry*]: and the chief captain also was afraid, after he knew that he was a Roman, and because he had bound him [*the Roman commander was also very worried because he had violated Paul's legal rights as a Roman citizen*].

30 On the morrow [*in the morning*], because he [*the Roman commander*] would have known the certainty wherefore he was accused of the Jews [*wanted to know exactly what the Jews had against Paul*], he loosed [*untied*] him [*Paul*] from his bands, and commanded the chief priests and all their council to appear [*he commanded the Jewish religious leaders to appear in court*], and brought Paul down, and set him before them.

Verses 29–30, above, are a bit confusing. The Roman commander was very concerned about having had Paul tied up illegally [*probably put in chains*], since Paul was a Roman citizen. Yet, he waited to set him free until the next morning (verse 30). The JST shows us what really happened as follows:

**JST Acts 22:29–30**

29 Then straightway they departed from him which should have examined him, and the chief captain also was afraid after he knew that he was a Roman, because he had bound him, and he loosed him [*set him free*] from his bands.

30 On the morrow, because he would have known the certainty wherefore he was accused of the Jews, he commanded the chief priests and all their council to appear, and brought Paul down, and set him before them.

Thus, the JST informs us that indeed the commander untied him immediately, then arranged for Paul to appear in court the next day, in front of the Jewish high priest and other leaders, assuring Paul of a fair trial according to Roman law.

# ACTS 23

The highest governing council, controlled by the Jews, was the Sanhedrin. The high priest presided over it. (See Bible Dictionary under "Sanhedrin.") The Roman commander instructed that the high priest and the Sanhedrin face Paul in a legal court setting. We will now watch as Paul defends himself and his actions in front of this council.

1 AND Paul, earnestly beholding [*sincerely looking at*] the council, said, Men and brethren, I have lived in all good conscience before God until this day [*I have done my best to live strictly according to God's commandments right up to this day*].

2 And the high priest Ananias commanded them that stood by him [*Paul*] to smite [*hit*] him on the mouth.

Ananias, the high priest, was an evil man who was later murdered during an uprising at Jerusalem. See Bible Dictionary under Ananias.

3 Then said Paul unto him, God shall smite thee, thou whited [*whitewashed*] wall [*in other words, you hypocrite; see Matthew 23:27*]: for sittest thou to judge me after the law, and commandest me to be smitten contrary to the law [*how can you claim to judge me according to the law and still command me to be hit which is against the law*]?

4 And they that stood by said, Revilest thou God's high priest [*how dare you speak to God's high priest like that*]?

5 Then said Paul, I wist not, brethren, that he was the high priest: for it is written, Thou shalt not speak evil of the ruler of thy people [*Exodus 22:28*].

**JST Acts 23:5**

5 Then said Paul, I did not know, brethren, that he was the high priest; for it is written, Thou shalt not speak evil of the ruler of thy people.

6 But when Paul perceived [*noticed*] that the one part [*part of the group of Jewish leaders there in court*] were Sadducees, and the other Pharisees, he cried out in the council, Men and brethren, I am a Pharisee, the son of a Pharisee: of the hope and resurrection of the dead I am called in question [*the real reason I have been arrested and brought here is because I believe in resurrection*].

Again, in these verses we see Paul's skill in using strategy. He is now going to pit the Pharisees against the Sadducees and get them arguing among themselves. The Pharisees believed in resurrection, but the Sadducees did not, and the topic of resurrection was a long-standing point of heated contention between them.

7 And when he had so said, there arose a dissension [*argument*] between the Pharisees and the Sadducees: and the

multitude [*crowd in the courtroom*] was divided [*took sides on the issue*].

8 For the Sadducees say [*teach*] that there is no resurrection, neither angel [*messengers from God*], nor spirit [*in other words, there is no such thing as a spirit, which leaves the body when it dies*]: but the Pharisees confess both [*believe in resurrection and in spirits*].

9 And there arose a great cry: and the scribes [*Pharisees who interpret the scriptures for the people*] that were of the Pharisees' part [*who belonged to the Pharisees*] arose, and strove [*argued*], saying, We find no evil in this man [*we do not find anything wrong with what Paul has taught*]: but if a spirit or an angel hath spoken to him, let us not fight against God.

10 And when there arose a great dissension [*a huge uproar*], the chief captain [*the commander of the Roman soldiers*], fearing lest Paul should have been pulled in pieces of them [*afraid that they would tear Paul apart physically*], commanded the soldiers to go down, and to take him by force from among them, and to bring him into the castle.

11 And the night following the Lord stood by him [*the Savior appeared to him*], and said, Be of good cheer [*cheer up*], Paul: for as thou hast testified of me in Jerusalem, so must thou bear witness also at Rome [*I need you to testify of Me in Rome, like you have done here in Jerusalem*].

12 And when it was day [*in the morning*], certain of the Jews banded together, and bound themselves under a curse [*made a vow, made an oath*], saying that they would neither eat nor drink till they had killed Paul.

In the Jewish culture of the day, to make a vow was the most serious commitment possible. Here, more than forty men promise each other that they will not eat or drink until they have killed Paul. It is a foolish vow. If they try to keep it, they will die of thirst and hunger.

13 And they were more than forty which had made this conspiracy [*plot*].

14 And they came to the chief priests and elders [*the main religious leaders of the Jews*], and said, We have bound ourselves under a great curse [*we have made an vow, and will come under a great curse if we fail to keep it*], that we will eat nothing until we have slain [*killed*] Paul.

15 Now therefore ye with the council [*you members of the council*] signify to [*make a request to*] the chief captain [*the chief Roman commander*] that he bring him [*Paul*] down unto you to morrow, as though ye would enquire something more perfectly concerning him [*ask the Roman commander to bring Paul to you again tomorrow and pretend that you want to get additional clarification from him on some matters*]: and we, or ever [*before*] he come near, are ready to kill him [*we will kill him before he arrives at the courtroom*].

**JST Acts 23:15**

15 Now therefore ye with the council signify to the chief captain that he bring him down unto you tomorrow, as though you would inquire something more perfectly concerning him; and we, before he come near, are ready to kill him.

16 And when Paul's sister's son heard of their lying in wait [*their plot to ambush him*], he went and entered into the castle [*the Antonia Fortress or castle, where the Roman soldiers in Jerusalem were headquarted*], and told Paul.

17 Then Paul called one of the centurions [*a Roman soldier in charge of 100 soldiers*] unto him, and said, Bring this

young man unto the chief captain [*take my nephew to the chief Roman captain*]: for he hath a certain thing to tell him.

18 So he took him, and brought him to the chief captain, and said, Paul the prisoner called me unto him, and prayed [*asked*] me to bring this young man unto thee, who hath something to say unto thee.

19 Then the chief captain took him by the hand, and went with him aside privately, and asked him, What is that thou hast to tell me?

20 And he said, The Jews have agreed [*plotted*] to desire thee [*to send a request to you*] that thou wouldest bring down Paul to morrow into the council, as though they would enquire somewhat of him more perfectly [*pretending that they want to ask him additional questions*].

21 But do not thou yield unto them [*don't let them do it*]: for there lie in wait for him of them more than forty men [*over forty men will be waiting in ambush for Paul*], which have [*who have*] bound themselves with an oath [*a vow*], that they will neither eat nor drink till they have killed him: and now are they ready, looking for a promise from thee.

22 So the chief captain then let the young man depart, and charged [*commanded*] him, See thou tell no man that thou hast shewed these things to me [*don't tell anyone that you have informed me about this*].

23 And he called unto him two centurions [*Roman soldiers in charge of one hundred soldiers each*], saying, Make ready two hundred soldiers to go to Cæsarea [*about 60 miles northwest of Jerusalem*], and horsemen threescore and ten [*70 horsemen*], and spearmen two hundred [*200 foot soldiers carrying spears*], at the third hour of the night [*at 9 PM tonight*];

24 And provide them beasts, that they may set Paul on [*make sure they have mounts for Paul to ride*], and bring him safe unto Felix the governor [*the chief Roman official in Caesarea*].

25 And he [*the Roman commander (Claudius Lysias) in Jerusalem*] wrote a letter after this manner [*which read as follows*]:

26 Claudius Lysias unto the most excellent governor Felix sendeth greeting [*greetings from Claudius Lysias to his excellency, Governor Felix*].

27 This man [*Paul*] was taken of [*grabbed by*] the Jews, and should have been killed of [*by*] them: then came I with an army, and rescued him, having understood that he was a Roman.

**JST Acts 23:27**

27 This man was taken of the Jews, and would have been killed of them; then came I with an army, and rescued him, having understood that he was a Roman.

28 And when I would have known the cause wherefore they accused him [*because I wanted to know what they had against him*], I brought him forth into their council [*I took him to appear before the Sanhedrin*]:

29 Whom I perceived to be accused of questions of their law, but to have nothing laid to his charge worthy of death or of bonds. [*As I watched them question him, it became clear that it had to do with their religious laws, but there was nothing he had done that was worthy of death or imprisonment.*]

30 And when it was told me how that the Jews laid wait for [*were waiting to ambush*] the man, I sent straightway [*immediately*] to thee, and gave commandment to his accusers also [*and commanded the Jews who brought charges against him*] to say before thee what they had against him [*to appear in your court*

*to bring charges against him*]. Farewell.

31 Then the soldiers, as it was commanded them, took Paul, and brought him by night to Antipatris [*a city near Caesarea, named after Herod the Great's father, Antipater*].

32 On the morrow [*in the morning*] they left the horsemen to go with him [*Paul*], and returned to the castle [*returned to Jerusalem*]:

33 Who [*the Roman soldiers who accompanied Paul on to Caesarea*], when they came to Cæsarea, and delivered the epistle [*the letter from Claudius Lysias; see verse 26, above*] to the governor [*Felix*], presented Paul also before him.

34 And when the governor had read the letter, he asked of what province he was [*he asked Paul which province he was from originally*]. And when he understood that he was of Cilicia [*would be in southeastern Turkey today*];

35 I will hear thee, said he, when thine accusers are also come [*I will convene the court and hear your case when the Jews who accuse you of criminal behavior arrive from Jerusalem*]. And he commanded him to be kept in Herod's judgment hall. [*He commanded that Paul be kept at Governor Felix's headquarters; see Acts 23:35, footnote a.*]

# ACTS 24

In this chapter, Paul's trial continues and he skillfully teaches the gospel as he provides his own defense.

1 AND after five days Ananias the high priest descended [*arrived from Jerusalem*] with the elders, and with a certain orator [*lawyer*] named Tertullus, who informed the governor against Paul [*who presented the case against Paul to Governor Felix*].

Watch now, as Tertullus attempts to flatter Felix with compliments and pretended loyalty of the Jewish religious leaders. In actuality, the Jews despised their Roman rulers.

2 And when he was called forth [*invited to speak*], Tertullus began to accuse him [*Paul*], saying, Seeing that by thee [*through you, Felix*] we enjoy great quietness [*we enjoy wonderful peace*], and that very worthy deeds are done unto this nation by thy providence [*you have done very noble things for our nation through your kindness and generosity*],

3 We accept it always, and in all places, most noble Felix, with all thankfulness [*we accept your leadership always and everywhere with deep gratitude*].

4 Notwithstanding [*however*], that I be not further tedious unto thee [*let me get right to the point, so that I don't waste your valuable time*], I pray thee that thou wouldest hear us of thy clemency a few words [*I humbly ask that you be so kind as to hear a few words from us*].

5 For we have found this man [*Paul*] a pestilent fellow [*to be a troublemaker*], and a mover of sedition [*who undermines leadership*] among all the Jews throughout the world, and a ringleader of the sect of the Nazarenes [*the followers of Jesus; see Strong's #3478*]:

6 Who also hath gone about to profane [*defile, to make unclean*] the temple: whom we took, and would have judged according to our law [*we arrested Paul and wanted to handle this matter ourselves. Remember that the way these Jews wanted to deal with Paul was to kill him on the spot after they dragged him out of the temple. See Acts 21:30–31.*]

7 But the chief captain Lysias came upon us, and with great violence took him away out of our hands [*but Lysias, commander of the Roman soldiers in Jerusalem, using unnecessary force, took Paul from us*],

The implication in Tertullus' words to

Felix is that if the Roman commander hadn't intervened in the Jews' private business, using inappropriate violence, then Felix wouldn't even have to be bothered with this whole thing.

8 Commanding his accusers to come unto thee [*Lysias commanded us to come to you to present our case against Paul*]: by examining of whom thyself mayest take knowledge of all these things, whereof we accuse him [*if you will now cross-examine Paul, you will see why we are so upset with him*].

9 And the Jews also assented, saying that these things were so [*the Jewish religious leaders confirmed that what Tertullus had told Felix was true*].

Watch now as Paul begins his own defense.

10 Then Paul, after that the governor had beckoned unto him [*had motioned for him*] to speak, answered [*responded*], Forasmuch as I know [*since I am aware*] that thou hast been of many years [*for many years*] a judge unto this nation, I do the more cheerfully answer for myself [*I am happy to defend myself because I know that you have had many years of experience judging cases brought before you by the Jews*]:

Paul will now tell Felix that he is not the cause of trouble and rioting, rather the religious leaders of the Jews themselves, who are in the courtroom now, are the ones who destroyed the peace and caused riots.

11 Because that thou mayest understand, that there are yet but twelve days since I went up to Jerusalem for to worship [*I want you to understand that I arrived in Jerusalem just twelve days ago*].

12 And they neither found me in the temple disputing with any man [*I was reverent in the temple, not arguing with anyone*], neither raising up the people [*I didn't stir the people up*], neither in the synagogues, nor in the city:

13 Neither can they prove the things whereof they now accuse me [*they can't prove any of the things they are accusing me of*].

14 But this I confess unto thee [*but I will admit this to you*], that after the way which they call heresy [*in opposition to what they believe*], so worship I the God of my fathers, believing all things which are written in the law and in the prophets [*I do indeed worship in the way they are accusing me of, namely, I worship the God of Abraham, Isaac and Jacob and believe very exactly all the things written by Moses and the other prophets in our scriptures*]:

15 And have hope toward God, which they themselves also allow [*I have the same hope and faith that my accusers claim to have in God*], that there shall be a resurrection of the dead, both of the just and unjust [*namely, that everyone, whether righteous or wicked, will be resurrected*].

You may wish to mark the important doctrine about the resurrection taught in verse 15, above, in your own scriptures. Many Christians believe that only the righteous will be resurrected. Here, Paul teaches clearly that both the righteous and the wicked will be resurrected.

16 And herein do I exercise myself [*I follow these religious beliefs very carefully*], to have always [*in order to always have*] a conscience void of offence toward God, and toward men.

17 Now after many years I came to bring alms to my nation, and offerings [*now, after many years I came to Jerusalem to bring money we collected for the poor*].

18 Whereupon certain Jews from Asia found me purified in the temple, neither with multitude, nor with tumult. [*While*

*I was purifying myself, according to the Law of Moses, in the temple, some Jews from Asia (Turkey today; see Acts 14, and who tried to stone Paul) found me, and I did not have a crowd around me nor was I causing a disturbance.*]

19 Who ought to have been here before thee, and object, if they had ought against me [*they are the ones who ought to be here bearing witness against me, if they have anything to say in your court.*].

20 Or else let these same here say, if they have found any evil doing in me, while I stood before the council [*since the Jews from Asia, who dragged me from the temple in Jerusalem are not here today, perhaps you could have these Jews who are here testify before you as to what evil they found in me when I stood before their council; see Acts 22:30 through Acts 23:1–9*],

21 Except it be for this one voice, that I cried standing among them [*there was one thing I said that apparently has bothered them*], Touching the resurrection of the dead [*I told them that I believe in the resurrection*] I am called in question by you this day. [*The only reason I am standing before you this day is because I told them I believe in the resurrection of the dead.*]

22 And when Felix heard these things, having more perfect knowledge of that way [*having a good understanding of the situation*], he deferred them [*he postponed the rest of the trial*], and said, When Lysias the chief captain [*the Roman commander in Jerusalem*] shall come down [*arrives from Jerusalem*], I will know the uttermost of your matter [*I will get the details I need to make a decision about your case*].

23 And he commanded a centurion to keep Paul [*to keep Paul under guard*], and to let him have liberty, and that he should forbid none of his acquaintance to minister or come unto him [*allow Paul's friends to come and go, visiting Paul whenever they wanted to*].

24 And after certain days [*a few days later*], when Felix came with his wife Drusilla, which [*who*] was a Jewess [*she was a Jew*], he sent for Paul, and heard him concerning the faith in Christ [*Felix asked Paul to teach them about Christ*].

25 And as he reasoned of [*as Paul taught them about*] righteousness, temperance [*self-control*], and judgment to come [*being judged by God for our actions here on earth*], Felix trembled, and answered [*responded*], Go thy way for this time [*leave for the time being because I can't handle any more*]; when I have a convenient season, I will call for thee [*when it is convenient for me, I will have you come and tell us more*].

26 He hoped also that money should have been given him of Paul, that he might loose him [*Felix was hoping that Paul would offer to bribe him to let him go free*]: wherefore he sent for him the oftener, and communed with him [*and so Felix sent for Paul quite often and talked with him*].

This went on for two years, after which Felix was replaced by Porcuis Festus. Festus was sent by Nero to take Felix's place, probably in the autumn of AD 60.

27 But after two years Porcius Festus came into Felix' room [*to take Felix's place*]: and Felix, willing to shew the Jews a pleasure, left Paul bound [*and, in order to please the Jews who hated Paul, he left Paul under guard rather than releasing him when he left office*].

## ACTS 25

In this chapter, in order to prevent being turned over to the Jews who would kill him, Paul, as a Roman citizen, exercises his right to appear before Caesar to be tried.

1 NOW when Festus was come into the province, after three days he ascended from Cæsarea to Jerusalem [*three days after Governor Festus arrived in Caesarea, to take Felix's place, he traveled up to Jerusalem*].

2 Then the high priest [*the highest Jewish religious leader*] and the chief of the Jews [*and other Jewish religious leaders*] informed him [*informed him of their charges*] against Paul, and besought him [*and urgently asked him*],

3 And desired favour against him [*Paul*], that he would send for him [*Paul*] to Jerusalem, laying wait in the way to kill him. [*In other words, the Jewish rulers tried to bias Festus against Paul and asked him to command that Paul be brought to Jerusalem so they could ambush and murder Paul as he came along the road.*]

4 But Festus answered, that Paul should be kept at Cæsarea, and that he himself would depart shortly thither [*but Festus turned down their request and told them that he himself would soon be leaving for Caesarea*].

5 Let them therefore, said he, which among you are able, go down with me, and accuse this man, if there be any wickedness in him. [*He invited the Jewish leaders, whoever could come with him, to come and present their case against Paul in Caesarea.*]

6 And when he had tarried [*stayed*] among them more than ten days, he went down unto Cæsarea; and the next day sitting on the judgment seat commanded Paul to be brought.

7 And when he was come [*when Paul arrived in the court room*], the Jews which came down from Jerusalem stood round about, and laid [*presented*] many and grievous [*serious*] complaints against Paul, which they could not prove.

8 While he answered for himself [*when Paul answered the charges, he said*], Neither against the law of the Jews, neither against the temple, nor yet against Cæsar, have I offended any thing at all [*I have done nothing at all against the law of the Jews, nor the temple, nor against Caesar*].

9 But Festus, willing to do the Jews a pleasure [*a favor*], answered Paul, and said, Wilt thou go up to Jerusalem, and there be judged of these things before me [*would you like me to take you to Jerusalem and hold court there on these charges against you*]?

As a Roman citizen, by birth, Paul will now exercise his legal right to trial in a Roman court, in person, in Rome, by appealing to Caesar. In this way, he will escape being turned back over to the Jews.

10 Then said Paul, I stand at Cæsar's judgment seat, where I ought to be judged [*I am where I belong, in a Roman courtroom*]: to the Jews have I done no wrong, as thou very well knowest [*you know very well that I have done no wrong to the Jews*].

11 For if I be an offender [*a lawbreaker*], or have committed any thing worthy of death, I refuse not to die [*if I have done anything worthy of death, I am willing to die for it*]: but if there be none of these things whereof these accuse me [*if the accusations against me are false*], no man may deliver me unto them [*the Jews*]. I appeal unto Cæsar.

12 Then Festus, when he had conferred with the council [*with his legal counselors*], answered, Hast thou appealed unto Cæsar? unto Cæsar shalt thou go [*since you have appealed to Caesar, to Caesar you will go*].

13 And after certain days [*after a few days*] king Agrippa and Bernice came

unto Cæsarea to salute [*to pay their respects to*] Festus.

> King Agrippa was the son of Herod Agrippa I, who is mentioned in Acts 12:1–23. Bernice was his sister. Drusilla, Felix's wife (Acts 24:24), was also his sister. See chart in Bible Dictionary under "Herod." We are dealing with members of the royal family, the ruling royal family in the Palestine area at the time, all of which was under Roman rule.

14 And when they had been there many days, Festus declared [*explained*] Paul's cause unto the king, saying, There is a certain man left in bonds by Felix: [*Felix left a prisoner here when he turned things over to me.*]

15 About whom, when I was at Jerusalem, the chief priests and the elders of the Jews informed me [*told me of several charges they had against him*], desiring to have judgment against him [*wanting me to turn Paul over to them*].

16 To whom I answered, It is not the manner of the Romans to deliver any man to die [*it is not legal, according to Roman law, to give any man to anyone to be executed*], before that he which is accused have the accusers face to face [*until they have faced the accused in our courts*], and have licence to answer for himself concerning the crime laid against him [*so that the accused has a chance to defend himself against the charges*].

> **JST Acts 25:16**
>
> 16 To whom I answered, It is not the matter of the Romans to deliver any man to die, before that he which is accused have the accusers face to face, and have license to answer for himself concerning the crime laid against him.

17 Therefore, when they [*the Jews*] were come hither [*arrived here in Caesarea*], without any delay on the morrow [*the next day*] I sat on the judgment seat [*I convened court*], and commanded the man [*Paul*] to be brought forth [*in*].

> **JST Acts 25:17**
>
> 17 Therefore, when they were come hither, without any delay on the day following I sat on the judgment seat, and commanded the man to be brought forth.

18 Against whom when the accusers stood up, they brought none accusation of such things as I supposed [*they didn't accuse Paul of any of the things I expected they would*]:

19 But had certain questions [*presented charges*] against him of their own superstition [*which came out of their own religious beliefs*], and of one Jesus, which was dead, whom Paul affirmed [*claimed*] to be alive.

20 And because I doubted of such manner of questions [*because I didn't feel qualified to deal with such questions, knowing nothing about such things*], I asked him whether he would go to Jerusalem, and there be judged of these matters [*I asked Paul if he would prefer to go to Jerusalem and appear in the Jews' court system where they would be more knowledgeable about such things*].

21 But when Paul had appealed to be reserved unto the hearing of Augustus [*when Paul demanded his right to be tried by Caesar Augustus (the Roman emperor)*], I commanded him to be kept [*in prison*] till I might send him to Cæsar.

22 Then Agrippa said unto Festus, I would also hear the man myself [*I would like to listen to Paul myself*]. To morrow, said he [*Festus*], thou shalt hear him.

23 And on the morrow [*the next day*], when Agrippa was come, and Bernice, with great pomp, and was entered into the place of hearing [*after King Agrippa and Bernice had arrived with*

*much pomp and ceremony*], with the chief captains, and principal men of the city, at Festus' commandment Paul was brought forth [*into the court room*].

24 And Festus said, King Agrippa, and all men which are here present with us, ye see this man [*now all of you can see this man, Paul, with your own eyes*], about whom all the multitude of the Jews have dealt with me, both at Jerusalem, and also here, crying that he ought not to live any longer [*about whom large numbers of Jews from Jerusalem as well as here have complained to me long and loud, saying he should be executed*].

25 But when I found that he had committed nothing worthy of death, and that he himself hath appealed to Augustus [*Caesar*], I have determined to send him [*to Caesar*].

26 Of whom I have no certain thing to write unto my lord [*I haven't been able to come up with anything definite to write to Caesar about him*]. Wherefore [*therefore*] I have brought him forth before you [*all the people gathered in the courtroom*], and specially before thee, O king Agrippa, that, after examination had [*so that, after today's court proceedings are over*], I might have somewhat to write [*I will have specific charges against Paul which I can include in a letter to Caesar*].

27 For it seemeth to me unreasonable to send a prisoner, and not withal [*along with him*] to signify [*to explain*] the crimes laid against him. [*In other words, it would be quite awkward to send a prisoner to Caesar without including specific charges against him.*]

## ACTS 26

As Paul defends himself before King Agrippa, he will again tell the story of his conversion. Paul is a great teacher and a skilled speaker and before this session is over, Agrippa will exclaim that Paul has almost persuaded him to become a Christian. Watch Paul's skill and inspiration now as he draws his listeners into his defense, which will focus on resurrection and on Christ.

1 THEN Agrippa said unto Paul, Thou art permitted to speak for thyself [*you are permitted to defend yourself now*]. Then Paul stretched forth the hand, and answered for [*defended*] himself:

2 I think myself happy, king Agrippa, because I shall answer for myself this day before thee touching all the things whereof I am accused of the Jews [*I consider myself fortunate to defend myself to you regarding each accusation which the Jews have brought against me*]:

3 Especially because I know thee to be expert in all customs and questions which are among the Jews: wherefore I beseech [*ask*] thee to hear me patiently.

4 My manner of life from my youth, which was at the first among mine own nation at Jerusalem, know all the Jews; [*The Jews know me and that I grew up in Jerusalem from the time of my youth.*]

5 Which knew me from the beginning, if they would testify, that after the most straitest sect of our religion I lived a Pharisee. [*Those who actually knew me from my youth, if they would tell you the truth about me, would testify that I was a Pharisee, the strictest religious group among the Jews.*]

6 And now I stand and am judged for the hope of the promise made of God unto our fathers: [*I am on trial here today because I believe in the promise God made to our ancestors.*]

7 Unto which promise our twelve tribes [*the descendants of Jacob*], instantly [*earnestly*] serving God day and night, hope to come. [*It is the same promise which all our people, the twelve tribes of Israel, hope to gain through faith-*

*fully serving God day and night.*] For which hope's sake, king Agrippa, I am accused of the Jews [*it is my belief in this promise and my hope for its fulfillment for which the Jews have brought me to trial*].

8 Why should it be thought a thing incredible with you, that God should raise the dead [*why should it be so difficult to believe that God can resurrect us*]?

9 I verily [*truly*] thought with myself, that I ought to do many things contrary to the name of Jesus of Nazareth [*In my earlier years, I was convinced that I ought to do everything possible to oppose Jesus and his followers*].

10 Which thing I also did in Jerusalem: and many of the saints [*the followers of Jesus*] did I shut up in prison, having received authority from the chief priests [*Jewish religious leaders*]; and when they [*Christians*] were put to death, I gave my voice against them [*I testified against them*].

11 And I punished them oft [*often*] in every synagogue [*congregation*], and compelled them to blaspheme [*say things which would justify their death*]; and being exceedingly [*very*] mad against them, I persecuted them even unto strange [*foreign*] cities [*I even went to foreign cities to round up and arrest Christians*].

12 Whereupon as I went [*in pursuit of this cause, I was traveling*] to Damascus [*about 140 miles north of Jerusalem, in Syria*] with authority and commission [*letters of authorization*] from the chief priests [*to arrest more Christians*],

13 At midday [*noon*], O king, I saw in the way [*while traveling along the road*] a light from heaven, above the brightness of the sun, shining round about me and them which journeyed with me.

14 And when we were [*when we had*] all fallen to the earth, I heard a voice speaking unto me, and saying in the Hebrew tongue [*language*], Saul, Saul, why persecutest thou me? it is hard for thee to kick against the pricks [*it is hard for you to keep going against your conscience*].

15 And I said, Who art thou, Lord? And he said, I am Jesus whom thou persecutest.

In verse 16, next, the Savior calls Paul to full-time service in the Church and tells him that he is to bear witness of this appearance of Jesus to him and also that more will be revealed to him in future appearances and revelations from Christ.

16 But rise, and stand upon thy feet: for I have appeared unto thee for this purpose, to make thee a minister and a witness both of these things which thou hast seen, and of those things in the which I will appear unto thee;

17 Delivering thee from the people, and from the Gentiles [*I will rescue you from the Jews and from the Gentiles*], unto whom now I send thee,

18 To open their eyes [*spiritually*], and to turn them from darkness [*spiritual darkness*] to light, and from the power of Satan unto God, that they may receive forgiveness of sins, and inheritance among them which are sanctified [*who obtain celestial glory; "sanctified" means being made clean, pure, holy, and fit to be in the presence of God*] by faith that is in me.

19 Whereupon, O king Agrippa, I was not disobedient unto the heavenly vision [*from that point on, I have been obedient to instructions given me in that vision*]:

20 But shewed first unto them of Damascus, and at Jerusalem, and throughout all the coasts [*borders*] of Judæa,

and then to the Gentiles, that they should repent and turn to God, and do works meet for repentance. [*I taught the people, beginning in Damascus, then at Jerusalem, and the Jews throughout the region of Judea, and then the Gentiles that they must repent and turn to God and demonstrate their sincere repentance by righteous living.*]

21 For these causes the Jews caught me in the temple, and went about to kill me [*these are the reasons the Jews grabbed me in the temple and tried to kill me*].

22 Having therefore obtained help of God [*because of God's help and protection*], I continue unto this day, witnessing both to small and great [*testifying to everyone I meet, both the little known and the famous*], saying none other things than those which the prophets and Moses did say should come [*saying nothing but what the prophets and Moses prophesied would happen, namely*]:

23 That Christ should suffer [*would suffer for our sins and be crucified*], and that he should be the first that should rise from the dead [*and that He would be the first to be resurrected*], and should shew light [*and would bring the light of the gospel*] unto the people [*the Jews*], and to the Gentiles [*everyone who is not a Jew or member of the Twelve Tribes*].

24 And as he [*Paul*] thus spake for himself [*spoke in his own defense*], Festus [*the Roman ruler over Judea, the Jerusalem area, whom King Agrippa was visiting*] said [*interrupted*] with a loud voice, Paul, thou art beside thyself; much learning doth make thee mad [*Paul, you are out of your mind! Too much education has made you crazy!*].

25 But he said, I am not mad, most noble Festus; but speak forth the words of truth and soberness.

26 For the king [*Agrippa*] knoweth of these things, before whom also I speak freely [*King Agrippa knows what I am talking about; that's why I have spoken so openly in front of him*]: for I am persuaded [*convinced*] that none of these things are hidden from him; for this thing was not done in a corner. [*I am convinced that he is very aware of the things about which I have spoken because all of this was done in public, not secretly.*]

27 King Agrippa, believest thou the prophets [*do you believe the words of the Old Testament prophets*]? I know that thou believest.

28 Then Agrippa said unto Paul, Almost thou persuadest me to be a Christian [*you have almost convinced me to become a Christian*].

29 And Paul said, I would to God [*I wish with all my heart*], that not only thou [*you*], but also all that hear me this day [*everyone in this room*], were both almost, and altogether such as I am [*were almost, in fact, exactly like me*], except these bonds [*except for being a prisoner*].

30 And when he had thus spoken, the king [*Agrippa*] rose up, and the governor [*Festus*], and Bernice [*Agrippa's sister*], and they that sat with them [*and other officials who were in their group*]:

31 And when they were gone aside [*had gone where they could talk privately*], they talked between themselves, saying, This man doeth nothing worthy of death or of bonds [*Paul has done nothing that justifies his being executed or even being held prisoner*].

32 Then said Agrippa unto Festus, This man might have been set at liberty, if he had not appealed unto Cæsar [*we could set Paul free right now if he had not made a formal request for a trial before Caesar; see Acts 25:11*].

# ACTS 27

Just a reminder (as previously noted) that when you see the word "we" in verse 1, next, it tells you that Luke (who wrote the Gospel of Luke as well as Acts) is with Paul and his companions at this time. In fact, it appears that Luke has been traveling with Paul since Acts 16:10. Paul's journey to Rome takes place in AD 55. As you will see, in this chapter, Paul's journey to Rome to be tried there before Caesar was just as eventful as most of his other travels, for him and his companions. Among other things, he will be shipwrecked.

1 AND when it was determined that we should sail into Italy [*to Rome*], they delivered Paul and certain other prisoners unto one named Julius, a centurion of Augustus' band.

> The "Augustus band" mentioned in verse 1, above, would probably be one of the elite detachments of Roman soldiers, who had been honored for valor and effective in fighting for the Roman Empire. See Strong's #4575. A "band" of soldiers has various definitions, but would quite likely be 600 Roman soldiers which would be one tenth of a Roman legion. Julius (verse 1, above), as a centurion, would be in charge of 100 Roman soldiers.

2 And entering into a ship of [*from*] Adramyttium [*a seaport in what would be far northwestern Turkey today*], we launched, meaning [*planning*] to sail by the coasts of Asia [*along the southern coasts of Turkey today*]; one Aristarchus, a Macedonian of Thessalonica [*a faithful member of the Church from Thessalonica, who will stay with Paul during his Roman imprisonment; see Colossians 4:10*], being with us.

3 And the next day we touched at Sidon [*a seacoast city about 130 miles north of Jerusalem on the Mediterranean Sea*]. And Julius [*the Roman centurion in charge of Paul and other prisoners on the ship*] courteously entreated Paul [*treated Paul very courteously*], and gave him liberty [*permission*] to go unto his friends [*to go ashore and visit friends*] and to refresh himself.

4 And when we had launched from thence [*set sail from there*], we sailed under Cyprus [*along the leeward side, or eastern side, of the Island of Cyprus; "leeward" means the side of the island which offers some protection from the wind*], because the winds were contrary [*not blowing in the right direction for us*].

5 And when we had sailed over the sea of Cilicia and Pamphylia [*along the coast of what would be southern Turkey today*], we came to Myra, a city of Lycia [*on the coast of southwestern Turkey today*].

6 And there the centurion found a ship of [*from*] Alexandria sailing into Italy; and he put us therein.

7 And when we had sailed slowly many days, and scarce were [*just barely had*] come over against Cnidus [*had only come about 150 miles and were approaching Cnidus, on the southwestern coast of southern Turkey today*], the wind not suffering us [*still not blowing in our favor*], we sailed under Crete [*for protection from the wind to the leeward side of Crete*], over against [*close to*] Salmone [*on the eastern end of Crete*];

8 And, hardly [*with much difficulty*] passing it, came unto a place which is called The fair havens [*on the southern coast of central Crete*]; nigh [*near*] whereunto was the city of Lasea.

9 Now when much time was spent [*we had already lost a lot of time*], and when sailing was now dangerous [*it was the dangerous time of year for sailing in this region because of*

*frequent storms*], because the fast was now already past, Paul admonished [*warned*] them,

The "fast" referred to in verse 9, above, which was already past, identifies the time of year when this dangerous sailing is taking place as autumn. This public fast was required by the Law of Moses. It was to be held on the tenth of the month of Tisri which is equivalent to mid-September to mid-October on our modern calendar. This "fast" in autumn, was held in conjunction with the Day of Atonement or Yom Kippur, as it is better known today on our calendars.

10 And said unto them, Sirs, I perceive [*I am inspired to tell you*] that this voyage will be with hurt and much damage [*that if we continue this journey now, it will result in disaster*], not only of [*for*] the lading [*cargo*] and ship, but also of [*for*] our lives.

11 Nevertheless the centurion [*the Roman commander*] believed the master [*captain*] and the owner of the ship, more than those things which were spoken by Paul.

12 And because the haven [*harbor where they were located at that time*] was not commodious [*suitable*] to winter in [*to stay in for the winter*], the more part [*the majority of the people on board*] advised to depart thence also [*counseled them to set sail from there*], if by any means they might attain to Phenice [*and try to sail to Phenice, on the southwestern end of Crete*], and there to winter [*and stay there for the winter*]; which is an haven of Crete, and lieth toward the south west and north west [*a harbor in western Crete which faced both southwest and northwest*].

13 And when the south wind blew softly [*and so, when a gentle south wind began to blow*], supposing that they had obtained their purpose [*thinking that luck was with them*], loosing thence [*taking up their anchor from there*], they sailed close by Crete [*they sailed along, keeping close to the shores of Crete*].

14 But not long after there arose against it [*their ship*] a tempestuous [*hurricane-like*] wind, called Euroclydon [*the "Northeaster" in other words, a severe north east wind which occurred often enough to be given a name; see Strong's #2148*].

15 And when the ship was caught, and could not bear up [*to sail*] into the wind, we let her drive [*we let the ship be driven with the wind*].

16 And running under [*using the island as a windbreak, in other words, on the lee side of*] a certain island which is called Clauda [*about 30 miles due south of Phenice, verse 12*], we had much work to come by the boat [*it was all we could do to get the lifeboat ready*]:

17 Which when they had taken up, they used helps, undergirding the ship [*the crew ran ropes under the ship and tied them together in an attempt to keep the ship from breaking apart*]; and, fearing lest they should fall into the quicksands [*afraid that they would be blown into the sandbars off the coast of northern Africa*], strake sail [*lowered the ships sails*], and so were driven [*and drifted with the wind*].

18 And we being exceedingly tossed with a tempest, the next day they lightened the ship [*because we were being so badly tossed about in the storm, the next day the crew began throwing cargo overboard to lighten the ship*];

19 And the third day we cast out [*threw overboard*] with our own hands the tackling [*equipment, furniture, and so forth*] of the ship.

20 And when neither sun nor stars in many days appeared [*we saw neither sun nor stars for many days*], and no

small tempest lay on us [*and the storm kept beating on us*], all hope that we should be saved was then taken away [*we lost all hope of surviving*].

21 But after long abstinence [NIV, *after the men had gone a long time without food*] Paul stood forth [*stood up*] in the midst [*middle*] of them, and said, Sirs, ye should have hearkened unto me [*you should have listened to me*], and not have loosed from Crete [*and not have left Crete*], and to have gained this harm and loss [*and then you would not have suffered this damage and loss of your cargo*].

22 And now I exhort you to be of good cheer [*however, cheer up*]: for there shall be no loss of any man's life among you, but of the ship [*none of you will lose your lives; all we will lose is the ship*].

23 For there stood by me this night the angel of God [*an angel of the Lord appeared to me last night*], whose I am, and whom I serve,

24 Saying, Fear not, Paul; thou must be brought before Cæsar [*you must appear before Caesar*]: and, lo, God hath given thee all them that sail with thee [*none who are sailing with you will die*].

25 Wherefore, sirs, be of good cheer [*cheer up*]: for I believe God, that it shall be even as it was told me [*I know that what God had the angel tell me will happen*].

26 Howbeit [*however*] we must be cast [*we will be shipwrecked*] upon a certain island.

27 But when the fourteenth night was come [*on the fourteenth night of the storm*], as we were driven up and down in Adria [*as we were driven back and forth on the Adriatic Sea, well south of Italy*], about midnight the shipmen [*sailors*] deemed [*felt*] that they drew near to [*were approaching*] some country [*land*];

28 And sounded [*lowered a weighted rope to determine how deep the water was*], and found it twenty fathoms [*120 feet d*eep]: and when they had gone a little further, they sounded again, and found it fifteen fathoms [*90 feet deep*].

29 Then fearing lest we should have fallen upon rocks [*afraid that the ship would hit rocks and be broken up*], they cast four anchors out of the stern [*the back of the ship*], and wished for the day [*wished that daylight would come*].

30 And as the shipmen were about to flee [*planning to escape*] out of the ship, when [*afte*r] they had let down the boat [*the lifeboat*] into the sea, under colour [*pretending*] as though they would have cast anchors out of the foreship [*pretending that they were going to do something with the forward anchors*],

31 Paul said to the centurion [*the Roman commander of the soldiers*] and to the soldiers, Except these abide in the ship, ye cannot be saved [*unless these sailors remain in the ship, none of you will survive*].

32 Then the soldiers cut off the ropes of the boat, and let her fall off [*so the soldiers cut the ropes that were holding the lifeboat and let it drift away so the sailors could not use it to escape the ship*].

33 And while the day was coming on [*at about dawn*], Paul besought [*encouraged*] them all to take meat [*to eat food, thus breaking their fast*], saying, This day is the fourteenth day that ye have tarried and continued fasting, having taken nothing [*this is the fourteenth day you have fasted to be saved from the storm*].

34 Wherefore I pray you [*I urge you*] to take some meat [*to eat some food*]: for this is for your health [*you must do this in order to survive*]: for there shall not an hair fall from the head of any of you [*if you follow my instructions, each of*

*you will be saved without injury*].

35 And when he had thus spoken, he took bread, and gave thanks to God in presence of them all: and when he had broken it, he began to eat.

36 Then were they all of good cheer, and they also took some meat [*then they cheered up and ate also*].

37 And we were in all in the ship two hundred threescore and sixteen souls [*there were 276 of us on board the ship*].

38 And when they had eaten enough, they lightened the ship, and cast out the wheat into the sea [*they threw more things overboard, including the wheat they were carrying*].

39 And when it was day [*when daylight came*], they knew not the land [*didn't recognize where they were*]: but they discovered a certain creek [*a bay where a river entered the sea*] with a shore [*beach*], into the which they were minded, if it were possible, to thrust in the ship [*they decided to try to get the wind to push the ship into the bay, if possible*].

40 And when they had taken up the anchors, they committed themselves unto the sea [*turned themselves over to the sea*], and loosed the rudder bands [*untied the ropes from the rudders*], and hoised [*hoisted, lifted*] up the mainsail to the wind, and made [*headed*] toward shore.

41 And falling into a place where two seas met, they ran the ship aground [*but the ship hit a sandbar before getting to the beach*]; and the forepart stuck fast, and remained unmoveable [*and the bow, the front of the ship was stuck and would not move*], but the hinder part was broken with the violence of the waves [*but the back of the ship was broken off by the pounding of the waves*].

42 And the soldiers' counsel [*plan*] was to kill the prisoners, lest any of them should swim out, and escape.

43 But the centurion [*the Roman commander of the soldiers*], willing [*wanting*] to save Paul, kept them from their purpose [*commanded the soldiers not to kill anyone*]; and commanded that they which could swim should cast themselves first into the sea, and get to land [*the centurion told all who were able to dive in and swim to shore*]:

44 And the rest, some on boards, and some on broken pieces of the ship [*the centurion told the rest, who were not good enough swimmers, to grab hold of boards and broken pieces of the ship and make their way to shore*]. And so it came to pass, that they escaped all safe to land [*thus, all of them arrived safely on the beach*].

## ACTS 28

As you have already seen, Paul is always a missionary. He will be bitten by a poisonous snake as he helps gather wood for the fire and it will turn into an excellent opportunity for spreading the gospel.

1 AND when they were escaped, then they knew [*found out*] that the island was called Melita [*Malta, south of Sicily in southern Italy; they had been blown about 600 miles by the storm*].

2 And the barbarous people [*native people of the island*] shewed us no little kindness [*were very kind to us*]: for they kindled a fire, and received [*welcomed*] us every one, because of the present [*continuing*] rain, and because of the cold.

In the following verses, the local people on the island will get quite an introduction to the Apostle Paul, and much good will be done by this great missionary.

3 And when [*after*] Paul had gathered a bundle of sticks, and laid them on the fire, there came a viper [*a very poisonous*

*snake*] out of the heat, and fastened on his hand [*and bit him on the hand and then continued to hang on to Paul's hand*].

4 And when the barbarians [*the inhabitants of the island*] saw the venomous [*poisonous*] beast [*snake*] hang on his hand, they said among themselves, No doubt this man is a murderer, whom, though he hath escaped the sea, yet vengeance suffereth not to live. [*They thought Paul must be a murderer and that although he escaped successfully from the ship, the gods were not going to let him get away; rather, they caused the snake to bite him so he would die.*]

Paul has an advantage over these people who believe that he will now die. Remember that Paul had been told by an angel (Acts 27:23–24) that he would be brought safely to Rome to appear in court before Caesar. One can almost imagine a bit of a twinkle in Paul's determined and energetic eyes as the people watch in rapt attention for him to die after the snake has been shaken off into the fire. He no doubt knew what they were waiting for, but simply went innocently about his activities on the beach.

5 And he shook off the beast [*snake*] into the fire, and felt no harm [*felt no negative effects from the bite*].

6 Howbeit [*in the meantime*] they looked when he should have swollen, or fallen down dead suddenly [*the people watched to see Paul's hand swell up or for him to drop dead*]: but after they had looked [*watched*] a great while, and saw no harm come to him, they changed their minds, and said that he was a god.

7 In the same quarters [*in that same area of the island*] were possessions of [*was an estate which belonged to*] the chief man [*probably the governor*] of the island, whose name was Publius; who received [*welcomed*] us, and lodged us [*had us stay at his place*] three days courteously.

8 And it came to pass, that the father of Publius lay sick of a fever and of a bloody flux [*bloody diarrhea, dysentery; see Strong's #1420*]: to whom Paul entered in [*Paul entered his room*], and prayed, and laid his hands on him [*administered to him*], and healed him.

9 So when [*after*] this was done, others also, which had diseases in the island, came, and were healed:

10 Who also honoured us with many honours; and when we departed, they laded us with such things as were necessary [*they provided us with necessities for our journey*].

11 And after three months we departed in a ship of [*from*] Alexandria, which had wintered in the isle [*which had spent the winter on Malta*], whose sign was Castor and Pollux [*the ship had figureheads of the gods Castor and Pollux*].

Castor and Pollux, in verse 11, above, were mythological gods, the twin sons of Jupiter and Leda, and were regarded as the gods who protected ships and sailors.

12 And landing at Syracuse [*in southeastern Sicily*], we tarried there three days.

13 And from thence we fetched a compass [*took a roundabout course*], and came to Rhegium [*on the southwestern tip of Italy, across the bay from the northeast tip of Sicily*]: and after one day the south wind blew, and we came the next day to Puteoli [*they covered about 230 miles and came to Puteoli, on the western coast of Italy, about 100 miles south of Rome*]:

14 Where we found brethren [*members of the Church*], and were desired to tarry with them seven days [*and stayed*

*with them, according to their request, for seven days*]: and so we went toward Rome.

15 And from thence [*from Rome*], when the brethren heard of us, they came to meet us as far as Appii forum, and The three taverns [*when the brethren at Rome heard we were coming, they came as far as Appii Forum and The Three Taverns, about 25 to 30 miles to meet us*]: whom when Paul saw, he thanked God, and took courage [*which was very encouraging to Paul*].

16 And when we came to Rome, the centurion [*Roman commander*] delivered the prisoners to the captain of the guard: but Paul was suffered [*allowed*] to dwell by himself with a soldier that kept [*guarded*] him. [*In other words, Paul was allowed to live in a place of his own, under house arrest, with a soldier assigned to watch him, rather than being put in prison.*]

Three days after his arrival in Rome, Paul will call the local leaders of the Jews together and explain how he ended up in Rome. He will explain that, even though he was innocent of any wrongdoing, he had to request a trial before Caesar in order to avoid being murdered by the Jews at home.

17 And it came to pass, that after three days Paul called the chief of the Jews [*the leaders of the Jews*] together: and when they were come together [*when they had assembled*], he said unto them, Men and brethren, though I have committed nothing against the people [*even though I am innocent of any crime*], or customs of our fathers [*ancestors*], yet was I delivered prisoner from Jerusalem [*I was arrested in Jerusalem*] into the hands of the Romans [*and turned over to the Romans*].

18 Who, when they had examined me [*had finished with my trial*], would have let me go, because there was no cause of death in me [*I had done nothing worthy of being executed*].

19 But when the Jews spake against it [*but when the Jews violently objected to the decision of the court*], I was constrained to [*I had to*] appeal unto Cæsar; not that I had ought to accuse my nation of [*not that I wanted to accuse my own nation of anything*].

20 For this cause therefore have I called for you [*this is why I've asked you to come here to me*], to see you, and to speak with you: because that for the hope of Israel I am bound with this chain [*the reason I am a prisoner, bound in chains, is that I believe in the God of Israel*].

21 And they said unto him, We neither received letters out of Judea concerning thee [*the Jewish religious leaders in the Jerusalem area have written nothing to us about you*], neither any of the brethren that came shewed or spake any harm of thee [*and none of our leaders who have visited us has said anything negative concerning you*].

22 But we desire to hear of thee what thou thinkest [*we would like to have you talk to us about your beliefs*]: for as concerning this sect [*the Christians*], we know that every where it is spoken against [*we have heard nothing but bad about the Christians*].

23 And when they had appointed him a day, there came many to him into his lodging [*on a day which they had decided upon, many Jews living in Rome came to Paul's quarters*]; to whom he expounded and testified the kingdom of God [*and he taught them and testified of the kingdom of God*], persuading [*teaching*] them concerning Jesus, both out of the law of Moses, and out of the prophets [*using the teachings of Moses and the other Old Testament prophets*], from morning till evening.

24 And some believed the things which were spoken, and some believed not.

25 And when they agreed not among themselves, they departed, after that Paul had spoken one word [*After discussing Paul's teachings among themselves, they couldn't agree about them, so they started to leave, after Paul had said this last thing, quoting Isaiah 6:9–10*], Well spake the Holy Ghost by Esaias [*through Isaiah*] the prophet unto our fathers [*ancestors*],

26 Saying, Go unto this people, and say, Hearing ye shall hear, and shall not understand [*you are spiritually deaf*]; and seeing ye shall see, and not perceive [*you are spiritually blind*]:

27 For the heart of this people is waxed gross [*the people are hard-hearted, spiritually insensitive*], and their ears are dull of hearing [*they are spiritually deaf*], and their eyes have they closed [*they don't want to understand spiritual things*]; lest they should see with their eyes, and hear with their ears, and understand with their heart, and should be converted, and I should heal them.

28 Be it known therefore unto you [*the Jews here in Rome*], that the salvation of God [*the gospel*] is sent unto the Gentiles [*is being taken to non-Jews*], and that they will hear it [*they will accept it*].

29 And when he had said these words, the Jews departed, and had great reasoning among themselves [*and had many arguments among themselves about Paul's teachings*].

30 And Paul dwelt two whole years in his own hired [*rented*] house, and received [*welcomed*] all that came in unto him [*who came to visit him*],

31 Preaching the kingdom of God, and teaching those things which concern the Lord Jesus Christ, with all confidence, no man forbidding him [*no one ordered him to stop teaching*].

As indicated by Luke in verse 30, above, Paul will spend two years as a prisoner in Rome. He will be under house arrest, living in his own rented quarters, at his own expense. Even though he is a prisoner, he will be given many freedoms and privileges, including the freedom to have people visit him whenever they want to and to teach anything he wants to. During this first Roman imprisonment, Paul will write at least four of his letters (called "epistles") to his converts in various locations along the routes of his missionary journeys. These four letters appear as books in our New Testament. They are: Philippians, Colossians, Ephesians, and Philemon. After two years, he will be released from prison and will visit members of the Church in many locations, traveling perhaps as far as Spain. After four years, he will again be taken prisoner to Rome and will be executed by Nero, the emperor or "Caesar" of the Roman Empire, about AD 65. See Bible Dictionary under "Paul."

## *A General Note about Paul's Writings*

Our Bible contains 14 epistles (letters) written by the Apostle Paul to members of the Church in various locations. Of the 14 letters, 13 of them, Romans through Philemon, are placed in the Bible generally according to length, the longest being Romans and the shortest being Philemon. The reason Hebrews is placed last is because some scholars question whether or not Paul is the author of Hebrews. See Bible Dictionary under "Pauline Epistles." We know that Paul did write Hebrews because the Prophet Joseph Smith said he did. In *Teachings of the Prophet Joseph Smith*, p. 59, he simply said, "It is said by Paul in his letter to the Hebrew brethren..."

# The Epistle of Paul the Apostle to the Romans

The epistle (letter) from the Apostle Paul to the Romans was written from Corinth (in southern Greece), probably in the winter of AD 57 to AD 58, near the end of Paul's third missionary journey. Major themes of Romans include a strong condemnation of every form of wickedness and Paul's teachings about the relationship between our own works and the grace of God. With respect to grace and works, or faith and works, many Christians use quotes from Romans to prove that one needs only grace in order to be saved. We will give some examples here:

**Example: Romans 3:27–28**

27 Where is boasting then? It is excluded. By what law? of works? Nay: but by the law of faith.

28 Therefore we conclude that a man is justified by faith without the deeds of the law.

Others quote Romans to show that works are also necessary in order to be saved.

**Example: Romans 2:13**

13 For not the hearers of the law are just before God, but the doers of the law shall be justified.

What is going on here? The answer is simple. We must keep Paul's writings in their context, in their setting in the scriptures. For instance, in our example, above, of Romans 3:27–28, Paul is speaking to Jewish members of the Church who, because of their past tradition and culture before their baptism, are going through the motions of religion, who do the rituals and sacrifices and works, etc., but don't have faith and are not living the true gospel. Therefore, Paul emphasizes faith to them, and downplays empty works, which won't save them. Also, the "law" in verse 28 refers to the Law of Moses, which was fulfilled by the Savior.

On the other hand, in Romans 2:13, quoted above, Paul's audience is Gentile members of the Church who are not as concerned as they should be about works, rather are thinking that since they have been baptized and are members, they don't need much else. Therefore, Paul's emphasis to them is that they must pay much closer attention to righteous works and deeds, and avoid sin and unrighteous behaviors.

## Romans 1

In Romans, chapter 1, Paul's emphasis is mainly on works, and on avoiding the evils of that day. You will notice that many in our world today are caught up in the same sins.

The Joseph Smith Translation of the Bible [*JST*] is very significant in helping us understand this chapter. The Prophet Joseph Smith made many changes, additions, and clarifications. We will include all of the changes he made for this chapter.

1 PAUL, a servant of Jesus Christ, called to be an apostle, separated [*set apart*] unto the gospel of God,

**JST Romans 1:1**
1 Paul, an apostle, a servant of God, called of Jesus Christ, and separated to preach the gospel,

2 (Which he [*God*] had promised afore [*in times past*] by [*through*] his prophets in the holy scriptures,)

**JST Romans 1:2**
2 (Which he had promised before by his prophets in the holy scriptures,)

3 Concerning his Son Jesus Christ our Lord, which was made of the seed of David [*was a descendant of* David] according to the flesh [*who was a descendant of King David, in terms of his mortal birth*];

4 And declared to be the Son of God with power, according to the spirit of holiness, by the resurrection from the dead: [*God testifies, with great power, through the Holy Ghost, that Christ is the Son of God, as witnessed by His resurrection from the dead.*]

**JST Romans 1:4**
4 And declared the Son of God with power, by the Spirit according to the truth through the resurrection from the dead;

5 By whom we have received grace and apostleship, for obedience to the faith among all nations, for his name:

**JST Romans 1:5**
5 By whom we have received grace and apostleship, through obedience, and faith in his name, to preach the gospel among all nations;

6 Among whom are ye also the called of Jesus Christ: [*You also are among those who have been called by Jesus Christ to bear witness of Him everywhere.*]

**JST Romans 1:6**
6 Among whom ye also are called of Jesus Christ;

7 To all [*the members of the Church*] that be in Rome, beloved of God, called to be saints: Grace to you and peace from God our Father, and the Lord Jesus Christ.

**JST Romans 1:7**
7 Wherefore I write to all who are in Rome, beloved of God, called saints; Grace to you, and peace, from God our Father, and the Lord Jesus Christ.

Verse 7, above, is one of many verses which are helpful in showing that the Father and Jesus are separate individuals.

8 First, I thank my God [*Heavenly Father*] through [*in the name of*] Jesus Christ for you all, that your faith is spoken of throughout the whole world [*the whole region of the Mediterranean Sea; the Roman "world"*].

**JST Romans 1:8**
8 First, I thank my God through Jesus Christ, that you all are steadfast, and your faith is spoken of throughout the whole world.

9 For God is my witness [*God knows that what I'm telling you is true*], whom I serve with my spirit in the gospel of his Son, that without ceasing I make mention of you always in my prayers [*that I pray for you continually*];

**JST Romans 1:9**
9 For God is my witness, whom I serve, that without ceasing I make mention of you always in my prayers, that you may be kept through the Spirit, in the gospel of his Son,

10 Making request, if by any means now at length [*in due time*] I might have a prosperous journey by the will of God to come unto you.

**JST Romans 1:10**
10 Making request of you, to remember me in your prayers, I now write unto you, that you will ask him in faith, that if by any means, at length, I may serve you with my labors, and may

have a prosperous journey by the will of God, to come unto you.

11 For I long to see you, that I may impart unto you some spiritual gift, to the end ye may be established [*I would like to visit you so that I can strengthen you spiritually for the rest of your lives*];

**JST Romans 1:11**
11 For I long to see you, that I may impart unto you some spiritual gift, that it may be established in you to the end;

12 That is, that I may be comforted together with you by the mutual faith both of you and me [*that we might strengthen and comfort each other; see Strong's #4837*].

**JST Romans 1:12**
12 That I may be comforted together with you by the mutual faith both of you and me.

13 Now I would not have you ignorant [*I want you to be aware*], brethren, that oftentimes I purposed [*planned*] to come unto you, (but was let hitherto) [*every time*], that I might have some fruit [*success*] among you also, even as among other Gentiles.

**JST Romans 1:13**
13 Now I would not have you ignorant, brethren, that oftentimes I purposed to come unto you, (but was hindered hitherto,) that I might have some fruit among you also, even as among other Gentiles.

14 I am debtor [*obligated*] both to the Greeks, and to the Barbarians [*people of other nations; this does not have a negative connotation–see Strong's #0915*]; both to the wise, and to the unwise. [*In other words, I owe all people my best efforts to teach them of Christ.*]

15 So, as much as in me is [*with my best efforts*], I am ready to preach the gospel to you that are at Rome also.

**JST Romans 1:15**
15 And, as much as in me is, I am ready to preach the gospel to you that are at Rome also.

The first 24 words of verse 16, next, are one of the most famous quotes from the Apostle Paul.

16 For I am not ashamed of the gospel of Christ: for it is the power of God unto salvation to every one that believeth; to the Jew first, and also to the Greek [*to the Gentiles*]. [*The gospel was given to the Jews first, then, after the Savior's resurrection, was taken to the Gentiles as well as the Jews.*]

17 For therein [*in the gospel of Jesus Christ*] is the righteousness [*the standard for personal righteousness*] of God revealed [*made known*] from faith to faith: as it is written, The just [*the righteous*] shall live by faith.

**JST Romans 1:17**
17 For therein is the righteousness of God revealed through faith on his name; as it is written, The just shall live by faith.

18 For the wrath [*anger*] of God is revealed from heaven against all ungodliness and unrighteousness of men, who hold the truth in unrighteousness [*who do not repent once they know the truth*];

**JST Romans 1:18**
18 For the wrath of God is revealed from heaven against all ungodliness and unrighteousness of men; who love not the truth, but remain in unrighteousness,

19 Because that which may be known of God is manifest in them; for God hath shewed it unto them. [*In other words, after they have been taught the gospel*]

**JST Romans 1:19**
19 After that which may be known of God is manifest to them.

20 For the invisible things of him from the creation of the world are clearly

seen [*evidence of the existence of God is everywhere to be seen*], being understood by the things that are made [*the earth and all creation bear witness of God*], even his eternal power and Godhead; so that they are without excuse: [*In other words, all creation clearly bears witness of God, therefore, the people described in verses 18–19 have no excuse for not believing in God and living His gospel.*]

**JST Romans 1:20**

20 For God hath revealed unto them the invisible things of him, from the creation of the world, which are clearly seen; things which are not seen being understood by the things that are made, through his eternal power and Godhead; so that they are without excuse;

21 Because that, when they knew God [*after they had been taught about God*], they glorified him not as God [*they did not worship Him as they should*], neither were thankful [*neither did they express gratitude; see D&C 59:21*]; but became vain in their imaginations [*they became corrupt in their thinking and desires*], and their foolish heart was darkened [*they became spiritually darkened*].

**JST Romans 1:21**

21 Because that, when they knew God, they glorified him not as God, neither were they thankful, but became vain in their imaginations, and their foolish hearts were darkened.

22 Professing [*claiming*] themselves to be wise, they became fools,

23 And changed [*reduced*] the glory of the uncorruptible [*immortal, eternal*] God into an image made like to corruptible man [*they brought God down to the level of man, as with Greek gods*], and to birds, and fourfooted beasts, and creeping things [*including making idols to worship*].

By way of warning from God, Paul will now describe some of the worst sins being committed by people in Rome at the time, including sexual immorality in many different forms such as masturbation, lesbianism, and homosexuality. See the heading to chapter 1 in our Bible, where it confirms that Paul is referring to homosexuality. See also Topical Guide, under "Homosexuality" for additional references to the sin of homosexual behavior.

24 Wherefore God also gave them up [*allowed them to use their agency and thus turned them over*] to uncleanness [*immorality*] through the lusts [*evil, immoral desires*] of their own hearts, to dishonour their own bodies between themselves [*by themselves; see* Strong's *#1722*; in other words, *masturbation*]:

25 Who changed the truth of God into a lie [*they changed the righteous use of the power of procreation into perversion*], and worshipped and served the creature [*lusts of the flesh*] more than the Creator, who is blessed [*is to be praised*] for ever. Amen.

26 For this cause [*because they desired wickedness*] God gave them up unto [*because of agency, God allowed them to become involved in*] vile [*unrighteous*] affections [*depraved passion; see Strong's #3806*]: for even their women did change the natural use [*of the powers of procreation*] into that which is against nature [*perversion; see Strong's #5449*]: [*In other words, women got involved in lesbianism, homosexuality, and so forth. See McConkie,* Doctrinal New Testament Commentary, *Vol. 2, p. 220.*]

27 And likewise also the men [*the men did similar things*], leaving the natural use of the woman [*departing from normal, proper sexual relations with their wives*], burned in their lust one toward another [*became inflamed with sexual attraction toward other men*]; men with men [*homosexuality; see Romans 1:27, footnote a*] working that which is unseemly [*shameful; involving nakedness; see Strong's #0808*], and receiving in themselves that recompence

of their error which was meet [*required by God's laws; in other words, setting themselves up for the punishment of God for their perversion*].

28 And even as they did not like [*choose*] to retain God in their knowledge [*to acknowledge God's laws*], God gave them over to a reprobate mind [*allowed them to exercise their agency leading toward failing the test*], to do those things which are not convenient [*which are improper*];

**JST Romans 1:28**
28 And even as they did not like to retain God according to some knowledge, God gave them over to a reprobate mind, to do those things which are not convenient;

29 Being filled with all unrighteousness [*with all kinds of sins*], fornication [*sexual immorality*], wickedness [*depravity; see Strong's #4189*], covetousness, maliciousness [*meanness*]; full of envy, murder, debate [*strife, arguing*], deceit [*dishonesty*], malignity [*plotting evil against others*]; whisperers [*gossipers*],

30 Backbiters [*slanderers; people who ruin other peoples' reputations*], haters of God, despiteful [*violent, overbearing*], proud, boasters, inventors of evil things [*thinking up more ways to be wicked*], disobedient to parents,

31 Without understanding [*foolish, stupid; see Strong's #0801*], covenantbreakers, without natural affection [*heartless*], implacable [*refuse to make covenants; see Strong's #0786*], unmerciful:

32 Who knowing the judgment of God [*they are sinning against knowledge*], that they which commit such things are worthy of death [*They know God's commandments and that people who commit such sins will die spiritually and will eventually be cut off from God*], not only do the same [*they not only commit such sins*], but have pleasure in them that do them [*they approve of and encourage others to commit such sins*]. [*In other words, members of the Church who have been taught the gospel and understand it, and still commit such sins, are very accountable. The effects on their spirituality are tragic. A major problem is that they not only commit such sins themselves, but they also encourage others to do the same.*]

**JST Romans 1:32**
32 And some who, knowing the judgment of God, that they which commit such things are worthy of death, are inexcusable, not only do the same, but have pleasure in them that do them.

# ROMANS 2

In verses 1–16, Paul will talk mainly to Gentiles who have joined the Church, counseling them to avoid hypocrisy and emphasizing good works. He then talks to Jewish converts in verses 17–29, counseling them to avoid merely going through the motions of true religion, while lacking faith and internal commitment to personal righteousness.

1 THEREFORE thou art inexcusable [*there is no excuse for the following behavior*], O man, whosoever thou art that judgest [*this warning applies to anyone who judges others unrighteously*]: for wherein thou judgest another, thou condemnest thyself [*when you criticize and judge others unrighteously you condemn yourself*]; for thou that judgest doest the same things [*because you do the same things you criticize them for*].

**JST Romans 2:1**
1 Therefore thou art inexcusable, O man, whosoever thou art that thus judgest; for wherein thou judgest another, thou condemnest thyself; for thou that judgest doest the same things.

Paul is teaching strongly against hypocrisy, which is defined as criticizing others for wrong things they do when we ourselves are secretly committing the same sins.

2 But we are sure that the judgment of God is according to truth against them which commit such things [*God's judgment against people who do such things is fair*].

3 And thinkest thou this, O man, that judgest them which do such things, and doest the same, that thou shalt escape the judgment of God [*do you really think that you can be hypocrites and God won't notice*]?

4 Or despisest thou the riches of his goodness and forbearance and longsuffering; not knowing that the goodness of God leadeth thee to repentance [*do you take God's goodness and tolerance and patience so lightly that you miss the chance to repent*]? [*In other words, do you misinterpret the fact that God hasn't smitten you yet to be a signal that the sins you are committing are not that bad?*]

5 But after thy hardness and impenitent heart treasurest up unto thyself wrath against the day of wrath and revelation of the righteous judgment of God [*but instead, you follow your hard and unrepentant heart and continue storing up reasons for God's righteous anger to eventually condemn you*];

6 Who will render to every man according to his deeds [*God will judge every man according to his deeds*]:

7 To them who by patient continuance in well doing seek for glory and honour and immortality, eternal life [*to those who patiently and constantly persevere in doing righteous deeds, faithfully seeking to develop the attributes of God, He will give eternal life, exaltation*]:

8 But unto them that are contentious [*those who like to cause contention*], and do not obey the truth, but obey unrighteousness [*and commit other sins also*], indignation and wrath [*will call the righteous anger of God upon themselves*],

9 Tribulation [*trouble*] and anguish [*sorrow*], upon [*will come upon*] every soul of man that doeth evil, of the Jew first, and also of the Gentile [*the Jews were first to hear the gospel, and now the Gentiles have the same accountability*];

10 But glory, honour, and peace, to every man that worketh good, to the Jew first, and also to the Gentile [*the rewards for righteous living will come to everyone who performs good works; this was taught first to the Jews and then to the Gentiles*]:

11 For there is no respect of persons with God [*because all people are of equal worth to God*].

12 For as many as have sinned without law [*without knowing the gospel*] shall also perish without law: and as many as have sinned in the law [*who continue sinning even though they know the gospel*] shall be judged by the law [*will be held accountable for what they know*];

Just so you know, the parenthesis in your Bible, at the beginning of verse 13, next, is closed at the end of verse 15.

13 (For not the hearers of the law are just before God [*it is not those who have heard the commandments of God whom God considers to be righteous*], but the doers of the law shall be justified [*but rather it is those who live the gospel who will be saved in celestial glory; "justified" means being exalted in celestial glory*].

In verses 14–15, next, Paul calls attention to an interesting and important truth, namely that all people are born with the Spirit of Christ, which includes a conscience. And when people follow the promptings of conscience, they naturally tend to live in

harmony with the principles and commandments of the gospel, or, as Paul puts it, the "law." Also, remember that the use of the word "Gentile" in Paul's writings, means everyone who is not a Jew.

14 For when the Gentiles, which have not the law [*who do not have the gospel of Christ*], do by nature the things contained in the law [*naturally live in harmony with the laws of the gospel*], these, having not the law, are a law unto themselves [*are doing what they consider to be right*]:

15 Which shew the work of the law written in their hearts [*as they live in harmony with the things their hearts tell them, their lives demonstrate the purpose and desired outcomes of the laws and commandments of the gospel*], their conscience also bearing witness [*being guided by their conscience*], and their thoughts the mean while accusing or else excusing one another;) [*in other words, being guided by their own conscience, they either approve or disapprove of each other's actions*]

It is easy to get confused as we go from verse 15 to verse 16. Verse 16 refers back to the judgment mentioned at the end of verse 12 and expands a bit on that subject. Verses 13 through 15 were enclosed in parentheses and contained a separate topic about the effects of following conscience in the lives of people who have not heard of the gospel.

16 In the day when God shall judge the secrets of men by Jesus Christ [*on Judgment Day, when the Father has Jesus judge the secret acts of people (see John 5:22)*] according to my gospel. [*In other words, going back to the end of verse 12 and then back to verse 16, those who know the gospel will be held accountable for their knowledge and actions on the final Judgment Day by the Savior, who serves as our final judge, under the direction of the Father.*]

**JST Romans 2:16**

16 In the day when God shall judge the secrets of men by Jesus Christ according to the gospel.

Did you notice that Joseph Smith changed only one word in verse 16, above? It is a little word that makes a big difference. He changed "my gospel" to "the gospel," making it the gospel of Jesus Christ rather than Paul's gospel.

Paul, who has been mainly addressing Gentile converts in this chapter so far, now specifically addresses the Jewish converts and warns them against inappropriate ethnic pride and the hypocrisy of telling everyone else exactly how to live the gospel but not practicing what they preach.

17 Behold, thou art called a Jew [*you are proud of your Jewish heritage*], and restest in the law [*you still rely on the Law of Moses*], and makest thy boast of God [*and boast of your fine relationship with God*],

18 And knowest his will [*you claim to know God's will*], and approvest the things that are more excellent, being instructed out of the law [*and you carefully compare all things against the standards of the Law of Moses in order to choose the best in your lives*] ;

19 And art confident that thou thyself art [*you thus have confidence in your ability to serve as*] a guide of the blind [*the spiritually blind*], a light of them which are in darkness [*who are in spiritual darkness*],

20 An instructor of the foolish, a teacher of babes [*those who know very little about the gospel*], which hast the form of knowledge and of the truth in the law [*you appear to have great gospel knowledge because of your knowledge of details of the Law of Moses*].

21 Thou therefore which teachest another [*you, who take it upon yourself to teach others*], teachest thou not thyself [*do you live the gospel yourself or*

*are you a hypocrite (see Romans 2:21, footnote a)*]? thou that preachest a man should not steal, dost thou steal [*do you steal*]?

22 Thou that sayest a man should not commit adultery, dost thou commit adultery? thou that abhorrest idols [*you who claim to be terribly offended by idol worship and claim to stay far away from idols and their associated shrines, so you don't get "contaminated" by them*], dost thou commit sacrilege [*are you among those who enter into those shrines and rob and plunder them; see Romans 2:22, footnote b; also see* Strong's *#2416*]?

23 Thou that makest thy boast of the law, through breaking the law dishonourest thou God [*you who boast that you keep the law of God, do you dishonor God by breaking His laws*]?

24 For the name of God is blasphemed among the Gentiles through you, as it is written [*God's name is ridiculed by Gentiles because of your poor example, just like it said in Isaiah 52:5 and Ezekiel 36:22*].

In verses 25–29, next, Paul brings up the topic of circumcision, which, in his day, is still held by many Jewish converts to be very important, even though Christ did away with that part of the Law of Moses and even though the Church leaders ruled that circumcision was not required of Gentile converts. See Acts 15:1–31. Also see Bible Dictionary under "Circumcision." Paul is a diplomat and a wise servant of God, so, instead of taking the Jews to task for still being adamant about circumcision, he simply teaches them to avoid the hypocrisy of making covenants and keeping them outwardly, but not keeping them with the heart.

25 For circumcision verily profiteth, if thou keep the law [*circumcision can have value, if you keep the covenant associated with it to be loyal and true to God*]: but if thou be a breaker of the law, thy circumcision is made uncircumcision [*but if you don't keep God's commandments, you might just as well not have been circumcised*].

26 Therefore if the uncircumcision [*if an uncircumcised convert*] keep the righteousness of the law [*keeps God's commandments as taught by Christ*], shall not his uncircumcision be counted for circumcision [*isn't it as if he were circumcised*]?

27 And shall not uncircumcision which is by nature, if it fulfil the law, judge thee, who by the letter and circumcision dost transgress the law? [*Won't you be condemned, who live the letter of the Law of Moses but don't live the gospel, by converts who naturally are not circumcised but do live the gospel?*]

Paul now drives home the point that outward appearance alone does not make a person a true member of God's covenant people.

28 For he is not a Jew [*he is not truly one of God's covenant people*], which is one outwardly [*who outwardly appears to be, but who merely goes through the outward motions of being righteous*]; neither is that circumcision, which is outward in the flesh [*neither is the outward surgery of being circumcised, true commitment to God; it does not automatically make one "circumcised of heart" or truly committed to God, inwardly righteous*]:

29 But he is a Jew [*he is truly a member of God's covenant people*], which is one inwardly [*who is one deep inside*]; and circumcision [*symbolic of true loyalty to God*] is that of the heart, in the spirit [*is a matter of heart and soul*], and not in the letter [*and not in outward appearance, conforming to the letter of the law*]; whose praise is not of men, but of God [*for those who look to God rather than men for approval*].

# ROMANS 3

As stated in the introduction to Romans in this study guide, chapter three can be taken out of context and used to show that works are not necessary and that faith and grace are all that count. In context, this chapter is addressed to Jews who have joined the Church in Rome. Many of them at the time of Paul's writing are still caught up in their previous culture and traditions before baptism. They still believe that strict adherence to the outward details and requirements of the Law of Moses will assure them salvation. Thus, Paul will emphasize the role of faith in Christ and the role of grace. He will emphasize that personal righteousness, not external appearance alone, enables the Savior's grace and mercy to cleanse us and save us. Examples of this emphasis are found, among others, in verses 24, 27 and 28. The first verses of chapter three are a continuation of the theme of the last verses of chapter two, namely that personal righteousness and covenant keeping, not outward appearance and empty ritual, are the things that lead to salvation in celestial glory.

The issue in verses 1 and 2 is whether or not a Jewish member of the Church, who strictly keeps the Law of Moses but is not a true follower of Christ in his heart, has any advantage over a Gentile member who is truly converted to Christ? Answer: Of course not!

The JST (Joseph Smith Translation of the Bible) is very important to our understanding of these two verses.

1 WHAT advantage then hath the Jew? or what profit is there of circumcision?

**JST Romans 3:1**
1 What advantage then hath the Jew over the Gentile? or what profit of circumcision, who is not a Jew from the heart?

2 Much every way: chiefly, because that unto them were committed the oracles of God.

**JST Romans 3:2**
2 But he who is a Jew from the heart, I say hath much every way; chiefly because that unto them were committed the oracles of God.

The word "Jew," as used here, can represent the covenant people of the Lord. In other words, anyone who is truly converted and makes and keeps covenants with God has the advantage in every way because they have been given the "oracles" or true words of God. The phrase "oracles of God" can also mean "the prophets of God;" see D&C 90:5, footnote 5a. See also Topical Guide, under "Oracle."

3 For what if some did not believe? shall their unbelief make the faith of God without effect? [*In other words, when have the wicked ever nullified God or made faith in Him of no value? Answer: Never!*]

4 God forbid [*that will never happen*]: yea, let God be true, but every man a liar [*even if everyone refused to obey God, it still would not change the fact that God is true*]; as it is written [*in Psalm 51:4*], That thou [*God*] mightest be justified [*will be proven right*] in thy sayings [*in everything You say*], and mightest overcome [*will triumph*] when thou art judged [*when people judge Your revelations to be of no value*].

In the next two verses, Paul says, in effect, that God's righteousness is constant, and that when people are wicked, God's righteousness shows up even more, by comparison and contrast with the wicked. He also points out that wicked people want God to "water down" His commandments so that they don't look so wicked. Paul asks the question, "How could God judge the world righteously if He yielded to the desires of the

wicked to do away with His commandments?"

5 But if our unrighteousness commend [*serves to point out*] the righteousness of God, what shall we say [*are we justified in asking*]? Is God unrighteous who taketh vengeance? (I speak as a man) [*In other words, if we say, "Isn't it unfair for God to punish the wicked who, in a helpful way, are serving to point out His righteousness?"*]

**JST Romans 3:5**

But if we remain in our unrighteousness and commend the righteousness of God [*thus demonstrate by contrast the righteousness of God*], how dare we say, God is unrighteous who taketh vengeance? (I speak as a man who fears God,) [*In other words, if we, through our unrighteousness, emphasize God's righteousness even more, because of the contrast between Him and us, how could we possibly criticize Him for judging us and punishing us?*]

6 God forbid [*never!*]: for then how shall God judge the world? [*How would God be able to judge the world properly if He gave in to peoples' criticism of Him?*]

Judging by what Paul is saying here, he has apparently heard that some members of the Church in Rome are excusing their sinful behavior by saying, in effect, there has to be opposition so we are just helping God's work by being the opposition.

Watch, next, as Paul continues to tackle this issue head on. He will, in effect, ask his readers, "If our unrighteousness serves to emphasize God's righteousness, is it fair for Him to punish us? Aren't we actually doing good?" In other words, the wicked are apt to say that somebody has to be wicked so that others can see God's righteousness. Therefore, is it fair for Him to punish the wicked?

7 For if the truth of God hath more abounded through my lie unto his glory; why yet am I also judged as a sinner?

**JST Romans 3:7**

7 For if the truth of God hath more abounded through my lie, (as it is called of the Jews,) unto his glory; why yet am I also judged as a sinner? and not received? Because we are slanderously reported;

8 And not rather, (as we be slanderously reported, and as some affirm that we say,) Let us do evil, that good may come? whose damnation is just.

**JST Romans 3:8**

And some affirm [*claim*] that we say, (whose damnation is just), Let us do evil that good may come. But this is false.

Apparently, as we learn in the JST above, Paul and the brethren have been falsely accused of teaching that it is okay to do evil because good comes from it. As you saw in the middle of JST verse 8, Paul said those false accusers deserved to be damned. And at the end of JST verse 8, Paul says this accusation is absolutely false.

In the next verses, Paul will teach clearly that no one is perfect, including Jews, Gentiles, Apostles, and members of the Church. Thus, all need the Atonement of Christ.

9 What then? are we better than they? No, in no wise [*no, not at all*]: for we have before proved both Jews and Gentiles [*all peo*ple], that they are all under sin [*everyone has committed sin, no one is perfect*];

**JST Romans 3:9**

9 If not so; what then are we better than they? No, in no wise; for we have proved before, that Jews and Gentiles are all under sin.

Paul, as a master teacher, and as one who knows the Old Testament very thoroughly, will now quote scripture to powerfully prove to his listeners that everyone is caught up in sin and thus all need the gospel of Christ and His Atonement.

In an even tighter context, Paul is

describing many of the self-righteous Jews of his day who engineered the crucifixion of Christ. They meticulously keep the details of the Law of Moses, and outwardly appear religious and righteous, when in reality their hearts are full of filth, corruption, and evil and they spew poison from their mouths (see verses 13–14, below) as they teach others to be like them.

10 As it is written [*in Psalm 14:1–3*], There is none righteous, no, not one [*everyone needs to repent*]:

11 There is none that understandeth, there is none that seeketh after God.

12 They are all gone out of the way, they are together become unprofitable; there is none that doeth good, no, not one [*absolutely no one is perfect*].

13 [*Next, quoting Psalm 5:9.*] Their throat is an open sepulchre [*their throat is like an open grave, accepting rot and corruption, sin and filth*]; with their tongues they have used deceit [*they lie with their tongues*]; the poison of asps [*poisonous snakes*] is under their lips [*poisonous things which kill spirituality spew forth from their lips*]:

14 [*Next, quoting Psalm 10:7.*] Whose mouth is full of cursing and bitterness:

15 [*Next, quoting Isaiah 59:7–8.*] Their feet are swift to shed blood [*they move quickly to execute prophets and other righteous people*]:

16 Destruction and misery are in their ways [*theirs is a lifestyle of destroying good and causing misery*]:

17 And the way of peace have they not known [*they don't even know what peace is*]:

18 [*Next, quoting Psalm 36:*1.] There is no fear of God before their eyes [*they don't even have enough sense to be afraid of God because of their wickedness*].

Having quoted several Old Testament scriptures, blasting the hypocrisy of Jewish religious leaders, and reminding all of us that we too have sins and shortcomings and all need Christ's grace, help, mercy and Atonement, he now goes on to teach that the preaching of the gospel makes everyone accountable.

19 Now we know that what things soever the law saith, it saith to them who are under the law [*those who have been taught the gospel*]: that every mouth may be stopped [*silenced*], and all the world may become guilty [*accountable*] before God.

20 Therefore by the deeds of the law [*the Law of Moses*] there shall no flesh [*person*] be justified [*be made worthy to enter into celestial glory*] in his sight: for by the law is the knowledge of sin [*knowledge of God's laws makes people accountable*]

**JST Romans 3:20**

20 For by the law is the knowledge of sin; therefore by the deeds of the law shall no flesh be justified in his sight.

Paul has emphasized, over and over in these verses, that one cannot be saved by complying with the Law of Moses, but rather must come unto Christ and comply with His laws and commandments in order to enter celestial glory. Remember, the Law of Moses was given as a "schoolmaster law" (Galatians 3:24) to elevate the people to a level where they would be capable of living the higher laws given by the Savior which lead to exaltation. The problem which Paul faces is the same as that faced by the Savior among the Jews. They have become so caught up in the tiny details of the Law of Moses that they have departed from the intent of that law, namely to point their minds toward the Messiah who was to come. They have strayed far away from the wonderful outcomes built into the Law of Moses such as those in Exodus 23: 1–13, Leviticus 19:18 [*"Thou shalt love thy neighbour as thyself:"*], Deuteronomy, chapter 8, and Deuteronomy 11:18–19.

21 But now the righteousness of God [*the standards required by God*] without [*outside of*] the law [*the Law of Moses; in other words, separate and apart from the Law of Moses*] is manifested [*has been revealed by Christ*], being witnessed by the law and the prophets [*the "law"—that is, the writings of Moses in Genesis, Exodus, Leviticus, Numbers, and Deuteronomy*—along *with other Old Testament prophets, all testified that Christ would come and restore the higher laws and ordinances necessary for exaltation*];

22 Even the righteousness of God [*God's standards and gospel*] which is by faith of Jesus Christ unto all and upon all them that believe [*which is available to all people who believe Christ*]: for there is no difference [*there is no difference between Jew and Gentile, they all need Christ*]:

23 For all have sinned, and come short of the glory of God [*everyone has sinned and fallen short of God's requirements for salvation*];

24 Being justified [*in this context, "justified" means to be lined up in harmony with God's laws, thus worthy to be ratified and approved for exaltation*] freely by his grace [*the help of Christ, ". . .after all we can do." (2 Nephi 25:23)*] through the redemption that is in Christ Jesus: [*In other words, the only way we can be made clean, free from sin, and fit to be in the presence of God again, is through Christ.*]

**JST Romans 3:24**

24 Therefore being justified only by his grace through the redemption that is in Christ Jesus;

25 Whom [*referring to Christ*] God hath set forth [*appointed*] to be a propitiation [*an atonement; a sacrifice for our sins*] through faith in his blood [*through our faith in His atoning sacrifice*], to declare [*announce; proclaim*] his righteousness [*Christ's Atonement*] for the remission of sins that are past [*so that we can be cleansed of past sins*], through the forbearance [*patience*] of God [*in other words, through the patience which God has with us, which gives us sufficient time to repent, do good and be cleansed from sin*];

26 To declare [*present to us*], I say, at this time his righteousness [*Christ and His Atonement*]: that he [*the sinner*] might be just [*might be made clean*], and the justifier [*and to present unto us Christ, the Atoner*] of him [*the sinner*] which [*who*] believeth in Jesus [*Christ's Atonement works for those who believe him*].

Paul will now summarize by reminding his audience that boasting of outwardly going through the motions of religion is of no value. In other words, going through the outward ritual and detail of the Law of Moses while the inward soul remains evil and corrupt, is worthless.

27 Where is boasting then [*what good does boasting of outward religious appearance do*]? It is excluded [*it is of no value*]. By what law? of works [*will empty, insincere, hypocritical outward show of complying with the Law of Moses save a person*]? Nay: but by the law of faith [*we are saved by faith in Christ, which requires sincere, deep, personal righteousness*].

28 Therefore we conclude that a man is justified by faith without [*outside of*] the deeds of the law [*in summary, we must conclude that a person is prepared to return to God by faith, which requires true personal righteousness, rather than merely going through the outward appearance of keeping the Law of Moses*].

**JST Romans 3:28**

28 Therefore we conclude that a man is justified by faith alone without the deeds of the law [*the performances, rites, and rituals of the Law of Moses*].

29 Is he the God of the Jews only? is he not also of the Gentiles? Yes, of the Gentiles also [*in other words, God is everybody's God*]:

30 Seeing it is one God [*since there is just one God for everyone*], which shall justify the circumcision [*the Jews*] by faith, and uncircumcision [*the Gentiles*] through faith [*everyone who is willing to follow Christ will be saved, justified, because of their faith in Him and keeping his commandments*].

> **JST Romans 3:30**
> 30 Seeing that God will justify the circumcision by faith, and uncircumcision through faith.

31 Do we then make void [*destroy*] the law [*the Law of Moses*] through faith? God forbid: yea, we stablish [*fulfill the purposes of*] the law. [*The whole purpose of the Law of Moses was to point our minds toward Christ. Therefore, when we demonstrate true faith in Jesus, which involves action and covenants, we are indeed fulfilling the major purpose of the Law of Moses, rather than destroying it.*]

# ROMANS 4

The word "faith" is used often in this chapter. One of the common mistakes that many people make in interpreting Paul's writings is that they assume that "faith" is passive, meaning simply believing in Christ, requiring no action on the part of the believer. To believe this about faith is not only false, but also terribly unfortunate. Faith is much more than mere belief. Joseph Smith said that faith is a "principal of action"—see *Lectures on Faith*, lecture number one. Thus, when Paul speaks of belief and faith, he is speaking of all the actions, ordinances, good works, repenting, and changing done by one who truly has faith in Jesus Christ and who desires to be cleansed by the Atonement. Generally speaking, in this chapter, when Paul refers to the "law" and to "works," he is referring to the detailed external behaviors and requirements of the Law of Moses, which the Jews had come to falsely believe would be sufficient to lead them to salvation.

Remember also that in this chapter Paul is speaking to Jewish converts to the Church, who still tend to be caught up in the details of the Law of Moses rather than see the need for faith in Christ and His grace which lead to personal, internalized, genuine righteousness.

1 WHAT shall we say then that Abraham our father, as pertaining to the flesh [*our mortal ancestor*], hath found? [*In other words, if Abraham, our common ancestor were here, what would he tell us about faith and works?*]

2 For if Abraham were justified by [*shown to be faithful by his*] works, he hath whereof to glory [*he has something to boast about*]; but not before God [*but it is not sufficient to save him as far as God is concerned*]

> **JST Romans 4:2**
> 2 For if Abraham were justified by the law of works, he hath to glory in himself; but not of God.

3 For what saith the scripture [*what does it say in the scriptures about Abraham*]? [*Answer*] *Abraham believed God, and it was counted unto him for righteousness.* [*He was given credit for being righteous because he believed God*].

4 Now to him that worketh is the reward not reckoned [*calculated*] of grace, but of debt. [*In other words, no matter how many "works" a person has, he is still in debt to God and cannot be saved without the grace of Christ. See Mosiah 2:24.*]

> **JST Romans 4:4**
> 4 Now to him who is justified by the law of works, is the reward reckoned, not of grace, but of debt.

As you have perhaps noticed already in your own Bible, verse 5, next, came through the various translations quite garbled and confusing. As it stands, it sounds like the "ungodly" are "justified" or saved. Without the help of the JST corrections given in brackets, we would be quite lost when it comes to understanding it. Remember that "justified," in this context, means to be made worthy of exaltation through the Atonement of Christ.

5 But to him that worketh not, but believeth on him that justifieth the ungodly, his faith is counted for righteousness.

**JST Romans 4:5**

5 But to him that seeketh not to be justified by the law of works, but believeth on him who justifieth not the ungodly, his faith is counted for righteousness. [*In other words, one does not have to live the Law of Moses (the law of works) in order to be exalted by God, who will not exalt the ungodly.*]

Paul is a master at quoting people from the Old Testament whom the Jewish converts highly respect, in order to prove his point about faith and works. He now quotes David from Psalm 32:1–2.

6 Even as David also describeth the blessedness of the man, unto whom God imputeth righteousness without works, [*In other words, David described the blessings which come to the righteous who do not live the Law of Moses.*]

**JST Romans 4:6**

6 Even as David also describeth the blessedness of the man, unto whom God imputeth righteousness without the law of works,

7 Saying, [*quoting Psalm 32:1*] Blessed are they whose iniquities are forgiven, and whose sins are covered [*JST, Psalm 32:1 "Blessed are they whose transgressions are forgiven, and who have no sins to be covered."*].

**JST Romans 4:7**

7 Saying, Blessed are they through faith whose iniquities are forgiven, and whose sins are covered.

8 [*Quoting Psalm 32:2.*] Blessed is the man to whom the Lord will not impute sin [*hold accountable for sins, because he has repented and has thus been forgiven*].

The phrase "the circumcision" is often used by Paul to refer to Jewish converts to the Church who have come from a background of living the Law of Moses. He uses the phrase "the uncircumcision" to refer to Gentile converts to the Church, who have not come from a background of living the Law of Moses. Knowing this helps understand verse 9, next.

9 Cometh this blessedness then upon the circumcision only [*do these blessings of being forgiven of sin come only upon Jewish converts*], or upon the uncircumcision also [*or are they available to Gentile converts also*]? for we say [*we have established, in this presentation to you*] that faith was reckoned to Abraham for righteousness [*God considered Abraham to be righteous because of his faith*].

10 How was it then reckoned [*under what circumstances was Abraham credited with being righteous by God*]? when he was in circumcision, or in uncircumcision [*before or after he was circumcised*]? Not in circumcision, but in uncircumcision [*Answer: before he was circumcised*].

Having established that Abraham was considered to be righteous by the Lord, before he was circumcised, Paul will now emphasize that point again in verse 11, next. Remember that what Paul is trying to get across to these Jewish converts to the Church in Rome is that it is indeed possible to be righteous without adhering to the Law of Moses, including circumcision, which the Jews considered to be extremely important in terms of loyalty to God. Paul points out

that Abraham received great promises and blessings, the blessings of exaltation with eternal posterity [*Genesis 17:1–8*], before he was actually circumcised [*Genesis 17:9–14*], thus emphasizing that it is possible to be very righteous and worthy of exaltation, without circumcision. His use of Abraham as an example of one who was considered by God to be righteous, without circumcision, in other words, without the Law of Moses, is designed to have real clout with these Jewish converts.

11 And he [*Abraham*] received the sign of circumcision [*great blessings promised to him by the Lord; see Genesis 17:1–8*], a seal of the righteousness of the faith which he had yet being uncircumcised [*a confirmation from God that he was righteous, before he was circumcised (in Genesis 17:9–11)* ]: that he might be the father of all them that believe [*so that all worthy believers, whether Jew or Gentile, could also receive the blessings promised to Abraham*], though they be not circumcised [*even if they were not living according to the Law of Moses*]; that righteousness might be imputed unto them also [*that they might be considered righteous in the eyes of the Lord also*]:

In verse 12, next, Paul will refer to Abraham as "the father of circumcision"—in other words, "the father (ancestor) of the covenant people." As mentioned in a note in verse 11, above, God chose Abraham to be the "father" of the covenant people, in other words, Abraham was called of God to make covenants of exaltation (see Genesis 17:1–8) and to carry the gospel and priesthood to all nations through his posterity. (See also Abraham 2:9–11.) His posterity became the "covenant" people. We, as members of the Church, are part of this covenant people. As stated in our patriarchal blessings, one way or another, we are entitled to the blessings of Abraham, Isaac, and Jacob, which are the blessings of exaltation, through our worthiness.

12 And the father of circumcision [*Abraham is the "father" or "ancestor" of all covenant people*] to them who are not of the circumcision only, but who also walk in the steps of that faith of our father Abraham, which he had being yet uncircumcised. [*In other words, Abraham is the one through whom the blessings of exaltation come, not only to his direct descendants, the Israelites, who lived the Law of Moses, but also to those who are not his direct descendants and did not keep the Law of Moses, but who faithfully live as Abraham did before he was circumcised.*]

13 For the promise, that he should be the heir of the world, was not to Abraham, or to his seed, through the law [*the Law of Moses*], but through the righteousness of faith. [*Abraham and his posterity did not receive the great promises of the Lord (Genesis 17:1–8) because of works alone, rather, also because of faith.*]

14 For if they which are of the law be heirs, faith is made void, and the promise made of none effect: [*If people were to automatically inherit the highest blessings of God merely because they are descendants of Abraham who live the Law of Moses, then faith would not be necessary and the promises of God to Abraham and his posterity would not effect or cause personal righteousness in people.*]

15 Because the law worketh wrath [*the Law of Moses brings accountability and punishment for those who know the law and violate it*]: for where no law is, there is no transgression [*people are not held accountable if they don't know the law*].

The JST is of great importance in helping us understand verse 16, next. The JST puts the word "works" back into the verse. As it stands in our Bible, the word "works" has been left out, and thus the powerful relationship between faith, works, and grace has been removed (faith, as a principle of action leads to good works

and to personal righteousness which enable the grace of Christ's Atonement to cleanse us).

16 Therefore it is of faith, that it might be by grace; to the end the promise might be sure to all the seed; not to that only which is of the law, but to that also which is of the faith of Abraham; who is the father of us all [*the ancestor of us all, whether literal or by "adoption," through whom all of us, Jew or Gentile, receive the blessings of exaltation, if worthy*],

**JST Romans 4:16**

Therefore ye are justified of [*saved by*] faith and works, through grace, to the end the promise might be sure to all the seed [*to all people*]; not to them only who are of the law [*not only to the Jews*], but to them also who are of the faith of Abraham [*but also to the Gentiles who have the faith that Abraham had*]; who is the father of us all [*the one through whom all of us can inherit the blessings of exaltation; see Abraham 2:9–11*],

17 (As it is written [*in Genesis 17:4*], I have made thee [*Abraham*] a father [*an ancestor*] of many nations,) before him [*in the presence of God*] whom he [*Abraham*] believed, even God, who quickeneth [*resurrects*] the dead, and calleth those things which be not as though they were [*and tells of things which have not yet happened as if they had already taken place*].

In verse 18, next, Paul continues emphasizing the role of faith and hope. He uses Abraham as an example of one who had great faith and hoped against all odds, who had faith in the promises of God against all obvious evidence to the contrary. Remember that Abraham and Sarah had been promised by the Lord that they would have posterity. See Genesis 17:19. Abraham was 62 years old and Sarah was 52 years old at the time the promise of posterity was given. (See Abraham 2:9 and 14.) Abraham was 100 and Sarah was 90 when Isaac was born. Sarah had already passed the time of life when she could be expected to bear a child. (See Genesis 18:11.) Thus, a "miracle child" was born to them, as promised by God.

18 [*Abraham*] Who against hope believed in hope, that he might become the father [*ancestor*] of many nations, according to that which was spoken [*according to the promise of numerous posterity spoken by the Lord; see Genesis 17:16*], So shall thy seed [*posterity*] be.

19 And being not weak in faith, he [*Abraham*] considered not his own body now dead [*didn't let the fact that his body was so old that it was nearly dead, shut down his faith that God's promise of posterity to him and Sarah would be fulfilled*], when he was about an hundred years old, neither yet the deadness of Sara's womb [*the physiological fact that Sarah was way past the age of childbearing*]:

20 He [*Abraham*] staggered not at the promise of God through unbelief [*he did not doubt the promise of God*]; but was strong in faith, giving glory [*praise and honor*] to God;

21 And being fully persuaded that, what he [*the Lord*] had promised, he [*the Lord*] was able also to perform.

22 And therefore it [*Abraham's faith*] was imputed to him for [*credited to him by the Lord as*] righteousness.

As you have already noticed, when Paul is trying to make an important point, he repeats it over and over. In this chapter, you have seen him do that with the topic of faith, using Abraham as the example. Remember that he is trying to convince Jewish converts to the Church that faith in Jesus Christ is an essential ingredient for salvation. As mentioned already, many of these converts still tended to think that strict adherence to the outward performances required by the traditions of the Jews would save them.

23 Now it was not written for his [*Abraham's*] sake alone, that it [*faith*] was imputed to him [*that he was given credit by the Lord for his great faith*];

24 But for us also, to whom it shall be imputed [*we also must demonstrate great faith in order to have it credited to us*], if we believe on him [*the true God*] that raised up Jesus our Lord from the dead;

25 Who was delivered [*who was turned over to suffer in Gethsemane and to be crucified*] for our offences [*because of our sins*], and was raised again [*resurrected*] for our justification [*was resurrected in order to complete the Atonement so that we can be "justified," that is, cleansed and made worthy to be exalted and to live again with God*].

# ROMANS 5

Paul uses the word "justified" often in his teaching. Generally speaking, "justified" means "saved," "ratified," "approved." Therefore, it can be considered to mean, in effect, "lined up in harmony with God's commandments." The word is used in a similar way in computer word processing. When typing a document on a computer, people usually "justify" the left margin and sometimes "justify" both margins. In other words, they do the key stroke sequence or the mouse click necessary to make the margins of the document line up perfectly. So it is with our lives. When we are "justified," it means that we have been faithful, have followed the promptings of the Holy Ghost who leads us to live righteously and participate in the saving ordinances and covenants of the gospel. Thus we become worthy to be cleansed by the Atonement and therefore are lined up in harmony with God such that we are worthy to live with Him forever. See Moses 6:59–60.

1 THEREFORE being justified by faith, we have peace with God [*the Father*] through our Lord Jesus Christ [*through Christ's Atonement*]:

2 By whom [*through Christ*] also we have access by faith into this grace [*"grace" can be considered to be the help and mercy of Christ*] wherein we stand [*which we are now enjoying*], and rejoice in hope of the glory of God [*and rejoice in anticipating exaltation, which is the glory in which God lives; see McConkie,* Doctrinal New Testament Commentary, *Vol. 2, p. 239*].

3 And not only so, but we glory in tribulations also [*we rejoice that we have problems here in mortality*]: knowing that tribulation [*trouble*] worketh patience [*develops patience, perseverance, and so forth in us*];

**JST Romans 5:3**

3 And not only this, but we glory in tribulations also; knowing that tribulation worketh patience;

4 And patience, [*develops*] experience; and experience, [*develops*] hope:

5 And hope maketh not ashamed [*keeps us from quitting in our efforts to live the gospel*]; because the love of God is shed abroad in our hearts by the Holy Ghost which is given unto us [*the Holy Ghost bears witness to us of God's love and encourages us to continue striving to live righteously*].

6 For when we were yet without strength [*before Christ's Atonement, we were helpless to save ourselves; see 2 Nephi 9:7–9*], in due time [*at the appropriate time in God's plan*] Christ died for the ungodly [*for all of us sinners*].

Paul will now point out how, on occasions among us mortals, some person gives his or her life for another, and that when this does take place, it is usually for someone who is righteous or at least good. The point is that it is truly amazing that someone (namely Christ) would give his life for

all people, including the wicked.

7 For scarcely for a righteous man will one die: yet peradventure [*perhaps*] for a good man some would even dare [*be willing*] to die.

8 But God commendeth [*shows*] his love toward us, in that, while we were yet sinners, Christ died for us.

9 Much more then [*and there is much more to what the Savior did for us*], being now justified [*cleansed, saved*] by his blood, we shall be saved from wrath [*from the punishments required by the Law of Justice*] through him.

10 For if, when we were enemies [*in opposition to God because of our sins*], we were reconciled to God [*the Atonement was put in place whereby we could be redeemed and placed in harmony with him*] by the death of his Son, much more, being reconciled, we shall be saved by his life [*by Christ's life and teachings*]. [*In other words, it is not only his death, but also His life which saves us. It is by following the teachings which Christ gave us during His mortal ministry that we bring the saving power of His Atonement into our lives.*]

11 And not only so [*And not only that*], but we also joy in God through our Lord Jesus Christ, by whom we have now received the atonement. [*In other words, the Atonement brings great joy into our lives and lets us enjoy a wonderful relationship with the Father.*]

Paul's teaching in verse 11, above, that we can have joy in our relationship with God, is more significant than many of us might realize. Typically, most Jews, by the time Paul came along, had been taught to fear God. They had been taught in their culture that God was a God of anger and vengeance. His mercy, kindness, patience, gentleness, etc., as taught in Deuteronomy 4:31, 2 Chronicles 30:9, Isaiah 54:7, Micah 7:18, and so forth, had been either downplayed or eliminated in the culture of the Jews.

12 Wherefore, as by one man [*Adam*] sin entered into the world, and death by sin [*see 1 Corinthians 15:21–22*]; and so death passed upon all men, for that all have sinned [*because everyone has sinned*]:

The parenthesis which you see at the beginning of verse 13, next in your Bible, is closed at the end of verse 17, in your Bible.

13 (For until the law sin was in the world: but sin is not imputed when there is no law [*people are not held accountable when they don't know the law and commandments*].

**JST Romans 5:13**

13 (For, before the law, sin was in the world; yet sin is not imputed to those who have no law.

14 Nevertheless death reigned [*ruled*] from Adam to Moses, even over them that had not sinned after the similitude of Adam's transgression, who [*referring to Adam*] is the figure of him [*is symbolic of Christ*] that was to come [*who would come sometime in the future*].

**JST Romans 5:14**

14 Nevertheless, death reigned from Adam to Moses, even over them that had not sinned after the similitude of Adam's transgression, who is the figure of him that was to come. For I say, that through the offense, death reigned over all.

Verse 14, above, is a bit complex. First of all, Paul's logic is that since people were living and dying for about 2500 years from Adam to Moses, and since the Law of Moses wasn't given until Moses came on the scene, there had to be a way for those people to be saved without knowing the Law of Moses, and the way is through Christ and His Atonement. Next, Paul says that Adam is "the figure of" or symbolic of Christ. We get some help with Paul's vocabulary by reading 1 Corinthians 15:45 where Paul refers to two "Adams," namely, "the first man Adam," who was Eve's husband,

and "the last Adam" (Christ), who is a "quickening spirit" or one who makes people come alive again. What Paul is teaching is that everyone will eventually die and thus, all of us need Christ's resurrection to free us from death. He also teaches that Adam was a "type" of Christ or symbolic of Christ, in the sense that Adam (and Eve) got things going for us to be born into mortality, and thus is a type of "savior" for us. In summary, Adam brought transgression, physical death, and the potential for spiritual death into the world. Christ brought forgiveness, immortality, and the potential for exaltation into the world.

15 But not as the offence, so also is the free gift. For if through the offence of one many be dead, much more the grace of God, and the gift by grace, which is by one man, Jesus Christ, hath abounded unto many.

**JST Romans 5:15**

15 But the offense is not as the free gift, for the gift aboundeth. For, if through the offense of one, many be dead; much more the grace of God, and the gift by grace, hath abounded by one man, Jesus Christ, unto many.

The "offense" spoken of above is the fall of Adam—see end of JST verse 14, above. The free gift is the Atonement of Christ. The gift includes the grace of Christ made available to us through His Atonement, which "aboundeth," in other words, continues to bless our lives abundantly forever. Among other things, Paul is saying, in effect, that the fall of Adam and the Atonement of Christ are not equal to each other. The Atonement is more powerful. The fall of Adam brought death into the world, but the Atonement overcomes physical death for everyone—see 1 Corinthians 15:22—and continues to give immeasurably to all the righteous as it enables them to attain eternal life].

16 And not as it was by one that sinned, so is the gift: for the judgment [*the condemnation which followed Adam's fall*] was by one to condemnation, but the free gift is of many offences unto justification. [*Again, the Atonement of Christ is far more powerful than Adam's transgression*];

**JST Romans 5:16**

16 And not as, by one that sinned, is the gift; for the judgment is by one to condemnation [*the fall of Adam was caused by one transgression*], but the free gift is of many offenses [*the Atonement is effective for innumerable sins*] unto justification [*and leads the righteous to exaltation*].

Through repetition, Paul is still emphasizing the fact that Christ's Atonement, which represents the grace of God to all who will live worthily, overcomes the fall of Adam. The main point is still that the Jewish converts to the Church must make the transition from their religious and cultural upbringing as followers of the Law of Moses to faithfully accepting Jesus of Nazareth as the promised Messiah. They will all be resurrected because of the Atonement, but must fully accept and follow the Savior's teachings in order to overcome spiritual death and to be redeemed by the grace of God, after all they can do (2 Nephi 25:23).

Paul's repetition of this topic continues in the next verses.

17 For if by one man's offence [*Adam's transgression*] death reigned by one [*death was caused by one man (Adam)*]; much more they which receive abundance of grace and of the gift of righteousness [*those who accept the gift of being made clean through the Atonement*] shall reign in life [*shall rule as Gods in eternal life*] by one, Jesus Christ [*because of one man, namely Jesus Christ*].)

By the way, as mentioned above, the parenthesis which ends verse 17 in your Bible, began with the parenthesis at the beginning of verse 13.

18 Therefore as by the offence of one [*Adam*] judgment came upon all men to condemnation [*therefore, because*

*of Adam's transgression, all people became subject to sin*]; even so by the righteousness of one [*Christ*] the free gift came upon all men unto justification of life [*the Atonement made eternal life available to all upon condition that they live worthy of being "justified," meaning to be cleansed from sin and "approved" to dwell in the presence of God forever.*]

19 For as by one man's disobedience many were made sinners [*because of Adam's transgression, many became involved in sin*], so by the obedience of one [*because of Christ's obedience to the Father*] shall many be made righteous [*many can become righteous through being cleansed from their sins*].

20 Moreover the law entered, that the offence might abound [*when the Law of Moses was given, it made people more accountable*]. But where sin abounded [*where there were abundant sins*], grace did much more abound [*the Atonement is more powerful than sins and can overcome them*]:

21 That as sin hath reigned unto death [*whereas sin leads toward spiritual death*], even so might grace reign through righteousness unto eternal life by Jesus Christ our Lord [*the grace of God, demonstrated by the Atonement, enables us to attain eternal life through personal righteousness*].

## ROMANS 6

Having taught that the Atonement of Jesus Christ overcomes the Fall of Adam, Paul will now turn his attention to the opportunity for these people to repent and be baptized, in order to benefit from the gospel of Jesus Christ, who fulfilled the Law of Moses.

1 WHAT shall we say then? Shall we continue in sin, that grace may abound [*should we go right on committing more and more sins so that there is more and more opportunity for God to bless our lives with his grace*]?

2 God forbid [*absolutely not*]. How shall we, that are dead to sin, live any longer therein [*how could we who are trying to stop sinning possibly be content to continue in our sins*]?

Paul will now give a beautiful explanation of why we are baptized, including the symbolism involved in baptism by immersion. Pay close attention to his careful use of highly descriptive vocabulary words as he teaches that when we are baptized, we, in effect, bury our old sinful selves with Christ in the grave. Then, we come forth with Christ as new people, "born again," starting a new life of dedication to the gospel and personal righteousness. Compare with Mosiah 27:26.

3 Know ye not, that so many of us as were baptized into Jesus Christ were baptized into his death [*are you aware that those of us who have been baptized were baptized so that Christ's death, resurrection, and so forth could cleanse us*]?

4 Therefore we are buried with him by baptism into death [*being buried in the waters of baptism is symbolic of accepting Christ's invitation to join Him in burying our old sinful selves and thus letting our sinful ways die*]: that like as Christ was raised up from the dead by the glory of the Father, even so we also should walk in newness of life [*so that, just as Christ came forth from the grave in glory, we can come forth from the waters of baptism into a new life filled with the glory and influence of the Father*].

5 For if we have been planted [*buried*] together in the likeness of his death [*if we have buried our old sinful lives, through His Atonement*], we shall be also in the likeness of his resurrection [*we will have a glorious new life in the gospel*]:

In verse 6, next, Paul uses a very strong word to describe the effort sometimes needed on our part to repent of sins. He uses the word "crucify." This implies that some sins require much pain and godly sorrow to be rid of. Indeed, changing friends, being cut off from family, going through withdrawals from chemical dependency, confessing serious sin to the bishop and facing possible consequences, refraining from Sabbath-breaking activities, cutting back on expenses in order to pay an honest tithe, and so forth, can be painful, but walking in "newness of life" (verse 4) makes it far more than worthwhile to "crucify" our sins.

6 Knowing this, that our old man [*our old lifestyle*] is crucified with him [*Christ*], that the body of sin [*our past sins*] might be destroyed, that henceforth [*from now on*] we should not serve sin.

The JST makes a very significant doctrinal change to verse 7, next.

7 For he that is dead is freed from sin.

**JST Romans 6:7**

7 For he that is dead to sin is freed from sin.

8 Now if we be dead with Christ [*if we follow Christ such that our sins die through His Atoning sacrifice*], we believe that we shall also live with him [*we will come alive in the sweetness of the gospel life here on earth and will live with Him eternally*]:

9 Knowing that Christ being raised from the dead dieth no more [*will never die again*]; death hath no more dominion [*power*] over him.

10 For in that he died, he died unto sin once [*in dying, the Savior suffered once for all sins; see 2 Nephi 9:21–22*]: but in that he liveth, he liveth unto God [*in being resurrected, He now joins the Father in eternal life*].

11 Likewise reckon ye also yourselves to be dead indeed unto sin [*consider your sins to be dead and buried*], but alive unto God through Jesus Christ our Lord [*and now you are alive spiritually and enjoy the blessings the Father has for you because of the Atonement of Jesus Christ*].

12 Let not sin therefore reign in your mortal body, that ye should obey it in the lusts thereof [*do not let sin rule over you here in mortality*].

In verse 13, next, Paul uses "members," meaning body parts such as head, arms, legs, eyes, ears, etc., to represent the possibility that some parts of your life and personality may be vulnerable to certain temptations.

13 Neither yield ye your members as instruments of unrighteousness unto sin [*don't allow yourself to give in to specific sins for which you may have particular weakness*]: but yield yourselves unto God [*give in to God's commandments rather than giving in to sin*], as those that are alive from the dead [*like those Saints have done who repented from sinful lifestyles and are now "alive" in Christ*], and your members as instruments of righteousness unto God [*exercise self-control such that your "members," in other words, all aspects of your life and personality, are in harmony with God*].

14 For sin shall not have dominion over you [*sin will not rule over you*]: for ye are not under the law [*because you are not living under the Law of Moses*], but under grace [*rather, you are living under the grace of God which allows the Atonement to cleanse you from sin*].

**JST Romans 6:14**

14 For in so doing sin shall not have dominion over you; for ye are not under the law, but under grace.

15 What then? shall we sin, because we are not under the law, but under grace [*do we have license to sin and not worry about "works" anymore because of "grace"*]? God forbid [*absolutely not*].

16 Know ye not, that to whom ye yield

yourselves servants to obey, his servants ye are to whom ye obey; whether of sin unto death [*spiritual death*], or of obedience unto righteousness [*don't you realize that if you yield to sin, you are sin's servants, and if you yield to God, you are God's servants*]? [*In other words, whose servants would you rather be?*]

17 But God be thanked, that ye were the servants of sin, but ye have obeyed from the heart that form of doctrine which was delivered you [*thanks be to God that you, who once had sin as your master, have now repented deep in your hearts and obeyed the true doctrine of Christ which was preached to you*].

> **JST Romans 6:17**
> 17 But God be thanked, that ye are not the servants of sin, for ye have obeyed from the heart that form of doctrine which was delivered you.

18 Being then made free from sin [*having repented and been cleansed from sin*], ye became the servants of righteousness.

19 I speak after the manner of men because of the infirmity of your flesh [*I have to put what I am saying in simple terms, using examples from your daily lives because you are still weak in the gospel of Christ*]: for as ye have yielded your members servants to uncleanness [*since you have yielded to various sins in the past and thus been servants of sin*] and to iniquity unto iniquity [*and your own wickedness then invited you to commit additional sins*]; even so now yield your members servants to righteousness unto holiness [*now exercise self-control and become servants of righteousness and holiness*].

> **JST Romans 6:19**
> 19 I speak after the manner of men because of the infirmity of your flesh; for as ye have in times past yielded your members servants to uncleanness and to iniquity unto iniquity; even so now yield your members servants to righteousness unto holiness.

20 For when ye were the servants of sin, ye were free from righteousness [*when you were ruled by your sins, you were free from the blessings of righteousness*].

21 What fruit [*results in your lives*] had ye then in those things whereof ye are now ashamed [*what good did your sins, of which you are now ashamed, do for you*]? for the end of those things [*the end result of sin and wickedness*] is death [*spiritual death*].

22 But now being made free from sin, and become servants to God, ye have your fruit unto holiness, and the end everlasting life. [*Having been cleansed from sin through faith, repentance, baptism, and so forth, and having become worthy servants of God, you have become holy, and your goal is now exaltation.*]

> Verse 23, next, is rather well-known and oft-quoted.

23 For the wages of sin is death [*the ultimate pay for unrepentant sin is spiritual death and being cut off from the presence of God forever*]; but the gift of God is eternal life [*exaltation*] through Jesus Christ our Lord.

# ROMANS 7

Paul will now teach that the Law of Moses is no longer in force, that it was fulfilled by Christ and that obedience to Christ's gospel is designed to develop and strengthen inward righteousness. He will use the imagery of marriage between a husband and wife, in Jewish culture, to represent the temporary nature and purpose of the Law of Moses. He will, in effect, teach that just as when her husband dies, the wife is no longer bound to him, so also with the Law of Moses. During the time it was in effect, from Moses to the beginning of Christ's mission, the people were bound to it. But with the coming of Christ, the

law "died," having fulfilled its purpose, and thus, people are no longer bound to it.

1 KNOW ye not, brethren, (for I speak to them that know the law,) [*the Law of Moses*] how that the law hath dominion over a man as long as he liveth?

**JST Romans 7:1**

1 Know ye not, brethren, (for I speak to them that know the law,) how that the law hath dominion over a man only as long as he liveth?

2 For the woman which hath an husband is bound by the law to her husband so long as he liveth; but if the husband be dead, she is loosed from the law of her husband [*she is no longer bound to her marriage vows made to her husband*].

**JST Romans 7:2**

2 For the woman which hath a husband is bound by the law to her husband only as long as he liveth; for if the husband be dead, she is loosed from the law of her husband.

3 So then if, while her husband liveth, she be married to another man [*if she were to marry another man while her husband is still alive*], she shall be called an adulteress [*she would be an adulteress*]: but if her husband be dead [*has died*], she is free from that law; so that she is no adulteress, though [*even though*] she be married [*gets married*] to another man.

4 Wherefore [*therefore*], my brethren, ye also are become dead to the law [*you are set free from the Law of Moses*] by the body of Christ [*by the death of Christ (in other words, by the Atonement of Christ)*]; that ye should be married to another [*it is time for you to "marry" another gospel*], even to him [*Christ*] who is raised [*who has been resurrected*] from the dead, that we should bring forth fruit [*worthy lives*] unto God [*so that we can live lives worthy of living with God*].

We will need a lot of help from the JST [*Joseph Smith Translation*] to understand verses 5 through 25. Remember, also, that Paul will continue to use much repetition to drive home the point that the Jews are no longer bound to the Law of Moses, which was a schoolmaster law to help prepare them for the full gospel taught by the Savior. Because he uses so much repetition, some readers begin to look for other meanings to what Paul is saying, thinking to themselves, "Surely he wouldn't keep saying the same thing over and over so many times, so there must be some additional meaning I am missing." Such is usually not the case. He is repeating because it is a tremendous transition for the Jews to change from an entire culture and upbringing, where the Law of Moses was everything to most people, to the gospel of Christ where inward, deep personal righteousness is the emphasis.

5 For when we were in the flesh [*carnally minded, living sinfully, not yet redeemed by Christ*], the motions of sins, which were by the law, did work in our members [*worked in us, caused us*] to bring forth fruit [*unworthy lives*] unto death [*which would ultimately lead to spiritual death*].

**JST Romans 7:5**

5 For when we were in the flesh, the motions of sin, which were not according to the law, did work in our members to bring forth fruit unto death.

6 But now we are delivered from the law [*In other words, we are now set free from the Law of Moses, to which we were previously bound, by the gospel of Christ.*], that being dead wherein we were held [*In other words, we are no longer bound to the Law of Moses*]; that we should serve in newness of spirit [*so that we can be "new people" serving Christ*], and not in the oldness of the letter [*and not be caught up in the old "letter of the law" which did not have power to save us*].

**JST Romans 7:6**

6 But now we are delivered from the law wherein we were held, being dead to the law, that we should serve in newness of spirit, and not in the oldness of the letter.

7 What shall we say then? Is the law sin [*was it a sin to live the Law of Moses*]? God forbid [*absolutely not*]. Nay, I had not known sin, but by the law [*I would not have known what sin was without the teachings of the Law of Moses*]: for I had not known lust [*unrighteous desire for something*], except the law had said, Thou shalt not covet [*without the Law of Moses, I would not have known that it is a sin to covet*].

8 But sin, taking occasion by the commandment, wrought [*caused*] in me all manner [*kinds*] of concupiscence [*strong desires for that which God forbids*]. [*In other words, once the Law of Moses pointed out to us what things were sinful and thus forbidden by God, it seems that those sins became all the more tempting.*] For without the law sin was dead [*when people don't know the law, they are not held accountable*].

9 For I was alive without the law once: but when the commandment came, sin revived, and I died. [*In other words, at one time in my life, I (Paul) lived the Law of Moses very strictly and felt spiritually alive. I was not accountable for Christ's gospel because I was not familiar with it. However, when I became aware of the commandments of Christ, I became accountable and thus was a sinner, and found myself to be spiritually dead.*]

**JST Romans 7:9**

9 For once I was alive without transgression of the law, but when the commandment of Christ came, sin revived, and I died.

10 And the commandment, which was ordained to life, I found to be unto death. [*When I heard the gospel and commandments of Christ, which lead to eternal life, but didn't yet believe, it made me accountable and thus condemned me to spiritual death and being separated from God forever.*]

**JST Romans 7:10**

10 And when I believed not the commandment of Christ which came, which was ordained to life, I found it condemned me unto death.

11 For sin, taking occasion by the commandment, deceived me, and by it slew me. [*Sin, taking advantage of my accountability, deceived me and tempted me to reject Christ and his gospel, thus killing me spiritually.*]

**JST Romans 7:11**

11 For sin, taking occasion, denied the commandment, and deceived me; and by it I was slain.

12 Wherefore the law is holy, and the commandment holy, and just, and good. [*In spite of the wrong way I was heading, I found out that Christ's gospel is holy, correct, and good.*]

**JST Romans 7:12**

12 Nevertheless, I found the law to be holy, and the commandment to be holy, and just, and good.

13 Was then that which is good [*Christ's gospel*] made death unto me [*did Christ's gospel ultimately cause spiritual death in me*]? God forbid [*absolutely not*]. But sin, that it might appear sin, working death in me by that which is good; that sin by the commandment might become exceeding sinful.

**JST Romans 7:13**

13 Was then that which is good made death unto me? God forbid. But sin, that it might appear sin by that which is good working death in me; that sin, by the commandment, might become exceeding sinful.

[JST "Was then that which is good made death unto me? God forbid. But sin, that it might appear sin by that which is good working death in me [*sin clearly shows up as sin in the*

*light of the gospel of Christ, and thus we see how dangerous it is*]; that sin, by the commandment, might become exceeding sinful [*as we compare sin against the gospel of Christ, we see all the better how dangerous sin is*]."

14 For we know that the law is spiritual:
but I am carnal, sold under sin.

**JST Romans 7:14**

14 For we know that the commandment is spiritual; but when I was under law, I was yet carnal, sold under sin.

[JST "For we know that the commandment (*the gospel of Christ*) is spiritual (*leads to worthiness for eternal life*); but when I was under law (*when I was living the Law of Moses*), I was yet carnal (*I was not redeemed, not living the higher law required for exaltation*), sold under sin (*still living under the burden of sin*)."]

Verse 15, next, seems to have been completely scrambled somewhere in the process of being put in our King James Bible. It provides a wonderful opportunity for us to witness the inspiration and power of God coming to us through the Prophet Joseph Smith. Through the Prophet's inspired translation, we see that Paul is telling the Roman Saints that he has gained great spiritual strength from the gospel of Christ.

15 For that which I do I allow not: for
what I would, that do I not; but what I
hate, that do I.

**JST Romans 7:15–16**

15 But now I am spiritual; for that which I am commanded to do, I do; and that which I am commanded not to allow, I allow not.

16 For what I know is not right, I would not do; for that which is sin, I hate.

16 If then I do that which I would not,
I consent unto the law that it is good.
[*I acknowledge by my actions that the gospel of Christ is good*]; and I am not condemned [*and thus I am not stopped in my progression toward eternal life with God*].

**JST Romans 7:17**

17 If then I do not that which I would not allow, I consent unto the law, that it is good; and I am not condemned.

17 Now then it is no more I that do it,
but sin that dwelleth in me. [*Now I am truly trying to live Christ's gospel and overcome and repent of my sins.*]

**JST Romans 7:18**

18 Now then, it is no more I that do sin; but I seek to subdue that sin which dwelleth in me.

18 For I know that in me [*that is, in my*
*flesh*,] dwelleth no good thing: for to will [*to want to do right*] is present with me; but how to perform that which is good I find not.

**JST Romans 7:19**

19 For I know that in me, that is, in my flesh, dwelleth no good thing; for to will is present with me, but to perform that which is good I find not, only in Christ.

[JST "For I know that in me, that is, in my flesh (*my mortal weaknesses*), dwelleth no good thing; for to will is present with me, but to perform that which is good I find not, only in Christ."] (*In other words, the flesh is weak; there is no good in yielding to my sins, imperfections, weaknesses, etc. I want to do good and be righteous. The only way to become righteous is through Christ and his Atonement.*)

19 For the good that I would I do not:
but the evil which I would not, that I do

**JST Romans 7:20–21**

20 For the good that I would have done when under the law, I find not to be good; therefore, I do it not.

21 But the evil which I would not do under the law, I find to be good; that, I do.

[JST "For the good that I would have done when under the law, I find not to be good; therefore, I do it not."] (*In other words, I have found out that all the good I wanted to do in*

*harmony with the Law of Moses, still couldn't save me and therefore was not good for me in the ultimate sense of gaining eternal life. Therefore, I no longer build my life around the Law of Moses.)*

[JST "But the evil which I would not do under the law, I find to be good; that, I do."] *(But the Law of Moses pointed out many sins which we should avoid. This is good, and I avoid those sins.)*

Remember that the Savior was constantly criticized by the Jewish religious leaders for violating the Law of Moses and their nit-picky interpretations of it. For example, they criticized Him for healing the sick on the Sabbath. They criticized Him for associating with sinners, for eating with them, for teaching that it is inward righteousness rather than outward appearance that saves us. They criticized Him and His disciples for not washing their hands ritually before eating, as prescribed by the Law of Moses and embellished by the traditions of the Jews. They criticized Him for teaching that the Law of Moses could not save them and that they must repent and be baptized and receive the Gift of the Holy Ghost in order to have eternal life. This cultural and religious background and setting is helpful in understanding Joseph Smith's corrections of what Paul says next in verse 20.

20 Now if I do that I would not, it is no more I that do it, but sin that dwelleth in me.

**JST Romans 7:22**
22 Now if I do that, through the assistance of Christ, I would not do under the law, I am not under the law; and it is no more that I seek to do wrong, but to subdue sin that dwelleth in me.

[JST "Now if I do that, through the assistance of Christ, I would not do under the law, I am not under the law; and it is no more that I seek to do wrong, but to subdue sin that dwelleth in me."] *(In other words, If, with the help of Christ and his gospel, I now do things that I would not have done under the Law of Moses, because I am no longer bound to the Law of Moses, it is because my focus has changed from constantly studying what sins to avoid according to the law, to simply wanting to be good deep down inside myself.)*

21 I find then a law, that, when I would do good, evil is present with me.

22 For I delight in the law of God after the inward man: [*note that JST verse 23, next, covers both verse 21 and 22 here.*]

**JST Romans 7:23**
23 I find then that under the law, that when I would do good evil was present with me; for I delight in the law of God after the inward man.

[JST "I find then that under the law, that when I would do good evil was present with me; for I delight in the law of God after the inward man."] *(I find that when I was living strictly according to the Law of Moses, focusing so intently on outward appearances, it still allowed me to be evil while appearing good. Now, I find delight in living the gospel of Christ which focuses on cleansing the inner man.)*

Remember that the word "members" as used next in verse 23, are members of the body such as eyes, ears, tongue, hands, feet, etc. which can get us into temptation and trouble.

23 But I see another law in my members, warring against the law of my mind, and bringing me into captivity to the law of sin which is in my members. [*In other words, the gospel of Christ is now firmly imprinted in my mind. I want to live true to it, but my weaknesses, imperfections, sins, etc. still make war against the righteous intent of my mind.*]

**JST Romans 7:24–25**
24 And now I see another law, even the commandment of Christ, and it is imprinted in my mind.

25 But my members are warring against the law of my mind, and bringing me into captivity to the law of sin which is in my members.

24 O wretched man that I am! who shall deliver me from the body of this death?

> **JST Romans 7:26**
> 26 And if I subdue not the sin which is in me, but with the flesh serve the law of sin; O wretched man that I am! who shall deliver me from the body of this death?
>
> [JST "And if I subdue not the sin which is in me (*if I do not control my tendencies to commit sin*), but with the flesh serve the law of sin (*but give in to my mortal weaknesses and thus commit sins*); O wretched man that I am! who shall deliver me from the body of this death (*from the sins and temptations of mortality which could lead me to spiritual death?*)"]

25 I thank God through Jesus Christ our Lord. So then with the mind I myself serve the law of God; but with the flesh the law of sin.

> **JST Romans 7:27**
> 27 I thank God through Jesus Christ our Lord, then, that so with the mind I myself serve the law of God.
>
> [JST "I thank God through Jesus Christ our Lord, then, that so with the mind I myself serve the law of God (*I rejoice in thanksgiving to the Father, that because of Christ and his Atonement, the desire of my mind to be righteous can be fulfilled as I serve and follow Christ's gospel*)."]

# ROMANS 8

Remember that Paul is addressing members of the Church, Jewish converts in Rome, who still tend to be very caught up in trying to keep the Law of Moses according to their culture and upbringing before joining the Church. Many of them struggle with the transition from the Law of Moses, with its exacting rites and daily spelled-out performances to the much less structured gospel brought by Christ which emphasizes genuine personal righteousness. They still believe that any convert who does not keep the Law of Moses, even though they have been baptized and have received the Gift of the Holy Ghost, will be condemned. Paul, with great teaching skill and inspiration, continues in this chapter to remind these Saints that salvation and eternal life come through Christ and His gospel, not in the Law of Moses. As mentioned previously, Paul is using much repetition in these chapters to drive home his main teaching points.

1 THERE is therefore now no condemnation [*being stopped in progression toward eternal life*] to them which are in Christ Jesus [*to those who follow Christ*], who walk not after the flesh [*who do not yield to the temptations of mortality nor follow the details of the Law of Moses*], but after the Spirit [*but yield to the guidance of the Holy Ghost*].

2 For the law of the Spirit of life in Christ Jesus [*Following the law of the Spirit which leads to eternal life through Christ's gospel*] hath made me free from the law of sin and death [*has set me free from the lasting effects of sin and spiritual death*].

3 For what the law [*the Law of Mo*ses] could not do, in that it was weak through the flesh [*it was given to people who were very weak and caught up in sins of the flesh, to strengthen them to the point, eventually, that they could accept Christ's gospel*], God [*the Father*] sending his own Son [*Jesus Christ*] in the likeness of sinful flesh [*in a mortal body*], and for sin [*to atone for our sins*], condemned sin in the flesh [*condemned all forms of wickedness*]:

4 That the righteousness of the law might be fulfilled in us [*so that the goal of the Law of Moses might find fulfillment in us, having helped us become righteous enough to accept Jesus and His higher laws*], who walk not after the flesh [*who have turned from sin*], but after the Spirit [*and are following the Spirit of Christ's gospel*].

5 For they that are after the flesh [*those who focus on desires of the mortal body*] do mind the things of the flesh [*yield to the temptations of the flesh*]; but they that are after the Spirit [*but those who are spiritual*] the things of the Spirit [*yield to the promptings of the Holy Ghost*].

6 For to be carnally minded is death [*to focus on bodily appetites and to give in to them leads us to spiritual death*]; but to be spiritually minded is life and peace [*but to focus on spiritual things brings peace now and eternal life in the world to come*].

7 Because the carnal mind is enmity against God [*to be focused on worldly sins pits us against God*]: for it is not subject to the law of God, neither indeed can be [*the carnal mind does not allow itself to be ruled by God's laws, therefore it is very dangerous to us and our potential for exaltation*].

8 So then they that are in the flesh cannot please God. [*In other words, those who yield to the temptations of the flesh cannot be pleasing to God.*]

**JST Romans 8:8**

8 So then they that are after the flesh cannot please God.

9 But ye [*you Jewish converts to the Church in Rome*] are not in the flesh, but in the Spirit, if so be that the Spirit of God dwell in you. [*In other words, you Saints in Rome are no longer following the desires of the flesh but are following the Spirit toward salvation.*] Now if any man have not the Spirit of Christ, he is none of his [*if anyone does not have and follow the Spirit of Christ, he does not yet belong to Christ*].

**JST Romans 8:9**

9 But ye are not after the flesh, but after the Spirit, if so be that the Spirit of God dwell in you. Now if any man have not the Spirit of Christ, he is none of his.

10 And if Christ be in you, the body is dead because of sin; but the Spirit is life because of righteousness.

**JST Romans 8:10**

10 And if Christ be in you, though the body shall die because of sin, yet the Spirit is life, because of righteousness [*If you allow Christ to rule your life, even though your body dies because of Adam's transgression, your personal righteousness will yet lead to eternal life*].

11 But if the Spirit of him [*Heavenly Father*] that raised up [*resurrected*] Jesus from the dead dwell in you, he [*Heavenly Father who*] that raised up Christ from the dead shall also quicken your mortal bodies [*will make you spiritually alive, born again, during your life on earth*] by his Spirit that dwelleth in you.

**JST Romans 8:11**

11 And if the Spirit of him that raised up Jesus from the dead, dwell in you, he that raised up Christ from the dead shall also quicken your mortal bodies by his Spirit that dwelleth in you.

12 Therefore, brethren, we are debtors, not to the flesh, to live after the flesh [*in other words, we have an obligation to avoid yielding to the temptations of the mortal body*].

13 For if ye live after the flesh, ye shall die [*if you submit to sin and live wickedly, you will die spiritually*]: but if ye through the Spirit [*with the help of the Spirit*] do mortify [*kill, do away with*] the deeds of the body [*the sins of the flesh*], ye shall live. [*In other words, if you follow the promptings of the Holy Ghost and thus keep repenting successfully, you will do away with evil in your lives and will be spiritually alive and will come unto Christ.*]

**JST Romans 8:13**

13 For if ye live after the flesh, unto sin, ye shall die; but if ye through the Spirit do mortify the deeds of the body, ye shall live unto Christ.

The phrase "sons of God" in verse 14, next, is a term for exaltation. See Mosiah 5:7 and D&C 76:24.

14 For as many as are led by the Spirit of God, they are the sons of God [*ultimately end up in exaltation, meaning the highest degree of glory in the celestial kingdom*].

15 For ye have not received the spirit of bondage again to fear [*with the gospel of Christ, you have not been given something which focuses on fear and bondage, as did the Law of Moses*]; but ye have received the Spirit of adoption [*through Christ's gospel, you receive the Spirit of being included in God's family, which is intimate, loving, and close*], whereby we cry [*which enables us to exclaim*], Abba, Father [*Abba is an intimate, familiar name for our Father in Heaven, see Bible Dictionary under "Abba."*]

The end of verse 15, above, is most beautiful indeed. Paul tells these converts that, through following the Savior's gospel, they will return to their rightful status of being true sons and daughters of God, belonging to Him and being privileged to call him "Daddy." This is a pleasant reminder that the family unit exists in exaltation.

16 The Spirit itself beareth witness with our spirit, that we are the children of God [*the Holy Ghost tells our spirit that we are indeed Heavenly Father's children; see Acts 17:28–29, Hebrews 12:9*]:

In verse 17, next, Paul uses vocabulary which specifically reminds the Roman Saints and us that we can literally become like God. This is one of the most important doctrinal verses in Paul's writings.

17 And if children [*since we are the Father's children*], then heirs; heirs of God [*then we stand to inherit all he has; see D&C 84:36–38*], and joint-heirs with Christ [*we inherit all things, jointly with Christ*]; if so be that we suffer with him [*if we sacrifice whatever in necessary to follow the Savior*], that we may be also glorified together [*that we may be received into celestial glory and exaltation with Him*].

18 For I reckon that the sufferings of this present time are not worthy to be compared with the glory which shall be revealed in us. [*There is no comparison between the small price we pay to attain exaltation and the actual glory of it.*]

**JST Romans 8:18**

18 For I reckon that the sufferings of this present time are not worthy to be named with the glory which shall be revealed in us.

19 For the earnest expectation of the creature [*creation, material universe; see Romans 8:19, footnote b*] waiteth for the manifestation of the sons of God. [*All creation is waiting anxiously for the righteous to become "sons of God." In other words, the whole purpose of the creation was to enable us to become exalted sons and daughters of God.*]

20 For the creature [*mankind*] was made subject to vanity, not willingly, but by reason of him [*Christ*] who hath subjected the same in hope, [*In other words, we, mankind, were given the trials and tribulations of mortality and were given hope of overcoming them through Christ who was subjected to all tribulations and overcame them, thus giving us the bright hope (2 Nephi 31:20) of overcoming them also with His help.*]

**JST Romans 8:20**

20 For the creature was made subject to tribulation not willingly, but by reason of him who hath subjected it in hope;

Next, in verse 21, Paul explains why we can have such an encouraging "hope."

21 Because the creature itself [*people who follow Christ*] also shall be delivered from the bondage of corruption

[*the captivity of sin*] into the glorious liberty of the children of God [*to the freedom which comes to the followers of God; see John 8:32*].

22 For we know that the whole creation [*all people*] groaneth and travaileth in pain together until now. [*All people groan and suffer in sin until they accept the redemption which is now being made available to you through Christ and His gospel.*]

23 And not only they, but ourselves also, which have the firstfruits of the Spirit [*even those of us who are among the first to have been baptized and received the Gift of the Holy Ghost*], even we ourselves groan within ourselves, waiting for the adoption [*struggling against sin as we await adoption as joint heirs with Christ, i.e., redemption and exaltation*], to wit [*namely*], the redemption of our body.

24 For we are saved by hope: but hope that is seen is not hope: for what a man seeth, why doth he yet hope for? [*In other words, if we could see the end result of our hope, we wouldn't have to have hope.*]

25 But if we hope for that we see not [*if we have hope to see God and live with Him eventually*], then do we with patience wait for it. [*Hope gives us the patience to wait for and live worthy of eternal life.*]

**JST Romans 8:25**

25 But if we hope for that we see not, then with patience we do wait for it.

26 Likewise the Spirit also helpeth our infirmities [*the Holy Ghost helps us overcome our sins, weaknesses, imperfections, etc.*]: for we know not what we should pray for as we ought [*even our prayers fall short of being what they should be*]: but the Spirit itself maketh intercession for us with groanings which cannot be uttered [*the Holy Ghost is very interested in helping us come unto Christ*].

27 And he [*Christ*] that searcheth the hearts [*who knows what is in our hearts, even though we fall short in expressing our feelings in prayer*] knoweth what is the mind of the Spirit, because he [*Christ*] maketh intercession [*performed the Atonement*] for the saints according to the will of God [*the Father*].

Next, in verses 28–31, Paul refers to the doctrine of foreordination and God's foreknowledge of us because we lived with him in premortal life. We understand that each person who comes to earth "is a beloved spirit son or daughter of heavenly parents" (Proclamation on the Family, September 23, 1995) and that as such, each is "called" or "foreordained" to come to earth and to successfully return to live with God forever. Unfortunately, the King James Bible translators chose to use the word "predestinate" instead of the word "foreordain," which reflects the meaning of the original Greek from which they translated. "Predestination" indicates loss of agency. "Foreordination" indicates being called and capable but preserves agency as to whether or not we live true to our potential. Because of this unfortunate use of "predestination" in these and other verses, many are burdened and shackled with the false belief that some have been chosen or "predestinated" by God to succeed, whereas others are predestinated by God to fail.

28 And we know that all things work together for good to them that love God, to them who are the called [*who are foreordained; see verses 29–30, next*] according to his purpose.

29 For whom he did foreknow [*which includes the noble and great in premortality, as mentioned in Abraham 3:22*], he also did predestinate [*foreordain*] to be conformed to the image of his Son [*to successfully follow the Savior and become "joint heirs" (Romans 8:17) with Him, and thus become like the Father*], that he might be the firstborn among many brethren [*that such might be exalted*].

**JST Romans 8:29**

29 For him whom he did foreknow, he also did predestinate to be conformed to his own image, that he might be the firstborn among many brethren.

30 Moreover whom he did predestinate [*foreordain*], them he also called: and whom he called, them he also justified: and whom he justified, them he also glorified.

**JST Romans 8:30**

30 Moreover, him whom he did predestinate, him he also called; and him whom he called, him he also sanctified [*meaning to be made pure and holy, fit to be in the presence of God, because of their worthiness to have the Atonement cleanse them*]; and him whom he sanctified, him he also glorified.

31 What shall we then say to these things [*how should we respond to these wonderful doctrines*]? [*Answer: with great hope and confidence in our potential for exaltation!*] If God be for us, who can be against us?

**JST Romans 8:31**

31 What shall we then say to these things? If God be for us, who can prevail against us?

32 He [*the Father*] that spared not his own Son [*Christ*], but delivered him up [*allowed Jesus to go through the suffering and humiliation of the Atonement*] for us all, how shall he not with him also freely give us all things? [*If the Father went through so much to give us the Atonement through His own Son, why wouldn't He also give us all things (meaning exaltation), which is the whole purpose of everything we have been talking about?*]

33 Who shall lay any thing to the charge of God's elect [*who could possibly hold the Saints of God back from exaltation*]? It is God that justifieth [*it is Christ who is the final judge; see John 5:22*].

34 Who is he that condemneth [*who is in charge of determining who does and who does not make it to exaltation*]? It is Christ that died, yea rather, that is risen again, who is even at the right hand of God, who also maketh intercession for us. [*In other words, in effect, we have great cause to hope for exaltation, in fact, to plan on it if we repent and follow the Savior, because Christ, who suffered and died and was resurrected for us is in a position of power at the right hand of the Father and wants us to succeed! In fact, He is our advocate with the Father, interceding between us and our sins as we repent.*]

35 Who shall separate us from the love of Christ [*who shall keep the Savior from helping us*]? shall tribulation, or distress, or persecution, or famine, or nakedness, or peril, or sword? [*The answer is given in verse 37.*]

36 As it is written [*in Psalm 44:22*], For thy sake we are killed all the day long; we are accounted as sheep for the slaughter [*we are all mortal and will die one way or another, so, in the eternal perspective, the tribulation, distress, persecution, etc., mentioned in verse 35 are not really important compared to whether or not we live righteously*].

37 Nay, in all these things we are more than conquerors through him that loved us [*we overcome all these things because of the Father's love as demonstrated in offering His Son for our sins*].

38 For I am persuaded, that neither death, nor life, nor angels, nor principalities, nor powers, nor things present, nor things to come,

39 Nor height, nor depth, nor any other creature, shall be able to separate us from the love of God, which is in Christ Jesus our Lord. [*If we are willing and faithful, nothing at all can prevent us from attaining exaltation through Jesus Christ.*]

# ROMANS 9

The heading for this chapter, in the Joseph Smith Translation of the Bible [*JST*] tells us that Paul has tender feelings for these new converts in Rome and in the opening verses of this chapter, he tells them he wishes that he could carry more of their burdens, sorrows, and troubles himself.

Paul will explain how the law of "election" (foreordination) works and will use Israel as an example.

1 I SAY the truth in Christ, I lie not, my conscience also bearing me witness in the Holy Ghost [*I am telling you the absolute truth when I tell you what I'm going to say to you next*],

2 That I have great heaviness and continual sorrow in my heart [*your sorrows and troubles weight heavily in my heart*].

3 For I could wish that myself were accursed from Christ for my brethren, my kinsmen according to the flesh [*in other words, for my fellow Israelites*]:

**JST Romans 9:3**

3 (For once I could have wished that myself were accursed from Christ,) for my brethren, my kinsmen according to the flesh; [*In other words, because of my tender feelings for you, I have felt at times that if you don't make it, I don't want to make it either. See Romans 9:3, footnote b, which refers you to Exodus 32:32 where Moses had similar feelings about his people, the children of Israel.*]

Paul uses the word "adoption" in verse 4, next. "Adoption" is another word for "election" or being "elected" by God to gain exaltation, because of personal worthiness. See Romans 9:4, footnote 4a. In the sense that Paul uses, the word "adoption" means to become part of the family of God, by joining the Church, becoming faithful Saints and to thus be "adopted" into the family of God and Christ in exaltation forever. Whereas we are all literal spirit children of God, and thus belonged to His family from the time of our spirit birth in premortality, we now must use our agency wisely, as mortals, to determine whether or not we are "adopted" back into His celestial family to live with Him forever.

4 Who are Israelites; to whom pertaineth the adoption, and the glory, and the covenants, and the giving of the law, and the service of God, and the promises;

**JST Romans 9:4**

4 Who are Israelites; of whom are the adoption, and the glory, and the covenants, and the giving of the law, and the service of God [*In other words, those who are "adopted," are adopted into God's Church and family through making and keeping covenants and receiving all the blessings of the gospel*],

5 Whose are the fathers, and of whom as concerning the flesh Christ came, who is over all, God blessed for ever. Amen.

**JST Romans 9:5**

5 And the promises which are made unto the fathers; and of whom, as concerning the flesh, Christ was, who is God over all, blessed forever. [*In other words, the promises of exaltation made to our ancestors, came from God. Christ was from God and came into mortality as the Son of God and has charge of all things on earth, under the Father's direction*]. Amen.

Some Jews held the belief that, because they were direct descendants of Abraham, to whom the blessings of exaltation were promised (Abraham 2:9–11; Genesis 12:1–3; 17:1–8), they were guaranteed entrance to heaven. Furthermore, they believed that all other people, because they were not direct descendants of Abraham, Isaac, and Jacob, would forever be second-class citizens in God's kingdom. Paul deals with that false belief, beginning in verse 6, next.

6 Not as though the word of God hath taken none effect. For they are not all Israel, which are of Israel [*all people who are blood-line Israelites are not necessarily true, covenant-keeping Israel, or God's people*]: [*In other words, it is not as if God's promises are not valid, in the fact that some of Abraham's descendants won't make it to heaven. It is simply that some of His descendants are not worthy of receiving God's promises of exaltation.*]

Paul uses repetition much, as a teaching tool, and will repeat the message of verse 6 again in verses 7 and 8.

7 Neither, because they are the seed of Abraham, are they all children [*in other words, just because they are all the descendants of Abraham doesn't necessarily mean they are all "children of God" or righteous Saints*]: but, In Isaac shall thy seed be called [*Isaac had the same blessings promised to him and his posterity*].

**JST Romans 9:7**

7 Neither, because they are all children of Abraham, are they the seed [*the Lord's people*]; but, In Isaac shall thy seed be called.

8 That is, They which are the children of the flesh [*those who are literal descendants of Abraham and Isaac*], these are not the children of God [*do not automatically get exaltation*]: but the children of the promise [*those who live righteously*] are counted for the seed [*are ultimately the Lord's people and the ones to whom the blessings promised to Abraham's seed or descendants will come*].

9 For this is the word of promise [*Here is what the Lord promised Abraham; see Genesis 17:16*], At this time will I come, and Sara [*Abraham's* wife] shall have a son.

10 And not only this; but when Rebecca [*Isaac's wife*] also had conceived by one, even by our father Isaac [*see Genesis 25:20–23*];

**JST Romans 9:10**

10 And not only Sarah; but when Rebecca also had conceived by one, our father Isaac,

11 (For the children being not yet born, neither having done any good or evil [*even though Rebecca and Isaac's twins had not been born yet, God told Rebecca about them*], that the purpose of God according to election [*foreordination*] might stand [*might take place*], not of works, but of him [*not merely because of genealogy, etc., but because of the will of God*] that calleth;)

12 It was said unto her [*Rebecca, the mother of twins, Esau and Jacob*], The elder [*the older twin*] shall serve the younger [*Esau will serve Jacob*].

13 As it is written [*Malachi 1:2–3*], Jacob have I loved, but Esau have I hated [*in effect, I was able to bless Jacob but had to withhold blessings from Esau*].

The word "hated" in verse 13, above, can cause problems. Obviously, God loves everyone. See John 3:16. Therefore, the word "hated" in this context has to mean people whom God can't bless as He would like to because of their personal wickedness.

14 What shall we say then? Is there unrighteousness with God [*Is God unrighteous? Is He prejudiced*]? God forbid [*Absolutely not!*].

15 For he saith to Moses, I will have mercy on whom I will have mercy, and I will have compassion on whom I will have compassion. [*In other words, I am the Judge and know how to strike the proper balance between justice and mercy.*]

16 So then it is not of him that willeth, nor of him that runneth, but of God that sheweth mercy. [*We do not dictate to God as to how He should run things, rather, He determines when mercy is appropriate and beneficial.*]

17 For the scripture [*Exodus 9:13–21*] saith unto Pharaoh, Even for this same

purpose have I raised thee up, that I might shew my power in thee, and that my name might be declared throughout all the earth. [*God used Pharaoh to show His power. Because of Pharaoh's arrogance and refusal to humble himself before God, God's power was dramatically displayed to the children of Israel.*]

18 Therefore hath he [*God*] mercy on whom he will have mercy, and whom he will he hardeneth [*leaves to his own stubbornness, hardheartedness; see Romans 9:18, footnote b*].

19 Thou wilt say then unto me [*in spite of what I have been teaching you so far, some of you Roman converts will still ask me*], Why doth he [*God*] yet find fault [*why does God still bless some people more than others*]? For who hath resisted his will [*who would go against God once they know His will*]?

20 Nay [*you know better than that*] but, O man, who art thou that repliest against God [*who do you think you are, criticizing God*]? Shall the thing formed say to him that formed it, Why hast thou made me thus [*is it proper for the thing that is made to say to the person who made it, "Why did you make me this way?"*] ?

21 Hath not the potter [*one who makes clay pots*] power over the clay, of [*with*] the same lump to make one vessel [*pot*] unto honour, and another unto dishonour?

Unless you think in terms of premortal life and our agency to choose there, and of mortal life and our agency to choose here, between right and wrong, you might end up believing in predestination because of what Paul says here. The potter in verse 21, above, symbolizes God, and the clay pots symbolize people. Taken out of the context of all the scriptures, this verse makes it sound like God makes some people good and some people evil in order to work out His plan for us here on earth. Such is definitely not the case. Jesus Christ is the righteous judge of all people (see John 5:22), and on final Judgment Day, He will, by virtue of His role as our final judge, "make" or designate some as righteous or "honorable" (end of verse 21) and some as unrighteous or "dishonorable" (verse 21), depending on how each used agency.

22 What if God, willing [*able*] to shew his wrath, and to make his power known, endured with much longsuffering [*patience*] the vessels of wrath [*the wicked*] fitted to destruction [*who are worthy of destruction*]: [*In other words, what if God showed great patience toward the wicked rather than destroying them when they seem to deserve it?*]

3 And that he might make known the riches of his glory on the vessels of mercy [*people to whom He shows mercy*], which he had afore prepared [*whom he had foreordained, not predestined*] unto glory,

24 Even us [*like each of us*], whom he hath called, not of the Jews only, but also of the Gentiles [*not just those of us who are Abraham's descendants, but all others too*]?

25 As he saith also in Osee [*Hosea 2:23; Zechariah 13:9*], I will call them my people, which were not my people; and her beloved, which was not beloved.

Paul's message here is that none of us is perfect, and all deserve punishment, but God is very patient and merciful and encouraging. He wants us each to return worthily to live with Him forever. Therefore, the Savior "stretches forth His hands unto [*us*] all the day long" (Jacob 6:4), encouraging us to repent, be faithful, and return to the Father through Him.

26 And it shall come to pass, that in the place where it was said unto them, Ye are not my people; there shall they be called the children of the living God. [*The Savior's Atonement will have much success, and many who once were not*

*worthy of returning to the Father, therefore were "not My people" at the time, will repent, be forgiven, and become "children of the living God," or, as Paul would put it, will be "adopted" into the family of God and live with Him in exaltation forever.*]

Paul is emphasizing the mercy of God now. He is reminding his readers that even though God could wipe out all of the wicked right now, He doesn't want to nor will He. Through His mercy and patience, He will yet save a large remnant of Israel.

27 Esaias [*Isaiah*] also crieth [*speaks out*] concerning Israel [*in Isaiah 10:22*], Though the number of the children of Israel be as the sand of the sea, a remnant shall be saved:

28 For he will finish the work [*of saving souls*], and cut it short in righteousness [*and bring it to an end with much power*]: because a short work will the Lord make upon the earth.

29 And as Esaias [*Isaiah*] said before [*in Isaiah 1:9*], Except the Lord of Sabaoth [*the Lord of Hosts, Jehovah, Christ; see Bible Dictionary under "Sabaoth"*] had left us a seed, we had been as Sodoma [*Sodom*], and been made like unto Gomorrha [*Gomorrah*]. [*In other words, if God had not intervened with mercy, Israel would have been destroyed as completely as Sodom and Gomorrah.*]

30 What shall we say then [*what conclusion should we draw from all this*]? [*Answer:*] That the Gentiles, which followed not after righteousness [*who did not live the Law of Moses*], have attained to righteousness [*can attain salvation*], even the righteousness which is of faith [*even the salvation which comes through faith in Jesus Christ*].

31 But Israel [*the "chosen" people, the descendants of Abraham, Isaac, and Jacob*], which followed after the law of righteousness [*who lived according to the Law of Moses*], hath not attained to the law of righteousness [*cannot attain salvation through it*]. [*In other words, one cannot be saved by the Law of Moses, but we must accept Christ and follow His gospel in order to be saved.*]

32 Wherefore [*why*]? Because they sought it [*salvation*] not by faith [*in Christ*], but as it were by the works of the law [*the Law of Moses*]. For they stumbled at that stumblingstone; [*In other words, the Law of Moses, which was designed to help them prepare for Christ's gospel, became a stumbling stone to them because of their hardheartedness and unbelief in Christ.*]

**JST Romans 9:32**

32 Wherefore they stumbled at that stumbling stone, not by faith, but as it were by the works of the law;

33 As it is written [*in Isaiah 8:14; 28:16*], Behold, I lay in Sion [*Zion*] a stumblingstone [*Christ*] and rock of offence [*Christ; in other words, many Israelites will be offended by Jesus and His gospel*]: and whosoever believeth on him shall not be ashamed [*will not be stopped in their progression toward eternal life*].

# ROMANS 10

Paul continues his letter to these members of the Church in Rome by emphasizing that salvation comes through living righteously and having faith in Jesus Christ. He will emphasize that the purpose of the Law of Moses was to lead people to accepting Christ and His gospel (see verse 4). We will point out that verses 9–11, when taken out of the context of the whole Bible, lead some Christians to believe that all they have to do to be saved is to verbally accept Christ as the Savior.

1 BRETHREN, my heart's desire and prayer to God for Israel [*all Israelites*] is, that they might be saved.

2 For I bear them [*Israel*] record that they have a zeal of God [*they are attempting to worship God properly*], but not according to knowledge [*but they don't have correct knowledge about Him and what He requires for salvation*].

3 For they being ignorant of God's righteousness [*they do not have correct knowledge of God and how he wants to go about saving them; see Strong's #1342*], and going about to establish their own righteousness [*they are going around making their own rules about how to be saved by God*], have not submitted themselves unto the righteousness of God [*therefore, they are not living the correct gospel*].

4 For Christ is the end of the law [*Christ is the whole purpose and end goal of the Law of Moses*] for righteousness to every one that believeth [*Christ's gospel leads to true righteousness for every one who believes in Him*].

5 For Moses describeth the righteousness which is of the law [*Moses gave us the Law of Moses to lead to a certain degree of righteousness*], That the man which doeth those things shall live by them [*and instructed his people to live according to the Law of Moses*].

In Deuteronomy 30:10–14, Moses told his people, the children of Israel, that they didn't have to hunt all over the place for the laws of God by which they should live. They didn't have to send someone to heaven to find God's laws, neither did they have to send beyond the sea for information. Rather, the laws and commandments were to be found in what Moses had written and they should be "in thy mouth" (verse 14) and "in thy heart" (verse 14). In other words, he told his people that God's laws and commandments should be in their conversation and in their heart always.

Next, in Romans 10:6–8, as he continues to instruct the Saints in Rome, Paul uses their knowledge of Deuteronomy 30:10–14 to remind them that they have the true gospel of Christ right in front of them and that they don't have to look far and wide for it.

6 But the righteousness which is of faith [*but the higher personal righteousness which comes through faith in Christ*] speaketh on this wise, Say not in thine heart, Who shall ascend into heaven? [*that is, to bring Christ down from above; in other words, you don't have to send someone to heaven to find out about Christ and then come back and report to you. Christ has already been here and given us His gospel.*]

7 Or, Who shall descend into the deep? [*in other words, you don't have to send someone across the sea to find God's will concerning you, as Moses said in Deuteronomy 30:13*].

8 But what saith it [*what did Moses say, in Deuteronomy 30:14*]? The word [*God's instruction to you*] is nigh thee [*near you; in fact, right here!*], even in thy mouth, and in thy heart: that is, the word of faith [*of faith in Jesus Christ*], which we preach;

As mentioned in the notes at the beginning of this chapter, verses 9–11, next, are often badly misused by taking them out of the bigger context of all Paul's writings as well as the rest of the scriptures. Some people use verses 9–11 to teach that all that is necessary to be "saved" is to believe in Jesus and to confess that he is the Christ with one's mouth. They forget that what Moses taught in Deuteronomy 30:10–14 and what Paul is teaching here is that, in order to be saved, in addition to ordinances, covenants, and so forth, we must have personal righteousness to the point that Jesus is constantly in our conversation and in our hearts.

9 That if thou shalt confess with thy mouth the Lord Jesus, and shalt believe in thine heart that God hath raised him from the dead, thou shalt be saved.

10 For with the heart man believeth unto righteousness [*when you truly believe in*

*Christ, it leads to personal righteousness*]; and with the mouth confession is made unto salvation.

11 For the scripture saith, Whosoever believeth on him shall not be ashamed [*will not be stopped in progressing to eventual exaltation*].

12 For there is no difference between the Jew and the Greek [*Gentile*]: for the same Lord over all is rich unto all that call upon him. [*The Lord gives all people the same rich blessings of exaltation, if they come unto Christ and live His gospel.*]

13 For whosoever shall call upon the name of the Lord shall be saved [*anyone who calls upon the name of Christ, meaning anyone who learns the gospel and lives it, will be saved*].

Next, Paul will say, in effect, that in order to properly worship Christ and keep His commandments, people have to be taught by authorized servants of God.

14 How then shall they call on him [*the true God*] in whom they have not believed? and how shall they believe in him of whom they have not heard? and how shall they hear without a preacher?

15 And how shall they preach, except they be sent [*who can teach the true gospel unless sent from God*]? as it is written [*in Isaiah 52:7*], How beautiful are the feet of them that preach the gospel of peace, and bring glad tidings of good things!

16 But they have not all obeyed the gospel [*every Israelite has not necessarily listened to God's messengers and obeyed*]. For Esaias [*Isaiah*] saith [*in Isaiah 53:1*], Lord, who hath believed our report [*in effect, who listens to us prophets, anyway*]?

17 So then faith cometh by hearing [*the only way we can exercise true faith is by hearing the true gospel*], and hearing by the word of God.

18 But I say, Have they not heard [*haven't the Israelites had a chance to hear the word of God*]? Yes verily [*absolutely yes*], their sound went into all the earth, and their words unto the ends of the world [*they have had prophets and more prophets who have taught them*].

19 But I say [*I ask the question again*], Did not Israel know [*Israel (the Israelites) heard, but did they understand with their hearts*]? First Moses saith, I will provoke you to jealousy by them that are no people, and by a foolish nation I will anger you. [*The answer to the question is "No." They did not understand with their hearts. They refused to. Therefore, Moses told them that the Lord would "provoke" them, or punish them to the point that they would return to Him.*]

**JST Romans 10:19**

19 But I say, Did not Israel know? Now Moses saith, I will provoke you to jealousy by them that are no people, and by a foolish nation I will anger you.

20 But Esaias [*Isaiah*] is very bold, and saith [*in Isaiah 65:1*], I was found of them that sought me not; I was made manifest unto them that asked not after me. [*JST Isaiah 65:1 "I am found of them who seek after me, I give unto all them that ask of me; I am not found of them that sought me not, or that inquireth not after me."*]

21 But to Israel he saith [*in Isaiah 65:2*], All day long I have stretched forth my hands unto a disobedient and gainsaying people [*a people who oppose and deny Me*]. [*In other words, "all day long" I continue to invite them to repent, even though they are wicked and oppose Me in everything I try to do for them. Compare with Jacob 6:4–5.*]

# ROMANS 11

One of the interesting pieces of information in this chapter is that Paul is from the tribe of Benjamin (verse 1), which, historically, was the smallest and least prestigious of all the tribes of Israel. Some members of the Church today feel a bit disappointed if their lineage is designated to be a tribe other than Ephraim, or Manasseh, or Judah or whatever they expected, when they receive their patriarchal blessing. Here we see that Paul, one of the greatest Apostles ever to have lived on earth, is from the tribe of Benjamin. Sometimes we forget that all of the tribes of Israel are given the charge to spread the gospel and blessings of the priesthood to all the world, as descendants of Abraham, Isaac, and Jacob (see Abraham 2:9–11). And the blessings of exaltation are promised to all of Israel if they are righteous, whether as direct descendants or as those who join Israel by making gospel covenants.

Paul continues his message to the Saints in Rome by discussing the foreordination of Israel and pointing out how Gentiles can become members of Israel in the kingdom of God. This is very important doctrine.

1 I SAY then [*I ask the question*], Hath God cast away his people [*has God deserted His people*]? God forbid [*absolutely not!*]. For I also am an Israelite, of the seed of Abraham, of the tribe of Benjamin [*I am a descendant of Abraham, coming through the tribe of Benjamin*].

2 God hath not cast away his people which he foreknew [*foreordained*]. Wot ye not what the scripture saith of Elias [*about Elijah*]? how he maketh intercession to God against Israel, saying [*in 1 Kings 19:10 and 14*],

**JST Romans 11:2**

2 God hath not cast away his people which he foreknew. Know ye not what the scripture saith of Elias? how he maketh complaint to God against Israel, saying,

3 Lord, they have killed thy prophets, and digged down thine altars; and I am left alone, and they seek my life.

4 But what saith the answer of God unto him [*what did God say when he answered Elijah's complaint*]? I have reserved to myself seven thousand men, who have not bowed the knee to the image of Baal [*there are still 7,000 righteous men in Israel, so you are not alone; see 1 Kings 19:18*].

5 Even so then at this present time also there is a remnant according to the election of grace [*even so there are many righteous Israelites now who are dedicated to God through the grace of Christ*].

6 And if by grace, then is it no more of works [*since they are being saved by the grace or help of Christ, then it is obvious that they are not being saved by the works of the Law of Moses*]: otherwise grace is no more grace [*otherwise, grace would not really be grace*]. But if it be of works, then is it no more grace [*if they were to be saved by compliance with the Law of Moses, there would be no need for the grace of Christ*]: otherwise work is no more work [*if they are being saved by grace, the works of the Law of Moses are not effective in saving them*].

7 What then [*so what is this all leading to*]? Israel hath not obtained that which he seeketh for; [*In other words, every one in Israel is not going to gain salvation.*] but the election hath obtained it [*those of Israel who honored their foreordination by living righteously have attained God's grace, through Christ, and are on their way to exaltation*], and the rest [*of Israel*] were blinded [*spiritually*]

**JST Romans 11:7**

7 What then? Israel hath not obtained that which they seek for; but the election hath obtained it, and the rest were blinded.

8 (According as it is written [*in Isaiah 29:10*], God hath given them the spirit of slumber, eyes that they should not see, and ears that they should not hear;) unto this day. [*In other words, God allows agency choice, and when used to choose wickedness, people end up being spiritually blind and deaf.*]

9 And David saith [*Psalm 69:22–23*], Let their table be made a snare, and a trap, and a stumbling block, and a recompence [*reward*] unto them: [*Let the wicked be rewarded appropriately for their wicked choices.*]

10 Let their eyes be darkened, that they may not see [*let them become spiritually blind*], and bow down their back alway [*and let the burdens of their wickedness bend them over always*].

11 I say then [*the next question is*:], Have they [*Israel*] stumbled that they should fall [*has Israel lost their chance for salvation forever*]? God forbid [*absolutely not!*]: but rather through their fall salvation is come unto the Gentiles [*because of their failure to keep the commandments and lead out in spreading the gospel, the gospel will be given to the Gentiles*, for to provoke them [*Israel*] to jealousy [*eventually Israel will be humbled, repent, and be gathered*].

12 Now if the fall of them [*Israel*] be the riches of the world [*if the failure of the Jews and Israelites in the Holy Land to be worthy of being the chosen people leads to the gospel being given to the rest of the world instead*], and the diminishing of them the riches of the Gentiles [*and leads to the taking of the gospel from them and giving it to the Gentiles (especially through Joseph Smith and the restoration)*]; how much more their fulness?

13 For I speak to you Gentiles [*Gentile converts to the Church*], inasmuch as [*since*] I am the apostle of the Gentiles, I magnify mine office [*I am carrying out my special calling to take the gospel to the Gentiles*]:

14 If by any means I may provoke to emulation [*following someone else's example*] them which are my flesh [*my fellow Israelites*], and might save some of them [*perhaps I can provoke some of my fellow Israelites to follow the good example of you Gentile converts and thus save some of them*].

15 For if the casting away of them [*if the casting off of Israel, because of their wickedness*] be the reconciling of the world [*leads to the teaching of the gospel of Christ to the whole world, so that they can be "reconciled"—made worthy through the Atonement*], what shall the receiving of them be, but life from the dead [*when Israel is finally restored and gathered in the last days, won't it be like bringing someone back from the dead*]?

**JST Romans 11:15**

15 For if the casting away of them is the reconciling of the world, what shall the restoring of them be, but life from the dead?

In order to understand what Paul says next in verses 16–26, one needs to understand the parable or allegory of the olive tree given in Jacob, chapter 5, in the Book of Mormon. The olive tree represents Israel, God's covenant people. Tame branches represent righteous people. Wild branches represent apostate, wicked people and can also represent Gentiles. Roots can represent gospel covenants. Branches, basically, represent various groups of people. You may wish to read Jacob 5 before continuing with Paul's sermon here.

16 For if the firstfruit [*the first lump of dough or loaf of bread made from the first grain harvested; see Numbers 15:17–21*] be holy, the lump is also holy

[*the rest of the harvest has the potential to be holy also*]: and if the root be holy, so are the branches. [*In other words, if Israel was once holy, a remnant of Israel can become holy again (and will in the last days after the restoration by Joseph Smith).*]

17 And if some of the branches be broken off [*if some of Israel goes into apostasy (falls away from God)*], and thou [*Gentiles*] being a wild olive tree, wert graffed [*grafted, joined*] in among them [*the people of God*], and with them partakest of the root and fatness of the olive tree [*and with them enjoy the blessings of being righteous, covenant people, in other words, Israel*];

18 Boast not against the branches. But if thou boast, thou bearest not the root, but the root thee. [*Don't become prideful and think you are better than other members of the Church. Remember that God is giving you strength through covenants, rather than you giving God strength by keeping covenants.*]

**JST Romans 11:18**

18 Boast not against the branches, for thou bearest not the root, but the root thee.

19 Thou [*Gentiles*] wilt say then, The branches were broken off, that I might be graffed in. [*Don't get caught up in thinking that you are worth more than those who get cut off the Church because of wickedness.*]

**JST Romans 11:19**

19 For if thou boast, thou wilt say, The branches were broken off, that we might be grafted in.

20 Well; because of unbelief they were broken off [*it is true that they, the wicked of Israel, were "cut off the olive tree" because of unbelief and resulting wickedness*], and thou standest by faith [*and you Gentile members are in good standing before God because of your faith*]. Be not highminded [*don't get cocky or prideful*], but fear:

21 For if God spared not the natural branches, take heed lest he also spare not thee [*if God cut off the natural branches (covenant Israel) from the olive tree, because of their wickedness, don't think for a moment that you can't get cut off too if you turn to wickedness*].

22 Behold therefore [*make sure you understand*] the goodness and severity of God: on them which fell, severity [*He has had to deal severely with those who fell away from the gospel*]; but toward thee, goodness, if thou continue in his goodness [*but you will receive of His goodness and blessings, if you continue faithful*]: otherwise thou also shalt be cut off.

23 And they [*those who fell away*] also, if they abide not still in unbelief [*if they repent*], shall be graffed [*grafted*] in [*brought back into the Lord's covenant people*]: for God is able to graff [*graft*] them in again.

24 For if thou [*you Gentiles*] wert [*were*] cut out of the olive tree which is wild by nature [*were taken from a Gentile culture which promotes lifestyles which are contrary to Christ's gospel*], and wert graffed contrary to nature into a good olive tree [*and were converted, seemingly against all odds, and brought into Christ's true Church*]: how much more shall these, which be the natural branches, be graffed into their own olive tree [*what do you think the chances are that wicked Israel will be brought back, gathered to Christ in the last days*]?

25 For I would not, brethren, that ye should be ignorant of this mystery [*I don't want you to remain ignorant about this matter*], lest ye should be wise in your own conceits [*for fear that you would become prideful about it*]; that blindness in part is happened to Israel, until the fulness of the Gentiles be come in [*namely, that through wickedness, Israel (particularly the Jews) have become spiritually blind and will remain that way until the last days after*

*the fulness of the Gentiles is fulfilled or, in other words, until the gospel has been preached to the Gentiles*].

The "fulness of the Gentiles" referred to in verse 25, above, is one of the signs of the times which is to be fulfilled before the Second Coming. Basically, it goes like this: In the days of the Savior's mortal mission, the Jews were "first" and the Gentiles "last," meaning that the gospel was taken first to the Jews, and then, after the Savior's crucifixion and resurrection, the Apostles took the gospel to the Gentiles. In the last days, the Gentiles will be "first" and the Jews "last," meaning that the gospel will go first to all the rest of the world, and then it will go to the Jews.

26 And so all Israel [*who repent; see Isaiah 59, heading*] shall be saved: as it is written [*in Isaiah 59:20–21; 27:9; Jeremiah 31:33–34*], There shall come out of Sion [*Zion*] the Deliverer [*the Redeemer*], and shall turn away ungodliness from Jacob [*and Jacob (Israel) will repent of wickedness*]:

**JST Romans 11:26**

26 And then all Israel shall be saved; as it is written, There shall come out of Sion the Deliverer, and shall turn away ungodliness from Jacob;

27 For this is my covenant unto them, when I shall take away their sins.

28 As concerning the gospel, they are enemies for your sakes [*the fact that the Jews reject the gospel actually works to your advantage because the prophecy gets fulfilled that the gospel is then taken to you, the Gentiles*]: but as touching the election [*but, speaking of Israel, who were foreordained to accept the gospel and take it to all the world*], they are beloved for the fathers' sakes [*the promises made to Abraham, Isaac, and Jacob will yet be fulfilled, and they will be successfully gathered into Christ's Church in the last days*].

29 For the gifts and calling of God are without repentance. [*In other words, God blesses sinners and calls them, through the preaching of the gospel, before they even start to repent. He does not wait until they have repented before He starts calling them to return to Him.*]

30 For as ye in times past have not believed God, yet have now obtained mercy through their unbelief [*it is just like with you: in times past you didn't believe in God either, but now you have joined the Church and obtained mercy and forgiveness because the Jews rejected it first and then it was preached to you*]:

31 Even so have these [*the Jews*] also now not believed, that through your mercy [*through the mercy of God to the Gentiles, they will get the gospel first in the last days*] they [*the Jews in the last days*] also may obtain mercy [*also will get the gospel, after the "fulness of the Gentiles" (verse 25) has taken place, before the Second Coming*].

32 For God hath concluded [*gathered, as fish are gathered in a net; see Strong's #4788*] them all [*will do everything possible to gather them all*] in unbelief [*despite their unbelief*], that he might have mercy upon all.

33 O the depth of the riches both of the wisdom and knowledge of God! how unsearchable are his judgments, and his ways past finding out! [*God's kindness, mercy, wisdom, knowledge, etc., are so far beyond man's capability to comprehend!*]

34 For who hath known the mind of the Lord? or who hath been his counsellor? [*Who can understand the mind of the Lord, or who can tell Him how to improve His reaching out to us?*]

35 Or who [*what person*] hath first given to him [*God*], and it shall be recompensed [*paid back*] unto him again? [*In other words, who has ever put God in his debt, or done things for God such*

*that God owes him? Answer: No one! See Mosiah 2:24*]

36 For of him, and through him, and to him, are all things [*we are forever indebted to Him*]: to whom be glory for ever. Amen.

# ROMANS 12

Since Satan has much success in luring people to follow him by giving in to the temptations to which the mortal body is subject, Paul now invites the members of the Church to exercise extra self-control over their physical bodies, "sacrificing" sins of the flesh such as impatience, temper, sexual immorality, jealousy, etc., and thus presenting their bodies as a living sacrifice to God. There is a bit of a play on words here. All animals used for sacrifices under the law of Moses, of course, ended up as dead bodies, symbolic of giving their "all" to God. Since the law of animal sacrifice has now been done away with by the Savior's Atonement, Paul invites the Saints to offer their bodies to God, in other words, to give their "all" to God, but their bodies stay alive, symbolic of the newness of life brought by the gospel of Christ.

In this chapter, Paul mentions a number of the gifts of the Spirit, including a number that members of the Church may not normally think of as being specific spiritual gifts. You may wish to mark these (verses 6–13) in your scriptures by way of emphasizing that there are many gifts of the Spirit in addition to the most commonly discussed ones.

Also, in this chapter, Paul gives us straightforward and simple advice on how to be good Christians.

1 I BESEECH you therefore, brethren, by the mercies of God [*through your using the mercies of God made available to you through the Atonement*], that ye present your bodies a living sacrifice, holy, acceptable unto God, which is your reasonable service [*this sacrifice shows up in your serving God*].

2 And be not conformed to this world [*don't live by the world's standards*]: but be ye transformed [*but let yourselves be changed*] by the renewing of your mind [*by the energizing and renewing of your minds which comes through the gospel of Christ*], that ye may prove [*recognize, discern*] what is that good, and acceptable, and perfect, will of God.

**JST Romans 12:2**

2 And be not conformed to this world; but be ye transformed by the renewing of your mind, that ye may prove what that good, and acceptable, and perfect will of God is.

3 For I say, through the grace given unto me [*through the help Christ has given me to understand these things*], to every man that is among you, not to think of himself more highly than he ought to think [*in other words, be humble*]; but to think soberly [*be serious minded about the gospel*], according as God hath dealt [*given out*] to every man the measure of faith.

4 For as we have many members in one body [*just as our physical bodies have many "members"—eyes, ears, head, feet, arms, hands, etc.*], and all members have not the same office [*and each of our body parts doesn't do the same thing for us, in other words, each has a different function*]:

5 So we [*members of the Church*], being many [*even though there are many of us and each is an individual*], are one body in Christ [*all work together in Christ's church*], and every one members one of another [*and each of us belongs to all the other members*]. [*In other words, it is very important that we work together with each other in unity for the good of the Church and each other.*]

Paul will now mention that there are different gifts of the Spirit, and one member has one and another has a different one. Working together in unity and harmony, all members of the Church benefit from each others' spiritual gifts. For a list of several gifts of the Spirit, see D&C 46:8–26; Moroni 10:8–19; 1 Corinthians 12:1–12.

As we continue, we will use **bold** to point out several of the spiritual gifts mentioned by Paul in verses 6–13.

## *Gifts of the Spirit*

6 Having then gifts differing according to the grace that is given to us, whether **prophecy** [*if we have the gift of prophecy*], let us prophesy according to the proportion of faith [*according to how much faith we have*];

7 Or **ministry** [*if we have the gift of serving others*], let us wait on [*attend to*] our ministering [*let us serve others*]: or he that **teacheth** [*he who has the gift of teaching*], on teaching [*let him teach*];

8 Or he that **exhorteth** [*he who has the gift of speaking and encouraging others to do right*], on exhortation: he that **giveth** [*he who has the gift of generosity*], let him do it with simplicity [*without drawing much attention to himself*]; he that **ruleth** [*has the gift of leadership*], with diligence [*let him be diligent in leading and fulfilling his duties*]; he that **sheweth mercy** [*he who has the gift of mercy*], with **cheerfulness** [*let him use it cheerfully*].

9 Let **love** be without dissimulation [*let the gift of love be used sincerely, without hypocrisy*]. **Abhor that which is evil** [*the gift of shunning evil*]; **cleave to that which is good** [*the gift of deeply desiring to be involved with good*].

<u>**JST Romans 12:9**</u>

9 Let love be without dissimulation. Abhor that which is evil and cleave to that which is good.

10 Be **kindly affectioned** one to another with **brotherly love**; in honour **preferring one another** [*the gift of leading by good example and honor*];

The word "preferring" in verse 10, above, is an example of Old English vocabulary which has changed in our day. "Pre" is used in association with going in advance. "Prefer" means "go before or show the way." See Strong's #4285. If we think of "prefer" in our modern English, we think of preferring one person over another and thus miss Paul's point completely. Another example of how words have changed drastically in meaning from Old English to modern American English is found in Matthew 17:25, where Jesus "prevented" Peter. It sounds like Jesus stopped Peter from doing something. Not so. Old English "prevented" means Christ spoke first, before Peter even had a chance to ask him about paying the temple tax. See Matthew 17:25, footnote a.

11 **Not slothful in business** [*the gift of being skilled in business*]; **fervent in spirit** [*the gift of spirituality*]; **serving the Lord**;

12 Rejoicing in **hope** [*the hope and confidence which comes through living Christ's gospel*]; **patient** in tribulation [*trials and troubles*]; **continuing instant in prayer** [*the gift of being in constant communication with God*];

13 **Distributing** [*the gift of sharing*] to the necessity of saints [*sharing according to the needs of the Saints*]; given to **hospitality**.

14 Bless them which persecute you: bless, and curse not.

15 Rejoice with them that do rejoice, and weep with them that weep.

16 Be of the same mind one toward another [*be united, live in harmony*]. Mind not high things [*don't be arrogant, conceited*], but condescend to men of low estate [*be willing to associate with people of low social status*]. Be not wise in your own conceits [*avoid pride*].

17 Recompense to no man evil for evil

[*don't try to get revenge*]. Provide things honest in the sight of all men [*be honest in your dealings with all people*].

18 If it be possible, as much as lieth in you [*as much as you possibly can*], live peaceably with all men.

19 Dearly beloved, avenge not yourselves [*please avoid getting revenge*], but rather give place unto wrath [*step aside and let God be the judge and take care of it; see D&C 64:11*]: for it is written [*in Deuteronomy 32:35*], Vengeance is mine; I will repay, saith the Lord.

20 Therefore if thine enemy hunger, feed him; if he thirst, give him drink: for in so doing thou shalt heap coals of fire on his head. [*In other words, in being kind to your enemies, in doing good to people who treat you badly, you save your own soul from bitterness and hatred and you shift the full burden of accountability for his behavior to your enemy.*]

21 Be not overcome of evil [*don't let evil overcome you*], but overcome evil with good.

# ROMANS 13

Paul now reminds the members in Rome how important it is for them to sustain and support the leaders of the Church. This same counsel applies to us today. If we sustain the leaders God has called to preside over us, we will not go astray and become subject to the punishments of God.

It is interesting to note that Joseph Smith made changes to seven out of the fourteen verses in this chapter in the JST.

1 LET every soul be subject unto the higher powers [*the leaders of the Church*]. For there is no power but of God: the powers that be [*the Church leaders*] are ordained of God.

**JST Romans 13:1**

1 Let every soul be subject unto the higher powers. For there is no power in the church but of God; the powers that be are ordained of God.

2 Whosoever therefore resisteth the power, resisteth the ordinance of God: and they that resist shall receive to themselves damnation. [*In other words, if you don't sustain and support the leaders of the Church, you are heading for the punishments of God.*]

**JST Romans 13:2**

2 Whosoever therefore resisteth the power, resisteth the ordinance of God; and they that resist shall receive to themselves punishment.

3 For rulers are not a terror to good works [*the leaders of the Church are not feared by those who are faithful*], but to the evil [*but the wicked often fear them*]. Wilt thou then not be afraid of the power [*do you desire not to be afraid of Church leaders*]? do that which is good [*then live righteously*], and thou shalt have praise of the same [*and you will have their praise and appreciation*]:

4 For he is the minister of God to thee for good [*the Church leaders are called by God for your benefit*]. But if thou do that which is evil [*if you choose to break God's commandments*], be afraid [*you should fear the leaders of the Church*]; for he beareth not the sword in vain [*for there are good reasons God has given leaders power and authority over you*]: for he [*each Church leader*] is the minister of God, a revenger [*judge*] to execute wrath upon him that doeth evil [*authorized leaders of the Church are judges and sometimes have to be strict with members involved in serious sin, even to the point of disfellowshipping or excommunicating them*].

**JST Romans 13:4**

4 For he is the minister of God to thee for good. But if thou do that which is evil be afraid; for he beareth not the

rod [*"rod" in the scriptures is often symbolic of authority*] in vain; for he is the minister of God, a revenger to execute wrath upon him that doeth evil.

5 Wherefore ye must needs be subject, not only for wrath, but also for conscience sake [*therefore you need to be subject to Church leaders, not only to avoid Church discipline, but also simply because your conscience tells you to*].

In verses 6–7, next, Paul reminds the Saints that many of the leaders of the Church are required by their callings to serve full time, much the same as our current First Presidency, Twelve, and Seventies do. Since they can't work for a living, they and their families are often supported out of funds donated to the Church by members.

6 For for this cause pay ye tribute [*tithes and offerings*] also; for they are God's ministers, attending continually upon this very thing [*many of our leaders serve full time*].

**JST Romans 13:6**
6 For, for this cause pay ye your consecrations also unto them; for they are God's ministers, attending continually upon this very thing.

Next, Paul counsels these members to pay their obligations, whether to the government, to other men, to the Church, or to anyone they owe.

7 Render therefore to all their dues [*give to everyone that which is properly due them*]: tribute [*tax*] to whom tribute [*tax*] is due; custom [*income*] to whom custom [*income is due*]; fear [*respect*] to whom fear [*respect is due*]; honour to whom honour.

**JST Romans 13:7**
7 But first, render to all their dues, according to custom, tribute to whom tribute, custom to whom custom, that your consecrations may be done in fear of him to whom fear belongs, and in honor of him to whom honor belongs.

8 Owe no man any thing [*don't let any debts remain outstanding or unpaid*], but to love one another [*except for the ongoing debt of loving one another*]: for he that loveth another hath fulfilled the law [*the whole purpose of the laws and commandments is to teach us to love one another*].

**JST Romans 13:8**
8 Therefore owe no man anything, but to love one another; for he that loveth another hath fulfilled the law.

9 For this [*the purpose of all the commandments, including*], Thou shalt not commit adultery, Thou shalt not kill, Thou shalt not steal, Thou shalt not bear false witness, Thou shalt not covet; and if there be any other commandment, it [*their purpose*] is briefly comprehended [*can be briefly summarized*] in this saying, namely, Thou shalt love thy neighbour as thyself.

10 Love worketh no ill to his neighbour [*if you truly love other people, you will do them no harm*]: therefore [*this is why*] love is the fulfilling of the law [*this is why you are fulfilling the laws of the gospel when you show love toward others*].

11 And that, knowing the time, that now it is high time to awake out of sleep [*it is time to wake up to the urgency of keeping the commandments*]: for now is our salvation nearer than when we believed [*we have more accountability now than when we first joined the Church*].

12 The night is far spent, the day is at hand: let us therefore cast off the works of darkness [*let us repent of our sins*], and let us put on the armour of light [*and put on the protection of the gospel light*].

13 Let us walk honestly [*let us behave decently; see Romans 13:13, footnote a*], as in the day; not in rioting [*wild parties in the night*] and drunkenness, not in chambering [*sleeping around, bed-hopping, as in sexual immorality*] and

wantonness [*whoredoms, lustfulness*], not in strife [*contention, arguing*] and envying [*jealousy*].

14 But put ye on the Lord Jesus Christ [*put on the full armor or protection of Christ and His gospel*], and make not provision for the flesh [*don't keep thinking of ways to satisfy your desires for sin and the lustful tendencies of your physical bodies*], to fulfil the lusts thereof.

> **JST Romans 13:14**
> 14 But put ye on the Lord Jesus Christ, and make not provision for the flesh, to gratify the lusts thereof.

# ROMANS 14

There is a great lesson for us in Paul's teaching about "doubtful disputations" in the next verses. "Doubtful disputations" are arguing, debating, criticizing, judging one another, and so forth, over trivial things and personal preferences. Often, members become critical of each other in such less significant or "doubtful" matters. For example, one member likes whole wheat bread, another prefers white bread, one prefers honey as a sweetener, another enjoys white sugar. One member finds great value in herbs and prefers mainly a vegetarian diet while another seems to enjoy and devour about anything that gets in the path of his knife and fork. Paul counsels members not to get caught up in the sin of being critical of each other in matters of individual preference, especially in reference to new members of the Church, whose preferences and tastes, over time, may well grow to reflect the finer details of scriptural counsel. Ultimately, this is a chapter counseling us not to judge one another unrighteously (compare with JST Matthew 7:1–2).

1 HIM that is weak in the faith receive ye, but not to doubtful disputations [*don't be critical of likes and preferences, etc., which are not priority at this point in their gospel progression*].

2 For one believeth that he may eat all things: another, who is weak, eateth herbs.

3 Let not him that eateth [*let not the member who likes to eat about anything and everything*] despise him that eateth not [*be critical of a member who is very choosy and particular about what he eats*]; and let not him which eateth not judge him that eateth [*on the other hand, the picky eater should avoid criticizing the member who eats everything*]: for God hath received him [*God accepts both types in His Church*].

4 Who art thou that judgest another man's servant? [*In other words, who are you to judge the Lord's servants who answer to Him, not you?*] to his own master he standeth or falleth [*it is the Master's job to judge His servants, not your job*]. Yea, he shall be holden up [*each of us is helped and supported by God, despite our weaknesses*]: for God is able to make him stand [*God is capable of helping each of us to come unto Him*].

5 One man esteemeth one day above another [*one convert considers special days under the Law of Moses to still be special*]: another esteemeth every day alike [*another convert considers each day to be a day dedicated to God's work*]. Let every man be fully persuaded in his own mind [*allow each person to act according to the convictions in his own mind*].

6 He that regardeth the day, regardeth it unto the Lord [*the person who considers a particular day to have religious significance, has his mind on the Lord that day*]; and he that regardeth not the day, to the Lord he doth not regard it [*but the member who no longer considers it to be a religious holiday (because it pertained to the Law of Moses), no longer*

*celebrates it as a special holy day*]. He that eateth [*he who eats everything (verses 2 and 3*), eateth to the Lord, for he giveth God thanks [*remembers the Lord and gives Him thanks as he eats*]; and he that eateth not [*he who doesn't eat everything, rather eats herbs* [*verses 2 and 3*], to the Lord he eateth not, and giveth God thanks [*even though there are many things he won't eat, he still gives thanks to the Lord for what he does eat*].

7 For none of us liveth to himself, and no man dieth to himself. [*We are not alone. We all need and receive God's help.*]

8 For whether [*if*] we live, we live unto the Lord; and whether [*if*] we die, we die unto the Lord: whether we live therefore, or die, we are the Lord's. [*Whether we live or die, we all belong to the Lord.*]

9 For to this end [*for this purpose*] Christ both died, and rose, and revived [*came back to life; was resurrected*], that he might be Lord both of the dead and living. [*Christ performed the Atonement in order to have all people be accountable to Him so He can help everyone and be everyone's judge.*]

10 But why dost thou judge thy brother [*So, why would any of you take it upon yourselves to judge one another*]? or why dost thou set at nought thy brother [*or why do you criticize each other and put each other down*]? for we shall all stand before the judgment seat of Christ.

11 For it is written [*in Isaiah 45:23*], As I live, saith the Lord, every knee shall bow to me, and every tongue shall confess to God. [*In other words, Christ is the final judge (see John 5:22) and everyone will ultimately acknowledge that Jesus is the Christ, whether or not they accept His gospel. See D&C 76:110.*]

**JST Romans 14:11**

11 For I live, saith the Lord, as it is written. And every knee shall bow to me, and every tongue shall swear to God.

12 So then every one of us shall give account of himself to God [*all of us will ultimately give an accounting of our lives to God. He, Christ will be our judge (John 5:22)*].

13 Let us not therefore judge one another any more: but judge this rather [*but judge ourselves on the following very important matter, namely*], that no man put a stumblingblock or an occasion to fall in his brother's way [*that we do not do things that would cause others to be less faithful to God or cause them harm or trouble of any kind*].

14 I know, and am persuaded by the Lord Jesus, that there is nothing unclean of itself: but to him that esteemeth any thing to be unclean, to him it is unclean. [*In other words, I realize that food, in and of itself, is neither clean nor unclean. But if a member considers certain foods to be unclean, then to him it is unclean. It is just that simple.*]

Paul gives some very wise counsel in verses 15–23, next. We would all do well to avoid offending new members or weak members or nonmembers by eating or drinking things which they believe "Mormons" don't use, even though they are a matter of personal choice rather than right or wrong. For instance, many members do not drink cola drinks, but many do. A faithful member can still get a temple recommend in spite of drinking cola drinks because the recommend questions do not prohibit cola drinks. However, a new convert or a nonmember might be offended or confused or bothered that a long-time member drinks such drinks. Another example might be that if you are eating at a restaurant with a Jewish friend, it would be insensitive for you to order pork and eat it in his presence. Paul counsels us to be sensitive and to do our best not

to offend or damage someone else's view of the Church by indulging in things which might offend. See especially verse 21.

15 But if thy brother be grieved with thy meat [*if an acquaintance is bothered from a religious standpoint by your choice of food*], now walkest thou not charitably [*you are not being charitable if you eat it in front of him*]. Destroy not him with thy meat [*don't destroy his respect for the Church and perhaps his potential testimony by your insensitive choice of food in his presence*], for whom Christ died. [*In other words, don't undo Christ's work to save him or her by your choice of foods around them.*]

**JST Romans 14:15**

15 But if thy brother be grieved with thy meat, thou walkest not charitably if thou eatest. Therefore destroy not him with thy meat, for whom Christ died.

16 Let not then your good be evil spoken of: [*Don't undo the good you can do by being unwise or insensitive in such matters.*]

17 For the kingdom of God is not meat and drink; but righteousness, and peace, and joy in the Holy Ghost. [*The ultimate focus of the kingdom of God is not on food or drink, but on personal righteousness, peace and joy from following the promptings of the Holy Ghost.*]

18 For he that in these things serveth Christ is acceptable to God, and approved of men. [*If you follow my counsel in these matters, you will be serving Christ, you will be acceptable to God and won't be offending others unnecessarily.*]

19 Let us therefore follow after the things which make for peace [*lets do everything we can to promote peace*], and things wherewith one may edify another [*and do things which build and strengthen one another*].

Just a reminder that the word "meat," as used by Paul in these verses, means "food." The word "flesh" is used in the Bible when referring to what we call meat, such as chicken, beef, lamb, etc.

20 For [*because of*] meat [*your choices of food*] destroy not the work of God [*don't destroy God's work with people by being insensitive about your choice of foods around them*]. All things indeed are pure [*all food is clean, since that part of the Law of Moses, Leviticus 14, is no longer in effect*] ; but it is evil for that man who eateth with offence [*but it is evil to offend people with insensitive choices of food in their presence*].

21 It is good [*better*] neither to eat flesh [*meat*], nor to drink wine, nor any thing whereby thy brother stumbleth, or is offended, or is made weak. [*It is better not to eat or drink anything, in the presence of others, which might weaken their testimony or commitment to God. In other words, don't offend others needlessly!*]

22 Hast thou faith? have it to thyself before God. [*If you have faith in the gospel of Christ, such that the dietary restrictions in the Law of Moses are no longer part of your life, keep it to yourself and between you and God, rather than offending others.*] Happy is he that condemneth not himself in that thing which he alloweth. [*You will be happier if you don't condemn yourself by offending others unnecessarily.*]

23 And he that doubteth is damned if he eat, because he eateth not of faith: for whatsoever is not of faith is sin. [*In other words, if a new member were to eat something forbidden by the Law of Moses, and doesn't yet have enough faith in the gospel of Christ to be convinced that the dietary laws of old are done away with, it could weaken his determination to follow God and thus stop his progress.*]

**JST Romans 14:23**

23 And he that doubteth is condemned if he eat, because it is not of faith; for whatsoever is not of faith is sin.

# ROMANS 15

As Paul begins to bring his letter to the Saints in Rome to a close (written from Corinth—see Bible Dictionary under "Pauline Epistles," "Epistle to the Romans"), he reminds them that the strong ought to support and help the weak in the Church. Among other things, he acknowledges that he has written very boldly to them (verse 15), and once again reminds them that the Gentile converts to the Church are entitled to every blessing of the gospel, through their faithfulness to the promptings of the Holy Ghost (verse 16). He tells them that he will now head for Jerusalem (verse 25) which will bring to a close his third missionary journey which has taken about three and a half years.

Once again, in this chapter, we see that Paul knew the Old Testament very well and was a master at using specific verses, with which the Jews would be familiar because of their upbringing in the tradition of the Law of Moses, to teach them the gospel of Jesus Christ. Here, he will especially use Old Testament prophesy to drive home the point to these Jewish converts that the Gentiles are to have the full gospel too.

1 WE then that are strong [*in the gospel*] ought to bear [*be patient with*] the infirmities [*shortcomings, weaknesses*] of the weak, and not to please ourselves [*not only be interested in our own needs*].

2 Let every one of us please [*be sensitive to the needs of*] his neighbour for his good to edification [*to build him up in the gospel*].

3 For even Christ pleased not himself [*did not give in to His own needs*]; but, as it is written [*in Psalm 69:9*], The reproaches of them that reproached thee fell on me [*the insults and caustic criticisms aimed at you came upon Me*].

4 For whatsoever things were written aforetime were written for our learning, that we through patience and comfort of the scriptures might have hope. [*Since ancient times, the scriptures have encouraged us to learn patience with others so that we might have hope of salvation ourselves.*]

5 Now the God of patience and consolation [*comfort*] grant you to be likeminded [*patient*] one toward another according to Christ Jesus [*like Jesus was with us*]:

**JST Romans 15:5**

5 Now the God of patience and consolation grant you to be likeminded one toward another according as was Christ Jesus;

6 That ye may with one mind and one mouth [*with unity*] glorify God, even the Father of our Lord Jesus Christ.

7 Wherefore receive ye one another [*accept one another with patience*], as Christ [*with great patience*] also received us to the glory of God.

As previously mentioned, the phrase "the circumcision" in Paul's writings means "the Jewish converts to the Church." We see this phrase in verse 8, next.

8 Now I say that Jesus Christ was a minister of the circumcision [*Jesus Christ was sent by the Father as a minister to the Jews*] for the truth of God, to confirm [*fulfill*] the promises made unto the fathers [*our ancestors*]:

9 And that the Gentiles [*the non-Jews*] might glorify [*be able to praise*] God for his mercy; as it is written [*in Psalm 18:49*], For this cause I will confess to thee among the Gentiles, and sing unto thy name. [*In other words, it was*

*prophesied that the gospel would be taken to the Gentiles too.*]

10 And again he saith [*in Deuteronomy 32:43*], Rejoice, ye Gentiles, with his people. [*The faithful Gentiles will join with the faithful covenant people and all will be the Lord's people in exaltation.*]

11 And again [*in Psalm 117:1*], Praise the Lord, all ye Gentiles; and laud him, all ye people.

12 And again, Esaias saith [*Isaiah prophesied, recorded in Isaiah 11:10*], There shall be a root of Jesse [*a descendant of Jesse (David's father), in other words, Christ; see Romans 15:12, footnote b*], and he that shall rise to reign over the Gentiles; in him shall the Gentiles trust [*the Gentiles will be brought into Christ's gospel*].

13 Now the God of hope fill you with all joy and peace in believing, that ye may abound in hope [*that you may have abundant hope*], through the power of the Holy Ghost.

14 And I myself also am persuaded of you, my brethren, that ye also are full of goodness, filled with all knowledge, able also to admonish one another. [*I am convinced by what I hear of you that you are wonderful Saints and are helping and strengthening each other.*]

15 Nevertheless, brethren, I have written the more boldly unto you in some sort, as putting you in mind, because of the grace that is given to me of God, [*Nevertheless, I have been quite blunt in what I have written you in this letter because of the responsibility God has given me.*]

16 That I should be the minister of Jesus Christ to the Gentiles [*namely, that I have been called to take the gospel to the Gentiles*], ministering the gospel of God, that the offering up of the Gentiles might be acceptable [*in order that the Gentiles might know the gospel too, and be able to live it*], being sanctified by the Holy Ghost [*"sanctified" means being made holy and fit to be in the presence of God by being led by the Gift of the Holy Ghost as members of the Church*].

17 I have therefore whereof I may glory through Jesus Christ in those things which pertain to God. [*I have great joy in the Savior and His teachings which point us to the Father.*]

18 For I will not dare to speak of any of those things which Christ hath not wrought by me [*I will not venture to speak of anything at this time except what Christ has accomplished, using me as His instrument*], to make the Gentiles obedient, by word and deed [*to bring the gospel to the Gentiles, so that they might be obedient to God in word as well as in their actions*],

19 Through mighty signs and wonders, by the power of the Spirit of God [*the Spirit of God has prepared the way and performed many miracles during my missionary journeys*]; so that from Jerusalem, and round about unto Illyricum [*all the way from Jerusalem through the eastern coast of the Adriatic Sea*], I have fully preached the gospel of Christ.

20 Yea, so have I strived to preach the gospel, not where Christ was named [*it has been my desire to preach the gospel in places where people hadn't even heard of Christ*], lest I should build upon another man's foundation [*because I didn't want to build upon what others had already started*]:

21 But as it is written [*you are familiar with what Isaiah said, in Isaiah 52:15, where he prophesied*], To whom he [*Christ*] was not spoken of, they shall see [*the gospel will be taken to people to whom Christ did not go*]: and they that have not heard shall understand [*and they who have never heard of Christ shall someday understand His gospel*].

22 For which cause also I have been much hindered from coming to you [*because of my involvement in taking*

*the gospel to the Gentiles, I have experienced many delays in coming to visit you in Rome*].

23 But now having no more place in these parts [*but now that I am no longer traveling and preaching in all those areas*], and having a great desire these many years to come unto you [*and having desired to visit you for many years*];

24 Whensoever I take my journey into Spain, I will come to you [*when I finally get on my way to Spain, I will stop by and visit you*]: for I trust to see you in my journey, and to be brought on my way thitherward [*toward Spain*] by you, if first I be somewhat filled with your company.

**JST Romans 15:24**
24 When I take my journey into Spain, I will come to you; for I trust to see you in my journey, and to be brought on my way thitherward by you, if first I be somewhat filled through your prayers.

25 But now I go unto Jerusalem to minister unto the Saints.

26 For it hath pleased them of Macedonia and Achaia to make a certain contribution for the poor Saints which are at Jerusalem. [*The members in northern and southern Greece have gathered a donation for the poverty-stricken Saints in Jerusalem.*]

27 It hath pleased them verily [*they were very pleased to gather up this donation*]; and their debtors they are [*and indeed they owe it to the Saints in Jerusalem*]. For if the Gentiles have been made partakers of their spiritual things, their duty is also to minister unto them in carnal things. [*Since the gospel came to the Gentiles through the Jews and Christ's ministry among them, the Gentiles certainly have a responsibility to help the Jewish Saints in their physical or temporal needs.*]

28 When therefore I have performed this, and have sealed to them this fruit [*after I have personally delivered the donation to the Saints in Jerusalem*], I will come by you into Spain [*I will come to you, and then go on to Spain from Rome*].

29 And I am sure that, when I come unto you, I shall come in the fulness of the blessing of the gospel of Christ.

30 Now I beseech you [*I have an urgent request*], brethren, for the Lord Jesus Christ's sake, and for the love of the Spirit, that ye strive together [*join together*] with me in your prayers to God for me;

31 That I may be delivered from them that do not believe in Judea [*that I be protected from those unbelievers in Judea and Jerusalem who want to arrest me*]; and that my service [*so that the contributions from the Saints in Greece*] which I have for Jerusalem may be accepted of the Saints [*might get into the hands of the Saints in Jerusalem*];

32 That I may come unto you with joy by the will of God, and may with you be refreshed.

33 Now the God of peace be with you all. Amen.

# ROMANS 16

As Paul finishes his letter to the members of the Church in Rome, he sends greetings to a number of individuals and leaves some final counsel about avoiding people who cause contention.

1 I COMMEND [*introduce and recommend*] unto you Phebe our sister, which is a servant [*a faithful member*] of the church which is at Cenchrea [*a city in the eastern harbor of Corinth*]: [*Paul is writing this letter to the Roman Saints from Corinth (in what today is in southern Greece) and Phebe is the one who carries it in person to the members*

*in Rome. See note in your King James Bible at the end of Romans 16.*]

2 That ye receive her in the Lord, as becometh saints [*please accept her among you as proper Saints would do*], and that ye assist her in whatsoever business she hath need of you [*and help her in whatever her needs are*]: for she hath been a succourer of many, and of myself also [*she has assisted many here in Corinth, including me*].

The word "succor," a form of which is used in verse 2, above, means "to hurry to help another."

3 Greet Priscilla and Aquila [*Priscilla is Aquila's wife*] my helpers in Christ Jesus:

4 Who have for my life laid down their own necks [*who risked their necks for me and many other members*]: unto whom not only I give thanks, but also all the churches [*wards and branches*] of the Gentiles.

5 Likewise greet the church [*the members*] that is in their house [*who meet in their home*]. Salute [*give my greetings to*] my wellbeloved Epænetus, who is the firstfruits of Achaia unto Christ [*who was the first convert to the Church in southern Greece*].

6 Greet Mary, who bestowed much labour on us.

7 Salute [*greet*] Andronicus and Junia, my kinsmen [*my relatives*], and my fellowprisoners [*who spent some time in prison with me*], who are of note among the apostles [*who are well known by the Apostles*], who also were in Christ before me [*who were converted to Christ before I was*].

8 Greet Amplias my beloved in the Lord.

9 Salute Urbane, our helper in Christ, and Stachys my beloved [*my dear friend*].

10 Salute Apelles approved in Christ [*who has proven faithful*]. Salute them which are of Aristobulus' household.

**JST Romans 16:10**

10 Salute Apelles approved in Christ. Salute them which are of Aristobulus' church.

11 Salute Herodion my kinsman [*relative*]. Greet them that be of the household of Narcissus, which are in the Lord [*who are members of the Church*].

**JST Romans 16:11**

11 Salute Herodian my kinsman. Greet them that be of the church of Narcissus, which are in the Lord.

12 Salute Tryphena and Tryphosa [*faithful women*], who labour in the Lord. Salute the beloved Persis [*another faithful sister*], which laboured much in the Lord.

13 Salute [*greet*] Rufus chosen in the Lord, and his mother and mine [*and his mother who is like a mother to me too*].

14 Salute Asyncritus, Phlegon, Hermas, Patrobas, Hermes, and the brethren which are with them.

15 Salute Philologus, and Julia, Nereus, and his sister, and Olympas, and all the saints which are with them.

16 Salute [*greet*] one another with an holy kiss. The churches of Christ salute you [*the members in other wards and branches of the Church send their greetings to you*].

**JST Romans 16:16**

16 Salute one another with a holy salutation. The churches of Christ salute you.

Next, Paul urges the members of the Church to avoid those who cause contention.

17 Now I beseech [*urge*] you, brethren, mark them which [*take note of those who*] cause divisions and offences contrary to the doctrine which ye have learned; and avoid them.

18 For they that are such [*those who cause contention*] serve not our Lord Jesus Christ, but their own belly [*their*

*own appetites and selfish interests*]; and by good words [*smooth talk*] and fair speeches [*flattery*] deceive the hearts of the simple [*the naive, easy to deceive*].

19 For your obedience is come abroad unto all men [*your reputation for being obedient is known far and wide*]. I am glad therefore on your behalf [*I have had much reason to be happy because of you*]: but yet I would have you wise unto that which is good, and simple concerning evil [*I still want to remind you to always be on guard to do good and avoid evil*].

20 And the God of peace shall bruise Satan under your feet shortly [*God will ultimately give you power over Satan and his influence*]. The grace of our Lord Jesus Christ be with you. Amen.

21 Timotheus [*Timothy, the one to whom Paul will later write two letters, known today as 1 and 2 Timothy*] my workfellow [*my companion*], and Lucius, and Jason, and Sosipater, my kinsmen [*my relatives*], salute you.

22 I Tertius [*Paul's scribe*], who wrote this epistle [*who wrote down this letter as Paul dictated it*], salute [*greet*] you in the Lord.

23 Gaius mine host, and of the whole church [*who has hosted us and the whole church here in Corinth*], saluteth [*greets*] you. Erastus the chamberlain of the city [*the city manager*] saluteth you, and Quartus a brother.

24 The grace [*help, mercy, and kindness*] of our Lord Jesus Christ be with you all. Amen.

Verses 25–27 can be confusing. If you look closely, you will see that they are one long sentence, with all kinds of clauses and phrases. If you were to take all the modifying clauses and phrases out, you would have, basically, "Now to him (the Father)," at the beginning of verse 25. . ." be glory through Christ and his gospel," at the end of verse 27.

By the way, as you compare verse 25 in the Bible to the JST verse 25, you will see that Joseph Smith changed the wording from "my gospel" in the Bible, to "the gospel" in the JST, because it is not Paul's gospel.

25 Now to him [*God*] that is of power to stablish you [*who has power to save you and establish you in his kingdom*] according to my gospel, and the preaching of Jesus Christ [*according to the gospel which Christ preached*], according to the revelation of the mystery [*Christ himself was a revelation from God, which to many remains a mystery*], which was kept secret since the world began [*which, unfortunately, many have remained unaware of since the beginning of history*],

**JST Romans 16:25**

25 Now to him that is of power to stablish you according to the gospel, and the preaching of Jesus Christ, according to the revelation of the mystery, which was kept secret since the world began,

26 But now is made manifest [*but now Jesus has come*], and by the scriptures of the prophets [*just as prophesied by ancient prophets*], according to the commandment of the everlasting God, made known to all nations [*being preached to all nations, Jew and Gentile*] for the obedience of faith [*to make obedience available to everyone who has faith in Jesus Christ*]:

27 To God only wise, be glory through Jesus Christ for ever. Amen.

# The First Epistle of Paul the Apostle to the Corinthians

This letter from the Apostle Paul to the members of the Church in Corinth [*in southern Greece today*], was probably written from Philippi [*in northeastern Greece*], probably in March or April of AD 57. Corinth was a wealthy commercial center, with ideas, philosophies, and religions from both East and West. Idol worship dominated the area, with 12 different temples in the city of Corinth alone. Sexual immorality was rampant everywhere. The people engaged in prostitution as part of their worship ceremonies in the temple of Aphrodite. In fact, leaders encouraged sexual immorality and other immoral behavior. Paul wrote three letters to the Corinthian Saints. We don't have the first one, referred to in 1 Corinthians 5:9. Thus, First Corinthians is actually the second letter Paul wrote to them. In it he responds to several issues and questions they asked him in the letter they sent to him in reply to his first (see 1 Corinthians 7:1).

Paul established the Church in Corinth during his second missionary journey, about AD 50. He had lived in Corinth himself for about a year and a half (see Acts 18:8–11).

## First Corinthians 1

Paul begins his letter by greeting the Saints at Corinth and greets them for members all over the Church. He will then teach these members to avoid contention and seek to be unified in the gospel. From his letter, we see that some apostasy had already made its way into the Church at Corinth.

1 PAUL, called to be an apostle of Jesus Christ through the will of God, and Sosthenes our brother [*Sosthenes, who was a member of the Church, had been publically beaten because of his association with Paul; see Acts 18:17*],

**JST 1 Corinthians 1:1**

1 Paul, an apostle, called of Jesus Christ through the will of God; and Sosthenes our brother,

2 Unto the church of God which is at Corinth, to them that are sanctified in [*Strong's #0037; who have dedicated themselves to*] Christ Jesus, called to be saints [*holy ones*], with all that in every place [*along with all other Saints who*] call upon the name of Jesus Christ our Lord, both theirs and ours [*their Lord and our Lord*]:

3 Grace be unto you, and peace, from God our Father, and from the Lord Jesus Christ.

Verse 3, above, is another good reminder that the Father and Son are separate individuals.

4 I thank my God always on your behalf, for the grace of God which is given you by Jesus Christ [*I give thanks constantly for the gospel and the Atonement, which the Father has given you through Jesus Christ*];

The only change made by Joseph Smith in both verses 4 and 5 was to change "by" to "of." We included these JST verses as a testimony that the Prophet paid much inspired attention to detail.

**JST 1 Corinthians 1:4**

4 I thank my God always on your behalf, for the grace of God which is given you of Jesus Christ;

5 That in every thing ye are enriched by
him, in all utterance, and in all knowledge [*which enriches and blesses every
aspect of your lives*];

**JST 1 Corinthians 1:5**

5 That in everything ye are enriched of him, in all utterance, and in all knowledge;

6 Even as the testimony of Christ was
confirmed [*strengthened*] in you:

7 So that ye come behind in no gift [*so
that you do not lack any spiritual gifts*];
waiting for the coming of our Lord
Jesus Christ:

8 Who shall also confirm you [*strengthen
you, make you strong and stable*] unto
the end, that ye may be blameless in the
day of our Lord Jesus Christ. [*Verses 7
and 8 are basically saying that you have
all that is necessary so that you can prepare to appear before Christ and have a
pleasant judgment day.*]

9 God is faithful [*you can rely on God*],
by whom ye were called unto the fellowship of his Son Jesus Christ our Lord
[*who called you to join with His son
Jesus Christ and be saved*].

10 Now I beseech you, brethren, by the
name of our Lord Jesus Christ, that ye
all speak the same thing [*stay true to the
gospel*], and that there be no divisions
among you [*that you don't start falling
away from the Church*]; but that ye be
perfectly joined together in the same
mind and in the same judgment [*that
you stick absolutely with the gospel that
we taught you*].

**JST 1 Corinthians 1:10**

10 Now I beseech you, brethren, in the name of our Lord Jesus Christ, that ye all speak the same thing, and that there be no divisions among you; but that ye be perfectly joined together in the same mind and in the same judgment.

11 For it hath been declared unto me of
you, my brethren, by them which are of
the house of Chloe, that there are contentions among you [*I have been told
by members of Chloe's household that
there are arguments among you as to
Church doctrines*].

All of the men mentioned along with the Savior in verse 12, next, were faithful members of the Church. Paul is warning the Saints against becoming part of splinter groups who break off from the true Church, using as their excuse that they prefer one leader or another in the Church.

12 Now this I say, that every one of you
saith [*I understand that some among you
are saying*], I am of Paul [*I follow Paul*];
and I of Apollos [*I follow Apollos (a
learned member of the Church; see Acts
18:24–19:5)*]; and I of Cephas [*I follow
Peter*]; and I of Christ [*I follow Jesus*].

**JST 1 Corinthians 1:12**

12 Now this I say, that many of you saith, I am of Paul; and I of Apollos; and I of Cephas; and I of Christ.

What Paul says next is strong evidence for the fact that there is one true church. Different churches with different doctrines cannot all lead to celestial glory and exaltation.

13 Is Christ divided [*What's going on
here? Did Christ preach several conflicting doctrines*]? was Paul crucified
for you? or were ye baptized in the name
of Paul? [*In other words, whose church
is this?*]

14 I thank God that I baptized none of
you, but Crispus and Gaius;

15 Lest any should say that I had baptized in mine own name. [*This is strong*

*language. Paul sounds disgusted that these members are so caught up in divisive arguing and doctrinal bickering that they are in danger of falling away from the Church.*]

16 And I baptized also the household of Stephanas: besides, I know not whether I baptized any other. [*I can't remember whether or not I personally baptized any others there in Corinth.*]

17 For Christ sent me not to baptize [*Christ didn't send me to baptize people in my own name to get converts for my church*], but to preach the gospel: not with wisdom of words [*not with the wisdom of man*], lest the cross of Christ should be made of none effect [*which would make the sacrifices required by Christ's gospel ineffective*].

18 For the preaching of the cross is to them that perish foolishness [*the gospel of Christ appears foolish to unbelievers*]; but unto us which are saved [*the Greek language gives this phrase as "to us who are being saved"*] it is the power of God.

> "We believe the Bible to be the word of God as far as it is translated correctly" (Article of Faith number 8). The phrase "unto us which are saved," in verse 18, above, appears to be one of those places where the Bible wording was deliberately changed to reflect the idea of predestination. It includes the idea that one can confess believing in Christ and thus be saved, with no other thoughts or concerns about salvation. In the original Greek, from which our New Testament was translated, this phrase clearly said "being saved," indicating an ongoing process of effort and learning, rather than "are saved," which could indicate no further concern about being saved in heaven.

19 For it is written [*in Isaiah 29:14*], I will destroy the wisdom of the wise, and will bring to nothing the understanding of the prudent. [*In other words, the pure gospel of Jesus Christ will expose false teachings, false philosophies, etc., and destroy them in the minds of faithful Saints so they are not led astray by such things.*]

20 Where is the wise? where is the scribe [*scribes were the religious scholars among the Jews who interpreted the scriptures and came up with all kinds of false doctrines*]? where is the disputer [*debater, scholar*] of this world? hath not God made foolish the wisdom of this world? [*In other words, hasn't the true gospel exposed the foolishness of man-made doctrines and philosophies*]?

21 For after that in the wisdom of God the world by wisdom knew not God [*since God has allowed people agency to follow man-made wisdom and make up their own false teachings to the point that they do not even believe in him*], it pleased God by the foolishness of preaching to save them that believe [*it pleased God to use what many worldly-wise people call "foolish preaching" of Christ to save those who will believe*] .

22 For the Jews require a sign [*the Jews always seem to say "show me a sign" to prove the gospel of Christ*], and the Greeks seek after wisdom [*and the Gentiles seem to always want to compare the gospel to their man-made philosophies to see if they should believe in Christ*]:

> Just a reminder, as stated previously, the word "Greek" is generally used here as a generic term for "Gentiles" no matter where the Gentiles mentioned live.

23 But we preach Christ crucified, unto the Jews a stumblingblock [*we preach the simple truth about the Savior's Atonement, and the Jews stumble all over it because Jesus didn't keep the Law of Moses*], and unto the Greeks foolishness [*and the Gentiles think our gospel teaching is foolish because it doesn't fit into their man-made false philosophies*];

24 But unto them which are called,

both Jews and Greeks [*Gentiles*], Christ the power of God, and the wisdom of God [*Christ represents the power and wisdom of the Father*].

> **JST 1 Corinthians 1:24**
> 24 But unto them who believe [*in other words, to those who are converted to Christ*], both Jews and Greeks, Christ the power of God, and the wisdom of God.

25 Because the foolishness of God is wiser than men [*the most foolish-looking aspect of God's teaching is wiser than the most impressive wisdom men can come up with*]; and the weakness of God is stronger than men. [*In other words, the wisdom of men can't even begin to compare with the wisdom of God.*]

26 For ye see your calling, brethren, how that not many wise men after the flesh, not many mighty, not many noble, are called: [*You see, with the perspective you have as members of the Church, that very few men who are wise, powerful, and high in society, in the eyes of the world, accept the gospel of Christ.*]

> **JST 1 Corinthians 1:26**
> 26 For ye see your calling, brethren, how that not many wise men after the flesh, not many mighty, not many noble, are chosen [*to preach the gospel (see verse 27) and ultimately to receive the blessings of the gospel because they choose not to accept it*];

27 But God hath chosen the foolish things of the world [*the humble Saints, whose beliefs look foolish and whose intellect appears weak to the so-called "wise" of the world*] to confound [*to successfully stand up to*] the wise; and God hath chosen the weak things of the world to confound the things [*the people*] which are mighty;

> **JST 1 Corinthians 1:27**
> 27 For God hath chosen the foolish things of the world to confound the wise; and God hath chosen the weak things of the world to confound the things which are mighty;

28 And base things of the world [*the lowly, simple, humble people, whom scholars, intellectuals, philosophers, etc., consider to be naive, unintelligent, so simple they can be easily led around without thinking*], and things which [*people who*] are despised, hath God chosen [*to be in His Church and to lead His Church*], yea [*indeed*], and things [*people*] which are not [*people whom the worldly wise consider to be nothing are chosen by God*], to bring to nought [*to destroy*] things that are: [*In other words, the humble Saints, upon whom the people of the world look down, will continue to carry the true gospel of Christ forth until it fills the whole earth (Daniel 2:35, 44–45) and until all the false, proud, arrogant teachings of the worldly-wise are put down in the light of truth.*]

> **JST 1 Corinthians 1:28**
> 28 And base things of the world, and things which are despised, hath God chosen, yea, and things which are not, to bring to naught things that are mighty;

29 That no flesh should glory in his presence [*so that no people who are arrogant and wise in their own opinion will be able to boast of themselves in the presence of God*].

30 But of him [*from the Father; in other words, because of the kindness of the Father*] are ye in Christ Jesus [*you have been brought to Christ*], who of God [*who was sent from God*] is made unto us [*who becomes our source of*] wisdom, and righteousness, and sanctification [*salvation*], and redemption [*being saved from our sins and the false philosophies of the world*]:

31 That, according as it is written [*in Jeremiah 9:24*], He that glorieth, let him glory in the Lord. [*In other words, because we have the true gospel, we can take pleasure and satisfaction

*in glorious truths from the Lord, rather than getting caught up in man-made philosophies and false worldly doctrines*]

# FIRST CORINTHIANS 2

Paul begins here by humbly confessing that he was very concerned by his lack of speaking and teaching ability when he first came to Corinth as a missionary on his second major missionary journey. He goes on to write a powerful sermon to these members of the Church in Corinth, teaching that the Holy Ghost is the real teacher when the gospel is preached. You may well recognize some verses here which are often quoted in sermons and lessons today. They include verses 9, 11, and 14.

1 AND I, brethren, when I came to you [*in Corinth*], came not with excellency of speech [*as a skilled speaker*] or of wisdom [*or with a lot of worldly wisdom*], declaring unto you the testimony of God [*as I taught you the gospel of Jesus Christ*].

2 For I determined not to know any thing among you, save Jesus Christ, and him crucified. [*Indeed, I kept my message very simple, focusing only on teaching you about Jesus and His Atonement.*]

3 And I was with you in weakness [*my weaknesses and imperfections were obvious to you and to me*], and in fear, and in much trembling.

4 And my speech and my preaching was not with enticing words of man's wisdom [*I did not use cunning, flattering words to teach you man's wisdom*], but in demonstration of the Spirit and of power [*rather, I came with the Holy Ghost and power of God*]:

5 That your faith should not stand in the wisdom of men [*so that your faith in Christ would not be based on the wisdom of men, intellectual, academic, etc.*], but in the power of God.

6 Howbeit [*however*] we speak wisdom among them that are perfect [*however, the spiritually mature among you will recognize the great wisdom contained in the gospel*]: yet not the wisdom of this world, nor of the princes [*leaders*] of this world, that come to nought: [*The wisdom contained in the gospel is not the wisdom of the world, which will ultimately come to nothing.*]

7 But we speak the wisdom of God in a mystery [*the wisdom of God and His teachings remain a mystery to unbelievers*], even the hidden wisdom [*the wisdom, the gospel, which is hidden from the worldly by their own unbelief*], which God ordained before the world unto our glory [*which the Father prepared for us clear back before the world was created to bring us back to Him in glory*]:

8 Which none of the princes [*the unbelieving leaders*] of this world knew [*accepted*]: for had they known [*accepted*] it, they would not have crucified the Lord of glory [*Jesus*].

9 But as it is written [*in Isaiah 64:4*], Eye hath not seen, nor ear heard, neither have entered into the heart of man, the things which God hath prepared for them that love him [*it is impossible to imagine the wonderful blessings the Father has in store for those who love Him enough to keep His commandments and thus return to live with Him someday*].

10 But God hath revealed them unto us by his Spirit [*God does reveal these things to us by the power of the Holy Ghost*]: for the Spirit searcheth [*helps us explore, investigate*] all things, yea, the deep things of God.

11 For what man knoweth the things of a man, save the spirit of man which is in him? even so the things of God knoweth no man, but the Spirit of God. [*In effect,*

*we understand other people because we are human, but we can only understand the things of God and gain a testimony of Him through the Holy Ghost.*]

**JST 1 Corinthians 2:11**

11 For what man knoweth the things of a man, save the spirit of man which is in him? even so the things of God knoweth no man, except he has the Spirit of God.

12 Now we [*as members of the Church*] have received, not the spirit of the world [*not the understanding which comes through worldly wisdom*], but the spirit which is of God [*rather, the understanding which comes from the Holy Ghost*]; that we might know [*understand and have testimonies of*] the things that are freely given to us of God.

13 Which things also we speak [*preach, teach*], not in the words which man's wisdom teacheth [*we don't use worldly vocabulary and wisdom to teach the gospel*], but which the Holy Ghost teacheth [*rather, we use special gospel vocabulary and wisdom, accompanied by the Holy Ghost*]; comparing spiritual things with spiritual.

14 But the natural man [*unbelievers who won't listen to the Holy Ghost*] receiveth not [*won't accept*] the things of the Spirit of God: for they are foolishness unto him [*they consider the gospel of Christ to be foolishness*]: neither can he know them [*understand them through intellectual and academic methods*], because they are spiritually discerned [*they can only be examined and understood with the help of the Holy Ghost*].

15 But he that is spiritual judgeth all things [*people who are spiritual are able to see all things in the light of the gospel and with the help of the Holy Ghost*], yet he himself is judged of no man [*the only judge he has to worry about is Christ*].

16 [*Paul now quotes Isaiah 40:13*] For who hath known the mind of the Lord, that he may instruct him [*who is wise enough to teach the Lord anything*]? [*Answer: No one, so don't let the wisdom and teachings of men take priority over the teachings of God in your lives.*] But we have the mind of Christ [*we know the mind of Christ, in other words, He has taught us His mind and will, and thus we don't have to get caught up in the confusion and falseness of much of the teaching and wisdom of men*].

## FIRST CORINTHIANS 3

Paul is very straightforward (some would even say he is blunt), but it is because of his love for these new members in Corinth as he encourages them to separate themselves from the worldly philosophies and lifestyles in Corinth. He tells them that he must speak to them as he would to children who are yet immature in the Church and urges them to build their lives upon the principles of the gospel, making their lives and bodies fit for the Spirit of the Lord to dwell in.

One of the better-known quotes in this chapter, among Latter-day Saints, is that found in verses 16–17, where Paul teaches us that our bodies are temples of God.

1 AND I, brethren, could not speak unto you as unto spiritual [*I can't yet speak to you as I would to spiritually mature members*], but as unto carnal [*rather, as to converts who are yet caught up much in worldly thinking and behaving*], even as unto babes in Christ [*in fact, I must speak to you as brand new in the gospel of Christ*].

2 I have fed you with milk [*I have given you the very basics of the gospel*], and not with meat [*not with advanced doctrines*]: for hitherto ye were not able to bear it, neither yet now are ye able

[*because you have not been able to handle it up to now and, in fact, you are still not able to handle it*].

**JST 1 Corinthians 3:2**

2 I have fed you with milk, and not with meat; for hitherto ye were not able to receive it, neither yet now are ye able.

3 For ye are yet carnal [*you are still too worldly*]: for whereas [*let me tell you what I mean*] there is among you envying [*jealousy*], and strife [*contention, arguing, bickering*], and divisions [*apostasy*], are ye not carnal, and walk as men [*isn't that sufficient evidence that you are still worldly, and acting like everyone else in Corinth*]?

4 For while [*as long as*] one saith, I am of Paul; and another, I am of Apollos; [*as long as you remain separated into factions—as mentioned in 1 Corinthians 1:11–13—rather than being united, following Christ*] are ye not carnal [*are you not proving that you have not yet been spiritually reborn*]?

5 Who then is Paul [*the Apostle*], and who is Apollos [*a faithful member and excellent teacher; see Acts 18:24–28*], but ministers by whom ye believed [*aren't we (Apollos and I) just servants of the Lord who brought you the gospel*], even as the Lord gave to every man [*simply following the Lord's instructions to teach you the gospel*]?

It may seem strange to us that these converts in Corinth would be dividing up into groups, some claiming to follow Paul, some claiming to be loyal to Apollos, or Peter (chapter 1, verse 12) or whomever. But if we remember that many different idols were worshiped in Corinth and that it was common in Corinthian culture for people to choose among several available "gods" for their family or neighborhood, school or business, etc., then it becomes more understandable as to what was going on among the members and why Paul had to repeat himself so many times in trying to get them to understand the principle of one God only, and His Son, Jesus Christ.

6 I have planted [*I came along first and preached the gospel to you, planting the seeds in your minds and hearts; compare with Alma 32*], Apollos watered [*then Apollos came among you and nourished the gospel seeds in you by his excellent teaching*]; but God gave the increase [*but God is the one who made them grow*].

7 So then neither is he that planteth any thing, neither he that watereth [*the servants of the Lord who plant the gospel seeds in your hearts and nourish them by teaching you are nothing compared to God*]; but God that giveth the increase [*God is everything and must be the focus of your loyalty as He causes the seeds to grow within you*].

8 Now he that planteth and he that watereth are one [*have just one purpose, that is, to bring the gospel to others*]: and every man shall receive his own reward according to his own labour [*the Lord's servants, missionaries, teachers, and so forth are rewarded by the Lord for their labors*].

9 For we are labourers together with God [*we work in unity with God*]: ye are God's husbandry [*you are His garden*], ye are God's building [*He is growing His gospel in you*].

10 According to the grace [*kindness and help*] of God which is given unto me, as a wise masterbuilder [*God is like a wise master builder*], I have laid the foundation, and another buildeth thereon [*other servants of the Lord come along after me and build upon the foundation which I have laid, under God's direction*]. But let every man take heed how he buildeth thereupon [*each of you must be very careful how you build upon the foundation of the gospel which has been laid for you*].

11 For other foundation can no man lay

than that is laid, which is Jesus Christ. [*If you choose to build your lives upon any foundation other than Christ, you will fail.*]

12 Now if any man build upon this foundation gold, silver, precious stones, wood, hay, stubble [*if you choose to try to build upon the foundation of wealth or any material priority*];

13 Every man's work shall be made manifest [*your work will eventually be exposed for what it is*]: for the day shall declare it [*the test of time will reveal it*], because it shall be revealed by fire [*the "trial by fire" eventually reveals whether or not we have built our lives on a firm foundation or not*]; and the fire shall try [*test*] every man's work of what sort it is [*and show what it is really made of*].

14 If any man's work abide [*stands through the trial by fire, in other words, if our lives stand up to trials, troubles, persecutions, etc., and we remain loyal to our covenants and commitments to Christ*] which he hath built thereupon, he shall receive a reward [*we will be well rewarded for building upon the foundation of Jesus Christ*].

Verse 15, next, is an example of the importance of the Joseph Smith Translation of the Bible (JST). The Prophet changed just one word in this verse, but it changes the meaning dramatically. Joseph Smith changed the word "shall" to "may." This is very important because it changes the meaning of the verse from saying that people who foolishly build their lives upon material things "shall be saved" to saying that they "may be saved," if they repent when they discover that they have built upon a foundation other than Christ.

15 If any man's work shall be burned [*if the things a person has built his life around are not in harmony with the gospel and thus don't survive the trials by fire*], he shall suffer loss: but he himself shall be saved; yet so as by fire [*if he will let the Holy Ghost "burn" the sins and imperfections out of his life by inspiring him to repent and use the Atonement*].

**JST 1 Corinthians 3:15**

15 If any man's work shall be burned, he shall suffer loss; but he himself may be saved; yet so as by fire.

16 Know ye not that ye are the temple of God, and that the Spirit of God dwelleth in you [*don't you realize that you are the temple of God and should take care of your mind and body in such a way that the Holy Ghost can dwell in you and direct you constantly*]?

Remember, as mentioned in notes at the beginning of First Corinthians in this study guide, that temples were a part of everyday life in Corinth. In fact, there were twelve temples set up in that area to worship various idols. Paul is very skillfully using this background and cultural setting to remind these relatively new members of the Church that each of them can be a "temple" in which the Holy Ghost will dwell, if they will build themselves upon the foundation of Jesus Christ, thus keeping their "temples" clean.

17 If any man defile the temple of God [*makes his temple unclean through sin, evil, personal corruption, crudeness, and so forth*], him shall God destroy [*if he doesn't repent*]; for the temple of God is holy, which temple ye are.

18 Let no man deceive himself [*don't fool yourselves*]. If any man among you seemeth to be wise in this world, let him become a fool [*let him humble himself*], that he may be wise [*that he may be taught by God and thus become truly wise*].

19 For the wisdom of this world is foolishness with God [*man's worldly wisdom becomes foolishness in the light of the gospel*]. For it is written [*in Job 5:13*], He taketh the wise in their own craftiness. [*In other words, those who think they are "crafty" or cunning*

*enough to work around God's laws will ultimately be "taken" or caught, trapped by the law of justice.*]

20 And again, The Lord knoweth the thoughts of the wise [*worldly wise*] are vain [*lead to no good*].

21 Therefore let no man glory in men [*don't get caught up in and trust the thinking of worldly people*]. For all things are yours [*exaltation is available to you, if you will just follow Christ*];

22 Whether Paul, or Apollos, or Cephas [*Peter*], or the world, or life, or death, or things present, or things to come; all are yours;

23 And ye are Christ's; and Christ is God's. [*See also Romans 8:17 where Paul teaches that we can become "joint heirs with Christ." In other words, through your faithfulness, you will belong to Christ (Mosiah 5:7), and He will belong to the Father (Revelation 3:21), thus you will belong to the Father and have exaltation.*]

## FIRST CORINTHIANS 4

The word "mysteries" as used next in verse 1, is commonly used in the scriptures to mean the simple basics of the gospel, such as the Ten Commandments, repentance, baptism, the Gift of the Holy Ghost, three degrees of glory, exaltation, eternal family units, life after death, the spirit world, and so forth, which remain a "mystery" to people who have never heard of the gospel or who do not believe it. Joseph Fielding Smith said "Until it is understood, however, a simple truth may be a great mystery." *Doctrines of Salvation*, Vol. 1, p. 296. In Mosiah 1:5, King Benjamin taught his sons that without the scriptures, they would not be able to understand the "mysteries." He said "I say unto you, my sons, were it not for these things, which have been kept and preserved by the hand of God, that we might read and understand of his mysteries, and have his commandments always before our eyes, that even our fathers would have dwindled in unbelief, and we should have been like unto our brethren, the Lamanites, who know nothing concerning these things, or even do not believe them when they are taught them, because of the traditions of their fathers, which are not correct."

1 LET a man so account of us, as of the ministers of Christ, and stewards of the mysteries of God. [*Please consider us to be ministers of Christ who bring you the simple basics of the gospel, which remain mysteries to unbelievers and those who have not heard the gospel.*]

2 Moreover it is required in stewards, that a man be found faithful. [*All ministers of Christ must be worthy.*]

**JST 1 Corinthians 4:2**

2 Moreover it is required of stewards, that a man be found faithful.

3 But with me it is a very small thing that I should be judged of you, or of man's judgment [*I really don't worry much about what you think of me or what others think of me*]: yea, I judge not mine own self [*I don't even judge myself*].

4 For I know nothing by myself; yet am I not hereby justified [*that doesn't mean that I can sit back and relax with respect to striving to be righteous*]: but he that judgeth me is the Lord [*what really counts is what the Lord thinks of me*].

**JST 1 Corinthians 4:4**

4 For though I know nothing against myself [*In other words, even though I have a clear conscience*]; yet I am not hereby justified; but he who judgeth me is the Lord.

5 Therefore judge nothing before the

time, [*I am careful not to judge anything or anyone prematurely*] until the Lord come [*but will wait for the Lord to Judge people*], who both will bring to light the hidden things of darkness [*who will expose all the hidden wickedness of people*], and will make manifest the counsels [*thoughts, plans, desires*] of the hearts: and then shall every man have praise of God. [*All who deserve it will then have the praise of God, when Christ Himself judges us.*]

**JST 1 Corinthians 4:5**

5 Therefore I judge nothing before the time, until the Lord come, who both will bring to light the hidden things of darkness, and will make manifest the counsels of the hearts; and then shall every man have praise of God.

6 And these things, brethren, I have in a figure transferred to myself and to Apollos [*I have, for example, applied these things to myself and to Apollos (a convert who was a great teacher among the Corinthian Saints)*] for your sakes [*for your benefit*]; that ye might learn in us [*by our example*] not to think of men above [*beyond*] that which is written [*that we should not judge one another unrighteously*], that no one of you be puffed up [*become proud, arrogant, and judgmental*] for one against another.

7 For who maketh thee to differ from another [*who makes one of you different from another; who makes one of you superior to another*]? and what hast thou that thou didst not receive [*What do you have that you did not receive from God? In other words, why should you think yourself superior to another, as if you truly earned what you have received from God*]? now if thou didst receive it [*since you receive everything you have from God*], why dost thou glory [*why should you think you are anything special above anyone else*], as if thou hadst not received it [*as if you had earned it completely yourself rather than receiving it from God*]? [*This is very similar to the message King Benjamin gave his people in Mosiah 4:19, namely, that we are all beggars and are completely dependant on God for everything we have.*]

8 Now ye are full [*you are very well off*], now ye are rich [*you are wealthy as to worldly goods there in Corinth*], ye have reigned as kings without us [*you are living like kings*]: and I would to God ye did reign, that we also might reign with you [*I wish that you really were kings of righteousness and that we could be there in Corinth with you*].

9 For I think that God hath set forth us the apostles last [*it sometimes seems to me that God has placed us Apostles last when it comes to money, wealth, homes, and so forth*], as it were appointed to death [*as if we were supposed to plan on trials, persecutions, even death as a result of our calling and service to others*]: for we are made a spectacle unto the world, and to angels, and to men [*we are often ridiculed in public for all to see, including angels as well as people*].

10 We are fools for Christ's sake [*we look like fools to many because of our commitment to Christ*], but ye are wise in Christ [*you will be made wise if you remain loyal to Christ*]; we are weak [*we have been weakened physically by persecutions and hard times*], but ye are strong [*you still have it good*]; ye are honourable [*many people still respect you*], but we are despised [*many unbelievers know and despise us*].

11 Even unto this present hour [*even now*] we both hunger, and thirst, and are naked, and are buffeted, and have no certain dwellingplace [*we suffer from hunger, thirst, inadequate clothing, and don't know for sure from day to day where we will be living*];

12 And labour, working with our own hands [*we earn our own way*]: being reviled, we bless [*we return good for evil*]; being persecuted, we suffer it [*we put up with a lot of persecution*]:

13 Being defamed [*slandered*], we intreat [*answer with kindness*]: we are made as the filth of the world [*we are treated as trash*], and are the offscouring of all things [*are treated as the scum of the earth*] unto this day.

14 I write not these things to shame you [*to make you feel ashamed that you have so good*], but as my beloved sons [*as my own much-loved children*] I warn you.

15 For though ye have ten thousand instructors in Christ [*even though you have many gospel teachers now*], yet have ye not many fathers [*I am like a father to you, because I first brought you life in the gospel of Christ*]: for in Christ Jesus I have begotten you through the gospel. [*You have become like family to me because of the gospel. I introduced it to you, and, in that sense, I am your father.*]

16 Wherefore I beseech [*urge*] you, be ye followers of me [*follow my example*].

17 For this cause have I sent unto you Timotheus [*Timothy, who became a missionary companion to Paul; see Acts 16:1*], who is my beloved son [*who has become like a son to me*], and faithful in the Lord, who shall bring you into remembrance of my ways which be in Christ, as I teach every where in every church. [*When Timothy arrives in Corinth, he will remind you about the things I taught you, which are the same things I teach in wards and branches everywhere.*]

18 Now some are puffed up [*have become arrogant and are preaching false doctrines, apostate doctrines*], as though I would not come to you [*as if they think I will not come to you in Corinth and straighten them out*].

19 But I will come to you shortly, if the Lord will, and will know, not the speech of them which are puffed up, but the power [*and will see first hand what actual influence and power these teachers of apostasy have among you*].

20 For the kingdom of God is not in word, but in power [*the true Church of God on earth is not sustained by the confusing and contentious words of men but by the power of God*].

21 What will ye? shall I come unto you with a rod, or in love, and in the spirit of meekness? [*What do you prefer, that I come to you, crashing down severely upon the false teachers and their followers among you, or would you prefer that I come in gentleness and love?*]

# FIRST CORINTHIANS 5

Remember that sexual immorality was very common in Corinthian society and culture and was considered normal behavior. Many members of the Church had the same attitudes about sexual involvements outside of marriage as their nonmember fellow citizens. Thus, in this chapter, Paul attacks this serious sinful behavior head on.

Just a note about the JST references given in this study guide. Not all of the JST changes are provided in our LDS Bible. Decisions had to be made as to what to include and what not to include because of space limitations. Therefore, you will not find some of the JST references we give in this study guide, in the Bible. But, you can find them in the full version of the Joseph Smith Translation of the Bible, which is available in most LDS book stores.

1 IT is reported commonly that there is fornication among you [*I understand that there is much sexual immorality among you*], and such fornication as is not so much as named among the Gentiles [*and even one type of sinful sexual intercourse that is not even known among Gentile nonmembers*],

that one should have his father's wife [*namely, incest, wherein one has sexual relations with his mother, his father's wife*].

2 And ye are puffed up [*are you so arrogant and prideful that you find this acceptable*!], and have not rather mourned, that he that hath done this deed might be taken away from among you [*whereas you should have been so shocked and saddened about such behavior that you would have excommunicated such sinners and no longer associated with them*].

3 For I verily, as absent in body, but present in spirit, have judged already, as though I were present, concerning him that hath so done this deed [*Even though I am physically away from you, I am there among you in spirit and have already passed judgment on those who are involved in this type of behavior*],

**JST 1 Corinthians 5:3**

3 For verily, as absent in body but present in spirit, I have judged already him who hath so done this deed, as though I were present.

4 In the name of our Lord Jesus Christ, when ye are gathered together, and my spirit, with the power of our Lord Jesus Christ,

**JST 1 Corinthians 5:4**

4 In the name of our Lord Jesus Christ, when ye are gathered together, and have the Spirit, with the power of our Lord Jesus Christ,

5 To deliver such an one unto Satan [*to excommunicate such members and turn them over to the buffetings of Satan*] for the destruction of the flesh [*which will cause them much anguish during the next part of their mortal lives*], that the spirit may be saved in the day of the Lord Jesus [*in order that they might repent and ultimately be saved on Judgment Day*].

**JST 1 Corinthians 5:5**

5 To deliver such a one unto Satan for the destruction of the flesh, that the spirit may be saved in the day of the Lord Jesus.

6 Your glorying is not good [*your boasting that "anything goes" among you is not good*]. Know ye not that a little leaven [*yeast*] leaveneth the whole lump [*of dough*]? [*If you do not deal properly with this terrible problem, it will continue to spread among you until everyone in the Church is affected by it, just as a little bit of yeast works through the whole lump of dough and affects it all.*]

7 Purge out therefore the old leaven [*get rid of the old sinful behaviors and attitudes which permeate the culture of Corinth, even to the extent of excommunicating some members if needed*], that ye may be a new lump [*so that you may be a new, pure and clean "lump of dough"*], as ye are unleavened [*and remain free of the old sins and corruption of your environment*]. For even Christ our passover is sacrificed for us [*Christ is our "unleavened bread" and was sacrificed for us that we may be freed from our enemies, including sin*]:

The reference in verse 7, above, to Passover, refers to the commandment Moses gave to the children of Israel (see Exodus 12:3–8) to prepare to be redeemed from their slavery in Egypt by putting lamb's blood (representing Christ's redeeming blood) on their door posts and eating unleavened bread (representing not being corrupted by the "leaven" or yeast of the society around them).

8 Therefore let us keep the feast [*of Passover*], not with old leaven [*not with old or past sins and wickedness*], neither with the leaven of malice [*evil intentions*] and wickedness; but with the unleavened bread [*the new influence of the gospel which is free from the corruption of the world*] of sincerity and truth.

9 I wrote unto you in an epistle not to company with fornicators [*I told you in a previous letter not to associate with people involved in sexual immorality*]:

10 Yet not altogether with the fornicators [*sexually immoral*] of this world, or with the covetous [*greedy*], or extortioners [*swindlers, cheaters*], or with idolaters [*but what I meant was not to allow them to have the privileges of Church membership, unless they repent*]; for then must ye needs go out of the world [*because if you never associated at all with such people, it would require that you leave this world, and that is not very practical*].

11 But now I have written unto you [*but now I am counseling you*] not to keep company [*not to associate with people*], if any man that is called a brother [*a member*] be a fornicator, or covetous, or an idolater, or a railer [*one who yells and screams at others or is always criticizing others*], or a drunkard, or an extortioner; with such an one no not to eat [*don't even eat with him or her*].

The message in the above verses about choosing friends and associates wisely is very important. Peer pressure causes many to commit sin.

12 For what have I to do to judge them also that are without [*outside of the Church*]? do not ye judge them that are within?

**JST 1 Corinthians 5:12**

12 For what have I to do to judge them also that are without? do not they judge them that are within [*aren't nonmembers critical of church members who won't join them in sinning*]?

13 But them that are without [*who are outside the Church, in other words, not members*] God judgeth. Therefore put away from among yourselves that wicked person [*you must do what is necessary to cleanse the Church from wickedness, even if it means excommunication; compare with D&C 42:24–26*].

# FIRST CORINTHIANS 6

Paul continues in this chapter by counseling the members of the Church in Corinth to avoid living like the world does. He counsels them to avoid the common practice in Corinth of taking each other to court to settle disputes, instead of working things out peaceably among themselves. In fact, he scolds them for using courts of law when they should be acting more like Saints and settling things with each other. He reminds them that they have the potential to someday be gods and thus are behaving far beneath their potential by being petty with each other.

1 DARE any of you, having a matter [*a dispute or disagreement*] against another, go to law [*take him or her to court*] before the unjust [*going before judges who often turn out to be corrupt*], and not before the saints [*rather than going to local leaders of the Church for help in settling things*]?

2 Do ye not know that the saints shall judge the world? [*This phrase has at least two meanings. First, the world will ultimately be judged by the standards of the gospel, which true Saints keep. Second, during the Millennium, the true Saints will rule and reign on earth with the Savior. See Revelation 20:4*] and if the world shall be judged by you, are ye unworthy to judge the smallest matters [*if you are someday going to judge the world, shouldn't you be able to take care of these relatively small or trivial matters among yourselves*]?

In the first phrase of verse 3, next, Paul clearly teaches that worthy Saints will someday have power over angels, in other words, they will someday become gods. Compare with D&C 132:20.

3 Know ye not that we shall judge

angels [*don't you know you will someday be gods*]? how much more things that pertain to this life [*shouldn't you be very capable then of handling disputes, etc., that come among you in this mortal life*]?

4 If then ye have judgments of things pertaining to this life, set them to judge who are least esteemed in the church. [*It would be better for you to take your disputes before the least respected judge who is a member of the Church than to go before worldly judges.*]

5 I speak to your shame [*shame on you for being so petty with each other!*]. Is it so, that there is not a wise man among you [*are there no wise men among you members there in Corinth*]? no, not one that shall be able to judge between his brethren [*not even one to whom you could go to get help in working out disagreements*]?

6 But brother goeth to law with brother, and that before the unbelievers [*one member takes another to court, and to make things worse, they do it in the court system of unbelievers*].

7 Now therefore there is utterly a fault among you, because ye go to law one with another [*you are way out of line in participating in this type of behavior*]. Why do ye not rather take wrong [*why don't you follow the Savior's council to turn the other cheek, to endure wrong; Matthew 5:38–48*]? why do ye not rather suffer yourselves to be defrauded [*why don't you allow yourselves to be cheated rather than getting all tied up with contention among yourselves*]?

8 Nay, ye do wrong [*you are the ones who are in the wrong, by not following the Savior's counsel*], and defraud [*you are the real cheaters!*], and that your brethren [*and the sad thing is that you are doing it to other members of the Church*].

In verses 9 and 10, next, Paul gives quite a list of sins which would qualify people for telestial glory, if not repented of.

9 Know ye not that the unrighteous shall not inherit the kingdom of God [*don't you realize that your contentious behavior puts you in the same category as the unrighteous and you will not get celestial glory if you continue*]? Be not deceived [*don't be fooled*]: neither fornicators [*those who break the law of chastity*], nor idolaters [*idol worshipers*], nor adulterers [*those who commit adultery*], nor effeminate [*men who use boys in homosexual acts; see Strong's #3120*], nor abusers of themselves with mankind [*male homosexuals*],

10 Nor thieves, nor covetous, nor drunkards, nor revilers [*people who are mean-tempered; who constantly criticize others; who mock and make fun of that which is good*], nor extortioners [*people who rob others through fear and intimidation*], shall inherit the kingdom of God.

In verse 11, next, we are reminded of the wonderful power of the Atonement to cleanse and heal. After naming several very serious and abominable sins, in the above verses, which were common behavior in Corinth, and which some members there have committed, Paul reminds them that they can be completely forgiven upon deep repentance.

11 And such were some of you [*some of you were involved in these kinds of sins*]: but ye are washed [*you have been baptized, cleansed*], but ye are sanctified [*you have been made holy and fit to be in the presence of God*], but ye are justified [*you have followed the promptings of the Holy Ghost and thus been lined up in harmony with God's commandments so that you are ratified and approved to be in the presence of God*] in the name of the Lord Jesus [*this has happened to you because of the Savior*], and by the Spirit of our God [*and because you have followed the promptings of the Holy Ghost*].

The Joseph Smith Translation of the Bible makes very significant changes in verse 12, next.

12 All things are lawful unto me, but all things are not expedient: all things are lawful for me, but I will not be brought under the power of any.

**JST 1 Corinthians 6:12**

12 All these things are not lawful unto me [*the commandments teach against all of these sins*], and all these things are not expedient [*there is no reason for any of us to commit such sins*]. All things are not lawful for me, therefore I will not be brought under the power of any [*therefore I will not allow any such sins to have power over me*].

13 Meats [*foods*] for the belly [*satisfy the stomach's hunger*], and the belly for meats: [*The Corinthians had a saying that just as it is permissible to eat food to satisfy the stomach's hunger, so also it is proper to satisfy one's sexual appetites by fornication, adultery, homosexuality, child sexual partners, etc. See also McConkie,* Doctrinal New Testament Commentary, *Vol. 2, p. 340.*] but God shall destroy both it and them. [*All such sinners who don't repent will be destroyed spiritually and eventually will be punished by God.*] Now the body is not for fornication, but for the Lord [*remember, the body is the temple of the Spirit of God (1 Corinthians 3:16) and should not be defiled by sexual immorality*]; and the Lord for the body [*the Spirit of the Lord would like to dwell in your bodies*].

14 And God [*the Father*] hath both raised up the Lord [*has exalted Christ*], and will also raise up us by his own power [*and will exalt us if we keep the commandments*].

15 Know ye not that your bodies are the members of Christ [*don't you realize that, as baptized members of the Church, you have joined yourselves to Christ, and, in a sense, have become part of His body*]? shall I then take the members of Christ, and make them the members of an harlot [*would it be proper to take part of Christ and have it involved with a prostitute*]? God forbid [*absolutely not!*].

16 What? know ye not that he which is joined to an harlot is one body [*don't you realize that when you join yourself to another in sexual immorality, you both become part of a body of sin*]? for two, saith he [*God, in Genesis 2:24*], shall be one flesh [*just as God said that a husband and wife become one flesh, in other words, one family unit and have children, so also those who get involved with each other in acts of sexual immorality become one unit of sin*].

17 But he that is joined unto the Lord is one spirit [*those who join with the Lord in purity and righteousness become united with Him and will be saved*].

Again, we must have the Prophet Joseph Smith's help to understand a verse. The JST makes significant changes to verse 18, next.

18 Flee fornication [*avoid sexual immorality at all costs!*]. Every sin that a man doeth is without the body; but he that committeth fornication sinneth against his own body. [*when you commit sexual sin, you are committing serious sin against yourself*].

**JST 1 Corinthians 6:18**

18 Flee fornication. Every sin that a man committeth is against the body of Christ, and he who committeth fornication sinneth against his own body.

19 What? know ye not that your body is the temple of the Holy Ghost which is in you, which ye have of God, and ye are not your own [*don't you realize that you can be a "temple" in which the Holy Ghost dwells, which gift you get from God, and that you have given yourselves to God? In other words, how would you dare defile and pollute a part of God, which you are, having given yourselves to him by covenant at baptism?*]

20 For ye are bought with a price [*Christ paid a heavy price to redeem you from your sins*]: therefore glorify God in your body [*worship God by treating your body as a temple, keeping it clean and pure*], and in your spirit [*and keep your mind clean and pure too*], which are God's [*both of which you have dedicated to God through the covenants you have made with Him*].

## FIRST CORINTHIANS 7

The JST makes changes in seventeen verses in this chapter. As you will see, without the Prophet's inspired changes, this chapter could lead to a number of damaging false doctrines. Indeed, many Christians have been confused or stumbled because of this chapter as it stands in the Bible.

Paul will deal with some issues which the Corinthian Saints brought up in the letter they wrote back to him in response to his first letter to them (which we don't have). See note about Paul's first letter to the Corinthians at the beginning of First Corinthians in this study guide.

Verse 1 contains what the Corinthian Saints said to Paul in their reply to him. They are wrong and have obviously misunderstood some basics of the gospel with respect to honorable relations between men and women, including marriage. Unfortunately, many in the world consider the powers of procreation to be inherently unclean and evil. This is not so. They are beautiful and wonderful and are key in happy marriages. They only become ugly, evil and destructive when misused. In fact, in the next life, after Judgment Day, when people have been placed in the three degrees of glory or outer darkness, the only ones who will have the powers of procreation and the privilege of using them will be those who become gods and bring forth spirit children to send to their own worlds. See Smith, *Doctrines of Salvation*, Vol. 2, pp. 286–288. Thus, the powers of procreation are pure, clean, holy, sacred, and wonderful when properly used in marriage between a man and a woman (see Proclamation on the Family, September 23, 1995, paragraph number 4). Just so you don't miss it, make sure you notice in verse 2 that Paul tells the members in Corinth that it is good to get married.

As we begin our study of this chapter, note that verse 1, as it stands, says that Paul says that it is good for a man not even to touch a woman. JST verse 1, however, changes the meaning completely. It informs us that it was the Corinthian Saints who said in their letter to Paul that "it is good for a man not to touch a woman." Paul will straighten out this false idea.

1 NOW concerning the things whereof ye wrote unto me [*JST "whereof ye wrote unto me saying"*]: It is good for a man not to touch a woman.

> **JST 1 Corinthians 7:1**
> Now concerning the things whereof ye wrote unto me, saying, It is good for a man not to touch a woman.

2 Nevertheless, to avoid fornication, let every man have his own wife, and let every woman have her own husband. [*In other words, in your letter back to me, you said that it would actually be best if men and women had nothing to do with each other. However, I say that marriage is fine and helps people avoid sexual immorality.*]

> **JST 1 Corinthians 7:2**
> 2 Nevertheless, I say, to avoid fornication, let every man have his own

wife, and let every woman have her own husband.

Paul now responds, teaching that marriage is not just something which is second best to never marrying, or something to get involved in by those who are so weak that they can't control sexual urges. Rather, marriage is honorable, and husbands and wives should treat each other with love and kindness and as equals.

3 Let the husband render unto the wife due benevolence [*proper kindness and respect*]: and likewise also the wife unto the husband.

4 The wife hath not power of her own body, but the husband: and likewise also the husband hath not power of his own body, but the wife. [*They have given themselves to each other and are equal partners. Sexual relations will be desired by each and it is proper for them to give themselves to each other in physical intimacy.*]

5 Defraud ye not one the other, except it be with consent for a time, that ye may give yourselves to fasting and prayer [*do not be apart from each other except by mutual agreement for brief periods of time when you want to dedicate some time to fasting and prayer*]; and come together again [*then resume sexual relations again; see Strong's #4905 "conjugal cohabitation"*], that Satan tempt you not for your incontinency [*so that you don't give Satan extra power to tempt you to become unfaithful to your spouse because of lack of self-control or because you are not finding physical satisfaction in your marriage*].

**JST 1 Corinthians 7:5**

5 Depart ye not one from the other, except it be with consent for a time, that ye may give yourselves to fasting and prayer; and come together again, that Satan tempt you not for your incontinency.

6 But I speak this by permission, and not of commandment [*I give this as my opinion and not by way of commandment from the Lord*].

**JST 1 Corinthians 7:6**

6 And now what I speak is by permission, and not by commandment.

Some people teach that Paul chose to remain single and use verses 7 and 8, next, to claim that he taught that it is better not to be married. Some groups use these verses to teach celibacy (deliberately remaining single as a form of devotion to God). Elder Spencer W. Kimball said that this is not so and explained it as follows: "Taking such statements in conjunction with others [*Paul*] made, it is clear that he is not talking about celibacy, but is urging the normal and controlled sex living in marriage and total continence [*refraining from sexual relations*] outside marriage. [*There is no real evidence that Paul was never married, as some students claim, and there are in fact indications to the contrary.*]" *Miracle of Forgiveness*, p. 64.

7 For I would that all men were even as I myself. [*Apostle Bruce R. McConkie explained that Paul was, in effect, saying: "I would that all men understood the law of marriage, that all had self-mastery over their appetites, and that all obeyed the laws of God in these respects." McConkie,* Doctrinal New Testament Commentary, *Vol. 2, p. 344.*] But every man hath his proper gift of God, one after this manner, and another after that [*each of us has gifts and strengths, one this and another that*].

**JST 1 Corinthians 7:7**

7 For I would that all men were even as myself. But every man hath his proper gift of God, one after this manner, and another after that.

8 I say therefore to the unmarried and widows, It is good for them if they abide even as I. [*Perhaps Paul is a widower and knows what it means to be single again and is counseling single members to be extra strong in controlling sexual*

*desires. Perhaps he is saying something else, namely, that being single allows him to devote full attention to his missionary labors.*]

9 But if they cannot contain, let them marry: for it is better to marry than to burn.

**JST 1 Corinthians 7:9**

9 But if they cannot abide, let them marry; for it is better to marry than that any should commit sin.

No matter how we explain or interpret verses 7–9, above, one thing is certain. Paul taught that celestial marriage is necessary. He said "Nevertheless neither is the man without the woman, neither the woman without the man, in the Lord." (1 Corinthians 11:11.) Also, there is no question as to whether or not Paul himself was or had been married (perhaps his wife had passed away). As a strict Pharisee (Acts 26:5), which he was before his conversion, he would have been required to be married, according to Jewish culture.

In verses 10 and 11, next, Paul counsels against divorce.

10 And unto the married I command, yet not I, but the Lord [*this is not my opinion, rather, it is what the Lord says*], Let not the wife depart from [*divorce*] her husband:

11 But and if she depart [*if she divorces him*], let her remain unmarried, or be reconciled to [*or work things out again with*] her husband: and let not the husband put away [*divorce*] his wife.

**JST 1 Corinthians 7:11**

11 But if she depart, let her remain unmarried, or be reconciled to her husband; but let not the husband put away his wife.

12 But to the rest speak I, not the Lord [*what I say next is my opinion, not a commandment from the Lord*]: If any brother [*member*] hath a wife that believeth not [*has a nonmember wife*], and she be pleased to dwell with him [*and she desires to stay with him, even though he joined the Church*], let him not put her away [*don't divorce her*].

13 And the woman [*member*] which hath an husband that believeth not [*who has a nonmember husband*], and if he be pleased to dwell with her [*and if he would like to stay married to her, even though she joined the Church*], let her not leave him [*don't divorce him*].

14 [*Be sure to look at the note after this verse.*] For the unbelieving [ *nonmember*] husband is sanctified [*saved*] by the wife [*who is a faithful member*], and the unbelieving [ *nonmember*] wife is sanctified [*saved*] by the husband [*who is a faithful member*]: else [*otherwise*] were your children unclean [*your children would not be saved*]; but now are they holy.

Having explained the wording in verse 14, above, we are now left to ask "Is that true doctrine?" Answer: "No." We would do well to suspect that something vital was left out in the translation. Article of Faith number eight reminds us that "We believe the Bible to be the word of God as far as it is translated correctly;" It is very likely that verse 14 is a quote from the letter the Corinthian Saints wrote Paul, expressing their beliefs on certain matters, as indicated in verse one of this chapter where Paul wrote "Now concerning the things whereof ye wrote unto me…" At any rate, the beliefs represented in verse 14 are not correct. This verse caused the Prophet Joseph Smith enough concern, when he was working on the Joseph Smith Translation of the Bible (JST), that he received D&C 74 by way of background for verse 14. You may wish to read section 74 now. You will find that nonmembers who were married to members in Corinth wanted their male children circumcised as required by the Law of Moses, which had been fulfilled by Christ. This was causing much contention in the Church. The net result was that when a member married a

nonmember, and the nonmember's religion was practiced in the home, the children generally grew up as non-believers in Christ. Thus, they were not "holy," in other words, they were not being saved. There was also a tradition among the Jews that little children were unholy, which is completely false doctrine and was apparently being perpetuated in these part-member homes. See D&C 137:10 where we are taught that all children who die before the years of accountability "are saved in the celestial kingdom of heaven." Perhaps, in the last two phrases of verse 14, Paul was responding and saying, in effect, "If things were indeed as is being taught in many of your part-member homes, little children would be unclean and thus lost. But, with the true gospel of Jesus Christ, we know that little children are holy, and thus, are saved."

15 But if the unbelieving depart [*if the nonmember spouse decides to divorce the spouse who is a member*], let him depart [*let him get a divorce*]. A brother or a sister is not under bondage [*is not guilty of sin*] in such cases: but God hath called us to peace [*to do our best to try to work things out and keep the peace*].

16 For what knowest thou, O wife, whether thou shalt save thy husband [*who knows but what your good example might someday cause your husband to be converted*]? or how knowest thou, O man, whether thou shalt save thy wife?

17 But as God hath distributed to every man [*but each case is different*], as the Lord hath called every one, so let him walk [*each member should follow the inspiration of the Lord in each individual situation*]. And so ordain I in all churches [*this is my advice to all the wards and branches of the Church who have to deal with these things*].

18 Is any man called being circumcised? let him not become uncircumcised. [*If a male convert was circumcised, according to the Law of Moses, don't worry about it.*] Is any called in uncircumcision? let him not be circumcised. [*If a man is converted to the Church, but was not circumcised, don't give in to the pressure from some members who still believe in the Law of Moses and circumcision.*]

19 Circumcision is nothing, and uncircumcision is nothing, but the keeping of the commandments of God. [*Circumcision and uncircumcision are not issues anymore. The issue is to keep the commandments given by the Savior.*]

Verses 20–24 deal with the legal status of slaves, or indentured servants or free people, etc., who join the Church. Paul counsels them that joining the Church doesn't necessarily change their legal status. This could obviously become a problem for some, because the gospel of Christ teaches of the equality and worth of all souls.

20 Let every man abide in the same calling wherein he was called [*remain in the same legal status as you were in at the time you joined the Church*].

21 Art thou called being a servant [*did you join the Church while a servant who belongs to someone*]? care not for it [*don't be overly concerned about it*]: but if thou mayest be made free, use it rather [*but if you can obtain your freedom, do it*].

22 For he that is called in the Lord, being a servant, is the Lord's freeman [*even if you are still a slave or a servant who still owes your owner a few more years of work before you are free, remember that if you live the gospel, you are free in the eternal sense that matters*]: likewise also he that is called, being free, is Christ's servant [*those who were free citizens when baptized, are now "servants" to Christ. In other words, living the gospel makes all of us free and living the gospel makes all of us servants*].

23 Ye are bought with a price; be not

ye the servants of men [*Christ paid an enormous price to purchase you from your sins, therefore, look upon yourselves as His servants, rather that being the servants of men*].

24 Brethren, let every man, wherein he is called, therein abide with God [*regardless of your social or legal status, be faithful to God*].

Paul now switches topics and deals with special issues concerning those involved in missionary service or other service which can require longer periods of time away from home. For instance, should engaged persons marry first, then go, or remain single? Also, would it be best for married members to get divorced, so that they can focus more effectively on their missionary service or whatever the calling may be? Paul is obviously answering questions raised by these members in their letter to him, as indicated in verse 1.

25 Now concerning virgins [*single sisters*] I have no commandment of the Lord [*I don't have any specific direction from the Lord*]: yet I give my judgment [*I will give my opinion*], as one that hath obtained mercy of the Lord to be faithful [*as one who has been helped much by the Lord and who is trustworthy*].

26 I suppose therefore that this is good for the present distress [*the current missionary work*], I say, that it is good for a man so to be.

**JST 1 Corinthians 7:26**

26 I suppose therefore that this is good for the present distress, for a man so to remain that he may do greater good [*In other words, I suppose that it is best for a man to remain single while he is involved fully in missionary work, so that he can be more effective*].

27 Art thou bound unto a wife? seek not to be loosed [*If you are married, don't seek a divorce so you can serve a full-time mission*]. Art thou loosed from a wife? seek not a wife. [*If you are already a widower or divorced, don't get married for the time being so you can focus on the missionary service to which you are called.*]

28 But and if thou marry, thou hast not sinned [*however, if you choose to marry, it is not a sin*]; and if a virgin marry [*and if a single sister gets married, rather than going into full-time missionary service*], she hath not sinned. Nevertheless such shall have trouble in the flesh: but I spare you.

**JST 1 Corinthians 7:28**

28 But if thou marry, thou hast not sinned; and if a virgin marry, she hath not sinned. Nevertheless, such shall have trouble in the flesh. For I spare you not [*No matter what you choose to do, you will not be spared the trials and tribulations that come with mortal life*].

29 But this I say, brethren, the time is short: it remaineth, that both they that have wives be as though they had none; [*In other words, for a short while yet, those of you who are married will have to be away from home so much that it will almost seem to you as if you were not married.*]

**JST 1 Corinthians 7:29**

29 But I speak unto you who are called unto the ministry. For this I say, brethren, the time that remaineth is but short, that ye shall be sent forth unto the ministry. Even they who have wives, shall be as though they had none; for ye are called and chosen to do the Lord's work.

30 And they that weep, as though they wept not; and they that rejoice, as though they rejoiced not; and they that buy, as though they possessed not; [*The intensity of the work and the fast pace of it will hardly give you time to weep for missionary efforts that failed, or to rejoice for very long because of successes, or to even enjoy material things.*]

**JST 1 Corinthians 7:30**
30 And it shall be with them who weep, as though they wept not; and them who rejoice, as though they rejoiced not, and them who buy, as though they possessed not;

31 And they that use this world, as not abusing it: for the fashion of this world passeth away.

**JST 1 Corinthians 7:31**
31 And them who use this world, as not using it; for the fashion of this world passeth away [*Because of the fast pace of the work, worldly concerns, likes and interests in material things will fade to the point that you don't hardly even feel like a part of the world*].

32 But I would have you without carefulness. He that is unmarried careth for the things that belong to the Lord, how he may please the Lord:

**JST 1 Corinthians 7:32**
32 But I would, brethren, that ye magnify your calling. I would have you without carefulness [*I would like you to be free from worldly cares during the time of your missionary service*]. For he who is unmarried, careth for the things that belong to the Lord [*a single person can focus more effectively on the things of missionary work*], how he may please the Lord; therefore he prevaileth [*has success*].

33 But he that is married careth for the things that are of the world, how he may please his wife. [*Single missionaries can focus more on the work, therefore, there is a difference between them and married members, because married members have more distractions and can't be as effective.*]

**JST 1 Corinthians 7:33**
33 But he who is married, careth for the things that are of the world, how he may please his wife; therefore there is a difference, for he is hindered.

34 There is difference also between a wife and a virgin. [*The same thing holds true for married women as opposed to single sisters, as holds for married men as opposed to single brethren.*] The unmarried woman careth for [*is better able to focus full-time on*] the things of the Lord, that she may be holy [*may be set apart and be spiritually focused*] both in body and in spirit: but she that is married careth for the things of the world [*has to devote time and energy to daily responsibilities of homemaking*], how she may please her husband.

**JST 1 Corinthians 7:34**
34 There is a difference also, between a wife and a virgin. The unmarried woman careth for the things of the Lord, that she may be holy both in body and in spirit; but she that is married careth for the things of the world, how she may please her husband.

By the way, the only difference between verse 34, above, and the JST is that the Prophet put a semicolon after "spirit" in place of the colon in verse 34. This is another example of Joseph Smith's inspired attention to detail.

35 And this I speak for your own profit [*I am giving you this counsel for your own good*]; not that I may cast a snare upon you [*not trying to cause trouble for you*], but for that which is comely [*honorable and appropriate*], and that ye may attend upon the Lord without distraction [*so that you can focus on temporary full-time service of the Lord without being distracted*].

36 But if any man think that he behaveth himself uncomely [*unkindly*] toward his virgin [*his fiancée*], if she pass the flower of her age [*the best years for her to bear children*], and need so require, let him do what he will, he sinneth not: let them marry. [*If a single man is engaged and thinks that going into full-time service of the Lord will cause his fiancée to be past the best years for child bearing when he returns, keep your promise to her. Stay home and marry her. It is not a sin to do so.*]

**JST 1 Corinthians 7:36**

36 But if any man think that he behaveth himself uncomely toward his virgin whom he hath espoused, if she pass the flower of age, and need so require, let him do what he hath promised, he sinneth not; let them marry.

37 Nevertheless, he that standeth stedfast in his heart [*who really wants to serve a mission*], having no necessity [*and his fiancee will not be too far along in years when he returns*], but hath power over his own will [*and has good self control*], and hath so decreed in his heart that he will keep his virgin and decides to remain espoused [*engaged*], doeth well.

The JST completely changes the meaning of the first phrase of verse 38.

38 So then he that giveth her in marriage [*who gives his fiancée to someone else to marry*] doeth well; but he that giveth her not in marriage doeth better. [*So, to summarize, if a man desires to go ahead and marry his fiancée, that is fine. But, if he could go on a mission first, that would be even better.*]

**JST 1 Corinthians 7:38**

38 So then he that giveth himself in marriage doeth well; but he that giveth himself not in marriage doeth better.

39 The wife is bound by the law [*the obligations that go along with marriage*] as long as her husband liveth [*so don't divorce your husbands so you can go on full-time missions*]; but if her husband be dead, she is at liberty to be married to whom she will; only in the Lord [*and in the case of a woman whose husband is a nonmember, if he dies, she of course can remarry, but she ought to marry a man who is a member of the Church*].

40 But she is happier if she so abide, after my judgment [*but, she will be happier if she remains faithful and marries a member of the Church, in my opinion*]: and I think also that I have the Spirit of God [*and I think that I have the Spirit of the Lord with me*].

# FIRST CORINTHIANS 8

It appears that one of the questions the Saints in Corinth asked Paul in their letter to him (see note at the beginning of chapter 7 in this study guide) had to do with whether or not it was okay for members to eat things left over from sacrifices offered by pagans to their idols. There were twelve temples to various idols in Corinth, consequently, there were many sacrifices. As a result, there was a significant market for leftover meat and whatever remained from these offerings. These Saints are apparently asking Paul if it is permissible for them to purchase such stuff in the open market and eat it.

1 NOW as touching [*concerning*] things offered unto idols, we know that we all have knowledge. Knowledge puffeth up [*knowledge can make us prideful*], but charity edifieth [*but the Christlike virtue of charity builds us up and strengthens us*].

2 And if any man think that he knoweth any thing, he knoweth nothing yet as he ought to know [*none of us knows near what we ought to know yet*].

3 But if any man love God, the same is known of him [*but God knows His faithful followers*].

4 As concerning therefore the eating of those things that are offered in sacrifice unto idols [*now, back to your question about eating things left over from pagan sacrifices*], we know that an idol is nothing in the world [*we know that idols are not really gods*], and that there is none other God but one [*and that there is only one true God*].

**JST 1 Corinthians 8:4**

4 As concerning therefore the eating of those things which are in the world offered in sacrifice unto idols, we know that an idol is nothing, and that there is none other God but one.

Before Paul continues to answer their questions about eating meat left over from pagan idol worship, he takes a minute to review the true doctrine of plurality of gods with them. We know from D&C 132:19–20, that all who are worthy will become gods over their own worlds, and will send their own spirit offspring to those worlds to go through the same plan of salvation as we are going through here. Therefore, because of the success of the Father's plan, there are many gods in the universe. But there is only one Heavenly Father for us. Thus, Paul reminds these Corinthian Saints that there actually are many gods out there.

5 For though there be that are called
gods, whether in heaven or in earth, (as
there be gods many, and lords many,)

The Prophet Joseph Smith tells us that the parentheses in verse 5, above, teach a marvelous doctrine, namely that there are many gods. This reminds us that we can all become gods. He taught that the word "gods" in verse 5 does not refer to idols or, in other words, heathen gods. He said: "Some say I do not interpret the Scripture the same as they do. They say it means the heathen's gods. Paul says there are Gods many and Lords many; and that makes a plurality of Gods, in spite of the whims of all men. . . You know and I testify that Paul had no allusion to the heathen gods. I have it from God, and get over it if you can. I have a witness of the Holy Ghost, and a testimony that Paul had no allusion to the heathen gods in the text." (Joseph Smith, *Teachings of the Prophet Joseph Smith*, selected and arranged by Joseph Fielding Smith, Salt Lake City: Deseret Book, 1976, p. 371.)

6 But to us [*but for us*] there is but one
God, the Father, of whom are all things
[*from whom all our blessings come*],
and we in him [*and we belong to Him*];
and one Lord Jesus Christ [*and there is
but one Savior*], by whom are all things
[*through whom the Father makes all His
blessings of exaltation available to us*],
and we by him [*we come to the Father
only through Jesus Christ*].

Having said, in verse 4, that idols are not actual gods, implying that there is nothing wrong with buying meat left over from pagan idol worship to help feed the family, Paul now cautions members that newer or weaker members of the Church might be shocked and offended to see members buying and eating such stuff, thinking that they are secretly or openly involved in idol worship themselves.

7 Howbeit [*however*] there is not in
every man that knowledge [*everyone
doesn't realize that idols are absurd and
are nothing, in and of themselves*]: for
some with conscience of the idol unto
this hour eat it as a thing offered unto
an idol [*many idol worshipers, even
now, eat such things as part of worshiping the idol*]; and their conscience
being weak is defiled [*and they are thus
defiled by it*].

8 But meat commendeth us not to God:
for neither, if we eat, are we the better;
neither, if we eat not, are we the worse.
[*Food by itself doesn't save us or condemn us with God.*]

9 But take heed lest by any means this
liberty of yours become a stumblingblock to them that are weak. [*But be
careful, for fear that the liberty which
this knowledge gives you (namely that
in and of themselves, various foods
used in idol worship are neither good
nor evil, so you can eat it if you want to)
could cause your behavior to become a
stumbling block for weaker members,
who don't understand these things as
you do.*]

10 For if any man see thee which hast
knowledge sit at meat in the idol's

temple [*if some weaker members see you (who understand this) sit down at a buffet in an idol worship temple for lunch*], shall not the conscience of him which is weak be emboldened to eat those things which are offered to idols [*isn't it possible that your example would make them think that they can be a member of our Church and still worship idols also*?];

11 And through thy knowledge shall the weak brother perish [*and thus, even though you know that the food itself is neither good nor evil, your example could cause a weaker member to lose salvation*], for whom Christ died [*thus undoing the work of the Savior which He did for them*]?

12 But when ye sin so against the brethren, and wound their weak conscience, ye sin against Christ [*if you go against the counsel of the Brethren and thus wound a member whose conscience and understanding is yet weak, it is a sin against the Savior*].

13 Wherefore, if meat make my brother to offend, I will eat no flesh while the world standeth, lest I make my brother to offend. [*Therefore, I will avoid things which I know are neither good or evil, but which might destroy another member's testimony.*]

## FIRST CORINTHIANS 9

Later in this chapter, Paul will continue with the theme in the last verses of chapter eight, namely that when we are in the presence of others, we need to be sensitive to their perceptions and feelings, so as to avoid offending them unnecessarily. But first, he will give a rather detailed treatment of the fact that Apostles and other full-time leaders in the Church need the support of the members for the physical needs of them and their families.

1 AM I not an apostle? am I not free? have I not seen Jesus Christ our Lord? are not ye my work in the Lord [*aren't you members of the Church because of the help the Lord gave me as a missionary to you*]?

2 If I be not an apostle unto others, yet doubtless I am to you [*even if others don't consider me to be an Apostle, at least you do*]: for the seal of mine apostleship are ye in the Lord [*you are the proof of my apostleship*].

3 Mine answer to them that do examine me is this [*my answer to those who challenge me about the counsel I just gave you is this*],

4 Have we [*the Apostles*] not power [*agency*] to eat and to drink?

5 Have we not power to lead about a sister, a wife [*don't we have the right to be married too*?], as well as other apostles [*just like other Apostles*], and as the brethren of the Lord, and Cephas [*including Peter, the president of the Church*]?

6 Or I only and Barnabas, have not we power to forbear working [*or are Barnabas and I the only ones who could quit working for the Lord if we chose to*]?

7 Who goeth a warfare any time at his own charges [*who else can you think of who serves as a soldier at his own expense*]? who planteth a vineyard, and eateth not of the fruit thereof [*who plants but never gets to be there to harvest*]? or who feedeth a flock, and eateth not of the milk of the flock [*who nourishes a ward or branch but doesn't get to be with them to enjoy the blessings with them in person*]?

8 Say I these things as a man [*am I just giving an opinion*]? or saith not the law the same also [*or is this what the Law of Moses said*]?

9 For it is written in the law of Moses, Thou shalt not muzzle the mouth of the ox that treadeth out the corn [*you are*

*not allowed to leave a muzzle on an ox which is working on the threshing floor*]. Doth God take care for oxen [*is God only concerned for oxen*]?

10 Or saith he it altogether for our sakes [*or is he telling us this for our sakes*]? For our sakes, no doubt, this is written: that he that ploweth should plow in hope; and that he that thresheth in hope should be partaker of his hope [*God expects us to plow and plant with the hope of a good harvest, and those who actually harvest the crops get to participate in the satisfaction of all involved in the whole process*].

11 If we have sown unto you spiritual things [*since we have planted spiritual seed, namely the seeds of the gospel of Christ among you*], is it a great thing if we shall reap your carnal things [*is it too much for us to expect your support in our physical needs as missionaries and full-time servants of God*]?

12 If others be partakers of this power over you, are not we rather [*if you support others among you, who need temporal and physical help from you, aren't we even more entitled to such help*]? Nevertheless we have not used this power [*we haven't used our authority to request such help*]; but suffer all things [*but often do without*], lest we should hinder the gospel of Christ [*for fear of offending some and thus hindering the work*].

13 Do ye not know that they which minister about holy things live of the things of the temple [*are you not aware that those who serve full-time in the temple are fed and taken care of by the donations to the temple*]? and they which wait [*those who serve*] at the alter [*in the temple*] are partakers with the alter [*take part of the flesh from the animal sacrifices to feed themselves and their families*]?

14 Even so hath the Lord ordained that they which preach the gospel should live of the gospel [*the Lord has commanded that his full-time servants should be supported by the members*].

15 But I have used none of these things [*but I have worked for my own living, rather than be supported by members*]: neither have I written these things, that it should be so done unto me [*and I am not writing these things to you for my own benefit, but so that you will be aware of God's will on this matter and will be more willing to support the physical needs of other leaders*] : for it were better for me to die [*I would rather die*], than that any man should make my glorying void [*than have my independence in earning my own way taken from me; see Acts 20:34*].

16 For though I preach the gospel, I have nothing to glory [*boast*] of: for necessity is laid upon me [*I am obligated to do it*]; yea, woe is unto me, if I preach not the gospel [*after all the blessings I have received from the Lord, I would be in deep trouble if I didn't preach the gospel*]!

17 For if I do this thing willingly, I have a reward [*I have the reward of extra joy and satisfaction*]: but if against my will [*if not willingly*], a dispensation of the gospel is committed unto me [*I still have an obligation to preach*].

18 What is my reward then? Verily that, when I preach the gospel, I may make the gospel of Christ without charge [*I preach without thought of monetary support*], that I abuse not my power in the gospel.

19 For though I be free [*am independent*] from all men, yet have I made myself servant unto all, that I might gain the more.

Paul now tells these members that he has always done his best to fit in with people, no matter who they were, so that he could avoid offending them and thus could gain their confidence in order to be effective in teaching the gospel. However, he assures his readers that he has never compromised the standards and commandments of the Savior in so doing.

20 And unto the Jews I became as a Jew, that I might gain the Jews [*while preaching to the Jews, I lived as much as possible like them so that they would be more willing to listen to me*]; to them that are under the law [*the Law of Moses*], as under the law, that I might gain them that are under the law;

21 To them [*Gentiles*] that are without law [*who do not live the Law of Moses*], as without law, (being not without law to God, but under the law to Christ,) [*I assure you I still kept the standards and commandments of the gospel as taught by Christ*] that I might gain them that are without law [*those who do not live the Law of Moses*].

22 To the weak became I as weak, that I might gain the weak: I am made all things to all men [*I try to fit in as well as possible with all people*], that I might by all means save some.

This "fitting in" as well as possible wherever he went would have been particularly hard for Paul because of his upbringing as a strict Pharisee, perhaps the strictest of all religious sects among the Jews. Most Pharisees were very judgmental of others who did not believe as they did and strictly avoided even associating with them. One must admire Paul for his willingness to quickly learn the Christ-like attribute of considering all people to be of equal worth.

23 And this I do for the gospel's sake, that I might be partaker thereof with you [*so that I might enjoy associating with you in the gospel*].

24 Know ye not that they which run in a race run all, but one receiveth the prize [*you know that lots of people run in a race, but only one is the winner*]? So run, that ye may obtain [*live the gospel so that you may get the prize, namely exaltation*].

**JST 1 Corinthians 9:24**

24 Know ye not that they which run in a race all run, but only one receiveth the prize? So run, that ye may obtain.

25 And every man that striveth for the mastery [*every participant in local athletic events*] is temperate [*goes through strict training*] in all things. Now they do it to obtain a corruptible crown [*they go through a lot to get a worldly honor*]; but we an incorruptible [*but we are training for an eternal crown*].

26 I therefore so run, not as uncertainly [*since the gospel crown is available to all who will live worthy, I do not run aimlessly*]; so fight I, not as one that beateth the air [*I do not fight for the prize like one who merely beats the air and puts on a show*]:

27 But I keep under my body, and bring it into subjection [*I control and discipline my body rigorously*]: lest that by any means [*for fear that through some temptation or another*], when I have preached to others, I myself should be a castaway [*my own soul should be lost*].

# FIRST CORINTHIANS 10

Paul will turn his attention to explaining that Jesus Christ was the God who let ancient Israel out of Egypt and into the promised land. This is crucial doctrine for those converts who are trying to understand why they should leave the Law of Moses rites and rituals and follow Christ as Paul has been teaching them to do. He will warn them not to fall into the same sins as the children of Israel did, which led many to destruction.

Verse 13 is one of the most often-quoted verses in the New Testament in our church meetings and lessons.

1 MOREOVER [*in addition*], brethren, I would not that ye should be ignorant [*I wouldn't want you to miss the fact*], how that all our fathers [*ancestors*] were

under the cloud [*were guided by the Lord by a "pillar of a cloud"; Exodus 13:21*], and all passed through the sea [*all passed to safety, escaping from Egypt through the Red Sea*];

Paul uses much symbolism in verses 2–4.

2 And were all baptized [*immersed*] unto Moses in the cloud and in the sea; [*Symbolically, they were "immersed" in God's leadership through Moses and "came up out of the waters of redemption," symbolic of being baptized in order to be freed from our enemies of sin and evil and led into the "promised land" (symbolic of heaven)*].

3 And did all eat the same spiritual meat [*they partook of the same manna, symbolic of being nourished by the gospel, sent down to them from heaven*];

4 And did all drink the same spiritual drink [*they were refreshed and saved by water which came out from the rock (Exodus 17:6), symbolic of the "living water" (John 4:10 and 14) which comes to us from Christ (the "Rock")*]: for they drank of that spiritual Rock [*the solid and sure foundation upon which we can safely build our lives*] that followed them: and that Rock was Christ.

5 But with many of them [*the children of Israel*] God was not well pleased: for they were overthrown [*destroyed*] in the wilderness.

6 Now these things were our examples, to the intent [*for the purpose of teaching us that*] we should not lust after evil things, as they also lusted.

7 Neither be ye idolaters [*don't be idol worshipers*], as were some of them; as it is written [*in Exodus 32:1–6*], The people sat down to eat and drink, and rose up to play [*to engage in pagan idol worship, including sexual immorality as part of the idol worship of the golden calf*].

8 Neither let us commit fornication [*let us avoid sexual immorality*], as some of them [*children of Israel*] committed, and fell in one day three and twenty thousand [*which caused 23,000 of them to get destroyed in one day*].

9 Neither let us tempt [*test or ignore*] Christ, as some of them also tempted [*did*], and were destroyed of serpents [*which led to their being destroyed by poisonous snakes*].

10 Neither murmur ye [*don't complain and mumble against the Lord and His leaders*], as some of them also murmured, and were destroyed of the destroyer [*were destroyed by the plague as recorded in Numbers 14:37*].

11 Now all these things happened unto them for ensamples [*all these things happened to them to try to teach them a lesson*]: and they are written for our admonition [*to warn us also*], upon whom the ends of the world are come.

**JST 1 Corinthians 10:11**

11 Now, all these things happened unto them for ensamples; and they were written for our admonition also, and for an admonition for those upon whom the end of the world shall come [*in other words, these things should serve as a warning to all those who will be destroyed if they don't repent, including those who live shortly before the Second Coming*].

12 Wherefore let him that thinketh he standeth take heed lest he fall. [*Let those who don't think these warnings apply to them think again and repent so they won't be destroyed.*]

13 There hath no temptation taken you but such as is common to man [*all of us are subject to temptation*]: but God is faithful, who will not suffer you to be tempted above that ye are able [*God will not allow you to be tempted beyond what you can resist*]; but will with the temptation also make a way to escape [*will help you overcome it*], that ye may be able to bear it [*so that you can handle it*].

Elder Joseph B. Worthlin, of the

Quorum of the Twelve, explained verse 13, above, in a talk given in the October 1989 General Conference. He said, "I suppose some of you, at one time or another, feel that you are 'hitting the wall', feeling an almost compelling urge to quit, give up, or give in to temptation. You will meet challenges, adversities, and temptations that seem to be more than you can bear. In times of sickness, death, financial need, and other hardships, you many wonder whether you have the strength, courage, or ability to continue. . . be sure you understand that God will not allow you to be tempted beyond your ability to resist (see 1 Corinthians 10:13). He does not give you challenges that you cannot surmount. He will not ask more than you can do but may ask right up to your limits so you can prove yourselves."

14 Wherefore, my dearly beloved, flee from idolatry [*avoid idol worship at all costs*].

15 I speak as to wise men [*I consider you to be wise men*]; judge ye what I say [*you be the judge of what I am teaching you*].

Paul will now compare the true sacrament with false "sacraments" partaken of by idol worshipers.

16 The cup of blessing [*the sacrament*] which we bless, is it not the communion [*sacrament*] of the blood of Christ? The bread which we break [*as we partake of the sacrament*], is it not the communion of the [*does it not represent*] body of Christ?

17 For we being many are one bread, and one body [*we are all united by Christ's sacrificing His body for us*]: for we are all partakers of that one bread [*we all partake of the gospel, represented by the sacrament bread*].

18 Behold Israel after the flesh [*think about the Israelites who have become so worldly*]: are not they which eat of the sacrifices partakers of the altar [*don't those apostate Israelites who eat the food used for the sacrifices to idols in effect participate in offering the sacrifice at the altar*]?

19 What say I then [*what am I saying*]? that the idol is any thing [*other than a piece of wood or stone*], or that which is offered in sacrifice to idols is any thing [*or that there is anything special about the food that is offered to it*]?

20 But I say, that the things which the Gentiles sacrifice, they sacrifice to devils [*the sacrifices the Gentiles offer to their idols are in effect sacrifices offered to false gods or devils*], and not to God: and I would not that ye should have fellowship with devils [*and I don't want you associating with devils*].

21 Ye cannot drink the cup of the Lord, and the cup of devils [*you can't worship the Lord and worship devils at the same time*]: ye cannot be partakers of the Lord's table, and of the table of devils [*you can't be nourished by the Lord and by devils at the same time*].

22 Do we provoke the Lord to jealousy [*is the Lord just another idol or god*]? are we stronger than he [*do we run His life like idol worshipers run the lives of their idols*]?

We would be lost and very confused by verse 23 without the JST.

23 All things are lawful for me, but all things are not expedient: all things are lawful for me, but all things edify not.

**JST 1 Corinthians 10:23**

23 All things are not lawful for me, for all things are not expedient; all things are not lawful, for all things edify not.

24 Let no man seek his own, but every man another's wealth.

**JST 1 Corinthians 10:24**

24 Let no man seek therefore his own, but every man another's good.

The word "shambles" in verse 25, next, refers to the meat markets in

Corinth where left over meat from idol worship was sold.

25 Whatsoever is sold in the shambles, that eat, asking no question for conscience sake [*don't worry about buying and eating meat that is left over from pagan idol worship*]:

26 For the earth is the Lord's, and the fulness thereof.

27 If any of them that believe not bid you to a feast, and ye be disposed to go; whatsoever is set before you, eat, asking no question for conscience sake [*if any nonmembers invite you to dinner, and you would like to accept their invitation, go ahead and eat whatever they serve*].

**JST 1 Corinthians 10:27**

27 If any of them that believe not bid you to a feast, and ye be disposed to eat; whatsoever is set before you, eat, asking no questions for conscience' sake.

28 But if any man say unto you, This is offered in sacrifice unto idols, eat not for his sake that shewed it, and for conscience sake [*but if the host or any others attending the feast tell you that eating this meat is part of their idol worship ceremonies, don't eat it as a matter of respect for him and his beliefs, and also as a matter of not participating in idol worship*]: for the earth is the Lord's, and the fulness thereof:

29 Conscience, I say [*let me explain a bit more of what I mean by conscience*], not thine own, but of the other [*I'm not referring to yours but rather to your host's or that of other dinner guests*]: for why is my liberty judged of another man's conscience [*why should my freedom to do as I please be limited by another man's beliefs*]?

30 For if I by grace be a partaker [*if through the kindness of God I am blessed with a good meal*], why am I evil spoken of for that for which I give thanks [*why do I get criticized for something I personally am thankful for*]?

31 Whether therefore ye eat, or drink, or whatsoever ye do, do all to the glory of God [*therefore, no matter what you do, make sure it furthers the work of God among your fellow beings*].

32 Give none offence, neither to the Jews, nor to the Gentiles, nor to the church of God [*do your best not to offend anyone*]:

33 Even as I please all men in all things [*just like I try not to offend anyone in anything*], not seeking mine own profits [*often not doing what I would prefer to do*], but the profit of many [*rather trying to do what will be best for many others*], that they may be saved [*so that they are encouraged to come to Christ and be saved*].

**JST 1 Corinthians 10:33**

33 Even as I please all men in all things, not seeking mine own profit, but of the many, that they may be saved.

# FIRST CORINTHIANS 11

In this chapter, the Apostle Paul will deal with a number of issues among the Corinthian Saints, including local customs of hair and grooming, marriage, and husband and wife roles, some of which he approves and some of which he disapproves. His counsel regarding some of these matters, if taken out of context, can become a problem. He will also give a beautiful written sermon regarding the sacrament.

1 BE ye followers of me, even as I also am of Christ [*follow me as I follow Christ*].

2 Now I praise [*compliment*] you, brethren, that ye remember [*for remembering*] me in all things, and keep the ordinances, as I delivered them to you [*and that you are keeping the ordinances*

*and teachings of the gospel just as I taught you to*].

In verse 3, next, Paul teaches the organization and relationship of husband and wife, which he compares to the organization and relationship of Christ and the Father, implying that the husband and wife should work together in love, unity, and harmony just as the Father and Son do.

Be sure to read the note provided after verse 9.

3 But I would have you know, that the head of every man is Christ; and the head of the woman is the man; and the head of Christ is God [*the Father*].

In verses 4–7, Paul deals with local customs used to show respect for God while worshiping. In Corinth, men took their hats or caps off as a way of showing respect for God while worshiping, whereas, local custom required women to wear head coverings while worshiping.

4 Every man praying or prophesying [*worshiping*], having his head covered, dishonoureth his head [*is showing disrespect*].

5 But every woman that prayeth or prophesieth with her head uncovered dishonoureth her head [*is showing disrespect*]: for that is even all one as if she were shaven [*it is just as if she had shaved her head bald, which, in Corinthian culture, was the sign of a woman who was an adulteress*].

**JST 1 Corinthians 11:5**

5 But every woman that prayeth or prophesieth with her head uncovered dishonoreth her head; for that is even all one as if she were shaven.

6 For if the woman be not covered [*if she is not willing to cover her head while worshiping*], let her also be shorn [*let her head be shaved*]: but if it be a shame for a woman to be shorn or shaven, let her be covered. [*In other words, even though this is just a local custom, there is wisdom in going along with it in order not to cause unnecessary distraction or criticism during worship.*]

**JST 1 Corinthians 11:6**

6 For if the woman be not covered, let her also be shorn; but if it be a shame for a woman to be shorn or shaven, let her be covered.

7 For a man indeed ought not to cover his head [*during worship*], forasmuch as he is the image and glory of God: but the woman is the glory of the man. [*The woman should bring glory and honor to her husband just as the husband should bring glory and honor to God.*]

8 For the man is not of the woman; but the woman of the man. [*Adam did not come from Eve, rather Eve came from Adam.*]

9 Neither was the man created for the woman; but the woman for the man.

Verses 8 and 9, above, can be misinterpreted to mean that men are superior to women in God's eyes. This is not true. James E. Faust said, "Nowhere does the doctrine of this Church declare that men are superior to women." (Conference Report, April 1988, p. 43.) We should study the word of the Lord through our modern First Presidency and Quorum of the Twelve given in "The Family, a Proclamation to the World," September 23, 1995, wherein they said "fathers and mothers are obligated to help one another as equal partners." You may wish to read the notes in this study guide that go along with Ephesians 5:21–33, which help with this topic.

D&C 132:19–20 also teaches us correct doctrine, namely, that worthy husbands and wives, sealed together for eternity, are gods and serve together and are "above all, because all things are subject unto them. . .and the angels are subject to them." Elder Bruce R. McConkie explained D&C 132:20 as follows: "Exaltation grows out of the eternal union of a man and his wife. Of those whose marriage endures in eternity, the Lord says, 'Then shall they be gods' (D&C

132:20); that is each of them, the man and the woman, will be a god. As such they will rule over their dominions forever." See *Mormon Doctrine*, p. 613.

10 For this cause ought the woman to have power on her head because of the angels. [*Out of respect for heaven.*]

**JST 1 Corinthians 11:10**
10 For this cause ought the woman to have a covering on her head because of the angels.

Next, in verse 11, Paul teaches eternal marriage, explaining that a man and a woman can remain married when they live with the Lord in His kingdom in heaven. Compare with D&C 132:19–20. Also, see Matthew 19:6.

11 Nevertheless neither is the man without the woman, neither the woman without the man, in the Lord.

12 For as the woman is of the man, even so is the man also by the woman [*Eve came from Adam, but all men come from women through birth*]; but all things of God [*and all things come from God*]. [*In other words, men and women should respect each other and sustain and build each other up, because they all come from God, and thus have great worth.*]

13 Judge in yourselves [*you be the judge*]: is it comely [*appropriate, fitting*] that a woman pray unto God uncovered [*with her head uncovered*]? [*In other words, in your local Corinthian culture, would it be appropriate for a righteous woman to pray with her head uncovered, since it would make everyone think she is an adulteress?*]

14 Doth not even nature itself teach you, that, if a man have long hair, it is a shame unto him?

Apparently, in the local Corinthian culture and society, there was something about men having long hair which was offensive and signaled that they were involved in evil or inappropriate behaviors. Thus, Paul counsels local Saints, in verse 14, above, to be sensitive to their culture and not wear hairstyles which directly associate them with wicked lifestyles. Certainly there was not anything inherently wrong with long hair on men. The Savior had long hair, signaling in His local culture that He was dedicated to God.

15 But if a woman have long hair, it is a glory to her [*it accentuates her beauty*]: for her hair is given her for a covering.

16 But if any man seem to be contentious [*if anyone gets upset about what I have just said*], we have no such custom, neither the churches of God [*remind them that we are dealing here with local customs, not a universal policy throughout the Church*].

17 Now in this that I declare unto you I praise you not [*now, in the next matter I am going to bring up, I can't compliment you*], that ye come together not for the better, but for the worse [*that when you meet together, you are causing more problems than you are solving.*].

18 For first of all, when ye come together in the church, I hear that there be divisions among you [*I hear that you are breaking up the Church into apostate groups and factions*]; and I partly believe it [*and I am inclined to believe that it is happening among you to some degree*].

19 For there must be also heresies among you, that they which are approved [*those who remain faithful to what I have taught you, and are thus approved by God*] may be made manifest [*may show up as steadfast Saints*] among you. [*In other words, as stated in 2 Nephi 2:11, "It must needs be that there is an opposition in all things" in order to test us.*]

**JST 1 Corinthians 11:19**
19 For there must be also divisions among you, that they which are approved may be made manifest among you.

20 When ye come together therefore into one place, this is not to eat the Lord's supper [*the sacrament*].

**JST 1 Corinthians 11:20**

20 When ye come together into one place, is it not to eat the Lord's supper?

In verses 21–22, next, Paul is apparently dealing with a specific problem which has developed among the Corinthian members. It appears that their meetings have degenerated into thoughtless and quarrelsome times of contention, where some selfishly eat while others go hungry, some get drunk, etc., all of which is contrary to the peaceful coming together of kind and faithful Saints to reverence the Savior through partaking of the sacrament.

21 For in eating every one taketh before other his own supper: and one is hungry, and another is drunken.

**JST 1 Corinthians 11:21**

21 But in eating everyone taketh before his own supper; and one is hungry, and another is drunken.

22 What? have ye not houses to eat and to drink in [*can't you eat and drink at home, instead of during sacred meetings*]? or despise ye the church of God, and shame them that have not [*are you so disrespectful of the Church of God that you bring expensive foods and then embarrass members who can't afford such lavish food by not sharing with them*]? What shall I say to you? shall I praise you in this? I praise you not.

Paul will now teach these members the background of the sacrament and thus illustrate to them why it is so sacred.

23 For I have received of the Lord [*I have been taught by the Lord*] that which also I delivered unto you [*that which I taught you*], That the Lord Jesus the same night in which he was betrayed took bread:

24 And when he had given thanks, he brake [*broke*] it, and said, Take, eat: this is my body, which is broken for you: this do in remembrance of me.

25 After the same manner [*in the same way*] also he took the cup, when he had supped [*after supper*], saying, This cup is the new testament [*the new covenant*] in my blood: this do ye, as oft as ye drink it, in remembrance of me.

26 For as often as ye eat this bread, and drink this cup, ye do shew the Lord's death [*you are remembering that Christ gave His life for you*] till he come. [*In other words, whenever you take the sacrament, you are bearing witness of Christ, and so it will continue until the Second Coming when He Himself will bear witness to everyone.*]

27 Wherefore whosoever shall eat this bread, and drink this cup of the Lord, unworthily [*whoever partakes of the sacrament unworthily*], shall be guilty of the body and blood of the Lord [*is guilty of being disrespectful or mocking the Savior's sacrifice of His body and blood for us*].

28 But let a man examine himself [*you judge yourselves carefully as to whether or not you are worthy to partake of the sacrament*], and so [*if he feels worthy*] let him eat of that bread, and drink of that cup.

29 For he that eateth and drinketh unworthily, eateth and drinketh damnation to himself, not discerning the Lord's body [*not being aware of how important the sacrament is and what it represents*].

**JST 1 Corinthians 11:29**

29 For he that eateth and drinketh unworthily, eateth and drinketh condemnation to himself, not discerning the Lord's body.

30 For this cause many are weak [*spiritually*] and sickly [*spiritually*] among you, and many sleep [*many have died spiritually*].

Based on what Paul counsels about the sacrament in the above verses, it would be easy for members to go too far and be afraid to ever take it. This is not the purpose of the sacrament. Bruce R. McConkie said, "This penalty [*referring to what Paul said in verse 27*] applies only to those who partake of the sacrament in total and complete unworthiness and rebellion." *Doctrinal New Testament Commentary*, Vol. 2, p. 365.

31 For if we would judge ourselves, we should not be judged [*if we were more careful not to take the sacrament unworthily, we wouldn't be in danger of being judged severely by God*].

32 But when we are judged, we are chastened of the Lord, that we should not be condemned with the world [*the Lord scolds us as needed so we can repent so we will not be condemned with the rest of the world*].

33 Wherefore, my brethren, when ye come together to eat, tarry [*wait*] one for another.

34 And if any man hunger, let him eat at home; that ye come not together unto condemnation [*so that you don't get condemned because of your contention and irreverence in your meetings*]. And the rest will I set in order when I come [*I will straighten out some other things when I get there*].

# FIRST CORINTHIANS 12

This chapter is well-known for mentioning several spiritual gifts. Each person who has received the gift of the Holy Ghost is given one or more gifts of the Spirit. Elder Orson Pratt described this privilege as follows: "Whenever the Holy Ghost takes up its residence in a person, it not only cleanses, sanctifies, and purifies him, in proportion as he yields himself to its influence, but also imparts to him some gift, intended for the benefit of himself and others . . . all Saints who constitute the Church of Christ, are baptized into the same Spirit; and each one, without any exception, is made a partaker of some spiritual gift. . . Each member does not receive all these gifts; [*they*] are distributed among the members of the Church, according to their faithfulness, circumstances, natural abilities, duties, and callings; that the whole may be properly instructed, confirmed, perfected, and saved." (*Masterful Discourses*, pp. 539–41. Institute of Religion *Doctrine and Covenants Student Manual*, p. 100.) Two other major references in the scriptures which also list a number of these gifts are Moroni 10:8–18 and D&C, 46:8–27. Romans 12:6–13 lists several additional gifts. These are gifts which are given by the Holy Ghost. See D&C 46:13. Many of the definitions of spiritual gifts, used in the notes for the following verses, derive from the Institute of Religion *Doctrine and Covenants Student Manual*, Religion 324–325, pp. 100–101.

We will use **bold** to point out specific gifts of the Spirit.

1 NOW concerning spiritual gifts, brethren, I would not have you ignorant [*not knowing about them*].

**JST 1 Corinthians 12:1**

1 Now concerning spiritual things, brethren, I would not have you ignorant.

2 Ye know that ye were Gentiles [*nonmembers*], carried away unto these dumb idols [*worshiping idols which can't talk*], even as ye were led [*having been led to do so by false religions and philosophies*].

3 Wherefore I give you to understand, that no man speaking by the Spirit of God calleth Jesus accursed [*no person*

*who has the Holy Ghost opposes Jesus*]: and that **no man can say that Jesus is the Lord, but by the Holy Ghost** [*you cannot have a full testimony of the Savior unless it is given you by the Holy Ghost*].

> In reference to the last phrase in verse 3, above, Joseph Smith said that it should be translated as "No man can know that Jesus is the Lord, but by the Holy Ghost." See *Teachings of the Prophet Joseph Smith*, p. 223.

4 Now there are diversities of gifts [*there are various spiritual gifts*], but the same Spirit [*but they all come from the Holy Ghost; see D&C 46:11 and 13*].

5 And there are [*one of these gifts is*] **differences of administrations** [*being able to use the organizations within the Church effectively, the gift of leadership in the Church*], but the same Lord [*each gift comes from the same God*].

> The last phrase in verse 5, above, may appear a bit unnecessary to those of us who have always believed in one Lord, but to the Corinthian Saints, who lived in an environment of many false gods, it is an important clarification. Otherwise, members might be tempted to believe that one spiritual gift came from one idol, and another from another god, etc.

6 And there are [*another gift is*] **diversities of operations** [*the ability to distinguish between truth and false philosophies and ideas*], but it is the same God which worketh all in all [*each of these gifts comes from God*].

7 But the manifestation of the Spirit is given to every man to profit withal. [*These gifts of the Spirit are given to individuals so that everyone can benefit.*]

8 For to one [*faithful member*] is given by the Spirit [*the Holy Ghost*] the word of **wisdom** [*the gift of wisdom*]; to another the word of **knowledge** [*the gift of acquiring and retaining knowledge, especially of the gospel*] by the same Spirit;

9 To another **faith** [*another member is given the gift of faith*] by the same Spirit; to another the **gifts of healing** by the same Spirit;

> With respect to the gift of healing, in verse 9, above, Joseph Smith taught that both men and women can have this gift. "These signs, such as healing the sick, casting out devils, etc., should follow all that believe, whether male or female." *Teachings of the Prophet Joseph Smith*, p. 224.

10 To another the **working of miracles**; to another **prophecy** [*the gift of knowing the future (which must be used properly within one's own stewardship)*]; to another **discerning of spirits** [*the gift of detecting evil which others don't see; also, the gift of seeing the good in others*]; to another divers [*various*] kinds of **tongues** [*the gift of tongues, which includes the ability to rather quickly learn a foreign language as a missionary*]; to another the **interpretation of tongues**:

> Joseph Smith warned that speaking in tongues is often used by Satan to deceive people. He said "Be not so curious about tongues, do not speak in tongues except there be an interpreter present; the ultimate design of tongues is to speak to foreigners, and if persons are very anxious to display their intelligence, let them speak to such in their own tongues. The gifts of God are all useful in their place, but when they are applied to that which God does not intend, they prove an injury, a snare, and a curse instead of a blessing." *History of the Church*, Vol. 5, pp. 31–32.

11 But all these worketh that one and the selfsame Spirit [*all these gifts come from the same Spirit, namely the Holy Ghost*], dividing [*giving*] to every man severally [*his own*] as he will.

12 For as the body is one [*is one unit*], and hath many members [*such as arms,*

*legs, hands, eyes, and so forth*], and all the members of that one body, being many, are one body: so also is Christ. [*Just as the body consists of many individual body parts, all belonging to the same body, so also is it with these gifts of the Spirit. Even though there are many different ones, given to various members of the Church, they all work together to bring us to unity in Christ's gospel.*]

13 For by one Spirit are we all baptized into one body, whether we be Jews or Gentiles, whether we be bond [*a slave or servant*] or free; and have been all made to drink into one Spirit. [*Regardless of our background, culture, etc., the same Spirit unites us in the gospel. In other words, the purpose of the gifts of the Spirit is to help us work in harmony as a team, each benefiting from the other's gifts. See D&C 46:11–12.*]

14 For the body is not one member, but many [*the body is not composed of just one part, but many parts*].

15 If the foot shall say, Because I am not the hand, I am not of the body; is it therefore not of the body? [*For instance, if a member who has the gift of faith but not the gift of knowledge were to say, "Since I don't have the gift of knowledge, I am left out," does that mean that he or she is not a valid member of the Church?*]

16 And if the ear shall say, Because I am not the eye, I am not of the body; is it therefore not of the body?

17 If the whole body were an eye, where were the hearing [*how would we hear*]? If the whole were hearing, where were the smelling [*how would we be able to smell things*]? [*The point is that we as a "body" of Saints need each member and the gifts which each member has been given.*]

18 But now hath God set the members every one of them in the body [*the Church*], as it hath pleased him [*God has given each member one or more gifts of the Spirit according to His will, and placed them in the Church*].

19 And if they were all one member, where were the body [*and if each of them were the same body part (such as a foot), what kind of a body would that be*]?

20 But now are they many members, yet but one body. [*God has given many different gifts of the Spirit, thus creating a well-balanced "body" of the Church.*]

By now you are probably quite used to the fact that Paul often uses much repetition to drive home his point when he is teaching.

21 And the eye cannot say unto the hand [*a member with one spiritual gift can't say to another*], I have no need of thee: nor again the head to the feet, I have no need of you.

22 Nay, much more [*on the contrary*] those members of the body, which seem to be more feeble [*weak; see 1 Corinthians 12:22, footnote a, in your Bible*], are necessary [*the weaker members of the Church are very necessary*]:

23 And those members of the body [*those members of the Church*], which we think to be less honourable [*not as capable; not as valuable to the Church—see* Teachings of the Prophet Joseph Smith, *pp. 223–224*], upon these we bestow more abundant honour [*we treat as more valuable*]; and our uncomely parts have more abundant comeliness [*and our members who are less influential and capable in the Church become more capable and thus more influential*].

The word "comely" has various meanings in the scriptures, depending on context. Strong's *Concordance* (definition #2158) defines it various ways, including "of elegant figure, shapely, graceful, bearing one's self becomingly in speech or behavior, of good standing, honourable, influential, respectable." In verse 23, above,

"uncomely" seems to have the connotation of being less influential or less experienced in the Church. In verse 24, next, "comely" seems to include the concept of "experienced," "influential," "bringing honor to the Church," and "being stable and solid in the Church." In speaking of these verses in 1 Corinthians, chapter 12, Joseph Smith warned members against being jealous of those called to leadership. In *Teachings of the Prophet Joseph Smith*, pp. 223–224, it tells us what the Prophet said about this. "He spoke of the disposition of many men to consider the lower offices in the Church dishonorable, and to look with jealous eyes upon the standing of others who are called to preside over them."

24 For our comely parts [*our stronger members*] have no need [*are already aware of their worth and value to God*]: but God hath tempered [*mixed*] the body [*members of the Church*] together, having given more abundant honour [*value, worth; Strong's #5092*] to that part [*weaker members; see verse 22*] which lacked: [*In other words, a major purpose of the Lord's mixing weaker members with stronger members is to increase the weaker members' self-esteem and sense of worth in God's eyes, as well as training them for future leadership callings.*]

25 That there should be no schism [*divisions*] in the body [*the Church*]; but that the members should have the same care one for another.

26 And whether one member suffer [*if one member is suffering*], all the members suffer with it; or one member be honoured, all the members rejoice with it. [*This is similar to Mosiah 18:8–9, which includes "willing to bear one another's burdens, that they may be light; . . . and are willing to mourn with those that mourn; and comfort those that stand in need of comfort, . . ."*]

27 Now ye are the body of Christ [*you all belong to Christ's Church*], and members in particular [*and each of you has individual skills, spiritual gifts, abilities, etc.*].

Next, Paul will summarize this chapter by emphasizing the importance of Church organization and the role each member has in strengthening the Church with his or her own unique gifts and abilities. He will also emphasize the importance of those who teach in the Church, placing them next in influence to Apostles and prophets.

28 And God hath set some in the church [*and God has organized the Church with*], first apostles, secondarily prophets, thirdly teachers, after that miracles, then gifts of healings, helps, governments, diversities of tongues [*the gift of tongues*].

29 Are all apostles? are all prophets? are all teachers? are all workers of miracles? [*Answer: No.*]

30 Have all the gifts of healing? do all speak with tongues? do all interpret? [*Answer: No.*]

31 But covet [*seek*] earnestly the best gifts [*D&C 46:8 ". . . seek ye earnestly the best gifts,"*]: and yet shew I unto you a more excellent way.

**JST 1 Corinthians 12:31**

31 I say unto you, Nay; for I have shown unto you a more excellent way, therefore covet earnestly the best gifts.

The "more excellent way" spoken of by Paul in verse 31, would seem to include the concept that spiritual gifts given to individual members open up the opportunity for unity, harmony, strengthening each other and all working together for the good of each other. Indeed, this "more excellent way" is the way to celestial glory and exaltation.

# FIRST CORINTHIANS 13

Having taught the Corinthian Saints about the role of spiritual gifts in strengthening the Church and its individual members, in chapter 12, Paul now focuses on the very essence of Christ like living for each of us, namely, having charity toward each other. He will teach us, in effect, that no matter how qualified we are in other areas, if we lack charity we are nothing.

The word "charity" in the original New Testament Greek is defined as "brotherly love, good will, love, benevolence." In Moroni 7:47, it is defined as "the pure love of Christ." This is one of the best known and beautiful of Paul's teachings. The Prophet Joseph Smith made no JST changes to this chapter.

1 THOUGH I speak with the tongues of men and of angels [*even though I speak many different languages and even speak like an angel*], and have not charity, I am become as sounding brass, or a tinkling cymbal [*I am nothing but a loud brass gong or a clanging cymbal*].

2 And though I have the gift of prophecy, and understand all mysteries, and all knowledge; and though I have all faith, so that I could remove mountains, and have not charity, I am nothing.

3 And though I bestow [*give*] all my goods [*material possessions*] to feed the poor, and though I give my body to be burned [*if I were to give my life for the gospel*], and have not charity, it profiteth me nothing.

4 Charity suffereth long [*is patient*], and is kind; charity envieth not [*does not resent others for what they have*]; charity vaunteth not itself [*does not brag*], is not puffed up [*is not prideful*],

5 Doth not behave itself unseemly [*indecently (see 1 Corinthians 13:5, footnote a), inappropriately, rudely*], seeketh not her own [*is not selfish*], is not easily provoked [*is not irritable; doesn't lose its temper*], thinketh no evil [*the word "thinketh" as used here, means "keeps a list of; keeps an account of"; Strong's #3049; see also the Institute of Religion New Testament student manual,* The Life and Teachings of Jesus and His Apostles, *p. 296. In other words, doesn't hold grudges, doesn't keep a list of wrongs done to him or her by others*];

6 Rejoiceth not in iniquity [*does not delight in or take pleasure in wickedness*], but rejoiceth in the truth;

7 Beareth all things [*keeps quiet about the errors and faults of others; see Strong's #4722; does not give in to resentment (see Institute New Testament student manual, p. 296)*], believeth all things [*is completely trusting of and committed to God and Christ; Strong's #4100*], hopeth all things [*in the Book of Mormon, the word "hope" implies "courage," "assurance," and "determination" (see Alma 58:11–12) and optimistically planning on success in following God, a "perfect brightness of hope" (see 2 Nephi 31:20)*], endureth all things [*never gives up in following Christ*].

The phrase "Charity never faileth" in verse 8, next, has many possible interpretations and lessons for us. For instance, it can mean that exercising charity never fails to make us a better person. It never fails to make the world a better place. Another lesson for us could be found in Strong's *Concordance* #1601, which defines "faileth" as being ineffective, in other words, "charity" is never ineffective. Even in the case where Christ like love and patience is rejected by others, charity still brings the one who has it back to God. Yet another use of the word "fail" is found in the phrase "Men's hearts failing them for fear," as used in Luke 21:26. Here, the word "failing" means "to run out of," as in running out of hope, courage, optimism, etc. Thus,

"Charity never faileth" could mean that a truly Christ like person never runs out of charity toward others. Still another help for understanding the word "faileth" is found in the Institute of Religion New Testament student manual, p. 296, where "faileth" is used in conjunction with a leaf falling off a tree or a flower. The message is that "charity" will never be removed from its place as a central focus of celestial, Christ like behavior.

8 Charity never faileth [*see note above*]: but whether there be prophecies [*in the case of prophecies*], they shall fail [*they eventually finish up by being fulfilled*]; whether there be tongues [*in the case of speaking various languages*], they shall cease [*it will no longer be necessary when we all learn the same language; it will no longer be necessary after the Second Coming because we will all speak the same language; see Zephaniah 3:9*]; whether there be knowledge [*in the case of knowledge*], it shall vanish away [*partial knowledge, false assumptions, philosophies, and opinions will vanish away in the light of truth*].

9 For we know in part, and we prophesy in part. [*In other words, we don't know all things, and the prophesying we do does not reveal all truth yet.*]

10 But when that [*Christ*] which is perfect is come, then that which is in part shall be done away. [*In other words, when Christ comes, He will "reveal all things." See D&C 101:32–34.*]

11 When I was a child, I spake [*spoke*] as a child, I understood as a child, I thought as a child: but when I became a man, I put away childish things. [*One of the messages in this verse is that as we develop Christ like charity, we put away "childish" or spiritually-immature behaviors, such as self-centeredness, selfishness, losing our temper, being impatient with others, gossiping, taking pleasure in wickedness, etc., as mentioned in the earlier verses in this chapter.*]

In order to better understand Paul's imagery about seeing "through a glass darkly" in the next verse, we need a bit of information about Paul's day. Page 296 of the Institute of Religion's New Testament student manual, *The Life and Teachings of Jesus and His Apostles*, has the following explanation: "The word translated glass is actually mirror. To those of us accustomed to the high quality mirrors of today, Paul's imagery is not clear. 'The thought of imperfect seeing is emphasized by the character of the ancient mirror, which was of polished metal, and required constant polishing, so that a sponge with pounded pumice-stone was generally attached to it.' (Vincent Word Studies, 2:795–96.") In other words, even with our best efforts, with our current limitations, we have a hard time seeing clearly who we are and what we can become as we develop charity and follow Christ. It is like looking at ourselves in a hazy, distorted mirror and saying, "That's the real me."

12 For now [*with our mortal limitations*] we see through a glass, darkly; but then face to face [*when we are face to face with God, and have become gods, we will see who we really are, that we are "like him"; see 1 John 3:2, where we are told "we shall be like him; for we shall see him as he is"; see also D&C 130:1*]: now I know in part [*now, I do not know all things*]; but then shall I know even as also I am known [*by God, in celestial exaltation; see D&C 76:94. In other words, via true doctrine, you must "see" your potential, and that you and I have the potential of becoming gods, and of knowing all things, just as our God, our Father knows us.*]

13 And now abideth faith, hope, charity, these three [*now, these three things are our main focus, faith, hope, and charity*]; but the greatest of these [*the character trait we need most, and to which faith in Christ and hope lead*] is charity.

In verse 13, above, faith, hope, and charity are a dynamic combination of

cause and effect, and might be summarized as follows: Faith in Jesus Christ leads to personal change and improvement, thus, to hope for ourselves as far as exaltation is concerned. Both faith and hope lead us to the essence of Christ like living, which is charity toward all others. Apostle Bruce R. McConkie explained verse 13, above, as follows: "But some things shall 'abide' forever. Among them: Faith, which is the very power of God himself; hope, which is the assurance of eternal life and everlasting progression; and charity, which is the pure love of Christ." *Doctrinal New Testament Commentary*, Vol. 2, p. 380.

# FIRST CORINTHIANS 14

Chapter 14 is a continuation of Paul's teachings dealing with gifts of the Spirit (chapter 12) and charity (chapter 13). By way of background, it would seem that many of the Corinthian members of the Church have gone overboard with speaking in tongues. It has become a matter of prestige among them and has become a type of false spirituality, leaving them subject to Satan's deceptions. Joseph Smith cautioned the members of the Church on several occasions about the dangers of deception when it comes to speaking in tongues and other so-called "manifestations of the Spirit." In *History of the Church*, Vol. 4, p. 572, he taught: "One great evil is, that men are ignorant of the nature of spirits; their power, laws, government, intelligence, &c., and imagine that when there is anything like power, revelation, or vision manifested, that it must be of God. Hence the Methodists, Presbyterians, and others frequently possess a spirit that will cause them to lie down, and during its operation, animation is frequently entirely suspended; they consider it to be the power of God, and a glorious manifestation from God—a manifestation of what? Is there any intelligence communicated? Are the curtains of heaven withdrawn, or the purposes of God developed? Have they seen and conversed with an angel—or have the glories of futurity burst upon their view? No! but their body has been inanimate, the operation of their spirit suspended, and all the intelligence that can be obtained from them when they arise, is a shout of 'glory,' or 'hallelujah,' or some incoherent expression; but they have had 'the power.' The Shaker will whirl around on his heel, impelled by a supernatural agency or spirit, and think that he is governed by the Spirit of God; and the Jumper will jump and enter into all kinds of extravagances. A Primitive Methodist will shout under the influence of that spirit, until he will rend the heavens with his cries; while the Quakers (or Friends) moved as they think, by the Spirit of God, will sit still and say nothing. Is God the author of all this? If not of all of it, which does He recognize? Surely, such a heterogeneous mass of confusion never can enter into the kingdom of heaven."

We will include other such cautions from the Prophet as we study this chapter.

1 FOLLOW [*eagerly pursue; seek*] after charity, and desire [*seek; see D&C 46:8*] spiritual gifts, but rather that ye may prophesy.

The word "prophesy" in verse 1, above, has more than one meaning in scripture. It usually means to foretell the future, especially predicting future events which pertain to the gospel. It can also mean to have the influence of the Holy Ghost upon you such that you know the gospel is true. Thus, for instance, you can "prophesy" that everyone will some day know that God exists. We are taught this in

the Bible Dictionary, p. 754, where it says "In a general sense a prophet is anyone who has a testimony of Jesus Christ by the Holy Ghost, as in Numbers 11:25–29; Revelation 19:10."

"Prophesying" can also mean "bearing one's testimony," for instance, in a church meeting. Yet another definition of "prophesy" is found in Strong's *Concordance* #4395, where it is defined as "to teach, refute, reprove, admonish, comfort others." This last definition may fit Paul's intent in verse 1 so that it basically says for us to seek to develop charity and to seek spiritual gifts so that we can more effectively teach and minister to one another by word and example. This seems to fit the context of verses 3 and 4.

2 For he that speaketh in an unknown tongue [*language*] speaketh not unto men, but unto God: for no man understandeth him [*perhaps meaning that it doesn't do anyone any good, because only God can understand him*]; howbeit [*however*] in the spirit he speaketh mysteries [*perhaps meaning that what he says while under the influence of such a spirit remains a mystery to others*].

**JST 1 Corinthians 14:2**

2 For he that speaketh in another tongue speaketh not unto men, but unto God; for no man understandeth him; howbeit in the spirit he speaketh mysteries.

It may be that the Prophet Joseph Smith's counsel about speaking in tongues fits in with this verse. He said:

"Not every spirit, or vision, or singing, is of God. The devil is an orator; he is powerful. . . Speak not in the gift of tongues without understanding it, or without interpretation. The devil can speak in tongues . . . he can tempt all classes; can speak in English or Dutch. Let no one speak in tongues unless he interpret, except by the consent of the one who is placed to preside; then he may discern or interpret, or another may." (*Teachings of the Prophet Joseph Smith*, p. 162.)

3 But he that prophesieth speaketh unto men to edification [*builds them up, strengthens them spiritually*], and exhortation [*encouragement*], and comfort.

4 He that speaketh in an unknown tongue edifieth himself [*builds himself up*]; but he that prophesieth [*teaches correct doctrine and ministers to others with the pure love of Christ; see note for verse 1*] edifieth [*builds and strengthens*] the church.

**JST 1 Corinthians 14:4**

4 He that speaketh in another tongue edifieth himself; but he that prophesieth edifieth the church.

As mentioned in the note at the beginning of this chapter, there seems to have been a problem among the Corinthian Saints with speaking in tongues. Paul appears to be trying to convince them to downplay speaking in tongues into its proper place as a gift of the Spirit as opposed to using it to build themselves up in the eyes of others. In verse 5, next, he is rather gentle and diplomatic with them.

5 I would that ye all spake with tongues [*it would be nice if you could all speak in different languages*], but rather that ye prophesied [*but I would rather have you teach and strengthen each other rather than yourselves*]: for greater is he that prophesieth than he that speaketh with tongues [*the member who humbly teaches others is actually greater than the member who speaks in tongues*], except he interpret [*unless the gift of interpretation of tongues is also present*], that the church may receive edifying [*may be strengthened*].

Joseph Smith addressed this issue as he explained Paul's teachings about gifts of the Spirit in 1 Corinthians, chapter 12. He said "There are several gifts mentioned here, yet which of them all could be known by an observer at the imposition of hands? The word of wisdom, and the word of knowledge, are as much gifts as any

> other, yet if a person possessed both of these gifts, or received them by the imposition of hands [*laying on of hands*], who would know it? Another might receive the gift of faith, and they would be as ignorant of it. Or suppose a man had the gift of healing or power to work miracles, that would not then be known; it would require time and circumstances to call these gifts into operation. Suppose a man had the discerning of spirits, who would be the wiser of it? Or if he had the interpretation of tongues, unless someone spoke in an unknown tongue, he of course would have to be silent; there are only two gifts that could be made visible—the gift of tongues and the gift of prophecy. These are the things that are the most talked about, and yet if a person spoke in an unknown tongue, according to Paul's testimony, he would be a barbarian to those present. They would say that it was gibberish; and if he prophesied they would call it nonsense. The gift of tongues is the smallest gift perhaps of the whole, and yet it is one that is the most sought after. (*Teachings of the Prophet Joseph Smith*, p. 246.) The Prophet went on to say, "Be not so curious about tongues, do not speak in tongues except there be an interpreter present; the ultimate design of tongues is to speak to foreigners, and if persons are very anxious to display their intelligence, let them speak to such in their own tongues. The gifts of God are all useful in their place, but when they are applied to that which God does not intend, they prove an injury, a snare and a curse instead of a blessing. (*Teachings of the Prophet Joseph Smith*, p. 247.)

6 Now, brethren, if I come unto you speaking with tongues, what shall I profit you [*what good will it do*], except [*unless*] I shall speak to you either by revelation, or by knowledge, or by prophesying, or by doctrine?

7 And even things without life giving sound, whether pipe or harp [*even in the case of lifeless things such as a flute or a harp which give out specific sounds*], except [*unless*] they give a distinction in the sounds [*if they all sounded the same, if notes were played indiscriminately, like when you speak in tongues and* no *one understands*], how shall it be known what is piped or harped [*how would a listener know what is being played*]?

8 For if the trumpet give an uncertain sound [*like when you are speaking in tongues and no one understands*], who shall prepare himself to the battle [*who would understand the message*]?

9 So likewise ye [*such is the case with you*], except ye utter by the tongue words easy to be understood [*unless you speak in words easy for others to understand*], how shall it be known what is spoken [*how would anyone understand the message*]? for ye shall speak into the air [*you are just talking into the wind*].

10 There are, it may be, so many kinds of voices [*languages; see Strong's #5456*] in the world, and none of them is without signification [*and each language has meaning*].

11 Therefore if I know not the meaning of the voice, I shall be unto him that speaketh a barbarian [*a foreigner*], and he that speaketh shall be a barbarian [*a foreigner*] unto me. [*In other words, it doesn't do us any good if we can't understand each other.*]

12 Even so ye [*it should be the case with you*], forasmuch as ye are zealous of spiritual gifts [*since you are anxious to obtain spiritual gifts*], seek that ye may excel to the edifying of the church [*seek gifts of the Spirit that will allow you to build up the Church and its members, rather than gifts such as the gift of tongues which build you up in their eyes*].

13 Wherefore let him that speaketh in an unknown tongue pray that he may interpret.

**JST 1 Corinthians 14:13**

13 Wherefore let him that speaketh in another tongue pray that he may interpret.

14 For if I pray in an unknown tongue, my spirit prayeth, but my understanding is unfruitful [*doesn't help anyone else*].

**JST 1 Corinthians 14:14**

14 For if I pray in another tongue, my spirit prayeth, but my understanding is unfruitful.

15 What is it then [*so what should I do*]? I will pray with the spirit, and I will pray with the understanding [*with my mind*] also: I will sing with the spirit, and I will sing with the understanding also.

16 Else [*otherwise*] when thou shalt bless with the spirit [*if you pray in tongues*], how shall he that occupieth the room of the unlearned say Amen at thy giving of thanks, seeing he understandeth not what thou sayest [*how would someone in the room with you, who does not understand that language, know whether or not to say "Amen," at the end of the prayer (which means "I agree.")*]?

17 For thou verily givest thanks well [*you did a right good job of praying in tongues*], but the other is not edified [*but it didn't do the person who couldn't understand any good*].

18 I thank my God, I speak with tongues more than ye all [*I am grateful that I can speak more languages than any of you*]:

19 Yet in the church I had rather speak five words with my understanding, that by my voice I might teach others also [*Yet, I would rather speak five words which members in the congregation can understand, and thus teach them something*], than ten thousand words in an unknown tongue.

**JST 1 Corinthians 14:19**

19 Yet in the church I had rather speak five words with my understanding, that by my voice I might teach others also, than ten thousand words in another tongue.

20 Brethren, be not children in understanding [*don't think like children; in other words, don't be so spiritually immature that you want to build yourselves up in the eyes of others by speaking in tongues*]: howbeit [*however*] in malice [*wickedness, depravity; see 1 Corinthians 14:20, footnote c*] be ye children [*be like little children who are pure, not wicked*], but in understanding be men [*think like men*].

21 In the law it is written [*in Isaiah 28:11–12*], With men of other tongues [*foreign languages*] and other lips [*other languages, including the inspiration of the Holy Ghost*] will I speak unto this people; and yet for all that will they not hear [*pay attention to*] me, saith the Lord.

22 Wherefore tongues are [*the gift of tongues is*] for a sign, not to them that believe [*not to members of the Church*], but to them that believe not [*but for nonmembers, such as on the Day of Pentecost (Acts 21:1–11) when people from many nations heard the preaching of Peter and the Apostles in their own language*] but prophesying serveth not for them that believe not, but for them which believe.

Joseph Smith spoke of the use of the gift of tongues in missionary work to enable missionaries to speak to people in their own mother tongue. He said, "I read the 13th chapter of First Corinthians, also a part of the 14th chapter, and remarked that the gift of tongues was necessary in the Church. . .the gift of tongues by the power of the Holy Ghost in the Church, is for the benefit of the servants of God to preach to unbelievers, as on the day of Pentecost. When devout men from every nation shall assemble to hear the things of

God, let the Elders preach to them in their own mother tongue, whether it is German, French, Spanish or Irish, or any other, and let those interpret who understand the language spoken, in their own mother tongue, and this is what the Apostle meant in First Corinthians 14:27." (*Teachings of the Prophet Joseph Smith*, p. 195.)

23 If therefore the whole church be come together into one place, and all speak with tongues, and there come in those that are unlearned, or unbelievers, will they not say that ye are mad [*if you are meeting together and all speaking in different languages, won't it make newer members or nonmembers who visit your meetings think you are all crazy*]?

24 But if all prophesy [*if all teach the gospel simply in the language of the members, and minister with Christ-like love*], and there come in one that believeth not [*if a nonmember visits your meetings*], or one unlearned [*or if one who doesn't understand the gospel very well visits your meetings*], he is convinced [*convicted, shamed; Strong's #1651*] of all [*in other words, when he sees your righteousness and hears you preach the gospel, he is ashamed of his lifestyle and convicted in his mind that he should change and join the Church*], he is judged of all [*he is "judged" by your righteous behaviors and clear teachings, and thus is motivated to change his lifestyle*]:

25 And thus are the secrets of his heart made manifest [*his unrighteousness and need for repentance become clear in his mind*]; and so falling down on his face [*in humility*] he will worship God, and report that God is in you of a truth [*that you members have the true gospel for sure*].

26 How is it then, brethren? when ye come together, every one of you hath a psalm [*a hymn*], hath a doctrine, hath a tongue, hath a revelation, hath an interpretation. Let all things be done unto edifying. [*In other words, each member has something good to contribute in your meetings. Things must be done in an orderly fashion so that all will be strengthened and built up in the gospel.*]

Obviously, Paul is very concerned about the wild, confusing, circus-like atmosphere that speaking in tongues has created in some of the meetings of the Corinthian Saints and he has said much about it so far in this chapter. Next, however, he assures these members that there is a place in the Church, on rare occasions, for speaking in tongues. When it comes from God, rather than from Satan, the gift of tongues will be done in an orderly fashion.

27 If any man speak in an unknown tongue, let it be by two, or at the most by three [*just two or at the most, three of you*], and that by course [*one at a time*]; and let one interpret.

**JST 1 Corinthians 14:27**

27 If any man speak in another tongue, let it be by two, or at the most by three, and that by course; and let one interpret.

28 But if there be no interpreter, let him keep silence in the church; and let him speak to himself, and to God.

29 Let the prophets speak two or three, and let the other judge [*listen attentively and weigh what is being said against the revealed word of God*].

The word "prophets" as used in verse 29, above, means members of the Church who have strong personal testimonies of the gospel. Referring to 1 Corinthians 14:29, Bruce R. McConkie explained this as follows: "Let those speak who have the testimony of Jesus, who know of spiritual things by revelation, who have tasted the good word of God; let those speak to whom the heavens have been opened, who can testify from personal knowledge, who have gained "words of wisdom. . . even by study and also by faith." (D&C 88:118.) Let

those speak who can tell what God has revealed to them about his glorious gospel, 'for one truth revealed from heaven is worth all the sectarian notions in existence.' (*Teachings of the Prophet Joseph Smith*, p. 338.)" *Doctrinal New Testament Commentary*, Vol. 2, p. 386.

30 If any thing be revealed to another that sitteth by [*if the Spirit reveals something to you and you want to share it with others in the meeting*], let the first hold his peace [*be courteous and let the one who is speaking finish what he has to say before you stand and bear your testimony*].

31 For ye [*members of the Church*] may all prophesy [*bear testimony; Revelation 19:10 says ". . . the testimony of Jesus is the spirit of prophecy."*] one by one, that all may learn, and all may be comforted.

32 And the spirits of the prophets [*the members of the Church*] are subject to the prophets [*are under the direction of the presiding priesthood authorities; see McConkie,* Doctrinal New Testament Commentary, *Vol. 2, p. 387*].

33 For God is not the author of confusion, but of peace, as in all churches [*wards, branches*] of the saints. [*In other words, God's true Church is run under the direction of presiding priesthood authorities in each ward, branch, stake, etc., which provides an atmosphere of confidence and peace rather than the confusion and wrangling for position which is often found in other organizations.*]

The next two verses can cause much trouble and misunderstanding unless kept very strictly in the context in which Paul gives them. What is the context? Answer: Verses 32 and 33, wherein Paul teaches the Corinthian Saints that God places presiding authorities in each congregation. Who are the presiding authorities in the true Church? Answer: The priesthood brethren, such as the First Presidency, Quorum of the Twelve, Seventies, Area Seventies, mission presidents, stake presidents, district presidents, bishops, and branch presidents, who preside over members, male and female, in Church units. What is Paul telling the Corinthian Saints in verses 34 and 35? As you will see, the JST changes give us the answer. Joseph Smith changed the word "speak" to "rule." President Spencer W. Kimball used the word "preside" in place of "rule" as he explained Genesis 3:16 "and he shall rule over thee." See *Ensign*, March 1976, p. 71. With these things in mind, Paul is telling the Corinthian Saints that women may not preside over Church units. Rather, it is the responsibility of the priesthood to do so.

34 Let your women keep silence in the churches [*wards, branches*]: for it is not permitted unto them to speak; but they are commanded to be under obedience, as also saith the law.

**JST 1 Corinthians 14:34**

34 Let your women keep silence in the churches; for it is not permitted unto them to rule; but to be under obedience, as also saith the law.

35 And if they will learn any thing, let them ask their husbands at home: for it is a shame [*not proper*] for women to speak in the church.

**JST 1 Corinthians 14:35**

35 And if they will learn any thing, let them ask their husbands at home; for it is a shame for women to rule in the church.

When confusion arises through such verses as 34 and 35 above, as they stand in the Bible, we would do well to remember that the Bible is not always complete nor is it always translated correctly. There is a simple and very important principle which can help members avoid hurt and confusion because of such incompleteness or incorrectness in the Bible. It is this: Simply ask, "What do the Brethren do or say on this matter?" There is

always safety in following the Brethren. And in this matter, do the Brethren allow women to speak, teach, serve as auxiliary presidents, bear testimony, etc., in church meetings? Answer: Yes! So, can women speak in the true Church, contrary to what the Bible says in these two verses? Answer: Yes.

36 What? came the word of God out from you [*did the word of God originate with you*]? or came it unto you only [*are you the only people it comes to*]?

37 If any man think himself to be a prophet, or spiritual [*if any of you has a true testimony*], let him acknowledge [*recognize*] that the things that I write unto you are the commandments of the Lord.

38 But if any man be ignorant, let him be ignorant [*wrong, mistaken; see Strong's #0050*]. [*In other words, if any members disagree with the counsel I have given, which comes from the Lord, realize that they are mistaken about it.*]

39 Wherefore, brethren, covet [*earnestly seek*] to prophesy [*emphasize orderly bearing of testimony, teaching and ministering in your meetings, under the inspiration of the Holy Ghost*], and forbid not to speak with tongues [*when it is appropriate*].

40 Let all things be done decently [*appropriately*] and in order.

# FIRST CORINTHIANS 15

This chapter is one of the better known ones as far as doctrine is concerned. We quote from it often in our missionary work and teaching in the Church. Among other things, Paul wrote of resurrection for everyone, baptism for the dead, and the three degrees of glory to the Corinthian Saints. It is interesting and significant to realize that these Saints in the early Church had the same true doctrines as we have. They are all a part of the great plan of happiness, the Father's plan of salvation for us.

Paul begins his review of what he has taught the Corinthians by bearing witness of the resurrected Christ.

1 MOREOVER [*in addition*], brethren, I declare unto you the gospel which I preached unto you [*when I was there in Corinth among you*], which also ye have received [*which you accepted*], and wherein ye stand [*as members of the Church*];

2 By which also ye are saved, if ye keep in memory what I preached unto you [*if you remember what I taught*], unless ye have believed in vain [*unless you are not living what you believe*].

Paul will now emphasize that Jesus fulfilled the scriptural prophecies about the promised Messiah.

3 For I delivered unto you first of all that which I also received, how that Christ died for our sins according to the scriptures [*according to Old Testament prophecies*];

4 And that he was buried, and that he rose again the third day according to the scriptures:

Just a quick comment about "rose again" in verse 4, above. Once in a while, a student will see the word "again" and start wondering if it means that Jesus had been resurrected previously on other earths and thus, was being resurrected "again" here on our earth, after performing an atonement for us. Furthermore, some start wondering if Jesus gets born, crucified, and resurrected over and over on each of Father's worlds. This is not true. The word "again" simply means that Jesus became alive "again" through the process of resurrection. We know from D&C 76:24, that the Atonement, which Jesus performed on our earth, works for all other worlds he has created or will create for the Father. He will never die again. Neither will we,

once we have been resurrected—see Hebrews 9:27.

5 And that he [*the resurrected Christ*] was seen of [*by*] Cephas [*Peter*], then of the twelve:

6 After that, he was seen of above [*more than*] five hundred brethren at once; of whom the greater part remain unto this present [*are still alive today*], but some are fallen asleep [*some have died*].

7 After that, he was seen of [*by*] James; then of all the apostles.

8 And last of all he was seen of me also [*as recorded in Acts 9:1–6*], as of one born out of due time [*as one born too late to see Him during His mortal ministry*].

9 For I am the least of the apostles, that am not meet to be called an apostle [*I am a very inadequate Apostle*], because I persecuted the church of God [*Acts 8:1–3*].

10 But by the grace of God [*because of the mercy, forgiveness, and help of God*] I am what I am [*I am a member of the Church and an Apostle*]: and his grace which was bestowed upon me was not in vain [*was not unproductive*]; but I laboured more abundantly than they all [*I had to work harder than any other convert to get my life in order and to take the gospel to others*]: yet not I, but the grace of God which was with me [*I do not take the credit, rather, I give all credit to God*].

**JST 1 Corinthians 15:10**

10 But by the grace of God I am what I am; and his grace which was bestowed upon me was not in vain; for I labored more abundantly than they all; yet not I, but the grace of God which was with me.

11 Therefore whether it were I or they, so we preach, and so ye believed [*it makes no difference whether I or others brought the gospel to you; the important thing is that you believed and joined the Church*].

There were apparently a number of members in Corinth who still did not believe in the resurrection of Christ or anyone else, because of their past traditions before joining the Church. You might remember that the Sadducees were an influential religious group among the Jews who did not believe in resurrection. See Bible Dictionary under "Sadducees." Paul will now address this issue.

12 Now if Christ be preached that he rose from the dead, how say some among you that there is no resurrection of the dead? [*In other words, you have been taught that Christ was resurrected from the dead, so why is it that some of you don't believe in resurrection?*]

13 But if there be no resurrection of the dead, then is Christ not risen [*if there were no resurrection from the dead, then Christ couldn't have resurrected*]:

14 And if Christ be not risen [*was not resurrected*], then is our preaching vain [*our preaching is worthless*], and your faith is also vain [*of no value*].

15 Yea, and we are found false witnesses of God [*and if that were the case, then we would be false witnesses of God because what we said about His resurrecting Christ (Acts 4:33) would have been false*]; because we have testified of God [*about the Father*] that he raised up Christ: whom he raised not up, if so be that the dead rise not [*are not resurrected*].

16 For if the dead rise not [*if there is no such thing as resurrection*], then is not Christ raised [*then Christ would not have been resurrected*]:

17 And if Christ be not raised, your faith is vain; ye are yet in your sins [*if Christ was not resurrected, then your faith in Him is worth nothing, and you have not been forgiven of your sins*].

18 Then they also which are fallen asleep in Christ [*furthermore, those who joined the Church and remained faithful until death*] are perished [*will

*not be resurrected nor saved in heaven because the Atonement they relied on would not be in effect*].

19 If in this life only we have hope in Christ [*if our belief in Christ only serves to give us hope during mortality, but is not based on eternal reality*], we are of all men most miserable [*we are to be pitied more than any other people because we have been so badly fooled*].

20 But now is Christ risen from the dead [*but, the truth of the matter is that Christ was indeed resurrected*], and become the firstfruits of them that slept [*and He was the first person from this earth to be resurrected, of all who had died up to the time of His resurrection*].

The reason we emphasize that Christ was the first person from this earth to be resurrected, in our note in verse 20, above, is that, obviously, Heavenly Father was resurrected long ago, before this earth was even created. And He had already had "worlds without number" created by the Son before our earth was created, which have already passed away. See Moses 1:32–35. Thus, there were already countless resurrections in the universe before our earth was even created.

Now let's come back down to earth and listen to more of Paul's teaching.

21 For since by [*because of*] man [*Adam*] came death, by man [*Christ; the "mortal" Messiah*] came also the resurrection of the dead. [*In other words, since physical death was introduced into the world through Adam and Eve, by the Fall, so also was the resurrection from the dead brought about by a mortal, namely the Savior.*]

Verse 22, next, is a rather famous and often-quoted verse in the New Testament by members of the Church. It teaches the wonderful true doctrine that everyone who has been or ever will be born will be resurrected. We will all get our bodies back and live forever. In fact, there is nothing anyone could do, no sin anyone could commit, including becoming a son of perdition during mortal life, which could prevent one from being resurrected. See D&C 88:97–102.

22 For as in Adam all die, even so in Christ [*because of Christ*] shall all be made alive [*all will be resurrected*].

23 But every man in his own order [*there is an order to the resurrection*]: Christ the firstfruits [*Christ is the first*]; afterward they that are Christ's at his coming [*then those who will go to the celestial kingdom*].

## *The Order of the Resurrection*

As Latter-day Saints, we are privileged to have considerable detail about the "order" of the resurrection, as referred to by Paul in verse 23, above. We know of five major groups and the order in which they have been or will be resurrected:

1. The first group resurrected on this earth consisted of the righteous, from Adam and Eve down to the time of Christ's resurrection. These are spoken of in D&C 133:54–55. This group, led by the Savior, included John the Baptist and involved only those worthy of celestial glory. Qualifications for celestial glory are given in D&C 76:50–53 and elsewhere.

2. Next comes the large group who will be resurrected first at the Second Coming of the Savior. This resurrection is spoken of in D&C 88:97–98. In our day, this group is often spoken of as "the morning of the first resurrection," "the resurrection of the just," "the resurrection of the righteous," and so on. It includes only those worthy of celestial glory who died after Christ's resurrection or who will have died up to the time of His Second Coming.

3. Next come those who are found worthy to enter terrestrial glory. Qualifications for terrestrial glory are given in D&C 76:71–80. They will be resurrected near the beginning of the Millennium, but after the celestials spoken of in #2, above, have

been resurrected. This resurrection is spoken of in D&C 88:99. This group consists of all those who will go to terrestrial glory who lived from the time of Adam and Eve up to the Second Coming. This will be the first time any terrestrials will have been resurrected. This group is sometimes referred to as "the afternoon of the first resurrection."

4. The next major group to be resurrected "in order" consists of those who will go to telestial glory. They are spoken of in D&C 88:100–101. They must wait for their resurrection until after the Millennium is over. No telestials have been resurrected yet. Qualifications for attaining telestial glory are given in D&C 76:81–85, 103–106; Revelation 22:15 and other places.

5. Last of all, those who were born on earth but who then became sons of perdition will be resurrected. This resurrection is referred to in D&C 88:102. Qualifications for becoming sons of perdition are detailed in D&C 76:31–35.

24 Then cometh the end [*of the mortal world*], when he [*Christ*] shall have delivered up the kingdom to God, even the Father [*see D&C 76:107–108*]; when he [*Christ*] shall have put down all rule [*brought to an end all earthly governments*] and all authority and power [*when Christ will have triumphed over all things; see D&C 76:106*].

**JST 1 Corinthians 15:24**

24 Afterward cometh the end, when he shall have delivered up the kingdom to God, even the Father; when he shall have put down all rule, and all authority and power.

The only change in the JST for verse 24, above, is the comma after "rule."

25 For he [*Christ*] must reign, till he hath put all enemies under his feet.

26 The last enemy that shall be destroyed is death.

**JST 1 Corinthians 15:26**

26 The last enemy, death, shall be destroyed.

27 For he [*Christ*] hath put all things under his feet [*has attained power over all things*]. But when he saith all things are put under him, it is manifest [*it is clear*] that he [*the Father; see verse 28*] is excepted, which did put all things under him. [*In other words, when we say that Christ will triumph over all things, we do not mean he will triumph over the Father, who gave Jesus power to overcome all things so that we can be exalted, if we so choose.*]

**JST 1 Corinthians 15:27**

27 For he saith, When it is manifest that he hath put all things under his feet, and that all things are put under, he is excepted of the Father who did put all things under him.

28 And when all things shall be subdued unto him [*Christ*], then shall the Son also himself be subject unto him [*the Father*] that put all things under him, that God [*the Father*] may be all in all [*may be over all things; see Ephesians 4:6*].

Verse 29, next, is another often-quoted verse of scripture. We use it to teach people that baptism for the dead was practiced in Bible times as well as in the latter days. It is interesting to note that the main point of these next verses is not baptism for the dead. Rather, Paul is emphasizing the point that people will be resurrected. Otherwise, Paul asks, what good does it do to get baptized for the dead if the dead are not resurrected? From this we gather that baptism for the dead was such a common practice that Paul used it as a backdrop to strengthen his teaching about resurrection.

29 Else what shall they do which are baptized for the dead, if the dead rise not at all [*are not resurrected*]? why are they then baptized for the dead?

30 And why stand we in jeopardy [*in danger*] every hour?

31 I protest [*promise you, confirm with an oath; Strong's #3513*] by your rejoicing which I have in Christ Jesus our Lord, I die daily.

**JST 1 Corinthians 15:31**
31 I protest [*testify*] unto you the resurrection of the dead; and this is my rejoicing which I have in Christ Jesus our Lord daily, though I die.

Paul's reference to fighting with wild beasts in the city of Ephesus, verse 32, next, may well imply that this was one of the things he suffered because of his loyalty to the Savior, and survived. There was a large stadium in Ephesus, which was the Roman capital in that part of Asia, which was 685 feet by 200 feet, and in which spectators gathered to watch as people were forced to fight ferocious beasts; see information in conjunction with Strong's #2181.

32 If after the manner of men I have fought with beasts at Ephesus [*as mentioned in the note above, Paul may be saying "When I was thrown to the wild beasts in Ephesus, because of my loyalty to Christ"*], what advantageth it me, if the dead rise not [*what good was it for me to be loyal to Christ if we don't get resurrected*]? let us eat and drink; for to morrow we die [*if there is no resurrection, then Christ was a fraud and we might just as well live it up in mortality because we won't exist after we die*].

33 Be not deceived [*don't be fooled into thinking that there is no life after death, and thus feeling free to live riotously, eating, drinking, and being merry*]: evil communications [*wicked associations and conversations; Strong's #3657*] corrupt good manners [*morals, character; Strong's #2239*].

34 Awake to righteousness, and sin not; for some [*of your members*] have not the knowledge of God: I speak this to your shame.

Paul will now be very direct with any members who challenge or do not believe in the doctrine of resurrection.

35 But some man will say, How are the dead raised up? and with what body do they come [*what kind of a body will they have when they are resurrected*]?

36 Thou fool, that which thou sowest [*the seed that you plant in the ground*] is not quickened [*does not grow and become a new plant*] except it die [*unless you bury it in the ground, just as our bodies are buried when we die*]: [*In other words, you are being foolish to challenge the doctrine of resurrection because there are examples of "death" and "resurrection" all around you in the daily world of agriculture.*]

37 And that which thou sowest [*and when you plant a seed*], thou sowest not that body that shall be [*you are not planting the plant which the seed will become*], but bare grain [*a mere seed, not the plant itself; Strongs #1131*], it may chance of wheat, or of some other grain [*whether it is wheat or any other type of grain*]:

**JST 1 Corinthians 15:37**
37 And that which thou sowest, thou sowest not that body which shall be, but grain, it may be of wheat, or some other;

38 But God giveth it a body as it hath pleased him, and to every seed his own body [*every seed that is planted and grows has a body unique to it, according to God's plan*].

Now Paul is focusing in on the question in verse 35, above, which asked what kind of a body people will have when they are resurrected. Paul's answer provides us with some very specific doctrine about types of bodies people will have in the resurrection. It tells us that there will be differences between the bodies of celestials and terrestrials and telestials. Let's see what he says.

39 All flesh is not the same flesh: but

there is one kind of flesh of men, another flesh of beasts, another of fishes, and another of birds.

40 There are also celestial bodies [*the bodies of those who are resurrected and go to celestial glory*], and bodies terrestrial [*bodies for those in the terrestrial kingdom*]: but the glory of the celestial is one, and the glory of the terrestrial is another [*there is a difference between the bodies of celestials and the bodies of terrestrials*].

**JST 1 Corinthians 15:40**

40 Also celestial bodies, and bodies terrestrial, and bodies telestial; but the glory of the celestial, one; and the terrestrial, another; and the telestial, another.

41 There is one glory of the sun, and another glory of the moon, and another glory of the stars: for one star differeth from another star in glory [*one of the differences between resurrected bodies is that there will be a difference in the glory radiating from the bodies of celestials, terrestrials, and telestials*].

The fact that there will be differences in resurrected bodies, depending on which kingdom of glory people go to, is taught in D&C 88:28–32. Apostle Joseph Fielding Smith explained these things as follows:

"KINDS OF RESURRECTED BODIES. In the resurrection there will be different kinds of bodies; they will not all be alike. The body a man receives will determine his place hereafter. There will be celestial bodies, terrestrial bodies, and telestial bodies. . . Elder Orson Pratt many years ago in writing of the resurrection and the kind of bodies which would be raised in these kingdoms said: '. . . There will be several classes of resurrected bodies; some celestial, some terrestrial, some telestial, and some sons of perdition. Each of these classes will differ from the others by prominent and marked distinctions;'

Continuing, Joseph Fielding Smith pointed out that procreation will be limited to those who gain exaltation. He said "Some will gain celestial bodies with all the powers of exaltation and eternal increase. These bodies will shine like the sun as our Savior's does, as described by John (in Revelation 1:16). Those who enter the terrestrial kingdom will have terrestrial bodies, and they will not shine like the sun, but they will be more glorious than the bodies of those who receive the telestial glory. In both of these kingdoms (terrestrial and telestial) there will be changes in the bodies and limitations. They will not have the power of increase, neither the power or nature to live as husbands and wives, for this will be denied them and they cannot increase. Those who receive the exaltation in the celestial kingdom will have the 'continuation of the seeds forever' (D&C 132:19.) They will live in the family relationship. In the terrestrial and in the telestial kingdoms there will be no marriage. Those who enter there will remain 'separately and singly' forever (D&C 132:17). Some of the functions in the celestial body will not appear in the terrestrial body, neither in the telestial body, and the power of procreation will be removed." (*Doctrines of Salvation*, Vol. 2, p. 286.)

The resurrection is, in fact, a partial judgment. We will know which degree of glory we will go to by what kind of a body we get in the resurrection.

42 So also is the resurrection of the dead [*this is how it will be in the resurrection of the dead*]. It is sown in corruption [*our mortal bodies will be buried and will decompose*]; it is raised in incorruption [*when we are resurrected, our resurrected bodies will never be subject to deterioration again*]:

43 It [*our mortal body*] is sown [*buried*] in dishonour [*having failed to sustain our life any longer*]; it is raised [*resurrected*] in glory: it is sown [*buried*] in weakness [*demonstrating mortal frailty*]; it is raised [*resurrected*] in power:

44 It is sown [*buried*] a natural [*mortal*] body; it is raised a spiritual body. [*Not a "spirit" body, rather, a "spiritual" body, meaning an immortal body of flesh, bone, and spirit.*] There is a natural body, and there is a spiritual body.

Apostle Howard W. Hunter, who later became the president of the Church, explained the meaning of the phrase "spiritual body" as used in verse 44, above. He taught "There is a separation of the spirit and the body at the time of death. The resurrection will again unite the spirit with the body, and the body becomes a spiritual body, one of flesh and bones but quickened [*made alive*] by the spirit instead of blood. Thus, our bodies after the resurrection, quickened by the spirit, shall become immortal and never die. This is the meaning of the statements of Paul that 'there is a natural body, and there is a spiritual body' and 'that flesh and blood cannot inherit the kingdom of God.' The natural body is flesh and blood, but quickened by the spirit instead of blood, it can and will enter the kingdom." [*General Conference, April 1969.*]

45 And so it is written, The first man Adam was made a living soul; the last Adam was made a quickening spirit.

We need some help with Paul's vocabulary in verse 45, above. Paul refers to two "Adams," namely, "the first man Adam," who was Eve's husband, and "the last Adam" (*Christ*), who is a "quickening spirit" or one who makes people come alive again, i.e., enables us to be resurrected. What Paul is teaching is that Adam's spirit was given a mortal body, and thus became a "living soul." The definition of "soul" is given in D&C 88:15 where it says "And the spirit and the body are the soul of man." Everyone will eventually die and thus, all of us need Christ's resurrection to free us from death.

46 Howbeit [*however*] that was not first which is spiritual, but that which is natural; and afterward that which is spiritual. [*In other words, first we get our mortal bodies. Next, we get our immortal, resurrected bodies.*]

**JST 1 Corinthians 15:46**

46 Howbeit, that which is natural first, and not that which is spiritual; but afterwards, that which is spiritual;

47 The first man [*Adam*] is of the earth, earthy [*Adam got a mortal body, first, made of earthly elements*]: the second man [*Christ*] is the Lord from heaven.

48 As is the earthy [*just like Adam*], such are they also that are earthy [*all of us mortals get a mortal body, subject to death*]: and as is the heavenly [*just as Christ received a resurrected celestial body*], such are they also that are heavenly [*so also will all the righteous get a celestial resurrected body*].

49 And as we have borne the image of the earthy [*we are just like Adam in the sense that our mortal bodies will die*], we shall also bear the image of the heavenly [*we will also be resurrected, like Christ was*].

50 Now this I say, brethren, that flesh and blood cannot inherit the kingdom of God [*physical, mortal bodies cannot go to heaven to be with God without being resurrected first, because mortal bodies could not survive in the fiery glory surrounding God. See* Teachings of the Prophet Joseph Smith*, pp. 367, 326, and 199–200.*]; neither doth corruption inherit incorruption [*mortal bodies, which are subject to decay upon burial, cannot inherit the presence of God*].

51 Behold, I shew you a mystery [*let me share an interesting exception to the general rule that all of us will be buried when we die, to await our resurrection*]; We shall not all sleep [*not everyone will be buried in the ground*], but we shall all be changed,

52 In a moment, in the twinkling of an eye [*those who live during the Millennium will not be buried when they die, rather, they will die and then be*

*resurrected instantly; see D&C 101:31 as referred to in 1 Corinthians 15:52, footnote c*], at the last trump: for the trumpet shall sound, and the dead shall be raised incorruptible [*with immortal bodies of flesh and bone*], and we shall be changed.

**JST 1 Corinthians 15:52**

52 In a moment, in the twinkling of an eye, at the sound of the last trump; for the trumpet shall sound, and the dead shall be raised incorruptible, and we shall be changed.

53 For this corruptible [*this mortal body*] must put on incorruption [*must be resurrected*], and this mortal must put on immortality.

54 So when this corruptible shall have put on incorruption [*so, when we are all resurrected*], and this mortal shall have put on immortality, then shall be brought to pass the saying that is written [*in Isaiah 25:8*], Death is swallowed up in victory.

55 O death, where is thy sting? O grave, where is thy victory?

56 The sting of death is sin [*the thing that really hurts us is unrepented of sin*]; and the strength of sin [*the power that sin has over us*] is the law [*of justice*].

57 But thanks be to God, which giveth us the victory through our Lord Jesus Christ [*we can triumph over sin through the Atonement of Christ*].

58 Therefore, my beloved brethren, be ye stedfast, unmoveable [*remain faithful*], always abounding in the work of the Lord [*remain active in the Church*], forasmuch as ye know that your labour is not in vain in the Lord.

## FIRST CORINTHIANS 16

Several of the members of the Church in the Jerusalem area had come upon hard times and needed welfare assistance from members elsewhere. Paul has been very active in taking up collections to be taken to these needy Saints. In the first few verses of this chapter, he gives instructions to the Corinthian Saints regarding collecting money for this cause.

1 NOW concerning the collection for the saints [*the donations being collected to be taken to the members of the Church who are in need of welfare help in the Jerusalem area*], as I have given order to the churches of Galatia, even so do ye [*please set things up for collecting donations from your wards and branches the same way I set things up among the Galatian Saints*].

2 Upon the first day of the week [*Sunday; see Acts 20:7; see also Bible Dictionary under "Sabbath"*] let every one of you lay by him in store, as God hath prospered him [*on each Sunday, gather up donations to the cause according to members' ability to give*], that there be no gatherings when I come [*so that I don't have to take time to gather up donations when I come*].

3 And when I come, whomsoever ye shall approve by your letters [*letters of recommendation*], them will I send to bring your liberality [*generosities; in other words, your donations*] unto Jerusalem.

4 And if it be meet [*and if it is necessary*] that I go also, they shall go with me.

5 Now I will come unto you, when I shall pass through Macedonia [*northern Greece, today*]: for I do pass through Macedonia.

6 And it may be that I will abide, yea, and winter with you [*it may be that I will spend the winter there with you*], that ye may bring me on my journey whithersoever [*wherever*] I go.

Paul is writing this letter to the Corinthians from Philippi, which is in the far northeastern part of Greece.

7 For I will not see you now by the way [*I don't want to visit you now, because I wouldn't have time to stay*]; but I trust to tarry [*stay*] a while with you, if the Lord permit.

8 But I will tarry at Ephesus [*in western Turkey, today*] until Pentecost [*a major religious celebration in Jerusalem, held fifty days after Passover; see Bible Dictionary under "Feasts"*].

9 For a great door and effectual is opened unto me [*I have many wonderful opportunities to serve that opened up for me*], and there are many adversaries [*and I have many enemies trying to stop me*].

10 Now if Timotheus [*Timothy*] come [*comes to Corinth*], see that he may be with you without fear: for he worketh the work of the Lord [*he is serving the Lord*], as I also do.

11 Let no man therefore despise him [*not take him seriously because he is so young; see 1 Timothy 4:12*]: but conduct him forth in peace [*help him get on his way without undue difficulties*], that he may come unto me: for I look for him with the brethren.

12 As touching our brother Apollos [*a faithful convert to the Church, who is with Paul as he writes this letter to the Corinthian members; see information given with Strong's #0625*], I greatly desired him to come unto you with the brethren: but his will was not at all to come at this time; but he will come when he shall have convenient time.

Just a reminder, that when we refer to "Strong's #" we mean the definition of a particular word as given in Strong's *Exhaustive Concordance of the Bible*.

13 Watch ye [*be alert*], stand fast [*firm*] in the faith, quit you [*behave*] like men, be strong.

14 Let all your things be done with charity.

15 I beseech [*urge*] you, brethren, (ye know the house [*the household*] of Stephanas [*the first people I baptized in Corinth, when I came through on my missionary journey*], that it is the firstfruits of Achaia [*the general area of southern Greece*], and that they have addicted [*devoted*] themselves to the ministry of the saints,)

16 That ye submit yourselves unto such [*listen to their advice and counsel; Strong's #5293*], and to every one that helpeth with us, and laboureth.

17 I am glad of the coming [*I am happy about the arrival here*] of Stephanas [*one of the first converts in Corinth, referred to in verse 15, above*] and Fortunatus [*apparently a convert from Corinth; Strong's #5415*] and Achaicus [*a convert from Corinth; see Strong's #0883*]: for that which was lacking on your part they have supplied [*they have supplied me with information I was lacking about you*].

18 For they have refreshed my spirit and yours: therefore acknowledge ye them that are such [*such men deserve recognition by you*].

19 The churches of Asia salute you [*send their greetings to you*]. Aquila and Priscilla salute you much in the Lord, with the church that is in their house [*along with the members of the Church who meet in their home*].

20 All the brethren greet you [*send their greetings to you*]. Greet ye one another with an holy kiss.

**JST 1 Corinthians 16:20**

20 All the brethren greet you. Greet ye one another with a holy salutation.

21 The salutation of [*greeting from*] me Paul with mine own hand [*which I have written with my own hand, rather than having it written by one of my scribes*].

22 If any man love not the Lord Jesus Christ, let him be Anathema Maranatha.

The two words, "Anathema" and "Maranatha", used in verse 22, are a bit puzzling to us. Some possible interpretations are given in the Institute of Religion New Testament student manual, *The Life and Teachings of Jesus and His Apostles*, p. 298, as follows:

"This strange inclusion of two Aramaic words together in Paul's closing words of the epistle [*letter*] has raised many questions. The meaning of both words is known, but the strange combination is what puzzles most scholars. Anathema means literally 'something set apart or consecrated,' and came to carry the meaning of 'cursed' or 'accursed.' This is the word Paul uses in Galatians 1:8 when he says that anyone preaching another gospel than the true one should be accursed. Maranatha has been variously translated as 'the Lord comes,' 'the Lord will come,' 'the Lord is at hand,' and so on. It seems to have been a common Christian greeting or watchword. As far as the combination of the two are concerned, two basic interpretations are made. Some versions assume that there should be a period between the two. Thus it reads: 'If anyone has no love for the Lord, let him be accursed. Our Lord, come!' Most scholars seem to prefer this separation. But one has suggested that Paul combines them deliberately, using an old Syriac exclamation, 'Let him be accursed, the Lord is at hand,' suggesting that at the Lord's coming, punishment will be meted out. (See Fallows, The Popular and Critical Bible Encyclopedia and Scriptural Dictionary, 1:104.)

23 The grace [*mercy, help, forgiveness, etc.*] of our Lord Jesus Christ be with you.

24 My love be with you all in Christ Jesus. Amen.

# The Second Epistle of Paul the Apostle to the Corinthians

This is Paul's follow up letter to First Corinthians. Most Bible scholars believe that it was written about AD 57 from Macedonia, which would be the northern area of modern-day Greece. The first nine chapters are comparatively conciliatory and kind. The last four chapters are somewhat strong and blunt like much of First Corinthians was.

## SECOND CORINTHIANS 1

In this opening chapter of his follow-up letter to what we know as 1 Corinthians, you will see that Paul is quite personal and down-to-earth with these members of the Church in Corinth. He will emphasize that these Saints are a valued comfort and support to him and his missionary companions, just as he hopes he and those with him have been a strength and comfort to them.

1 PAUL, an apostle of Jesus Christ by the will of God, and Timothy our brother, unto the church of God which is at Corinth, with all the saints which are in all Achaia [*southern Greece*]:

2 Grace be to you and peace from God our Father, and from the Lord Jesus Christ. [*Another reminder that the Father and the Son are separate personages.*]

3 Blessed be [*praised be*] God, even the Father of our Lord Jesus Christ, the Father of mercies, and the God of all comfort;

An important message for us all is found in verse 4, next. It is that since we are blessed with comfort from above, we should also be willing to comfort and help others.

4 Who comforteth us in all our tribulation [*trials and troubles*], that we may be able to comfort them [*others*] which are in any trouble, by the [*because of the*] comfort wherewith [*with which*] we ourselves are comforted of [*by*] God.

5 For as the sufferings of Christ abound in us [*we are persecuted because we believe in Christ*], so our consolation also aboundeth by Christ [*we receive much comfort from Christ as we go through persecutions*].

6 And whether [*if*] we [*Paul and his direct associates*] be afflicted [*are persecuted*], it is for your consolation and salvation, which is effectual in the enduring of the same sufferings which we also suffer [*our suffering helps you endure similar suffering because of your faithfulness to Christ*]: or whether [*if*] we be [*are*] comforted, it is for your consolation and salvation [*it helps to comfort you and strengthen your testimonies, leading to salvation*].

7 And our hope of you is stedfast [*we have full confidence in you*], knowing, that as ye are partakers of the sufferings, so shall ye be also of the consolation [*knowing that just as you suffer because of your loyalty to Christ, so also you will be comforted and strengthened by Him*].

8 For we would not, brethren, have you ignorant of our trouble which came to us

in Asia [*and, speaking of suffering, may we remind you of the troubles we went through in Asia (western Turkey today)*], that we were pressed out of measure, above strength [*how we had troubles, seemingly far beyond our ability to survive*], insomuch that we despaired even of life [*to the point that we expected to die*]:

9 But we had the sentence of death in ourselves [*we felt in our hearts that we were facing certain death*], that we should not trust in ourselves, but in God which raiseth the dead [*we knew that we could not rely on our own abilities, rather that we must trust in God who can raise the dead*]:

10 Who delivered us from so great a death [*who saved us from the life-threatening dangers we faced in Asia*], and doth deliver [*and continues to deliver us from such perils*]: in whom we trust that he will yet deliver us [*and we trust that he will yet deliver us from additional dangers*];

11 Ye also helping together by prayer for us [*your prayers for us are a great help*], that for the gift bestowed upon us by the means of many persons thanks may be given by many on our behalf.

12 For our rejoicing is this [*consists of this*], the testimony of our conscience [*in good conscience*], that in simplicity [*with no other motive*] and godly sincerity, not with fleshly wisdom [*not with the wisdom of man*], but by the grace of God, we have had our conversation [*our associations*] in the world, and more abundantly to you-ward [*and our rejoicing is because of our association with you*].

13 For we write none other things unto you, than what ye read or acknowledge [*we write nothing to you but what you can easily understand*]; and I trust ye shall acknowledge [*understand*] even to the end;

14 As also ye have acknowledged [*understood*] us in part [*to some degree*], that we are your rejoicing [*that we are the source of your rejoicing because we brought you the gospel*], even as ye also are ours [*even as you are the source of great rejoicing in our hearts*] in the day of the Lord Jesus [*as we all look forward to returning to be with Jesus*].

15 And in this confidence [*assurance that you are glad that we brought you the gospel*] I was minded [*I intended*] to come unto you before [*earlier*], that ye might have a second [*additional*] benefit [*that I might help you understand even more of the gospel*];

16 And to pass by you into Macedonia [*and to stop by and visit you on my way to Macedonia—northern Greece*], and to come again out of Macedonia unto you, and of you to be brought [*and to have your help in getting*] on my way toward Judea [*the Jerusalem area*].

17 When I therefore was thus minded [*when my intention was to come visit you*], did I use lightness [*do you think I was being overly light-minded, optimistic, or unrealistic*]? or the things that I purpose, do I purpose according to the flesh [*or do you think that I am being a bit selfish, desiring the personal pleasure which it would bring me to be among you again*], that with me there should be yea yea, and nay nay [*do you think I am too indecisive*]?

18 But as God is true [*just as surely as God is trustworthy*], our word toward you was not yea and nay [*there was nothing indecisive in our message to you about Christ*].

19 For the Son of God, Jesus Christ, who was preached among you by us, even by me and Silvanus and Timotheus [*Timothy*], was not yea and nay [*Christ, whom we preached to you, was not indecisive*], but in him was yea [*in Christ was definitely the one road to salvation*].

20 For all the promises of God [*the Father*] in him [*through Christ*] are yea

[*positive*], and in him Amen [*Christ; Christ is often referred to as "the Amen"; see Bible Dictionary under "Amen"*], unto the glory of God by us [*our salvation through Christ adds to the glory of God*].

21 Now he which establisheth us with you in Christ [*who establishes us with you in his kingdom via Christ*], and hath anointed us [*and who has given us the Gift of the Holy Ghost, with its accompanying gifts; see Strong's #5548*], is God [*is the Father*];

22 Who hath also sealed us [*who has put His seal of ownership upon us*], and given the earnest of the Spirit in our hearts [*and has put "earnest money," so to speak, on us in the form of the Gift of the Holy Ghost, which, if followed, assures that we will someday belong to the Father in exaltation forever*].

As indicated in the note in verse 22, above, the word "earnest" as used in verse 22, above, is the same as the phrase "earnest money" as used today. It means to pay earnest money to secure the right to purchase a car, or house or whatever at a later date. Symbolically, the Gift of the Holy Ghost is given to members of the Church to secure the right for Christ's Atonement to purchase us for the Father, later, on Judgment Day, to live with Him forever in exaltation, if we will hearken to the promptings of the Holy Ghost.

23 Moreover [*furthermore*] I call God for a record upon my soul [*I call upon God as my witness that I am telling you the truth*], that to spare you I came not as yet unto Corinth. [*In other words, the reason I haven't yet come to Corinth is to spare you further preaching from me which might cause you more pain (see 2 Corinthians 2:1–5). In other words, Paul realizes that what he wrote them in 1 Corinthians was very direct and no doubt caused many of them considerable pain. Paul is obviously a very sensitive, though energetic, Apostle, and doesn't like to hurt people's feelings, even though it is sometimes necessary in order to open their eyes and hearts to the need for change.*]

24 Not for that we have dominion over your faith [*not that we want to dominate you*], but are helpers of your joy [*rather, we want to help your faith and joy grow*]: for by faith ye stand [*faith in Christ is the key to your remaining faithful in the Church and being in good standing with God*].

# SECOND CORINTHIANS 2

As previously mentioned, it was hard on Paul to be as direct and blunt with these members of the Church as he sometimes had to be, as seen in 1 Corinthians. Now his deep tenderness and gentleness emerges as he shows forth "an increase of love toward [*those*] whom [*he has*] reproved" (Compare with D&C 121:43.)

1 BUT I determined this with myself, that I would not come again to you in heaviness [*scolding you and causing you grief and worry*].

2 For if I make you sorry, who is he then that maketh me glad, but the same which is made sorry by me? [*In other words, if I make you unhappy, who is left to make me happy? Answer: only you whom I have made sad, and that doesn't seem to work.*]

3 And I wrote this same unto you, lest, when I came, I should have sorrow from them of whom I ought to rejoice [*the reason I wrote rather harsh things to you in my last letter is that I was worried for fear you would continue going in wrong directions, thus causing me sorrow instead of joy because of you*]; having confidence in you all, that my joy is the joy of you all [*having confidence that the joy which obedience to*

*Christ brings me is the same joy which such obedience will bring you*].

4 For out of much affliction and anguish of heart I wrote unto you with many tears [*I was deeply worried about you*]; not that ye should be grieved [*I didn't want to cause you grief*], but that ye might know the love which I have more abundantly unto you [*I just wanted you to know how much I love you and care about your salvation*].

5 But if any have caused grief [*if some among you have caused trouble in the Church there in Corinth*], he hath not grieved me, but in part [*they haven't caused me as much grief as they have you*]: that I may not overcharge you all [*I need to be careful not to blame all of you for the misdeeds and apostasy of some among you*].

6 Sufficient to such a man is this punishment, which was inflicted of many [*the punishment inflicted upon such by the majority of you, who are faithful, should be sufficient*].

We don't know what the "punishment" in verse 6, above, was. Perhaps it was something as simple as disapproval or as strong as withdrawing from associating with them. Whatever it was, Paul considers it sufficient and now counsels these Saints to forgive one another and show increased love for those members who had caused trouble.

7 So that contrariwise [*instead*] ye ought rather to forgive him, and comfort him, lest perhaps [*for fear that*] such a one should be swallowed up with overmuch [*too much*] sorrow. [*Compare this with D&C 121:43.*]

8 Wherefore [*therefore*] I beseech [*urge*] you that ye would confirm [*demonstrate*] your love toward him.

9 For to this end also did I write [*another reason I wrote to you is*], that I might know the proof of you [*that I might receive evidence from you*], whether ye be obedient in all things.

10 To whom ye forgive any thing, I forgive also [*whomever you forgive, I will forgive*]: for if I forgave any thing [*in any cases where I needed to forgive anything*], to whom I forgave it, for your sakes forgave I it in the person of Christ [*I forgave them under the direction of Christ*];

11 Lest Satan should get an advantage of us: for we are not ignorant of his devices. [*In other words, we know how Satan works, and it is essential that we forgive one another so that he doesn't get the advantage over us.*]

12 Furthermore [*let me mention another thing now*], when I came to Troas [*on the western tip of northern Turkey*] to preach Christ's gospel, and a door was opened unto me of the Lord [*and the Lord opened up many opportunities for successful preaching there*],

13 I had no rest in my spirit [*I couldn't relax*], because I found not Titus my brother [*because I couldn't locate Titus*]: [*Titus was one of Paul's favorite and most faithful associates in the Church. He was a Greek convert and was very familiar with the Saints in Corinth; see information associated with Strong's #5103*] but taking my leave of them, I went from thence into Macedonia [*so I left Troas and went to northern Greece*].

14 Now thanks be unto God [*the Father*], which always causeth us to triumph in Christ [*because of Christ and his Atonement*], and maketh manifest the savour of his knowledge by us in every place.

Paul will use the word "savour" several times as this chapter comes to a close. It is translated from the Greek and means "smell," "odor" or "fragrance." The smell of sacrifices in Old Testament times would remind God's people of Him and their loyalty to Him. Incense was also used in worshiping God and was symbolic of the prayers of the Saints. See Bible Dictionary under "Incense," and also Revelation 5:8. Thus, when the Saints would smell the fragrance of

incense, it would remind them of the Lord. Paul refers to the members of the Church, symbolically, as "savour" or fragrance.

15 For we are unto God [*the Father*] a sweet savour of Christ, in them that are saved [*in Greek, it says "are being saved"*], [*In other words, righteous Saints are like a sweet "fragrance," i.e., a pleasant result of Christ's mission to save us*], and in them that perish [*standing out among those who will not come to Christ*]: [*Another way to say this might be "Our righteous lives, based on Christ, are a prayer of gratitude rising up like incense to the Father," in contrast to those who will not return to Him through Christ.*]

16 To the one we are the savour of death unto death [*to those who reject our example as followers of Christ, we become the smell of spiritual death and damnation, because our example will help condemn them on Judgment Day*]; and to the other the savour of life [*of being "born again"*] unto life [*eternal life*]. And who is sufficient for these things [*how many of us are up to the task, equal to the opportunities before us to spread the pleasant fragrance of the gospel to others*]?

17 For we are not as [*like*] many, which corrupt the word of God [*peddle for personal gain and financial profit; see Strong's #2585*]: [*Paul seems to be referring to "priestcraft," as defined in Alma 1:16.*] but as of sincerity [*but we teach the word of God sincerely, without thought of personal gain or profit*], but as of God [*as servants sent from God*], in the sight of God speak we in Christ [*God is our witness that we speak the truth about Christ*].

# SECOND CORINTHIANS 3

Paul will now reemphasize that the gospel, as brought by Christ, takes the place of the Law of Moses. He will begin by asking if he and the brethren who are with him need additional identification as authorized servants of the Lord. He uses this as the background for complimenting them and telling them that their lives as members of the Church are all the recommendation others need to see that the gospel brought to them by Paul is true.

1 DO we begin again to commend ourselves [*are our names sufficient recommendation for you*]? or need we, as some others, epistles of commendation to you [*or do we need, as some others do, letters of recommendation*], or letters of commendation [*of recommendation*] from you?

2 Ye are our epistle written in our hearts, known and read of all men: [*In other words, the answer is "No." Your righteous lives are all the "letter of recommendation" necessary, witnessing that the gospel we brought to you, as authorized servants of God, is true. Your lives are the "letter of recommendation" which others read to find out about God.*]

3 Forasmuch as [*since*] ye are manifestly [*obviously*] declared to be the epistle of Christ [*you are the "letter" from Christ to be "read" by others*] ministered by us, written not with ink, but with the Spirit of the living God [*not literally a letter written with ink, but rather you are a "letter" which radiates the Spirit of the living God for others to "read"*]; not in tables of stone, [*not written in stone tablets like the Ten Commandments were*], but in fleshy tables of the heart [*but written deep in your hearts*].

4 And such trust have we through Christ to God-ward:

**JST 2 Corinthians 3:4**

4 And such trust have we through Christ toward God.

5 Not that we are sufficient of ourselves to think any thing as of ourselves; but our sufficiency is of God; [*Not that we are capable of doing the work of God because of any great talents or abilities we ourselves have, rather we are instruments in God's hand, and He makes us adequate to do His work.*]

You may wish to mark "the letter killeth, but the spirit giveth life," found in verse 6, next, in your own scriptures. It is a very important part of the gospel of Jesus Christ.

6 Who also [*God*] hath made us able ministers of the new testament [*the new covenant, brought by Christ, which replaces the Law of Moses*]; not of the letter [*the detailed performances required by the Law of Moses*], but of the spirit [*the "spirit" or "intent" of all God's commandments is to make us Christ like*]: for the letter killeth, but the spirit giveth life. [*Those who pay attention only to the "letter of the law" eventually die spiritually; whereas, those who strive to grow spiritually, understanding the intent of all God's laws for us, grow spiritually toward eternal life.*]

7 But if the ministration of death [*if the Law of Moses, followed exclusively, would still lead to spiritual death*], written and engraven in stones, was glorious [*yet was a relatively high law*], so that the children of Israel could not stedfastly behold [*look directly at*] the face of Moses [*it still didn't enable the children of Israel to look directly at Moses' face when it shined*] for [*because of*] the glory of his countenance [*because his face shined with glory after he had been in the presence of the Lord for 40 days in the mountain; see Exodus 34:29–35*]; which glory was to be done away [*which glory was not the full glory which God has*]:

Verse 7, above, is saying, in effect, that if we were to follow only the Law of Moses, which included the Ten Commandments engraved in stone, and which was glorious indeed compared to the depraved lifestyles the children of Israel learned in Egypt, we would not be able to return to the presence of God in celestial glory and would thus suffer spiritual death (meaning being cut off from the direct presence of God forever); see Bible Dictionary under "Death" for the definition of spiritual death. The Law of Moses didn't even get the children of Israel to the point where they could stand to be in the presence of Moses after he had been in the presence of the Lord. And the light radiating from Moses' face was nothing compared to the light you would have to be able to stand if you go to celestial glory.]

8 How shall not the ministration of the spirit be rather glorious [*don't you think the Spirit which attends Christ's gospel will be even more glorious*]?

9 For if the ministration of condemnation be glory [*if the Law of Moses had much glory along with it*], much more doth the ministration of righteousness exceed in glory [*the personal righteousness which comes through following Christ will lead to much more glory*].

10 For even that which was made glorious had no glory in this respect, by reason of the glory that excelleth [*when you compare the glory brought by following the Law of Moses to the glory which will come through following Christ, it is as if there were not glory at all accompanying the Law of Moses*].

11 For if that which is done away was glorious [*if the Law of Moses, which has been done away with now, was glorious, which it was*], much more that which remaineth is glorious [*the glory attained by following Christ far exceeds it*].

In 2 Corinthians 4:17, Paul will emphasize again the tremendous difference in glory between those who attain celestial glory and all others, when he says they will obtain "a far more exceeding and eternal weight of glory."

12 Seeing then that we have such hope [*because we know what God has in store for us*], we use great plainness of speech [*we speak plainly with boldness; see 2 Corinthians 3:12, footnote a*]:

13 And not as Moses [*who had to hold back*], which put a vail over his face [*symbolically, we are not hiding the glory of God from you, like Moses had to because of their unbelief*], that the children of Israel could not stedfastly look to the end [*see the purpose*] of that which is abolished [*of the Law of Moses*]:

14 But their minds were blinded [*they were spiritually blind and could not see the purpose of the Law of Moses*]: for until this day remaineth the same vail untaken away in the reading of the old testament [*it is as if, even today, the same veil were still in place, hiding the glory of God from spiritually blind Israel who are still stuck in Old Testament times*]; which vail is done away in Christ [*even though that "veil" has been removed by the gospel which Christ brought*].

15 But even unto this day, when Moses is read [*when they read the Old Testament*], the vail is upon their heart [*Israelites today are still spiritually blind and hard-hearted*].

16 Nevertheless when it [*Israel*] shall turn to the Lord, the vail shall be taken away. [*When Israelites repent and turn to Christ, the veil of spiritual darkness and hard-heartedness will be taken from them.*]

> **JST 2 Corinthians 3:16**
> 16 Nevertheless, when their heart shall turn to the Lord, the veil shall be taken away.

17 Now the Lord is that Spirit: and where the Spirit of the Lord is, there is liberty [*there is freedom from spiritual darkness and bondage*].

> In verse 18, next, Paul says, in effect, that we are just beginning to catch a glimpse of the glory which will be ours as we progress toward becoming "joint heirs" with Christ (Romans 8:17), in other words, exalted beings, through the help of the Holy Ghost.
>
> Paul uses a clever play on words here as he refers to our faces which are beginning to shine just a bit.

18 But we all, with open face beholding as in a glass the glory of the Lord [*seeing, as if in an imperfect mirror*], are changed [*Greek: "are being transformed"*] into the same image [*to look like Christ*] from glory to glory [*with continually increasing glory and light*], even as by the Spirit of the Lord [*by the power of the gift of the Holy Ghost*].

# SECOND CORINTHIANS 4

After reminding the Corinthian Saints that he and his companions are authorized servants of God, Paul will continue, warning them against such things as dishonesty, and reminding them that troubles for the righteous in mortality are nothing compared to the blessings of eternity with God.

1 THEREFORE seeing we have this ministry, as we have received mercy [*the fact that we have been called of God to do this work, along with the fact that we, ourselves, have been blessed by the Atonement, gives us strength and courage so that*], we faint not [*we do not give up*];

2 But have renounced the hidden things of dishonesty [*we have turned away from the hidden evils which come from dishonesty*], not walking in craftiness [*not deceiving others*], nor handling the word of God deceitfully [*nor corrupting (Strong's #1389) God's word to make it more acceptable to people*]; but by manifestation of the truth [*we teach the true gospel plainly*] commending ourselves to every man's conscience in the sight of God [*presenting ourselves*

*and our message to all people so that they can follow their conscience and come to God.*]

3 But if our gospel be hid, it is hid to them that are lost [*if it seems to some that our message is hard to understand, be aware that it only seems so to those who are spiritually lost*]:

4 In whom the god of this world [*the devil, Satan*] hath blinded the minds of them which believe not [*it is because the "god of this world," the devil (see 2 Corinthians 4:4, footnote a), has blinded their minds because of their unbelief*], lest [*for fear that*] the light of the glorious gospel of Christ, who is the image of God [*who literally looks like the Father (Hebrews 1:3) and also represents the Father*], should shine unto them [*those who are under Satan's influence*].

5 For we preach not ourselves [*about ourselves and our own ideas*], but Christ Jesus the Lord [*the Messiah; Strong's #2962*]; and ourselves your servants [*as your servants*] for Jesus' sake [*sent by Christ*].

6 For God, who commanded the light to shine out of darkness [*Genesis 1:3–5*], hath shined in our hearts [*has shined the gospel light into our hearts*], to give the light of the knowledge of the glory of God in the face of Jesus Christ [*and has let us see His glory as it shined from Him to us through the face of Christ*].

7 But we have this treasure [*the gospel light*] in earthen vessels [*in our mortal lives*], that the excellency of the power may be of God, and not of us [*the source of this powerful gospel light is God, not us*].

8 We are troubled on every side [*every way we turn, we run into trouble as we fulfill our missions*], yet not distressed [*yet we are not detoured, stopped*]; we are perplexed, but not in despair;

9 Persecuted, but not forsaken [*not abandoned by the Lord*]; cast down, but not destroyed;

10 Always bearing about in the body the dying of the Lord Jesus [*always remembering that Jesus went through trials in His mortal life also*], that the life also of Jesus might be made manifest in our body [*that, through our faithfulness, we might be resurrected to eternal life with Christ; see McConkie,* Doctrinal New Testament Commentary, *Vol. 2, p. 419*].

11 For we which live are alway [*always*] delivered unto death for Jesus' sake [*are always repenting because of Christ*], that the life also of Jesus [*that the newness of life from Jesus, being "born again" constantly*] might be made manifest in our mortal flesh [*might happen to us during our mortal lives*].

Verse 11, above, seems to tie in with Romans 6:4–6, where we continue going through the process of dying or repenting, "burying" our old sinful ways, and "crucifying" our sins in order to "walk in newness of life" through the Atonement. It also ties in with Alma 5:14, where, through repentance, we "receive his image in [*our*] countenances." All of this is an ongoing process during our mortal lives.

12 So then death worketh in us, but life in you. [*Perhaps Paul is saying in effect, based on the context of previous verses, "So, then, the gospel inspires us to put our own sins and worldly ways to death, so that we can more effectively bring the gospel of Christ to you, which brings new life to you."*]

**JST 2 Corinthians 4:12**

12 So then it worketh death unto us, but life unto you.

13 We having the same spirit of faith, according as it is written [*like it says in Psalm 116:10*], I believed, and therefore have I spoken; we also believe [*in Christ*], and therefore speak [*of Christ*];

14 Knowing that he [*the Father*] which raised up [*resurrected*] the Lord Jesus shall raise up us also by Jesus [*will resurrect us also, through Jesus*], and shall present us with you [*and we will meet*

*together at the judgment bar of God (compare with 2 Nephi 33:15)*].

15 For all things are for your sakes, that the abundant grace might through the thanksgiving [*gratitude*] of many redound [*overflow; see Strong's #4052*] to the glory of God. [*In other words, we put up with whatever we have to in order to help you understand the gospel so that there will be many who are grateful for the Atonement to the point that their gratitude overflows in praising God and bringing glory to Him.*]

**JST 2 Corinthians 4:15**

15 For we bear all things for your sakes, that the abundant grace might, through the thanksgiving of many, redound to the glory of God.

16 For which cause we faint not [*we never give up in this cause*]; but though our outward man perish [*even though our physical bodies get exhausted*], yet the inward man is renewed day by day [*our minds and spirits are constantly being strengthened and refreshed*].

17 For our light affliction [*the little suffering we are called to endure*], which is but for a moment, worketh for us [*prepares for us*] a far more exceeding and eternal weight of glory [*exaltation in the kingdom of God; see D&C 132:16*];

18 While we look not at the things which are seen, but at the things which are not seen [*we prioritize on spiritual things rather than on the things of the world*]: for the things which are seen are temporal [*temporary; Strong's #4340*]; but the things which are not seen [*the things of God*] are eternal.

# SECOND CORINTHIANS 5

In this chapter, Paul starts out by teaching the doctrine of the resurrection of our mortal bodies. He emphasizes how wonderful it will be to eventually get a resurrected body. He will go on to teach the doctrine that we will all appear before the Lord on Judgment Day, and then teach the Atonement of Jesus Christ.

1 FOR we know that if our earthly house [*our mortal body*] of this tabernacle [*mortal body*] were dissolved [*decomposed when we die*], we have a building [*we will have a resurrected body*] of [*from*] God, an house [*a body*] not made with hands [*not mortal*], eternal in the heavens [*which will last forever; see McConkie,* Doctrinal New Testament Commentary, *Vol. 2, p. 420*].

2 For in this we groan, earnestly desiring to be clothed upon with our house which is from heaven [*we sigh in anticipation, looking forward to our resurrected bodies*]:

3 If so be that being clothed [*with a resurrected body*] we shall not be found naked.

4 For we that are in this tabernacle [*this mortal body*] do groan [*sigh*], being burdened [*burdened with the pains, sicknesses, weariness, etc., to which our mortal bodies are subject*]: not for that we would be unclothed [*not that we want to die right now*], but clothed upon [*but look forward to the resurrection*], that mortality might be swallowed up of life [*when our mortal bodies will become resurrected bodies which live for ever*].

5 Now he that hath wrought us for the selfsame thing [*He who made it possible for us to be resurrected*] is God [*the Father; see notes with 2 Corinthians 1:21–22 in this study guide*], who also hath given unto us the earnest of the Spirit [*who, in effect, put "earnest money" on us in the form of the Holy Ghost to ensure that we return to Him*].

6 Therefore we are always confident [*cheerful; see 2 Corinthians 5:6, footnote a*], knowing that, whilst we are

at home in the body [*while we live in our mortal bodies*], we are absent from the Lord [*we are merely absent for a while longer from living with the Lord in heaven*]:

7 (For we walk by faith, not by sight)

8 We are confident [*cheerful, of good courage; Strong's #2292*], I say, and willing [*looking forward*] rather to be absent from the body [*to leave the mortal body*], and to be present with the Lord [*to live with the Lord*].

9 Wherefore we labour, that, whether present or absent, we may be accepted of him [*we strive to be worthy to be acceptable to the Lord, whether alive or dead*].

10 For we must all appear before the judgment seat of Christ; that every one may receive the things done in his body, according to that he hath done [*may be rewarded or punished, according to what we did in mortality*], whether it be good or bad.

**JST 2 Corinthians 5:10**

10 For we must all appear before the judgment seat of Christ, that everyone may receive a reward of the deeds done in the body; things according to what he hath done, whether good or bad.

11 Knowing therefore the terror of the Lord [*since we know what fear the wicked will have when they face the Lord*], we persuade men [*we try to persuade them to follow Christ*]; but we are made manifest unto God [*God knows that we are trying*]; and I trust also are made manifest in your consciences [*and I trust that we have had a positive impact on you*].

12 For we commend not ourselves again unto you [*we are not going to talk ourselves up or brag to you*], but give you occasion to glory on our behalf [*but you can judge us by our works and praise us if you so choose*], that ye may have somewhat to answer them which glory in appearance [*people who want to look righteous*], and not in heart [*but don't want to be righteous in their hearts*].

13 For whether [*if*] we be beside ourselves [*out of our minds; Strong's #1839*], it is to God: or whether we be sober, it is for your cause.

**JST 2 Corinthians 5:13**

13 For we bear record that we are not beside ourselves [*we assure you that we are not out of our minds*]; for whether we glory, it is to God, or whether we be sober [*sober-minded, serious*], it is for your sakes.

14 For the love of Christ constraineth us [*keeps us from coming apart, giving up; Strong's #4912*]; because we thus judge, that if one died for all [*if Christ had to die for everyone*], then were all dead [*then everyone must have needed His Atonement, otherwise they would all remain spiritually dead*]:

15 And that he [*Christ*] died for all, that they which live [*all people*] should not henceforth live unto themselves [*should not live according to their own knowledge and rules*], but unto him [*Christ*] which died for them, and rose again.

**JST 2 Corinthians 5:15**

15 And he died for all, that they which live should not henceforth live unto themselves, but unto him which died for them, and rose again.

16 Wherefore henceforth know we no man after the flesh: yea, though we have known Christ after the flesh, yet now henceforth know we him no more.

**JST 2 Corinthians 5:16**

Wherefore, henceforth live we no more after the flesh [*from now on, we no longer live according to worldly standards*]; yea, though we once lived after the flesh [*though we were once worldly*], yet since we have known Christ [*since we are now converted to Christ*], now henceforth live we no more after the flesh [*we no longer live according to the ways of the world*].

17 Therefore if any man be in Christ [*if anyone has been converted and come unto Christ*], he is a new creature [*he becomes a new person, born again*]: old things are passed away [*old lifestyles are gone*]; behold, all things are become new [*he has a new life*].

**JST 2 Corinthians 5:17**
17 Therefore if any man live in Christ, he is a new creature; old things are passed away; behold, all things are become new,

18 And all things are of God [*all these things come from the Father*], who hath reconciled us to himself by Jesus Christ [*who brings us back to his presence through Jesus Christ*], and hath given to us the ministry of reconciliation [*and has given us the Atonement*];

**JST 2 Corinthians 5:18**
18 And receiveth all the things of God [*". . . all that my Father hath shall be given unto him."; D&C 84:38; in other words, exaltation*], who hath reconciled us to himself by Jesus Christ, and hath given to us the ministry of reconciliation;

19 To wit [*namely; in other words, the "ministry of reconciliation" spoken of in verse 18, above, is*], that God [*the Father*] was in Christ [*was made known to us by Christ*], reconciling the world unto himself [*in order to bring us back to His presence*], not imputing their trespasses unto them [*not holding us accountable for sins we repent of*]; and hath committed unto us the word [*the gospel*] of reconciliation [*of the Atonement*].

20 Now then we are ambassadors [*messengers*] for Christ, as though God did beseech you by us [*what we say to you is the same as if God were speaking to you; compare with "whether by mine own voice or by the voice of my servants, it is the same." D&C 1:38*]: we pray you in Christ's stead [*we urge you, standing in for Christ*], be ye reconciled to God [*be brought into harmony with the Father through the Atonement of Christ*].

Next, in verse 21, Paul tells us, in effect, that Christ, the Sinless One, was made to bear all our sins as if He, personally, had committed them all.

21 For he [*the Father*] hath made him [*Christ*] to be sin for us [*the Father has given us the Savior to pay for our sins*], who knew no sin [*Christ was perfect*]; that we might be made the righteousness of God in him. [*that we might be sanctified, made clean, pure, holy, righteous, through Christ*].

# SECOND CORINTHIANS 6

Paul reminds these Corinthian members of the Church that now is the time for them to accept the gospel, since the opportunity is now being given to them. He reminds them to be good examples so that they don't hurt the work of spreading the gospel. He recounts the many things he and his missionary companions have gone through in order to bring the gospel to many.

1 WE then, as workers together with him, beseech you [*urge you*] also that ye receive not the grace of God in vain [*that you not fail to take full advantage of the Father's grace in giving us the Atonement of Christ*].

**JST 2 Corinthians 6:1**
1 We then, as workers together with Christ, beseech you also that ye receive not the grace of God in vain.

2 (For he saith [*in Isaiah 49:8*], I have heard thee in a time accepted, and in the day of salvation have I succoured thee [*rushed to your aid; in other words, the Lord will gather people in to the gospel as described in Isaiah 49:6*]: behold, now is the accepted time; behold, now is the day of salvation.) [*Paul is telling these members of the Church in*

*Corinth that this time is their opportunity to accept the gospel; don't waste the opportunity.*]

3 Giving no offence in any thing, that the ministry be not blamed [*be good examples so you don't hurt the work of the Lord*]:

4 But in all things approving ourselves [*we (Paul and his companions) have always tried to be good examples*] as the ministers of God, in much patience, in afflictions [*troubles*], in necessities [*in times of need*], in distresses,

5 In stripes [*we have been beaten*], in imprisonments [*we have been in prisons*], in tumults [*we have been attacked by mobs during riots*], in labours [*hard work*], in watchings [*in sleepless nights; Strong's #0070*], in fastings;

6 By pureness, by knowledge, by longsuffering [*not seeking revenge; Strong's #3115*], by kindness, by the Holy Ghost, by love unfeigned [*love which is genuine, not pretended*],

7 By the word of truth, by the power of God, by the armour of righteousness on the right hand and on the left,

8 By [*through*] honour and dishonour [*slander*], by evil report [*lies told about us*] and good report: as deceivers [*being thought of by many as deceivers*], and yet true [*yet as true servants of God*];

9 As unknown [*not known by most*], and yet well known [*by some*]; as dying [*going through times when it looked like we would not survive*], and, behold, we live [*and, as you see, we are still alive*]; as chastened [*beaten; Strong's #3811*], and not killed;

10 As sorrowful [*sad and mourning at times*], yet alway rejoicing [*because of Christ*]; as poor [*often having to ask for alms, financial help, etc.*], yet making many rich [*by bringing them the gospel*]; as having nothing [*in terms of worldly possessions and riches*], and yet possessing all things [*the gospel and potential exaltation*].

11 O ye Corinthians, our mouth is open unto you [*we have spoken clearly and straightforward to you*], our heart is enlarged [*swells with love and compassion for you*].

In the next verse, Paul uses the word "bowels." This word is used differently in modern English than in Old English. Strong's *Exhaustive Concordance of the Bible* defines this word as used by Paul here, as "inward affection, tender mercy, kindness, benevolence, compassion."

12 Ye are not straitened in us [*there is much room in our hearts for you*], but ye are straitened in your own bowels [*but there is not as much love and compassion in your hearts as there needs to be*].

13 Now for a recompence in the same [*now, in order to correct this*], (I speak as unto my children [*I'm speaking to you as I would to my children*],) be ye also enlarged [*make more room in your hearts for Christlike love of others*].

Next, Paul will warn the Corinthian Saints and all of us about the dangers of trying to merge our LDS lifestyles in with the lifestyles of the world around us, through commitments and relationships which could lead us away from Christ.

14 Be ye not unequally yoked together with unbelievers [*don't get yourselves tied up in dealings and commitments with nonmembers which would lead you to be unfaithful to Christ; this could even include marrying out of the Church*]: for what fellowship hath righteousness with unrighteousness [*what business would righteousness have in trying to make unholy alliances with sin*]? and what communion [*association*] hath light with darkness [*are light and darkness compatible*]?

15 And what concord [*harmony, agreement; Strong's #4857*] hath Christ with

Belial [*Satan; Strong's #0955*]? or what part hath he that believeth with an infidel [*a faithless unbeliever; Strong's #0571*]?

16 And what agreement hath the temple of God with idols [*in what way could true temples of God be compatible with idols and their temples*]? for ye are the temple of the living God; as God hath said [*in Leviticus 26:12*], I will dwell in them, and walk in them; and I will be their God, and they shall be my people.

17 Wherefore come out from among them [*leave associations which take you away from Christ*], and be ye separate, saith the Lord, and touch not the unclean thing; and I will receive you,

**JST 2 Corinthians 6:17**

17 Wherefore come out from among them, and be ye the separate, saith the Lord, and touch not the unclean thing; and I will receive you,

18 And will be a Father unto you, and ye shall be my sons and daughters, saith the Lord Almighty. [*This is a beautiful reminder to us that if we will leave the ways of the world, whatever the cost, we will become "family" with God, becoming His "sons and daughters," which is a scriptural phrase which means exaltation. See D&C 76:24 and Mosiah 5:7.*]

# SECOND CORINTHIANS 7

This chapter is one of the more famous and oft-quoted of Paul's writings, because it defines "godly sorrow" (being truly sorry for sins committed, rather than merely being sorry you got caught) in verses 9–11. Godly sorrow is an essential part of true repentance and coming unto Christ.

The JST makes no corrections in this chapter.

1 HAVING therefore these promises [*including the promises in verse 18 of chapter 6, above*], dearly beloved, let us cleanse ourselves [*let us repent*] from all filthiness of the flesh and spirit [*of body and mind*], perfecting holiness in the fear of God [*working toward perfection with a realization that we are accountable to God*].

2 Receive us [*please accept our efforts in your behalf*]; we have wronged no man, we have corrupted no man, we have defrauded [*deceived for personal gain*] no man.

3 I speak not this to condemn you [*I am not comparing you to us to make you feel inferior*]: for I have said before, that ye are in our hearts to die and live with you.

4 Great is my boldness of speech toward you [*I have spoken very plainly to you*], great is my glorying of you [*I have great confidence in you*]: I am filled with comfort [*I am greatly encouraged by your progress*], I am exceeding joyful in all our tribulation [*I have much joy in spite of persecutions*].

5 For, when we were come [*when we came*] into Macedonia [*northern Greece*], our flesh had no rest [*we were physically exhausted*], but we were troubled on every side [*we were persecuted on every side*]; without were fightings [*externally, we were fighting for survival*], within [*inside of us*] were fears.

6 Nevertheless God, that comforteth those that are cast down [*discouraged*], comforted us by the coming of Titus; [*When Titus (one of Paul's favorite missionary companions) came, it cheered us up.*]

7 And not by his coming only, but by the consolation wherewith he was comforted in you, when he told us your earnest desire, your mourning, your fervent mind toward me; so that I rejoiced the more. [*Not only were we*

*cheered up by Titus' coming, but I was cheered up even more when he told us about your concerns and worries for my well-being.*]

8 For though I made you sorry with a letter [*even though I caused you sorrow when I scolded you in my last letter to you (First Corinthians)*], I do not repent [*I don't take back what I said because you needed it*], though I did repent [*though I did regret hurting your feelings*]: for I perceive that the same epistle [*that letter*] hath made you sorry, though it were but for a season [*even though you got over it after while*].

9 Now I rejoice, not that ye were made sorry [*I'm not happy because I caused you pain*], but that ye sorrowed to repentance [*but because you actually repented because of what I said to you*]: for ye were made sorry after a godly manner [*my letter caused you to have "godly sorrow" so that you truly repented*], that ye might receive damage by us in nothing [*so that, as it ultimately turned out, we did not hurt you in any way*].

Paul now defines "godly sorrow," which is a vital part of truly repenting.

10 For godly sorrow worketh repentance [*causes us to repent*] to salvation [*and thus obtain exaltation*] not to be repented of [*and leaves us with no regrets*]: but the sorrow of the world [*being sorry you got caught, or sorry because you are embarrassed, or sorry that your opportunity to continue committing that sin has been taken away, etc.*] worketh death [*leads to spiritual death*].

Now, Paul describes some components of "godly sorrow," which make it so effective in cleansing us from sin and leading us to truly change and become more righteous.

11 For behold this selfsame thing [*this godly sorrow, the very thing I'm teaching you about, namely*], that ye sorrowed [*were sorry for sins*] after a godly sort [*in the way God wants you to be*], what carefulness [*sincerity, anxiety*] it wrought [*caused*] in you, yea, what clearing of yourselves [*eagerness to become clear of the sin*], yea, what indignation [*irritation, anger at yourself for committing the sin*], yea, what fear [*alarm*], yea, what vehement desire [*strong desire to change*], yea, what zeal [*enthusiasm to change*], yea, what revenge [*punishment; suffering whatever is necessary to make permanent change*]! In all things ye have approved yourselves to be clear in this matter [*in everything you have done, you have demonstrated that you understand godly sorrow*].

12 Wherefore, though I wrote unto you [*even though I wrote to all of you*], I did it not for his cause that had done the wrong [*I did not write it only to the members guilty of sinning*] , nor for his cause that suffered wrong [*nor did I write only to support the victims of others' sins*], but that our care for you in the sight of God might appear unto you [*but so that all of you would know that we care about you, with God as our witness*].

13 Therefore we were comforted in your comfort [*we were comforted by your concern for our comfort and well-being*]: yea, and exceedingly the more joyed we for the joy of Titus, because his spirit was refreshed by you all [*and we had all the more joy because of your kindnesses to Titus when he was among you*].

14 For if I have boasted any thing to him of you, I am not ashamed [*I told him what great Saints you are, and what he found when he visited you proved me right*]; but as we spake all things to you in truth, even so our boasting, which I made before Titus, is found a truth. [*In other words, when Titus arrived among us (see verse 6), and we talked about you and his visit among you, he verified that all the good things we said about you were true.*]

15 And his [*Titus'*] inward affection is more abundant toward you [*his affection for you swells up in his heart*], whilst he remembereth the obedience of you all [*as he talks to us about you and your obedience to the gospel*], how with fear and trembling ye received him [*and how you humbly and respectfully welcomed him in your midst*].

16 I rejoice therefore that I have confidence in you in all things [*it brings me great joy that I can have such confidence in you in all these things*].

# SECOND CORINTHIANS 8

Paul has been raising funds from members of the Church everywhere to take back to the impoverished Saints in the Jerusalem area. He now mentions to the members in Corinth the contributions made by members in northern Greece.

1 MOREOVER, brethren, we do you to wit of the grace of God bestowed on the churches [*wards and branches*] of Macedonia [*the area known as northern Greece today*];

**JST 2 Corinthians 8:1**

1 Moreover, brethren, we would have you to know of the grace of God bestowed on the churches of Macedonia;

2 How that in a great trial of affliction [*even though they have many afflictions themselves*] the abundance of their joy and their deep poverty abounded unto the riches of their liberality [*they were still very liberal and generous in joyfully giving money, despite their own poverty, to the fund for the Saints in Jerusalem*].

3 For to their power, I bear record, yea, and beyond their power they were willing of themselves [*they went far beyond their ability to contribute*];

4 Praying us with much intreaty [*asking us, indeed pleading with us*] that we would receive the gift [*accept their donations to the fund*], and take upon us the fellowship of the ministering to the saints [*and thus allow them to join in ministering to their fellow Saints*].

5 And this they did, not as we hoped, [*In other words, they did not do it because we required it of them.*] but first gave their own selves to the Lord [*rather, they did it because they had dedicated themselves to the Lord*], and unto us by the will of God [*and thus, they recognized the will of God and gave generously to us for the fund*].

**JST 2 Corinthians 8:5**

5 And this they did, not as we required, but first gave their own selves to the Lord, and unto us by the will of God.

6 Insomuch that we desired Titus, that as he had begun, so he would also finish in you the same grace also [*so we asked Titus, who had helped raise money for this fund elsewhere, to work with you to raise money for this fund*].

7 Therefore, as ye abound [*since you excel*] in every thing, in faith, and utterance [*in doctrine; see Strong's #3056*], and knowledge, and in all diligence, and in your love to us, see that ye abound in this grace also [*see that you excel in contributing to this fund also*].

8 I speak not by commandment [*I am not commanding you to do this*], but by occasion of the forwardness of others [*but since others elsewhere have been so generous*], and to prove the sincerity of your love [*I think this is a test of your sincerity and love to see if you will contribute as generously as they have*].

9 For ye know the grace of our Lord Jesus Christ, that, though he was rich [*in heaven*], yet for your sakes [*in order to help you*] he became poor [*He came to earth*], that ye through his poverty [*through His sacrifices*] might be rich [*gain eternal life*]. [*In other words,*

*you know that the Savior gave His all in order to make you rich in eternity, indeed, to give you the Atonement.*]

10 And herein I give my advice [*here is my advice to you about raising money for this fund*]: for this is expedient [*this advice is necessary*] for you, who have begun before [*who were the first to start contributing to this fund*], not only to do, but also to be forward [*desirous; Strong's #2309*] a year ago. [*In other words, you were the first to express a desire to contribute, and to actually start contributing to this fund a year ago.*]

11 Now therefore perform the doing of it [*now I counsel you to finish the job*]; that as there was a readiness to will [*since you were so willing to begin with*], so there may be a performance also out of that which ye have [*let's have your performance match your expressed commitment, according to your ability to pay*].

12 For if there be first a willing mind [*if the desire to contribute is in your hearts in the first place*], it is accepted according to that a man hath, and not according to that he hath not [*the actual amount you contribute must be according to what you have, not according to what you don't have*]. [*This reminds us of King Benjamin's counsel about giving to the poor in Mosiah 4:24.*]

13 For I mean not that other men be eased, and ye burdened [*I do not mean to imply that you should be overburdened in contributing in order to ease the needs of the Saints in Jerusalem and the surrounding area*]:

14 But by an equality [*I just think there should be a type of equality produced between you and them by your generosity*], that now at this time your abundance may be a supply for their want [*you help them now*], that their abundance also may be a supply for your want [*perhaps they will be the ones to help you another day*]: that there may be equality:

The principle of helping each other, as given in verse 14, above, is one of the guiding principles for our welfare system today within the Church.

15 As it is written [*in Exodus 16:18*], He that had gathered much had nothing over [*left over*]; and he that had gathered little had no lack [*had plenty*].

16 But thanks be to God, which put the same earnest care into the heart of Titus for you [*I am thankful that Titus cares for you as much as I do*].

17 For indeed he accepted the exhortation [*he accepted the challenge we gave him to collect these funds*]; but being more forward [*but being very enthusiastic about it himself*], of his own accord [*on his own initiative*] he went unto you [*he is coming to you*].

18 And we have sent with him the brother [*Bible scholars don't know who this brother is, but he has a good reputation*], whose praise is in the gospel throughout all the churches [*who is very well thought of by all the members here*];

19 And not that only, but who was also chosen of the churches [*wards and branches*] to travel with us with this grace [*with the money that has been raised so far*], which is administered by us to the glory of the same Lord [*which we are raising to honor the principles taught us by the Savior*], and declaration of your ready mind [*and because we understand that you are ready to finish the fundraising project among yourselves*]:

20 Avoiding this, that no man should blame us in this abundance [*money which has been raised*] which is administered by us [*we don't want to do anything in this matter of raising money for the impoverished Saints in Jerusalem and in taking it to them that would set us up for valid criticism*]:

21 Providing for honest things, not only in the sight of the Lord, but also in the

sight of men [*we want to be considered honest by God and also by our fellow men*].

22 And we have sent with them our brother [*we have also sent another brother with Titus and his companion (verse 18)*], whom we have oftentimes proved diligent [*enthusiastic; Strong's #4707*] in many things [*who has proven his enthusiasm to us already in many things*], but now much more diligent [*even more enthusiastic*], upon [*because of*] the great confidence which I have in you.

23 Whether any do enquire of Titus, he is my partner and fellowhelper concerning you: or our brethren be enquired of, they are the messengers of the churches, and the glory of Christ.

The JST combines portions of verses 22 and 23 as follows:

**JST 2 Corinthians 8:23**
23 Therefore we send him unto you, in consequence of the great confidence which we have in you, that you will receive the things concerning you, to the glory of Christ; whether we send by the hand of Titus, my partner and fellow laborer, or our brethren, the messengers of the churches.

24 Wherefore shew ye to them [*Titus and those traveling with him, plus any others Paul might send to them*], and before the churches [*wards and branches*], the proof of your love, and of our boasting on your behalf. [*In other words, we've bragged a lot about you, so please don't let us down.*]

# SECOND CORINTHIANS 9

In this chapter, Paul will continue the theme he started in chapter 8 He will tell the members of the Church in Corinth who are being asked to continue donating to the fund for helping poverty-stricken Saints in Jerusalem, that the Lord loves people who give willingly and cheerfully (verse 7).

1 FOR as touching [*regarding*] the ministering to the saints [*this fundraising for the needy Saints in Jerusalem*], it is superfluous [*unnecessary*] for me to write to you:

2 For I know the forwardness of your mind [*I know how eager you are to participate in it*], for which I boast of you to them of Macedonia [*for which I have already bragged about you to the members in northern Greece*], that Achaia [*the area known as southern Greece today, including Corinth*] was ready [*to start contributing*] a year ago; and your zeal [*enthusiasm*] hath provoked very many [*inspired many to action already*].

3 Yet have I sent the brethren [*however, I have sent Titus (2 Corinthians 8:6) and his companions to follow up with you in this collection*], lest our boasting of you should be in vain in this behalf [*just in case you are not coming through with the needed contributions*]; that, as I said, ye may be ready [*so that you can have the job done when he gets there*]:

4 Lest haply [*for fear*] if they [*any members*] of Macedonia [*northern Greece today*] come with me, and find you unprepared, we (that we say not, ye) [*let alone you*] should be ashamed [*embarrassed, disappointed*] in this same confident boasting [*because of how we talked you up to others*].

5 Therefore I thought it necessary to exhort [*urge*] the brethren [*Titus and his companions*], that they would go before [*ahead of me and my companions*] unto you, and make up beforehand your bounty [*and make sure the welfare collection for the needy members in the Jerusalem area*], whereof ye had notice before [*about which we previously talked*], that the same might be ready [*might be in place*], as a matter of bounty [*as a generous gift, given over*

*a longer period of time*], and not as of covetousness [*rather than a gift given grudgingly because of too short a time to collect it*].

6 But this I say, He which soweth sparingly shall reap also sparingly; and he which soweth bountifully shall reap also bountifully. [*But let me remind you that those who donate little will harvest fewer blessings from God and those who donate generously will have a bounteous harvest of blessings from God.*]

7 Every man according as he purposeth in his heart [*it is up to each person to decide how much he will give to this cause*], so let him give; not grudgingly, or of necessity [*or because he feels forced*]: for God loveth a cheerful giver.

8 And God is able to make all grace abound toward you [*God can bless you abundantly*]; that ye, always having all sufficiency in all things, may abound to every good work [*so that you can give abundantly to help others*]:

9 (As it is written [*in Psalm 112:9*], He hath dispersed abroad; he hath given to the poor: his righteousness remaineth for ever.

10 Now he [*God*] that ministereth [*provides*] seed to the sower [*planter, farmer*] both minister [*supplies*] bread for your food, and multiply your seed sown [*multiplies your harvest*], and increase the fruits of your righteousness [*and multiplies the rewards given to you because of your righteousness*];)

11 Being enriched in every thing to all bountifulness [*you will be blessed in every way by God so that you can be generous in giving to this fund*], which causeth through us thanksgiving to God [*which, when we bring it to the destitute members in Jerusalem, will cause them to give thanksgiving to God*].

12 For the administration of this service [*your giving of this money*] not only supplieth [*takes care of*] the want of the saints [*in the Jerusalem area*], but is abundant also by many thanksgivings unto God [*but will be the cause of much gratitude to God*];

13 Whiles by the experiment of this ministration [*meanwhile, the result of your ministry to them is that*] they glorify God for [*because of*] your professed subjection [*observable loyalty*] unto the gospel of Christ, and for your liberal distribution [*contribution*] unto them, and unto all men;

14 And by their prayer for you [*and in their prayers for you*], which long after you [*which reach out to you*] for [*because of*] the exceeding grace of God in you [*the great blessings of God which came to them through you*].

15 Thanks be unto God for his unspeakable [*indescribable*] gift.

# SECOND CORINTHIANS 10

Paul is apparently concerned about criticism aimed at him by some who say his letters strike terror in people (see verse 9), but that he is less than impressive in person (see verse 10) and, furthermore, listening to him talk is of no value at all (see verse 10). It might be interesting here to read the Prophet Joseph Smith's description of Paul so that we can better understand why some unthinking people might be critical of him. The Prophet said, "He is about five feet high; very dark hair; dark complexion; dark skin; large Roman nose; sharp face; small black eyes, penetrating as eternity; round shoulders; a whining voice, except when elevated, and then it almost resembled the roaring of a lion. He was a good orator, active and diligent, always employing himself in doing good to his fellow man."

(*Teachings of the Prophet Joseph Smith*, p. 180.)

1 NOW I Paul myself beseech [*urge*] you by the meekness and gentleness of Christ [*in meekness and gentleness as taught by Christ*], who in presence [*when I am in your presence*] am base [*I am humble; Strong's #5011*] among you, but being absent am bold toward you [*but since I am away from you now, I have written rather boldly about issues and concerns to you*]:

2 But I beseech you [*I urge you to follow the counsel I have given you*], that I may not be bold when I am present [*so that I don't have to be too bold with you when I come to you*] with that confidence, wherewith I think to be bold against some, which think of us as if we walked according to the flesh [*like I think I will have to be with some who think of us as living according to the ways of the world*].

Paul will now use the imagery of war and weapons to describe the "war" against evil in which the members of the Church are involved.

3 For though we walk in the flesh [*though we live in the world*], we do not war after the flesh [*the war we fight is not like that of the world*]:

4 (For the weapons of our warfare are not carnal [*worldly*], but mighty through God [*but mighty because of God's power*] to the pulling down of strong holds [*and able to destroy the strongholds of the devil*];)

5 Casting down imaginations [*false doctrines and philosophies*], and every high [*prideful*] thing that exalteth itself [*rises up to fight*] against the knowledge of God, and bringing into captivity every thought to the obedience of Christ [*and overcoming every inappropriate thought or idea and making it subject to Christ*];

6 And having in a readiness to revenge [*punish*] all disobedience [*we are prepared to punish any disobedience on the part of others*], when your obedience is fulfilled [*once you yourselves have obeyed the counsel we have given you*].

7 Do ye look on things after the outward appearance [*do you really think that outward appearance is all that important*]? If any man trust to himself that he is Christ's, let him of himself think this again [*if anyone who is being critical of us thinks that he belongs to Christ, he should rethink it*], that, as he is Christ's, even so are we Christ's [*that we have just as much right to belong to Christ as he does*].

8 For though I should boast somewhat more of our authority, which the Lord hath given us for edification, and not for your destruction, I should not be ashamed: [*It wouldn't embarrass me to remind you that the Lord has given us authority over you, but He didn't give us this authority with the intent that we should tear you down, rather that we should use it to build you up.*]

9 That I may not seem as if I would terrify you by letters. [*I don't want it to seem as if I am trying to frighten you with my letters.*]

10 For his letters, say they [*some people say Paul's letters*], are weighty [*severe; Strong's #0926*] and powerful [*too forceful; Strong's #2478*]; but his bodily presence is weak, and his speech contemptible. [*Some say that my letters are too severe and forceful, and they say that, in person, I am less than impressive, and my voice and speech are to be despised.*]

11 Let such an one [*let those who criticize*] think this, that, such as we are in word by letters when we are absent, such will we be also in deed when we are present [*we will be just as bold when we are among you as we are in letter writing*].

12 For we dare not make ourselves of the number [*we would not want to be numbered among those*], or compare ourselves with some that commend themselves [*who think too highly

12 But what I do, that I will do [*what I have been doing I will continue to do. In other words, I have been speaking boldly against things which pose a spiritual danger to you, and I will continue to do so*], that I may cut off occasion [*the opportunity to deceive you*] from them which desire occasion [*from those who seek such opportunity among you*]; that wherein they glory, they may be found even as we [*in order to take away their advantage among you*].

13 For such are false apostles, deceitful workers, transforming themselves into the apostles of Christ [*trying to make you think they are true Apostles of Jesus Christ*].

14 And no marvel [*and it is no wonder that they are trying to do this*]; for Satan himself is transformed into [*appears as*] an angel of light.

Paul's statement that Satan can transform himself into an angel of light in order to deceive people is a very important matter for us to understand. D&C 129:8 was given by Joseph Smith to inform members of this danger. Furthermore, Joseph Smith said, "One great evil is, that men are ignorant of the nature of spirits; their power, laws, government, intelligence, etc., and imagine that when there is anything like power, revelation, or vision manifested, that it must be of God." (*Teachings of the Prophet Joseph Smith*, p. 203.)

The Prophet further warned that "nothing is a greater injury to the children of men than to be under the influence of a false spirit when they think they have the Spirit of God." He continued in the same sermon to say, "There have also been ministering angels in the Church which were of Satan appearing as an angel of light. A sister. . .saw a glorious personage descending, arrayed in white, with sandy colored hair;" (*Teachings of the Prophet Joseph Smith*, p. 205 and 214.)

Now, one last comment about avoiding such cunning and, in some cases, spectacular deception: How can we tell the difference between Satan and his evil spirits appearing as angels of light and angels from God? Answer: We have the Gift of the Holy Ghost. Furthermore, we have the gifts of the Spirit, which are given to enable us to avoid deception as explained in D&C 46:8.

15 Therefore it is no great thing [*therefore, it is not surprising*] if his [*Satan's*] ministers also be transformed as [*also try to make us think that they are*] the ministers of righteousness; whose end [*punishment*] shall be according to their works.

Next, Paul will use a little play on words to emphasize a point. He will use variations of the word "fool" and, in effect, say that some consider those who believe in Christ to be fools, yet, these so-called fools are wiser than those who don't believe, and thus allow themselves to become real fools, deceived by Satan.

16 I say again, Let no man think me a fool [*let no one consider me to be a fool*]; if otherwise [*but if they can't bring themselves to not consider me a fool*], yet as a fool receive me [*if it is foolish to believe in Christ, then accept me as a fool*], that I may boast myself a little [*that I may show how smart a "fool" can be*].

17 That which I speak [*what I am now going to say*], I speak it not after the Lord [*I do not speak in the manner the Lord would normally have me speak*], but as it were foolishly, in this confidence of boasting [*rather in a way that may sound foolish and a bit boastful*].

18 Seeing that many glory after the flesh, I will glory also [*since many boast of some of their own accomplishments, I will do a little boasting also, about some of the things I have survived—see verses 23–28*].

19 For ye suffer [*listen to*] fools gladly, seeing ye yourselves are wise.

20 For ye suffer [*put up with it*], if a man bring you into bondage [*enslaves you*], if a man devour [*destroys*] you, if a man take of you [*takes advantage of you*], if a man exalt himself [*lords it over you*], if a man smite [*slaps*] you on the face.

21 I speak as concerning reproach, as though we had been weak [*we are not strong enough to put up with some of the things you put up with*]. Howbeit [*however*] whereinsoever any is bold [*when it comes to things in which others are bold*], (I speak foolishly) [*I speak as a fool*], I am bold also [*I will be bold also*].

In order to accomplish what he did, Paul had to have a very strong personality. He was very humble and obedient to the Lord. He was sweet and gentle and tender. He was brilliant, energetic, powerful, and virtually unstoppable when he made up his mind to do something. He was also feisty, and we see this side of his personality in the next verses.

22 Are they Hebrews? so am I. Are they Israelites? so am I. Are they the seed [*descendants*] of Abraham? so am I.

23 Are they ministers of Christ? (I speak as a fool) [*you will think I have lost my mind when I say what I say next*] I am more; in labours more abundant [*I have worked harder than they have*], in stripes above measure [*I can't even count how many times I have been whipped*], in prisons more frequent [*I have spent more time in prison than they have*], in deaths oft [*I have been nearly killed time and time again*].

**JST 2 Corinthians 11:23**

23 Are they ministers of Christ? (I speak as a fool.) so am I; in labors more abundant, in stripes above measure, in prisons more frequent, in deaths oft.

24 Of the Jews five times received I forty stripes [*lashes of a whip*] save one [*five times, the Jews flogged me with 39 lashes of the whip*].

Under Jewish law, it was illegal to flog a person with a whip more than 40 times (see Deuteronomy 25:3), therefore, they never struck a person more than 39 times with a whip in order to avoid breaking the law if they slipped up and miscounted. A description of this whipping is as follows: "Both of (the victim's) hands were tied to . . . a stake a cubit and a half high (about 27 inches high). The public officer then tore down his robe until his breast was laid bare. The executioner stood on a stone behind the criminal. The scourge consisted of two thongs, one of which was composed of four strands of calfskin, and one of two strands of ass's-skin, which passed through a hole in a handle. . . . The prisoner bent to receive the blows, which were inflicted with one hand, but with all the force of the striker, thirteen on the breast, thirteen on the right, and thirteen on the left shoulder. While the punishment was going on, the chief judge read aloud (Deuteronomy 28:58, 59; 24:9; and Psalm 78:38, 39 which dealt with God's commandments, the punishment for their nonobservance, and the Lord's compassion on the sinner) . . . If the punishment was not over by the time that these three passages were read, they were again repeated, and so timed as to end exactly with the punishment itself. Meanwhile a second judge numbered the blows, and a third before each blow exclaimed 'Hakkehu' (strike him)." (Farrar, *The Life and Works of St. Paul*, pp. 715–16. Quoted in the Institute of Religion New Testament student manual, *The Life and Teachings of Jesus and His Apostles*, p. 303.)

25 Thrice [*three times*] was I beaten with rods, once was I stoned [*see Acts 14:19 where Jews stoned Paul and left him for dead*], thrice I suffered shipwreck [*I was shipwrecked three times*], a night and a day I have been in the deep [*I spent a night and a day in the sea*];

26 In journeyings often [*I have been constantly on the go*], in perils of [*in dangers from*] waters, in perils of

robbers, in perils by mine own countrymen [*in dangers from the Jews*], in perils by the heathen [*in dangers from the Gentiles*], in perils in the city, in perils in the wilderness [*the country*], in perils in the sea, in perils among false brethren [*in dangers because of members who betrayed me*];

27 In weariness [*I have gone through much toil and trouble*] and painfulness [*and pain*], in watchings often [*I have often gone without sleep*], in hunger and thirst [*I have been hungry and thirsty*], in fastings often [*I have often fasted; can also mean he had gone without food*], in cold and nakedness [*I have endured cold and nakedness (perhaps when he was in prison)*].

28 Beside those things that are without [*in addition to these things which are matters of physical suffering*], that which cometh upon me daily, the care of all the churches [*I have had the daily worries and concerns of caring for all the wards and branches of the Church under my stewardship*].

29 Who is weak, and I am not weak [*when a member shows weakness, does it not require energy from me*]? who is offended, and I burn not? [*In other words, the daily needs of members take a lot out of me.*]

> **JST 2 Corinthians 11:29**
> 29 Who is weak, and I am not weak? who is offended, and I anger not?

30 If I must needs glory [*if I am going to rejoice; Strong's #2744*], I will glory of the things which concern mine infirmities [*I will rejoice in the fact that God has given me weaknesses; compare to Ether 12:27; see also 2 Corinthians 12:10, where Paul says "I take pleasure in infirmitie. . .for when I am weak, then am I strong."*]

31 The God and Father of our Lord Jesus Christ, which is blessed [*praised*] for evermore, knoweth that I lie not.

32 In Damascus the governor under Aretas the king kept the city of the Damascenes with a garrison, desirous to apprehend me: [*In other words, let me mention one more hardship I have been through, namely, that some years ago, I was hiding from soldiers in Damascus who were under orders to arrest me.*]

33 And through a window in a basket was I let down by the wall, and escaped his hands [*and I had to be let down the outside wall of the city from a window, in a basket, to escape*].

# SECOND CORINTHIANS 12

This chapter is very important doctrinally, because it mentions the "third heaven" in verse 2, in other words, the celestial kingdom. Paul shares some sacred experiences with us that strengthen our testimonies.

1 IT is not expedient [*not necessary*] for me doubtless to glory [*to keep talking about these things*]. I will come to visions and revelations of the Lord [*I will mention more important things, namely visions and revelations from the Lord*].

> Joseph Smith confirms that the "man in Christ" referred to next, in verse 2, is Paul himself. See *Teachings of the Prophet Joseph Smith*, pp. 301, 304–305. Paul is being modest and doesn't give his name, initially, as he tells of the experience. But when he uses the word "I" in verses 2 and 3, it becomes obvious that he is the man.

2 I knew a man in Christ above fourteen years ago [*over fourteen years ago*], (whether in the body, I cannot tell; or whether out of the body, I cannot tell [*I couldn't tell whether or not I was in my body when this happened*]: God knoweth;) such an one caught up to the third heaven [*one who was taken up to the celestial glory*].

3 And I knew such a man, (whether in

the body, or out of the body, I cannot
tell: God knoweth;)

4 How that he was caught up into
paradise [*the third heaven*], and heard
unspeakable words, which it is not
lawful for a man to utter [*talk about*].

Joseph Smith explained a bit of what Paul saw during this experience as follows: "Paul ascended into the third heavens, and he could understand the three principal rounds of Jacob's ladder—the telestial, the terrestrial, and the celestial glories or kingdoms, where Paul saw and heard things which were not lawful for him to utter." (*Teachings of the Prophet Joseph Smith*, p. 304.)

5 Of such an one will I glory [*I can
rejoice about such a person*]: yet of
myself I will not glory, but in mine
infirmities [*I don't want to boast about
myself, rather, I will limit myself to
rejoicing in my shortcomings and weaknesses which allow God to teach and
strengthen me; see verses 7 and 9,
next*].

6 For though I would desire to glory
[*even if I wanted to boast a bit*], I shall
not be a fool; for I will say the truth [*I
would be telling the truth*]: but now I
forbear [*I will hold back*], lest any man
should think of me above that which he
seeth me to be, or that he heareth of me
[*for fear that people would hold me up
higher than I am*].

**JST 2 Corinthians 12:6**

6 For though I would desire to glory, I shall not be a fool; for I will say the truth; but now I forbear, lest any man should think of me above that which he seeth of me, or that he heareth of me.

7 And lest I should be exalted above
measure through the abundance of the
revelations [*and just in case I were to
become prideful because of the many
revelations I have been given*], there
was given to me a thorn in the flesh, the
messenger of Satan to buffet me [*strike
me down, hit me; Strong's #2852; this
"thorn in the flesh" serves to pound me
down and keep me humble*], lest I should
be exalted above measure [*for fear that
I should become prideful*].

We do not know what Paul's "thorn in the flesh" was. Whether it was some physical problem or spiritual difficulty or persistent difficulty with someone close to him or whatever, it served to keep him humble as he explains in verses 9 and 10.

There is comfort for us in what Paul tells us next. Many humble members pray with great faith for God to heal them or a loved one, or to remove a problem from their lives, etc., but it doesn't happen. It is comforting to know that someone with as much faith as Paul had didn't get what he asked for either. The Lord's will is done in such matters, and that is important for us to understand so that we do not get bitter or angry with God.

8 For this thing [*my "thorn in the flesh"*]
I besought the Lord thrice, that it might
depart from me [*I pleaded with the Lord
on three different occasions to remove
this from me*].

9 And he said unto me, My grace [*My
will, My mercy, My understanding*] is
sufficient for thee: [*In other words, My
will for you in this matter will be better
for you than My granting your desire*]
for my strength is made perfect in weakness [*my weaknesses keep me humble
and allow God to strengthen me as I
grow toward perfection*]. Most gladly
therefore will I rather glory [*rejoice*]
in my infirmities [*problems and weaknesses*], that the power of Christ may
rest upon me.

The message in verse 9, above, is very similar to what Moroni said in Ether 12:27 when he quoted the Lord who said, "And if men come unto me I will show unto them their weakness. I give unto men weakness that they may be humble; and my grace is sufficient for all men that humble themselves before me; for if they humble

themselves before me, and have faith in me, then will I make weak things become strong unto them."

10 Therefore I take pleasure in infirmities, in reproaches [*insults*], in necessities [*hardships*], in persecutions, in distresses [*difficulties*] for Christ's sake [*because of my commitment to Christ*]: for when I am weak, then am I strong [*then I become strong; Compare with Ether 12:27*].

11 I am become a fool in glorying [*I have overdone it in telling you all this*]; ye have compelled me [*but you encouraged me to do it*]: for I ought to have been commended of you [*it is proper for me to be well-thought of by you*]: for in nothing am I behind the very chiefest apostles [*because I have taught you and dealt with you exactly like the senior Apostles would have if they had been here in my place*], though I be nothing [*even though I am nothing compared to them*].

12 Truly the signs of an apostle were wrought [*done*] among you in all patience, in signs, and wonders, and mighty deeds [*truly, I have ministered among you as a true Apostle*].

13 For what is it wherein ye were inferior to other churches, except it be that I myself was not burdensome to you [*can you think of any way in which you are inferior to other members elsewhere, except in that you had to put up with me*]? forgive me this wrong.

14 Behold, the third time I am ready to come to you [*when I come to you again, it will be for the third time*]; and I will not be burdensome to you [*and I will not be a burden to you*]: for I seek not yours, but you [*I do not seek material support from you, rather to help you*]: for the children ought not to lay up for the parents, but the parents for the children [*the children are not supposed to have to take care of the parents, rather, the parents take care of the children; in other words, you (my "children") should not have to take care of me (your "parent" in the gospel)*].

15 And I will very gladly spend and be spent [*be worn out*] for you; though the more abundantly I love you, the less I be loved.

16 But be it so, I did not burden you: nevertheless, being crafty, I caught you with guile.

17 Did I make a gain [*take advantage*] of you by any of them whom I sent unto you?

18 I desired Titus, and with him I sent a brother. Did Titus make a gain of you [*take advantage of you in any way*]? walked we not in the same spirit? walked we not in the same steps [*isn't it true that Titus and I treat you the same*]?

19 Again, think ye that we excuse ourselves unto you [*do you think we owe you an apology for being too hard on you*]? we speak before God in Christ [*God is our witness that we teach you what Christ wants us to*]: but we do all things, dearly beloved, for your edifying [*but everything we do is designed to build you up and strengthen you*].

20 For I fear, lest, when I come, I shall not find you such as I would [*I worry that when I come to you, I will not find everything in order*], and that I shall be found unto you such as ye would not [*and that I will not be as pleasant to you as you would like*]: lest there be [*I worry that you still have among you*] debates [*quarreling*], envyings [*jealousy*], wraths [*uncontrolled tempers; outbursts of anger; Strong's #2372*], strifes [*dividing into factions*], backbitings [*slander*], whisperings [*gossiping*], swellings [*pride*], tumults [*disorder*]:

21 And lest [*I worry for fear that*], when I come again, my God will humble me among you, and that I shall bewail [*be saddened because of*] many which have sinned already, and have not repented of the uncleanness and fornication and

lasciviousness [*sexual immorality in thought and deed*] which they have committed.

## SECOND CORINTHIANS 13

Paul now concludes this letter to the members of the Church living in Corinth. He begins by reminding them about the law of witnesses.

1 THIS is the third time I am coming to you [*this will be the third time I have visited you*]. In the mouth of two or three witnesses shall every word be established [*Deuteronomy 19:15*].

2 I told you before, and foretell you, as if I were present, the second time [*I warned you when I was visiting you for the second time, and I repeat the warning now*]; and being absent now [*in my absence*] I write to them which heretofore [*in the past*] have sinned, and to all other, that, if I come again, I will not spare: [*In other words, I am warning you that when I come for this next visit, I will once again speak out boldly against sin among you as I have in times past.*]

3 Since ye seek a proof of Christ speaking in me [*since some of you are still seeking proof that Christ is speaking to you through me*], which to you-ward is not weak, but is mighty in you [*Christ does not demonstrate weakness toward you as He deals with you; rather, He shows His mighty power among you*].

4 For though he was crucified through weakness [*because He was mortal*], yet he liveth [*has been resurrected*] by the power of God [*the Father*]. For we also are weak in him [*we are weak compared to Him*], but we shall [*be resurrected and*] live with him by the power of God toward you [*because of the power which the Father has demonstrated to you*].

5 Examine yourselves, whether ye be in the faith [*look at yourselves to see whether or not you are being faithful to Christ*]; prove your own selves. Know ye not your own selves, how that Jesus Christ is in you, except ye be reprobates [*don't you realize that Christ can help you unless you are unfit, unless you fail the test; Strong's #0096*]?

6 But I trust that ye shall know that we are not reprobates [*unfit for the kingdom of God*].

7 Now I pray to God that ye do no evil; not that we should appear approved [*not so that people praise us for bringing you the gospel*], but that ye should do that which is honest, though we be as reprobates [*you should do right whether or not we do right*].

8 For we can do nothing against the truth, but for the truth [*everything we do is in harmony with the truth*].

9 For we are glad, when we are weak, and ye are strong [*we are happy when you live the gospel even better than we do*]: and this also we wish, even your perfection [*because we want you to progress toward perfection*].

10 Therefore I write these things being absent, lest being present I should use sharpness, according to the power which the Lord hath given me to edification, and not to destruction. [*In effect, I'm writing these things in advance, before my third visit to you, so that you can work on any problems before I arrive so that I won't have to be sharp with you. That way, I can build you up and strengthen you, rather than having to tear you down to try to get you to repent.*]

11 Finally, brethren, farewell. Be perfect [*keep working toward perfection*], be of good comfort, be of one mind [*be united*], live in peace; and the God of love and peace shall be with you.

12 Greet one another with an holy kiss.

**JST 2 Corinthians 13:12**

12 Greet one another with a holy salutation [*greeting*].

13 All the saints salute [*greet*] you.

14 The grace of the Lord Jesus Christ, and the love of God, and the communion [*companionship*] of the Holy Ghost, be with you all. Amen.

# THE EPISTLE OF PAUL THE APOSTLE TO THE GALATIANS

Galatia was in what is now central Turkey. Paul had many converts in Galatia during his first missionary journey and wrote this letter to them somewhere around AD 57, which would be about 23 years after the crucifixion of the Savior. We do not know for sure where he was when he wrote this epistle (letter). Some scholars believe it was Rome, others believe he wrote it to the Galatian Saints while in Corinth.

The main theme of this letter is that the Gospel of Jesus Christ is the only source of true freedom. A major problem which Paul addresses in this letter is the "Judaizers." These were Jewish converts to the Church who insisted on keeping the Law of Moses in spite of the fact that they had joined the Church and had been taught that the Law of Moses had been fulfilled by Christ. Thus, the higher laws taught by Christ and the accompanying freedom from letter-of-the-law daily ritual were being undermined by the Judaizers. We encounter similar problems today when some members attempt to emphasize the words of dead prophets over the words of the current living prophets.

## GALATIANS 1

In this chapter we learn that the prophesied apostasy is already under way. Paul warns these members that those among them who are attempting to change the true gospel are already in apostasy. No one is authorized to change the true gospel. Among other things, Paul will review his conversion for these Galatian members of the Church.

1 PAUL, an apostle, (not of men, neither by man, but by Jesus Christ, and God the Father, who raised him from the dead;) [*In other words, Paul, an Apostle who was called of God.*]

2 And all the brethren which are with me, unto the churches [*wards and branches*] of Galatia:

> Verse 3, below, is another scriptural verification that the Father and the Son are separate beings.

3 Grace be to you and peace from God the Father, and from our Lord Jesus Christ,

4 Who gave himself for our sins [*who gave us the Atonement*], that he might deliver us from this present evil world, according to the will of God and our Father [*who is our Father*]:

5 To whom be glory for ever and ever. Amen.

6 I marvel that ye are so soon removed from him that called you into the grace of Christ unto another gospel [*I am amazed that you are going into apostasy (falling away from the Church) so soon*]:

7 Which is not another [*actually, there is no such thing as "another gospel"*]; but there be [*are*] some that trouble you, and would pervert [*corrupt, change*] the gospel of Christ.

8 But though [*even if*] we, or an angel

from heaven, preach [*were to preach*] any other gospel unto you than that which we have preached unto you, let him be accursed [*let him be doomed to destruction; Strong's #0331*].

9 As we said before, so say I now again, If any man preach any other gospel unto you than that ye have received, let him be accursed [*damned for eternity*].

10 For do I now persuade men, or God [*do you think I am trying to win the approval of men, or of God*]? or do I seek to please men [*the approval of men*]? for if I yet pleased men [*if my goal were to gain the approval of men*], I should not [*could not*] be the servant of Christ.

**JST Galatians 1:10**

10 For do I now please men, or God? or do I seek to please men? for if I yet pleased men, I should not be the servant of Christ.

11 But I certify [*assure*] you, brethren, that the gospel which was preached of me is not after man [*does not come from the philosophies of men*].

12 For I neither received it of man, neither was I taught it, but by [*through*] the revelation of Jesus Christ.

13 For ye have heard of my conversation [*behavior, lifestyle; Strong's #0391*] in time past in the Jews' religion [*as a Pharisee who strictly kept the Law of Moses and saw the new "Christian" church as a threat to the established Jewish religion*], how that beyond measure [*without limits*] I persecuted the church of God, and wasted it [*destroyed it wherever I could*]:

14 And profited [*I was a success*] in the Jews' religion above many my equals [*over and above my peers*] in mine own nation, being more exceedingly zealous of the traditions of my fathers [*I was stricter than most Jews in keeping the Law of Moses and the religious traditions of my ancestors*].

Paul will now briefly tell of his conversion.

15 But when it pleased God [*when it was God's will*], who separated me from my mother's womb [*who gave me life*], and called me by his grace [*and showed mercy and kindness to me*],

16 To reveal his Son in me [*to use me as an instrument to reveal His Son to others*], that I might preach him [*Christ*] among the heathen [*Gentiles*]; immediately I conferred not with flesh and blood [*I did not consult with men*]:

17 Neither went I up [*neither did I go*] to Jerusalem to them which were apostles before me [*to those who were called to be Apostles before I was*]; but I went into Arabia, and returned again unto Damascus [*in Syria*].

It is worth noting that it usually takes time for real change to take place. Paul needed a period of at least three years to let the gospel sink deeply into his soul and lifestyle, then he went to the Apostles for instructions, as indicated in verse 18, next.

18 Then after three years I went up to Jerusalem to see Peter [*who was the president of the Church*], and abode [*stayed*] with him fifteen days.

19 But other of the apostles saw I none, save James the Lord's brother [*the only other Apostle I saw was Jesus' half-brother James*].

Jesus' brother, James, mentioned in verse 19, above, is generally considered to be the author of the Book of James in the New Testament. See Bible Dictionary under "James."

20 Now the things which I write unto you, behold, before God [*as God is my witness*], I lie not.

21 Afterwards [*after that*] I came into the regions of Syria and Cilicia [*southeastern Turkey today*];

22 And was unknown by face unto the churches of Judæa which were in Christ

[*so none of the members there even knew what I looked like*]:

23 But they had heard only, That he which persecuted us in times past now preacheth the faith which once he destroyed. [*All they knew was that the man who once tried to destroy the Church was now preaching to convert others to Christ.*]

24 And they glorified [*praised*] God in me [*because of me*].

**JST Galatians 1:24**
24 And they glorified God on account of me.

# GALATIANS 2

Paul continues reviewing his ministry, talking about two of his missionary companions named Barnabas and Titus.

1 THEN fourteen years after [*later*] I went up again to Jerusalem with Barnabas, and took Titus with me also.

Barnabas was a faithful Jewish convert who served as a missionary companion to Paul. See Bible Dictionary under "Barnabas" for more information about him. Titus was a Gentile convert, possibly from the area of south central Turkey, today, who likewise was a missionary companion of Paul. See Bible Dictionary under "Titus."

2 And I went up by revelation [*as directed in a revelation I received*], and communicated unto them that gospel which I preach among the Gentiles [*and explained to the members in Jerusalem what I was preaching among the Gentiles*], but privately to them which were of reputation [*to the leaders of the Church*], lest by any means I should run, or had run, in vain [*in order to have their approval of what I was teaching and doing among the Gentiles*].

In Paul's writings, the word "Greek" is a general reference to all Gentiles.

3 But neither Titus [*not even Titus*], who was with me, being a Greek [*a Gentile; Strong's #1672*], was compelled to be circumcised: [*In other words, the Brethren did not require Titus to be circumcised, which validated what I had been teaching about that issue.*]

The Judaizers, as mentioned in the opening note for Galatians, were Jewish converts who insisted that Jewish Christians should still keep the Law of Moses, especially the law of circumcision. This demand from them caused much controversy in the early Church, as mentioned in Bible Dictionary under "Circumcision." These members caused much trouble for Paul, who taught that Gentile male converts did not have to be circumcised in order to join the Church. Much of the rest of this chapter deals with Paul's battle against converts who believed that the Law of Moses should still be lived.

4 And that because of false brethren unawares brought in, who came in privily to spy out our liberty which we have in Christ Jesus, that they might bring us into bondage:

**JST Galatians 2:4**
4 Notwithstanding [*even though the Brethren said Titus didn't have to be circumcised*], there were some brought in by false brethren [*apostates*] unawares, who came in privily [*who infiltrated among us*] to spy out our liberty [*to verify that we were not living the Law of Moses and to destroy the freedom*] which we have in Christ Jesus, that they might bring us into bondage [*in an attempt to put us under the requirements of the Law of Moses again*];

5 To whom we gave place by subjection, no, not for an hour [*and we did not give in to them for even a moment*]; that the truth of the gospel might continue with you [*so that they could not destroy the gospel we taught to you*].

6 But of these [*apostates*] who seemed

to be somewhat [*who seemed to think they were pretty important*], (whatsoever they were, it maketh no matter to me: God accepteth no man's person [*does not show favoritism*]:) for they who seemed to be somewhat in conference added nothing to me [*didn't persuade me at all*]:

7 But contrariwise [*on the contrary*], when they saw that the gospel of the uncircumcision [*the gospel which did not require keeping the Law of Moses*] was committed unto me [*when they saw that I was to be the Apostle to the Gentiles*], as the gospel of the circumcision was unto Peter [*just as Peter was the apostle to the Jews*];

8 (For he [*Christ*] that wrought effectually in Peter to the apostleship of the circumcision [*who worked effectively through Peter with the Jews*], the same [*Christ*] was mighty in me toward the Gentiles [*worked effectively through me with the Gentiles*])

9 And when James, Cephas [*Peter*], and John, who seemed to be pillars [*who were obviously pillars in the Church*], perceived the grace that was given unto me [*saw that I was working under Christ's direction*], they gave to me and Barnabas the right hands of fellowship [*their full approval*]; that we should go unto the heathen [*that we should preach the gospel among the Gentiles*], and they unto the circumcision [*and they would continue teaching the gospel among the Jews*].

The phrase "the right hand of fellowship" used in verse 9, above, is a saying in both Greek and Hebrew, which means full partnership, agreement and unity. See p. 309 of the Institute of Religion New Testament student manual. It is interesting to note that this is the phrase the Prophet Joseph Smith used in a letter welcoming William W. Phelps (who wrote several hymns including *Praise to the Man*, *The Spirit of God*, *Now Let Us Rejoice*, and *If You Could Hie to Kolob*) back into the Church. See *History of the Church*, Vol 4, p. 162.

10 Only they would that we should remember the poor; the same which I also was forward to do. [*All they asked was that we remember to collect money for the impoverished Saints in the Jerusalem area (see the note at the beginning of 2 Corinthians 8 in this study guide) which I was already eager to do.*]

11 But when Peter was come [*came*] to Antioch [*a Gentile city in what is central Turkey today, where Paul and his companions had baptized many Gentile converts*], I withstood him to the face [*I stood up to him*], because he was to be blamed [*because he was wrong*].

Apostle Bruce R. McConkie explained the situation in verse 11, above, as follows: "Peter and Paul—both of whom were apostles, both of whom received revelations, saw angels, and were approved of the Lord, and both of whom shall inherit the fulness of the Father's kingdom—these same righteous and mighty preachers disagreed on a basic matter of church policy. Peter was the President of the Church; Paul, an apostle and Peter's junior in the church hierarchy, was subject to the direction of the chief apostle. But Paul was right, and Peter was wrong. Paul stood firm, determined that they should walk "uprightly according to the truth of the gospel"; Peter temporized (rationalized) for fear of offending Jewish semi-converts who still kept the law of Moses. The issue was not whether the Gentiles should receive the gospel. Peter himself had received the revelation that God was no respecter of persons, and that those of all lineages were now to be heirs of salvation along with the Jews. (Acts 10:21–35.) Further, the heads of the Church, in council assembled, with the Holy Ghost guiding their minds and directing their decisions, had determined that the Gentiles who received the gospel should not be subject to the law of Moses. (Acts 15:1–35.) The Jewish members of the

Church, however, had not been able to accept this decision without reservation. They themselves continued to conform to Mosaic performances, and they expected Gentile converts to do likewise. Peter sided with them; Paul publicly withstood the chief apostle and won the debate, as could not otherwise have been the case. Without question, if we had the full account, we would find Peter reversing himself and doing all in his power to get the Jewish Saints to believe that the law of Moses was fulfilled in Christ and no longer applied to anyone, Jew or Gentile. (*Doctrinal New Testament Commentary*, Vol. 2: pp. 463–464.)

Beginning with verse 12, next, Paul explains what caused him to challenge Peter.

12 For before that certain came from James [*before some Jewish converts (Judaizers; see note after verse 3 of Galatians, chapter 2 in this study guide) came to Antioch*], he [*Peter*] did eat with the Gentiles [*associated freely with our Gentile converts, including eating with them*]: but when they [*the Jewish converts who felt strongly that all Gentile converts should live the Law of Moses*] were come [*arrived on the scene*], he [*Peter*] withdrew and separated himself [*and wouldn't eat with Gentile converts*], fearing them which were of the circumcision [*fearing what the Jewish converts thought*].

13 And the other Jews dissembled likewise with him [*followed Peter's example*]; insomuch that Barnabas [*a Jewish convert and one of Paul's missionary companions*] also was carried away with their dissimulation [*hypocrisy; Strong's #5272*].

14 But when I saw that they walked not uprightly according to the truth of the gospel [*when I saw that they were not living according to Christ's teachings*], I said unto Peter before them all [*in front of all of them*], If thou, being a Jew, livest after the manner of [*live like the*] Gentiles, and not as do the Jews [*and not like a Jew*], why compellest thou [*why do you require*] *the Gentiles to live as do the Jews* [*according to Jewish customs*]?

**JST Galatians 2:14**

14 But when I saw that they walked not uprightly according to the truth of the gospel, I said unto Peter before them all, If thou, being a Jew, livest after the manner of the Gentiles, and not as do the Jews, why compellest thou the Gentiles to live as do the Jews?

15 We who are Jews by nature [*by birth*], and not sinners of the Gentiles [*and not sinners who come from the Gentiles*], [*In other words, every one of us is a sinner, and even we Jews know that we will not get to heaven by the Law of Moses. This explanation includes the first part of verse 16, next.*]

16 Knowing that a man is not justified by the works of the law [*the Law of Moses*], but by the faith of Jesus Christ, even we [*Jews*] have believed in Jesus Christ, that we might be justified [*brought into full harmony with God*] by the faith of Christ, and not by the works of the law [*the Law of Moses*]: for by the works of the law shall no flesh be justified [*the Law of Moses won't get anyone to heaven*].

17 But if, while we seek to be justified by Christ, we ourselves also are found sinners [*if, while we are striving for salvation through Christ, we are still found to be sinners*], is therefore Christ the minister of sin [*does that mean that Christ supports sin*]? God forbid.

18 For if I build again the things which I destroyed, I make myself a transgressor [*if I go back to my old ways, after having repented and having started following Christ, I make myself a sinner*]. [*In other words, Paul is, in effect, saying "Peter, if you, who know better, decide to side with the Jews and not eat with Gentile converts, because of peer pressure, in spite of what Christ showed you*

*in your vision about taking the gospel to the Gentiles (Acts, chapter 10), you are making yourself a sinner.*]

19 For I through the law [*of Christ*] am dead to the law [*have quit living the Law of Moses*], that I might live unto God [*in order that I might progress to exaltation with God*].

20 I am crucified with Christ [*I crucified my old self, with my sins, through Christ's Atonement; see Romans 6:4–6*]: nevertheless I live [*but I am not literally dead*]; yet not I, but Christ liveth in me [*Christ is alive in me*]: and the life which I now live in the flesh [*in mortality*] I live by the faith of the Son of God, who loved me, and gave himself for me [*because of Christ's confidence in me, so much in fact that He died for me*].

21 I do not frustrate [*set aside; Strong's #0114*] the grace of God: for if righteousness come by the law [*because if we can be saved from our sins by the Law of Moses*], then Christ is dead in vain [*then Christ died for nothing*].

# GALATIANS 3

Paul will now give a masterful discourse explaining the role of the Law of Moses as a "schoolmaster law," given to bring the children of Israel up to the point where they can accept the higher laws of Christ's full gospel which will lead them to exaltation.

1 O FOOLISH Galatians, who hath bewitched [*deceived*] you, that ye should not obey the truth, before whose eyes Jesus Christ hath been evidently set forth, crucified among you [*before whose very eyes Christ and His crucifixion was obviously and clearly taught*]?

2 This only would I learn of you [*just answer one question for me*], Received ye the Spirit by the works of the law, or by the hearing of faith [*did you get the Holy Ghost through the Law of Moses or through the gospel of faith in Christ*]?

3 Are ye so foolish [*how could you be so foolish*]? having begun in the Spirit [*having begun a new life in the gospel of Christ and started to feel the effects of the Holy Ghost*], are ye now made perfect by the flesh [*how can you revert back to the Law of Moses*]?

4 Have ye suffered so many things in vain [*have you gone through the persecutions heaped upon you as Christians in vain*]? if it be yet in vain [*if indeed it is in vain*].

5 He [*God*] therefore that ministereth to you the Spirit [*who gives you the Holy Ghost*], and worketh miracles among you, doeth he it by the works of the law [*does He give you these things through the Law of Moses*], or by the hearing of faith [*or because of your faith in Christ*]?

Next, Paul will use the logic that Abraham (one of the most respected prophets among the Jews) did not have the Law of Moses, and yet God considered him to be righteous.

6 Even as Abraham [*who did not have the Law of Moses*] believed God, and it was accounted to him for righteousness [*and God considered him to be righteous*].

7 Know ye therefore [*you must realize*] that they which are of faith [*who have faith in Christ*], the same are the children of Abraham [*will have the same reward as Abraham*].

The phrase "children of" as used in verse 7, above, is a scriptural phrase which means "followers of" and, in context, usually means "they will receive the same reward as." Paul uses it in this sense in Romans 8:16–17, where he says "children of God" will be "heirs of God" and "joint heirs with Christ."

8 And the scripture, foreseeing [*prophesying*] that God would justify [*save*] the heathen [*the Gentiles*] through faith

[*in Christ*], preached before [*back then*] the gospel unto Abraham, saying [*in Genesis 12:3*], In thee shall all nations be blessed.

9 So then they which be of faith are blessed with faithful Abraham [*therefore, those who believe in Christ will be blessed like Abraham was*].

10 For as many as are of the works of the law are under the curse [*those who try to gain salvation through the Law of Moses, will be stopped in progression*]: for it is written [*in Deuteronomy 27:26*], Cursed is every one that continueth not in all things which are written in the book of the law to do them.

11 But that no man is justified by the law [*no one is saved by the Law of Moses*] in the sight of God, it is evident [*is obvious*]: for, The just [*the righteous*] shall live by faith [*Habakkuk 2:4*].

12 And the law is not of faith [*the Law of Moses does not emphasize faith*]: but, The man that doeth them shall live in them [*quoting Leviticus 18:5*].

As evidenced above and elsewhere, Paul has a remarkably detailed knowledge of the Old Testament and is thus able to quote from the very sources that the Judaizers hang on to in order to justify their continuing to live the Law of Moses.

13 Christ hath redeemed us from the curse of the law [*Christ has freed us from the bondage of the Law of Moses*], being made a curse for us: for it is written [*in Deuteronomy 21:22–23*], Cursed is every one that hangeth on a tree: [*In other words, Christ subjected Himself to the curse of being hung on a tree (the cross).*]

14 That [*so that*] the blessing of Abraham [*the blessings of exaltation; see Abraham 2:9–11*] might come on the Gentiles through Jesus Christ; that we might receive the promise of the Spirit through faith.

**JST Galatians 3:14**

14 That the blessing of Abraham might come on the Gentiles through Jesus Christ; that they might receive the promise of the Spirit through faith.

15 Brethren, I speak after the manner of men [*I'm going to use an example from everyday life so you can understand me*]; Though it be but a man's covenant, yet if it be confirmed, no man disannulleth, or addeth thereto [*when two men make a legal contract or covenant, no one can change or nullify it*].

**JST Galatians 3:15**

15 Brethren, I speak after the manner of men; Though it be but a man's covenant, yet when it be confirmed, no man disannulleth, or addeth thereto.

16 Now to Abraham and his seed were the promises made. He saith not [*God didn't say*], And to seeds, as of many [*meaning many people*]; but as of one, And to thy seed [*but just one*], which is Christ [*meaning Christ*].

17 And this I say, that the covenant [*the covenant with Abraham*], that was confirmed before [*before Moses came along*] of God in Christ, the law, which was four hundred and thirty years after [*the Law of Moses which was given 430 years after God's covenant with Abraham*], cannot disannul [*nullify God's covenant with Abraham*], that it should make the promise [*God's promise to Abraham*] of none effect. [*In other words, it wouldn't be fair for God to tell Abraham, "Sorry, I've changed My mind. The covenant I made with you is void. The only way for people to be saved is through the Law of Moses."*]

18 For if the inheritance be of the law [*if the only way we can get to heaven is through the Law of Moses*], it is no more of promise [*the promise God gave to Abraham is broken*]: but God gave it to Abraham by promise [*but God did promise Abraham*]. [*In other words, God doesn't break promises.*]

**JST Galatians 3:18**

18 For if the inheritance is of the law, then it is no more of promise; but God gave it to Abraham by promise.

19 Wherefore then serveth the law [*what is the purpose of the Law of Moses*]? It was added because of transgressions, till the seed should come to whom the promise was made; and it was ordained by angels in the hand of a mediator.

**JST Galatians 3:19**

19 Wherefore then [*this, then, is the reason that*], the law was added because of transgressions [*of the children of Israel*], till the seed should come to whom the promise was made in the law given to Moses, who was ordained by the hand of angels to be a mediator of this first covenant, (the law [*meaning the Law of Moses*].

20 Now a mediator is not a mediator of one, but God is one.

**JST Galatians 3:20**

20 Now this mediator was not a mediator of the new covenant; but there is one mediator of the new covenant, who is Christ, as it is written in the law concerning the promises made to Abraham and his seed. Now Christ is the mediator of life [*the one who brings eternal life, exaltation*]; for this is the promise which God made unto Abraham.

Next, in verse 21, Paul clarifies that the Law of Moses did not work against the promises of God to Abraham. In fact, if properly understood, the Law of Moses was designed to point the peoples' minds toward Christ, and his great last sacrifice, in opening the door of exaltation to all.

21 Is the law then against the promises of God [*does the Law of Moses work against God's promises of exaltation to Abraham*]? God forbid [*absolutely not!*]: for if there had been a law given which could have given life [*if it had been possible to give a law to the children of Israel, through Moses, which would have brought them to eternal life*], verily righteousness should have been by the law [*such a law would have been given*]. [*In other words, the children of Israel were so far into wickedness that it was impossible to give them a law high enough to bring them exaltation at that point in their lives.*]

22 But the scripture hath concluded all under sin [*the scriptures verify that all are guilty of sinning; see D&C 49:8*], that the promise by faith of Jesus Christ might be given to them that believe [*therefore, all who want to receive the blessings from Christ which come through faith must believe in Him*].

23 But before faith came [*before the gospel of Christ came to us*], we were kept under the law [*we were bound by the Law of Moses*], shut up unto the faith [*held back from Christ's full gospel*] which should afterwards be revealed [*which was to be taught to us at a later date*].

Note: This next verse sums up everything Paul has been teaching in this chapter.

24 Wherefore [*therefore*] the law was our schoolmaster [*the Law of Moses was our teacher*] to bring us unto Christ, that we might be justified [*saved*] by faith [*in Christ*].

**JST Galatians 3:24**

24 Wherefore the law was our schoolmaster until Christ, that we might be justified by faith.

25 But after that faith is come [*once we have come to the point of having faith in Christ*], we are no longer under a schoolmaster [*we don't need the schoolmaster (Law of Moses) any more*].

26 For ye are all the children of God by faith in Christ Jesus [*all of you may become saved by faith in Jesus Christ*].

**JST Galatians 3:26**

26 For ye are all the children of God by faith in Jesus Christ.

27 For as many of you as have been baptized into Christ have put on Christ

[*all of you who have been baptized have taken upon you the name of Christ*].

28 There is neither Jew nor Greek, there is neither bond nor free, there is neither male nor female: for ye are all one in Christ Jesus [*we are all the same in Christ's eyes when we join His Church*].

29 And if ye be Christ's [*if you belong to Christ*], then are ye Abraham's seed [*then you also belong to Abraham*], and heirs according to the promise [*and are entitled to the promises given to him; see Abraham 2:9–11 for these promises*].

# GALATIANS 4

Next, Paul will emphasize the fact that all of us are still "children" in comparison to God, and that, even though we can become "heirs" and inherit "all that my Father hath" (D&C 84:38), we still have to be treated as children and servants, governed and tutored along the way to becoming gods. The point is, that the Law of Moses was given to the children of Israel to tutor and govern them so that they could progress to the point of receiving the higher laws of Christ's gospel which eventually lead the faithful to exaltation and being gods, in other words, to being "heirs of God, and joint-heirs with Christ" (Romans 8:17), invited to "sit with me in my throne, even as I also overcame, and am set down with my Father in his throne" (Revelation 3:21). Paul teaches very clearly here that we can become gods.

1 NOW I say, That the heir [*the one who will someday inherit the whole estate*], as long as he is a child, differeth nothing from a servant [*is no different than a servant*], though he be lord of all [*even though he will someday own the whole estate*];

2 But is under [*is subject to*] tutors and governors until the time appointed of the father [*until his father gives him his estate*].

3 Even so we, when we were children [*still immature in spiritual things, and thus were given the Law of Moses to tutor us and prepare us for Christ's gospel*], were in bondage under the elements of the world [*were in the captivity of sin because we were involved in the ways of the world*]:

4 But when the fulness of the time was come [*when the time was right*], God [*the Father*] sent forth his Son [*Christ*], made of a woman [*born to a mortal woman*], made under the law [*born while the Law of Moses was still in effect*],

5 To redeem them that were under the law [*to redeem those who were under the bondage of the Law of Moses*], that we might receive the adoption of sons [*that we might become gods*].

6 And because ye are sons [*because you are heirs*], God [*the Father*] hath sent forth the Spirit of his Son into your hearts, crying, Abba, Father [*you have been inspired in your hearts to feel that Heavenly Father is literally your father and that you have an intimate child to father relationship with Him such that you could feel to call him "Daddy"*].

The term "Abba" is an intimate, familial name for our Father in Heaven. See Bible Dictionary under "Abba." It can be translated as "Daddy" and is the same term the Savior used during His suffering in the Garden of Gethsemane when He asked that, if possible, He might not drink the bitter cup. See Mark 14:36. An explanation of the term "Abba" is given in the Institute of Religion New Testament student manual, *The Life and Teachings of Jesus and His Apostles*, p. 311, as follows: "Paul suggested that through the atonement of Christ we can be adopted as sons of God, and then the Spirit shall help us cry 'Abba,

> Father.' Abba is Aramaic (a cognate of Hebrew) and carries more than just the connotation of father. It is the intimate and personal diminutive of the word father used by children in the family circle. The closest equivalent we have is papa or daddy, although neither can really convey fully the impact of the word. The point is that God is not only Father (the formal title and name), but he is also Abba, the parent of love and guidance that knows us intimately and whom we can approach without fear."

7 Wherefore [*therefore*] thou art no more a servant, but a son [*the gospel of Christ elevates you from being a servant under the Law of Moses to the level of being a family member*]; and if a son, then an heir of God through Christ [*through Christ's gospel, including the Atonement*].

8 Howbeit [*however*] then [*back then*], when ye knew not God, ye did service unto them which by nature are no gods [*you worshiped idols*].

9 But now, after that ye have known God [*now that you know about the plan of salvation brought by Christ*], or rather are known of God, how turn ye again to the weak and beggarly [*powerless to accomplish the goal; Strong's #4434*] elements [*of the Law of Moses*], whereunto [*to which*] ye desire again to be in bondage [*how can you possibly turn back to the Law of Moses and its accompanying bondage; do you really want to be in bondage again*]?

10 Ye observe days, and months, and times, and years [*you have gone back to the rituals of the Law of Moses; see Bible Dictionary under "New Moon"*]. [*Bruce R. McConkie explains "days, and months, and times, and years" as "The various feasts, fasting periods, and sabbatical years which were part of the worship of ancient Israel."* Doctrinal New Testament Commentary, *Vol. 2, p. 476.*]

11 I am afraid of [*for*] you, lest I have bestowed upon you labour in vain [*for fear that all my work among you has done no good*].

12 Brethren, I beseech [*urge*] you, be as I am; for I am as ye are: ye have not injured me at all.

> **<u>JST Galatians 4:12</u>**
>
> 12 Brethren, I beseech you to be perfect as I am perfect; for I am persuaded as ye have a knowledge of me [*you have gained knowledge about Christ from me*], ye have not injured me at all by your sayings.

13 Ye know how through infirmity of the flesh I preached the gospel unto you at the first [*you know that I was sick when I first arrived among you to teach you the gospel*].

14 And my temptation [*trial*] which was in my flesh [*my illness*] ye despised not, nor rejected; but received me as an angel of God, even as Christ Jesus [*you accepted me as a messenger of God in spite of my being ill when I arrived*].

15 Where is then the blessedness ye spake of [*where is the commitment and spirituality you had back then*]? for I bear you record, that, if it had been possible, ye would have plucked out your own eyes, and have given them to me [*your commitment to the gospel I taught you was so strong that you would have done anything for me*].

16 Am I therefore become your enemy, because I tell you the truth [*have I offended you because I have told you the truth about your status now*]?

17 They [*those who want you to go back to living the Law of Moses*] zealously affect you, but not well [*are very energetic but not good for you*]; yea, they would exclude you [*they want to alienate you from us*], that ye might affect them [*in order to make you loyal to them*].

18 But it is good to be zealously affected always in a good thing [*it is good to*

*be enthusiastically involved in a right cause*], and not only when I am present with you.

19 My little children, of whom I travail in birth again until Christ be formed in you [*my dear, immature children in the gospel, I feel like I am having to go through the pains of childbirth again in order to get you "born" or established in the gospel of Christ again*],

20 I desire to be present with you now [*I wish I were with you now*], and to change my voice [*my tone of voice*]; for I stand in doubt of you [*I am worried about you*].

21 Tell me, ye that desire to be under the law, do ye not hear the law [*tell me, you who want to go back to living under the Law of Moses again, don't you realize what that law says*]?

22 For it is written [*in Genesis, chapters 16 and 21*], that Abraham had two sons, the one by a bondmaid [*a servant wife, named Hagar*], the other by a freewoman [*Sarah*].

23 But he [*Ishmael; Genesis 16:15*] who was of the bondwoman [*Hagar*] was born after the flesh [*was born normally*]; but he [*Isaac; Genesis 21:3*] of the freewoman [*Sarah*] was by promise [*as a result of a special promise and covenant*].

24 Which things are an allegory [*these things are symbolic*]: for these are the two covenants [*Ishmael and Isaac represent the two covenants (the Law of Moses and the higher gospel given to Abraham)*]; the one [*the Law of Moses*] from the mount Sinai, which gendereth [*leads*] to bondage, which is Agar [*which came through Hagar*].

25 For this Agar is mount Sinai in Arabia, and answereth to Jerusalem which now is, and is in bondage with her children. [*In other words, the Law of Moses came from Mount Sinai, through Moses, and is still going strong in Jerusalem where the Jews hold tightly to it, in spite of Christ's teachings.*]

26 But Jerusalem which is above is free, which is the mother of us all. [*But the New Covenant, which Christ taught in Jerusalem, is the higher, spiritual gospel, which is superior to the Law of Moses and is designed to set us free from it. Christ's gospel is our new "mother" and through her, we are born again and set free from the old Law of Moses.*]

27 For it is written [*in Isaiah 54:1*], Rejoice, thou barren that bearest not; break forth and cry, thou that travailest not: for the desolate hath many more children than she which hath an husband.

> Isaiah 54:1, quoted in verse 27, above, appears in the Old Testament as follows (with notes in brackets added to help with understanding): "Sing, O barren [*one who has not produced children, i.e., Israel who has not produced many righteous children up to now*], thou that didst not bear; break forth into singing, and cry aloud, thou that didst not travail [*go into labor*] with child [*i.e., in former days, you did not succeed in bringing forth righteous children, loyal to Christ*]: for more are the children [*righteous converts*] of the desolate [*perhaps meaning the Gentiles*] than the children of the married wife [*perhaps meaning the Jews who insist on holding on to the Law of Moses; in other words, you've got more righteous converts than you ever thought possible, almost all the converts coming from outside the land of Israel*], saith the LORD.

28 Now we, brethren, as Isaac was, are the children of promise [*we are the covenant descendants of Abraham, coming through Isaac*].

29 But as then he [*Ishmael and his descendants*] that was born after the flesh persecuted him [*Isaac and his posterity*] that was born after the Spirit [*who are children of the covenant*], even so it is now.

30 Nevertheless what saith the scripture [*Genesis 21:10*]? Cast out the bondwoman and her son: for the son of the bondwoman shall not be heir with the son of the freewoman. [*In other words, Paul, speaking symbolically, is saying that just as Hagar and Ishmael, who represent the Law of Moses in this discussion, were cast out, so also will God cast out all who adhere to the Law of Moses now, rather than being baptized and remaining true to the higher law and spiritual covenants given by Christ, which can make us heirs in heaven with Abraham, Isaac, and Jacob.*]

31 So then, brethren, we are not children of the bondwoman, but of the free. [*Therefore, we are not under the Law of Moses, rather, we are made free from it by making and keeping covenants given to us by Christ.*]

# GALATIANS 5

Paul continues his skillful and inspired sermon, counseling the Galatian Saints to resist the efforts of some apostates among them to get them to revert back to the Law of Moses. He urges them to hold tightly to the freedoms which come with the gospel of Jesus Christ.

A beautiful summary of the whole gospel given us by the Savior is found at the end of verse 14. You will no doubt recognize it.

There are no JST changes for this chapter.

1 STAND fast therefore in the liberty [*the gospel of Christ*] wherewith Christ hath made us free, and be not entangled again with the yoke of bondage [*the Law of Moses*].

2 Behold, I Paul say unto you, that if ye be circumcised [*if you live the Law of Moses*], Christ shall profit you nothing [*you will not benefit from Jesus Christ*].

3 For I testify again to every man that is circumcised [*who submits to circumcision as required of those who live the Law of Moses*], that he is a debtor to do the whole law [*that you are committing yourself to the whole Law of Moses*].

4 Christ is become of no effect unto you [*in so-doing, you reject Christ*], whosoever of you are justified by the law [*any of you who go back to the Law of Moses in order to be saved*]; *ye are fallen from grace* [*can no longer be saved by Christ's Atonement, thus, you will not be saved.*].

5 For we through the Spirit [*we who believe in Christ*] wait [*patiently wait; Strong's #0553*] for the hope of righteousness [*becoming acceptable to God; Strong's #1343*] by faith [*exercise faith in Christ toward salvation*].

6 For in Jesus Christ [*for if you are going to follow Christ*] neither circumcision [*being a Jew*] availeth any thing, nor uncircumcision [*nor being a Gentile*]; [*In other words, in the true gospel, brought by Christ, merely being a Jew or a Gentile does you no good, as far as salvation is concerned.*] but faith which worketh by love [*the only thing that counts is faith in Christ, who came because of the Father's love for us*].

7 Ye did run well [*you were doing well in the gospel I brought to you*]; who did hinder you that ye should not obey the truth [*what happened to take you back to living the Law of Moses*]?

8 This persuasion cometh not of him that calleth you [*whoever is persuading you to leave the Church is not from God*].

9 A little leaven leaveneth the whole lump [*a little yeast works its way through the whole lump of dough*]. [*In other words, if you go back to requiring circumcision, you will soon have the Law of Moses in every aspect of your life again.*]

10 I have confidence in you through the Lord, that ye will be none otherwise minded [*I have confidence that you will listen to what I am saying and not be led astray*]: but he that troubleth you shall bear his judgment, whosoever he be [*whoever is trying to lead you astray will have to face God and will be held accountable*].

11 And I, brethren, if I yet preach circumcision [*if my preaching included that you should still live the Law of Moses*], why do I yet suffer persecution [*why would I continue to be persecuted*]? then is the offence of the cross ceased [*if that were the case, our teachings about Christ would not be offensive to those who continue to live the Law of Moses*].

12 I would they were even cut off which trouble you [*I think that you should excommunicate those among you who are trying to lead you astray*].

13 For, brethren, ye have been called unto liberty [*you have been called to come unto Christ and thus be set free of the Law of Moses*]; only use not liberty for an occasion to the flesh [*but do not misunderstand this freedom and use it to justify sin*], but by love serve one another.

The word "law" (Strong's #3551), as used next in verse 14, is the same word as "law" in Galatians 6:2, which is the "law of Christ," in other words, His whole gospel.

14 For all the law is fulfilled in one word, even in this [*the whole gospel, including all the commandments could be summed up as follows*]; Thou shalt love thy neighbour as thyself.

15 But if ye bite and devour one another [*if you keep picking each other apart, bit by bit*], take heed that ye be not consumed one of another [*watch out or you will eventually destroy each other*].

16 This I say then [*in summary, this is what I'm telling you*], Walk in the Spirit [*follow the Holy Ghost (see Galatians 5:17, footnote a), which teaches you to be loyal to Christ*], and ye shall not fulfil the lust of the flesh [*and you won't get caught up in sin, including sexual immorality*].

17 For the flesh lusteth against the Spirit [*the natural man (Mosiah 3:19) fights against the Holy Ghost*], and the Spirit against the flesh: and these are contrary the one to the other [*the Spirit and the natural man are opposites*]: so that ye cannot do the things that ye would [*you can't just do whatever you want to*].

18 But if ye be led of the Spirit, ye are not under the law [*if you follow the promptings of the Spirit, you will not be under the Law of Moses; see Acts 15:5, footnote a*].

19 Now the works of the flesh are manifest, which are these [*now here are some of the worldly sins you must avoid*]; Adultery, fornication, uncleanness, lasciviousness [*lustful thinking and talking and all sexual immorality, including pornography*],

20 Idolatry [*idol worship*], witchcraft, hatred, variance [*disharmony*], emulations [*rivalry, etc., based on jealousy and worldly ambitions*], wrath [*anger, loss of temper*], strife, seditions [*stirring up unrighteous discontent with those in power, including government leaders and church leaders*], heresies [*false doctrines*],

21 Envyings, murders, drunkenness, revellings [*riotous, drunken parties and lifestyles*], and such like: of the which I tell you before [*I forewarn you*], *as I have also told you in time past, that they which do such things shall not inherit the kingdom of God* [*the celestial kingdom*].

Verses 22–23, next, contain one of the most often quoted scriptures in Galatians, by members of the Church.

22 But the fruit of the Spirit [*the result of following the promptings of the Holy*

*Ghost*] is love, joy, peace, longsuffering, gentleness, goodness, faith,

23 Meekness [*mildness, gentleness*], temperance [*self control*]: against such there is no law [*there are no commandments of God against such personal character traits*].

24 And they that are Christ's have crucified the flesh with the affections and lusts [*those who belong to Christ are those who have learned to control the passions and lusts of the body*].

25 If we live in the Spirit, let us also walk in the Spirit. [*In other words, let our actions be in harmony with our beliefs.*]

26 Let us not be desirous of vain glory [*let us not be prideful*], provoking one another, envying one another.

## GALATIANS 6

As Paul concludes his letter to the members of the Church in Galatia, he gives clear advice for righteous daily living.

There are no JST changes for this chapter.

1 BRETHREN, if a man be overtaken in a fault, ye which are spiritual, restore such an one in the spirit of meekness [*when you see others' sins, you who are stronger in the gospel should help them in love and kindness so they can also become strong in the gospel*]; considering thyself [*watching yourself*], lest thou also be tempted [*for fear that you might commit sins yourself*].

2 Bear ye one another's burdens [*compare with Mosiah 18:8–9*], and so fulfil the law of Christ.

3 For if a man think himself to be something, when he is nothing, he deceiveth [*fools*] himself.

4 But let every man prove his own work [*consider his own behaviors and deeds carefully and make sure they are in harmony with the gospel*], and then shall he have rejoicing in himself alone, and not in another [*then he will not be dependent on others for status*].

5 For every man shall bear his own burden [*each person is accountable for his own doings*].

6 Let him that is taught in the word communicate unto [*share with*] him that teacheth in all good things.

7 Be not deceived [*fooled*]; God is not mocked [*what God says will happen*]: for whatsoever a man soweth, that shall he also reap [*whatever you plant, you will harvest*]. [*In other words, you will be rewarded on Judgment Day for how you live. This is known as the "law of the harvest."*]

8 For he that soweth to his flesh [*he who plants or lives according to the worldly desires of the flesh*] shall of the flesh reap corruption [*will receive the punishments of God for his corrupt lifestyle*]; but he that soweth to the Spirit shall of the Spirit reap life everlasting [*but those who "plant" righteousness will harvest a reward of exaltation, in other words, eternal life*].

9 And let us not be weary in well doing [*let's not get tired of doing good, thus living the gospel*]: for in due season we shall reap [*when the time comes to be judged, we will harvest a reward of eternal life*], if we faint not [*if we don't give up and quit living the gospel*].

10 As we have therefore opportunity, let us do good unto all men, especially unto them who are of the household of faith [*those who are fellow members of the Church*].

11 Ye see how large a letter I have written unto you with mine own hand.

12 As many as [*those who*] desire to make a fair shew [*a good outward impression among Jews who keep the Law of Moses*] in the flesh, they constrain you to be circumcised [*are trying*

*to make you submit to circumcision*]; only lest they should suffer persecution for the cross of Christ [*the only reason they do this is that they are afraid of being persecuted for following Christ*].

13 For neither they themselves who are circumcised keep the law [*not even those who are circumcised truly understand and keep the Law of Moses*]; but desire to have you circumcised, that they may glory in your flesh [*but still they want to convert you back to the Law of Moses so they can brag to others about getting you back*].

14 But God forbid that I should glory [*brag*], save [*except*] in the cross [*about the gospel*] of our Lord Jesus Christ, by whom the world is crucified unto me [*through which gospel I overcome my sins*], and I unto the world [*and through which I become unavailable to the sins of the world*].

15 For in Christ Jesus [*in the Savior's gospel*] neither circumcision availeth any thing, nor uncircumcision [*it makes no difference whether one is circumcised or not*], but a new creature [*the only thing that counts is whether or not they have been born again, thus becoming a new "creature" or "creation," in other words, a new person, loyal to Christ and thus freed from sin, kind, pleasant, patient, etc., as mentioned in Galatians 5:22–23*].

16 And as many as walk according to this rule [*what Paul said in verse 15*], peace be on them, and mercy, and upon the Israel [*the covenant people*] of God.

17 From henceforth let no man trouble me [*never let it be said that I am not loyal to Christ*]: for I bear in my body the marks of the Lord Jesus [*because I have many scars from beatings, whippings, stonings, etc., which I received because I was loyal to Him*]. [*Paul could also be saying that his body bears the marks of Jesus in a symbolic sense, meaning that he has exercised self-control over the lusts of the flesh and thus has the effects of the Atonement in his mortal life now.*]

18 Brethren, the grace of our Lord Jesus Christ be with your spirit. Amen.

# THE FIRST EPISTLE OF PAUL THE APOSTLE TO THE EPHESIANS

According to Ephesians 3:1, 4:1, and 6:20, Paul is in prison when he writes to the members of the Church in Ephesus (on the western coast of what we know as western Turkey today). Most scholars agree that it was during his first imprisonment in Rome when he wrote to these members, and most agree that this letter was written between AD 61 and AD 63. Paul was eventually executed, probably in the spring of AD 65. See Bible Dictionary under "Paul."

Ephesians does not seem to have a particular theme responding to specific false doctrines or apostasy or wickedness as is the case with most of Paul's letters. Rather, it seems to be written to more spiritually mature members of the Church who are living the gospel and are capable of understanding and appreciating doctrines such as premortality, foreordination, the dispensation of the fulness of times, being sealed by the Holy Spirit of Promise (the Holy Ghost), the vital role of Apostles and prophets and other offices in the organization of the true Church, the fact that there is only one true Church, family, family life, and so forth. The letter to the Ephesians is one of the most helpful of Paul's writings for us as we do missionary work among Christians, because it contains so many doctrines which are usually thought of as being distinctive doctrines of The Church of Jesus Christ of Latter-day Saints.

## EPHESIANS 1

As Paul begins this letter, among other things, he touches on foreordination, the restoration of the gospel in the last days, the dispensation of the fullness of times, and being sealed by the Holy Spirit of Promise. It is exciting and refreshing to us as Latter-day Saints to realize that these important doctrines were taught in the true church in Paul's day. It is a reminder to us that we indeed belong to the "restored" Church of Jesus Christ.

There are no JST changes for this chapter.

1 PAUL, an apostle of Jesus Christ by the will of God [*called of God*], to the saints which are at Ephesus, and to the faithful in Christ Jesus [*who are being faithful to the gospel of Jesus Christ*]:

2 Grace be to you, and peace, from God our Father, and from the Lord Jesus Christ.

Verse 2, above, is another reminder that the Father and the Son are two distinct, separate personages. As previously noted, one of the exciting things about Ephesians is that Paul teaches so many "LDS" doctrines in it. For instance, the context of verses 3 and 4, next, is our premortal life, our life "before the foundation of the world" (verse 4). With this in mind, we see, in verse 3, that we were blessed with "all spiritual blessings" there, and that these blessings came to us through Christ. In other words, we had the gospel of Jesus Christ

there. We know from Moses 4:1–3 and Abraham 3:27–28 that Christ was chosen there to be our Savior. In teaching us that we were blessed with "all spiritual blessings in heavenly places in Christ," Paul teaches that the Atonement of Christ worked for us already in premortality.

While we may not understand how it can be that the Atonement worked for us before it was actually performed here on earth, we do know that the Atonement is "infinite" and that it worked for many who lived before Christ, for instance Alma and the sons of Mosiah. In October 1995 General Conference, Elder Jeffrey R. Holland taught that the Atonement worked for us in premortality when he said, referring to the premortal Jesus Christ, "We could remember that even in the Grand Council of Heaven He loved us and was wonderfully strong, that we triumphed even there by the power of Christ and our faith in the blood of the Lamb."

Another quote reminding us that the Atonement of Christ was already working for us in premortality is found in the institute of religion New Testament student manual, *The Life and Teachings of Jesus and His Apostles*, p. 336, where it says "We were given laws and agency, and commandments to have faith and repent from the wrongs that we could do there." "Man could and did in many instances, sin before he was born."

In summary, one of the marvelous teachings of Paul here is that we were taught the gospel in premortality under the direction of the Father and that the Atonement of Christ worked for us there already, helping us to progress.

3 Blessed [*praised*] be the God and Father of our Lord Jesus Christ, who hath blessed us with all spiritual blessings in heavenly places [*in premortality*] *in Christ* [*through Christ*]:

In verse 4, Paul teaches the doctrine of foreordination, which means that those who were valiant and faithful in the premortal life were chosen and foreordained to perform particular missions and service when they came to earth. We are often told what some aspects of our foreordained missions are in our patriarchal blessings. Joseph Fielding Smith said the following about foreordination and premortal life: "There must be leaders, presiding officers, and those who are worthy and able to take command. During the ages in which we dwelt in the premortal state we not only developed our various characteristics and showed our worthiness and ability, or the lack of it, but we were also where such progress could be observed. It is reasonable to believe that there was a Church organization there. The heavenly beings were living in a perfectly arranged society. Every person knew his place. Priesthood, without any question, had been conferred and the leaders were chosen to officiate. Ordinances pertaining to that preexistence were required and the love of God prevailed. Under such conditions it was natural for our Father to discern and choose those who were most worthy and evaluate the talents of each individual. He knew not only what each of us could do, but also what each of us would do when put to the test and when responsibility was given us. Then, when the time came for our habitation on mortal earth, all things were prepared and the servants of the Lord chosen and ordained to their respective missions." (Smith, *The Way to Perfection*, pp. 50–51.)

4 According as he [*the Father*] hath chosen [*foreordained*] us in him [*in Christ; in other words, we were foreordained because of our obedience to the gospel of Christ in premortality*] before the foundation of the world [*in premortality*], that we should be holy [*sanctified*] and without blame before him in love [*because of the Father's love for us*]:

5 Having predestinated [*foreordained; Strong's #4309*] us unto the adoption

of children [*to become sons of God; Strong's #5206*] by [*through*] Jesus Christ to himself [*to become "begotten sons and daughters unto God" (in other words, exalted), D&C 76:24*], according to the good pleasure of his will [*according to the kindness of the Father*],

The word "predestinated" as used in verse 5, above, is an incorrect translation. The correct translation from the Greek is "foreordination," which is the word used in most modern translations of the Bible.

6 To the praise of the glory of his [*the Father's*] grace, wherein he [*the Father*] hath made us accepted [*has made it possible for us to return to His presence*] in the beloved [*through His Beloved Son*].

7 In whom we have redemption [*through whom we can be redeemed*] through his [*Christ's*] blood, the forgiveness of sins, according to the riches of his [*the Father's*] grace;

8 Wherein [*in Christ*] he [*the Father*] hath abounded toward us [*provided us with bounteous blessings*] in all wisdom and prudence [*understanding of our needs*];

9 Having made known unto us the mystery of his will [*the teachings of the gospel which remain a "mystery" to people who will not come unto Christ*], according to his good pleasure [*kindness toward us; Strong's #2107*] which he hath purposed [*planned*] in himself [*according to the plan of salvation which the Father has planned for us*]:

10 That in the dispensation of the fulness of times [*in the latter-days, when all things have been restored*] he [*the Father*] might gather together in one all things in Christ [*the restoration of the gospel of Jesus Christ, through Joseph Smith*], both which are in heaven, and which are on earth; even in him [*Christ*]:

Verse 10, above, is the only place in the Bible where the phrase "dispensation of the fulness of times" is used. It is an important doctrinal phrase. The word "dispensation" means "period of time." We know from D&C 27:13 that this dispensation is the last time that the gospel will be restored, and we know from Daniel 2:44 that there will not be another apostasy, rather, the Church, as restored by Joseph Smith, will continue right up to the Second Coming and then, of course, on through the Millennium.

11 In whom [*through Christ*] also we have obtained an inheritance [*we have the opportunity to inherit exaltation; see Romans 8:17*], being predestinated [*foreordained; see verse 5, above*] according to the purpose [*plan*] of him [*the Father*] who worketh all things after the counsel [*plan*] of his own will [*who does all things according to His own will*]: [*In other words, all things are done according to the Father's plan.*]

12 That we should be to the praise of his glory [*in other words, the Father's glory is "to bring to pass the immortality and eternal life of man." Moses 1:39*], who first trusted in Christ [*who trusted Christ to be the Redeemer; see Moses 4:1–3*].

Notice the skillful transition from verse 12, above, to verse 13, next, by which Paul says, in effect, that just as these Ephesian Saints heard and accepted the gospel of Jesus Christ in premortality, so also they have now heard and accepted it here on earth.

13 In whom ye also trusted [*you Ephesian members also trusted in Christ*], after that ye heard the word of truth, the gospel of your salvation [*after the gospel was preached to you*]: in whom also after that ye believed, ye were sealed with that holy Spirit of promise [*the Holy Ghost*],

The phrase "ye were sealed with that holy Spirit of promise" in verse 13, above, is important doctrinally. D&C 132 verses 7 and 19 remind us that all ordinances and covenants between us and God must be sealed by the "Holy Spirit of promise," in

other words, by the Holy Ghost. One of the functions of the Holy Ghost is to ratify and approve all such ordinances and covenants. Another way of saying this is that all such covenants and ordinances must be "justified" by the Spirit (see Moses 6:60). Since the Holy Ghost knows all things, if a person lies as he or she seeks approval from the bishop and other authorized priesthood holders to participate in the ordinances of the Church, the Holy Ghost will simply not ratify or approve or seal the ordinance. Thus, the ordinance does the person no good. In fact, the deception can hurt the person spiritually, and if not repented of, can cause eternal damage. On the other hand, if a person, who has been dishonest about qualifying to receive such ordinances, repents, confesses, and gets his or her life in order, the Holy Ghost can then "seal" the ordinance so that it is now valid for that person.

14 Which is the earnest of our inheritance [*the Holy Ghost is the "earnest money" which the Father gives as a "down payment" toward our exaltation*] until the redemption of the purchased possession [*until we are "fully paid for" by our own efforts in combination with the Atonement of Christ; see 2 Nephi 25:23*], unto the praise of his glory [*which brings glory to the Father; see Moses 1:39*].

15 Wherefore I also, after I heard of your faith in the Lord Jesus, and love unto all the saints,

16 Cease not to give thanks for you, making mention of you in my prayers;

17 That the God of our Lord Jesus Christ, the Father of glory, may give unto you the spirit of wisdom and revelation in the knowledge of him [*Christ*]:

18 The eyes of your understanding being enlightened [*your whole being has been enlightened by the gospel*]; that ye may know what is the hope of his calling [*so that you realize the wonderful hope and confidence in salvation which comes through Christ's calling to be our Savior*], and what the riches of the glory of his inheritance in the saints [*and you see the incredibly rich blessings and glory which await the faithful Saints as they inherit exaltation*],

19 And what is the exceeding greatness of his power to us-ward who believe, according to the working of his mighty power, [*In other words, you also see the unbelievably wonderful power of God as it comes into your lives.*]

20 Which he wrought in Christ [*which the Father gave us through Christ*], when he [*the Father*] raised him [*Christ*] from the dead, and set him at his own right hand in the heavenly places [*in heaven; see Acts 7:55–56*],

21 Far above all principality, and power, and might, and dominion, and every name that is named, not only in this world, but also in that which is to come [*Christ has overcome all things (see D&C 76:106–108) and has power over all things, next to the Father*]:

22 And hath put all things under his feet [*the Father has given Christ power over all things*], and gave him to be the head over all things to the church, [*In other words, Christ is the head of all things in the Church, under the direction of the Father.*]

23 Which is his body [*symbolically, the Church represents the body of Christ*], the fulness of him that filleth all in all [*and thus Christ influences every aspect of the Church*].

An additional explanation of verse 23, above, is given by Bruce R. McConkie as follows: "In the *Lectures on Faith*, Joseph Smith describes the Father and the Son as 'filling all in all' because the Son, having overcome, has 'received a fulness of the glory of the Father,' and possesses 'the same mind with the Father.' Then he announces the conclusion to which Paul here only alludes: 'And all those who keep his commandments shall grow up from grace to grace, and

become heirs of the heavenly kingdom, and joint-heirs with Jesus Christ; possessing the same mind, being transformed into the same image or likeness, even the express image of him who fills all in all; being filled with the fulness of his glory, and become one in him, even as the Father, Son and Holy Spirit are one.' (*Lectures on Faith*, pp. 50–51." *Doctrinal New Testament Commentary*, Vol. 2, p. 497.)

# EPHESIANS 2

Here, among other things, Paul will address the doctrines of mercy, grace, and faith, coupled with the cleansing blood of Christ and being faithful in the Church, which is built upon the foundation of Apostles and prophets. You may well be familiar with verses 19–21, which are often used in our missionary work.

1 AND you hath he [*Christ*] quickened [*made spiritually alive*], who were dead [*spiritually dead*] in trespasses and sins;

2 Wherein in time past ye walked according to the course of this world [*lived according to the ways of the world*], according to the prince of the power of the air [*Satan; see McConkie,* Doctrinal New Testament Commentary, *Vol. 2, p. 499*], the spirit [*evil spirit; Strong's #4151*] that now worketh [*operates*] in the children of disobedience [*in wicked people*]:

The word "conversation," as used in New Testament English, usually means "behavior." An example of this in found in verse 3, next.

3 Among whom also we all had our conversation [*we behaved like they did*] in times past in the lusts [*sins*] of our flesh, fulfilling the desires of the flesh [*physical desires*] and of the mind; and were by nature the children of wrath [*people facing the punishments of God*], even as others [*just like everyone else*].

4 But God [*the Father*], who is rich in mercy, for his great love wherewith [*with which*] he loved us,

5 Even when we were dead in sins [*even when we were spiritually dead, caught up in sin*], hath quickened us [*has given us new spiritual life*] together with [*through*] Christ, (by grace ye are saved;)

In reference to Paul's parentheses (by grace ye are saved;) in verse 5, above, we know that without God's grace, we could not be saved. In fact, without it, we would eventually be completely subject to the devil and would have become devils. See 2 Nephi 9:7–9. However, we also know that we must do as much as we can in order to qualify for grace, as stated in 2 Nephi 25:23, where it says "For we know that it is by grace that we are saved, after all we can do."

6 And hath raised us up together, and made us sit together in heavenly places in Christ Jesus [*has made it possible for us to enter the celestial kingdom with Christ; see Romans 8:17 and Revelation 3:20–21*]:

7 That in the ages to come [*throughout the eternities*] he might shew [*show*] the exceeding riches of his grace in his kindness toward us through Christ Jesus.

Verses 8 and 9, next, are often used out of context to teach that we do not need works in order to be saved. This is false and Paul himself constantly counsels his people to show by the lives they live that they truly believe in Christ. In fact, in verse 10, he tells them that they should walk in good works. The point is that works alone cannot save us. The Law of Moses, as modified and added to by the Jews over many centuries, had led many to believe that works alone could save them. They placed all the emphasis on strictly following the details of their religious laws, and failed to become personally righteous. For example, the Savior scolded them severely in

Matthew 23:23 when he said "Woe unto you, scribes and Pharisees, hypocrites! for ye pay tithe of mint and anise and cummin, and have omitted the weightier matters of the law, judgment, mercy, and faith: these ought ye to have done, and not to leave the other undone." In this context, then, Paul teaches the Ephesian members that works alone cannot save them.

8 For by grace are ye saved through faith [*in Christ*]; and that not of yourselves [*you can't save yourselves*]: it is the gift of God [*the Father has given us the gift of his Son and the Atonement*]:

**JST Ephesians 2:8**

8 For by grace are ye saved through faith; and that not of yourselves; but it is the gift of God;

9 Not of works [*works alone can't save us*], lest any man should boast [*lest any people should become prideful, thinking that they can save themselves*].

10 For we are his [*the Father's*] workmanship, created in Christ Jesus [*becoming new people, made spiritually alive, through Jesus Christ*] unto good works [*to do the good works Jesus taught us to do*], which God [*the Father*] hath before ordained that we should walk in them [*which the Father planned in advance for us to do*].

Remember, as previously explained, that "Uncircumcision" means Gentiles, and "Circumcision" means Jews.

11 Wherefore remember, that ye being in time past Gentiles in the flesh [*think back to the time before you joined the Church*], who are called Uncircumcision [*when you were called outsiders, Gentiles*] by that which is called the Circumcision [*by the Jews who kept the Law of Moses*] in the flesh made by hands [*because you hadn't been circumcised*];

12 That at that time ye were without Christ, being aliens from the commonwealth of Israel [*not belonging to God's covenant people*], and strangers from the covenants of promise [*and having no knowledge about the covenants which lead to fulfillment of the promises of exaltation*], having no hope [*of attaining exaltation*], and without God in the world [*and living without God's true gospel in your daily lives*]:

13 But now in [*through*] Christ Jesus ye who sometimes were far off [*who were so far away from God*] are made nigh [*are brought near to Him*] by the blood of Christ [*by the Atonement of Christ*].

14 For he is our peace [*He is the source of our peace*], who hath made both one [*who has made both Jews and Gentiles into one covenant people*], and hath broken down the middle wall of partition [*and has broken down the barrier*] between us;

15 Having abolished in his flesh [*by His mortal ministry*] the enmity [*the opposition*], even the law of commandments [*the Law of Moses*] contained in ordinances; for to make in himself of twain one new man [*in order to make, through His mission, two peoples (Jews and Gentiles) into one people*], so making peace [*and thus making peace between Jews and Gentiles, as they both join His Church*];

16 And that he [*Christ*] might reconcile [*bring into harmony; atone for*] both [*Jews and Gentiles*] unto God in one body [*uniting them together*] by the cross [*through His Atonement*], having slain the enmity [*destroyed the animosity between Jewish members and Gentile members*] thereby [*through bringing them into His true church*]:

17 And came and preached peace to you which were afar off [*to you Gentiles*], and to them that were nigh [*and to the Jews*].

18 For through him [*Christ*] we both [*both Jews and Gentiles*] have access by one Spirit [*through the Holy Ghost; Strong's #4151*] unto the Father.

19 Now therefore ye are no more strangers [*without knowledge of Christ*] and foreigners [*without citizenship in God's kingdom; Strong's #3941*], but fellowcitizens [*equal partners*] with the saints, and of the household of God [*and members of God's family*];

Next, in verse 20, Paul teaches that members are privileged and blessed to build their lives upon the foundation and teachings of Apostles and prophets, which are available only in the Church of Jesus Christ.

20 And are built [*and your lives are built*] upon the foundation of the apostles and prophets, Jesus Christ himself being the chief cornerstone [*with Jesus Himself at the head of the Church*];

21 In whom all the building [*the whole Church*] fitly framed together [*properly put together and guided*] groweth unto an [*becomes a*] holy temple in the Lord [*directed by the Savior*]:

22 In whom ye also are builded together for an habitation of God through the Spirit [*as members of the Church, your lives are put in order so that you become temples (1 Corinthians 3:16) in which the Spirit of God can reside*].

# EPHESIANS 3

As you have no doubt sensed already in Paul's sermons and writings, the reluctance of many Jewish converts to accept Gentile converts as being of equal status in the eyes of God is a strong concern. In this chapter, he will speak to Gentile converts, assuring them that they are indeed on equal footing with any other converts.

1 FOR this cause I Paul, the prisoner of Jesus Christ for you Gentiles [*it is because I brought the gospel to you Gentiles that I, Paul, am currently in Prison in Rome*],

**JST Ephesians 3:1**

For this cause, I, Paul, am the prisoner of Jesus Christ among you Gentiles.

2 If ye have heard of the dispensation [*responsibility, stewardship, Strong's #3622*] of the grace of God which is given me to you-ward [*which God gave to me to bring you the gospel*]:

**JST Ephesians 3:2**

2 For the dispensation of the grace of God which is given me to you-ward;

3 How that by revelation he made known unto me the mystery [*the gospel of Christ, which is a mystery to those who know nothing of Christ*]; (as I wrote afore in few words [*as I wrote previously to you in a brief letter*],

**JST Ephesians 3:3**

3 As ye have heard that by revelation he made known unto me the mystery of Christ; as I wrote before in few words;

4 Whereby, when ye read [*so that when you read it*], ye may understand my knowledge in the mystery of Christ)

The brief letter referred to by Paul in verses 3 and 4, above, is missing, and serves to remind us that the Bible is not complete. For more about missing scripture, see Bible Dictionary under "Lost Books."

5 Which in other ages [*in some ages past, the gospel*] was not made known unto the sons of men [*was not revealed to people*], as [*in the way that*] it is now revealed unto his holy apostles and prophets by the Spirit;

6 That the Gentiles should be fellowheirs, and of the same body, and partakers of his promise in Christ by the gospel [*namely, that Gentiles are invited to join the Church and become full partners with the covenant people and become heirs of exaltation through Christ's gospel*]:

7 Whereof I was made a minister [*it was*

*this gospel which I was called to bring to you*], according to the gift of the grace of God given [*by the kindness and mercy of God*] unto me by the effectual working of his power [*which caused the gospel to work effectively in me*].

8 Unto me, who am less than the least of all saints, is this grace [*help and stewardship*] given, that I should preach among the Gentiles the unsearchable riches of Christ [*the infinite blessings of the gospel of Christ*];

9 And to make all men see what is the fellowship of the mystery [*and to plainly teach what some consider to be a mystery, namely that both Jews and Gentiles are to be fellowshipped together as equals in the Church of Jesus Christ*], which from the beginning of the world hath been hid in God [*has not been revealed by the Father because people were not ready to accept it*], who created all things by Jesus Christ: [*Christ created the world under the direction of the Father.*]

10 To the intent that now unto the principalities and powers in heavenly places might be known by the church the manifold wisdom of God, [*In other words, the Father has revealed these things with the intent that members of the Church might now be able to understand the many aspects of God's wisdom as revealed in celestial doctrines.*]

11 According to the eternal purpose [*the plan of salvation*] which he [*the Father*] purposed [*planned for us*] in [*through*] Christ Jesus our Lord:

12 In whom we have boldness and access with confidence by the faith of him [*through faith in Christ we gain confidence to approach the Father*].

13 Wherefore I desire that ye faint not at my tribulations for you [*I hope you don't get too discouraged by what I am now going through in prison because of what I did for you*], which is your glory [*which is for your benefit*].

14 For this cause I bow my knees unto the Father of our Lord Jesus Christ, [*I humbly pray to the Father (this thought is continued in verse 16)*]

15 Of whom the whole family in heaven and earth is named [*who can name every one of His family members, in other words, who knows every one of his children in heaven and earth*],

What Paul says about Heavenly Father in verse 15, above, is similar to what the Lord told Moses in Moses 1:35, wherein He said "All things are numbered unto me, for they are mine and I know them."

16 That he would grant you, according to the riches of his glory, to be strengthened with might by his Spirit in the inner man [*that the Holy Ghost will strengthen your inward self according to the rich blessings available from the Father*];

17 That Christ may dwell in your hearts by faith; that ye, being rooted and grounded [*being solidly based*] in love,

18 May be able to comprehend with all saints what is the breadth [*width*], and length, and depth, and height [*of the Father's plan for us*];

19 And to know [*feel*] the love of Christ, which passeth knowledge [*exceeds our ability to understand*], that ye might be filled with all the fulness of God [*that you might be blessed with all blessings the Father has in store for us*].

20 Now unto him [*the Father*] that is able to do exceeding abundantly above all that we ask or think [*the Father is able to do far more with us than we ask or even think; in other words, he can help us attain exaltation*], according to [*through*] the power [*of God*] that worketh in us,

21 Unto him [*the Father*] be glory in the church by Christ Jesus throughout all ages, world [*worlds; see D&C 76:112*] without end [*in other words, forever*]. Amen.

# EPHESIANS 4

This chapter contains strong Biblical evidence that there is one true church. Paul also clearly teaches that the true church will have Apostles, prophets, evangelists, teachers, and so forth, through which the Saints can receive guidance as they progress toward perfection. You may well be familiar with verses 11–14.

1 I THEREFORE, the prisoner of the Lord [*in prison in Rome because of loyalty to Christ*], beseech [*urge*] you that ye walk worthy of the vocation [*responsibilities of membership in the Church*] wherewith [*to which*] ye are called,

2 With all lowliness and meekness [*in humility*], with longsuffering [*patience*], forbearing one another [*being patient with one another*] in love;

3 Endeavouring [*striving*] to keep the unity of the Spirit in the bond of peace [*to live in unity and peace*].

Next, Paul explains that there is just one true church, only one Holy Ghost, only one valid baptism, and only one God. In other words, there can't be more than one true church. If there were more than one, that would mean that there is more than one Holy Ghost and more than one God who are giving conflicting revelations to people everywhere, telling them that their churches are true.

4 There is one body [*there is one true church*], and one Spirit [*and one Holy Ghost*], even as ye are called [*and this is what you have been called by God to participate in*] in one hope [*you only have hope of attaining exaltation in one church, namely the true Church*] of your calling [*to which you have been called to work toward*];

**JST Ephesians 4:4**

4 In one body, and one Spirit, even as ye are called in one hope of your calling;

5 One Lord, one faith, one baptism,

6 One God and Father of all [*we are all His spirit children; Hebrews 12:9*], who is above all, and through all, and in you all.

7 But unto every one of us is given grace according to the measure of the gift of Christ [*the Atonement is available to all of us*].

8 Wherefore [*this is why*] he saith [*in Psalm 68:18*], When he [*Christ*] ascended up on high, he led captivity captive [*overcame the captivity of sin*], and gave gifts unto men [*and gave the gift of resurrection and potential for eternal life to all*].

9 (Now that he [*Christ*] ascended [*to heaven, having finished the Atonement*], what is it but [*isn't it true*] that he also descended first into the lower parts of the earth [*that he had to first descend below all things—see D&C 122:8*]?

10 He that descended is the same also [*the same one*] that ascended up far above all heavens [*rose above all things that stood in His way*], that [*in order that*] he might fill [*fulfil*] all things.)

**JST Ephesians 4:10**

10 He who descended, is the same also who ascended up into heaven, to glorify him who reigneth over all heavens, that he might fill all things.)

Paul has been teaching that there is only one true church. Now he teaches that that Church will have specific priesthood offices in it.

11 And he gave some, apostles; and some, prophets; and some, evangelists [*patriarchs; see Ephesians 4:11, footnote d*]; and some, pastors [*bishops; see Ephesians 4:11, footnote e*] and teachers;

12 For the perfecting of the saints, for the work of the ministry, for the edifying of the body of Christ [*the members of the Church*]:

Next, Paul teaches how long we will

need this specific church organization.

13 Till we all come in the unity of the faith, and of the knowledge of the Son of God, unto a perfect man [*until we become perfect*], unto the measure of the stature of the fulness of Christ [*until we measure up to the perfection which Christ has attained*]:

**JST Ephesians 4:13**

13 Till we, in the unity of the faith, all come to the knowledge of the Son of God, unto a perfect man, unto the measure of the stature of the fullness of Christ;

Paul next gives us another reason why we need Apostles, prophets, and so forth.

14 That we henceforth be no more children [*immature in the gospel*], tossed to and fro [*thrown all over the place*], and carried about with every wind of doctrine [*all kinds of conflicting teachings*], by the sleight [*deception; Strong's #2940*] of men, and cunning craftiness, whereby they lie in wait to deceive [*they try to take us away from Christ by deceiving us*];

15 But speaking the truth in love, may grow up into him [*Christ*] in all things, which [*who*] is the head [*of the Church*], even Christ:

16 From whom the whole body [*Church*] fitly joined together [*properly working together*] and compacted [*helped*] by that which every joint [*office; member*] supplieth, according to the effectual working in the measure of every part [*according to the capacity of each officer and member*], maketh increase of the body [*strengthens the Church*] unto the edifying [*strengthening and building up*] of itself in [*through*] love.

17 This I say therefore [*to teach you these things*], and testify in the Lord, that ye henceforth [*from now on*] walk [*live*] not as other Gentiles walk, in the vanity of their mind [*in pride, arrogance*],

18 Having the understanding darkened [*losing spiritual understanding*], being alienated [*pushed away*] from the life of God through [*because of*] the ignorance that is in them, because of the blindness of their heart [*because they are spiritually blind*]:

19 Who being past feeling have given themselves over unto lasciviousness [*sexual immorality*], to work all uncleanness with greediness [*who are greedy for all kinds of wickedness*].

20 But ye have not so learned Christ [*this is not the way Christ taught you to be*];

21 If so be that ye have heard him [*if it happens that you have listened well to Christ*], and have been taught by him, as the truth is in Jesus [*since Jesus is the source of truth*]:

**JST Ephesians 4:21**

21 If so be that ye have learned him [*if it happens that you have learned the gospel well*], and have been taught by him, as the truth is in Jesus;

22 That ye put off concerning the former conversation [*lifestyle*] the old man [*that you do away with your old, corrupt lifestyles and associations*], which is corrupt according to the deceitful lusts [*your old lifestyles were corrupt because you were fooled by worldly desires*];

**JST Ephesians 4:22**

22 And now I speak unto you concerning the former conversation [*way of life*], by exhortation, that ye put off the old man, which is corrupt according to the deceitful lusts;

23 And be renewed in the spirit of your mind [*be spiritually renewed in your minds, in other words, be "born again" through following the promptings of the Spirit*];

**JST Ephesians 4:23**

23 And be renewed in the mind of the Spirit;

24 And that ye put on the new man

[*become "born again," as new, righteous people*], which after God is created in righteousness and true holiness [*made righteous and truly holy by following Christ*].

25 Wherefore putting away lying [*stop lying*], speak every man truth with his neighbour: for we are members one of another [*for we belong to each other*].

26 Be ye angry, and sin not: let not the sun go down upon your wrath:

**JST Ephesians 4:26**

26 Can ye be angry, and not sin? let not the sun go down upon your wrath;

27 Neither give place to the devil [*don't make room in your lives for the devil*].

28 Let him that stole steal no more: but rather let him labour, working with his hands the thing which is good [*earn his own living*], that he may have to give to him that needeth [*so that he can give to the poor*].

**JST Ephesians 4:28**

28 Let him that stole steal no more; but rather let him labor, working with his hands for the things which are good, that he may have to give to him that needeth.

29 Let no corrupt communication [*evil speech*] proceed out of your mouth, but that which is good to the use of edifying [*say only things which strengthen and build up*], that it may minister grace unto the hearers [*so that it strengthens those who hear you*].

30 And grieve not the holy Spirit of God [*don't offend the Holy Ghost*], whereby ye are sealed unto the day of redemption. [*In other words, don't do things that will make it so that the Holy Spirit of Promise (the Holy Ghost) can't seal you to exaltation. See Ephesians 1:13.*]

31 Let all bitterness, and wrath [*rage*], and anger, and clamour [*irreverent noise*], and evil speaking [*slander*], be put away from you, with [*along with*] all malice [*depravity, naughtiness; Strong's #2549*]:

32 And be ye kind one to another, tenderhearted, forgiving one another, even as God for Christ's sake [*through Christ's Atonement*] hath forgiven you.

# EPHESIANS 5

As Paul continues to encourage the Ephesian Saints to live the gospel in their daily lives, he counsels them to develop Christ like love for one another. He also warns them about specific sins which are all around them in society.

1 BE ye therefore followers of God, as dear children [*like dearly beloved children; Strong's #0027*];

2 And walk in love, as Christ also hath loved us, and hath given himself for us an offering [*as an offering*] and a sacrifice to God for a sweetsmelling savour [*as a sacrifice which was pleasing to God; Strong's #2175*].

3 But fornication, and all uncleanness, or covetousness, let it not be once named among you [*don't even have a hint of it among you*], as becometh saints; [*In other words, behave like Saints.*]

4 Neither [*nor*] filthiness [*obscenity; Strong's #0151*], nor foolish talking, nor jesting [*course joking; Strong's #2160*], which are not convenient [*not appropriate; Strong's #0433*]: but rather giving of thanks [*gratitude to God*].

Next, Paul teaches against sins which, if not repented of, will lead to telestial glory (see D&C 76:103).

5 For this ye know, that no whoremonger [*one who intentionally seeks sexual immorality as a lifestyle*], nor unclean person, nor covetous man [*one who covets*], who is an idolater [*who worships idols*], hath any inheritance in the kingdom of Christ and of God [*in the celestial kingdom*].

6 Let no man deceive you with vain [*flattering*] words: for because of these things [*these sins*] cometh the wrath [*punishments*] of God upon the children of disobedience [*people who disobey God's commandments*].

7 Be not ye therefore partakers with them [*don't participate in such sins*].

8 For ye were sometimes darkness [*in spiritual darkness*], but now are ye light in the Lord [*you have spiritual light from Christ*]: walk as children of light [*followers of Christ*]:

9 (For the fruit [*product*] of the Spirit is in [*is observed in*] all goodness and righteousness and truth;)

10 Proving [*test, evaluate*] what is acceptable unto the Lord.

11 And have no fellowship with [*do not participate in*] the unfruitful [*unproductive*] works of darkness [*evil*], but rather reprove [*expose; Strong's #1651*] them.

12 For it is a shame even to speak of those things which are done of them in secret [*it is a shame to even talk about such secret works of darkness*].

13 But all things that are reproved [*exposed*] are made manifest by the light [*are exposed by the light of the gospel*]: for whatsoever doth make manifest is light [*anything that exposes evil and wickedness is light*].

14 Wherefore [*this is why*] he saith, Awake thou that sleepest, and arise from the dead [*the spiritually dead*], and Christ shall give thee light.

15 See then that ye walk circumspectly [*exercise wisdom in how you live your lives*], not as fools, but as wise,

16 Redeeming the time [*making the best use of your time*], because the days are evil [*because there is plenty of wickedness around*].

17 Wherefore be ye not unwise, but understanding what the will of the Lord is.

**<u>JST Ephesians 5:17</u>**

17 Wherefore be ye not unwise, but understanding what is the will of the Lord.

18 And be not drunk with wine, wherein is excess [*which leads to lustful wickedness*]; but be filled with the Spirit;

19 Speaking to yourselves in psalms and hymns and spiritual songs, singing and making melody in your heart to the Lord;

In verse 20, next, we are reminded that we are to pray to the Father in the name of Jesus Christ. This may seem simple and obvious to us, but there are many in the world who do not know how to pray and wish they did.

20 Giving thanks always for all things unto God and the Father [*unto God the Father*] in the name of our Lord Jesus Christ;

21 Submitting yourselves one to another [*cooperating with one another; Strong's #5293*] in the fear of [*out of respect, reverence for; Strong's #5401*] God.

Various translations and explanations of Paul's words in verses 22–24, next, often cause confusion and resentment. When we come to such verses in the Bible, where misinterpretation and misunderstanding is possible, we need to step back and ask ourselves, "What do our current prophets teach us respecting this topic?" In this case, the topic concerns the relationship between husband and wife. There is safety in "following the Brethren." What do the "Brethren" say on the topic of equality of husbands and wives? The answer is clear.

James E. Faust said, "Nowhere does the doctrine of this Church declare that men are superior to women" (In Conference Report, April 1988, p. 43). President Faust also said, "Every father is to his family a patriarch and every mother a matriarch as coequals in their distinctive parental roles" ("The Prophetic Voice," April 1996 General Conference). President Joseph F. Smith said, referring to

parents, "They stand as the head of the family, the patriarch, the mother, the rulers" (*Gospel Doctrine*, published by Deseret Book, 1977, p. 161).

Thus, it becomes obvious that there is a difference between how priesthood holders "preside" in the Church and the role of priesthood in the home. In the Proclamation on the Family, given September 23, 1995, the First Presidency and the Quorum of the Twelve said, ". . . fathers and mothers are obligated to help one another as equal partners." Thus, our modern prophets have spoken clearly on the relationship between husbands and wives. President Spencer W. Kimball used the word "cooperate" (see verse 22, below) in describing the relationship between woman and man. (See *Ensign*, March 1976, p. 71.)

22 Wives, submit yourselves unto
[*voluntarily cooperate with; Strong's*
Exhaustive Concordance of the Bible,
*#5293*] your own husbands, as unto the
Lord.

Ephesians 5:22, footnote a, in our Bible, suggests that continuing courtship is an important ingredient in correct understanding of verse 22.

23 For the husband is the head of the
wife, even as Christ is the head of the
church [*see verse 25*]: and he is the saviour of the body [*the marriage*].

24 Therefore as the church is subject
unto Christ, so let the wives be to their
own husbands in every thing.

We are blessed to be led by inspired prophets of God, members of the First Presidency and the Twelve. We will use their teachings to offer yet additional clarification for these verses.

In "The Family: A Proclamation to the World," the First Presidency and Council of the Twelve Apostles said, "By divine design, fathers are to preside over their families in love and righteousness and are responsible to provide the necessities of life and protection of their families."

Perhaps you are aware that there is a difference between the role of priesthood in the Church as an organization and the role of the priesthood in the family unit. In the Church it provides order, a definite vertical line of government, a hierarchy of leadership, a definite "person in charge." Whereas, in the family, it serves in full partnership and equality with the wife. It is when the role of priesthood in the Church is imposed upon the family, or vice versa, that trouble arises. Elder Boyd K. Packer explained this difference between how the priesthood functions in the Church and in the home. He said, "There is a difference in the way the priesthood functions in the home as compared to the way it functions in the Church . . . . In the Church there is a distinct line of authority . . . . In the home it is a partnership with husband and wife equally yoked together, sharing in decisions, always working together." (See talk entitled, "The Relief Society," April 1998 General Conference.)

25 Husbands, love your wives, even as
Christ also loved the church, and gave
himself for it [*men should treat their
wives as the Savior would treat them*];

26 That he [*Christ*] might sanctify
[*make it pure and holy*] and cleanse
it [*the Church*] with the washing of
water [*through baptism of converts and
through the recommitment which should
accompany partaking of the sacrament*]
by the word [*through His gospel*],

27 That he might present it to himself
a glorious church, not having spot, or
wrinkle, or any such thing; but that it
should be holy and without blemish.
[*The Savior works with the members
of the Church through His gospel and
Atonement, so that He can eventually
make them pure and spotless and fit to
enter celestial glory.*]

28 So ought men to love their wives as their
own bodies. He that loveth his wife loveth
himself [*he who loves his wife is doing the
very best possible thing for himself*].

29 For no man ever yet hated his own flesh; but nourisheth and cherisheth it, even as the Lord the church [*the same as the Lord treats the Church*]:

30 For we are members of his body, of his flesh, and of his bones [*we are united with Christ through the gospel*].

31 For this cause [*for the purpose of having happy marriages*] shall a man leave his father and mother, and shall be joined unto his wife [*make his wife top priority*], and they two shall be one flesh [*shall work together in unity and cooperation*].

32 This is a great mystery [*this may sound like a deep mystery*]: but I speak concerning Christ and the church [*but Christ and the Church are symbolic of a good marriage between a man and a woman*].

33 Nevertheless let every one of you in particular so love his wife even as himself; and the wife see that she reverence her husband [*treat her husband with courtesy and respect (see Ephesians 5:33, footnote b, in our Bible)*].

# EPHESIANS 6

In this chapter, Paul continues offering counsel that will strengthen families. Also, you will probably recognize verses 11–17 because they are rather famous and often quoted in sermons and lessons.

There are no JST changes for this chapter.

1 CHILDREN, obey your parents in the Lord [*as the Lord would have you do*]: for this is right.

2 Honour thy father and mother; (which is the first commandment with promise [*which is the first of the Ten Commandments with a positive promise attached; see Exodus 20:12*];)

3 That it may be well with thee, and thou mayest live long on the earth [*the promise attached to that commandment*].

4 And, ye fathers, provoke not your children to wrath [*rage*]: but bring them up in the nurture and admonition [*teachings*] of the Lord.

As we move on to verse 5, it helps to know that in Paul's day there was slavery. There were also numerous servants who had sold themselves to owners for a certain number of years in order to satisfy obligations or improve their own status, etc.

5 Servants, be obedient to them that are your masters according to the flesh [*here on earth, even though your ultimate loyalty should be to God*], with fear and trembling [*with respect and humility*], in singleness of your heart [*with pure motives*], as unto Christ;

6 Not with eyeservice [*not only when your masters are watching you*], as menpleasers [*to look good when you have to*]; but as the servants of Christ, doing the will of God from the heart; [*In other words, do a good job of whatever you are asked to do and do it from your heart.*]

7 With good will doing service, as to the Lord, and not to men [*serve with all your heart, as if you were serving God, not men*]:

8 Knowing that whatsoever good thing any man doeth, the same shall he receive of the Lord, whether he be bond or free [*you will be rewarded by God for whatever good you do, whether you are a slave, servant, or free citizen*].

9 And, ye masters, do the same things unto them [*and you who own slaves or servants should treat them the same as I have told them to treat you*], forbearing threatening [*avoiding threatening them*]: knowing that your Master [*God*] also is in heaven; neither is there respect of persons with him [*God respects each person for who he or she is, not because of social status or position*].

10 Finally, my brethren, be strong in the Lord, and in the power of his might [*in His mighty power*].

Verses 11–17, next, are often quoted and constitute one of Paul's more famous teachings using symbolism. He uses the symbolism of preparing for a serious battle and thus warns us that we need to put on the full gospel of Jesus Christ in order to be protected from the devil and come out triumphant in celestial glory.

11 Put on the whole armour of God, that ye may be able to stand against the wiles [*cunning temptations*] of the devil.

12 For we wrestle not against flesh and blood [*we are not only fighting against evil people*], but against principalities, against powers, against the rulers of the darkness of this world, against spiritual wickedness in high places.

13 Wherefore [*therefore*] take unto you [*put on*] the whole armour of God [*the protection of the whole gospel*], that ye may be able to withstand [*come out the winner*] in the evil day, and having done all, to stand [*to remain standing, as a soldier who survives in battle does when the battle is over*].

"Gird up your loins" is a scriptural phrase which usually means "prepare for action." Or, "don't get caught off guard." We see one form of this used by Paul in verse 14, next.

14 Stand [*win*] therefore, having your loins girt about with truth [*be prepared for action with truth*], and having on the breastplate [*the protection*] of righteousness;

15 And your feet shod with the preparation of the gospel of peace;

16 Above all, taking the shield of faith, wherewith ye shall be able to quench all the fiery darts of the wicked.

Faith is indeed a great and fundamental power in our lives. Joseph Smith, in *Lectures on Faith*, lecture number one, emphasizes that faith is a principle of action as well as a principle of power. In other words, faith compels us to action, to good works, to faithful church attendance, to forgiving others, to repenting, to fleeing evil company, and so on. In Hebrews, chapter 11, Paul teaches the power of faith in the lives of many great people, including Enoch, Noah, Abraham, Sarah, and others, who triumphed over "all the fiery darts of the wicked" spoken of in verse 16 above.

17 And take the helmet of salvation, and the sword of the Spirit, which is the word of God:

The imagery of the "word of God" being like a "sword" is used often in the scriptures. See Topical Guide under "Sword." Thus, the "word of God" cuts through false doctrines and mistaken thinking like a "sword."

For instance, some teach that little children who are not baptized and who die in infancy, are doomed forever. The true "word of God" cuts quickly and completely through this terrible false doctrine and gives comfort by teaching clearly that this is not so (see D&C 137:10 plus Moroni, chapter 8.) Many nowadays, as was the case in the days of Paul, teach that premarital or extramarital sex is just fine. The "word of God" cuts right through this evil falsehood in numerous scriptural passages as well as through modern prophets. Thus, a person who is "armed" with the "word of God" and who uses that mighty "sword" does not fall prey to such evil.

18 Praying always with all prayer [*in all your prayers*] and supplication [*requests to God*] in the Spirit [*as directed by the Holy Ghost*], and watching thereunto [*to that end*] with all perseverance and supplication [*keep praying faithfully*] for all saints;

19 And for me, that utterance may be given unto me [*that I may know what to teach and how to teach it*], that I may open my mouth boldly, to make known the mystery of the gospel [*the simple truths of the gospel which are still a mystery to so many*],

20 For which I am an ambassador in bonds [*I am a messenger of the gospel who is still in prison in Rome*]: that therein I may speak boldly, as I ought to speak [*and I need your faith and prayers for me so that I can write clearly and boldly to teach the gospel*].

21 But that [*so that*] ye also may know my affairs, and how I do, Tychicus [*a faithful member who accompanied Paul on some of his missionary journeys; see Strong's #5190*], a beloved brother and faithful minister in the Lord, shall make known to you all things:

22 Whom I have sent unto you for the same purpose, that ye might know our affairs, and that he might comfort your hearts. [*In other words, I've sent Tychicus to visit you, and he will fill you in on everything that is going on with me.*]

23 Peace be to the brethren, and love with faith, from God the Father and the Lord Jesus Christ.

24 Grace be with all them that love our Lord Jesus Christ in sincerity. Amen.

# The Epistle of Paul the Apostle to the Philippians

As was the case with Paul's letter to the Ephesian Saints, it seems that the Philippian members of the Church were living the gospel. Thus, there seems to be no real dominant problem among them which Paul addresses. At the time Paul wrote this letter to the Saints at Philipp (in what would be known as northeastern Greece today), Paul was still a prisoner in Rome. Thus, most scholars agree that this letter was written and sent sometime in AD 63. They also believe that this was probably the last letter written by Paul during his first imprisonment in Rome, before he was released. Philippi was the first city on what we now refer to as the European continent to receive the gospel. Paul was told in a vision to go there (Acts 16:9).

## PHILIPPIANS 1

1 PAUL and Timotheus [*Timothy*], the servants of Jesus Christ, to all the saints in Christ Jesus [*to all the members of the Church*] which are at Philippi, with the bishops and deacons:

2 Grace be unto you, and peace, from God our Father, and from the Lord Jesus Christ.

Verse 2, above, is another reminder that the Father and Son are two separate personages.

3 I thank my God upon every remembrance of you [*I give thanks to God every time I think of you*],

4 Always in every prayer of mine for you all making request [*praying for you*] with joy,

**JST Philippians 1:4**

4 Always in every prayer of mine, for the steadfastness of you all, making request with joy,

5 For your fellowship [*I thank God for your association with me*] in the gospel from the first day until now;

6 Being confident of this very thing, that he [*the Father*] which hath begun a good work in you [*who has introduced the gospel to you*] will perform it [*will continue working with you*] until the day of Jesus Christ [*until Judgment Day; see McConkie,* Doctrinal New Testament Commentary, *Vol. 2, p. 528*]:

7 Even as it is meet [*necessary*] for me to think this of you all, because I have you in my heart; inasmuch as both in my bonds [*while I am in prison here in Rome*], and in the defence and confirmation of the gospel [*and as I defend and bear testimony of the gospel*], ye all are partakers of my grace [*you are participants with me in the grace of God*].

8 For God is my record [*God is my witness*], how greatly I long after you all [*how my heart yearns for you*] in the bowels [*the tender affection; Strong's #4698*] of Jesus Christ.

9 And this I pray, that your love may abound [*increase*] yet more and more in knowledge and in all judgment [*wisdom*];

10 That ye may approve [*recognize: Strong's #1381*] things that are excellent; that ye may be sincere and without

offence [*and set a good example to others; Strong's #0677*] till the day of Christ;

11 Being filled with the fruits [*end results*] of righteousness, which are by Jesus Christ [*which come as a result of following Christ*], unto the glory and praise of God [*and which bring glory and honor to the Father*].

12 But I would ye should understand, brethren, that the things which happened unto me have fallen out rather unto the furtherance of the gospel [*I want you to understand that the seemingly bad things that have happened to me have actually helped further the gospel cause*];

13 So that my bonds in Christ [*so that my being in prison because of my faith in Christ*] are manifest in all the palace, and in all other places [*has called attention to the gospel throughout the Roman emperor's palace and everywhere else*];

14 And many of the brethren in the Lord [*many of the members*], waxing [*growing*] confident by my bonds [*because I am here in prison*], are much more bold to speak the word [*spread the gospel*] without fear. [*In other words, many members are not so afraid anymore to share the gospel because of my being here in prison.*]

Even though much good is being done because Paul is there in Rome under house arrest (he was there for two years under such conditions), there are still some members who do not teach the gospel out of love, but rather because they enjoy stirring up contention. Paul refers to them in the next verses.

15 Some indeed preach Christ [*preach the gospel*] even of envy and strife [*because they enjoy creating contention*]; and some also of good will [*and some preach it with good motives*]:

16 The one preach Christ of contention [*the ones who create contention with the gospel*], not sincerely, supposing to add affliction to my bonds [*are trying to make life more miserable for me*]:

17 But the other of love [*but others preach out of love*], knowing that I am set [*knowing that I am called of God; Strong's #2749*] for the defence of the gospel [*to defend the gospel*].

Paul's attitude about the fact that some of his enemies ridicule him and the gospel of Christ, while others teach the gospel with testimony and conviction, is a good lesson for us. His attitude, as seen in verse 18, next, is that either way, people are becoming aware of Christ and His Church. So they also are in our day. Enemies and unknowing people write unkind things in national magazines about the Church. People who don't like the Church make films and videos, write editorials, appear on local or national TV, criticizing us. Paul would probably say, "Don't let it upset you. It is all free advertising!" Indeed, missionaries usually find more success after intense efforts on the part of our enemies and detractors to discredit the Church.

18 What then [*what does it matter*]? notwithstanding [*regardless*], every way [*either way*], whether in pretence [*with evil motives*], or in truth [*or with good motives*], Christ is preached [*Christ and the Church get more public recognition*]; and I therein do rejoice [*and that makes me happy*], yea, and will rejoice.

19 For I know that this shall turn to my salvation through your prayer [*your prayers for me will help all this opposition work toward my salvation*], and the supply of the Spirit of Jesus Christ [*and it will also help the Spirit of Christ, which every person who is born into the world has (see John 1:9) to guide people to the true Church*],

20 According to my earnest [*sincere*] expectation and my hope, that in nothing I shall be ashamed [*that I will not fail in anything*], but that with all boldness, as always, so now also Christ shall

be magnified in my body, whether it be by life, or by death. [*I trust that I will not let anyone down, rather that I will continue to represent Christ boldly, whether I live or die.*]

21 For to me to live is Christ, and to die is gain.

22 But if I live in the flesh, this is the fruit of my labour: yet what I shall choose I wot not.

Joseph Smith switched the order of verses 21 and 22, above, and gave them as follows in the JST:

**JST Philippians 1:21**
21 But if I live in the flesh, ye are the fruit of my labor [*if I am not executed, I will have the advantage of being with you whom I brought into the Church*]. Yet what I shall choose [*what will happen to me*] I know not.

**JST Philippians 1:22**
22 For me to live, is to do the will of Christ; and to die, is my gain.

23 For I am in a strait betwixt two [*I am caught between two desirable alternatives*], having a desire to depart, and to be with Christ [*I would love to die and thus be with Christ*]; which is far better:

**JST Philippians 1:23**
23 Now I am in a strait betwixt two, having a desire to depart, and to be with Christ; which is far better;

24 Nevertheless to abide in the flesh is more needful for you [*but if I remain here on earth, I can be more helpful to you*].

25 And having this confidence [*and knowing this is true*], I know that I shall abide [*I know that I will not die for a while*] and continue with you all for your furtherance and joy of faith;

26 That your rejoicing may be more abundant in Jesus Christ for me by my coming to you again.

**JST Philippians 1:26**
26 That your rejoicing with me may be more abundant in Jesus Christ, for [*because of*] my coming to you again.

27 Only let your conversation [*your behavior, your lives; Strong's #4176*] be as it becometh [*be in harmony with*] the gospel of Christ: that whether I come and see you, or else be absent, I may hear of your affairs [*doings*], that ye stand fast in one spirit [*that you are solidly united*], with one mind [*in harmony with each other*] striving [*working*] together for the faith of the gospel;

**JST Philippians 1:27**
27 Therefore let your conversation be as it becometh the gospel of Christ; that whether I come and see you, or else be absent, I may hear of your affairs, that ye stand fast in one spirit, with one mind striving together for the faith of the gospel;

28 And in nothing terrified by your adversaries: which is to them an evident token of perdition, but to you of salvation, and that of God.

**JST Philippians 1:28**
28 And in nothing terrified by your adversaries, who reject the gospel, which bringeth on them destruction; but you who receive the gospel, salvation; and that of God.

29 For unto you it is given in the behalf of Christ, not only to believe on him, but also to suffer for his sake; [*In other words, it is a privilege for you to not only believe in Christ, but also to suffer in behalf of Christ just as it is for me to do so.*]

30 Having the same conflict which ye saw in me, and now hear to be in me. [*In other words, you have the privilege of having the same struggles you saw me have in times past and know that I am still enduring now.*]

**JST Philippians 1:30**

30 Having the same conflict which ye saw in me, and now know to be in me.

# PHILIPPIANS 2

Paul is a master teacher, and he starts off this segment of his letter to the Philippians by saying, in effect, "If the gospel has proven beneficial to you in any way, I hope you will make my joy full by being united together in kindness and love for each other."

1 IF there be therefore [*because of the gospel I brought to you*] any consolation [*comfort, solace; Strong's #3874*] in Christ, if any comfort of love [*because of His love for you*], if any fellowship of the Spirit [*companionship of the Holy Ghost*], if any bowels [*tender feelings*] and mercies,

2 Fulfil ye my joy [*make my joy complete*], that ye be likeminded [*live in harmony with one another*], having the same love, being of one accord [*united*], of one mind [*united in thought*].

3 Let nothing be done through strife [*contention*] or vainglory [*foolish pride; Strong's #2754*]; but in lowliness of mind [*humility*] let each esteem other better than themselves [*consider the needs of others to be more important than their own needs*].

4 Look not every man on his own things [*don't only be concerned about your own needs, in other words, don't be selfish*], but every man also on the things of others [*but be concerned about the needs of others also*].

5 Let this mind [*attitude*] be in you, which was also in Christ Jesus: [*In other words, learn to think like Christ.*]

6 Who, being in the form of God [*who looks just like the Father; see Hebrews 1:3*], thought it not robbery [*not taking anything away from the Father's status*] to be equal with God: [*In other words, even though Christ, during His mortal ministry, constantly taught that the Father was greater than He (example: John 14:28), He now has been resurrected and is equal with the Father in the sense that He has completed what the Father asked Him to do and thus, the Father has given Him "all things" (D&C 76:55). Therefore, He has entered into His exaltation, just as all faithful Saints will when "all that my Father hath shall be given unto (them)." (D&C 84:38.)*]

7 But made himself of no reputation [*did not seek glory for Himself*], and took upon him the form of a servant [*and became the servant of all, providing the Atonement for them*], and was made in the likeness of men [*and took upon Himself a mortal body*]:

8 And being found in fashion as a man [*and having taken upon Himself mortality*], he humbled himself, and became obedient unto death [*He was humbly obedient to the Father*], even the death of the cross [*even to the point of suffering crucifixion*].

9 Wherefore [*because of that*] God [*the Father*] also hath highly exalted him [*has given Him exaltation*], and given him a name which is above every name [*and given Him power to judge all people; see John 5:22*]:

10 That at the name of Jesus every knee should bow [*everyone will ultimately acknowledge that Jesus is the Christ; see D&C 76:112*], of things in heaven, and things in earth, and things under the earth [*all things have thus become subject to Christ*];

11 And that every tongue should confess [*acknowledge*] that Jesus Christ is Lord, to the glory of God the Father.

12 Wherefore [*therefore*], my beloved, as ye have always obeyed, not as in my presence only, but now much more in my absence, work out your

own salvation with fear and trembling [*acute awareness of how important it is to be righteous*].

President David O. McKay explained verse 12, above, as follows: "To work out one's salvation is not to sit idly by dreaming and yearning for God miraculously to thrust bounteous blessings into our laps. It is to perform daily, hourly, momentarily, if necessary, the immediate task or duty at hand, and to continue happily in such performance as the years come and go, leaving the fruits of such labors either for self or for others to be bestowed as a just and beneficent Father may determine." (David O. McKay in Conference Report, Apr. 1957, p. 7.)

13 For it is God which worketh in you both to will and to do of his good pleasure. [*It is God who works with you to help you to want to truly be good as well as to do good.*]

14 Do all things without murmurings [*complaining*] and disputings [*contentions*]:

15 That ye may be [*Greek Bible says "become"*] blameless [*innocent of sin*] and harmless, the sons of God [*followers of God*], without rebuke [*of good reputation*], in the midst of a crooked and perverse [*corrupt; Strong's #1294*] nation [*generation; Strong's #1074*], among whom ye shine as lights in the world;

16 Holding forth the word of life [*holding up the gospel for all to see*]; that I may rejoice in the day of Christ [*on Judgment Day*], that I have not run in vain, neither laboured in vain [*that my work in bringing you the gospel may not have been without good results*].

17 Yea, and if I be offered upon the sacrifice and service of your faith [*even though I am now in prison, being in effect "sacrificed" because of bringing the gospel of Christ to you and others*], I joy, and rejoice with you all.

**<u>JST Philippians 2:17</u>**

17 Yea, and if I be offered a sacrifice upon the service of your faith, I joy, and rejoice with you all.

18 For the same cause [*you also have to sacrifice for the gospel*] also do ye joy [*which brings joy to you*], and rejoice with me [*and, thus, you can rejoice with me*].

19 But I trust in the Lord Jesus [*I trust that the Lord will enable me*] to send Timotheus [*Timothy*] shortly [*soon*] unto you, that I also may be of good comfort [*that I may be cheered up*], when I know your state [*when I find out how you are getting along*].

20 For I have no man likeminded, who will naturally care for your state [*there is no one else who cares for you like Timothy does, who will take such a genuine interest in your well-being*].

21 For all seek their own [*most people seek to do as they please*], not the things which are Jesus Christ's [*rather than prioritizing on what Christ taught*].

22 But ye know the proof of him [*you know that Timothy has "passed the test"*], that, as a son with the father [*that, like a son working with his father*], he hath served with me in the gospel.

23 Him therefore I hope to send presently, so soon as I shall see how it will go with me [*as soon as I get an idea of what is going to happen to me here in Rome, I hope to send Timothy to you*].

24 But I trust in the Lord that I also myself shall come shortly [*I hope to visit you myself soon*].

Most scholars think that when Paul was finally released from his two-year house arrest in Rome, he went to Philippi to rest there for a while, then went on from there to visit the members of the Church in Ephesus.

25 Yet I supposed it necessary [*I found it necessary*] to send to you Epaphroditus [*to send Epaphroditus back home to you*], my brother, and companion in

labour, and fellowsoldier, but your messenger [*whom you sent to me to help take care of my needs here in Rome*], and he that ministered to my wants [*he performed great service for me while he was here*].

26 For he longed after you all [*because he became very homesick for you*], and was full of heaviness [*and got depressed*], because that ye had heard that he had been sick [*because, as you have heard, he became very sick*].

27 For indeed he was sick nigh unto death [*in fact, he nearly died*]: but God had mercy on him; and not on him only, but on me also, lest I should have sorrow upon sorrow [*because if he had died, it would have been almost more than I could bear*].

28 I sent him therefore the more carefully [*the more quickly*], that, when ye see him again, ye may rejoice, and that I may be the less sorrowful [*less worried about him*].

29 Receive him therefore in the Lord with all gladness; and hold such in reputation [*and hold such men as he in high regard*]:

30 Because for the work of Christ [*because of his work for the Lord*] he was nigh unto death [*he almost died*], not regarding his life [*willing to give his life*], to supply your lack of service toward me [*to do for me what you couldn't do because I am so far away from you*].

# PHILIPPIANS 3

The wording here, at the beginning of chapter 3 indicates that Paul is repeating some counsel he has given these members of the Church previously. However, we have no record of when he gave it.

1 FINALLY, my brethren, rejoice in the Lord [*find joy in living the gospel*]. To write the same things to you, to me indeed is not grievous [*I don't mind writing the same things to you again*], but for you it is safe [*and it will help safeguard you against evil*].

**JST Philippians 3:1**

1 Finally, my brethren, rejoice in the Lord. To write the same things to you, to me indeed is not grievous, and for you it is safe.

2 Beware of dogs, beware of evil workers, beware of the concision.

An explanation of verse 2, above, is given in the Institute of Religion New Testament student manual, *The Life and Teachings of Jesus and His Apostles*, 1979, p. 361, as follows: "Paul was attacking the Judaizers—those Jewish Christians who demanded complete obedience to the Mosaic law as a condition for salvation. He used the word dogs to imply that they were unclean and unholy. His use of the words evil workers indicates those who thought they were righteous and in fact were not. In sarcasm he used the word concision, which means mutilation, instead of circumcision, which is the normal adjective used to define Jews."

3 For we are the circumcision [*we are Jews*], which worship God in the spirit, and rejoice in Christ Jesus, and have no confidence in the flesh [*and have no confidence in being saved by the Law of Moses*].

4 Though I might also have confidence in the flesh [*although I am one who could very well have continued to live the Law of Moses*]. If any other man thinketh that he hath whereof he might trust in the flesh, I more [*in fact, I probably have more reason to stay with the Law of Moses than most men; in other words, I was raised in a very strict Jewish home, where the Law of Moses was lived to the letter.*]

5 Circumcised the eighth day, of the stock of Israel [*a descendant of Abraham, Isaac, and Jacob*], of the tribe of Benjamin, an Hebrew of the Hebrews

[*I was a "Hebrew's Hebrew," in other words, a model Jew*]; as touching the law, a Pharisee [*as far as the Law of Moses was concerned, I was a Pharisee*];

> Among the Jews, the Pharisees were the strictest of all in adhering to the Law of Moses. See Bible Dictionary under "Pharisees."

6 Concerning zeal, persecuting the church [*I was a most energetic persecutor of this new church started by Jesus*]; touching the righteousness which is in the law, blameless [*I lived the Law of Moses down to the very tiniest details*].

7 But what things were gain to me, those I counted loss for Christ [*and that was a big social advantage to me among the Jews, but I gave it all up to follow Christ*].

8 Yea doubtless [*that was absolutely the case*], and I count all things but loss for the excellency of the knowledge of Christ Jesus my Lord [*I would indeed be the loser if I put anything else above the gospel of Christ*]: for whom I have suffered the loss of all things [*I have lost basically everything because of my loyalty to Christ*], and do count them but dung [*and consider what I have lost to be nothing but rubbish; Strong's #4657*], that I may win Christ [*that I may win the real prize, which is Christ and His gospel in my life*],

9 And be found in him [*and be found loyal to Christ*], not having mine own righteousness, which is of the law [*not appearing righteous to others, which is often the goal of those who keep the Law of Moses*], but that [*true righteousness*] which is [*comes*] through the faith of Christ, the righteousness which is of God [*which comes from the Father*] by faith [*through faith in Christ*]:

10 That I may know him [*Christ*], and the power of his resurrection, and the fellowship of his sufferings, being made conformable unto his death [*conforming to the gospel which lets His Atonement work for me*];

11 If by any means I might attain unto the resurrection of the dead.

> **JST Philippians 3:11**
> 11 If by any means I might attain unto the resurrection of the just.
>
> The change made in the Joseph Smith Translation in verse 11, above, is very significant doctrinally. Some Christians who read verse 11 as it stands in our Bible, claim that this proves that all people will not be resurrected., whereas, what Paul was teaching is that he hopes to be resurrected with those who attain celestial exaltation, in other words, the "resurrection of the just." Thus, some Christians dispute our doctrine that everyone who has ever been born will be resurrected. Of course, Paul taught that all will be resurrected, in 1 Corinthians 15:22.

12 Not as though I had already attained, either were already perfect [*it is not as if I have already attained exaltation or were already perfect*]: but I follow after [*but I am pressing forward in that direction*], if that [*in the hope that*] I may apprehend that [*obtain that*] for which also [*for which purpose*] I am apprehended of Christ Jesus [*Christ has taken me in*].

13 Brethren, I count not myself to have apprehended [*I have not attained this goal yet*]: but this one thing I do, forgetting those things which are behind, and reaching forth unto those things which are before, [*In other words, here is how I plan to attain this goal. I leave the past behind and take advantage of the opportunities to do better which lie before me*].

14 I press toward the mark for the prize of the high calling of God in Christ Jesus [*I continue pressing forward toward the prize of exaltation*].

15 Let us therefore, as many as be perfect [*are mature enough to understand what I am saying; Strong's #5046*], be

thus minded [*keep this in mind*]: and if in any thing ye be otherwise minded [*and if you think otherwise, with respect to anything I have said*], God shall reveal even this unto you [*God will help you understand*].

16 Nevertheless, whereto we have already attained, let us walk by the same rule, let us mind the same thing [*but let's stick with the progress we have already made in the gospel*].

17 Brethren, be followers together of me [*be united in following me*], and mark them which walk so as ye have us for an ensample [*and take note of those who follow what we taught you and use them for an example*].

18 (For many walk, of whom I have told [*warned*] you often, and now tell you even weeping, that they are the enemies of the cross of Christ [*many are not living exemplary lives and have thus become enemies of Christ's gospel*]:

> **JST Philippians 3:18**
> 18 (For many walk, of whom I have told you often, and now tell you even weeping, as the enemies of the cross of Christ;

19 Whose end is destruction [*they will eventually be destroyed*], whose God is their belly [*who worship the "gods" of physical desires*], and whose glory is in their shame, who mind earthly things [*who think only of worldly things*].)

> **JST Philippians 3:19**
> 19 Whose end is destruction, whose God is their belly, and who glory in their shame, who mind earthly things.)

20 For our conversation is in heaven [*we are governed by heaven; Strong's #4175*]; from whence also we look for the Saviour, the Lord Jesus Christ [*and we look to the Savior for guidance*]:

21 Who shall change [*resurrect*] our vile body [*lowly mortal body*], that it may be fashioned [*become*] like unto his glorious body, according to the working whereby he is able even to subdue all things unto himself [*because of the power He has over all things*].

> For Paul to teach that we can have glorious resurrected bodies like the Savior has is marvelous doctrine indeed! In 1 Corinthians 15:40, he spoke of "celestial bodies." In verse 21, above, and in the verses preceding it, he assures the Philippian Saints that they can have celestial bodies. D&C 88:28–32 explains that celestial bodies will be "natural" bodies, whereas, those who go to other kingdoms of glory will have terrestrial bodies or telestial bodies or son of perdition bodies, as the case may be. Joseph Fielding Smith taught about the differences in resurrected bodies as follows: "In the resurrection there will be different kinds of bodies; they will not all be alike. The body a man receives will determine his place hereafter. There will be celestial bodies, terrestrial bodies, and telestial bodies, and these bodies will differ as distinctly as do bodies here. . . Bodies will be quickened (resurrected) according to the kingdom which they are judged worthy to enter. . . Some will gain celestial bodies with all the powers of exaltation and eternal increase. These bodies will shine like the sun as our Savior's does, as described by John. Those who enter the terrestrial kingdom will have terrestrial bodies, and they will not shine like the sun, but they will be more glorious than the bodies of those who receive the telestial glory. In both of these kingdoms there will be changes in the bodies and limitations. They will not have the power of increase, neither the power or nature to live as husbands and wives, for this will be denied them and they cannot increase. Those who receive the exaltation in the celestial kingdom will have the 'continuation of the seeds forever.' They will live in the family relationship. In the terrestrial and in the telestial kingdoms there will be no marriage. Those who enter there will remain 'separately and singly' forever. Some of the functions

in the celestial body will not appear in the terrestrial body, neither in the telestial body, and the power of procreation will be removed." (*Doctrines of Salvation*, Vol. 2, pp. 286–288.)

# PHILIPPIANS 4

Paul now finishes his letter to the Philippian Saints, reminding them that the things he has written to them are designed to help them remain strong in the gospel. Verse 8 will likely sound familiar to you.

1 THEREFORE, my brethren dearly beloved and longed for, my joy and crown, so stand fast in the Lord [*what I have written above in this letter to you is how to remain firm and faithful in the gospel of Christ*], my dearly beloved.

2 I beseech [*urge*] Euodias, and beseech Syntyche [*two female members of the Church in Philippi*], that they be of the same mind in the Lord [*that they get along with each other in the gospel*].

3 And I intreat thee also, true yokefellow [*associate; see Philippians 4:3, footnote a*], help those women which laboured [*worked*] with me in the gospel, with Clement [*probably a male member of the Church in Philippi*] also, and with other my fellowlabourers, whose names are in the book of life.

The "book of life" means those whose names are recorded in heaven as being faithful. See Bible Dictionary under "Book of Life."

4 Rejoice in the Lord alway [*always*]: and again I say, Rejoice.

You may recognize the words "again I say, Rejoice" as being part of Hymn #66, "Rejoice, the Lord Is King!," in our current hymn book.

5 Let your moderation [*fairness, mildness, patience; Strong's #1933*] be known unto all men. The Lord is at hand [*the Lord is not far from us*].

6 Be careful for nothing; [*In other words, don't worry too much about things of the world.*] but in every thing by prayer and supplication with thanksgiving let your requests be made known unto God [*pray to God with gratitude about all your concerns*].

**JST Philippians 4:6**

6 Be afflicted for nothing; but in everything by prayer and supplication with thanksgiving let your requests be made known unto God.

7 And the peace of God [*which comes from the Father*], which passeth all understanding [*which is beyond comparison to anything else*], shall keep [*guard and protect; Strong's #5432*] your hearts and minds through Christ Jesus [*through Christ and His gospel*].

You will immediately see the connection between verse 8, next, and the thirteenth Article of Faith, which says: "We believe in being honest, true, chaste, benevolent, virtuous, and in doing good to all men; indeed, we may say that we follow the admonition of Paul—We believe all things, we hope all things, we have endured many things, and hope to be able to endure all things. If there is anything virtuous, lovely, or of good report or praiseworthy, we seek after these things."

8 Finally, brethren, whatsoever [*whatever*] things are true, whatsoever things are honest, whatsoever things are just [*righteous*], whatsoever things are pure, whatsoever things are lovely, whatsoever things are of good report [*are excellent*]; if there be any virtue, and if there be any praise [*if there is anything that is praiseworthy*], think on these things [*keep such things on your mind constantly*].

9 Those things, which ye have both learned, and received, and heard, and seen in me, do: and the God of peace shall be with you.

10 But I rejoiced in the Lord greatly,

that now at the last your care of me hath flourished again; wherein ye were also careful, but ye lacked opportunity. [*In other words, I know you have been worried about me, but you have not had any opportunity to help me.*]

11 Not that I speak in respect of want [*not that I am trying to make you think that I am in any great need*]: for I have learned, in whatsoever state I am, therewith to be content [*because I have learned to be content with whatever conditions I find myself in*].

12 I know both how to be abased [*I know how to live with many unmet needs*], and I know how to abound [*and I can get along fine when surrounded by plenty*]: every where and in all things I am instructed both to be full and to be hungry [*I have experienced having a full stomach and being hungry*], both to abound [*have plenty*] and to suffer need [*and to be in need*].

13 I can do all things through Christ which strengtheneth me.

14 Notwithstanding [*nevertheless*] ye have well done, that ye did communicate with my affliction [*in that you shared with me in my times of need*].

15 Now ye Philippians know also, that in the beginning of the gospel [*in the early days when you were just getting started in the gospel*], when I departed from Macedonia [*when I was leaving your area*], no church [*no other members*] communicated [*worked*] with me as concerning giving and receiving, but ye only.

16 For even in Thessalonica ye sent once and again unto my necessity [*even while I was in Thessalonica, you sent assistance to me time and time again*].

17 Not because I desire a gift [*not that I am looking for assistance from you now*]: but I desire fruit that may abound to your account [*but I want that which is best for you*].

18 But I have all, and abound [*all my needs are now being met*]: I am full, having received of Epaphroditus [*a faithful member of the Church who worked with Paul*] the things which were sent from you [*Epaphroditus brought me the things you sent*], an odour of a sweet smell [*an offering acceptable to God*], a sacrifice acceptable, wellpleasing to God.

19 But my God shall supply all your need according to his riches in glory by Christ Jesus [*God will take care of all your needs as He has mine*].

20 Now unto God and our Father be glory [*praises*] for ever and ever. Amen.

21 Salute [*greet*] every saint in Christ Jesus. The brethren which are with me greet you.

22 All the saints [*members of the Church*] salute [*greet*] you, chiefly they that are of Cæsar's household [*especially those who belong to Caesar's household*].

23 The grace of our Lord Jesus Christ be with you all. Amen.

# THE EPISTLE OF PAUL THE APOSTLE TO THE COLOSSIANS

Most Bible scholars agree that Paul's letter to the Colossians in the small city of Colosse (about 11 miles southeast of Laodicea and about 90 to 100 miles east of Ephesus, in what is today western Turkey) was written about AD 62, during Paul's first imprisonment in Rome (see note at the end of Acts 28:31 in this study guide). The church in Colosse was established during Paul's third missionary journey during the three years he spent in Ephesus. It appears that one of Paul's converts named Epaphras (Colossians 1:7, 12, and 13), who was a citizen of Colosse and who was probably converted while visiting Ephesus, was sent by Paul to actually establish the Church in Colosse, although it may be that Paul himself established it there with the help of Epaphras.

In this letter, Paul expresses love and appreciation for the Colossian members and expresses concern that some of them seem to be reverting back to mechanically going through the motions of religion (2:16), rather than internalizing the gospel. He cautions against believing that angels can serve as mediators ("patron saints," etc.) between us and God (2:18.) He repeatedly reminds these members that it is only through Christ and His Atonement that we can attain celestial glory. He also explains that Jesus is the firstborn spirit child of the Father (1:15.)

## COLOSSIANS 1

In this chapter, Paul gives one of the most beautiful and powerful testimonies ever given about Jesus Christ. You may want to mark several passages in chapter one in your own scriptures as well as make notes therein. Paul gives much doctrine about Christ which Latter-day Saints are in a position to understand better than any other people on earth. In fact, you may be aware that many Christian churches no longer agree with much of what Paul says here and other places about Christ and His commandments to us. Thus, it is a simple fact that faithful Latter-day Saints actually believe the Bible much more faithfully than any other Christians.

As mentioned above, one of the significant doctrines taught in this chapter is that Jesus Christ was the firstborn spirit child of the Father (verses 13–15). Thus, He is our "Elder Brother," and indeed is our oldest spirit brother.

1 PAUL, an apostle of Jesus Christ by the will of God [*called of God*], and Timotheus [*Timothy, one of Paul's favorite missionary companions who was like a son to Paul*] our brother,

2 To the saints and faithful brethren in Christ which are at Colosse [*a small city in what would be in western Turkey today, about 11 miles south of Laodicea*]: Grace be unto you, and peace, from God our Father and the Lord Jesus Christ.

3 We give thanks to God [*the Father*] and the Father [*who is the Father*] of our Lord Jesus Christ, praying always for you,

4 Since we heard of your faith in Christ Jesus, and of the love which ye have to [*toward*] all the saints [*members of the Church*],

**JST Colossians 1:4**

4 Since we heard of your faith in Christ Jesus, and of your love to all the saints,

The word "Saints" as used often by Paul in referring to members of the Church, means "holy" according to Strong's #0040. Thus, when we hear ourselves referred to as "Latter-day Saints," we are reminded that we should be trying to be "holy ones," people who are trying to faithfully follow the Savior and properly represent Him at all times and under all circumstances.

5 For the hope [*the prospect of attaining exaltation*] which is laid up [*which is in store*] for you in heaven, whereof ye heard before [*which you were taught in times past*] in the word of the truth of the gospel [*when you heard the truths of the gospel*];

6 Which is come [*has been brought*] unto you, as it is in all the world; and bringeth forth fruit [*and produces exaltation for the faithful*], as it doth also in you, since the day ye heard of it, and knew the grace of God in truth [*and you knew the truth, that the kindness and mercy of the Father are made available to us through the Atonement of Christ*]:

**JST Colossians 1:6**

6 Which is come unto you, as in all generations of the world; and bringeth forth fruit, as it doth also in you, since the day ye heard of it, and knew the grace of God in truth;

7 As ye also learned of [*as you were taught by*] Epaphras our dear fellowservant, who is for you a faithful minister of Christ [*see note about Epaphras at the beginning of Colossians in this study guide*];

8 Who also declared unto us [*who told us about*] your love in the Spirit [*because of the Spirit which is with you*].

9 For this cause we also [*this is why we*], since the day we heard it, do not cease to pray for you, and to desire that ye might be filled with the knowledge of his will in all wisdom and spiritual understanding [*understanding which comes through the Holy Ghost*];

10 That ye might walk worthy of the Lord unto all pleasing [*that you might be pleasing to the Lord in all you do*], being fruitful in every good work [*accomplishing good with every aspect of the gospel*], and increasing in the knowledge of God;

11 Strengthened with all might [*with God's power*], according to his glorious power, unto all [*leading you to have*] patience and longsuffering [*endurance; Strong's #3115*] with joyfulness;

12 Giving thanks unto the Father, which hath made us meet [*enabled us*] to be partakers of the inheritance of the saints in light [*through the light of the gospel*]:

13 Who hath delivered us [*redeemed us*] from the power of darkness, and hath translated us [*transferred us*] into the kingdom of his dear Son:

14 In whom we have redemption through his blood [*Christ's Atonement*], even the forgiveness of sins:

15 Who is the image of the invisible God [*Christ looks just like His Father; see Hebrews 1:3; also, the Father is invisible in the sense that He can't be seen by people unless He chooses to appear to them; Stephen saw Him in Acts 7:55–56. Joseph Smith saw Him.*], the firstborn of every creature [*the firstborn spirit child of our Heavenly Father*]:

Verse 15, above, has important doctrines. First, the Savior looks just like

His Father. Apostle Bruce R. McConkie explained this as follows: "Christ is the image of the Father physically and spiritually, in person and in personality. . . They look alike; in appearance one could pass for the other. Spiritually our Lord is 'in the form of God' (Philip. 2:6); he has acquired all of the attributes of godliness in their perfection; as it is with the Father, so it is with him; he is the embodiment of justice, mercy and truth, of faith, hope and charity, of wisdom, virtue and knowledge, and of every good thing; thus he is in the likeness of and a projection of the personality of the Father." (*Doctrinal New Testament Commentary*, Vol. 3, p. 25.)

Second, the Savior is the firstborn of all Heavenly Father's spirit children. President Joseph F. Smith taught this as follows: "Among the spirit children of Elohim, the first-born was and is Jehovah, or Jesus Christ, to whom all others are juniors." (*Improvement Era*, Vol. 19, p. 940.)

16 For by him [*Christ*] were all things created, that are in heaven, and that are in earth, visible and invisible [*things that we can see with our eyes and things that we can't see with our eyes, such as other worlds in the universe, etc.*], whether they be thrones, or dominions, or principalities, or powers: all things were created by him, and for him [*for the Father; see Moses 1:33*]:

17 And he is before [*above; Strong's #4253*] all things, and by him all things consist [*are held together; see D&C 88:40–45*].

18 And he is the head of the body, the church [*Christ stands at the head of the Church*]: who is the beginning [*who has helped us from the beginning in premortal life*], the firstborn from the dead [*the first one resurrected on this earth*]; that in all things he might have the preeminence [*in order that all things might be subject to Him*].

19 For it pleased the Father [*it was the Father's will*] that in him [*Christ*] should all fulness dwell [*the fullness of the gospel would be made available to all people*];

20 And, having made peace through the blood of his cross [*having made it possible for us to be at peace through forgiveness of sin through Christ's Atonement*], by him [*through Christ*] to reconcile [*harmonize*] all things unto himself [*the Father*]; by him [*through Christ*], I say, whether they be things in earth, or things in heaven [*in other words, everything*].

21 And you, that were sometime [*in times past*] alienated [*from God*] and enemies in your mind by wicked works [*because of your wicked deeds*], yet now hath he reconciled [*Christ has atoned for your sins*]

22 In the body of his flesh through death [*by giving His life for you*], to present you holy [*sanctified*] and unblameable [*without sin*] and unreproveable [*no one can accuse you of any wrongdoing*] in his sight:

23 If ye continue in the faith grounded and settled [*on the firm foundation of the gospel*], and be not moved away from the hope of the gospel [*the exaltation which is available to you*], which ye have heard, and which was preached to every creature which is under heaven [*which has been or will be preached to everyone everywhere*]; *whereof* [*of which gospel*] I Paul am made a minister;

24 Who now rejoice in my sufferings for you [*it is a joy and a privilege to be a prisoner here in Rome because I made the gospel available to you*], and fill up that which is behind of the afflictions of Christ in my flesh [*and to continue to fill my cup with more suffering here in mortality*] for his body's sake [*for the sake of you members*], which is the church: [*The Church is symbolic of the body of Christ, to which all the "members" belong.*]

25 Whereof [*of which*] I am made a minister, according to the dispensation of God [*calling from God*] which is given to me for you, to fulfil the word of God [*to fulfill the prophecies God made that the gospel would be taken to the Gentiles; see verse 27, below*];

26 Even the mystery [*the gospel of Jesus Christ which replaces the Law of Moses*] which hath been hid from ages and from generations, but now is made manifest [*is taught and testified*] to his saints:

27 To whom God [*the Father*] would make known what is the riches of the glory of this mystery [*that which contains the fulness and glory of the gospel*] among the Gentiles; which is Christ in you, the hope of glory [*the hope for celestial glory*]:

28 Whom we preach [*we preach of Christ*], warning every man, and teaching every man in all wisdom; that we may present every man perfect in Christ Jesus [*that everyone may become perfect by following the gospel of Jesus Christ*]:

29 Whereunto I also labour [*I am also striving for perfection*], striving according to his working [*working with God's help*], which worketh in me mightily [*which influences and helps me strongly*].

# COLOSSIANS 2

Paul continues by reminding these Saints that the only safety lies in the gospel sent by the Father through His Son Jesus Christ. He counsels them to avoid sin, especially the type that gains acceptance through unrighteous traditions.

1 FOR I would that ye knew what great conflict I have for you [*I hope you know how much I have worried about you*], and for them at Laodicea [*about 11 miles north of Colosse*], and for as many as have not seen my face in the flesh [*and also for all those with whom I have not visited personally*];

2 That their hearts might be comforted, being knit together in love, and unto all riches of the full assurance of understanding, to the acknowledgement of the mystery of God, and of [*from*] the Father, and of Christ;

**JST Colossians 2:2**

2 That their hearts might be comforted, being knit together in love, and unto all riches of the full assurance of understanding, to the acknowledgment of the mystery of God and of Christ, who is of God, even the Father;

3 In whom are hid all the treasures of wisdom and knowledge. [*We can gain all the treasures of wisdom and knowledge which the Father has for us if we follow Christ and His gospel.*]

4 And this I say, lest any man should beguile [*deceive*] you with enticing [*cunning, attractive*] words.

5 For though I be absent in the flesh [*even though I am not physically present with you*], yet am I with you in the spirit, joying and beholding [*seeing and understanding*] your order [*you are trying to put your lives in order*], and the stedfastness [*firmness*] of your faith in Christ.

6 As [*since*] ye have therefore received [*accepted*] Christ Jesus the Lord, so walk ye in him [*live according to His teachings*]:

7 Rooted [*you have put down roots in the gospel*] and built up [*edified*] in him, and stablished [*established*] in the faith [*gospel*], as ye have been taught, abounding therein [*receiving many blessings*] with thanksgiving.

8 Beware lest any man spoil you through philosophy [*the philosophies of men, especially Greek philosophy for these members*] and vain deceit

[*worthless deception*], after [*according to*] the tradition of men, after the rudiments [*worldly thinking*] of the world, and not after [*according to*] Christ.

9 For in him dwelleth all the fulness of the Godhead bodily [*in Christ, all the goals and desires of the Godhead are made available to us*].

10 And ye are complete in him [*you can become exalted by following Christ*], which is the head of all principality and power [*who has risen above all things*]:

11 In whom [*through whom*] also ye are circumcised [*dedicated to God; through whom you make covenants with God; see Bible Dictionary under "Circumcision"*] with the circumcision made without hands [*through covenants which come from God, rather than being rooted in man-made philosophies*], in putting off the body of the sins of the flesh [*overcoming sins which tempt us here in mortality*] by the circumcision of [*the covenants we make with*] Christ:

12 Buried with him in baptism [*through proper baptism, we "bury" our old sinful selves; see Romans 6:4–6*], wherein also ye are risen with him [*and come forth "born again," new people*] through the faith of the operation of God [*because of your faith in the Father's plan*], who hath raised him [*Christ*] from the dead.

13 And you, being dead in your sins and the uncircumcision of your flesh [*and you, who were spiritually dead because of your sins*], hath he [*the Father*] quickened [*given new life*] together with him [*along with Christ*], having forgiven you all trespasses [*sins*];

14 Blotting out the handwriting of ordinances that was against us [*doing away with the Law of Moses*], which was contrary to us [*which could not save us*], and took it out of the way [*made it so it was no longer an obstacle to us*], nailing it to his cross [*fulfilling the Law of Moses through His crucifixion and Atonement*];

15 And having spoiled [*disarmed; Strong's #0554*] principalities and powers [*things that hold us back from salvation*], he made a shew of them openly [*He exposed them to public view*], triumphing over them in it [*through His Atonement*].

16 Let no man therefore judge you in meat, or in drink, or in respect of an holyday, or of the new moon, or of the sabbath days: [*In other words, don't worry if people criticize you for not participating in various aspects of the Law of Moses. For instance, there were special rituals and sacrifices required by the Law of Moses in conjunction with the new moon; see Bible Dictionary under "New Moon."*]

17 Which are a shadow [*a "type" or symbolic*] of things to come; but the body is of Christ [*the real purpose of the Law of Moses was fulfilled by Christ*].

The animal sacrifices and rituals contained in the Law of Moses were designed to be "shadows" and "types" or symbols which would point the mind and spirit of the children of Israel toward the coming Messiah. See Bible Dictionary under "Law of Moses."

18 Let no man beguile [*fool, deceive*] you of your reward in a voluntary humility and worshipping of angels [*and strip you of your eternal reward by talking you into worshiping "go-between" angels, "patron saints," and the like*], intruding into those things which he hath not seen [*who supposedly intervene for people between them and God whom they say can't be seen*], vainly puffed up by his fleshly mind [*foolishly caught up in philosophies hatched in their worldly minds*],

Greek philosophy had apparently worked its way into the thinking of some early converts to the Church in Colosse, or else, they still held onto it despite their baptism into Christ's gospel. At any rate, one of these philosophies was that God was

totally unapproachable by man. Thus, people needed to contact God by means of angels who were mediators between man and God. This false philosophy is described in the Institute of Religion New Testament student manual entitled *The Life and Teachings of Jesus and His Apostles*, published in 1979, p. 345, as follows: "The Gnostic philosophy held that God was not directly approachable by man but had to be contacted through a series of angelic mediators or less divine spirits. Paul is here denouncing this idea of worshiping angels, which led the Saints away from allegiance to the true head (Christ), and only true mediator between man and God."

19 And not holding [*sticking with*] the Head [*Christ; see Ephesians 4:15*], from which all the body [*the whole Church, symbolically*] by joints and bands [*sinews*] having nourishment ministered [*receive nourishment from Christ*], and knit together [*held together*], increaseth [*continues to grow*] with the increase [*nourishment and blessings*] of God.

20 Wherefore [*therefore*] if ye be dead with Christ from the rudiments of the world [*if you have put worldliness out of your lives by joining with Christ's true Church*], why, as though living in the world, are ye subject to ordinances [*why are you behaving as if you did not have the true gospel by submitting to the ordinances of the Law of Moses, or to the belief that you need patron saints, etc.*],

21 (Touch not; taste not; handle not; [*don't even touch such things!*]

22 Which all are to perish with the using) [*which will lead to spiritual death and loss of salvation for all who get involved with them*]; after the commandments and doctrines of men?

23 Which things have indeed a shew [*an appearance*] of wisdom in will worship [*in forms of worship which reflect man's will*], and humility [*and have an appearance of promoting humility*], and neglecting of the body [*and sound good to some because they teach to subdue physical needs*]; not in any honour [*which brings no honor to God*] to the satisfying of the flesh.

The JST changes verses 21–23, above, as follows:

**JST Colossians 2:21**
21 Which are after the doctrines and commandments of men, who teach you to touch not, taste not, handle not; all those things which are to perish with the using?

**JST Colossians 2:22**
22 Which things have indeed a show of wisdom in will-worship, and humility, and neglecting the body as to the satisfying the flesh, not in any honor to God.

# COLOSSIANS 3

Basically, what Paul is saying in the following verses is, "How can you even think of returning to the doctrines and philosophies of men after having heard the true gospel of Christ and repenting, being baptized, and coming forth in newness of life, with the happy prospect of living with God forever?" He then counsels them to live the gospel and avoid evil in their daily lives.

There are no JST changes for this chapter.

1 IF ye then be risen [*if you have come out of the waters of baptism*] with Christ [*thus joining Christ's church*], seek those things which are above, where Christ sitteth on the right hand of God [*seek to be guided by Him still, rather than reverting back to false philosophies, ordinances of men, and so forth*].

2 Set your affection [*loyalties and desires*] on things above, not on things on the earth.

3 For ye are dead [*you have buried your*

*old selves and lifestyles through repentance and baptism; see Romans 6:4–6*], and your life is hid [*safe*] with Christ in God [*with Christ who has returned to the Father*].

4 When Christ, who is our life [*who has opened the door for eternal life to us*], shall appear, then shall ye also appear with him in glory [*you will be with Him in celestial glory*].

5 Mortify [*do away with, kill*] therefore your members [*sins; see Romans 6:13 and JST Matthew 5:30*] which are upon the earth [*which tempt you here on earth, such as*]; fornication, uncleanness [*immoral, reckless living; Strong's #1067*], inordinate affection [*lust; Strong's #3806*], evil concupiscence [*evil, lustful desires; Strong's #1939*], and covetousness, which is idolatry [*which are forms of idol worship*]:

6 For which things' sake the wrath of God cometh on the children of disobedience [*which things bring the punishments of God upon those who disobey his commandments*]:

7 In the which ye also walked some time, when ye lived in them. [*You used to be involved in such things.*]

8 But now ye also put off all these [*but now, in addition to the sins mentioned in verse 5, you also avoid*]; anger, wrath [*rage*], malice [*desire to hurt others*], blasphemy [*evil speaking of God or sacred things*], filthy communication out of your mouth [*filthy language*]. [*In other words, you are living a much higher law now.*]

9 Lie not one to another, seeing that ye have put off the old man with his deeds [*you have repented of your previous lifestyle and sins*];

10 And have put on the new man [*you have become new, spiritually reborn*], which is renewed in knowledge after the image of him that created him [*and you are now being helped and shaped to become Christ like*]:

11 Where there is neither Greek nor Jew, circumcision [*Jew*] nor uncircumcision [*Gentile*], Barbarian, Scythian [*rough, rude, ignorant, low in social status; Strong's #4658*], bond nor free: but Christ is all, and in all. [*In other words, living the gospel makes us all equal and brings exaltation to all who become worthy, regardless of race, origins, former status, etc.*]

12 Put on therefore, as the elect of God [*as God's chosen people*], holy [*Saints*] and beloved, bowels of mercies [*tender feelings toward others; Strong's #4698*], kindness, humbleness of mind, meekness [*not quickly angered*], longsuffering [*patience; endurance in a good cause*];

13 Forbearing [*hold up, sustain; Strong's #0430*] one another, and forgiving one another, if any man have a quarrel against any: even as Christ forgave you, so also do ye [*forgive one another just like Christ forgave you of your former sins*].

14 And above all these things put on charity [*see 1 Corinthians 13*], which is the bond of perfectness [*which leads to perfect, Christ like relationships*].

15 And let the peace of [*from*] God rule in your hearts [*control your hearts*], to the which also ye are called in one body [*as members of the Church*]; and be ye thankful [*have and express gratitude; see D&C 59:21*].

16 Let the word of Christ dwell in you richly [*fill your souls*] in all wisdom; teaching and admonishing [*urging toward righteousness*] one another in psalms and hymns and spiritual songs, singing with grace [*gratitude and God's goodness; Strong's #5485*] in your hearts to the Lord.

17 And whatsoever ye do in word or deed, do all in the name of the Lord Jesus, giving thanks to God and the Father by him.

Look again at the last phrase of verse

17, above. There are a number of verses where the Prophet Joseph Smith changed the phrase "to God and the Father" to "to God, the Father" or "unto God, his Father" and such like. For example: Revelation 1:6 is changed from "unto God and his Father" to "unto God, his Father."

18 Wives, submit [*a voluntary attitude of cooperating; Strong's #5293*] yourselves unto your own husbands, as it is fit in the Lord [*appropriate in a gospel-centered home*]. [*See notes in Ephesians 5:21–33 in this study guide.*]

19 Husbands, love your wives, and be not bitter against them [*don't make them bitter by your behaviors; Strong's #4087*].

20 Children, obey your parents in all things: for this is well pleasing unto the Lord.

21 Fathers, provoke not your children to anger, lest they be discouraged [*for fear that you will break their spirit; Strong's #0120*].

22 Servants, obey in all things your masters according to the flesh [*be a good example to your masters, as followers of Christ*]; not with eyeservice [*not just when they are watching you*], as menpleasers [*trying to look good in their eyes*]; but in singleness of heart [*but sincerely*], fearing God [*living the gospel*]:

23 And whatsoever ye do, do it heartily [*energetically, wholeheartedly*], as to the Lord [*as if you were doing it for the Lord*], and not unto men;

24 Knowing that of [*from*] the Lord ye shall receive the reward of the inheritance [*you will inherit exaltation, if faithful*]: for ye serve the Lord Christ [*Christ is your real master*].

25 But he that doeth wrong shall receive for the wrong which he hath done [*if you commit wrongs against your masters, you will be punished by God*]: and there is no respect of persons [*it makes no difference who your are or what you are, God expects personal integrity and righteousness from all members of the Church*].

# COLOSSIANS 4

One particularly interesting thing about this chapter is that we discover that Luke, who wrote Luke and Acts is with Paul at the time he wrote this letter. We are also told that Luke is a physician. See verse 14. Perhaps Luke is attending to some of Paul's health needs during Paul's two years of house arrest imprisonment in Rome.

There are no JST changes for this chapter.

1 MASTERS [*you owners of slaves or servants who are members of the Church*], give unto your servants that which is just and equal; knowing that ye also have a Master in heaven [*knowing that God is your Master*].

It was common in the days of Paul for people to own slaves. It was also common for people to sell themselves to wealthier people for a time in order to pay debts or to improve their status and opportunities in life.

2 Continue in prayer, and watch in the same with thanksgiving [*and express gratitude to God in your prayers*];

3 Withal [*at the same time; Strong's #0260*] praying also for us, that God would open unto us a door of utterance [*the opportunity to continue to preach*], to speak the mystery of Christ [*the gospel, which is a mystery to all who do not know about Christ*], for which I am also in bonds [*which is the cause of my being in prison here in Rome*]:

The phrase "for which I am also in bonds" in verse 3, above, could also mean "to whom I am obligated because of His bounteous blessings to me."

4 That I may make it [*the gospel*] manifest, as I ought to speak [*so that I can preach the gospel as I ought to*].

5 Walk in wisdom toward them that are without [*behave wisely toward those who are not members of the Church*], redeeming the time [*making the best of every opportunity to teach them*].

6 Let your speech [*conversations with nonmembers*] be alway [*always*] with grace [*with the help of God*], seasoned with salt [*making everything go better*], that ye may know [*be inspired as to*] how ye ought to answer every man.

7 All my state shall Tychicus declare unto you [*Tychicus will give you more details about conditions here in Rome*], who is a beloved brother, and a faithful minister and fellowservant in the Lord:

8 Whom I have sent unto you for the same purpose, that he might know your estate [*that he might see how things are going there in Colosse with you*], and comfort your hearts;

9 With Onesimus [*Tychicus is traveling with Onesimus—see Philemon for information about Onesimus*], a faithful and beloved brother, who is one of you [*who is from your city*]. They shall make known unto you all things which are done here [*they will fill you in with all the details of what is happening here*].

10 Aristarchus my fellowprisoner saluteth [*greets*] you, and Marcus, sister's son to Barnabas, (touching whom ye received commandments [*you already received instructions about him*]: if he come unto you, receive [*welcome*] him;)

In the next verse, Paul mentions a Jewish member of the Church, named Jesus. Jesus was a common name among the Jews at the time. See Bible Dictionary under the second listing for "Jesus."

11 And Jesus, which [*who*] is called Justus, who are of the circumcision [*who are Jewish converts*]. These only are my fellowworkers unto the kingdom of God, which have been a comfort unto me [*these are the only Jewish converts who have been helping me here*].

12 Epaphras, who is one of you [*who is from your city*], a servant of Christ, saluteth [*greets*] you, always labouring fervently for you in prayers [*he constantly prays for you with all his heart*], that ye may stand perfect [*that you will be spiritually mature; Strong's #5046*] and complete in all the will of God [*paying attention to all the details of living the gospel*].

13 For I bear him record [*I am his witness*], that he hath a great zeal [*that he works very hard*] for you, and them that are in Laodicea, and them in Hierapolis [*cities a few miles northwest of Colosse*].

14 Luke, the beloved physician, and Demas, greet you.

15 Salute the brethren which are in Laodicea, and Nymphas [*a wealthy and energetic member of the Church in Laodicea; Strong's #3564*], and the church which is in his house [*the members in his household*].

16 And when this epistle [*letter*] is read among you [*when you receive this letter*], cause that it be read also in the church of the Laodiceans [*in the Laodicean ward*]; and that ye likewise read the epistle from Laodicea [*and make sure that you read the letter the Laodicean members wrote*].

17 And say to Archippus [*a member of the Church in Colosse, perhaps a member of Philemon's family: see Philemon 1:2; Strong's #0751*], Take heed to the ministry [*pay attention to the calling*] which thou hast received in the Lord, that thou fulfil it.

18 The salutation by the hand of me Paul [*I personally greet you in my own handwriting*]. Remember my bonds [*don't forget me*]. Grace be with you. Amen.

# THE FIRST EPISTLE OF PAUL THE APOSTLE TO THE THESSALONIANS

Just a reminder, as mentioned earlier, that Paul's epistles (letters) are arranged in the Bible according to length rather than in chronological order (see Bible Dictionary under "Pauline Epistles"). The exception is his letter to the Hebrews, which was placed at the end of his letters because there was disagreement among scholars as to whether or not Paul wrote it. We know he did write it because the Prophet Joseph Smith informed us that he did (see *Teachings of the Prophet Joseph Smith*, p. 59).

Paul's first and second letters to the Thessalonian members of the Church were written around AD 50–52 from Corinth during Paul's second missionary journey. He and his companion missionaries had recently been driven out of Thessalonica, in what is known today as northeastern Greece, by an angry mob of Jews. See Acts 17:1–15. After they were driven out, they journeyed to Berea, then to Athens and from there to Corinth, in southern Greece, where they were met by Silas and Timothy. Timothy was then sent back to Thessalonica to check on conditions in the ward or branch there and to help them as relatively new members of the Church, most of whom appear to have been Gentile converts rather than Jewish converts. After spending some time among them, Timothy returned to Corinth and reported conditions among the Thessalonian members to Paul. With this information plus Paul's own experience with these Saints, he wrote First and Second Thessalonians to them. These were the first letters written by Paul which are included in our New Testament.

## FIRST THESSALONIANS 1

Paul's relief and gratitude upon Timothy's safe return from visiting the Saints in Thessalonica, plus his gratitude for the sincere efforts of the relatively new converts there to live the gospel, are very evident in this chapter.

1 PAUL, and Silvanus [*another form of the name "Silas," see Acts 15:32–34, a missionary companion of Paul on his second missionary journey, Acts 15:40*], and Timotheus [*Timothy*], unto the church [*ward or branch*] of the Thessalonians which is in God the Father and in the Lord Jesus Christ: Grace be unto you, and peace, from God our Father, and the Lord Jesus Christ.

> **JST 1 Thessalonians 1:1**
> 1 Paul, and Silvanus, and Timotheus, servants of God the Father and the Lord Jesus Christ, unto the church of the Thessalonians; grace unto you, and peace from God our Father, and the Lord Jesus Christ.

2 We give thanks to God always for you all, making mention of [*remembering*] you in our prayers;

> **JST 1 Thessalonians 1:2**
> 2 We give thanks always, making mention of you all, in our prayers to God for you.

3 Remembering without ceasing your work of faith, and labour of love, and patience of hope in our Lord Jesus Christ, in the sight of God and our Father [*who is our Father*];

4 Knowing, brethren beloved, your election of God. [*In other words, you know that you have been chosen and set apart, because of your baptism, to be a peculiar people and to forsake the world; compare with D&C 53:1–2.*]

5 For our gospel came not unto you in word only [*you didn't just hear the gospel from us with your ears*], but also in power, and in the Holy Ghost, and in much assurance [*but the Holy Ghost bore powerful witness to you*]; as ye know what manner of men we were among you for your sake.

6 And ye became followers of us, and of the Lord, having received the word [*gospel*] in much affliction [*persecution*], with joy of [*from*] the Holy Ghost:

7 So that ye were ensamples [*examples*] to all that believe in Macedonia [*northern Greece today*] and Achaia [*central and southern Greece today*].

8 For from you sounded [*spread*] out the word of the Lord not only in Macedonia and Achaia, but also in every place your faith to God-ward is spread abroad; so that we need not to speak any thing [*we don't have any need to comment on it*].

**JST 1 Thessalonians 1:8**

8 For from you sounded out the word of the Lord not only in Macedonia and Achaia, but also in every place your faith toward God is spread abroad; so that we need not to speak anything.

9 For they themselves [*your good example and spreading of the gospel*] shew [*show*] of us what manner of entering in we had unto you [*what kind of reception you gave us when we came to you*], and how ye turned to God [*Heavenly Father*] from idols to serve the living and true God;

Often, Heavenly Father is referred to in scripture as "the living God." This is obvious to us, but in a culture of idol worship, where people rebelliously or foolishly or unknowingly worship "dead gods" made of wood and stone, the phrase "living God" is a major doctrinal statement.

10 And to wait for his Son from heaven [*and to prepare for the Second Coming; Acts 1:11*], whom he [*the Father*] raised from the dead [*resurrected*], even Jesus, which delivered us from the wrath to come [*whose gospel makes it possible for us to escape the punishments of God which will come upon the wicked*].

It may seem like a bit of a stretch for these Saints to prepare for the Second Coming of Christ, which, for them, is a minimum of approximately 2000 years in the future. But, D&C 88:97–98 reminds us that all the righteous dead, from after Christ's resurrection to the Second Coming, will be privileged to be resurrected and caught up to join Him in His Second Coming, and actually descend to the earth with Him at that time. Thus, these Saints can prepare during their lifetime to be part of that group.

## FIRST THESSALONIANS 2

In this chapter, Paul discusses the missionary work he and his companions have done and some of the persecutions they endured in order to do it. Among other things, he discusses how true missionaries go about the work, using himself and his companions as examples.

There are no JST changes for this chapter.

1 FOR yourselves, brethren, know our entrance in unto you [*our coming to you*], that it was not in vain:

2 But even after that we had suffered

before [*previously*], and were shamefully entreated [*treated outrageously; Strong's #5195*], as ye know, at Philippi [*where Paul and Silas were beaten and placed in prison in stocks; Acts 16:19–24*], we were bold [*we were made bold by our confidence*] in our God to speak unto you the gospel of God with much contention [*in spite of much opposition*].

3 For our exhortation [*teaching*] was not of deceit [*based on deception*], nor of uncleanness [*unworthiness*], nor in guile [*ulterior motives*]:

4 But as we were allowed of God to be put in trust with the gospel [*since we were entrusted by God with the gospel*], even so we speak; not as pleasing men, but God [*we do not teach things pleasing to worldly people, rather, we speak the words of God*], which trieth our hearts [*who examines our hearts and motives*].

5 For neither at any time used we flattering words [*we didn't use words which would please worldly people*], as ye know, nor a cloke of covetousness [*nor were we secretly covering up greed for gain and power*]; God is witness [*God is our witness*]:

6 Nor of men sought we glory [*neither did we seek for the praise of men*], neither of you, nor yet of others, when we might have been burdensome, as the apostles of Christ [*we could have come across pretty strong as Apostles*].

7 But we were gentle among you, even as a nurse cherisheth her children [*cherishes little children placed in her care*]:

8 So being affectionately desirous of you [*we developed such tender feelings for you*], we were willing to have imparted unto you, not the gospel of God only [*that we didn't just give you the gospel*], but also our own souls, because ye were dear unto us.

9 For ye remember, brethren, our labour and travail [*how hard we worked*]: for labouring night and day, because we would not be chargeable unto any of you [*we worked night and day so we would not be a burden to you*], we preached unto you the gospel of God.

10 Ye are witnesses, and God also, how holily [*holy*] and justly [*living the gospel exactly*] and unblameably [*giving no reason for criticism*] we behaved ourselves among you that believe:

11 As ye know how we exhorted and comforted and charged [*instructed*] every one of you, as a father doth his children,

12 That ye would walk [*live*] worthy of God, who hath called you unto his kingdom and glory.

13 For this cause also thank we God without ceasing, because, when ye received the word of God which ye heard of [*from*] us, ye received [*accepted*] it not as the word of men [*not as the philosophies of men*], but as it is in truth [*as it really is*], the word of God, which effectually worketh also [*which works very effectively*] in you that believe.

14 For ye, brethren, became followers of the churches of God which in Judæa are in Christ Jesus [*you followed in the footsteps of members of the Church in the wards and branches in Judea who follow Jesus Christ*]: for ye also have suffered like things of your own countrymen [*you have suffered similar persecutions by your fellow citizens*], even as they [*the members in Judea*] have of [*through*] the Jews:

15 Who both killed [*who killed both*] the Lord Jesus, and their own prophets, and have persecuted us; and they [*the Jews who persecute Christians*] please not God, and are contrary [*hostile; Strong's #1727*] to all men [*everyone*]:

16 Forbidding us to speak [*teach the gospel*] to the Gentiles that they might be saved, to fill up their sins alway [*the Jews seem to want to constantly add more sins upon their own heads*]:

for the wrath [*punishment of God*] is come upon them to the uttermost [*to the extreme*].

17 But we, brethren, being taken from you [*away from you*] for a short time in presence [*in physical presence*], not in heart, endeavoured the more abundantly [*tried all the more*] to see your face with great desire [*to visit you and see you to satisfy the desire of our hearts*].

18 Wherefore we would have come unto you, even I Paul, once and again [*repeatedly*]; but Satan hindered [*stopped*] us.

19 For what is our hope, or joy, or crown of rejoicing [*what is the source of so much joy and happiness for us*]? [*Answer: You are!*] Are not even ye in the presence of our Lord Jesus Christ at his coming? [*We have confidence that you will be with the Savior at His Second Coming.*]

> Sometimes people read the last phrase of verse 19, above, and wonder why Paul expected the Second Coming clear back then. But if we correctly understand from Paul's writings in general, that he understood the plan of salvation very well, we might do well to think that he was saying something else. We know from D&C 88:96–98 that the righteous, living and dead, will accompany the Savior as He comes for the Second Coming. Thus, what Paul may well be saying is, in effect, that the righteous members of the Church in Thessalonica should plan on coming with the Savior, at the time when He returns to earth in the last days to preside during the Millennium.

20 For ye are our glory and joy.

## FIRST THESSALONIANS 3

Paul is complimentary to these members as he speaks of their faith and charity. He counsels them to strive to increase in love for one another and to get the gospel deep in their hearts.

There are no JST changes for this chapter.

1 WHEREFORE [*so*] when we could no longer forbear [*when we could stand it no longer*], we thought it good [*best*] to be left at Athens alone;

> Just a reminder that some angry Jews in Thessalonica assembled a mob to oppose Paul and his companions there (Acts 17:1–9), and, as a result, faithful members quickly helped Paul and Silas escape by sending them to Berea (a few miles south of Thessalonica) that night (Acts 17:10.) However, the Jews in Thessalonica soon found out that Paul and Silas were preaching the gospel successfully in Berea, and so they rushed to that city and stirred up the people there (Acts 17:13). Consequently, worried members quickly sent Paul on his way toward Athens, while Silas and Timothy remained in Berea (Acts 17:14–15). Ultimately, Silas and Timothy caught up with Paul in Corinth, and Paul sent Timothy back to check on conditions among the Saints at Thessalonica.

2 And sent Timotheus, our brother, and minister of God, and our fellowlabourer in the gospel of Christ, to establish you [*to strengthen you in the gospel*], and to comfort you concerning your faith:

3 That no man should be moved [*disturbed or discouraged*] by these afflictions: for yourselves know that we are appointed thereunto. [*In other words, Paul does not want the members in Thessalonica and the surrounding area to lose their testimonies or become discouraged because of the persecutions Paul and his associates are going through.*]

4 For verily, when we were with you, we told you before [*ahead of time*] that we should [*would*] suffer tribulation [*trials and troubles*]; even as it came to pass

[*just as it has happened*], and ye know.

5 For this cause [*this is the reason*], when I could no longer forbear [*when I couldn't stand it any longer*], I sent to know your faith [*I sent Timothy to you to find out how your faith was holding up*], lest by some means [*for fear that in some way*] the tempter [*the devil*] have tempted you [*might have succeeded in tempting you to quit the Church*], and our labour be in vain [*and thus our work among you would have been ineffective*].

6 But now when Timotheus came from you unto us [*but now that Timothy has returned from visiting you*], and brought us good tidings [*news*] of your faith and charity, and that ye have good remembrance of us always [*and that you have pleasant memories of us*], desiring greatly to see us [*and that you would love to see us again*], as we also to see you [*as we would love to see you again*]:

7 Therefore, brethren, we were comforted over you in all our affliction and distress by your faith [*we were comforted to the point that we didn't even think of our own troubles when we heard of your faithfulness*]:

8 For now we live, if ye stand fast in the Lord [*you bring new life and energy to us if you remain faithful to the Lord*].

9 For what thanks can we render to God again [*how could we possibly express more gratitude to God*] for you, for all the joy wherewith we joy for your sakes before our God [*because of all the joy you have brought to us*];

10 Night and day praying exceedingly that we might see your face [*we are constantly praying that we might see you again*], and might perfect that which is lacking in your faith [*and fill in some weak spots in your understanding of the gospel*]?

11 Now God himself and [*who is*] our Father, and our Lord Jesus Christ, direct our way unto you [*guide us toward you*].

12 And the Lord make you to increase and abound [*flourish*] in love one toward another, and toward all men, even as we do toward you:

13 To the end [*for the purpose that*] he may stablish [*establish*] your hearts unblameable [*to become pure and free from sin*] in holiness before God, even our Father, at the coming of our Lord Jesus Christ with all his saints. [*See D&C 88:96–98.*]

# FIRST THESSALONIANS 4

In this chapter, as is the case with other letters of Paul to various congregations of the Church in other cities, this great Apostle to the Gentiles will encourage these members to live righteously and will warn them against getting caught up in sins accepted by the culture in which they lived. We face similar threats to our living the gospel today. Among other doctrines he teaches them, he will give some detail about the Second Coming.

1 FURTHERMORE [*in addition*] then we beseech [*ask*] you, brethren, and exhort [*urge*] you by the Lord Jesus, that as ye have received of us how ye ought to walk and to please God [*since you accepted the gospel from us*], so ye would abound more and more [*that you keep increasing in your ability to live it more and more faithfully*].

2 For ye know what commandments we gave you by [*from*] the Lord Jesus.

3 For this is the will of God, even your sanctification [*your salvation depends on this*], that ye should abstain from fornication [*avoid sexual immorality*]:

One of the serious problems among

the Thessalonian converts came as a result of the culture in which they lived. Sexual immorality, in many varieties, was commonplace. Thus, many new converts had a difficult time seeing what was so wrong with it. If they had come from a Jewish background, they would have at least had the Law of Moses, including the Ten Commandments and would have been trained and warned from the time they were young that any sexual relations, including intercourse, outside of marriage was wrong, being forbidden by God. This would have included homosexuality also (see Leviticus 20:13; Bible Dictionary under "Homosexuality"). Most of the converts in Thessalonica were Gentiles and had no such upbringing or background. Thus, Paul must often emphasize the law of chastity among them.

4 That every one of you should know how to possess his vessel [*body*] in sanctification and honour; [*In other words, every one of you should know how to keep your body pure and chaste.*]

5 Not in the lust of concupiscence [*not getting involved in sexual immorality*], even as [*like*] the Gentiles which know not God:

6 That no man go beyond [*take advantage of*] and defraud [*wrong*] his brother in any matter: because that the Lord is the avenger of all such [*because the Lord will punish those who do*], as we also have forewarned [*warned*] you and testified.

7 For God hath not called us unto uncleanness [*to remain unclean*], but unto holiness [*but to become holy, to become Saints*].

8 He therefore that despiseth [*rejects this counsel*], despiseth not man, but God [*is not rejecting us but is rejecting God*], who hath also given unto us his holy Spirit.

9 But as touching [*now, speaking of*] brotherly love ye need not that I write unto you [*you don't need me to say anything to you about it*]: for ye yourselves are taught of [*by*] God to love one another.

10 And indeed ye do it toward all the brethren which are in all Macedonia [*northern Greece today*]: but we beseech [*urge*] you, brethren, that ye increase more and more [*develop more and more brotherly love*];

11 And that ye study to be quiet [*learn how to live quiet, peaceful lives*], and to do your own business [*and to mind your own business*], and to work with your own hands [*and to provide for your own living*], as we commanded [*instructed*] you;

12 That ye may walk honestly toward them that are without [*that you may earn the respect of nonmembers*], and that ye may have lack of nothing [*and that you may be self-reliant*].

Paul will now teach these new members more about the resurrection of the righteous.

13 But I would not have you to be ignorant, brethren, concerning them which are asleep [*those who have died*], that ye sorrow not [*don't keep mourning for them*], even as others which have no hope [*like others do who don't believe as we do*].

14 For if we believe that Jesus died and rose again, even so them also which sleep in Jesus [*those who died who were faithful to Jesus*] will God [*the Father*] bring [*to heaven*] with him [*Christ*].

We definitely need the help of the JST to understand verse 15, next. We will use **bold** to point out the main changes.

15 For this we say unto you by the word of the Lord [*this is what the Lord says*], that **we** which are alive and remain unto the coming of the Lord shall not prevent [*have any advantage over*] them **which are asleep** [*have died already*].

**JST 1 Thessalonians 4:15**
15 For this we say unto you by the word of the Lord, that they [*the righteous*] who are alive at the coming of the Lord, shall not prevent them [*have any advantage over those*] who remain [*in their graves*] unto [*until*] the coming of the Lord, who are asleep [*who are dead*].

The word "prevent" in verse 15, above, is key in understanding the verse. "Prevent" is an Old English word which has changed meaning over time. It originally meant "precede" or "to be first" or "to have an advantage over" or "to progress over." See 1 Thessalonians 4:15, footnote c. For another example of how the word "prevent" is used in King James English, see Matthew 17:25, including footnote a, where Peter was coming into the house to ask the Savior a question about paying the temple tax, but Jesus spoke to him first ("Jesus prevented him"), meaning Jesus "preceded" him, in other words, spoke to him before he even had a chance to ask his question.

16 For the Lord [*Christ*] himself shall descend from heaven [*at the Second Coming*] with a shout, with the voice of the archangel, and with the trump of God: and the dead in Christ [*the righteous dead*] shall rise [*be resurrected*] first:

The JST changes made to verse 17, next, are essential for correct understanding. This verse needs to be read along with JST verse 15, above, for correct understanding.

17 Then **we** which are alive and remain shall be caught up together with them in the clouds, to meet the Lord in the air: and so shall we ever be with the Lord.

**JST 1 Thessalonians 4:17**
17 Then they who are alive, shall be caught up together into the clouds with them who remain [*who are dead and in the grave*], to meet the Lord in the air; and so shall we be ever with the Lord.

Without the JST, above, it sounds like Paul is teaching that the Second Coming will be in his day. You may wish to read D&C 88:96–98, where the same doctrine is taught.

18 Wherefore [*therefore*] comfort one another with these words.

# FIRST THESSALONIANS 5

In this chapter, Paul gives a few more details about the Second Coming and counsels the members to live as Saints (meaning "holy ones"). He warns them not to get so comfortable that they start slipping in living the gospel. He counsels them to arm themselves with the gospel as protection against the damaging effects of sin and to strengthen each other.

1 BUT of the times and the seasons [*the signs of the times which will indicate the approximate time of the Second Coming*], brethren, ye have no need that I write unto you.

2 For yourselves know perfectly that the day of the Lord [*the Second Coming which ushers in the Millennium*] so cometh as a thief in the night [*the wicked will be caught off guard, see D&C 106:4, but the righteous will not, see verse 4, below, as well as D&C 106:5*].

3 For when they [*the wicked*] shall say, Peace and safety [*when they claim that there is peace and safety in wickedness*]; then sudden destruction cometh upon them, as travail [*labor pains come*] upon a woman with child [*who is expecting a baby*]; and they shall not escape [*the destruction at the Second Coming*].

The imagery of a woman in labor, which Paul uses to describe the time of the Second Coming is very fitting. A woman who is expecting knows the approximate timing of the birth of her

child, because she knows "the times and seasons" or the "signs of the times" that indicate that the birth is close. But she doesn't know exactly when it will occur. So it is with the Second Coming. There are many "signs of the times" which will indicate to the righteous who pay attention to them that the Savior's coming is getting close, but no one knows the exact time. See Matthew 24:36. Also, once the labor pains begin, there is no way in Paul's day to avoid the birth of the baby. So also there is no way for the wicked to escape destruction, once the Second Coming starts.

4 But ye, brethren, are not in darkness [*spiritual darkness, wickedness*], that that day [*the Second Coming*] should overtake you as a thief [*that you would be caught off guard; D&C 106:5*] .

5 Ye are all the children of light [*you are the righteous, who have the light and revelations of the gospel*], and the children of the day: we are not of the night, nor of darkness.

6 Therefore let us not sleep [*fall into a false sense of security*], as do others; but let us watch and be sober [*and be serious about the gospel*].

Next, Paul uses the habits of people as a comparison between the wicked and foolish, and the righteous. In effect, he says that people who don't study about and live the gospel, live in spiritual darkness and are asleep. He also says, in effect, that people who don't take the gospel seriously and choose to "party" instead, do it in the night, symbolic of doing foolish and evil deeds in spiritual darkness.

7 For they that sleep sleep in the night; and they that be drunken are drunken in the night.

8 But let us, who are of the day [*who live in the light of the gospel*], be sober [*be serious-minded*], putting on the breastplate [*spiritual protection; Ephesians 6:11–18*] of faith and love; and for an helmet [*spiritual protection*], the hope [*anticipation*] of salvation.

9 For God hath not appointed us to wrath [*be punished*], but to obtain salvation by [*through*] our Lord Jesus Christ,

10 Who died for us, that, whether we wake or sleep [*live or die*], we should live together with him [*in celestial glory*].

11 Wherefore comfort yourselves together [*comfort one another*], and edify [*strengthen and build up in the gospel*] one another, even as also ye do [*as you have already been doing*].

12 And we beseech [*urge*] you, brethren, to know [*pay attention to; Strong's #1492*] them which labour among you, and are over you [*who are your leaders*] in the Lord [*called of God*], and admonish you;

13 And to esteem [*respect*] them very highly in love for their work's sake [*because of the work they do in your behalf*]. And be at peace among yourselves [*avoid contention*].

14 Now we exhort [*warn*] you, brethren, warn them that are unruly [*who refuse to work; see 2 Thessalonians 3:11*], comfort [*encourage*] the feebleminded [*those who are discouraged; see 1 Thessalonians 5:14, footnote d*], support the weak [*those who are spiritually weak; 1 Thessalonians 5:14, footnote f*], be patient toward all men.

15 See that none render evil for evil [*get revenge*] unto any man; but ever follow that which is good, both among yourselves, and to all men.

16 Rejoice evermore.

17 Pray without ceasing.

18 In every thing give thanks [*express gratitude in all things; see D&C 59:21*]: for this is the will of God [*the Father*] in Christ Jesus concerning you.

19 Quench not the Spirit [*don't hold back in following the Holy Ghost*].

20 Despise not [*don't ignore or ridicule; Strong's #1848*] prophesyings [*the word

*of God, including prophecies; Strong's #4394*].

Verses 21 and 22, next, are quoted quite often in sermons and classes in the Church.

21 Prove all things [*test everything in comparison to the word of God*]; hold fast that which is good.

22 Abstain [*avoid*] from all appearance of [*kinds of; see 1 Thessalonians 5:22, footnote b*] evil.

23 And the very God of peace sanctify you wholly [*cleanse you from all sin*]; and I pray God your whole spirit and soul and body be preserved blameless unto the coming of our Lord Jesus Christ [*so that you will be worthy to come with the Savior at His Second Coming; see D&C 88:97–98*].

24 Faithful is he [*Christ*] that calleth you [*to come unto him*], who also will do it [*Christ is capable of making you clean and can and will do it if you live worthily*].

25 Brethren, pray for us.

26 Greet all the brethren with an holy kiss.

**JST 1 Thessalonians 5:26**

26 Greet all the brethren with a holy salutation.

27 I charge [*instruct*] you by the Lord [*in the name of the Lord*] that this epistle be read unto all the holy brethren [*to all the Saints*].

Remember that the word "holy" as used in verse 27, above, is the same as the word "saint" in Greek which essentially means "holy ones." See Strong's *Exhaustive Concordance of the Bible*, #0040.

28 The grace of our Lord Jesus Christ be with you. Amen.

# THE SECOND EPISTLE OF PAUL THE APOSTLE TO THE THESSALONIANS

As mentioned in the note at the beginning of First Thessalonians, this letter was written by Paul from Corinth, probably between AD 50–52.

## SECOND THESSALONIANS 1

In this chapter, Paul continues teaching these members in Thessalonica about the Second Coming of Jesus Christ. He reminds them that the day of the Savior's coming will not be pleasant for the wicked.

1 PAUL, and Silvanus [*Silas*], and Timotheus [*Timothy*], unto the church [*ward or branch*] of the Thessalonians in God our Father and the Lord Jesus Christ:

> **JST 2 Thessalonians 1:1**
> 1 Paul, and Sylvanus, and Timotheus, the servants of God the Father and our Lord Jesus Christ, unto the church of the Thessalonians;

2 Grace unto you, and peace, from God our Father and the Lord Jesus Christ.

3 We are bound [*obligated*] to thank God always for you, brethren, as it is meet [*appropriate, Strong's #0514*], because that your faith groweth exceedingly, and the charity of every one of you all toward each other aboundeth [*is abundant*];

4 So that we ourselves glory in you in the churches of God [*we have bragged about you in many other wards and branches*] for [*because of*] your patience and faith in all your persecutions and tribulations that ye endure:

5 Which is a manifest token of the righteous judgment of God [*which shows obviously that you have God's approval*], that ye may be counted worthy of the kingdom of God [*the celestial kingdom*], for which ye also suffer [*for which you are going through persecutions*]:

6 Seeing it is a righteous thing with God to recompense [*pay back*] tribulation [*punishments*] to them that trouble you; [*In other words, God will punish those who persecute you.*]

7 And to you who are troubled rest with us [*in God's kingdom*], when the Lord Jesus shall be revealed from heaven [*at the Second Coming*] with his mighty angels,

8 In flaming fire [*with His full glory*] taking vengeance on them that know not God [*punishing the wicked*], and that obey not the gospel of our Lord Jesus Christ:

9 Who shall be punished with everlasting destruction from the presence of the Lord, and from the glory of his power [*In other words, the glory of the Lord will destroy the wicked at the Second Coming; see D&C 5:19; 2 Nephi 12:10, 19, 21.*]

> **JST 2 Thessalonians 1:9**
> 9 Who shall be punished with destruction from the presence of the Lord, and from the glory of his everlasting power;

10 When he [*Christ*] shall come to be glorified in [*praised and adored*

*by; Strong's #1740*] his saints, and to be admired in all them that believe [*because our testimony among you was believed*] in that day [*at the time of the Second Coming and the Millennium*].

11 Wherefore also we pray always for you, that our God would count you worthy of this calling [*being worthy to join with Christ at the time of His Second Coming*], and fulfil all the good pleasure of his goodness [*and give you all the rewards He has in store for you, according to His will*], and the work of faith with power [*because of your faith and the power of God that is in you*]:

12 That the name of our Lord Jesus Christ may be glorified in you [*praised by others because of your faithfulness*], and ye in him [*and that you might be praised by Him*], according to the grace of our God [*the Father*] and the Lord Jesus Christ.

## SECOND THESSALONIANS 2

It appears that some of the Saints in Thessalonica had come to believe that the Second Coming of the Savior was very near and would come in their lifetime. Paul tells them that they should not believe such a thing, no matter what the source of their information. He informs them that there will be an apostasy from the Church before the Second Coming. We often use verses 1–3 in teaching investigators that the Great Apostasy (the falling away from the Church), as it is called, was prophesied by the Apostles in the New Testament. Thus it was necessary that there be a restoration of the gospel, which the Lord accomplished through the Prophet Joseph Smith, beginning with the First Vision in the spring of 1820.

1 NOW we beseech [*urge*] you, brethren, by the coming of our Lord Jesus Christ, and by our gathering together unto him,

2 That ye be not soon shaken in mind [*that you not begin to believe false doctrines*], or be troubled, neither by spirit, nor by word [*no matter what anyone says*], nor by letter as from us, as that the day of Christ is at hand [*that the Second Coming is about to take place*].

**JST 2 Thessalonians 2:2**

2 That ye be not soon shaken in mind, or be troubled by letter, except ye receive it from us; neither by spirit, nor by word, as that the day of Christ is at hand.

3 Let no man deceive you [*don't let anyone fool you*] by any means: for that day [*the Second Coming*] shall not come, except there come a falling away [*apostasy*] first, and that man of sin [*the devil*] be revealed, the son of perdition [*Satan*];

**JST 2 Thessalonians 2:3**

3 Let no man deceive you by any means; for there shall come a falling away first, and that man of sin be revealed, the son of perdition;

4 Who opposeth [*who opposes everything from God*] and exalteth himself [*lifts himself up in pride*] above all that is called God [*that has anything to do with God*], or that is worshipped; so that he as God sitteth in the temple of God [*Satan tries to take over God's position; compare with Isaiah 14:12–14*], shewing himself [*trying to make people believe*] that he is God.

5 Remember ye not, that, when I was yet with you, I told you these things?

6 And now ye know what withholdeth [*what you should beware of; Strong's #2722*] that he [*Satan*] might be revealed in his time [*will be exposed for what he is, when the timing is right*].

7 For the mystery of iniquity doth already work [*Satan's deception about the timing of the Second Coming is*

*already going around*]: only he who now letteth will let, until he be taken out of the way.

**JST 2 Thessalonians 2:7**
7 For the mystery of iniquity doth already work, and he [*Satan*] it is who now worketh, and Christ suffereth [*allows*] him to work, until the time is fulfilled that he shall be taken out of the way [*for 1,000 years at the Second Coming, see D&C 101:28, as well as permanently, after the final battle at the end of the Millennium, see D&C 88:11–15*].

8 And then shall that Wicked [*Satan*] be revealed [*exposed*], whom the Lord shall consume [*overpower*] with the spirit of his mouth [*with His authority*], and shall destroy with the brightness of his coming [*with His glory*]:

**JST 2 Thessalonians 2:8**
8 And then shall that wicked one be revealed, whom the Lord shall consume with the spirit of his mouth, and shall destroy with the brightness of his coming.

9 Even him, whose coming is after the working of Satan with all power and signs and lying wonders,

**JST 2 Thessalonians 2:9**
9 Yea, the Lord, even Jesus, whose coming is not until after there cometh a falling away [*after the prophesied apostasy*], by the working of Satan with all power, and signs and lying wonders,

10 And with all deceivableness of unrighteousness [*with every conceivable form of wickedness*] in them that perish [*in those who will be destroyed at the Second Coming*]; because they received not [*they would not accept*] the love of the truth, that they might be saved.

11 And for this cause [*because they deliberately chose wickedness*] God shall send them strong delusion [*God allows Satan to deceive them*], that they should believe a lie:

12 That they all might be damned [*stopped from progressing toward heaven*] who believed not the truth, but had pleasure in unrighteousness.

13 But we are bound to [*we must*] give thanks alway [*always*] to God for you, brethren beloved of the Lord, because God hath from the beginning [*from the time you were converted and baptized*] chosen you to [*toward*] salvation through sanctification of the Spirit [*has given you the help of the Holy Ghost to lead you toward sanctification (being worthy to dwell in celestial glory)*] and belief of the truth [*because of your accepting the truth of the gospel*]:

14 Whereunto he called you by our gospel [*the Father called you to come unto Him through the gospel we preached to you*], to the obtaining of the glory of our Lord Jesus Christ [*so that you can obtain exaltation in the celestial kingdom*].

15 Therefore, brethren, stand fast [*be firm and faithful*], and hold the traditions [*of living the gospel*] which ye have been taught, whether by word [*what we have said*], or our epistle [*letter*].

16 Now our Lord Jesus Christ himself, and God, even our Father, which hath loved us, and hath given us everlasting consolation and good hope through grace,

17 Comfort your hearts, and stablish you [*establish; help you to become strong and faithful*] in every good word and work.

## SECOND THESSALONIANS 3

There are no JST changes for this chapter.

1 FINALLY, brethren, pray for us, that the word of the Lord may have free course [*may spread freely and rapidly;*

*see 2 Thessalonians 3:1, footnote a*], and be glorified [*praised by others*], even as it is with you:

2 And that we may be delivered from unreasonable and wicked men [*men who are harmful, way off base, Strong's #0824*]: for all men have not faith [*in Christ*].

3 But the Lord is faithful, who shall stablish [*strengthen, Strong's #4741*] you, and keep you from evil [*the evil one, the devil; see 2 Thessalonians 3:3, footnote a in our Bible*].

4 And we have confidence in the Lord touching you [*as regarding you*] that ye both do and will do the things which we command you.

5 And the Lord [*may the Lord*] direct your hearts into the love of God [*"to serve him with all your heart and with all your soul" Deuteronomy 11:13*], and into the patient waiting for Christ [*into being steadfast and loyal to Christ; Strong's #5281*].

6 Now we command you, brethren, in the name of our Lord Jesus Christ, that ye withdraw yourselves from every brother that walketh disorderly [*who does not try to live the gospel, which includes being lazy and working to provide for his own needs, and who causes contention and divisiveness among you; see Romans 16:17*], and not after the tradition [*teachings; tradition of following Christ*] which he received of [*from*] us.

7 For yourselves know how ye ought to follow us [*you ought to follow our example*]: for we behaved not ourselves disorderly [*we did not neglect our duty; we worked to provide for ourselves; Strong's #0812*] among you;

The word "disorderly" as used in verses 7 and 8 above, often means "laziness," "idleness," "unwillingness to work," etc., and thus, Paul is warning his people against the dole, inappropriate use of welfare funds, etc. This is evident when we read verses 10–12, below.

8 Neither did we eat any man's bread for nought; but wrought with labour and travail night and day, that we might not be chargeable to any of you [*we didn't ask for handouts, rather we worked day and night to pay our own way so that we would not be a burden to any of you*]:

9 Not because we have not power [*not that we couldn't justifiably accept donations*], but to make ourselves an ensample [*example*] unto you to follow us.

10 For even when we were with you, this we commanded you, that if any would not work, neither should he eat. [*Compare with D&C 42:42.*]

11 For we hear that there are some which walk [*live*] among you disorderly [*who refuse to work*], working not at all, but are busybodies [*prying into peoples' personal affairs, gossips, etc.*].

12 Now them that are such we command and exhort [*urge*] by our Lord Jesus Christ [*in the name of Jesus Christ*], that with quietness they work [*that they settle down from running around minding everyone else's business and go to work*], and eat their own bread [*provide for themselves*].

13 But ye, brethren, be not weary in well doing [*doing good*].

14 And if any man obey not our word [*instructions*] by this epistle [*given in this letter*], note that man, and have no company with him [*don't associate with him*], that he may be ashamed.

15 Yet count him not as an enemy, but admonish him as a brother [*but don't treat him like an enemy, rather, counsel him and help him understand the importance of work, as you would a brother*].

16 Now the Lord of peace himself give you peace always by all means. The Lord be with you all.

17 The salutation [*greeting*] of Paul
with mine own hand [*in my own hand-*
*writing*], which is the token in every
epistle [*which is something by which*
*you can recognize me in every letter I*
*write*]: so I write.

18 The grace of our Lord Jesus Christ
be with you all. Amen.

# THE FIRST EPISTLE OF PAUL THE APOSTLE TO TIMOTHY

Paul's letters to Timothy, known as First and Second Timothy, are thought to have been written around AD 64 to AD 65 (see Bible Dictionary under "Pauline Epistles") and, chronologically, are the last of Paul's letters contained in our Bible. First Timothy was written during a brief interval of freedom for Paul after he was set free from his first Roman imprisonment. See Bible Dictionary under "Pauline Epistles," and then keep looking ahead until you find "The Fourth Group." Timothy was a young missionary companion of Paul and was treated tenderly like a son by this great Apostle of the Lord. He was probably Paul's most capable and relied upon companion and assistant. His father was a Greek and his mother (Eunice) was Jewish. See Bible Dictionary under "Timothy." Timothy accompanied Paul on many of his missionary travels, including to Corinth, Macedonia, Troas, Rome, and Ephesus. Paul left Timothy in Ephesus to serve the members of the Church there. In First Timothy, among other things, Paul gives Timothy advice concerning his leadership duties and repeats the Church's stand on many sinful behaviors common in society at that time.

## FIRST TIMOTHY 1

In this chapter, Paul counsels Timothy to keep the doctrines of the Church pure and to stand up against some who are trying to get members to return to living the Law of Moses. He explains that the Law of Moses was designed to pull people away from grievous sins in preparation for accepting the gospel of Jesus Christ. Paul then reviews the doctrines of repentance and mercy.

1 PAUL, an apostle of Jesus Christ by the commandment of God our Saviour, and Lord Jesus Christ [*I have been called of God*], which is our hope [*our hope and optimism comes because of Christ*];

**JST 1 Timothy 1:1**

1 Paul, an apostle of Jesus Christ by the commandment of God and the Lord Jesus Christ, our Savior and our hope;

2 Unto Timothy, my own son [*who is like a son to me*] in the faith [*in the gospel*]: Grace, mercy, and peace, from God our Father and Jesus Christ our Lord.

Verse 2, above, is another reminder that the Father and the Son are separate personages.

3 As I besought thee to abide still at Ephesus [*I asked you to stay in Ephesus*], when I went into Macedonia [*when I traveled on to northern Greece*], that thou mightest charge some that they teach no other doctrine [*so that you could instruct some members there not to teach false doctrine*],

4 Neither give heed to fables [*falsehoods; Strong's #3454*] and endless genealogies, which minister questions

[*which generate more questions than they answer*], rather than godly edifying [*rather than building up the Church and its members*] which is in faith [*which comes through faith*]: so do.

The phrase "endless genealogies" in verse 4, above, has been used by some enemies of the Church to attack our emphasis on family history and genealogy work. We understand that Paul was referring to the common practice among some Jews of his day of proving at great lengths that they were descendants of Abraham, claiming that they were thus automatically saved above any Gentiles, no matter what the Gentiles did by way of faithfulness and personal righteousness. In the next verses, Paul will continue his emphasis on the requirement that people are saved individually, through personal righteousness and faithfulness, rather than based on who their ancestors are.

5 Now the end of [*purpose of; end goal of*] the commandment [*the gospel of Christ*] is charity out of a pure heart, and of a good conscience, and of faith unfeigned [*faith which is genuine, not pretended*]:

6 From which some having swerved [*having gone off course*] have turned aside unto vain jangling [*empty talk; Strong's #3150*];

7 Desiring to be teachers of the law [*wanting to teach us that we should go back to living the Law of Moses; see verse 9, footnote a in our Bible*]; understanding neither what they say, nor whereof they affirm [*they don't know what they are saying nor what they bear witness of*].

8 But we know that the law [*of Moses*] is good, if a man use it lawfully [*according to the purposes for which God gave it to Moses*];

Next, Paul will emphasize that the Law of Moses was given as a "schoolmaster" law (see Galatians 3:24), to elevate the children of Israel out of a very corrupt environment of sin and crude behavior, and to prepare them for the higher laws Christ would give during His mortal ministry.

9 Knowing this, that the law [*of Moses*] is not made for a righteous man [*one who is living the higher laws given by Christ*], but for the lawless and disobedient, for the ungodly [*unrighteous*] and for sinners, for unholy and profane [*irreverent; disrespectful toward sacred things*], for murderers of fathers and murderers of mothers, for manslayers [*murderers*],

10 For whoremongers [*for people whose lives are built around sexual immorality*], for them that defile themselves with mankind [*homosexuals; see Topical Guide, p. 216, under "Homosexuality,"* *for menstealers* [*kidnappers*], for liars, for perjured persons [*covenant breakers*], and if there be any other thing that is contrary to sound [*correct*] doctrine;

11 According to the glorious gospel of the blessed God, which was committed to my trust [*according to the gospel which God entrusted me to preach*].

12 And I thank Christ Jesus our Lord, who hath enabled me [*made it possible for me to preach and teach*], for that he counted me faithful, putting me into the ministry [*for considering me trustworthy enough to call to this ministry*];

13 Who [*Paul*] was before [*in times past*] a blasphemer [*totally disrespectful of Christ*], and a persecutor [*of Christians; see Acts 9, where Paul, known at that time as Saul, was persecuting early Christians*], and injurious [*doing much damage to Christ's Church*]: but I obtained mercy, because I did it ignorantly in unbelief [*I was forgiven because I didn't know it was wrong*].

14 And the grace [*help, mercy, forgiveness, etc.*] of our Lord [*of the Savior*] was exceeding [*very*] abundant with faith and love which is in Christ Jesus. [*In other words, when I found out that*

*I was wrong in persecuting Christians and repented, I felt the abundant mercy of the Lord.*]

15 This is a faithful saying [*what I say next is absolutely true*], and worthy of all acceptation [*and should be accepted by everyone*], that Christ Jesus came into the world to save sinners; of whom I am chief [*one of the worst*].

16 Howbeit [*however*] for this cause I obtained mercy [*the reason I was forgiven was*], that in me first Jesus Christ might shew forth all longsuffering [*might exhibit incredible patience*], for a pattern [*for an example*] to them which should hereafter believe on him to life everlasting [*to all others who believe in His Atonement, which leads to exalt*ation].

17 Now unto the King eternal [*Christ*], immortal, invisible [*can only be seen by those who are worthy; see JST, 1 Timothy 6:9, 15–16*], the only wise God, be honour and glory for ever and ever. Amen.

Next, Paul gives Timothy a specific charge, to fight against evil. Paul will explain more of this charge, beginning in verse 1 of chapter 2.

18 This charge I commit unto thee [*these instructions I give to you*], son Timothy [*Timothy, my son*], according to the prophecies [*the blessings and setting apart; see 1 Timothy 4:14*] which went before on thee [*which you were given previously*], that thou by them mightest war a good warfare [*fight a good fight against evil*];

19 Holding faith, and a good conscience; which some having put away concerning faith have made shipwreck [*which some have abandoned and have thus been spiritually shipwrecked*]:

20 Of whom is Hymenæus [*a member who denied the truth of the resurrection; see Strong's #5211*] and Alexander; whom I have delivered unto Satan [*turned him over to the buffetings of Satan, which means being turned over to Satan without any of the protective power of God to hold Satan back from tormenting them for a season; see McConkie,* Mormon Doctrine*, p. 108. Compare with D&C 78:12*], that they may learn not to blaspheme [*break covenants and intentionally teach terrible false doctrines*].

# FIRST TIMOTHY 2

Paul continues his letter to Timothy by instructing that members of the Church should pray for all people, including leaders of governments and all who have authority over them. He also gives counsel regarding local customs in Ephesus for women and their hairstyles, use of jewelry, etc., some of which we must make sure we leave in local context rather than giving it universal application.

1 I EXHORT [*urge*] therefore, that, first of all, supplications [*requests to God*], prayers, intercessions [*pleadings*], and giving of thanks, be made for all men;

**JST 1 Timothy 2:1**

1 I exhort therefore, that, first of all, supplications, prayers, intercessions, and giving thanks, be made for all men;

2 For kings, and for all that are in authority; that we may lead a quiet and peaceable life in all godliness and honesty [*dignity, respectability; see 1 Timothy 2:2, footnote d, in our Bible*].

For some whose religious beliefs do not permit them to support governments, this teaching from the Apostle Paul to pray for government leaders could serve to inspire them to rethink their position and to give appropriate support and respect, especially in view of verse 3, next.

3 For this is good and acceptable in the sight of God our Saviour [*our Father in*

*Heaven, whose plan of salvation gives all of us the opportunity to be saved*];

4 Who will have all men to be saved, and to come unto the knowledge of the truth.

**JST 1 Timothy 2:4**

4 Who is willing to have all men to be saved, and to come unto the knowledge of the truth which is in Christ Jesus, who is the Only Begotten Son of God, and ordained to be a Mediator between God [*the Father*] and man; who is one God, and hath power over all men.

5 For there is one God [*Heavenly Father*], and one mediator between God and men, the man Christ Jesus;

The word "mediator" as used in verses 4 and 5, above, is very important. By definition, a mediator works out differences between people or groups of people. Christ is the Mediator between us and the Father, meaning that He helps us work out the differences, in other words, our sins, imperfections, shortcomings, etc., which stand between us and the Father. Since the Father is perfect, and thus does not need to change, we are the ones who must change in order to "work out the differences" between us. The Savior is our Mediator, and His Atonement opens the door for us to overcome these differences and to eventually become like our Father.

6 Who gave himself a ransom for all [*who paid the cost of redeeming us from sin*], to be testified in due time.

There are various possible interpretations for the phrase "to be testified in due time" in verse 6, above. One possibility is that everyone who chooses to follow Christ can eventually have a strong testimony of Christ and His Atonement, wherein He ransomed us from sin. Another possibility is that "in due time" everyone will know who Jesus is and that "every knee should bow. . . and every tongue confess that Jesus Christ is Lord," Philippians 2:10–11.

7 Whereunto [*to whom*] I am ordained a preacher, and an apostle, (I speak the truth in Christ, and lie not;) a teacher of the Gentiles in faith and verity [*truth*].

8 I will [*desire*] therefore that men pray every where, lifting up holy hands [*a form used in praying in some cultures*], without wrath [*anger*] and doubting [*contention, arguing; Strong's #1261*].

9 In like manner also, that women adorn themselves in modest apparel [*clothing*], with shamefacedness [*reverence and respect for others; Strong's #0127*] and sobriety [*a sense of what is appropriate*]; not with broided hair, or gold, or pearls, or costly array [*expensive, showy things*];

**JST 1 Timothy 2:9**

9 In like manner also, that women adorn themselves in modest apparel, with shamefacedness and sobriety; not with braided hair, or gold, or pearls, or costly array;

It is obvious that Paul's counsel regarding women's hairstyles, jewelry, etc., in verse 9, above, is given in the context of local culture. It should not, for instance, be taken out of context and used to demand that women in our culture not be allowed to braid their hair. Perhaps braided hair in the local culture in which the Ephesian Saints lived represented a sinful lifestyle just as a woman with a shaved head represented that she was an adultress in Corinth (see note accompanying 1 Corinthians 11:5–6, in this study guide.)

10 But (which becometh [*is appropriate for*] women professing godliness) [*claiming to be reverent toward God; Strong's #2317*] with good works.

Verses 11–15, next, can become a source of contention and hurt if not read in the larger context of the scriptures and the words of the modern prophets. You may wish to review notes accompanying 1 Corinthians 11:1–16 and Ephesians 5:21–33 in this study guide, on the subject of men and women. Specifically, verses

11 and 12 do not reflect the teachings of the modern prophets and Apostles with respect to women and their vital role in our society and the Church, including teaching and leading in many ways. Therefore, we are left to assume that Paul was counseling Timothy with respect to rather drastic local problems where women were being very contentious or exercising unrighteous dominion over men. (The phrase "usurp authority over the man" in verse 12, below, may be a clue to what is going on in the Ephesus Ward.) A possible interpretation for verses 11 and 12 is given by the notes in parentheses. You may well be able to come up with a better one.

11 Let the woman learn in silence [*learn to listen, rather than being contentious and constantly interrupting*] with all subjection [*with proper respect toward local priesthood leaders*].

12 But I [*Paul*] suffer not [*do not allow*] a woman to teach, nor to usurp authority over the man, [*take what properly belongs to another; to domineer; see 1 Timothy 2:12, footnote b*] but to be in silence [*not meddling in the affairs of others; Strong's #2271*].

**JST 1 Timothy 2:12**

12 For I suffer not a woman to teach, nor to usurp authority over the man, but to be in silence.

For many centuries in many cultures verses 13–15, below, have sometimes been used by men as the "scriptural justification" for abuse of women. Many cultures and religions criticize and condemn Eve for her role in the fall of Adam and Eve. Our true gospel teaches us great respect for Eve and her role in furthering the purposes of God and making it possible for us to come to earth.

Eve was no doubt deceived in some ways, as indicated in verse 14, below. Perhaps Satan deceived her into believing that mortality and raising children would not ever be difficult. Perhaps he fooled her into believing that it was not that hard to cook for that many people, or to deal with 27 children who had the stomach flu at the same time, or to help Adam prepare a family home evening lesson and activity when she was bone weary from having been up with sick children nightly for two weeks.

Whatever the case, we are taught that Eve was actually not completely deceived when it came to the choice presented to her and Adam in the Garden of Eden. In Moses 4:6, we read that Satan "sought" to deceive Eve. "Sought" means that he "tried to." It implies that Lucifer was not completely successful. Apostle John A. Widtsoe explained this as follows: "Such was the problem before our first parents: to remain forever at selfish ease in the Garden of Eden, or to face unselfishly tribulation and death, in bringing to pass the purposes of the Lord for a host of waiting spirit children. They chose the latter . . . This they did with open eyes and minds as to consequences. The memory of their former estates may have been dimmed, but the gospel had been taught them during their sojourn in the Garden of Eden . . . the choice that they made raises Adam and Eve to preeminence among all who have come on earth." *Evidences and Reconciliations*, pp. 193–194.

In Encyclopedia of Mormonism, under the topic "EVE," we are taught: "Satan was present to tempt Adam and Eve, much as he would try to thwart others in their divine missions: 'and he sought also to beguile Eve, for he knew not the mind of God, wherefore he sought to destroy the world' (Moses 4:6). Eve faced the choice between selfish ease and unselfishly facing tribulation and death (Widtsoe, *Evidences and Reconciliations*, p. 193). As befit her calling, she realized that there was no other way and deliberately chose mortal life so as to further the purpose of God and bring children into the world."

13 For Adam was first formed [*God created Adam first*], then Eve.

14 And Adam was not deceived, but the woman being deceived was in the transgression.

Regarding the word "transgression," as used in connection with the fall of Adam, Joseph Fielding Smith said: "I'm very, very grateful that in the Book of Mormon, and I think elsewhere in our scriptures, the fall of Adam has not been called a sin. It wasn't a sin. . . . What did Adam do? The very thing the Lord wanted him to do; and I hate to hear anybody call it a sin, for it wasn't a sin. Did Adam sin when he partook of the forbidden fruit? I say to you, no, he did not! Now, let me refer to what was written in the book of Moses in regard to the command God gave to Adam. (Moses 3:16–17.) Now this is the way I interpret that: The Lord said to Adam, here is the tree of the knowledge of good and evil. If you want to stay here, then you cannot eat of that fruit. If you want to stay here, then I forbid you to eat it. But you may act for yourself, and you may eat of it if you want to. And if you eat it, you will die. I see a great difference between transgressing the law and committing a sin." (Joseph Fielding Smith, "Fall—Atonement—Resurrection—Sacrament," in Charge to Religious Educators, p. 124.) See Institute of religion *Doctrines of the Gospel Student Manual*, Religion 431 and 432, p. 20.

The JST makes a most significant change in verse 15, next. The Prophet changed the word "she" to "they," thus the verse applies to Adam and Eve, not just to Eve in a subservient role.

15 Notwithstanding she shall be saved in childbearing [*supported and strengthened in their role as parents*], if they [*Adam and Eve*] continue in faith and charity and holiness with sobriety [*taking their responsibilities seriously; with soberness; Strong's #4997*].

**JST 1 Timothy 2:15**

15 Notwithstanding they shall be saved in childbearing [*supported and strengthened in their role as parents*], if they [*Adam and Eve*] continue in faith and charity and holiness with sobriety.

# FIRST TIMOTHY 3

Paul now gives Timothy instructions regarding what kind of men he should look for in calling bishops and deacons. He also gives qualifications for the wife of a bishop and the wife of a deacon.

1 THIS is a true saying, If a man desire the office of a bishop, he desireth a good work.

2 A bishop then must be blameless [*must have a good reputation; Strong's #0423*], the husband of one wife [*must not be practicing polygamy, which was still done to some extent among the Jews in New Testament times*], vigilant [*temperate; Strong's #3524*], sober [*exercising good self-control; Strong's #4998*], of good behaviour, given to hospitality, apt to teach [*skilled at teaching; Strong's #1317*];

3 Not given to wine [*not a drunkard*], no striker [*not violent or overbearing*], not greedy of filthy lucre [*not greedy where money is involved*]; but patient, not a brawler [*not contentious, not inclined to pick fights; Strong's #0269*], not covetous;

4 One that ruleth well his own house [*one who presides appropriately over his own family*], having his children in subjection with all gravity [*one whose children respect and honor him because he earns their respect; Strong's #4587*];

5 (or if a man know not how to rule his own house, how shall he take care of the church of God?)

6 Not a novice [*not a very recent convert; Strong's #3504*], lest being lifted

up with pride [*for fear that he might become prideful and exercise unrighteous dominion*] he fall into the condemnation of the devil [*and thus becomes a tool in the devil's hand*].

7 Moreover he must have a good report of them which are without [*he must have a good reputation among nonmembers in the community*]; lest he fall into reproach [*be criticized*] and the snare [*trap*] of the devil.

Next, in verse 8, Paul gives counsel concerning deacons. Keep in mind that in the culture of the day, men had to be 30 years old or older in order to be ministers in a church. Thus, deacons would have been mature men at least 30 years old.

8 Likewise must the deacons be grave [*dignified; respected because of their good character; Strong's #4586*], not doubletongued [*saying one thing to one person but a different thing to another; deceitful*], not given to much wine [*not given to drunkenness*], not greedy of filthy lucre [*not greedy where money is involved; dishonest in business dealings*];

9 Holding the mystery of the faith [*sticking with the doctrines of the Church*] in a pure conscience.

10 And let these also first be proved [*let them be thoroughly interviewed before calling them to serve as deacons*]; then let them use the office of a deacon, being found blameless [*maintaining a good reputation*].

11 Even so must their wives be grave [*respected because of their good character: Strong's #4586*], not slanderers [*not gossipers*], sober [*self-controlled*], faithful [*trustworthy: Strong's #4103*] in all things.

12 Let the deacons be the husbands of one wife [*must not be practicing polygamy*], ruling [*presiding over*] their children and their own houses well [*appropriately*].

13 For they that have used the office of a deacon well purchase to themselves a good degree [*earn themselves a reputation of being a good influence in the Church; Strong's #0898*], and great boldness in the faith [*and are able to teach the gospel openly and frankly; Strong's #3954*] which is [*which exists*] in Christ Jesus.

14 These things write I [*Paul*] unto thee [*Timothy*], hoping to come unto thee shortly [*soon*]:

15 But if I tarry long [*if I end up remaining here for a long time*], that thou mayest know how thou oughtest to behave thyself in the house of God [*in your leadership responsibilities in the Church*], which is the church of the living God [*the God who is actually alive, not an idol carved of wood, made of stone, etc.*], the pillar and ground of the truth.

16 And without controversy [*without a doubt*] great is the mystery of godliness [*this remains a great mystery to unbelievers, namely that*]: God [*Christ*] was manifest in the flesh [*came to earth to live*], justified in the Spirit [*was testified of by the Holy Ghost*], seen of angels [*was pointed out to many mortals by angels*], preached unto the Gentiles [*was preached about to the Gentiles*], believed on in the world [*many now believe in him*], received up into glory [*was received into celestial glory in heaven*].

The JST combines the last phrase of verse 15 into verse 16. This change emphasizes that the Savior is the "pillar" and "ground (foundation) of the truth."

**JST 1 Timothy 3:16**

16 The pillar and ground of the truth is, (and without controversy, great is the mystery of godliness,) God was manifest in the flesh, justified in the Spirit, seen of angels, preached unto the Gentiles, believed on in the world, received up into glory.

# FIRST TIMOTHY 4

Paul now will prophesy about conditions in the world in the last days before the Second Coming of the Savior.

1 NOW the Spirit speaketh expressly [*the Spirit tells me specifically*], that in the latter times [*in the last days*] some shall depart from the faith [*some will abandon the gospel of Christ*], giving heed to seducing spirits [*evil spirits who deceive*], and doctrines of devils [*false doctrines and philosophies*];

2 Speaking lies in hypocrisy; having their conscience seared with a hot iron; [*In other words, their consciences will no longer work.*]

**JST 1 Timothy 4:2**

2 Speaking lies in hypocrisy; having their conscience seared as with a hot iron;

3 Forbidding to marry [*see note below*], and commanding to abstain from meats [*and requiring not to eat meat, for religious reasons*], which God hath created to be received with thanksgiving of them which believe and know the truth.

"Forbidding to marry" in verse 3, above, can happen in many ways as described in the following quote: "Celibacy, living together out of wedlock, homosexuality, adultery, abortion, and birth control are but a few of the many methods employed to pervert men's minds and prevent the creation and continuance of this holy union. In the words of President Harold B. Lee, 'Satan's greatest threat today is to destroy the family, and to make mockery of the law of chastity and the sanctity of the marriage covenant' (Church News, 19 Aug. 1972, 3.)" See Institute of Religion New Testament student manual, Life and Teachings of Jesus and His Apostles, p. 363.

Verse 3, above, is also significant in conjunction with our Word of Wisdom, D&C 89:13–14, regarding the eating of meat. Some members mistakenly believe that faithful members should not eat meat at all, except in times of famine or extreme cold. Paul prophesied that some would teach this as a matter of religious doctrine and would thus lead some astray. In the Word of Wisdom, the key word regarding meat is "sparingly" (D&C 89:12.) That the Word of Wisdom is not a system of vegetarianism is clearly taught in D&C 49:18–19, including footnote 18a. Apostle John A. Widtsoe emphasized this when he said, "The Word of Wisdom is not a system of vegetarianism. Clearly, meat is permitted (see D&C 42:18). Naturally, that includes animal products, less subject than meat to putrefactive and other disturbances, such as eggs, milk, and cheese. These products cannot be excluded simply because they are not mentioned specifically. By that token most of our foodstuffs could not be eaten." (Widtsoe, *Evidences and Reconciliations*, 3:156–57. Quoted in the Institute of Religion *Doctrine and Covenants Student Manual*, p. 210.)

4 For every creature of [*everything created by*] God is good, and nothing to be refused [*rejected; Strong's #0579*], if it be received with thanksgiving [*with gratitude*]:

Under the Law of Moses, many foods were to be rejected by faithful Israelites. They had, indeed, a rather strict "Word of Wisdom," including several kinds of meat, fish, poultry, and bugs which were not to be eaten. See Leviticus, chapter 11. In verses 4 and 5, next, Paul reminds Timothy that under the gospel of Christ, these restrictions were done away with.

5 For it is sanctified [*made acceptable*] by the word of God [*the gospel of Jesus Christ*] and prayer.

6 If thou put the brethren in remembrance of [*if you will remind the brethren about*] these things, thou shalt be a good minister of Jesus Christ, nourished up in the words of faith and of good doctrine, whereunto thou hast

attained [*of which you have attained a good understanding*].

7 But refuse [*reject*] profane [*the wisdom of men rather than of God*] and old wives' fables [*tales*], and exercise thyself rather unto godliness [*keep learning what God says about such matters*].

8 For bodily exercise profiteth little [*for a little while, in other words, does some good; see 1 Timothy 4:8, footnote a*]: but godliness [*exercising God's word in your life*] is profitable unto all things [*applies to all aspects of living*], having promise of the life that now is [*has benefits during our mortal lives*], and of that which is to come [*and is beneficial into eternity*].

9 This is a faithful saying and worthy of all acceptation [*of being accepted fully*].

10 For therefore [*for the gospel*] we both labour [*work*] and suffer reproach [*endure criticism*], because we trust in the living God, who is the Saviour of all men, specially of those that believe [*who wants to save all people, and will save those who live the gospel*].

11 These things command and teach.

In verse 12, next, we find that Timothy is relatively young. No doubt there were members of the Church in Ephesus who were much older than he, including some of the priesthood leaders.

12 Let no man despise thy youth [*show disrespect for you because of how young you are*]; but be thou an example of the believers, in word, in conversation [*conduct, behavior; Strong's #0391*], in charity, in spirit, in faith, in purity.

13 Till I come [*until I can manage to visit you in Ephesus*], give attendance [*apply yourself*] to reading, to exhortation [*to teaching*], to doctrine.

14 Neglect not the gift that is in thee, which was given thee by prophecy, with the laying on of the hands of the presbytery [*do not neglect to use the blessing that was given you under inspiration when you were set apart to your position by the elders*].

15 Meditate upon [*think about*] these things; give thyself wholly [*completely*] to them; that thy profiting [*progress*] may appear to all [*may be easily recognizable by the members there*].

16 Take heed unto thyself, and unto the doctrine [*watch what you do and hold to correct doctrine*]; continue in them: for in doing this thou shalt both save thyself, and them that hear thee.

# FIRST TIMOTHY 5

Since Timothy is a relatively young priesthood leader, Paul now counsels him to be careful how he deals with older members under his stewardship.

1 REBUKE not an elder [*don't correct an older man harshly*], but intreat him as a father [*but offer correction gently as if he were your father*]; and the younger men as brethren [*as if they were your brothers*];

2 The elder [*older*] women as mothers; the younger as sisters, with all purity [*with pure motives to help them*].

In the next several verses, Paul will give Timothy instructions concerning welfare assistance to needy members. These principles hold true for us today.

3 Honour widows that are widows indeed [*respond to the welfare needs of widows who are actually in need of assistance because they have no family to help them*].

4 But if any widow have children or nephews [*grandchildren, descendants; see 1 Timothy 5:4, footnote b*], let them [*her children and relatives*] learn first to shew [*show*] piety [*live their religion*] at home, and to requite [*pay back*] their parents [*for taking care of them when*

*they were growing up*]: for that is good and acceptable before God.

5 Now she that is a widow indeed [*has no one to help her*], and desolate [*and is in need of assistance*], trusteth in God [*has faith in God*], and continueth in supplications [*asking God for help*] and prayers night and day.

6 But she [*the widow*] that liveth in pleasure [*who indulges in worldly pleasures*] is dead [*spiritually dead*] while she [*the widow who humbly relies on God for help*] liveth [*is spiritually alive*].

7 And these things give in charge [*instruct all the members in these matters*], that they may be blameless [*so that they don't make mistakes in the matter of welfare assistance*].

8 But if any provide not for his own, and specially for those of his own house [*if anyone who is capable does not provide for the needs of his own, including his relatives; Strong's #3609*], he hath denied the faith [*he has rejected the gospel*], and is worse than an infidel [*one who does not believe in God; Strong's #0571*].

9 Let not a widow be taken into the number under threescore years old [*don't put any widow on the list of widows to receive welfare assistance unless she is at least 60 years old*], having been the wife of one man [*and was faithful to her husband while he was alive*],

10 Well reported of for good works [*and has a reputation for doing good deeds*]; if she have brought up children [*such as raising children*], if she have lodged strangers [*providing shelter and food for strangers in need*], if she have washed the saints' feet, if she have relieved the afflicted [*given aid to people in distress*], if she have diligently followed every good work [*and has done all sorts of good deeds*].

**JST 1 Timothy 5:10**

10 Well reported of for good works; if she have brought up children, if she have lodged strangers, if she have washed the Saints' clothes, if she have relieved the afflicted, if she have diligently followed every good work.

Based on what Paul says next about younger widows, there must have been some problems among the members in Ephesus with younger widows desiring sexual relations but not wanting to remarry. It would seem that some things must have been left out of the next verses, so we will make a guess, based on what we know from other scriptures.

11 But the younger widows refuse [*don't put them on welfare assistance*]: for when they have begun to wax wanton [*have become lustful*] against Christ [*against the teachings of Christ*], they will marry [*they marry for lustful reasons rather than out of desire to raise children, be good homemakers, etc.*];

12 Having damnation, because they have cast off their first faith [*because they have rejected the gospel*].

13 And withal [*at the same time they reject the gospel; Strong's #0260*] they learn to be idle, wandering about from house to house; and not only idle, but tattlers [*gossips*] also and busybodies [*minding everybody's business*], speaking things which they ought not.

14 I will [*prefer*] therefore that the younger women [*widows*] marry, bear children, guide the house [*take care of their homes*], give none occasion [*reason*] to the adversary [*enemies of the Church*] to speak reproachfully [*to criticize*].

15 For some are already turned aside after Satan [*some have already left the Church and are following Satan*].

16 If any man or woman that believeth have widows [*if any adult members of the Church have relatives who are widows*], let them relieve them [*render assistance to them*], and let not the church be charged [*don't leave it up to the Church to help them*]; that it may

relieve them that are widows indeed [*so that Church funds and resources can be used for those widows who have no other means of support*].

Verses 17 and 18, next, refer to Church leaders and missionaries who are serving full-time and thus need assistance for them and their families while they are serving.

17 Let the elders that rule well [*who serve honorably*] be counted worthy of double honour [*not only respect but also financial and other assistance as needed*], especially they who labour in the word and doctrine [*especially those serving full-time missions*].

18 For the scripture saith [*in Deuteronomy 25:4*], Thou shalt not muzzle the ox that treadeth out the corn [*make sure the ox has plenty to eat while he is working to harvest the grain*]. And, The labourer is worthy of his reward [*Luke 10:7. In other words, the faithful worker deserves to be well taken care of.*]

19 Against an elder receive not an accusation, but before two or three witnesses [*don't take any disciplinary action against a leader unless there are at least two or three witnesses that he has done wrong*].

20 Them that sin rebuke [*correct*] before all [*publicly*], that others also may fear [*will be afraid to commit such sins*]. [*This apparently refers to those who sin openly and, as a result, many know about it. See D&C 42:90–91. D&C 42:92 instructs us to deal privately with people whose sins were done secretly or privately, so that we don't embarrass them unnecessarily*]

21 I charge [*instruct*] thee before God, and the Lord Jesus Christ, and the elect angels, that thou observe these things without preferring one before another, doing nothing by partiality. [*In other words, make sure you are fair and impartial as you deal with such matters.*]

22 Lay hands suddenly on no man [*don't set anyone apart for a church calling or ordain any man to the priesthood without making sure they are prepared and ready for it*], neither be partaker of [*don't participate in*] other men's sins: keep thyself pure.

In verse 23, next, Paul gives Timothy a bit of personal medical advise for stomach problems he apparently has. Some enemies of the Church delight in quoting this verse to us in order to discredit the Word of Wisdom. What they don't realize and what some members today don't remember is that the Word of Wisdom was not given until 1833, and that it was given because of special problems and concerns which would exist in the last days (see D&C 89:4). Therefore, whether the "wine" referred to by Paul was fresh fruit juice or was fermented wine, it is not a problem because the Word of Wisdom had not yet been given.

23 Drink no longer water, but use a little wine for thy stomach's sake and thine often infirmities [*and for your frequent sicknesses*].

Verse 24, next, seems to be a continuation of the counsel given in verse 22, above. It appears that Paul is giving Timothy counsel about interviewing potential priesthood holders or men for particular callings in the Church, before he lays hands on them to set them apart.

24 Some men's sins are open beforehand, going before to judgment [*some men's sins are already well known before they come to an interview*]; and some men they follow after [*and some men's sins show up later*].

25 Likewise also the good works of some are manifest beforehand [*likewise, you will already be familiar with the good works of some men before you interview them*]; and they that are otherwise cannot be hid [*and some will blossom and surprise people after they have been interviewed and called to serve*].

# FIRST TIMOTHY 6

In Paul's day, many people had slaves and many had servants. Some of those who were servants or slaves apparently joined the Church. Paul counsels them to be good examples to their masters so that the masters would have a favorable opinion of the gospel of Christ.

1 LET as many servants as are under the yoke [*who are owned by their masters*] count their own masters worthy of all honour [*show honor and respect toward their masters*], that [*in order that*] the name of God and his doctrine be not blasphemed [*might not be mocked*].

2 And they that have believing masters [*and those who have masters who have joined the Church*], let them not despise them, because they are brethren [*don't become too informal with them because they are members*]; but rather do them service [*serve them well*], because they are faithful and beloved, partakers of the benefit [*partakers of the blessings of the gospel*]. These things teach and exhort [*urge; counsel*].

3 If any man teach otherwise [*if any of your members teach against what I have told you*], and consent not to wholesome words [*and won't accept correction*], even [*according to*] the words of our Lord Jesus Christ, and to the doctrine which is according to godliness [*which leads to godly behavior*];

4 He is proud, knowing nothing [*then you will know that he is prideful and knows nothing*], but doting [*is sick in the head; Strong's #3552*] about questions and strifes of words, whereof cometh envy, strife, railings, evil surmisings [*and will cause doubts and arguments which will lead to envy, contention, vicious criticism, false assumptions*],

5 Perverse disputings [*twisted debates*] of men of corrupt minds, and destitute of the truth [*who do not know the truth*], supposing that gain is godliness [*supposing that dishonest profit in business is righteousness*]: from such withdraw thyself.

6 But godliness with contentment is great gain [*is very profitable*].

7 For we brought nothing into this world, and it is certain we can carry nothing out.

8 And having food and raiment [*clothing*] let us be therewith content.

9 But they that will be rich [*whose top priority is to get rich*] fall into temptation and a snare [*a trap*], and into many foolish and hurtful lusts [*damaging temptations*], which drown men in destruction and perdition [*and lead them to spiritual death*].

Verse 10, next, is one of the most often-quoted verses in the Bible. However, it is very often miss-quoted as follows: "Money is the root of all evil." As you can see, Paul says "**the love of money** is the root of all evil." Many people handle money just fine and remain righteous. It is when people love money more than honesty or integrity or God or covenants or people, and so forth, that they get into trouble.

10 For the love of money is the root of all evil: which while some coveted after, they have erred from the faith [*which has caused some to fall away from the gospel*], and pierced themselves through with many sorrows [*and caused themselves much heartache*].

11 But thou, O man of God [*but if you want to be a true man of God*], flee these things; and follow after righteousness, godliness, faith, love, patience, meekness.

12 Fight the good fight of faith [*remain faithful at all costs*], lay hold on eternal life [*hang on to things which will lead to exaltation*], whereunto [*to which*]

thou art also called, and hast professed a good profession before many witnesses [*and of which you have born testimony before many people*].

13 I give thee charge in the sight of God [*I tell you in the strongest possible terms, with God as my witness*], who quickeneth all things [*who gives life to all things*], and before Christ Jesus [*and with Jesus Christ as my witness*], who before Pontius Pilate [*the Roman ruler who turned Jesus over to the crowd to be crucified; see John 18:29–40*] witnessed a good confession [*bore strong testimony of who he was*];

14 That thou keep this commandment without spot [*with absolutely no compromising*], unrebukeable [*allowing no room for being scolded*], until the appearing of our Lord Jesus Christ:

15 Which in his times [*when the time is right*] he shall shew, who is the blessed and only Potentate [*the Supreme Authority*], the King of kings, and Lord of lords;

**JST 1 Timothy 6:15**

15 Which in his times he shall show, who is the blessed and only Potentate, the King of kings, and Lord of lords, to whom be honor and power everlasting;

The JST makes very important changes in verse 16, next. Without the Prophet's help on this, a terribly damaging false doctrine might go unchecked, namely, that no one has seen nor can see God, nor can people ever even approach becoming like God. Unfortunately, such tragic false doctrine is taught by many who use this mistranslation in the Bible as their doctrinal foundation.

16 Who only hath immortality, dwelling in the light which no man can approach unto; whom no man hath seen, nor can see: to whom be honour and power everlasting. Amen.

**JST 1 Timothy 6:16**

16 Whom no man hath seen, nor can see, unto whom no man can approach, only he who hath the light and the hope of immortality dwelling in him [*in other words, only those who live the gospel can have such blessings*].

Even honest people who don't believe in the Prophet Joseph Smith but do believe in the Bible would be compelled to conclude that verse 16, as it stands in the Bible, is not correct. All they have to do is read scriptures such as Acts 7:55–56 where Stephen did see both God and Jesus standing on His right side. Also, they can know that God is approachable by reading such scriptures as Matthew 5:48 where we are told to become perfect like God, or read 1 John 3:2 where we are told in the Bible that the "sons of God," in other words "the righteous" will someday see that they are just like Jesus.

17 Charge [*instruct*] them that are rich in this world, that they be not highminded [*prideful; Strong's #5309*], nor trust in uncertain riches [*wealth, which is unreliable*], but in the living God, who giveth us richly all things to enjoy;

18 That they do good, that they be rich in good works, ready to distribute [*share their wealth*], willing to communicate [*be generous with others; Strong's #2843*];

19 Laying up in store for themselves a good foundation against the time to come [*storing up for themselves blessings in heaven for the future*], that they may lay hold on eternal life [*so that they can obtain exaltation*].

By the way, the phrase "eternal life," used in verse 19, above, always means "exaltation."

20 O Timothy, keep that which is committed to thy trust [*be faithful in your stewardship, your responsibilities*], avoiding profane and vain babblings [*avoiding commonplace, useless, time-wasting*

*talk*], and oppositions of science falsely so called [*and so-called science which opposes our religion*]:

21 Which some professing have erred concerning the faith [*which have caused some who get caught up in it to not believe the gospel*]. Grace be with thee. Amen.

# The Second Epistle of Paul the Apostle to Timothy

For background information on Timothy, see note at the beginning of First Timothy in this study guide. Second Timothy was written during Paul's second imprisonment, shortly before he was executed during the extreme persecution of Christians under Nero, Emperor of Rome. Bible Scholars estimate that Paul was killed somewhere between about AD 65 to AD 68 in Rome. As you will sense as you study Second Timothy, Paul knew that his time was short.

## SECOND TIMOTHY 1

In the first verse of this chapter, Paul preaches that eternal life is available through Jesus Christ. In this case, "life" means "eternal life." In the scriptures, eternal life always means "exaltation." Exaltation refers to those who attain the highest degree of glory in the celestial kingdom—see D&C 132:19–20.

Later in this chapter, we learn that Paul is rather lonely at this point of his last imprisonment in Rome, not long before his execution (verse 15).

There are no JST changes for this chapter.

1 PAUL, an apostle of Jesus Christ by the will of God [*having been called of God*], according to the promise of life [*eternal life*] which is in [*comes through*] Christ Jesus,

2 To Timothy, my dearly beloved son [*Paul considers Timothy to be like a son to him*]: Grace, mercy, and peace, from God the Father and Christ Jesus our Lord.

3 I thank God, whom I serve from my forefathers [*as my ancestors did*] with pure conscience, that without ceasing I have remembrance of thee in my prayers [*I remember you in my prayers*] night and day;

4 Greatly desiring to see thee, being mindful of thy tears, that I may be filled with joy;

5 When I call to remembrance the unfeigned faith that is in thee [*when I think back on your pure faith*], which dwelt first in thy grandmother Lois, and thy mother Eunice [*which your grandmother and mother had also*]; and I am persuaded that in thee also [*I am convinced that you have that kind of pure faith also*].

6 Wherefore I put thee in remembrance that thou stir up the gift of God, which is in thee by the putting on of my hands [*I want to remind you to be faithful to the spiritual gift which was given to you when I set you apart*].

7 For God hath not given us the spirit of fear; but of power, and of love, and of a sound mind.

8 Be not thou therefore ashamed of [*embarrassed by*] the testimony of our Lord, nor of me his prisoner: but be thou partaker of the afflictions of the gospel according to the power of God [*but endure afflictions, troubles, trials, and so forth, with the help of our Father in Heaven*];

9 Who hath saved us [*from the ways of the world*], and called us with an holy calling [*and called us to serve Him*], not according to our works [*not because we are that worthy or capable*], but according to his own purpose and grace [*according to His plan of salvation*], which was given us in Christ Jesus before the world began [*which the Father gave us through Jesus Christ in premortality*],

As noted above, the last of verse 9, above, contains an important doctrine, namely, that the Savior's Atonement was already working for us in our premortal life. We had agency there (D&C 29:35–36) and could thus make choices. If we made a mistake, we could repent and be forgiven and continue to progress in premortality, because of the infinite Atonement (just as the Atonement also worked before it was performed for Alma, Alma the Younger, and so many others who lived here on earth before the Atonement was done by Jesus.)

Elder Jeffrey R. Holland, of the Quorum of the Twelve, referred to the fact that the Atonement was already working for us in premortality in his General Conference address in October, 1995 when he said, referring to premortality, "We could remember that even in the Grand Council of Heaven He loved us and was wonderfully strong, that we triumphed even there by the power of Christ and our faith in the blood of the Lamb."

10 But [*the Father's plan*] is now made manifest [*made clear to us*] by the appearing of our Saviour Jesus Christ, who hath abolished [*overcome*] death, and hath brought life and immortality to light through the gospel [*and has taught us about eternal life and resurrection through His gospel*]:

11 Whereunto [*for which gospel*] I am appointed [*I have been called to be*] a preacher, and an apostle, and a teacher of the Gentiles.

12 For the which cause I also suffer these things [*and this is the reason I am now in prison in Rome*]: nevertheless I am not ashamed: for I know whom I have believed [*in other words, I believe in Christ*], and am persuaded [*convinced*] that he is able to keep that which I have committed unto him against that day. [*In other words, I am convinced that the sacrifices I have made and continue to make for the gospel will be there on Judgment Day to bless me.*]

13 Hold fast the form of sound words, which thou hast heard of me [*adhere strictly to the words of counsel I have given you*], in faith and love which is in Christ Jesus [*which I gave you in the faith and love which come from the Savior*].

14 That good thing which was committed unto thee keep by the Holy Ghost which dwelleth in us [*use the promptings of the Holy Ghost to help you carry out the responsibilities you were given*].

During Paul's first imprisonment in Rome, which lasted two years, he was under "house arrest," living in a house he rented, and he had many privileges not usually given to prisoners. But now, imprisoned again in Rome and soon to be executed, his conditions are poor. Bible scholars believe that Luke was still with him, but apparently few, if any, others were allowed to visit him or even dared to visit him in prison. His loneliness is felt in verse 15, next.

15 This thou knowest, that all they which are in Asia [*the wards and branches of the Church in what would be western Turkey today*] be turned away from me [*have forgotten me*]; of whom are [*including*] Phygellus and Hermogenes.

16 The Lord give mercy unto the house of Onesiphorus; for he oft refreshed me, and was not ashamed of my chain [*was not afraid to visit me here in prison*]:

17 But, when he was in Rome, he sought

me out [*looked for me*] very diligently, and found me.

18 The Lord grant unto him that he may find mercy of the Lord in that day [*on Judgment Day*]: and in how many things he ministered unto me at Ephesus, thou knowest very well.

# SECOND TIMOTHY 2

Paul will now compare the work Timothy has before him to the work of a valiant soldier, a well-trained athlete, a skilled farmer who raises fine crops. The imagery is that when we serve the Lord with skill and dedication, we accomplish the work effectively and bring the rewards of the gospel upon ourselves.

1 THOU therefore, my son, be strong in the grace [*merciful kindness; Strong's #5485*] that is in [*comes from*] Christ Jesus.

2 And the things [*the words of counsel*] that thou hast heard of [*from*] me among many witnesses, the same commit thou [*teach the same things*] to faithful men, who shall be able to teach others also.

3 Thou therefore endure hardness, as a good soldier of Jesus Christ.

Paul will now compare the work Timothy has to do to the work which a valiant soldier must do to be worthy of his captain's approval.

4 No man that warreth [*no good soldier*] entangleth himself with the affairs of this life [*lets his attention be diverted to other cares*]; that he may please him who hath chosen him to be a soldier [*so that he can remain pleasing to the leader who chose him to join his army*].

The imagery used in verse 5, next, is that of an athlete in training to compete in an event. In the actual competition, the athlete must follow the rules of the game in order to earn the victor's crown.

5 And if a man [*an athlete*] also strive for masteries [*competes in an athletic event; see 2 Timothy 2:5, footnote a, in our Bible*], yet is he not crowned [*he is not given the victor's crown*], except he strive lawfully [*unless he has followed the rules of the game*].

**JST 2 Timothy 2:5**

5 And if a man also strive for masteries, he is not crowned, except he strive lawfully.

Next, in verse 6, Paul uses the imagery of a hardworking farmer who is the first to receive a share of the harvest. In other words, if Timothy continues to labor diligently in the "field," he will enjoy the "harvest" of his own soul.

6 The husbandman [*farmer*] that laboureth [*who works diligently to produce a good harvest*] must be first partaker of the fruits [*harvests salvation for his own soul*].

7 Consider [*think carefully about*] what I say; and the Lord give thee understanding in all things.

8 Remember that Jesus Christ of the seed of David [*who was a descendant of King David*] was raised from the dead according to my gospel [*JST "according to the gospel"*]:

**JST 2 Timothy 2:8**

8 Remember that Jesus Christ of the seed of David was raised from the dead, according to the gospel;

9 Wherein I suffer trouble [*my preaching of the gospel has caused me much trouble*], as an evil doer [*and has made many people think I am an evil man*], even unto bonds [*and is the cause of my being in prison, in chains, here in Rome*]; but the word of God is not bound [*but the gospel can still go forth*].

10 Therefore I endure all things for the elect's sakes [*for the sake of those who are willing to make and keep covenants with God; see D&C 84:34–38*], that they may also obtain the salvation which is

in Christ Jesus with eternal glory [*in the celestial kingdom*].

11 It is a faithful saying [*you can trust the following saying completely*]: For if we be dead with him [*if we "bury" our sins through baptism and through his Atonement; see Romans 6:4–6*], we shall also live with him [*we will live with him in celestial glory*]:

**JST 2 Timothy 2:11**

11 For this is a faithful saying, If we be dead with him, we shall also live with him;

12 If we suffer [*remain faithful, no matter what*], we shall also reign with him [*we will rule with him during the Millennium; see Revelation 20:4*]: if we deny [*reject*] him, he also will deny us:

13 If we believe not [*whether or not we remain faithful*], yet he abideth faithful [*Christ remains faithful to the Father*]: he cannot deny himself.

14 Of these things put them in remembrance [*teach your people these things*], charging [*instructing*] them before the Lord that they strive not about words to no profit [*don't argue about trivial things*], but to the subverting of the hearers [*which only serves to damage the testimonies of those who hear such arguing*].

15 Study to shew thyself approved unto God [*do all you can to stay in harmony with God*], a workman [*a servant in God's kingdom*] that needeth not to be ashamed [*who has no need to be ashamed of what he is doing*], rightly dividing [*teaching; Strong's #3718*] the word of truth.

16 But shun [*avoid*] profane [*irreverent*] and vain [*worthless*] babblings [*talk*]: for they will increase unto [*lead to*] more ungodliness.

17 And their word will eat as doth a canker [*will spread to others like an infection with gangrene; see Strong's #1044*]: of whom is [*for example*] Hymenæus and Philetus;

18 Who concerning the truth have erred [*who are teaching false doctrine*], saying that the resurrection is past already [*has already happened, so it is too late for us*]; and overthrow [*undermine*] the faith of some.

19 Nevertheless the foundation of God standeth sure [*if we build on the sure foundation of Christ, which the Father has given us*], having this seal [*we positively know this*], The Lord knoweth them that are his [*the Lord will reward the faithful*]. And, Let every one that nameth [*who have taken upon them*] the name of Christ depart from iniquity.

20 But in a great [*large*] house there are not only vessels of gold and of silver, but also of wood and of earth; and some to honour, and some to dishonour. [*In other words, even in the Church which is a "big house," there are righteous and unrighteous people, and some will be rewarded by God and some will be punished by him.*]

21 If a man therefore purge himself from these [*the sins, etc., which I have mentioned to you, Timothy*], he shall be a vessel unto honour [*a "container" of righteousness, worthy of being honored by God*], sanctified [*made clean and pure by the Atonement*], and meet [*fit*] for the master's use [*and a worthy instrument in the hand of the Lord*], and prepared unto every good work [*and properly prepared to do much good*].

22 Flee also youthful lusts [*avoid sins and lustful desires which trap many younger people*]: but follow righteousness, faith, charity, peace, with them that call on the Lord out of a pure heart.

23 But foolish and unlearned questions avoid [*avoid getting caught up in foolish, shallow controversies*], knowing that they do gender strifes [*knowing that they lead to contention*].

24 And the servant of the Lord must not strive [*argue with people*]; but be gentle unto all men, apt to teach, patient,

25 In meekness [*slow to anger*] instructing those that oppose themselves [*who argue against them*]; if God peradventure [*perhaps*] will give them repentance to the acknowledging of the truth [*the opportunity to repent and accept the true gospel*];

26 And that they may recover themselves [*so that they can turn their lives around*] out of the snare [*trap*] of the devil, who are taken captive by him at his will [*who are easy for the devil to capture because they don't live the gospel*].

## SECOND TIMOTHY 3

In these next verses, Paul describes in considerable detail conditions and evils which will take place in the last days, before the Savior's Second Coming.

1 THIS know also, that in the last days [*before the Savior's Second Coming*] perilous [*dangerous*] times shall come.

2 For men shall be lovers of their own selves [*selfish*], covetous [*wanting what belongs to others*], boasters [*empty pretenders; Strong's #0213*], proud, blasphemers [*disrespectful of sacred things*], disobedient to parents, unthankful [*ungrateful*], unholy [*unreligious*],

3 Without natural affection [*involved in homosexuality; see 2 Timothy 3:3, footnotes a and b*], trucebreakers [*breaking their word*], false accusers [*ruining the good reputations of others*], incontinent [*lacking self-control*], fierce [*savage; Strong's #0434*], despisers of those that are good,

4 Traitors, heady [*rash, reckless, not thinking ahead*], highminded [*conceited*], lovers of pleasures more than lovers of God;

5 Having a form of godliness [*claiming to be religious*], but denying the power thereof: from such turn away [*avoid such behaviors and people*].

6 For of this sort are they which [*these are the types who*] creep into houses [*who work their way into people's houses and lives*], and lead captive [*gain control over*] silly women laden with sins [*already loaded with sins*], led away with divers [*various*] lusts [*wicked, evil passions*],

7 Ever learning, and never able to come to the knowledge of the truth.

8 Now as Jannes and Jambres [*two Egyptian magicians in Pharaoh's court who, according to Jewish tradition, imitated Aaron's miracles when Moses was trying to get Pharaoh to let the children of Israel go; Strong's #2389*] withstood [*opposed*] Moses, so do these also resist the truth: men of corrupt minds, reprobate [*failing the test; Strong's #0096*] concerning the faith [*with respect to the gospel*].

9 But they shall proceed no further [*they won't get very far*]: for their folly [*foolishness*] shall be manifest [*exposed*] unto all men, as theirs [*Jannes and Jambres in verse 8*] also was.

10 But thou hast fully known [*you are thoroughly familiar with*] my doctrine, manner of life, purpose, faith, longsuffering [*enduring trials and tribulations*], charity, patience,

11 Persecutions, afflictions, which came unto me at Antioch, at Iconium, at Lystra; what persecutions I endured: but out of them all the Lord delivered [*rescued*] me.

12 Yea, and all that will live godly in Christ Jesus [*everyone who lives the gospel*] shall suffer persecution.

13 But evil men and seducers [*deceivers*] shall wax worse and worse [*will become worse and worse*], deceiving, and being deceived.

**JST 2 Timothy 3:13**

13 For evil men and seducers shall wax worse and worse, deceiving, and being deceived.

14 But continue thou in the things which thou hast learned and hast been assured of, knowing of whom thou hast learned them; [*In other words, but you, Timothy, stay on the "strait and narrow path."*]

15 And that from a child [*and remember that from your youth*] thou hast known the holy scriptures, which are able to make thee wise unto salvation through faith which is in Christ Jesus.

16 All scripture is given by inspiration of God, and is profitable [*beneficial*] [JST "And all Scripture given by inspiration of God is profitable"], for doctrine, for reproof [*rebuke when needed*], for correction, for instruction in righteousness:

**JST 2 Timothy 3:16**

16 And all scripture given by inspiration of God, is profitable for doctrine, for reproof, for correction, for instruction in righteousness;

17 That the man of God [*the person who wants to be righteous*] may be [*become*] perfect, throughly furnished [*equipped*] unto all good works [*to do all kinds of good works*].

**JST 2 timothy 3:17**

17 That the man of God may be perfect, thoroughly furnished unto all good works.

The only difference in JST verse 17, above, is changing "throughly" to "thoroughly."

## SECOND TIMOTHY 4

1 I CHARGE thee therefore before God, and the Lord Jesus Christ [*I give you instructions, with the Father and the Lord Jesus Christ as my witnesses*], who shall judge the quick [*the living*] and the dead at his appearing and his kingdom; [*In other words, Christ will judge the living and the dead when he comes; see John 5:22 where we are told that the Father has turned all judging over to Christ.*]

2 Preach the word; be instant in season [*be ready to preach the gospel when the opportunity presents itself*], out of season; reprove, rebuke, exhort with all longsuffering [*patience*] and doctrine.

JST verse 2 is given next, with punctuation according to the original JST manuscript research done by Robert J. Matthews as per the Institute of Religion New Testament student manual, *The Life and Teachings of Jesus and His Apostles*, p. 377.

**JST 2 Timothy 4:2**

Preach the word. Be instant in season. Those who are out of season [*who are not prepared*], reprove, rebuke, exhort [*urge them to get ready*] with all long-suffering and doctrine.

Next, Paul predicts the apostasy from the Church which the Savior set up during his mortal ministry.

3 For the time will come when they will not endure [*put up with or tolerate*] sound [*correct*] doctrine; but after their own lusts [*according to their own sinful lifestyles*] shall they heap to themselves teachers, having itching ears [*they will select preachers and ministers who will preach what they want to hear, in order to profit by preaching*];

4 And they shall turn away their ears from the truth, and shall be turned unto fables [*and will accept false doctrines and philosophies*].

5 But watch thou in all things [*watch out for such things in everything you do*], endure [*put up with*] afflictions, do the work of an evangelist [*a father or patriarch of a family, in other words, be like a "patriarch" or "father" to the leaders and members under your stewardship*], make full proof of [*complete*] thy ministry.

6 For I am now ready to be offered [*I am*

*ready to be sacrificed, executed, for the gospel*], and the time of my departure is at hand [*my death is getting close*].

7 I have fought a good fight, I have finished my course [*I have finished my work*], I have kept the faith [*I have kept my covenants*]:

8 Henceforth there is laid up for me a crown of righteousness [*I know that I will receive exaltation*], which the Lord, the righteous judge [*Christ*], shall give me at that day: and not to me only, but unto all them also that love his appearing [*not only to me but to all who love his gospel which he gave us when he came to earth to live*].

9 Do thy diligence to come shortly unto me [*finish your duties and come visit me soon*]:

10 For Demas hath forsaken [*deserted*] me [*Demas was a faithful member and companion to Paul during his first imprisonment in Rome; see Strong's #1214*], having loved this present world [*having become worldly*], and is departed [*has gone*] unto Thessalonica; Crescens to Galatia, Titus unto Dalmatia [*northern Albania or southern Yugoslavia today*].

11 Only Luke is with me. Take Mark, and bring him with thee: for he is profitable [*very helpful*] to me for the ministry.

12 And Tychicus have I sent to Ephesus.

13 The cloke [*the long coat used for protection against the weather; Strong's #5341*] that I left at Troas with Carpus, when thou comest, bring with thee, and the books [*my small books or scrolls; Strong's #0975*], but especially the parchments [*tanned animal skins used to write upon*].

14 Alexander the coppersmith did me much evil [*opposed me much in my work*]: the Lord reward him according to his works:

15 Of whom be thou ware also [*watch out for him*]; for he hath greatly withstood our words [*he is a dangerous enemy to the gospel we have preached*].

**JST 2 Timothy 4:15**

15 Of whom be thou ware; for he hath greatly withstood our words.

16 At my first answer no man stood with me [*no one came with me this time when I went to my first court hearing in conjunction with this second imprisonment*], but all men forsook me [*everyone deserted me*]: I pray God that it may not be laid to their charge [*I hope and pray that God will not hold it against them*].

17 Notwithstanding [*however*] the Lord stood with me [*the Lord was with me*], and strengthened me; that by me the preaching might be fully known [*so that I might complete my mission in preaching the gospel*], and that all the Gentiles might hear [*the gospel*]: and I was delivered out of the mouth of the lion [*I was saved once more*].

18 And the Lord shall deliver me from every evil work, and will preserve me unto his heavenly kingdom [*the Lord will bring me safely to him in his kingdom*]: to whom be glory for ever and ever. Amen.

19 Salute [*greet*] Prisca and Aquila, and the household of Onesiphorus.

20 Erastus abode [*stayed*] at Corinth: but Trophimus have I left at Miletum sick.

21 Do thy diligence to come before winter [*do your best to get here before winter sets in*]. Eubulus greeteth thee, and Pudens, and Linus, and Claudia, and all the brethren.

22 The Lord Jesus Christ be with thy spirit. Grace be with you. Amen.

**JST 2 Timothy 4:22**

22 The Lord Jesus Christ be with you, and grace be with you all. Amen.

Have you noticed the notes at the

end of Paul's epistles in your Bible which give information about where and when the letters were written? For instance, in the case of Second Timothy, the note says: "The second epistle unto Timotheus, ordained the first bishop of the church of the Ephesians, was written from Rome, when Paul was brought before Nero the second time."

# THE EPISTLE OF PAUL TO TITUS

Most Bible scholars believe that Titus was a Greek who was converted to the Church by Paul, and that he accompanied Paul on his third missionary journey. See Bible Dictionary under "Titus." This letter was probably written sometime between AD 65 and AD 68, between Paul's first and second Roman imprisonments. Sometime before writing this letter, Paul and Titus had visited the Island of Crete in the Mediterranean Sea. When Paul had to leave, he left Titus to help the Church there continue to get established. Sometime later, he wrote this epistle (letter) to him, giving counsel on various organizational and doctrinal matters.

## TITUS 1

One of the important doctrines in this chapter is the doctrine of premortality (verse 2). Few, if any, Christian religions in the world today teach that we had a premortal existence before coming to earth. Jeremiah 1:5 teaches this same doctrine.

1 PAUL, a servant of God, and an apostle of Jesus Christ, according to the faith of God's elect [*according to the gospel which those who strive for exaltation follow*], and the acknowledging of the truth which is after [*leads to*] godliness;

2 In hope of eternal life [*exaltation*], which God [*the Father*], that cannot lie, promised before the world began [*promised us in premortality*];

3 But hath in due times [*when the time was right*] manifested his word [*revealed His plan of salvation*] through preaching, which is committed [*assigned*] unto me according to the commandment of God our Saviour;

4 To Titus, mine own son [*who is like a son to me and is my own convert to the gospel*] after the common faith [*in the gospel which is available to all*]: Grace, mercy, and peace, from God the Father and the Lord Jesus Christ our Saviour.

5 For this cause left I thee in Crete [*this is why I left you in Crete*], that thou shouldest [*so that you can*] set in order the things that are wanting [*that are not as they should be*], and ordain elders in every city, as I had appointed thee [*as I assigned you to do*]:

Next, Paul gives Titus some qualifications which a man should have in order to be called to serve as a bishop. You will note that one of the qualifications is that he must not be practicing polygamy. Polygamy was obviously still being practiced by some people in the Middle East at this time. According to Jacob 2:27 and 30, the Lord controls when plural marriage is to be practiced and when it should not be practiced. Plural marriage is not required for exaltation. See McConkie, *Mormon Doctrine*, p. 578.

6 If any be blameless [*has a good reputation; Strong's #0423*], the husband of one wife [*does not practice polygamy*], having faithful children not accused of riot [*wild, partying lifestyle; Strong's #0810*] or unruly [*will not submit to authority; Strong's #0506*].

7 For a bishop must be blameless [*have a good reputation*], as the steward of God [*as one who takes care of others for*

*God*]; not selfwilled [*stubborn, arrogant; Strong's #0829*], not soon angry [*controls his temper*], not given to wine [*not a drunkard*], no striker [*not a bully, not quick to argue with people; Strong's #4131*], not given to filthy lucre [*is not greedy for wealth*];

8 But a lover of hospitality [*is pleasant and hospitable*], a lover of good men [*loves that which is good; see Titus 1:8, footnote b*], sober [*temperate; self-controlled; Strong's #4998*], just [*lives the gospel with exactness*], holy, temperate [*has self-mastery; Strong's #1468*];

9 Holding fast [*holding firmly to*] the faithful word [*the true gospel*] as he hath been taught, that he may be able by sound doctrine both to exhort [*teach*] and to convince [*expose; Strong's #1651*] the gainsayers [*those who teach false doctrine or rebel against the Church for their own personal gain*].

10 For there are many unruly [*disobedient; Strong's #0506*] and vain talkers [*what they say has nothing of value; Strong's #3151*] and deceivers [*apostates, people who are falling away from the Church*], specially they of the circumcision [*especially the Judaizers, Jewish converts to the Church who insist that the Law of Moses should still be lived*]:

11 Whose mouths must be stopped [*who must be stopped in their preaching of this false doctrine*], who subvert [*undermine*] whole houses [*whole families*], teaching things which they ought not, for filthy lucre's sake [*preaching what people want to hear in order to get wealthy themselves.*] [*In other words, beware of those who practice "priestcraft," as defined in 2 Nephi 26:29.*]

12 One of themselves, even a prophet of their own said [*even one of these apostates' own false prophets said*], The Cretians [*those who live on the Island of Crete*] are alway liars, evil beasts [*savage and brutal; Strong's #2342*], slow bellies [*lazy gluttons; Strong's #0692 and #1064*].

13 This witness is true [*what I'm telling you is true*]. Wherefore rebuke them sharply, that they may be sound in the faith [*so that they can repent and be solid in the gospel*];

14 Not giving heed to Jewish fables [*do not give in to Jews or Jewish converts who teach false doctrines; see verse 10, above*], and commandments of men, that turn [*depart*] from the truth.

15 Unto the pure [*in mind and body, including sexual purity*] all things are pure [*all things in the gospel lead to personal purity*]: but unto them that are defiled [*corrupt*] and unbelieving [*don't believe in gospel standards*] is nothing pure [*nothing is sacred*]; but even their mind and conscience is defiled [*they have filthy and corrupt minds and their conscience doesn't work*].

**JST Titus 1:15**

15 Unto the pure, let all things be pure; but unto them who are defiled and unbelieving, nothing is pure; but even their mind and conscience is defiled.

16 They profess that they know God [*they claim to believe in God*]; but in works they deny him [*their actions prove otherwise*], being abominable [*detestable; Strong's #0947*], and disobedient, and unto every good work reprobate [*unfit for doing anything good; Strong's #0096*].

# TITUS 2

In this chapter Paul continues his counsel to Titus, emphasizing that he should teach the members of the Church under his jurisdiction the importance of personal righteousness in daily living.

1 BUT speak thou the things which become sound doctrine [*you be sure to*

*teach things which are in harmony with correct doctrine*]:

2 That the aged men be [*teach the older men to be*] sober [*serious-minded; can also mean not drinking any wine at all or not drinking too much; Strong's #3524*], grave [*worthy of respect; Strong's #4586*], temperate [*self-controlled*], sound in faith, in charity, in patience.

3 The aged women likewise, that they be in behaviour as becometh holiness [*that their behavior should be fitting for Saints*], not false accusers [*ruining the reputations of others; Strong's #1228*], not given to much wine [*not drunkards*], teachers of good things;

4 That they may teach the young women to be sober, to love their husbands, to love their children,

5 To be discreet [*self-controlled; Strong's #4998*], chaste [*keep the law of chastity*], keepers at home [*good homemakers*], good, obedient to their own husbands [*cooperating with their husbands; Strong's #5293; see also notes in this study guide, for Ephesians 5:21–33*], that the word of God be not blasphemed [*so that they do not bring criticism and disrespect to the gospel of Christ*].

6 Young men likewise exhort [*teach young men likewise*] to be sober minded.

7 In all things shewing thyself a pattern of good works [*making sure that you are a good example in all things*]: in doctrine shewing uncorruptness [*preaching uncorrupted, pure doctrine*], gravity [*taking serious things seriously*], sincerity,

8 Sound speech [*teaching that is based on correct doctrine*], that cannot be condemned [*that can't be set aside by honest people*]; that he that is of the contrary part may be ashamed [*so that those who criticize you may realize their mistakes and repent*], having no evil thing to say of you.

9 Exhort [*teach*] servants to be obedient unto their own masters, and to please them well in all things; not answering again; [*In other words, teach servants who are members of the Church to set a good example for their masters.*]

10 Not purloining [*not stealing things for their own use from their masters*], but shewing all good fidelity [*but being trustworthy in all things*]; that they [*servants*] may adorn the doctrine of God our Saviour in all things [*may be a good example for the gospel in everything*].

11 For the grace of God that bringeth salvation hath appeared to all men [*the kindness, mercy, and help from the Father is for everyone*],

**JST Titus 2:11**

11 For the grace of God which bringeth salvation to all men, hath appeared;

12 Teaching us that, denying ungodliness and worldly lusts [*that when we avoid wickedness and worldly desires*], we should live soberly, righteously, and godly, in this present world;

13 Looking for that blessed hope [*looking forward to salvation*], and the glorious appearing of the great God and our Saviour Jesus Christ;

14 Who gave [*sacrificed*] himself for us [*who gave us the Atonement*], that he might redeem us [*set us free*] from all iniquity [*from all wickedness*], and purify unto himself a peculiar people [*a people who belong to Him; Strong's #4041*], zealous of good works [*eager to do good works; Strong's #2207*].

15 These things speak, and exhort [*teach*], and rebuke [*correct*] with all authority. Let no man despise thee [*don't let people who think they know more than you try to exercise authority over you; Strong's #4065*].

## TITUS 3

On occasions we find Christians who come to believe that if they are truly

loyal to God, they must not be loyal to presidents, kings, governments or government entities, and so forth. Some of them base this belief on the first of the Ten Commandments, namely, "Thou shalt have no other gods before me." [See Exodus 20:3.] They believe that any loyalty to government is breaking this commandment. They would do well to take to heart what Paul says in verse 1, next, on this matter.

There are no JST changes for this chapter.

1 PUT them in mind [*teach them*] to be subject to principalities [*governments; see Titus 3:1, footnote b.*] and powers [*the rule of government authorities; Strong's #1849*], to obey magistrates [*rulers; Strong's #3980*], to be ready to every good work [*to be involved in whatever is good*],

2 To speak evil of no man, to be no brawlers [*to not be quarrelsome or contentious*], but gentle, shewing [*showing; pronounced "showing"*] all meekness [*mildness; slow to anger*] unto all men.

3 For we ourselves also were sometimes [*in times past*] foolish, disobedient, deceived, serving divers lusts and pleasures [*giving in to various passions and pleasures*], living in malice [*with unkind thoughts*] and envy, hateful [*showing hatred, detesting others; Strong's #4767*], and hating one another [*detesting others; Strong's #3404*]. [*In other words, when you are correcting others, be gentle and meek, keeping in mind that we ourselves are not perfect.*]

4 But after that the kindness and love of God our Saviour toward man appeared [*but then, the kindness and love of the Savior came into our lives as we found out about the gospel*],

5 Not by works of righteousness which we have done, but according to his mercy he saved us [*no matter how many works of righteousness we have done, we still could not be saved if it were not for His mercy*], by the washing of regeneration [*through baptism which allows us to become new people*], and renewing of [*which comes through the Gift of*] the Holy Ghost;

6 Which he [*the Father*] shed on us abundantly [*generously*] through Jesus Christ our Saviour;

7 That being justified by his grace [*through the process of repentance and change made available by the Atonement*], we should be made heirs [*we can inherit exaltation; see Romans 8:17*] according to the hope of eternal life [*as found in God's promises to the righteous*].

8 This is a faithful saying [*these things are true*], and these things I will that thou affirm constantly [*and I want you to teach and bear witness of them constantly*], that they which have believed in God might be careful to maintain good works [*so that your members there in Crete are encouraged to watch themselves carefully and remain faithful*]. These things are good and profitable unto men.

9 But avoid foolish questions [*foolish controversies*], and genealogies [*many Jews studied their genealogy for the purpose of proving that they were descendants of Abraham and thus were better than Gentiles; compare with Matthew 3:9*], and contentions, and strivings about the law [*arguments about the Law of Moses*]; for they are unprofitable and vain [*they do no one any good and are worthless*].

10 A man that is an heretick [*one who is teaching false doctrine intentionally*] after the first and second admonition [*after warning him twice*] reject;

The word "reject" in verse 10, above, could mean "not associate with anymore." It could also mean taking action as severe as excommunication as indicated in Matthew 18:17.

11 Knowing that he that is such is subverted [*knowing that a person who continues to teach false doctrine after repeated warnings is in apostasy*], and sinneth, being condemned of himself [*and is condemning himself*].

Paul now brings this letter to Titus to a close with a few final personal notes and instructions.

12 When I shall send Artemas unto thee, or Tychicus, be diligent [*try your best*] to come unto me to Nicopolis [*most Bible scholars agree that this was a city in what is known as northwestern Greece today; see Strong's #3533*]: for I have determined there to winter [*I plan on staying there for the winter*].

13 Bring Zenas the lawyer and Apollos on their journey diligently, that nothing be wanting [*lacking*] unto them [*take good care of them while they are traveling*].

14 And let ours [*let our members*] also learn to maintain [*keep doing*] good works for necessary uses [*for good causes*], that they be not unfruitful [*so that they don't become unproductive; symbolically, "unfruitful" can mean "lose their salvation"*].

15 All that are with me salute [*greet*] thee. Greet them that love us in the faith [*say "hello" to the members of the Church there in Crete for us*]. Grace be with you all. Amen.

# The Epistle of Paul to Philemon

This brief letter consists of just one chapter and gives us a rather delightful insight into Paul's tenderness, pleasant sense of humor, and spunk. It teaches forgiveness and repentance. It deals with a runaway slave, Onesimus (verse 10,) who stole some things (see Bible Dictionary under "Epistle to Philemon") from his master, Philemon, then ran away to Rome, probably planning on hiding successfully among the crowds there. Somehow, he met Paul in Rome and was converted to the Church. Philemon, his owner, was already a member of the Church and was very well acquainted with this humble and powerful Apostle. Paul was apparently responsible for converting him some time previously when he was in Ephesus (verse 19.) In fact, Philemon was a citizen of Colosse, a city near Ephesus. By the time this letter was written, Paul has convinced Onesimus to return to his owner (verse 12), Philemon, and make restitution. The penalty for a runaway slave was death, but Paul asks Philemon to forgive Onesimus and accept him back as a brother and fellow member of the Church (verses 15–16). Just in case Philemon has difficulty in so doing, Paul asks him to accept Onesimus back as he would Paul himself (verse 17), and if Philemon is too concerned about the financial losses incurred in the whole situation, Paul says "Charge it to my account" (verse 18). Additionally, just in case Philemon still can't bring himself to forgive Onesimus, Paul mentions, in effect, "Remember, you owe me" (verse 19). Paul sends the letter with a trusted member of the Church named Tychicus who accompanies Onesimus back to Colosse to make peace with Philemon.

## PHILEMON 1

1 PAUL, a prisoner of Jesus Christ [*a prisoner in Rome because of his preaching the gospel*], and Timothy our brother [*in the gospel*], unto Philemon our dearly beloved, and fellowlabourer [*fellow worker in the Church*],

2 And to our beloved Apphia [*possibly Philemon's wife; Strong's #0682*], and Archippus our fellowsoldier, and to the church in thy house [*possibly meaning the members of the Church who meet in Philemon's home, or perhaps other members of Philemon's household who belong to the Church*]:

3 Grace to you, and peace, from God our Father and the Lord Jesus Christ.

4 I thank my God, making mention of thee always in my prayers [*I always remember you in my prayers*],

5 Hearing of thy love and faith, which thou hast toward the Lord Jesus, and toward all saints;

6 [*I pray*] That the communication [*spreading; Strong's #2842*] of thy faith [*that your spreading of the gospel*] may become effectual [*powerful; Strong's #1756*] by the acknowledging of every good thing which is in you in Christ Jesus [*through others' acknowledging the value of the gospel by seeing your good example*] .

7 For we have great joy and consolation [*comfort*] in thy love, because

the bowels [*tender affections; Strong's #4698*] of the saints are refreshed by thee, brother.

Next, Paul gets to the main point of his letter to Philemon, namely, asking him to forgive his runaway slave, Onesimus, and take him back.

8 Wherefore, though I might be much bold in Christ to enjoin thee [*even though I could be so bold as to command you; Strong's #2004*] that which is convenient [*in the matter at hand*],

9 Yet for love's sake I rather beseech thee [*yet I would rather beg a favor of you, in light of the love we have for each other*], being such an one as Paul the aged [*as one who is getting quite old*], and now also a prisoner of Jesus Christ [*and currently is in prison because I dared to be loyal to Christ*].

10 I beseech thee for my son Onesimus [*I have a big favor to ask for my convert, Onesimus*], whom I have begotten in my bonds [*whom I have converted while here in Rome in prison*]:

11 Which in time past was to thee unprofitable [*who has caused you much trouble in the past*], but now profitable to thee and to me [*but who is now very valuable to both you and me as a new member of the Church*]:

12 Whom I have sent again [*whom I have asked to return to you*]: thou therefore receive him [*I ask you, therefore, to welcome him*], that is, mine own bowels [*for whom I have the deepest affection; Strong's #4698*]:

13 Whom I would have retained with me [*I would like to have kept him here with me*], that in thy stead [*in place of you*] he might have ministered unto me in the bonds of the gospel [*he could have helped me here as a brother in the gospel*]:

14 But without thy mind would I do nothing [*but I didn't want to do any such thing without your permission*]; that thy benefit [*so that any help from you*] should not be as it were of necessity, but willingly [*would not come as a matter of obligation but as a matter of choice*].

15 For perhaps he therefore departed for a season [*perhaps the reason he ran away from you*], that thou shouldest receive him for ever [*was so that he could be converted and return to you as a brother in the gospel forever*];

16 Not now as a servant [*he comes back to you not as a servant*], but above a servant [*but much more than a servant*], a brother beloved [*a beloved brother in the gospel*], specially to me, but how much more unto thee [*but even more so to you*], both in the flesh, and in the Lord [*both as your brother here on earth as well as in the gospel*]?

17 If thou count me therefore a partner [*if you consider me worthy to be your partner in this situation*], receive him as myself [*welcome him as you would me*].

18 If he hath wronged thee, or oweth thee ought, put that on mine account [*if he has harmed you or owes you anything, send the bill to me*];

19 I Paul have written it with mine own hand, I will repay it: albeit I do not say to thee how thou owest unto me even thine own self besides [*although I probably don't need to remind you that you owe me for saving your soul*].

20 Yea, brother, let me have joy of thee in the Lord [*bring joy to me by living the gospel in this matter*]: refresh my bowels in the Lord [*reaffirm the tender feelings I have for you*].

21 Having confidence in thy obedience [*knowing that you would do the right thing in this matter*] I wrote unto thee, knowing that thou wilt also do more than I say [*in fact, I know that you will do more even than I am asking*].

22 But withal [*while you are at it*] prepare me also a lodging [*a guest room*]: for I trust that through your prayers I shall be given unto you [*for I trust*

*that your prayers in my behalf will be answered and that I will be freed from prison and come to stay with you for a while*].

23 There salute thee Epaphras, my fellowprisoner in Christ Jesus [*Epaphras sends his greeting to you also*];

24 [*along with greetings from*] Marcus, Aristarchus, Demas, Lucas, my fellow-labourers.

25 The grace of our Lord Jesus Christ be with your spirit. Amen.

**JST Philemon 1:25**

25 The grace of our Lord Jesus Christ be with you. Amen.

# THE EPISTLE OF PAUL THE APOSTLE TO THE HEBREWS

There is uncertainty and disagreement among Bible scholars as to who wrote Hebrews. That is why it was placed in the New Testament at the end of Paul's letters. As you can see, Paul is given as the writer of Hebrews in the King James Version of the Bible (the one we use for English speaking areas of the Church). (Look at the beginning of Hebrews in your Bible.) We have the advantage of having a true prophet, Joseph Smith, who told us that Paul is indeed the author of Hebrews. See *Teachings of the Prophet Joseph Smith*, p. 59.

Hebrews is a letter from the Apostle Paul to Jewish members of the Church, who were commonly referred to in his day as "Hebrews," meaning descendants of Abraham, in other words, Israelites. The letter was probably written sometime between AD 62 and AD 65. It is a masterpiece designed to persuade Jewish converts to the Church to accept the fact that Christ fulfilled the Law of Moses, and therefore they should no longer practice the Law of Moses. So-called "Judaizers," who were Jewish members of the Church, continued to insist that the Law of Moses, with all of its detailed requirements, should continue to be lived by both Gentile and Jewish converts. They caused much trouble among members in the early Church as it struggled after Christ's crucifixion.

Paul, who spent most of his ministry taking the gospel to the Gentiles (non-Jews), turns his attention to Jewish members as he writes this magnificent letter pointing out the fallacies of continuing to live the Law of Moses. He uses his extensive knowledge of Old Testament writings and prophecies to present his message about Christ, and, as a result, Hebrews becomes one of our best resources for understanding the Old Testament. Hebrews is especially helpful to us in pointing out Old Testament references to the Savior and His Atonement. Hebrews is full of rich doctrine as well as Atonement symbolism.

## HEBREWS 1

Paul begins his letter by bearing witness that Jesus is the Son of God and that He is the focus of many Old Testament prophecies and writings. He gives many details as to who Christ actually is.

1 GOD [*the Father*], who at sundry [*various*] times and in divers manners [*different ways*] spake [*spoke*] in time past unto the fathers [*to our ancestors*] by the prophets,

2 Hath in these last days [*has recently*] spoken unto us by his Son [*Jesus*], whom he hath appointed heir of all things, by whom also he made the worlds [*the Father had Jesus create the worlds*];

Next, Paul teaches us that the Savior has the Father's glory upon Him and that the Father and Son are exact lookalikes.

3 Who being the brightness of his glory, and the express image of his person [*looks just like the Father; compare with John 14:7*], and upholding all things by the word of his power [*and that the Savior used His authority to fulfill everything the Father asked Him to do*], when he had by himself purged our sins [*when He alone had accomplished the Atonement and paid for our sins*], sat down on the right hand of the Majesty on high [*took His rightful place in heaven on the right side of the Father*];

"The right hand" is symbolic of covenants, and the symbolism here includes that Jesus kept all of the covenants He made with the Father.

4 Being made so much better than the angels [*Christ is higher in authority than the angels*], as he hath by inheritance obtained a more excellent name than they. [*In other words, Christ, as the literal Son of the Father, has a name which is superior to any other, namely the "Son of God".*]

5 For unto which of the angels said he at any time, Thou art my Son, this day have I begotten thee [*as prophesied about Christ in Psalm 2:7*]? [*In other words, can you think of any angels to whom the Father said, "You will be my Son?"*] And again [*I repeat, can you think of anyone else to whom God said, as prophesied about Christ in 2 Samuel 7:14 and 1 Chronicles 17:13*], I will be to him a Father, and he shall be to me a Son?

Next, in verse 6, Paul will use the term "firstbegotten." Remember that Jesus was the firstborn spirit child of our Heavenly Father (see Colossians 1:15 and accompanying notes in this study guide.)

6 And again, when he [*the Father*] bringeth in the firstbegotten into the world, he saith, And let all the angels of God worship him. [*In other words, when Jesus was born, all the angels worshiped him, and angels have great glory, which is another reminder of who Jesus was.*]

**JST Hebrews 1:6**

6 And again, when he bringeth in the first begotten into the world, he saith, And let all the angels of God worship him, who maketh his ministers as a flame of fire.

7 And of the angels he saith [*in Psalm 104:4*], Who maketh his angels spirits, and his ministers a flame of fire.

**JST Hebrews 1:7**

7 And of the angels he saith, Angels are ministering spirits.

8 But unto the Son he saith, Thy throne, O God, is for ever and ever: a sceptre of righteousness is the sceptre of thy kingdom. [*In other words, combining verse 7 with verse 8, Paul says, in effect, that the Father uses angels as ministering spirits but the Son is a God with power and authority given only to Gods.*]

Verse 9, next, is a continuation of the first line of verse 8, above, "But unto the Son he [*the Father*] saith . . ." [*As recorded in Psalm 45:7.*]

9 Thou [*Jesus*] hast loved righteousness [*you have been completely faithful to me*], and hated iniquity [*and you are without sin*]; therefore God [*the Father*], even thy God [*thy Father*], hath anointed thee with the oil of gladness above thy fellows [*more than anyone else*].

The phrase "oil of gladness" is a beautiful description of the satisfaction and joy the Savior receives when we accept His gift of the Atonement and repent and come unto the Father through Him. Isaiah 53:11 emphasizes this satisfaction and joy which comes to the Savior as He sees the results of the Atonement in so many lives, as follows: "He [*Christ*] shall see the travail of his soul [*will look back on His Atonement*], and shall be satisfied:"

Paul continues to bear testimony to the Hebrews about Jesus and who He

really was, continuing the sentence he used at the beginning of verse 5, "But unto the Son he [*the Father*] saith"

10 And, Thou, Lord [*Christ*], in the beginning hast laid the foundation of the earth [*created the earth*]; and the heavens are the works of thine hands [*created the heavens*]:

11 They [*the heavens and the earth*] shall perish; but thou remainest [*but Christ is eternal*]; and they [*the heavens and the earth*] all shall wax [*grow*] old as doth a garment [*as does a piece of clothing*];

12 And as a vesture [*robe*] shalt thou fold them up, and they shall be changed [*at the time of the Second Coming, and again, at the end of the little season after the end of the Millennium; see D&C 88:26 and 130:6–9*]: but thou art the same [*You will remain the same, exalted as a God; see D&C 76:107–108*], and thy years shall not fail [*Your years will never end*].

13 But to which of the angels said he at any time [*as was written about Christ in Psalm 110:1*], Sit on my right hand, until I make thine enemies thy footstool [*until all Your enemies have been overcome*]?

14 Are they not all ministering spirits, sent forth to minister for them who shall be heirs of salvation [*who receive exaltation*]?

The reference to "angels" in verse 13, above, and the reference to "ministering spirits" in verse 14, above, are references to those who do not earn exaltation, and thus remain "ministering servants" for those who receive exaltation. Compare with D&C 132:16–17.

# HEBREWS 2

In this chapter, Paul continues to bear witness to the Jews as to who Christ is. He again uses many Old Testament references to Christ with which the Jews would be familiar.

1 THEREFORE we ought to give the more earnest heed to [*we ought to be all the more careful to pay attention to*] the things which we have heard [*about Christ*], lest at any time we should let them slip [*for fear that we might be disobedient to them*].

2 For if the word spoken by angels was stedfast [*solid, trustworthy*], and every transgression and disobedience received [*has been assigned*] a just recompence of reward [*a fair punishment*];

3 How shall we escape [*how can we escape fair punishment*], if we neglect so great salvation [*if we neglect the opportunity we have been given for salvation*]; which at the first began to be spoken by the Lord [*which Christ Himself taught during His mortal ministry at the first of this dispensation*], and was confirmed [*witnessed*] unto us by them [*including the Apostles*] that heard him;

4 God also bearing them witness [*Christ showed His Apostles and others who He was; see McConkie,* Doctrinal New Testament Commentary, *Vol. 3, p. 143*], both with signs and wonders, and with divers [*various*] miracles, and gifts of the Holy Ghost, according to his own will?

5 For unto the angels hath he not put in subjection the world to come, whereof we speak. [*In other words, "Don't we talk of angels being given responsibilities by Christ in the world to come?" Example: D&C 132:16–17, 19.*]

In the following 3 verses, Paul teaches the wonderful and powerful doctrine that we can actually eventually become gods, with all things "in subjection under [*our*] feet," which means to have power over all things. See verse 8 and also D&C 132:20. For further scriptural evidence that we can indeed become gods, see 1 Corinthians 15:27, where a similar

phrase, "all things under his feet" is used to describe Christ.

6 But one [*King David*] in a certain place [*Psalm 8:4–6*] testified, saying, What is man, that thou art mindful of him? or the son of man [*mortal men; Strong's #5207*], that thou visitest him?

7 Thou madest him a little lower than the angels [*we were placed here on earth as mortals with mortal weaknesses and limitations*]; thou crownedst him with glory and honour [*the same phrase used in connection with Christ in verse 9, below*], and didst set him over the works of thy hands:

8 Thou hast put all things in subjection under his feet [*we have the potential to become gods; compare with D&C 132:19–20*]. For in that he put all in subjection under him, he left nothing that is not put under him. But now we see not yet all things put under him [*but we are not gods yet*].

9 But we see Jesus, who was made a little lower than the angels [*Jesus became mortal*] for the suffering of death [*in order to suffer death*], crowned with glory and honour; that he by the grace of God should taste death for every man [*so that every person ever born will be resurrected; see 1 Corinthians 15:22*].

10 For it became him [*it was according to the Father's will*], for whom are all things, and by whom are all things, in bringing many sons unto glory [*in order to bring many to exaltation in celestial glory*], to make the captain of their salvation [*to make Christ*] perfect through sufferings.

11 For both he [*Christ*] that sanctifieth [*who makes it possible for people to become worthy to enter celestial glory*] and they [*faithful Saints*] who are sanctified are all of one [*are united*]: for which cause he is not ashamed to call them brethren [*they are full "brothers" and "sisters," in other words, "joint heirs with Christ" as Paul describes them in Romans 8:17.*]

12 Saying [*as stated in Psalm 22:22*], I will declare thy name unto my brethren, in the midst of the church will I sing praise unto thee. [*In other words, Christ will acknowledge and accept the faithful members into celestial glory.*]

13 And again [*as stated in Psalm 18:2*], I will put my trust in him. And again [*as stated in Isaiah 8:18*], Behold I and the children [*faithful followers*] which God [*the Father*] hath given me [*compare with D&C 27:14*].

14 Forasmuch then as [*since*] the children [*the Father's spirit children*] are partakers of flesh and blood [*are born into mortality*], he [*Christ*] also himself likewise took part of the same [*was born into mortality also*]; that through death he might destroy [*completely overcome*] him that had the power of death, that is, the devil;

15 And deliver [*redeem*] them who through fear of death [*spiritual death*] were all their lifetime subject to bondage [*were subject to sin as mortals*].

16 For verily he took not on him the nature of angels; but he took on him the seed of Abraham. [*In other words, Christ took mortality upon Himself in order to suffer, die, and resurrect for us (see verses 9, 10, 14, and 18), and to fulfill the covenants made to Abraham.*]

**JST Hebrews 2:16**

16 For verily, he took not on him the likeness of angels; but he took on him the seed of Abraham.

17 Wherefore in all things it behoved him [*it was necessary for Christ*] to be made like unto his brethren [*to become mortal*], that he might be a merciful and faithful high priest in things pertaining to God, to make reconciliation [*to atone*] for the sins of the people.

18 For in that he [*Christ*] himself hath suffered being tempted, he is able to

succour [*help*] them that are tempted.

The word "succor," used in verse 18, above, literally means "to rush to the aid of."

# HEBREWS 3

Remember that one of Paul's major objectives in writing this letter to the Hebrews (Jewish converts to the Church) was to convince them to accept Christ fully and to discontinue living the Law of Moses. Many Jews considered Moses to be the most important prophet of all. Here Paul shows that Moses was indeed a very significant prophet, but that he was Christ's servant.

1 WHEREFORE, holy brethren, partakers of the heavenly calling [*who have been called to hold the holy Melchizedek Priesthood*], consider the Apostle and High Priest of our profession, Christ Jesus [*think about Christ who is the chief High Priest of all high priesthood holders*];

2 Who was faithful to him [*the Father*] that appointed him, as also Moses was faithful in all his house [*just as Moses was faithful in all his responsibilities in God's "house" or Church; Strong's #3624; see also verse 6, below, where members of the Church are referred to as Christ's "house"*].

3 For this man was counted worthy of more glory than Moses [*was above Moses in authority*], inasmuch [*since*] as he who hath builded the house hath more honour than the house [*since the one (Christ) who built the house (God's kingdom) is more important than the house itself*].

**JST Hebrews 3:3**
3 For he was counted worthy of more glory than Moses, inasmuch as he who hath builded the house hath more honor than the house.

It is important to remember here that Jesus was the God of the Old Testament, and was known as Jehovah. See Bible Dictionary under "Jehovah." For example, Jesus is the one who gave Moses the Ten Commandments. He did all these things as the God of the Old Testament while He was still a spirit personage, because He had not yet been born and received a mortal body.

4 For every house is builded by some man; but he that built all things is God [*God has power and authority over all things, including His prophets*].

5 And Moses verily was faithful in all his house [*Moses was very faithful in carrying out the responsibilities given him by Christ*], as a servant [*as a servant of Christ*], for a testimony of those things which were to be spoken after [*as a testimony and teaching tool, pointing the peoples' minds toward the coming of Jesus at a later time*];

6 But Christ as a son over his own house [*as the Son of God placed in charge of His own kingdom here on earth*]; whose house are we [*whose church we are*], if we hold fast [*if we are faithful to*] the confidence and the rejoicing of the hope [*which the gospel brings*] firm unto the end [*and remain faithful to the end*].

7 Wherefore [*as the Holy Ghost saith, in Psalm 95:7–11*], To day if ye will hear his voice,

8 Harden not your hearts, as in the provocation, in the day of temptation in the wilderness: [*In other words, don't harden your hearts like the children of Israel did when they provoked God and He caused them to wander 40 years in the wilderness until the older generation died out; see Numbers 14:2–23.*]

9 When your fathers tempted [*provoked; see verse 16, below*] me, proved me [*tried My patience*], and saw my works forty years.

10 Wherefore I was grieved [*made sad*] with that generation, and said, They do alway [*always*] err in their heart [*they do*

*not want to be righteous*]; and they have not known my ways [*they don't try to learn the gospel*].

11 So I sware [*promised them*] in my wrath [*My righteous anger*], They shall not enter into my rest [*they will not enter into the promised land; symbolic of heaven*]. [*This is the end of the quote from Psalms begun in verse 7, above.*]

12 Take heed [*watch out*], brethren, lest there be in any of you an evil heart of unbelief, in departing from the living God [*which would cause you to apostatize and leave the gospel of Christ*].

13 But exhort [*teach*] one another daily, while it is called To day [*while you have the chance*]; lest any of you be hardened [*for fear that your hearts could be hardened*] through the deceitfulness of sin [*through being fooled by sin*].

14 For we are made partakers of Christ [*we can be saved with Christ*], if we hold the beginning of our confidence stedfast unto the end [*if we hold onto the faith we had when we first joined the Church*];

15 While it is said [*as I just said, quoting from Psalm 95:7–8*], To day if ye will hear his voice, harden not your hearts, as in the provocation.

16 For some, when they had heard, did provoke [*disobeyed God and provoked Him to anger*]: howbeit [*however*] not all that came out of Egypt by Moses [*not all who were led out of Egypt by Moses provoked God*].

17 But with whom was he grieved forty years [*who was it that grieved God and thus caused the children of Israel to wander 40 years in the wilderness*]? was it not with them that had sinned [*wasn't it the sinners among them*], whose carcases [*dead bodies*] fell in the wilderness?

18 And to whom sware he [*to whom did God say*] that they should not enter into his rest [*that they would not enter exaltation; see D&C 84:24, where "rest" is defined*], but to them that believed not [*wasn't He speaking to the unbelievers*]?

19 So we see that they could not enter in because of unbelief [*thus we see that they could not enter into the presence of God because they refused to believe in Him*].

# HEBREWS 4

It is very helpful in understanding this chapter to be aware that the word "rest" ultimately means "the fulness of his glory." See D&C 84:24. In other words, "rest" means to return to the presence of God and receive the "fulness" which He has for us, that is, exaltation. Obviously, it also means to have peace of conscience and strength from God in this life. Also, along with other important doctrines about Christ in this chapter, it teaches that Jesus was completely without sin, even though He was tempted in all things (*verse 15*.)

1 LET us therefore fear [*let us be very careful*], lest, a promise being left us of entering into his rest [*since God's promise that we can enter into exaltation with Him still stands*], any of you should seem to come short of it [*for fear any of you would fail to achieve that goal*].

2 For unto us was the gospel preached, as well as unto them: but the word preached did not profit them [*but they did not benefit from it*], not being mixed with faith in them that heard it [*because they did not have faith in it*].

**JST Hebrews 4:2**

2 For unto us was the rest [*the doctrine of exaltation*] preached, as well as unto them; but the word preached did not profit them, not being mixed with faith in them that heard it.

The JST makes very significant changes in verse 3, next. Also,

remember that the word "believe" in this context means to live the gospel faithfully.

3 For we which have believed do enter into rest, as he said, As I have sworn in my wrath, if they shall enter into my rest: although the works were finished from the foundation of the world.

**JST Hebrews 4:3**

3 For we who have believed do enter into rest [*exaltation—see D&C 84:24*], as he said, As I have sworn in my wrath, If they harden their hearts they shall not enter into my rest; also, I have sworn, If they will not harden their hearts, they shall enter into my rest; although the works of God were prepared, [*or in place*], from the foundation of the world [*In other words, the Father's plan of salvation for us was planned completely in premortality.*]

4 For he spake in a certain place [*in Genesis 2:2*] of the seventh day on this wise, And God did rest the seventh day from all his works.

5 And in this place again, If they shall enter into my rest.

**JST Hebrews 4:5**

5 And in this place again, If they harden not their hearts they shall enter into my rest.

6 Seeing therefore it remaineth that some must enter therein [*some will enter into exaltation*], and they to whom it was first preached [*many to whom it has been preached in times past, including the children of Israel*] entered not in [*did not enter into God's presence*] because of unbelief:

7 Again, he limiteth a certain day [*he appoints a certain day*], saying in David [*in Psalm 95:7–8*], To day, after so long a time; as it is said, To day if ye will hear his voice, harden not your hearts.

8 For if Jesus [*Joshua; see Acts 7:45, footnote a, in our Bible*] had given them rest [*if the children of Israel had become a righteous people when Joshua was their leader*], then would he [*God*] not afterward have spoken of another day. [*In other words, the majority of the children of Israel were not righteous under Moses or Joshua. Therefore, God prophesied through His prophets that the day would yet come when Israel would become righteous and enter into God's rest. See Isaiah 29:22–24.*]

9 There remaineth therefore a rest to the people of God [*there will come a time when Israel will become righteous and enter into God's rest*].

10 For he that is entered into his rest [*the person who enters into exaltation*], he also hath ceased from his own works [*has finished his labors toward exaltation*], as God did from his [*just as God ceased from His labors when He finished creating the earth; see Genesis 2:2 as referred to in verse 4, above*].

11 Let us labour [*work*] therefore to enter into that rest, lest any man fall after the same example of unbelief [*for fear that we might fall away into unbelief like the children of Israel did*].

12 For the word of God [*the gospel of Jesus Christ*] is quick [*alive; Strong's #2198*], and powerful, and sharper than any two-edged sword, piercing even to the dividing asunder of soul and spirit, and of the joints and marrow, and is a discerner of [*and reveals*] the thoughts and intents of the heart.

**JST Hebrews 4:12**

12 For the word of God is quick, and powerful, and sharper than any two-edged sword, piercing even to the dividing asunder of body and spirit, and of the joints and marrow, and is a discerner of the thoughts and intents of the heart.

13 Neither is there any creature that is not manifest [*revealed*] in his sight [*none of our thoughts and intents are hidden from God*]: but all things are

naked [*completely exposed*] and opened unto the eyes of him [*God*] with whom we have to do.

14 Seeing then that we have a great high priest [*Hebrews 3:1*], that is passed into the heavens [*who has gone to heaven*], Jesus the Son of God, let us hold fast our profession [*let us hold firmly to our testimonies and live the gospel we profess to believe*].

Next, in verse 15, Paul reminds us that the Savior has gone through everything we go through, including temptations, and understands us, and is indeed "touched" with deep feelings and mercy for us.

15 For we have not an high priest [*Christ; see Hebrews 3:1*] which cannot be touched [*can't relate to our mortal weaknesses*] with the feeling of our infirmities; but was in all points tempted like as we are, yet without sin [*Christ was perfect*].

16 Let us therefore come boldly [*with confidence: Strong's #3954*] unto the throne of grace [*unto our merciful Father in Heaven*], that we may obtain mercy [*through Christ's Atonement*], and find grace to help in time of need.

# HEBREWS 5

This chapter contains one of our most important scripture references used in missionary work, namely, verse 4. It deals with the necessity of having proper priesthood authority in the true Church of Jesus Christ. It emphasizes that we can't just "feel" called to set up a church or whatever; rather, God's kingdom is a kingdom of order and those who hold positions of authority in it must be called by God through the laying on of hands in the same way Aaron was. In this chapter Paul continues to teach the Jewish converts (the Hebrews) about Christ and His role as "the Great High Priest," and begins by comparing Christ with men who are called as high priests.

There are no JST changes for this chapter.

1 FOR every high priest taken from among men [*every mortal man who is called and ordained to be a high priest*] is ordained for men in things pertaining to God [*is called to serve his fellow beings in God's work here on earth*], that he may offer both gifts and sacrifices for sins [*and is authorized to perform priesthood functions for the people*]:

2 Who can have compassion on [*for*] the ignorant, and on them that are out of the way [*those who are going astray*]; for that [*because*] he himself also is compassed with [*surrounded by*] infirmity [*has shortcomings and imperfections*].

3 And by reason hereof [*and because of this*] he ought, as for the people, so also for himself, to offer for sins [*he ought to work on his own salvation as well as on the salvation of the people whom he serves*].

4 And no man taketh this honour unto himself, but he that is called of God, as was Aaron. [*In other words, no one takes this priesthood upon himself without being properly called of God and having it conferred upon him by the laying on of hands as was the case with Aaron. See Numbers 27:18–23.*]

5 So also Christ glorified not himself to be made an high priest [*Christ did not want to bring glory to Himself as a high priest*]; but he [*to the Father*] that said unto him [*in Psalm 2:7*], Thou art my Son, to day have I begotten thee [*you are my Only Begotten Son in the flesh*].

6 As he saith also in another place [*Psalm 110:4*], Thou art a priest for ever after the order of Melchisedec. [*In other words, Christ was a high priest in the Melchizedek Priesthood. Melchizedek*

*was the great prophet and leader to whom Abraham paid tithing (Genesis 14:20.) For more about Melchizedek, see Bible Dictionary under "Melchizedek."*]

Verses 7 and 8, next, refer to Melchizedek. See Hebrews 5:7, footnote a, in our Bible.

7 Who in the days of his flesh, when he [*Melchizedek*] had offered up prayers and supplications with strong crying and tears unto him [*God*] that was able to save him from death [*perhaps referring to the event in JST Genesis 14:26, where Melchizedek, when he was a child, "stopped the mouths of lions, and quenched the violence of fire."*], and was heard in that he feared [*was heard because he had reverence for God; Strong's #2124*];

Verse 8 refers to both Melchizedek and Christ. See McConkie, *Doctrinal New Testament Commentary*, Vol. 3, p. 157.

8 Though he were a Son, yet learned he obedience by the things which he suffered;

9 And being made perfect, he [*Christ*] became the author [*provider*] of eternal salvation unto all them that obey him;

10 Called of God an high priest [*called by the Father to be a high priest*] after the order of Melchisedec.

11 Of whom we have many things to say [*we have much to say about this*], and hard to be uttered [*but it is hard to explain*], seeing ye are dull of hearing [*because you are spiritually out of tune and slow to learn*].

12 For when for the time ye ought to be teachers [*considering the time you have already had to learn about this, you should be teaching it to others*], ye have need that one teach you again [*but you have to be taught it again and again yourselves*] which be the first principles [*these are basic principles*] of the oracles of God [*words of God; Strong's #3051*]; and are become such as have need of milk, and not of strong meat [*you have become the type of members who have to be fed milk because you are not ready for meat*]. [*In other words, you can't be given the deeper doctrines of the gospel because you have not yet mastered the basics.*]

13 For every one that useth milk [*everyone who can only handle milk*] is unskilful [*inexperienced; Strong's #0552*] in the word of righteousness [*in the gospel*]: for he is a babe [*he must be treated as a small child as far as what we can teach him*].

14 But strong meat [*more advanced doctrine and truth*] belongeth to them that are of full age [*mature in the gospel*], even those who by reason of use have their senses exercised [*developed*] to discern both good and evil [*to distinguish between good and evil, true doctrine and false doctrine*].

# HEBREWS 6

Paul continues by encouraging these members to go on to perfection, and warns against becoming sons of perdition. Among other things, he describes sons of perdition as those members whose hatred toward Christ is such that they would gladly crucify Him again if they could (verse 6).

The JST for verse one makes an important change. It says "Therefore not leaving. . ." as opposed to "Therefore leaving. . ." in the Bible.

1 THEREFORE leaving the principles of the doctrine of Christ, let us go on unto perfection [*let us continue growing toward exaltation*]; not laying again the foundation of repentance from dead works, and of faith toward God, [*In other words, let's keep growing in the gospel, not having to relearn again and again the basics or the "first principles" of the gospel (Hebrews 5:12)*

*including those things mentioned in verse 2, next.*]

**JST Hebrews 6:1**
1 Therefore not leaving the principles of the doctrine of Christ, let us go on unto perfection; not laying again the foundation of repentance from dead works, and of faith toward God.

2 Of the doctrine of baptisms, and of laying on of hands, and of resurrection of the dead, and of eternal judgment.

**JST Hebrews 6:2**
2 Of the doctrine of baptisms, of laying on of hands, and of the resurrection of the dead, and of eternal judgment.

3 And this will we do, if God permit. [*In other words, we will continue advancing until we reach exaltation if God judges us worthy of it.*]

**JST Hebrews 6:3**
3 And we will go on unto perfection if God permit.

Next, in verses 4–6, Paul briefly describes what it takes to become a son of perdition, assigned to outer darkness forever. Compare with D&C 76: 31–35.

4 For it is impossible, and have tasted of the heavenly gift [*have participated in temple endowments*], and were made partakers of the Holy Ghost [*who had the Gift of the Holy Ghost and who had strong testimonies*],

**JST Hebrews 6:4**
4 For he hath made it impossible for those who were once enlightened, and have tasted of the heavenly gift, and were made partakers of the Holy Ghost,

5 And have tasted the good word of God, and the powers of the world to come, [*In other words, they have participated fully in the gospel and understand the plan of salvation and the possibility of exaltation in the world to come.*]

6 If they shall fall away, to renew them again unto repentance [*God cannot bring them back again through the process of repentance*]; seeing they crucify to themselves the Son of God afresh, and put him to an open shame [*since they have become just like Satan and would gladly crucify Christ again if they could and would openly condemn Him again in front of the whole world*].

**JST Hebrews 6:6**
6 If they shall fall away, to be renewed again unto repentance; seeing they crucify unto themselves the Son of God afresh, and put him to an open shame.

President Joseph F. Smith explained the concepts given in verses 4–6, above, as follows: "And he that believes, is baptized, and receives the light and testimony of Jesus Christ, and walks well for a season, receiving the fulness of the blessings of the gospel in this world, and afterwards turns wholly unto sin, violating his covenants, he will be among those whom the gospel can never reach in the spirit world; and all such go beyond its saving power, they will taste the second death, and be banished from the presence of God eternally." (*Gospel Doctrine*, Deseret Book, 1939, p. 476.)

7 For the earth which drinketh in the rain that cometh oft upon it, and bringeth forth herbs [*plants*] meet [*necessary*] for them by whom it is dressed, receiveth blessing from God:

**JST Hebrews 6:7**
7 For the day cometh that the earth which drinketh in the rain that cometh oft upon it, and bringeth forth herbs meet for them who dwelleth thereon, by whom it is dressed, who now receiveth blessings from God, shall be cleansed with fire.

8 But that which beareth thorns and briers is rejected, and is nigh unto cursing; whose end is to be burned.

> **JST Hebrews 6:8**
> 8 For that which beareth thorns and briers is rejected, and is nigh unto cursing; therefore they who bring not forth good fruits, shall be cast into the fire; for their end is to be burned.

9 But, beloved, we are persuaded better things of you [*we are convinced that you will be found among the righteous*], and things that accompany salvation [*and doing things that lead to salvation*], though we thus speak [*even though we speak and warn against becoming sons of perdition*].

10 For God is not unrighteous to forget your work and labour of love, which ye have shewed [*showed*] toward his name, in that ye have ministered to the saints, and do minister. [*In other words, God is aware of your righteousness and that you have done many good deeds to the Saints and continue to do so.*]

> **JST Hebrews 6:10**
> 10 For God is not unrighteous, therefore he will not forget your work and labor of love, which ye have showed toward his name, in that ye have ministered to the saints, and do minister.

11 And we desire that every one of you do shew the same diligence to the full assurance of hope [*leading to the full assurance of salvation*] unto the end: [*In other words, we desire that each of you continue faithful to the end so that you make your salvation sure.*]

12 That ye be not slothful [*lazy*], but followers of them who through faith and patience inherit the promises [*inherit salvation*].

13 For when God made promise to Abraham, because he could swear [*make covenants*] by no greater, he sware by himself [*he made promises to Abraham in His own name; see Genesis 22:16*],

14 Saying, Surely blessing I will bless thee [*"I will bless thee above measure"; see Abraham 2:9 (In other words, I will bless you with exaltation)*], and multiplying I will multiply thee [*you will have descendants as numerous "as the sand which is upon the sea shore;" see Genesis 22:17*].

15 And so, after he [*Abraham*] had patiently endured [*after he waited until he was 100 years old; see Genesis 21:5*], he obtained the promise [*he and Sarah had Isaac, through whom the promises made to Abraham would be fulfilled; see Genesis 21:2*].

16 For men verily swear by the greater [*make promises by someone or something greater than themselves*]: and an oath for confirmation is to them an end of all strife [*when men give their word by making an oath, there is no more debating over the matter*].

17 Wherein God, willing more abundantly to shew unto the heirs of promise the immutability of his counsel [*willing to give even more abundant evidence of the unchangeable nature of His plan of salvation for us*], confirmed it by an oath [*God made an unchangeable oath with Abraham to bless his descendants*]:

> In verse 18, next, Paul speaks of "two immutable things." They are two unchangeable promises given to Abraham in Genesis 22:17, as follows: (1) "That in blessing I will bless thee [*I will give you innumerable blessings leading to exaltation*], and (2) in multiplying I will multiply thy seed as the stars of the heaven, and as the sand which is upon the sea shore [*I will give you innumerable posterity*]."

18 That by two immutable things, in which it was impossible for God to lie, we might have a strong consolation [*comfort*], who have fled for refuge [*who have fled to God*] to lay hold upon the hope set before us [*to take hold of the promise of exaltation through righteousness and covenant making which He has made available to us*]:

19 Which hope we have as an anchor

of the soul [*this hope for exaltation through Jesus Christ is an anchor for our souls*], both sure and stedfast [*absolutely dependable*], and which entereth into that within the veil [*this hope for exaltation penetrates the veil between earth and heaven*];

20 Whither [*to which*] the forerunner [*Christ*] is for us entered, even Jesus, made an high priest for ever after the order of Melchisedec. [*In other words, Christ was the "forerunner" who prepared the way for us to go through the veil into the presence of God. The symbolism is of the high priest serving in the temple in Jerusalem going through the veil into the Holy of Holies, which is symbolic of entering into celestial glory and into the presence of God.*]

# HEBREWS 7

Paul will now teach more about Melchizedek, who was the king of Salem, to whom Abraham paid tithing and for whom the high priesthood was named. One of Paul's overall goals in this chapter is to point out to the Jewish (Hebrew) converts to the Church in his day what Christ's position was compared to Abraham (whom the Jew's held in highest esteem as their great ancestor) and Melchizedek. The logic that Paul uses is this: The Levites were under Moses. Moses was under Abraham. Abraham was under Melchizedek. Melchizedek was under Christ. The point is that Christ is above them all. All of this will lead up to the point that salvation cannot be attained through living the Law of Moses. Rather, it is attained through Christ.

1 FOR this Melchisedec, king of Salem [*Jerusalem; see Bible Dictionary under "Salem"*], priest of the most high God, who met Abraham returning from the slaughter of the kings, and blessed him [*see Genesis 14:17–19*];

Verse 2, next, can be used to teach the law of tithing as well as to teach what the name "Melchizedek" means.

2 To whom also Abraham gave a tenth part of all [*to whom Abraham paid tithing; Genesis 14:20*]; first being by interpretation King of righteousness [*first of all, the name, "Melchizedek," means "King of righteousness"*], and after that also King of Salem, which is, King of peace [*secondly, Melchizedek was the King of Salem, which means King of peace*];

The two definitions of the name "Melchizedek," given in verse 2, above, are reminders to all Melchizedek Priesthood holders that they should be righteous and should be peacemakers. Alma 13:17–19 gives us more details about Melchizedek as follows: "Now this Melchizedek was a king over the land of Salem; and his people had waxed strong in iniquity and abomination; yea, they had all gone astray; they were full of all manner of wickedness; But Melchizedek having exercised mighty faith, and received the office of the high priesthood according to the holy order of God, did preach repentance unto his people. And behold, they did repent; and Melchizedek did establish peace in the land in his days; therefore he was called the prince of peace, for he was the king of Salem; and he did reign under his father. Now, there were many before him, and also there were many afterwards, but none were greater; therefore, of him they have more particularly made mention."

Without the help of the JST, verse 3, next, sounds like Melchizedek did not have a father or mother, nor did he have posterity, neither did he die. The JST tells us that this verse refers to the Melchizedek Priesthood, rather than Melchizedek himself.

3 Without father, without mother, without descent, having neither beginning of days, nor end of life; but made like unto the Son of God; abideth a priest continually.

**JST Hebrews 7:3**

3 For this Melchizedek was ordained a priest after the order of the Son of God [*which is the priesthood held by the Savior*], which order [*which priesthood*] was without father, without mother, without descent, having neither beginning of days, nor end of life. And all those who are ordained unto this priesthood are made like unto the Son of God, abiding a priest continually [*hold the same priesthood as the Savior, and will hold it forever*].

4 Now consider how great this man [*Melchizedek*] was, unto whom even the patriarch Abraham gave the tenth of the spoils [*unto whom Abraham paid tithing*].

Paul next refers to the Levites who were the men who held the Aaronic Priesthood among the children of Israel under Moses. Among other duties, these "sons of Levi" collected tithing from the Israelites.

5 And verily they that are of the sons of Levi, who receive the office of the priesthood [*the Aaronic Priesthood*], have a commandment to take tithes of the people according to the law [*the Law of Moses*], that is, of [*from*] their brethren, though they come out of the loins of Abraham [*even though they are descendants of Abraham*]:

6 But he [*Melchizedek*] whose descent is not counted from them [*who was not an Israelite and did not descend from Abraham*] received tithes of [*from*] Abraham, and blessed him [*Abraham*] that had the promises [*with whom God had made the covenants; see Genesis 12:1–3; 17:1–8; 22:17–18; Abraham 2:9–11*].

The JST, Genesis 14:36–40 expands upon verse 6, above, as follows: "And this Melchizedek, having thus established righteousness, was called the king of heaven by his people, or, in other words, the King of peace. And he lifted up his voice, and he blessed Abram [*Abraham*], being the high priest, and the keeper of the storehouse of God; Him whom God had appointed to receive tithes for the poor. Wherefore, Abram paid unto him tithes of all that he had, of all the riches which he possessed, which God had given him more than that which he had need. And it came to pass, that God blessed Abram, and gave unto him riches, and honor, and lands for an everlasting possession; according to the covenant which he had made, and according to the blessing wherewith Melchizedek had blessed him."

7 And without all contradiction the less [*Abraham*] is blessed of [*by*] the better [*Melchizedek*]. [*In other words, it is not a contradiction that Melchizedek was higher in authority than Abraham, because Abraham paid tithes to him.*]

8 And here men that die receive tithes [*and here, on the one hand, we are dealing with mortal men who receive tithing from other mortals*]; but there [*on the other hand*] he [*Christ*] receiveth them [*receives tithes from all*], of whom it is witnessed that he [*Christ*] liveth [*has been resurrected and is alive*]. [*In other words, Christ is above all, because, ultimately, He is the one to whom all pay tithes. For more on this, see McConkie,* Doctrinal New Testament Commentary, *Vol. 3, p. 169.*]

Verse 9, next, refers back to "the sons of Levi" mentioned in verse 5.

9 And as I may so say [*and if I may stretch your minds a bit*], Levi also, who receiveth tithes, payed tithes in Abraham [*Levi, a descendant of Abraham, was there with Abraham when he paid tithes to Melchizedek*].

10 For he [*Levi*] was yet in the loins of his father [*his ancestor*], when Melchisedec met him [*Abraham*]. [*In other words, in a sense, Levi was still inside Abraham, as a seed, and thus was there when Abraham paid tithes to Melchizedek.*]

Paul will now make the transition from the above doctrines, about

Christ's position above all prophets and people, to the fact that the Law of Moses is under the gospel of Christ, and that salvation cannot be obtained through the Law of Moses. Remember, he is talking to Jews who have joined the Church of Jesus Christ but still think that they should live the Law of Moses completely.

11 If therefore perfection were by [*if exaltation came through*] the Levitical [*Aaronic*] priesthood, (for under it the people received the law,) [*in other words, the Law of Moses was administered under the Aaronic* Priesthood] what further need was there that another priest [*Christ*] should rise [*come to us*] after the order of Melchisedec [*why would we need someone who held the Melchizedek Priesthood*], and not be called after the order of Aaron? [*In other words, if we could attain exaltation through the ordinances of the Aaronic Priesthood, as had in the Law of Moses, why would we need another priest, who was a Melchizedek Priesthood high priest? In other words, why would we need Christ and His gospel if the Law of Moses could save us in celestial glory?*]

12 For the priesthood being changed, there is made of necessity a change also of the law. [*Since we have gone from the Aaronic Priesthood to the Melchizedek Priesthood, it means that we have gone from Aaronic Priesthood laws and ordinances (associated with the Law of Moses) to the higher laws and ordinances of the Melchizedek Priesthood (Associated with Christ and His gospel) which lead to exaltation.*]

13 For he [*Christ*] of whom these things are spoken pertaineth to another tribe [*comes from a different tribe of Israel (namely, the tribe of Judah)*], of which no man gave attendance at the altar [*and no men from the tribe of Judah held the Aaronic Priesthood and officiated at the altar in the temple under the Law of Moses*].

14 For it is evident [*clear*] that our Lord [*Christ*] sprang out of Juda [*came from the tribe of Judah*]; of which tribe Moses spake nothing concerning priesthood [*and Moses did not give the priesthood to the men of the tribe of Judah*].

15 And it is yet far more evident [*clear*]: for that after the similitude of Melchisedec there ariseth another priest [*that we have been given a High Priest (Christ) of whom Melchizedek was symbolic (as "King of righteousness" and "King of peace" in verse 2, above)*],

16 Who is made [*who comes to us*], not after the law of a carnal commandment [*not with the Aaronic Priesthood and the laws and commandments of the Law of Moses*], but after the power of an endless life [*but with the higher priesthood power to bring us to exaltation*].

17 For he [*David*] testifieth [*in Psalm 110:4*], Thou [*Christ*] art a priest for ever after the order of Melchisedec.

Are you impressed with Paul's command of the scriptures? As pointed out previously, Paul has an amazing memory for the prophecies about the Messiah contained in the Old Testament, which, of course, was the book of scripture for the Jews. Not only does he recall these passages of scripture, but he has marvelous inspired skill in using them in making convincing arguments as he teaches the gospel of Jesus Christ.

18 For there is verily [*truly*] a disannulling of the commandment going before [*there is a doing away with the Law of Moses*] for the weakness and unprofitableness thereof [*because it is weak and unprofitable in the sense that it cannot bring us to exaltation*].

19 For the law [*of Moses*] made nothing perfect [*was not capable of bringing us to perfection in exaltation*], but the bringing in of a better hope did; by the which we draw nigh unto God.

**JST Hebrews 7:19**

19 For the law [*the Law of Moses*] was administered without an oath [*did not have the oath and covenant of the Melchizedek Priesthood, as explained in D&C 84:33–42*] and made nothing perfect [*could not lead us to perfection*], but was only the bringing in of a better hope [*rather was only the means of pointing our minds to Jesus Christ*]; by the which we draw nigh unto God [*through whom we can return to the presence of the Father*].

20 And inasmuch as not without an oath he was made priest:

**JST Hebrews 7:20**

20 Inasmuch as this high priest [*Christ*] was not without an oath [*did not function without the Melchizedek Priesthood*], by so much [*all the more*] was Jesus made the surety [*the guarantee*] of a better testament [*covenant*]. [*In other words, Jesus Christ as the Great High Priest became the anchor or foundation of a "better" covenant, because the ordinances of the Melchizedek Priesthood involve covenants which guarantee exaltation for the faithful.*]

21 (For those [*Aaronic, Levitical; see verse 11*] priests were made without an oath [*the Levitical priests were not called with an oath*]; but this with an oath [*but Christ was made a high priest*] by him that said unto him, The Lord sware [*promised*] and will not repent [*will not go back on His word*], Thou [*Christ*] art a priest for ever after the order of Melchisedec:)

22 By so much was Jesus made a surety [*the guarantee*] of a better testament [*of the "New Testament," in other words, the "new and everlasting covenant," which, when faithfully kept, leads to exaltation*].

23 And they [*Levitical priests; verse 5*] truly were many priests, because they were not suffered [*allowed*] to continue by reason of death [*because they eventually died*]:

24 But this man [*Christ*], because he continueth ever [*lives forever*], hath an unchangeable priesthood [*will hold His priesthood authority forever*].

25 Wherefore he [*Christ*] is able also to save them to the uttermost [*to and including exaltation*] that come unto God by him [*who come unto the Father through Him*], seeing he ever liveth to make intercession for them [*since His Atonement continues forever with its power to intercede and save them*].

26 For such an high priest became us [*was needed by us*], who is holy, harmless, undefiled, separate from sinners [*sinless*], and made higher than the heavens;

**JST Hebrews 7:25**

25 For such an high priest became us, who is holy, harmless, undefiled, separate from sinners, and made ruler over the heavens;

A little background will help you in understanding the next verses. In Old Testament times, before the Levitical priests went to perform sacrifices for the cleansing of the people of Israel, they were required first to offer sacrifices for their own cleansing and purification. Christ, of course, did not need to cleanse Himself from sin first, before offering Himself as a sacrifice for us whereby we can become clean and pure from our sins.

27 Who needeth not daily, as those high priests, to offer up sacrifice, first for his own sins, and then for the people's: for this he did once, when he offered up himself.

**JST Hebrews 7:26**

26 And not as those high priests who offered up sacrifice daily, first for their own sins, and then for the sins of the people; for he needeth not offer sacrifice for his own sins, for he knew no sins; but for the sins of the people. And this [*atoning for the sins of the people*] he did once, when he offered up himself.

28 For the law [*of Moses*] maketh men high priests which have infirmity [*who have imperfections*]; but the word of the oath [*the covenants administered by the Melchizedek Priesthood*], which was since the law [*which were given after the Law of Moses was given*], maketh the Son [*were given by Christ*], who is consecrated for evermore [*who is our Savior for evermore*].

# HEBREWS 8

Paul will now summarize what he has taught in the previous chapters, as he continues to teach the need for the Savior, Jesus Christ.

1 NOW of the things which we have spoken this is the sum [*now, to summarize what I have said in this letter so far*]: We have such an high priest [*Christ*], who is set on the right hand of the throne of the Majesty in the heavens [*who has returned to heaven and sits at the right hand of the Father*];

2 A minister of the sanctuary, and of the true tabernacle, which the Lord pitched, and not man. [*In other words, Christ is our High Priest who serves for us in heaven. He has gone on to prepare a place for us.*]

3 For every high priest is ordained to offer gifts and sacrifices: wherefore it is of necessity that this man [*Christ*] have somewhat also to offer [*something to offer as a sacrifice also*].

4 For if he were on earth, he should not be a priest, seeing that there are priests that offer gifts according to the law:

**JST Hebrews 8:4**

4 Therefore while he was on the earth, he offered for a sacrifice his own life for the sins of the people. Now every priest under the law [*who served under the Law of Moses*], must needs [*must of necessity*] offer gifts, or sacrifices, according to the law.

5 Who serve unto the example and shadow [*whose service is symbolic*] of heavenly things, as Moses was admonished of God [*instructed by God in Exodus 25:40*] when he was about to make the tabernacle: for, See, saith he, that thou make all things according to the pattern shewed to thee in the mount [*while you were on Mount Sinai*].

6 But now hath he [*Christ*] obtained a more excellent [*a superior*] ministry, by how much also he is the mediator of a better [*higher*] covenant, which was established upon better [*higher*] promises. [*In other words, the ministry of Jesus is as superior to the ministry of the priests of the Aaronic Priesthood mentioned in verses 4 and 5, above, as the Melchizedek Priesthood covenants and ordinances are to the ordinances of the Law of Moses.*]

7 For if that first covenant [*the Law of Moses*] had been faultless [*had been able to lead us to perfection*], then should no place have been sought for the second [*then there would have been no need for the new covenant brought by Christ*].

8 For finding fault with them [*pointing out that the requirements of the Law of Moses were not able to bring us salvation in heaven*], he saith [*God said, in Jeremiah 31:31–34*], Behold, the days come [*the time will come in the future*], saith the Lord, when I will make a new covenant with the house of Israel and with the house of Judah [*and with the Jews*]:

9 Not according to the covenant [*the Law of Moses*] that I made with their fathers [*ancestors*] in the day when I took them by the hand to lead them out of the land of Egypt; because they continued not in my covenant [*because they broke the higher gospel laws I had given them*], and I regarded them not [*I had to withdraw some blessings from them*], saith the Lord.

10 For this is the covenant [*I will*

*describe the covenant*] that I will make with the house of Israel after those days [*in a future time*], saith the Lord; I will put my laws into their mind, and write them in their hearts: and I will be to them a God, and they shall be to me a people [*as prophesied in Jeremiah 31:33*]: [*In other words, the new covenant (the gospel of Jesus Christ) which I make with them will involve personal righteousness of heart and mind and testimony, rather than a law of performances and daily ritual and sacrifices, as was the case with the Law of Moses.*]

Next, in verse 11, Paul teaches that because of the new covenant brought in the gospel of Jesus Christ, the day will come in which everyone will follow Christ. We understand this to be referring to the Millennium. See D&C 84:98.

11 And they shall not teach every man his neighbour, and every man his brother, saying, Know the Lord: for all shall [*because everyone will*] know me, from the least to the greatest.

Next, Paul explains how such widespread acceptance of and loyalty to Christ can happen. The answer is simple. It will happen because people will take advantage of the gift of the Atonement.

12 For I will be merciful to their unrighteousness, and their sins and their iniquities will I remember no more. [*In other words, I will forgive them when they repent.*]

13 In that he saith, A new covenant, he hath made the first old [*the simple fact that God mentions a "new covenant" tells us that the "old covenant" (Law of Moses) will someday become obsolete*]. Now that which decayeth and waxeth old is ready to vanish away. [*In other words, the Law of Moses is on its way out because Christ fulfilled it.*]

# HEBREWS 9

Paul will continue here with the comparison between the symbolism contained in the rituals and sacrifices required by the Law of Moses and the sacrifice given by Christ as He carried out the Atonement. A brief description of the portable tent used by the children of Israel, which was very elaborate and ornate and was known as the "tabernacle," is helpful in understanding this chapter. We will use a description given in the Institute of Religion New Testament student manual, *The Life and Teachings of Jesus and His Apostles*, 1979 edition, p. 390. It is: "During Israel's wanderings and prior to the building of a temple in Solomon's day (about 970 B.C.), the priests of Israel performed the sacred ordinances in behalf of their people in a portable tent known as the tabernacle. This edifice, constructed in such a way that it could be quickly moved from place to place, was the first item set up in any new place of encampment. The tabernacle was composed of two parts. There was an outer compartment into which the Levites and sons of Aaron might enter daily to perform the sacred ordinances prescribed by the Mosaic law. There was also an inner compartment separated by a veil and considered to be the most holy place, into which the high priest might enter but once a year to perform his sacred duties on the Day of Atonement. As explained by Paul, the outer division of the tabernacle contained the sacred candlestick, twelve loaves of shewbread, and an altar of incense; in the inner chamber known as the Holy of Holies was located the ark of the covenant, a chest somewhat equivalent to a good-sized modern trunk. In the ark were kept the golden censer, the golden pot containing manna, Aaron's rod, and the

tablets on which were inscribed the Ten Commandments."

1 THEN verily the first covenant [*the Law of Moses; see notes in chapter 8, above*] had also ordinances of divine service, and a worldly sanctuary [*an earthly tabernacle, temple*].

2 For there was a tabernacle made [*by Moses for the children of Israel; see heading to Exodus 26 in our Bible*]; the first [*the first room in the tabernacle*], wherein was the candlestick, and the table, and the shewbread; which is called the sanctuary [*this room in the tabernacle was called "the sanctuary"*].

3 And after the second veil, the tabernacle, [*behind the second veil in the tabernacle made by Moses was the room*] which is called the Holiest of all [*the "Holy of Holies" or the "Most Holy Place"*];

4 Which had the golden censer, and the ark of the covenant overlaid round about with gold, wherein [*in the Ark of the Covenant*] was the golden pot that had manna, and Aaron's rod that budded, and the tables of the covenant [*the stone tablets which had the Ten Commandments on them*];

5 And over it [*above the Ark of the Covenant*] the cherubims of glory shadowing the mercyseat; of which we cannot now speak particularly [*about which we will not give details at this time*].

6 Now when these things were thus ordained [*when the tabernacle was being used among the Israelites*], the priests went always [*all of the priests could go*] into the first tabernacle [*into the first room*], accomplishing [*performing*] the service of God.

7 But into the second went the high priest alone [*but only the high priest could go into the Holy of Holies*] once every year, not without blood, which he offered for himself, and for the errors of the people [*not without offering a blood sacrifice to atone for his own sins and for the sins of the people*]:

8 The Holy Ghost this signifying, that the way into the holiest of all was not yet made manifest, while as the first tabernacle was yet standing: [*In other words, the Holy Ghost tells us that, under the Law of Moses, the way to the "Holy of Holies," (symbolic of the celestial kingdom) was not shown to the people.*]

**JST Hebrews 9:8**

8 The Holy Ghost signifying this that the way into the holiest of all was not yet made manifest, while as yet the first tabernacle was standing;

9 Which was a figure [*served as symbolism*] for the time then present [*for that time among the Israelites*], in which were offered both gifts and sacrifices [*when they were following the Law of Moses*], that could not make him that did the service perfect [*which could not make the priests who were performing the rituals or the people providing the sacrifices perfect*], as pertaining to the conscience [*with respect to the deep, inner soul*];

10 Which stood only in [*the Law of Moses consisted only of*] meats [*foods*] and drinks, and divers [*various*] washings, and carnal [*earthly*] ordinances, imposed on them until the time of reformation [*until the time when Christ would restore the higher laws and ordinances of His gospel*].

**JST Hebrews 9:10**

10 Which consisted only in meats and drinks, and divers washings, and carnal ordinances, imposed on them until the time of reformation.

11 But Christ being come an high priest of good things to come, by a greater and more perfect tabernacle, not made with hands, that is to say, not of this building; [*In other words, Christ has already come and performed the role of a high priest for us, sacrificing Himself as a blood sacrifice for us so that we can*

*enter into a "more perfect tabernacle," in other words, the celestial kingdom.*]

12 Neither by the blood of goats and calves [*as used by the high priests in the tabernacle to symbolically cleanse themselves and their people from sin*], but by his own blood [*by giving His own life for us*] he entered in once into the holy place [*he entered into the "Holy of Holies," in other words, the celestial kingdom*], having obtained eternal redemption for us [*having made eternal exaltation available to us*].

13 For if the blood of bulls and of goats, and the ashes of an heifer sprinkling the unclean, sanctifieth to the purifying of the flesh: [*If, according to the Law of Moses, the blood of sacrificial animals and the ashes of burnt offerings can be ceremonially sprinkled upon a person to make him ritually "clean."*]

14 How much more shall the blood of Christ, who through the eternal Spirit offered himself without spot [*as a perfect sacrifice, without sin or blemish*] to God, purge your conscience from dead works to serve the living God? [*In other words, don't you think that if people can be made outwardly clean through ritual cleansing in the Law of Moses, you can become inwardly clean through purging you mind of notions of following the dead works of the Law of Moses and following Christ?*]

15 And for this cause [*this is the purpose for which*] he is the mediator [*the one who helps us return to the Father*] of the new testament, that by means of death [*by offering Himself as a sacrifice*], for the redemption of the transgressions that were under the first testament, [*in other words, to redeem us from personal sins which remained upon us when we were living the Law of Moses*], they which are called [*the Israelites*] might receive the promise of eternal inheritance [*the promise of exaltation*].

**JST Hebrews 9:15**

15 And for this cause he is the mediator of the new covenant, that by means of death, for the redemption of the transgressions that were under the first covenant, they which are called might receive the promise of eternal inheritance.

16 For where a testament is, there must also of necessity be the death of the testator.

**JST Hebrews 9:16**

16 For where a covenant is, there must also of necessity be the death of the victim.

The word "testator," as used in the King James Bible, means a person who is making out a will to leave an inheritance to someone else. Thus, the "testator" must die before the heir can inherit the gift. So also, says Paul in effect, the Savior had to die in order for us to be able to inherit His gift to us, which is eternal life, provided we live His gospel.

17 For a testament is of force after men are dead [*the will transfers the gift or inheritance to the heir only after the person who made the will is dead*]: otherwise it is of no strength at all while the testator liveth.

**JST Hebrews 9:17**

17 For a covenant is of force after the victim is dead; otherwise it is of no strength at all while the victim liveth.

The word "victim," used by Joseph Smith in these verses, carries the connotation of one who is innocent suffering for the sins of others.

18 Whereupon neither the first testament was dedicated without blood. [*This is why even the Law of Moses was not put into effect without the shedding of blood.*]

**JST Hebrews 9:18**

18 Whereupon neither the first covenant was dedicated without blood.

19 For when Moses had spoken every

precept [*teaching and commandment*] to all the people according to the law [*see Exodus 24:7–8*], he took the blood of calves and of goats, with water, and scarlet wool, and hyssop, and sprinkled both the book [*scroll*], and all the people,

There is much symbolism in verse 19, above, which relates to Christ's Atonement. Blood, water, scarlet fabric, and hyssop were all present during Christ's atoning sacrifice for us. Blood came from every pore in Gethsemane. Water gushed forth from the wound in His side after He had died upon the cross. The soldiers mocked Him with a scarlet robe upon His back, before He was crucified. Hyssop was used in putting vinegar to Christ's mouth while He was on the cross; see John 19:29.

20 Saying, This is the blood of the testament which God hath enjoined [*commanded; Strong's #1781*] unto you.

**JST Hebrews 9:20**

20 Saying, This is the blood of the covenant which God hath enjoined unto you.

21 Moreover he [*Moses*] sprinkled with blood both the tabernacle, and all the vessels of the ministry [*containers used in the services and rituals*].

**JST Hebrews 9:21**

21 Moreover he sprinkled likewise with blood both the tabernacle, and all the vessels of the ministry.

Next, Paul points out that virtually everything was cleansed by blood, in the rites and rituals of the Law of Moses. This, of course, is symbolic of the cleansing and healing that comes into every aspect of our lives through the cleansing blood of Christ.

22 And almost all things are by the law [*of Moses*] purged [*cleansed*] with blood; and without shedding of blood is no remission [*of sins*].

23 It was therefore necessary that the patterns of [*the "types" or things in the Law of Moses that are symbolic of*] things in the heavens should be purified with these [*with the blood of sacrificial animals*]; but the heavenly things themselves with better sacrifices than these [*but the things which lead to exaltation in the celestial kingdom must be made available to us with a better sacrifice than animal sacrifices, namely, Christ*].

24 For Christ is not entered into the holy places made with hands [*for Christ's sacrifice did not take place in the tabernacle or the temple made by men*], which are the figures of the true [*which are symbolic of the true "holy places," namely, celestial glory*]; but into heaven itself, now to appear in the presence of God for us [*and now He is in the presence of the Father as our Mediator*]:

25 Nor yet that he should offer himself often, as the high priest entereth into the holy place every year with blood of others [*Christ's sacrifice does not have to be repeated every year for us*];

26 For then must he often have suffered since the foundation of the world [*if that were the case, He would have had to have suffered, been crucified and resurrected over and over again ever since the beginning of the world*]: but now once in the end of the world hath he appeared to put away sin by the sacrifice of himself. [*Jesus only had to die once to atone for us.*]

**JST Hebrews 9:26**

26 For then must he often have suffered since the foundation of the world; but now once in the meridian of time hath he appeared to put away sin by the sacrifice of himself.

27 And as it is appointed unto men once to die, but after this the judgment [*men die just once and then will appear before God on Judgment Day*]:

28 So Christ was once offered to bear the sins of many; and unto them that look for him shall he appear the second time without sin unto salvation.

**JST Hebrews 9:28**

28 So Christ was once offered to bear the sins of many; and he shall appear the second time, without sin unto salvation unto them that look for him.

There are some important doctrines contained in verses 27 and 28, above. First of all, many people believe in reincarnation, meaning that they believe that we have many lives here on earth. We live one life, for instance as a peasant, then another as a wealthy person, then another life as a soldier, etc., until we overcome evil and are worthy of heaven. This cannot be so, according to verse 27, above, because "it is appointed unto men once to die." In other words, we only have one mortal life here on earth. Another doctrine of interest especially to Latter-day Saints, is taught in verse 28. Occasionally, members of the Church who are aware that the Savior's Atonement works for the inhabitants of other worlds belonging to Heavenly Father (see D&C 76:24), ask whether or not Jesus has to be born, crucified, and die on each of those worlds. The answer is "No." Verse 28, above, informs us that Christ was sacrificed "once," and we know that His sacrifice occurred on our earth.

# HEBREWS 10

Paul will continue in this chapter with the theme that the Law of Moses cannot make us perfect, but the gospel brought by Christ can.

1 FOR the law [*of Moses*] having a shadow of good things to come [*is symbolic of the complete gospel to come*], and not the very image of the things [*and is not the full gospel*], can never with those sacrifices which they offered year by year continually make the comers thereunto perfect [*the Law of Moses cannot bring those who come unto it to exaltation*].

**JST Hebrews 10:1**

1 For the law having a shadow of good things to come, and not the very image of the things, can never with those sacrifices, which they offered continually year by year make the comers thereunto perfect.

2 For then would they not have ceased to be offered [*if it could, wouldn't the sacrifices have ceased to be offered*]? because that the worshippers once purged [*once cleansed and made perfect*] should have had no more conscience of sins [*would have had no more guilty conscience for sins*].

3 But in those sacrifices [*in the sacrifices required by the Law of Moses*] there is a remembrance again made of sins every year [*the sacrifices for sins continue to be made year after year*].

4 For it is not possible that the blood of bulls and of goats should take away sins [*animal sacrifices cannot take away sins*].

5 Wherefore when he [*Christ*] cometh into the world, he saith [*as recorded in Psalm 40:6–8*], Sacrifice and offering thou [*God*] wouldest not, but a body [*a mortal body*] hast thou prepared me [*Christ*]:

6 In burnt offerings and sacrifices for sin thou hast had no pleasure [*compare with Isaiah 1:11*].

7 Then said I, Lo, I come (in the volume of the book it is written of me,) to do thy will, O God [*O Father*].

8 Above when he said [*and, more importantly, He said*], Sacrifice and offering and burnt offerings and offering for sin thou [*Father*] wouldest not [*do not like*], neither hadst pleasure therein; which are offered by the law [*which are part of the Law of Moses*]; [*In other words, Paul explains that the Savior explained that the Father does not like or enjoy animal sacrifices and burnt offerings. His goal is to have people become truly personally*

*righteous through the Atonement of Christ.*]

9 Then said he [*Christ*], Lo, I come to do thy will, O God [*Father*]. He taketh away the first [*the Law of Moses*], that he may establish the second [*the gospel of Christ*].

10 By the which will we are sanctified [*made clean, pure, holy and fit to be in the presence of the Father*] through the offering of the body [*through the sacrifice*] of Jesus Christ once [*only once*] for all.

**JST Hebrews 10:10**

10 By which will we are sanctified through the offering once of the body of Jesus Christ.

11 And every priest [*in the Law of Moses*] standeth daily ministering and offering oftentimes the same sacrifices, which can never take away sins: [*No matter how many sacrifices are offered by how many priests, they still cannot take away our sins.*]

12 But this man [*Christ*], after he had offered one sacrifice for sins for ever [*after offering just one eternal sacrifice for sin*], sat down on the right hand of God;

13 From henceforth expecting till his enemies be made his footstool [*In other words, until He has overcome all things.*]

**JST Hebrews 10:13**

13 From henceforth to reign until his enemies be made his footstool.

14 For by one offering [*sacrifice*] he [*Christ*] hath perfected for ever them that [*has brought eternal exaltation to those who*] are sanctified [*made worthy to enter celestial glory*].

15 Whereof the Holy Ghost also is a witness to us [*the Holy Ghost bears witness to us of this*]: for after that he [*Christ*] had said before [*in the past, as recorded in Jeremiah 31:33–34*],

16 This is the covenant that I will make with them after those days [*after the Law of Moses has done its job*], saith the Lord, I will put my laws into their hearts, and in their minds will I write them; [*In other words, the day will come when I will have a righteous people.*]

17 And their sins and iniquities will I remember no more [*compare to D&C 58:42–43*].

18 Now where remission of these is, there is no more offering for sin [*when sins have been forgiven, there is no more need for additional sacrifices for sin*].

19 Having therefore, brethren, boldness [*confidence*] to enter into the holiest [*to enter into the heavenly "Holy of holies," in other words, the celestial kingdom*] by the blood of Jesus [*because of Christ's Atonement*],

20 By a new and living way [*through the new and living gospel of Christ rather than the old, dead Law of Moses*], which he [*Christ*] hath consecrated [*prepared*] for us, through the veil [*so that we can pass through the veil into the celestial kingdom*], that is to say, his flesh [*because Christ sacrificed His mortal life for us*];

21 And having an high priest over the house [*kingdom*] of God;

**JST Hebrews 10:21**

21 And having such an high priest over the house of God;

22 Let us draw near [*let us approach the Father*] with a true heart [*a pure heart, focused on righteousness*] in full assurance of faith [*with full confidence*], having our hearts sprinkled [*cleansed by the blood of Christ*] from an evil [*guilty*] conscience, and our bodies washed [*baptized*] with pure water.

23 Let us hold fast the profession of our faith [*let us hold firmly to what we profess (claim) to believe*] without wavering; (for he [*God*] is faithful [*is completely reliable*] that promised

[*who promised that we could attain exaltation through Christ*];)

24 And let us consider one another to provoke unto love and to good works: [*In other words, let us help one another, reminding each other to show love and to do good works.*]

25 Not forsaking the assembling of ourselves together [*not missing church meetings*], as the manner of some is [*like some are doing*]; but exhorting [*teaching and warning*] one another: and so much the more, as ye see the day [*the Second Coming and final judgment; Strong's #2250*] approaching.

Next, Paul warns them not to wait until it is too late to repent and faithfully follow Christ.

26 For if we sin wilfully [*if we refuse to repent*] after that we have received the knowledge of the truth, there remaineth no more sacrifice for sins [*the Savior's sacrifice cannot cleanse us from our sins*],

27 But [*all we will have left will be*] a certain fearful looking for of judgment and fiery indignation, which shall devour the adversaries [*the burning of the wicked at the Second Coming*].

28 He that despised [*rejected, disregarded; Strong's #0114*] Moses' law died without mercy under two or three witnesses [*when testified against by two or three witnesses*]:

29 Of how much sorer [*worse*] punishment, suppose ye, shall he be thought worthy, who hath trodden under foot [*who has despised, rejected*] the Son of God, and hath counted [*considered*] the blood of the covenant [*the Savior's blood which he shed for us*], wherewith he was sanctified, an unholy thing [*who has mocked the Savior's sacrifice*], and hath done despite unto the Spirit of grace [*and has despised the Atonement*]?

30 For we know him [*Jehovah*] that hath said [*in Deuteronomy 32:35*], Vengeance belongeth unto me, I will recompense [*repay*], saith the Lord. And again [*in Deuteronomy 32:36*], The Lord shall judge his people.

31 It is a fearful thing to fall into the hands of [*to be punished by*] the living God.

32 But call to remembrance the former days, in which, after ye were illuminated, ye endured a great fight of afflictions [*think back to the days when you were converted and had to endure many persecutions*];

33 Partly, whilst ye were made a gazingstock both by reproaches and afflictions [*sometimes you were insulted and persecuted in public*]; and partly, whilst ye became companions of them that were so used [*and sometimes you accompanied those who were so treated*].

34 For ye had compassion of me in my bonds [*you sympathized with me while I was in prison*], and took joyfully the spoiling of your goods [*and you cheerfully submitted to being plundered and ruined financially*], knowing in yourselves [*because of the inner assurance*] that ye have in heaven a better and an enduring substance [*that a better reward awaits you in heaven*].

35 Cast not away therefore your confidence [*don't set aside your faith in Christ*], which hath great recompence of reward [*through which you have a great reward in store for you*].

36 For ye have need of patience [*you will need to have patience in afflictions*], that, after ye have done the will of God [*that after you have endured faithfully to the end*], ye might receive the promise [*you will receive the promised exaltation*].

37 For yet a little while, and he [*Christ*] that shall come will come, and will not tarry [*when the time is right, Christ will not wait any longer, but will come again to earth; see Habakkuk 2:3*].

38 Now the just shall live by faith [*as written in Habakkuk 2:4*]: but if any man draw back [*if anyone apostatizes*], my soul shall have no pleasure in him.

39 But we are not of them who draw back unto perdition [*but we are not among those who will become sons of perdition*]; but of them that believe to the saving of the soul [*rather, we will remain among those who will stay faithful and thus save our souls*].

# HEBREWS 11

This chapter contains one of the most important, most beautiful, and most skillfully taught sermons about faith anywhere in scripture. So far in this letter, the Apostle Paul has prepared the Hebrew Saints with much skill and inspiration to receive the crowning principle which will help them attain exaltation. What is this crowning principle? Answer: Faith. We are taught in the Articles of Faith that faith is indeed the first principle of the gospel (see Fourth Article of Faith). Paul now teaches us why this is so.

1 NOW faith is the substance of things hoped for, the evidence [*the proof, conviction; Strong's #1650*] of things not seen.

**JST Hebrews 11:1**

1 Now faith is the assurance of things hoped for, the evidence of things not seen.

The words "substance," "evidence," and "assurance" (JST) in verse 1, above, are powerful words defining faith. "Substance," as defined in Strong's *Exhaustive Concordance of the Bible*, #5287, means "confidence, foundation." This is in harmony with the Prophet Joseph Smith's word "assurance." When we are "assured" in our hearts and minds that our course of action is in harmony with God's will, our lives are built upon that foundation. Thus, faith is the foundation upon which our whole lives are based.

Joseph Smith defined faith as both a "principle of action" and also a "principle of power." (See *Lectures on Faith*, Lecture First, published by Deseret Book Company, 1985, p. 7.) When we build our lives upon faith as a "principle of action," it influences every aspect of life. It gets us to church on Sunday. It urges us to "action" in doing good, paying tithing, fleeing filth, reading scriptures, praying, even if we don't feel like it, and on and on. It motivates us to attend the temple, to go on missions, to be honest when everyone around us is lying. It compels us to accept callings in the Church, to agree to speak in sacrament meeting when such things frighten us. In short, faith truly becomes the "substance" around which our lives are built. And, when such is the case, we are constantly given "evidence" or "proof" and "conviction," in other words, the Holy Ghost constantly bears testimony to us "assuring" us that the direction of our lives is correct and is leading us on a path which will lead to exaltation.

As mentioned above, Joseph Smith taught that faith is a principle of action and also a principle of power. For our lives, it is primarily a principle of action which will lead to our eventually having the power of gods. However, it gives us power right now to overcome evil and fear. It gives us power, when it is God's will, to have miracles performed in our behalf or in behalf of others. You may wish to pay special attention to the examples of faith given by Paul in the following verses and note which ones are primarily examples of faith as a principle of action and which are primarily examples of faith as a principle of power.

2 For by it [*faith*] the elders [*ancient prophets*] obtained a good report [*obtained strong testimonies; Strong's #3140; also see Hebrews 11:39, footnote a, in your Bible*].

3 Through faith we understand that the worlds were framed [*created*] by the word of God, so that things which are seen [*God's creations*] were not made of things which do appear [*were not created by powers which are visible to common man*].

4 By faith Abel offered unto God a more excellent sacrifice than Cain [*Abel offered an acceptable sacrifice, whereas Cain did not; see Moses 5:16–23*], by which he [*Abel*] obtained witness that he was righteous, God testifying of his gifts: and by it he [*Abel*] being dead yet speaketh.

The Prophet Joseph Smith adds much to our understanding of verse 4, above. He explains that Abel was taught by God concerning the Atonement and the symbolism of blood sacrifices. (See *Teachings of the Prophet Joseph Smith*, p. 58.) Thus, Abel offered one of the firstlings of his flock as a blood sacrifice to God. (See Moses 5:20.) Cain, on the other hand, in a rebellious mood and commanded by Satan, offered a sacrifice of garden produce rather than an animal sacrifice. (See Moses 5:18–19.)

Joseph Smith also explained what Paul meant in verse 4 when he said, referring to Abel, "he being dead yet speaketh," as follows: "How doth he yet speak? Why he magnified the Priesthood which was conferred upon him, and died a righteous man, and therefore has become an angel of God by receiving his body from the dead, holding still the keys of his dispensation; and was sent down from heaven unto Paul to minister consoling words, and to commit unto him a knowledge of the mysteries of godliness. And if this was not the case, I would ask, how did Paul know so much about Abel, and why should he talk about his speaking after he was dead? Hence, that he spoke after he was dead must be by being sent down out of heaven to administer." (*Teachings of the Prophet Joseph Smith*, selected and arranged by Joseph Fielding Smith [Salt Lake City: Deseret Book, 1976], p. 168.)

5 By faith Enoch was translated [*taken up to heaven without dying first*] that he should not see death; and was not found [*on earth*], because God had translated him: for before his translation he had this testimony [*he was given the assurance*], that he pleased God [*he knew that he was acceptable to God*].

Enoch and his entire city were translated (see Bible Dictionary under "Enoch.") He and his people in the City of Enoch were resurrected at the time of the Savior's resurrection (see D&C 133:54–55), and they will return to earth at the time of the Second Coming.

6 But without faith it is impossible to please him [*to become acceptable to God*]: for he that cometh to God must believe that he is, and that he is a rewarder of them that diligently seek him.

7 By faith Noah, being warned of God of things not seen as yet, moved with fear [*motivated by fear because he had faith in what God had told him about the coming flood*], prepared an ark to the saving of his house [*family*]; by the which he condemned the world [*Noah became a witness that obedience to God saves us, and thus his good example condemned those who disobeyed*], and became heir of the righteousness [*received exaltation*] which is by faith [*which comes through faith*].

8 By faith Abraham, when he was called to go out into a place [*the Land of Canaan; see Abraham 2:3–4*] which he should after receive for an inheritance, obeyed; and he went out, not knowing whither he went [*where he was going*].

9 By faith he sojourned in the land of promise, as in a strange country, dwelling in tabernacles [*tents; Strong's #4633*] with Isaac and Jacob, the heirs with him of the same promise [*who had been given the same promises of*

*exaltation through their faithfulness; see Abraham 2:9–11; Genesis 26:1–4; Genesis 28:13–15*]:

10 For he looked for a city [*the "celestial city," the celestial kingdom; Revelation 21:2*] which hath foundations, whose builder and maker is God. [*In other words, Abraham built his life on the sure foundation of faith in God which would lead him to the celestial kingdom and exaltation.*]

11 Through faith also Sara [*Sarah, Abraham's wife*] herself received strength to conceive seed [*see Genesis 18:10–11*], and was delivered of a child [*and had a baby who was named Isaac*] when she was past age [*when she was beyond childbearing age*], because she judged him [*God*] faithful who had promised.

12 Therefore sprang there even of one [*from Abraham*], and him as good as dead [*he was about 100 years old when Isaac was born; see Genesis 17:1 and 15–16*], so many [*posterity as many*] as the stars of the sky in multitude, and as the sand which is by the sea shore innumerable. [*In other words, through faith, no matter what other obstacles or circumstances get in the way, the promises of God will ultimately be completely fulfilled.*]

**JST Hebrews 11:12**

12 Therefore sprang there even of one, and him as good as dead, as many as the stars of the sky in multitude, and as the sand which is by the seashore innumerable.

13 These all [*all of these great people*] died in faith, not having received the promises [*not having received exaltation yet*], but having seen them afar off [*but knowing the promised blessings were coming far off in the future*], and were persuaded of them [*and were convinced they would receive those blessings*], and embraced them [*and made covenants with God in order to receive them*], and confessed [*acknowledged*] that they were strangers and pilgrims on the earth [*that this earth is not their final destination, rather it is just a station en route to exaltation; see verse 16, below*].

14 For they [*righteous "strangers" and "pilgrims" in verse 13, above*] that say such things declare plainly that they seek a country [*a final home where they can stay forever; see Hebrews 11:14, footnote a; in other words, they are seeking a permanent home in celestial exaltation*].

15 And truly, if they had been mindful of that country from whence they came out, they might have had opportunity to have returned. [*If they had only thought of this mortal life and what is available to them on earth, they might have been satisfied.*]

16 But now [*because they know about celestial glory and have that for perspective*] they desire a better country, that is, an heavenly [*the celestial kingdom*]: wherefore God is not ashamed to be called their God [*God has accepted them*]: for he hath prepared for them a city [*the celestial kingdom; see Revelation 21, heading plus that whole chapter where the celestial kingdom is described*].

Next, we gain insight into how faith helped Abraham when he was given the commandment to sacrifice Isaac, his only covenant son through Sarah. See Genesis 22:1–19 for more details.

17 By faith Abraham, when he was tried [*tested*], offered up Isaac: and he [*Abraham*] that had received the promises [*who had been promised posterity as numerous as the sands of the sea through his only covenant son, Isaac; see Genesis 21:12*] offered up his only begotten son [*Isaac*],

18 Of whom it was said, That in Isaac shall thy seed be called [*Genesis 21:12*]:

19 Accounting that God was able to raise him up, even from the dead [*knowing that, if necessary, God would bring*

*Isaac back to life after he had been sacrificed*]; from whence also he [*Abraham*] received him [*Isaac*] in a figure [*figuratively or symbolically speaking*].

20 By faith Isaac blessed Jacob and Esau concerning things to come [*prophesying about the future*].

21 By faith Jacob, when he was a dying [*Genesis 48:2*], blessed both the sons of Joseph; and worshipped, leaning upon the top of his staff [*using his staff for support*].

22 By faith Joseph [*who was sold into Egypt*], when he died [*when he was dying*], made mention of the departing of the children of Israel [*prophesied that the children of Israel would be delivered out of Egyptian bondage (see JST Genesis 50:24 in the Joseph Smith Translation section, at the back of your Bible*]; and gave commandment concerning his bones [*and instructed that his bones be carried out of Egypt and that he be buried in the promised land when the time came for the children of Israel to be set free from Egyptian bondage; see Genesis 50:24–25*].

23 By faith Moses, when he was born, was hid three months of [*by*] his parents, because they saw he was a proper child; [*In other words, Moses' parents knew that he was a special child and it was their faith which preserved his life*] and they were not afraid of the king's [*Pharaoh's*] commandment [*to kill all the male Hebrew babies when they were born*].

**JST Hebrews 11:23**

23 By faith Moses, when he was born, was hid three months of his parents, because they saw that he was a peculiar [*special*] child; and they were not afraid of the king's commandment.

Thanks to Stephen, in Acts 7:20–25, we know that Moses actually knew that he was to be the one who would lead the children of Israel out of Egypt. In the next verses here, Paul emphasizes the role of faith in Moses' carrying out his mission.

24 By faith Moses, when he was come to years [*in other words, when he grew up*], refused to be called the son of Pharaoh's daughter [*refused to continue the privileged life of royalty in Pharaoh's court*];

**JST Hebrews 11:24**

24 By faith Moses, when he was come to years of discretion, refused to be called the son of Pharaoh's daughter;

25 Choosing rather to suffer affliction with the people of God [*choosing instead to join with the Hebrew slaves and help them*], than to enjoy the pleasures of sin for a season [*rather than enjoying the pleasures of sin and luxury for a time which was available to him in Pharaoh's palace*];

26 Esteeming the reproach of Christ [*the burden of being loyal to Christ*] greater riches [*to be of greater worth*] than the treasures in Egypt: for he had respect unto the recompence of the reward [*he understood the rewards which come to the righteous*].

27 By faith he forsook [*left*] Egypt, not fearing the wrath of the king [*Pharaoh*]: for he endured, as seeing him who is invisible [*he endured because he saw God, who is not seen by most people*].

28 Through faith he kept the passover [*when the destroying angel "passed over" the firstborn of the Israelites in Egypt*], and the sprinkling of blood [*on the doorposts and lintel (top of the door frame); see Exodus 12:21–23*], lest he [*the destroying angel*] that destroyed the firstborn [*in Egypt*] should touch them [*the children of Israel*].

29 By faith they passed through the Red sea as by dry land: which the Egyptians assaying to do [*attempting to do, as they continued pursuing the Israelites*] were drowned.

30 By faith the walls of Jericho fell down, after they were compassed about [*marched around*] seven days.

31 By faith the harlot Rahab perished not with them that believed not [*Rahab was not killed with the unbelievers in Jericho when the walls tumbled down (verse 30, above) because of her faith*], when she had received the spies [*who were sent out by Joshua; see Joshua 2:1*] with peace.

> Some people are not comfortable with the word "harlot" used in reference to Rahab in verse 31, above. This should not be a problem to those who believe that the Atonement provides forgiveness for such people when they repent. If you read Joshua 2:1–11, you will see that Rahab had apparently gained a testimony of the gospel and acted accordingly. Both Paul, here, and James in James 2:25, use her as a good example of faith. For additional discussion of this, see the *Institute of Religion Old Testament Student Manual, Genesis–2 Samuel*, pp. 236–237.

32 And what shall I more say [*what more shall I say*]? for the time would fail me to tell of [*I don't have time to tell you about*] Gedeon [*Gideon; see Judges, chapters 6–8*], and of Barak [*Judges, chapter 4*], and of Samson [*Judges, chapters 13–16*], and of Jephthae [*Jephthah; see Judges, chapter 11*]; of David also, and Samuel, and of the prophets:

33 Who through faith subdued [*conquered*] kingdoms, wrought [*caused*] righteousness, obtained promises, stopped the mouths of lions,

34 Quenched the violence of fire, escaped the edge of the sword, out of weakness were made strong, waxed [*grew*] valiant [*mighty; Strong's #2478*] in fight, turned to flight the armies of the aliens [*foreigners; Strong's #0245*].

35 Women received their dead raised to life again: and others were tortured, not accepting deliverance; that they might obtain a better resurrection:

> **JST Hebrews 11:35**
> 35 Women received their dead raised to life again; and others were tortured, not accepting deliverance; that they might obtain the first resurrection [*meaning those who will go to celestial glory*];

36 And others had trial of cruel mockings and scourgings [*whippings*], yea, moreover of bonds [*captivity*] and imprisonment:

37 They were stoned, they were sawn asunder [*cut in two with saws*], were tempted [*tested; Strong's #3985*], were slain [*killed*] with the sword: they wandered about in sheepskins and goatskins [*had insufficient wealth to even afford fabric for clothing*]; being destitute [*in extreme poverty*], afflicted, tormented;

38 (Of whom the world was not worthy:) they wandered in deserts, and in mountains, and in dens and caves of the earth.

39 And these all, having obtained a good report [*having obtained a strong testimony; see Hebrews 11:39, footnote a*] through faith, received not the promise [*were not given exaltation while they were still on earth*]:

40 God having provided some better thing for us, that they without us should not be made perfect.

> **JST Hebrews 11:40**
> 40 God having provided some better things for them through their sufferings, for without sufferings they could not be made perfect.

# HEBREWS 12

As Paul continues his letter to the Jewish converts to the Church (the "Hebrew" members of the Church), he counsels them to avoid sin and look to Jesus Christ for salvation, rather than to the Law of Moses.

One of the great doctrinal verses of this

chapter is verse 9, in which Paul teaches that we are the spirit children of our Father in Heaven.

1 WHEREFORE seeing we also are compassed [*surrounded*] about with so great a cloud [*large dense multitude; Strong's #3509*] of witnesses, let us lay aside every weight [*anything which would hold us back; Strong's #3591*], and the sin which doth so easily beset [*surround; Strong's #2139*] us, and let us run with patience the race that is set before us,

2 Looking unto Jesus the author and finisher of our faith [*the one who helps us complete our quest for exaltation*]; who for [*because of*] the joy that was set before him [*that was available to Him*] endured the cross [*crucifixion*], despising [*not paying attention to*] the shame, and is set down at the right hand of the throne of God [*is now in heaven in a position of authority with the Father*].

3 For consider him [*just think about Christ*] that endured such contradiction [*opposition*] of sinners against himself, lest ye be wearied and faint in your minds [*when you start feeling tired and discouraged because of the opposition you face*].

4 Ye have not yet resisted unto blood [*you have not given your lives yet, as Christ did*], striving [*fighting*] against sin.

5 And ye have forgotten the exhortation [*encouragement; Strong's #3874*] which speaketh unto you as unto children [*in Proverbs 3:11–12*], My son, despise not thou the chastening of the Lord [*do not take the Lord's discipline lightly*], nor faint [*become too discouraged*] when thou art rebuked of [*by*] him:

6 For whom the Lord loveth he chasteneth [*disciplines*], and scourgeth [*punishes as needed*] every son whom he receiveth [*whom He accepts into celestial glory*].

7 If ye endure chastening [*put up with discipline*], God dealeth with you as with sons; for what son is he whom the father chasteneth not [*how would a son turn out if his father did not discipline him*]?

8 But if ye be without chastisement [*if you do not accept discipline from the Father*], whereof all are partakers [*which all people get*], then are ye bastards [*then you are not covenant children*], and not sons [*and you cannot return to Him*].

9 Furthermore we have had fathers of our flesh [*we have had our mortal fathers*] which corrected [*disciplined*] us, and we gave them reverence [*respect*]: shall we not much rather [*shouldn't we even more*] be in subjection unto [*in obedience to*] the Father of spirits [*the Father of our spirit bodies*], and live [*receive exaltation*]?

10 For they [*our mortal fathers*] verily for a few days [*for our relatively short mortal lives*] chastened [*disciplined*] us after their own pleasure [*according to what they thought best*]; but he [*the Father of our spirits*] for our profit [*knows exactly what is best for us*], that we might be partakers of his holiness [*so that we can become like Him in exaltation; compare with D&C 88:107 which says, "and the Saints shall be filled with his glory, and receive their inheritance and be made equal with him."*].

11 Now no chastening for the present seemeth to be joyous [*being disciplined is not particularly pleasant while it is going on*], but grievous [*rather, it is miserable*]: nevertheless afterward [*when it is finished*] it yieldeth [*produces*] the peaceable fruit of righteousness unto them which are exercised [*trained, disciplined; see Hebrews 12:11, footnote b*] thereby.

12 Wherefore lift up the hands which hang down, and the feeble knees [*strengthen yourselves and one another*];

**JST Hebrews 12:12**

12 Wherefore lift up the hands which hang down, and strengthen the feeble knees;

13 And make straight paths for your feet [*follow a straight course in the gospel*], lest that which is lame [*for fear that members who are weak*] be turned out of the way [*might lose the way*]; but let it rather be healed [*let weaker members be healed by your good deeds and example*].

14 Follow peace with all men, and holiness, without which no man shall see the Lord:

15 Looking [*watching over one another*] diligently lest any man fail of the grace of God [*so that no one misses out on the help and mercy provided by the Atonement*]; lest any root of bitterness springing up [*for fear that apostasy might come up among you and*] trouble you, and thereby many be defiled [*and thus, many members become unclean*];

16 Lest there be any fornicator [*guilty of sexual immorality*], or profane [*worldly*] person, as [*like*] Esau, who for one morsel of meat sold his birthright [*sold his salvation*].

17 For ye know how that afterward, when he would have inherited the blessing [*when he decided he wanted the birthright blessings after all*], he was rejected [*he was turned down*]: for he found no place of repentance [*because he refused to repent of his wicked lifestyle*], though he sought it [*the birthright*] carefully [*with much emotion*] with tears.

Next, Paul reminds the Hebrews that they should not be like the children of Israel who could not stand the glory of God on Mount Sinai or even the glory which was upon Moses when he came down from talking with the Lord on Sinai.

18 For ye are not come unto the mount [*Mount Sinai; see Exodus 19, starting with verse 12*] that might be touched [*that can be touched, physically*], and that burned with fire, nor unto blackness, and darkness, and tempest,

19 And the sound of a trumpet, and the voice of words; which voice they that heard intreated [*pleaded*] that the word should not be spoken to them any more [*see Exodus 20:19*]:

20 (For they could not endure that which was commanded, And if so much as a beast touch the mountain, it shall be stoned, or thrust through with a dart [*compare with Exodus 19:12–13*]:

21 And so terrible was the sight, that Moses said, I exceedingly fear and quake [*compare with Deuteronomy 9:19*]):

Next, Paul uses several vocabulary words and phrases which mean "celestial glory" and most often mean "exaltation in the presence of God." Compare with D&C 76:66–69. We will put these words and phrases in bold print in order to point them out to you.

22 But ye are come unto **mount Sion**, and unto **the city of the living God**, the **heavenly Jerusalem**, and to **an innumerable company of angels**,

23 To **the general assembly** and **church of the firstborn**, which are written in heaven [*whose names are written in heaven; D&C 76:68*], and to God the Judge of all, and to the spirits of **just men made perfect**,

24 And to Jesus the mediator of the new covenant [*to Jesus, who works with us to help us take advantage of the "new covenant" or gospel of Jesus Christ, which replaces the "old covenant" or the Law of Moses*], and to the blood of sprinkling [*the Atonement, which was made available to us by the shedding of the Savior's blood*], that speaketh better things than that of Abel.

The phrase "and to the blood of sprinkling, that speaketh better things than that of Abel" in verse 24, above,

needs explaining. Apostle Bruce R. McConkie gave his explanation as follows: "But whatever the then prevailing views of the Hebrews may have been (including the false doctrine that Abel's blood was an atonement for the sins of others), Paul is here teaching: 'The blood of righteous Abel' (Matt. 23–35), together 'with the innocent blood of all the martyrs under the altar that John saw (D&C 135:7; Rev. 6:9–11) cries unto the Lord for vengeance against the wicked; the blood of Christ, on the other hand, was poured out as a propitiation for sins, and through it men are empowered to repent and be reconciled to God. Thus the voice of Abel's blood is one of death and separation and sorrow; the voice of our Lord's blood is one of life and reunion and eternal joy. Truly his blood speaketh better things than that of Abel!" (McConkie, *Doctrinal New Testament Commentary*, Vol. 3, pp. 231–32.)

25 See that ye refuse not him that speaketh [*don't reject the Lord*]. For if they [*the children of Israel*] escaped not who refused him that spake on earth [*who rejected Jehovah (Christ) when He spoke from Sinai*], much more shall not we escape, if we turn away from him [*if we reject Christ*] that speaketh from heaven [*as He speaks to us now from heaven, and including when He comes at the Second Coming*]:

26 Whose voice then shook the earth [*on Sinai; see Exodus 19:18*]: but now he hath promised, saying, Yet once more I shake not the earth only, but also heaven [*the heavens and the earth will shake at the time of the Second Coming*].

27 And this word, Yet once more [*and this phrase, "Yet once more"*], signifieth [*indicates*] the removing of those things that are shaken, as of things that are made, that those things which cannot be shaken may remain. [*In other words, the phrase "Yet once more" points out that all corruptible things which do not belong on earth during the Millennium will be done away with at the time of the Second Coming, when the Lord "shakes" the earth, and cleanses it from all wickedness, so that the things that belong on earth during the Millennium can remain in an environment of peace and righteousness.*]

28 Wherefore we receiving a kingdom which cannot be moved [*we, belonging to the kingdom of Christ, which cannot be done away with*], let us have grace, whereby we may serve God acceptably with reverence and godly fear:

**JST Hebrews 12:28**

28 Wherefore we receiving a kingdom which cannot be moved, should have grace, whereby we may serve God acceptable with reverence and godly fear [*we can serve God acceptably because of the Atonement*];

29 For [*as it says in Deuteronomy 4:24*] our God is a consuming fire. [*In other words, when the Savior comes again, all the wicked and all corrupt things will be consumed or burned by his glory. See D&C 5:19.*]

# HEBREWS 13

Paul now concludes by counseling these members of the Church to love one another and live the gospel in their daily lives. He reminds them to be constantly aware of Christ and to let their daily sacrifices be those of righteous deeds and kind treatment of others.

1 LET brotherly love continue.

2 Be not forgetful to entertain strangers [*do not forget to be hospitable toward strangers; Strong's #5381*]: for thereby [*by so doing*] some have entertained angels unawares [*without being aware of it*].

Bruce R. McConkie suggests that many of these "angels," spoken of in verse 1, above, are righteous mortals who are involved in the service of God. (See *Doctrinal New Testament*

*Commentary*, Vol. 3, p. 235.) In addition, we might consider the words of the Savior in Matthew 25:34–40 wherein the righteous ask, "Lord, when saw we thee an hungred, and fed thee? Or thirsty, and gave thee drink?" The Master answered, "Inasmuch as ye have done it unto one of the least of these my brethren, ye have done it unto me."

3 Remember them that are in bonds [*in prison*], as bound with them [*as if you were in prison with them*]; and them which suffer adversity, as being yourselves also in the body [*as if you were suffering their adversity with them*].

**JST Hebrews 13:3**

3 Remember them that are in bonds, as bound with them; and them which suffer adversity, as being yourselves also of the body.

Next, Paul teaches that marriage is approved by God. This shows that celibacy as a means of showing loyalty to God is wrong. He also teaches that sexual relations between husband and wife do not make them unclean. In other words, such a relationship is clean and righteous, but he warns that such relations between those who are not married are wicked.

4 Marriage is honourable in all, and the bed undefiled: but whoremongers [*those who make sexual immorality a major focus of their lives*] and adulterers [*those who have sexual relations outside of marriage*] God will judge [*punish*].

5 Let your conversation be without covetousness [*give willingly to the Lord's work; in other words, don't "covet" what you are dedicating to the Lord*]; and be content with such things as ye have: for he [*the Lord*] hath said [*in Deuteronomy 31:6; Joshua 1:5*], I will never leave thee, nor forsake thee.

**JST Hebrews 13:5**

5 Let your consecrations be without covetousness; and be content with giving such things as ye have; for he hath said, I will never leave thee, nor forsake thee.

6 So that we may boldly say [*we may say with confidence; Strong's #2292; as stated in Psalm 118:6–7*], The Lord is my helper, and I will not fear what man shall do unto me.

7 Remember them which have the rule over you [*remember your leaders in the Church*], who have spoken unto you the word of God: whose faith follow [*follow their example*], considering the end of their conversation [*behavior, way of life; Strong's #0391*]. [*In other words, being aware of where their way of life is taking them.*]

8 Jesus Christ the same yesterday, and to day, and for ever. [*The doctrines and ordinances of the gospel, which lead to exaltation, remain the same throughout eternity.*]

9 Be not carried about with divers [*various*] and strange [*false*] doctrines. For it is a good [*meet, necessary; Strong's #2570*] thing that the heart [*the center of spiritual life; Strong's #2588*] be established [*made firm; Strong's #0950*] with grace [*the Atonement of Christ*]; not with meats [*not with the ceremonial foods and rituals of the Law of Moses*], which have not profited them that have been occupied therein [*which do not lead to exaltation*].

As he finishes his letter to the Jewish converts to the Church (the Hebrews), Paul will now emphasize once more that the Law of Moses does not have the power to bring people to exaltation. The gospel of Jesus Christ does.

10 We have an altar [*in other words, we have the sacrament which commemorates His body and blood sacrificed for us*], whereof they [*the Levitical priests spoken of in Hebrews 9:1–10 and elsewhere, who offer sacrifices in the tabernacle and temple, under the Law of Moses*] have no right to eat which serve the tabernacle [*are not authorized to eat because they haven't joined the Church*].

11 For the bodies of those beasts [*sacrificial animals*], whose blood is brought into the sanctuary [*speaking both of the tabernacle while the Israelites traveled in the wilderness etc., and also the temple in Jerusalem*] by the high priest for sin [*as an offering for sin, as required by the Law of Moses*], are burned without [*outside of*] the camp [*outside of the camp of the children of Israel, in other words, outside of the city*].

12 Wherefore [*for this reason*] Jesus also, that he might sanctify [*cleanse*] the people with his own blood, suffered without the gate [*Jesus was likewise crucified outside of the city*].

13 Let us go forth therefore unto him without the camp, bearing his reproach. [*Let us depart from the Law of Moses and the people who still insist on living it and go forth unto Christ.*]

14 For here have we no continuing city, but we seek one to come. [*In a way, this leaves us without a "home" among men here on earth, but we strive to attain the celestial kingdom in the future.*]

15 By him [*through Christ*] therefore let us offer the sacrifice of praise to God [*the Father*] continually, that is, the fruit of our lips [*the words which come out of our mouths*] giving thanks to his name.

16 But to do good and to communicate [*spread the gospel*] forget not: for with such sacrifices God is well pleased.

17 Obey them [*your church leaders*] that have the rule over you, and submit yourselves: for they watch [*watch out*] for your souls, as they that must give account [*they have that stewardship and are accountable to God*], that they may do it with joy, and not with grief [*when you obey them, it makes their job more pleasant*]: for that [*disobedience which brings them grief*] is unprofitable for you [*is not good for you*].

18 Pray for us: for we trust we have a good conscience, in all things willing to live honestly.

19 But I beseech you the rather to do this [*please pray for me*], that I may be restored to you the sooner [*so that I can come visit you sooner*].

20 Now the God of peace [*Heavenly Father*], that brought again from the dead our Lord Jesus [*who resurrected Jesus Christ*], that great shepherd of the sheep, through the blood of the everlasting covenant,

21 Make you perfect [*prepare you; equip you; Strong's #2675*] in every good work to do his will, working in you that which is wellpleasing in his sight, through Jesus Christ; to whom be glory for ever and ever. Amen.

22 And I beseech you, brethren, suffer the word of exhortation [*please accept my counsel to you*]: for I have written a letter unto you in few words.

23 Know ye that our brother Timothy is set at liberty [*has been released*]; with whom, if he come shortly, I will see you.

24 Salute all them that have the rule over you [*greet all your local leaders for me*], and all the saints. They of Italy salute you [*the members here in Italy send their greetings to you*].

25 Grace be with you all. Amen.

# THE GENERAL EPISTLE OF JAMES

It is the general belief of many Bible scholars that James is the half brother of Jesus and is the son of Joseph and Mary. See Bible Dictionary under "James," definition #3, and also under "James, Epistle of." This is a "general epistle" or "general letter," so named because it is not written to any specific location, as is the case with most of Paul's letters. It is written to the twelve tribes of Israel (see chapter 1, verse 1) and consists of a series of "mini" sermons and contains valuable counsel for us to follow in our daily lives. It is not known when this letter was written, but a best guess might put the date of writing around AD 50–51, possibly written from Jerusalem.

## JAMES 1

This chapter contains one of the best-known verses among members of the Church, namely verse 5. Joseph Smith read this and was thus motivated to go into the Sacred Grove and pray, which led to the First Vision. See Joseph Smith–History 1:11–20.

1 JAMES, a servant of God and of the Lord Jesus Christ, to the twelve tribes which are scattered abroad, greeting.

2 My brethren, count it [*consider it*] all joy when ye fall into divers temptations;

**JST James 1:2**

2 My brethren, count it all joy when ye fall into many afflictions;

3 Knowing this, that the trying [*testing*] of your faith worketh [*builds*] patience.

4 But let patience have [*do*] her perfect work, that ye may be perfect and entire, wanting [*lacking*] nothing.

**JST James 1:4**

4 But let patience have its perfect work, that ye may be perfect and entire, wanting nothing.

5 If any of you lack wisdom, let him ask of God, that giveth to all men liberally, and upbraideth not [*will not scold you for asking*]; and it shall be given him.

6 But let him ask in faith, nothing wavering [*not doubting*]. For he that wavereth is like a wave of the sea driven with the wind and tossed. [*In other words, is unstable.*]

7 For let not that man [*whose faith wavers*] think that he shall receive any thing of the Lord.

8 A double minded [*wavering, uncertain, doubting; Strong's #1374*] man is unstable in all his ways [*in all he does*].

9 Let the brother [*member of the Church*] of low degree [*who is in humble circumstances*] rejoice in that he is exalted [*in that the gospel makes him of equal worth with all other members*]:

10 But the rich, in that he is made low [*let the rich member rejoice that he is made humble by the gospel*]: because as the flower of the grass he shall pass away [*because his worldly wealth will pass away like grass and be of no value to him when he dies*].

11 For the sun is no sooner risen with a burning heat, but it withereth the grass, [*In other words, wealth is very temporary.*] and the flower thereof falleth,

and the grace of the fashion of it [*its beauty*] perisheth: so also shall the rich man fade away in his ways [*such will be the case with the rich man who lets his wealth corrupt him*].

12 Blessed is the man that endureth temptation [JST "that resisteth temptation"]: for when he is tried [*proven worthy*], he shall receive the crown of life [*he will receive exaltation*], which the Lord hath promised to them that love him.

**JST James 1:12**

12 Blessed is the man that resisteth temptation; for when he is tried, he shall receive the crown of life, which the Lord hath promised to them that love him.

13 Let no man say when he is tempted, I am tempted of God: for God cannot be tempted with evil, neither tempteth he any man: [*In other words, God does not tempt people to do evil.*]

14 But every man is tempted, when he is drawn away of his own lust, and enticed [*when he allows himself to be pulled away by the desire for sexual immorality*].

15 Then when lust hath conceived [*when he allows sexual temptation to remain in his mind and grow*], it bringeth forth sin [*it eventually causes him to commit such sin*]: and sin, when it is finished [*when it has finished its work*], bringeth forth death [*brings spiritual death*].

16 Do not err [*don't be mistaken*], my beloved brethren.

17 Every good gift and every perfect gift is from above, and cometh down from the Father of lights [*from God, who created the stars; Strong's #3962*], with whom is no variableness [*who does not change*], neither shadow of turning [*not even the slightest bit*].

18 Of his own will begat he us with the word of truth [*he gave us new life by giving us the gospel of Christ*], that we should be a kind of firstfruits [*superior in excellence; Strong's #0536*] of his creatures. [*In other words, so that we could become exalted.*]

19 Wherefore, my beloved brethren, let every man be swift to hear [*listen*], slow to speak, slow to wrath [*anger*]:

20 For the wrath [*extreme anger*] of man worketh not the righteousness of God [*does not lead to personal righteousness*].

21 Wherefore lay apart [*set aside*] all filthiness and superfluity of naughtiness [*the evil, especially hatred and bitterness toward others, which is so prevalent around you*], and receive with meekness the engrafted word [*the gospel which has been implanted in you; Strong's #1721*], which is able to save your souls.

**JST James 1:21**

21 Wherefore lay aside all filthiness and superfluity of naughtiness, and receive with meekness, the engrafted word, which is able to save your souls.

22 But be ye doers of the word [*live the gospel*], and not hearers only [*don't merely listen to it*], deceiving [*fooling*] your own selves.

23 For if any be a hearer of the word [*if anyone hears the gospel*], and not a doer [*but does not live it*], he is like unto a man beholding [*looking at*] his natural face in a glass [*a mirror; Strong's #2072*]:

24 For he beholdeth [*sees*] himself, and goeth his way, and straightway [*immediately*] forgetteth what manner of man he was [*what he looked like*].

25 But whoso looketh into the perfect law of liberty [*whoever sees himself reflected in the light of the perfect gospel*], and continueth therein [*and continues to walk in that light*], he being not a forgetful hearer [*not as one who forgets about the gospel*], but a doer of

the work [*but one who lives it*], this man shall be blessed in his deed [*in what he does*].

26 If any man among you seem [*appears*] to be religious, and bridleth not [*doesn't control*] his tongue, but deceiveth [*fools*] his own heart, this man's religion is vain [*is worthless to him*].

Next, in verse 27, James gives a rather famous definition of what pure religion is.

27 Pure religion and undefiled before God and the Father is this, To visit the fatherless [*orphans*] and widows in their affliction, and to keep himself unspotted from the world [JST "unspotted from the vices of the world"].

**JST James 1:27**
27 Pure religion and undefiled before God and the Father is this, To visit the fatherless and widows in their affliction, and to keep himself unspotted from the vices of the world.

# JAMES 2

This chapter is very important doctrinally, because it teaches the necessity of works to go along with faith.

You will see that the Prophet Joseph Smith not only changed wording in some verses, but also rearranged the order of some of them in the JST.

1 MY brethren, have not the faith of our Lord Jesus Christ, the Lord of glory, with respect of persons [*In other words, if you are truly living the gospel, you cannot show prejudice toward others; see verses 2–4, below.*]

**JST James 2:1**
1 My brethren, ye cannot have the faith of our Lord Jesus Christ, the Lord of glory, and yet have respect to persons.

2 For if there come unto your assembly a man [*if a man comes into your meetings*] with a gold ring, in goodly apparel [*wearing fine clothes*], and there come in also a poor man in vile raiment [*and a poor man comes in wearing dirty, shabby clothing*];

**JST James 2:2**
2 Now if there come unto your assembly a man with a gold ring, in goodly apparel, and there come in also a poor man in vile raiment;

3 And ye have respect [*show preferential treatment*] to him that weareth the gay [*fine*] clothing, and say unto him, Sit thou here in a good place; and say to the poor, Stand thou there, or sit here under my footstool [*sit on the floor by my chair*]:

4 Are ye not then partial in yourselves, and are become judges of evil thoughts? [*In other words, haven't you just become unrighteous judges?*]

**JST James 2:4**
4 Are ye not then in yourselves partial judges, and become evil in your thoughts?

5 Hearken [*listen to me*], my beloved brethren, Hath not God chosen the poor of this world [*who are*] rich in faith, and heirs of the kingdom which he hath promised to them that love him? [*In other words, doesn't God give righteous poor people exaltation also, who show their love to Him by faithfully living the gospel*?]

6 But ye have despised the poor [*treated them with contempt; Strong's #0818*]. Do not rich men oppress you, and draw you before the judgment seats? [*Have you forgotten what it feels like to be treated with contempt yourselves?*]

7 Do not they [*the men of high position in the community who oppress members of the Church*] blaspheme [*mock*] that worthy name [*the name of Christ*] by the which ye are called [*which you have taken upon you*]?

8 If ye fulfil [*obey*] the royal law according to the scripture [*Leviticus 19:18*],

Thou shalt love thy neighbour as thyself, ye do well:

9 But if ye have respect to persons [*if you show unrighteous favoritism*], ye commit sin, and are convinced of the law [*convicted by the law of God*] as transgressors.

In the next verses, James teaches a very important gospel doctrine, namely that if we claim to be living the whole gospel, but intentionally disobey a certain obvious part of it, it is as if we were violating the whole gospel. For instance, if a person holds a temple recommend, and is doing well at keeping all the requirements of it, however, he or she decides to drink wine on occasions for social reasons, it voids the recommend and the person's worthiness to attend the temple.

10 For whosoever shall keep the whole law [*keeps all the commandments*], and yet offend in one point [*and intentionally breaks just one of the commandments*], he is guilty of all [*it is as if he broke all the commandments*].

**JST James 2:10**

10 For whosoever shall, save in one point, keep the whole law, he is guilty of all.

11 For he [*the Lord*] that said, Do not commit adultery, said also, Do not kill. Now if thou commit no adultery, yet if thou kill, thou art become a transgressor of the law [*you will still go to the telestial kingdom; see D&C 76:103 and Revelation 22:15*].

12 So speak ye, and so do, as they that shall be judged by the law of liberty. [*In other words, you should speak and act like those who will be shown mercy on Judgment Day.*]

13 For he shall have judgment without mercy, that hath shewed no mercy [*the person who showed no mercy to others will be shown no mercy on Judgment Day, because the law of justice will take over in their case*]; and mercy rejoiceth against judgment [*if you are merciful, you will be able to rejoice on Judgment Day; see Alma 41:14*].

14 What doth it profit, my brethren, though a man say he hath faith, and have not works? can faith save him? [*In other words, what good does it do to claim to have faith but not have good works to go along with it?*]

**JST James 2:14**

14 What profit is it, my brethren, for a man to say he hath faith, and hath not works? can faith save him?

15 If a brother or sister be naked [*inadequately clothed*], and destitute [*has run out*] of daily food,

16 And one of you [*who claim to have faith in Christ's gospel*] say unto them, Depart in peace, be ye warmed and filled; notwithstanding [*but*] ye give them not those things which are needful to the body; what doth it profit [*what good does it do*]?

JST James 2:16, given next, covers both verses 15 and 16 above.

**JST James 2:16**

16 For if a brother or sister be naked and destitute, and one of you say, Depart in peace, be warmed and filled; notwithstanding he give not those things which are needful to the body; what profit is your faith unto such?

Verses 17 and 20, next, are much-used in teaching the restored gospel in the mission field.

17 Even so faith, if it hath not works [*if we don't have deeds to go along with it, which demonstrate our faith*], is dead, being alone.

**JST James 2:17**

17 Even so faith, if it have not works is dead, being alone. [*The only change in this verse is "have" in place of "hath" in the Bible.*]

18 Yea, a man may say, Thou hast faith, and I have works: shew [*show*] me thy faith without thy works, and I will shew [*demonstrate*] thee my faith by my works.

**JST James 2:15**

15 Yea, a man may say, I will show thee I have faith without works; but I say, Show me thy faith without works, and I will show thee my faith by my works.

19 Thou believest that there is one God; thou doest well: the devils also believe, and tremble. [*In other words, you are just like the evil spirits from the premortal existence who know who Christ is but have no righteous works to go along with it.*]

**JST James 2:19**

19 Thou believest there is one God; thou doest well; the devils also believe, and tremble; thou hast made thyself like unto them, not being justified.

20 But wilt thou know, O vain [*foolish, prideful*] man, that faith without works is dead?

**JST James 2:18**

18 Therefore wilt thou know, O vain man, that faith without works is dead and cannot save you?

21 Was not Abraham our father justified [*was made acceptable to God*] by works, when he had offered Isaac his son upon the altar?

22 Seest thou how faith wrought [*went along*] with his works, and by works was faith made perfect [*complete; Strong's #5048*]?

23 And the scripture [*Genesis 15:6*] was fulfilled which saith, Abraham believed God, and it was imputed [*credited: Strong's #3049*] unto him for [*as*] righteousness: and he was called the Friend of God [*Isaiah 41:8*].

24 Ye see then how that by works a man is justified [*placed in harmony with God*], and not by faith only.

**JST James 2:23**

23 Ye see then that by works a man is justified, and not by faith only.

25 Likewise also was not Rahab the harlot justified [*made right with God*] by works, when she had received the messengers [*the spies sent out by Joshua in Joshua 2:1*], and had sent them out another way?

**JST James 2:24**

24 Likewise also Rahab the harlot was justified by works, when she had received the messengers and sent them out another way.

For some thoughts about Rahab, see the note which follows Hebrews 11:31 in this study guide.

26 For as the body without the spirit is dead, so faith without works is dead also.

**JST James 2:25**

25 For, as the body without the spirit is dead, so faith without works is dead.

# JAMES 3

James continues by urging members to control their tongues. He gives many examples of how much damage an uncontrolled tongue can cause.

1 MY brethren, be not many masters, knowing that we shall receive the greater condemnation. [*Strong's #1320 defines "masters" as "teachers" and "the teachers of the Jewish religion." Perhaps, one interpretation of this may be "Don't debate about who is the greatest teacher among you. If we, who are supposed to be teaching others the gospel of peace, have contention among ourselves about such things, we will receive the greater condemnation."*]

**JST James 3:1**

1 My brethren, strive not for the mastery, knowing that in so doing we shall receive the greater condemnation.

James will now lead up to the importance of controlling our tongues, in other words, controlling the words which come out of our mouths.

2 For in many things we offend all [*we all offend others at one time or another*]. If any man offend not in word [*does not ever offend others in what he says*], the same is a perfect [*complete*] man, [*In other words, he "has his act together."*] and able also to bridle the whole body [*is able to exercise self-control over the whole self*].

3 Behold, we put bits [*bridle bits*] in the horses' mouths, that they may obey us; and we turn about their whole body [*we control the whole horse with just a small bit in its mouth*].

4 Behold [*consider*] also the ships, which though they be so great [*even though they are so large*], and are driven of fierce winds, yet are they turned about [*they are controlled*] with a very small helm [*rudder; Strong's #4079*], whithersoever [*wherever*] the governor listeth [*wherever the captain wants*].

5 Even so the tongue is a little member [*is a small part of the body*], and boasteth great things [*and has great power*]. Behold, how great a matter [*forest; Strong's #5208*] a little fire kindleth [*consider how big of a forest fire a small fire can start*]!

6 And the tongue is a fire, a world of iniquity [*the tongue is like a fire and can cause a world of wickedness*]: so is the tongue among our members [*our body parts*], that it defileth [*corrupts*] the whole body [*it can ruin us spiritually*], and setteth on fire the course of nature [*it inflames the passions of the "natural man"; see verse 15, below, as well as Mosiah 3:19 and Moses 6:49*]; and it is set on fire of hell [*and is often inspired by hell*].

7 For every kind of beasts, and of birds, and of serpents, and of things in the sea, is tamed, and hath been tamed of [*by*] mankind:

8 But the tongue can no man tame; it is an unruly [*uncontrollable; see James 3:8, footnote b, in our Bible*] evil, full of deadly poison.

9 Therewith bless we God [*with the tongue, we praise God*], even the Father; and therewith curse we men [*and with it we hurl insults at our fellow men*], which are made after the similitude of God [*which deserve more respect than that because they are God's children*].

10 Out of the same mouth proceedeth blessing and cursing. My brethren, these things ought not so to be. [*In other words, we ought to control our tongues and not use them to make ourselves hypocrites.*]

11 Doth a fountain [*spring of water*] send forth at the same place [*out of the same source*] sweet water and bitter?

12 Can the fig tree, my brethren, bear olive berries [*produce olives*]? either a vine, figs [*or a grape vine produce figs*]? so can no fountain [*spring of water*] both yield salt water and fresh [*produce salt water and fresh water at the same time*].

13 Who is a wise man and endued with knowledge among you [*who wants to be endowed with knowledge (including wisdom—see verse 17) among you*]? let him shew [*show, demonstrate*] out of a good conversation [*by righteous behavior; Strong's #0391*] his works with meekness of wisdom [*the self-control produced by wisdom*].

14 But if ye have bitter envying and strife [*contention*] in your hearts, glory not [*don't boast*], and lie not against [*don't deny*] the truth [*which is that this kind of behavior does not come from heaven, rather is as described in verse 15, next*].

15 This wisdom descendeth not from above [*does not come from heaven*], but is earthly, sensual, devilish.

16 For where envying and strife [*contention; selfish ambition; Strong's #2052*] is, there is confusion and every evil work [*and every form of evil as a result*].

17 But the wisdom that is from above

[*which comes down to us from heaven*] is first [*above all*] pure, then peaceable, gentle, and easy to be intreated [*humble and teachable*], full of mercy and good fruits, without partiality [*favoritism*], and without hypocrisy.

18 And the fruit of righteousness is sown [*planted*] in peace of [*by*] them that make peace.

# JAMES 4

James now explains the root causes of contention and wickedness.

There are no JST changes for this chapter.

1 FROM whence come wars [*quarreling; Strong's #4171*] and fightings among you [*what causes quarreling and fighting among you*]? come they not hence, even of your lusts that war in your members [*don't they ultimately come from the evil desires that battle for control within each of you*]?

2 Ye [*worldly people*] lust, and have not [*you covet what others have and haven't obtained it*]: ye kill, and desire to have [*and want others' possessions*], and cannot obtain [*and still don't end up getting them*]: ye fight and war, yet ye have not [*you fight and war among yourselves but are never satisfied*], because ye ask not [*because you don't consult God as to how to attain true satisfaction in life*].

3 Ye ask, and receive not [*some of you do pray to God, but still don't get what you want*], because ye ask amiss [*because you are not asking with the right attitude and for the right reasons*], that ye may consume it upon your lusts [*you are asking so that you may satisfy your own evil lusts and ambitions*].

4 Ye adulterers and adulteresses, know ye not that the friendship of the world [*joining in with wicked and lustful people*] is enmity with God [*is antagonism toward God*]? whosoever therefore will be a friend of the world [*participates in worldly wickedness*] is the enemy of God.

5 Do ye think that the scripture saith in vain, The spirit that dwelleth in us lusteth to envy?

Bruce R. McConkie deals with verse 5, above, as follows: "There is no scripture to this effect in our present Old Testament. As here given, the meaning must be that man in this mortal probation is subject to envy and other lusts. (*Doctrinal New Testament Commentary*, 3 Vols. [Salt Lake City: Bookcraft, 1965–1973], Vol. 3, p. 266.)

6 But he giveth more grace [*help; mercy and kindness; Strong's #5485*]. Wherefore he saith [*in Proverbs 3:34*], God resisteth [*opposes*] the proud, but giveth grace unto the humble.

7 Submit yourselves therefore to God. Resist the devil, and he will flee from you.

8 Draw nigh [*near*] to God, and he will draw nigh to you. Cleanse your hands [*repent*], ye sinners; and purify your hearts, ye double minded [*you who cannot decide whether to serve God or the devil*].

9 Be afflicted, and mourn, and weep: let your laughter be turned to mourning, and your joy to heaviness.

It appears that verse 9, above, refers back to verse 8 and the issue of being "double minded." With this in mind, one interpretation of verse 9 might be: "Allow yourselves to feel godly sorrow (2 Corinthians 7:8–11) for your sins, and weep for them; let your riotous living be turned into mourning for your sins, and your shallow happiness to solemn thinking about your sins." Another possible interpretation might be, referring to those who resist the devil in verse 7, above: "You Saints will suffer and mourn and weep because of the wickedness around you; much sadness will replace your laughter, and your joy will turn to depression

because of the wickedness in this world."

10 Humble yourselves in the sight of the Lord, and he shall lift you up [*encourage you and eventually exalt you in the celestial kingdom*].

11 Speak not evil one of another [*don't slander or criticize*], brethren. He that speaketh evil of [*slanders*] his brother, and judgeth [*passes judgment against*] his brother, speaketh evil of the law [*is going against the laws of God*], and judgeth the law [*is, in effect, acting as if he had power to be above the law himself*]: but if thou judge the law, thou art not a doer of the law, but a judge. [*In other words, what right have you to be a judge?*]

12 There is one lawgiver [*God*], who is able to save and to destroy: who art thou that judgest another [*who do you think you are, judging one another, in other words, taking over God's job*]?

13 Go to now [*listen carefully*], ye that say, To day or to morrow we will go into such a city, and continue there a year, and buy and sell, and get gain: [*In other words, listen carefully, you who think you are in control of life and can go about your daily affairs without having God in your lives.*]

14 Whereas ye know not what shall be on the morrow [*you don't even know what will happen tomorrow, let alone a year from now*]. For what is your life [*what is your mortal life; how long do your think it will last*]? It is even a vapour [*it is like a bit of mist in the morning*], that appeareth for a little time [*it is there for a moment*], and then vanisheth away [*and then it is gone*].

15 For that ye ought to say [*what you ought to say is*], If the Lord will [*if it is the Lord's will*], we shall live, and do this, or that [*we will do thus and such*].

16 But now ye rejoice in your boastings [*in your prideful living without God*]: all such rejoicing is evil.

Next, James teaches about what we often call "sins of omission," as opposed to "sins of commission," meaning that we need to repent not only of sins we commit, but of things we are not doing (omitting) and should be doing.

17 Therefore to him that knoweth to do good, and doeth it not, to him it is sin.

# JAMES 5

This chapter is of particular interest to Latter-day Saints because it contains verse 14, which deals with administering to the sick. First, in verses 1–6, James warns rich people about a miserable future if they keep setting their hearts on wealth rather than on God. He speaks of the future of corrupt rich people as if it had already come upon them. After that, he gives encouragement and counsel to the righteous.

There are no JST changes for this chapter.

1 GO to now [*listen carefully*], ye rich men, weep and howl for your miseries that shall come upon you [*if you don't repent*].

2 Your riches are corrupted [*have become rotten and dissolved away*], and your garments [*luxurious clothes*] are motheaten [*have turned to rags*].

3 Your gold and silver is cankered [*has rusted; Strong's #2728; in other words, has lost its value*]; and the rust of them shall be a witness against you, and shall eat your flesh [*will destroy you*] as it were fire [*as if it were fire*]. Ye have heaped treasure together for the last days [*you have foolishly stockpiled your worldly treasures as a means of surviving the last days*].

4 Behold [*look ahead into the future and see*], the hire [*wages*] of the labourers [*workers*] who have reaped down your fields [*whom you hired to harvest*

*your fields*], which is of you kept back by fraud [*which wages you dishonestly refused to pay*], crieth [*shout against you*]: and the cries of them which have reaped are entered into the ears of the Lord of sabaoth [*the Lord has heard the cries of the workers you cheated out of their wages*].

The phrase "the Lord of sabaoth" in verse 4, above, is defined in D&C 95:7 as follows: "Lord of Sabaoth; which is by interpretation, the creator of the first day," in other words, it means "Jesus" or "Jehovah." See also Bible Dictionary under "Sabaoth."

5 Ye have lived in pleasure [*luxury and excess; Strong's #5171*] on the earth, and been wanton [*voluptuous; have given in to sensual, lustful pleasures: Strong's #4684*]; ye have nourished your hearts, as in a day of slaughter [*you have fattened yourselves up as if in preparation to be slaughtered*].

6 Ye have condemned and killed the just [*murdered the righteous*]; and he doth not resist you [*and he was not doing anything against you; Strong's #0498*].

James now switches his attention from the wicked wealthy to the humble righteous.

7 Be patient therefore, brethren, unto the coming of the Lord [*until the Savior returns*]. Behold [*think about it*], the husbandman [*farmer*] waiteth for the precious fruit of the earth [*waits for the harvest*], and hath long patience for it, until he receive the early and latter rain [*and patiently waits for the spring and fall rains*].

8 Be ye also patient; stablish your hearts [*and stand firm in the gospel*]: for the coming of the Lord draweth nigh [*is getting close*].

9 Grudge not one [*don't hold grudges*] against another, brethren, lest ye be condemned: behold, the judge standeth before the door [*the time when you will be judged is getting close*].

10 Take, my brethren, the prophets [*use the prophets*], who have spoken in the name of the Lord [*who have taught us as authorized servants of the Lord*], for an example of suffering affliction, and of patience.

11 Behold, we count [*consider*] them happy which endure [*remain faithful in the gospel*]. Ye have heard of the patience of Job, and have seen the end [*purposes*] of the Lord; that the Lord is very pitiful [*full of pity; Strong's #4184; compassionate*], and of tender mercy.

12 But above all things, my brethren, swear not [*don't make contracts, agreements, and so forth*], neither by heaven, neither by the earth, neither by any other oath [*don't make your agreements with others so complex with legalistic language, etc., that no one can understand it*]: but let your yea be yea [*if you say "Yes," let it mean "Yes,"*] and your nay, nay [*in other words, be honest and simply keep your word when you give it to someone*]; lest ye fall into condemnation [*or you will be punished by God*].

13 Is any among you afflicted [*in trouble*]? let him pray. Is any merry? let him sing psalms.

Next, James gives instructions regarding administering to the sick.

14 Is any sick among you? let him call for the elders of the church [*Melchizedek Priesthood holders*]; and let them pray over him [*administer to him*], anointing him with oil [*pure, consecrated olive oil*] in the name of the Lord [*in the name of Jesus Christ*]:

15 And the prayer of faith shall save the sick, and the Lord shall raise him up [*either literally heal him here on earth or bring him to celestial glory, eventually if he has lived righteously*]; and if he have committed sins, they shall be forgiven him.

The phrase "if he have committed sins, they shall be forgiven him" in verse 15, above, needs to be handled

with care. It is very comforting and truly significant just as it stands, when applied to the lives of righteous and faithful Saints. However, there is no such thing as "automatic salvation" or "automatic forgiveness of sins" through merely performing a particular ordinance or having one performed for you. If a member who is administered to is healed, but has not repented of sins nor is trying to do so, he would still need to go through the repentance process in order to be forgiven.

16 Confess your faults one to another, and pray one for another, that ye may be healed. The effectual fervent prayer of a righteous man availeth much [*is very effective*].

The phrase "Confess your faults one to another" in verse 16, above, needs explaining. It obviously does not mean that we should confess all our faults, shortcomings, sins, and so forth, to every member we meet. Spencer W. Kimball said the following regarding this matter: "The confession of. . . major sins to a proper Church authority is one of those requirements made by the Lord. These sins include adultery, fornication, other sexual transgressions, and other sins of comparable seriousness. This procedure of confession assures proper controls and protection for the Church and its people and sets the feet of the transgressor on the path of true repentance. When one has wronged another in deep transgression or in injuries of lesser magnitude, he, the aggressor, who gave the offense, regardless of the attitude of the other party, should immediately make amends by confessing to the injured one and doing all in his power to clear up the matter and again establish good feelings between the two parties." (Kimball, *Miracle of Forgiveness*, pp. 179, 186.)

17 Elias [*Elijah*] was a man subject to like passions [*temptations and imperfections*] as we are [*just like we are*], and he prayed earnestly [*this is referring back to the last half of verse 16, above*] that it might not rain: and it rained not on the earth by the space of [*for*] three years and six months [*see 1 Kings 17:1*].

18 And he prayed again, and the heaven gave rain, and the earth brought forth her fruit [*see 1 Kings 18:41–45*].

19 Brethren, if any of you do err [*stray; Strong's #4105*] from the truth, and one convert him [*bring him back; Strong's #1994*];

20 Let him know, that he which converteth the sinner from the error of his way shall save a soul from death [*from spiritual death*], and shall hide a multitude of sins.

Regarding the phrase "and shall hide a multitude of sins" in verse 20, above, it is interesting to note that Joseph Smith changed the phrase "cover the multitude of sins" in 1 Peter 4:8, to "preventeth a multitude of sins" in JST 1 Peter 4:8.

# THE FIRST EPISTLE GENERAL OF PETER

The Apostle Peter became the president of the Church after the Savior was taken up into heaven. Most Bible scholars believe that he wrote this letter from Rome, sometime around AD 63 or AD 64. It is a general epistle [*letter*] addressed to members of the Church in many locations. At this time in Christian history, Nero, emperor of Rome, was undertaking severe persecutions of the Christians. In this letter, Peter, as the leader of the Church, prepares the Saints to endure much persecution and trouble by reminding them who they are, a "chosen generation" with a "royal priesthood." He reminds them that they were chosen in the premortal life to come to earth and become members of the Lord's Church and that because of this heritage, they can be strong and remain faithful at all costs. Peter's writings are of particular interest to Latter-day Saints because, among other things, he clearly teaches premortal life and foreordination (1 Peter 1:2), work for the dead (1 Peter 3:18–21), and also he teaches about making one's calling and election sure (2 Peter 1:10.)

## FIRST PETER 1

In this chapter, Peter teaches the doctrine of foreordination and the bright hope for the future that the Atonement of Christ brings to the faithful.

1 PETER, an apostle of Jesus Christ, to the strangers [*members of the Church who are exiles from society*] scattered throughout Pontus, Galatia, Cappadocia, Asia, and Bithynia,

2 Elect [*chosen, foreordained*] according to the foreknowledge of God the Father [*the knowledge which the Father has about us from our premortal life with Him*], through sanctification of the Spirit [*through the guidance of the Holy Ghost*], unto obedience and sprinkling of the blood of Jesus Christ [*to the point of being blessed and cleansed by the Atonement of Christ*]: Grace unto you, and peace, be multiplied.

The Prophet Joseph Smith taught about God's foreknowledge of us, mentioned in verse 2, above. We often refer to this in conjunction with the doctrine of foreordination (being chosen and foreordained in our premortal life to come to earth and carry out certain responsibilities in the Lord's work here.) The Prophet taught, "Every man who has a calling to minister to the inhabitants of the world was ordained to that very purpose in the Grand Council of heaven before this world was. I suppose I was ordained to this very office in that Grand Council." (*Teachings of the Prophet Joseph Smith*, p. 365.) Apostle Bruce R. McConkie also taught concerning this doctrine. He said, "To bring to pass the salvation of the greatest possible number of his spirit children, the Lord, in general, sends the most righteous and worthy spirits to earth through the lineage of Abraham and Jacob. This course is a manifestation of his grace or in other words his love, mercy, and condescension toward his children. This election to a chosen lineage is based on preexistent worthiness and is thus made 'according to the foreknowledge of God.' (1 Pet. 1:2.) Those so grouped together during their mortal probation have more abundant opportunities to make and keep the covenants of salvation, a right which they earned by

preexistent devotion to the cause of righteousness. As part of this election, Abraham and others of the noble and great spirits were chosen before they were born for the particular missions assigned them in this life. . . . (Abraham 3:22–24; Rom. 9.) Actually, if the full blessings of salvation are to follow, the doctrine of election must operate twice. First, righteous spirits are elected or chosen to come to mortality as heirs of special blessings. Then, they must be called and elected again in this life, an occurrence which takes place when they join the true Church. (D&C 53:1.) Finally, in order to reap eternal salvation, they must press forward in obedient devotion to the truth until they make their 'calling and election sure' (2 Pet. 1), that is, are 'sealed up unto eternal life.' (D&C 131:5.)" (McConkie, *Mormon Doctrine*, pp. 216–17.)

3 Blessed [*praised*] be the God and Father of our Lord Jesus Christ, which according to his abundant mercy hath begotten us again [*has given us spiritual rebirth, in other words, we are "born again*"] unto a lively hope [*unto a joyful and confident expectation of eternal salvation: Strong's #1680; compare also with 2 Nephi 31:20 where Nephi calls this "a perfect brightness of hope"*] by the resurrection of Jesus Christ from the dead,

4 To an inheritance [*exaltation, being "heirs of God, and joint-heirs with Christ"; Romans 8:17*] incorruptible [*eternal*], and undefiled [*pure*], and that fadeth not away, reserved in heaven [*celestial glory*] for you,

5 Who are kept [*preserved*] by the power of God through faith [*if they keep the commandments*] unto salvation [*exaltation*] ready to be revealed in the last time [*prepared to receive exaltation on final Judgment Day; compare with Strong's #2078*].

The word "salvation," as used in verse 5, above, with very few exceptions in the scriptures, means "exaltation."

6 Wherein ye greatly rejoice [*which you can look forward to with great joy*], though now for a season [*during the coming days*], if need be, ye are in heaviness [*you may be burdened down*] through manifold temptations [*because of trials and afflictions; see 1 Peter 1:6, footnote b*]:

Peter, as a prophet of God, is warning the members of the Church that very difficult times are coming, during which they will be severely persecuted. He strengthens them by giving them perspective, reminding them of the glorious reward of exaltation which awaits the faithful in eternity.

7 That the trial [*testing*] of your faith, being much more precious than of gold that perisheth [*faith is much more precious than gold*], though it be [*even though your faith is*] tried with fire [*is tested by severe troubles*], might be found unto praise and honour and glory [*might be found strong and worthy of God's praise and respect and worthy of your exaltation*] at the appearing of Jesus Christ:

8 Whom having not seen, ye love; in whom, though now ye see him not, yet believing [*having faith in Christ*], ye rejoice with joy unspeakable and full of glory: [*In other words, you love Christ, whom you have not seen. The faith which you have in Him brings you inexpressible and glorious joy.*]

9 Receiving the end of your faith, even the salvation of your souls [*the end result of your faith will be exaltation*].

**JST 1 Peter 1:9**
9 Receiving the object of your faith, even the salvation of your souls.

10 Of which salvation the prophets have enquired and searched diligently, who prophesied of the grace that should come unto you: [*The prophets of old studied diligently and asked God many questions about salvation.*]

**JST 1 Peter 1:10**

10 Concerning which salvation the prophets who prophesied of the grace bestowed upon you, inquired and searched diligently;

11 Searching what, or what manner of time the Spirit of Christ which was in them did signify [*following the promptings of the Spirit*], when it testified beforehand the sufferings of Christ [*when it testified to them about the Atonement of Christ, before it happened*], and the glory that should follow

**JST 1 Peter 1:11**

11 Searching what time, and what manner of salvation the Spirit of Christ which was in them did signify, when it testified beforehand the sufferings of Christ, and the glory which should follow.

The "Spirit of Christ," as used in verse 11, above, can refer to the Holy Ghost or the Spirit of Christ or both. See McConkie, *Doctrinal New Testament Commentary*, Vol. 3, pp. 286–287. We know from D&C 84:45–47, that the Spirit of Christ [*which many people refer to as our "conscience," but which is far more than that*] "giveth light to every man that cometh into the world;" and that "every one that hearkeneth to the voice of the Spirit cometh unto God, even the Father." From this we understand that the Spirit of Christ works with all people to help them eventually come into the true Church so that they can receive the Gift of the Holy Ghost (which is a far more powerful influence) which will testify to them of the Father and Son and will teach them and testify to them of all things necessary for exaltation.

12 Unto whom [*referring to the prophets spoken of in verses 10 and 11*] it [*the gospel of Christ which leads to salvation*] was revealed, that not unto themselves, but unto us they did minister [*teach and prophesy*] the things, which are now reported [*taught*] unto you by them [*the Apostles and missionaries*] that have preached the gospel unto you with the Holy Ghost [*by the power of the Holy Ghost*] sent down from heaven; which things the angels desire to look into [*even the angels want to learn as much as possible about these things*].

13 Wherefore gird up the loins of your mind [*prepare your minds to handle the coming trials and persecutions*] be sober [*be serious about living righteously; circumspectly; Strong's #3225*], and hope to the end [*keep your hopes high so that you can reach the goal of exaltation*] for the grace that is to be brought unto you [*which exaltation will be given you*] at the revelation of Jesus Christ [*when Christ shows forth His power to all*];

14 As obedient children [*keep your hopes high through being obedient followers of Christ*], not fashioning yourselves according to the former lusts in your ignorance [*not returning to your former lifestyles before you were converted and repented*]:

15 But as he [*God*] which hath called you is holy, so be ye holy in all manner of conversation [*conduct; Strong's #0391*];

16 Because it is written [*in Leviticus 11:44–45*], Be ye holy; for I am holy.

17 And if ye call on the Father, who without respect of persons [*who, without prejudice; in other words, who is fair and impartial*] judgeth according to every man's work, pass the time of your sojourning here in fear [*spend your time here in mortality with high respect for God*]:

18 Forasmuch as ye know [*since you know*] that ye were not redeemed with corruptible [*temporary, perishable*] things, as [*like*] silver and gold, from your vain [*unsuccessful as far as salvation is concerned; Strong's #3152*] conversation [*lifestyle; Strong's #0391*] received by tradition from your fathers;

19 But [*rather*] with the precious blood of Christ, as of a lamb [*like a sacrificial

*lamb*] without blemish and without spot [*who was perfect*]:

20 Who [*Christ*] verily was foreordained before the foundation of the world [*was called to be our Savior in premortality; see Moses 4:1–3 and Abraham 3:27*], but was manifest [*came to earth*] in these last times [*recent times*] for you,

21 Who by him [*Christ*] do believe in God [*Heavenly Father*], that raised him [*Christ*] up from the dead, and gave him [*Christ*] glory; that your faith and hope might be in God [*the Father*]. [*In other words, Jesus came to you and was glorified by the Father so that you could have truth and correct understanding about Heavenly Father.*]

22 Seeing [*since*] ye have purified your souls in [*by*] obeying the truth through the Spirit [*with the help of the Holy Ghost*] unto unfeigned [*genuine*] love of the brethren, see that ye love one another with a pure heart fervently [*deeply*]:

23 Being born again [*having been spiritually reborn*], not of corruptible seed [*not by mortal parents, or doctrines or philosophies*], but of incorruptible [*rather a rebirth that can last forever*], by the word of God [*through the gospel of Christ*], which liveth and abideth for ever [*which lasts eternally*].

24 For all flesh is as grass [*mortal life is very temporary*], and all the glory of man as the flower of grass [*like blossoms which soon fade away and die*]. The grass withereth, and the flower [*blossoms*] thereof falleth away: [*Compare this with Isaiah 40:6–8.*]

25 But the word of the Lord endureth [*lasts*] for ever. And this is the word which by the gospel is preached unto you.

## FIRST PETER 2

Peter will now remind these Saints what they must do in order to be "born again," in other words, what they must do in order to become spiritual and worthy for exaltation.

1 WHEREFORE [*and so,*] laying aside all malice [*evil intentions toward others*], and all guile [*deceptiveness; Strong's #1388*], and hypocrisies, and envies [*jealousies*], and all evil speakings [*slandering, gossiping*],

2 As newborn babes [*be like newborn babies*], desire the sincere milk of the word [*seek to be nourished by the simple basics of the gospel*], that ye may grow thereby [*so that you can grow up in the gospel*]:

3 If so be ye have tasted that the Lord is gracious [*I hope you have noticed that the Lord is kind, merciful and gracious*].

> Next, Peter will compare Christ to a large, solid rock, or foundation upon which we can safely build. He will also invite these Saints to become "rock solid" in their faithfulness to God and to become solid foundations for others to rely on as they come to Christ.

4 To whom coming, as unto a living stone [*as you come to Christ, which is like coming to a living foundation*], disallowed indeed of men [*who was rejected by worldly men*], but chosen of God [*but was God's chosen Son*], and precious,

5 Ye also, as lively stones [*as foundations who are alive spiritually*], are built up a spiritual house [*are being built up spiritually*], an holy priesthood [*you are a holy priesthood*], to offer up spiritual sacrifices [*and you are sacrificing whatever is necessary in order to become spiritually in tune with God*], acceptable to God by Jesus Christ [*you are becoming acceptable to the Father through the Atonement of Christ*].

6 Wherefore also it is contained in the scripture [*this is the purpose of Isaiah 28:16, which says*], Behold, I lay in Sion [*Zion*] a chief corner stone [*Christ*], elect [*foreordained in premortality*],

precious: and he that believeth on him [*Christ*] shall not be confounded [*confused, disappointed, or stopped in progressing to exaltation*].

7 Unto you therefore which believe he is precious [*to you who believe in Christ, He is precious, dear, tender, and loving*]: but unto them which be disobedient [*who do not keep the commandments*], the stone [*Christ*] which the builders [*the Jews*] disallowed [*rejected*], the same [*Christ*] is made [*has been made*] the head of the corner [*the ruler over all things*],

8 And a stone of stumbling, and a rock of offence, even to them which stumble at the word, being disobedient: whereunto also they were appointed.

The JST combines and changes verses 7 and 8 as follows:

**JST 1 Peter 2:7–8**

Unto you therefore who believe, he [*Christ*] is precious; but unto them who are disobedient, who stumble at the word [*Christ's gospel*] through disobedience [*because of disobedience*], whereunto they were appointed [*they were invited to live the gospel*], a stone of stumbling [*to them the gospel gets in their way*], and a rock of offense [*and is offensive to them*]. For the stone [*Christ*] which the builders [*the Jews and anyone who rejects Christ*] disallowed [*rejected*], is become the head of the corner [*has become the ruler over all things*].

Next, in verse 9, Peter uses powerful, symbolic, and beautiful language to describe who the faithful Saints are. We are included in this description if we too are striving to be righteous.

9 But ye are a chosen generation [*a people chosen to carry the blessings of the gospel and the priesthood to all people; see Abraham 2:9*], a royal priesthood [*we have the Melchizedek Priesthood of God, with all its saving ordinances, which can ultimately make us "royalty," in other words kings and queens in exaltation*], an holy nation [*a holy people*], a peculiar people [*a special possession of the Lord; see 1 Peter 2:9, footnote f, in our Bible*]; that ye should shew forth [*tell everyone; declare abroad; Strong's #1804*] the praises of him [*God*] who hath called you out of darkness [*spiritual darkness*] into his marvellous light [*into the marvelous light of the gospel*] :

**JST 1 Peter 2:9**

9 But ye are a chosen generation, a royal priesthood, a holy nation, a peculiar people; that ye should show forth the praises of him who hath called you out of darkness into his marvelous light;

10 Which in time past were not a people [*before you received the gospel and joined the Church, you were not a part of this group of chosen people*], but are now the people of God: which had not obtained mercy, but now have obtained mercy.

11 Dearly beloved, I beseech [*urge*] you as strangers and pilgrims [*as temporary inhabitants of this earth here in mortality; see note in Hebrews 11:13 in this study guide*], abstain from fleshly lusts [*do not give in to physical appetites and passions*], which war against the soul [*which threaten your exaltation*];

12 Having your conversation; honest among the Gentiles [*nonmembers of the Church*]: that, whereas they speak against you as evildoers [*that even though they accuse you of being wicked*], they may by your good works, which they shall behold, glorify God in the day of visitation [*so that they can, through your good example, be converted and be among the righteous who will join with the Lord and praise Him when He comes*].

**JST 1 Peter 2:12**

12 Having your conduct honest among the Gentiles; that, whereas they speak against you as evildoers, they may by your good works, which they shall behold, glorify God in the day of visitation.

There are some, who for religious reasons, refuse to submit to Kings, presidents, government or civic leaders, and so forth. They would do well to follow Peter's counsel here in the next verses. Allegiance to government authority is very necessary for law and order and to prevent anarchy and chaos. See D&C 134 for more about the Lord's counsel on this matter.

13 Submit yourselves to every ordinance [*government, institution; Strong's #2937*] of man for the Lord's sake: whether it be to the king, as supreme [*as the supreme authority*];

14 Or unto governors, as unto them [*as well as to those*] that are sent by him [*the governor*] for the punishment of evildoers [*those who break the law*], and for the praise of them that do well.

15 For so is the will of God [*this is the will of God*], that with well doing [*good behavior*] ye may put to silence the ignorance of foolish men:

16 As free [*as free people*], and not using your liberty for a cloke of maliciousness [*not misusing your freedom as a coverup for evil deeds*], but as the servants of God [*use your liberty as becomes servants of God*].

17 Honour all men [*show proper respect to all people*]. Love the brotherhood [*show love to all members of the Church*]. Fear [*show reverence to, respect; Strong's #5399*] God. Honour the king [*show proper respect to political authorities*].

18 Servants, be subject to your masters with all fear [*reverence for one who has authority over you; Strong's #5401*]; not only to the good and gentle, but also to the froward [*also toward masters who are crooked, wicked; Strong's #4646*].

19 For this is thankworthy [*commendable; worthy of being rewarded by God; Strong's #5485*], if a man for conscience toward God [*because of his belief in God*] endure grief, suffering wrongfully [*innocent of wrongdoing*].

20 For what glory is it [*what special honor should you receive*], if, when ye be buffeted [*if, when you are made to suffer*] for your faults [*for your own sins and mistakes*], ye shall take it patiently? but if, when ye do well [*when you are living righteously*], and suffer for it, ye take it patiently, this is acceptable with God.

21 For even hereunto were ye called [*when you joined the Church, you were, in effect, called to suffer persecution*]: because Christ also suffered for us [*just as Christ suffered for being righteous*], leaving us an example, that ye should follow his steps:

22 Who [*Christ*] did no sin, neither was guile [*deception*] found in his mouth:

23 Who, when he was reviled [*mocked and insulted*], reviled not again [*did not retaliate*]; when he suffered, he threatened not; but committed himself to him [*the Father*] that judgeth righteously:

24 Who [*Christ*] his own self [*all alone*] bare [*took*] our sins in his own body [*took our sins upon Himself*] on the tree [*on the cross*], that we, being dead to sins [*when we repent*], should live unto righteousness [*will be spiritually reborn and brought back unto God*]: by whose stripes [*the painful welts on the Savior's back as a result of the scourging He was given before He was crucified*] ye were healed [*you were forgiven and healed through the punishment which Christ took for your sins*].

25 For ye were as [*like*] sheep going astray; but are now returned unto the Shepherd and Bishop [*overseer, guardian; Strong's #1985*] of your souls [*but through the Atonement, you have now returned to the Good Shepherd (Christ) who is the Overseer, the Guardian, of your souls*].

# FIRST PETER 3

This chapter contains the marvelous and comforting doctrine that the gospel is taught to the spirits of the dead in the spirit world. This is very significant doctrine and ties in with 1 Corinthians 15:29 which mentions baptism for the dead. It also ties in with 1 Peter 4:6 which teaches that after they have been taught the gospel, the dead will be judged by the same standards by which we will be judged. So far in his epistle (letter), Peter has given the members of the Church much counsel regarding humbly submitting to the Savior as well as submitting to governments and government leaders, masters, and so forth. As noted in Ephesians 5:21 in this study guide, the word "submit" carries with it the connotation of "voluntary cooperation" rather than slave-like subservience. You may wish to review the notes given for Ephesians 5:21–33 as you read Peter's counsel to wives in the next several verses.

1 LIKEWISE [*just as I counseled your husbands to humbly submit to Christ and their leaders*], ye wives, be in subjection to [*voluntarily submit; cooperate with; Strong's #5293*] your own husbands; that [*so that*], if any obey not the word [*if they are not living the gospel*], they also may without the word [*without understanding the gospel*] be won [*won over to the gospel*] by the conversation of the wives;

**JST 1 Peter 3:1**
1 Likewise, ye wives, be in subjection to your own husbands; that, if any obey not the word, they also may without the word be won by the conduct of the wives;

2 While they behold your chaste conversation coupled with fear.

**JST 1 Peter 3:2**
2 While they behold your chaste conduct [*in other words, when they see your righteous conduct*] coupled with fear [*coupled with the respect they will have for you*].

3 Whose adorning [*beauty*] let it not be that outward adorning of plaiting [*braiding*] the hair, and of wearing of gold [*wearing costly jewelry*], or of putting on of apparel [*or in the type of clothing you wear*]; [*In other words, let your true beauty not depend on hairstyles, jewelry, clothing styles, etc.*]

**JST 1 Peter 3:3**
3 Let your adorning be not that outward adorning of plaiting the hair, and wearing of gold, or putting on of apparel;

4 But let it be the hidden man of the heart [*let your true beauty be the hidden beauty that dwells in the heart*], in that which is not corruptible [*in qualities and character traits which have eternal value*], even the ornament of [*beauty, such as*] a meek and quiet spirit [*a self-controlled and peaceful nature*], which is in the sight of God of great price [*of great value*].

5 For after this manner [*this is the way*] in the old time [*in times past*] the holy women also [*the women who were true Saints*], who trusted in God, adorned [*beautified*] themselves, being in subjection unto [*respecting and cooperating with*] their own husbands:

**JST 1 Peter 3:5**
5 For after this manner in old times the holy women, who trusted in God, adorned themselves, being in subjection unto their own husbands;

6 Even as Sara [*even as Sarah did when she*] obeyed Abraham, calling him lord [*when she treated him with respect and reverence; Strong's #2962*]: whose daughters [*descendants*] ye are, as long as ye do well [*as long as you live the gospel*], and are not afraid with any

amazement [*and do not give in to fears and pressures of the world*].

Peter pays Sarah a very high compliment in verse 6, above. The phrase, "whose daughters ye are," is symbolic of exaltation. "Daughters of" means "followers of" in the same way that "sons of" means "followers of." See Mosiah 5:7 where "sons" and "daughters" are symbolic words meaning "exalted."

7 Likewise [*in the same way*], ye husbands, dwell with them [*live with your wives*] according to knowledge [*according to what God has taught; footnote b in our Bible for 1 Peter 3:7 which refers us to D&C 121:41–42 which includes persuasion, patience, gentleness, meekness, genuine love, kindness, pure knowledge, no hypocrisy, and no deception*], giving honour unto [*showing respect to*] the wife, as unto the weaker vessel, and as being heirs together of the grace of life; that your prayers be not hindered [*otherwise, bad behavior toward your wives will get in the way of your prayers to God*].

The phrase "as unto the weaker vessel" in verse 7, above, does not agree with the teachings of our prophets today. They clearly teach that "fathers and mothers are obligated to help one another as equal partners" in The Family: A Proclamation To The World, given September 23, 1995. Thus, we are left to conclude that either Peter's statement was not properly translated or that it reflected cultural tradition of his time rather than the eternal status of women.

8 Finally, be ye all of one mind [*be united*], having compassion one of another, love as brethren, be pitiful [*full of compassion; Strong's #2155*], be courteous:

9 Not rendering [*returning*] evil for evil, or railing [*insult*] for railing: but contrariwise blessing [*doing just the opposite, thus blessing each other*]; knowing that ye are thereunto called [*knowing that you have been called by Christ*], that ye should inherit a blessing [*to inherit the blessings of eternal life*].

10 For he that will love life, and see good days, let him refrain his tongue from evil, and his lips that they speak no guile [*no deception; Strong's #1388*]:

11 Let him eschew [*avoid*] evil, and do good; let him seek peace, and ensue it [*do his best to achieve it*].

12 For the eyes of the Lord are over [*upon*] the righteous, and his ears are open unto their prayers: but the face of the Lord is against them that do evil.

13 And who is he that will harm you [*who can do you any permanent harm, eternally*], if ye be followers of that which is good?

14 But and if ye suffer for righteousness' sake [*because of being righteous*], happy are ye: and be not afraid of their terror [*don't fear their threats*], neither be troubled;

15 But sanctify the Lord God [*make the Lord God the top priority*] in your hearts: and be ready always to give an answer to every man that asketh you a reason of the hope that is in you with meekness and fear [*be ready to humbly and respectfully tell anyone about the gospel, who asks you why you are so optimistic and happy*]:

**JST 1 Peter 3:15**

15 But sanctify the Lord God in your hearts; and be ready always to give an answer with meekness and fear to every man that asketh of you a reason for the hope that is in you:

16 Having a good conscience [*having a clear conscience*]; that, whereas they speak evil of you, as of evildoers [*when they accuse you of being evil*], they may be ashamed [*they will be put to shame*] that falsely accuse your good conversation in Christ.

**JST 1 Peter 3:16**

16 Having a good conscience; that, whereas they speak evil of you, as of

evildoers, they may be ashamed that falsely accuse your good conduct in Christ.

17 For it is better, if the will of God be so [*if it is in harmony with God's will that you suffer*], that ye suffer for well doing, than for evil doing [*that you suffer for doing good rather than for doing evil*].

Next, Peter uses the Savior as the supreme example of one who suffered for doing good. In so doing, he teaches tremendous doctrine about work for the dead.

18 For Christ also hath once suffered for sins [*suffered once and for all for all sins; compare with 2 Nephi 9:21–22*], the just for the unjust [*the Perfectly Righteous One suffered for the guilty ones (all of us)*], that he might bring us to God [*so that He could bring us to exaltation in the presence of the Father*], being put to death in the flesh [*having His mortal body crucified*], but quickened by the Spirit:

**JST 1 Peter 3:18**

18 For Christ also once suffered for sins, the just for the unjust, being put to death in the flesh, but quickened [*resurrected*] by the Spirit, that he might bring us to God [*so that He could bring us home to the Father*].

19 By which also he went and preached unto the spirits in prison; [*In other words, for the same cause, offering people exaltation, Christ also went and preached to the spirits in prison in the spirit world.*]

**JST 1 Peter 3:19**

19 For which cause also, he went and preached unto the spirits in prison;

20 Which sometime were disobedient, when once the longsuffering of God waited in the days of Noah, while the ark was a preparing [*while the ark was being prepared*], wherein few, that is, eight souls were saved by water. [*Those in the spirit prison included those who had been wicked in the days of Noah and who were drowned in the flood. Only eight people were saved on Noah's ark.*]

**JST 1 Peter 3:20**

20 Some of whom were disobedient in the days of Noah, while the long-suffering of God waited, while the ark was preparing, wherein few, that is, eight souls were saved by water.

We know from D&C 138:18–20 and 29–30 that the Savior only appeared to the righteous in the spirit world. He organized a great missionary force among the righteous who were then sent to the spirit prison to teach the gospel to those spirits. We also know from Moses 7:27 that many people were converted by Noah and were taken up to join the City of Enoch before the flood occurred.]

21 The like figure [*the flooding of the earth by water, mentioned at the end of verse 20, above, is symbolic of baptism*] whereunto even baptism doth also now save us [*baptism, even now, opens the door to our being saved*] not the putting away of the filth of the flesh [*we are not referring to physically washing dirt off of our bodies*], but the answer of a good conscience [*rather to having a clear conscience*] toward God,) by the resurrection of Jesus Christ [*through the Atonement of Christ*]:

22 Who is gone into heaven, and is on the right hand of God [*the Father*]; angels and authorities and powers being made subject unto him [*Christ*].

## FIRST PETER 4

Without the help of the JST, people could misinterpret verse 1, below, as saying that Christ "ceased from sin," thus implying that the Savior was not perfect. Such is not the case. As you will see, next, in verse 1, the JST takes the last phrase from verse 1 and adds it to verse 2. The Prophet Joseph Smith also makes significant changes in verse 2.

1 FORASMUCH [*since*] then as Christ hath suffered for us in the flesh, arm yourselves likewise with the same mind [*prepare yourselves to suffer also*]: for he that hath suffered in the flesh hath ceased from sin;

**JST 1 Peter 4:1**

1 Forasmuch then as Christ hath suffered for us in the flesh, arm yourselves likewise with the same mind;

2 That he no longer should live the rest of his time in the flesh to the lusts of men, but to the will of God.

**JST 1 Peter 4:2**

2 For you who have suffered in the flesh [*here in mortality*] should cease from sin [*should repent*], that you no longer the rest of your time in the flesh [*so that for the rest of your mortal lives*], should live to the lusts of men [*you no longer give in to the worldly passions of mortal men*], but to the will of God.

The JST changes in the next verse take away the implication that Peter lived a wicked lifestyle before he was converted and followed the Savior.

3 For the time past of our life may suffice us to have wrought the will of the Gentiles, when we walked in lasciviousness, lusts, excess of wine, revellings, banquetings, and abominable idolatries: when ye walked in lasciviousness [*all kinds of sexual immorality*], lusts [*uncontrolled passions*], excess of wine [*drunkenness*], revellings [*wild parties; Strong's #2970*], banquetings [*carousing; Strong's #4224*], and abominable idolatries [*wicked idol worship*];"]

**JST 1 Peter 4:3**

3 For the time past of life may suffice to have wrought the will of the Gentiles [*you have spent enough time in the past living like people who don't know the gospel*], when ye walked in lasciviousness, lusts, excess of wine, revellings, banquetings, and abominable idolatries;

4 Wherein they [*the Gentiles, non-Christians*] think it strange that ye run not with them to the same excess of riot [*don't understand why you won't participate in their wicked lifestyle anymore*], speaking evil of you [*and so they mock and criticize you*]:

**JST 1 Peter 4:4**

4 Wherein they speak evil of you, thinking it strange that you run not with them to the same excess of riot;

5 Who [*the wicked who continue in this wicked lifestyle*] shall give account to him [*God*] that is ready to judge the quick [*the living; Strong's #2198*] and the dead.

6 For for this cause was the gospel preached also to them that are dead [*this is the reason that the gospel is being taught to the dead in the spirit world prison*], that they might be judged according to men in the flesh [*so that they can be judged by the same standards as mortal people who are taught the gospel*], but live according to God in the spirit [*and can accept the gospel and become spiritually alive*].

**JST 1 Peter 4:6**

6 Because of this, is the gospel preached to them who are dead, that they might be judged according to men in the flesh, but live in the spirit according to the will of God.

7 But the end of all things is at hand [*But for you, this is the time to prepare to meet God; compare with Alma 34:32–33*]: be ye therefore sober [*serious-minded and self-controlled; Strong's #4993*], and watch unto prayer [*watch yourselves so that you can pray successfully*].

**JST 1 Peter 4:7**

7 But to you, the end of all things is at hand; be ye therefore sober, and watch unto prayer.

Joseph Smith made a very important change in verse 8, next, namely, that charity does not cover up many sins,

rather, it prevents many sins.

8 And above all things have fervent [*continuous; Strong's #1618*] charity among yourselves: for charity shall cover the multitude of sins.

**JST 1 Peter 4:8**

8 And above all things have fervent charity among yourselves; for charity preventeth a multitude of sins.

9 Use hospitality one to another without grudging [*without murmuring*].

10 As every man hath received the gift [*since you have received various spiritual gifts; compare with D&C 46:11–12*], even so minister the same one to another [*use them to help each other*], as good stewards of the manifold grace of God [*as good stewards of the grace of God which is demonstrated in so many different ways*].

11 If any man speak, let him speak as the oracles of God [*In other words, teach under the direction of the Spirit*]; if any man minister, let him do it as of [*according to*] the ability which God giveth: that God [*the Father*] in all things may be glorified through Jesus Christ, to whom be praise and dominion for ever and ever. Amen.

**JST 1 Peter 4:11**

11 If any man speak, let him speak as an oracle of God; if any man minister, let him do it as of the ability which God giveth; that God in all things may be glorified through Jesus Christ; to whom be praise and dominion forever and ever. Amen.

12 Beloved, think it not strange concerning the fiery trial which is to try you [*do not be surprised at the severe trials that are coming upon you*], as though some strange thing happened unto you [*as if such trials were something new for the righteous*]:

13 But rejoice, inasmuch as ye are partakers of Christ's sufferings [*take comfort that you are able to join Christ in suffering because of righteousness*]; that, when his glory shall be revealed [*that when Christ rules over all things here*], ye may be glad also with exceeding joy [*you can rejoice with Him that all wickedness is gone*].

14 If ye be reproached [*mocked*] for the name of Christ [*because you have taken the name of Christ upon you*], happy are ye; for the spirit of glory and of God resteth upon you: on their part he is evil spoken of [*the wicked speak evil of God*], but on your part he is glorified [*but you glorify God*].

Next, Peter again reminds the Saints that it is one thing to suffer because you are trying to be righteous, but quite another thing to suffer because you are wicked.

15 But let none of you suffer as a murderer, or as a thief, or as an evildoer, or as a busybody in other men's matters.

16 Yet if any man suffer as a Christian [*because he is a follower of Christ*], let him not be ashamed; but let him glorify God on this behalf [*because of it*].

17 For the time is come that judgment must begin at the house of God [*the time has come when great trials and tribulation will come upon the members of the Church*]: and if it first begin at us [*and if it starts with us*], what shall the end be of them that obey not the gospel of God [*imagine what will happen to the wicked who deserve punishment because they reject the gospel*]?

18 And if the righteous scarcely be saved [*and if it is hard for the righteous to be saved*], where shall the ungodly and the sinner appear [*can you imagine where the wicked fit into the picture*]?

19 Wherefore let them that suffer according to the will of God commit the keeping of their souls to him in well doing [*through doing good*], as unto a faithful Creator [*as one who can be completely trusted*].

# FIRST PETER 5

Peter finishes this letter by reminding the local priesthood of their responsibility to take care of the members under their care. He teaches them that one of the most important ways of leading is to be a good example. He also counsels younger members to show respect for their leaders and to follow them.

There are no JST changes for this chapter.

1 THE elders [*Melchizedek Priesthood holders, local leaders of the Church*] which are among you I exhort [*counsel*], who am also an elder, and a witness of the sufferings of Christ [*and as a witness who personally saw the suffering of the Savior*], and also a partaker of the glory that shall be revealed [*and as one who has partaken of the gospel*]:

2 Feed the flock [*nourish the members of the Church*] of God which is among you [*of God, who is among you; compare with D&C 38:7 wherein the Savior says "But behold, verily, verily, I say unto you that mine eyes are upon you. I am in your midst and ye cannot see me;"*], taking the oversight thereof [*supervising the work of the Lord*], not by constraint [*not because you are obligated to*], but willingly; not for filthy lucre [*not for money*], but of a ready mind [*but willingly*];

3 Neither as being lords over God's heritage [*not as masters or bosses*], but being ensamples to the flock [*but as good examples to your members*].

4 And when the chief Shepherd [*Christ*] shall appear, ye shall receive a crown of glory that fadeth not away [*you will receive a crown of exaltation which will never end*].

5 Likewise, ye younger [*you younger members*], submit [*respect; cooperate; Strong's #5293*] yourselves unto the elder [*cooperate with your leaders*]. Yea, all of you be subject one to another [*cooperate with one another*], and be clothed with humility: for God resisteth [*opposes*] the proud, and giveth grace to the humble.

6 Humble yourselves therefore under the mighty hand of God, that he may exalt you [*give you exaltation*] in due time:

7 Casting all your care upon him; for he careth for you.

8 Be sober, be vigilant [*be watchful*]; because your adversary the devil, as a roaring lion, walketh about, seeking whom he may devour:

9 Whom resist stedfast in the faith [*resist the temptations from the devil by carefully living the gospel*], knowing that the same afflictions are accomplished in your brethren that are in the world [*knowing that other members of the Church throughout the world are going through similar troubles.*]

10 But the God [*may the Father*] of all grace [*of all mercy, kindness, forgiveness, and salvation*], who hath called us unto his eternal glory [*to celestial exaltation*] by [*through*] Christ Jesus, after that ye have suffered a while [*after you have passed the test*], make you perfect [*bring you into exaltation*], stablish [*make you firm in the gospel*], strengthen, settle you [*make you well-grounded in the gospel; Strong's #2311*].

11 To him [*the Father*] be glory and dominion for ever and ever. Amen.

12 By Silvanus, a faithful brother unto you, as I suppose, I have written briefly, exhorting, and testifying that this is the true grace of God wherein ye stand. [*I have sent this letter to you with the help of Silvanus, a faithful member of the Church.*]

13 The church that is at Babylon [*probably meaning that Peter was writing from Rome, where members of the Church are being particularly severely*

*persecuted*], elected together with you [*chosen by God to spread His gospel abroad, as you are*], saluteth [*greets*] you; and so doth Marcus [*Mark, who later wrote the Gospel of Mark*] my son [*my son in the gospel*].

14 Greet ye one another with a kiss of charity. [*Joseph Smith replaced the word "kiss" with "salutation" in several other places, for instance, 1 Thessalonians 5:26*]. Peace be with you all that are in Christ Jesus [*who have taken upon you the name of Jesus Christ*]. Amen.

# THE SECOND EPISTLE GENERAL OF PETER

Second Peter seems to have been written after the persecutions heaped upon the Christians by Nero, Emperor of Rome, had died off somewhat (see notes at the beginning of First Peter, in this study guide). Consequently, many Bible scholars set the approximate date of this letter to be around AD 65 to AD 68, shortly before Peter's death. It was apparently written to the same general audience of Saints to whom First Peter was written. See Bible Dictionary under "Peter, Epistles of." Some scholars believe it was written from Rome. It seems that the real danger to the Church at this time is internal apostasy. Peter is the President of the Church and as such, strengthens the members by teaching them how to make their calling and elections sure (chapter 1), how to avoid personal apostasy by recognizing false teachings and apostate doctrines being taught by some members of the Church (chapter 2), and by warning them not to get caught up in false teachings about the Second Coming (chapter 3.)

## SECOND PETER 1

The Prophet Joseph Smith said that "Peter penned the most sublime language of any of the apostles." See *History of the Church*, Vol. 5, p. 392. Certainly, this chapter is a wonderful example of the "sublime language" of this humble and powerful Apostle of the Lord. In it, Peter teaches the Saints how to become Christ like, thus making their callings and elections sure, in other words, how to make sure that they attain exaltation.

1 SIMON Peter, a servant and an apostle of Jesus Christ, to them [*to members of the Church*] that have obtained like precious faith with us [*who have obtained the same precious faith in Christ which we have*] through the righteousness of God [*the Father*] and our Saviour Jesus Christ:

> Next, in verse 2, Peter emphasizes that knowledge about the Father and about Jesus Christ is power. Joseph Smith said "Knowledge is the power of salvation." (*Teachings of the Prophet Joseph Smith*, p. 306—you may wish to read pp. 304–306.) This ties in with D&C 131:6 which says, "It is impossible for a man to be saved in ignorance" meaning ignorance of the gospel.

2 Grace and peace be multiplied unto you through the knowledge of God, and of Jesus our Lord,

3 According as his divine power hath given unto us all things that pertain unto life and godliness [*God has taught us everything we need to gain exaltation and to become gods*], through the knowledge of him [*the Father*] that hath called us to glory and virtue [*who has called us by His Son Jesus Christ to join Him in eternal glory and righteousness*]:

4 Whereby are given unto us exceeding great and precious promises [*through the teachings we have been given, we receive the promises of exaltation*]: that by these ye might be partakers of the divine nature [*that through these teachings and promises you can become like God*], having escaped [*overcome*] the

corruption [*wickedness*] that is in the world through lust [*which comes from uncontrolled worldly passions*].

Next, Peter will give a detailed set of steps which can lead to making our "calling and election sure" (verse 10). First, though, we need a very basic explanation of what the phrase "calling and election made sure" means. In its most basic sense, it means to "make our exaltation certain." Exaltation means becoming like our Father in Heaven (D&C 76:95) through entering into the highest degree of glory in the celestial kingdom (D&C 131:1–4), becoming gods, having our own spirit offspring (D&C 132:19–20), creating worlds for them, and making exaltation available to them in the same way our Father has made it available to us. Our Father in Heaven "calls" all of His children to make themselves worthy to return to Him in exaltation, through the gospel of His Son, Jesus Christ. Those of His children who heed this "calling" and do all they can to make themselves worthy are cleansed and qualified by the Atonement, "after all they can do" (2 Nephi 25:23), to be "elected by God" to enter exaltation. Thus, they are "called" by their Father to return to Him. If they follow the course requirements for exaltation, they are eventually "elected" by Him to receive it.

Technically, the Father has turned it over to the Savior to be our final judge. "The Father judgeth no man, but hath committed all judgment unto the Son" (John 5:22.) Thus, when the Savior "elects" or "votes" for you to enter exaltation, you are in! Another way to put it is this: "Calling and election" is another way of saying "exaltation." If we live righteously and repent and use the Atonement completely, we make our exaltation "sure" or "certain." Peter gives us instructions on how to do this, in verses 5–12. You may wish to pay special attention to how he sequenced these attributes and how they build off each other.

5 And beside this, giving all diligence, add to your faith virtue [*moral goodness; chastity; purity*]; and to virtue knowledge [*knowledge of the gospel; see verse 3*];

6 And to knowledge temperance [*self-control*]; and to temperance patience; and to patience godliness [*Christ-like attributes; reverence toward God*];

7 And to godliness brotherly kindness; and to brotherly kindness charity [*see 1 Corinthians 13*].

8 For if these things be in you, and abound [*if these attributes are thoroughly ingrained in your personality and your life*], they make you that ye shall neither be barren [*unproductive*] nor unfruitful in the knowledge of our Lord Jesus Christ [*they will produce the highest possible results of the gospel, namely, exaltation*]. [*In other words, you will be on your way to exaltation.*]

9 But he that lacketh these things is blind [*spiritually blind*], and cannot see afar off [*and has no wisdom*], and hath forgotten that he was purged [*cleansed*] from his old sins.

10 Wherefore the rather, brethren, give diligence [*therefore, be all the more anxious*] to make your calling and election sure: for if ye do these things, ye shall never fall: [*In other words, if you do these things, you can plan on obtaining exaltation.*]

11 For so [*thus*] an entrance [*into exaltation*] shall be ministered [*given*] unto you abundantly [*with all the promised blessings*] into the everlasting kingdom [*celestial exaltation*] of our Lord and Saviour Jesus Christ.

12 Wherefore I will not be negligent to put you always in remembrance of these things [*this is why I will keep emphasizing these things to you*], though ye know them [*even though you already know them*], and be established in the present truth [*and are already living them*].

13 Yea, I think it meet [*necessary*], as

long as I am in this tabernacle [*as long as I live*], to stir you up by putting you in remembrance [*to keep reminding you of these things*];

14 Knowing that shortly I must put off this my tabernacle [*knowing that I will soon die*], even as our Lord Jesus Christ hath shewed me [*in the way which the Lord Jesus Christ showed me I would die*].

According to John 21:18–19, we understand that the Savior told Peter that he, too, would be crucified because of his faithfulness to the gospel. Tradition has it that Peter was crucified upside down in Rome as early as AD 64 or as late as AD 68.

15 Moreover I will endeavour [*attempt*] that ye may be able after my decease [*after my death*] to have these things always in remembrance.

16 For we have not followed cunningly devised fables [*cleverly made up false doctrines*], when we made known unto you the power and coming of our Lord Jesus Christ, but were eyewitnesses of his majesty [*we (Peter, James, and John) saw the Savior personally, including His glory when He was transfigured; see verses 17–18*].

17 For he received from God the Father honour and glory, when there came such a voice to him from the excellent glory, This is my beloved Son, in whom I am well pleased [*see Matthew 17:1–5*].

18 And this voice which came from heaven we heard, when we were with him in the holy mount [*the Mount of Transfiguration*].

19 We have also a more sure word of prophecy [*See D&C 131:5*]; whereunto ye do well that ye take heed [*to which you would be wise to pay close attention*], as unto a light that shineth in a dark place [*as if it were a light lighting the way for you through the darkness*], until the day dawn [*until the morning comes*], and the day star arise in your hearts:

**JST 2 Peter 1:19**

19 We have therefore a more sure knowledge of the word of prophecy, to which word of prophecy ye do well that ye take heed, as unto a light which shineth in a dark place, until the day dawn, and the day star arise in your hearts;

Bruce R. McConkie explained the phrase "until the day dawn, and the day star arise in your hearts" in verse 19, above, as follows: "Until the Second Coming of the Lord; until the Millennial day dawns; until the day when 'the root and the offspring of David' who is 'the bright and morning star' (Rev. 22:16) shall reign personally on earth and be the companion, confidant, and friend of those whose calling and election is sure and who are thus called forth as 'kings and priests' to live and 'reign on earth' (Rev. 5:10) with him a thousand years." (Bruce R. McConkie, *Doctrinal New Testament Commentary*, 3 vols. [Salt Lake City: Bookcraft, 1965–1973], Vol. 3, p. 355.)

20 Knowing this first, that no prophecy of the scripture is of any private interpretation. [*In other words, you must not twist the meaning of the scriptures to suit your own purposes.*]

**JST 2 Peter 1:20**

20 Knowing this first, that no prophecy of the scriptures is given of any private will of man.

21 For the prophecy [*scriptures which include prophecies*] came not in old time [*in ancient times*] by the will of man: but holy men [*prophets*] of God spake [*spoke*] as they were moved [*inspired*] by the Holy Ghost.

## SECOND PETER 2

As mentioned in the general introduction to Second Peter, above, it appears that many false doctrines were working their way into the Church at the time Peter wrote this epistle (letter.) In this chapter, Peter warns the Saints about

such things. He will use strong language as he condemns the wicked practices found among unrighteous people.

1 BUT there were false prophets also among the people [*in the past; see 2 Peter 1:21, above*], even as there shall be false teachers among you, who privily [*secretly; cunningly; Strong's #3919*] shall bring in damnable heresies [*false doctrines which will make you lose eternal life; Strong's #0684*], even denying the Lord that bought them, and bring upon themselves swift destruction.

**JST 2 Peter 2:1**

1 But there were false prophets also among the people, even as there shall be false teachers among you who privily shall bring in abominable heresies, even denying the Lord that bought them, and bring upon themselves swift destruction.

2 And many shall follow their [*the teachers of false doctrines in verse 1, above*] pernicious [*evil, destructive*] ways; by reason of whom the way of truth shall be evil spoken of [*which will cause the true gospel of Christ to be referred to as false*].

3 And through covetousness [*because of greed and desire for worldly gain*] shall they with feigned [*pretended*] words make merchandise of you [*take advantage of you*]: whose judgment now of a long time lingereth not, and their damnation slumbereth not [*they will soon be caught up with by the judgments and punishments of God*].

**JST 2 Peter 2:3**

3 And through covetousness shall they with feigned words make merchandise of you; whose judgment now of a long time lingereth not, and their destruction slumbereth not.

4 For if God spared not the angels that sinned [*the one third who were cast out as a result of the war in heaven; see Revelation 12:4 and 7–9*], but cast them down to hell, and delivered them into chains of darkness, to be reserved unto judgment;

5 And spared not the old world [*and punished the wicked at the time of Noah and the flood*], but saved Noah the eighth person [*one of the eight people who survived the flood by entering the ark; see 1 Peter 3:20*], a preacher of righteousness, bringing in the flood upon the world of the ungodly [*the wicked*];

6 And turning the cities of Sodom and Gomorrha into ashes condemned them with an overthrow [*with complete destruction*], making them an ensample [*example*] unto those that after should live ungodly [*as an example to the wicked who came along later*];

7 And delivered just Lot [*and only saved Lot from the destruction of Sodom and Gomorrah*], vexed with [*oppressed, offended by*] the filthy conversation [*filthy behavior; Strong's #0391*] of the wicked:

8 (For that righteous man dwelling among them, in seeing and hearing, vexed his righteous soul from day to day with their unlawful [*evil*] deeds;)

9 The Lord knoweth how to deliver the godly out of temptations, and to reserve the unjust [*the wicked*] unto the day of judgment to be punished:

10 But chiefly [*mainly*] them [*the wicked*] that walk after the flesh in the lust of uncleanness [*who live lustful and evil lives*], and despise government [*hate rules and regulations*]. Presumptuous [*boastful, daring; Strong's #5113*] are they, selfwilled [*arrogant: Strong's #0829*], they are not afraid to speak evil of dignities [*of angels; of the things of God; Strong's #1391*].

11 Whereas angels, which are greater in power and might [*than the wicked men spoken of in the above verses*], bring not railing accusation against them [*do not lower themselves to rant and rave, like the wicked themselves do against the*

*righteous, (see verse 12, next)*] before the Lord [*in the presence of the Lord*].

12 But these [*the wicked*], as natural brute beasts [*are like animals who follow their base instincts*], made to be taken and destroyed, speak evil of the things [*things of righteousness*] that they understand not; and shall utterly perish in their own corruption [*will cause their own destruction; see Mormon 4:5*];

13 And shall receive the reward of unrighteousness [*and will receive the punishment which comes to the wicked*], as they that count it pleasure to riot [*live riotously*] in the day time [*in broad daylight; in other words, they take evil satisfaction in flaunting their wickedness in public*]. Spots they are and blemishes [*they are defects and blemishes on society*], sporting [*amusing*] themselves with their own deceivings [*cunning deceptiveness*] while they feast with you [*even while associating with you*];

14 Having eyes full of adultery [*always lusting after women and looking for opportunities to break the law of chastity*], and that cannot cease from sin; beguiling unstable souls [*seducing insecure people*]: an heart they have exercised with covetous practices [*their hearts are filled with evil greed*]; cursed children [*immature people who are bringing the punishments of God upon themselves*]:

15 Which have forsaken the right way [*who have left the gospel*], and are gone astray [*and have strayed away*], following the way of Balaam [*see Numbers 22*] the son of Bosor, who loved the wages of unrighteousness [*was trying to profit from wickedness and going against the Lord*];

16 But was rebuked for his iniquity: the dumb ass [*the donkey who normally could not talk*] speaking with man's voice forbad the madness of the prophet [*told Balaam not to do what he was foolishly planning to do*].

17 These are wells without water [*the wicked are like empty wells, they produce nothing of value to others*], clouds that are carried with a tempest [*they have nothing to anchor them and are blown all around by their evil lusts*]; to whom the mist of darkness is reserved for ever [*eternal punishments in hell are being prepared for them; compare with D&C 19:3–12*].

18 For when they [*the apostates, false teachers and wicked people spoken about in the above verses*] speak great swelling words of vanity [*long, empty speeches which draw attention to themselves*], they allure through the lusts of the flesh [*they use lustful physical desires to attract*], through much wantonness [*especially sexual passions*], those that were clean escaped from them who live in error [*who had successfully gotten away from them and their wicked lifestyles*]; [*In other words, wicked people are quite successful at deceiving and destroying others, who would normally not join in wickedness, through the use of pornography and lustful living.*]

19 While they promise them liberty [*while they promise them freedom from rules and regulations, commandments, etc.*], they themselves are the servants of corruption [*they themselves are enslaved by their own wickedness*]: for of whom a man is overcome, of the same is he brought in bondage. [*In other words, whatever overpowers a person becomes his or her master.*]

20 For if after they have escaped the pollutions [*wickedness*] of the world through the knowledge of the Lord and Saviour Jesus Christ [*through the Atonement of Christ*], they are again entangled therein, and overcome [*they get tangled up in sin again and are overpowered by it*], the latter end is worse with them than the beginning [*they are worse off than they were before they repented the first time; compare with D&C 82:3 and 7*].

21 For it had been [*would have been*] better for them not to have known the way of righteousness, than, after they have known it, to turn from the holy commandment delivered unto them.

22 But it is happened unto them according to the true proverb [*but what has happened to them is just like the old saying in Proverbs 26:11, which says*], The dog is [*has*] turned to [*is eating*] his own vomit again; and the sow [*pig*] that was washed [*was clean*] to [*has returned to* ] her wallowing in the mire.

# SECOND PETER 3

In this chapter, Peter will prophesy that when the time of the Second Coming is getting near, many will scoff at it and will not believe in it. He will teach that the Second Coming will catch many people off guard, reminding them that the same attitude prevailed at the time of the flood. He will teach that one day in heaven is a thousand years here on earth. He will give additional details about the Second Coming and the beginning of the Millennium. The JST (The Joseph Smith Translation of the Bible) will be tremendously helpful to us in understanding this last chapter of Peter's second letter to the Saints. Joseph Smith made changes to all but one verse (verse 14). In some cases, the changes are minor wording changes (or even punctuation changes, as in verse 16, where a semicolon is replaced by a comma), but the changes in other verses are crucial to correct understanding of Peter's message.

1 THIS second epistle [*letter*], beloved, I now write unto you; in both which [*in both of which letters*] I stir up your pure minds by way of remembrance [*in which I am going to remind you of several important things*]:

**JST 2 Peter 3:1**

1 This second epistle, beloved, I now write unto you; in which I stir up your pure minds by way of remembrance;

2 That ye may be mindful of [*remember*] the words which were spoken before [*in times past*] by the holy prophets, and of the commandment of [*and I am going to remind you about the commandments you have received from the Savior through*] us the apostles of the Lord and Saviour:

3 Knowing this first, that there shall come in the last days scoffers [*mockers of righteousness*], walking after their own lusts [*who make their own rules and live in wickedness*],

**JST 2 Peter 3:3**

3 Knowing this first, that in the last days there shall come scoffers, walking after their own lusts.

4 And saying, Where is the promise of his coming [*where is this much talked about Second Coming*]? for since the fathers [*ancestors*] fell asleep [*died*], all things continue [*everything keeps right on going*] as they were from the beginning of the creation. [*In other words, they have been talking about this "Second Coming" since way back, and nothing has happened. Life keeps right on going. There is nothing to worry about.*]

**JST 2 Peter 3:4**

Denying the Lord Jesus Christ, and saying, Where is the promise of his coming? for since the fathers fell asleep, all things must continue as they are, and have continued as they are from the beginning of the creation.

Next, Peter will remind them that people didn't expect the flood to happen either.

5 For this they willingly are ignorant of [*there is one thing that they are intentionally ignoring*], that by the word of God the heavens were of old, and the

earth standing out of the water and in the water: [*In other words, they are ignoring the fact that God created the earth and that when He says something will happen, it will happen!*]

**JST 2 Peter 3:5**
5 For this they willingly are ignorant of, that of old the heavens, and the earth standing in the water and out of the water, were created by the word of God;

6 Whereby the world that then was, being overflowed with water, perished: [*In other words, when God gave the "word," the earth was flooded and the wicked perished.*]

**JST 2 Peter 3:6**
6 And by the word of God, the world that then was, being overflowed with water, perished;

7 But the heavens and the earth, which are now, by the same word are kept in store, reserved unto fire against the day of judgment and perdition [*utter destruction; Strong's #0684*] of ungodly men.

**JST 2 Peter 3:7**
7 But the heavens, and the earth which are now [*which currently exist*], are kept in store [*are preserved*] by the same word [*by that same power*], reserved unto fire against the day of judgment and perdition of ungodly men [*being saved until it is time to burn the wicked*].

8 But, beloved, be not ignorant of this one thing, that one day [*in heaven*] is with the Lord as a thousand years [*on earth*], and a thousand years [*on earth*] as one day [*is as one day in heaven*]. [*In other words, what seems like a long time to us on earth is just a short time in heaven. The point is that even though wicked men claim that it has been "forever" that prophets have been saying that Jesus will come again, and so it is just an empty threat, yet it surely will come, and it will be just a "little while longer" in the Lord's time system.*]

**JST 2 Peter 3:8**
8 But concerning the coming of the Lord, beloved, I would not have you ignorant of this one thing, that one day is with the Lord as a thousand years, and a thousand years as one day.

9 The Lord is not slack [*being slow, Strong's #1019*] concerning his promise, as some men count slackness [*like some people think*]; but is longsuffering to us-ward [*In other words, He is very patient, giving us plenty of time to repent*], not willing that any should perish [*He doesn't want any of us to be destroyed*], but that all should come to repentance [*rather, He wants everyone to repent*].

**JST 2 Peter 3:9**
9 The Lord is not slack concerning his promise and coming, as some men count slackness; but long-suffering toward us, not willing that any should perish, but that all should come to repentance.

Notice in the JST of verse 10 that Joseph Smith points out that only "corruptible" things (people and things which deal with and represent evil and wickedness) will be burned. The verse, as it stands in our Bible, would lead the reader to believe that everything on the earth ("the works that are therein") will be destroyed by the burning which accompanies the Second Coming.

10 But the day of the Lord will come as a thief in the night [*the wicked will be caught off guard*]; in the which [*at which time*] the heavens shall pass away with a great noise, and the elements shall melt with fervent heat, the earth also and the works that are therein shall be burned up.

**JST 2 Peter 3:10**
10 But the day of the Lord will come as a thief in the night, in the which the heavens shall shake, and the earth also shall tremble, and the mountains shall melt, and pass away

with a great noise, and the elements shall be filled with fervent heat; the earth also shall be filled, and the corruptible works which are therein shall be burned up.

D&C 106:4 teaches us that the wicked will be caught off guard by the Second Coming; however, D&C 106:5 teaches us that the righteous will be expecting the Second Coming and thus will not be caught off guard when it actually happens.

11 Seeing then that all these things shall be dissolved, what manner of persons ought ye to be in all holy conversation and godliness, [*In other words, since all these wicked people and evil things, which could include pornography, Satanic rites, evil literature, evil media, etc., are going to be destroyed, what kind of people do you think you ought to be?*]

**JST 2 Peter 3:11**
11 If then all these things shall be destroyed, what manner of persons ought ye to be in holy conduct and godliness,

12 Looking for and hasting unto the coming of the day of God, wherein the heavens being on fire shall be dissolved, and the elements shall melt with fervent heat?

**JST 2 Peter 3:12**
12 Looking unto, and preparing for the day of the coming of the Lord wherein the corruptible things of the heavens being on fire, shall be dissolved, and the mountains shall melt with fervent heat?

13 Nevertheless we, according to his promise, look for new heavens and a new earth, wherein dwelleth righteousness. [*In other words, we are looking forward to the Millennium and the celestial kingdom.*]

**JST 2 Peter 3:13**
13 Nevertheless, if we shall endure, we shall be kept [*preserved*] according to his promise. And we look for a new heavens, and a new earth wherein dwelleth righteousness.

14 Wherefore, beloved, seeing that ye look for such things, be diligent that ye may be found of [*by*] him [*Christ*] in peace, without spot, and blameless [*having been cleansed by His Atonement*].

15 And account [*keep in mind*] that the longsuffering of our Lord is salvation; even as our beloved brother Paul also according to the wisdom given unto him hath written unto you; [*In other words, keep in mind what Paul wrote you about how the Lord is so patient and gives us plenty of time to work out our salvation.*]

**JST 2 Peter 3:15**
15 And account, even as our beloved brother Paul also, according to the wisdom given unto him, hath written unto you, the long-suffering and waiting of our Lord, for salvation.

16 As also in all his epistles [*Paul's letters*], speaking in them of these things; in which are some things hard to be understood [*some of Paul's writings are hard to understand*], which they that are unlearned and unstable wrest [*and so some who do not know the gospel very well or who are not committed to the Church misinterpret and twist what Paul wrote*], as they do also the other scriptures [*just like they do other scriptures*], unto their own destruction [*which will lead to their destruction*].

**JST 2 Peter 3:16**
16 As also in all his epistles, speaking in them of these things, in which are some things hard to be understood, which they who are unlearned and unstable wrest, as they do also the other scriptures, unto their own destruction.

17 Ye therefore, beloved, seeing ye know these things before [*ahead of time because of prophecies*], beware lest ye also, being led away with the error of

the wicked [*mistakes in interpreting the scriptures*], fall from your own stedfastness [*from your faithfulness in the Church*].

**JST 2 Peter 3:17**

17 Ye therefore, beloved, seeing ye know before the things which are coming, beware lest ye also being led away with the error of the wicked, fall from your own steadfastness.

18 But grow in grace, and in the knowledge of our Lord and Saviour Jesus Christ. To him be glory both now and for ever. Amen.

**JST 2 Peter 3:18**

18 But grow in grace and the knowledge of our Lord and Savior Jesus Christ. To him be glory both now and for ever. Amen.

# THE FIRST EPISTLE GENERAL OF JOHN

Bible scholars do not know when this letter was written, but many believe it was written around AD 96. This epistle was written by the Apostle John, who, with Peter and James, served as the First Presidency of the Church after the Savior was taken up into heaven. John wrote five of the books which are contained in our New Testament, namely, The Gospel of John, First John, Second John, Third John, and The Book of Revelation. This great Apostle was translated and is still on earth, helping with the work of the Lord (see D&C 7). In 1831, Joseph Smith told the early members of the Church that John was, at that time, working with the lost ten tribes, getting them ready for their return (see *History of the Church*, Vol. 1, p. 176.) John was with Peter and James when they gave Joseph Smith and Oliver Cowdery the Melchizedek Priesthood (see D&C 27:12.)

## FIRST JOHN 1

It seems that by the time this letter was written, many Christians were beginning to doubt that Jesus had actually been born into a mortal body and that He had actually lived as a mortal being on earth. They were teaching that such could not be the case because God is holy and certainly would not lower Himself to be so closely associated with unclean mankind. Thus, they were teaching that the birth, baptism, mortal mission, suffering in the Garden of Gethsemane, crucifixion, resurrection, and ascension into heaven did not literally happen, because such things could not actually happen to God. John, who was an eyewitness to the Savior's mortal mission, Atonement, resurrection, and ascension bears strong witness that these things did literally happen.

1 THAT which was from the beginning, which we have heard, which we have seen with our eyes, which we have looked upon, and our hands have handled, of the Word of life;

> **JST 1 John 1:1**
> 1 Brethren, this is the testimony which we give of that which was from the beginning [*in other words, Jesus Christ*], which we have heard [*to whom we have personally listened*], which we have seen with our eyes, which we have looked upon, and our hands have handled [*whom we have personally touched*], of the Word of life;

2 (For the life was manifested [*Christ was here on earth*], and we have seen it [*Him*], and bear witness [*and testify of Him*], and shew unto you [*point out to you*] that eternal life, which was with the Father, and was manifested [*clearly shown*] unto us;)

3 That [*the things*] which we have seen and heard declare we unto you, that [*so that*] ye also may have fellowship with us [*so that you may join with us*]: and truly our fellowship is with the Father [*and indeed we have joined with the Father*], and with his Son Jesus Christ.

4 And these things write we unto you, that your joy may be full.

5 This then is the message which we have heard of him [*which we have heard from the Father through Christ*], and declare unto you, that God is light, and

in him is no darkness at all [*as Jesus said, "I am the light of the world; he that followeth me shall not walk in darkness, but shall have the light of life"; John 8:12*].

6 If we say that we have fellowship with him [*if we claim that we worship the Father*], and walk in darkness, we lie, and do not the truth:

7 But if we walk in the light, as he is in the light, we have fellowship one with another [*we are truly united as brothers and sisters in the gospel*], and the blood of Jesus Christ his Son cleanseth us from all sin.

8 If we say that we have no sin [*if we say that we are perfect*], we deceive ourselves, and the truth is not in us.

9 If we confess our sins [*and repent*], he is faithful and just [*fair*] to forgive us our sins, and to cleanse us from all unrighteousness.

10 If we say that we have not sinned, we make him a liar [*because He said we all need to repent of sins; see D&C 49:8*], and his word is not in us.

# FIRST JOHN 2

1 MY little children, these things write I unto you, that ye sin not [*I am writing this to you to help you avoid sinning*]. And if any man sin, we have an advocate with the Father, Jesus Christ the righteous [*compare with D&C 45:3–5*]:

**JST 1 John 2:1**

1 My little children, these things write I unto you, that ye sin not. But if any man sin and repent, we have an advocate with the Father, Jesus Christ the righteous;

2 And he is the propitiation [*the Atonement*] for our sins: and not for ours only, but also for the sins of the whole world.

3 And hereby we do know that we know him, if we keep his commandments [*here is how you demonstrate that you know Him, you keep His commandments*].

4 He that saith, I know him, and keepeth not his commandments, is a liar, and the truth is not in him.

5 But whoso keepeth his word [*keeps His commandments*], in him verily is the love of God perfected [*the love of God as shown in the gospel will work with him until he reaches exaltation*]: hereby know we that we are in him [*and this is how we ourselves know that we are in harmony with God*].

6 He that saith he abideth in him [*he who claims to follow Christ*] ought himself also so to walk, even as he walked [*ought to follow in Christ's footsteps*].

7 Brethren, I write no new commandment unto you, but an old commandment which ye had from the beginning. The old commandment is the word which ye have heard from the beginning.

**JST 1 John 2:7**

7 Brethren, I write a new commandment unto you, but it is the same commandment which ye had from the beginning [*which you have had all along*]. The old commandment is the word which ye have heard from the beginning.

8 Again, [*I repeat*] a new commandment I write unto you, which thing is true in him and in you: because the darkness is past, and the true light now shineth.

**JST 1 John 2:8**

8 Again, a new commandment I write unto you, which thing was of old ordained of God [*which is what God gave us long ago*]; and is true in him, and in you; because the darkness is past in you [*you have repented and changed and the spiritual darkness has left you*], and the true light now shineth.

9 He that saith he is in the light [*someone who claims to be a faithful member of the Church*], and hateth his brother,

is in darkness even until now [*is still in spiritual darkness*].

10 He that loveth his brother abideth in the light [*is living as Christ would have him live*], and there is none occasion of stumbling in him [*and there is nothing holding him back*].

11 But he that hateth his brother is in darkness [*is living in spiritual darkness*], and walketh in darkness, and knoweth not whither he goeth [*and does not realize where he is heading*], because that darkness hath blinded his eyes [*because he has become spiritually blind and insensitive*].

12 I write unto you, little children, because your sins are forgiven you for his name's sake [*because little children are not accountable for sins because of Christ's Atonement; see Mosiah 3:16; D&C 29:46–47*].

13 I write unto you, fathers, because ye have known him [*Christ*] that is from the beginning. I write unto you, young men, because ye have overcome the wicked one [*because you have overcome the temptations of the devil*]. I write unto you, little children, because ye have known the Father.

14 I have written unto you, fathers, because ye have known him [*Christ*] that is from the beginning. I have written unto you, young men, because ye are strong, and the word of God abideth in you [*and you are living the gospel*], and ye have overcome the wicked one.

15 Love not the world, neither the things that are in the world [*don't become involved in worldly wickedness*]. If any man love the world [*participates in the wickedness of worldly people*], the love of the Father is not in him [*the Father cannot bless him as he would like to; see "Divine Love" by Elder Russell M. Nelson of the Quorum of the Twelve Apostles,* Ensign, *February 2003, pp. 20–25*].

**JST 1 John 2:15**

15 Love not the world, neither the things that are of the world. If any man love the world, the love of the Father is not in him.

16 For all that is in the world, the lust of the flesh, and the lust of the eyes, and the pride of life, is not of the Father, but is of the world. [*In other words, all of the wickedness in the world does not come from the Father, rather comes from other sources.*]

**JST 1 John 2:16**

16 For all in the world that is of the lusts of the flesh, and the lust of the eyes, and the pride of life, is not of the Father, but is of the world.

17 And the world passeth away [*the wicked and the wickedness on the world will be done away with at the Second Coming and again after the little season at the end of the Millennium; see D&C 5:19 and 88:111–114*], and the lust thereof: but he that doeth the will of God abideth for ever [*will attain the celestial kingdom and will live on earth forever when it becomes their celestial kingdom; see D&C 130:9–11*].

18 Little children, it is the last time [*we know that the church which Christ established is entering its last days, because the great apostasy is underway; compare with 2 Thessalonians 2:1–3*]: and as ye have heard that antichrist [*false prophets; see 2 Peter 2:18, footnote a*] shall come, even now are there many antichrists [*apostates and false prophets*]; whereby [*this is how*] we know that it is the last time.

19 They went out from us [*many of them were members of the Church*], but they were not of us [*but they were not faithful*]; for if they had been of us [*if they had been faithful*], they would no doubt have continued with us: but they went out, that they might be made manifest that they were not all of us [*they left us and it has become obvious that they were apostates*].

20 But ye have an unction [*an anointing; Strong's #5545; in other words, you have the Gift of the Holy Ghost; see McConkie, Doctrinal New Testament Commentary, Vol. 3, p. 383*] from the Holy One [*given to you by Christ*], and ye know all things [*and you have a testimony of what I am telling you*].

21 I have not written unto you because ye know not the truth, but because ye know it, and that no lie is of the truth [*no lie can be part of truth*].

22 Who is a liar but he that denieth that Jesus is the Christ? He is antichrist, that denieth the Father and the Son.

23 Whosoever denieth the Son, the same hath not the Father [*will not be accepted by the Father*]: [*but*] he that acknowledgeth the Son hath the Father also.

24 Let that therefore abide in you, which ye have heard from the beginning [*stand firm and steadfast in what you heard originally from us*]. If that which ye have heard from the beginning shall remain in you, ye also shall continue in the Son, and in the Father [*you will continue faithful to the Savior and the Father*].

> **JST 1 John 2:24**
> 24 Let that therefore abide in you, which ye have heard from the beginning. If that which ye have heard from the beginning shall remain in you, ye shall continue in the Son, and also in the Father.

25 And this is the promise that he hath promised us, even eternal life [*exaltation*].

26 These things have I written unto you concerning them [*false prophets and teachers*] that seduce [*deceive*] you.

27 But the anointing [*see verse 20, above*] which ye have received of him [*from Christ*] abideth in you [*you have the Gift of the Holy Ghost*], and ye need not that any man teach you [*and you have no reason to be led astray by false teachings*]: but as the same anointing teacheth you of all things [*but since the Holy Ghost teaches you all things; John 14:26*], and is truth, and is no lie, and even as it hath taught you, ye shall abide in him [*do as the Holy Ghost teaches you and remain true to Christ*].

28 And now, little children, abide in him [*remain true to Christ*]; that, when he shall appear, we may have confidence, and not be ashamed before him [*in His presence*] at his coming.

29 If ye know that he is righteous, ye know that every one that doeth righteousness is born of him [*is "born again" and becomes a "son" or "daughter" of Christ; compare with Mosiah 5:7*].

# FIRST JOHN 3

1 BEHOLD [*consider*], what manner of [*kind of*] love the Father hath bestowed upon us, that we should be called the sons of God: [*In other words, consider the incredible love which the Father has given us, to allow us to someday become like He is, in other words, to be exalted. The terms "sons of God" and "daughters of God" are scriptural terms which mean exaltation; see Mosiah 5:7 and D&C 76:24.*] therefore the world knoweth us not [*worldly people don't understand us*], because it knew him not [*because they don't understand the Father*].

> Verse 2, next, teaches very clearly that we can become like Christ, just as Paul taught in Romans 8:17.

2 Beloved, now are we the sons of God [*followers of Christ, who will be exalted if we remain faithful*], and it doth not yet appear what we shall be [*and we don't understand everything about exaltation*]: but we know that, when he [*Christ*] shall appear, we shall be like him; for we shall see him as he is.

3 And every man that hath this hope in

him [*everyone who hopes for exaltation*] purifieth himself, even as he [*Christ*] is pure.

4 Whosoever committeth sin transgresseth also the law: for sin is [*defined as*] the transgression of the law.

5 And ye know that he [*Christ*] was manifested [*sent*] to take away our sins; and in him is no sin [*and that He was perfect*].

6 Whosoever abideth in him [*whoever is faithful to Christ*] sinneth not: whosoever sinneth hath not seen him, neither known him [*whoever commits sin and does not repent, does not understand Christ's mission*].

**JST 1 John 3:6**

6 Whosoever abideth in him sinneth not; whosoever continueth in sin hath not seen him, neither known him.

7 Little children, let no man deceive [*fool*] you: he that doeth righteousness is righteous, even as he is righteous [*he who follows Christ becomes righteous, just like Christ is righteous*].

8 He that committeth sin is of the devil; for the devil sinneth from the beginning. For this purpose the Son of God was manifested [*came to earth*], that he might destroy the works of the devil.

**JST 1 John 3:8**

8 He that continueth in sin is of the devil; for the devil sinneth from the beginning. For this purpose the Son of God was manifested, that he might destroy the works of the devil.

9 Whosoever is born of God doth not commit sin; for his seed remaineth in him: and he cannot sin, because he is born of God.

**JST 1 John 3:9**

9 Whosoever is born of God doth not continue in sin; for the Spirit of God remaineth in him; and he cannot continue in sin, because he is born of God, having received that holy Spirit of promise.

10 In this the children of God are manifest, and the children of the devil [*this is how you can tell the true followers of God from the followers of the devil*]: whosoever doeth not righteousness is not of God, neither he that loveth not his brother.

11 For this is the message that ye heard from the beginning [*this is what the gospel is all about*], that we should love one another.

12 Not as Cain, who was of that wicked one [*who was inspired by Satan; see Moses 5:18–33*], and slew his brother [*Abel*]. And wherefore slew he him [*and why did he kill him*]? Because his own works were evil, and his brother's righteous.

13 Marvel not [*don't be surprised*], my brethren, if the world hate you [*if worldly, wicked people hate you*].

14 We know that we have passed from death [*from being spiritually dead*] unto life [*to being spiritually alive*], because we love the brethren [*because we love one another*]. He that loveth not his brother abideth in death [*remains spiritually dead*].

15 Whosoever hateth his brother is a murderer [*in his heart*]: and ye know that no murderer hath eternal life abiding in him.

16 Hereby perceive we the love of God, [*In other words, this is how we know that Christ loved us*] because he laid down his life for us: and we ought to lay down our lives for the brethren [*for each other*].

**JST 1 John 3:16**

16 Hereby perceive we the love of Christ, because he laid down his life for us; and we ought to lay down our lives for the brethren.

17 But whoso hath this world's good [*but a person who has plenty*], and seeth his brother have need [*and sees that his brother is in need*], and shutteth up his

bowels of compassion from him [*and refuses to feel compassion toward him*], how dwelleth the love of God in him [*how could he have Christ-like love in his heart*]?

18 My little children, let us not love in word, neither in tongue [*let us not merely claim that we have Christ-like love*]; but in deed and in truth [*but let us show it through our good works*].

**JST 1 John 3:18**

18 My little children, let us not love in word, neither in tongue only; but in deed and in truth.

19 And hereby [*and if we do this*] we know that we are of the truth [*that we are genuine in the gospel*], and shall assure our hearts before him [*and we will have confidence someday in the presence of the Lord*].

20 For if our heart condemn us [*if the content of our heart condemns us*], God is greater than our heart, and knoweth all things [*God knows what is in our heart*].

21 Beloved, if our heart condemn us not [*if our heart is clean and pure*], then have we confidence toward God [*then we can approach God in confidence*].

22 And whatsoever we ask, we receive of him, because we keep his commandments, and do those things that are pleasing in his sight. [*In other words, if we are keeping His commandments, we can have faith when we pray and thus receive the blessings we need, provided it is in harmony with His will. See D&C 46:30 and 50:30 where it tells us that if we are pure before God, the Holy Ghost will tell us what we can ask for in prayer and thus we will receive what we ask for.*]

23 And this is his [*the Father's*] commandment, That we should believe on the name of his Son Jesus Christ, and love one another, as he gave us commandment [*like He commanded us to*].

24 And he that keepeth his commandments dwelleth in him, and he in him [*is close to Him and He is close to them*]. And hereby we know that he abideth in us, by the Spirit which he hath given us [*the way we can tell if God is close to us is that it will be manifest to us by the Holy Ghost*].

# FIRST JOHN 4

Next, the Apostle John gives counsel to the Saints about detecting false spirits and false doctrine. You may wish to read D&C 129 also, with respect to detecting false spirits.

1 BELOVED, believe not every spirit [*don't believe everything you hear*], but try the spirits whether they are of God [*test the doctrines and spirits to see if what you are hearing is in harmony with the gospel*]: because many false prophets are gone out into the world [*because there are many false prophets around*].

2 Hereby know ye [*here is how you can recognize*] the Spirit of God: Every spirit that confesseth [*testifies*] that Jesus Christ is come in the flesh [*that Jesus Christ literally was born into mortality*] is of God:

As mentioned in the general introduction to First John, one of the "false spirits" or false doctrines at the time John wrote this letter was the teaching that Christ, as a God, could not possibly have literally been born into a mortal body, because God would not lower Himself to associate so closely with corrupt mankind. Thus, John, in verse 2, above, states very clearly that one way to tell the difference between false teachers and those who teach truth is to listen to see if they bear testimony that Jesus literally came to earth in a mortal body.

3 And every spirit that confesseth not [*all who do not testify*] that Jesus Christ

is come in the flesh is not of God: and this is that spirit of antichrist [*deceivers, false prophets, false teachers; compare with 2 John 1:7*], whereof ye have heard that it should come; and even now already is it in the world [*you have heard that the time would come when there are many antichrists (deceivers) and that time has come*].

**JST 1 John 4:3**

And every spirit that confesseth not that Jesus Christ is come in the flesh is not of God; and this is that spirit of antichrist, whereof ye have heard that it should come; and even now it is already in the world.

4 Ye are of God, little children, and have overcome them [*teachers of false doctrines*]: because greater is he [*God*] that is in you, than he [*the false teacher*] that is in the world.

5 They [*antichrists, false teachers*] are of the world [*are worldly*]: therefore speak they of the world, and the world [*worldly and wicked people*] heareth them [*listen to them*].

6 We are of God [*we are in tune with God*]: he that knoweth God heareth us [*people who are spiritually in tune listen to us*]; he that is not of God heareth not us [*will not listen to our message*]. Hereby know we [*this is how we tell the difference between*] the spirit of truth, and the spirit of error.

7 Beloved, let us love one another: for love is of God; and every one that loveth is born of God [*has the Spirit with them and is "born again"*], and knoweth God.

8 He that loveth not [*who doesn't love his fellow men*] knoweth not God; for God is love.

9 In this was manifested [*demonstrated, made clear*] the love of God toward us, because that God sent his only begotten Son into the world, that we might live [*that we might be born "spiritually" and have eternal life*] through him [*Christ*].

10 Herein is love [*the love the Father has for us is shown by this*], not that we loved God, but that he loved us, and sent his Son to be the propitiation [*sacrifice; Atonement*] for our sins.

11 Beloved, if God [*the Father*] so loved us, we ought also to love one another.

12 No man hath seen God at any time. If we love one another, God dwelleth in us, and his love is perfected in us.

**JST 1 John 4:12**

12 No man hath seen God at any time, except them who believe. If we love one another, God dwelleth in us, and his love is perfected in us.

13 Hereby know we that we dwell in him, and he in us, because he hath given us of his Spirit [*the Holy Ghost tells us when we are in harmony with God*].

14 And we have seen and do testify that the Father sent the Son to be the Saviour of the world.

15 Whosoever shall confess [*accept*] that Jesus is the Son of God, God dwelleth in him, and he in God.

16 And we have known [*felt*] and believed the love that God hath to us. God is love; and he that dwelleth in love dwelleth in God, and God in him.

17 Herein is our love made perfect [*this is how our love becomes Christ-like love*], that we may have boldness [*confidence in the presence of God*] in the day of judgment: because as he is, so are we in this world [*because we have become clean through the Atonement*].

18 There is no fear [*of God*] in love; but perfect love casteth out fear: because fear hath torment [*fear of God comes from a guilty conscience*]. He that feareth is not made perfect in love.

19 We love him, because he first loved us.

20 If a man say, I love God, and hateth his brother, he is a liar: for he that loveth not his brother whom he hath seen, how

can he love God whom he hath not seen?

21 And this commandment [*see Matthew 22:37–39*] have we from him, That he who loveth God love his brother also.

# FIRST JOHN 5

As John concludes this letter, he, in effect, defines the term "born again."

1 WHOSOEVER [*whoever*] believeth that Jesus is the Christ is born of God [*experiences spiritual rebirth; compare with Alma 5:14*]: and every one that loveth him [*Heavenly Father*] that begat [*who is the Father of Jesus*] loveth him [*Jesus*] also that is begotten of him [*who is Heavenly Father's Son*].

2 By this we know that we love the children of God [*our fellow beings*], when we love God, and keep his commandments [*compare with John 14:15 where the Savior said, "If ye love me, keep my commandments"*].

3 For this is the love of God, that we keep his commandments: and his commandments are not grievous [*are not difficult to keep, are not a burden*].

4 For whatsoever is born of God overcometh the world [*anyone who experiences spiritual rebirth successfully overcomes the evils and temptations of the world*]: and this is the victory that overcometh the world, even our faith [*and it is our faith in Christ which enables us to successfully overcome the world*].

5 Who is he that overcometh the world, but [*can anyone successfully overcome the temptations of the world except*] he that believeth that Jesus is the Son of God?

Next, the Apostle John uses the terms "water," "blood," and "Spirit" both literally and symbolically. You may wish to read Moses 6:59–60 in which this symbolism is also used. Basically, each of us, including the Savior, literally came into this world by the process of physical birth, which involved "water" (in the womb,) "blood" (involved in the birth process,) and "spirit" (our spirit bodies gave life to our physical, mortal bodies.) Symbolically, in order to be "born again," this time spiritually, we must be baptized by "water." We must receive the "Spirit," the Gift of the Holy Ghost." And we are saved from our sins, through repentance, by the "blood" of Christ. Note also the literal application to the Savior's crucifixion itself, wherein His spirit left His body when He was finished on the cross (John 19:30) and blood and water came forth from the wound in His side when the soldier pierced His side (John 19:33–34.)

6 This [*Christ*] is he that came by water and blood [*who was born into a mortal body by the birth process*], even Jesus Christ; not by water only, but by water and blood. And it is the Spirit [*the Holy Ghost*] that beareth witness, because the Spirit is truth [*the Holy Ghost guides us to the truth in all things; see John 16:13*].

7 For there are three that bear record in heaven, the Father, the Word [*Christ, the Son*], and the Holy Ghost: and these three are one [*work in complete unity and harmony with each other*].

8 And there are three that bear witness in earth [*there are three things here on earth which show us the way to salvation and enable us to achieve it, namely*], the Spirit [*the Holy Ghost*], and the water [*baptism*], and the blood [*the blood of Christ*]: and these three agree in one [*bring us into unity and harmony with God*].

9 If we receive the witness [*accept the testimony*] of men [*who bring us the gospel message*], the witness of God is greater [*we will receive a greater testimony from God*]: for this [*the testimony given by the Holy Ghost; see verse 6*] is the witness of God [*from the Father*] which he hath testified of his Son.

10 He that believeth on the Son of God hath the witness in himself [*receives the testimony of the Holy Ghost into his*

*soul; see Joseph Smith's correction of 1 Corinthians 12:3 in which he says, "no man can know that Jesus is the Lord, but by the Holy Ghost" (*Teachings of the Prophet Joseph Smith, *p. 223)*]: he that believeth not God hath made him a liar [*anyone who rejects the testimony of Christ given them by the Holy Ghost, is, in effect, calling God a liar*]; because he believeth not the record [*the testimony given by the Holy Ghost*] that God [*the Father*] gave of his Son.

11 And this is the record [*what the Holy Ghost witnesses to us*], that God hath given to us eternal life [*that the Father has made exaltation available to us*], and this life is in his Son [*and this exaltation comes to us through Jesus Christ*].

12 He that hath the Son hath life [*he who is faithful to Christ receives exaltation*]; and he that hath not the Son of God hath not life [*he who is not faithful to Christ does not receive exaltation*].

13 These things have I written unto you that believe on the name of the Son of God; that ye may know that ye have eternal life [*that you can achieve exaltation*], and that ye may believe on the name of the Son of God.

**JST 1 John 5:13**

13 These things have I written unto you that believe on the name of the Son of God; that ye may know that ye have eternal life, and that ye may continue to believe on the name of the Son of God.

14 And this is the confidence that we have in him [*the assurance we receive from the Father*], that, if we ask any thing according to his will [*D&C 46:30; 50:30*], he heareth us [*he will give it to us*]:

15 And if we know that he hear us, whatsoever we ask [*if it is "according to His will" (verse 14, above)*], we know that we have the petitions [*things we were asking*] that we desired of him.

Next John indicates that there is such thing as sin which cannot be forgiven. He refers to this as "sin unto death." You may wish to read D&C 76:31–35 where it reviews the sins which would lead one to become a son of perdition. You may also wish to read D&C 42:18, 76:103 and Revelation 22:15 wherein it indicates that first degree murder is unforgivable in the sense that such murderers will go to the telestial kingdom.

16 If any man see his brother sin a sin which is not unto death, he shall ask, and he shall give him life for them that sin not unto death [*forgiveness, through repentance, is available except for unforgivable sins*]. There is a sin unto death: I do not say that he shall pray for it [*pray for forgiveness from it*].

17 All unrighteousness is sin: and there is a sin not unto death [*there are sins which can be forgiven*].

18 We know that whosoever is born of God sinneth not; but he that is begotten of God keepeth himself, and that wicked one toucheth him not.

**JST 1 John 5:18**

We know that whosoever is born of God [*anyone who is "born again"*] continueth not in sin; but he that is begotten of God [*who is "born again"*] and keepeth himself [*and is always on guard against committing sin; Strong's #5083*], that wicked one overcometh him not [*Satan will not overcome him*].

19 And we know that we are of God [*are following God*], and the whole world lieth in wickedness.

20 And we know that the Son of God is come [*came to earth*], and hath given us an understanding, that we may know him [*the Father*] that is true, and we are in him [*and we are following Christ*] that is true, even in his Son Jesus Christ. This is the true God, and eternal life [*and this is how we gain exaltation*].

21 Little children, keep yourselves from idols [*avoid idol worship*]. Amen.

# THE SECOND EPISTLE OF JOHN

This brief letter by John seems to be an intimate note to family members, perhaps even to his wife and children. We don't know for sure. It was probably written about the same time as First John, but, again, Bible scholars don't know for sure.

There are no JST changes for this book.

## SECOND JOHN 1

1 THE elder [*John*] unto the elect lady and her children, whom I love in the truth; and not I only, but also all they [*the faithful members of the Church*] that have known the truth;

2 For the truth's sake, which dwelleth in us, and shall be with us for ever.

3 Grace be with you, mercy, and peace, from God the Father, and from the Lord Jesus Christ, the Son of the Father, in truth and love.

4 I rejoiced greatly that I found of thy children walking in truth [*I am grateful that your children are living the gospel faithfully*], as we have received a commandment from the Father [*according to the commandments we have received from Heavenly Father*].

5 And now I beseech thee [*I urge you*], lady, not as though I wrote a new commandment unto thee [*not as if I were telling you anything you don't already know*], but that which we had from the beginning, that we love one another.

6 And this is love [*this is what truly helps us love one another, namely*], that we walk after his commandments [*keeping His commandments*]. This is the commandment, That, as ye have heard from the beginning, ye should walk in it [*keep it*].

7 For many deceivers are entered into the world, who confess not that Jesus Christ is come in the flesh [*there are many false prophets and false teachers in the world now who do not accept the fact that Jesus Christ came to us in a mortal body*]. This is a deceiver and an antichrist [*such people are deceivers and apostates; see 1 John 2:18, footnotes a and b*].

8 Look to yourselves [*watch out*], that we lose not those things which we have wrought [*already accomplished in the gospel*], but that we receive a full reward [*exaltation*].

9 Whosoever [*anyone who*] transgresseth, and abideth not [*does not remain faithful*] in the doctrine of Christ, hath not God [*does not have God in their lives*]. He that abideth in the doctrine of Christ, he hath both the Father and the Son [*he will obtain the full blessings promised to the faithful by the Father and the Son*].

10 If there come any unto you, and bring not this doctrine [*if any people come to you and their teachings are not in harmony with what Christ taught*], receive him not into your house, neither bid him God speed [*don't have anything to do with them*]:

11 For he that biddeth him God speed is partaker of his evil deeds [*if you lead him to believe that you agree with what he is teaching, you are a partner with him in his evil work*].

12 Having many things to write unto you, I would not write with paper and ink: but I trust to come unto you, and speak face

to face [*I have many more things to say which I want to tell you in person, rather than writing them in this letter*], that [*so that*] our joy may be full.

13 The children of thy elect sister greet thee. Amen.

# THE THIRD EPISTLE OF JOHN

In this brief letter, John commends a member of the Church named Gaius for the good work he has accomplished.

There are no JST changes for this book.

## THIRD JOHN 1

1 THE elder [*John*] unto the wellbeloved Gaius, whom I love in the truth.

2 Beloved, I wish above all things that thou mayest prosper and be in health, even as thy soul prospereth [*I wish you prosperity and health to match your spiritual prosperity*].

3 For I rejoiced greatly, when the brethren came and testified of the truth that is in thee, even as thou walkest in the truth [*I rejoiced when I received word from the brethren that you are faithfully living the gospel*].

4 I have no greater joy than to hear that my children walk in truth.

5 Beloved, thou doest faithfully whatsoever thou doest to the brethren, and to strangers [*you perform faithful service to our traveling elders as well as nonmembers*];

6 Which have borne witness of [*who have told me about*] thy charity before the church: whom if thou bring forward on their journey after a godly sort, thou shalt do well [*and it would be wonderful if you would continue helping them on their way in their missionary travels and so forth*]:

7 Because that for his name's sake they went forth, taking nothing of the Gentiles [*because they are in the service of God and they do not receive assistance from nonmembers*].

8 We therefore ought to receive such [*we ought to be hospitable to them*], that we might be fellowhelpers to the truth [*so that we, ourselves, are involved in helping spread the gospel*].

9 I wrote unto the church [*I wrote to the ward there*]: but Diotrephes, who loveth to have the preeminence among them, receiveth us not [*but Diotrephes, who thinks himself to be a very important person, rejected us*].

It would appear that Diotrephes was a Gentile convert to the Church who held a powerful political position in the community and who had been called to be a leader in one of the wards but who now had gone into apostasy. See *Strong's* #1361.

10 Wherefore, if I come, I will remember his deeds which he doeth, prating against us [*making false accusations against us: Strong's #5396*] with malicious [*vicious*] words: and not content therewith [*it is not enough in his mind to speak evil against us, but in addition*], neither doth he himself receive the brethren [*he will not allow the Lord's servants to come to him*], and forbiddeth them that would [*but he also forbids the members in his area to welcome them*], and casteth them out of the church [*and has them cast out of the church*].

11 Beloved, follow not [*do not get involved with*] that which is evil, but that which is good. He that doeth good is of God [*is in harmony with God*]: but he that doeth evil hath not seen God [*compare with JST 1 John 4:12; see 1 John 4:12, footnote a*].

12 Demetrius hath good report [*has a good reputation*] of all men, and of the

truth itself: yea, and we also bear record; and ye know that our record is true.

13 I had many things to write, but I will not with ink and pen write unto thee:

14 But I trust I shall shortly see thee, and we shall speak face to face. Peace be to thee. Our friends salute [*greet*] thee. Greet the friends by name.

# THE GENERAL EPISTLE OF JUDE

Jude identifies himself as the "brother of James" (see verse 1, below.) Thus, it appears quite possible to some Bible scholars that Jude was the "Juda," who was one of Jesus' half-brothers, spoken of in Mark 6:3. In his epistle (letter), Jude warns members of the Church to beware of people who claim to be Christians but who were giving in to sexual immorality which was widely accepted in the culture in which they lived. Jude also uses the term "first estate," which we use often in our doctrinal discussions concerning our premortal life and the war in heaven. Jude also mentions something not mentioned elsewhere in scripture, namely an event in which Michael (Adam) and Satan contend "over the body of Moses." See Bible Dictionary, p. 719, under "Jude, Epistle of."

## JUDE 1

1 JUDE, the servant of Jesus Christ, and brother of James, to them that are sanctified [*in process of being made worthy to enter celestial glory*] by God the Father, and preserved in [*in process of being saved by*] Jesus Christ, and called [*called by the Father to come unto him through Jesus Christ*]:

**JST Jude 1:1**

1 Jude, the servant of God, called of Jesus Christ, and brother of James; to them who are sanctified of the Father; and preserved in Jesus Christ;

2 Mercy unto you, and peace, and love, be multiplied.

3 Beloved, when I gave all diligence to write unto you of the common salvation, it was needful for me to write unto you, and exhort [*warn*] you that ye should earnestly contend [*stand up*] for the faith [*gospel*] which was once [*originally*] delivered unto the saints. [*In other words, there is much apostasy that is creeping into the Church and we must stick to the original teachings of the Savior and Apostles.*]

4 For there are certain men crept in unawares [*who have infiltrated the Church*], who were before of old ordained to this condemnation [*who are those spoken of in the scriptures who will be condemned for what they are doing*], ungodly [*wicked*] men, turning the grace of our God into lasciviousness [*turning from the gospel to sexual immorality*], and denying the only Lord God, and our Lord Jesus Christ [*and thus rejecting the only One who can save them*].

5 I will therefore put you in remembrance [*remind you*], though ye once knew this [*though you have already been taught this*], how that the Lord, having saved the people out of the land of Egypt, afterward destroyed them that believed not [*wicked Pharaoh and his armies were drowned in the Red Sea*].

6 And the angels [*the wicked spirits, in other words, the one third (Revelation 12:4)*] which kept not their first estate [*who did not earn the right to be born on earth, into this "second estate" (Abraham 3:26)*], but left their own habitation [*rejected the opportunity to have physical bodies of their own*], he [*God*] hath reserved in everlasting chains [*they will be sons of perdition forever*] under darkness [*in total spiritual darkness*]

unto the judgment of the great day [*as their final judgment*].

The phrase "left their own habitation" in verse 6, above, in Greek, means that they do not have a physical body as a dwelling place for the spirit. Joseph Smith used the word "habitation" in teaching that Satan will not have a physical body. He said, "The punishment of the devil was that he should not have a habitation like men." In referring to the privilege spirits have of obtaining physical bodies, Joseph Smith said that the spirits "who kept not their first estate" do not receive physical bodies. *Teachings of the Prophet Joseph Smith*, pp. 305–306.

7 Even as [*just like*] Sodom and Gomorrha, and the cities about them in like manner, giving themselves over to fornication [*sexual immorality*], and going after strange flesh [*homosexuality; see Jude 1:7, footnote c, in our Bible*], are set forth for [*are given as*] an example, suffering the vengeance of eternal fire.

8 Likewise also these filthy dreamers [*people who do not face reality*] defile the flesh [*pollute their bodies*], despise dominion [*despise being ruled by God, Priesthood leaders, etc.*], and speak evil of dignities [*and mock God, angels, Church leaders, and so forth*].

9 Yet Michael [*Adam*] the archangel, when contending with the devil he disputed about the body of Moses [*see note in the introduction to this chapter, above*], durst not bring against him a railing [*slanderous; Strong's #0988*] accusation, but said, The Lord rebuke thee.

Joseph Smith spoke of Moses not "railing" against the devil when he said, "The spirits of good men cannot interfere with the wicked beyond their prescribed bounds, for Michael, the Archangel, dared not bring a railing accusation against the devil, but said, 'The Lord rebuke thee, Satan.'" See *History of the Church*, vol. 4, pp. 575–76.

10 But these [*such people, filthy dreamers in verse 8, above*] speak evil of those things [*gospel truths and commandments*] which they know not [*which they do not understand or which they intentionally reject*]: but what they know naturally [*as carnal, sensual, and devilish, "natural men;" see Mosiah 3:19*] as brute beasts [*like animals*], in those things they corrupt [*destroy*] themselves.

11 Woe unto them! for they have gone in the way of Cain [*who opposed God and killed Abel; see Moses 5:16–33*], and ran greedily after the error of Balaam [*Numbers 22*] for reward, and perished in the gainsaying [*rebelling against God*] of Core [*Korah, who rebelled against Moses as recorded in Numbers 16*].

12 These are spots [*blemishes*] in your feasts of charity, when they feast with you, feeding themselves without fear [*with no qualms; boldly, as if they belonged among the righteous; Strong's #0870*]: clouds they are without water [*they are like clouds that don't carry rain to benefit others*] carried about of winds [*blown every which way by the winds of passion and greed*]; trees whose fruit withereth, without fruit [*they are barren trees*], twice dead [*they are already dead spiritually and will die physically and be condemned*], plucked up by the roots;

13 Raging waves of the sea [*dangerous like wild crashing waves*], foaming out their own shame [*foaming at the mouth with their shameful wickedness*]; wandering stars, to [*for*] whom is reserved the blackness of darkness [*of hell*] for ever.

Jude next quotes a prophecy given by Enoch, which does not appear elsewhere in scripture except perhaps a brief reference in Moses 7:65.

14 And Enoch also, the seventh [*generation*] from Adam, prophesied of these [*about these kinds of wicked people*], saying, Behold, the Lord cometh with

ten thousands of his saints [*at the Second Coming*],

15 To execute judgment upon all, and to convince all that are ungodly [*wicked*] among them of all their ungodly deeds which they have ungodly [*wickedly*] committed, and of all their hard [*wicked*] speeches which ungodly sinners have spoken against him.

16 These are murmurers, complainers, walking after their own lusts [*living in wickedness*]; and their mouth speaketh great swelling words [*they give long, empty explanations in which they attempt to justify their wickedness*], having men's persons in admiration [*they are admired by wicked people*] because of advantage [*because they stand to gain from the admiration of others*].

17 But, beloved, remember ye the words which were spoken before [*in the past*] of [*by*] the apostles of our Lord Jesus Christ;

18 How that they told you there should [*would*] be mockers in the last time [*in the last days*], who should walk after their own ungodly lusts [*wicked desires and passions*].

19 These be they who separate themselves [*who leave the Church*], sensual [*involved in sexual immorality*], having not the Spirit [*who have become insensitive to the Spirit*].

20 But ye, beloved, building up yourselves on your most holy faith, praying in the Holy Ghost [*as directed by the Holy Ghost; see 1 John 5:14; D&C 46:30 and 50:30*],

21 Keep yourselves in the love of God, looking for the mercy of our Lord Jesus Christ [*using the Atonement of Christ*] unto [*which leads to*] eternal life [*exaltation*].

22 And of some have compassion, making a difference [*show compassion to those who need it, thus making a difference in their lives*]:

23 And others save with fear, pulling them out of the fire [*saving their souls from punishment*]; hating even the garment spotted by the flesh ["*Touch not their unclean things." (Alma 5:57)*].

24 Now unto him [*Christ*] that is able to keep you from falling, and to present you faultless before the presence of his [*the Father's*] glory with exceeding joy [*compare with D&C 45:3–5*],

25 To the only wise God our Saviour, be glory and majesty, dominion and power, both now and ever. Amen.

# THE REVELATION OF ST JOHN THE DIVINE

The Prophet Joseph said, "The book of Revelation is one of the plainest books God ever caused to be written" (*Teachings of the Prophet Joseph Smith*, p. 290). This statement by the Prophet is a reminder that this marvelous book of scripture can be understood. In fact, we are greatly blessed to have much inspired help as we seek to understand the Revelation of John. Elder Bruce R. McConkie, of the Quorum of the Twelve Apostles, said the following:

"As a matter of fact, we are in a much better position to understand those portions of Revelation which we are expected to understand than we generally realize. Thanks be to the interpretive material found in sections 29, 77, 88, and others of the revelations in the Doctrine and Covenants; plus the revisions given in the Inspired Version of the Bible [*the Joseph Smith Translation of the Bible*]; plus the sermons of the Prophet; plus some clarifying explanations in the Book of Mormon and other latter-day scripture; plus our overall knowledge of the plan of salvation—thanks be to all of these things (to say nothing of a little conservative sense, wisdom and inspiration in their application), the fact is that we have a marvelously comprehensive and correct understanding of this otherwise hidden book." (Bruce R. McConkie, *Doctrinal New Testament Commentary*, 3 vols. [Salt Lake City: Bookcraft, 1965–1973], 3: 431.)

One of our real advantages in studying the Book of Revelation is that we recognize that it presents the Plan of Salvation, especially as seen against the background of the last days, when evil and wickedness will finally come to an end as the Millennium is ushered in by the Second Coming of the Savior. Since we have been taught the Plan of Salvation, we are in a much better position to understand Revelation than others who are not familiar with the restored gospel.

The JST makes changes in over 80 verses of the Book of Revelation, and thus becomes one of our most valuable keys for understanding John's writings in this book of the New Testament.

Still, for most members of the Church, the Book of Revelation is somewhat intimidating when it comes to reading it and trying to understand it. Therefore, as is the case elsewhere in this study guide, our notes will be rather simple, brief, and straightforward, allowing you to concentrate mostly on the scriptures themselves. It is hoped that you will mark your own scriptures and make many notes in the margins so that your study of Revelation will bless you throughout your life.

### *Background*

The Book of Revelation was written by the Apostle John about AD 95. He was the brother of James and was one of the original twelve called by Jesus. He came to be known as John the Beloved because of the special fondness Jesus felt for him (John 13:23). He was in the presidency of the early Church with Peter and James. He is the author of the Gospel of John, the three epistles

of John, and the book of Revelation. He was given the special privilege of being allowed to live on the earth as a translated being until the Savior's Second Coming. (See John 21:21–23; D&C 7.) Little more is recorded of his life except for the brief mention in Revelation of his being on the isle of Patmos (Revelation 1:9), to which he was probably banished during the wave of Christian persecution under the emperor Domitian. In 1831 the Prophet Joseph Smith indicated that John was then laboring among the lost ten tribes. (See HC, 1:176.)

Revelation, chapters 1–3, deal mainly with John's day. Chapters 4–22 deal mainly with the future, including our day, and include glimpses back into premortality as well as visions of the last days, the Second Coming, the Millennium, and celestial glory.

## *Symbolism*

The use of symbolism in the Book of Revelation is one of several things which make it hard for us to understand. While we use much symbolism in our own culture, the symbolism used by John is difficult for us because we are not familiar with the culture of his day.

One of the great things about symbolism is that it is "infinitely deep," meaning that through symbolism, the Holy Ghost can teach you one thing during one reading of a verse or set of verses, then, the next time your read the same thing, you can be given a different message. For instance, suppose you are reading Revelation 1:18 where the Savior says "I. . . have the keys of hell and of death." The symbolism used is "keys," meaning the power to lock up or unlock, to condemn or to set free. During this reading of this verse, the Holy Ghost impresses your mind that the Savior is our final Judge and can, if necessary, smite wicked people and transfer them to hell in order to cleanse the earth and free it from their wicked influence. Thus, in your heart, you say to yourself, "I'd better be good!" However, the next time you read this verse, with its symbolism of "the keys of hell and of death," your mind is on personal progress and improvement. This time, the Holy Ghost whispers that the Savior has the "keys," through His Atonement, to free you from hell and from spiritual death. Thus, you are impressed and encouraged to repent and accept the cleansing and healing power of the Atonement in your own life.

The following list of symbols can be helpful to us in understanding the scriptures:

# Symbolism Often Used in the Scriptures

## Colors

| | |
|---|---|
| **white** | purity; righteousness; exaltation (Example: Rev. 3:4–5) |
| **black** | evil; famine; darkness (Example: Rev. 6:5–6) |
| **red** | sins; bloodshed (Example: Rev. 6:4; D&C 133:51) |
| **blue** | heaven; godliness; remembering and keeping God's commandments (Example: Numbers 15:37–40) |
| **green** | life; nature (Example: Rev. 8:7) |
| **amber** | sun; light; divine glory (Example: D&C 110:2, Rev. 1:15, Ezek. 1:4, 27; 8:2) |
| **scarlet** | royalty (Example: Dan. 5:29; Matt. 27:28–29) |
| **silver** | worth, but less than gold (Example: Ridges, *Isaiah Made Easier*, Isa. 48:10 notes) |
| **gold** | the best; exaltation (Example: Rev. 4:4) |

## Body parts

| | |
|---|---|
| **eye** | perception; light and knowledge |
| **head** | governing |
| **ears** | obedience; hearing |
| **mouth** | speaking |
| **hair** | modesty; covering |
| **members** | offices and callings |
| **heart** | inner man; courage |
| **hands** | action, acting |
| **right hand** | covenant hand; making covenants |
| **bowels** | center of emotion; whole being |
| **loins** | posterity; preparing for action (gird up your loins) |
| **liver** | center of feeling |
| **reins** | kidneys; center of desires, thoughts |
| **arm** | power |
| **foot** | mobility; foundation |
| **toe** | associated with cleansing rites (Example: Lev. 14:17) |

| | |
|---|---|
| **nose** | anger (Example: 2 Samuel 22:16; Job 4:9) |
| **tongue** | speaking |
| **blood** | life of the body |
| **knee** | humility; submission |
| **shoulder** | strength; effort |
| **forehead** | total dedication, loyalty (Example: Rev. 14:1 [loyalty to God]; Rev. 13:16 [loyalty to wickedness, Satan]) |

## NUMBERS

| | |
|---|---|
| **1** | unity; God |
| **3** | God; Godhead; A word repeated 3 times means superlative, "the most" or "the best." (See Isa. 6:3) |
| **4** | mankind; earth (See Smith's Bible Dictionary, p. 456) (Example: Rev. 7:1. Four angels over four parts of the earth) |
| **7** | completeness; perfection. When man lets God help, it leads to perfection. (man + God = perfection) 4 + 3 = 7 |
| **10** | numerical perfection (Example: Ten Commandments, tithing); well-organized (Example: Satan is well-organized, Rev. 13:1) |
| **12** | divine government; God's organization (Example: JST Rev. 5:6) |
| **40 days** | literal; sometimes means "a long time" as in 1 Samuel 17:16 |
| **forever** | endless; can sometimes be a specific period or age, not endless (see *BYU Religious Studies Center Newsletter*, Vol. 8, No. 3, May 1994) |

## OTHERS

| | |
|---|---|
| **horse** | victory; power to conquer (Example: Rev. 19:11; Jer. 8:16) |
| **donkey** | peace (Example: Christ came in peace at the Triumphal Entry) |
| **palms** | joy; triumph, victory (Example: John 12:13; Rev. 7:9) |
| **wings** | power to move, act etc. (Example: Rev. 4:8; D&C 77:4) |
| **crown** | power; dominion; exaltation (Example: Rev. 2:10; 4:4) |
| **robes** | royalty; kings, queens; exaltation (Example: Rev. 6:11, 7:14; 2 Ne. 9:14; D&C 109:76; 3 Ne. 11:8) |

# REVELATION 1

As mentioned in the introductory material above, chapters 1–3 deal mainly with things in John's day, while chapters 4–22 deal mainly with the future.

1 The Revelation of Jesus Christ, which God gave unto him, to show unto his servants things which must shortly come to pass; and he sent and signified it by his angel unto his servant John:

**JST Revelation 1:1**

1 The Revelation of John, a servant of God, which was given unto him of Jesus Christ, to show unto his servants things which must shortly come to pass, that he sent and signified by his angel unto his servant John, [*This is an example of what is known as "divine investiture" where an angel speaks directly for Christ. See Rev. 19:9–10.*]

### *Divine Investiture*

Often in the scriptures, without so indicating, the Savior speaks for the Father (example: D&C 29:1, 42, 46), the Holy Ghost speaks for the Savior (example: Moses 5:9), an angel speaks for the Savior (example: Revelation 1:1), and so forth. This is known as "divine investiture." Apostle Joseph Fielding Smith explained this divine investiture of authority as follows: "In giving revelations our Savior speaks at times for himself; at other times for the Father, and in the Father's name, as though he were the Father, and yet it is Jesus Christ, our Redeemer who gives the message. So, we see, in Doctrine and Covenants 29:1, that he introduces himself as 'Jesus Christ, your Redeemer,' but in the closing part of the revelation he speaks for the Father, and in the Father's name as though he were the Father, and yet it is still Jesus who is speaking, for the Father has put his name on him for that purpose." (*Doctrines of Salvation*, 3 vols., edited by Bruce R. McConkie [Salt Lake City: Bookcraft, 1954–56], Vol. 1, p. 27.)

Apostle Jeffrey R. Holland also explained divine investiture. "Christ can at any time and in any place speak and act for the Father by virtue of the 'divine investiture of authority' the Father has given him. (Jeffrey R. Holland, *Christ and the New Covenant: The Messianic Message of the Book of Mormon* [Salt Lake City: Deseret Book, 1997], 183–84.)

2 Who [*John*] bare record of the word of God, and of the testimony of Jesus Christ, and of all things that he [*John*] saw.

**JST Revelation 1:2**

2 Who bore record of the word of God, and of the testimony of Jesus Christ, and of all things that he saw.

3 Blessed is he that readeth, and they that hear the words of this prophecy, and keep those things which are written therein: for the time is at hand.

**JST Revelation 1:3**

3 Blessed are they who read, and they who hear and understand the words of this prophecy, and keep those things which are written therein, for the time of the coming of the Lord draweth nigh.

4 John to the seven churches [*to the leaders of the seven "branches" or "wards" of the Church*] which are in Asia [*modern day western Turkey*]: Grace be unto you, and peace, from him [*Christ*] which is, and which was, and which is to come; and from the seven Spirits which are before his throne;

**JST Revelation 1:4**

4 Now this is the testimony of John to the seven servants who are over the seven churches in Asia. Grace unto you, and peace from him who is, and who was, and who is to come; who hath sent forth his angel from before his throne, to testify unto those who are the seven servants over the seven churches.

5 And from Jesus Christ, who is the faithful witness, and the first begotten of the dead [*the first resurrected*], and

the prince of [*the leader over*] the kings of the earth. [*The JST puts the rest of verse 5 with verse 6.*] Unto him [*Christ*] that loved us, and washed us from our sins in his own blood [*the Atonement*],

**JST Revelation 1:5**

5 Therefore, I, John, the faithful witness, bear record of the things which were delivered me of the angel, and from Jesus Christ the first begotten of the dead, and the Prince of the kings of the earth.

The phrase, "washed us from our sins in his own blood," in verse 5, above is symbolic of being cleansed by the Atonement. It is interesting to note the cleansing role of blood in our own physical bodies. It constantly cleans out the toxins from each individual cell, and thus continually gives each cell newness of life.

6 And hath made us kings and priests [*terms meaning exaltation*] unto God [*Heavenly Father*] and his Father; to him be glory and dominion for ever and ever. Amen.

**JST Revelation 1:6**

6 And unto him who loved us, be glory; who washed us from our sins in his own blood, and hath made us kings and priests unto God, his Father. To him be glory and dominion, for ever and ever. Amen.

Bruce R. McConkie explains verse 6, above, as follows: "If righteous men have power through the gospel and its crowning ordinance of celestial marriage to become kings and priests to rule in exaltation forever, it follows that the women by their side (without whom they cannot attain exaltation) will be queens and priestesses (Rev. 1:6; 5:10). Exaltation grows out of the eternal union of a man and his wife. Of those whose marriage endures in eternity, the Lord says, 'Then shall they be gods' (D&C 132:20); that is, each of them, the man and the woman, will be a god. As such they will rule over their dominions forever." (Bruce R. McConkie, *Mormon Doctrine*, 2nd ed. [Salt Lake City: Bookcraft, 1966], 613.)

7 Behold, he [*Christ*] cometh with clouds [*symbolic of the presence of the Lord; see Exodus 13:21 and Exodus 19:9*]; and every eye shall see him, and they also which pierced him [*even those who participated in his crucifixion will see him at the Second Coming; see Orson Pratt,* Journal of Discourses, *Vol. 18, p. 170*]: and all kindreds [*the wicked*] of the earth shall wail because of him. Even so, Amen.

**JST Revelation 1:7**

7 For behold, he cometh in the clouds with ten thousands of his saints in the kingdom, clothed with the glory of his Father. And every eye shall see him; and they who pierced him, and all kindreds of the earth shall wail because of him. Even so, Amen.

8 I am Alpha and Omega [*the beginning and ending letters of the Greek alphabet*], the beginning and the ending, saith the Lord, which is, and which was, and which is to come, the Almighty [*In other words, I have been involved with you since the beginning, premortality and creation, and I will be around at the end of the earth as I judge you and finish all things the Father has asked Me to do*].

**JST Revelation 1:8**

8 For he saith, I am Alpha and Omega, the beginning and the ending, the Lord, who is, and who was, and who is to come, the Almighty.

Having set the stage now, John proceeds to tell us what the circumstances in his life were at the time he received this revelation.

9 I John [*the Beloved Apostle*], who also am your brother, and companion in tribulation [*I've got problems too; I understand you*], and in the kingdom and patience of Jesus Christ, was in the isle that is called Patmos [*he was in a prison colony just off the west coast of Turkey, just below the island of Samos; (see E 2 on map 13 of your Bible or Map 22 in the 1989 LDS Bible for the location of Samos), then put a dot just*

*under Samos and label it Patmos*], for the word of God, and for the testimony of Jesus Christ [*I am in prison because I wouldn't stop teaching and living the gospel*].

10 I was in the Spirit on the Lord's day [*Sunday, Acts 20:7*], and heard behind me a great voice, as of a trumpet,

Trumpet is used often in the scriptures to represent a clear, easy to recognize message from God, just as a trumpet is a clear, easy-to-recognize musical instrument for us today.

Revelation 19:10 informs us that an angel is speaking for Jesus Christ here. As mentioned earlier, this is known as "divine investiture."

11 Saying, I [*Christ*] am Alpha and Omega, the first and the last: and, What thou seest, write in a book, and send it unto the seven churches [*"wards" or "branches"*] which are in Asia [*western Turkey today*]; unto Ephesus, and unto Smyrna, and unto Pergamos, and unto Thyatira, and unto Sardis, and unto Philadelphia, and unto Laodicea [*listed in geographical order*].

12 And I turned to see the voice that spake with me. And being turned, I saw seven golden candlesticks [*representing the seven "wards" or "branches"*];

Symbolism is involved here and carries an important message. Gold symbolizes the best, i.e., the true gospel. Candlesticks don't give light, rather, they carry the source of light, which is Christ and His gospel, to the world.

**JST Revelation 1:12**

12 And I turned to see from whence the voice came that spake to me; and being turned, I saw seven golden candlesticks;

13 And in the midst [*D&C 38:7 reminds us that Christ is often in our midst*] of the seven candlesticks one like unto the Son of man [*Christ*], clothed with a garment down to the foot, and girt about the paps [*breast, chest*] with a golden [*symbolic of the best, celestial*] girdle.

The phrase "one like unto the Son of man" in verse 13, above, needs explaining. The question is, why don't they just say "Jesus Christ," rather than using an oblique reference to Him? In order to keep the commandment "Thou shalt not take the name of the Lord thy God in vain;" (Exodus 20:7), the Jews developed rules and standard practices which kept them far away from taking the name of the Lord in vain. For instance, rather than saying the Lord's name directly, they would use an indirect reference such as "one like unto," and then the name. Thus, they avoided even coming close to breaking the commandment. There are many examples of this practice of showing reverence and respect toward the name of Deity. For instance, see Daniel 3:25, 7:13; Revelation 14:14; Abraham 3:27; 1 Nephi 1:8.

The phrase "Son of man," in reference to Christ in verse 13, above, and elsewhere in the scriptures is explained in Moses 6:57 as follows: ". . . in the language of Adam, Man of Holiness is his name, and the name of his Only Begotten is the Son of Man, even Jesus Christ. . . " In other words, "Man of Holiness" refers to Heavenly Father. Jesus is, therefore, the "Son of Man of Holiness," which, in the Bible, is shortened to "Son of man."

14 His head and his hairs were white like wool, as white as snow; and his eyes were as a flame of fire [*this is similar to the description of the Savior in D&C 110:3*];

It is interesting to notice that the word "wool" and the phrase "white as snow," used in verse 14, above, are also used in Isaiah 1:18 in describing the power of the Atonement to cleanse and heal from sin. Isaiah 1:18 says, "Come now, and let us reason together, saith the LORD: though your sins be as scarlet, they shall be as white as snow; though they be red like crimson, they shall be as wool." The use here is no doubt a tie-in with

Isaiah 1:18 and a reminder to us of the power of the Atonement.

15 And his feet like unto fine brass, as if they burned in a furnace; and his voice as the sound of many waters.

16 And he had in his right hand [*covenant hand*] seven stars [*the leaders of the seven "wards"; stars are symbolic. We rely on them, like we rely on our Church leaders, to guide us through darkness to our desired destination.*]: and out of his [*Christ's*] mouth went a sharp twoedged sword [*perhaps symbolic of the fact that the Savior can both defend the righteous and destroy the wicked; see 2:16. It is our choice. Also, a two edged sword, representing the word of God as in JST Rev. 19:15, can cut quickly through falsehood and error.*]: and his countenance was as the sun shineth in his strength.

**JST Revelation 1:16**

16 And he had in his right hand seven stars; and out of his mouth went a sharp two-edged sword; and his countenance was as the sun shining in his strength.

Next, in verse 17, John tells us how seeing the resurrected Savior (see heading to this chapter in your Bible) affected him at this moment.

17 And when I [*John*] saw him, I fell at his feet as dead [*completely overwhelmed*]. And he laid his right hand [*covenant hand; symbolizing that via making and keeping covenants, we can feel at ease in Christ's presence*] upon me, saying unto me, Fear not; I am the first and the last [*i.e., I am Jesus Christ your Savior; you don't need to be afraid of Me.*]:

18 I am he that liveth, and was dead [*I have been literally resurrected!*]; and, behold, I am alive for evermore [*I will continue to live forever*], Amen; and have the keys of hell and of death [*i.e., I overcame all things and thus have all power to save you; I am fully qualified to be your Savior*].

19 Write the things which thou hast seen, and the things which are, and the things which shall be hereafter [*write this vision down*];

The angel, speaking for Christ, now explains to John some of the imagery used so far in the vision.

20 The mystery of the seven stars which thou sawest in my right hand, and the seven golden candlesticks. The seven stars are the angels of the seven churches [*wards or branches*]: and the seven candlesticks which thou sawest are the seven churches.

**JST Revelation 1:20**

20 This is the mystery of the seven stars which thou sawest in my right hand, and the seven golden candlesticks. The seven stars are the servants [*leaders, presiding elders*] of the seven churches; and the seven candlesticks which thou sawest are the seven churches.

# REVELATION 2

The Savior here and in chapter 3 gives personal messages through John the Revelator to the Saints in the various "wards" or "branches" spoken of in Revelation 1:11, which were located in what is known as western Turkey, today. Watch for symbolism representing the celestial kingdom at the end of each of these messages.

The first message is the Savior's message to the members of the Ephesus "ward" in verses 1–7, next.

1 Unto the angel [*presiding elder, leader*] of the church [*"ward"*] of Ephesus write; These things saith he [*Christ*] that holdeth the seven stars [*"branch presidents" or "bishops"; the Savior similarly helps our church leaders today*] in his right hand [*covenant hand*], who walketh in the midst of the seven golden candlesticks [*the Savior is in our midst, D&C 38:7; he is not an absentee Savior*];

**JST Revelation 2:1**

1 Unto the servant of the church of Ephesus write; These things saith he that holdeth the seven stars in his right hand, who walketh in the midst of the seven golden candlesticks;

In the next few verses, the Savior will first compliment these Saints and then express some concerns to them.

2 I know thy works, and thy labour, and thy patience, and how thou canst not bear them which are evil: and thou hast tried [*tested*] them which say they are apostles, and are not, and hast found them liars [*you have faced issues and dealt properly with apostates among you*];

3 And hast born, and hast patience, and for my name's sake hast laboured, and hast not fainted [*you haven't given up when the going was difficult*].

4 Nevertheless I have somewhat against thee [*I have a serious concern*], because thou hast left thy first love [*i.e., your enthusiasm for the gospel when you were first converted; now you are diminishing in zeal and getting weak in the faith*].

5 Remember therefore from whence thou art fallen, and repent, and do the first works [*return to your former level of commitment and enthusiasm*]; or else I will come unto thee quickly, and will remove thy candlestick out of his place, except thou repent [*your "ward" will die out much faster than you might think possible, if you don't repent*].

6 But this thou hast [*here is another compliment, something you are doing right*], that thou hatest the deeds of the Nicolaitans [*D&C 117:11; people who want the prestige of Church membership but who are not fully committed to the gospel; they secretly want to follow the ways of the world*], which I also hate.

7 He that hath an ear, let him hear what the Spirit saith unto the churches [*listen carefully to the promptings of the Holy Ghost who teaches and warns members of the Church constantly*]; To him that overcometh will I give to eat of the tree of life, which is in the midst of the paradise of God. [*Celestial glory is the reward of the righteous. Perhaps this reflects back to Lehi's dream in 1 Nephi 8. Also note that the Nicolaitans in verse 6 of Rev. 2 seem to tie in with the "great and spacious building" in 1 Nephi 8:26–27 while verse 5 above might tie in with 1 Nephi 8:25, where members have tasted the gospel but then let peer pressure make them ashamed of it.*]

Next, the Savior gives John a message for the Saints in Smyrna.

8 And unto the angel [*presiding elder*] of the church ["*ward*"] in Smyrna write; These things saith the first and the last [*the Savior*], which was dead, and is alive [*is resurrected*];

**JST Revelation 2:8**

8 And unto the servant of the church in Smyrna write; These things saith the first and the last, which was dead, and is alive;

9 I know thy works, and tribulation, and poverty, [*but thou art rich; i.e., you are well-off because you have the gospel*] and I know the blasphemy of them which say they are Jews [*who claim to be "the chosen people of the Lord"*], and are not [*i.e., they are not faithful and have rejected Christ and are persecuting the Saints in Smyrna*], but are the synagogue of Satan [*the church of the Devil; 1 Nephi 14:10; 1 Nephi 13:6–9*].

10 Fear none of those things which thou shalt suffer [*you will have some suffering as part of your "curriculum" here on earth, but don't fear it*]: behold, the devil shall cast some of you into prison, that ye may be tried [*tested*]; and ye shall have tribulation ten days [*perhaps meaning a short time compared to eternity*]: be thou faithful unto death [*endure to the end*], and I will give thee a crown of life [*you will be a god in exaltation*].

11 He that hath an ear [*he who is willing*

*to listen*], let him hear what the Spirit saith unto the churches; He that overcometh [*who overcomes evil through the Atonement of Christ*] shall not be hurt of the second death [*will not suffer spiritual death and be cut off from the presence of God forever; in other words, you will receive a celestial reward*].

The next message from the Savior goes to the Saints in Pergamos.

12 And to the angel [*leader*] of the church [*"ward"*] in Pergamos [*a center for Roman emperor worship*] write; These things saith he [*Christ*] which hath the sharp sword with two edges [*Rev. 1:16*];

**JST Revelation 2:12**

12 And to the servant of the church in Pergamos write; These things saith he which hath the sharp sword with two edges;

13 I know thy works, and where thou dwellest [*I know your situation*], even where Satan's seat is [*you live in an area where evil and false religion is very strong*]: and thou holdest fast my name [*and are remaining faithful to the covenants you made when you took My name upon you*], and hast not denied my faith [*a compliment*], even in those days wherein Antipas was my faithful martyr [*gave his life for the gospel*], who was slain among you, where Satan dwelleth [*where Satan has great power over many*].

14 But I have a few things against thee [*I have some concerns about you*], because thou hast there them that hold the doctrine of Balaam [*priestcraft; preaching for popularity, money, and approval of men; see Numbers 22*], who taught Balac to cast a stumblingblock before the children of Israel, to eat things sacrificed unto idols [*participating in idol worship*], and to commit fornication [*sexual immorality used as part of idol worship in many Bible cults; "fornication" can also mean breaking covenants, intense and total disloyalty to God. See Jer. 3:8, Rev. 14:8; also see Bible Dictionary under "Adultery"*].

15 So hast thou also them that hold the doctrine of the Nicolaitans [*some members of the Church in your area are thinking like Nicolaitans; see verse 6, above*], which thing I hate.

16 Repent; or else I will come unto thee quickly, and will fight against them with the sword of my mouth [*the two edged sword in 1:16 can destroy the wicked as well as protect the righteous*].

17 He that hath an ear, let him hear what the Spirit saith unto the churches; To him that overcometh [*who overcomes sin and evil through repentance and the Atonement*] will I give to eat of the hidden manna [*i.e., nourishment from heaven*], and will give him a white stone [*symbolic of celestial glory, D&C 130:11*], and in the stone a new name [*symbolic of celestial glory; see also Rev. 3:12*] written, which no man knoweth saving he that receiveth it [*a key word, D&C 130:11*].

**JST Revelation 2:17**

17 He that hath an ear, let him hear what the Spirit saith unto the churches; To him that overcometh will I give to eat of the hidden manna, and will give him a white stone, and in the stone a new name written, which no man knowest saving he that receiveth it.

Isaiah mentions "a new name, which the mouth of the Lord shall name" in Isaiah 62:2. Additional information about the term "new name," as used in verse 17, above, is given in the Doctrine and Covenants. According to D&C 130:10–11, a "white stone" is given to each of those who attains the celestial kingdom. In D&C 130:11, the "new name" is "the key word" used in conjunction with celestial glory.

Brigham Young explained the term "key word," in conjunction with temple endowments, as follows: "Your endowment is, to receive all those ordinances in the house of the Lord, which are necessary for you, after you

have departed this life, to enable you to walk back to the presence of the Father, passing the angels who stand as sentinels, being enabled to give them the key words, the signs and tokens, pertaining to the holy Priesthood, and gain your eternal exaltation in spite of earth and hell." (Discourses of Brigham Young, p. 416.)

It is interesting to note that people anciently had new names given them upon making additional covenants with the Lord. Examples include Abram, whose name was changed to Abraham when he made covenants of exaltation with the Lord (Genesis 17:5.) In the heading to JST Genesis 17, the term "new name" appears again as "Abram's new name." Likewise, Sarai's name was changed to Sarah (Genesis 17:15–16.) Jacob's name was changed to Israel (Genesis 32:28.) Saul's name was changed to Paul (Acts 13:2–3, 9 and 13.) King Mosiah promised his people another name if they would be diligent "in keeping the commandments of the Lord" (Mosiah 1:11). The name he gave them was the name of Jesus Christ (Mosiah 5:8 and 11) which is the name through which we receive exaltation if worthy (see Mosiah 5:7.)

Robert L. Millet spoke of this name which King Benjamin gave his people as follows: "As members of the family of Christ, they were required to take upon them a new name, the name of Christ; they thereby became Christians in the truest sense of the word and were obligated by covenant to live by the rules and regulations of the royal family, to live a life befitting the new and sacred name they had taken." (Robert L. Millet, *Alive in Christ: The Miracle of Spiritual Rebirth* [Salt Lake City: Deseret Book, 1997], p. 77.)

Next, the Lord gives John a message for the members in Thyatira.

18 And unto the angel [*leader*] of the church in Thyatira write; These things saith the Son of God, who hath his eyes like unto a flame of fire, and his feet are like fine brass;

**JST Revelation 2:18**

18 And unto the servant of the church in Thyatira write; These things saith the Son of God, who hath his eyes like unto a flame of fire, and his feet are like fine brass;

19 I know thy works, and charity, and service, and faith, and thy patience, and thy works [*a compliment*]; and the last to be more than the first [*in effect, your recent works are greater than your previous works, in other words, you continue to progress in living the gospel*].

20 [*A concern:*] Notwithstanding I have a few things against thee, because thou sufferest [*you allow*] that woman Jezebel, which calleth herself a prophetess, to teach [*major message: There are limits as to what you can tolerate in the Church. You leaders shouldn't allow her to do this teaching in your congregation.*] and to seduce my servants to commit fornication [*can be literal; also means apostasy, total disloyalty—see Rev. 14:8; Bible Dictionary under "Adultery"*], and to eat things sacrificed unto idols [*i.e., participating in idol worship*].

21 And I gave her space to repent of her fornication [*she had plenty of chances to repent*]; and she repented not.

**JST Revelation 2:21**

21 And I gave her space to repent of her fornications; and she repented not.

22 Behold, I will cast her into a bed, and them [*her followers*] that commit adultery [*who are in apostasy*] with her into great tribulation, except [*unless*] they repent of their deeds.

**JST Revelation 2:22**

22 Behold, I will cast her into hell, and them that commit adultery with her into great tribulation, except they repent of their deeds.

23 And I will kill her children [*followers*] with death [*spiritual death*]; and

all the churches [*"wards"*] shall know that I am he which searcheth [*knows*] the reins [*kidneys, loins; symbolically the center of thoughts and desires, i.e., the inner person*] and hearts: and I will give unto every one of you according to your works.

24 But unto you [*the presiding officer*] I say, and unto the rest in Thyatira, as many as have not this doctrine [*who haven't become followers of Jezebel*], and which have not known the depths of Satan [*haven't gone deep into apostasy*], as they speak; I will put upon you none other burden [*i.e., I will not express any other concerns about you at this time; just work on this one*].

25 But that which ye have already [*the things in which you are being faithful*] hold fast till I come [*endure to the end*].

26 And he that overcometh, and keepeth my works unto the end, to him will I give power over the nations [*celestial reward; i.e., they will become gods, D&C 132:20*]:

**JST Revelation 2:26**

26 And to him who overcometh, and keepeth my commandments unto the end, will I give power over many kingdoms;

27 And he [*those who overcome all things*] shall rule them [*nations, i.e., future worlds; D&C 132:20*] with a rod of iron [*the word of God—see JST below, also, 1 Nephi 11:25*]; as the vessels [*clay pots*] of a potter shall they be broken to shivers [*broken to bits, if they are disobedient*]: even as I received of my Father [*just as is the case with me and my work on this earth*].

**JST Revelation 2:27**

27 And he shall rule them with the word of God; and they shall be in his hands as the vessels of clay in the hands of a potter; and he shall govern them by faith, with equity and justice, even as I received of my Father.

28 And I will give him [*the righteous in verse 26*] the morning star [*the brightest, best, symbolic of exaltation*].

29 He that hath an ear, let him hear what the Spirit saith unto the churches [*i.e., pay close attention and obey what I say to you through the Holy Ghost*].

# REVELATION 3

As the revelation and vision continue, John is given messages from the Savior to three more units of the Church, namely Sardis, Philadelphia, and Laodicea. Among other things in this chapter, we are taught about the book of life (verse 5) and the fact that worthy people can become gods (verse 21).

1 And unto the angel [*presiding officer*] of the church [*"ward"*] in Sardis write; These things saith he [*the Savior*] that hath the seven Spirits of God, and the seven stars [JST "the seven stars, which are the seven servants of God," i.e., I'm holding the seven "bishops" of the seven "wards" in the hollow of my hand; I am directing them]; I know thy works, that thou hast a name that thou livest [*i.e., you have a reputation for being good*], and art dead [*see JST change below*].

**JST Revelation 3:1**

1 And unto the servant of the church in Sardis, write; These things saith he who hath the seven stars, which are the seven servants of God [*in other words, the Savior is holding the seven "bishops" of the seven "wards" in the hollow of His hand; He is directing them*]; I know thy works, that thou hast a name that thou livest, and art not dead [*in effect, you still have some spirituality left—see verse 2, next*].

2 Be watchful, and strengthen the things which remain, that are ready to die: for I have not found thy works perfect before God. [*An understatement of concern!*]

**JST Revelation 3:2**

2 Be watchful therefore, and strengthen those who remain, who

are ready to die [*spiritually*]; for I have not found thy works perfect before God.

3 Remember therefore how thou hast received and heard [*the gospel*], and hold fast [*keep your commitments*], and repent. If therefore thou shalt not watch, I will come on thee as a thief [*unexpectedly; Strong's #2240*], and thou shalt not know what hour I will come upon thee.

4 Thou hast a few names [*you have a few members*] even in Sardis which have not defiled their garments [*a compliment; you still have a few righteous members*]; and they shall walk with me in white [*symbolic of exaltation*]: for they are worthy.

5 He that overcometh [*he who overcomes sin through Christ's Atonement*], the same shall be clothed in white raiment [*white clothing; symbolic of exaltation*]; and I will not blot out his name out of the book of life, but I will confess [*acknowledge, praise*] his name before my Father [*as in D&C 45:3–5*], and before his angels [*i.e., they will receive celestial reward*].

The term "book of life" referred to in verse 5, above, is referred to as the "Lamb's Book of Life" in D&C 132:19. It represents the records kept in heaven in which the names of those worthy of exaltation are written. See McConkie, *Mormon Doctrine*, second edition, 1966, p. 97.

6 He that hath an ear, let him hear what the Spirit saith unto the churches.

7 And to the angel [*presiding officer*] of the church in Philadelphia write; These things saith he [*Christ*] that is holy, he that is true, he that hath the key of David [*Isaiah 22:22; i.e., power to command and be obeyed; who holds the priesthood keys of exaltation*], he that openeth, and no man shutteth; and shutteth, and no man openeth [*i.e., Christ's Atonement can set us free from death and hell, in spite of Satan's efforts against us, or He can condemn us on Judgment Day*];

**JST Revelation 3:7**

7 And to the servant of the church in Philadelphia write; These things saith he that is holy, he that is true, he that hath the key of David, he that openeth, and no man shutteth; and shutteth, and no man openeth;

8 I know thy works: behold, I have set before thee an open door [*I have prepared the way for you to come unto Me*], and no man can shut it [*no man can stop you*]: for thou hast a little strength, and hast kept my word [*i.e., you are improving, and you are keeping your commitments to Me*], and hast not denied my name [*and you have not rejected Me*].

9 Behold, I will make them of the synagogue of Satan [*the church of the Devil, 1 Nephi 14:10; Rev. 2:9*], which say they are Jews [*i.e., claim to be covenant people*], and are not, but do lie [*through their personal wickedness*]; behold, I will make them to come and worship before thy feet [*you will be exalted and have power over them; see D&C 132:20*], and to know that I have loved thee [*I have been privileged to bless you because of your righteousness; see* Ensign, *Feb. 2003 article "Divine Love" by Elder Russell M. Nelson, pp. 20–25*].

10 Because thou hast kept the word of my patience [*i.e., you have patiently kept your commitments, Heb. 10:36*], I also will keep thee from the hour of temptation [*help and protect you during temptation*], which shall come upon all the world, to try [*test*] them that dwell upon the earth.

11 Behold, I come quickly [*not "soon," rather, when I do come, it will be "quickly" (see Strong's #5035) and the wicked will not have time to repent and escape*]: hold that fast which thou hast [*keep your commitments*], that no man take thy crown [*exaltation*].

Notice the various ways exaltation is described in verse 12, next.

12 Him that overcometh will I make a

pillar in the temple of my God [*you will receive exaltation in my "temple," in other words, in the celestial kingdom; see Revelation 21:22*], and he shall go no more out [*exaltation lasts forever*]: and I will write upon him the name of my God [*symbolism meaning he will belong to God, i.e., exaltation; Rev. 14:1, 22:4*], and the name of the city of my God, which is new Jerusalem [*i.e., your eternal "address" will be New Jerusalem, Celestial Kingdom*], which cometh down out of heaven from my God: and I will write upon him my new name [*symbolic of celestial glory, D&C 130:11*].

**JST Revelation 3:12**

12 Him that overcometh will I make a pillar in the temple of my God, and he shall go no more out; and I will write upon him the name of my God, and the name of the city of my God, this is New Jerusalem, which cometh down out of heaven from my God; and I will write upon him my new name.

The phrase "new name" has meaning understood only by endowed members of the Church of Jesus Christ of Latter-day Saints. See the note after Revelation 2:17 in this study guide.

13 He that hath an ear, let him hear what the Spirit saith unto the churches.

To this next "ward" or "branch" of the Church, the Savior expresses only "concerns." From what Christ tells them, we should learn that one of the most serious concerns of all is indecision about whether or not to be completely committed to God.

14 And unto the angel [*presiding officer*] of the church of the Laodiceans write; These things saith the Amen [*Christ*], the faithful and true witness, the beginning [*the firstborn spirit child of our Heavenly Father, Colossians 1:15*] of the creation of God [*the Father*];

**JST Revelation 3:14**

14 And unto the servant of the church of the Laodiceans write; These things saith the Amen, the faithful and true witness, the beginning of the creation of God;

15 I know thy works, that thou art neither cold nor hot [*i.e., you won't make a commitment or take a stand*]: I would [*wish that*] thou wert cold or hot.

16 So then because thou art lukewarm [*you won't make a solid commitment*], and neither cold nor hot, I will spue [*vomit; see Rev. 3:16, footnote b in our Bible*] thee out of my mouth [*i.e., I will reject you*].

17 Because thou sayest, I am rich, and increased with goods [*I have lots of worldly possessions; Strong's #4147*], and have need of nothing [*you are materialistic*]; and knowest not that thou art wretched, and miserable, and poor, and blind, and naked [*you don't realize how spiritually poor you really are!*]:

Next, the Savior explains how such people can repent. This counsel applies to all of us.

18 I counsel thee to buy [*through your actions*] of me gold [*symbolic of the best, i.e., the gospel, the Atonement, exaltation*] tried in the fire [*proven to be good*], that thou mayest be [*truly*] rich; and white raiment [*buy white robes; symbolic of purity and exaltation*], that thou mayest be clothed, and that the shame of thy nakedness do not appear [*i.e., you need to repent and be clothed with righteousness, so you do not stand naked, i.e., without excuse for your sins, and embarrassed on Judgment Day*]; and anoint thine eyes [*prepare your spiritual eyes*] with eyesalve, that thou mayest see. [*Eye salve often hurts at first and then heals; so also with the Holy Ghost. His counsel sometimes hurts at first, but when heeded, it heals.*]

19 As many as I love, I rebuke and chasten [*D&C 95:1*]: be zealous [*pursue the "gold" in verse 18 earnestly; Strong's #2206*] therefore, and repent.

Perhaps you have seen paintings depicting verse 20, next. If so, did

you notice that the artist did not put a doorknob on the outside of the door? It is symbolic of the fact that the Savior knocks, but we must let Him in to our hearts and lives.

20 Behold, I [*the Savior*] stand at the door [*your door; your life*], and knock [*waiting humbly*]: if any man hear [*pay attention to*] my voice, and open the door [*we have the agency to or not to*], I will come in to him, and will sup [*eat the evening meal; can be symbolic of the Last Supper, sacrament; in other words, making covenants*] with him, and he with me.

"Throne," as used in verse 21, next, symbolizes exaltation, in other words, attaining the highest degree of glory in the celestial kingdom and becoming gods. See D&C 132:20.

21 To him that overcometh [*overcomes wickedness and temptation*] will I grant to sit with me in my throne [*i.e., we will be joint-heirs with Christ (Romans 8:17), exalted*], even as I also overcame, and am set down with my Father in his throne [*compare with D&C 76:107–108*].

22 He that hath an ear, let him hear what the Spirit saith unto the churches.

# REVELATION 4

As mentioned previously, chapters 1–3 of Revelation deal mainly with John's day. Starting with this chapter, John will primarily be shown things which will take place in the future. Verse 1 specifically says that John will now be shown the future.

Among other things, he will be shown Heavenly Father seated on His throne of power and glory.

1 After this I [*John*] looked, and, behold, a door was opened in heaven: and the first voice which I heard was as it were of a trumpet [*a clear, definite sound whose source is unmistakable, and whose message is clear*] talking with me; which said, Come up hither, and I will shew [*pronounced "show"*] thee things which must be hereafter [*now we will talk about the future*].

**JST Revelation 4:1**

1 After this I looked, and behold, a door was opened into heaven; and the first voice which I heard was as it were of a trumpet talking with me; which said, Come up hither, and I will show thee things which must be hereafter.

Did you notice the JST change? It changes "opened in heaven" to "opened into heaven," giving the sense that John was invited to look into heaven, where he will see the Father.

2 And immediately I was in the spirit: and, behold, a throne was set in heaven, and one [*Heavenly Father, see 5:7*] sat on the throne.

John now uses highest descriptive terms, superlatives, precious jewel stones, and so forth in attempting to describe the Father.

3 And he that sat [*upon the throne*] was to look upon like a jasper and a sardine stone [*a very hard, deep orange-red jewel stone symbolic of something one would look upon with total awe and wonder*]: and there was a rainbow [*depicting glory and beauty*] round about the throne, in sight like unto an emerald.

**JST Revelation 4:3**

3 And he that sat there was to look upon like a jasper and a sardine stone; and there was a rainbow round about the throne, in sight like unto an emerald.

The JST changes for verse 4, next, are doctrinally very significant because they show that faithful Saints can become gods, rather than existing eternally as angels.

4 And round about the throne were four and twenty seats: and upon the seats

I saw four and twenty elders [*faithful elders from the seven "wards" mentioned in Rev. 1:11 who had died; see D&C 77:5*] sitting, clothed in white raiment [*white robes; Strong's #2440; symbolic of exaltation*]; and they had on their heads crowns [*symbolic of authority and power*] of gold [*gold represents the best, i.e., exaltation*].

**JST Revelation 4:4**

4 And in the midst of the throne [*symbolizing becoming "joint heirs" with God, rather than forever being "on-the-outside-looking-in" worshipers*] were four and twenty seats [*thrones; symbolic of royalty, in other words, exaltation—see Revelation 3:21*]; and upon the seats I saw four and twenty elders sitting, clothed in white raiment, and they had on their heads crowns like gold.

5 And out of the throne proceeded lightnings and thunderings [*symbolic of God's presence, as on Mt. Sinai; Exodus 20:18*] and voices: and there were seven lamps of fire [*the seven leaders of the seven "wards"*] burning [*shining*] before the throne [*in front of the throne of the Father*], which are the seven Spirits [*JST "seven servants," in other words, the presiding officers of the seven "wards"; see Rev. 1:4*] of God.

**JST Revelation 4:5**

5 And out of the throne proceeded lightnings and thunderings and voices; and there were seven lamps of fire burning before the throne, which are the seven servants of God [*in other words, the presiding officers of the seven "wards" mentioned in Revelation 1:4*].

6 And before [*in front of*] the throne there was a sea of glass [*the celestialized earth; see D&C 77:1, 130:9*] like unto crystal: and in the midst of the throne, and round about the throne, were four beasts [*see D&C 77:2–3*] full of eyes [*representing light and knowledge; D&C 77:4*] before and behind [*in front and back*].

**JST Revelation 4:6**

6 And before the throne there was a sea of glass like unto crystal; and in the midst of the throne were the four and twenty elders; and round about the throne, were four beasts full of eyes before and behind.

7 And the first beast was like a lion, and the second beast like a calf, and the third beast had a face as a man, and the fourth beast was like a flying eagle [*D&C 77:4*].

8 And the four beasts had each of them six wings [*representing power to move, act, etc. in the service of God; D&C 77:4*] about him; and they were full of eyes within [*full of knowledge; D&C 77:4*]: and they rest not day and night [*never stop being loyal to God*], saying, Holy, holy, holy [*in Hebrew culture, repeating something three times makes it the highest superlative, i.e., the very best*], Lord God Almighty [*Elohim*], which was, and is, and is to come [*i.e., is eternal*].

9 And when those beasts give glory and honour and thanks to him [*the Father*] that sat on the throne, who liveth for ever and ever [*indicating that all created things respect and worship the Father*],

**JST Revelation 4:9**

9 And when those beasts give glory and honor and thanks to him that sits on the throne, who liveth forever and ever,

10 The four and twenty elders fall down before him that sat on the throne, and worship him that liveth for ever and ever [*i.e., these faithful elders are eternally loyal to God*], and cast their crowns before the throne [*show submission and respect to the Father and His authority*], saying,

**JST Revelation 4:10**

10 The four and twenty elders fall down before him that sits on the throne, and worship him that liveth forever and ever, and cast their crowns before the throne, saying,

11 Thou art worthy, O Lord, to receive glory [*praise; Strong's #1391*] and honour and power: for thou hast created all things, and for thy pleasure [*according to Thy will; Strong's #2307*] they are and were created.

# REVELATION 5

Chapter five is the most complete description we have in the scriptures of the premortal council wherein Christ was chosen to be our Savior and Redeemer. Most Christian religions do not believe in a premortal life. If someone is willing to believe the Bible, this chapter, in conjunction with Job 38:4–7, and Jeremiah 1:5, presents a chance to help them understand that we did live before we came to earth.

This chapter also contains one of the greatest collections of significant symbolic words and phrases anywhere in the scriptures. You may find it helpful to become familiar with these. A partial list follows:

## Symbolic words and Phrases

### Verse 1

**right hand:** covenant hand

**him that sat on the throne:** Heavenly Father (see verse 7)

**a book:** the Father's plan for us to be sent to this mortal world (Note that in Revelation 10:2, 8–10, "book" is a mission for John, see D&C 77:14, thus, "a book" can also be symbolic here of Christ's mission to be our Redeemer.)

**written within and on the backside:** **a** complete plan **sealed with seven seals:** the 7000 years of the earth's mortal existence (see D&C 7:7)

### Verse 2

**a strong angel:** a mighty angel (we don't know who this is)

**Who is worthy to open the book, and loose the seals thereof?** Who can carry out the Father's plan for us?

### Verse 3

**neither to look thereon:** No one could even come close to being our Savior and carrying out the Father's plan.

### Verse 4

**read the book:** carry out the Father's plan for us

### Verse 5

**the Lion of the tribe of Juda:** Christ (Jesus was from the tribe of Judah. See Heb. 7:14)

**the Root of David:** Christ (see Revelation 22:16)

**hath prevailed:** can carry out the Father's plan

### Verse 6

**in the midst:** the central focus

**a Lamb:** Christ; symbolic of being sacrificed

**as it had been slain:** The Atonement worked for us even in premortality, as if it had already been accomplished. See Elder Jeffery R. Holland, General Conference, Oct. 1995. See also quote in the Institute of Religion New Testament Student manual, published in 1978, p. 336.

**seven horns (JST "twelve horns"):** Horn symbolizes power. See scriptural examples in Topical Guide, p. 218, under "horn".

**seven (JST "twelve") Spirits of God sent forth into all the earth:** Twelve Apostles

**eyes:** light and knowledge, see D&C 7:4

### Verse 7

**he came and took the book:** Jesus accepted the mission to be our Savior.

**out of the right hand of him that sat upon the throne**: Jesus covenanted with the Father

1 And I saw in the right hand [*the covenant-making hand*] of him [*the Father; 5:7*] that sat on the throne a book [*containing the Father's plan; also a specific mission for Jesus*] written within [*on the inside*] and on the backside, sealed with seven seals [*containing information about the 7,000 years of the earth's temporal existence; see D&C 77:7*].

**JST Revelation 5:1**

1 And I saw in the right hand of him that sits on the throne a book written within and on the back side, sealed with seven seals.

We use Rev. 10:2, 8–9 plus D&C 77:14 to show us that "book," as used in verse 1, above, is symbolic of a mission or stewardship.

2 And I saw a strong angel [*one high in authority*] proclaiming with a loud voice, Who is worthy to open the book, and to loose the seals thereof [*i.e., who can carry out the Father's plan of salvation, including the Atonement, for us*]?

**JST Revelation 5:2**

2 And I saw a strong angel, and heard him proclaiming with a loud voice, Who is worthy to open the book, and loose the seals thereof?

3 And no man [*no common man*] in heaven, nor in earth, neither under the earth, was able to open the book, neither to look thereon [*i.e., there was no one to carry out the Father's plan and perform the Atonement; this was a dramatic moment in the vision (a very effective teaching technique) which created the "need" to know in John's mind*].

4 And I [*John*] wept much [*John has become deeply emotionally involved in the vision*], because no man was found worthy to open and to read the book, neither to look thereon [*none of God's spirit children was even close to being worthy or able to carry out the Father's plan or perform the Atonement*].

5 And one of the elders [*mentioned in Rev. 4:4*] saith unto me, Weep not: behold [*look!*], the Lion of the tribe of Juda [*Christ*], the Root of David [*Christ*], hath prevailed to open the book, and to loose the seven seals thereof. [*Jesus Christ can do it!*]

6 And I beheld [*I looked*], and, lo, in the midst of the throne and of the four beasts, and in the midst of the elders, stood a Lamb [*Christ*] as it had been slain [*symbolic of Christ's atoning blood, shed for us*], having seven horns and seven eyes, which are the seven Spirits of God sent forth into all the earth.

**JST Revelation 5:6**

6 And I beheld, and, lo, in the midst of the throne and of the four beasts, and in the midst of the elders, stood a Lamb as it had been slain, having twelve horns and twelve eyes, which are the twelve servants of God [*symbolic of the Twelve Apostles*], sent forth into all the earth.

If you will refer back to the symbolism notes included at the beginning of Revelation, in this study guide, you will note that the number 12 symbolizes God's divine organization here on earth.

7 And he [*Christ*] came and took the book [*i.e., accepted the calling*] out of the right hand [*covenant hand*] of him [*Elohim*] that sat upon the throne [*in other words, Jesus Christ made a covenant with the Father to be the Redeemer*].

Next, In verses 8–14, John beautifully describes all of heaven praising Christ for His willingness to perform the Atonement and be our Redeemer, thus carrying out the Father's plan.

8 And when he [*Christ*] had taken the book, the four beasts and four and twenty elders fell down before the Lamb, having every one of them harps [*harps symbolize being in the presence of God in biblical culture*], and golden vials [*containers*] full of odours [*incense; symbolic of prayers which rise up to*

*God*], which are the prayers of saints.

The phrase "they sung a new song," in verse 9, next, is a scriptural phrase which means, in effect, that they could now rejoice over something that they could not rejoice about before. In other words, they can now sing praises to our Redeemer, whereas, they couldn't before. They can now rejoice about blessings of the Atonement which are now available which were not available before. Another example of "new song" can be found in D&C 84:98–102, where a "new song" can be sung about the Millennium which has finally come.

9 And they sung a new song, saying, Thou [*Christ*] art worthy to take the book [*see verse 1, i.e., the mission to be the Savior and work out the Father's plan*], and to open the seals thereof [*and to carry out the work planned for each of the 1,000 year periods of the earths temporal history*]: for thou wast slain [*speaking of the Atonement as if it were already accomplished*], and hast redeemed us to God [*brought us to the Father*] by thy blood out of every kindred, and tongue, and people, and nation [*the gospel covenants are for all peoples of the world; the Pharisees of Jesus' day didn't like this concept because they felt that the Jews were superior to all other people and, consequently, all other people would be "second class" citizens in heaven*];

10 And hast made us unto our God kings and priests [*celestial glory; see Rev. 1:6*]: and we shall reign on the earth [*both during the Millennium (Rev. 20:4) and when it becomes the celestial kingdom; see D&C 132:20*].

11 And I beheld, and I heard the voice of many angels round about the throne [*of the Father; see Rev. 4:2 and 5:1*] and the beasts and the elders: and the number of them was ten thousand times ten thousand [*a hundred million*], and thousands of thousands [*plus millions more*];

The emphasis in verse 11, above, that there will be a great number of people in the celestial kingdom is very comforting. You may wish to cross-reference verse 11 with Revelation 7:9 and also with D&C 76:67 in which we learn that there will be "innumerable" people in celestial glory. This is not surprising when we consider the missionary work that is being done in the spirit world as well as the fact that "all children who die before they arrive at the years of accountability are saved in the celestial kingdom of heaven." See D&C 137:10.

12 Saying with a loud voice, Worthy is the Lamb [*Christ*] that was slain to receive power, and riches, and wisdom, and strength, and honour, and glory, and blessing.

13 And every creature which is in heaven [*birds, etc.*], and on the earth, and under the earth [*animals that burrow underground*], and such as are in the sea [*fish, etc.*], and all that are in them, heard I saying, Blessing, and honour, and glory, and power, be unto him [*the Father*] that sitteth upon the throne, and unto the Lamb [*Christ*] for ever and ever [*all animals, birds, fish, etc., will be resurrected too as a result of Christ's Atonement; see D&C 29:23–24*].

14 And the four beasts said, Amen [*"We agree."*]. And the four and twenty elders fell down and worshipped him that liveth for ever and ever.

# REVELATION 6

This is one of the most famous and well known chapters in the Book of Revelation. In it, the Lamb, Christ, opens six of the seven seals mentioned in Revelation 5:1. Joseph Smith tells us, in D&C 77:7, that each of the seals represents one thousand years of the earth's temporal or mortal existence. We understand this to mean that the earth has a total of 7,000 years from the time of the Fall of Adam and Eve to the end of the "little season" at the end of the Millennium (see D&C

77:6). It is important to remember that we do not know the exact date of Adam's Fall (see Bible Dictionary under "Chronology," p. 635, where it says, "Many dates cannot be fixed with certainty.") Thus, we cannot tell exactly where we are in relation to the 7,000 years.

In Revelation, chapter 6, we are given a very, very brief overview of each of the first six thousand year periods of the earth's temporal existence. In the following chapters of Revelation, many more details will be given, which are to be fulfilled near the end of the sixth thousand year period and in the beginning of the seventh thousand year period, before the Savior's Second Coming (see D&C 7:12–13).

The fact that the Lamb, the Savior, opens the seals is symbolic of the fact that Christ is in charge of things here on earth, under the Father's direction, and is carrying out the Father's plan as shown in Revelation, chapter five [*see notes for Revelation 5:1–4 and 5:5–7*]. There are four "horsemen" in this chapter, which are rather famous among Christians who study their Bibles. With the aid of symbolism given in the introduction of Revelation in this study guide, we can see major insights and descriptions given for each of these one thousand year periods as summarized in the following chart:

## Verses 1–2
## The First Thousand Years (ca. 4,000 to 3,000 BC):

"White" is symbolic of righteousness, purity, etc., and "horse" is symbolic of victory, might, triumph, etc. Thus, there is a great triumph of righteousness during the first thousand years. We don't know who this horseman is, but two good possibilities would be Adam and Enoch.

## Verses 3–4
## The Second Thousand Years (ca. 3,000 to 2,000 BC):

A red horse could symbolize the triumph of war, bloodshed, etc., possibly representing the wickedness during Noah's day. This horseman has a "great sword," representing terrible destruction.

## Verses 5–6
## The Third Thousand Years (ca. 2,000 to 1,000 BC):

A black horse and its rider could symbolize evil, spiritual darkness, etc., as well as the blackness and depression which accompanies famine. This period of the earth's history would include the days of Abraham, Joseph in Egypt, and the years of captivity in Egypt for the children of Israel. Famine was a major aspect of life during this one thousand year period. Abraham's brother, Haran, starved to death during this period (see Abraham 2:1). In fact, the rider of the black horse is holding "a pair of balances in his hand" which can be symbolic of famine and can represent that every morsel of food must be carefully measured out during times of famine (see Leviticus 26:26). Additional famine symbolism is found in the phrases "A measure of wheat for a penny," and "three measures of barley for a penny." Here, a "penny" represents a day's wages (see Matt. 20:2) and a "measure of wheat" is about one quart (see McConkie, *Doctrinal New Testament Commentary*, Vol. 3, p. 480).

## Verses 7–8
## The Fourth Thousand Years (ca. 1,000 to 0 BC):

The fourth horse is pale and its rider is named "Death." "Hell" seems to be following this horseman around and

could symbolize that spirit prison is gaining many new inmates during this thousand year period. The pale horse could represent that, after the riders of the red horse and the black horse have taken their toll, not much quality of life remains for those who have chosen wickedness as a lifestyle. It is during this time in history that we see Israel divided by civil war, Assyria carries the lost ten tribes away, Lehi and his family flee Jerusalem, the Babylonians conquer Jerusalem, Daniel is thrown into the lions' den, and the Romans become the rulers of the Holy Land.

The next two 1000-year periods do not involve "horsemen" but do give a very brief overview of events during those times.

## Verses 9–11 The Fifth Thousand Years (ca. AD 0 to 1,000):

The fifth seal would include the Savior's birth, the early Church, the persecutions of the Christians and the beginning centuries of the dark ages. In verses nine through eleven, John was shown early martyrs, members of the church organized by the Savior during His mortal mission who had been killed because they would not deny their testimonies. According to symbolism in verse 11, these righteous Saints were given "white robes" indicating that they had earned exaltation.

## Verses 12–16 The Sixth Thousand Years (ca. AD 1,000 to 2,000):

In these verses, John sees the Savior open the sixth seal, and is shown some signs of the times, including a great earthquake (verse 12). Perhaps, as a result of this earthquake, "every mountain and island were moved out of their places." These and other signs of the times occurring in the sixth seal appear to make the wicked think that the end of the world has come. Whatever the case, events which occur in the sixth seal cause the wicked to wish for anything necessary to prevent them from seeing God. These verses remind us that "wickedness never was happiness" (Alma 41:10), and that the wicked, when faced with the evil and foolishness of their agency choices, will be in great agony.

We will now study Revelation, chapter 6.

1 And I saw when the Lamb [*Christ*] opened one of the seals [*the first one, representing the first thousand years of the earth's temporal existence, i.e., approximately 4,000–3,000 BC; (D&C 77:7)*], and I heard, as it were the noise of thunder, one of the four beasts saying, Come and see.

**JST Revelation 6:1**

1 And I saw when the Lamb opened one of the seals, one of the four beasts, and I heard, as it were, the noise of thunder, saying, Come and see.

2 And I [*John*] saw, and behold a white horse [*symbolically, white can mean righteousness and horse represents victory*]: and he that sat on him had a bow; and a crown [*authority*] was given unto him: and he went forth conquering, and to conquer [*one possible interpretation could be Adam. Another, Enoch and his victories with the City of Enoch*].

3 And when he [*Christ*] had opened the second seal [*3,000–2,000 BC*], I heard the second beast say, Come and see.

4 And there went out another horse that was red [*bloodshed, war*]: and power was given to him [*perhaps Satan and wicked worldly leaders during the days of Noah*] that sat thereon to take peace from the earth, and that they should kill one another: and there was given unto him a great sword [*representing terrible destruction*].

5 And when he [*Christ*] had opened the third seal [*2,000–1,000 BC*], I heard the third beast say, Come and see. And I beheld [*I looked*], and lo a black horse [*evil, darkness, despair*]; and he that sat on him had a pair of balances [*representing famine; food had to be carefully measured and meted out*] in his hand. [*During this seal, Abraham went to Egypt because of famine; Joseph's brothers later came to him in Egypt because of famine; also, the Israelites were held as slaves in Egypt during this period.*]

6 And I heard a voice in the midst of the four beasts say, A measure [*two U.S. pints*] of wheat for a penny [*a day's wages*], and three measures of barley for a penny; and see thou hurt not [*don't waste*] the oil and the wine [*i.e., terrible famine*].

**JST Revelation 6:6**

6 And I heard a voice in the midst of the four beasts say, A measure of wheat for a penny, and three measures of barley for a penny; and hurt not thou the oil and the wine.

7 And when he [*Christ*] had opened the fourth seal [*1,000–0 BC; Assyrian captivity, ten tribes lost about 722 BC; Babylonian captivity about 588 BC; Daniel in lion's den; Romans take over prior to Christ's birth*], I heard the voice of the fourth beast say, Come and see.

8 And I looked, and behold a pale horse [*not much left of Israel, few righteous people, terrible conditions among the wicked, etc.*]: and his name that sat on him was Death, and Hell followed with him. And power was given unto them over the fourth part [*perhaps meaning not quite as severe destruction as in the wind up scenes of the world in Rev. 9:15*] of the earth, to kill with sword [*military destruction*], and with hunger, and with death [*pestilence, plagues*], and with the beasts of the earth.

9 And when he [*Christ*] had opened the fifth seal [*AD 0–1,000*], I saw under the altar [*altar represents sacrifice*] the souls of them that were slain for the word of God [*for the gospel*], and for the testimony which they held [*i.e., those who gave their lives for the gospel's sake*]:

10 And they [*the people who had given their lives for the gospel*] cried with a loud voice, saying, How long, O Lord, holy and true, dost thou not judge and avenge our blood on them [*the wicked*] that dwell on the earth [*i.e., when will the wicked get what's coming to them?; the same question is asked by Joseph Smith in D&C 121 and by Habakkuk in Habakkuk 1*]?

11 And white robes [*exaltation; 3:5*] were given unto every one of them [*the righteous martyrs in verse 9*]; and it was said unto them, that they should rest yet for a little season, until their fellowservants also and their brethren, that should be killed as they were, should be fulfilled [*i.e., others would have similar fates throughout earth's remaining history*].

12 And I beheld when he [*Christ*] had opened the sixth seal [*roughly AD 1,000–2,000*], and, lo, there was a great earthquake; and the sun became black as sackcloth of hair [*perhaps meaning black goat's hair used in weaving fabric*], and the moon became as blood [*i.e., great signs in heaven and earth during this period of time*];

13 And the stars of heaven [*perhaps including satellites, airplanes, etc., in our day*] fell unto the earth, even as a fig tree casteth her untimely figs, when she is shaken of a mighty wind.

John now jumps ahead to the Second Coming for a few verses. Caution, do not put the Second Coming in the sixth seal. See headings to Rev. 8 and 9 and D&C 77:13.

14 And the heaven departed as a scroll when it is rolled together; and every mountain and island were moved out of their places [*one continent, one ocean again; D&C 133:22–24, Gen. 10:25*].

**JST Revelation 6:14**

14 And the heavens opened as a scroll is opened when it is rolled together; and every mountain, and island, was moved out of its place.

15 And the kings [*wicked political leaders*] of the earth, and the great men, and the rich men, and the chief captains, and the mighty men, and every bondman, and every free man [*i.e., all the wicked*], hid themselves in the dens [*caves*] and in the rocks of the mountains [*like Isaiah said the wicked would do at the Second Coming; see Isaiah 2:19, and 2 Nephi 12, verses 10, 19 and 21*];

16 And said to the mountains and rocks, Fall on us, and hide us from the face of him [*the Father; Rev. 5:1, 7, 13*] that sitteth on the throne, and from the wrath [*anger*] of the Lamb [*Christ*]:

17 For the great day of his [*the Savior's*] wrath is come; and who shall be able to stand [*i.e., who will be able to survive the Second Coming*]? [*Answer: those living a terrestrial or celestial lifestyle. D&C 5:19 plus 76:81–85 and 88:100–101 tell us that those who live the wicked lifestyle of telestials, which includes lying, stealing, sexual immorality, and murder (and of course, sons of perdition) will be destroyed by the Savior's glory at the Second Coming and will not be resurrected until after the Millennium is over.*]

# REVELATION 7

John now returns to the 6th seal and tells more about it. He will show us that great missionary work will take place during the sixth 1,000 year period of the earth's temporal existence. He will also show that many will eventually be exalted out of all nations. This chapter is perhaps best known for verse 4 in which the 144,000 are mentioned. We will say more about them when we come to that verse.

As we begin with verse 1, it helps to know that "wind," as used in the scriptures, is often symbolic of destruction.

1 And after these things I saw four angels [*with power and authority to save life or destroy, and to oversee the preaching of the gospel to the whole earth; D&C 77:8*] standing on the four corners of the earth, holding the four winds [*north, east, south, and west winds which symbolically have power to bless mankind from all directions or cause great destruction from all directions*] of the earth, that the wind should not blow on the earth, nor on the sea, nor on any tree [*i.e., these four angels hold massive destruction back until the restoration and ensuing gathering of the righteous have taken place; see verse 3*].

2 And I saw another angel [*Elias; D&C 77:9; represents several angels with keys, see McConkie,* Doctrinal New Testament Commentary, *Bookcraft, Inc., 1973, Vol 3, p. 492*] ascending from the east [*"east" typically represents coming from heaven, since the sun, representing celestial glory and heaven, appears first from the east*], having the seal of the living God: and he cried with a loud voice to the four angels, to whom it was given to hurt the earth and the sea [*they are not just destroying angels; they save life too, D&C 77:8*],

**JST Revelation 7:2**

2 And I saw another angel ascending from the east, having the seal of the living God; and I heard him cry with a loud voice to the four angels, to whom it was given to hurt the earth and the sea,

3 Saying, Hurt not the earth, neither the sea, nor the trees [*do not allow the final destructions prior to the Second Coming*], till we have sealed the servants of our God [*the righteous*] in their foreheads [*i.e., the faithful will be gathered to the gospel before the final*

*destruction; anciently, some cultures literally marked their foreheads indicating which religion they were loyal to*].

4 And I heard the number of them which were sealed: and there were sealed an hundred and forty and four thousand [*these are not the only ones saved; see verse 9*] of all the tribes of the children of Israel.

**JST Revelation 7:4**

4 And the number of them who were sealed, were an hundred and forty and four thousand of all the tribes of the children of Israel.

Who are the 144,000? Joseph Smith answered this question for us in D&C 77:11. He said that these are high priests, 12,000 out of each of the tribes of Israel, who will "bring as many as will come to the church of the Firstborn." The "church of the Firstborn" is the Church of Jesus Christ of Latter-day Saints and often includes the connotation of being exalted. Thus, we see this great group of high priests much involved in the gathering of the righteous spoken of in verses 1–3, above.

5 Of the tribe of Juda were sealed twelve thousand. Of the tribe of Reuben were sealed twelve thousand. Of the tribe of Gad were sealed twelve thousand.

6 Of the tribe of Aser were sealed twelve thousand. Of the tribe of Nepthalim were sealed twelve thousand. Of the tribe of Manasses were sealed twelve thousand.

7 Of the tribe of Simeon were sealed twelve thousand. Of the tribe of Levi were sealed twelve thousand. Of the tribe of Issachar were sealed twelve thousand.

8 Of the tribe of Zabulon were sealed twelve thousand. Of the tribe of Joseph were sealed twelve thousand. Of the tribe of Benjamin were sealed twelve thousand.

If you look very carefully at verses 5–8, above, you will see that the tribes of Dan and Ephraim are missing. We have no idea why they are left out here and speculation doesn't help. We know for sure that they are not "left out" as far as the Lord's blessings are concerned, because many members of the Church are from the lineage of Ephraim, and quite a number are from the tribe of Dan.

9 After this I beheld, and, lo, a great multitude, which no man could number [*i.e., many more than 144,000 are saved; see also D&C 76:67*], of all nations, and kindreds, and people, and tongues, stood before the throne [*of the Father*], and before the Lamb, clothed with white robes [*symbolic of exaltation*], and palms [*symbolic of joy and triumph, victory*] in their hands;

10 And cried with a loud voice, saying, Salvation to our God [*the Father*] which sitteth upon the throne, and unto the Lamb.

11 And all the angels stood round about the throne, and about the elders and the four beasts [*see notes in chapter 4*], and fell before the throne on their faces [*a way of showing humility and worship in Biblical culture*], and worshipped God,

12 Saying, Amen ["*We agree.*"]: Blessing, and glory, and wisdom, and thanksgiving, and honour, and power, and might, be unto our God for ever and ever. Amen.

John is now invited to become an active participant in the vision, as one of the elders asks him a question about what he has just seen. Notice his wise and careful answer.

13 And one of the elders answered [*asked a question*], saying unto me [*John*], What are these which are arrayed in white robes? and whence came they [*i.e., who are the people dressed in white in verse 9*]?

14 And I said unto him, Sir, thou knowest [*please tell me*]. And he said to me, These are they which came out of great tribulation [*trials and persecutions*], and

have washed their robes [*had their sins cleansed by the Atonement of Christ; something each of us must do in our own lives, i.e., symbolic of repentance, obedience*], and made them white [*i.e., become clean*] in the blood of the Lamb [*i.e., the Atonement can cleanse completely; compare with Isaiah 1:16–18*].

15 Therefore are they [*this is the reason they are*] before the throne of God [*they are in celestial glory*], and serve him day and night [*keep His commandments day and night*] in his temple: and he that sitteth on the throne shall dwell among them.

16 [*John now briefly and beautifully describes some benefits of celestial glory.*] They shall hunger no more, neither thirst any more; neither shall the sun light on them, nor any heat.

17 For the Lamb [*the Savior*] which is in the midst of the throne shall feed them, and shall lead them unto living fountains of waters: and God shall wipe away all tears from their eyes [*the final state of the righteous; in other words, it is worth repenting and returning to God's presence!*].

# REVELATION 8

Many people think that the Savior's Second Coming will occur at the end of the sixth seal. According to the Lord, this is not so. In D&C 77:12, Joseph Smith tells us that the things prophesied in Revelation, chapter 8, will happen "in the beginning of the seventh thousand years," before the coming of the Lord. Indeed, we who live in the last days live in a day when prophecies are being fulfilled all around us. It is a glorious time to be alive, a time when testimonies can be strengthened by observing the fulfillment of many ancient prophecies known as the signs of the times, which will lead up to the actual Second Coming of the Lord. Let's watch now and see some of the things that will take place early in the seventh seal, before the Savior comes to usher in the Millennium.

1 And when he had opened the seventh seal [*roughly AD 2,000–3,000*], there was silence in heaven about the space of half an hour.

This "silence" is also mentioned in D&C 88:95. We have not been told yet what this means. So far in the opening of the seals, we have been dealing with the earth's time system. Some people speculate about this half hour of silence and suggest that it might be about 21 years in the Lord's time system, and thus we would be 21 years without revelation. This has no merit, especially in view of Daniel 2:35, 44–45, in which we are assured that this restored Church "shall stand forever" and thus we will have continuous revelation right up to the Second Coming.

2 And I saw the seven angels which stood before God; and to them were given seven trumpets [*perhaps symbolic of perfecting or finishing his work; in Biblical number symbolism, "seven" represents being complete or perfection*].

We will pause to mention an interesting possibility in conjunction with Biblical numerical symbolism. As indicated in the symbolism notes at the beginning of Revelation in this study guide, the number three represents God, and the number four represents man. Therefore, 3 (God) plus 4 (man) equals 7 (perfection), i.e., when man works with God, the result is perfection, ultimately, exaltation.

3 And another angel came and stood at the altar [*worshiped*], having a golden censer [*symbolic of worship*]; and there was given unto him much incense [*incense rises, prayers "rise;" hence incense is symbolic of prayers*], that he should offer it with the prayers of all saints upon the golden altar which was before the throne [*in front of the throne*

*of the Father; see Rev. 4:4 and 5:5; in other words, Saints and angels worship God*].

4 And the smoke of the incense, which came with the prayers of the saints, ascended up [*rose up*] before God out of the angel's hand [*the prayers reached God*].

5 And the angel took the censer, and filled it with fire [*punishments of God*] of the altar, and cast it into the earth [*punishments of God pour out upon the earth early in the seventh seal, before Second Coming*]: and there were voices, and thunderings, and lightnings, and an earthquake [*more signs of the times*].

6 And the seven angels [*in verse 2, above*] which had the seven trumpets [*since "seven" is symbolic of completeness or perfection, this could be symbolic of the completing, perfecting, or finishing of all things necessary before the Second Coming; see D&C 77:12*] prepared themselves to sound.

Just a thought about verses 7–12, next. There is much use of symbolism. Symbolism can be understood many ways and thus can present many different messages to us as directed by the Holy Ghost. So it is with the symbolism in these next verses. One could easily look at the damage to earth, trees, grass, sea, rivers, fountains of waters, waters, sun, moon, and stars, as shown in this chapter, and consider it to be prophetic reference to severe ecological damage in the last days prior to the Second Coming.

Another possibility is that one could consider "trees" and "grass" to represent people, as is often the case in the scriptures. If so, the prophetic symbolism here could refer to damage done to people by evil in the last days. We could look at the "rivers," "fountains of waters" and "waters" and consider John 4:10 and 14 wherein the Savior teaches of the "living water" (the gospel, including the Atonement) and its cleansing and refreshing power in our lives. Then we could see prophetic reference to the damage done to the "living water" in people's lives by the wickedness in the last days. Again, we could look at the "sun, moon, and stars" as representing spiritual light from above and the darkening of them as spiritual darkness increases in the last days.

Chapter 8 also mentions hail, fire, blood, and so forth. It is interesting to observe that some of these plagues and pestilences to be poured out upon the earth in the last days, prior to the coming of the Lord, are reminiscent of some which took place in order to prepare the way for Moses and the children of Israel to gain freedom from Egyptian bondage. Revelation chapter 16 contains a number of these plagues also. We will make a brief list of these plagues from both chapters 8 and 16, which lead us to realize that the ten plagues are, in effect, to be repeated in the last days before the Second Coming, and for the same purpose (to serve as a wake up call to repent and be delivered from spiritual bondage).

**From Revelation Chapter 8:**

Verse 7: **hail and fire** (Exodus 9:23)

Verse 7: **blood** (Exodus 7:17)

Verse 8: **sun. . . darkened** (Exodus 10: 21–22)

**From Revelation Chapter 16:**

Verse 2: **sores** (Exodus 9:9)

Verse 3: **blood** (Exodus 7:17)

Verse 8: **fire** (Exodus 9:23–24)

Verse 10: **darkness** (Exodus 10:21–22)

Verse 13: **frogs** (Exodus 8:2)

Verse 21: **hail** (Exodus 9:18)

7 The first angel sounded, and there followed hail and fire mingled with blood [*similar to plagues in Egypt whose purpose likewise was to humble the wicked and prepare Israelites for redemption from wickedness*], and they were cast

upon the earth: and the third part of trees was burnt up, and all green grass was burnt up [*perhaps indicating that significant amounts of earth's greenery will be destroyed prior to the Second Coming, rain forests razed, acid rain damage, etc.*].

8 And the second angel sounded, and as it were a great mountain burning with fire was cast into the sea: and the third part of the sea became blood [*similar to the plague in Egypt; Exodus 7:17*];

9 And the third part of the creatures which were in the sea, and had life, died; and the third part of the ships were destroyed [*much destruction everywhere*].

10 And the third angel sounded, and there fell a great star [*Lucifer; Isaiah 14:12, D&C 76:25–27*] from heaven, burning as it were a lamp, and it fell upon the third part of the rivers, and upon the fountains of waters [*Satan has counterfeit "living water," i.e., false religions and philosophies*];

11 And the name of the star is called Wormwood [*a very bitter substance; see Bible Dictionary under "Wormwood;" i.e., followers of Satan have a "bitter" fate*]: and the third part of the waters became wormwood; and many men died of the waters, because they were made bitter.

12 And the fourth angel sounded, and the third part of the sun was smitten, and the third part of the moon, and the third part of the stars; so as the third part of them was darkened [*perhaps symbolizing that there would be great spiritual darkness upon the earth in the last days before the coming of the Savior*], and the day shone not for a third part of it, and the night likewise [*perhaps referring in part to spiritual darkness as well as physical darkness caused by burning oil fields, pollution, volcanic ash, etc., in the last days*].

**JST Revelation 8:12**

12 And the fourth angel sounded, and the third part of the sun was smitten, and the third part of the moon, and the third part of the stars; so that the third part of them was darkened, and the day shone not for a third part of it, and the night likewise.

The "one third" used in the above verses might be a symbolic tie in with the "one third" who were cast out with Satan (Rev. 12:4), thus symbolizing their destructive influence upon the earth in the last days.

13 And I beheld, and heard an angel flying through the midst of heaven, saying with a loud voice, Woe, woe, woe, to the inhabiters [*inhabitants*] of the earth by reason of [*because of*] the other voices of the trumpet of the three angels [*in verse 2, above*], which are yet to sound [*i.e., worse is yet to come*]!

# REVELATION 9

This chapter continues with prophecies of events which will take place in the seventh seal, prior to the Second Coming.

The JST makes a very significant change to verse 1. As it stands in the Bible, it sounds like Lucifer is given the "key" to the bottomless pit. However, the JST informs us that the key is given to a powerful angel, through whose power and authority limits are placed upon Satan and his kingdom (see verse 4).

1 And the fifth angel sounded, and I saw a star [*Lucifer*] fall from heaven unto the earth: and to him was given the key of the bottomless pit.

**JST Revelation 9:1**

1 And the fifth angel sounded, and I saw a star fall from heaven unto the earth; and to the angel was given the key of the bottomless pit.

In verses 2 and 3, next, we see all

of the forces of hell unleashed in the final days before the coming of the Lord. There is much imagery here. We see "the bottomless pit" representing hell, Satan's kingdom, etc. We see "smoke." In a house fire, "smoke" gets into everything and causes much damage. Thus, "smoke," as used here, can be symbolic of evil and wickedness permeating every aspect of society. It arises out of the pit and darkens the light of the sun, reminding us that Satan's goal is to obscure the spiritual light which comes from above and leave us in spiritual darkness. "Locusts" bring to mind one of the plagues in Egypt (Exodus 10:4) and can symbolize seemingly countless hordes of the wicked working their evil designs upon the earth in the last days.

2 And he [*the angel in JST verse 1*] opened the bottomless pit [*allowed Satan to unleash all the forces of hell!*]; and there arose a smoke [*Satan's "dark" influence*] out of the pit, as the smoke of a great furnace; and the sun and the air were darkened by reason of the smoke of the pit [*Satan and his evil hosts have great influence in the last days*].

3 And there came out of the smoke [*Satan's influence; see verse 2*] locusts [*symbolic of countless numbers of wicked in the last days*] upon the earth: and unto them was given power, as the scorpions of the earth have power [*scorpions have power to cause much suffering if people get close enough to them; so also is the case with wickedness*].

It is very important that we know that God has power over Satan and his wicked followers. He sets limits on them, as we see in verse 4, next.

4 And it was commanded them [*Satan and his hosts have limits put upon them by God*] that they should not hurt the grass of the earth, neither any green thing [*perhaps representing those who are still growing toward heaven*], neither any tree [*protection for the righteous; trees often represent people, for instance Isaiah 10:19*]; but only those men which have not the seal of God in their foreheads [*i.e., Satan only has power to "hurt" the spirituality of the wicked who do not have God's seal, i.e., who are not loyal to God*].

5 And to them [*Satan and his hosts*] it was given that they should not kill them [*the wicked in verse 4 who have not the seal of God in their foreheads*], but that they should be tormented five months [*through this torment, hopefully, some of them would see Satan for what he is and repent*]: and their torment was as the torment of a scorpion, when he striketh a man.

What is the significance of "five months" as seen in chapter nine? Answer: We don't know. We do know that the life cycle of a locust is about five months (see Jay and Donald Parry, *Understanding the Book of Revelation*, p. 118), so it could symbolize that Satan and his evil forces have a limited time, as stated in Revelation 12:12. It could also be a symbolical tie in with the "fifth angel" in verse 1.

6 And in those days [*the last days*] shall men seek death, and shall not find it; and shall desire to die, and death shall flee from them [*some plagues are worse than death*].

7 And the shapes of the locusts were like unto horses [*horse is symbolic of military victory, i.e., Satan had much success; there are almost countless people involved in military actions in the last days*] prepared unto battle; and on their heads were as it were crowns like gold [*Satan's counterfeit rewards of power and wicked temporary glory lead many to follow him*], and their faces were as the faces of [*wicked*] men.

8 And they had hair as the hair of women [*perhaps long hair might cause people in New Testament times to think of Samson's long hair and great strength and his destructive misuse of power; Judges 14–16*], and their teeth were as [*like*] the

teeth of lions [*lion is symbolic of great power, i.e., they were able to inflict much damage, destruction*].

9 And they had breastplates [*armor*], as it were breastplates of iron; and the sound of their wings [*airplanes*?] was as the sound of chariots of many horses running to battle [*noises of modern military machinery in action?*].

10 And they had tails like unto scorpions [*modern warfare, tanks, flame throwers, rifles, etc.?*], and there were stings in their tails: and their power was to hurt men five months. [*We don't know for sure what the five months symbolize here or in verse 5. Perhaps it might simply be symmetry tying in with the fifth angel in verse one, thus meaning the "five months" or time spoken of by the fifth angel during which Satan rages in the last days.*]

11 And they had a king [*Satan*] over them, which is the angel of the bottomless pit, whose name in the Hebrew tongue is Abaddon [*ruin, destruction; Strong's #0003*], but in the Greek tongue hath his name Apollyon [*Destroyer; Strong's #0623*].

Moses 5:24 gives another name for Satan. It is "Perdition" which means "utter loss" or "destruction." See also 2 Thessalonians 2:3.

12 One woe is past [*of the three woes spoken of in 8:13*]; and, behold, there come two woes more hereafter.

Just a bit more about the woes spoken of in verse 12, above. In chapter eight, verse 13, John was told that there were "three angels, which are yet to sound," in other words, three more "woes" or plagues to come. Revelation 9, verses 1–11, have described one of the three "woes" for us, which leaves two more to come.

13 And the sixth angel sounded [*still dealing with occurrences in the beginning of the seventh seal, before the Lord comes; see heading to chapter 9 in our Bible*], and I heard a voice from the four horns [*of the altar, see 1 Kings 1:50; symbolic of a place of safety, refuge, protection; in other words, heaven*] of the golden [*heavenly*] altar which is before God [*i.e., he heard a voice from heaven*],

14 Saying to the sixth angel [*the sixth of the seven angels in Rev. 8:2*] which had the trumpet, Loose the four angels [*Satan's angels of destruction; counterfeits of God's four righteous angels in Rev. 7:1; i.e., Satan is the great counterfeiter*!] which are bound [*by God's power*] in the great river Euphrates.

**JST Revelation 9:14**

14 Saying to the sixth angel which had the trumpet, Loose the four angels which are bound in the bottomless pit.

15 And the four angels [*evil angels*] were loosed, which were prepared for an hour, and a day, and a month, and a year, for to slay the third part of men. [*Perhaps one third ties in symbolically with the one third wicked in Rev. 12:4 indicating that Satan and his hosts will devastate a great number of people on earth, just as he did in the war in heaven.*]

16 And the number of the army of the horsemen [*Satan's wicked followers*] were two hundred thousand thousand [*200 million, i.e., innumerable*!]: and I heard the number of them.

**JST Revelation 9:16**

16 And the number of the army of the horsemen were two hundred thousand thousand; and I saw the number of them.

17 And thus I saw the horses [*symbolic of military victory*] in the vision, and them that sat on them [*Satan and his followers*], having breastplates of fire, and of jacinth [*a precious stone, perhaps symbolizing that materialism will lead many to follow Satan; could also mean that misuse of wealth will cause much sorrow and destruction in the last*

*days*], and brimstone [*molten sulphur; symbolic of destruction*]: and the heads of the horses were as the heads of lions [*capable of much destruction*]; and out of their mouths issued fire and smoke and brimstone [*i.e., terrible devastations will occur in the last days*].

18 By these three [*fire, smoke and brimstone in verse 17, above*] was the third part of men killed, by the fire, and by the smoke, and by the brimstone, which issued out of their mouths.

19 For their power is in their mouth [*perhaps including, symbolically, the power of the media in the last days to destroy*], and in their tails [*perhaps referring to "scorpion" in verse 5, which could symbolize military weapons, tanks, flame throwers, missiles, etc.*]: for their tails were like unto serpents, and had heads, and with them they do hurt.

20 And the rest of the men which were not killed by these plagues yet repented not [*a sad fact*] of the works of their hands, that they should not worship devils, and idols of gold, and silver, and brass, and stone, and of wood: which neither can see, nor hear, nor walk [*i.e., the remaining wicked went right on with their wicked lifestyles in spite of the destruction all around them*]:

21 Neither repented they of their murders, nor of their sorceries [*witchcraft, etc.*], nor of their fornication [*sexual immorality*], nor of their thefts.

# REVELATION 10

This chapter is particularly touching when one realizes that by this time (approximately AD 95) John has long been the only Apostle remaining from the Church which Jesus established in the Holy Land. He was told that he would "tarry" (see John 21:21–23 combined with D&C 7:3), but, as far as we know, nothing had yet transpired with respect to that promise. He is now an old man, likely in his nineties, and a prisoner on the Isle of Patmos. Imagine his feelings when he is told that he would yet prophesy before the nations and carry out a great mission among the people of the earth! We know that he was translated and has not yet died, rather, has continued assisting with the work of the Lord here on earth. He will continue to do so until the Second Coming, at which time he will be resurrected.

1 And I saw another mighty angel [*this appears to be the seventh of the angels in 8:2; if so, it might be Adam, the "seventh angel" in D&C 88:106, 110, 112*] come down from heaven, clothed with a cloud: and a rainbow was upon his head, and his face was as it were the sun, and his feet as pillars of fire [*quite a description of Michael or Adam, if he is the seventh angel spoken of here*]:

> The "rainbow upon his head" in verse 1, above, could tie in with the "rainbow round about the throne" of the Father, in Rev. 4:3. If so, it might be symbolic of the splendid power of God and of exaltation.

2 And he had in his hand a little book [*a mission for John; see verses 8–10, also D&C 77:14*] open: and he set his right foot upon the sea, and his left foot on the earth [*D&C 88:110; i.e., this angel has a large jurisdiction*],

3 And cried with a loud voice, as when a lion roareth: and when he had cried, seven thunders uttered their voices [*seven angels with seven seals; D&C 88:108–110*].

4 And when the seven thunders had uttered their voices, I [*John*] was about to write: and I heard a voice from heaven saying unto me, Seal up those things which the seven thunders uttered, and write them not [*in other words, they are not yet to be revealed to the world in the scriptures*].

**JST Revelation 10:4**

4 And when the seven thunders had uttered their voices, I was about to write; and I heard a voice from heaven saying unto me, Those things are sealed up which the seven thunders uttered, and write them not.

5 And the angel [*in verses 1 and 2, above*] which I saw stand upon the sea and upon the earth lifted up his hand to heaven,

6 And sware [*promised*] by him that liveth for ever and ever [*spoke with authority from God*], who created heaven, and the things that therein are, and the earth, and the things that therein are, and the sea, and the things which are therein, that there should be time no longer [*that there will be no more delay, in other words, "Let the Millennium begin."*]:

7 But in the days of the voice of the seventh angel, when he shall begin to sound, the mystery [*plans; Strong's #3466*] of God should be finished [*completed; Strong's #5055*], as he hath declared to his servants the prophets.

8 And the voice which I heard from heaven spake unto me again, and said, Go and take the little book [*a mission for John; D&C 77:14*] which is open in the hand of the angel which standeth upon the sea and upon the earth.

9 And I went unto the angel, and said unto him, Give me the little book [*i.e., I accept the mission*]. And he said unto me, Take it, and eat it up [*i.e., "internalize" it, make it a part of you*]; and it shall make thy belly bitter, but it shall be in thy mouth sweet as honey [*being a servant of God to the people has both bitter and sweet aspects*].

10 And I took the little book out of the angel's hand, and ate it up [*"internalized it"; made it a part of me*]; and it was in my mouth sweet as honey: and as soon as I had eaten it, my belly was bitter [*working with stubborn, unrepentant people can sometimes cause indigestion indeed!*].

11 And he said unto me, Thou must prophesy again before many peoples, and nations, and tongues, and kings [*i.e., you have a great mission yet to perform on earth, a very significant and encouraging statement, since John at this time, about AD 95, was banished on the Isle of Patmos in a prison colony. In D&C 7, we are told that John will "tarry" or remain until the Second Coming. In June, 1831, Joseph Smith said "that John the Revelator was then among the ten tribes of Israel . . . to prepare them for their return." See* History of the Church, *vol. 1, p. 176.*]

# REVELATION 11

We are not alone in the Christian world in believing that the events of the last days spoken of in this chapter will take place. This chapter is one of the most famous among Christians throughout the world. They, like we, believe that the mission of these two prophets, ending with their martyrdom and being brought back to life, will signify that the Second Coming of the Savior is close. Revelation 11:3 refers to them as "two witnesses" and Revelation 11:10 refers to them as "two prophets." In D&C 77:15, the Prophet Joseph Smith calls them "two prophets." Therefore, we see them as two witnesses, fulfilling the law of witnesses (D&C 6:28) and as two prophets holding the keys to control the elements, etc., as shown in verse 6.

It is interesting to point out several parallels between the ministry of these two prophets and the ministry of the Savior. For instance, Christ's formal mission was carried out in the Holy Land and lasted about three years. The mission of these two prophets in the last days will be to the Holy Land and will last about three years. The Savior is the "light of the world." The two prophets are

"candlesticks" (verse 4) which carry the light from the Savior to the world. Jesus demonstrated His power over the elements during His mortal ministry. The two prophets will be given power over the elements during their ministry (verse 6). Christ was crucified when He had completed His mortal mission. The two prophets will be killed after they have completed their mission (verse 7). The wicked rejoiced in the Savior's death. The wicked will rejoice in the slaying of the two prophets (verses 8–10). Jesus was resurrected after three days. The two will be resurrected [*see heading to chapter 11*] after three days. Great destruction accompanied the death of the Savior. Great destruction will accompany the resurrection of the two prophets [*verse 13*]. Many were converted by Christ's resurrection. Many will be converted after the resurrection of these two prophets [*verse 13, last phrase.*]

1 [*John is the only living apostle remaining in the eastern hemisphere at this time. He is told here to see how the Church is doing in his day.*] And there was given me [*John*] a reed [*a measuring device*] like unto a rod: and the angel stood, saying, Rise, and measure the temple of God, and the altar, and them that worship therein [*i.e., study current conditions among the Saints, see how they "measure up"*].

2 But the court [*the courtyard or temple grounds*] which is without [*outside of*] the temple leave out, and measure it not; for it is given unto the Gentiles [*apostasy is coming*]: and the holy city [*Jerusalem*] shall they tread under foot forty and two months [*perhaps referring to the 42 months spoken of in verse 3. Jerusalem will be downtrodden by Gentiles for hundreds of years. The universal apostasy alluded to here will end in the spring of 1820 when Joseph Smith has his first vision.*]

3 And I will give power unto my two witnesses [*two prophets to the Jews in the last days; D&C 77:15*], and they shall prophesy [*serve, minister, prophesy, etc.*] a thousand two hundred and threescore days [*42 months or 3 1/2 years, about the same length as Christ's ministry*], clothed in sackcloth [*in humility*].

4 These are the two olive trees [*olive trees provide olive oil for lamps so people can be prepared to meet Christ; compare with the parable of the ten virgins in Matthew 25:1–13*], and the two candlesticks [*hold light so people can see clearly*] standing before the God of the earth.

5 And if any man will hurt them [*the two prophets*], fire [*the power of God to destroy*] proceedeth out of their mouth, and devoureth their enemies [*the two prophets will be protected during their mission*]: and if any man will hurt them, he must in this manner be killed [*he will be killed by the power of God; Strong's #1163*].

6 These [*two prophets*] have power to shut heaven [*have the power of God; compare with the Prophet Nephi in Helaman 10:5–10 and 11:1–6*], that it rain not in the days of their prophecy: and have power over waters to turn them to blood, and to smite the earth with all plagues [*to encourage people to repent; to deliver from evil, bondage, as with the plagues in Egypt*], as often as they will.

7 And when they shall have finished their testimony [*ministry*], the beast [*Satan*] that ascendeth out of the bottomless pit [*Rev. 9:1–2*] shall make war against them [*the two prophets*], and shall overcome them, and kill them.

8 And their dead bodies shall lie in the street of the great city [*Jerusalem*], which spiritually is called Sodom and Egypt [*i.e., is very wicked*], where also our Lord was crucified.

9 And they [*the wicked*] of the people and kindreds and tongues and nations shall see their dead bodies three days and an half [*perhaps symbolically tying in with their 3 1/2 year ministry as well as the Savior's three days in the tomb; the Savior was killed, too, by the wicked for trying to save them*], and shall not suffer [*allow*] their dead bodies to be put in graves [*many in eastern cultures believed that if the body is not buried, the spirit is bound to wander the earth in misery forever*].

10 And they that dwell upon the earth [*not just people in Jerusalem; implies that knowledge of the death of the two prophets will be known worldwide*] shall rejoice over them, and make merry, and shall send gifts one to another [*people all over the world will cheer and send gifts to one another to celebrate the deaths of these two prophets*]; because these two prophets tormented them [*the wicked*] that dwelt on the earth [*implies that these prophets' influence was felt and irritated the wicked far beyond Jerusalem*].

11 And after three days and an half the Spirit of life from God entered into them [*they are resurrected at this time; McConkie,* Doctrinal New Testament Commentary, *Bookcraft, Inc., 1973, Vol. 3, p. 511*], and they stood upon their feet; and great fear fell upon them which saw them.

12 And they [*the wicked who were celebrating*] heard a great voice from heaven saying unto them [*the two slain prophets*], Come up hither. And they ascended up to heaven in a cloud; and their enemies beheld [*saw*] them.

13 And the same hour [*immediately*] was there a great earthquake, and the tenth part of the city fell, and in the earthquake were slain of men seven thousand: and the remnant were affrighted, and gave glory to the God of heaven [*perhaps implying that some of the wicked were converted as was the case with the Savior's resurrection and also when Lazarus was brought back from the dead; if so, the deaths of the two prophets bore immediate fruit in helping some begin returning to God*].

14 The second woe [*Rev. 9:12–21; 10; 11:1–13*] is past [*one more to go; Rev. 8:13*]; and, behold, the third woe [*the burning at the Second Coming*] cometh quickly.

15 And the seventh angel sounded; and there were great voices in heaven, saying, The kingdoms of this world are become the kingdoms of our Lord, and of his Christ [*i.e., Christ will now come to rule and the Millennium will begin*]; and he shall reign for ever and ever.

**JST Revelation 11:15**

15 And the seventh angel sounded; and there were great voices in heaven, saying, The kingdoms of this world are become the kingdom of our Lord, and of his Christ; and he shall reign for ever and ever.

Even though the JST change for verse 15, above consisted only of changing "kingdoms" to "kingdom," the change is doctrinally significant. When the Savior comes to rule and reign on earth for the thousand years, He will have just one kingdom on earth, and it will be a time of unity and peace.

16 And the four and twenty elders [*who had asked how long they must wait for justice to be done upon the wicked; Rev. 6:10*], which sat before God on their seats, fell upon their faces [*a show of humility and respect in Bible culture*], and worshipped God,

17 Saying, We give thee thanks, O Lord God Almighty, which art, and wast, and art to come [*in other words, the Lord is eternal*]; because thou hast taken to thee thy great power [*i.e., have finally taken over*], and hast reigned [*finally will rule the earth, during the Millennium*].

18 And the nations were angry, and thy wrath [*righteous anger at the wicked*] is come, and the time of the dead, that

they should be judged, and that thou shouldest give reward unto thy servants the prophets, and to the saints, and them that fear [*respect and honor*] thy name, small and great [*the hardly-known righteous as well as the widely-known righteous*]; and shouldest destroy them [*the wicked*] which destroy [*corrupt*] the earth.

19 And the temple of God was opened in heaven, and there was seen in his temple the ark of his testament [*the ark of the covenant was behind the veil in the Holy of Holies in Israel's temple, and when the high priest passed through the veil into the presence of the ark, it symbolized entering into the presence of God; thus, the symbolism here is that the righteous may now enter the presence of the Lord*]: and there were lightnings, and voices, and thunderings, and an earthquake, and great hail [*perhaps this last phrase is a brief review of woes and events leading up to the Second Coming as mentioned in verses 13 and 15 above as well as elsewhere, rather than being a prophesy of things yet to come*].

## REVELATION 12

This is the most revised chapter in the JST version of Revelation. The Prophet changed the verse sequence in several places. For your convenience, at the end of this chapter, we will include the entire Joseph Smith Translation of chapter 12.

1 And there appeared a great wonder in heaven; a woman [*the true Church—see JST verse 7*] clothed with the sun, and the moon under her feet [*symbolic of beauty and glory*], and upon her head a crown [*symbolic of power*] of twelve stars [*the twelve Apostles*]:

**JST Revelation 12:1**

1 And there appeared a great sign in heaven, in the likeness of things on the earth; a woman clothed with the sun, and the moon under her feet, and upon her head a crown of twelve stars.

2 And she [*the Church*] being with child [*the kingdom of God—see JST 12:7*] cried, travailing in birth and pained to be delivered [*labor pains; symbolic of the fact that there are labor and pain involved in bringing forth the kingdom of God*].

**JST Revelation 12:2**

2 And the woman being with child, cried, travailing in birth, and pained to be delivered.

3 And there appeared another wonder in heaven; and behold a great red dragon [*Lucifer; see verse 9*], having seven heads and ten horns, and seven crowns upon his heads [*i.e., Satan has great power, has many "front" organizations behind which he hides*].

4 And his tail drew the third part of the stars of heaven [*1/3 followed Satan in the war in heaven; D&C 29:36*], and did cast them to the earth [*the spirits who followed Lucifer are here on earth!*]: and the dragon [*Satan*] stood before the woman [*the Church*] which was ready to be delivered [*ready to bring forth the kingdom of God*], for to devour her child [*the kingdom of God*] as soon as it was born [*started*].

The JST combines verses 3 and 4, above.

**JST Revelation 12:4**

4 And there appeared another sign in heaven; and behold, a great red dragon, having seven heads and ten horns, and seven crowns upon his heads. And his tail drew the third part of the stars of heaven, and did cast them to the earth. And the dragon stood before the woman which was delivered, ready to devour her child after it was born.

5 And she [*the Church; JST 12:3, 7*] brought forth a man child [*the kingdom of God and his Christ; JST 12:7*], who was to rule all nations with a rod of iron

[*i.e., during the Millennium (which John has just seen in the vision, 11:15–19), the kingdom of God will be established, and the iron rod (or the word of God), will be in full effect*]: and her child was caught up unto God, and to his throne.

**JST Revelation 12:3**

3 And she brought forth a man child, who was to rule all nations with a rod of iron; and her child was caught up unto God and his throne.

6 And the woman fled into the wilderness [*symbolic of the great apostasy, when the Church was gone for many centuries*], where she hath a place prepared of God, that they should feed her there a thousand two hundred and threescore days.

**JST Revelation 12:5**

5 And the woman fled into the wilderness, where she had a place prepared of God, that they should feed her there a thousand two hundred and threescore years.

Did you notice that the JST changes "days" to "years" at the end of the verse?

7 And there was war in heaven [*a war of opinions, words, truth, error, light, darkness, and so forth, which continues here on earth today*]: Michael [*Adam*] and his angels [*righteous spirits*] fought against the dragon [*Satan*]; and the dragon fought and his angels [*the evil spirits who followed Satan*],

**JST Revelation 12:6**

6 And there was war in heaven; Michael and his angels fought against the dragon; and the dragon and his angels fought against Michael;

8 And prevailed not; neither was their [*Satan and his followers*] place found any more in heaven.

**JST Revelation 12:7**

7 And the dragon prevailed not against Michael, neither the child, nor the woman which was the church of God, who had been delivered of her pains, and brought forth the kingdom of our God and his Christ.

9 And the great dragon was cast out, that old serpent, called the Devil, and Satan, which deceiveth the whole world: he was cast out into the earth, and his angels were cast out with him.

**JST Revelation 12:8**

8 Neither was there place found in heaven for the great dragon, who was cast out; that old serpent called the devil, and also called Satan, which deceiveth the whole world; he was cast out into the earth; and his angels were cast out with him.

10 And I heard a loud voice saying in heaven, Now is come salvation [*in other words, now people will be able to go down to earth and live and choose between good and evil, and thus earn salvation; see 2 Nephi 2:11*], and strength, and the kingdom of our God, and the power of his Christ: for the accuser [*Satan*] of our brethren is cast down, which accused them before our God day and night.

The JST breaks verse 10, above, into two verses.

**JST Revelation 12:9–10**

9 And I heard a loud voice saying in heaven, Now is come salvation, and strength, and the kingdom of our God, and the power of his Christ;

10 For the accuser of our brethren is cast down, which accused them before our God day and night.

11 And they [*the righteous*] overcame him [*Satan and his evil*] by the blood of the Lamb [*through the Atonement of Christ*], and by the word of their testimony [*they kept their covenants*]; and they loved not their lives unto the death [*i.e., they were willing to give all to gain exaltation*].

12 Therefore rejoice, ye heavens, and ye that dwell in them. Woe to the inhabiters of the earth [*there will be trouble because Satan is here, and you will*

*have to choose right from wrong under severe pressure*] and of the sea! for the devil is come down unto you, having great wrath [*Satan is really "turning up the pressure"*], because he knoweth that he hath but a short time.

The JST rearranges verses 11–12, above, as follows:

**JST Revelation 12:11–12**
11 For they have overcome him by the blood of the Lamb, and by the word of their testimony; for they loved not their own lives, but kept the testimony even unto death. Therefore, rejoice O heavens, and ye that dwell in them.

12 And after these things I heard another voice saying, Woe to the inhabiters of the earth, yea, and they who dwell upon the islands of the sea! for the devil is come down unto you, having great wrath, because he knoweth that he hath but a short time.

13 And when the dragon saw that he was cast unto the earth, he persecuted the woman [*the Church; i.e., this is the time of Satan's power*] which brought forth the man child [*the kingdom of God*].

**JST Revelation 12:13**
13 For when the dragon saw that he was cast unto the earth, he persecuted the woman which brought forth the man-child.

14 And to the woman were given two wings of a great eagle, that she might fly into the wilderness [*universal apostasy*], into her place, where she is nourished for a time, and times, and half a time [*we don't know what this means; perhaps it could be 1 time plus 2 times plus 1/2 a time, i.e., 3 1/2 times which might symbolically tie in with other uses of 3 1/2, such as in Rev. 11:3 where the Lord preserves the two prophets for three and a half years*], from the face of the serpent [*Satan*].

**JST Revelation 12:14**
14 Therefore, to the woman were given two wings of a great eagle, that she might flee into the wilderness, into her place, where she is nourished for a time, and times, and half a time, from the face of the serpent.

15 And the serpent cast out of his mouth water as a flood after the woman [*symbolically, just as flood waters reach and surround everything in their path, so also Satan tries to get to us from every angle*], that he might cause her to be carried away of [*destroyed by*] the flood.

**JST Revelation 12:15**
15 And the serpent casteth out of his mouth water as a flood after the woman, that he might cause her to be carried away of the flood.

16 And the earth helped the woman [*earth is designed and created to help us return to the Father; all things in it bear witness of Him to us; Moses 6:63*], and the earth opened her mouth, and swallowed up the flood which the dragon cast out of his mouth.

**JST Revelation 12:16**
16 And the earth helpeth the woman, and the earth openeth her mouth, and swalloweth up the flood which the dragon casteth out of his mouth.

17 And the dragon [*Satan*] was wroth [*angry*] with the woman [*the Church*], and went to make war with the remnant of her seed [*the Saints in the last days*], which keep the commandments of God, and have the testimony of Jesus Christ.

**JST Revelation 12:17**
17 Therefore, the dragon was wroth with the woman, and went to make war with the remnant of her seed, which keep the commandments of God, and have the testimony of Jesus Christ.

**JST Revelation 12:1–17.**
As mentioned above, we are including the complete JST of Revelation, chapter 12, here, in order that you might read straight through it in the order in which Joseph Smith arranged the verses. We have included some notes for teaching purposes.

1 And there appeared a great sign in heaven, in the likeness of things [*symbolic of things*] on the earth; a woman [*the Church, see verse 7*] clothed with the sun [*symbolic of beauty, glory, and power to bring us to exaltation*] and the moon under her feet, and upon her head a crown [*symbolic of power, authority; exaltation*] of twelve stars [*the Twelve Apostles*].

In this imagery, woman brings forth the greatest, highest good. In contrast, in Satan's work, see Revelation 17:1–6 and elsewhere, the woman "the whore of all the earth," (1 Nephi 14:11) brings forth the greatest evil. Perhaps this is symbolic of the power of women, both for good and for evil.

2 And the woman being with child [*verse 7, the kingdom of God and his Christ*], cried, travailing in birth [*labor pains*], and pained to be delivered [*i.e., it requires much pain and effort to establish God's kingdom on earth*].

Some might think that the "man child" in verse 7, next, refers to Christ. Such is not the case. Mary brought forth Christ. The Church did not bring Christ forth. Rather, He brought forth the Church.

3 And she [*the Church, verse 7*] brought forth a man child [*verse 7, the kingdom of God*], who was to rule all nations with a rod of iron [*the word of God, 1 Nephi 11:25*]; and her child [*see verse 7, the kingdom of God and the righteous Saints who belong to it*] was caught up unto God and his throne [*i.e., the righteous are eventually taken up to live in celestial glory with God*].

4 And there appeared another sign [*John is seeing actual events in premortality and on earth in vision*] in heaven; and behold, a great red dragon [*Satan*], having seven heads [*symbolic of counterfeiting God's work*] and ten [*a number often associated with being well-organized*] horns [*horns are symbolic of power*], and seven crowns [*Satan has authority in his own realm*] upon his heads. And his tail drew the third part of the stars of heaven [*a third part of the premortal spirits in our group;*], and did cast them to the earth. And the dragon stood before the woman which was delivered [*gave birth to the Kingdom of God, verse 7*], ready to devour her child [*the Kingdom of God, verse 7*] after it was born. [*Satan has tried to destroy God's work from the beginning.*]

Apostle James E. Talmage indicates that there was a certain number of spirits assigned to our group to come to this earth. See *Articles of Faith*, by James E. Talmage, printed in 1977, p. 194. Thus, we understand the "third part" in verse 4, above, to be a third part of our group of spirits.

5 And the woman fled into the wilderness [*symbolic of the great apostasy; the Church is gone for many centuries until the restoration by Joseph Smith*], where she had a place prepared of God, that they should feed [*nourish, take care of*] her there a thousand two hundred and threescore years.

6 And there was war in heaven [*a war of words, ideas, truth, error, loyalties, etc.*]; Michael [*Adam*] and his angels [*righteous spirits*] fought against the dragon [*Satan*]; and the dragon and his angels [*wicked spirits*] fought against Michael;

7 And the dragon [*Satan*] prevailed not [*did not win*] against Michael, neither the child [*the kingdom of our God*], nor the woman [*the Church*] which was the church of God, who had been delivered of her pains, and brought forth the kingdom of our God and his Christ. [*This is a great prophecy that Satan will not ultimately win against Christ and the forces of good.*]

8 Neither was there place found in heaven for the great dragon [*Lucifer, Satan*], who was cast out; that old serpent called the devil, and also called Satan, which deceiveth the whole world; he was cast out into the earth; and his angels were cast out with him. [*They are here on earth and in the spirit world prison, tempting, and fighting against that which is good.*

*See Teachings of the Presidents of the Church: Brigham Young, 1997, p. 282. (study course for priesthood and Relief Society)*]

9 And I heard a loud voice saying in heaven, Now is come salvation, and strength, and the kingdom of our God, and the power of his Christ; [*In other words, the earth is set up and "school is in session;" worthy spirits can go down to earth, have opportunities to choose between good and evil, join the kingdom of God via the gospel of Jesus Christ, and gain exaltation because of the Atonement of Christ–see verse 11.*]

10 For the accuser [*Satan*] of our brethren is cast down, which accused them before our God day and night [*continuously*].

11 For they [*the righteous*] have overcome him [*Satan*] by the blood of the Lamb [*using the Atonement of Christ*], and by the word of their testimony [*keeping their covenants*]; for they loved not their own lives, but kept the testimony even unto death [*endured faithful to the end*]. Therefore, rejoice O heavens, and ye that dwell in them [*righteous people bring joy to the inhabitants of heaven*].

12 And after these things I heard another voice saying, Woe to [*a warning, caution to*] the inhabiters of the earth, yea, and they who dwell upon the islands of the sea [*all continents; everybody on earth*]! for the devil is come down unto you, having great wrath, because he knoweth that he hath but a short time [*beware of Satan; he is really "turning up the heat"*].

13 For when the dragon [*Satan*] saw that he was cast unto the earth, he persecuted the woman [*the Church*] which brought forth the man-child [*the kingdom of God—see verse 7*].

The "great eagle" in verse 14, next, could possibly symbolize the role which the United States of America would play in providing a safe place for the Church to start and then grow, when the time was right.

14 Therefore, to the woman were given two wings of a great eagle, that she might flee into the wilderness, into her place, where she is nourished for a time, and times, and half a time, from the face of the serpent [*Satan, who wants to destroy the Church in its infancy, see verse 4*].

15 And the serpent [*Satan*] casteth out of his mouth water as a flood [*a wicked flood of filthiness designed to get into every aspect of life. This may tie in with the "filthy water" in 1 Nephi 12:16*], after the woman [*the Church, verse 7*], that he might cause her to be carried away of the flood [*destroyed by a flood of wickedness*].

16 And the earth helpeth the woman [*example: Moses 6:63, "all things bear witness*], and the earth openeth her mouth, and swalloweth up the flood which the dragon [*Satan*] casteth out of his mouth [*the earth is set up to help us overcome Satan and gain exaltation*].

17 Therefore, the dragon was wroth [*angry*] with the woman [*the Church*], and went to make war with the remnant of her seed [*the Saints in the last days*], which keep the commandments of God, and have the testimony of Jesus Christ [*who make and keep covenants with God*].

# REVELATION 13

This chapter contains one of the most notable and often talked about topics contained in the Bible. It is the mark of the beast, mentioned in verses 16 and 17.

We don't have exact interpretations of many of the things John saw in this chapter. It is easy to get caught up in trying to figure out details and thus miss the rather obvious and simple messages. For instance, we may not know who or what the beast is or what his seven heads and ten horns are. However, it is obvious that evil is being

represented in the vision as vicious and destructive, something for us to avoid. The beast's seven heads might represent Satan's attempted counterfeits of God's perfect work since the number seven represents perfection in Bible symbolism. Or the seven heads could represent attempts by Lucifer to confuse us. (For example, which one is really Satan or his front organizations or what?) Or perhaps the seven heads could symbolize Satan's ability to come at us from several different directions, using many different types of temptations. The head wounded, that was then healed in verse 3, could remind us that just when we think we have overcome Satan's temptations, he bounces back and tries for us again. The important thing is for us to be reminded that Satan is a very capable enemy and we must do all that we can to avoid getting the "mark of the beast" in our foreheads [*verse 16*], i.e., to avoid becoming followers of Satan.

1 And I stood upon the sand of the sea, and saw a beast rise up out of the sea, having seven heads and ten horns [*perhaps symbolizing that Satan is well-organized but not as powerful as Christ's 12 horns, 12 eyes and 12 servants or Apostles in JST 5:6*], and upon his horns ten crowns [*symbolizing power over kingdoms*], and upon his heads the name of blasphemy [*symbolic of total disrespect for God*].

**JST Revelation 13:1**

1 And I saw another sign, in the likeness of the kingdoms of the earth; a beast rise up out of the sea, and he stood upon the sand of the sea, having seven heads and ten horns; and upon his horns ten crowns; and upon his heads the name of blasphemy.

The phrase "sand of the sea" in the JST, above, reminds us that Satan's kingdom is built upon "sand." As depicted by the Savior in Matthew 7:24–27, sand is not a good foundation upon which to build. It will eventually crumble out from under the "kingdom" and the kingdom will be destroyed.

2 And the beast which I saw was like unto a leopard, and his feet were as the feet of a bear, and his mouth as the mouth of a lion [*i.e., he has great ability to destroy*]: and the dragon [*the devil*] gave him [*Satan's degenerate earthly kingdoms*] his power, and his seat, and great authority.

3 And I saw one of his heads as it were wounded to death; and his deadly wound was healed: and all the world wondered after the beast [*the majority of the world will admire and desire wickedness in the last days*].

4 And they worshipped the dragon [*Satan*] which gave power unto the beast [*representing degenerate earthly kingdoms controlled by Satan; see heading to Revelation 13 in our Bible*]: and they [*the wicked*] worshipped the beast, saying, Who is like unto the beast? who is able to make war with him [*i.e., isn't he wonderful!*]?

5 And there was given unto him a mouth speaking great things and blasphemies [*God allows Satan to wield power that we might be properly tested*]; and power was given unto him to continue forty and two months. [*42 months; a thousand two hundred and threescore days represented the time allocated to the two prophets in Rev. 11:3 to do God's work. Perhaps the use of 42 months again here simply implies that whenever God is doing His work, Satan is allowed to provide opposition at the same time. Such will be the case until the Millennium.*]

6 And he opened his mouth in blasphemy [*mocking God and all that is sacred and good*] against God, to blaspheme his name, and his tabernacle, and them that dwell in heaven [*Satan and*

*his followers will mock all that is sacred on earth and in heaven*].

Some read verse 7, next, and think that all the righteous will eventually be overcome by Satan in the last days. Such is obviously not the case. They need to read verse 8, also, where we see that Satan overcomes those who worship or follow him. In other words, he overcomes those who do not overcome him by following Christ and accessing His Atonement in their lives.

7 And it was given unto him [*allowed him*] to make war with the saints, and to overcome them [*only the unfaithful Saints whose names are not written in the book of life will be overcome; see verse 8*]: and power was given him over all kindreds, and tongues, and nations [*i.e., he is allowed to tempt people everywhere*].

At the risk of being redundant, we will again emphasize that Satan will not overcome all of the righteous. Note that "all," in verse 8, next, refers to those "whose names are not written in the book of the . . . Lamb," as defined in the note following verse 8.

8 And all [*the wicked*] that dwell upon the earth shall worship him, whose names are not written in the book of life of the Lamb slain from the foundation of the world [*i.e., those who do not follow the Savior are worshiping Satan; compare with Matthew 12:30*].

"The book of life of the Lamb" in verse 8, above, is symbolic of the record kept in heaven which contains the names of those who will be exalted. See D&C 132:19.

9 If any man have an ear, let him hear [*i.e., you would be very wise to heed these warnings about Satan*].

10 He [*the powerful wicked*] that leadeth into captivity shall go into captivity [*the wicked will be destroyed by the wicked; Mormon 4:5; also could mean that the wicked who lead others to the captivity of hell will go into the captivity of hell themselves*]: he [*the wicked*] that killeth with the sword must be [*will be*] killed with the sword. Here is the patience and the faith of the saints [*perhaps meaning that through being surrounded by opposition in the mortal world, the patience and faith of the Saints are developed*].

11 And I beheld another beast coming up out of the earth; and he had two horns like a lamb [*"like a lamb," not "the Lamb," perhaps meaning a powerful "false Christ," a counterfeit by Satan*], and he spake as a dragon [*like Satan; see Rev. 12:9*].

12 And he exerciseth all the power of the first beast before him [*just when you think you've seen Satan at his worst, worse will come!*], and causeth the earth and them [*the wicked*] which dwell therein to worship the first beast [*in verse 3, above*], whose deadly wound was healed.

13 And he doeth great wonders [*Satan and his angels can do miracles*], so that he maketh fire come down from heaven on the earth in the sight of men [*a counterfeit of Elijah's miracle, 1 Kings 18:38*],

14 And deceiveth them [*the wicked and foolish*] that dwell on the earth by the means of those miracles which he had power to do in the sight of the beast; saying to them that dwell on the earth, that they should make an image to [*i.e., worship*] the beast, which had the wound by a sword, and did live. [*In other words, Satan will do all he can to get all people to follow him, to "worship" him by living wickedly in the last days.*]

15 And he had power to give life [*make wickedness attractive*] unto the image of the beast [*which the wicked made in verse 14 by following Satan's instructions*], that the image of the beast should both speak, and cause that as many as would not worship the image of the beast should be killed [*people's "idols" can take over their lives and cause them*

*to die spiritually, as well as physically in wars, plagues, etc. Also, the wicked can cause great trouble, temporarily, for the righteous*].

Verses 16 and 17, next, are an example of the importance of carefully considering context when interpreting verses of scripture. If one were to read only these verses, the conclusion would be that, in the last days, "all" (verse 16) people will eventually come under the power of Satan and wicked people under his control. This would be very depressing and could cause people to give up hope. However, if we examine other verses in Revelation, we see the truth. For example, read Revelation 14:1, where we see 144,000 with the Father's name in their foreheads, rather than the mark of the beast in their foreheads. Furthermore, in Revelation 20:4, we see righteous people "which had not worshipped the beast, neither his image, neither had received his mark upon their foreheads, or in their hands." Thus we see that "all" (Rev. 13:16) do not come under Satan's control, rather "all" the foolish or wicked do who "wondered after the beast" (verse 3).

Verse 17 implies much of financial bondage in the last days. If we follow the council of the Brethren, we will not come under this bondage. For example, Elder L. Tom Perry counseled: "Live strictly within your income and save something for a rainy day. Incorporate in your lives the discipline of budgeting that which the Lord has blessed you with . . . avoid excessive debt. Necessary debt should be incurred only after careful, thoughtful prayer and after obtaining the best possible advice. We need the discipline to stay well within our ability to pay. Wisely we have been counseled to avoid debt as we would avoid the plague . . . It is so easy to allow consumer debt to get out of hand. If you do not have the discipline to control the use of credit cards, it is better not to have them. A well-managed family does not pay interest—it earns it. The definition I received from a wise boss at one time in my early business career was 'Thems that understands interest receives it, thems that don't pays it.'. . .Acquire and store a reserve of food and supplies that will sustain life. Obtain clothing and build a savings account on a sensible, well-planned basis that can serve well in times of emergency. As long as I can remember, we have been taught to prepare for the future and to obtain a year's supply of necessities. I would guess that the years of plenty have almost universally caused us to set aside this counsel. I believe the time to disregard this counsel is over. With events in the world today, it must be considered with all seriousness." (L. Tom Perry, *Ensign*, November 1995, p. 36.)

16 And he causeth all [*who follow Satan; the righteous are not part of this group because they have the seal of God in their foreheads as seen in Rev. 7:3*], both small and great, rich and poor, free and bond, to receive a mark in their right hand, or in their foreheads [*symbolically indicating that they are loyal to Satan and the wickedness he sponsors*]:

In the culture of the Bible, "forehead" was symbolic of "loyalty" (see symbolism notes at the beginning of Revelation in this study guide.) Thus we see faithful Jews wearing phylacteries even today (see Bible Dictionary under "Phylacteries") tied to their foreheads, symbolizing loyalty and obedience to their God. Notice also in Revelation 14:1 that there are a 144,000 righteous who have the "Father's name written in their foreheads," which symbolizes loyalty and obedience to the Father.

17 And that no man might buy or sell, save he that had the mark, or the name of the beast, or the number of his name [*Satan exercises great control over economies where the majority are wicked or allow wickedness; the righteous today would do well to follow the*

*counsel of the prophets regarding self-sufficiency and staying out of unnecessary debt, etc.*].

18 Here is wisdom. Let him that hath understanding count the number of the beast: for it is the number of a man; and his number is Six hundred threescore and six [*i.e., 666; we don't yet know what this means*].

## REVELATION 14

In this chapter, the Apostle John sees the restoration of the gospel (verses 6–7), then sees the fall of Satan's kingdom (verses 8–11), including the final gathering and the destruction of the wicked (verses 14–20).

1 And I [*John*] looked, and, lo, a Lamb [*Christ*] stood on the mount Sion [*this is representative of many appearances; D&C 133:18–20*], and with him an hundred forty and four thousand [*Rev. 7:4*], having his Father's name written in their foreheads [*i.e., who were loyal to the Father*].

**JST Revelation 14:1**

1 And I looked, and, lo, a Lamb stood on the mount Sion, and with him a hundred forty and four thousand, having his Father's name written in their foreheads.

2 And I heard a voice from heaven, as the voice of many waters [*D&C 110:3*], and as the voice of a great thunder [*symbolic of a voice from heaven as on Sinai; Exodus 19:16–19*]: and I heard the voice of harpers harping with their harps [*in Bible symbolism, harps are symbolic of heaven*]:

3 And they sung as it were a new song [*i.e., one that couldn't be sung before the Millennium and the destruction of the wicked came; see note with Rev. 5:9 in this study guide*] before the throne [*in front of the throne of God*], and before the four beasts, and the elders: and no man could learn that song but the hundred and forty and four thousand [*plus many others as mentioned in Rev. 7:9*], which were redeemed from the earth. [*In other words, only the righteous, those who were saved by the Atonement, could sing the words of the "new song" in the presence of God in celestial splendor, which words applied to them. The words of the "new song" are, in effect, given in D&C 84:99–102.*]

4 These are they which were not defiled with women [*i.e., they are morally clean*]; for they are virgins [*i.e., pure and clean, keeping the law of chastity; does not mean unmarried*]. These are they which follow the Lamb whithersoever he goeth [*who follow Christ at all costs*]. These were redeemed from among men, being the firstfruits [*the "highest quality fruit"; i.e., those who will attain exaltation*] unto God and to the Lamb.

5 And in their mouth was found no guile [*deceit; Strong's #1388*]: for they are without fault [*blameless; without sin, pure and clean because of the Atonement*] before the throne of God.

6 And I saw another angel [*Angel Moroni plus many other angels who helped with the restoration; D&C 128:20–21; 133:36*] fly in the midst of heaven, having the everlasting gospel to preach unto them that dwell on the earth, and to every nation, and kindred, and tongue, and people [*the restoration of the Church*],

7 Saying with a loud voice, Fear [*respect, reverence; Strong's #5399*] God, and give glory to him; for the hour of his judgment is come: and worship him that made heaven, and earth, and the sea, and the fountains of waters.

8 And there followed another angel, saying, Babylon [*symbolic of Satan and his earthly kingdom*] is fallen, is fallen, that great city [*Satan's kingdom*], because she made all nations drink of the wine of [*i.e., the results of*] the

wrath of her fornication [*fornication as used here includes apostasy (see Bible Dictionary under "Adultery"), disloyalty, all manner of wickedness, breaking of covenants and commitments*].

9 And the third angel followed them, saying with a loud voice, If any man worship the beast and his image [*Rev. 13:14*], and receive his mark in his forehead, or in his hand [*i.e., is a loyal follower of Satan, in other words, is wicked*],

10 The same shall drink of the wine [*results of, i.e., punishments*] of the wrath of God, which is poured out without mixture [*undiluted*] into the cup of his indignation; and he [*the wicked*] shall be tormented with fire and brimstone in the presence of the holy angels, and in the presence of the Lamb [*i.e., will not be able to stand the presence of God; D&C 88:22*]:

11 And the smoke of their torment ascendeth up for ever and ever: and they have no rest day nor night, who worship the beast and his image, and whosoever receiveth the mark of his name [*applies eternally only to the sons of perdition, D&C 76:33; all others will eventually suffer for their own sins, D&C 19:17, and then be redeemed into the telestial kingdom*].

12 Here is the patience of the saints [*when the righteous see the fall of Satan's kingdom as mentioned in the above verses, they will see that their patience, in waiting for God to destroy Lucifer's kingdom, has paid off*]: here are they that keep the commandments of God, and the faith of Jesus.

13 And I heard a voice from heaven saying unto me, Write, Blessed are the dead which die in the Lord [*i.e., who have lived righteously*] from henceforth: Yea, saith the Spirit, that they may rest from their labours; and their works do follow them [*they will be rewarded for their righteousness*].

14 And I looked, and behold a white cloud [*symbolic of heaven*], and upon the cloud one [*Christ*] sat like unto the Son of man [*Christ*], having on his head a golden crown [*celestial*], and in his hand a sharp sickle [*i.e., it is "harvest" time*].

The phrase "like unto the Son of man" is explained in two notes following Revelation 1:13 in this study guide.

15 And another angel came out of the temple [*where Heavenly Father is; Rev. 3:12; 7:15*], crying with a loud voice to him [*Christ*] that sat on the cloud [*giving instructions to the Savior from the Father*], Thrust in thy sickle, and reap: for the time is come for thee to reap; for the harvest of the earth is ripe [*"the field is white already to harvest;" D&C 6:3, in other words, the Father is telling Christ that it is time for the final gathering, prior to the Second Coming*].

First the righteous are gathered out of all the earth.]

16 And he [*Christ*] that sat on the cloud thrust in his sickle on the earth; and the earth was reaped [*Christ supervised the final gathering of the righteous; compare with D&C 86:7, in which the "wheat" is gathered first, and then the "tares" are burned*].

Now the wicked will be "harvested" and cast into the fire. See verses 18 and 19.

17 And another angel [*the "destroying angel;" see verses 18–20*] came out of the temple [*from the presence of the Father*] which is in heaven, he also having a sharp sickle.

18 And another angel came out from the altar [*i.e., from the presence of the Father*], which had power over fire; and cried with a loud cry to him [*the destroying angel in verse 17*] that had the sharp sickle, saying, Thrust in thy sharp sickle, and gather the clusters of the vine of the earth; for her grapes

[*wicked people*] are fully ripe [*ripe in iniquity, thoroughly wicked*].

19 And the angel thrust in his sickle into the earth, and gathered the vine of the earth [*the wicked*], and cast it into the great winepress of the wrath of God [*the destruction of the wicked*].

20 And the winepress was trodden without [*outside of*] the city, and blood came out of the winepress, even unto the horse bridles [*in other words, many wicked are destroyed when the Savior comes again*], by the space of a thousand and six hundred furlongs [*the blood ran for over 200 miles in the vision seen by John; symbolic of terrible destruction accompanying the Battle of Armageddon and the Second Coming*].

> **JST Revelation 14:20**
> 20 And the winepress was trodden without the city, and blood came out of the winepress, even unto the horses' bridles, by the space of a thousand and six hundred furlongs.

# REVELATION 15

This is a beautiful part of the vision in which John was shown the reward of the righteous who have overcome evil through the Atonement. He sees them on "a sea of glass," representing a celestial world (D&C 77:1 and 130:7) with "harps," symbolizing that they spend the rest of eternity in the presence of God. They are singing "the song of Moses. . . and the song of the Lamb," meaning that they have received the same reward which Moses receives from Christ and His Father, in other words, exaltation. Some of the words they "sing" in verses three and four are contained in our hymn # 267.

There are no JST changes for this chapter.

1 And I saw another sign in heaven, great and marvellous, seven angels having the seven last plagues [*as described in chapters 16, 17, and 18, and which will take place prior to the Millennium*]; for in them is filled up [*concluded*] the wrath of God.

2 And I saw as it were a sea of glass mingled with fire [*celestial glory; D&C 130:7*]: and them [*the righteous*] that had gotten the victory over the beast [*in chapter 13*], *and over his image* [*13:14*], and over his mark [*13:16–17*], and over the number of his name [*13:17, i.e., the righteous who had overcome all attempts of Satan to trap them*], stand on the sea of glass, having the harps of God [*i.e., they were standing in the presence of God; the harps could symbolize that they were found in "harmony" with God*].

3 And they sing the song of Moses the servant of God [*they sing God's praises like Moses did*], and the song of the Lamb [*Christ*], saying, Great and marvellous are thy works, Lord God Almighty; just and true are thy ways, thou King of saints [*praising God*].

4 Who shall not fear thee, O Lord, and glorify thy name? for thou only art holy: for all nations shall come and worship before thee; for thy judgments are made manifest.

5 And after that I looked, and, behold, the temple [*see Rev. 11:19*] of the tabernacle of the testimony in heaven was opened:

6 And the seven angels came out of the temple, having the seven plagues [*spoken of in verse 1*], clothed in pure and white linen [*i.e., celestial beings; fine linen represents personal righteousness in Rev. 19:8*], and having their breasts girded with golden girdles [*symbolic of the best, celestial*].

7 And one of the four beasts gave unto the seven angels seven golden vials [*representing the final seven plagues*] full of the wrath of God, who liveth for ever and ever.

8 And the temple was filled with smoke [*symbolic of God's glory as on Sinai; Exodus 19:18*] from the glory of God, and from his power; and no man was able to enter into the temple, till the seven plagues of the seven angels were fulfilled [*i.e., millennial conditions won't start until the final seven plagues are finished*].

# REVELATION 16

This chapter will review plagues which will sweep the earth, leading up to the Battle of Armageddon and the Second Coming of Christ. A major message here is that there will be widespread destruction before the Millennium. You may also note that there seems to be terrible damage to the ecology of the earth in the last days prior to the Second Coming.

1 And I [*John*] heard a great voice out of the temple [*from heaven*] saying to the seven angels, Go your ways, and pour out the vials of the wrath of God upon the earth [*i.e., start the final plagues*].

2 And the first [*angel*] went, and poured out his vial [*the first plague during the final scenes*] upon the earth; and there fell a noisome [*destructive: Strong's #2556*] and grievous [*evil, devastating; Strong's #4190*] sore upon the men which [*who*] had the mark of the beast [*who were loyal to Satan, evil, wickedness*], and upon them which worshipped his image [*i.e., upon the wicked*].

3 And the second angel poured out his vial [*the second plague*] upon the sea; and it became as the blood [*similar to the plague of blood in Egypt; Exodus 7:20*] of a dead man [*in other words, the waters were polluted, like a corpse*]: and every living soul died in the sea.

4 And the third angel poured out his vial [*the third plague*] upon the rivers and fountains of waters [*springs*]; and they became blood.

5 And I heard the angel of the waters [*the angel who poured the plague upon the waters in verse 4, above*] say, Thou art righteous, O Lord, which art, and wast, and shalt be, because thou hast judged thus [*i.e., this punishment is fair and just because of the wickedness of men*].

6 For they have shed the blood of saints and prophets, and thou hast given them blood to drink [*symbolic of forbidden evils, pollution; in other words, this is the "Law of the Harvest;" what you have "planted" comes back to you at "harvest time" or Judgment Day*]; for they are worthy [*they deserve such punishment*].

7 And I heard another out of the altar [*from heaven; Rev. 8:3*] say, Even so, Lord God Almighty, true and righteous are thy judgments. [*In other words, a second witness, according to the law of witnesses, that God is completely fair and just in punishing the wicked.*]

> **JST Revelation 16:7**
> 7 And I heard another angel who came out from the altar saying, Even so, Lord God Almighty, true and righteous are thy judgments.

8 And the fourth angel poured out his vial [*plague*] upon the sun; and power was given unto him to scorch men with fire [*perhaps similar to our modern saying, "turn up the heat," to see if we can get some of them to repent*].

9 And men were scorched with great heat [*terrible calamities*], and blasphemed [*mocked*] the name of God, which hath power over these plagues [*God could stop these plagues if men would repent*]: and they repented not to give him glory.

10 And the fifth angel poured out his vial [*the fifth plague*] upon the seat [*headquarters*] of the beast [*Satan*]; and his kingdom was full of [*spiritual*] darkness; and they [*the wicked*] gnawed their tongues for [*because of*] pain [*the*

*wicked will suffer greatly, both physically and spiritually, because they refuse to repent and let Christ's Atonement pay for their sins; D&C 19:15–18*],

11 And blasphemed [*mocked*] the God of heaven because of their pains and their sores, and repented not of their deeds [*their wickedness*].

12 And the sixth angel poured out his vial [*the sixth plague*] upon the great river Euphrates [*included in modern-day Iraq and the Persian Gulf*]; and the water thereof was dried up, that the way of the kings of the east might be prepared [*perhaps symbolic of world leaders gathering for the Battle of Armageddon; see verse 16, below*].

13 And I saw three unclean [*evil*] spirits like frogs [*frogs represent unclean spirits in some cultures; perhaps this harks back to the plague of frogs in Egypt, Exodus 8:6, with the same purpose, i.e., to encourage people to repent and obey God*] come out of the mouth of the dragon [*Satan; Rev. 12:9*], and out of the mouth of the beast, and out of the mouth of the false prophet [*i.e., evil spirits are much involved in all Satan-sponsored evil and wickedness*].

14 For they are the spirits of devils, working miracles [*Satan and his evil spirits have much power, although limited by God*], which go forth unto the kings [*wicked political leaders*] of the earth and of the whole world, to gather them to the battle of that great day of God Almighty [*the battle of Armageddon; see verse 16*].

15 Behold, I [*Christ*] come as a thief [*unexpectedly, i.e., will catch the wicked off guard, but not the righteous, D&C 106:4–5*]. Blessed is he that watcheth, and keepeth his garments [*who keeps himself unspotted from the sins of the world (D&C 59:9); who keeps clean via the Atonement*], lest he walk naked [*his wickedness is no longer "covered" by excuses on Judgment Day*], and they see his shame [*embarrassment for his wicked deeds*].

16 And he [*the sixth angel in verse 12*?] gathered them together into a place called in the Hebrew tongue Armageddon [*also called "Megiddo," geographically located in a valley about 60 miles north of Jerusalem in northern Israel, today*].

17 And the seventh angel [*probably Adam; see D&C 88:110 and 112*] poured out his vial [*plague*] into the air; and there came a great voice [*Heavenly Father's voice*] out of the temple of heaven, from the throne, saying, It is done [*the end is here; Rev. 11:15*].

18 And there were voices, and thunders, and lightnings; and there was a great earthquake [*great destruction, perhaps including that caused by putting the land masses back together. D&C 133:23–24*], such as was not since men were upon the earth, so mighty an earthquake, and so great [*final destruction before the Millennium*].

19 And the great city [*Babylon, Satan's kingdom; see middle of this verse*] was divided into three parts [*perhaps meaning 1/3, 1/3, and 1/3, symbolic of Satan and his 1/3 completely dominating the wicked in the last days*], and the cities of the nations fell [*all worldly kingdoms have fallen; "a full end of all nations" (see D&C 87:6)*]: and great Babylon came in remembrance before God [*God "remembered" Babylon*], to give unto her the cup of the wine of the fierceness of his wrath [*gave the wicked the punishments they had earned*].

20 And every island fled away, and the mountains were not found [*geographical changes in conjunction with the Second Coming; D&C 133:22–24*].

21 And there fell upon men a great hail out of heaven, every stone about the weight of a talent [*in Old Testament weight, about 75 pounds; Bible Dictionary, p. 789, but we don't know what a*

*"talent" was in New Testament times*]: and men blasphemed [*mocked and criticized*] God [*they didn't repent*] because of the plague of the hail; for the plague thereof was exceeding great.

## REVELATION 17

The description of the final seven plagues is continued here. This is a chapter of Revelation which makes use of many symbols and images introduced previously in the vision. Assuming that you have become somewhat familiar with many of them, studying this part of the vision will be a rather rewarding experience, as far as understanding Biblical symbolism is concerned. In it, we see "the great whore" (Satan, in verse 1) sitting on the "many waters" (representing the wicked in all nations; verse 15). He has been highly successful among the leaders and inhabitants of the earth, and they are "drunk" (out of control) with wickedness (verse 2). The woman in verse 3 is the complete opposite of the woman (the Church) in JST Revelation 12:7, symbolizing Satan's skill at being attractive while blaspheming and prostituting all that is good, pure and righteous. The beast ridden by the woman has "seven heads" and "ten horns" (Revelation 13:1), symbolizing, among other things, Satan's counterfeiting of God's work and his power to attack us from several different directions.

The woman in this chapter has "MYSTERY" (Secret combinations —see footnote 5a) written upon her forehead (forehead here symbolizes loyalty, dedication to Satan's goals) along with several other terms describing Satan's kingdom. In verse 8 we see the wicked, those "whose names were not written in the book of life," astonished that "the beast . . . was, and is not," perhaps meaning that Babylon was once powerful, but now is not, i.e., has fallen at the Second Coming. At the end of verse eight, these same wicked are astonished "when they behold the beast that was, and is not, and yet is," perhaps meaning Satan's kingdom was here, but is not here now, yet is still in existence in outer darkness (after the final battle at the end of the Millennium).

In verse 16, the "ten horns" take on additional symbolic identity as parts of Satan's kingdom which "hate the whore and . . . make her desolate and naked, and shall eat her flesh, and burn her with fire." In other words, "That great and abominable church, which is the whore of all the earth, shall turn upon their own heads; for they shall war among themselves" (1 Nephi 22:13).

A very comforting prophetic fact in verse 14 is that "the Lamb (Christ) shall overcome them (the wicked, including Satan and his evil spirits)." Thus, those who remain faithful to the Lord are assured that they will be on the winning side.

1 And there came one of the seven angels [*Rev. 15:1*] which had the seven vials [*representing the final seven plagues before the Millennium*], and talked with me [*John*], saying unto me, Come hither; I will shew unto thee the judgment [*punishment*] of the great whore [*a word that means perversion, terrible abuse of that which is good; the great whore is the church or kingdom of the devil; 1 Nephi 14:10–11*], that sitteth upon many waters [*representing peoples and nations of the earth; Rev. 17:15*]:

2 With whom the [*wicked*] kings of the earth have committed fornication [*they have "stepped out" on the true God, have been unfaithful to Him*], and the inhabitants of the earth have been made

drunk [*gone out of control*] with the wine [*symbolizing the attractiveness of Satan's temptations*] of her fornication [*terrible wickedness of all kinds*].

3 So he [*one of the seven angels*] carried me away in the spirit into the wilderness [*the apostate world*]: and I saw a woman [*symbolizing Satan's counterfeits for the true Church which was represented by a righteous woman in JST Rev. 12:1 and 7*] sit upon a scarlet [*symbolic of royalty, governing power*] coloured beast [*the beast is controlled by Satan; Revelation 13 heading*], full of names of blasphemy [*i.e., full of mocking, disrespect for God, sacred things, truth, etc.*], having seven heads and ten horns [*the number, ten, in symbolism represents ordinal perfection, i.e., well-ordered or well organized; in other words, Satan's kingdom is well organized*].

4 And the woman was arrayed [*dressed*] in purple and scarlet colour, and decked with gold and precious stones and pearls [*all symbolic of royalty, wealth, power, glory, materialism, etc., i.e., Satan's kingdom has its "hour of glory" on the earth*], having a golden cup [*counterfeiting God's "best"*] in her hand full of abominations and filthiness [*the things Satan "pours" out upon the earth*] of her fornication:

5 And upon her forehead was a name written, MYSTERY [*secret combinations*], BABYLON THE GREAT [*Satan and his kingdom; Isaiah 14:4 and 12*], THE MOTHER OF HARLOTS [*the "producer of terrible wickedness;" just as a harlot, prostitute, appears desirable to wicked men, so also Satan's ways appear desirable to the wicked*] AND ABOMINATIONS OF THE EARTH.

6 And I saw the woman drunken with the blood of the saints [*i.e., Satan's forces have caused much suffering for the Saints*], and with the blood of the martyrs of Jesus: and when I saw her, I wondered [*marveled; Strong's #2296*] with great admiration [*surprise, astonishment; see Rev. 17:6, footnote c, in our Bible*].

7 And the angel said unto me, Wherefore didst thou marvel [*why were you so astonished*]? I will tell [*explain*] thee the mystery of the woman, and of the beast [*in Revelation 13*] that carrieth her, which hath the seven heads and ten horns.

8 The beast [*Satan and his forces; Rev. 9:1–2*] that thou sawest was, and is not; and shall ascend out of the bottomless pit, and go into perdition [*Rev. 20:1–3; D&C 76:26*]: and they that dwell on the earth shall wonder [*i.e., will be amazed when they see Satan and his forces "trimmed down to size" as told in Isaiah 14:12–16*], whose names were not written in the book of life [*the wicked*] from the foundation of the world [*because of disobedience to the gospel which was established before the foundation of the world*], when they behold the beast that was, and is not, and yet is [*perhaps meaning Satan was here on earth, is not here anymore, because he is in perdition*].

9 And here is the mind which hath wisdom [*if you have wisdom, you will understand this*]. The seven heads are seven mountains [*could refer to Rome, which persecuted the Saints in John's day; see also notes in verse 18*], on which the woman sitteth.

We don't know the interpretation of many of the following images and events in John's vision.

10 And there are seven kings: five are fallen, and one is, and the other is not yet come; and when he cometh, he must continue a short space.

11 And the beast that was, and is not, even he is the eighth, and is of the seven, and goeth into perdition.

12 And the ten horns which thou sawest are ten kings, which have received no kingdom as yet; but receive power as

kings one hour with the beast [*perhaps meaning that they will have very temporary power and glory in Satan's organizations*].

13 These have one mind [*perhaps meaning they are united in evil*], and shall give their power and strength [*i.e., loyalty*] unto the beast.

14 These shall make war with the Lamb [*Christ*], and the Lamb shall overcome them [*a wonderfully comforting statement of fact*]: for he is Lord of lords, and King of kings: and they that are with him are called, and chosen [*a word meaning "elected" by God for eternal happiness*], and faithful.

As stated in verse 14, above, Christ is "Lord of lords, and King of kings." It is interesting to note that "Lord" with a capital "L" refers to Christ as does "King" with a capital "K." We (hopefully) the righteous, who will rule with Him during the Millennium are the "lords" and "kings," spelled with small "l" and small "k."

15 And he saith unto me, The waters [*verse 1*] which thou sawest, where the whore sitteth, are peoples, and multitudes, and nations, and tongues.

Just as water gets into everything, for instance when a home's basement is flooded, so also the "waters" symbolizing a flood of wickedness in the last days get into all aspects of society.

16 And the ten horns which thou sawest upon the beast, these shall hate the whore, and shall make her desolate and naked, and shall eat her flesh, and burn her with fire [*perhaps a reminder that Satan's followers often turn on each other; Isaiah 49:26*].

17 For God hath put in their [*the wicked*] hearts [*Probably a mistranslation similar to Exodus 4:21 that was corrected in the JST to read "but Pharaoh will harden his heart." God does not inspire people to do evil, rather allows them agency to chose between good and evil.*] to fulfil his [*Satan's?*] will, and to agree, and give their kingdom unto the beast, until the words of God shall be fulfilled [*i.e., until the Millennium comes and judgment catches up with the wicked*].

18 And the woman which thou sawest is that great city, which reigneth over the kings of the earth [*this city could be Rome in John's day but in a general sense would seem to symbolize "Babylon" or the "church of the devil" as stated in 1 Nephi 14:10–11*].

# REVELATION 18

The description of the final seven plagues (described, starting in Revelation 16:1) is continued in this chapter.

Chapter 17 gave considerable detail about Babylon, which is Satan and his wicked earthly kingdom. Now, in chapter 18, John sees the fall of Babylon, described as "the woman . . . that great city" in Revelation 17:18. The actual ancient city of Babylon is used in scripture to symbolize Satan's huge kingdom. Babylon was an enormous city, straddling the Euphrates River and was said to have had walls 335 feet high, 85 feet wide and 56 miles long surrounding the square city (see Bible Dictionary under "Babylon").

One of the sad things in this part of John's vision is that the wicked who "have committed fornication and lived deliciously (in lustful, riotous sin) with her (Babylon)" will mourn Babylon's downfall, rather than repenting and worrying about their status with God. See verses 10–19. They have no "godly sorrow" as described in 2 Corinthians 7:10.

There are no JST changes for this chapter.

1 And after these things I saw another

angel come down from heaven, having great power; and the earth was lightened [*brightened, lit up*] with his glory.

2 And he cried mightily with a strong voice, saying, Babylon the great is fallen, is fallen [*Satan's kingdom on earth has come to an end via the Second Coming*], and is [*has*] become the habitation of [*dwelling place for*] devils, and the hold [*prison; Strong's #5438*] of every foul [*wicked*] spirit, and a cage [*prison; the unrighteous have been "caged" by their wickedness and ultimately "trapped" by Satan*] of every unclean and hateful [*detestable; Strong's #3404*] bird [*i.e., the wicked are destroyed and are turned over to Satan to pay for their own sins; 2 Nephi 12:10, D&C 101:24, 19:17*].

3 For all nations have drunk of the wine [*intentionally and skillfully produced temptations*] of the wrath of her fornication [*i.e., people in all nations of the earth have joined Satan in gross wickedness and disloyalty to God*], and the kings [*leaders, people of power and influence*] of the earth have committed fornication [*symbolic of "stepping out" on God, breaking covenants and promises, extreme disloyalty*] with her, and the merchants of the earth are waxed [*have grown*] rich through the abundance of her ["*Babylon's*"] delicacies [*i.e., much wealth has been acquired by exploiting people's wicked and lustful desires*].

4 And I heard another voice from heaven, saying, Come out of her, my people, that ye be not partakers of her sins, and that ye receive not of her plagues [*the righteous are warned not to participate in the gross evils of the last days*].

5 For her sins have reached unto heaven, and God hath remembered her iniquities [*God is fully aware of what is going on and the wicked will be punished*].

6 Reward her even as she rewarded you [*the "law of the harvest"*], and double unto her double according to her works: in the cup which she hath filled fill to her double [*i.e., Babylon's cup of wickedness is completely full, therefore, punish her and her followers accordingly*].

7 How much [*to the degree that*] she hath glorified herself, and lived deliciously [*wickedly, riotously*], so much [*to the same degree*] torment and sorrow give her [*an equation of justice; D&C 1:10*]: for she [*Babylon; the wicked*] saith in her heart [*the wicked fool themselves by thinking . . .* ], I sit a queen [*I am untouchable, I have great power*], and am no widow [*i.e., I won't be cut off from support and admiration*], and shall see no sorrow [*I won't get caught up with or be punished*].

8 Therefore shall [*this is why*] her plagues come in one day [*i.e., suddenly*], death, and mourning, and famine; and she shall be utterly burned with fire [*the wicked will be burned at the Second Coming, utterly destroyed by the Savior's glory; D&C 5:19*]: for strong [*powerful*] is the Lord God who judgeth her [*God has power over Satan*].

9 And the kings [*powerful, wicked leaders*] of the earth, who have committed fornication [*who have been extremely wicked*] and lived deliciously [*riotously*] with her [*the "whore," Satan's kingdom, Babylon*], shall bewail her [*mourn losing her; Strong's #2799*], and lament for her [*instead of repenting*], when they shall see the smoke of her burning [*i.e., the wicked will be devastated by the destruction of their lifestyle*],

10 Standing afar off for the fear of her torment, saying, Alas, alas, that great city Babylon, that mighty city! for in one hour is thy judgment come [*i.e., the Second Coming will change things quickly; they can't believe how fast she was destroyed!*].

11 And the merchants of the earth shall weep and mourn over her [*rather than repenting*]; for no man buyeth their merchandise any more [*because Satan's kingdom has fallen*]:

12 [*In verses 12 and 13, idolatry and accompanying wickedness are described along with materialism.*] The merchandise of gold, and silver, and precious stones, and of pearls, and fine linen, and purple, and silk, and scarlet, and all thyine wood, and all manner vessels of ivory, and all manner vessels of most precious wood, and of brass, and iron, and marble,

13 And cinnamon, and odours [*incense*], and ointments, and frankincense, and wine, and oil, and fine flour, and wheat, and beasts [*domestic animals*], and sheep, and horses, and chariots, and slaves, and souls of men. [*In other words, everything Satan does has the ultimate goal of trapping the "souls of men."*]

14 And the fruits [*the wickedness*] that thy soul lusted [*sinfully chased*] after are departed from thee [*are gone*], and all [*wicked*] things which were dainty and goodly [*i.e., which you considered pleasurable*] are departed from thee [*are gone*], and thou shalt find them no more at all [*they are gone permanently*].

You have no doubt noticed that repetition is often used in the scriptures to drive home a point. What you are seeing in John's vision here is an example of this teaching technique.

15 The merchants of these things [*wickedness*], which [*who*] were made rich by her [*Babylon*], shall stand afar off for the fear of her torment, weeping and wailing,

16 And saying, Alas, alas, that great city [*Babylon, i.e., the wickedness of the world sponsored by Satan*], that was clothed in fine linen, and purple, and scarlet, and decked with gold, and precious stones, and pearls!

17 For in one hour [*suddenly*] so great riches is come to nought [*destroyed completely*]. And every shipmaster, and all the company in ships, and sailors, and as many as trade by sea, stood afar off,

18 And cried when they saw the smoke of her burning, saying, What city is like unto this great city! [*i.e., we thought Babylon (verse 21), Satan's kingdom, was indestructible!*]

19 And they cast dust on their heads [*a sign of extreme mourning in New Testament culture and society*], and cried, weeping and wailing, saying, Alas, alas, that great city, wherein were made rich all that had ships in the sea by reason of her costliness! for in one hour is she made desolate [*our wicked businesses have been destroyed*].

20 Rejoice over her, thou heaven, and ye holy apostles and prophets; for God hath avenged you on her [*i.e., all you righteous who have asked how long it will be before the wicked get what's coming to them (Habakkuk 1:4, D&C 121:2, Rev. 6:10) can now rejoice that the Savior has finally come*].

21 And a mighty angel took up a stone like a great millstone [*a stone used to grind wheat, commonly used to represent the fate of the wicked; Matthew 18:6*], and cast it into the sea, saying, Thus with violence shall that great city Babylon [*symbolic of Satan's kingdom and his followers*] be thrown down, and shall be found no more at all.

22 And the voice of harpers, and musicians, and of pipers, and trumpeters, shall be heard no more at all in thee [*Babylon*]; and no craftsman, of whatsoever craft he be, shall be found any more in thee; and the sound of a millstone shall be heard no more at all in thee [*i.e., the destruction of Satan's kingdom will be absolute*];

23 And the light of a candle shall shine no more at all in thee; and the voice of the bridegroom and of the bride shall be heard no more at all in thee [*absolute destruction*]: for [*because*] thy [*Babylon's*] merchants were the great men of the earth; for by thy sorceries [*Satan's deceptions*] were all nations deceived.

24 And in her [*Babylon*] was found the blood of prophets, and of saints, and of all that were slain upon the earth [*i.e., Babylon is guilty as charged*].

# REVELATION 19

After witnessing the destruction of Babylon, as shown in chapter 18, John now sees the faithful Saints praising God for His righteous judgment upon the wicked which has prepared the way for the Millennium to begin (verses 1–6). The righteous are invited to the marriage supper of the Lamb (verses 7–9), symbolic in this context of being invited to join the Savior for the Millennium. John sees the glory, power, and authority of the Savior symbolically coming on a white horse (verse 11) to reign as "KING OF KINGS, AND LORD OF LORDS" (verse 16).

Perhaps you have noticed already that things in Revelation are often not given in chronological order. Such is also the case in this chapter. For example, you will see the arrival of the Millennium, but later, in verse 19, you will read about the final wars and battles on the earth before the Millennium.

1 And after these things [*after the destruction of Satan and his kingdom, Babylon, spoken of in Revelation 18*] I [*John*] heard a great voice of much people in heaven, saying, Alleluia [*"Praise ye the Lord," see Bible Dictionary under "Alleluia"*]; Salvation, and glory, and honour, and power, unto the Lord our God [*the righteous rejoice*]:

2 For true [*exactly on the mark*] and righteous are his judgments: for he hath judged the great whore [*Satan's kingdom; D&C 29:21, 1 Nephi 14:10*], which did corrupt the earth with her fornication [*total disloyalty to God, wickedness, breaking covenants*], and hath avenged the blood of his servants at her hand [*has punished the wicked for killing the Saints; Revelation 18:20*].

**<u>JST Revelation 19:2</u>**

2 For true and righteous are his judgments; for he hath judged the great whore, which did corrupt the earth with her fornication, and hath avenged the blood of his saints at her hand.

3 And again they said, Alleluia. And her smoke rose up for ever and ever [*Babylon's destruction is complete; Rev. 18:18*].

4 And the four and twenty elders [*the 24 faithful Elders from John's day, who had died; Rev. 4:4, D&C 77:5*] and the four beasts [*defined in D&C 77:2–4*] fell down and worshipped God that sat on the throne, saying, Amen; Alleluia.

5 And a voice came out of the throne, saying, Praise our God, all ye his servants [*the righteous*], and ye that fear [*respect*] him, both small and great.

**<u>JST Revelation 19:5</u>**

5 And a voice came out of the throne, saying, Praise our God, all ye his saints, and ye that fear him, both small and great.

6 And I heard as it were the voice of a great multitude, and as the voice of many waters, and as the voice of mighty thunderings, saying, Alleluia: for the Lord God omnipotent reigneth. [*Finally, the Millennium is here and Jesus is our King!*]

7 Let us be glad and rejoice, and give honour to him: for the marriage of the Lamb is come [*i.e., the Savior has come to join with the righteous for a thousand years*], and his wife [*the Church, the righteous Saints*] hath made herself ready [*i.e., they are prepared for him, they have "oil in their lamps;" Matthew 25:4*].

8 And to her [*the Church, the righteous*] was granted that she should be arrayed in fine linen, clean and white [*dressed*

*in white robes, symbolic of exaltation*]: for the fine linen is the righteousness of saints [*i.e., they are clothed with personal righteousness; the Savior's Atonement can do this for us, after all we can do; 2 Nephi 25:23*].

9 And he [*the angel in Rev. 1:1*] saith unto me [*John*], Write, Blessed are they which are called unto the marriage supper of the Lamb [*i.e., the righteous who are called up to meet and be with the Savior at his coming; D&C 88:96*]. And he saith unto me, These are the true sayings of God [*the angel bears his testimony to John*].

10 And I [*John*] fell at his [*the angel's*] feet to worship him. And he said unto me, See thou do it not: I am thy fellowservant, and of thy brethren that have the testimony of Jesus: worship God [*i.e., don't worship me, worship God; I am one of you, one of the prophets (Rev. 22:9)*]: for the testimony of Jesus is the spirit of prophecy.

**JST Revelation 19:10**

10 And I fell at his feet to worship him. And he said unto me, See that thou do it not; I am thy fellow servant, and of thy brethren that have the testimony of Jesus; worship God; for the testimony of Jesus is the spirit of prophecy.

11 And I saw heaven opened, and behold a white horse [*symbolic of the triumph of righteousness*]; and he [*Christ*] that sat upon him was called Faithful and True, and in righteousness he doth judge [*the Father turns all judgment over to the Son; John 5:22*] and make war [*destroy the wicked with Satan's kingdom*].

**JST Revelation 19:11**

11 And I saw heaven opened, and behold a white horse; and he that sat upon him is called Faithful and True, and in righteousness he doth judge and make war;

12 His [*Christ's*] eyes were as a flame of fire, and on his head were many crowns [*Christ rules over many kingdoms; D&C 88:50–61*]; and he had a name written [*new name, Rev. 2:17; symbolic of celestial glory; D&C 130:11*], that no man knew, but he himself.

**JST Revelation 19:12**

12 His eyes as a flame of fire; and he had on his head many crowns; and a name written, that no man knew, but himself.

13 And he was clothed with a vesture dipped in blood [*He wore red at his coming, D&C 133:48, symbolic of the blood of the wicked as judgment falls upon them, D&C 133:50–51*] : and his name is called The Word of God [*i.e., Christ; John 1:1*].

**JST Revelation 19:13**

13 And he is clothed with a vesture dipped in blood; and his name is called The Word of God.

14 And the armies which were in heaven [*the hosts of heaven*] followed him upon white horses [*symbolic of righteous victory*], clothed in fine linen [*righteousness; Rev. 19:8*], white and clean.

15 And out of his mouth goeth a sharp sword, that with it he should smite the nations: and he shall rule them with a rod of iron [*the word of God; 1 Nephi 11:25*]: and he treadeth the winepress of the fierceness and wrath of Almighty God [*He destroys the wicked*].

**JST Revelation 19:15**

15 And out of his mouth proceedeth the word of God, and with it he will smite the nations; and he will rule them with the word of his mouth; and he treadeth the winepress in the fierceness and wrath of Almighty God.

16 And he hath on his vesture [*robe: Strong's #2440*] and on his thigh [*German Bible: "hip." Symbolic of great slaughter at Christ's coming. See Judges 15:8 where a terrible slaughter is described as "smote them hip and thigh with a great slaughter."*] a name written, KING OF KINGS, AND LORD

OF LORDS [*i.e., He is Jesus Christ!*].

**JST Revelation 19:16**

16 And he hath on a vesture, and on his thigh a name written, KING OF KINGS, AND LORD OF LORDS.

17 And I saw an angel standing in the sun [*symbolic of power and authority in heaven*]; and he cried with a loud voice, saying to all the fowls that fly in the midst of heaven, Come and gather yourselves together unto the supper of the great God [*symbolically, many carrion birds are needed to clean up the carcasses of the wicked who will be destroyed in the final wars before the Second Coming*];

18 That ye may eat the flesh of kings [*wicked, influential leaders*], and the flesh of captains, and the flesh of mighty men, and the flesh of horses [*horses are symbolic of military might, weapons of war and destruction*], and of them that sit on them, and the flesh of all men, both free and bond, both small and great [*i.e., all the wicked*].

**JST Revelation 19:18**

18 That ye may eat the flesh of kings, and the flesh of captains, and the flesh of mighty men, and the flesh of horses, and of them that sit on them, and the flesh of all who fight against the Lamb, both bond and free, both small and great.

19 And I saw the beast [*perhaps referring back to Revelation 13:1*], and the [*wicked*] kings of the earth, and their armies, gathered together to make war against him [*Christ; verse 11*] that sat on the horse, and against his army [*the final battles*].

20 And the beast was taken [*conquered*], and with him the false prophet that wrought miracles before him [*Revelation 13:14*], with which he deceived them that had received the mark of the beast [*Revelation 13:16*], and them that worshipped his image [*i.e., his followers; Revelation 13:14*]. These both were cast alive into a lake of fire burning with brimstone [*i.e., you can't imagine how miserable it will be for the wicked; compare with D&C 19:15*].

21 And the remnant [*those wicked who survive the horrible final battles before the Second Coming*] were slain with the sword of him that sat upon the horse, [*i.e., destroyed at the Second Coming*] which sword proceeded out of his mouth: and all the fowls [*the carrion birds in verse 17*] were filled with their flesh [*the carcasses of the slain wicked in verse 18*].

**JST Revelation 19:21**

21 And the remnant were slain with the word of him that sat upon the horse, which word proceeded out of his mouth; and all the fowls were filled with their flesh.

# REVELATION 20

In this chapter, we see the binding of Satan for the duration of the Millennium. We see the righteous, resurrected Saints reigning with Christ a thousand years. Then we see Satan "loosed a little season" at the end of the Millennium which leads to the battle of Gog and Magog. At the end of this battle, we see the total defeat of the devil and the hosts of the wicked. Finally, we see the last resurrection and final judgment.

1 And I saw an angel come down from heaven, having the key of the bottomless pit and a great chain in his hand [*i.e., fully equipped to bind Satan*].

**JST Revelation 20:1**

1 And I saw an angel come down out of heaven, having the key of the bottomless pit and a great chain in his hand.

2 And he laid hold on the dragon, that old serpent, which is the Devil, and Satan, and bound him a thousand years [*during the Millennium*],

From verse 2, above, we see that Satan is bound for the duration of the Millennium and is not even allowed to try to tempt the people living on the earth during the thousand years. This doctrine is taught clearly in D&C 101:28.

3 And cast him into the bottomless pit [*the depths of hell*], and shut him up, and set a seal upon him, that he should deceive the nations no more, till the thousand years should be fulfilled [*i.e., are over*]: and after that he must be loosed a little season [*D&C 88:110–115*].

4 And I saw thrones [*symbolic of being joint heirs with Christ; Romans 8:17; i.e., exaltation*], and they [*the righteous*] sat upon them, and judgment was given unto them: and I saw the souls [*resurrected bodies*] of them that were beheaded for the witness of Jesus [*i.e., righteous martyrs*], and for the word of God, and which had not worshipped the beast [*Revelation 13, i.e., who had not followed Satan*], neither his image [*Revelation 13:14*], neither had received his mark upon their foreheads, or in their hands [*Revelation 13:16*]; and they [*the righteous*] lived and reigned with Christ a thousand years.

5 But the rest of the dead [*the wicked*] lived not again [*were not resurrected*] until the thousand years were finished. This [*the resurrection of the righteous indicated in verse 4—see D&C 88:97–98*] is the first resurrection [*which takes place at the beginning of the Millennium*].

6 Blessed and holy is he that hath part in the first resurrection: on such the second death [*spiritual death*] hath no power, but they shall be priests of God and of Christ, and shall reign with him a thousand years.

**JST Revelation 20:6**

6 Blessed and holy are they who have part in the first resurrection; on such the second death hath no power, but they shall be priests of God and of Christ, and shall reign with him a thousand years.

7 And when the thousand years are expired, Satan shall be loosed out of his prison [*D&C 88:111*],

8 And shall go out to deceive the nations which are in the four quarters of the earth, Gog and Magog [*symbolic of wicked nations and their leaders; for a definition of Gog, see Bible Dictionary under "Gog," and for Magog, under "Magog"*], to gather them together to battle: the number of whom is as the sand of the sea [*i.e., there will be great numbers of wicked during the little season, after the end of the Millennium*].

9 And they [*the wicked; Gog and Magog*] went up on the breadth of the earth, and compassed the camp of the saints about [*made war against the Saints; D&C 88:112–115*], and the beloved city [*the Lord's kingdom*]: and fire came down from God out of heaven, and devoured them.

10 And the devil that deceived them was cast into the lake of fire and brimstone, where the beast and the false prophet are, and shall be tormented day and night for ever and ever [*Satan and his wicked hosts are cast out forever (D&C 76:32–36, 44–45)*].

11 And I saw a great white throne, and him [*Christ; Rev. 21:5–6*] that sat on it, from whose face the earth and the heaven fled away; and there was found no place for them [*i.e., there will be a new heaven after the Millennium and little season are over, perhaps referring to the fact that "This earth will be rolled back into the presence of God, and crowned with celestial glory." (*Teachings of the Prophet Joseph Smith*, Deseret Book, 1977, p. 181)*] and new earth; [*not a different one, but a resurrected earth; D&C 88:26, 130:9*].

12 And I saw the dead, small and great, stand before God; and the books were opened: and another book was opened, which is the book of life: and the dead were judged out of those things which were written in the books, according to their works [*the final judgment*].

13 And the sea gave up the dead which were in it; and death and hell delivered up the dead which were in them [*all the wicked were finally resurrected also; D&C 88:101–102*]: and they were judged every man according to their works.

14 And death and hell were cast into the lake of fire. This is the second death [*only sons of perdition will suffer this forever; D&C 76:36–37*].

15 And whosoever was not found written in the book of life was cast into the lake of fire [*all except sons of perdition are saved at least to some degree, by Christ, into the telestial, terrestrial or celestial kingdoms; D&C 76:37–39, 81–87*].

## REVELATION 21

In this chapter John describes the earth as it attains celestial glory.

1 And I saw a new heaven and a new earth [*D&C 29:23–24; see also notes for Rev. 20:11*]: for the first heaven and the first earth were passed away; and there was no more sea.

2 And I John saw the holy city, new Jerusalem, coming down from God out of heaven, prepared as a bride adorned for her husband [*i.e., dressed in her finest i.e., celestial*].

3 And I heard a great voice out of heaven saying, Behold, the tabernacle [*physical body*] of God is with men [*i.e., the Savior is literally, physically, here with us*], and he will dwell with them, and they shall be his people, and God himself shall be with them, and be their God [*Christ will dwell with the righteous on the celestialized earth; D&C 130:9*].

Referring to verses 2 and 3, above, we see that, according to Ether 13:8–10, a city called "New Jerusalem" will be built upon the American continent (see also the tenth Article of Faith). Moses 7:22 tells us that this New Jerusalem will be built up by the righteous as they look forward to the coming of Christ. In his vision, John saw "the holy city, new Jerusalem, coming down from God out of heaven" (verse 3). We understand the "new Jerusalem" which John saw here to be a different city than the New Jerusalem described in Ether and Moses. The "new Jerusalem" seen by John seems to be symbolic of this earth as it is celestialized and as it becomes the abode of the Savior and the righteous Saints forever (see verse 3). Bruce R. McConkie said: "When this earth becomes a celestial sphere 'that great city, the holy Jerusalem,' shall again descend 'out of heaven from God,' as this earth becomes the abode of celestial beings forever. (Rev. 21:10–27.)" (McConkie, *Doctrinal New Testament Commentary*, 3:580–81.)

4 And God shall wipe away all tears from their eyes; and there shall be no more death, neither sorrow, nor crying, neither shall there be any more pain [*a beautiful description of celestial glory*]: for the former things [*past troubles*] are passed away.

5 And he [*Christ; Rev. 20:11, 21:6*] that sat upon the throne said, Behold, I make all things new. And he said unto me, Write: for these words are true and faithful [*Christ bears testimony to John of the truthfulness of the things he is seeing and hearing*].

6 And he [*Christ*] said unto me [*John*], It is done [*everything is fulfilled; D&C 1:38*]. I am Alpha and Omega, the beginning and the end. I will give unto him [*the righteous*] that is athirst of the fountain of the water of life freely [*living water; John 4:14*].

7 He that overcometh [*overcomes sin and wickedness*] shall inherit all things

[*i.e., will receive exaltation, D&C 132:20*]; and I will be his God, and he shall be my son.

8 But the fearful [*perhaps meaning those who are afraid to do right*], and unbelieving, and the abominable, and murderers, and whoremongers, and sorcerers, and idolaters, and all liars, shall have their part [*will receive their punishment*] in the lake which burneth with fire and brimstone: which is the second death [*an important message for John to give during his remaining ministry on earth*].

9 And there came unto me one of the seven angels [*Revelation 15:1*] which had the seven vials full of the seven last plagues, and talked with me, saying, Come hither, I will shew thee the bride, the Lamb's wife [*there are many possible meanings for this, including the Church, the righteous, the City of Enoch, the celestial city or kingdom described in verses 11–27 of this chapter*].

10 And he carried me away in the spirit to a great and high mountain, and shewed me that great city, the holy Jerusalem [*symbolic of the celestial kingdom*], descending out of heaven from God,

In other words, John is now shown the beauty and glory of the celestial kingdom.

11 Having the glory of God: and her light [*the city's light*] was like unto a stone most precious, even like a jasper stone, clear as crystal;

12 And had a wall great and high [*symbolic of security, safety*], and had twelve [*symbolic of divine government—see symbolism notes at the beginning of Revelation in this study guide*] gates, and at the gates twelve angels, and names written thereon, which are the names of the twelve tribes of the children of Israel:

13 On the east three gates; on the north three gates; on the south three gates; and on the west three gates [*perhaps the use of sets of "three" symbolizes that the whole celestial city or kingdom is blessed with the presence of the Godhead—see symbolism notes referred to above*].

14 And the wall of the city had twelve foundations, and in them the names of the twelve apostles of the Lamb [*perhaps symbolizing that the city is indeed built upon the righteous principles and priesthood covenants taught by the twelve Apostles*].

15 And he that talked with me had a golden reed [*perhaps a celestial measuring device similar to the reed in Revelation 11:1, used here to show John that things indeed "measure up" just as promised*] to measure the city, and the gates thereof, and the wall thereof.

16 And the city lieth foursquare, and the length is as large as the breadth: and he measured the city with the reed, twelve thousand furlongs [*if a furlong is about 220 yards, Bible Dictionary under "Weights and Measures," and the length and breadth are twelve thousand furlongs each, the city which John saw was about 1,500 U.S. miles in length, width and height, or about 3 billion, 375 million cubic miles of living space, perhaps symbolizing to John that there is plenty of glorious living space for the "great multitude" of the righteous which he saw in heaven in Revelation 7:9; see also D&C 76:67*]. The length and the breadth and the height of it are equal.

17 And he [*the angel talking to John in verse 15*] measured the wall thereof, an hundred and forty and four cubits, according to the measure of a man, that is, of the angel.

**JST Revelation 21:17**

17 And he measured the wall thereof, a hundred and forty and four cubits, according to the measure of a man, that is, of the angel.

18 [*John now attempts almost the impossible, i.e., to describe to us the beauty of celestial glory.*] And the building of the wall of it was of jasper: and the city was pure gold, like unto clear glass.

19 And the foundations of the wall of the city were garnished with all manner of precious stones. The first foundation was jasper; the second, sapphire; the third, a chalcedony; the fourth, an emerald;

20 The fifth, sardonyx; the sixth, sardius; the seventh, chrysolite; the eighth, beryl; the ninth, a topaz; the tenth, a chrysoprasus; the eleventh, a jacinth; the twelfth, an amethyst.

21 And the twelve gates were twelve pearls; every several gate was of one pearl: and the street of the city was pure gold, as it were transparent glass.

22 And I saw no temple therein [*a temple is not needed*]: for the Lord God Almighty and the Lamb are the temple of it.

23 And the city had no need of the sun, neither of the moon, to shine in it: for the glory of God did lighten it, and the Lamb [*Christ*] is the light thereof.

24 And the nations of them which are saved [*i.e., the righteous*] shall walk in the light of it: and the kings of the earth do bring their glory and honour into it.

25 And the gates of it shall not be shut at all by day: for there shall be no night there.

26 And they shall bring the glory and honour of the nations into it.

27 And there shall in no wise enter into it any thing that defileth, neither whatsoever worketh abomination, or maketh a lie [*i.e., no unclean thing can enter the kingdom; 3 Nephi 27:19*]: but they which are written in the Lamb's book of life [*i.e., the righteous who have been made clean through the Atonement of Christ; Alma 34:36*].

# REVELATION 22

John's vision draws to a close with symbolism and doctrines which summarize major messages of the Book of Revelation, including that the reward of the righteous is wonderful beyond our ability to comprehend and that the wicked are left out of these priceless blessings.

As we start verse 1, we see that it is a continuation of the description of celestial glory from chapter 21.

1 And he [*one of the seven angels; Revelation 21:9*] shewed me a pure river of water of life, clear as crystal, proceeding out of the throne of God and of the Lamb.

2 In the midst of the street of it [*the celestial city (chapter 21), i.e., celestial glory*], and on either side of the river, was there the tree of life [*1 Nephi 8:10, Revelation 22:14*], which bare twelve manner of fruits, and yielded her fruit every month [*i.e., the benefits of the gospel are not "seasonal," rather continue constantly forever*]: and the leaves of the tree were for the healing of the nations [*what the gospel can do for people*].

3 And there shall be no more curse [*on the earth, Genesis 3:17, which will then be the celestial kingdom, D&C 130:9; 88:25*]: but the throne of God and of the Lamb shall be in it; and his servants shall serve him:

4 And they shall see his face; and his name shall be in their foreheads [*Revelation 3:12; i.e., they have taken His name upon them and kept their covenants, therefore they will be with Him in celestial glory*].

5 And there shall be no night there; and they need no candle, neither light of the sun; for the Lord God giveth them light: and they shall reign for ever and ever [*i.e., they will be Gods; D&C 132:20*].

6 And he said unto me, These sayings are faithful and true [*the angel bears his testimony to John*]: and the Lord God of the holy prophets sent his angel to shew unto his servants the things which must shortly be done [*the vision is now coming to a close and the angel is summarizing for John*].

7 Behold, I [*Christ*] come quickly [*not "soon," rather, when the time is right, He will come suddenly upon the wicked as a thief in the night; D&C 106:4–5*]: blessed is he that keepeth [*obeys*] the sayings of the prophecy of this book.

8 And I John saw these things, and heard them. And when I had heard and seen, I fell down to worship before the feet of the angel [*as mentioned in Revelation 19:10*] which shewed me these things.

9 Then saith he unto me, See thou do it not [*don't worship me*]: for I am thy fellowservant, and of thy brethren the prophets [*I am one of you*], and of them which keep the sayings of this book: worship God.

**<u>JST Revelation 22:9</u>**

9 Then saith he unto me, See that thou do it not; for I am thy fellowservant, and of thy brethren the prophets, and of them which keep the sayings of this book; worship God.

10 And he saith unto me, Seal not the sayings of the prophecy of this book [*i.e., let these things be read*]: for the time is at hand.

11 He that is unjust, let him be unjust still: and he which is filthy, let him be filthy still: and he that is righteous, let him be righteous still: and he that is holy, let him be holy still [*when final judgment comes you will be judged according to what you are*].

12 And, behold, I [*Christ*] come quickly; and my reward is with me, to give every man according as his work shall be.

13 I am Alpha and Omega [*Revelation 1:11*], the beginning and the end, the first and the last [*i.e., I am the "A" and the "Z"; I know the beginning from the end; I was there at the beginning of creation, and I will be there at the end of the earth to judge you; I am in charge of all things under the direction of the Father*].

14 Blessed are they that do his commandments, that they may have right to the tree of life [*spoken of in verse 2*], and may enter in through the gates into the city [*the celestial kingdom*].

15 For without [*i.e., outside of the celestial glory, i.e., telestial glory; see D&C 76:103*] are dogs [*an unclean beast under the Law of Moses, perhaps symbolic here of people who refused to make themselves clean through the Atonement*], and sorcerers, and whoremongers [*people who constantly seek opportunities for immorality*], and murderers, and idolaters, and whosoever loveth and maketh a lie [*people who are dishonest, love to lie*].

Next, the Savior bears His testimony to John that He is the Redeemer, about whom the Old Testament prophesied.

16 I Jesus have sent mine angel to testify unto you these things in the churches [*probably the seven churches or "wards" referred to in Rev. 1:11*]. I am the root [*that came out of dry ground, i.e., apostate Judaism, as stated by Isaiah in Isaiah 53:2*] and the offspring of David [*a descendent of David*], and the bright and morning star [*the first and the brightest, i.e., I am the Savior*].

17 And the Spirit [*the Holy Ghost*] and the bride [*the righteous members of the Church; see Rev. 21:2*] say, Come. And let him that heareth say, Come. And let him that is athirst come. And whosoever will, let him take the water of life freely [*an open invitation to all to come unto Christ*].

Perhaps you have run into the argument by other Christians that our Book of Mormon and other scriptures

in addition to the Bible, violate Revelation 22:18. They suggest that nothing should be added to the Bible. Pay close attention to the notes in verses 18–19, next, for the solution to this challenge.

18 For I testify unto every man that heareth the words of the prophecy of this book [*the Book of Revelation, not the whole Bible; John wrote the Gospel of John after Revelation*], If any man shall add unto these things [*i.e., intentionally twists meanings or adds false doctrines*], God shall add unto him the plagues that are written in this book:

19 And if any man shall take away from the words of the book of this prophecy, God shall take away his part out of the book of life, and out of the holy city, and from the things which are written in this book [*i.e., don't intentionally twist the meanings, delete doctrines, etc., from this book*].

20 He which testifieth these things saith, Surely I come quickly. Amen. Even so, come, Lord Jesus.

21 The grace of our Lord Jesus Christ be with you all. Amen.

# SOURCES

*Doctrine and Covenants Student Manual, Religion 324 and 325.* Salt Lake City: The Church of Jesus Christ of Latter-day Saints, 2001.

*Ensign*. March 1976 and November 1995.

*Hymns of The Church of Jesus Christ of Latter-day Saints*. Salt Lake City: The Church of Jesus Christ of Latter-day Saints, 1985.

*Improvement Era*. Vol. 19.

*Journal of Discourses*. Vol 18. London: Latter-day Saints' Book Depot, 1854–86.

Parry, Jay A. and Donald W. *Understanding the Book of Revelation*. Salt Lake City: Deseret Book, 1998.

Kimball, Spencer W. *The Miracle of Forgiveness*. Salt Lake City: Bookcraft, 1969.

McConkie, Bruce R. *Doctrinal New Testament Commentary*. 3 vols. Salt Lake City: Bookcraft, 1965–73.

McConkie, Bruce R. *Mormon Doctrine*. 2d ed. Salt Lake City: Bookcraft, 1966.

Millet, Robert L. *Alive in Christ: The Miracle of Spiritual Rebirth*. Salt Lake City: Deseret Book, 1997.

Pratt, Orson. *Masterful Discourses and Writings of Orson Pratt*. Compiled by N. B. Lundwall. Salt Lake City: Bookcraft, 1962.

Smith, Joseph. *History of The Church of Jesus Christ of Latter-day Saints*. Edited by B. H. Roberts. 2d ed. rev., 7 vols., Salt Lake City: The Church of Jesus Christ of Latter-day Saints, 1932–51.

Smith, Joseph. *Joseph Smith's "New Translation" of the Bible* (JST). Independence, Missouri: Herald Publishing House, 1970.

Smith, Joseph. *Lectures on Faith*. Salt Lake City: Deseret Book, 1985.

Smith, Joseph. *Teachings of the Prophet Joseph Smith*. Selected by Joseph Fielding Smith. Salt Lake City: Deseret Book, 1976.

Smith, Joseph F. *Gospel Doctrine: Selections from the Sermons and Writings of Joseph F. Smith.* Salt Lake City: Deseret Book, 1971.

Smith, Joseph Fielding. *Doctrines of Salvation*. Compiled by Bruce R. McConkie. 3 vols. Salt Lake City: Bookcraft, 1954–56.

Strong, James. *The Exhaustive Concordance of the Bible*. Nashville: Abingdon, 1890.

*The Life and Teachings of Jesus and His Apostles,* The New Testament Student Manual, Religion 211. Salt Lake City: The Church of Jesus Christ of Latter-day Saints, 1979.

Widtsoe, John A. *Evidences and Reconciliations*. Salt Lake City: Bookcraft, 1943.

Various translations of the Bible, including the Martin Luther edition of the German Bible, which Joseph Smith said was the most correct of any then available.

# About the Author

David J. Ridges taught for the Church Educational System for thirty-five years and has taught for several years at BYU Campus Education Week. He taught adult religion classes and Know Your Religion classes for BYU Continuing Education for many years. He has also served as a curriculum writer for Sunday School, Seminary, and Institute of Religion manuals.

He has served in many callings in the Church, including Gospel Doctrine teacher, bishop, stake president, and patriarch. He and Sister Ridges served a full-time eighteen-month mission, training senior CES missionaries and helping coordinate their assignments throughout the world.

Brother Ridges and his wife, Janette, are the parents of six children and make their home in Springville, Utah.

www.ingramcontent.com/pod-product-compliance
Lightning Source LLC
LaVergne TN
LVHW050152080826
844660LV00002B/177

* 9 7 8 0 2 5 3 0 4 0 5 3 4 *

# FOREWORD

In more than forty-two years of teaching in the Church and for the Church Educational System, I have found that members of the Church encounter some common problems when it comes to understanding the scriptures. One problem is understanding the language of the scriptures themselves. Another is understanding symbolism. Another is how best to mark scriptures and perhaps make brief notes in them. Yet another concern is how to understand what the scriptures are actually teaching. In other words, what are the major messages being taught by the Lord through His prophets?

This book is designed to address each of the concerns mentioned above for Acts through Revelation in the New Testament. The Bible text of each book is included in its entirety and serves as the basic text for this work.

The format is intentionally simple, with some license taken with respect to capitalization and punctuation in order to minimize interruption of the flow. The format is designed to help readers to:

- Quickly gain a basic understanding of these scriptures through the use of brief explanatory notes in brackets within the verses as well as notes between some verses. This paves the way for even deeper testimony and understanding later.
- Better understand the beautiful language of the scriptures. This is accomplished in this book with in-the-verse notes that define difficult scriptural terms.
- Mark their scriptures and put brief notes in the margins that will help them understand now and remember later what given passages of scripture teach.
- Better understand the symbolism, especially in the writings of Paul and in the book of Revelation
- Get a feel for the background and setting in which events and teachings take place

Over the years, one of the most common expressions of gratitude from my students has been, "Thanks for the notes you had us put in our scriptures." This book is dedicated to that purpose.

Sources for the notes given in this work are as follows:

- The standard works of The Church of Jesus Christ of Latter-day Saints.
- Footnotes in the Latter-day Saint version of the King James Bible.
- The Joseph Smith Translation of the Bible.
- The Bible Dictionary in the back of the Latter-day Saint version of the Bible.
- Strong's *Exhaustive Concordance of the Bibl*e, shown as [*Strong's* #].
- Various Bible dictionaries.
- The New Testament Student Manual provided for our institutes of religion.
- Various translations of the Bible, including the Martin Luther edition of the German Bible, which Joseph Smith said was the most correct of any then available.
- *Doctrinal New Testament Commentary*, Vol. 2 and 3, by Apostle Bruce R. McConkie.
- *Understanding the Book of Revelation*, by Jay A. Parry and Donald W. Parry.
- *New International Version of the Bible*, Zondervan Publishing House, 1984.
- Other sources as noted in the text and in the "Sources" section.

I hope that this study guide will serve effectively as a "teacher in your hand" to members of the Church as they seek to increase their understanding of the writings and teachings of the Savior's Apostles. Above all, if this work serves to bring increased understanding and testimony of the Atonement of Christ, all the efforts to put it together will have been far more than worth it. A special thanks goes to my wife, Janette, and my children who have encouraged me every step of the way.

# THE ACTS OF THE APOSTLES

It is helpful to know that Luke wrote both the Gospel of Luke and Acts (The Acts of the Apostles). As mentioned at the beginning of Luke in this study guide series, he was a physician, apparently a Greek convert to the gospel. Many believe that Luke addressed his writings to the Gentiles. See Bible Dictionary (at the back of our LDS Bible), under "Luke." Both Luke and Acts were written to "Theophilus" (see Luke 1:3 and Acts 1:1). Theophilus is a Greek name meaning "friend of God" or "beloved of God." Some Bible scholars suggest that "Theophilus" could mean anyone who is a friend of God. However, most consider Theophilus to have been an actual person, probably a Greek official of high rank.

Acts deals mainly with the growth of the Church after the Savior had ascended up to heaven. In it Luke writes of the ministries of Peter and the other Apostles and especially gives us much detail about Paul's teaching and missionary journeys to the Gentiles.

We will include verses from the JST (the Joseph Smith Translation of the Bible) frequently for clarification. As we do so, you will be able to gain an even stronger testimony of the inspired work of the Prophet Joseph Smith.

## ACTS 1

As this chapter begins, Luke explains that this account is a continuation of his former account (the Book of Luke) to Theophilus. After a very brief review of Luke, he proceeds to tell Theophilus what took place with the Church and spread of the gospel after the Savior's ascension into heaven. Among other things, you will see that Peter has now taken on his role as president of the Church, and you will see a new Apostle chosen to take the place of Judas Iscariot.

1 THE former treatise [*the former account, namely, the Gospel of Luke*] have I made, O Theophilus, of all that Jesus began both to do and teach,

2 Until the day in which he was taken up [*Acts 1:9–11*], after that he through the Holy Ghost had given commandments unto the apostles whom he had chosen:

In verse 3, next, you will see the word "passion." As used here it refers to the Savior's suffering for us, and includes His agony in the Garden of Gethsemane and on the cross. You will see that the Prophet Joseph Smith uses "sufferings" in place of "passion," as you read the JST [*Joseph Smith Translation of the Bible*], quoted after verse 3.

3 To whom also he shewed [*showed, pronounced "showed"*] himself alive after his passion by many infallible [*absolute*] proofs, being seen of them forty days, and speaking of the things pertaining to the kingdom of God:

**JST Acts 1:3**

3 To whom also he showed himself alive after his sufferings by many infallible proofs, being seen of them forty days, and speaking of the things pertaining to the kingdom of God;

In verse three, above, we learn that

the Savior associated with His Apostles during the forty days following His resurrection. They saw Him and spent time with Him as He taught and instructed them in preparation for the time when they would lead the Church, after His departure.

4 And, being assembled together with them, commanded them that they should not depart from Jerusalem, but wait for the promise of the Father [*that they would receive the full power of the Gift of the Holy Ghost; see John 14:16–17, 26, etc.*], which, saith he, ye have heard of me [*which, Jesus reminded them, they had heard of from Him*].

**JST Acts 1:4**

3 And, being with them when they were assembled together, commanded them that they should not depart from Jerusalem, but wait for the promise of the Father, which, saith he, ye have heard of me.

5 For John truly baptized with water; but ye shall be baptized with the Holy Ghost not many days hence [*from now*]. [*This will happen on the day of Pentecost. See Acts 2:1–4.*]

We know from Luke 4:1, Matthew 3:13–17 and many other references that the Holy Ghost was actively functioning during the Savior's mortal ministry. Yet, in verse 5, above, the Apostles are told that, in a few days, they would be "baptized with the Holy Ghost." We understand that the full power of the Gift of the Holy Ghost was not given these men while the Savior was with them, and that it is what was given to them after the Savior departed. See Bible Dictionary under "Holy Ghost."

6 When they therefore were come together [*when they had met together, at the end of the forty days, to be instructed some more by the resurrected Savior*], they asked of him, saying, Lord, wilt thou at this time restore again the kingdom to Israel [*in other words, is the time for the Second Coming about here, when Israel will be restored and the gospel taught upon the whole earth*] ?

7 And he said unto them, It is not for you to know the times or the seasons [*the exact timing of these things*], which the Father hath put in his own power [*the Father is the one who will say when these things will happen; see Matthew 24:36, Mark 13:32, Revelation 15:15*].

8 But ye shall receive power, after that the Holy Ghost is come upon you [*in full power; see note following verse 5, above*]: and ye shall be witnesses unto me both in Jerusalem, and in all Judea, and in Samaria, and unto the uttermost [*most distant*] part of the earth.

9 And when he had spoken these things, while they beheld [*watched*], he was taken up; and a cloud received him out of their sight.

10 And while they looked stedfastly [*in rapt attention*] toward heaven as he went up, behold, two men [*angels*] stood by them in white apparel [*clothing*];

11 Which also said, Ye men of Galilee, why stand ye gazing up into heaven? this same Jesus, which is taken up from you into heaven, shall so come in like manner as ye have seen him go into heaven. [*The Savior will come in clouds of glory at the time of His Second Coming.*]

It is interesting to note that the Second Coming is mentioned over 1500 times in the Old Testament and over 300 times in the New Testament.

12 Then returned they unto Jerusalem from the mount called Olivet [*the Mount of Olives, just outside Jerusalem*], which is from Jerusalem a sabbath day's journey [*about 3,000 feet; see Bible Dictionary under "Sabbath"*].

13 And when they were come in [*had come into the building*], they went up into an upper room, where abode [*lived*] both Peter, and James, and John, and Andrew, Philip, and Thomas, Bartholomew, and Matthew, James the son

of Alphæus, and Simon Zelotes, and Judas the brother of James. [*All eleven remaining Apostles were apparently staying temporarily in Jerusalem, as commanded in verse 4, above.*]

14 These all continued with one accord [*in unity of purpose*] in prayer and supplication [*asking God for things they desired*], with the women, and Mary the mother of Jesus, and with his brethren [*Jesus' half brothers—He had at least four; see Mark 6:3*].

Next, beginning with verse 15, we see Peter take charge, indicating to us that he is now serving as the president of the Church. He will explain what happened to Judas Iscariot and the need to find a replacement for him to serve in the Quorum of the Twelve.

15 ¶ And in those days [*at a certain point during those days*] Peter stood up in the midst of the disciples, and said, (the number of names together [*the total number who were meeting together*] were about an hundred and twenty,)

16 Men and brethren, this scripture [*Psalm 41:9*] must needs have been fulfilled [*had to be fulfilled*], which the Holy Ghost by the mouth of [*through*] David spake before [*spoke in the past*] concerning Judas [*Iscariot*], which [*who*] was guide to them that took Jesus [*who guided the soldiers to arrest Jesus*].

17 For he was numbered with us [*he was one of the Twelve*], and had obtained part of this ministry. [*Judas Iscariot worked with us as one of the twelve Apostles.*]

18 Now this man [*Judas*] purchased a field with the reward of iniquity [*money obtained through wickedness; the thirty pieces of silver Judas was paid for betraying Jesus was used to buy a field*]; and falling headlong, he burst asunder in the midst, and all his bowels gushed out.

Matthew 27:3–8 tells us that Judas hanged himself. From verse 18, above, we would conclude that the rope broke, or was cut later, and that Judas' body fell headfirst down a steep incline and burst open.

19 And it was known unto all the dwellers at Jerusalem [*everybody in Jerusalem knew about Judas Iscariot's awful death*]; insomuch as that field is called in their proper [*own*] tongue, Aceldama, that is to say, The field of blood.

20 For it is written in the book of Psalms [*69:25*], Let his habitation be desolate, and let no man dwell therein: and his bishoprick [*church calling; Psalm 109:8*] let another take.

21 Wherefore of these men which have companied with [*who have accompanied*] us all the time that the Lord Jesus went in and out [*came and went*] among us,

22 Beginning from the baptism of John [*beginning at the time John the Baptist baptized Jesus*], unto that same day that he [*Jesus*] was taken up from us, must one be ordained to be a witness with us of his resurrection. [*We need an Apostle to replace Judas Iscariot.*]

23 And they appointed two [*selected two men*], Joseph called Barsabas, who was surnamed [*whose family name was*] Justus, and Matthias.

24 And they prayed, and said, Thou, Lord, which knowest the hearts of all men, shew whether [*show which*] of these two thou hast chosen,

25 That he [*the new Apostle*] may take part of this ministry and apostleship, from which Judas by transgression fell, that he [*Judas*] might go to his own place [*reward*].

26 And they gave forth their lots; and the lot fell upon Matthias; and he was numbered with the eleven apostles. [*Matthias became a member of the twelve Apostles.*]

Praying, and then casting lots, sticks of wood, or whatever, with one being shorter than the other, such that the and signs, which God did by him [*through Jesus*] in the midst of [*among*] you, as ye yourselves also know:

23 Him, being delivered by the determinate counsel [*according to the plan presented in the council in heaven where Christ was chosen to be our Redeemer*] and foreknowledge of God, ye have taken, and by wicked hands have crucified and slain:

24 Whom God hath raised up [*resurrected*], having loosed the pains of death [*having freed Jesus from the pains of death*]: because it was not possible that he [*Jesus*] should be holden of it [*it was not possible that Christ should be held captive by death and the grave*].

25 For David speaketh concerning him [*Psalm 16:8–11*], I foresaw the Lord always before my face, for he is on my right hand, that I should not be moved: [*"Right hand" is symbolic of making covenants. Being on the "right hand" of God is symbolic of being saved.*]

26 Therefore did my heart rejoice, and my tongue was glad; moreover also my flesh shall rest in hope:

27 Because thou wilt not leave my soul in hell, neither wilt thou suffer thine Holy One to see corruption.

**JST Acts 2:27**

27 Because thou wilt not leave my soul in prison, neither wilt thou suffer thine Holy One to see corruption.

28 Thou hast made known to me the ways of life; thou shalt make me full of joy with thy countenance. [*End of quote from Psalm.*]

29 Men and brethren, let me freely speak unto you of the patriarch [*of our ancestor*] David, that he is both dead and buried, and his sepulchre [*tomb, grave*] is with us unto this day. [*In other words, David is still dead and buried, meaning that he did not get resurrected with the righteous at the time of Christ's resurrection. See D&C 133:54–55 to see who was resurrected with the Savior.*]

30 Therefore being a prophet [*King David*], and knowing that God had sworn [*promised*] with an oath [*with a covenant*] to him, that of the fruit of his loins [*from his posterity*], according to the flesh [*here on earth*], he would raise up Christ to sit on his throne; [*David was promised that Christ would be one of his descendants and would be King.*]

31 He seeing this before [*David, having seen this before it happened*] spake [*spoke*] of the resurrection of Christ, that his soul was not left in hell, neither his flesh did see corruption.

The phrase "that his soul was not left in hell" in verse 31, above, seems to have a dual meaning, as is often the case in the scriptures. One meaning is that Satan and all the powers of hell would not succeed in overcoming Christ or preventing His resurrection. In this sense, the word "hell" in verse 31 would mean the spirit world. See Bible Dictionary under the topic "Hell," first four lines, where "hell," "Sheol," and "Hades" all refer to the world of departed spirits. In other words, Christ would not remain, as others had, in the world of departed spirits, but would be resurrected after a short three days.

A second meaning of the phrase "his soul was not left in hell" refers to King David. After having committed adultery with Uriah's wife, Bathsheba, and then being told that she was expecting his child, (2 Samuel 11:2–5), David arranged to have Uriah killed in battle and then quickly married Bathsheba, thus attempting to cover up with murder his adultery. This was a tragedy, and David pled with the Lord not to leave his soul in hell. Joseph Smith tells us that David got a promise that his soul would not be left in hell (*Teachings of the Prophet Joseph Smith*, p. 339). We understand the "hell" spoken of by David in reference to his own status to be perdition, meaning "outer darkness" as we commonly use the term. See McConkie,

*Doctrinal New Testament Commentary*, Vol. 2, p. 39. According to D&C 42:18, murderers cannot be forgiven as far as gaining exaltation is concerned, but D&C 76:103 combined with Revelation 22:15 informs us that such murderers will go to telestial glory, and thus are out of Satan's grasp eternally. Tragically, David was a murderer, and will apparently go to telestial glory. D&C 132:39 confirms that David will not obtain exaltation. It also assures us that David's wives were not penalized eternally because of their husband's wickedness. They would be blessed to marry someone else and thus be exalted.

32 This Jesus hath God raised up [*resurrected*], whereof we all are witnesses.

33 Therefore being by the right hand [*covenant hand*] of God exalted [*Christ kept His covenants and the Father exalted him*], and having received of [*from*] the Father the promise of the Holy Ghost, he hath shed forth this, which ye now see and hear [*He sent the Holy Ghost, as promised, and this is why you witnessed the speaking in tongues which has amazed you so*].

34 For David is not ascended into the heavens [*David didn't make it to heaven; see footnote 34a in your Bible, which refers to D&C 132:39*]: but he saith himself [*but he prophesied; Psalm 110:1*], The LORD [*Heavenly Father*] said unto my Lord [*Christ*], Sit thou on my right hand [*sit down with Me in heaven*],

35 Until I make thy foes thy footstool [*until the Second Coming when You will triumph over all enemies of righteousness*].

36 Therefore let all the house of Israel know assuredly, that God [*the Father*] hath made that same Jesus, whom ye have crucified, both Lord and Christ.

Above, in verse 36, Peter lays the blame for the Savior's crucifixion directly upon the Jews of that day, rather than upon the Romans. However, watch in verse 39, below, as repentance and forgiveness are extended to the Jews.

37 ¶ Now when they [*the people in the crowd who had heard the Apostles speak in tongues with the power of the Holy Ghost upon them*] heard this, they were pricked [*deeply touched*] in their heart, and said unto Peter and to the rest of the apostles, Men and brethren, what shall we do?

38 Then Peter said unto them, Repent, and be baptized every one of you in the name of Jesus Christ for the remission of sins [*to be forgiven of your sins*], and ye shall receive the gift of the Holy Ghost.

39 For the promise [*of forgiveness of sins*] is unto you [*is available to you*], and to your children, and to all that are afar off [*to everyone*], even as many as the Lord our God shall call.

Verse 39, above, is most significant. In verse 36, Peter boldly told the Jews that they had crucified Christ. Yet, in this verse, mercy is still extended to them as they are invited to repent and be forgiven. This is a strong reminder of how patient and kind the Lord is and how anxious He is to forgive us and help us progress.

40 And with many other words did he [*Peter*] testify and exhort [*strongly counsel*], saying, Save yourselves from this untoward [*wicked and rebellious*] generation.

41 ¶ Then they that [*who*] gladly received his word were baptized: and the same day there were added unto them about three thousand souls. [*About 3,000 converts joined the Church that day.*]

42 And they [*the new converts*] continued stedfastly [*faithfully*] in the apostles' doctrine [*teachings*] and fellowship, and in breaking of bread [*the sacrament*], and in prayers.

43 And fear came upon every soul [*everyone was filled with awe*]: and

many wonders [*miracles and amazing things*] and signs were done by the apostles.

44 And all that believed were together [*were united and harmonious*], and had all things common [*they lived a united order*];

45 And sold their possessions and goods, and parted them to all men [*shared with everyone*], as every man had need [*according to each person's needs*].

46 And they, continuing daily with one accord [*in unity and peace*] in the temple, and breaking bread from house to house, did eat their meat [*food*] with gladness and singleness of heart,

Just a quick reminder. The word "meat" as used in verse 46, above, means "food." When the Bible refers to beef, chicken, lamb, etc., it uses the word "flesh."

47 Praising [*worshiping*] God, and having favour with all the people. And the Lord added to the church daily such as should be saved. [*With the help of the Lord, many people who wanted to be saved were baptized daily.*]

# ACTS 3

Watch now as Peter and John fearlessly and faithfully go forth in their calling as Apostles of Jesus Christ. Imagine the excited talk among the people as these great servants of the Lord carry on the work of the Master. You will probably recognize verses 19–21, which prophesy of the restoration of the gospel in the latter-days.

1 NOW Peter and John went up together into the temple at the hour of prayer, being the ninth hour [*about 3 PM*].

**JST Acts 3:1**

1 Now Peter and John went up together into the temple at the ninth hour, for prayer.

2 And a certain man lame from his mother's womb [*who had been crippled since he was born*] was carried, whom they laid daily at the gate of the temple which is called Beautiful, to ask alms [*donations*] of them that entered into the temple;

There were several "gates" or doorways into the temple grounds. One of these was named "Beautiful," and it was here that friends left the cripple each day so he could beg for a living.

3 Who seeing Peter and John about to go into the temple [*into the inner courtyard of the temple complex*] asked an alms [*a donation*].

4 And Peter, fastening his eyes upon him with John, said, Look on us.

**JST Acts 3:4**

4 And Peter and John, fastening their eyes upon him, said, Look on us.

5 And he [*the crippled man*] gave heed unto them, expecting to receive something of them.

6 Then Peter said, Silver and gold have I none; but such as I have give I thee: In the name of Jesus Christ of Nazareth rise up and walk.

7 And he took him by the right hand, and lifted him up: and immediately his feet and ankle bones received strength.

8 And he [*the crippled man*] leaping up stood, and walked, and entered with them into the temple, walking, and leaping, and praising God.

9 And all the people saw him walking and praising God:

10 And they knew that it was he which [*who*] sat for alms at the Beautiful gate of the temple: and they were filled with wonder and amazement at that which had happened unto him.

11 And as the lame man which was healed held [*held onto*] Peter and John, all the people ran together unto them

in the porch that is called Solomon's, greatly wondering [*astonished*].

12 ¶ And when Peter saw it, he answered unto [*responded to*] the people, Ye men of Israel, why marvel ye at this? or why look ye so earnestly on us [*so seriously at us*], as though by our own power or holiness we had made this man to walk?

> **JST Acts 3:12**
> 12 And when Peter saw this, he answered and said unto the people, Ye men of Israel, why marvel ye at this? or why look ye so earnestly on us, as though by our own power or holiness we had made this man to walk?

13 The God of Abraham, and of Isaac, and of Jacob, the God of our fathers, hath glorified his Son Jesus; whom ye delivered up [*whom you told Pilate to crucify*], and denied him [*you said "Crucify Him!"*] in the presence of Pilate, when he was determined to let him go.

14 But ye denied the Holy One [*Christ*] and the Just, and desired a murderer [*Barabbas; Luke 23:16–25*] to be granted [*released*] unto you;

15 And killed the Prince of life [*Jesus*], whom God hath raised from the dead; whereof we are witnesses. [*We are witness of the resurrected Christ whom you insisted be crucified.*]

16 And his name through faith in his [*Christ's*] name hath made this man strong, whom ye see and know: yea, the faith which is by him [*the faith which comes through Christ*] hath given him [*the crippled man*] this perfect soundness [*complete healing*] in the presence of you all.

> **JST Acts 3:16**
> 16 And this man, through faith in his name, hath been made strong, whom ye see and know; yea, the faith which is in him hath given him this perfect soundness in the presence of you all.

17 And now, brethren, I wot that through ignorance ye did it, as did also your rulers.

> **JST Acts 3:17**
> 17 And now, brethren, I know that through ignorance ye have done this, as also your rulers.

18 But those things, which God before had shewed by the mouth of all his prophets, that Christ should suffer, he hath so fulfilled. [*Jesus fulfilled all the prophecies about Christ.*]

19 ¶ Repent ye therefore, and be converted, that your sins may be blotted out, when the times of refreshing shall come [*the Second Coming; see footnote 19a in your Bible*] from the presence of the Lord;

20 And he [*the Father; see Mark 13:32*] shall send Jesus Christ [*the Second Coming*], which [*who*] before [*in the Old Testament*] was preached unto you:

> **JST Acts 3:20**
> 20 And he shall send Jesus Christ, which before was preached unto you, whom ye have crucified;
>
> Just a note to emphasize that Peter has grown much in strength since the night he denied knowing Jesus three times before the rooster crowed. See Matthew 26:69–75. He now boldly preaches of Christ to the Jews in the face of certain arrest.

21 Whom the heaven must receive [*who will dwell in heaven*] until the times of restitution of all things [*the restoration of the gospel through the Prophet Joseph Smith and the fulfillment of all the signs of the times*], which God hath spoken by the mouth of all his holy prophets since the world began.

22 For Moses truly said [*Deuteronomy 18:15–19*] unto the fathers [*our ancestors in Old Testament times*], A prophet [*Jesus Christ*] shall the Lord your God raise up unto you of your brethren, like unto me; him shall ye hear in all things whatsoever he shall say unto you.

23 And it shall come to pass, that every soul, which will not hear that prophet [*Christ*], shall be destroyed from among the people.

24 Yea, and all the prophets from Samuel and those that follow after, as many as have spoken, have likewise foretold [*prophesied*] of these days.

25 Ye are the children of [*descendants of*] the prophets, and of the covenant which God made with our fathers, saying unto Abraham [*Genesis 12:3*], And in thy seed shall all the kindreds of the earth be blessed.

26 Unto you first [*the Jews received the gospel first from Jesus, then it went to the Gentiles*] God, having raised up his Son Jesus, sent him to bless you, in turning away every one of you from his iniquities [*in giving every one of you the opportunity to turn away from your sins*].

## ACTS 4

Opposition will continue increasing as the Adversary seeks to stop the work of the Lord. Luke describes how Peter and John are arrested and threatened with serious consequences if they don't stop teaching about Jesus Christ. They don't stop.

1 AND as they [*Peter and John; see chapter three, verse one*] spake unto the people, the priests, and the captain of the temple, and the Sadducees, came upon them,

2 Being grieved [*disappointed, angry*] that they [*the Apostles*] taught the people, and preached through Jesus the resurrection from the dead.

The religious leaders of the Jews, mentioned in verse 1, above, were the main force behind getting the Savior crucified. They had hoped in their evil hearts to have stopped the religious movement started by Jesus. Now they find that the Apostles are continuing to teach about Jesus and His gospel, including the resurrection from the dead. The Sadducees did not believe in resurrection (see Bible Dictionary under "Sadducees"), therefore, such preaching is particularly irritating to them. Furthermore, a crippled man, whom many people knew, has been healed by Peter and John (Acts 3:6–7) and everybody is talking about it. These wicked religious rulers of the Jews are alarmed because they find that the people are excited about the Apostles' teachings and miracle, and many are joining the Church.

3 And they laid hands on them [*they arrested Peter and John*], and put them in hold [*in jail*] unto [*until*] the next day: for it was now eventide [*evening*].

4 Howbeit [*however*] many of them which heard the word [*the preaching*] believed; and the number of the men was about five thousand. [*5,000 more are ready to join the Church.*]

5 ¶ And it came to pass on the morrow, that their rulers [*the Jews' religious leaders*], and elders, and scribes,

6 And Annas the high priest, and Caiaphas [*who presided at the illegal trial of Christ during the night. See Matthew 26:57*], and John, and Alexander, and as many as were of the kindred [*relatives*] of the high priest, were gathered together [*had met in council*] at Jerusalem.

Israel was part of the Roman Empire at this time. However, the Romans allowed the Jews to pretty much have their own government and to govern their own affairs, with the exception that they were not allowed to execute anyone without Roman permission. The Jewish religious leaders mentioned in verses 5 and 6, above, represented the highest governing body of Jews. The fact that they quickly gathered together in council is evidence of how alarmed they were about Peter and John and their influence among the people. Watch now as they proceed to interrogate Peter and John.

7 And when they had set them [*Peter and John*] in the midst [*in the center of the court chambers*], they asked, By what power, or by what name, have ye done this [*by whose authority did you heal this lame man*]?

8 Then Peter, filled with the Holy Ghost, said unto them, Ye rulers of the people, and elders of Israel,

9 If we this day be examined of [*be placed on trial because of*] the good deed done to the impotent [*crippled*] man, by what means he is made whole [*as to how he was healed*];

10 Be it known unto you all, and to all the people of Israel, that by the name of Jesus Christ of Nazareth, whom ye crucified, whom God raised from the dead, even by him doth this man stand here before you whole. [*In other words, we healed him in the name of Jesus Christ, whom you crucified and who is now resurrected. It is through Christ's power that the man is healed.*]

11 This [*Christ*] is the stone which was set at nought of [*which was rejected by*] you builders, which is become the head of the corner [*the capstone; the finishing of the whole building*].

Peter is quoting Psalm 118:22, where it was prophesied that builders would foolishly reject the very stone (Christ) or rock upon which God's work is built, in other words, upon which their salvation depends. The imagery is that wicked builders would foolishly refuse to use a solid foundation upon which to build, rather, would build their own kingdom, with no foundation, which guarantees that it will crumble. It reminds us of the "great and spacious building" in Lehi's dream (1 Nephi 8:26) which had no foundation at all. Peter tells these high rulers that they are the "builders" who have rejected the Stone, and have thus fulfilled the prophecy in Psalms!

Next, Peter bears testimony to those who have him on trial that Jesus Christ is the only source of salvation.

12 Neither is there salvation in any other [*there is no other way to be saved, other than through Christ*]: for there is none other name under heaven given among men, whereby we must be saved.

13 ¶ Now when they saw the boldness of Peter and John, and perceived [*were aware*] that they were unlearned [*hadn't had the formal training which the Jewish religious leaders had had*] and ignorant men [*common, ordinary men*], they marvelled; and they took knowledge of them [*they took note*], that they had been with Jesus.

14 And beholding [*seeing*] the man which was healed standing with them, they could say nothing against it.

15 But when they had commanded them [*Peter and John*] to go aside out of the council [*to step outside the courtroom*], they conferred [*counseled*] among themselves,

16 Saying, What shall we do to these men? for that indeed a notable miracle hath been done by them is manifest to all them that dwell in Jerusalem [*everybody in Jerusalem knows that Peter and John have done a great miracle*]; and we cannot deny it [*we can't make it go away*].

17 But that it spread no further among the people, let us straitly [*strictly*] threaten them, that they speak henceforth [*from now on*] to no man in this name. [*Let's threaten them with most serious consequences if they do any more such things in the name of Jesus Christ.*]

18 And they called them [*back into the courtroom*], and commanded them not to speak at all nor teach in the name of Jesus.

19 But Peter and John answered and said unto them, Whether it be right in the sight of God to hearken unto you [*to obey you*] more than unto [*to obey*] God, judge ye [*you decide*].

20 For we cannot but speak the things

which we have seen and heard. [*In other words, we will obey God rather than you.*]

21 So when they had further threatened them, they let them go, finding nothing how they might punish them, because of the people: for all men glorified God for that which was done. [*They were afraid to do more than threaten Peter and John for fear of causing a riot among the people, because of their popularity.*]

> **JST Acts 4:21**
> 21 So when they had further threatened them, they let them go, finding nothing how they might punish them, because of the people; for many glorified God for that which was done.

22 For the man was above [*over*] forty years old, on whom this miracle of healing was shewed [*showed*]. [*People had known of this crippled man for over forty years, so there were too many witnesses as to the miracle for the chief priests and elders to squelch it successfully.*]

23 ¶ And being let go, they [*Peter and John*] went to their own company [*to their group of Church members*], and reported all that the chief priests and elders had said unto them.

24 And when they [*the members*] heard that, they lifted up their voice to God with one accord [*in unity*], and said, Lord, thou art God, which hast made heaven, and earth, and the sea, and all that in them is:

25 Who by the mouth of thy servant David hast said [*Psalm 2:1–2*], Why did the heathen rage, and the people imagine vain things?

26 The kings of the earth stood up, and the rulers were gathered together against the Lord, and against his Christ.

27 For of a truth [*just as was stated in David's prophecy,*] against thy holy child Jesus, whom thou hast anointed, both Herod, and Pontius Pilate, with the Gentiles, and the people of Israel, were gathered together, [*King Herod, Pontius Pilate, etc. have fulfilled the prophecy that they would gather together against Jesus.*]

28 For to do whatsoever thy hand and thy counsel determined before to be done. [*They did exactly as it was prophesied that they would do.*]

29 And now, Lord, behold [*consider*] their [*the rulers*] threatenings [*against Peter and John*]: and grant unto thy servants, that with all boldness they may speak thy word,

30 By stretching forth thine hand to heal; and that signs and wonders may be done by the name of thy holy child Jesus.

31 ¶ And when they had prayed, the place was shaken where they were assembled together; and they were all filled with the Holy Ghost, and they spake [*spoke*] the word of God with boldness.

32 And the multitude of them that believed were of one heart and of one soul: neither said any of them that ought of the things which he possessed was his own; but they had all things common. [*They lived in harmony, in a united order.*]

33 And with great power gave the apostles witness of [*the Apostles bore testimony with great power of*] the resurrection of the Lord Jesus: and great grace [*help from the Lord*] was upon them all.

> In verses 34–37, next, we see these early Saints practicing the law of consecration in conjunction with their united order.

34 Neither was there any among them that lacked: for as many as were possessors of lands or houses sold them, and brought the prices of the things that were sold,

35 And laid them down at the apostles'

feet [*they gave the money they received from selling their possessions to the Apostles*]: and distribution was made unto every man according as he had need.

36 And Joses, who by the apostles was surnamed Barnabas, (which is, being interpreted, The son of consolation,) a Levite, and of the country of Cyprus,

37 Having land, sold it, and brought the money, and laid it at the apostles' feet.

# ACTS 5

Luke begins this chapter by informing us that a certain man and his wife were intentionally dishonest with the Lord. They attempted to deceive the Apostles, claiming to be consecrating all they had to the Lord, but secretly holding back a portion for themselves.

1 BUT a certain man named Ananias, with Sapphira his wife, sold a possession [*some land; see verse 8*],

2 And kept back part of the price [*the money received*], his wife also being privy to it [*being fully aware of what he was doing*], and brought a certain part [*just part of the money*], and laid it at the apostles' feet [*donated it to the Apostles for the united order*].

3 But Peter said, Ananias, why hath Satan filled thine heart to lie to the Holy Ghost, and to keep back part of the price of the land? [*Why have you secretly kept back part of the money for yourself and pretended to donate all of it to the Church for the united order?*]

4 Whiles it remained, was it not thine own [*didn't it belong to you before you sold it*]? and after it was sold, was it not in thine own power [*wasn't all the money you got for it in your control*]? why hast thou conceived this thing [*hatched this plot*] in thine heart? thou hast not lied unto men, but unto God.

Those who lie to their bishop or stake president during an interview would do well to read and take to heart the last two phrases of verse 4, above.

5 And Ananias hearing these words fell down, and gave up the ghost [*died*]: and great fear came on all them that heard these things.

6 And the young men arose, wound him up [*wrapped him in strips of burial cloth*], and carried him out, and buried him.

7 And it was about the space of three hours after [*about three hours later*], when his wife, not knowing what was done [*not knowing what had happened to her husband*], came in.

Have you noticed that "answered unto" someone is quite often used in King James English (the language of our English version of the Bible) ifor "asked" or "responded to" a person? We see an example of this at the beginning of verse 8, next.

8 And Peter answered unto her [*asked her*], Tell me whether ye sold the land for so much [*is it true you sold the land for this much money*]? And she said, Yea, for so much [*yes, that's correct*].

9 Then Peter said unto her, How [*why*] is it that ye [*you and your husband*] have agreed [*plotted*] together to tempt [*test*] the Spirit of the Lord [*to find out whether or not we are inspired by the Holy Ghost*]? behold, the feet of them which have buried thy husband are at the door, and shall carry thee out.

10 Then fell she down straightway [*immediately*] at his feet, and yielded up the ghost [*died*]: and the young men came in, and found her dead, and, carrying her forth, buried her by her husband.

11 And great fear came upon all the church, and upon as many as heard these things.

This is a rather strong reminder to us that it is a serious thing to lie to the

Lord's servants. For most members who lie to their bishop or stake president, the penalty is not so final as with Ananias and Sapphira. However, it is equally as deadly and immediate in terms of spiritual damage to the liar.

12 ¶ And by the hands of the apostles were many signs and wonders wrought [*done*] among the people; and they were all with one accord [*gathered together in unity of purpose*] in Solomon's porch [*a part of the outer courtyard of the temple grounds in Jerusalem*].

13 And of the rest durst [*dared*] no man join himself to them: [*In other words, none of the religious rulers of the Jews dared join with them.*] but the people magnified them [*held the Apostles in very high regard*].

**JST Acts 5:13**

13 And of the rulers durst no man join himself to them; but the people magnified them.

14 And believers were the more added to the Lord [*many more converts joined the Church*], multitudes both of men and women."

15 Insomuch that [*as a result*] they brought forth the sick into the streets, and laid them on beds and couches, that at the least the shadow of Peter passing by might overshadow [*might touch*] some of them.

16 There came also a multitude [*large crowds of people*] out of the cities round about unto Jerusalem, bringing sick folks, and them which were vexed [*troubled*] with unclean [*evil*] spirits: and they were healed every one.

17 ¶ Then the high priest [*the chief religious leader of the Jews*] rose up, and all they that were with him [*along with his associates*], (which is the sect of the Sadducees,) and were filled with indignation [*anger*],

18 And laid their hands on [*arrested*] the apostles, and put them in the common prison [*the public jail*].

19 But the angel of the Lord by night [*during the night*] opened the prison doors, and brought them forth [*out*], and said,

20 Go, stand and speak in the temple to the people all the words of this life. [*Go back to the temple grounds and continue teaching the gospel.*]

21 And when they heard that [*the angel's instructions*], they [*the Apostles who had been freed from jail*] entered into the temple early in the morning, and taught. But the high priest came, and they that were with him [*the high priest and his associates came to their offices the next morning*], and called the council [*the Sanhedrin, the highest government body run by the Jews*] together, and all the senate [*senators*] of the children of Israel, and sent to the prison to have them brought [*to have the Apostles brought to appear before the rulers*].

22 But when the officers came, and found them not in the prison, they returned, and told,

23 Saying, The prison truly found we shut with all safety [*the jail doors were all locked and secure*], and the keepers [*the men who guarded the jail*] standing without [*outside the jail*] before [*in front of*] the doors: but when we had opened [*the doors to the jail cells*], we found no man within [*inside*].

24 Now when the high priest and the captain of the temple and the chief priests heard these things, they doubted of them whereunto this would grow [*they were puzzled and worried as to what would happen when the people found about it and word of it spread*].

25 Then came one [*someone*] and told them, saying, Behold, the men whom ye put in prison are standing in the temple [*on the Jerusalem temple grounds*], and teaching the people.

26 Then went the captain [*of the police*] with the officers, and brought them

without violence [*arrested the Apostles, handling them gently*]: for they feared the people, lest they should have been stoned. [*The police were worried that the people might throw rocks at them when they arrested the Apostles.*]

27 And when they [*the police*] had brought them [*the Apostles*], they set them before the council: and the high priest asked [*questioned*] them,

28 Saying, Did not we straitly [*strictly, strongly*] command you that ye should not teach in this name [*didn't we command you not to teach about Jesus*]? and, behold, ye have filled Jerusalem with your doctrine [*you have everyone in Jerusalem filled with excitement about Jesus*], and intend to bring this man's blood upon us [*you are trying to make us look guilty for crucifying Jesus*].

29 ¶ Then Peter and the other apostles answered and said, We ought to obey God rather than men.

30 The God of our fathers [*ancestors*] raised up [*sent*] Jesus, whom ye slew [*killed*] and hanged on a tree [*crucified on a cross*].

31 Him [*Jesus*] hath God [*the Father*] exalted [*lifted up*] with his right hand [*to sit at his right hand; see Acts 5:31, footnote a*] to be a Prince and a Saviour, for to give repentance [*for the purpose of making repentance available*] to Israel, and forgiveness of sins.

32 And we are his witnesses of these things; and so is also the Holy Ghost, whom God hath given to them that obey him.

33 ¶ When they [*the High Priest and his associates*] heard that, they were cut to the heart, and took counsel [*made plans*] to slay them [*to kill the Apostles*].

In verse 34, next, you will see that not all Pharisees were wicked and corrupt. Gamaliel was a Pharisee who had wisdom and integrity and was not afraid to stand up to peer pressure. Acts 22:3 informs us that Paul, in his younger days, was one of Gamaliel's students.

34 Then stood there up one in the council, a Pharisee, named Gamaliel, a doctor of the law, had in reputation [*highly respected*] among all the people, and commanded to put the apostles forth a little space [*ordered the Apostles to be taken out of the room for a few minutes*];

As mentioned in the note above, Gamaliel seems to have been a rare exception among the members of the Sanhedrin (the highest governing council of the Jews). Here, he has enough influence and confidence to successfully challenge the prevailing feeling in the Sanhedrin to execute the Apostles. The Bible Dictionary also tells us that the Apostle Paul was one of Gamaliel's students. See Bible Dictionary under "Gamaliel." Watch the logic Gamaliel uses to try to persuade his fellow council members to beware of what they do to these Apostles.

35 And [*Gamaliel*] said unto them [*the other members of the Sanhedrin*], Ye men [*rulers*] of Israel, take heed to yourselves [*stop and think about*] what ye intend to do as touching [*concerning*] these men [*Apostles*].

36 For before these days rose up Theudas [*remember back to the time when a fellow named Theudas came along*], boasting himself to be somebody [*claiming to be someone special*]; to whom a number of men, about four hundred, joined themselves [*about four hundred men became his loyal followers*]: who was slain [*Theudas was killed*]; and all, as many as obeyed him, were scattered, and brought to nought [*his followers were scattered and his influence among the people died out*].

37 After this man rose up Judas of Galilee [*after Theudas was gone, a man named Judas, from Galilee, came along*] in the days of the taxing [*census*], and

drew away much people after him [*Judas led a revolt at the time the Romans ordered that a census be taken among us for the purpose of taxation*]: he also perished [*he was also killed*]; and all, even as many as obeyed him, were dispersed [*all his followers scattered and nothing came of what he tried to start*].

38 And now I [*Gamaliel*] say unto you [*members of the Sanhedrin*], Refrain from these men, and let them alone [*don't do anything to these Apostles of Jesus*]: for if this counsel or this work be of men, it will come to nought [*if what Jesus started is man-made, it will eventually die out, like the movements started by Theudas and Judas*]:

39 But if it be of God [*if Jesus and His gospel are from God*], ye cannot overthrow it [*you can't stop it*]; lest haply [*perhaps*] ye be found even to fight against God.

**JST Acts 5:39**

39 But if it be of God, ye cannot overthrow it; be careful, therefore, lest ye be found even to fight against God.

As you will see in verse 40, next, these evil rulers of the Jews backed off some because of Gamaliel's counsel, but they still didn't get it.

40 And to him they agreed: and when they had called the apostles, and beaten them, they commanded that they should not speak in the name of Jesus, and let them go.

41 ¶ And they [*the Apostles*] departed from the presence of the council, rejoicing that they were counted worthy to suffer shame [*to be persecuted*] for his name [*for Christ*].

42 And daily in the temple, and in every house, they ceased not [*did not stop*] to teach and preach Jesus Christ.

# ACTS 6

As you will see in this chapter, the Church continues to experience rapid growth, and the Apostles can't keep up with everything. As a result, the Seventy were established and seven righteous men, including Stephen (who will be martyred in chapter 7) were called to serve. In a way, they experienced what we are experiencing in our day as the gospel expands into all the world and the quorums of general authority Seventy have been expanded to fill the needs.

1 AND in those days, when the number of the disciples was multiplied [*as the Church continued to grow*], there arose a murmuring [*a complaint*] of the Grecians [*the Greek members of the Church*] against the Hebrews [*the Jewish members*], because their widows were neglected in the daily ministration [*they felt that their widows were not being properly taken care of in the united order by the Church leaders*].

2 Then the twelve called the multitude of the disciples unto them [*the Twelve called a meeting of the members*], and said, It is not reason [*wise*] that we should leave the word of God [*stop preaching and handling administrative matters*], and serve tables [*spend all our time taking care of individual member needs*].

3 Wherefore [*therefore*], brethren, look ye out [*seek out*] among you seven men of honest report, full of the Holy Ghost and wisdom, whom we may appoint over this business [*managing the daily needs of the united order, taking care of widows etc.*].

4 But we will give ourselves continually to prayer, and to the ministry of the word.

5 ¶ And the saying pleased the whole multitude: and they chose Stephen, a man full of faith and of the Holy Ghost, and Philip, and Prochorus, and Nicanor, and Timon, and Parmenas, and Nicolas

a proselyte of Antioch [*a convert from Antioch*]:

6 Whom they set before the apostles: and when they had prayed, they laid their hands on them [*ordained them and set them apart for that work*].

7 And the word of God increased [*the gospel continued to spread*]; and the number of the disciples [*converts*] multiplied [*increased*] in Jerusalem greatly; and a great company [*a large group*] of the priests [*Jewish priests who were converted*] were obedient to the faith.

8 And Stephen, full of faith and power, did great wonders and miracles among the people.

9 ¶ Then there arose certain of the synagogue, which is called the synagogue of the Libertines [*Freed-men*], and, Cyrenians, and Alexandrians, and of them of Cilicia and of Asia, disputing [*debating, arguing against him*] with Stephen.

**JST Acts 6:9**

9 And there arose certain of the synagogue, who are called Libertines, and also Cyrenians, and Alexandrians, and of them of Cilicia, and of Asia, disputing with Stephen.

10 And they were not able to resist [*could not successfully contradict*] the wisdom and the spirit by which he spake.

11 Then they suborned men [*secretly bribed false witnesses*], which [*who*] said, We have heard him [*Stephen*] speak blasphemous words against Moses, and against God.

"Blasphemous words" or "blasphemy," meaning speaking mockingly or disrespectfully of God or prophets, was a sin which was punishable by death in the Jewish legal system.

12 And they [*the angry Jews mentioned in verse 9, above*] stirred up the people, and the elders, and the scribes, and came upon him, and caught him [*arrested Stephen*], and brought him to the council [*the Sanhedrin, the "supreme court" run by the Jews; see Bible Dictionary under "Sanhedrin."*],

13 And set up false witnesses, which said, This man ceaseth not to speak [*refuses to quit speaking*] blasphemous words against this holy place, and the law [*the Law of Moses, as given in Genesis, Exodus, Leviticus, Numbers, and Deuteronomy*]:

14 For we have heard him say, that this Jesus of Nazareth shall destroy this place [*Jerusalem*], and shall change the customs which Moses delivered us.

15 And all that sat in the council, looking stedfastly on [*intently at*] him, saw his face as it had been the face of an angel. [*Stephen was transfigured in front of them so that his face shined with glory, and all the Sanhedrin and others there saw it happen.*]

# ACTS 7

This chapter contains one of the finest reviews of the history of Israel, beginning with Abraham, found anywhere in the scriptures. Included in it is a rather detailed history of Moses. The review is given by Stephen during his trial in answer to the Jewish high priest who asked if he was guilty of the accusations against him recorded in chapter 6, above.

1 THEN said the high priest [*the highest ruling official among the Jews*], Are these things so?

2 And he [*Stephen*] said, Men, brethren, and fathers [*leaders of the Jews*], hearken [*pay very close attention to what I say*]; The God of glory appeared unto our father [*ancestor*] Abraham, when he was in Mesopotamia [*the Persian*

*Gulf area*], before he dwelt in Charran [*Haran; southern part of Turkey*],

3 And said unto him, Get thee out of thy country, and from thy kindred [*relatives*], and come into the land which I shall shew [*show*] thee.

4 Then came he [*Abraham*] out of the land of the Chaldaeans [*Babylon; Persian Gulf area*], and dwelt in Charran: and from thence [*from there*], when his father was dead, he removed him [*he traveled*] into this land [*the Holy Land*], wherein [*in which*] ye now dwell.

5 And he [*God*] gave him [*Abraham*] none [*no*] inheritance in it, no, not so much as to set his foot on: yet he promised that he would give it to him for a possession, and to his seed [*descendants*] after him, when as yet he had no child.

6 And God spake on this wise [*God said*], That his seed [*Abraham's posterity*] should sojourn [*would live temporarily*] in a strange [*foreign*] land; and that they [*the inhabitants of that foreign land; in other words, Egypt*] should [*would*] bring them into bondage [*slavery*], and entreat them evil [*treat them very badly*] four hundred years.

7 And the nation to whom they shall be in bondage will I judge [*punish*], said God: and after that [*after Abraham's posterity had spent four hundred years as slaves in Egypt*] shall they come forth [*leave Egypt*], and serve me [*God*] in this place [*in Israel*].

8 And he [*God*] gave him [*Abraham*] the covenant of circumcision [*see Bible Dictionary under "Circumcision."*]: and so Abraham begat [*fathered, sired*] Isaac, and circumcised him the eighth day [*eight days after Isaac was born*]; and Isaac begat Jacob; and Jacob begat [*was the father of*] the twelve patriarchs [*heads of the twelve tribes*]. [*Jacob had twelve sons, and that was the beginning of the twelve tribes of Israel.*]

9 And the patriarchs [*Joseph's older brothers*], moved with envy [*being jealous of him*], sold Joseph into Egypt [*Genesis, chapter 37*]: but God was with him,

10 And delivered him out of all his afflictions [*troubles*], and gave him favour and wisdom in the sight of Pharaoh king of Egypt; and he made him [*Joseph*] governor over Egypt and all his [*Pharaoh's*] house.

11 Now there came a dearth [*famine*] over all the land of Egypt and Chanaan [*where Joseph's father and eleven brothers were living; basically Israel or the Holy Land today*], and great affliction: and our fathers [*Jacob and his eleven sons and their families*] found no sustenance [*were starving up in Israel*].

12 But when Jacob heard that there was corn [*grain*] in Egypt, he sent out our fathers [*ancestors; Joseph's older brothers*] first. [*Jacob sent his ten oldest sons to Egypt to see if they could buy food there and bring it back home to Israel.*]

13 And at the second time Joseph was made known to his brethren [*when Joseph's brothers came the second time to Egypt (Genesis 43–45,) Joseph told them who he was*]; and Joseph's kindred was [*relatives were*] made known unto Pharaoh [*were introduced to Pharaoh*].

14 Then sent Joseph, and called his father Jacob to him, and all his kindred, threescore and fifteen souls. [*Joseph brought his father, Jacob, and all seventy five of his father's family to Egypt to help them survive the famine.*]

15 So Jacob went down into Egypt, and died, he, and our fathers [*our ancestors*],

16 And were carried over into Sychem [*in southern Israel*], and laid in the sepulchre [*grave*] that Abraham bought for a sum of money of [*from*] the sons of Emmor the father of Sychem.

17 But when the time of the promise drew nigh [*when it came time for God to*

# The JST References in Study Guides by David J. Ridges

Note that some of the JST (The Joseph Smith Translation of the Bible) references I use in my study guides are not found in our LDS Bible in the footnotes or in the Joseph Smith Translation section in the reference section in the back. The reason for this, as explained to me while writing curriculum materials for the Church, is simply that there is not enough room to include all of the JST additions and changes to the King James Version of the Bible (the one we use in the English speaking part of the Church). As you can imagine, as was likewise explained to me, there were difficult decisions that had to be made by the Scriptures Committee of the Church as to which JST contributions were included and which were not.

The Joseph Smith Translation of the Bible in its entirety can generally be found in or ordered through LDS bookstores. It was originally published under the auspices of the Reorganized Church of Jesus Christ of Latter Day Saints in Independence, Missouri. The version of the JST I prefer to use is a parallel column version, *Joseph Smith's "New Translation" of the Bible*, published by Herald Publishing House, Independence, Missouri, in 1970. This parallel column version compares the King James Bible with the JST side by side and includes only the verses that have changes, additions, or deletions made by the Prophet Joseph Smith.

By the way, some members of the Church have wondered whether or not we can trust the JST since it was published by a breakaway faction from our Church. They worry that some changes from Joseph Smith's original manuscript might have been made to support doctrinal differences between us and the RLDS Church. This is not the case. Many years ago, Robert J. Matthews of the Brigham Young University Religion Department was given permission by leaders of the RLDS Church to come to their Independence, Missouri, headquarters and personally compare the original JST document word for word with their publication of the JST. Brother Matthews was thus able to verify that they had been meticulously true to the Prophet's original work.

# CONTENTS

# INTRODUCTION

Welcome to the Second Edition of *The New Testament Made Easier.* This second edition is a substantial rewrite of the first edition. It contains hundreds of additional notes and explanations, plus a great many additional verses from the Joseph Smith Translation of the Bible, which were not included in the first edition. It has been reformatted to make it easier to follow.

Continuing on from where Part 1 of *The New Testament Made Easier* left off, this volume studies Acts through Revelation. This study guide uses the King James version of the Bible as published and used by the Church of Jesus Christ of Latter-day Saints as the basic text. As is the case with other volumes in this Gospel Studies Series, it is anticipated that you will use your own copy of the scriptures as the main text for your studies.

This is intended to be a quick-reference, user-friendly, basic study of this portion of the New Testament. The notes given in brackets within the verses, and the brief notes between verses are provided as helps toward understanding, and also for you to use as desired to make notes in your own scriptures. The entire Bible text of Acts through Revelation is included, with brief notes of explanation between and within the verses to clarify and help with understanding. We encourage you to underline or otherwise mark words and phrases which are significant to you in your study of these scriptures.

—David J. Ridges

# Books
## by David J. Ridges

### The Gospel Studies Series:

- *Isaiah Made Easier, Second Edition*
- *The New Testament Made Easier, Part 1 (Second Edition)*
- *The New Testament Made Easier, Part 2 (Second Edition)*
- *Your Study of The Book of Mormon Made Easier, Part 1*
- *Your Study of The Book of Mormon Made Easier, Part 2*
- *Your Study of The Book of Mormon Made Easier, Part 3*
- *Your Study of The Doctrine and Covenants Made Easier, Part 1*
- *Your Study of The Doctrine and Covenants Made Easier, Part 2*
- *Your Study of The Doctrine and Covenants Made Easier, Part 3*
- *The Old Testament Made Easier, Part 1*
- *The Old Testament Made Easier—Selections from the Old Testament, Part 2*
- *The Old Testament Made Easier—Selections from the Old Testament, Part 3*
- *Your Study of the Pearl of Great Price Made Easier*
- *Your Study of Jeremiah Made Easier*
- *Your Study of The Book of Revelation Made Easier, Second Edition*

### Additional titles by David J. Ridges:

- *Our Savior, Jesus Christ: His Life and Mission to Cleanse and Heal*
- *Mormon Beliefs and Doctrines Made Easier*
- *The Proclamation on the Family: The Word of the Lord on More Than 30 Current Issues*
- *65 Signs of the Times and the Second Coming*
- *Doctrinal Details of the Plan of Salvation: From Premortality to Exaltation*

These titles will soon be available through
Cedar Fort as e-books and on CD.